Basque-English
English-Basque
Dictionary

D0595878

The Basque Series

Basque-English
English-Basque
Dictionary

Gorka Aulestia
and
Linda White

University of Nevada Press
Reno   Las Vegas   London

Basque Series Editor: William A. Douglass

Library of Congress Cataloging-in-Publication Data

Aulestia, Gorka, 1932–
    Basque-English English-Basque dictionary / Gorka Aulestia and
Linda White.
        p. cm. — (The Basque series)
    ISBN 0-87417-178-4
    1. Basque language—Dictionaries—English. 2. English language—
Dictionaries—Basque. I. White, Linda, 1949–   . II. Title.
III. Series.
PH5177.E5A954   1992
499'.92321—dc20   91–44306
                                                              CIP

Published in the United States
by the University of Nevada Press, Reno, Nevada 89557
Copyright © 1992 by Gorka Aulestia and Linda White
All rights reserved

Published in the Basque Country by Elkar S.A., Esterlines 10, 20003 Donostia,
Gipuzkoa, as *Euskara-Ingelesa Ingelesa-Euskara Hiztegia*

Designed by Kaelin Chappell

3 5 7 9 8 6 4 2

Contents

Preface   vii

Hitzaurrea   ix

Abbreviations   xi

Basque-English Dictionary   1

English-Basque Dictionary   411

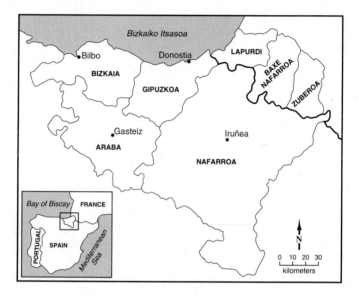

The Basque Country

Preface

This *Basque-English English-Basque Dictionary* represents the culmination of twelve years of effort and dedication to a task. The creation of a pocket version from the larger *Basque-English Dictionary* and *English-Basque Dictionary* was one of our goals from the earliest moments of our collaboration. We both feel that the primary purpose of the pocket dictionary is to help students involved in the study of either Basque or English.

The limitations of space forced on us during creation of the pocket dictionary have prompted the removal of many of the entries that appeared in our larger dictionaries. However, we were very selective about our reductions, and we are confident that the words included here will be more than sufficient to help the student of Basque or English take those first tentative steps toward communication. We also feel that the more advanced student, as well, will find the volume highly useful.

We would like to thank those who helped make this work a reality. Dr. William A. Douglass, coordinator of the Basque Studies Program, was behind the project from the beginning, providing organizational support and making the dictionary a first priority. Jill Berner, also with the Basque Studies Program, spent many long hours assisting in the preparation of the text for publication as a pocket dictionary.

After twelve years we are pleased to present this useful reference tool to all students of the Basque and English languages.

Gorka Aulestia
and
Linda White

Hitzaurrea

Esku artean daukazun *Euskara-Ingelesa Ingelesa-Euskara Hiztegia* hamabi urtetako ahaleginaren ondorio duzu. Gure elkarlanaren hasierako helburuetako bat, *Euskara-Ingelesa* eta *Ingelesa-Euskara Hiztegia* zabalagoetatik esku-hiztegi bat ateratzea izan zen. Esku-hiztegi honen helbururik nagusiena, bai euskara eta bai ingelesa ikasten diharduten ikasleei laguntza eskeintzea dela uste dugu biok.

Esku-hiztegi hitzaren definizioak berak ezarri zigun murrizketak, gure hiztegi zabalagoetan agertzen diren hitzen laurden bat edo, ezabatzera behartu gaitu. Halere, murrizketak egiteko orduan oso zorrotzak izan gara eta hemen agertzen diren hitzak euskara edo ingelesa ikasten ari denari komunikazioaren bidean lehenengo urratsak ematen laguntzeko nahikoak izango direla espero dugu. Hizkuntza maila hobea duen ikasleari ere, hiztegia guztiz lagungarria gertatuko zaiolakoan gaude.

Honako hiztegi hau gauzatzen lagundu diguten guztiei eskerrak eman nahi genizkieke. Dr. William A. Douglass, Euskal Mintegiaen koordinatzailea, proiektuaren bultzatzaile izan da hasiera batetik, antolaketa lanetan lagundu eta hiztegiari lehentasuna emanaz. Jill Berner-ek ere, hau ere Euskal Mintegikoa, ordu asko eman ditu testua esku-hiztegi

moduan argitara zedin. Esku-hiztegi hau Euskara eta
ingelesa ikasten ari diren guztiei lagungarri izango
zaielakoan argitaratzen dugu hamabi urte ondoren.

Gorka Aulestia
eta
Linda White

ABBREVIATIONS

abbr.	abbreviation, *laburdura*	masc.	masculine, *maskulino*
abl.	ablative, *ablatibo*	math.	mathematics, *matematika*
acc.	accusative, *akusatibo*	mech.	mechanics, *mekanika*
adj.	adjective, *izenlagun*	med.	medicine, *sendagintza*
adv.	adverb, *adizlagun*	mil.	military, *militar*
anat.	anatomy, *anatomia*	min.	mineralogy, *mineralogia*
arch.	archaic, *behinolako*	mus.	music, *musika*
archit.	architecture, *arkitektura*	n.	noun, *izen*
arith.	arithmetic, *aritmetika*	N.	north, *iparralde*
art.	article, *mugizki*	naut.	nautical, *itsasjakintza*
astron.	astronomy, *astronomia*	neg.	negative, *ezezkoi*
augm.	augmentative, *handikari*	neol.	neologism, *hitz berri*
biol.	biology, *biologia*	no.	number, *zenbaki*
bot.	botany, *botanika*	nom.	nominative, *nominatibo*
cap.	capitalized, *letra nagusi*	onomat.	onomatopoeia, *hotsizen*
cf.	confer, *gonbara*	p.	past, *lehenaldi*
chem.	chemistry, *kimika*	part.	participate, *partizipio*
colloq.	colloquial, *hitzaspertu*	perf.	perfect, *bukatu*
comp.	comparative, *gonbaraziozko*	pers.	person, *pertsona*
compl.	complement, *osagarri*	phil.	philosophy, *filosofia*
conj.	conjunction, *lokarritz*	pl.	plural, *plural zenbaki*
contr.	contraction, *laburtzapen*	pol.	politics, *politika*
dat.	dative, *datibo*	poss.	possessive, *jabekor*
def.	definite, *mugatu*	pref.	prefix, *aurrizki*
dim.	diminutive, *tipigarri*	prep.	preposition, *hitzaurreko*
eccl.	ecclesiastical, *elizaren*	pres.	present, *orainaldi*
econ.	economics, *ekonomia*	pret.	preterite, *lehenaldi*
e.g.	for example, *adibidez*	pron.	pronoun, *izenorde*
elec.	electrical, *elektrizitate*	prov.	proverb, *atsotitz*
Eng.	English, *ingeles*	psych.	psychology, *psikologia*
etc.	and so forth, *etab.*	refl.	reflexive, *norberekiko*
exclam.	exclamation, *oihu*	rel.	religion, *erlijio*
f.	feminine, *femenino*	R.C.Ch.	Roman Catholic Church, *Err. El.*
fam.	familiar, *familiarki*		*Katolikoa*
fig.	figuratively, *idurizko zentzuan*	S.	south, *hegoalde*
Fr.	French, *frantzes*	sing.	singular, *banako zenbaki*
fut.	future, *geroaldi*	sociol.	sociology, *soziologia*
genit.	genitive, *genitibo*	Span.	Spanish, *espainiera*
geog.	geography, *geografia*	subj.	subjunctive, *subjuntiboera*
geol.	geology, *geologia*	suff.	suffix, *atzizki*
geom.	geometry, *geometria*	superl.	superlative, *gehieneko*
Gr.	Greek, *greko*	syn.	synonymous, *izenkide*
gram.	grammar, *gramatika*	theat.	theater, *antzerki*
imp.	imperative, *aginkera*	theol.	theology, *teologia*
imperf.	imperfect, *bukagabe*	var.	variant of, *aldakin*
ind.	indicative, *egite era*	v.aux.	auxiliary verb, *aditz laguntzaile*
indef.	indefinite, *mugagabe*	vb.	verb, *aditz*
inf.	infinitive, *infinitibo*	v.i.	intransitive verb, *aditz*
int.	interjection, *hitz asperen*		*iragangaitz*
inter.	interrogative, *galderazko*	voc.	vocative, *bokatibo*
Lat.	Latin, *latin*	v.t.	transitive verb, *aditz iragankor*
lit.	literary, *hitzezitz*	vulg.	vulgar, *arruntki*

Basque-English
Dictionary

A

a *n.* first letter of the Basque alphabet. *int.* exclamation which denotes surprise, admiration.

-a *(gram).* the. Singular definite article. **Gizona.** The man.

-aba *suff.* Usually appears in compound words which express a family or work relationship. **Asaba.** Ancestor. **Izeba.** Aunt. **Osaba.** Uncle. **Ugazaba.** Boss, master.

abade *n.* priest.

abagadune *n.* chance, occasion.

abaildu *v.i.* to get tired, to become exhausted, to become fatigued.

abaildura *n.* fatigue, weariness, tiredness.

abailgarri *adj.* tiring.

abantaila *n.* advantage.

abantailadun *adj.* privileged.

abantailatu *v.t.* to advance, to surpass.

abantailatuki *adv.* advantageously.

abantailezko *adj.* advantageous, profitable.

abar *n.* branch of a tree. *n.* residue, rest, remnant. *adv.* so on. **Eta abar.** Et cetera, and so on and so forth.

abaraska *n.* honeycomb.

abariz *n.* (bot.) kermes oak.

abarka *n.* shoe of leather or rubber very typical in the Basque Country.

abarkatu *v.t.* to put on typical Basque rubber or leather shoes.

abarkaziri *n.* punch, point.

abarketa *n.* rope-soled shoe with a canvas top.

abaroan egon *v.i.* to take refuge (livestock).

abarreria *n.* bunch of firewood.

abarreztatu *v.t.* to cover with branches.

abartsu *adj.* having many branches (tree).

abata *n.* abbot.

abe *n.* beam. *n.* column, pillar, support. *n.* supporter of the family. *n.* stanchion. *n.(fig.)* cross.

abegi *n.* reception of someone (good or bad).

abegi egin *v.t.* to receive, to accept, to welcome.

abegikor *adj.* hospitable.

abegikortasun *n.* hospitality.

abegion *n.* hospitality.

abegitasun *n.* fondness.

abegitsu *adj.* hospitable.

abel *n.* var. of *abere* (animal). Used in certain compound words.

abelazkuntza *n.* cattle raising.

abelburu *n.* head of cattle.

abeletxe *n.* sheepshed; stable, stall.

abelgorri *n.* cattle.

abelongarri *n.* dung, excrement.

abelsendagile *n.* veterinarian.

abelsendagintza *n.* veterinary science.

abeltalde *n.* flock, herd, group of animals.

abeltegi *n.* stable. *n.* sheepfold.

abeltzain *n.* herdsman.

abeltzaintza *n.* tending of flocks.

abendu *n.* December. *n.* Advent, season before Christmas.

aberasgarri *adj.* enriching.

aberasketa *n.* enrichment.

aberaski *adv.* elegantly, sumptuously.

aberastasun *n.* wealth, richness.

aberastu *v.t.* to enrich (someone), to make (someone) rich or wealthy. *v.i.* to get rich, to become rich.

aberats *adj.* rich, wealthy, well-to-do. *adj.* abundant, rich. *n.* rich.

abere *n.* animal, brute, beast.

abereborda *n.* sheepshed, sheepfold.

aberekeria *n.* brutality, savageness, brutishness, bestiality.

abereki *adv.* brutally, roughly, brusquely.

aberetasun *n.* brutality, bestiality.

aberetu *v.i.* to become brutish.

aberkide *n.* fellow countryman.

aberkoi *adj.* patriotic.

aberri *n.* fatherland, homeland.

aberrikeria *n.* chauvinism.

aberrikoi *adj.* patriotic.

aberriratu *v.i.* to return to one's country.

aberritasun *n.* patriotism.

abertzale *n./adj.* patriot, nationalist.

abertzalekeria *n.* chauvinism.

abertzaletasun *n.* patriotism.

abertzaletu *v.i.* to become a patriot.

abesbatza *n.* choir, chorus.

abeslari *n.* singer.

abesti *n.* song.

abestisorta *n.* song-book.

abestu *v.t.* to sing.

abi *n.(bot.)* cranberry.

abiada *n.* speed; impulse.

abiadore *n.* pilot.

abiadura *n.* speed.

abiaketa *n.* departure.

abialdi *n.* departure. *n.* moment of departure.

abian *adv.* about to, on the point of.

abiapuntu *n.* point of departure.

abiarazi *v.t.* to cause to move, to initiate.

abiarazle *n.* person who causes to move, initiator.

abiatu *v.i.* to be ready to. *v.i.* to start walking, to set out. *v.i.* to go to, to go towards.

abil *adj.* skillful.

abildu *v.i.* to become skillful.

abilezia *n.* ability, talent, skill.

abilitate *n.* ability, talent, skill.

abilki *adv.* skillfully.

abiltasun *n.* ability, talent.

abio *n.* (bot.) cranberry.

abioi *n.* airplane.

abizen *n.* last name, surname.

abizendu *v.t.* to give a last name to.
abogadu *n.* lawyer.
abogadutza *n.* law (profession).
abstentzio *n.* abstention.
abstraktu *adj.* abstract.
abstrakzio *n.* abstraction.
aburu *n.* opinion.
aburu eman *v.t.* to express one's opinion.
aburukide *n.* person who agrees.
aburupen *n.* opinion.
abuztua *n.* August.
ada- *(gram.)* Prefix used in certain compound words as a variation of *adar*, branch, horn.
-ada *(gram.)* Suffix used in onomat. words. It represents the noise of the action.
adabaketa *n.* mending, patching.
adabaki *n.* patch, mending-piece.
adabakitu *v.t.* to patch, to mend.
adabatu *v.t.* to patch, to mend.
adabegi *n.* knot of a tree.
adabu *n.* patch, mending-piece.
adaburu *n.* top of a tree.
adar *n.* branch. *n.* horn. *n.(mus.)* hunting horn.
adarbakar *adj.* having a single horn (animal).
adardun *adj.* having many branches (tree). *adj.* having horns (animal), horned.
adardura *n.* branching, branching out.
adargabetu *v.t.* to remove branches.
adarka *adv.* goring, by goring.
adarkada *n.* thrust with a bull's horn, goring, butt.
adarka egin *v.t.* to gore.
adarkari *adj.* (one)that gores (with horns).
adarkatu *v.t.* to gore (with horns).
adarketa *n.* action of goring. *n.* branching out.
adarki *n.* firewood. *n.* piece of horn; piece of branch.
adarmozketa *n.* dehorning.
adarmoztu *v.t.* to cut (horns or branches).
adarno *n.(dim.)* small branch. *n.* (dim.) small horn.
adarra jo *v.t.(colloq.)* to kid, to tease.
adarra sartu *v.t.* to gore. *v.t.(fig.)* to deceive.
adarreztatu *v.i.* to be covered with branches.
adarrots *n.* rustle of branches. *n.* sound of a trumpet.
adartsu *adj.* having horns (animal). *adj.* having branches (tree).
adartu *v.t.* to gore. *v.i.* to sprout branches.
adartxo *n.(dim.)* small horn. *n.(dim.)* small branch.
adats *n.* long hair.
adei *n.* deference.
adeigabeko *adj.* impolite, rude.
adeigabetasun *n.* rudeness.

adeitasun *n.* courtesy, good manners.
adeitsu *adj.* courteous, gentle, polite.
adi *adj.* attentive.
adi-adi *adv.* attentively.
adiarazi *v.i.* to explain. *v.t.* to announce, to express. *v.t.* to mean.
adibide *n.* example, pattern.
adibidez *adv.* for instance, for example.
adi egon *v.i.* to pay attention.
adiera *n.* meaning. *n.* hearing. *n.* explanation, interpretation.
adieratzaile *n.* interpreter.
adierazburu *n.* title, headline.
adierazi *v.t.* to explain.
adierazkailu *n.* indicator, detector, recorder (instrument).
adierazkera *n.* form of expression.
adierazkor *adj.* significant, meaningful. *adj.* expressive.
adierazkorki *adv.* expressively.
adierazkortasun *n.* expressiveness.
adierazle *n.* expositor, interpreter.
adierazpen *n.* interpretation, explanation, exposition.
adierazpide *n.* means of expression.
adiezin *n.* discrepancy, disagreement. *adj.* incomprehensible.
adiezintasun *n.* incomprehensibility.
adigabe *adj.* negligent, careless, inattentive, absent-minded.
adigabetu *v.i.* to be absent-minded, to be inattentive.
adigabezia *n.* distraction.
adigai *adj.* logical, reasonable. *n.* meaning.
adigaitz *adj.* incomprehensible.
adigaiztasun *n.* incomprehension, unintelligibleness.
adigalkor *adj.* distracted, inattentive.
adigarri *adj.* comprehensible, intelligible, clear. *n.* explanation, meaning.
adigarriki *adv.* intelligibly.
adigarritasun *n.* intelligibility, comprehensibility.
adikor *adj.* capable of understanding; understandable, comprehensible. *adj.* attentive, watchful.
adikuntza *n.* discernment, discretion. *n.* comprehension, understanding.
adimen *n.* intelligence, mind, capability to understand.
adimendun *adj.* intelligent.
adimenezko *adj.* rational.
adimengabeko *adj.* irrational.
adimentsu *aj.* intelligent.
adin *n.* age.
adina *conj./adv.* as much as, as many as; so much, so many.
adinaro *n.* period when a person attains full legal rights.
adinbereko *adj.* coetaneous, contemporary.
adindu *v.i.* to be middle aged. *v.i.* to reach middle age.
adineko *adj.* contemporaneous. *adj.*

adult, of older age.

adingabeko *adj./n.* minor. *adj.* irrational.

adingabetasun *n.* state of being a minor.

adinkide *adj.* contemporary, of the same age. *n.* person having the same age as another.

adin-nagusitasun *n.* coming of age.

adintsu *adj.* aged, old.

adio! *int.* good-bye, bye-bye.

adiskidantza *n.* friendship.

adiskide *n.* companion, friend.

adiskidegaitz *adj.* irreconcilable, incompatible.

adiskidegarri *adj.* friendly.

adiskidegisa *adv.* amicably, in a friendly way.

adiskidego *n.* friendship, fellowship.

adiskideki *adv.* amicably, in a friendly way.

adiskiderazi *v.t.* to reconcile.

adiskidetasun *n.* fellowship, comraderie, friendship.

adiskidetsu *adj.* friendly, amicable.

adiskidetu *v.t.* to make friends. *v.i.* to reconcile.

adiskidetza *n.* reconciliation.

adiskidetzaile *adj.* conciliating. *n.* conciliator.

aditasun *n.* attention.

aditu *v.t.* to pay attention, to listen, to hear. *v.i.* to get along with, to understand each other.

aditz *n.(gram.)* verb. **Aditz iragangaitz.** Intransitive verb. **Aditz iragankor.** Transitive verb. **Aditz jasale.** Passive verb. **Aditz laguntzaile.** Auxiliary verb.

aditzaile *n.* listener.

aditzaldi *n.(gram.)* verb tense.

aditz-atzizki *n.(gram.)* verb suffix.

aditz-aurrizki *n.(gram.)* verb prefix.

aditzera *n.(gram.)* verbal mood.

aditzera eman *v.t.* to explain, to present, to make something understood.

adizjokera *n.(gram.)* verbal mood.

adizjoko *n.* conjugation (of a verb).

adizkera *n.(gram.)* verbal mood.

adizki *n.* (gram.) verbal element.

adizlagun *n.(gram.)* adverb.

adiztegi *n.* list of verbs.

adoba *n.* patch. *n.* condiment, sauce.

adobatu *v.t.* to mend, to patch. *v.t.* to dress (food), to season.

adore *n.* courage, encouragement.

adoregabe *adj.* discouraged.

adoregabetasun *n.* discouragement, depression.

adoregabetu *v.i.* to discourage, to depress.

adoregarri *adj.* encouraging.

adoretsu *adj.* courageous, brave.

adoretu *v.i./v.t.* to animate, to encourage, to stimulate, to cheer up.

adoretzaile *adj.* encouraging,

cheering, stimulating, animating.

ados *adj.* agreeing, agree, in agreement.

ados egon *v.i.* to agree.

adosezintasun *n.* incompatibility, nonagreement.

adostasun *n.* agreement.

adostezin *n.* disagreement.

adostezintasun *n.* incompatibility, discrepancy.

adostu *v.i.* to agree.

adreilatu *v.t.* to pave with bricks.

adreilu *n.* brick.

adreiluztatu *v.t.* to cover with bricks, to brick up, to brick over.

aduana *n.* customs house.

aduanagela *n.* customs house.

aduanazain *n.* customs house officer, customs officer.

adur *n.* slobber, spittle, drool, saliva that dribbles involuntarily out of the mouth.

adurretako *n.* bib, chin-cloth.

adurreztatu *v.i.* to drool.

adurti *adj.* dribbling, drooling.

adurzapi *n.* bib, chin-cloth.

aeroneska *n.* stewardess, female flight attendant, air hostess.

afa! *int.* exclamation which expresses happiness, joy.

afal *n.* var. of *afari*, dinner, supper. Used in compound words.

afalaurre *n.* short period of time before dinner or supper.

afalburuko *n.* dinner dessert.

afaldu *v.t.* to have dinner or supper, to eat dinner or supper.

afalondo *n.* period of time after dinner or supper (during which people are still sitting at the table talking).

afalordu *n.* dinner time, supper time.

afaltegi *n.* dining room, room where dinner or supper is served.

afaltiar *n.* dinner guest.

afari *n.* supper, dinner, late meal usually eaten around 10 p.m.

afarimerienda *n.* early evening meal.

afarino *n.(dim.)* light dinner, light supper.

-aga *(gram.)* Suffix which expresses abundance of or place of.

agaka *n.* Basque alphabet.

agentzia *n.* agency.

agerbide *n.* index, table of contents. *n.* declaration. *n.* public demonstration. *n.* sign, symbol, signal. *n.* certificate. *n.* proof, reason.

agerbidezko *adj.* declarative.

agergarri *adj.* showable, that which can be shown.

ageri *v.t.* to declare, to testify. *n.* declaration, document, manifest. *adj./adv.* evident, patent, public, obvious, clear; in evidence.

agerian *adv.* evidently, clearly, openly.

ageri izan *v.i.* to appear; to be obvious, to be evident.

ageriko *adj.* public, notorious.
agerkai *n.* document. *n.* proof, evidence.
agerkari *n.* document. *n.* periodical.
agerkera *n.* apparition, vision.
agerkeria *n.* bragging.
agerketa *n.* discovery. *n.* revelation.
agerkunde *n.* apparition. *n.* revelation. *n.* Feast of the Epiphany (January 6).
agerkuntza *n.* apparition.
agernahi *n.* exhibitionism, tendency to call attention to oneself.
agerpen *n.* presentation. *n.* revelation, vision. *n.* show.
agerraldi *n.* visit. *n.(theat.)* scene. *n.* apparition.
agerrarazi *v.t.* to cause to appear, to make appear. *v.t.* to show, to manifest.
agerrune *n.* clearing in a grove.
agertaldi *n.* apparition.
agertoki *n.* theater-box. *n.* stage.
agertu *v.i.* to appear. *v.t.* to declare, to show, to present, to explain. *v.t.* to manifest.
agertzaile *n.* explainer.
agian *adv.* maybe, perhaps.
aginbide *n.* authority, power to give orders.
agindu *v.t.* to order *v.t.* to promise. *n.* order, commandment. *n.* promise.
aginduagiri *n.* order, decree.
aginduarazi *v.t.* to issue precepts, to give orders.
aginduhausketa *n.* lawbreaking, transgression, trespassing.
agindupe *n.* submission, dependency.
agindutako *adj.* promised; ordered.
aginduz *prep.* by order of.
aginduzko *adj.* prescriptive.
aginkeria *n.* despotism.
aginketa *n.* order, precept.
aginkor *adj.* imperious, commanding.
aginpe *n.* authority.
aginpeko *n./adj.* subordinate.
aginpetu *v.t.* to dominate, to subordinate.
aginpetza *n.* dominating, subordinating.
aginpide *n.* authority, power to give orders.
agintaldi *n.* period during which a person holds power. *n.(gram.)* imperative mood.
agintari *n.* chief, authority, head.
agintariorde *n.* delegate.
agintaritza *n.* dignity and office of a chief, person in power.
agintza *n.* promise.
agintzaile *n.* promiser.
agiri *n.* document.
agirian *adv.* openly, manifestly, publicly.
agirika *adv.* reprimanding.
agirika egin *v.t.* to reproach, to reprimand, to rebuff.
-ago *comp.* Suffix which means: more.

Used with verbs, adjectives and adverbs. **Ederrago.** More beautiful, prettier. **Goizago.** Earlier. **Txikiago.** Smaller.
agor *adj.* dry. *adj.* unproductive, sterile.
agorgaitz *adj.* inexhaustible.
agorgarri *adj.* exhaustible, ending.
agorketa *n.* desiccation, dryness. *n.* sterilization.
agorki *adv.* unfruitfully, barrenly.
agorkor *adj.* drying.
agorraldi *n.* drought, time of drought.
agorreria *n.* dryness.
agorrezin *adj.* inexhaustible.
agorril *n.* August.
agortasun *n.* drought. *n.* sterility.
agorte *n.* drought.
agortezin *adj.* inexhaustible.
agortu *v.i.* to dry, to dry up, to go dry (fountain, river, etc.). *v.i.* to become unproductive, to be sterile.
agortzaile *adj.* sterilizing. *n.* sterilizer. *n.* drier.
agudo *adj.* quick. *adj.* diligent.
agudoki *adv.* quickly.
agudotasun *n.* quickness, promptness, rapidity.
agudotu *v.i.* to become active.
agur *int.* good-bye. *n.* greeting.
agure *n.* old man.
agur egin *v.t.* to greet. *v.t.* to say goodbye.
aguretasun *n.* old age (man).
aguretu *v.i.* to become an old man.
aguretzar *n.(augm.)* big old man.
agurgarri *adj.* respectable, venerable, distinguished.
agurgarriro *adv.* respectfully.
agurgarritasun *n.* respectability.
agurgile *n.* greeter.
agurka *adv.* greeting.
agurregile *n.* greeter. *n.* person who says goodbye.
agurritzak *n.(pl.)* salutation, greeting. *n.* farewell words.
agurtu *v.t.* to greet. *v.t.* to say goodbye.
agurtza *n.* salutation, greeting.
agurtza donea *n.* *(R. C. Ch.)* Holy Rosary.
agurtzaile *n.* person who greets.
agurtzapen *n.* salutation, greeting.
ah! *int.* exclamation which shows admiration.
ahabi *n.* *(bot.)* cranberry.
ahaide *n.* relative.
ahaidego *n.* kinship, kindred.
ahaidekeria *n.* incest.
ahaideria *n.* kinship, kindred.
ahaidetasun *n.* kinship. *n.* affinity
ahaidetu *v.i.* to become a relative of someone (by marriage).
ahal *n.* capacity, power, ability. *int.* I hope, I wish. *adj.* possible.
ahala *adv.* as much as possible.
ahalbide *n.* possibility.
ahaldun *adj.* capable *adj.* powerful,

mighty.

ahalduntasun n. capacity, capability. n. power.

ahalegin n. effort, trial, attempt, try, endeavor.

ahaleginak egin v.t. to do everything within one's power.

ahalegindu v.i. to do one's best, to try.

ahalegintsu adj. diligent.

ahalezin adj. incapable, impotent, unable. n. inability, incapacity.

ahalezko adj. optional adj. possible.

ahalgabe adj. impotent, incapable.

ahalgabetasun n. inability, impotence, incapacity, incapability.

ahalgarri adj. possible.

ahalguzti n. omnipotence, unlimited power.

ahalguztidun adj. almighty, omnipotent.

ahalik adv. as . . . as possible.

ahal izan v.i./v.t. to be possible, can, to be able to.

ahalke n. shame, shyness.

ahalkegabe adj. bold, impudent, cynical.

ahalkegabekeria n. shamelessness.

ahalkegabeki adv. shamelessly.

ahalkegarri adj. shameful, modest, indecent.

ahalkegarriki adv. shamefully, bashfully.

ahalketu v.i. to be ashamed, to feel shame, to blush.

ahalmen n. capacity, power, ability, capability.

ahalmendu v.t./v.i. to potentiate, to empower. v.t. to authorize.

ahalmenera n. (gram.) potential mood.

ahalmenez adv. powerfully, mightily.

ahalpide n. ability. n. possibility.

ahaltsu adj. powerful, mighty.

ahaltsuki adv. powerfully, mightily.

ahal ukan v.t. can, to be able to.

ahamen n. mouthful, bite.

ahantzarazi v.t. to cause to forget.

ahantzezin adj. unforgettable.

ahantzi v.t./v.i. to forget.

ahanzgarri adj. that which causes to forget. adj. easy to forget.

ahanzkor adj. forgetful, short of memory.

ahanzkortasun n. tendency to forget.

ahanztura n. forgetfulness.

ahapaldi n. strophe. n. stanza.

ahapeka adv. whispering, in a low voice.

ahardi n. (zool.) sow.

ahari n.(zool.) ram.

ahariki n. mutton.

ahariko n. (dim.) young ram.

aharitalde n. flock of rams.

aharito n. (dim.) young ram.

aharitopeka n. fight between male sheep held in a public place as entertainment.

aharra n. disturbance, mess, dispute.

aharrari n. trouble-maker; disputer, scolder.

aharratu v.i. to argue, to get angry.

aharrausi n. yawn.

aharrausi egin v.t. to yawn.

aharrausika adv. yawning.

ahate n. (zool.) duck.

ahateki n. duck meat.

ahateme n. female duck.

ahatetxo n. (dim.) duckling.

ahausi n. bark, yelp.

ahausi egin v.t. to bark.

ahausika adv. barking.

ahausilari adj. barking.

ahazgarri adj. forgettable, that causes to forget.

ahazkor adj. forgetful.

ahaztu v.i./v.t. to forget.

ahaztukor adj. forgetful.

aheria n. disease of the mouth.

ahi n. kind of mush, a sweet made with flour, milk and sugar, usually for infants.

ahidura n. exhaustion, fatigue, tiredness.

ahigaitz adj. inexhaustible.

ahigarri adj. exhausting. adj. exhaustible.

ahipen n. exhaustion.

ahitu v.i. to become exhausted, to be finished.

ahizpa n. sister (of a woman or girl).

ahizpatasun n. sisterhood.

ahizperdi n. stepsister.

ahizporde n. stepsister.

aho n. mouth. n. entrance of a cave. n. mouth of a river, bell, etc. n. one of a pair of swinging doors.

ahobatasun n. unanimity.

ahobateko adj. unanimous.

ahobatez adv. unanimously.

ahobero adj. indiscreet.

ahoberokeria n. exaggeration.

ahobete n. mouthful.

ahobetean adv. openly.

ahobeteko adj. tasteful, appetizing, savory.

ahobizar n. cutting edge.

ahodun n. sharp.

ahoeder adj. eloquent, fluent.

ahoeri n. disease of the mouth.

ahogain n.(anat.) palate, roof of the mouth.

ahogaizto adj. bold, impudent, talkative.

ahogaiztotu v.i. to speak impudently; to be impudent, to become impudent.

ahogarbi adj. well-spoken.

ahogarbiketa n. cleaning or rinsing of the mouth.

ahogozagarri adj. delicious, flavorful.

ahogozo n. good taste, good flavor.

ahohandi adj. indiscreet, exaggerating.

ahohizkuntza n. spoken language.

ahokada n. bite, morsel of food. n.

mouthful, puff of smoke. *n.* exaggeration.

ahokadura *n.* engaging of gears, connection, link, interlocking (ideas, etc.).

ahokari *adj.* oral, vocal. *n.* shouter.

ahokats *n.* bad breath.

ahokatu *v.t.* to plug in, to connect. *v.t.* to fit the end of one tube into another. *v.t.* to imbricate, to overlap.

ahoko *adj.* relating to the mouth. *n.* punch in the mouth. *adj.* vocal.

ahokomin *n.* pain of the mouth.

ahokorapilo *n.* tongue twister.

aholkatu *v.t.* to advise, to counsel.

aholku *n.* advice, counsel.

aholkuemale *n.* counselor, advisor.

aholku eman *v.t.* to advise, to counsel, to give advice.

aholkugarri *adj.* advisable.

aholkulari *n.* advisor, counselor.

ahoneko *adj.* gourmet.

ahopats *n.* burp.

ahopean *adv.* secretly, whispering, in whispers.

ahopeka *adv.* whispering, secretly.

ahopekatu *v.t.* to whisper.

ahopeko *n.* secret, confidence.

ahopetik *adv.* whispering, secretly.

ahoratu *v.t.* to raise something to the mouth. *v.t.* to put something into the mouth. *v.i.* to come to mind, to occur to.

ahosabai *n.(anat.)* palate, roof of the mouth.

ahosabaiko *adj.* palatine.

ahosabaitu *v.t.* to palatize.

ahoskatu *v.t.* to pronounce, to vocalize, to articulate, to utter.

ahotan erabili *v.t.* to mention.

ahotik-ahora *adv.* mouth to mouth.

ahots *n.* voice.

ahotxar *n.* bad taste in the mouth.

ahotz *n.* chaff.

ahotzar *n.* big mouth. *adj.* big mouth, talkative.

ahoz *adv.* orally.

ahozabal *adj.* chatterbox. *adj.* impudent, exaggerative.

ahozabalik *adv.* astonished, in an astonished manner.

ahozabalka *adv.* yawning.

ahozeru *n.(anat.)* palate, roof of the mouth.

ahozgora *adv.* lying on one's back.

ahozkera *n.* way of speaking.

ahozko *adj.* oral.

ahozpez *adv.* lying face down, in a face down position.

ahozpezka *adv.* face down.

ahozpeztu *v.i.* to kneel down, to prostrate, to lie flat.

ahozuri *n.* flatterer. *adj.* flattering. *n./adj.* gourmet, gourmand.

ahul *adj.* weak.

ahulaldi *n.* period of weakness, depression.

ahuldu *v.i.* to become weak. *v.t.* to weaken.

ahuldura *n.* weakness, feebleness, attenuation. *n.* depression.

ahuleria *n.* weakness, feebleness, debility.

ahulezia *n.* weakness.

ahuleziadun *adj.* weak, asthenic.

ahulgarri *adj.* depressing; causing weakness, debilitating.

ahulkeria *n.* weakness, feebleness.

ahulki *adv.* weakly, feebly.

ahultasun *n.* weakness, feebleness, debility.

ahuntz *n.(zool.)* female goat.

ahuntzadar *n.* female goat horn. *n.(bot.)* terebinth tree.

ahuntzain *n.* goatherd.

ahuntzume *n.* kid, young goat.

ahunzbizar *n.* goatee.

ahunzkara *n.* mating period of female goats.

ahunzki *n.* female goat's meat.

ahunzlarru *n.* female goatskin, leather made from female goatskin.

ahunztalde *n.* herd of goats.

ahunztegi *n.* hut for goatherds.

ahuna *n.* small female goat.

Ahunamendi *n.* Mt. Anie (the highest mountain in the Basque Country).

ahur *n.* palm of the hand, cavity of the hand. *adj.* concave.

ahurbiko *adj.* biconcave.

ahurbikotasun *n.* biconcavity, quality of being concave on both sides.

ahurka *adv.* by the handful (seed, etc.).

ahurtasun *n.* concavity.

ahutz *n.* cheek.

ai *int.* ouch! Exclamation which denotes pain, sorrow, grief. *n.* sigh. *int.* I hope. Expression which denotes strong desire.

aida! *int.* exclamation to encourage cattle to move.

aiduru *adv.* expecting.

aieka *adv.* groaning.

aienatu *v.i.* to disappear.

aiene *n.* lament; complaint.

ai ene! *int.* exclamation of depression, loneliness, sorrow, grief. Groan!

aiene egin *v.t.* to groan, to grieve.

aieneka *adv.* groaning, grieving, moaning, complaining.

aieru *n.* conjecture, assumption. *n.* sign.

aierukor *adj.* suspicious.

aierukortasun *n.* suspiciousness.

aierupen *n.* conjecture, suspicion.

aierutsu *adj.* suspicious.

aieruz *adv.* suspiciously.

aiezka *adv.* groaning, grieving, moaning.

aihen *n.* branch of the grapevine.

aihenadar *n.* branch of the grapevine.

aihendu *v.i.* to climb (grapevine).

aihenondo *n.* main trunk of the

grapevine.

aihentsu *adj.* full of vine shoots, viney.

aiher *n.* inclination, tendency. *n.* hatred. *n.* revenge.

aiherbide *n.* cause for hating someone.

aihergo *n.* strong dislike.

aiher izan *v.i.* to be revengeful. *v.i.* to feel like, to long to, to have a tendency to.

aiherki *adv.* revengefully, hatefully.

aiherkor *adj.* vindictive, revengeful, resentful.

aiherkunde *n.* tendency, inclination.

aiherkuntza *n.* hatred. *n.* revenge.

aihertsu *adj.* vindictive, revengeful, resentful, unforgiving.

aihertu *v.i.* to be up to, to be inclined to, to tend to. *v.t.* to hate.

aihotz *n.* kind of scythe to cut branches or shrubs.

aihozkatu *v.t.* to scythe.

aika *adv.* groaning, grieving, moaning.

aika ari *v.i.* to grieve, to lament.

aiko-maiko *n.* pretext, excuse.

aina *adv.* as much as.

aingeru *n.(theol.)* angel. *n.* little boy (girl) dressed in white. *n.* dead baby.

aingeru-belar *n.(bot.)* angelica garden.

aingerugisa *adv.* angelically.

aingeru-kanpai *n.* small church bell tolled when a child dies.

aingeruki *adv.* angelically.

aingerukote *n.* large figure of an angel.

aingerulili *n.(bot.)* marigold.

aingerutalde *n.* group of angels, host of angels.

aingerutan hil *v.i.* to die immediately after birth.

aingerutar *adj.* angelical.

aingerutxo *n.(dim.)* little angel. *n.(fig.)* baby.

aingeruxka *n.(dim.)* little angel.

aingeruzko *adj.* angelic.

aingira *n.(zool.)* eel.

aingiraki *n.* eel meat.

aingirakume *n.(dim.)* small eel.

aingirategi *n.* eel hatchery.

aingiratxo *n.(dim.)* young eel.

aingura *n.* anchor.

ainguraketa *n.* casting anchor.

ainguraleku *n.* anchoring-ground.

ainguratu *v.t.* to anchor, to drop anchor, to cast anchor.

ainguratxo *n.(dim.)* small anchor.

ainguratzar *n.(augm.)* big anchor.

aintza *n.* glory. *n.* fame.

aintzadun *adj.* glorious.

aintzagabeko *adj.* inglorious.

aintzagarri *adj.* glorious, glorifiable.

aintzakotzat hartu *v.t.* to take into consideration.

aintzaldu *v.t.* to glorify.

aintzalgarri *adj.* glorious, glorifiable.

aintzapen *n.* glorification.

aintzat hartu *v.t.* to take into consideration.

aintzatsu *adj.* glorious; famous, illustrious.

aintzigar *n.* frost.

aintzina *adv.* a long time ago, in ancient times.

aintzinako *adj.* ancient.

aintzinaro *n.* Ancient Age.

aintzinatasun *n.* quality of being ancient, antiquity.

aintzinate *n.* ancient times, antiquity.

aintzindari *n.* pioneer, predecessor.

aintzindarigo *n.* leadership.

aintzindaritasun *n.* quality of being chief; power, authority.

aintzindaritza *n.* leadership.

aintzindu *v.t.* to anticipate, to foresee, to forestall. *v.t.* to surpass. *v.i.* to go forward.

aintzinean *adv.* in ancient times, a long time ago, before.

aintzineko *adj.* preceding. *n.* ancestor. *adj.* ancient.

aintzinkari *n.* antiquarian, antiquary.

aintzin solas *n.* foreword.

aintzintasun *n.* antecedence; quality of being ancient. *n.* advance, progress. *n.* superiority.

aipa *v.t.* to mention. Var. of the verb *aipatu.*

aipabide *n.* mention.

aipaera *n.* mention, citation.

aipaezin *n.* unmentionable.

aipagabe *adv.* virtually, implicitly. *adv.* without mentioning.

aipagarri *adj.* mentionable. *adj.* famous, illustrious, celebrated.

aipagarriro *adv.* memorably.

aipaketa *n.* enunciation, declaration.

aipakizun *n.* mention.

aipaldi *n.* time to mention. *n.* act of mentioning, reference, allusion.

aipamen *n.* mention, honorary mention, reference, quote, citation. *n.* fame.

aipari *n.* citer, quoter.

aipatu *v.t.* to mention, to make reference to, to name.

aipatzaile *n.* person who mentions or makes a reference to, citer, quoter.

aipu *n.* fame, reputation; mention.

aipuera *n.* mention, reference, quotation, citation, allusion.

aipugabe *adj.* discredited.

aipugabetu *v.i.* to discredit, to lose one's reputation.

aipugabezia *n.* failure to mention.

aipu galdu *v.t.* to discredit, to disgrace.

aipugalketa *n.* discredit, disgrace.

aipuoneko *adj.* distinguished, accredited, reputable.

airatu *v.i.* to raise in the air. *v.i.* to leave from, to go from.

aire *n.* air. *n.* overhanded blow. *n.* resemblance, likeness, similarity, appearance, aspect.

aireaketa *n.* ventilation.

airealdi *n.* exposure to air, ventilation, aeration.

airean *adv.* in the air.

airean egon *v.i.* to be uncertain, to be up in the air.

aireberritu *v.t.* to expose to air, to aerate, to ventilate.

airebide *n.* air route.

airegabeki *adv.* ungracefully, awkwardly.

airegailu *n.* fan.

aireketa *n.* ventilation, aeration.

aireko *adj.* aerial, airy, air, pertaining to air. *adj.* similar.

aireneurkin *n.* aerometer.

aireontzi *n.* plane, airplane, airship.

aireplanu *n.* plane, airplane.

aireportu *n.* airport.

aireraketa *n.* takeoff, taking off.

aireratu *v.t.* to take off, to blow away in the wind.

airestatu *v.t.* to ventilate, to aerate, to oxygenate.

airetu *v.t.* to ventilate, to aerate, to expose to fresh air, to air out.

aireuntzi *n.* airship, dirigible, plane.

aireztabide *n.* ventilation system, ventilation duct.

aireztaketa *n.* ventilation.

aireztapen *n.* ventilation.

aireztatu *v.t./v.i.* to ventilate, to be ventilated.

airos *adj.* joyful, jolly, lively, merry.

airosketa *n.* grace of form or movement.

airoski *adv.* gracefully, lightly.

aise *n.* ease. *adv.* easy, easily, with ease.

aiseki *adv.* easily, with ease, comfortably.

aisetasun *n.* ease, facility. *n.* comfort.

aita *n.* father.

aitabesoetako *n.* godfather.

aitabitxi *n.* godfather.

aitagandiko *adj.* paternal, fatherly.

aitaginarreba *n.* father-in-law.

aitagisako *adj.* paternal.

aitagoi *n.* patriarch. *n.* grandfather.

aitagoigo *n.* patriarchy, patriarchate.

aitagurea *n.* the Our Father (prayer), the Lord's Prayer.

aitahilketa *n.* parricide; patricide.

aitalehen *n.* progenitor, ancestor, forefather. *n.* patriarch.

aitalehenaldi *n.* age of the patriarchs.

aitalehengo *n.* position of being a patriarch.

aitamak *n.* parents.

aitaponteko *n.* godfather.

aitaren *adj.* paternal, fatherly. *n.* sign of the cross.

aitaren egin *v.t.* to cross oneself, to make the sign of the cross.

aitasaindu *n.* Pope.

aitasaindugo *n.* papacy.

aitasaindutasun *n.* papacy.

aitasaindutza *n.* papacy, pontificate.

aitasantu *n.* Pope.

aita-semeak *n.* father and son.

aitasun *n.* fatherhood, paternity.

aitatar *adj.* resembling the father.

aitatasun *n.* paternity, parenthood.

aitatxo *n.(dim.)* daddy.

aitatzako *adj.* reputed, commonly considered as father.

aitazale *adj.* fond of one's father.

aitazaletu *v.i.* to be or become attached to one's father.

aitazulo *adj.* extremely attached to one's father.

aitazulotu *v.i.* to be or become extremely attached to one's father.

aitita *n.* grandfather.

aitona *n.* grandfather.

aiton-amonak *n.* grandparents.

aiton-seme *n.* nobleman.

aitor *n.* declaration. *n.* confession, testimony. *n.* legendary patriarch of the Basque Country considered to be the father of all the Basques.

aitorbide *n.* way of declaring, way of confessing.

aitorde *n.* stepfather. *n.* legal guardian.

aitordego *n.* co-guardianship.

aitoren seme *n.* nobleman.

aitoren semetasun *n.* nobility.

aitorgaitz *adj.* difficult to confess.

aitorgarri *adj.* avowable, confessable.

aitorgile *n.* testifier, witness.

aitorketa *n.* confession; declaration.

aitorkide *n.* witness who confirms the evidence presented by another witness, acollaborating witness.

aitorkizun *n.* declaration, confession (to be declared in the future).

aitorkuntza . declaration. *n.* confession.

aitorlari *n.* confessor. *n.* witness.

aitorleku *n.* confessional.

aitormen *n.* testimony, declaration. *n.* confession.

aitorpen *n.* declaration, testimony. *n.* confession.

aitorraldi *n.* testimony, declaration; confession. *n.* time or turn to confess, time or turn to declare.

aitorrarazi *v.t.* to cause someone to declare, to confess.

aitorrarazle *n.* wheedler, one who gets information out of another.

aitorregile *n.* witness, confessor.

aitorrentzule *n.* person who listens to a declaration. *n.* confessor (priest).

aitorrerazle *n.* wheedler, one who gets information out of another.

aitorrezin *adj.* unconfessable, undeclarable.

aitortu *v.t.* to declare. *v.t.* to confess.

aitortza *n.* declaration. *n.* confession.

aitortzaile *n.* witness. *n.* confessor.

Aitortzako Sakramendu *n.(eccl.)* Sacrament of Confession.

aitzakia *n.* excuse.

aitzaki-maitzaki *n.* excuse.

aitzakitu *v.t.* to make an excuse.
aitzakizale *adj.* fond of making excuses.
aitzin *adv.* before. *prep.* in front of.
aitzin- *(gram.)* Prefix signifying before, fore-, pre-, proto-.
aitzina *adv.* from now on.
aitzinadanik *adv.* previously, in anticipation.
aitzinago *adv.* from now on. *adv.* farther.
aitzinagoko *adj.* preceding, foregoing.
aitzinalde *n.* facade, front part.
aitzinaldean *prep.* in front of.
aitzinalderatu *v.t./v.i.* to move forward, to advance.
aitzinaldi *n.* progress, advance.
aitzinapen *n.* anticipation. *n.* advance, progress.
aitzinaratu *v.i.* to pass, to move forward, to advance.
aitzinarazi *v.t.* to cause to move forward, to make an advance, to cause to advance.
aitzindari *n.* chief, boss. *n.* predecessor, pioneer.
aitzindaritza *n.* job of a guide, leadership.
aitzindegi *n.* facade.
aitzindu *v.t.* to advance. *v.i.* to anticipate, to initiate, to go forward. *v.t.* to prevent, to foresee.
aitzinean *prep.* in front of. *adv.* in ancient times, before, a long time ago.
aitzineratu *v.i.* to advance, to take the lead, to move to the front.
aitzinerazi *v.t.* to advance, to make (someone) advance.
aitzineuskara *n.* old Basque, proto-Basque.
aitzinjakite *n.* prescience, foreknowledge.
aitzinkontu *n.* estimation, estimate. *n.(econ.)* budget.
aitzin solas *n.* foreword, prologue, preface.
aitzintasun *n.* antecedence, precedence, priority.
aitzur *n.* hoe.
aitzurkada *n.* blow with a hoe.
aitzurkatu *v.t.* to till with a hoe.
aitzurketa *n.* tillage, cultivation with a hoe.
aitzurkintza *n.* digging.
aitzurkula *n.* two-pronged hoe.
aitzurlari *n.* digger, hoer, excavator.
aitzurraldi *n.* digging time.
aitzurtu *v.t.* to dig with a hoe.
aitzurtxo *n.(dim.)* small hoe.
aizkol- Var. of *aizkora.* Used in compound words.
aizkolari *n.* woodcutter.
aizkora *n.* ax.
aizkoraburu *n.* head of an ax.
aizkoraho *n.* cutting edge of an ax.
aizkorajoko *n.* wood chopping (with ax) contest.

aizkorakada *n.* blow with an ax.
aizkorakirten *n.* handle of the ax.
aizkoratu *v.t.* to cut with an ax.
aizkoratxo *n.(dim.)* small ax.
aizto *n.* knife. Contr. of *aitz + to.*
aiztogile *n.* knife maker, razor maker.
aiztogintza *n.* manufacture of knives.
aiztogirten *n.* handle of the knife.
aiztokada *n.* cut, slash.
aiztokatu *v.t.* to stab.
aiztotzar *n. (aug.)* big knife.
aiztur *n.* shearing scissors.
aizun *adj.* false, pseudo.
ajaja *int.* exclamation which denotes laughing. Ha, ha, ha.
aje *n.* deterioration. *n.* an upset; hangover.
ajedun *adj.* defective. *adj.* upset.
ajetu *v.i.* to be upset.
-ak *art.* suffix which expresses the plural of the definite article. **Umeak etorri dira.** The children have come. *art.* suffix which expresses one agent. **Gizonak jan du.** The man has eaten.
akademia *n.* academy.
akara *n. (bot.)* spikenard.
akasdun *adj.* notched, indented. *adj.* defective, imperfect.
akasdura *n.* chip, dent.
akastsu *adj.* chipped, dented.
akastu *v.t.* to notch, to dent, to chip.
akats *n.* notch, indentation, nick, chip. *n.* fault, defect
akelarre *n.* meeting of witches and wizards.
aker *n.(zool.)* male goat.
akerbizar *n.* pointed beard of a goat.
aketo *n.* kid, young male goat.
aketz *n.* male pig.
akiakula *n.* pretext, excuse.
akialdi *n.* fatigue, tiredness, exhaustion.
akiarazi *v.t.* to fatigue, to tire, to exhaust.
akitu *v.i.* to be tired.
akordeoi *n.* accordion.
akordio *n.* agreement. *n.* pact, contract.
akordiogarri *adj.* agreeable, in conformity with.
akordiotu *v.i.* to agree. *v.i.* to consent, to contract.
akordiozko *adj.* conventional.
akordu *n.* memory.
akorgabetu *v.i.* to disagree.
akorgabezia *n.* disagreement.
akuilaketa *n.* spurring.
akuilari *n.* person who spurs the oxen in contests (popular Basque sport).
akuilatu *v.t.* to incite; to spur. *v.t. (fig.)* stimulate.
akuilatzaile *n.* inciter, one who spurs. *n.(fig.)* stimulator.
akuilu *n.* spur, goad.
akuilukada *n.* a strike with a spur.

akuilukari *n.* spurrer.
akula *n.(zool.)* garfish, fish which resembles a small sword-fish.
akura *n.* to rent, to lease, to rent out, to let. *n.* rental
akuragarri *adj.* rentable.
akuratu *v.t.* to rent; to hire.
akuri *n.(zool.)* guinea pig.
akusatibo *(gram.)* the accusative case.
akustika *n.* acoustics.
al *adv.* perhaps, maybe. Word used to make questions. **Etorri al da?** Has he come?
ala *conj.* or. Implies a choice; usually used in interrogative sentences. **Bai ala ez?** Yes or no?
-ala *(gram.)* Verbal suffix meaning as.
alaba *n.* daughter; native of (woman).
alababakar *n.* only daughter.
alabaina *int.* of course, indeed. *conj.* however, although. *conj.* in fact.
alabanagusi *n.* eldest, first-born (woman).
alabaponteko *n.* goddaughter.
alabatasun *n.* state of being a daughter.
alabatxi *n.* goddaughter.
alabatxo *n.* (dim.) small daughter.
alabatzako *n.* adopted daughter.
alabatzat hartu *v.t.* to adopt a daughter.
alabehar *n.* fate, destiny.
alabeharreko *adj.* unavoidable, necessary.
alabeharrez *adv.* casually. *adv.* fatally.
alaborde *n.* stepdaughter.
alafede! *int.* I swear to!
alai *adj.* happy, joyful, rejoicing, content, merry, gay.
alaiarazi *v.t.* to make (someone) happy, to fill (someone) with joy.
alaigarri *adj.* cordial, comforting, happy, joyful.
alaiki *adv.* merrily, happily, joyfully, joyously.
alaikiro *adv.* merrily, happily, joyfully, joyously.
alaitasun *n.* happiness, joy.
alaitsu *adj.* happy, merry, joyful, joyous.
alaitu *v.i.* to be or become happy, to be joyful. *v.t.* to make happy, to fill with joy.
alaitzaile *adj.* joyful, happy, joyous, spreading of joy or happiness.
alajaina! *int.* wow!, by Jove!
alajainkoa! *int.* exclamation to ascertain.
alanbratu *v.t.* to fence with wire.
alanbre *n.* wire
alanbresi *n.* wire fence.
alarao *n.* outcry, shout, howl, scream.
alargun *n.* widow. *n.* widower. *adj.* widowed.
alargundu *v.i.* to become a widow(er).
alargunketa *n.* act of becoming a widow or a widower.

alarguntasun *n.* widowhood. *n.* widowerhood.
alarguntsa *n.* widow.
alarguntza *n.* widowhood. *n.* widowerhood.
alarguntzaro *n.* time of widowhood or widowerhood.
alartze *n.* threshold.
alatu *v.t.* to swear. *v.t.* to cause pain, to torment. *v.t.* to feed, to graze.
alatzaile *n.* feeder, person who feeds.
alba *n.* dawn.
albain *n.* basting.
albaindu *v.t.* to baste.
albaindura *n.* act of basting.
albainorratz *n.* basting needle.
albainu *n.* basting.
albaitari *n.* veterinarian.
albaitaritza *n.* veterinary medicine.
albarikoke *n.(bot.)* apricot.
albarikondo *n.(bot.)* apricot tree.
albate *n.* side door.
alberri . neighboring village.
albistari *n.* reporter. *n.* magazine, newspaper.
albistaritza *n.* reporting.
albiste *n.* news.
albo *n.* side. *n.* aspect. *n.(bot.)* planer tree.
albo-alboka *adv.* stumbling, staggering.
alboan *prep.* beside, next to. *adv.* close, near.
alboka *n.* type of Basque horn (musical instrument).
albokada *n.* hitting with the side of the body.
albokari *n.* person who plays the Basque horn.
alboko *adj.* neighbor. *n.* blow in the side (body, ship, etc.) *adj.* adjacent, close, neighboring.
albokomin *n.* pain in the side of the body.
albora egin *v.t.* to move aside, to move over.
alboraketa *n.* proximity, approaching.
alborapen *n.* approaching, approach. *n.* slant; slope.
alboratu *v.i.* to approach, to come close to. *v.i.* to move aside. *v.t.* to put aside.
aldaba *n.* door knocker.
aldabakada *n.* loud knocking.
aldabera *adj.* variable. *adj.* inconstant.
aldaberatasun *n.* variability.
aldabide *n.* manner of transition.
aldaera *n.* variation. *n.* moving.
aldaerazi *v.t.* to transform, to mutate.
aldaerazpen *n.* modification, transformation, mutation.
aldaezin *adj.* unchangeable, invariable, constant.
aldaezinez *adv.* invariably, inmutably, unalterably.
aldaezinezko *adj.* invariable, unchangeable.

aldaezinik *adv.* invariably.
aldaezintasun *n.* inmutability, invariability.
aldagabe *adj.* invariable, constant, unaltered.
aldagai *n.* variant, variable. *adj.* variable.
aldagaitz *adj.* invariable, unchangeable.
aldagaizkiro *adv.* unalterably, invariably, inmutably.
aldagaiztasun *n.* invariability, inmutability.
aldagarri *adj.* changeable, variable; inconstant. *n,* extra change of clothes.
aldagarritasun *n.* variability.
aldagela *n.* dressing-room, locker room, fitting room.
aldagune *n.* time of change. *n.* transition area.
aldakaitz *adj.* invariable, constant, unchangeable.
aldakera *n.* manner of changing. *n.* change, modification, mutation.
aldakeria *n.* frivolity; versatility.
aldaketa *n.* change, mutation, transformation.
aldakoi *adj.* versatile, variable.
aldakor *adj.* changeable, fickle, variable, versatile.
aldakortasun *n.* versatility, inconstancy; variability.
aldakortu *v.i.* to become inconsistent.
aldakuntza *n.* change, alteration, transformation.
aldamen *n.* vicinity, side. *n.* place beside a person.
aldamenak *n. (pl.)* surroundings, outskirts (of a town).
aldamenean *prep.* close to, near, next to.
aldameneko *adj.* adjacent, neighboring.
aldameneratu *v.i.* to place oneself at the side, to place onself at one's side.
aldamio *n.* scaffold.
aldapa *n.* slope, hill; ramp.
aldapabehera *n.* downhill.
aldapadun *adj.* steep.
aldapagabe *adj.* flat, slopeless, without steep slopes.
aldapagora *n.* steep slope. *n.* uphill.
aldapatsu *adj.* steep.
aldaragarri *adj.* detachable, separatable.
aldaratu *v.i.* to leave, to move away from.
aldare *n.* altar.
aldaregile *n.* altar-maker.
aldareko Jaun *n.* Eucharist.
aldaremahai *n.* altar.
aldarenagusi *n.* main altar.
aldaretxo *n.(dim.)* small altar.
aldarezapi *n.* altar-cloth.
aldarri *n.* announcement, edict,

decree. *n.* clamor.
aldarri egin *v.t.* to proclaim publicly, to announce publicly.
aldarrika *adv.* shouting, shoutingly, clamorously.
aldarrikaketa *n.* declaration, proclamation, promulgation.
aldarrikapen *n.* declaration, proclamation, promulgation.
aldarrikari *n.* town crier.
aldarrikatu *v.t.* to proclaim, to announce, shouting.
aldarriketa *n.* proclamation, promulgation.
aldarrilari *n.* town crier.
aldarte *n.* chance, occasion, opportunity, free time. *n.* physical condition. *n.* humor, wit.
aldatoki *n.* fitting room, locker room. *n.* place where one changes (trains, planes, etc.)
aldats *n.* slope, hill, rising ground with slope.
aldatu *v.t.* to change, to alter. *v.t.* to change clothes. *v.t.* to move
aldatzaile *n.* changer.
alde *n.* area, region. *prep.* in favor of, for. *int.* go! move away! leave! *prep.* on behalf of.
-alde *(gram.)* Suffix indicating proximity, nearness. **Elizalde.** Area near the church.
aldean *prep.* with oneself, next to, beside. *prep.* in comparison with, in comparison to.
aldean eraman *v.t.* to take, to carry with oneself.
aldeaskodun *adj.* multilateral.
aldeaskotako *adj.* multilateral.
aldebakar *adj.* unilateral, one-sided.
aldebateko *adj.* unilateral, one-sided.
aldebatekotasun *n.* unilaterality, one-sidedness, unilateralism.
alde batera *adv.* on one hand.
aldebateratu *v.t.* to separate, to segregate, to exclude.
alde batetik *adv.* on one hand.
aldebiko *adj.* bilateral, two-sided.
aldebitako *adj.* bilateral.
aldebitakotasun *n.* bilateralism.
alde egin *v.t.* to run away, to escape, to leave.
alde eragin *v.t.* to force to leave.
aldegite *n.* escape.
aldekaitz *adj.* inseparable.
aldekeria *n.* partiality, favoritism.
aldekide *n.* follower, supporter, partisan. *adj.* equilateral.
aldeko *adj.* close, adjacent, lateral. *adj.* favorite, favorable. *n.* neighbor.
aldekortasun *n.* partiality.
aldendu *v.i.* to be or become lost. *v.t.* to separate, to divide.
aldera *prep.* towards.
alderagarri *adj.* avoidable.
alderantzi *n.* reverse side.
alderantzikatu *v.t.* to reverse, to

invert, to turn over.

alderantziketa *n.* inverse, inversion.

alderantzitu *v.t.* to reverse, to invert.

alderantziz *adv.* vice versa, in reverse, backwards.

alderantzizko *adj.* backwards, in reverse.

alderanzkarri *adj.* reversible.

alderanzketa *n.* inversion.

alderatu *v.i.* to come closer, to approach. *v.i.* to leave, to move away from. *v.i.* to turn on one side.

alderatzaile *n.* excluder, discriminator, segregator.

alderazi *v.t.* to cause to leave. *v.t.* to reject; to separate.

alderazle *n.* separator.

alderdi *n.* side; direction. *n.* political party; the Basque political party E.A.J.-P.N.V. *n.* side of the body. *n. (anat.)* limb.

alderdikatu *v.i.* to lean to one side.

alderdikeria *n.* partiality, bias, prejudice.

alderdikide *n.* partisan, supporter, follower of a political party. *n.* fellow partisan.

alderdikidetu *v.i.* to affiliate with a political party.

alderdiko *adj.* belonging to a political party. *n.* slap (in the face).

alderdikoi *adj.* partial, partisan.

alderdikoitasun *n.* partiality, partisanship.

alderdikor *adj.* biased, prejudiced, sectarian.

alderditar *adj.* partisan.

alderditu *v.i.* to turn on one side.

alderditxar *n.* difficulty, obstacle, inconvenience.

alderkide *n.* fellow-partisan.

aldetik *prep.* on behalf of, on the part of.

aldetxar . disadvantage, drawback. *n.* con (as in the pros and cons).

aldez *prep.* on behalf of, in the name of.

aldez edo moldez *adv.* in one way or another.

aldezin *adj.* unavoidable.

aldezkari *n.* follower, supporter, partisan; protector.

aldezkatu *v.t.* to defend, to protect, to support.

aldezketa *n* defense, support.

aldezlari *n.* protector, defender.

aldezpen *n.* defense.

aldeztu *v.t.* to defend, to protect, to support.

aldi *n.* time, occasion, session.

-aldi *(gram.)* suffix which means turn. **Ikustaldi.** Visit.

aldia eman *v.t.* to spend time.

aldiak *n. (pl.)* periods of whims, fancies, less severe mental disorders.

aldiak izan *v.t.* to have periods of whims.

aldian-aldian *adv.* periodically, from time to time.

aldi bakoitzean *adv.* each time.

aldiberean *adv.* simultaneously.

aldibereko *adj.* coetaneous. *adj.* simultaneous.

aldiberetasun *n.* simultaneousness, simultaneity.

aldiberetu *v.t.* to synchronize.

aldibiko *adj.* biphasic.

aldigaiztu *v.i.* to faint, to lose consciousness.

aldika *adv.* every now and then. *adv.* in turn, by turns, taking turns.

aldikada *n.* period of time, epoch.

aldikako *adj.* alternative.

aldikatu *v.t.* to alternate; to substitute.

aldiko *adj.* contemporary, of the same age or epoch. *adj.* temporary, temporal.

aldikotasun *n.* temporality.

aldikotu *v.t.* to bring up to date, to update, to modernize.

aldioro *adv.* every time.

alditsu *adj.* versatile, inconsistent. *adj.* lunatic.

alditxar *n.* slight indisposition. *n.* misfortune, disgrace.

alditxarreko *adj.* unfortunate, unlucky.

aldiune *n.* interval.

aldiuneko *adj.* instantaneous.

aldiz *conj.* but, on the other hand, on the contrary, however, although, nevertheless.

aldizka *adv.* in lots, in threes. *adv.* alternately, at intervals.

aldizkako *adj.* temporal, temporary. *adj.* intermittent.

aldizkakotasun *n.* intermittence.

aldizkari *n.* periodical, magazine.

aldizkatu *v.t.* to take turns, to alternate, to change.

aldizko *adj.* variable, alternative, inconstant. *adj.* occasional, recurrent, periodical.

aldizkotasun *n.* periodicity, recurrence, intermittence.

aldra *n.* group, crowd, bunch.

aldrebes *adv.* vice versa, in the opposite way, backwards.

aldrebeskeria *n.* awkwardness, clumsiness. *n.* mistake, blunder, usually in speaking.

aldrebestu *v.t./v.i.* to confuse, to disorder, to disarrange.

ale *n.* grain, seed; unit of fruit (grape, apple, etc.). *n.* sample, unity of countable nouns.

-ale *(gram.)* suffix which indicates agent in some verbs which end in -an (jan, edan, etc.). **Jale.** Eater.

alebanatu *v.t.* to shell out grain from an ear of corn etc.

aledun *adj.* full of grains.

alegabe *adj.* without grains.

alegeratu *v.i./v.t.* to be or become

happy.

alegia *n.* fable, allegory, parable. *n.* simulation, fake. *adv.* certainly. *conj.* That is to say.

alegiaz *adv.* allegorically.

alegiazko *adj.* allegorical. *adj.* fake, simulated.

alegiaztu *v.t.* to allegorize, to turn into allegory.

alegikeria *n.* fake.

alegilari *n.* fabulist, writer of fables.

alejale *adj.* graniverous, grain-eating.

aleketa *n.* abundance of grain.

alemaniera *n.* German (language).

aletegi *n.* barn.

aletsu *adj.* full of grains.

aletu *v.t.* to shake out grain.

aletxo *n. (dim.)* small grain.

aleztatu *v.i.* to mature, to form grains.

alfabeta *n.* alphabet.

alfabetagabe. *adj.* illiterate.

alfabetatu *v.t.* to teach elementary knowledge.

alfer *adj./n.* lazy, idle; idler, loafer.

alferkeria *n.* laziness.

alferki *adv.* lazily, indolently, languidly.

alferlan *n.* useless work.

alferraldi *n.* lazy time; period of laziness.

alferrarena egin *v.t.* to be lazy.

alferreko *adj.* useless, worthless.

alferrik *adv.* in vain, fruitlessly.

alferrikako *adj.* useless, superfluous.

alferrik izan *v.i.* to be in vain.

alfertasun *n.* laziness.

alfertu *v.i.* to become lazy.

alfertzar *adj. (augm.)* very lazy.

alga *n. (bot.)* alga.

algara *n.* loud laughter, noisy laugh, guffaw.

algaraka *adv.* laughing loudly.

algarroba *n. (bot.)* carob bean.

algebra *n.* algebra.

algodoi *n.* cotton.

algodoigile *n.* cotton manufacturer, cotton miller.

algodoigintza *n.* cotton manufacture, cotton milling.

alguazil *n.* peace-officer.

alienatu *v.t./v.i.* to destroy someone's personality.

alienazio *n.* destruction of someone's personality.

aliketak *n.(pl.)* pliers.

alkandora *n.* shirt.

alkate *n.* mayor.

alkatekeria *n.* despotism or vile act performed by the mayor.

alkatesa *n.* female mayor. *n.* mayor's wife.

alkatetasun *n.* office or job of the mayor, mayoralty.

alkatetu *v.i.* to become mayor, to be mayor.

alkatetxe *n.* city hall, town hall.

alkatetza *n.* position of mayor, job of mayor, mayoralty.

alkatorde *n.* acting mayor.

alkatxofa *n.(bot.)* artichoke.

alkohol *n.* alcohol.

alkoholdun *adj.* alcoholic.

alkoholezko *adj* alcoholic.

alkoholeztatu *v.t.* to alcoholize.

alkoholkeria *n.* alcoholism.

alkoholontzi *n.* bottle or container of alcohol.

alkoholtsu *adj.* alcoholic.

alkoholtzale *adj./n.* alcoholic, person fond of alcohol.

alkoholtzaletu *v.i.* to become fond of alcohol.

almaiz *n.* mortar.

almidoi *n.* starch.

almidoidun *adj.* starched.

almidoitsu *adj.* starched.

almidoizko *adj.* starched.

almidoiztu *v.t.* to starch (clothing).

almitz *n. (bot.)* amaranth.

aloger *n.* salary, wage.

alogeratu *v.t.* to hire.

alogereko *n.* wage earner. *n.* mercenary.

alogerekotu *v.t.* to give (someone) a salary; to hire by the day.

aloka *n.(bot.)* marine algae.

alokairu *n.* rent.

alokari *n.* renter.

alokatu *v.t.* to rent.

alondegi *n.* building where wine is stored.

alor *n.* field (prepared to be sown).

alpesarunzko *adj.* transalpine.

alpesetako *adj.* alpine.

alpestar *adj.* alpine.

alproja *adj.* low, mean, despicable. *n.* cur, swine, despicable person, rabble, riffraff.

alprojakeria *n.* despicable act, lowness, meanness.

alprojatalde *n.* rabble, riffraff, low despicable group of people.

alprojatu *v.i.* to be a despicable person, to become low or mean.

alta *conj.* however.

altu *adj.* tall, high.

altuera *n.* height

altxagarri *adj.* which can be lifted or raised.

altxaketa *n.* act of lifting something up. *n.* uprising, rebellion, revolution.

altxaketari *n.* revolutionary, rebel.

altxaldi *n.* act of lifting, lift. *n.* uprising, rebellion, revolution.

altxamendu *n.* raising. *n.* revolutionary revolt, insurrection.

altxatu *v.t.* to lift, to raise. *v.i.* to rebel, to revolt. *v.i.* to get up, to rise.

altxor *n.* treasure, treasury, hoard.

altxortu *v.t.* to hoard.

altxorzain *n.* treasurer.

altxuma *n.* sprout, shoot.

altzairu *n.* steel.

altzairugintza *n.* steel making, production of steel.

altzairumolde *n.* die.
altzairutegi *n.* steel works, steel factory.
altzairutsu *adj.* steel, steely, made of steel.
altzairutu *v.t.* to cover with steel, to point or edge with steel.
altzo *n.* lap.
altzokada *n.* apronful, apron full of something.
altzoratu *v.t.* to put into one's lap.
alu *n.(anat.)* female genitals, vulva. *adj.* stupid.
alukeria *n.(colloq.)* bad action, repulsive action.
ama *n.* mother. *int.* exclamation of pain.
ama-alabak *n.* mother and daughter.
amaberri *n.* woman who has just given birth.
amabesoetako *n.* godmother.
Ama Birjina *n.* Our Lady, Virgin Mother.
amabitxi *n.* godmother.
amaeraile *n.* murderer of one's own mother.
amaerailketa *n.* matricide, murder of one's own mother.
amai *n.* end.
amaiera *n.* end, termination, ending.
amaiezin *adj.* interminable, endless.
amaigabe *adj.* without end, endless, infinite; unfinished.
amaigabeko *adj.* infinite, endless; unfinished.
amaigabetasun *n.* endlessness, infinity.
amaigarri *adj.* finishable, terminable.
amaitu *v.t./v.i.* to finish, to end.
amakoi *adj.* affectionate towards one's mother.
amakoitu *v.i.* to be very attached to one's mother.
amakor *adj.* affectionate towards one's mother.
amaldeko *adj.* maternal.
Ama-Lur *n.* motherland.
amandre *n.* grandmother.
amantal *n.* apron.
amaponteko *n.* godmother.
amaraun *n.(zool.)* cobweb.
amarausare *n.* cobweb.
amarru *n.* cunning, shrewdness, astuteness.
amarrudun *adj.* shrewd, cunning, astute.
amarrukeria *n.* cunning, shrewdness.
amarruki *adv.* cunningly.
amarruti *adj.* cunning, shrewd.
amarrutsu *adj.* cunning, shrewd.
amasabel *n.(anat.)* uterus, womb.
ama-semeak *n.* mother and son.
amatar *adj.* maternal. *adj.* resembling one's mother.
amatasun *n.* motherhood, maternity.
amatau *v.t.* to turn off, to switch off, to extinguish.

amatiar *adj.* resembling one's mother.
amatu *v.i.* to become a mother, to have a child. *v.t.* to conceive.
amatxi *n.* grandmother.
amatxo *n. (dim.)* mommy.
amazale *adj.* emotionally very attached to one's mother.
amazaletu *v.i.* to be very attached to one's mother.
amazulo *n./adj.* spoiled child; child very attached to his mother.
Amerika *n. (geog.)* America.
amerikak egin *v.t.* to make a fortune.
amerikanu *adj./n.* Basque who went to America and returned to the Basque Country.
amerikar *adj.* American.
Ameriketak. *n.* The Americas.
Ameriketako Estatu Batuak *n.(geog.)* United States of America. **A.E.B.** U.S.A.
ameriketar *adj./n.* American.
amesgaitz *n.* nightmare.
amesgaizto *n.* nightmare.
amesgarri *adj.* dream inducing.
amesgile *n.* dreamer.
amesgin *n.* dreamer.
ameskaitz *n.* nightmare.
ameskaizto *n.* nightmare.
ameskeria *n.* chimera, fantasy, impossible or idle fancy.
ameskeriatsu *adj.* dreamy.
ameskeriaz *adv.* impossibly, fancifully, chimerically.
ameskeriazko *adj.* imaginary, fanciful; chimerical.
ameskile *adj.* visionary, fanciful. *n.* dreamer.
ameskoi *adj.* dreaming, daydreaming, dreamy.
ameskoikeria *n.* delirium. *n.* extravagant speech.
ameslari *adj.* idealist. *n.* dreamer.
amestxar *n.* nightmare.
ameszoro *n.* impossible dream, fancy, whim.
amets *n.* dream.
ametsaldi *n.* period of dreams.
amets egin *v.t.* to dream.
ametsezko *adj.* chimerical, whimsical.
ametsuts *n.* chimera.
ametsutzez *adv.* illusively, chimerically.
ametz *n.(bot.)* muricated oak, variety of oak.
amezki *n.* wood of a muricated oak.
amezti *n.* place of muricated oaks.
amiamoko *n.(zool.)* stork.
amilarazi *v.t.* to cause to fall down a ravine.
amildegi *n.* ravine, chasm, gorge. *n.* place of ravines.
amildu *v.i.* to fall down a ravine.
amildura *n.* act of throwing something or somebody down a precipice.
amilera *n.* fall from a precipice.
aministralgo *n.* administration, management.

aminifistrari n. administrator.
aminifistratu v.t. to administer, to manage.
aminifistratzaile n. administrator, manager.
aminifistrazio n. administration, management.
amnistia n. amnesty.
amodio n. love.
amodiogabe adj. without love, heartless.
amodiotsu adj. loving, affectionate.
amodioz adv. for love.
amodiozko adj. loving, affectionate.
amoltsu adj. affectionate, kind, amiable.
amoltsuki adv. affectionately.
amona n. grandmother.
amonatu v.i. to become a grandmother.
amonatxo n.(dim.) little grandmother, dear grandmother.
amor n. act of giving in.
amorante n. mistress.
amoratu v.t. to cause to give in. v.t./v.i. to gain affection by gallantry.
amorde n. stepmother.
amordeko n. stepmother. n. wet nurse.
amore n. giving in, acquiescence, indulgence, yielding. n. love
amoregile adj. obliging, acquiescent.
amor egin v.t. to give in, to compromise, to condescend.
amoregaitz adj. rigid, inflexible, strict, intransigent.
amoregaiztasun n. intransigence.
amoregite n. act of giving in, acquiescence, condescension.
amorekeria n. excessive acquiescence.
amoremale adj. tolerant, condescending, transigent.
amor eman v.t. to give in.
amoremate n. act of giving in.
amorra n. fury, rage. Used in compound words.
amorragarri adj. troublesome.
amorraldi n. moment of fury, rage.
amorrarazi v.t. to molest, to annoy, to irritate.
amorratu v.i. to be or become furious, to be angry. adj. mad, rabid, furious. adj. (fig.) impetuous, fervent, raging, avid.
amorratuz adv. fervently, ragingly, rabidly.
amorrazio n. fury, rage, anger.
amorro n. rage, fury, anger. n. (fig.) determination, firmness.
amorrubizi n. fury, rage, anger.
amorruz adv. furiously, angrily.
amortizagarri adj. refundable, payable.
amortizapen n. refund, payment.
amortizatu v.t. to refund, to pay off.
amortizazio n. refund, payment.
amotz adj. blunt, dull.
amoztu v.i./v.t. to become blunt or dull;
to dull, to blunt.
amu n. hook, fishing hook.
amuzki n. bait.
-an suffix indicating in, inside. **Etxean.** In the house.
anaia n. brother.
anaialdeko adj. brotherly.
anai-arrebak n. brother(s) and sister(s).
anaiarte n. congregation, fraternity.
anaiartekotasun n. brotherhood.
anaide n. fellow member of a brotherhood.
anaidetasun n. brotherhood.
anaieraile n. fratricide, murderer of a brother.
anaierailtza n. fratricide, murder of a brother.
anaigiarreba n. brother-in-law.
anaigo n. congregation, brotherhood.
anaihilketa n. murder of a brother, fratricide.
anaihiltzaile n. one who murders his own brother, fratricide.
anaiki adv. fraternally, brotherly.
anaikide n. fellow member of a brotherhood.
anaikidego n. confraternity, brotherhood.
anaikidetasun n. confraternity, brotherhood.
anaikoi adj. fraternal, brotherly.
anaikor adj. brotherly.
anaiorde n. stepbrother.
anaitar adj. fraternal, brotherly.
anaitasun n. brotherhood, fraternity.
anaitu v.t./v.i. to unify, to unite, to consider as a brother.
anaitxo n. (dim.) little brother, dear brother.
anaizale adj. brotherly, fraternal.
anarkia n. anarchy.
anarkiko adj. anarchical.
anarkikoki adv. anarchically.
anarkismo n. anarchism.
anarkista n./adj. anarchist.
anatomia n. anatomy.
anbulo n.(bot.) daffodil.
anburu n.(med.) hemorrhoids.
anda n. litter, handbarrow, coffin.
andagin n. barrow-maker.
andana n. group. n. troop.
andanaka adv. in groups; in bulk, in large quantities.
andazain n. stretcher-bearer.
andea n. spoilage, corruption, putrefaction.
andeaezin adj. incorruptible, unspoilable.
andeagabe a. uncorrupted, unspoiled.
andeagarri adj. spoilable, corruptible.
andeakaitz adj. incorruptible, unspoilable.
andeakor adj. corruptible, spoilable, capable of rotting.
andeakortasun n. corruptibility, putrescence, rot, spoilability.

andeamendu *n.* corruption, spoilage, rot.

andeari *n.* corruptor, spoiler.

andeatu *v.t.* to spoil, to damage.

andere *n.* woman. *n.* young lady *n.* housewife.

andereno *n.* young lady. *n.* Basque school teacher (woman).

anderetu *v.i.* to be effeminate, to be woman-like, to become feminine.

andesandiko *adj.* transandine.

andetar *adj./n.* native of the Andes.

andraketa *n.* fornication.

andrakila *n.* doll.

Andra Mari *n.* Our Lady (the Virgin Mary). **Andramariak.** Annual celebrations starting on August 15 in honor of Our Lady.

andramin *n.(med.)* venereal disease.

andraundi *n.(augm.)* large woman.

andre *n.* lady, woman; madam; Mrs.

andregai *n.* fiancée.

andrekari *adj.* fond of women, womanizing.

andrekoi *adj.* fond of women; dissolute, libertine, licentious.

andrekoitu *v.i.* to become fond of women, to be fond of women.

andretsai *n.* misogynist; person, especially a man, who hates women.

andrezale *adj.* fond of women; libertine.

anega *n.* grain measure (about 1.5 bushels or 12 gallons).

angaila *n.* handbarrow, litter.

angailari *n.* stretcher-bearer.

angelu *n.(geom.)* angle.

angeluar *adj.* angular.

angeluarki *adv.* angularly.

angelukide *adj.(geom.)* equiangular.

angelutsu *adj.* angular.

angeluzuzen *n.(geom.)* right angle.

angeluzuzendun *adj.* rectangular.

anglikanismo *n.(eccl.)* Anglicanism.

anglikar *adj.(eccl.)* Anglican.

angula *n.(zool.)* baby eel.

angurri *n.(bot.)* watermelon.

anil *n.(bot.)* indigo plant. *n.* indigo dye, indigo blue.

anildu *v.t.* to dye in indigo.

animalia *n.* beast, animal.

anis *n.* anisette.

anitz *adv./adj.* much, many.

anitzetan *adv.* often, frequently.

anizkarri *adj.(arith.)* multiplicable, multipliable.

anizkoitz *n.(arith.)* multiple.

anizkoiztasun *n.(arith.)* multiplicity.

aniztasun *n.* plurality, multitude. *n.* pluralism.

aniztu *v.t./v.i.* to pluralize, to multiply, to increase.

anker *adj.* cruel, brutal, ruthless.

ankerki *adv.* cruelly, mercilessly, ruthlessly.

ankertu *v.t./v.i.* to be cruel, to be ruthless, to become cruel or

ruthless.

ano *n.* portion, food supply. *n.* wine. *n.* animal feed.

anonimo *adj.* anonymous. *n.* anonymous letter.

anormal *adj.* abnormal.

anpulu *n.* bubble. *n.* tear.

antena *n.* aerial, antenna.

antiernari *n.* contraceptive.

antigorpuzki *n.* antibody.

antilapurkin *n.* safety device against thieves, burglar alarm.

antoisin *n.* holy water container.

antolabide *n.* arrangement, adjustment, agreement, settlement, solution.

antolaezin *adj.* not arrangeable, unsolvable, impossible to settle; incompatible.

antolagabe *adj.* disordered, unorganized.

antolagabetu *v.t.* to mess up, to disorganize, to unsettle, to put in disarray.

antolagaitz *adj.* difficult to settle or arrange.

antolagarri *adj.* reparable, repairable, reformable.

antolaketa *n.* preparation, organization.

antolakizun *n.* organization. *n.* arrangement, settlement.

antolakuntza *n.* preparation, organization.

antolamendu *n.* settlement, preparation, organization.

antolapen *n.* settlement, arrangement.

antolarazi *v.t.* to make (someone) organize (something), to make (someone) arrange (something).

antolatu *v.t.* to arrange, to prepare, to organize. *v.t.* to repair.

antolatzaile *n.* organizer.

antologia *n.* anthology.

antsia *n.* care, diligence. *n.* groan, moan.

antsiatsu *adj.* careful, diligent.

antsiatu *v.i.* to be diligent, to be careful, to be gentle.

antsikabe *adj.* careless, negligent.

antsikabekeria *n.* negligence, carelessness.

antsikabeki *adv.* carelessly, negligently.

antsikabetasun *n.* negligence, carelessness, neglect.

antsikabetu *v.i.* to be careless, to be negligent.

antxeta *n.(zool.)* seagull.

antxintxinketan *adv.* running.

antxoa *n.(zool.)* anchovy.

antz *n.* likeness, similarity, resemblance.

-antz *(gram.)* suffix which indicates direction.

antza *v.i.* it seems, it appears.

antzaldagarri *adj.* changeable,

transformable.

antzaldaketa n. transfiguration, transformation.

antzaldatu v.i./v.t. to be transfigured, to transfigure, to transform.

antzaldatze n. act of transforming.

antzandobi n.(zool.) shrike.

antzara n.(zool.) goose, gander.

antzarle n. imitator.

antzarpen n. imitation.

antzartu v.t. to look like, to resemble. v.t. to imitate, to copy.

antze-antzeko adj. very similar.

antzegabe adj. unskillful, awkward, clumsy.

antzegabetasun n. ineptitude, lack of skill, lack of ability.

antzeko adj. similar, alike, resembling.

antzekotasun n. similarity, affinity, likeness.

antzekotu v.i. to resemble, to look like. v.t. to imitate, to copy.

antzeman v.t. to foresee, to guess, to form a conjecture, to infer. v.t. to identify, to recognize.

antzera adv. in the way of, in the same way, like, likewise, in the manner of.

antzera egin v.t. to imitate, to copy.

antzerki n. play, stage play, drama for the stage, theater (genre).

antzerkigile n. playwright, dramatist.

antzerkilari n. actor, actress (on the stage).

antzerkitxo n.(dim.) kind of burlesque, one-act farce.

antzezlari n. actor, actress (on the stage).

antzezlaritza n. theatrical profession, actor's profession, acting.

antzezpen n.(theat.) play, show, presentation.

antzeztoki n. stage, theater (building).

antzeztu v.t. to imitate. v.t. to perform, to play on the stage, to act.

antzgabeko adj. dissimilar, unlike.

antzgarri adj. imitable, copyable.

antzi n. sigh.

antzirudi n. imitation, copy, image.

antzirudiko adj. similar, alike, resembling.

antzitxuratu v.t./v.i. to symbolize.

antzo n. way, manner; likeness.

antzoki n. theater (building).

antzu adj. infertile, sterile.

antzudura n. sterility, unfruitfulness.

antzuketa n. sterilization.

antzuki adv. barrenly, unfruitfully.

antzukin n. sterilizer.

antzutasun n. sterility.

antzutu v.i. to become sterile. v.t. to sterilize, to castrate, to neuter.

antzutzaile n. sterilizer.

anu n. fainting, passing out, faintness.

anu egin v.t. to fall back in fear, to be faint with fear.

ana n. baby-sitter. n. wet nurse.

apa n. kiss. v.t. to sit down (children's language).

apaburu n. (zool.) tadpole.

apa egin v.t. to sit down (children's language).

apailatu v.t. to prepare, to get ready, to organize. v.t. to cook.

apain adj. elegant, dressed up, fancy, smart.

apaindegi n. beauty parlor.

apaindu v.t. to embellish, to ornament, to beautify, to decorate, to adorn. v.i. to make up.

apaindura n. embellishment, ornamentation, decoration, ornament.

apaingabetu v.t. to remove ornaments or decoration.

apaingai n. ornament.

apaingailu n. ornament.

apaingarri n. decorative object, decoration, ornament. adj. decorative, ornamental.

apaingarriztu v.i. to adorn oneself profusely. v.t. to adorn, to ornament, to embellish.

apaingela n. bathroom.

apainjantzi v.t./v.i. to dress up.

apainkera n. fashion, style.

apainkeria n. excess of ornamentation, ostentation.

apainketa n. act of decorating, ornamenting.

apainki adv. ornamentally, gaudily, sumptuously. n. ornament.

apainmahi n. dressing-table.

apainpoltza n. toilet case.

apaintasun n. decoration.

apaintsu adj. ornamented.

apaintzaile n. ornamenter.

apaiz n. priest.

apaka adv. kissing.

apakatu v.t. to kiss.

apal adj. humble. n. shelf. adj. low.

apalaldi n. depression, weakness. n. descent.

apalarazi v.t. to cause to go down, to cause to descend.

apalategi n. shelving unit.

apaldura n. humiliation.

apalerazi v.t. to humiliate, to embarrass, to put down.

apaletsi v.t. to despise, to scorn.

apalgarri adj. humiliating, humbling, embarrassing.

apalgune n. ravine, glen.

apalkeria n. servility, false humility.

apalketa n. humiliation, embarrassment.

apalki adv. meekly. adv. humbly.

apalkiro adv. humbly.

apalkor adj. depressive.

apalkuntza n. humiliation, embarrassment.

apaltasun n. humility.

apaltegi n. shelves, shelving.

apapuan adv. in poverty.

apar n. foam.

apardun adj. foamy.
aparkaleku n. parking lot.
aparkatu v.t. to park.
aparta adj. excellent, superior.
aparte adj. special, particular. adv. separately, apart.
apartsu adj. foamy.
apeta n. whim, fancy, caprice. n. tendency, inclination.
apetaldi n. whim, fancy, caprice.
apetatsu adj. whimsical, fanciful, capricious.
apetatu v.i. to be capricious, to give in to a whim.
apez n. priest.
apezberri n. new priest.
apezbiltzar n. gathering of priests.
apezeria n. clergy.
apezetxe n. rectory.
apezgai n. seminarian.
apezgaitegi n. seminary.
apezgintza n. ordination into the priesthood.
apezgisa adv. priestly, in a priestly manner.
apezgo n. priesthood, job of a priest.
apezketa n. group of priests.
apezki adv. priestly.
apezkide n. fellow priest.
apezkoi adj. clerical.
apezkoikeria n. clericalism.
apezkunde n. priesthood, job of a priest.
apezlagun n. friend of priests. n. fellow priest.
apezlegez adv. priestly, in a priestly manner.
apeznagusi n. head priest.
apezpiku n. bishop.
apezpikualdi n. time of a bishop's pontificate.
apezpikuburu n. archbishop.
apezpikuburutza n. primateship, the office of the highest ranking bishop in a country.
apezpikueraz adv. in the manner of a bishop.
apezpikugo n. office of the bishop, bishopric.
apezpikutar adj. pertaining to the bishop; fond of the bishop.
apezpikutasun n. quality of being a bishop.
apezpikutegi n. place where the bishop lives.
apezpikuteria n. group of bishops.
apezpikutu v.t. to govern as a bishop.
apezpikutza n. state of being a bishop, bishopric.
apeztalde n. group of priests.
apeztasun n. quality of being a priest.
apeztiar adj. fond of priests.
apeztu v.i. to become a priest. v.t. to ordain into the priesthood.
apika adv. maybe, perhaps.
apikako adj. accidental.
apirila n. April.

apo n.(zool.) toad. n. hoof.
apobelar n.(bot.) great mullein.
apodun adj. ungulate, having a hoof, hoofed.
apokeria n.(fig.) insult, filthy word or deed.
apokume n.(dim.) tadpole.
apopilu n. lodger.
apopiluetxe n. lodging house.
apostolu n. apostle.
apostu n. bet.
apostugile n. one who makes bets, bettor, wagerer.
apostuka adv. betting, making bets, wagering.
apostuzale adj. fond of betting.
apotzar n.(augm.) large toad.
apropos adv. intentionally, on purpose.
aproposa adj. adequate.
apropostasun n. capability, ability.
apropostu v.t./v.i. to adapt, to make adequate.
apur n. bread crumb, small fragment. adv. a little bit, bit.
apurgailu n. grater.
apurgarri adj. triturable, breakable, fragile.
apurgarritasun n. brittleness.
apurjale adj. frugal, sparing.
apurka adv. little by little adv. at retail.
apurka saldu v.t. to sell at retail, to retail.
apurkatu v.t. to chip, to shred, to crumble.
apurkeria n. meanness, avarice, insignificant thing.
apurketa n. breakage, destruction, fragmentation. n. division, separation.
apurkor adj. fragile, breakable.
apurreria n. smallness. n. residue, rest, remains.
apurtezin adj. unbreakable.
apurtu v.t. to break, to destroy. v.t. to grind.
apurtxo adv. a little bit. n. (dim.) small crumb, small fragment, tiny bit.
apurtzaile n. breaker, destroyer, crusher. adj. breaking, destroying, crushing.
ar n./adj. male. n. (fig.) remorse, regret.
-ar (gram.) Suffix which indicates the male of the species. (gram.) Suffix which indicates native of.
Araba n. (geog.) One of the four provinces of the southern Basque Country. Its capital is Vitoria.
arabera n. proportion. prep. according to.
araberako adj. proportionate, regular.
araberatasun n. conformity, agreement, accordance.
araberatu v.t. to adapt, to adjust, to arrange.
araberaz prep. according to.
araberazko adj. apt, adequate. adj.

proportionate.

arabi *n. (bot.)* cranberry.

arabi-sagar. *n.(bot.)* grapefruit.

araka *n.* knot on the trunk of a tree.

arakagarri *adj.* investigable, examinable.

arakakor *adj.* inquisitive, curious.

arakapen *n.* investigation, scrutiny.

arakatu *v.t.* to investigate, to examine, to scrutinize, to find out, to dig out, to look into.

arakatzaile *n.* investigator, researcher.

araketa *n.* investigation, examination.

araketari *n.* examiner, investigator.

aralde *n.* large group.

aran *n.(bot.)* plum, prune.

arana *n.* echo. *n.* plum tree.

arandi *n.* abundance of plum-trees.

aranondo *n.(bot.)* plum tree.

arantza *n.(bot.)* thorn. *n.(bot.)* hawthorn.

arantzadi *n.* field of hawthorns.

arantzadun *adj.* thorny.

arantzatsu *adj.* thorny.

arantzatu *v.i.* to become covered with thorns. *v.t.* to cover something with thorns. *v.t.* to prick.

arantzazko *adj.* thorny.

arantzesi *n.* fence made of hawthorns.

arantzeta *n.* field of hawthorns.

arantzurde *n.(zool.)* porcupine.

ararte *n.* interval, space between two points.

arartegabeko *adj.* immediate, without intermediary.

arartekari *n.* intermediary, mediator.

ararteko *n.* intermediary, mediator.

arartekotasun *n.* mediation, intercession.

arasa *n.* shelf. *n.* closet, cupboard, cabinet.

araseria *n.* shelving units, bookcase.

arau *n.* rule, norm, regulation.

arauaz *prep.* according to.

araubide *n.* discipline, order. *n.* method, system.

araubidez *adv.* systematically, orderly, lawfully.

araubidezko *adj.* systematic, lawful, ordered.

araudi *n.* code, rules and regulations.

araudiz *adv.* legitimately, legally, lawfully.

araudun *adj.* systematic, methodical.

arauemaile *adj.* normative *n.* one who gives precepts.

arauera *prep.* according to.

araueratu *v.t.* to legislate.

araueraz *adv.* preceptively.

araugabeko *adj.* irregular, abnormal, anomalous.

araugabetasun *n.* irregularity, anomaly.

araugabezia *n.* irregularity, anomaly.

arauhausle *n.* violator, infractor.

arauhauspen *n.* infraction, violation.

arauhauste *n.* infraction, infringement, violation.

arauketa *n.* regulation; system of laws and regulations.

araukontrako *adj.* antiregulatory.

araupeko *adj.* regulated, subject to a rule.

araupetu *v.t.* to regulate, to adjust, to govern according to a rule.

arausail *n.* code of laws.

arautegi *n.* code of laws.

arauteria *n.* set of rules and regulations.

arautu *v.t.* to legislate, to issue rules and regulations.

arauz *adv.* proportionally, orderly. *prep.* according to.

arauzko *adj.* preceptive, regulative, systematic, methodic.

-arazi *(gram.)* suffix meaning to make (someone) do (something), to cause (someone) to do (something).

arazketa *n.* purification.

arazo *n.* job, occupation, work, task. *n.* problem, preoccupation, worry. *n.* question, matter, issue.

arazodun *adj.* busy.

arazogabetu *v.i.* to be unemployed.

arazopetu *v.t.* to employ, to hire. *adj.* busy.

arazotu *v.i.* to be worried. *v.i.* to be busy.

araztasun *n.* cleanliness.

araztegi *n.* refinery, place where oil is processed.

araztu *v.t.* to purify, to refine.

arbaso *n.* ancestor.

arbasta *n.* pitchfork.

arbatza *n.* frame, skeleton of the roof or ceiling.

arbel *n.* slate. *n.* blackboard.

arbelaitz *n.* slate.

arbelezko *adj.* slatey.

arbeleztatu *v.t.* to cover with slate, to tile with slate.

arbelgin *n.* slater, slate-cutter.

arbelgintza *n.* slate making.

arbeltegi *n.* slate quarry.

arbeltsu *adj.* slatey.

arbi *n.(bot.)* turnip. *n.* bait.

arbilore *n.* flower of the turnip.

arbin *n.* anguish, distress.

arbindu *v.i.* to worry. *v.i.* to be quick to anger.

arbintasun *n.* worry, affliction. *n.* state of anger.

arbisail *n.* turnip field.

arbisolo *n.* turnip field.

arbitxo *n.(dim.)* small turnip.

arbola *n.* tree.

arbolaburu *n.* top part of the tree.

arboladi *n.* plantation or grove of trees.

arbolagerri *n.* trunk of a tree.

arbolatsu *adj.* full of trees.

arbolazain *n.* person who takes care of trees, arboriculturist.

arbolazaintza *n.* arboriculture.

arbuiagarri *adj.* despisable,

despicable, worthless.

arbuiakor adj. disdainful, contemptuous.

arbuiatu v.t. to despise, to disdain.

arbuitzaile n. despiser, scorner.

arbuio n. disdain, contempt, scorn.

arbuiotsu adj. disdainful, contemptuous.

arbuioz adv. disdainfully.

arbuiozko adj. disdainful.

ardan n. wine. Used in compound words.

ardandegi n. tavern, pub. n. wine market or shop.

ardangela n. tavern. n. wine cellar.

ardantza n. vineyard. n. vintage, gathering of grapes, grape harvest.

ardantzale adj. fond of wine.

ardao n. wine.

ardatz n. axis, axle.

ardatzaire adj. fusiform, spindle-shaped.

ardatzantzeko adj. fusiform, spindle-shaped.

ardatzeusle n.(mech.) bearing, part of a machine in or on which another part revolves.

ardazlari n. spinner, weaver.

ardaztu v.t. to spin.

ardi n.(zool.) sheep, ewe.

ardiantzu n. sheep which cannot produce milk, sterile sheep.

ardiborda n. sheep pen, sheep shed.

ardiesne n. sheep's milk.

ardigaldu adj.(fig.) vagabond, solitary, isolated, late-comer, straggler.

ardijabe n. owner of sheep.

ardiketa n. group of sheep.

ardiki n. sheep's meat.

ardikide n. member of the sheep family (sheep, lamb, ram).

ardilarru n. sheepskin.

arditegi n. sheepfold.

arditoki n. sheepfold.

arditxabola n. sheep shed.

ardizakur n. sheep dog.

ardizko adj. ovine, pertaining to sheep.

ardo n. wine.

ardoantz n. vinosity, the state or quality of having the characteristics of wine.

ardoantzeko adj. wine-like.

ardoedale n. wine drinker.

ardo edan v.t. to drink wine.

ardoegile n. wine maker.

ardo egin v.t. to make wine.

ardogin n. viniculturist.

ardogintza n. viniculture.

ardogorriska n. rosé wine.

ardoketa n. supply of wine. n. wine selling.

ardoketari n. wine provider, supplier.

ardokoi adj. fond of wine.

ardontzi n. wine container.

ardosaltzaile n. wine seller, tavern keeper.

ardotegi n. tavern, bar.

ardotsu adj. having an abundance of wine.

ardotzar n. strong wine.

ardoxka n. weak wine.

ardozale adj. fond of wine.

ardozalekeria n. excess in drinking, addiction to wine.

ardozaletu v.i. to become fond of wine.

ardozko adj. wine, made of wine.

ardoztatu v.t. to soak in wine.

ardura n. care, diligence, solicitude, responsibility.

arduradun adj. diligent, careful, responsible. n. manager, person in charge.

arduraeza n. carelessness, negligence, indolence.

arduragabe adj. negligent, careless, indolent, neglectful.

arduragabekeria n. carelessness, negligence, neglectfulness.

arduragabeki adv. carelessly, negligently.

arduragabeko adj. negligent, careless, neglectful.

arduragabetasun n. negligence, carelessness, neglectfulness.

arduragabetu v.i. to neglect, to be careless.

arduragabezia n. carelessness, negligence, neglectfulness.

arduragarri adj. interesting, attractive. adj. deserving of care.

ardura izan v.t. to be careful, to take care of. v.t. to administer, to manage.

arduraldi n. management, administration.

ardurape n. protection.

ardurapeko adj. recommended.

ardurapetu v.t. to recommend. v.i. to take charge.

arduratasun n. care, diligence.

ardu[rati adj. diligent, careful, responsible.

arduratsu adj. diligent, responsible, careful.

arduratu v.i. to look after, to take care, to be interested. v.i. to take charge of, to take responsibility for.

arduraz adv. carefully, attentively.

are n. rake. n.(anat.) pancreas.

areago adv. more, more so.

areagotu v.t./v.i. to intensify, to grow, to augment, to multiply, to increase.

areko adj. pancreatic.

aremeta n. dune, sand dune.

aremin n.(med.) inflammation of the pancreas.

arerio n. enemy, foe.

areriotasun n. rivalry, enmity, hostility, animosity.

areriotu v.i. to become an enemy. v.t. to make an enemy.

aresti n. moment, instant.

arestian adv. recently, a short time ago.

areto *n.* salon, lounge, large room.

argal *adj.* thin, skinny, slender.

argalbera *adj.* having a tendency for slenderness or weakness.

argaldu *v.i.* to lose weight, to get thin, to become thin.

argaldura *n.* slenderness, thinness; weakness, debility.

argalgarri *adj.* producing weight loss or weakness, debilitating.

argalkeria *n.* exhaustion, great fatigue.

argalketa *n.* loss of weight, thinness; weakness.

argaltasun *n.* thinness. *n.* weakness.

argazki *n.* picture, photograph.

argazkia egin *v.t.* to take pictures.

argazkidenda *n.* camera shop.

argazkietxe *n.* photographic studio.

argazkigile *n.* photographer.

argazkilari *n.* photographer.

argazkimakina *n.* camera.

argazkin *n.* photographer.

argazkintza *n.* photographer's profession.

argaztu *v.t.* to take pictures.

argi *n.* light. *adj.* intelligent, bright. *adj.* clear, obvious.

argi- - Used in compound words.

argiago *adj.(comp.)* clearer, lighter, brighter, more intelligent.

argiagotu *v.t.* to clarify further, to make clearer.

argialdi *n.* illumination, clarity, brightness. *n.* perspicacity, penetration.

argiarazi *v.t.* to elucidate, to explain. *v.t.* to cause to illuminate.

argiarazpen *n.* elucidation.

argi-argi *adj.* very clear, evident, obvious. *adv.* very clearly.

argibegi *n.* dawn.

argibelar *n.(bot.)* alfalfa.

argibelardi *n.* alfalfa field.

argibide *n.* document, proof, evidence. *n.* information, direction, instruction. *n.* skylight.

argibidedun *adj.* documented.

argibidegabe *adj.* undocumented.

argibidetu *v.t.* to clarify, to clear up, to prove.

argibidez *adv.* documentarily, as proof.

argibidezko *adj.* explanatory, clarifying.

argibizi *n.* high intensity light.

argibotoi *n.* push button.

argidistira *n.* brightness of light.

argidun *adj.* bright, luminous, shining. *n.* electrician.

argidura *n.* illumination, brightness.

argi egin *v.t.* to light, to give light, to illuminate. *v.t.* to clarify, to decipher.

argi egon *v.i.* to be alert, to be vigilant.

argiemale *n.* lighter.

argieman *v.t.* to light, to lighten.

argierazi *v.t.* to elucidate, to clarify, to explain; to make (someone) explain.

argierazle *n.* clarifier, elucidator, explainer.

argiezkila *n.* early morning tolling of church bells.

argigabe *adj.* dark, deprived of light, shady.

argigarri *adj.* explanatory. *n.* proof, evidence.

argigile *n.* lighter (person).

argi ibili *v.i.* to be careful, to pay attention, to be watchful.

argikari *n.* electrician.

argiketa *n.* beam of light. *n.* investigation, inquest.

argiki *adv.* clearly, explicitly.

argikiro *adv.* clearly, explicitly.

argikor *adj.* luminous, brilliant, bright.

argikorronte *n.(elec.)* light current.

argikortasun *n.* luminescence.

argikuntza *n.* illumination, lighting.

argikusle *n.* discerning person. *adj.* clairvoyant.

argikusmen *n.* clear-sightedness, discernment, perspicacity.

argikuste *n.* clairvoyance.

argilabur *n.* low beam (headlight).

argimutil *n.* candleholder.

arginabar *n.* sunrise.

argindar *n.* electricity.

argineurketa *n.* photometry.

argineurkin *n.(elec.)* lightmeter, photometer.

arginirnir *n.* flash.

argino *n. (dim.)* small light.

argiontzi *n.* lamp.

argipen *n.* illustration, interpretation, explanation.

argiragarri *adj.* publishable.

argiratu *v.t.* to give birth to.

argiro *adv.* clearly, explicitly.

argirudi *n.* luminous image (as a neon sign). *n.* picture.

argisorta *n.* light beam.

argi ta garbi *adv.* clearly, openly.

argitaldari *n.* editor. *n.* publishing firm.

argitaldi *n.* edition.

argitaldu *v.t.* to publish.

argitaletxe *n.* publishing house.

argitalgarri *adj.* worthy of publishing.

argitalpen *n.* edition.

argitan *adv.* openly, publicly.

argitapen *n.* elucidation, interpretation.

argitara eman *v.t.* to publish. *v.t.* to show, to display.

argitaragabeko *adj.* unpublished.

argitaragarri *adj.* publishable.

argitarapen *n.* edition, publication.

argitaratu *v.t.* to publish.

argitaratzaile *n.* publisher. *n.* editor.

argitarazi *v.t.* to publish. *v.t.* to shine, to make (something) shine.

argitarazle *n.* publisher. *n.* editor.

argitasun *n.* light. *n.* glow. *n.* clarity, clearness, luminosity. *n.* illustration, explanation.

argiteria *n.* set of lights.

argitoki *n.* candleholder.

argitsu adj. clear, bright, luminous. adj. intelligent, bright.

argitto n. (dim.) small light.

argitu v.t. to shine, to give light, to light, to illuminate. v.t. (fig.) to illustrate, to explain, to clarify. v.t. to inform, to show, to instruct.

argiturri adj. bright, knowledgeable. n. light source.

argitza n. luminosity. n. group of lights.

argitzaile. n. lighter. n. (fig.) expositor, explainer, informer.

argitzapen n. explanation, illustration, clarification.

argiune n. moment of light. n. clearing in a grove.

argixka n. (dim.) small light.

argizagi n. wax, candle.

argizale adj. fond of light. adj. fond of clarification.

argizari n. wax.

argizarigile n. wax candle maker, chandler.

argizarigintza n. job of a wax candle maker, chandlery.

argizariohol n. a decorative carved wooden block wrapped with candle wax which is unraveled and burned as a funerary vigil light.

argizarizko adj. made of wax.

argizko adj. luminous, bright, clear.

argizpi n. beam of light.

argiztadura n. illumination.

argiztagarri adj. illuminating, lighting. adj. xplanatory, clarifying.

argiztapen n. illumination, lighting. n. clarification, explanation.

argiztatu v.t. to clarify, to explain. v.t. to light, to illuminate.

argizulo n. skylight.

argose n. mating period of a female animal, oestrus, heat.

argosetu v.i. to go into heat (female animals), to be in oestrus.

argudiaezin adj. incontrovertible, indisputable.

argudiagaitz adj. undeniable, indisputable.

argudiaketa n. argument. n. reasoning.

argudiatu v.t. to allege, to adduce. v.t. to argue.

argudiatzaile n. arguer.

argudio n. allegation. n. argument, dispute, controversy. n. reasoning.

argudioka adv. controversially.

-ari (gram.) Suffix which indicates agent, profession, job. **Pelotari.** Jai-alai player. (gram.) Verb suffix which indicates material object. **Janari.** Food. (dat.) Suffix which indicates to whom, ind. obj. **Gizonari.** To the man.

ari v.i. to be occupied, to be doing something.

ariel n. custom duty.

arieletxe n. customhouse.

ari izan. v.i./v.aux. to be active, to be busy with, to be occupied, to be doing something.

arik eta conj. until.

ariketa n. exercise, drill; activity. n. assignment.

arima n. soul. n. person.

arimadun adj. alive, living.

arimagabeko adj. inert, lifeless.

arin adj. light, venial, not heavy. adj. stupid, thoughtless adv. quickly, fast.

arinagotu v.i./v.t. to accelerate, to hasten. v.t. to lighten (a burden).

arinaldi n. alleviation, lightening, mitigation. n. improvement. n. sprint, short and fast run.

arinarazi v.t. to hasten, to expedite.

arinari eman v.t. to escape.

arin-arin adv. very quickly, very fast. n. popular Basque dance.

arindu v.t. to lighten, to make light. v.t. to alleviate.

arindura n. mitigation, alleviation.

arineketa n. race. n. haste, hurry, speed.

arineketaldi n. race.

aringarri adj. laxative. n. sedative.

arinka adv. quickly, fast. adv. running.

arinkari n. runner.

arinkeria n. frivolity, triviality.

arinkerizko adj. ephemeral, transient, momentary, fleeting.

arinketa n. alleviation, mitigation. n. acceleration.

arinki adv. superficially. adv. quickly, fast, immediately, rapidly.

arinkor adj. laxative.

arintasun n. levity, lightness. n. speed, velocity, fastness.

arintzaile n. mitigator, alleviator. adj. alleviating, mitigating.

aritmetika n. arithmetic.

aritu v.i. to be busy with, to be occupied, to be active, to be doing something.

arkaldu v.i. to be in heat (referring to a female sheep).

arkara n. mating period of sheep.

arkara egon v.i. to be in the mating period (for sheep).

arkaratu v.i. to be in the mating period (for sheep).

arkasats n.(bot.) sarsaparrilla plant.

arkatz n. pencil.

arkatzontzi n. pencil holder.

arkazi n. (bot.) acacia tree.

arkeologari n. archaeologist.

arkeologia n. archaeology.

arkeologiko adj. archaeological.

arkitekto n. architect.

arku n. (archit.) arch.

arkudantza n. Basque folk dance performed with wooden arcs.

arkugiltza n. (archit.) keystone.

arkuharri n. (archit.) vousoir of an arch, archstone.

arkuharritu v.t. to hew a stone in

curves for an arch.

arkume *n.* young lamb.

arkumeki *n.* lamb's meat.

arkumetalde *n.* flock of lambs.

arkupe *n.* portico. *n.* porch (of the church).

arkuzorrotz *n. (archit.)* ogival arch.

arlanka *n.(naut.)* anchor.

arlanpa *n.* drydock.

arlo *n.* task, matter, affair. *n.* subject, theme, field.

arlote *adj.* ragged, shabby, untidy, dirty, sloppy.

arlotekeria *n.* vulgarity, crudeness.

arloteki *adv.* extravagantly.

arloteria *n.* untidiness, dirt, squalor.

arlotetasun *n.* untidiness, slovenliness.

arlotetu *v.i.* to become vulgar. *v.i.* to be untidy.

arma *n.* weapon, firearm. *int.* exclamation used to alert somebody.

armada *n.* army.

armadenda *n.* gun shop.

armadore *n.* shipowner.

armaetxe *n.* gun factory.

armagabeko *adj.* unarmed.

armagabetu *v.i./v.t.* to disarm, to prohibit the carrying of arms.

armagile *n.* gunsmith.

armagin *n.* gunsmith.

armagintza *n.* manufacture of guns.

armagizon *n.* soldier, warrior.

armarri *n.* coat-of-arms.

armasaltzaile *n.* seller of weapons, seller of guns.

armategi *n.* gun factory. *n.* armory.

armatu *v.i./v.t.* to arm.

armazale *adj.* bellicose; fond of guns.

armazoi *n.* framework, rigid structure.

armiarma *n.(zool.)* spider.

armiarmasare *n.* cobweb.

arnari *n.* fruit.

arnasa *n.* breathing, respiration.

arnasa bota *v.t.* to exhale.

arnasa egin *v.t.* to breathe.

arnasa hartu *v.t.* to breathe. *v.t.(fig.)* to relax, to take a breather.

arnasaldi *n.* breath.

arnasats *n.* bad breath.

arnasbehar *n.* panting, difficult breathing.

arnasbehera *n.* exhalation.

arnasbide *n.(anat.)* trachea. *n.* breathing-hole, vent.

arnasbotaketa *n.* act of exhaling.

arnasdun *adj.* breathing.

arnasemaldi *n.* exhalation.

arnasestu *n.* suffocation.

arnasestuka *adv.* panting, out of breath.

arnasestutu *v.i.* to pant, to be out of breath, to choke.

arnasezin *adj.* unbreathable, unfit for respiration.

arnasezko *adj.* respiratory.

arnasgabe *adj.* without breathing, out of breath.

arnasgabetu *v.i.* to pant, to have difficulty breathing.

arnasgailu *n.* respirator, inhalator.

arnasgarri *adj.* breathable, suitable for breathing.

arnasgora *n.* inhalation.

arnasgoratu *v.t.* to inhale.

arnasgoratzaile *n.* inhaler.

arnaska egin *v.t.* to pant, to heave.

arnasketa *n.* respiration, breathing, respiratory exercise.

arnasneke *n.(med.)* asthma.

arnasnekedun *adj.* asthmatic.

arnasots *n.* panting sound, sound of labored breathing.

aro *n.* weather. *n.* season, time for, epoch. *n. (geol.)* era, age.

aroberri *n.* modern age.

arotz *n.* carpenter. *n.* blacksmith

arotzeria *n.* carpenter's shop.

arotzeritza *n.* carpentry, carpenter's job.

arotzmahai *n.* carpenter's bench.

arotzmutil *n.* carpenter's apprentice.

arozgo *n.* job of blacksmith.

arozkintza *n.* carpentry, carpenter's job. *n.* job of blacksmith.

arpoi *n.* harpoon.

arpoilari *n.* harpooner.

arpoindu *v.t.* to throw the harpoon, to harpoon.

arra *n.* palm (unit of measure, 8 1/4 inches)

arraba *n.* fish ovary.

arrabete *n.* palm (unit of measure, 8 1/4 inches).

arrabeteko *adj.* handful, palm's width of (unit of measurement).

arrabita *n. (mus.)* violin.

arrabitari *n.* violinist.

arrabota *n.* jack-plane (carpenter's tool).

arrago *n.* crucible.

arragotu *v.t.* to refine metals.

arraia *n.(zool.)* ray, skate. *n.* line.

arrailadura *n.* crack, fissure, crevice.

arrailagarri *adj.* crackable, splittable.

arrailatu *v.i.* to split, to crack, to cleave.

arraildu *v.i.* to begin to open, to split, to break apart.

arrailgune *n.* crevice, fissure, crack.

arrain *n.* fish

arrainaire *adj.* pisciform, fish-shaped.

arrainandre *n.* mermaid.

arrainazketa *n.* fish culture.

arrainazkuntza. *n.* fish culture.

arraindegi *n.* fish-market, fish shop.

arrainegaldun *n. (zool.)* flying fish.

arrainegalak *n. (pl.)* fins.

arrainezpata *n. (zool.)* sword fish.

arrainezur *n.* fishbone.

arraingorri *n. (zool.)* red gurnard, fish found in rocky areas of the sea.

arrainjale *n.* fish-eater.

arrainketa *n.* a lot of fish. *n.* fishing.

arrainontzi n. fish tank.
arrainotzara n. basket for fish.
arrainsaltzaile n. fish seller.
arrainsare n. fishing net.
arraintsu adj. abundant in fish.
arraintxo n. (dim.) small fish.
arrainzale adj. fond of fish.
arrainzopa n. fish soup.
arraio int. hell!
arraioka adv. cursing, swearing.
arraitasun n. happiness, joyfulness. n. kindness, gentleness.
arrakala n. fissure, crack, split, crevice.
arrakaladura n. fissure, crack, split.
arrakalagarri adj. crackable, splittable.
arrakalakor adj. fragile, brittle.
arrakalatsu adj. split, cracked.
arrakalatu v.i. to crack, to split. adj. cracked, split.
arrakasta n. successful sale. n. success.
arrakastatsu adj. successful.
arrakastatu v.t. to look for, to seek. v.t. to desire, to covet strongly.
arrakero adj. cheating. n. cheater.
arrama n. howl, moo, growl, sound made by an animal (dog, bear, wolf, cow, etc.).
arramaka adv. shouting, crying, howling, wailing.
arran n. bell worn by cattle or sheep. n. Used in compound words. Derived from arrain, fish.
arranak jo v.t. to ring (a bell), to clang, to jingle.
arrandegi n. fish market.
arrandi n. ostentation.
arrandikeria n. ostentation, show of vanity.
arrandiro adv. ostentatiously.
arranditasun n. ostentation.
arranditsu adj. ostentatious, pretentious, boastful.
arranditu v.i. to be vain, to be ostentatious, to be boastful.
arrankari n.(zool.) trout.
arrano n.(zool.) eagle.
arranobeltz n.(zool.) vulture.
arranokume n.(dim.) young eagle.
arranopola! int. gosh!, goodness gracious!
arranotzar n.(augm.) large eagle.
arranoxka n.(dim.) small eagle.
arrantxu n. ranch.
arrantza n. fishing, action of fishing. n. fish, amount of fish caught. n. braying of an ass.
arrantza egin v.t. to bray. v.t. to weep.
arrantzaka adv. braying.
arrantzaldi n. fishing season; fishing, time spent fishing. n. braying.
arrantzale n. fisherman.
arrantzan egin v.t. to fish.
arrantzatoki n. fishing-ground, fishing spot.
arrantzatu v.t. to fish, to catch (fish).

arrantzu n. large amount of fish, catch.
arranume n.(dim.) young eagle, eaglet.
arrapalada n. rush, haste, bustle; gallop, running.
arrapaladan adv. hastily, precipitately, in a hurry, in a rush, at a gallop.
arraro adj. rare, infrequent, strange, odd.
arras adv. completely, totally.
arrast n. match.
arraste n. fishing technique in which the net is dragged along the ocean floor.
arrastero n. ship which fishes by dragging the net.
arrasti n. afternoon.
arrasto n. track, vestige, trace.
arrastu v.i. to become dark at nightfall, to get dark.
arratoi n.(zool.) rat.
arrats n. early evening, late afternoon.
arratsalde n. afternoon.
arratsaldeko adj. evening, of the evening.
arratsalderdi n. mid-afternoon.
arratsaldero adv. every afternoon, every evening.
arrats beheran adv. at sunset, in the evening.
arratseko adj. evening, of the evening.
arrauki n. caviar.
arraultza n. egg.
arraultzadenda n. store where eggs are sold.
arraultzagorringo n. yolk.
arraultzaldi n. ovulation.
arraultzaro n. spawning season.
arraultzazal n. egg shell.
arraun n. oar.
arraunean egin v.t. to row.
arraunketan adv. rowing.
arraunaldi n. stroke with an oar. n. rowing time.
arraunka adv. rowing.
arraunkada n. stroke with an oar.
arraunkatu v.t. to row.
arraunketa n. rowing. n. regatta (rowing).
arraunlari n. rower, oarsman.
arraza n. race, breed.
arrazaz adv. ethnically, racially.
arrazarteko adj. interracial.
arrazaskotako adj. multiracial, interracial.
arrazazalekeria n. racism.
arrazazko adj. racial.
arrazoi n. reason, right.
arrazoiak eman v.t. to reason, to give reasons, to explain.
arrazoi izan v.t. to be right.
arrazoinamendu n. reasoning.
arrazoinbide n. reasoning, allegation.
arrazoinbidez adv. reasonably, judiciously, prudently.
arrazoindun adj. rational.
arrazoingabe adj. irrational.
arrazoingabekeria n. absurdity,

irrationality.

arrazoingabeki adv. irrationally, absurdly, for no reason, without a reason.

arrazoingabeko adj. absurd, irrational. adj. arbitrary.

arrazoinkeria n. faulty reasoning.

arrazoinketa n. reasoning, argumentation.

arrazoinketatu v.t. to give reasons, to show the reason, to prove.

arrazointzaile n. reasoner.

arrazoizko adj. rational.

arre int. exclamation used to encourage donkeys to move forward. adj. gray; turbid.

arreba n. sister (of a man).

arreborde n. man's stepsister.

arre esan v.t. to encourage donkeys to move forward.

arreme n. bisexual, hermaphrodite.

arremeak n.(pl.) male and female.

arren int. please! n. petition, request, begging. n. prayer.

arrenbizi n. earnest petition.

arrendu v.t. to beg, to implore, to request.

arrengura n. complaint.

arrenguratsu adj. lamenting, plaintive, mournful.

arrenka adv. begging, imploring, asking earnestly, entreating.

arrenkari n. petitioner, supplicant.

arrenkatu v.t. to implore, to beg, to ask for earnestly.

arrenkura n. anxiety, anguish, affliction. n. complaint.

arrenkuratsu adj. lamenting, complaining.

arrenkuratu v.i. to become vexed, to be afflicted. v.i. to become impatient.

arrenkuraz adv. impatiently. adv. cautiously, carefully.

arreo n. trousseau, equipment (linen, furniture, etc.) that a bride contributes to the marriage.

arreta n. care, diligence, concern, attention.

arretatsu adj. careful, attentive, diligent.

arretazko adj. careful, diligent, attentive.

arretasun n. turbidity.

arretatu v.t. to prevent, to foresee. v.i. to be careful.

arretaz adv. carefully, attentively.

arretu v.i. to become turbid, to become greyish.

arriskatu v.t./v.i. to risk, to expose oneself to danger.

arrisku n. risk, danger, hazard.

arriskuan egon v.i. to be in danger.

arriskudun adj. risky, hazardous, dangerous.

arriskugabe. adj. safe, secure, without danger.

arriskugarri adj. hazardous, risky, dangerous.

arriskugarritasun n. dangerousness, riskiness, hazardousness.

arriskuratu v.t./v.i. to risk, to be in danger, to hazard.

arriskutsu adj. hazardous, dangerous, risky.

arriskuz adv. dangerously, hazardously.

arriskuzko adj. risky, hazardous, dangerous.

arrosa n.(bot.) rose.

arrosadi n. rose garden.

arrosaire adj. rosy, rosaceous.

arrosalore n. rose (flower).

arrosantzeko adj. rosy, like a rose, rosaceous.

arrosario n.(eccl.) rosary.

arrosatxo n.(dim.) small rose.

arrosazko adj. rosy, rosaceous.

arrostiar adj. hospitable.

arrotz n. stranger, foreigner.

arrotzale adj. fond of foreigners.

arrotzari n. innkeeper.

arrotzetxe n. inn.

arroz n.(bot.) rice.

arrozdun adj. made of rice.

arrozesko adj. made of rice.

arrozesne n. type of rice pudding.

arrozjale n. rice-eater.

arrozsoro n. rice field.

arroztasun n. quality of being a foreigner, alienism, foreignness.

arroztegi n. inn.

arroztetxe n. inn.

arrozti n. rice field.

arroztiar adj. hospitable.

arroztu v.t./v.i. to exile, to banish. v.t. to introduce foreign customs.

arrubio n.(zool.) salamander.

arrunkeria n. vulgarity, coarseness. n. triviality (of speech), prosaic conversation, pleasantry.

arrunt adj. vulgar, coarse, unrefined. adj. common, simple.

arruntasun n. vulgarity, coarseness. n. simplicity, plainness.

arruntatu v.i. to become vulgar, coarse. v.i./v.t. to become current usage, to make (some word or expression) part of the vernacular.

arruntki adv. commonly, simply.

art- var. of ardi (sheep). Used in compound words.

arta- var. of arto (corn) and arte (evergreen oak). Used in compound words.

artabizar n. corn silk.

artaburu n. ear of corn.

artadi n. evergreen oak forest.

artaereite n. act of sowing corn.

artagarau n. grain of corn.

artairin n. corn flour.

artajorra n. act of weeding.

artajorratu v.t. to weed corn.

artalanda n. cornfield.

artalandara n. corn plant.

artalasto *n.* stalk of corn plant.
artalde *n.* flock of sheep.
artaldekeria *n.(fig.)* gregariousness.
artaldetxo *n.(dim.)* small flock of sheep.
artale *n.* grain of corn.
artalore *n.* corn flower.
artamaluta *n.* corn husk.
artasoro *n.* corn field.
artasun *n.* masculinity, manhood.
artatxori *n.(zool.)* sparrow (of the corn field).
artatza *n.* cornfield.
artazi(ak) *n.* scissors.
artazuriketa *n.* act of removing the corn husk.
artazuritzaile *n.* corn husk remover.
artazuritu *v.t.* to remove the corn husk.
arte *prep.* until. *n.* interval of time, time. *prep.* between, among. *n.(bot.)* evergreen oak tree, holm oak. *n.* trap.
-arte *(gram.)* Suffix used with expressions of place which signifies space between. *n.* beam made of evergreen oak. *n.* forest of evergreen oaks.
artean *adv.* meanwhile. *prep.* between, among.
artega *adj.* restless, agitated, nervous, impatient.
artegabeko *adj.* continuous, uninterrupted.
artegatasun *n.* restlessness, anxiety.
artegatsu *adj.* restless, uneasy, anxious.
artegatu *v.i.* to become restless, uneasy, anxious.
artegintza *n.* artistic production.
arteka *adv.* alternately, every so often.
artekadura *n.* insertion, introduction, putting in.
arteka-marteka *adv.* in one's free time.
artekari *n.* mediator, intermediary. *n.* agent, broker.
artekaritza *n.* brokerage, business of a broker.
artekatu *v.t.* to insert, to interpose, to put or place in between.
arteki *n.* wood of the evergreen oak. *n.* bacon.
arteko *adj.* medium. *n.* mediator, intermediary.
artelan *n.* work of art. *n.* community work.
artelari *n.* artist.
artetik *prep.* from the space between two or among several.
artetsu *adj.* skillful, expert. *adj.* abundant in evergreen oaks.
artetu *v.t.* to intervene, to interfere, to mediate. *v.i.* to manage, to find a way to, to contrive to.
artetxe *n.* sheepfold. *n.* house in the middle, middle house.
artetza *n.* grove of evergreen oaks.
arteune *n.* interruption, intermission.

artez *adv.* straight, directly. *adj.* honest, fair. *adj.* straight, unbent.
artezale *adj.* fond of art.
artezarketa *n.* insertion, interposition.
artez-artez *adv.* straight ahead, directly, straight away.
artezgarri *adj.* straightenable. *adj.* reformable.
artezko *adj.* artistic.
arteztu *v.t.* to straighten, to rectify, to correct.
artikulu *n.* article. *n.(gram.)* article.
artile *n.* sheep's wool.
artiledun *adj.* woolly.
artilegin *n.* wool dealer.
artilegintza *n.* wool industry.
artiletsu *adj.* woolly, woolen.
artilezko *adj.* wool, woolen, made of wool.
artileztu *v.t.* to cover with wool.
artirin *n.* corn flower.
artista *n.* artist.
artizar *n.(astron.)* Venus, morning star.
artizki *n.(gram.)* infix. **Contr. of** *arte* + *izki*.
arto *n.(bot.)* corn, maize.
artola *n.* sheepfold. *n.* evergreen oak forest. *n.* type of saddle.
artxibagailu *n.* filing cabinet.
artxibari *n.* archivist.
artxibatu *v.t.* to file.
artxibo *n.* archive, card catalog.
artxibozain *n.* archivist.
artxiduke *n.* archduke.
artxidukego *n.* office or position of an archduke.
artximiloidun *adj.* multimillionaire.
artxo *n.(dim.)* young lamb, small sheep.
artzain *n.* sheepherder, shepherd.
artzainborda *n.* sheepherder's hut.
artzaindu *v.t.* to herd sheep.
artzaineraz *adv.* rustically, pastorally.
artzaineria *n.* group of sheepherders.
artzainezko *adj.* pertaining to a sheepherder.
artzaingo *n.* job of sheepherding.
artzainmutil *n.* young sheepherder, shepherd boy.
artzainsoinu *n.(mus.)* pastorale, sheepherder's melody. *n.* shepherd's whistle, whistle by a shepherd.
artzaintsa *n.* female sheepherder, sheepherdess.
artzaintxo *n.(dim.)* young shepherd.
artzaintza *n.* shepherding, sheepherding, tending flocks, the job of a sheepherder.
artzainzakur *n.* sheepherder's dog, sheepdog.
artzakume *n.(dim.)* bear cub.
artzan- Used in compound words.
artzaneska *n.* woman sheepherder, shepherdess.
artzanor *n.* sheepherder's dog, sheepdog.

artzapez *n. (eccl.)* archpriest.
artzapezgo *n.(eccl.)* office of the archpriest.
artzapezpiku *n.(eccl.)* archbishop.
artzapezpikugo *n.(eccl.)* office of the archbishop.
artzapezpikutar *adj.* archiepiscopal.
artzapezpikutegi *n.* archbishopric.
artzapezpikutu *v.i.* to become archbishop.
asaba *n.* ancestor.
asaben *adj.* ancestral.
asabetxe *n.* ancestral house.
asaldagarri *adj.* alarming, shocking, frightening, upsetting.
asaldagarriki *adv.* alarmingly, frighteningly, shockingly.
asaldaketa *n.* agitation, excitement.
asaldakuntza *n.* riot, revolt, mutiny.
asaldapen *n.* riot, tumult, disturbance.
asaldarazi *v.t.* to mutiny, to riot, to incite to riot.
asaldari *n.* disturber, botherer, perturber.
asaldatu *v.i.* to be scared, to be perturbed. *v.t.* to disturb. *v.t.* to mutiny.
asaldatzaile *n.* disturber, agitator, botherer.
ase *v.i.* to be full, to be satiated. *adj.* abundant, full, satiated, sufficient.
asealdi *n.* act of gorging, overeating, satiety.
asearazi *v.t.* to satiate, to stuff, to overeat.
ase-ase *adj.* oversatiated, over full, stuffed, gorged.
asebete *n.* gorging, binge, overeating. *v.i./v.t.* to be satiated, to satiate, to satisfy hunger.
asebetean *adv.* by gorging, oversatiating.
asedura *n.* satiety, fullness.
asegabe *adj.* insatiate, unsatisfied.
asegabeki *adv.* greedily.
asegabetasun *n.* insatiableness, insatiateness.
asegaitz *adj.* insatiable, craving, greedy.
asegarri *adj.* satiable; filling.
asegurantza *n.* insurance.
aseguratu *v.t.* to insure.
aseguratzaile *n.* insurer, underwriter.
aseguru *n.* insurance.
asegurudun *adj.* insured.
asekada *n.* satiety, fullness.
asekai *adj.* satiable.
asekaitz *adj.* insatiable, craving.
asekaldi *n.* gorging, binge, overeating.
asekari *n.* glutton.
aseketa *n.* overeating, fill.
aseki *adv.* abundantly.
asekuntza *n.* satisfaction, fullness.
asetasun *n.* satiety, fullness, full satisfaction of a desire.
asete *n.* period of abundance, satiety.
asetu *v.i./v.t.* to become full, to

become satiated; to fill (someone) up (with food). *v.t.* to feed, to nourish.
asetzaile *n.* satiator, filler.
asezin *adj.* insatiable, craving, greedy, glutton.
asezindako *adj.* insatiable, craving.
asezinez *adv.* voraciously, greedily, gluttonously.
asezinik *adv.* greedily, insatiably.
asezintasun *n.* insatiableness, greediness, gluttony.
asezkor *adj.* insatiable, greedy, craving.
aska *n.* watering-place for cattle. *n.* manger, crib.
askabide *n.* liberation process, way of setting (something) loose.
askadura *n.* liberation, act of setting loose.
askaezin *adj.* impossible to free, impossible to untie, unsolvable.
askaezintasun *n.* unsolvability.
askagaitz *adj.* difficult to untie.
askagarri *adj.* freeable, loosenable. *adj.* liberating.
askagintza *n.* liberating activity.
askaketa *n.* liberation, act of freeing. *n.* untying, setting loose.
askakor *adj.* easily loosened.
askaldegi *n.* place to have an afternoon meal, snack bar.
askaldu *v.t.* to have a mid-afternoon snack.
askalondo *n.* period of time after a mid-afternoon snack.
askaltiar *n.* guest for mid-afternoon snack.
askamin *n.* strong desire for liberation.
askapen *n.* liberation, freeing.
askarazi *v.t.* to liberate, to free, to set free.
askari *n.* mid-afternoon snack.
askasari *n.* ransom.
askatasun *n.* freedom, liberty.
askatasunez *adv.* freely, spontaneously, independently.
askatu *v.t.* to untie, to loosen, to unfasten, to untangle. *v.t./v.i.* to free, to liberate.
askatxo *n.(dim.)* small cattle trough, manger, crib.
askatzaile *n.* liberator, freer.
askaurre *n.* front part of a manger.
askazi *n.* relative. *n.* race.
askazgo *n.* clan, kinship.
aske *adj.* free, independent. *adj.* loose.
askespen *n.* pardon, absolution, forgiveness.
aski *adv.* enough, sufficiently, quite.
askietsi *v.t.* to think (something) is sufficient or enough.
aski izan *v.t.* to be enough, to be sufficient.
askiki *adv.* sufficiently, enough.
asko *adj./adv.* many, much, a lot, a great deal of.
askodun *adj.* owning many things.

askoka adv. whole sale, bulk.
askokari n. wholesaler.
askoren adj. common, general.
askotako adj. diverse, multiple.
askotan adv. many times, often, frequently, generally.
askotara adv. in many ways, in different manners.
askotariko adj. complex, varied, diverse.
askotarikotza n. diversity, variety, multiplicity.
askotasun n. multiplicity, variety, diversity.
askotsu adj. varied, diverse, multiple.
askotu v.i./v.t. to multiply, to increase, to grow in number.
askotxo adv. slightly too much, a little too much.
askoz adv. by far, by a large difference, much.
askozko adj. multiple, diverse. adj.(gram.) plural.
asmabide n. manner of inventing. n. discernment, judgment.
asmaezin adj. impossible to invent. adj. unconceivable, unbelievable, unthinkable.
asmagai n. puzzle, enigma, riddle.
asmagaitz adj. difficult to invent; enigmatic, inconceivable.
asmagarri adj. imaginable, predictable, guessable.
asmagin n. guesser.
asmaginkeria n. witchcraft, sorcery, black magic.
asmagintza n. job of guesser. n. magic, adivination.
asmakeria n. divination, augury, prediction. n. vain illusion, fiction.
asmaketa n. invention, riddle. n. thought, reflection.
asmakizun n. invention, riddle. n. reflection, thought, intellectual conception.
asmakor adj. original, imaginative.
asmakunde n. invention, discovery.
asmakuntza n. invention, creation.
asmalari n. guesser, inventor, discoverer.
asmamen n. discernment, creativity, talent, inventiveness. n. imagination, fantasy.
asmapen n. discovery, invention.
asmari n. inventor. n. diviner, guesser.
asmatu v.t. to invent, to devise, to plan, to think of, to make up. v.t. to guess, to conjecture, to imagine, to figure out.
asmatzaile n. inventor, improviser. n. guesser, diviner.
asmo n. intention, plan, idea, purpose.
asmobakarreko adj. having a fixed idea, single-minded.
asmogabez adv. unintentionally, unpremeditatedly, without plans.
asmogabeko adj. unintentional,

unplanned, unpremeditated.
asmogaiztoko adj. ill-disposed, ill-intentioned.
asmo izan v.t to intend, to pretend, to try.
asmoz adv. on purpose, intentionally, deliberately.
aspaldi adv. a long time ago, long ago.
aspaldian adv. for a long time, it is a long time since.
aspaldidanik adv. for a long time.
aspaldiko adj. old, ancient.
aspaldikotasun n. antiquity, oldness.
aspaldion adv. lately, in the recent past.
aspalditasun n. oldness, antiquity.
aspalditik adv. for a long time.
aspalditxoan adv. for some time.
aspaldiz adv. for some time.
asperdura n. boredom, tediousness.
aspergaitz adj. indefatigable, untiring.
aspergaiztasun n. indefatigability, untiringness.
aspergarri adj. fastidious, bothersome, inopportune, boring.
aspergarriro adv. boringly, bothersomely, fastidiously, inopportunely.
asperkeria n. tediousness, boredom.
asperketa n. boredom, tediousness.
asperraldi n. boring time, boredom. n. act of vengeance, revenge.
aspertasun n. tediousness, boredom. n. revenge, vengeance.
asperterazi v.t. to bore, to annoy, to bother, to molest.
aspertu v.i. to be bored, to get bored. v.t. to bore. v.i. to take revenge, to avenge.
aspertzaile n. boring person. n. avenger, one who takes revenge.
aspiltzeta n. grove of hawthorns.
aspirina n.(med.) aspirin.
asta- Used in compound words. Derived from asto, ass, donkey.
astabelar n. evening primrose.
astaburu n. head of an ass.
astajoko n. donkey race.
astakeria n. brutishness, stupidity, foolishness.
astakilo n.(dim.) young donkey. adj.(fig.) foolish, silly, stupid.
astakirten adj.(colloq.) stupid, foolish, silly.
astakume n.(dim.) young ass.
astalarranga n. rolling on the back (donkey).
astalasterketa n. ass race.
astalkatu v.t. to reel, to wind a spool, to wind thread into skeins.
astalketa n. reeling, winding.
astalketari n. reeler, winder.
astalko n. skein, hank.
astama n. mother donkey.
astanabar n.(zool.) zebra.
astapotro adj.(colloq.) foolish, stupid; brutish, brute.

astaputz adj.(colloq.) stupid, foolish, silly; rude, vulgar, coarse.

astapuztu v.i. to become foolish, to become stupid.

astar n. male donkey.

astasaski n. pair of saddlebags usually made of wicker.

astatalde n. group of donkeys.

astatu v.i. to become brutish.

astazain n. ass keeper, donkey keeper.

astazakil adj. foolish, stupid.

aste n. week.

asteamai n. weekend.

astearte n. Tuesday.

asteazken n. Wednesday.

astebete n. one whole week.

astebiko adj. biweekly.

astebukaera n. weekend.

astegun n. working day.

asteka adv. every other week.

astekari n. weekly publication.

asteko adj. of the week, weekly. n. weekly wage. n. person in charge of a weekly duty.

astelehen n. Monday.

asteme n. female donkey.

astenagusi n. week of annual celebrations in a city.

asterdi n. middle of the week.

astero adv. weekly, each week.

asteroko adj. weekly. n. weekly publication.

Aste Saindu n. Holy Week.

astesari n. weekly wage.

asti n. free time, time, a while.

astia eman v.t. to pass the time.

astialdi n. free time, time.

astidun adj. slow, tardy, sluggish.

astigabe adj. impatient, anxious.

astigar n.(bot.) maple tree.

astigarraga n. grove of maples.

astikoi adj. slow, tardy.

astikor adj. slow, calm, tardy.

astinaldi n. beating, whipping, flogging. n. reprimand, scolding. n. shake.

astindari n. beater, pounder.

astindu v.t. to shake off; to shake; to sift. v.t. to beat, to whip, to flog. v.t. to shake (someone) up, to affect (someone) emotionally.

astindura n. shaking, beating, pounding.

astingarri adj. beatable, punishable.

astinkada n. blow, beat.

astinkari n. beater, pounder, whipper.

astinketa n. shaking, beating.

astintasun n. fluffiness.

astintsu adj. fluffy.

astintzaile n. beater, flogger, whipper.

astiro adv. slowly, calmly.

astirotasun n. slowness, tardiness, calmness.

astitsu adj. slow, tardy, calm.

astiune n. free time.

asto n.(zool.) donkey, ass. adj.(colloq.)

stupid, foolish, silly. adj.(colloq.) rude, brute. n. A-shaped wooden construction which supports a scaffold.

astoantzeko adj. brutish.

astoarrantza n. braying.

astoketa n. group of burros.

astoki n. meat of an ass. adv.(colloq.) foolishly, stupidly.

astokilo adj.(colloq.) foolish, stupid, silly.

astoko adj.(colloq.) brutish.

astolan n. hard work.

astolapiko adj.(colloq.) stupid, fool, silly.

astolaster n. donkey race.

astolasterketa n. donkey race.

astopotro adj.(colloq.) foolish, stupid; brutish, bestial, brute.

astotxo n.(dim.) small donkey.

astotzar n.(augm.) large ass. adj.(fig.) stupid, foolish, brutish.

astotzara n. saddlebag or basket carried by a donkey.

astrapala n. noise, clamor.

astrapalada n. deafening noise, crash, clamor.

astrapaladaka adv. noisily.

astro n. star.

astrologari n. astronomer.

astrologia n. astrology.

astun adj. heavy. adj. mortal. adj. serious, grave.

astunagotu v.t. to make heavier.

astundu v.i./v.t. to get heavy, to add weight to, to increase the weight of. v.i. to become heavy.

astungabezia n. weightlessness, lightness, lack of weight.

astungarri adj. burdensome, heavy.

astunketa n. heaviness, weight.

astunki adj. heavily, weightily.

astuntasun n. heaviness, weightiness.

asturu n. luck, fate, fortune.

asturuz adv. by chance, accidentally.

asun n.(bot.) nettle.

asundegi n. field of nettles.

ata- Used in compound words. Derived from ate, door.

atabaka n. small box used by fishermen to keep tobacco.

atabal n.(mus.) drum.

atabalari n. drummer.

atabalatu v.t. to play the drum. v.t. to announce by means of a drum.

atabaldun n. drummer, tambour player.

atabalkari n. drummer, percussionist.

atabalmakila n. drumstick.

atabaltxo n.(dim.) small drum.

ataburu n. lintel.

ataga n. wooden bar across a door.

atagatu v.t. to bar a door.

ataka n. narrow door, narrow passage.

atal n. piece, fragment, chunk.

atal- Used in compound words. Derived from ate, door.

atalarri n. lintel.

atalaurre n. space in front of the main entrance.

atalbanaketa n. decomposition, division into parts, fragmentation.

atalbanatu v.t. to divide into pieces, to fragment.

atalbiko adj. having two members.

atalburu n. lintel. n. chapter of a book.

ataldu v.t. to divide into pieces or parts.

ataldun adj. composed of pieces or parts, patched, pieced.

ataleiho n. peephole, small grate or door in a larger door.

atalera n. manner of dividing.

atalgabeko adj. whole, entire, in one piece, undivided, simple.

atalgai adj. divisible, dividable.

atalgaitasun n. divisibility.

atalgaitz adj. indivisible, difficult to divide.

atalgarri adj. divisible, dividable.

atalgarritasun n. divisibility.

atalgarrizko adj. dividing, divisional.

atalka adv. in pieces, in parts, in segments, in sections.

atalkatu v.t. to fragment, to cut up into pieces.

atalkatzaile n. dissector; divider, one who fragments (something).

atalketa n. parceling, dividing, fragmentation; dissection.

atalkide n. member, integral part.

atalkin n. integral part.

atalkor adj. dividing, separating.

atalondo n. porch, vestibule.

ataltxo n.(dim.) small piece, small part.

atari n. front door, doorway, main entrance, vestibule.

ataritxo n.(dim.) small entrance door.

atarramendu n. advantage, benefit.

atarte n. vestibule, porch.

ataska n. hatch door.

ataurre n. vestibule, porch. n.(fig.) introduction.

ataurreko adj. pertaining to the vestibule. adj.(fig.) introductory, preliminary.

ate n. door, gate.

atenagusi n. main entrance, front door.

atera v.t. to take out. v.i. to go out, to get out, to exit, to leave.

aterabide n. exit, way out. n. solution, alternative.

ateradura n. act of leaving, going out.

ateraegun n. departure day.

ateragarri adj. extracting, taking out.

ateraketa n. act of taking out, extraction.

aterakin n. extract, that which has been taken out.

ateraldi n. witty saying, remark. n. extraction.

aterapen n. taking out. n. result, consequence, outcome.

aterarazi v.t. to cause to take out.

aterarazle n. wheedler, enticer, coaxer.

ateratu v.i. to go out, to walk out, to leave. v.t. to take advantage of, to make a profit. v.i. to go to the door.

ateratzaile n. person who takes out something. n. server, person who serves in the game (tennis, jai-alai, etc.).

atergabe adj. continual, incessant, constant, continuous. adv. constantly, incessantly.

atergabeki adv. constantly, uninterruptedly, incessantly, continuously.

atergabeko adj. uninterrupted, continuous, continual, incessant.

ateri adj. clear, calm (weather).

aterki n. umbrella.

aterkiontzi n. umbrella stand.

aterpe n. penthouse, pent roof; porch; shelter, refuge.

aterperatu v.i. to get out of the rain, to be protected from the rain.

aterpetu v.i. to take shelter, to shelter.

aterraldi n. clearing up (of weather).

aterrezin adj. incessant, continuous (rain).

aterrune n. clearing up (of weather), break in the weather.

atertu v.t. to clear up, to interrupt raining. v.i. to cease, to end, to stop.

atesari n. toll, fee.

atetxo n.(dim.) small door.

atetzar n.(augm.) large door.

atexka n. (dim.) small door.

atezain n. doorkeeper, gate-keeper, usher of the court, doorman. n. goalie, goalkeeper, goaltender.

atezaindegi n. doorkeeper's office.

atezaingela n. doorkeeper's room, doorman's room.

atezaintzaile n. doorkeeper.

atezakur n. guard dog, watchdog.

atez-ate adv. from door to door.

atezatu v.t. to tighten. v.t. to stretch out.

atlantiko adj. Atlantic.

atlas n. (geog.) atlas.

atletismo n. athleticism.

atoi n. tow, trailer.

atoiontzi n. tugboat.

atoitu v.t. to drag, to tow.

atomiko adj. atomic.

atomo n. (phys.) atom.

atomozko adj. atomic.

atondu v.t. to prepare, to fix; to put in order, to arrange. v.i. to make up, to get ready, to dress up.

atonketa n. preparation.

atontzaile n. preparer, arranger, organizer.

ator n. shirt.

atorluze n. nightgown, nightshirt.

atrakaldi n. act of docking, approaching the pier.

atrakaleku *n.* dock, pier, wharf.

atrakatu *v.t.* to berth, to dock, to come alongside a pier. *v.t.* to rob (armed robbery).

atrakatzaile *n.* robber (armed).

atraku *n.* armed robbery.

atralaka *n.* fight, quarrel, dispute, contention.

atralakari *n.* person inclined to fight, quarrelsome.

atseden *n.* relaxation, rest.

atsedenaldi *n.* relaxation, rest time, break.

atsedenartu *v.t.* to rest, to relax, to take a rest.

atsedendu *v.i.* to rest, to relax.

atsedenez *adv.* restedly, in a relaxed manner.

atsedengarri *adj.* relaxing, resting, soothing.

atsedenleku *n.* place to rest.

atsedentoki *n.* place to rest.

atsegin *n.* pleasure, satisfaction, joy, delight. *n.* rest, relief. *adj.* pleasing, pleasant.

atseginaldi *n.* pleasure, joy, time of satisfaction.

atseginarazi *v.t.* to cause pleasure for another.

atsegindu *v.t.* to please, to delight, to entertain.

atsegindura *n.* pleasure, delight.

atseginez *adv.* gladly, with pleasure.

atseginezko *adj.* pleasing, pleasant, agreeable.

atsegingarri *adj.* delightful, agreeable, pleasant.

atsegingarriro *adv.* pleasantly, agreeably.

atsegingarritasun *n.* agreeableness, pleasantness.

atsegingose *n.* sensuality, lust.

atsegin izan *v.t./v.i.* to like, to please.

atseginkeria *n.* lust, sensuality.

atseginkoi *adj.* voluptuous, lascivious, libertine, lustful.

atseginkoitasun *n.* voluptuousness, lustfulness, lasciviousness.

atseginkor *adj.* agreeable, amiable, pleasant.

atseginkortasun *n.* gentleness, amiability.

atsegintasun *n.* pleasure, delight, delectation.

atsegintsu *adj.* nice, pleasant, delightful, agreeable.

atseginzale *adj.* voluptuous, sensual, sensuous.

atsegintzalekeria *n.* voluptuousness, sensuality, sybaritism.

atsekabe *n.* affliction, anxiety, suffering, sorrow, anguish, grief.

atsekabedun *adj.* hurt, aching, suffering.

atsekabeki *adv.* sadly, sorrowfully, painfully.

atsekabekor *adj.* likely to be hurt, morose, depressed. *adj.* painful.

atsekabetsu *adj.* painful, full of anguish, sorrowful. *adj.* sad.

atsekabetu *v.t.* to afflict, to distress, to sadden, to cause sorrow. *v.i.* to sadden, to become sad.

atsekabetzaile *adj.* sorrowful, distressing, heartbreaking.

atsekabez *adv.* painfully, sorrowfully.

atsekabezko *adj.* condoling, comforting.

atso *n.* old woman

atsokeria *n.* old woman's whim, frenzy, extravagance, eccentricity.

atsotasun *n.* quality of being an old woman.

atsoteria *n.* group of old ladies.

atsotitz *n.* proverb, saying. (lit.) old lady's word.

atsotitzale *adj.* fond of proverbs.

atsotitz-bilduma *n.* collection of proverbs or refrains.

atsotitzez *adv.* proverbially.

atsotu *v.i.* to grow old (for women), to become old.

atsotxo *n.(dim.)* little old lady.

atsotzar *n.(augm.)* strong and husky old woman.

atun *n.(zool.)* tuna fish.

atunaldi *n.* tuna fishing season (July to October).

atunari *n.* tuna fisherman.

atunketa *n.* season of tuna fishing. *n.* act of fishing tuna. *n.* great amount of tuna.

atunketari *n.* tuna fisherman.

atunki *n.* tuna meat.

atunontzi *n.* boat for fishing tuna, tuna boat.

atunzale *adj.* fond of tuna.

atxiki *v.t.* to retain. *v.t.* to grab, to catch, to seize.

atxikidura *n.* adhesion, attachment. *n.* family tie or link.

atxikiezin *adj.* impossible to adhere to, nonadhesive.

atxikigarri *adj.* adhesive, adhering, sticking.

atxikimendu *n.* adhesion, attachment.

atxikitasun *n.* adhesion, adhesiveness. *n.* constancy, steadiness, tenacity.

atxikitzaile *n.* catcher, apprehender. *n.* maintainer, supporter.

atxilotu *v.t.* to arrest.

atximur *n.* pinch.

atximurkada *n.* pinch.

atximurkari *n.* pincher.

atximurkatu *v.t.* to pinch.

atximurkatxo *n.(dim.)* small pinch, gentle pinch.

atxis! *n.* onomatopoeic sound of sneezing, achoo!

atzapar *n.* claw.

atzaparkada *n.* scratch; mauling.

atzaparkatu *v.t.* to scratch. *v.t.* to scrape.

atzaparketa n. scratching.

atzapartu v.t. to scratch.

atze n. back part, posterior part (of house, boat, etc.). n.(anat.) bottom of the body.

atzea eman v.t. to disdain.

atzealde n. back part, rear, posterior part.

atzean adv./prep. in the back, behind.

atzearazi v.t. to cause to go back. v.t. to dissuade, to advise against.

atze-atzeka adv. backwards, toward the rear, backing up.

atzebegirada n. act of looking back on, retrospection.

atzebegiraz adv. retrospectively.

atzeikuspen n. retrospection.

atzeispilu n. rearview mirror.

atzejaile n. detractor.

atzejarrera n. postposition.

atzekalde n. back side. n. rear part of anything (boat, car, house, etc.). n.(anat.) bottom, fanny.

atzekaldeko adj. back.

atzeko adj. posterior, rear, back. n. back player in the game of jai-alai. n. skipper, tillerman (in a boat).

atzekoaurrez adv. backwards.

atzelari n. back player at the game of jai-alai. n./adj.(colloq.) homosexual.

atzemaile n. seizer, grabber, catcher.

atzeman v.t. to capture, to seize, to catch, to arrest. v.t. to reach, to get hold of.

atzemanarazi v.t. to cause to seize, to cause to catch.

atzemangarri adj. apprehensible, capable of being seized.

atzemansari n. reward for finding something.

atzemate n. capture, seizure.

atzera adv. again. adv. backwards, to the back.

atzera-aurrera n. round trip.

atzerabide n. deferment, postponement, delay. n. obstacle, hindrance.

atzeradei n. bugle call for retreat.

atzera egin v.t. to go back, to recede, to go backwards, to retreat. v.t. to revoke, to go back upon one's word.

atzera ekarri v.t. to bring again, to bring back, to return.

atzera eman v.t. to give back.

atzeraeragineko adj. retroactive.

atzeraeragintasun n. retroactivity, quality of being retroactive.

atzeraerazi v.t. to make (someone) go back, to cause to retreat.

atzeraezin adj. irrevocable, irreversible.

atzeragarri adj. hindering, impeding. n. obstacle, difficulty, hindrance.

atzeragotu v.t. to postpone, to delay, to prolong.

atzera jo v.t. to recede, to go back, to return.

atzeraka adv. receding, going back.

atzerakada n. backward motion, recession, receding, retreating.

atzeraka egin v.t. to go back, to return, to recede, to retreat.

atzerakari n. person who recedes, person who backs out.

atzeraketa n. act of receding, recession, retreat, backing up, backing away.

atzerakoi adj. strongly conservative, reactionary. adj. fond of being last, laggardly, backwards, tardy.

atzerakor adj. regressive, recessive.

atzerakotasun n. retroactivity, regressiveness.

atzerakuntza n. backward motion, retrogression, step backward.

atzeraldi n. backward motion, regression. n. withdrawal.

atzerapen n. delay, postponement. n. obstacle, hindrance, drawback. n. retrogression, recession.

atzera saldu v.t. to resell.

atzeratasun n. shyness. n. underdevelopment.

atzeratu v.t. to pull back, to move back, to push back. v.i./v.t. to postpone, to delay, to be delayed, to defer, to get behind.

atzeratzaile adj. dissuasive.

atzerri n. foreign country.

atzerrialdi n. period of time in a foreign country. n. time in exile, expatriation.

atzerrikeria n. fondness of foreign customs.

atzerriko adj. foreign.

atzerriraketa n. exodus, exile, banishment, expatriation.

atzerrirapen n. exile, exodus, banishment, expatriation.

atzerriratu v.i. to emigrate, to go abroad. v.t. to banish, to exile.

atzerritar n./adj. foreigner, stranger.

atzerrizale adj. fond of foreign customs.

atzerrizaletasun n. strong fondness for foreign customs.

atzerrizaletu v.i. to adopt foreign manners.

atzetik prep. from the back, behind.

atzez adv. backward.

atzezarketa n. postponement, delay.

atzezarri v.t. to postpone, to delay.

atzezka adv. backward, on one's back, face up.

atzipetsu adj. deceitful, false, fraudulent.

atzipetu v.t. to deceive, to cheat, to trick.

atzipez adv. fraudulently, falsely, deceitfully.

atzizki n. (gram.) suffix.

atzo adv. yesterday.

aufa! int. exclamation of happiness.

auhen n. complaint, lament.

auhendari n. complainer.

auhendatu *v.i.* to lament, to complain.

auhengarri *adj.* deplorable.

aukera *n.* election; choice, selection. *n.* abundance. *n.* opportunity, chance, possibility.

aukerabide *n.* option, chance, opportunity, choice.

aukerabidezko *adj.* optional, selective.

aukeragarri *adj.* eligible, choosable, selectable.

aukeraketa *n.* election; choice.

aukerakizun *n.* possibility to choose or elect.

aukerako *adj.* select, elected, chosen. *adj.* convenient, appropriate.

aukeraldi *n.* election time; time of choosing.

aukeramen *n.* free will, faculty to choose.

aukeratasun *n.* possibility to choose.

aukeratu *v.t.* to choose, to select; to elect, to vote.

aukeratzaile *n.* person who chooses or selects.

aukerazko *adj.* optional, elective.

aulki *n.* small bench, stool, chair. *n.* throne.

aulkiratu *v.i.* to go to one's chair.

aulkitxo *n.(dim.)* small stool.

Aunamendi *n.* Mount Anie in the Basque Pyrenees. (The highest mountain in the Basque country.)

aupa! *int.* exclamation used for cheering. *int.* exclamation used when lifting heavy weights.

aupada *n.* challenge, provocation, defiance.

aupa egin *v.t.* to pick up (children's language).

aupagarri *adj.* praiseworthy.

aupagile *n.* challenger, defier.

aupaka *adv.* challenging, defying.

aupaka egin *v.t.* to challenge, to defy.

aupakari *n.* challenger, defier.

aupakatu *v.t.* to challenge, to provoke.

aupatu *v.t.* to promote, to praise, to glorify. *v.t.* to lift up, to raise up.

aupatzaile *n.* praiser.

aurka *prep.* against. *prep.* face to face, in front of.

aurka egin *v.t.* to challenge, to defy. *v.t.* to fight, to oppose.

aurkagarri *adj.* opposing.

aurkagile *n.* opponent, contradictor, antagonist, adversary.

aurkako *adj.* contrary, opposed, opposite, antagonistic, opponent.

aurkakotasun *n.* antagonism, opposition.

aurkalari *n.* adversary, contradictor, antagonist, opponent.

aurkari *n.* adversary, antagonist, contradictor, opponent.

aurkatasun *n.* antagonism, opposition.

aurkatzaile *adj.* imputing, refuting, challenging, attacking. *n.* imputer, refuter, challenger, attacker.

aurkazko *adj.* contrary, adverse.

aurkezgarri *adj.* presentable.

aurkezkizun *n.* requisition, summons.

aurkezkunde *n.* presentation, exhibition, personal introduction.

aurkezlari *n.* presenter, demonstrator, shower, introducer.

aurkezle *n.* presenter, demonstrator, shower.

aurkezpen *n.* presentation, exhibition, personal introduction. *n.* appearance (before a judge, etc.).

aurkeztatu *v.t.* to present, to introduce. *v.t.* to show, to exhibit.

aurkeztatzaile *n.* presenter, introducer, demonstrator, shower.

aurkeztezin *adj.* irrepresentable, unshowable, undemonstrable.

aurkeztu *v.t.* to present, to introduce. *v.i.* to introduce oneself.

aurki *adv.* soon, immediately. *adv.* surely, undoubtedly.

aurkiarazi *v.t.* to cause to find.

aurkibide *n.* index, table of contents.

aurkigune *n.* point of encounter.

aurkiketa *n.* discovery, invention.

aurkikunde *n.* discovery; finding.

aurkikuntza *n.* discovery.

aurkileku *n.* meeting place.

aurkintza *n.* group of young people. *n.* finding; discovery, invention.

aurkipen *n.* discovery; finding.

aurkitu *v.i.* to be, to find oneself, to feel. *v.t.* to find.

aurkitzaile *n.* finder; discoverer.

aurpegi *n.* face.

aurpegi eman *v.t.* to face, to confront, to defend, to counterattack, to face up to.

aurpegiera *n.* facial expression, feature, look.

aurpegiestalketa *n.* act of covering the face.

aurpegihandi *adj.* bold, insolent, petulant.

aurpegi izan *v.t.* to have guts, to be bold, to be daring, to have nerve.

aurpegiko *n.* slap in the face. *adj.* facial, pertaining to the face.

aurpegilun *n.* serious-looking face.

aurpegiordeko *n.* mask.

aurpegira bota *v.t.* to incriminate, to accuse.

aurpegiratu *v.t.* to accuse. *v.t.* to confront.

aurpegiz-aurpegi *adv.* face to face.

aurre *n.* front part. *conj.* before.

aurre- *(gram.)* Prefix meaning before, front, face, fore-, pre-; progress.

aurreadierazpen *n.* forecast, prediction.

aurrea eman *v.t.* to face, to confront.

aurrealde *n.* facade, front part.

aurrean *adv.* ahead. *prep.* in front of.

aurrean egon *v.i.* to witness, to attend, to be present at, to be in front of.

aurrean erabili *v.t.* to harass, to

oppress, to persecute.

aurrean joan *v.i.* to go before, to precede.

aurreasmo *n.* forethought, premeditation.

aurrebaldintza *n.* condition, prerequisite.

aurre egin *v.t.* to face, to confront.

aurregun *n.* eve.

aurreiritzi *n.* prejudice, bias.

aurreirizle *n.* previous or last speaker.

aurrejarrera *n.* prevention. *n.* act of placing before.

aurrejarri *v.t.* to place before. *v.i.* to face, to confront.

aurrekalde *n.* facade, front part.

aurrekari *adj.* preceding, previous.

aurreko *adj.* previous, anterior to, before. *n.* predecessor, ancestor.

aurrekontu *n.(econ.)* budget.

aurrekontu egin *v.t.* to budget.

aurrekontuzko *adj.* budgetary.

aurrekotasun *n.* precedence, priority, antecedence.

aurrelan *n.* preliminary work or task.

aurrelari *n.* foreplayer in jai-alai. *adj.* progressive, leading, vanguard. *n.* precursor, pioneer, predecessor.

aurrelaritza *n.* primacy, leadership.

aurren *adj.* main, principal. *adj.* previous, preceding. *adj.* first.

aurrenik *adv.* first of all.

aurreohar *n.* premonition, forewarning, warning.

aurrera *int.* go! go on! go ahead! *adv.* forward, ahead.

aurrerabaki *n.* predetermination, deciding beforehand.

aurrerabide *n.* process, development. *n.* stimulus, incentive.

aurrerabideak *n.* preliminary actions.

aurrerabidez *adv.* progressively.

aurrera egin *v.t.* to make progress, to advance, to move forward, to keep going.

aurreragarri *adj.* progressive.

aurreragoko *adj.* previous, former, preceding.

aurreragotu *v.t./v.i.* to advance, to take a lead, to move (something) ahead.

aurrerakada *n.* advance, progress, forward movement. *n.* improvement.

aurreraketa *n.* advancement, passing.

aurrerakin *n.(econ.)* advance (money).

aurrerakoan *adv.* from now on.

aurrerakoi *adj.* progressive, innovative.

aurrerakor *adj.* progressive. *adj.* prosperous, successful.

aurrerakortasun *n.* progressiveness.

aurrerakuntza *n.* progress, advancement, advance, improvement.

aurreraldi *n.* progress, advancement, improvement.

aurrerantzean *adv.* from now on.

aurrerantzeko *adj.* forthcoming, future, upcoming, successive.

aurrerapen *n.* progress, advance, advancement.

aurrerapide *n.* progress, advance, advancement.

aurreratu *v.i.* to advance, to move forward, to get ahead. *v.t.* to anticipate, to foresee. *v.t.* to make progress, to promote.

aurreratzaile *n.* anticipator, forecaster. *n.* saver.

aurrerazale *adj.* progressive.

aurrerazaletasun *n.* progressiveness.

aurrerazle *adj.* progressive.

aurreritzi *n.* prejudice, bias.

aurreruntz *adv.* forward

aurresale *n.* forecaster, prognosticator.

aurresan *v.t.* to predict, to foretell. *n.* prediction, guess.

aurresku *n.* typical Basque dance.

aurreskulari *n.* dancer in the *aurresku.*

aurresortu *v.t.* to preconceive.

aurresusmo *n.* suspicion, presentiment, foresight.

aurretasun *n.* priority, preference.

aurretiazko *adj.* preventive.

aurretik *adv.* before, beforehand. *prep.* away, out of here.

aurretikan *adv.* previously, in advance.

aurretiko *adj.* previous, precedent, former. *n.* ancestor.

aurreuste *n.* presentiment, suspicion, foresight.

aurrez *adv.* previously, in advance. *prep.* in front of, facing, opposite.

aurrez-aurre *adv.* face to face.

aurrez-aurreko *adj.* opposed, faced, confronted.

aurrez-aurretu *v.t.* to confront, to oppose.

aurrez eman *v.t.* to loan in advance.

aurrezki *n.* savings.

aurrezkibide *n.* way of saving (money).

aurrezkigile *n.* one who saves money.

aurrezkikontu *n.* savings account.

aurrezki kutxa *n.* savings and loan bank.

aurrezte *n.* anticipation, foresight.

aurrizki *n. (gram.)* prefix.

aurrizkiztatu *v.t.* to prefix.

aurten *adv.* this year, in this year, during this year.

aurtengo *adj.* pertaining to this year, of this year, this year's.

aurtengoz *adv.* for this year.

ausardia *n.* courage, bravery, intrepidity, boldness, resolution.

ausarditsu *adj.* courageous, brave, bold, intrepid.

ausarkuntza *n.* courage, bravery.

ausarpen *n.* courage, bravery, audacity.

ausarta *adj.* brave, courageous.

ausartasun *n.* courage, intrepidity, fearlessness, bravery.

ausartatu *v.i.* to dare, to be fearless, to

venture.

ausarti *adj.* courageous, brave, bold.

ausartkeria *n.* bragging, arrogance, insolence.

ausartki *adv.* bravely, courageously, boldly, audaciously.

ausartsu *adj.* fearless, brave, courageous.

ausartu *v.i.* to dare, to be fearless, to venture.

ausartzia *n.* bravery, courage, fearlessness.

ausaz *adv.* maybe, perhaps. *adv.* accidentally, by chance.

ausikari *n.* biter.

ausiki *v.t.* to bite.

auskalo! *int.* who knows!

auto *n.* car, automobile.

autoaldakin *n.* any spare parts for cars.

autoargi *n.* car light, headlight.

autoargiteria *n.* group of headlights.

autobide *n.* road

autobidezabal. *n.* highway.

autobus *n.* bus.

autogidari *n.* driver.

autogobernu *n.(pol.)* self-government.

autoikustegi *n.* place for auto exhibitions, automobile showroom.

autokrata *adj.* autocratic.

autokrazia *n.* autocracy.

autolasterketa *n.* car race.

automatiko *adj.* automatic.

automatizatu *v.t.* to automate.

autonomia *n.(pol.)* autonomy.

autonomizale *adj.* fond of autonomy.

autopista *n.* highway, freeway.

autoseguru *n.* car insurance.

autostop *n.* hitch-hike.

autotoki *n.* garage, parking garage.

autozale *adj.* fond of cars.

autozerbitzu *n.* self-service.

autu *n.* conversation, talk.

autulari *n.* gossip, gossiper, person who likes rumors and spreads them.

autu-mautuak *n.* anecdotes, chatter, joke, spicy tale.

auzabide *n.* secondary road usually unpaved, village path, bridle path.

auzakide *n.* next-door neighbor, neighbor, one who lives in the same neighborhood.

auzalagun *n.* one who lives in the same neighborhood.

auzalan *n.* community work.

auzalur *n.* community land.

auzapez *n.* mayor.

auzatasun *n.* neighborhood, quality of being a neighbor.

auzatu *v.i.* to be a neighbor, to live next door.

auzi *n.* trial, lawsuit, litigation, contest, dispute.

auziagindu *n.* court order.

auzialdi *n.* prosecution, the conducting of a lawsuit.

auziareto *n.* courtroom.

auziaurre *n.* hearing, judicial investigation or trial as before court.

auziaurreko *adj.* prior to the trial, pre-trial.

auzibide *n.* procedure of a trial.

auzibidetu *v.t.* to prosecute.

auziegun *n.* day in court, trial date.

auziepai *n.* judicial sentence.

auziepaile *n.* judge.

auzietendura *n.* suspension or postponement of a trial.

auzigai *n.* litigation, carrying on a legal contest by judicial process.

auzikanpoko *adj.* extrajudicial.

auzikatu *v.t.* to litigate, to contend, to plead (a case).

auziketa *n.* litigation.

auzikide *n.* litigant, opposing party of a lawsuit.

auziko *adj.* belonging to a lawsuit, of a trial.

auzikor *adj.* litigating.

auzilagun *n.* litigant, party in a lawsuit.

auzilan *n.* legal procedure.

auzilari *n.* litigant, pleader.

auzilege *n.* judicial law.

auzimahai *n.* table at which a tribunal sits.

auzipeko *adj.* accused, prosecuted.

auzipetu *v.t.* to prosecute, to sue.

auzitan ari *v.i.* to prosecute, to sue.

auzitan ibili *v.i.* to sue, to prosecute.

auzitan sartu *v.i.* to prosecute, to sue.

auzitara eraman *v.t.* to prosecute, to take someone to court.

auzitaraketa *n.* incrimination, prosecution, inculpation.

auzitaratu *v.t.* to accuse, to prosecute.

auzitari *n.* contentious, litigious person.

auzitegi *n.* tribunal, court.

auzitu *v.t.* to prosecute.

auzizale *adj.* litigant, litigating.

auzo *n.* neighbor. *n.* neighborhood.

auzobide *n.* secondary or local road usually unpaved.

auzodi *n.* district.

auzogabe *adj.* uninhabited, deserted, unpopulated.

auzogabetu *v.i.* to vacate, to abandon, to be disinhabited, to move away.

auzokide *n.* neighbor.

auzoko *n.* neighbor. *adj.* nearby, adjacent, next door.

auzokotu *v.i.* to dwell close by, to be a neighbor, to live next door.

auzolan *n.* community work.

auzolur *n.* community land.

auzo-ondasunak *n.* property belonging to a community or neighborhood.

auzoraketa *n.* settling, dwelling, taking up residence in a neighborhood.

auzotar *n.* neighbor, next-door neighbor.

auzotasun *n.* quality of being a neighbor, neighborhood.

auzotegi n. neighborhood, vicinity. n. number of inhabitants in one place.
auzune n. district, neighborhood, ward, limits of a neighborhood.
axola n. care, concern, solicitude, interest, worry.
axoladun adj. careful, diligent, worried.
axolagabe adj. careless, heedless, negligent, unconcerned.
axolagabekeria n. carelessness, negligence, thoughtlessness, heedlessness.
axolagabeki adv. carelessly, negligently, heedlessly, unworriedly.
axolagabeko adj. careless, heedless, negligent.
axolagabetasun n. carelessness, heedlessness, negligence, lack of worry.
axolagabetu v.i. to become negligent, to become unconcerned, to be careless.
axola izan v.t./v.i. to care, to care about.
axolati adj. careful, solicitous, thoughtful, attentive, vigilant.
axolatsu adj. careful, solicitous, attentive, vigilant, thoughtful.
axolatu v.i. to be concerned, to be worried.
axolaz adv. carefully, diligently, attentively.
axolazko adj. worried, preoccupied, grave.
axubeta n. shoelace.
aza n. (bot.) cabbage.
azaburu n. head of cabbage.
azal n. bark of a tree; crust. n. skin. n. water surface. n. cover, peel. n. envelope. adj. shallow.
azalak n.(pl.) peelings, peels.
azalandare n. cabbage plant.
azalapaindu v.t. to make up.
azalapaingarri n. cosmetic.
azalapainketa n. make-up.
azalbide n. explanation, clarification.
azalbidezko adj. declarative, explanatory.
azaldaketa n. explanation, clarification.
azaldu v.t. to discover, to invent. v.t. to explain, to declare, to present. v.i. to appear, to appear in front of, to turn up. v.i. to scab, to cover with skin or bark (trees, etc.)
azalduezin adj. inexplicable, unexplainable.
azaldun adj. having a crust, crusty, having skin, covered.
azaldura n. explanation, clarification.
azaleko adj. superficial. adj. apparent, visible.
azaleratu v.t./v.i. to rise to the surface, to appear on the surface. v.t. to manifest, to show, to exhibit.
azalerazi v.t. to make (someone) show (something).
azaleri n.(med.) skin disease.

azalez adv. superficially, externally, lightly.
azalezko adj. apparent, visible. adj. pertaining to the skin.
azaleztadura n. act of covering, binding.
azaleztapen n. binding (books).
azaleztatu v.t. to bind (a book).
azaleztu v.t. to cover with a case or book cover, to line. v.i. to cover with skin, to scar, to scab over, to form a scab.
azalgabetu v.t./v.i. to strip or remove the bark, crust, cover, etc.
azalgaitz adj. difficult to explain, inexplicable, unexplainable.
azalgarri adj. explainable, manifestable.
azalgogortu v.i. to harden the skin.
azalili n.(bot.) cauliflower.
azalitxura n. external aspect.
azalkatu v.t. to explain. v.t. to peel.
azalkera n. appearance, way in which one shows oneself.
azalkeria n. superficiality. n. hypocrisy, pharisaism.
azalki n. piece of peel or bark.
azalkor adj. showy, flashy.
azalkuntza n. declaration, explanation, manifestation.
azalmintz n.(anat.) epidermis, skin.
azalore n.(bot.) cauliflower.
azalpen n. declaration, explanation, manifestation.
azaltasun n. superficialness, superficiality.
azaltsu adj. having lots of skin, having crust, having bark.
azaltzaile adj. declaring. n. declarer, expositor, explainer.
azaluskeria n. hypocrisy.
azaluts adj. insincere, hypocritical. n. hypocrite.
azalutsezko adj. apparent. adj. false, feigned.
azantz n. noise.
azantzio n.(bot.) wormwood, absinthe.
azaro n. season to sow, planting season. n. drops of dew. n. November.
azauto n.(dim.) small sheaf.
azeleragailu n.(mech.) starter, accelerator.
azelerapen n. acceleration.
azeleratu v.t./v.i. to accelerate, to speed up.
azenario n.(bot.) carrot.
azentu n.(gram.) accent (diacritical mark).
azentuapen n. accentuation.
azentuatu v.t. to accent, to accentuate, to stress.
azentudun adj. accentuated, accented, stressed.
azentugabe adj. unaccentuated.
azentuketa n. accentuation.
azeri n.(zool.) fox. adj.(fig.) shrewd,

mischievous.

azeriantzeko adj. fox-like, foxy.

azeribuztan n.(bot.) equisetum, foxtail.

azerieme n. female fox.

azerikeria n.(fig.) cunning, astuteness, artfulness, foxiness.

azeriki n. fox meat.

azeriko n.(dim.) fox cub.

azerikume n.(zool.) fox cub.

azeritegi n. fox den.

azerizko adj. fox-like, vulpine.

azerizulo n. burrow, hole made by the fox.

azido n.(chem.) acid.

azidotasun n.(chem.) acidity.

azienda n. livestock; landed property. n. wealth, property (boats, nets, fishing gear).

aziendatsu adj. rich in livestock.

azkar adj. active, strong, vigorous. adj. fast, quick, swift. adv. quickly, fast. adj. clever, bright.

azkara n. estrus, mating period of a female goat.

azkargarri adj. fortifying, vivifying, life-giving. n. fortifier.

azkar ibili v.i. to act quickly. v.i. to walk quickly.

azkarketa n. acceleration, speeding-up, hastening.

azkarki adv. actively. adv. fast, quickly, rapidly, swiftly.

azkartasun n. quickness, promptness, agility, haste, speed. n. sagacity, brightness, intelligence.

azkartu v.t./v.i. to urge, to press. v.t./v.i. to hasten, to hurry, to hurry up.

azken n. end, conclusion. adj. (the) last (one), final.

azkena eman v.t. to finish.

azkenagiri n. last will and testament.

azkenagur n. good-bye, a final farewell, goodbye forever.

azkenahi n. will, last will and testament.

azkenahiko adj. testamentary, pertaining to a will.

azkenalde n. last part, end.

azkenaldeko adj. final, last, ultimate.

azkenaldi n. last time.

azkenaldiak n.(theol.) death, judgment, hell and heaven.

azkenaldiko adj. finalist.

azkenarnasa n. last breath, agony.

azkenats n. last breath, agony.

azken-aurreko adj. next to the last.

azken-aurren adj. next to the last.

azken-azken adj. very last.

azken-azkeneko adj. very last.

azken batez adv. finally, at last, ultimately.

azkenburu n. end, conclusion.

azkenburuan adv. finally, at the end.

azkenburuko adj. terminal, final.

azkendu v.t. to finish, to end, to complete, to terminate.

azkenean adv. finally, at last, in the end.

azkenegun n. deadline.

azkeneko adj. final, last. adj. finalist.

azkenekoz adv. finally, ultimately.

azkenepai n. Final Judgment, Last Judgment, end of the world.

azkenepe n. final deadline.

azkenerabaki n. final decision.

azkeneratu v.i. to reach the end.

azkeneren adj.(gram.) accented on the antepenultimate syllable of a word.

azkenetan egon v.i. to be dying.

azkenez adv. finally, at last, ultimately.

azkengabe adj. infinite, unending, interminable, endless, unlimited.

azkengabeki adv. endlessly, unlimitedly.

azkengabeko adj. unlimited, unending.

azkengabetasun n. infinitude, infinity, greatness.

azkenigurtzi n.(eccl.) last rites, extreme unction.

azkenik adv. finally, lastly.

azkenitz n. peroration, the last part of a speech.

azkenizki n. last letter.

azkenohar n. last warning.

azkentasun n. final stage.

azkenune n. last part.

azkenurren adj. next to the last.

azkon n. arrow, dart.

azkonaga n. place of yew trees.

azkonar n.(zool.) badger.

azoka n. open-air market, local market.

azokaegun n. market day.

azokalari n. merchant.

azokari n. merchant.

azondo n. stem of cabbage.

azorri n. cabbage leaf.

azosto n. cabbage leaf.

azpi n. lower part. prep. under, beneath, below. n. sole. n. cattle bed.

azpi- (gram.) prefix meaning under-, sub-, infra-.

azpialde n. bottom, lower part.

azpian prep. under, underneath. adv. below.

azpibabes n. protecting cover, cover, binding.

azpibabestu v.t. to cover, to bind.

azpibatzorde n. subcommittee.

azpiberritu v.t. to renew the foundation, to repair the foundation (of a building).

azpiberrizte n. act of renewing the foundation.

azpibide n. underpass, subway, underground passage.

azpidatzi v.t. to subtitle.

azpidazkari n. undersecretary.

azpiegitura n. infrastructure, substructure.

azpiezarri v.t. to subdue. v.i. to be contingent upon.

azpigona n. slip, a woman's

undergarment.

azpigoratu *v.t./v.i.* to invert, to turn upside down.

azpijale *n.* underminer, traitor.

azpijan *n.* conspiracy, treason. *v.t.* to undermine.

azpijarri *v.i.* to put oneself under something or somebody. *v.t.* to put something under something or somebody.

azpijo *v.t.* to undermine.

azpijokalari *n.* traitor, underminer.

azpijokatu *v.t.* to conspire, to commit treason, to betray.

azpijoko *n.* dirty play.

azpikalde *n.* reverse side of anything, lower part, back part.

azpikari *adj.* cunning, sly.

azpikeria *n.* fraud, deceit, cheating, treason.

azpikeriaz *adv.* fraudulently, deceitfully.

azpikeriazko *adj.* cunning, sly.

azpiko *adj./n.* subordinate, inferior. *adj.* submissive, obedient. *n.* cattle bed. *n.* protective cover.

azpikogona *n.* slip, woman's undergarment.

azpikotasun *n.* submissiveness, subordination, inferiority.

azpikotu *v.t.* to subdue, to subjugate.

azpikozgora *adv.* upside down, in disorder.

azpil *n.* large dish, serving platter. *n.* fold. *n.(bot.)* azarole, haw (fruit of the hawthorne).

azpilan *n.* undermining, treason.

azpilandu *v.t.* to conspire, to deceive.

azpilan egin *v.t.* to conspire, to plot, to commit treason, to betray.

azpildu *v.t.* to fold. *v.t.* to hem, to border.

azpildura *n.* hem. *n.(fig.)* malice, ill will.

azpilduratu *v.t.* to hem.

azpimarra *n.* underline, emphasize.

azpimarratu *v.t.* to underline, to emphasize.

azpiohar *n.* post script, P.S.

azpirakatu *v.t.* to destroy, to tear down, to demolish.

azpiraketa *n.* domination. *n.* demolition, destruction, act of tearing down. *n.* act of throwing to the ground.

azpirapen *n.* subjection, submission.

azpiratu *v.t.* to subdue, to dominate, to defeat, to beat, to conquer, to subjugate.

azpiratzaile *n.* oppressor, subjugator.

azpisalketa *n.* treason.

azpisuge *adj.* disloyal, traitorous.

azpisugekeria *n.* treason.

azpitalde *n.* subgroup.

azpitik *adv.* surreptitiously, clandestinely, secretly.

azpizale *adj.* insidious, sly, guileful, deceitful, traitorous.

azpizenburu *n.* subtitle.

azpizulatu *v.t.* to excavate underground, to undermine.

azpizulo *n.* excavation, underground tunnel.

aztal *n.(anat.)* heel.

aztarna *n.* track, footprint, trace, vestige, mark.

aztarnaketa *n.* act of following a track, inquiry, inquest.

aztarnari *n.* tracker.

aztarnatu *v.t.* to trail, to scent, to track.

aztarren *n.* track, trail, trace, footprint, vestige, mark.

azterbide *n.* poll. *n.* analytical method.

azterbidezko *adj.* analytical.

aztergai *n.* subject of an examination, examination topic, subject matter being tested.

aztergaitz *adj.* inscrutable.

aztergarri *adj.* explorable, researchable, investigable, scrutable.

aztergile *n.* investigator, examiner, researcher.

azterka *adv.* scratching the earth, scraping the earth.

azterkaldi *n.* analysis, examination.

azterkapen *n.* act of scratching the earth.

azterkari *n.* investigator, inquirer, examiner.

azterkatu *v.t.* to examine, to investigate, to research.

azterkatzaile *n.* examiner, inquirer, investigator.

azterketa *n.* exam, examination, research, investigation. *n.* excavation.

azterkor *adj.* inquisitive, curious.

azterkuntza *n.* investigation, examination, research.

azterlan *n.* seminar, research.

azterlari *n.* examiner, investigator, researcher.

aztermahai *n.* examining tribunal, judicial bench.

azterpen *n.* examination, exam, investigation, research.

azterraldi *n.* examination, investigation, scrutiny.

aztertu *v.t.* to examine, to inquire, to analyze, to investigate, to study. *v.t.* to scrape, to scratch, to dig out.

aztertzaile *n.* analyst. *n.* examiner, investigator.

azti *n.* wizard, sorcerer.

aztiatu *v.t.* to guess, to foresee.

aztigai *n.* apprentice of a sorcerer.

aztigaizkile *n.* person who uses black magic, sorcerer, wizard, magician.

aztikeria *n.* black magic, divination, wizardry, sorcery.

aztikeriazko *adj.* pertaining to black magic.

aztiketa *n.* divination, prediction, augury, fortunetelling.

aztizale adj. superstitious, fond of witches.
aztoragarri adj. disconcerting, confusing.
aztorapen n. confusion, disorientation.
aztoratu v.t. to confuse, to disturb.
aztore n.(zool.) hawk, goshawk.
aztura n. habit.
azturazko adj. habitual.
azturatu v.i. to become familiar with. v.t. to get used to.
azukre n. sugar.
azukredun adj. sugared, sweet.
azukregintza n. sugar processing.
azukrekainabera n.(bot.) sugar cane.
azukrekoskor n. sugar cube.
azukreola n. sugar factory.
azukreontzi n. sugar container, sugar bowl.
azukretsu adj. sweet, sugary.
azukrezko adj. made of sugar, sweet.
azukreztatu v.t. to sweeten with sugar.
azukreztu v.t. to sugar, to add sugar, to sweeten.

B

b n. second letter in the Basque alphabet. Pronounced like the b in English bat.
ba adv. already. **Ba al dator?** Is he already coming? conj. so. Contr. of bada. **Kontuz ba!** So be careful! int. exclamation which expresses irony, skepticism.
ba- (gram.) verbal prefix meaning condition. **Balego.** If he were. **Balu.** If he had. adv. already. **Badator.** He is already coming.
baba n.(bot.) broad bean. n. blister on the skin.
bababeltz n.(bot.) small broad beans.
babaleka n. pod of broad beans.
babalore n. broad bean flower.
babarrun n.(bot.) bean (white, kidney).
babazale n. fond of broad beans.
babazorri n.(zool.) grubworm.
babazuri n.(bot.) white bean.
babazuza n. hail.
babes n. protection; shelter, refuge.
babesdun adj. fortified, protected, defended.
babesdura n. preservation, protection.
babes egin v.t. to defend, to protect, to preserve, to shelter.
babesemale n. protector, guardian, defender.
babesetxe n. asylum, shelter, refuge.
babeseko adj. protective, defensive.
babesgabe adj. defenseless, unprotected.
babesgabeko adj. defenseless, unprotected.
babesgabetasun n. defenselessness, lack of protection, lack of support.
babesgabetu v.t. to abandon, to forsake.
babesgabezia n. abandonment, helplessness, defenselessness.
babesgailu n. safeguard, protective device.
babesgaitz adj. indefensible, unprotectable, unsupportable.
babesgarri adj. protecting, sheltering.
babesgune n. shelter, fortified place.
babesiri n. stronghold, fortress.
babesketa n. defense, act of defending.
babeski n. rampart, parapet, defense, shelter. n. shield.
babeskor adj. preservative, protective, defensive.
babeskuntza n. protection, preservation.
babeslan n. protective or preservative function.
babesle n. protector, defender.
babesleku n. asylum, shelter, refuge.
babeslerro n. defensive line, line of defense.
babespe n. refuge, protection, defense.
babespean hartu v.t. to patronize, to take under one's protection.
babespeko adj. sponsored, protected.
babespen n. protection, refuge.
babespetu v.t. to protect. v.i. to shelter behind a parapet, to take refuge.
babespide n. defense, fortification.
babeste n. patronage, sponsorship.
babestezin adj. indefensible, undefendable, unprotectable.
babestoki n. fortress, stronghold. n. shelter, refuge. n. asylum.
babestu v.i. to take refuge. v.t. to protect, to defend, to give shelter, to take care of.
babestzaile n. protector, sponsor, patron, supporter. adj. protecting.
bada conj. so, well, then.
badaezbada n. eventuality. adv. just in case.
badaezbadako adj. eventual, contingent, dubious; commonplace. adj. rude, having bad manners.
badia n.(geog.) bay.
bagoi n. wagon.
bagoiketa n. wagon train.
bagoilerro n. wagon train, row of wagons.
bahe n. sieve.
bahegile n. sieve maker.
baheketa n. sieving, sifting.
bahestatu v.t. to sift.
bahetu v.t. to sift, to winnow.
bahetzaile. n. winnower; sifter.
baheztadura n. sifting; winnowing.
baheztaketa n. winnowing; sifting.
bahi n. bail. n. mortgage.
bahiemale n. guarantor.
bahigarri adj. mortgageable.
bahikunde n. mortgage.
bahikuntza n. mortgage. n. kidnapping.

bahimendu n. kidnapping.

bahipen n. legal attachment of property.

bahitegi n. pawnshop.

bahitu v.t. to pawn.

bahitugarri adj. pawnable. adj. confiscatable.

bahitura n. mortgage. n. kidnapping.

bahituretxe n. pawnshop.

bahituri n. hostage.

bahitzaile n. mortgager.

bai adv. yes, indeed. conj. both . . . and. n. affirmation, agreement.

baiemale n. person who agrees, authorizer.

baieskarri adj. approvable.

baiesle adj. acquiescent, agreeable.

baiespen n. agreement, affirmation, permission.

baietsi v.t. to approve (of), to confirm, to agree.

baietz adv. yes, so.

baietza n. agreement, conformity, affirmation.

baietza eman v.t. to agree, to assent, to give one's approval.

baietzean adv. if yes, if the answer is yes.

baietz esan v.t. to affirm, to agree, to assent, to concede, to say yes, to give one's approval.

baiezgarri adj. grantable, approvable, permissible.

baiezka adv. affirmatively.

baiezko adj. affirmative. n. assent, agreement, consent, approbation.

baieztakor adj. assertive.

baieztapen n. agreement, approbation, ratification, approval.

baieztari n. affirmer, agreer, approver.

baieztatu v.t. to ratify, to confirm, to approve.

baieztu v.t. to affirm, to approve, to assent, to confirm, to ratify, to permit.

baikor adj. affirmative, positive. adj. optimist.

baikortasun n. optimism, quality of being optimistic.

bailara n. suburb, section of the town.

bailaraune n. section of a suburb.

baimen n. approbation, authorization, permission, agreement.

baimena eman v.t. to permit, to consent, to authorize, to give permission.

baimena eskatu v.t. to ask for permission.

baimenagiri n. written document of authorization.

baimena lortu v.t. to obtain permission, to get permission.

baimena ukatu v.t. to deny permission.

baimendu v.t. to allow, to consent, to permit.

baimendura n. permission, authorization.

baimengabetu v.t. to withdraw authority.

baimengarri adj. permissible, authorizable.

baimenkor adj. permissive, indulgent.

baina conj. but (before the verb). conj. though, although (at the end of the sentence).

baino conj. but. Used in negative sentences. **Ez du besterik nahi bere ama ikustea baino.** He wants nothing but to see his mother. conj. than (comparative) **Elurra baino zuriago.** Whiter than snow.

baino lehen conj. before.

bainu n. bath, bathroom.

bainuetxe n. health spa.

bainugela n. bathroom.

bainujantzi n. bathing suit, swimsuit.

bainulari n. bather.

bainuontzi n. bathtub.

baioneta n. bayonette.

bait- (gram.) verbal prefix meaning because, used with conjugated verbs.

-bait (gram.) suffix for interrogative words. It indicates an indefinite idea. **Noizbait.** Some time.

baita adv./prep. also, too, even. n. home, within.

baita . . . ere adv. also, too, even, as well, in addition.

baitan adv. inside, internally.

bai zera! int. exclamation which expresses doubt or hesitation, no way, not at all, come on!

baizik conj. but. Used in negative sentences, generally at the end of the sentence. **Ez da gorria beltza baizik.** It is not red but black.

bakailo n.(zool.) codfish.

bakailontzi n. dish of codfish.

bakaldun n. king.

bakan adj. scarce, singular, few. adv. seldom.

bakandu v.i. to be scarce. v.i. to scatter. v.t./v.i. to isolate, to separate. v.t.(chem.) to separate into components.

bakanezin adj. inseparable.

bakangaitz adj. difficult to separate.

bakangarri adj. separatable, isolatable.

bakanka adv. seldom, rarely, from time to time.

bakanketa n. separation. n. scarcity.

bakanki adv. rarely, infrequently, from time to time.

bakantasun n. scarcity, rarity, lack. n. solitude, retreat.

bakantzaile n. separator, divider.

bakantza(k) n. vacation.

bakar adj. isolated, alone, just one. adj. unique, singular. adj. only, sole.

bakardade n. solitude, loneliness.

bakardun adj. possessing one thing, possessing one of a kind.

bakargailu *n.* insulator.
bakargela *n.* secluded room.
bakarjoko *n.* solitary game.
bakarka *adv.* privately.
bakarkatu *v.t.* to space, to lay out, to place evenly.
bakarkeria *n.* excessive solitude, hermitism.
bakarketa *n.* isolation, incommunication.
bakarlan *n.* individual work.
bakarlari *n.* soloist.
bakarleku *n.* solitary place, remote place.
bakarmin *n.* nostalgia, longing.
bakarmindu *v.i.* to long, to feel homesick.
bakarmintzatu *v.i.* to talk to oneself.
bakarraldi *n.* time for retreat or solitude.
bakarrean *adv.* privately, by oneself, alone.
bakarreko *adj.* singular, unique. *adj.* private.
bakarreratu *v.i.* to isolate oneself, to seclude oneself, to become isolated.
bakarrezko *adj.* private, singular.
bakarrik *adv.* privately, solitarily, alone. *adv./conj.* only.
bakarrizketa *n.* monologue, soliloquy.
bakarrizketari *n.* monologist.
bakartade *n.* solitude.
bakartaldi *n.* retreat, solitude, seclusion.
bakartar *adj.* solitary, lonely.
bakartasun *n.* solitude, isolation, loneliness. *n.* singularity, uniqueness.
bakartegi *n.* retreat, lonely place.
bakartegun *n.* day of retreat.
bakartetxe *n.* retirement home.
bakarti *adj.* solitary, shy, reclusive, withdrawn.
bakartiar *adj.* solitary, reclusive, withdrawn.
bakartoki *n.* secluded place, remote place.
bakartsu *adj.* solitary, lonely, remote (people or place).
bakartu *v.t.* to isolate, to insulate, to separate. *v.i.* to be or become isolated, to isolate oneself.
bakartzale *n.* recluse, loner. *adj.* misanthropic, hating mankind, fond of solitude.
bakarzulo *n.* remote place, solitary place.
bakaulki *n.* throne.
bakaulkitu *v.t.* to place on the throne, to enthrone.
bake *n.* peace, tranquility.
bakeak egin *v.t.* to reconcile, to make peace.
bakealdi *n.* period of peace, truce, cease-fire.
bakearazle *n.* conciliator, peace-maker.

bakearazpen *n.* propitiation, reparation, reconciliation, expiation.
bakebide *n.* way or means of reconciliation.
bakedun *adj.* peaceful, having peace.
bakegarri *adj.* propitiatory, conciliatory, pacifying.
bakegile *n.* peacemaker.
bakehauste *n.* disturbance of the peace.
bakekarle *n.* peace maker.
bakekor *adj.* conciliatory, pacifying.
bakekuntza *n.* pacification, peace making.
bakelari *n.* peace maker, pacifier.
bakeopari *n.* propitiatory sacrifice, peace offering.
bakerazi *v.t.* to pacify, to make peace.
bakerazle *n.* pacifier, peace maker.
bakerazpen *n.* pacification, peace making.
baketan *adj.* peacefully, in peace.
baketasun *n.* tranquility, peacefulness, calmness.
bakete *n.* period of peace, truce.
baketiar *n.* pacifist.
baketsu *adj.* quiet, calm, peaceful.
baketu *v.t./v.i.* to reconcile, to make peace, to pacify.
baketuezin *adj.* irreconcilable.
baketxe *n.* house of peace.
baketzaile *n.* pacifier, reconciler, peace maker. *adj.* pacifying, conciliating.
bakeune *n.* truce, cease fire, period of peace.
bakez *adv.* peacefully, quietly, calmly.
bakezale *adj.* pacifistic, fond of peace.
bakezaletasun *n.* pacifism.
bakezko *adj.* pacific, calm, tranquil, peaceful, serene, quiet.
bakeztatu *v.t.* to reconcile.
bakoitz *pron.* each one. *adj.* each.
bakoitzaren *adj.* particular, individual.
bakoitzean *adv.* each (time).
bakoitzeko *adj.* of each (time)
bakoizka *adv.* separately, one by one.
bakoizpen *n.* individuation.
bakoiztasun *n.* individuality, characteristic, peculiarity, property.
bakoiztu *v.i./v.t.* to personalize, to individualize, to become unique.
bakun *adj.* simple, not compound.
bakundu *v.t.* to simplify, to make easier. *adj.* simplified.
bakungaitz *adj.* unsimplifiable.
bakungarri *adj.* simplifiable.
bakuntasun *n.* oneness.
bakunzale *adj.* tending to simplify.
bala *n.* bullet.
bala-bala *adv.* onomatopoeic sound which indicates a great deal, profusion.
balakada *n.* shot, hit with a projectile.
balakagarri *adj.* flattering, cajoling.
balakaldi *n.* adulation, flattery.
balakari *adj./n.* flattering, adulating;

cajoler, flatterer, sycophant.

balakatu *v.t.* placate, appease. *v.t.* to flatter, to cajole.

balaketa *n.* ammunition dump, pile of bullets.

balaku *n.* flattery, cajolery, adulation.

balakuz *adv.* with flattery, with adulation, in a flattering way.

balanka *n.* lever, crowbar.

balankari *n.* thrower of an iron bar (popular Basque sport).

balantza *n.* scale, balance.

balantzaka *adv.* staggering, swinging, swaying, moving from one side to another.

balantzaketa *n.* stagger, tottering movement.

balantzatu *v.i.* to stagger, to totter, to sway.

balazta *n.* bridle.

balaztatu *v.t.* to bridle, to control an animal using the bridle, to rein in.

balda *n.* shelf.

baldan *adj.* slow, negligent, apathetic, sluggish.

baldandu *v.i.* to be negligent, to be careless (with one's appearance or actions).

baldankeria *n.* negligence, carelessness, apathy, slowness, sluggishness.

baldanki *adv.* sluggishly, slowly, rudely.

baldar *adj.* clumsy, crude, unskillful, unskilled; negligent, careless.

baldargarri *adj.* obstructive, delaying.

baldarkeria *n.* sluggishness, negligence.

baldarki *adv.* clumsily, sluggishly.

baldarkiro *adv.* slowly, sluggishly.

baldartasun *n.* sluggishness, clumsiness.

baldartu *v.i.* to become sluggish, inactive.

baldin *conj.* word which emphasizes the conditional sentence but has no direct translation.

baldindu *v.t.* to condition, to stipulate, to be contingent upon, to depend on.

baldinezko *adj.* hypothetic, conditional.

baldingabe *adj.* unconditional.

baldinkizun *n.* condition, requirement.

baldinkor *adj.* conditional, hypothetical.

baldinpeko *adj.* conditional.

baldinpetu *v.t.* to make conditional, to make contingent upon, to be contingent upon, to depend on.

baldintasun *n.* condition, requirement.

baldintza *n.* condition, requirement.

baldintzapen *n.* condition, act of making conditional.

baldintzapetu *v.t.* to condition, to stipulate.

baldintzatu *v.t.* to condition, to stipulate.

baldintzazko *adj.* conditional, dependent on.

baldintzazkotasun *n.* conditionality.

baldintzera *n.(gram.)* conditional mood.

baldres *adj.* untidy, crude, slovenly.

baldreskeria *n.* untidiness, slovenliness.

baldreski *adv.* untidily, slovenly.

baldrestu *v.i.* to be untidy. *v.t.* to become sluggish.

balea *n.(zool.)* whale.

baleakari *n.* whaler.

baleaki *n.* whale meat.

baleatzale *n.* whaler.

baleazale *adj.* fond of whales.

balebizar *n.* whalebone, baleen.

balekume *n.(dim.)* whale calf.

balentria *n.* bravery, prowess.

baleontzi *n.* whaleboat, whaling ship.

baliabide *n.* manner of using something; resource.

baliadura *n.* worth, value.

baliaezin *adj.* useless, unworthy.

baliagaitz *adj.* useless, worthless.

baliagarri *adj.* useful, worthy, available.

baliagarritasun *n.* usefulness, utility.

baliaketa *n.* utilization.

baliakizun *n.* resource.

baliapide *n.* resource.

baliarazi *v.t.* to make (something) valuable. *v.t.* to make (someone) use (something).

baliatu *v.i.* to use, to utilize. The object of this verb takes *z* as a suffix.
Liburuaz baliatuko da. He will use the book.

baliatzaile *n.* user.

balio *n.* value, worth; profit. *n.* validity. *n.* price, cost.

balioaldi *n.* period of validity.

balioaskodun *adj.(chem.)* polyvalent, multivalent.

baliobakar *adj.(chem.)* univalent.

balioberdineko *adj.* equivalent, of the same value.

balioberritu *v.t.* to increase the value of.

baliobiko *adj.(chem.)* bivalent; having two values.

baliodun *adj.* valid, in force. *adj.* valuable, of great value.

balio eman *v.t.* to value, to appraise.

balio eragin *v.t.* to make valuable.

balioeza *n.* invalidity. *n.* worthlessness.

baliogabe *adj.* invalid, null, having no force or efficacy, void.

baliogabeki *adv.* invalidly, without validity.

baliogabetasun *n.* invalidity, lack of validity, nullity.

baliogabetu *v.t.* to invalidate, to cancel, to annul.

baliogabez *adv.* invalidly.

baliogabezia *n.* nullity, invalidity.

baliogarri *adj.* valued, valuable. *adj.*

useful.

baliogarritasun *n.* utility, usefulness.

balio izan *v.t.* to cost, to be worth. *v.t.* to be useful.

balioketa *n.* use, utility, benefit.

baliokide *adj.* equivalent.

baliokidetasun *n.* equivalency.

baliokidetu *v.i.* to be equivalent.

baliokidetza *n.* equivalence.

balioko *adj.* valuable, valid, worthy.

baliopen *n.* evaluation.

balios *adj.* valuable, precious.

balioski *adv.* usefully.

baliostasun *n.(econ.)* value.

baliotsu *adj.* valuable, expensive.

balio ukan *v.t.* to cost, to be worth.

baliozko *adj.* worthy, worthwhile, valuable.

balioztadura *n.* evaluation.

balioztapen *n.* appraisal, evaluation.

balioztatu *v.t.* to appraise, to value, to evaluate.

balioztatzaile *n.* appraiser.

balkoi *n.* balcony.

balkoipe *n.* place under the balcony. *n.* underside of the balcony.

baloi *n.* ball.

baloraezin *adj.* invaluable, inestimable.

baloragabe *adj.* unestimated, unvalued, unappraised.

baloragarri *adj.* appraisable, estimatable, evaluatable.

baloratu *v.t.* to evaluate; to value.

balorazio *n.* valuation; evaluation.

balore *n.* audacity, boldness. *n.(econ.)* share, stock, bond.

baltsa *n.* school of fish. *n.* guild. *n.* fund raised by a group for a common purpose. *n.* slush; partially melted snow.

baltsamo *n.* balsam, lotion.

baltsatu *v.t.* to put together, to mix. *v.i.* to become slushy.

bana *pron.* one for each person. *adj.* each.

bana-banaka *adv.* one by one.

banagailu *n.* separator.

banagarri *adj.* distributable, separable, divisible; distributing, separating, divisive.

banaka *adv.* one by one, one at a time, individually.

banakatu *v.t.* to distribute, to divide. *v.t.* to separate, to segregate, to isolate.

banakatzaile *adj./n.* distributor.

banakera *n.* manner of distributing.

banaketa *n.* distribution, allotment. *n.* dissemination. *n.* discrimination. *n.(arith.)* division.

banako *adj.* unique, singular, individual. *n.* Basque dance where one of eight dancers is dancing.

banakor *adj.* distributive.

banakortasun *n.* quality of distributing.

banakuntza *n.* division, separation, distribution. *n.* dissension, discord.

banalerro *n.* dividing line.

banana *n.(bot.)* banana.

banandu *v.t./v.i.* to separate, to isolate, to distribute, to segregate; to discriminate. *v.i.* to get a divorce.

banangarri *adj.* separating; separable.

banangarritasun *n.* separableness.

banatasun *n.* variety, diversity.

banatu *v.t.* to distribute, to give out, to disseminate, to propagate, to spread, to disperse, to separate.

banatutako *adj.* separated, divorced.

banatzaile *n./adj.* distributor; distributing. *n./adj.* disseminator, propagator; disseminating, spreading.

banatzaldi *n.* distribution, dissemination, spreading.

banazale *adj.* separatist.

banda *n.* band (music). *n.*

bandera *n.* flag.

banderadun *n.* flag bearer.

banderamakila *n.* flagpole.

banderatu *v.t.* to decorate with flags.

banderatxo *n.(dim.)* small flag.

bankari *n.* banker.

banketxe *n.* bank.

bankorde *n.* branch office of a bank.

banku *n.* bench. *n.* bank.

bankubalio *n.(econ.)* bank paper.

bankudiru *n.* money in the bank.

bankukontu *n.* bank account.

bankuporroketa *n.* bankruptcy.

bankutxartel *n.* bank note.

bapatean *adv.* suddenly. *adv.* at once, simultaneously.

bapateko *adj.* sudden, instantaneous. *adj.* simultaneous.

bapo *adv.* opulently, very well, abundantly.

barakuilantzeko *adj.* snail-like.

baranda *n.* balustrade, railing, bannister.

baratxuri *n.(bot.)* garlic.

baratxuriatal *n.* clove of garlic.

baratxuriburu *n.* head of garlic.

baratxurikorda *n.* string of garlic.

baratxurisaltza *n.* garlic sauce.

baratxurizopa *n.* garlic soup.

baratz *adj.* slow, careful. *adj.* lazy. *adv.* slowly.

baratzain *n.* gardener.

baratze *n.* vegetable garden.

baratzelan *n.* horticulture, gardening.

baratzereintza *n.* act of sowing a vegetable garden.

barau *n.* fast, fasting, abstinence from food, either total or partial.

baraua hautsi *v.t.* to break the fast.

baraualdi *n.* time of fasting.

barau egin *v.t.* to fast.

barauegun *n.* day of fasting.

baraugile *n.* one who fasts.

baraugorri *n.* total abstinence from food, total fast.

barauhauste *n.* break of the fast.

baraurik *adv.* without eating.

barautasun *n.* fasting, without eating.
barautsi *v.t.* to have breakfast.
barazki *n.* vegetable.
barazkijale *n./adj.* vegetarian.
barazkijate *n.* vegetarianism.
barazkintza *n.* horticulture, vegetable gardening.
barazkisaltzaile *n.* vegetable seller.
barazlangile *n.* vegetable gardener.
barbarin *n.(zool.)* red mullet.
barberu *n.* barber.
barbo *n.(zool.)* barbel.
bare *adv./adj.* calm. *n.(zool.)* slug. *n.(anat.)* spleen.
barealdi *n.* period of calm seas. *n.* period of tranquility and quietness.
bare-bare *adj./adv.* calmly, very calm.
baregarri *adj.* mitigant, calmative.
bareketa *n.* mitigation, sedation, attenuation.
bareki *adv.* peacefully, calmly, quietly.
barekin *n.* tranquilizer, pain-reliever.
bareko *adj.* pertaining to the spleen.
baremin *n.(med.)* pain of the spleen.
baresare *n.(anat.)* mesentery.
baretasun *n.* quietness, tranquility, calm, stillness.
baretegi *n.* place abundant in slugs.
baretsu *adj.* calm, quiet, placid.
baretu *v.i.* to become calm, to calm down. *v.t.* to tranquilize, to quiet, to pacify, to calm.
baretzaile *n.* tranquilizer, pacifier, soother. *adj.* tranquilizing, pacifying, soothing.
bareune *n.* short period of calm on the sea.
bargosta *n.(zool.)* young sow.
barik *prep.* without.
barka *n.* pardon, forgiveness, mercy.
barkabera *adj.* indulgent, forgiving, merciful.
barkaberatasun *n.* indulgence, forgiveness, tendency to forgive easily.
barkaezin *adj.* unexcusable, unpardonable, irremissible.
barkaezinezko *adj.* unpardonable, unexcusable, unforgivable.
barkagaitz *adj.* unpardonable, difficult to excuse, unforgivable.
barkagarri *adj.* excusable, pardonable.
barkakoi *adj.* merciful, indulgent, forgiving.
barkakoitasun *n.* mercy, clemency, forgiveness.
barkaldi *n.* pardon, indulgence.
barkamen *n.* pardon, mercy, forgiveness.
barkamenurte *n.(eccl.)* jubilee, concession of plenary indulgence.
barkapen *n.* pardon, forgiveness, absolution.
barkapenezko *adj.* acquitting, absolving, absolutory, absolvatory.
barkarazi *v.t.* to cause to pardon.
barkatiar *adj.* merciful, absolving, pardoning, forgiving.

barkatu *v.t.* to pardon, to absolve, to forgive, to excuse. *v.t.* to cancel someone else's debts.
barkatzaile *n.* pardoner, forgiver, absolver. *adj.* merciful, absolving, pardoning, forgiving.
barkazale *adj.* merciful, indulgent, forgiving.
barkazaletasun *n.* mercifulness, forgiveness, clemency.
barkazio *n.* pardon, forgiveness, amnesty.
barkilu *n.* sweet biscuit.
barna *adj.* profound, deep.
barne *n.* interior, inside. *adj.* deep, interior, internal, inner, inside. *n.* depth. *prep.* including, even, also.
barnealde *n.* interior side, inside.
barnean *prep./adv.* within, inside.
barneazterpen *n.* introspection.
barne-barneko *adj.* innermost, intrinsic.
barnebehaketa *n.* self-observation.
barnebelarri *n.(anat.)* inner ear.
barnebide *n.* interior corridor, Inside passageway, indoor hallway.
barnebizitza *n.* inner life.
barne-eragin *n.* internal impulse.
barnegatazka *n.* internal conflict.
barnegitura *n.* internal structure.
barneikusketa *n.* introspection.
barnejario *n.* internal secretion.
barnekalde *n.* inner part, inside.
barneketa *n.* inclusion.
barneki *adv.* profoundly, deeply, intimately.
barnekidetasun *n.* interpenetration, compenetration.
barnekidetu *v.i.* to penetrate mutually.
barnekiro *adv.* internally
barneko *adj.* inherent, intrinsic, interior.
barnekoi *adj.* introverted, thoughtful.
barnekor *adj.* deep, profound, intimate, introvert, penetrating.
barnekotasun *n.* inherence, intrinsicalness.
barnelotura *n.* coherence.
barnemerkataritza *n.(econ.)* domestic trade.
barnemerkatu *n.(econ.)* domestic market.
barnemin *n.* resentment, grudge.
barnemugida *n.* commotion, upheaval, emotional upset.
barnemuin *n.(anat.)* marrow.
barneragaitz *adj.* inscrutable, unsearchable; unfathomable.
barneraketa *n.* act of deepening, act of going inside. *n.* importation.
barnerakoi *n.* introvertive, introverted.
barnerakoitasun *n.* introversion.
barnerapen *n.* introversion, introvertedness, ingoingness.
barneratu *v.t./v.i.* to search, to investigate; to insert; to enter, to go

inside. *v.i.* to concentrate one's mind.

barnesusmaketa *n.* intuition.

barnetasun *n.* quality of being inner or inward; depth, interior, inside.

barnetiko *adj.* internal, intimate.

barnetu *v.t./v.i.* to penetrate, to go inside, to prove, to examine.

barnez *adv.* internally.

baroi *n.* baron.

barra *n.* pier, dock.

barrabas *adj.* naughty, rascally, mischievous. *n.* rascal; scoundrel.

barrabaskeria *n.* serious mischief.

barrabil *n.(anat.)* testicle.

barrabildun *adj./n. (colloq.)* brave, courageous.

barrabilzorro *n.(anat.)* scrotum.

barraskilo *n.(zool.)* snail.

barre *n.* laughter, laugh.

barrealdi *n.* time to laugh.

barrealgara *n.* loud laughter, guffaw.

barre egin *v.t.* to laugh, to smile. *v.t.* to make fun of, to ridicule, to laugh at someone.

barre eragin *v.t.* to cause to laugh, to make (someone) laugh.

barregarri *adj.* funny. *adj.* ridiculous, hilarious, laughable.

barregarrikeria *n.* extravagance, eccentricity, grotesqueness.

barregarriro *adv.* ridiculously, eccentrically, grotesquely.

barregarritasun *n.* quality of being humorous, funniness.

barregarrizko *adj.* humorous, funny, hilarious, ridiculous.

barregile *n.* clown, comedian.

barregura *n.* desire to laugh.

barreiadura *n.* spreading, scattering, dispersion.

barreiagarri *adj.* publishable; spreadable, dispersable.

barreiaketa *n.* divulgation, publication. *n.* act of scattering or spreading, dispersion.

barreialdi *n.* dispersion, scattering, spreading.

barreiapen *n.* discrimination; separation. *n.* scattering, dispersion.

barreiari *n.* town crier. *adj.* wasteful, spendthrifty, squandering.

barreiatu *v.t.* to spread, to disperse; to publish. *v.i.* to disperse, to scatter. *v.t.* to break into pieces. *v.t.* to spend lavishly.

barreiatzaile *n.* squanderer. *adj.* squandering, wasteful.

barreka *adv.* laughing.

barrekari *n.* clown.

barrekera *n.* way of laughing.

barrelari *n.* mocker, ridiculer.

barren *prep.* inside, within. *adj.* interior, internal. *n.* inside, interior; inner self, conscience. *n.* inferior part, lower part.

-barren Used in compound words.

Signifies inside, interior, lower part.

barrenalde *n.* inner part, inside.

barrenaldeko *adj.* interior, inner; intimate.

barrenate *n.* inner door.

barrenatsekabe *n.* sorrow, grief, sadness, affliction.

barrenatu *v.t.* to deepen, to penetrate.

barrenazal *n.(anat.)* endodermis.

barrenazterketa *n.* inner searching, examination of one's conscience.

barrenazterpen *n.* introspection.

barrenaztertu *v.t.* to find out, to investigate, to examine.

barrenbake *n.* peace of mind, interior calm.

barren-barrendik *adv.* from the deepest part; from within; deeply, profoundly.

barren-barrengo *adj.* interior, inner, intimate.

barrenbide *n.* corridor, gallery.

barrendamu *n.* remorse, regret, contrition, repentance.

barrendari *n.* spy, intruder.

barrendatu *v.t.* to spy, to watch.

barrendatzaile *n.* spy.

barrendei *n.* inspiration.

barrendik *adv.* from the inner part; from within, internally.

barreneko *adj.* interior, inner; deep. *adj.* secret, intimate.

barreneratu *v.i.* to go in; to come in.

barrenetik *prep./adv.* from within; internally; from the low part.

barrengaitz *adj.* impenetrable, inscrutable.

barrengaizto *adj.* inhuman, merciless, ruthless.

barrengaltzak *n.* men's underpants.

barrengarri *adj.* capable of being probed, sounded, or fathomed.

barrengo *adj.* inner, interior, intimate.

barrengotasun *n.* intimacy.

barrenikusle *adj.* clairvoyant.

barrenkale *n.* lower street.

barrenkezka *n.* scruple; remorse.

barrenkezkatu *v.i.* to be worried, to become restless.

barrenkoi *adj.* introvert.

barrenkor *adj.* penetrant, penetrative.

barrenleiho *n.* window blind.

barrenlotura *n.* coherence.

barrenloturazko *adj.* coherent.

barrenmugida *n.* commotion, emotional upheaval.

barrensusmakor *adj.* intuitive.

barrensusmaketa *n.* intuition.

barrensusmatu *v.t.* to know or learn by intuition, to intuit.

barrentasun *n.* intimacy. *n.* depth.

barreragile *n.* comedian, humorist.

barrez *adv.* laughing, smilingly.

barrezale *adj.* laughing, jolly, fond of laughing.

barru *adv.* inside. *n.* inner part, inside, interior. *n.* conscience, heart, inner

self. *prep.* within, inside, in.
barrualde *n.* inner part, inside, interior.
barruan *prep./adv.* inside, within, in.
barru-barruko *adj.* innermost; intrinsic.
barru-barruratu *v.t./v.i.* to sink deeply, . to go far into.
barruestu *adj.* restless, worried, agitated, uneasy.
barrugaizto *adj.* insensitive, wicked.
barrugogor *adj.* hard, severe, cruel, hard-hearted.
barrukalde *n.* inner part, inside, interior.
barruko *adj.* inner, familiar, interior, intimate.
barrukoi *adj.* introverted, thoughtful, pensive.
barrukor *adj.* deep in thought; introvert; profound, thoughtful, intimate.
barrukotasun *n.* intimacy, familiarity; membership. *n.* inherence, intrinsicalness.
barruleiho *n.* window shutter.
barrunbe *n.* cavity; a hollow place.
barruragotu *v.i.* to go deeply into, to go further in.
barruraketa *n.* retreat, seclusion.
barrurapen *n.* act of going inside.
barruratu *v.t./v.i.* to bring in, to put in, to penetrate; to go in. *v.i.* to be deep in thought, to meditate.
barruti *n.* district; zone, area, precinct.
barrutik *prep./adv.* from the inside, from within.
barrutiko *adj.* internal, interior, intimate. *adj.* territorial.
bart *adv.* last night.
bartz *n.* louse egg.
basa *n.* mud. *adj.* wild, not domesticated. *adj.* primitive, rustic. *adj.* brutal.
basa- *(gram.)* Prefix which means rustic, wild, pseudo. Derived from *baso.*
basabere *n.* wild animal.
basaberetalde *n.* group of wild animals.
basabide *n.* path, wilderness trail.
basabizitza *n.* wildlife.
basagizon *n.* mountain man, country man, rustic man.
basahate *n.(zool.)* wild duck.
basahuntz *n.(zool.)* wild female goat, deer.
basajaun *n.* Basque mythological man who inhabits the forest as lord.
basakatu *n.(zool.)* mountain cat, kind of genet.
basakeria *n.* brutality, savageness.
basalan *n.* forest work.
basalore *n.* wild flower.
basalur *n.* uninhabited place, untilled land.
basamahats *n.(bot.)* wild grape.
basamaisu *n.* rural teacher; wild teacher. *n.* inexperienced teacher.

basamortu *n.* desert.
basamortuko *adj.* desert, deserty.
basandere *n.* Basque mythological woman; wife of *basajaun.*
basapiztia *n.* wild animal; beast.
basasendagile *n.* rural physician. *n.* inexperienced physician.
basatasun *n.* state of being wild. *n.* barbarism, savagery.
basati *adj.* ferocious, cruel, inhuman. *adj.* wild, brutal, rustic, savage.
basatiar *n.* inhabitant of the desert.
basatikeria *n.* savagery.
basatu *v.i.* to become wild.
basatxakur *n.(zool.)* wild dog.
basatxori *n.(zool.)* wild bird.
basauso *n.(zool.)* wild dove.
basazain *n.* forest ranger.
basazezen *n.(zool.)* wild bull. *n.(zool.)* buffalo, bison.
baseliza *n.* small church in the mountains.
baserri *n.* farmhouse, homestead.
baserrikeria *n.* rusticity, rudeness.
baserriko *adj.* rural.
baserritar *n./adj.* farmer, country dweller, peasant.
baserritarkeria *n.* rudeness, rusticity.
baserritartu *v.i.* to become a farmer, to become rural.
baserritxo *n.(dim.)* small farm house.
basetxe *n.* house in the forest.
basezti *n.* wild honey.
basko *n./adj.* Basque.
baso *n.* forest, wild place. *n.* glass.
basoerdi *n.* half a glass of wine.
basoilanda *n.(zool.)* pheasant.
basoilar *n.(zool.)* capercaillie, wild cock.
basoilo *n.(zool.)* bustard, wild hen.
basokada *n.* contents of a glass, glassful.
basoko *adj.* wild, forestal.
basoneurle *n.* land surveyor.
basotsu *adj.* rich in forests, thickly forested or wooded.
basta *n.* packsaddle.
bastagin *n.* maker of packsaddles, saddle maker.
bastarketa *n.* retirement.
bastatu *v.t.* to put a packsaddle on (an animal), to saddle.
basto *n.* club (in cards). *adj.* crude, unpolished, vulgar.
bastokeria *n.* crudeness, vulgarity.
bastoki *adv.* rudely.
bastorratz *n.* large needle used to sew mattresses.
bastotu *v.i.* to become vulgar, crude.
basurde *n.(zool.)* boar.
basurdekume *n.(dim.)* young boar.
basurdeme *n.* female boar.
basurdetzar *n.(augm.)* enormous boar.
basuso *n.(zool.)* wild dove.
bat *adj./n.* one. The only numeral that goes after the noun in all Basque dialects. *adj.* some. *art.* a, an. *adv.*

about, approximately, more or less.
Hogei bat. About twenty.
bata *n.* the one, one.
bataiari *n.* baptizer.
bataiategi *n.* baptistery.
bataiatu *v.t.* to baptize. *v.t.(colloq.)* to water the milk.
bataiatzaile *n.* baptizer.
bataiharri *n.* baptismal font.
bataio *n.* baptism.
bataioiturri *n.* baptismal font.
bataioizen *n.* Christian name.
bataioko *adj.* baptismal.
bataioliburu *n.* book of baptisms.
batak *pron.* one, the one.
batan *n.(bot.)* wild mint.
batasun *n.* union, unification, connection; harmony; agreement.
batasunzale *adj.* unionist.
batasunzaletasun *n.* unionism.
bataz-beste *adv.* on the average.
bataz-besteko *adj.* proportional.
bat-batean *adv.* suddenly. *adv.* simultaneously, at once.
bat-bateko *adj.* unforeseen, sudden, improvised; simultaneous.
bat-batera *adv.* at the same time, simultaneously. *adv.* suddenly, all of a sudden.
batean *adv.* simultaneously, at the same time. *adv.* in common, together, as a group, as one.
bat edo bat *pron.* someone.
bat edo beste *pron.* one or another; some, one or two, a few.
bat egin *v.t.* to associate (with). *v.t.* to join, to connect, to combine, to unify, to fuse together.
bategina *adj.* joined, connected, united, associated.
bategite *n.* merger, union, joining, connection, association.
batek *pron./adj.* one (as a subject with transitive verbs).
batekin *adj./pron.* with one.
bateko *n.* ace (in cards). *n.* traditional Basque dance where one of eight dancers is dancing. *n.* solitaire (card game).
-bateko Used in compound words. Signifies uni-, one.
batel *n.* rowboat, small boat.
batelari *n.* rower.
batelzain *n.* one who takes care of the boat, boatman.
baten *adv.* once. *adj./pron.* in one. *adj./pron.* of one, one, a.
batera *adv.* simultaneously, at the same time. *adv.* jointly, together. *adv.*
batera egon *v.i.* to agree. *v.i.* to be together.
batera etorri *v.i.* to come together. *v.i.* to agree.
bateraezin *adj.* incompatible, irreconcilable.
bateraezintasun *n.* incompatibility.
bateragaitz *adj.* irreconcilable.

bateragarri *adj.* compatible.
bateragarritasun *n.* compatibility.
bateraketa *n.* unification, the act of unifying.
baterakide *adj.* joining, confluent.
baterako *adj.* synchronous, simultaneous.
baterakoi *adj.* tending to unify, tending to agree.
baterakoitasun *n.* agreeableness.
baterakor *adj.* convergent. *adj.* compatible
baterakuntza *n.* unity. *n.* convergence.
bateratasun *n.* simultaneity. *n.* unification. *n.* convergence, confluence.
bateratu *v.t.* to unify, to gather, to associate, to join. *v.i.* to converge, to fit together.
bateratzaile *adj.* coordinating, centralizing.
batere *adv.* not . . . any, not . . . at all, none at all, nothing.
bat ere ez *adj./pron.* nobody, not one, no one, not any.
batetik *adv.* from one (place).
bat etorri *v.i.* to agree, to converge.
batez *adv.* collectively, unanimously.
batez-beste *adv.* on the average.
batez-besteko *adj.* average, mean.
batez ere *adv.* particularly, especially, above all.
batezin *adj.* irreconcilable, incompatible.
bati *pron./adj. (dat.)* to one, to a.
batik-bat *adv.* especially, particularly.
bat izan *v.i.* to be united; to agree.
batu *v.t.* to join, to unify, to unite. *v.i.* to get together, to gather, to meet. *v.t. (arith.)* to add. *adj.* unified; coagulated.
batugai *n.(arith.)* addend.
batugarri *adj.* unitive, unifying; addable.
batuketa *n.(arith.)* addition, summation.
batukor *adj.* additive.
batukortasun *n.* quality of being additive.
batura *n.(arith.)* sum, result.
baturazi *v.t.* to congregate, to cause to gather.
batutzaile *adj.* unifying, joining.
batxiler *n.* high school student, secondary school student.
batxilergo *n.* period of secondary school.
batza *n.* society, guild, union.
batzaile *n./adj.* unifier, collector, gatherer; unifying.
batzalde *n.* association, society, corporation.
batzaldi *n.* meeting, assembly, conference.
batzar- Used in compound words.
batzarburu *n.* chairperson.
batzargela *n.* conference room.

batzarkide *n.* companion at a meeting.
batzarleku *n.* meeting place, conference room.
batzarragiri *n.* minutes of a meeting.
batzarraldi *n.* session.
batzarre *n.* meeting, conference, assembly.
batzarre egin *v.t.* to hold a meeting.
batzarreko *adj.* pertaining to a meeting.
batzarreratu *v.i.* to go to a meeting, to attend a meeting. *v.i.* to gather, to get together.
batzarretxe *n.* building for meetings, convention center.
batzartegi *n.* meeting place, conference room.
batzartoki *n.* conference room.
batzartu *v.i.* to gather, to get together.
batzoki *n.* meeting place. *n.(pol.)* Basque meeting places for political purposes founded by the Basque Nationalist Party.
batzorde *n.* committee.
batzordekide *n.* committee member.
batzu *pron./adj.* some. Can be used as a subject with v.i. and as a direct object.
batzuek *pron.* some. Used as subject with v.t.
batzuen *pron./adj. (genit.)* of some, belonging to some.
batzuetan *adv.* sometimes, every so often.
batzuk *pron./adj.* some.
baxera *n.* set of clay dishes or stoneware.
baxeragile *n.* potter.
baxerakintza *n.* trade of a potter.
baxerategi *n.* dish rack, dish cupboard, china hutch.
baxu *n.(mus.)* bass. *adj.* low, short.
baxuki *adj.* lowly.
baxura *n.* surface (fishing).
bazka *n.* food. *n.* fodder; pasture.
bazkabelar *n.* pasture grass.
bazkal- Used in compound words. Derived from *bazkari*, main meal between 1 and 2 p.m.
bazkalagur *n.* toast (drinking) at the midday meal.
bazkalarre *n.* pasture.
bazkalaurre *n.* time before the main midday meal.
bazkalaurreko *n.* appetizers, hors d'oeuvres before the main midday meal.
bazkalazkeneko *n.* dessert of the main midday meal.
bazkalburuko *n.* dessert of the midday meal.
bazkaldar *n.* guest for the main midday meal.
bazkaldei *n.* invitation for the main midday meal.
bazkaldu *v.t.* to have the main meal between 1 and 2 p.m.; to have lunch.
bazkaleku *n.* pasture.

bazkalgarai *n.* time of the main midday meal.
bazkalkide *n.* table companion.
bazkalondo *n.* time after the main midday meal.
bazkalordu *n.* hour of the main midday meal (between 1 and 2 p.m.).
bazkaltiar *n.* guest for the main midday meal.
bazkaltoki *n.* dining room.
bazkari *n.* main meal between 1 and 2 p.m.; lunch.
bazkaritxo *n.(dim.)* small lunch.
bazkatoki *n.* grazing field.
bazkatu *v.t.* to pasture, to graze, to eat (animals). *v.i.* to graze.
bazkatzaile *n.* shepherd, herdsman.
bazkide *n.* member of a society.
bazkide izan *v.i.* to belong, to be a member of a society.
bazkidetasun *n.* quality of being a member of a society.
bazkidetu *v.i.* to become a member of a society.
bazko *n.* Easter.
bazkoargizari *n.(eccl.)* paschal candle.
bazkun *n.* meeting, assembly. *n.* society.
baztanga *n.(zool.)* fish similar to a ray or skate. *n.(med.)* smallpox.
baztangadun *adj.* variolous, having smallpox.
bazter *n.* corner, place. *n.* margin.
bazterdura *n.* seclusion.
baztergaitz *adj.* unavoidable.
baztergarri *adj.* avoidable.
baztergela *n.* secluded room, storeroom.
bazterketa *n.* retirement, seclusion.
bazterralde *n.* corner.
bazterraldi *n.* confinement, relegation, putting in a corner.
bazterreko *adj.* marginal; distant, remote, out of the way.
bazterreratu *v.t.* to corner; to put in the corner. *v.t.* to eliminate, to exclude, to put away, to put out of the way.
bazterrezineko *adj.* unforgettable, unavoidable.
bazterrune *n.* secluded place.
baztertu *v.t.* to corner, to put in the corner. *v.t.* to exclude; to deny admission. *v.i.* to retreat; to retire; to move over; to seclude.
baztertzaile *n./adj.* excluder; excluding.
bazterzulo *n.* secluded corner.
be- *(gram.)* Verbal prefix used with the 3rd. pers. sing. imp. of *edin*, to be. Used with v.i. **Betor.** Have him come.
-be *(gram.)* Suffix which indicates lower part. **Mendibe.** Lower part of the mountain.
bedeinkagarri *adj.* blessed.
bedeinkapen *n.* blessing.
bedeinkatzaile *n./adj.* blesser; blessing.

bedeinkazio *n.* blessing.
bederatzi *n./adj.* nine.
bederatzigarren *adj.* ninth.
bederatzika *adv.* in groups of nine.
bederatzikoitz *adj.* ninefold.
bederatzina *adv.* nine to each one. *adv.* nine to nine (a game score).
bederatzinaka *adv.* in groups of nine.
bederatzinakatu *v.t.* to distribute in groups of nine.
bederatzirehun *adj./n.* nine hundred.
bederatziren *adj.* one-ninth.
bederatziurren *n.(eccl.)* novena.
bederen *conj./adv.* at least; at any rate. *conj.* as for, concerning.
bee *egin v.t.* to bleat.
begi *n.(anat.)* eye. *n.* hole through which a handle can be fitted. *n.(bot.)* bud. *n.* skin abscess. *n.(arch.)* span (of a bridge).
begia bete *v.t.* to like, to please.
begia bota *v.t.* to choose, to select.
begialde *n.* area around the eyes.
begiarte *n.* face.
begiarteko *adj.* facial; between the eyes.
begibakar *adj.* one-eyed.
begibarne *n.* eye socket.
begibarren *n.* eye socket.
begibazter *n.* corner of the eye.
begi-begi egon *v.i.* to stare.
begi-belarri *adj.* alert.
begibeteko *adj.* pleasant, agreeable.
begibitarte *n.* face.
begiburu *n.(anat.)* eyebrow.
begiederreko *adj.* good looking.
begieri *n.(med.)* eye disease, ophthalmia.
begierre *adj.* having irritated eyes.
begiertz *n.* corner of the eye.
begiespen *n.* act of observing, contemplating.
begiestalki *n.* eye patch.
begietako *adj.* visual, ophthalmic. *adj.* evident, obvious. *adj.* pleasant, agreeable, dear.
begietaratu *v.i.* to be evident, to be obvious. *v.t.* to show, to present.
begietsi *v.t.* to look at, to watch, to contemplate.
begiezkel *adj.* cross-eyed.
begigaizto *n.* bewitching, fascination, casting a spell. *adj.* sly, cunning.
begigorri *adj.* having irritated eyes, red eyed.
begigorritu *v.i.* to get red eyes.
begikada *n.* look, glance.
begikari *n.* eye doctor, ophthalmologist.
begikizkur *n.* squinty eyelid, squinted eye.
begiko *adj.* ocular, visual, pertaining to the eye. *adj.* appreciated, pleasant, agreeable, preferred. *n.* grudge, ill will, spite.
begikoile *n.(anat.)* eyelash.
begiko izan *v.i./v.t.* to like, to please,

to prefer.
begikokeria *n.* favoritism.
begikolpe *n.* glance, look.
begikomin *n.* eye disease, ophthalmia.
begikotasun *n.* preference, predilection, favor; affection.
begilarri *adj.* goggle-eyed.
begilauso *n.(med.)* cataract.
begilausotu *v.i.* to become cloudy (the eye), to develop cataracts.
begilun *adj.* sad-looking, having sad-looking eyes.
begiluze *adj.* curious, nosy.
begimakur *adj.* cross-eyed.
begimin *n.(med.)* ophthalmia, eye disease.
begimoteltasun *n.* near-sightedness, myopia.
begineke *n.(med.)* presbyopia, tired eye.
beginini *n.(anat.)* iris.
begininieri *n.(med.)* iritis.
begino *n.(dim.)* small eye.
begioker *adj.* cross-eyed.
begiokertu *v.t.* to cross one's eyes. *v.i.* to become cross-eyed.
begion *n.* sympathy, affection.
begionez *adv.* friendly, amicably, lovely.
begira *v.t.* Imp. of the verb *begiratu*, look, pay attention. *int.* look, pay attention. *adv.* waiting; watching, looking.
begira-begira *adv.* looking attentively, staring.
begirada *n.* look, glance.
begira egon *v.i.* to contemplate, to consider; to pay attention. *v.i.* to wait. *v.i.* to be spying, to be staring, to be watching attentively.
begiragabe *adj.* disrespectful. *adj.* inattentive.
begiragarri *adj.* worth seeing, admirable.
begiragarrizko *adj.* admirable.
begirakada *n.* look, glance.
begiraketa *n.* inspection, survey, examination.
begirakoi *adj.* curious.
begirakor *adj.* discreet, prudent, respectful, attentive.
begirakorki *adv.* cautiously, carefully, prudently.
begirakortasun. *n.* prudence, moderation, caution, carefulness.
begirakune *n.* severe look.
begiraldi *n.* glance, look.
begirale *n.* observer, watcher. *n.* keeper, guardian.
begiramen *n.* deference, consideration, courtesy; esteem, appreciation, respect.
begiramendu *n.* discretion, moderation. *n.* reverence, respect.
begiramenez *adv.* moderately, discretely; respectfully, reverently.
begiramen izan *v.t.* to respect, to

revere, to esteem.

begiramentsu *adj.* respectful, courteous, deferent.

begirapen *n.* discretion, circumspection; deference, respect.

begiratasun *n.* caution, vigilance, prudence, discretion, judiciousness.

begiratu *v.t.* to look at, to stare, to watch. *v.t.* to observe (a fast, a rule, etc.), to keep, to comply with. *v.t.* to protect, to preserve, to keep.

begiratzaile *n./adj.* watcher, inspector, guardian, keeper; protecting, watching.

begirazale *adj.* curious. *adj.* protective, defensive.

begirune *n.* respect, deference, consideration, circumspection.

begirunegabe *adj.* disrespectful, impolite.

begirunetsu *adj.* respectful, courteous.

begirunez *adj.* respectfully.

begirunezko *adj.* respectful, courteous.

begisare *n.(anat.)* retina.

begisaremin *n.(med.)* retinitis.

begisendagile *n.* ophthalmologist, eye doctor.

begisendagiletza *n.* ophthalmology.

begisendatzaile *n.* ophthalmologist, eye doctor.

begitako *n.* visor cap. *n.* binoculars.

begitandu *v.i.* to imagine, to figure out.

begitan hartu *v.t.* to hate, to dislike strongly.

begitazio *n.* fantasy, illusion.

begitsu *adj.* having many knots.

begiurdin *adj.* blue-eyed.

begiz *adv.* visually.

begizain *n.(anat.)* optic nerve.

begiz-begi *adv.* face to face.

begiz jo *v.t.* to take a look, to glance. *v.t.* to choose, to elect, to select.

begizko *n.* enchantment, witchery, spell, evil eye. *n.* eye witness.

begizorrotz *adj.* acute, sagacious, discerning.

begiztaketa *n.* act of sighting, act of taking aim (guns).

begiztatu *v.t.* to take a look, to glance. *v.t.* to choose, to select.

begiztatzaile *n.* observer, watcher.

begizulo *n.* eye socket.

begizuri *adj.* having light-colored eyes. (lit.) white eye.

begizuringo *n.(anat.)* cornea.

bego *v.i.* have him be, let him stay. *(egon,* to be, to stay, to rest)

beha egon *v.i.* to be looking, to be watching.

behaketa *n.* observation.

behar *v.t.* must, should, to have to. *n.* need, necessity. *n.* poverty.

beharbada *adv.* maybe, perhaps.

behar-beharrez *adv.* necessarily, compulsorily.

behar-beharrezko *adj.* urgent, absolutely necessary, indispensable.

beharbezala *adv.* properly, correctly, adequately.

behargabe *adj.* unnecessary, superfluous.

behargabeko *adj.* unnecessary, useless.

behargorri *n.* extreme poverty, penury, indigence.

behar izan *v.t.* to need, to have to.

beharki *n.* duty, obligation. *n.* necessity.

beharkor *adj.* coercive, restraining, compulsory.

beharkuntza *n.* requirement, exigency.

beharrarazi *v.t.* to force, to oblige, to constrain, to compel.

beharrean *conj.* instead of.

beharrez *adv.* necessarily, compulsorily, coercively, forcibly.

beharrezko *adj.* necessary, urgent, indispensable. *adj.* compulsory, obligatory, mandatory.

beharrizan *n.* need, necessity.

behartasun *n.* necessity, poverty, indigence.

behartsu *adj.* needy, poor. *n.* beggar; needy.

behartu *v.t.* to oblige, to compel, to constrain, to force. *v.t.* to require.

behartzaile *n.* oppressor, tyrant.

behar ukan *v.t.* to need. *v.t.* to have to, must, should, ought to.

behatoki *n.* observatory; look-out point, place for viewing, observation point.

behatu *v.t.* to take a look.

behatz *n.(anat.)* toe. *n.(anat.)* toenail.

behatzaile *n.* observer, watcher.

behatzarteko *adj.* interdigital, between the toes.

behatzeko *adj.* related to the toe.

behatzezur *n.(anat.)* phalanx.

behazale *n.* sentinel, sentry. *adj.* curious.

behaztopa *n.* obstacle, hindrance, difficulty; trip, stumble.

behaztopabide *n.* hindrance, obstacle.

behaztopa egin *v.t.* to stumble, to trip over.

behaztopagarri *n.* obstacle, hindrance.

behaztoparazi *v.t.* to cause to stumble, to trip. *v.t.(fig.)* to scandalize.

behaztopari *n.* tripper, stumbler.

behaztoparri *n.* obstacle.

behaztopatu *v.i.* to stumble, to trip over.

behaztopatzaile *n./adj.* stumbler.

behazun *n.* bile, gall. *n.(fig.)* pain, suffering.

behazunbide *n.(anat.)* bile duct.

behazunezko *adj.* biliary.

behazuntsu *adj.* bilious, full of bile.

behe *n.* floor, ground. *n.* lower part,

bottom.

behe- *(gram.)* prefix meaning lower, sub, under.

behea jo *v.t.* to touch the bottom. *v.t.* to be bankrupt, to go broke, to ruin.

behealde *n.* lower part, low place. *n.* cellar, basement.

behean *adv.* below, down, under, underneath, downstairs.

behegela *n.* room on the ground floor.

beheititu *v.i.* to bend over. *v.t.* to reduce (the price, etc.).

beheko *adj.* lower (space).

behemaila *n.* lower level, low level.

behemailako *adj.* lower in status or rank; inferior.

behera *adv.* below, down, under. *int.* down with.

beherabide *n.* slope, downhill. *n.* way of decreasing.

beheradura *n.* reducing, lowering.

beheragarri *adj.* decreasing.

beheragoko *adj.* inferior.

beheragotu *v.t./v.i.* to decrease, to diminish. *v.i.* to humble oneself. *v.i./v.t.* to go lower, to put lower, to lower.

beherakada *n.* emotional depression, slump; fall, decline, deterioration.

beheraketa *n.* discount. *n.* depreciation. *n.* descent.

beherakor *adj.* decadent. *adj.* decreasing.

beheraldi *n.* decadence, decay. *n.* decrease. *n.* depreciation.

beherapen *n.* descent, decrease, ebb, wane. *n.* discount.

beherarazi *v.t.* to demolish, to overthrow, to destroy.

beheratu *v.t./v.i.* to lower, to decrease, to bring down, to go down, to fall. *v.t./v.i.* to depreciate, to cheapen. *v.i.* to fall in price.

behetasun *n.* inferiority, lowness.

behetik *adv.* from below.

beheuskalki *n.* Basque subdialect.

behezarri *v.t.* to subordinate, to be contingent upon.

behezatiketa *n.* subdivision, fraction.

behezatitu *v.t.* to subdivide, to fractionate.

behezuzendari *n.* assistant director.

behezuzendaritza *n.* assistant management.

behi *n.(zool.)* cow.

behiketa *n.* herd of cows.

behiki *n.* beef, cow's meat.

behilarru *n.* cowhide.

behin *adv.* once. *adv.* once upon a time.

behin batean *adv.* once upon a time.

behin batez *adv.* once, one time.

behin bederen *adv.* at least once.

behin-behinean *adv.* temporarily.

behin-behineko *adj.* temporary, provisional, transient.

behinbetiko *adj.* definitive. *adv.* once

and for all.

behin edo behin *adv.* sometimes, once in a while, from time to time.

behin edo beste *adv.* sometimes; every so often.

behinen *adj.* main, principal, most important.

behinepein *adv.* at least.

behinere *adv.* never.

behin eta berriro *adv.* again and again, frequently, repetitiously, many times.

behin eta berriz *adv.* repetitiously, many times, repeatedly.

behingo *adj.* momentary; occurring once.

behingoan *adv.* suddenly, rapidly.

behingo batean *adv.* once; on a certain occasion. *adv.* suddenly.

behingo batez *adv.* for good.

behingoz *adv.* once and for all, for once.

behinik-behin *adv.* at least.

behinola *adv.* once; on a certain occasion.

behinolako *adj.* old, ancient, archaic.

behintzat *conj./adv.* at least.

behitalde *n.* herd of cows.

behitegi *n.* stable; cattle barn.

behixka *n.(zool.)* small cow.

behizain *n.* cowboy.

behizaintza *n.* act or job of herding cattle.

behobide *n.* path of mares.

behor *n.(zool.)* mare.

behorketa *n.* herd of mares.

behorkume *n.(zool.)* young mare, filly.

behortalde *n.* herd of mares.

behortegi *n.* stable for mares.

behorzain *n.* herdsman (for mares).

behorzaintza *n.* act of herding mares.

behorzaintzaile *n./adj.* keeper of mares, herdsman.

beila *n.* vigil.

beilari *n./adj.* he who keeps a vigil.

beilatu *v.t.* to keep a vigil.

beira *n.* glass.

beiragarri *adj.* vitrifiable, crystallizable.

beiragile *n.* glass dealer.

beiragintza *n.* manufacture of glass.

beiraki *n.* piece of glass. *n.* glass object.

beirakuntza *n.* crystallization, vitrification, changing into glass.

beirategi *n.* glass shop. *n.* glass factory.

beirateria *n.* glass window, stained glass window; group of windows or glass.

beiratu *v.t.* to vitrify.

beirazko *adj.* glassy, vitreous.

beiraztu *v.t.* to vitrify, to change into glass.

beireria *n.* set of glass pieces.

beita *n.* bait.

beitatu *v.t.* to bait.

beka *n.* scholarship, fellowship.

bekadun n./adj. holder of a scholarship.

bekain n. eyebrow.

bekainandi adj. having large eyebrows.

bekaineko adj. superciliary.

bekainondo n. part of the forehead above the eyebrows.

bekaitz adj. envious.

bekaizdun adj. envious.

bekaizgarri adj. enviable.

bekaizkeria n. envy.

bekaizki adv. enviously.

bekaizkoi adj. envious.

bekaizti adj. envious.

bekaiztu v.t. to envy. v.i. to be or become envious.

bekatari n./adj. sinner.

bekatu n. sin.

bekatu egin v.t. to sin.

bekatuezin adj. impeccable, incapable of sin.

bekatugabezia n. lack of sin, freedom from sin, impeccability.

bekatuzko adj. sinful, pertaining to sin.

bekoki n.(anat.) forehead.

bekokihezur n.(anat.) frontal; bone of the forehead.

bekokiko adj. frontal; pertaining to the forehead.

bekorotz n. excrement, dung.

bekosua n. fireplace.

bela n. sail. n.(zool.) raven, crow.

belabeltz n.(zool.) carrion crow.

beladun adj. having sails, sail.

belagile n. sail maker.

belagin n. sail maker.

belaki n. sponge.

belakitsu adj. spongy.

belakume n.(zool.) young raven.

belaontzi n. sailboat.

belar n.(bot.) grass.

belardi n. barn. n. pasture, meadow, field, prairie.

belardun adj. grassy.

belari n. thread for sewing sails.

belarjale adj. herbivorous, grass-eating.

belarketa n. harvest or abundance of grass, a lot of grass.

belarmeta n. haystack.

belarpilo n. mound of grass, pile of grass or hay.

belarrezko adj. herbaceous, grassy.

belarri n.(anat.) ear. n. buckle.

belarribarne n.(anat.) inner ear.

belarribarren n.(anat.) inner ear.

belarribarru n. inner ear.

belarridun adj. having ears.

belarrigogor adj. hard-of-hearing.

belarrihandi adj. having large ears.

belarriko n. headphones, headset. adj. pertaining to the ear, ear.

belarriluze adj. long-eared. adj.(fig.) curious.

belarrimin n.(med.) otitis; inflammation of the ear.

belarrimingarri adj. dissonant, discordant, bad sounding.

belarrimintz n.(anat.) eardrum, tympanum.

belarrimotz adj. short eared. adj. word used to designate Spaniards who used to settle in the Basque country.

belarriondoko n. slap in the face, blow.

belarriratu v.i. to hear, to reach one's ears. v.t. to put (something) to one's ear.

belarritako n. earring.

belarrizulo n. ear duct.

belarrondo n.(anat.) cheek.

belarrondoko n. blow, slap in the face.

belartegi n. barn. n. pasture, meadow, field.

belartsu adj. grassy.

belartu v.i. to become grassy.

belartza n. pile of grass, grass.

belarzale adj. herbivorous.

belarzelai n. meadow, field.

belasko n.(zool.) small raven.

belategi n. place of ravens.

belatxiki n.(zool.) small raven.

belatxikieta n. place of small ravens.

belatxinga n.(zool.) crow.

belatz n.(zool.) sparrow-hawk.

belaun n.(anat.) knee.

belaunaldi n. generation.

belaunaulki n. praying stool, chair.

belaunazpi n.(anat.) back of the knee.

belaunbabes n. knee guard, kneepad.

belaunburu n.(anat.) knee bone, kneecap.

belaunetako n. kneepad, knee guard.

belaunezur n.(anat.) knee bone, kneecap.

belaunikaketa n. genuflection, bending of the knee.

belaunikaldi n. genuflection.

belaunikarazi v.t. to cause to kneel.

belaunikatu v.i. to kneel.

belauniko adv. kneeling.

belaunkada n. hit in the knee.

belaunkonkor n.(anat.) knee bone, kneecap.

belaunpe n.(anat.) back of the knee; ham.

belaunpeko n. cushion of a praying stool or chair.

belaunzulo n.(anat.) back of the knee; ham.

beldar n.(zool.) larva of an insect.

beldur n. fear.

beldurbera adj. easily frightened.

beldurgabe adj. fearless, brave, courageous.

beldurgabeki adv. bravely, courageously, fearlessly.

beldurgabetasun n. courage, bravery, fearlessness.

beldurgarri adj. terrible, awful, frightful, dreadful.

beldurgarriro adv. awfully, terribly, dreadfully.

beldurgarritasun n. awfulness,

fearfulness.

beldurgarrizko *adj.* terrible, awful, fearful.

beldurgorri *n.* intense fear, terror.

beldur izan *v.i.* to fear, to be frightened, to be afraid.

beldurkeria *n.* cowardice.

beldurkoi *adj.* fearful, easily scared, easily frightened.

beldurkoitasun *n.* fearfulness.

beldurkor *adj.* fearful. *adj.* shy.

beldurkortasun *n.* shyness.

beldurrarazi *v.t.* to cause fear, to frighten.

beldurrarazle *adj./n.* frightening, scaring, scary; frightener.

beldurrez *adv.* fearfully, in fear of; shyly.

beldurrikara *n.* panic, awe, terror.

beldurtasun *n.* state of being afraid.

beldurti *adj.* fearful. *adj.* shy. *adj.* coward, cowardly.

beldurtu *v.i.* to be scared, to be frightened. *v.t.* to scare.

beldurtzaile *n.* threatener.

bele *n.(zool.)* raven, crow.

belen *n.* nativity scene.

belorratz *n.* needle for sewing sails.

beltz *n./adj.* black. *adj.* tanned, tan. *n.* red (wine). *n.(mus.)* quarter note.

beltzaile *n./adj.* blackener, blackening.

beltzaldi *n.* blackening.

beltzantzeko *adj.* blackish.

beltzaran *adj.* brown.

beltzarandu *v.i.* to tan, to get tan.

beltzeria *n.* group of black people.

beltzilun *adj.* sombre, gloomy.

beltziska *adj.* blackish.

beltzune *n.* black spot; bruise.

beltzura *n.* blackness.

beltzurdin *adj.* dark blue, navy blue.

beltzuri *n.* frown.

beltzuritsu *adj.* frowning.

beltzuritu *v.i.* to frown.

belzjantzi *v.t./v.i.* to dress in black, to dress in mourning.

belzkeria *n.* infamous action, treason.

belzketari *n.* slave-dealer.

belztalde *n.* group of black people.

belztasun *n.* blackness, darkness.

belztu *v.i.* to blacken, to darken, to grow black, to become dark.

bemol *n.(mus.)* flat.

benabartar *n./adj.* native of Low Navarra.

benda *n.* bandage.

bendatu *v.t.* to bandage.

benedikatu *v.t.* to bless.

beneditar *n./adj.* Benedictine.

benetako *adj.* real, genuine, serious, sincere, true, truthful.

benetakotasun *n.* authenticity.

benetan *adv.* sincerely, truly, truthfully, really, honestly.

benetasun *n.* authenticity, seriousness.

beno *int.* well; let's see.

benta *n.* inn.

bentari *n.* innkeeper.

bentura *n.* chance.

benturaz *adv.* maybe, perhaps, by chance.

bepuru *n.(anat.)* eyebrow.

ber- *(gram.)* prefix which indicates repetition, duplication, equivalent to English re-, bi-.

-bera *(gram.)* suffix which denotes sensitivity.

beraganatu *v.t.* to take possession of. Used only in 3rd pers. sing.

beragan egon *v.i.* to depend on (him or her).

beragarri *adj.* softening.

beraiek *pron.* they themselves.

beraien *adj./pron.(genit.)* their; theirs.

berak *pron.* he, she. Used as subject with v.t.

berandu *adv.* late.

beranduko *adj.* late, tardy.

berandukor *adj.* tardy, late.

berandupen *n.* delay, deferral, postponement.

berandutasun *n.* lateness, tardiness.

berandutu *v.i.* to be late, to become late.

berandutxo *adv.* a bit late, a little late, slightly late.

berangarri *adj.* delayable, deferrable, postponable.

berankoi *adj.* tardy, late, slow.

berankor *adj.* slow, tardy, late.

berant *adv.* late. *adj.* late, tardy, slow.

berant- Used in compound words. Signifies lateness, tardiness.

berantaro *n.* late season.

berantegi *adv.* too late.

berantetsi *v.t.* to become impatient (while waiting for something).

berantiar *adj.* late, delayed, tardy.

berantordu *n.* late hour.

berarazi *v.t.* to cause to soften, to make soft.

beratasun *n.* softness, tenderness. *n.* sensitivity.

berati *adj.* benign, merciful.

beratu *v.t./v.i.* to soften. *v.t./v.i.* to soak.

berau *pron.* emphatic pronoun meaning he himself, she herself, this one.

beraz *conj.* therefore, consequently, so, thus.

berba *n.* word.

berbera *pron.* he himself, she herself, it itself. *adj.* same.

ber-berau *pron.* this (person) and no other.

berbihurketa *n.* reconversion.

berbihurtu *v.t./v.i.* to reconvert.

berbikoizketa *n.* reduplication.

berbikoiztu *v.t.* to reduplicate.

berbizkunde *n.* revival, resurrection.

berbizle *n.* resuscitator, reviver.

berbizte *n.* revival, resurrection.

berbiztu v.i./v.t. to revive, to resuscitate. v.t. to light again, to turn on again.

berde adj. green.

berdebizi adj. intense green, bright green.

berdegune n. green area, green belt.

berdekeria n. dirty story, dirty joke, blue humor.

berdel n.(zool.) kind of mackerel, a salt water fish about one foot long, dark blue color on top.

berdemin adj. very green.

berdeska adj. greenish.

berdetasun n. greenness.

berdetu v.i. to become green, to turn green.

berdeztatu v.t./v.i. to cover with green.

berdilun adj. dark green.

berdin adj. same, equal, identical. n. tie, even score. n. equal sign. adv. equally. adj. flat, smooth, leveled.

berdindu v.t./v.i. to level; to make even. v.i. to tie (a score).

berdindura n. symmetry.

berdinean adv. under identical conditions; in equal circumstances.

berdineza n. difference, inequality.

berdineztasun n. dissimilarity, unlikeness, differentness.

berdingabe adj. incomparable, unequaled, extraordinary, matchless.

berdingabeki adv. incomparably.

berdingabeko adj. unequal. adj. odd, unpaired. adj. unique, incomparable, excellent, exceptional, extraordinary.

berdingabetu v.i./v.t. to make uneven, to unmatch.

berdingailu n. leveling harrow.

berdingaitz adj. incomparable, unable to be equaled.

berdingarri adj. comparable, equaled. adj. matching, equalling.

berdin izan v.i. to equal, to be equal, to be the same.

berdinkatu v.t. to compare. v.t. to level.

berdinketa n. leveling. n. comparison.

berdinki adv. equally, similarly, indistinguishably.

berdinkuntza n. similitude, likeness.

berdintasun n. equality, evenness, sameness.

berdintsu adj. similar, almost identical, analogous.

berdintza n. comparison; equation.

berdintzaile n./adj. leveler, equalizer; leveling, equalizing.

berdinzale adj. egalitarian, equalitarian.

berdinzki adv. equally, similarly.

berdizka adj. greenish.

bere adj. his (own), her (own), its (own).

berebaitan adv. in his mind, heart, conscience.

berebat adv. the same, equally.

berebateko adj. uniform, equal, equitable.

berebiziko adj. excellent, extraordinary, fantastic, special.

berebizikotasun n. originality, particularity, singularity, uniqueness.

bereburu adj. independent.

bereburuz adv. spontaneously.

beregain adv. on his own.

beregaindu v.t. to appropriate (for himself or herself). v.t. to attract.

beregaintasun n. individuality, particularity.

bereganaketa n. appropriation. n. attraction towards him.

bereganatu v.t. to appropriate, to seize. v.t. to attract to him.

beregandu v.t. to attract, to appropriate. Used only in 3rd pers. sing.

beregisako adj. individual, particular, peculiar, characteristic.

beregizko adj. original, individual, singular, particular.

berehala adv. quickly, soon, hastily, in a hurry, right away.

berehalako adj. sudden, quick, immediate, instantaneous.

berehalatasun n. diligence, celerity, swiftness.

berehalaxe adv. immediately, soon, at once, quickly, instantly, right away.

berejabe adj. autonomous, independent, self-sufficient. (Used with 3rd pers. sing.)

berejabetasun n. autonomy, independence.

berekabuz adv. on his (or her) own initiative, on his (or her) own.

berekautan adv. in his conscience. adv. spontaneously.

berekeria n. caprice, fancy, whim.

berekiko adj. own, proper.

berekoi adj. selfish, self-centered (Used with 3rd pers. sing.).

berekoikeria n. selfishness.

berekoiki adv. egotistically, selfishly (used with 3rd pers. sing.).

berekoitasun n. selfishness (used with 3rd pers. sing.).

berekoitu v.i. to become selfish (3rd pers.).

berekor adj. selfish.

beren adj./pron. their, theirs.

berendia n. Mr. so-and-so.

berenganatu v.t./v.i. to appropriate (for themselves).

berera etorri v.i. to regain consciousness.

bereratu v.i. to regain consciousness.

beretar adj. selfish, self-centered.

bereter n. church assistant, altar boy. n. clergyman.

bereteretxe n. parish house.

beretergo n. job of church assistant.

beretertsa n. priestess.

beretu v.t. to appropriate, to seize

(used only in the 3rd per. sing.).
beretzakotu *v.t.* to monopolize, to seize (used only in the 3rd pers. sing.)
berez *adv.* spontaneously, instinctively; by nature, in itself.
berezale *adj.* selfish, lonely.
berezgabe *adj.* indistinctive.
berezgabeki *adv.* indifferently, indistinctly, indiscriminately, without classifying.
berezgaitz *adj.* inseparable.
berezgarri *adj.* distinguishable, specifiable. *adj.* separable, distinct. *n.* differentiator.
berezi *v.t./v.i.* to separate; to divorce. *v.t.* to choose, to select, to elect. *adj.* special, particular, distinct.
berezikeria *n.* favoritism, nepotism.
bereziki *adv.* separately. *adv.* especially, particularly.
berezitasun *n.* state of separation. *n.* specialty, singularity, characteristic, distinctness.
berezitu *v.t.* separate, to divide.
berezitzaile *n.* separator, segregator, discerner. *adj.* separating, segregating, discerning.
berezkeria *n.* egotism, self-centeredness (used with 3rd pers. sing.).
berezketa *n.* selection; segregation, discrimination.
berezko *n.* natural, spontaneous, innate.
berezkoi *adj.* self-centered, selfish.
berezkor *adj.* separating, dividing.
berga *n.* rod, twig, club. *n.* pole used to hang fishing nets for drying. *n.* penis of animals.
berjabe *adj.* independent, autonomous, free.
berjabetasun *n.* independence, autonomy, freedom.
berjabetu *v.i.* to reconquer.
berjabetza *n.* autonomy, independence.
berjaiotza *n.* rebirth.
bermagarri *adj.* guaranteeable, warrantable.
bermatu *v.t.* to guarantee, to warrant.
bermatzaile *n.* guarantor.
berme *n.* bail; guarantee; collateral.
bermedun *adj.* guaranteed, having a guarantee.
bermetasun *n.* guarantee.
berna *n.(anat.)* calf of the leg.
bernahezur *n.(anat.)* tibia, shin.
bernazaki *n.(anat.)* tibia, bone of the leg.
bernoker *adj.* crooked-legged, bow-legged, pigeon-toed, knock-kneed.
bero *n.* heat. *adj.* hot. *adj.(fig.)* ardent, vehement.
beroagotu *v.t.* to reheat, to warm up; to make hotter.

beroalde *n.* hot region, tropic region, tropics.
beroaldeko *adj.* tropical.
beroaldi *n.* hot season, hot weather.
beroarazi *v.t.* to inflame, to set on fire, to kindle. *v.t.* to excite, to cheer up.
beroarazle *n.* person who cheers (someone) up.
bero-bero *adj.* very hot. *adj.* very excited, very agitated.
beroberdindun *adj.* isothermal.
bero-berotu *v.i.* to get very excited.
berodura *n.* reheating.
bero egin *v.t.* to be hot.
beroeragile *n.* heater. *n.* person whose work is to heat something.
berogailu *n.* heater.
berogarri *adj.* suffocating; ardent, burning. *adj.* giving off heat.
berogintza *n.* thermal activity.
berogorri *n.* suffocating heat.
beroindar *n.* calory (thermodynamics).
beroindarrezko *adj.* thermodynamic.
beroketa *n.* heating.
beroki *n.* overcoat. *adv.* ardently, warmly.
berokitu *v.i.* to protect oneself with clothes.
berokor *adj.* warm.
beromaila *n.* degree of temperature.
beronen *pron.(genit.)* of this one, this one's.
beroneurketa *n.* thermometry.
beroneurkin *n.(phys.)* thermometer.
beroneurtailu *n.(phys.)* calorimeter.
beroneurri *n.(phys.)* thermometer.
beroni *pron.(dat.)* to this one.
berontzi *n.* small pan to hold coals; fire pan.
berorekin *pron.(abl.)* with you (formal usage).
berori *pron.(nom.)* you (formal usage).
berorrek *pron.(nom.)* you (formal usage, used with v.t.).
berorren *pron.(genit.)* of you, your (formal usage).
berosendabide *n.* thermotherapy.
berosortzaile *adj.* thermogenic, thermogenus.
berotasun *n.* heat, warmth. *n.* affection, cordiality.
berote *n.* hot season.
berotsu *adj.* hot, warm.
berotu *v.t./v.i.* to heat up, to warm up. *v.i./v.t.* to get excited; to excite. *v.i.* to get angry. *v.t.* to beat up; to flog. *v.t.* to hatch, to incubate.
berotzaile *n.* heater (person who heats something). *n.* person who cheers; cheerleader.
berozko *adj.* thermic, thermal.
berr- *(gram.)* prefix which denotes repetition, duplication, doubling. Equivalent to the English prefixes bi-, re-.
berrabiadura *n.* reactivation.
berrabiatu *v.t./v.i.* to reactivate, to

start again, to continue (a movement).

berragerketa n. reappearance.

berragerpen n. reappearance.

berragertu v.i. to reappear.

berraitona n. great-grandfather.

berraldagarri adj. transplantable.

berraldaketa n. reexchange. n. transplant.

berraldatu v.t. to transplant. v.t./v.i. to move again.

berraldatzaile n. transplanter.

berramona n. great-grandmother.

berrantolaketa n. reorganization, rearrangement.

berrantolamendu n. reorganization.

berrantolatu v.t. to repair. v.t. to reorganize.

berrantolatzaile n. reorganizer, rearranger, repairman.

berrargitaraldi n. new or further edition; reprint.

berrargitarapen n. reprint, second printing.

berrargitaratu v.t. to reprint.

berraukeragarri adj. reeligible.

berraukeraketa n. reelection.

berraukeratu v.t. to reelect.

berraurkikunde n. rediscovery.

berraurkitu v.t. to rediscover.

berrautagarri adj. reeligible.

berrautaketa n. reelection.

berrautamen n. reelection.

berrautapen n. reelection.

berrautatu v.t. to reelect.

berrazterketa n. revision, reexamination, double check.

berregin v.t. to redo, to remake, to do again, to copy. v.t. to embellish, to ornament.

berregintza n. rebuilding, restoration.

berregitaratu v.t. to restructure.

berregite n. act of redoing; repetition.

berregitura n. reorganization, restructuralization.

berregituraketa n. restructuralization, reorganization.

berregiturapen n. reorganization.

berregituratu v.t. to reorganize.

berregosi v.t. to boil again.

berregozketa n. act of boiling again.

berrehun n./adj. two hundred.

berrehungarren adj. two hundredth.

berrelkarketa n. reincorporation. n. reconciliation.

berrelkartu v.t./v.i. to reconcile. v.i. to meet again.

berreragiketa n. reactivation.

berreragin v.t. to reactivate.

berreraiketa n. reconstruction.

berreraiki v.t. to rebuild, to reconstruct.

berreraikuntza n. rebuilding, reconstructing.

berreraso v.t. to counterattack.

berrerasoketa n. counterattack.

berreratu v.t. to reorganize, to

rearrange, to restructure.

berrerori v.i. to fall again.

berrerorketa n. relapse, fall further.

berrerorpen n. relapse, fall further.

berrerosgarri adj. redeemable, easily bought back.

berrerosi v.t. to buy secondhand. v.t. to buy back. v.t. to redeem. v.t. to rescue.

berrerosketa n. second-hand purchase. n. redemption. n. rescue.

berrerosle n. second-hand buyer. n. redeemer.

berrerospen n. repurchase. n. redemption.

berreroste n. act of rebuying. n. act of buying back.

berreskuko adj. secondhand.

berreskuraezin adj. irrecoverable, irretrievable.

berreskuragarri adj. recoverable, retrievable, recuperable.

berreskuraketa n. rescue, recovery.

berreskurapen n. rescue, recovery.

berreskuratu v.t. to rescue, to recover, to get back, to recuperate.

berreskuratzaile n. rescuer.

berrestaldu v.t. to recover.

berrestalketa n. recovery.

berretorri v.i. to return, to come back.

berretu v.t. to repeat. v.t. to increase.

berretura n. renovation, renewal. n. augmentation, increase. n. relapse.

berreuskaraketa n. act of using the Basque language and reviving the Basque culture again.

berreuskaratu v.t. to revive Basque language and culture.

berrezagutu v.t. to recognize.

berrezarketa n. restoration, replacement.

berrezarle n. restorer.

berrezarpen n. restoration, reestablishment, reinstatement.

berrezarri v.t. to reinstate, to replace, to reestablish.

berrezi v.t. to re-educate.

berreziera n. re-education.

berreziketa n. re-education.

berrezkondu v.i./v.t. to marry for the second time, to remarry.

berrezkontza n. second marriage.

berri adj. new. adj. recent. n. news. Usually used in the plural.

berriago adj.(comp.) newer.

berriarazi v.t. to make (someone) renew (something).

berribanatzaile n. journalist, reporter.

berridatzi v.t. to copy, to rewrite.

berridazki n. copy.

berridazle n. copier, transcriber, one who copies something.

berridun adj. having news, informed.

berridura n. renovation, restoration.

berriekarle n. messenger.

berriemaile n. journalist, reporter, correspondent.

berrieman *v.t.* to bring up to date; to inform.
berriemate *n.* reporting the news, giving the news.
berrieramaile *n.* messenger.
berrigarri *adj.* renewable, reformable. *v.t.* to perceive again.
berrikari *n.* messenger; reporter.
berriketa *n.* gossip, idle, talk. *n.* amount of news. *n.* search for news.
berriketaldi *n.* conversation, chat, talk.
berriketan ari *v.i.* to talk, to chat, to converse.
berriketan ibili *v.i.* to talk, to chat.
berriketan jardun *v.t.* to talk, to chat.
berriketari *n.* chatter, talker.
berriketazale *adj.* fond of gossiping, talkative.
berriketontzi *adj.* talkative, loquacious.
berriki *adv.* recently, modernly, newly.
berrikitasun *n.* novelty, innovation.
berrikizale *adj.* modernist, fond of modern ideas or things.
berrikunde *n.* renovation, remodeling, innovation, reform.
berrikuntza *n.* renovation, remodeling, reform, innovation.
berrikuntzari *n.* innovator, reformer, restorer.
berrikusi *v.t.* to see again.
berrikusketa *n.* act of seeing again; review.
berrikuspen *n.* review, revision.
berrikustapen *n.* review.
berrikustatu *v.t.* to review.
berrindartu *v.t./v.i.* to strengthen, to reinforce, to fortify.
berrion *n.* good news. *n.* gospel.
berripen *n.* renovation, restoration.
berrirakin *v.t.* to boil again.
berrirakurri *v.t.* to reread.
berriro *adv.* again, once again.
berritan *adv.* at the beginning; being new. *adv.* twice; again.
berritasun *n.* novelty, innovation, renovation.
berritsu *adj.* almost new. *adj.* talkative, loquacious, gossipy.
berritsukeria *n.* gossip, idle talk.
berritu *v.t./v.i.* to renew, to reform. *v.t.* to repair, to restore, to renovate, to remodel. *v.t.* to repeat.
berritura *n.* renovation, change.
berritzaile *n./adj.* innovator, restorer, remodeler, reformer, renovator; restoring, reforming.
berritzuli *v.i.* to revert; to reverse.
berritzulketa *n.* restitution, devolution.
berritzulpen *n.* revolt. *n.* second turn, return.
berrixka *adj.* almost new, quite new. *n.* story, joke, short chronicle, anecdote.
berriz *adv.* again, once again. *conj.* but, however, yet, on the other hand.
berrizale *adj.* fond of news. *adj.* fond of novelties.

berrizalekeria *n.* snobbism.
berrizkagarri *adj.* restorable.
berrizkakor *adj.* reiterative, repetitious.
berrizkatu *v.t.* to reiterate, to repeat. *v.t.* to copy, to reproduce. *v.t.* to renew.
berrizketa *n.* restoration, reform, renovation.
berrizkunde *n.* reiteration, repetition. *n.* renovation.
berriztadura *n.* renovation, restoration, reform.
berriztaketa *n.* restoration, renovation, reform.
berriztapen *n.* renovation, reform, restoration.
berriztari *n./adj.* reformer, renewer, renovator; renewing.
berriztasun *n.* renovation, reformation.
berriztatu *v.t.* to renew, to reform, to remodel, to renovate, to repair, to restore.
berriztatzaile *n.* restorer, repairer, remodeler.
berrizte *n.* renovation, renewal, repair, rearrangement. *n.* repetition. *n.* reform.
berriztu *v.t./v.i.* to renew, to restore, to remodel. *v.t.* to repeat.
berro *n.(bot.)* bush.
berrogei *n./adj.* forty.
berrogeigarren *adj.* fortieth.
berrogeiko *n.* period of forty (days, years).
berrogeitamar *n./adj.* fifty.
berrogeitamargarren *adj.* fiftieth.
berrogeiurteko *adj.* forty years old, forty year old.
berrontziraketa *n.* reembarkation, reembarkment.
berrontziratu *v.i./v.t.* to reembark.
berrugeta *n.(zool.)* seabass.
bersalketa *n.* resale.
bertako *adj.* local, native.
bertakotu *v.i.* to naturalize. *v.i.* to settle down, to install oneself. *v.i.* to get used to a place.
bertan *adv.* right there.
bertanbehera utzi *v.t.* to abandon, to give up.
bertarakotu *v.i.* to get used to (a place), to become acclimatized.
bertaratu *v.i./v.t.* to approach, to come closer.
bertatik *adv.* from right there.
berton *adv.* right here.
bertso *n.(poet.)* stanza. *n.* verse.
bertso egin *v.t.* to versify, to make verses.
bertsogile *n.* versifier, Basque troubadour.
bertsogintza *n.* versification.
bertsolari *n.* Basque troubadour.
bertsolarisaio *n.* contest of Basque troubadours.
bertsolaritza *n.* profession of Basque troubadours, Basque troubadourism.

n. popular oral literature created by the Basque troubadours.

bertsoneurketa *n.* scansion; the analysis of verse into rhythmic components.

bertsoneurtu *v.t.* to scan verses.

bertsopaper *n.* piece of paper on which Basque troubadours' poems were written,especially in the 19th century.

bertsoz *adv.* in verse.

bertsozale *adj.* fond of popular poems.

bertute *n.* virtue.

bertutedun *adj.* virtuous.

bertutez *adv.* virtuously.

bertz *n.* bucket, pail.

berun *n.* lead. *n.* sounding line, plummet, sound.

berunaire *adj.* leaden.

berunantzeko *adj.* leaden, lead-like.

berunari *n.* person who works with lead; plumber.

berundegi *n.* storehouse of leaden goods.

berundu *v.t.* to solder with lead.

berundun *adj.* leaden, lead.

beruneria *n.* lead trim, lead edging, lead border.

berunezko *adj.* leaden, made of lead, lead.

beruneztapen *n.* solder with lead.

beruneztatu *v.t.* to solder with lead.

berungile *n.* plumber.

berunkari *n.* plumber.

berunki *n.* lead ore, piece of lead.

berunkintza *n.* job of a plumber.

beruntsu *adj.* leaden.

berunztatu *v.t.* to fill with lead.

berunztatzaile *n.* plumber.

berzkada *n.* bucketful, pailful.

berzkin *n.* tinker, boiler maker, pot maker.

berzkintza *n.* manufacture of pots. *n.* pot maker's job.

besa- Used in compound words. Derived from *beso*, arm.

besaburu *n.(anat.)* shoulder, shoulder blade.

besaeragin *v.t.* to move the arms.

besagain *n.(anat.)* shoulder.

besahezur. *n.(anat.)* humerus.

besakada *n.* armful.

besaldi *n.* armful.

besamotz *adj.* having short arms. *adj.* missing part of one's arm.

besamutur *n.(anat.)* wrist.

besanga *n.* largest branch of the tree. *n.* stanchion.

besape *n.(anat.)* armpit, axilla, underarm.

besapeko *adj.* pertaining to the armpit.

besapetu *v.t.* to carry (something) under the arm, to put under one's arm.

besarka *adv.* embracing.

besarkada *n.* embrace, hug.

besarkaldi *n.* embrace, hug.

besarkatu *v.t./v.i.* to embrace, to hug.

besarkatzaile *n.* hugger, embracer; person who embraces.

besarketa *n.* embracing, hugging.

besarte *n.* space surrounded by the arms.

besartean *adv.* between the arms.

besaulki *n.* armchair.

besaurre *n.(anat.)* forearm.

besazpi *n.(anat.)* armpit, axilla.

besazulo *n.* sleeve opening, shirt cuff.

besigu *n.(zool.)* sea bream.

beso *n.(anat.)* arm.

besobakar *adj.* armless; missing one arm, one-armed.

besodun *adj.* having arms.

besoetako *n.* godchild.

besondo *n.(anat.)* arm from the shoulder to the elbow.

besozabalik *adv.* with open arms.

besozabalka *adv.* with open arms.

besoz-beso *adv.* arm in arm.

besta *n.* feast, celebration, holiday.

bestaberri *n.(eccl.)* feast of Corpus Christi.

bestaburu *n.* main feast.

bestaegun *n.* festivity, feast, holiday.

bestalde *n.* other side; opposite side. *adv.* moreover, furthermore, in addition.

bestaldean *prep.* beyond, on the other side of.

bestaldeko *n.* neighbor. *adj.* of the other side, neighboring. *adj.* opposing, contrary, opposite.

bestaldi *n.* festivity, feast.

bestazale *adj.* fond of feasts.

beste *adj./pron.* another, other. *adv.* as much as.

bestegabe *adv.* without further comment, with nothing more.

bestegangarri *adj.* transferable.

besteganatu *v.t.* to transmit property to another person, to transfer; to expropriate.

beste hainbeste *adv.* the same amount, as much, as many.

bestela *adv.* in a different manner, in another manner, in another way. *conj.* otherwise, if not.

bestelako *adj.* different, another kind of, diverse.

bestelakotasun *n.* variety, diversity.

bestelakotu *v.t.* to transform, to vary, to change. *v.i.* to fade, to lose color.

bestemunduko *adj.* pertaining to the afterlife, other worldly. *adj.* special, outstanding, exceptional.

besteren *adj./pron.* belonging to another, someone else's, of others.

besterendu *v.t.* to transmit property to another person; to expropriate.

besterenganatu *v.t.* to transmit (something) to another person; to pass on to.

besterik *conj.* but, other than, only.

bestetik *adv.* on the other hand.
bestetasun *n.* heterogeneity, diversity.
bestondo *n.* hangover.
besuts *n.* naked arm.
besutsik *adv.* with naked arms.
bet- Used in compound words. Derived from *begi*, eye and *behi*, cow (changing the *g* to *t*).
beta *n.* free time (to do something). *n.(min.)* vein. *n.* ring of a tree.
betagin *n.(anat.)* canine tooth; tusk.
betalde *n.* herd of cows.
betargi *adj.* having a happy face.
betargitsu *adj.* jovial, happy, content.
betarte *n.(anat.)* face, brow.
betaurreko(ak) *n.(pl.)* eyeglasses.
betazal *n.(anat.)* eyelid.
betazaleko *adj.* ciliary, belonging to the eyelids.
betazpi *n.* ring under the eye.
betazpidun *adj.* having rings under one's eyes.
betazpitsu *adj.* having many rings under one's eyes.
bete *v.t./v.i.* to fill; to satiate. *v.t.* to fulfill, to complete. *adj.* one, an, a. Used instead of *bat* in expressions of time, measurement, etc. **Ordu bete.** One hour, an hour.
betealdi *n.* fulfillment, completion. *n.* excess, great abundance, saturation. *n.* indigestion.
betebehar *n.* obligation, duty, requirement.
betebeharreko *adj.* compulsory, obligatory.
bete-betean *adv.* totally, fully, completely. *adv.* justly.
bete-beterik *adj.* completely full.
betedura *n.* fullness. *n.* completion, fulfillment.
betegailu *n.* instrument used to fill something (gun, etc.).
betegabe *adj.* unsatisfied, unfulfilled; vacant.
betegaitz *adj.* difficult to fulfill, difficult to observe, difficult to carry out.
betegarri *n.* complement, supplement. *adj.* satisfying, saturating. *adj.* overly sweet.
betekada *n.* excess eating; indigestion.
beteketa *n.* act of filling.
betekizun *n.* duty, obligation.
betekor *adj.* fruitful, productive.
betekuntza *n.* fulfillment, realization.
betelur *n.* filling soil, land fill.
beteria *n.(med.)* ophthalmia, inflammation of the eyeball. *n.* sleep (secretion of the eyes).
beterik *adv./adj.* full, satiated, satisfied.
beteriko *adj.* executed, completed, carried out.
beterre *adj.* having irritated eyes.
beterri *n.* lowland. *n.* lowland region of Guipuzcoa.

beterriko *adj./n.* inhabitant of the lowlands, plainsman.
beterritar *adj./n.* inhabitant of the lowlands.
betertz *n.* corner of the eye.
betetasun *n.* satisfaction, fullness. *n.* fulfillment.
betetzaile *n./adj.* one who carries out or fulfills plans, etc. *n./adj.* saturator.
betezin *adj.* insatiable, voracious, greedy. *adj.* unfillable, unfulfillable.
beti *adv.* always.
beti bat *adv.* invariably, as usual.
betibateko *adj.* unchangeable, invariable.
beti-betiko *adv.* forever. *adj.* eternal.
betidanik *adv.* always, always in the past, since always.
betidaniko *adj.* eternal, perpetual.
betiere *adv.* always. *n.* eternity, perpetuity.
betiereko *adj.* eternal, perpetual, perennial.
betierekotasun *n.* eternity, perpetuity.
betiko *adj.* eternal, perpetual, everlasting.
betikor *adj.* eternal, lasting, perpetual.
betikotasun *n.* eternity, perpetuity, long period of time.
betikotu *v.t./v.i.* to perpetuate, to immortalize.
betikoz *adv.* forever, eternally.
betile *n.(anat.)* eyelash.
betiletsu *adj.* having thick eyelashes.
betilun *adj.* frowning. *adj.(fig.)* unfriendly; sad.
betilundu *v.i.* to frown.
betirako *adv.* forever, for good.
betiraun *adj.* perpetual, eternal, everlasting. *v.t.* to last forever, to perpetuate, to make (something) last forever.
betiraunez *adv.* perpetually.
betiraungarri *adj.* immortal, everlasting, perpetuable.
betiraunpen *n.* perpetuation.
betiraute *n.* eternity.
betiro *adv.* permanently, always.
betitasun *n.* perpetuity, eternity.
betoker *adj.* cross-eyed.
betokertasun *n.* cross-eye, convergent strabismus.
betokertu *v.t./v.i.* to be cross-eyed.
betondo *n.* area around the eyes, part of the forehead above the eyebrow.
betondoilun *n.* frown.
betondoko *n.* hit near the eye. *adj.* superciliary.
betor *v.i.* have him come (*etorri*, to come).
betorde *n.* false eye.
betortz *n.(anat.)* canine tooth.
betsare *n.(anat.)* retina.
betsaremin *n.(med.)* disease of the retina.
betule *n.* eyelash.
betun *n.* shoe polish.

betzain *n.* cowboy. *n.(anat.)* optic nerve.

betzulo *n.* eye socket.

betzuringo *n.(anat.)* cornea.

bezain *conj.* as . . . as. Used with adj. and adv.

bezainbat *conj./adv.* as much . . . as, as many . . . as; so much.

bezainbeste *conj./adv.* so much, so many.

bezala *conj.* as, like.

bezalakatu *v.i.* to resemble.

bezalako *adj.* similar, alike, like, resembling.

bezalatsu *adj.* almost identical.

bezera *n.* milkwoman.

bezeria *n.* clientele, customers.

bezero *n.* customer, client, patient.

bezin *conj.* as . . . as.

bezpera *n.* eve, the day before.

bezperak *n.(eccl.)* vespers. A church service held in the late afternoon.

bezperan *adv.* the day before.

bezperaurre *n.* two days before.

beztidura *n.* shroud.

beztitu *v.t.* to shroud (a corpse), to dress (a corpse).

beztitzaile *n.* person who shrouds (a corpse).

bi *adj./n.* two. *n.* number two.

biago *n.* siesta, nap.

biago egin *v.t.* to take a nap.

biagotan *adv.* taking a nap.

biak *adj.* both, both of them.

bialdedun *adj.* having two sides, two-sided.

bialdeko *adj.* bilateral, having two sides, two-sided.

bialdizko *adj.(elec.)* diphase, diphasic, two-phase.

bialdu *v.t.* to send.

biangeluzko *adj.* biangular, having two angles.

biastekari *n.* biweekly magazine.

biasteko *adj.* biweekly.

biasteroko *adj.* biweekly, once every two weeks (publication).

Biblia *n.* Bible.

bibliako *adj.* biblical.

biblialari *n.* exegete, interpreter of the Holy scriptures.

bibolin *n.(mus.)* violin, fiddle.

bibote *n.* moustache.

bibotedun *adj.* having a moustache.

biburudun *adj.* having two heads, two-headed.

biburuko *adj.* bicephalous, having two heads.

bida- Used in compound words. Derived from *bide*, road.

bidagintza *n.* building and repair of roads.

bidaia *n.* journey, trip.

bidaia egin *v.t.* to travel, to take a trip.

bidaiari *n.* traveler, passenger. *adj.* migratory.

bidaide *n.* traveling companion.

bidaizorro *n.* handbag, tote bag.

bidalarazi *v.t.* to cause to send, to make (someone) send (something).

bidalari *n.* walker.

bidalezin *adj.* untransmissible, unsendable.

bidalgailu *n.* transmitter.

bidalgarri *adj.* transmissible, sendable.

bidali *v.t.* to send. *v.t.* to transmit. *n.* apostle.

bidalketa *n.* act of sending.

bidalpen *n.* shipment, sending (of goods).

bidaltzaile *n.* sender.

bidari *n.* walker, traveler. *n.* price of the trip, toll.

bidaro *n.* weather for walking.

bidarri *n.* stone-paved road.

bidarte *n.* crossroad, junction.

bidaso *n.* stream, brook.

bidaurreko *n.* pioneer; guide.

bidazain *n.* road man. *n.* traffic policeman.

bidazti *n.* traveler.

bide *n.* road, path, trail, way, route. *n.* distance, trip. *adv.* certainly, surely, probably, apparently.

-bide *(gram.)* suffix meaning road, route, means, job, occupation, duct, tract.

bideadar *n.* branch of the road.

bidebasle *n.* highway robber, highway bandit.

bidebazter *n.* shoulder of the road, corner of the road. *n.* turnout.

bidebieta *n.* crossroads.

bide egin *v.t.* to advance, to progress, to move along, to walk. *v.t.* to build roads.

bide eman *v.t.* to give an opportunity, chance.

bidegabe *n.* injustice, iniquity. *adj.* unjust, unfair. *adj.* astray.

bidegabekeria *n.* injustice, inequity, unfairness.

bidegabeki *adv.* unfairly, unjustly.

bidegabeko *adj.* arbitrary. *adj.* unjust, unfair, inappropriate.

bidegabetasun *n.* illegitimacy, illegality.

bidegabetu *v.i.* to get or become lost. *v.i.* to be unfair.

bidegabez *adv.* unfairly.

bidegain *n.* upper part of the road or trail. *n.* above the trail.

bidegaitz *n.* difficult or dangerous road or trail.

bidegaiztoz *adv.* perversely.

bidegalketa *n.* deviation, losing one's way.

bidegidari *n.* guide, leader.

bidegile *n.* road builder.

bidegintza *n.* road construction.

bidegite *n.* act of building roads.

bidegune *n.* stretch of road.

bidegurutze *n.* crossroads, junction.

bidehandi *n.* freeway, highway.

bidekari *n.* walker, traveler.
bideketa *n.* abundance of roads.
bideko *adj.* pertaining to a trip.
bidelagun *n.* traveling companion.
bidelan *n.* road construction.
bidelapur *n.* highwayman, robber.
bidelapurketa *n.* robbery, brigandage.
bidemale *n.* person who provides an
    opportunity for something.
bideman *v.t.* to give occasion to, to
    provide an opportunity.
bidenabar *adv.* as well. *adv.* on the
    way; halfway, midway.
bideohe *n.* cot, narrow bed that can be
    folded.
bideokerketa *n.* act of going astray.
bider *n.* time, times.
bideraezin *adj.* unfeasible, not viable.
bideragarri *adj.* viable, possible,
    feasible.
bideragarritasun *n.* viability, likelihood,
    feasibility.
bideraketa *n.* act of channeling.
biderakusle *n.* guide, leader.
biderapen *n.* act of arriving at the road.
bideratu *v.t.* to guide, to lead. *v.i.* to
    meet, to wait for, to encounter. *v.i.* to
    arrive at the road or trail, to get to the
    road.
biderdi *n.* halfway, midway.
biderdiko *adj.* equidistant, halfway.
biderdura *n.(arith.)* times, multiplied
    by.
bidergai *n.(arith.)* multiplicand.
biderkaketa *n.(arith.)* multiplication.
biderkakor *adj.* multiplicative.
biderkatu *v.t.* to multiply.
biderkatzaile *n./adj.* multiplier.
biderketa *n.(arith.)* multiplication.
biderki *n.(arith.)* factor.
biderreten *n.* canal, trench, drain.
bidertz *n.* shoulder of the road.
bidertu *v.t./v.i.* to multiply.
bidertzaile *n.(arith.)* multiplier,
    multiplicator.
bidesare *n.* network of roads.
bidesari *n.* toll, fee, payment.
bideseinale *n.* traffic signal.
bidetxo *n.(dim.)* short trail.
bidexka *n.(dim.)* path, short trail.
bidez *prep.* through, via, by means of.
    prep. by dint of.
bidezabal *n.* avenue.
bidezain *n.* road man. *n.* traffic
    policeman.
bidezaingo *n.* traffic inspection.
bidez-bide *adv.* straight ahead. *adv.*
    from road to road.
bidezidor *n.* shortcut.
bidezidortu *v.t.* to open up trails, to
    blaze a trail.
bidezko *adj.* reasonable, fair,
    legitimate. *adj.* convenient. *adj.*
    evident, obvious, manifest.
bidezoko *n.* corner of the road.
bidezorro *n.* satchel, backpack.
bidezulo *n.* pothole.

biegaleko *adj.* dipterous, two-winged,
    dipteran.
bien *adj.(genit.)* belonging to two,
    belonging to those two.
bienarteko *adj.* between two, mutual.
bienbitartean *conj.* meanwhile.
bieskudun *adj.* ambidextrous.
bietan *adj.* in the two. *adv.* twice.
bietara *adv.* in both ways. *adj.* to the
    two.
biga *adj.* two. *n.(zool.)* young cow, two
    year old cow.
bigantxa *n.(zool.)* calf, young cow
    (three to twelve months old).
bigarren *adj.* second. *n.* double,
    replica.
bigarrenaro *n.(geol.)* secondary era.
bigarrendu *v.i.* to become the second
    one. *v.t.* to put in second place.
bigarrenean *adv.* for the second time.
bigarreneko *adj.* second.
bigarrenez *adv.* for the second time.
bigarrengo *adj.* second.
bigarrengoz *adv.* for the second time.
bigun *adj.* soft. *adj.* sensitive.
bigunaldi *n.* softening.
bigunbera *adj.* tender, soft.
bigundu *v.t.i./v.i.* to soften, to get soft.
    v.i./v.t. to mitigate, to alleviate, to
    relieve, to lessen. *v.i./v.t.* to move to
    compassion, to move (emotionally).
bigundura *n.* softening.
bigungarri *n.* softener. *adj.* relieving,
    mitigating. *adj.* touching, moving
    (emotionally).
bigunkeria *n.* easy life; life of
    pleasures.
bigunketa *n.* softening.
bigunki *adv.* softly, delicately, tenderly,
    gently.
bigunkiro *adv.* softly, delicately,
    tenderly, gently.
bigunkor *adj.* mollient, softening,
    lessening.
biguntasun *n.* softness.
biguntzaile *n.* softener.
bihar *adv.* tomorrow.
biharamon *n.* the next day, the
    following day.
biharamonean *adv.* on the next day,
    the next day.
biharko *adv.* for tomorrow. *adj.* of
    tomorrow, tomorrow's.
bihi *n.* grain, seed.
bihigabe *adj.* seedless, grainless.
bihika *adv.* grain by grain.
bihikatu *v.t.* to shake out grain, to
    winnow.
bihiketa *n.* abundance of grain.
bihikor *adj.* fertile, giving many grains.
bihileko *adj.* bimonthly (every two
    months).
bihitegi *n.* barn, granary.
bihitoki *n.* threshing floor.
bihitsu *adj.* abundant in grain.
bihitu *v.t.* to shake out grain, to remove
    seeds, to remove kernels. *v.i.* to form

grains, to form seeds or kernels, to be full of grains, seeds or kernels.

bihitzaile *n.* person who shakes out grain from wheat or kernels from an ear of corn, etc.

bihortz *n.* two-pronged pitchfork.

bihotz *n.* heart. *n.(fig.)* inner part, middle.

bihotzagur *n.* warm greeting.

bihotzalde *n.* side of the heart.

bihotzaldi *n.* intuition, premonition, feeling, presentiment, foreboding.

bihotzandi(ko) *adj.* generous, magnanimous, big-hearted.

bihotzanditasun *n.* generosity, magnanimity, big-heartedness.

bihotzandiz *adv.* generously, magnanimously.

bihotzeko *adj.* cardiac. *adj.* cordial. *adj.* dear, darling, beloved.

bihotzeragile *adj.* moving, touching.

bihotzeratu *v.t.* to bring towards the heart, to attract.

bihotzerdiragarri *adj.* moving, stirring emotions.

bihotzerre *n.* heartburn, acid indigestion.

bihotzestu *n.(med.)* angina pectoris.

bihotzestura *n.* anguish, distress, sorrow, grief.

bihotzez *adv.* cordially, affectionately, lovingly.

bihotzikara *n.* emotion, feeling.

bihotzirrara *n.* emotion, feeling.

bihotzondo *n.* lower part of the heart, deepest part of the heart, innermost part of the heart.

bihotzondoko *n.* emotion, feeling.

bihotzoneko *adj.* kind, good-hearted.

bihotzonez *adv.* kindly, gently, favorably.

bihotzunkigarri *adj.* stirring emotions, moving.

bihoz- Used in many compound words when the following syllable begins with a consonant. Derived from *bihotz*, heart.

bihozbatez *adv.* unanimously.

bihozbeltz *adj.* cruel, merciless, black-hearted.

bihozbera *adj.* sentimental, tender, compassionate, soft-hearted.

bihozberakeria *n.* sentimentalism, soft-heartedness.

bihozberatasun *n.* mercy, pity, compassion, tenderness.

bihozberatu *v.i.* to have pity, to feel sorry for, to be compassionate.

bihozbero *adj.* generous.

bihozberotasun *n.* compassion; generosity.

bihozbigun *adj.* soft-hearted, merciful, kind, compassionate.

bihozbiguntasun *n.* compassion, mercy.

bihozdun *adj.* tender, compassionate, lenient, indulgent.

bihozgabe *adj.* cruel, merciless, ruthless. *adj.* discouraged.

bihozgabekeria *n.* cruelty, inhumanity, atrocity.

bihozgabeki *adv.* cruelly, mercilessly, ruthlessly.

bihozgabetasun *n.* inhumanity, cruelty. *n.* discouragement.

bihozgabetu *v.i.* to become cruel, to be cruel. *v.i.* to be discouraged.

bihozgabezia *n.* discouragement.

bihozgarbitasun *n.* chastity, pureness of heart.

bihozgogor *adj.* cruel, inhuman, ruthless, hard-hearted, merciless.

bihozgogorkeria *n.* cruelty, inhumanity, ruthlessness, mercilessness.

bihozgogorreko *adj.* cruel, inhuman, ruthless.

bihozgogortasun *n.* cruelty, inhumanity, ruthlessness, mercilessness.

bihozkada *n.* heartbeat, palpitation. *n.* intuition, premonition. *n.* feeling.

bihozkari *n.(med.)* cardiologist.

bihozkoi *adj.* affectionate, friendly.

bihozleun *adj.* benevolent, kind, gentle.

bihozmin *n.(med.)* heart disease. *n.* affliction, sorrow.

bihozmindun *adj.* suffering from heart disease.

bihozmingarri *adj.* moving, touching, heartbreaking.

bihozmintasun *n.* predilection, favoritism.

bihozpilpira *n.* heartbeat, palpitation, throbbing.

bihozsare *n.(anat.)* pericardium.

bihoztaupada *n.* palpitation, heartbeat.

bihoztasun *n.* cordiality, friendliness.

bihozti *adj.* affectionate.

bihoztsu *adj.* brave, courageous.

bihoztun *adj.* courageous, brave. *adj.* compassionate.

bihoztxarreko *adj.* malignant, malevolent, malicious.

bihur *adj.* crooked, curved, twisted, bent. *adj.(fig.)* cruel, ruthless.

bihurbide *n.* manner of returning, means of returning.

bihurdikatu *v.t.* to equivocate, to shuffle, to twist (meanings), to distort (statements).

bihurdura *n.* twisting, distortion, bending, curving. *n.* delivery.

bihurgaitz *adj.* difficult to bend.

bihurgarri *adj.* twistable. *adj.* returnable; convertible.

bihurgarritasun *n.* reversibility, convertibility.

bihurgune *n.* turn, curve.

bihurgunetsu *adj.* winding, bending, crooked, sinuous.

bihurkada *n.* twist, contortion.

bihurkatu *v.t.* to twist, to bend.

bihurketa n. conversion. n. mutation. n. devolution, return.

bihurkin n. screwdriver.

bihurkoi adj. twistable, bendable.

bihurkor adj. changeable, unstable, flexible, reflexive.

bihurpen n. conversion. n. devolution.

bihurrarazi v.t. to give back, to return. v.t. to make (someone) return (something).

bihurrera n. devolution, restitution, return.

bihurri adj. bent, curved, crooked. adj.(fig.) mischievous, rascally, naughty. adj.(fig.) rebellious. n.(med.) dislocation, luxation, sprain.

bihurrialdi n. revolution, riot, mutiny.

bihurriantzeko adj. looking like a rascal.

bihurri izan v.i. to be a rascal.

bihurrikada n. mischievous trick, villainy, prank.

bihurrikatu v.t. to twist, to bend. v.i. to turn.

bihurrikeria n. mischief, fraud, trick, trickery.

bihurriki adv. deceitfully, trickily, mischievously, maliciously, malevolently.

bihurripen n. riot, rebellion, revolt, uprising.

bihurritalde n. group of rascals, scoundrels.

bihurritasun n. rebelliousness, mischievousness.

bihurritu v.i. to revolt, to rebel, to mutiny. v.t. to twist, to bend.

bihurritxo adj.(dim.) rascally, naughty, mischievous.

bihurritza n. sedition, insurrection, revolution, revolt, riot, rebellion.

bihurtezin adj. irreversible.

bihurtezintasun n. irreversibility.

bihurtu v.i. to convert, to turn into, to change into, to become. v.i. to return, to come back. v.t./v.i. to twist, to bend. v.t. to give back, to return, to restore.

bihurtza n. sedition, rebellion, revolution. n. bending, winding, torsion.

bihurtzaile n. returner. n. transformer.

bihurtzapen n. act of giving back.

bikain adj. excellent, extraordinary, gorgeous.

bikaindu v.t. to improve, to better, to perfect.

bikainen(a) adj.(superl.) the most select, the best.

bikainki adv. extraordinarily.

bikaintasun n. excellence.

bikarbonato n. bicarbonate of soda.

bikario n. rector of a parish, vicar.

bikaritza n. vicarship.

bike n. tar, pitch.

bikedun adj. tarred.

bikelari n. person who works with tar

or pitch.

biketsu adj. having tar, tarry.

biketu v.t. to tar, to cover with pitch.

bikeztaldi n. act of tarring or covering with pitch.

bikeztapen n. act of tarring.

bikeztatu v.t. to tar, to cover with pitch.

bikeztu v.t. to cover with pitch, to tar.

biki adj./n. twin.

biko n. couple. (lit.) of two. n. deuce (cards).

bikoitz adj. twin. adj. double. adj. two-fold.

bikoizketa n. act of doubling.

bikoizpen n. duplication, act of doubling.

bikoiztasun n. duality, duplicity.

bikoizte n. duplication, doubling.

bikoiztu v.t./v.i. to duplicate.

bikondo n.(bot.) fig tree.

bikor n. lump. n. grain of cereal.

bikordun adj. granulous, granulated, granular.

bikorketa n. granulation.

bikortatu v.i. to granulate. v.i. to curdle (milk).

bikortsu adj. granulous, lumpy.

bikortu v.i. to granulate.

bikortxo n.(dim.) small granule.

bikote n. pair, couple, duo.

bikoteka adv. in pairs, in twos.

bikotu v.t./v.i. to pair up.

biku n. fig.

bikun adj. double, two-fold.

bikundu v.t. to duplicate. adj. duplicate, doubled.

bikunketa n. duplication.

bikuntasun n. quality of being doubled.

bikuntza n. act of doubling in amount or size.

bikuntzaile adj. duplicating.

bila n. search, searching, looking for, seeking.

bilabetekari n. bimonthly publication.

bilagarri adj. worth looking for.

bilaka adv. in search of, looking for.

bilakabide n. process of evolution.

bilakaera n. process, evolution, development.

bilakagaitz adj. difficult to evolve.

bilakagarri adj. capable of evolution.

bilakaketa n. evolution.

bilakakor adj. evolutionary.

bilakari n. explorer, seeker, searcher.

bilakatu v.i. to become, to change into, to develop into.

bilakaune n. stage of development.

bilaketa n. search, scrutiny.

bilaketari n. searcher.

bilakuntza n. investigation, search, probe, scrutiny.

bilatu v.t. to look for, to search, to seek.

bilatzaile n. searcher.

bilau adj. vile, cruel, despicable.

bilaukeria n. vileness, cruelty.

bilauki *adv.* villainously.
bilautasun *n.* quality of being vile, villainy, cruelty.
bilautu *v.t.* to become a villain.
bilbapen *n.* act of weaving.
bilbatu *v.t.* to weave.
bilbe *n.* weft, woven fabric.
Bilbo *n.* Bilbao, capital city of the province of Biscay. **Bilbotar.** Native of Bilbao.
bildegi *n.* storage place, warehouse.
bildei *n.* invitation to a meeting, meeting announcement, call for a meeting.
bildos- Used in compound words in which the following syllable begins with a consonant. Derived from *bildots*, lamb.
bildoski *n.* lamb's meat, lamb.
bildostalde *n.* flock of lamb.
bildostegi *n.* lamb fold.
bildots *n.* lamb.
bildotsile *n.* lamb's wool.
bildu *v.t.* to gather, to collect. *v.t.* to fold. *v.i./v.t.* to join, to unite, to meet, to gather. *v.t.* to pack, to wrap.
bilduketa *n.* gathering, collection, meeting.
bildukin *n.* wrapping.
bilduma *n.* collection, gathering, accumulation. *n.* meeting, assembly.
bilduma egin *v.t.* to collect, to gather.
bildumari *n.* gatherer, collector, compiler.
bildumatu *v.t.* to collect, to gather, to add.
bildumatzaile *n.* collector, gatherer. *adj.* compiling.
bildupen *n.* summary, abstract.
bildura *n.* meeting, reunion, gathering.
bilera *n.* meeting, reunion, gathering, assembly.
bileragiri *n.* minutes of a meeting.
bileraldi *n.* session.
bilerazi *v.t.* to call a meeting.
bilgarri *adj.* collectible.
bilgor *n.* lard.
bilgorjario *n.(med.)* seborrhea.
bilgorreria *n.(med.)* seborrhea.
bilgorrezko *adj.* made of tallow, fat.
bilgortsu *adj.* sebaceous, fatty.
bilin-balan *adv.* swaying, swinging, to and fro.
bilin-balatu *v.i.* to sway, to swing.
bilin-balaunka *adv.* swaying, swinging.
bilin-bolaka *adv.* tumbling, somersaulting.
bilioi *adj./n.* billion.
bilketa *n.* act of collecting or gathering, recruitment. *n.* collection.
bilketari *n.* collector, gatherer.
bilkor *adj.* convergent.
bilkordun *adj.* sebaceous, fatty.
bilkortsu *adj.* sebaceous, fatty.
bilkunde *n.* meeting, gathering.
bilkuntza *n.* storage. *n.* meeting, gathering.

bilkura *n.* meeting, assembly.
bilo *n.* hair.
biloba *n.* great-grandchild.
bilodun *adj.* hairy.
bilogabe *adj.* beardless, clean-shaven.
bilotsu *adj.* hairy.
biltegi *n.* storage place.
biltegiratu *v.t.* to store.
biltegizain *n.* warehouse keeper.
biltoki *n.* meeting place, conference room.
biltzaile *n.* collector, gatherer.
biltzar Used in compound words. Derived from *biltzazarre*, meeting.
biltzarburu *n.* chairperson of a meeting.
biltzargela *n.* conference room.
biltzari *n.* collector.
biltzarre *n.* meeting, gathering, assembly.
biltzarreratu *v.i.* to meet, to gather.
biltzartegi *n.* meeting place, conference room.
biltzartoki *n.* conference room.
biluzdura *n.* nakedness, nudity.
biluzgorri *adj.* stark naked, nude.
biluzgorritasun *n.* complete nakedness, nudity.
biluzi *adj.* nude, naked.
biluzik *adv.* nakedly, naked.
biluzkeria *n.* nudism, indecent exposure, exhibitionism.
biluztasun *n.* nudism.
biluztu *v.t./v.i.* to undress, to strip, to disrobe.
bimargodun *adj.* two-colored, having two colors.
bimintzotasun *n.* bilingualism.
binaka *adv.* in twos, two by two, two at a time.
binakatu *v.t./v.i.* to couple, to pair up, to pair off.
binaketa *n.* pairing, coupling, matching.
binako *adj.* coupled, paired up, paired off. *n.* a Basque folk dance.
binan *adv.* two at a time, in twos.
binbilikatu *v.i.* to shake, to sway, to swing, to jolt.
binbiliketa *n.* shaking, jolting.
biokimika *n.* biochemistry.
biokimiko *adj.* biochemical.
biola *n.(mus.)* viola.
biologari *n.* biologist.
biologia *n.* biology.
biolontxelo *n.(mus.)* cello.
biper *n.(bot.)* red or green pepper. *n.(fig.)* wit, humor.
biperbeltz *n.(bot.)* black pepper.
biperdun *adj.* hot, spicy. *adj.(fig.)* funny.
biper egin *v.t.(fig.)* to cut class, to play hooky.
bipergorri *n.(bot.)* red pepper.
biperlandare *n.(bot.)* pepper plant.
bipermin *n.(bot.)* hot pepper, chili pepper. *n.(fig.)* quick-tempered

person.
biperrada n. fried peppers.
biperrauts n. any ground pepper. n. paprika.
biperrezko adj. peppery, having the taste of pepper.
biperrontzi n. pepper box, pepper shaker.
biperropil n. pepper omelet.
biperztatu v.t. to season with pepper, to pepper.
bipi n.(zool.) wood-borer. n.(zool.) moth.
bipiadura n. becoming moth-eaten.
bipiatu v.i. to corrode (by the wood-borer); to damage (clothes, by moths).
bipi jo v.t./v.i. to corrode (by the wood-borer).
bipil adj. courageous, brave. adj. plucked, depilated.
bipildu v.t./v.i. to pull out hair. v.t. to pluck. v.t.(fig.) to sack, to pillage.
bipildura n. act of plucking. n. vivacity, audacity, frankness, openness.
bipilki adv. frankly, openly, straightforwardly, bluntly.
bipiltasun n. audacity, boldness, daring, frankness.
bipitsu adj. moth-eaten.
bir- (gram.) Prefix which indicates repetition or duplication. Used before a consonant.
bira n. quick maneuver, quick turn.
birabarki n. brace and bit, hand-held drill.
bira-biraka adv. winding, moving like a snake, slithering.
biradura n. quick turn. n. pirouette.
bira egin v.t. to turn around.
biraerraz adj. easily turnable.
biragailu n. rotor.
biragune n. turn, curve.
biraka adv. turning around, rotating, turning.
birakari adj. rotative, rotating, rotatory, gyrating.
birakatu v.i. to turn, to rotate, to gyrate.
biraketa n. rotation, revolution, turning. n.(mech.) gyration.
birakoi adj. rotating.
birakor adj. easily rotating, turning with ease.
birakuntza n. rotation, quick maneuver.
biraldi n. turn, rotation.
birao n. blasphemy, curse.
birao bota v.t. to blaspheme.
biraogarri adj. detestable, abominable, blasphemous.
biraogile n. blasphemer, curser.
biraoka adv. blaspheming, cursing.
biraokatu v.t. to blaspheme, to curse, to swear, to cuss.
biraolari n. blasphemer.
biraoti adj. having a tendency to curse.

biraotsu adj. cursing, blaspheming.
biraotu v.t. to blaspheme, to curse, to swear, to cuss.
biraotzaile n. blasphemer.
biraozale adj. cursing, cussing, blaspheming.
biratu v.i. to turn, to revolve, to rotate, to spin. v.t. to turn.
biratzaile adj. gyrating, turning, rotating.
birbaietsi v.t. to confirm, to ratify.
birbaiezpen n. ratification, confirmation, assurance.
birbaieztu v.t. to confirm, to ratify, to reassure.
birbaliodura n.(econ.) increase in value, appreciation.
birbalioketa n.(econ.) increase in value, appreciation.
birbaliopen n.(econ.) increase in value, appreciation.
birbaliotu v.t./v.i. to increase in value, to revalue, to appreciate.
birbalioztapen n. revaluation.
birbalioztatu v.t. to revalue, to make a new valuation of.
birbanaketa n. redistribution.
birbanatu v.t. to redistribute.
birbanatzaile n. one who redistributes.
birbatu v.t. to reunify, to gather something. v.i. to gather again.
biren adj. dual; of those two, belonging to two.
birgaldaketa n. recasting; remelting.
birgaldatu v.t. to remelt; to recast.
birgogorapen n. remembering again.
biribil adj. round. adj.(fig.) categorical, definite, decisive; striking. adj. stout.
biribildu v.t./v.i. to round, to round off (edges).
biribildura n. roundness.
biribilgarri adj. roundable. adj. coilable, rollable.
biribilka adv. coiling.
biribilkakor adj. twistable, coilable, spirable.
biribilkapen n. coiling.
biribilkatu v.t./v.i. to coil.
biribilketa n. coiling. n. Basque folk dance.
biribilki adv. categorically.
biribiltasun n. roundness. n. touch. n. categoricalness, absoluteness, positiveness.
birigarro n.(zool.) red-wing, thrush.
birika n.(anat.) lung.
birikadun adj. having lungs.
birikako adj. pulmonary, pertaining to the lungs.
birikeri n.(med.) tuberculosis.
biriketako adj. pulmonary. n.(med.) tuberculosis (especially in animals).
birikomin n.(med.) pneumonia.
birilkatu v.t. to coil.
birilketa n. coiling.
biritxi n. twin.
birjabeketa n. reconquest.

birjabetu *v.t.* to reconquer. *v.t.* to recover, to recuperate.
birjaio *v.i.* to be born again.
birjaiotza *n.* act of being born again; rebirth.
birjarpen *n.* restoration, replacement, reestablishment.
birjarri *v.t./v.i.* to replace, to reestablish, to restore.
birjaso *v.t.* to restore, to rebuild. *v.t.* to recover (money), to reimburse.
birjina *adj./n.* virgin. *n.* young unmarried woman.
birjintasun *n.* virginity.
birla *n.* bowling pin.
birlaleku *n.* bowling alley.
birlandagarri *adj.* transplantable, capable of being transplanted.
birlandaketa *n.* transplantation, transplant.
birlandatu *v.t.* to transplant.
birlandu *v.t.* to weed again. *v.t.* to rework.
birlari *n.* bowler.
birlatu *v.t.* to bowl.
birlehengusin *n.* second cousin (female).
birlehengusu *n.* second cousin (male).
birloba *n.* great-grandchild.
birloraketa *n.* act of blooming again, reblooming.
birloraldi *n.* reblooming.
birloratu *v.i.* to bloom again, to rebloom.
birlore *n.* second bloom.
birloretu *v.i.* to bloom again.
birlorpen *n.* recovery, recuperation, revival.
birlortu *v.t.* to recover, to regain, to recuperate, to revive.
birlotu *v.t.* to bind again, to tie again.
birlotura *n.* rebinding, retying.
birmargotu *v.t.* to repaint.
birmoldaketa *n.* remodeling.
birmoldapen *n.* remodeling.
birmoldatu *v.t.* to remodel.
birpiztu *v.t./v.i.* to relight; to revive, to reanimate.
birr- *(gram.)* Prefix which indicates duplication or repetition. Used before vowels. Loses the second *r* when used before consonants.
birraitona *n.* great-grandfather.
birramona *n.* great-grandmother.
birrin *n.* bran.
birrindu *v.t.* to granulate, to powder, to crush, to grind. *v.t.* to destroy, to annihilate, to crush.
birringailu *n.* grinder, mortar and pestle.
birringarri *adj.* pulverizable, grindable, crushable.
birrintsu *adj.* having bran, full of bran. *adj.* powdered, ground.
birrintzaile *adj.* grinding, crushing. *adj.* demolishing, annihilating.
birritan *adv.* twice.

birsaldu *v.t.* to resell.
birsalmenta *n.* resale.
birsaltzaile *n.* reseller.
birsorketa *n.* reproduction, regeneration.
birsorkuntza *n.* reproduction, regeneration.
birsortu *v.t./v.i.* to regenerate, to reproduce. *v.i.* to be born again. *v.i./v.t.* to multiply.
birsortzaile *n.* regenerator. *adj.* regenerating, reproducing.
birtute *n.* virtue.
birtutedun *adj.* virtuous.
biru *n.* fiber, thread.
birzatigarri *adj.* divisible, subdividable.
birzatiketa *n.* subdivision.
birzatitu *v.t.* to subdivide.
birzenbaketa *n.* recount.
birzenbatu *v.t.* to recount.
bis *adv.* bi-, twice.
bisonte *n.(zool.)* bison.
bista *n.* view, scenery. *n.* eyesight, vision. *n.* presence, sight.
bistako *adj.* evident, obvious.
bistan *adv.* clearly, evidently, obviously.
bistaratu *v.t.* to put in plain sight, to make visible. *v.i.* to come into view, to come into sight.
bisteder *n.* good view.
bisuts *n.* blizzard, storm.
bisutsu *adj.* stormy.
bitan *adv.* twice. *adv.* in two parts.
bitar *adj.(phys.)* binary.
bitariko *adj.* of two kinds, two kinds of.
bitarte *n.* space between two. *n.* interval, period of time. *n.* occasion, opportunity.
bitartean *conj.* while. *adv.* meanwhile. *prep.* between, among.
bitartegune *n.* place between (two objects).
bitartekari *n.* middleman, intermediary, go-between.
bitarteko *n.* mediator, intermediary, middleman, go-between. *adj.* temporary. *adj.* intermediary.
bitarteko izan *v.i.* to intercede, to mediate, to intervene.
bitartekotasun *n.* mediation, intervention, intercession.
bitartekotu *v.i./v.t.* to intercede, to mediate, to intervene.
bitartekotza *n.* mediation, intervention, intercession.
bitartetu *v.i.* to mediate, to intervene, to intercede.
bitartetza *n.* mediation, intervention, intercession.
bitartez *prep.* through the intervention of, through.
bitasun *n.* dualism; duality.
bitika *n.(zool.)* young male goat.
bits *n.* foam.
bitsadera *n.* skimmer, colander.
bitsetan *adv.* foaming.

bitsu *adj.* foamy.
bitu *v.t./v.i.* to duplicate.
bitxi *n.* jewel. *adj.* very pretty. *adj.* original, unusual, exotic.
bitxidenda *n.* jeweler's, jewelry store.
bitxigile *n.* jeweler.
bitxigintza *n.* manufacture of jewels.
bitxikeria *n.* extravagant thing or saying. *n.* futile ornamentation.
bitxilore *n.(bot.)* daisy.
bitxiontzi *n.* jewelry box, jewel case.
bitxisaltzaile *n.* jeweler. *n.* fake jewelry peddler.
bitxitegi *n.* jewelry shop.
bitxiteria *n.* abundance of jewelry.
bitxitu *v.t.* to ornament with jewels, to bejewel.
bitxixka *n.* jewel of little value.
bitxiztatu *v.i./v.t.* to wear jewels, to decorate with jewels.
biurtealdi *n.* biennium.
biurteko *adj.* biennial, having two years, two-year-old.
biurtero *adv.* biennially, every two years.
biurteroko *adj.* biennial.
bizar *n.* beard.
bizardo *adj.* having a beard.
bizardun *adj.* having a beard, bearded.
bizargabe *adj.* beardless.
bizargabeko *adj.* beardless.
bizargabetu *v.t./v.i.* to shave off a beard.
bizargile *n.* barber.
bizargin *n.* barber.
bizargintza *n.* barber's profession.
bizargorri *adj.* having a red beard.
bizargorridun *adj.* having a red beard, red-bearded.
bizarkentzaile *n.* barber.
bizarlabaina *n.* razor blade.
bizarmakina *n.* electric razor.
bizarmotz *adj.* having a thin beard.
bizarmozketa *n.* act of cutting the beard, trimming the beard, shaving.
bizarmozle *n.* barber.
bizarmoztaile *n.* barber.
bizarmoztailu *n.* razor blade.
bizarmoztaldi *n.* shaving.
bizarmozte *n.* shaving.
bizarrontzi *n.* shaving dish, barber's basin.
bizartegi *n.* barber shop.
bizarti *adj.* having a beard, bearded.
bizartsu *adj.* having a thick beard, having a heavy beard, heavily bearded.
bizartu *v.i.* to grow a beard.
biz-biz *int.* here, kitty, kitty! Expression for calling cats..
bizi *v.i.* to live; to live off. *adj.* alive, living. *adj.* ardent. *adj.* fresh. *adj.* fast, quick. *n.* strength, vigor. *adj.* strong.
biziagotu *v.t./v.i.* to intensify, to revive, to vivify.
bizialdi *n.* duration of life, lifetime, course of one's life.
bizialdiko *adj.* lifetime.
biziarazi *v.t.* to cause to live, to animate, to vivify, to activate.
biziarazle *adj.* life-giving, invigorating, vivifying.
bizi-aseguru *n.* life insurance.
bizibehar *n.* need to live.
biziberritu *v.i./v.t.* to revivify, to revive.
bizibide *n.* job, profession, occupation.
bizi-bizi *adj.* very lively. *adj.* very fresh.
bizi-bizitu *v.i.* to recover completely. *v.t.* to revive.
bizidun *adj.* alive, living.
bizidura *n.* intensity.
biziebaketa *n.* vivisection.
biziemale *adj.* viviparous.
biziemangarri *adj.* life-giving, vivifying.
biziera *n.* way of life; act of living.
bizieragile *adj.* vivifying, activating, life-giving.
bizieragin *v.t.* to cause to live, to animate, to vivify, to activate.
bizierrule *adj.* ovoviviparous.
biziezin *adj.* uninhabitable, inhospitable.
bizigabe *adj.* lifeless, inanimate, inert.
bizigaitz *adj.* uninhabitable, inhospitable.
bizigarri *adj.* exciting, stimulating. *adj.* habitable, inhabitable, livable. *adj.* vital, pertaining to life. *n.* incentive. *n.* food, nourishment.
bizigarritasun *n.* habitableness, inhabitableness.
bizigiro *n.* environment, atmosphere.
bizigogo *n.* desire to live, will to live.
bizigura *n.* desire to live, will to live.
biziguztiko *adj.* for life, lifelong, lasting for life.
bizikai *n.* nourishment, nutritious food.
biziki *adv.* lively, dearly, intensively. *adv.* very, really, entirely, completely, totally.
bizikide *n.* life companion; spouse.
bizikidego *n.* coexistence, living together.
bizikidekeria *n.* concubinage, illicit cohabitation.
bizikidetasun *n.* living with others, cohabitation.
bizikidetu *v.i.* to live together.
bizikidetza *n.* relationship; cohabitation, living together with others. *n.* symbiosis.
bizikiro *adv.* lively, dearly, intensively.
bizikleta *n.* bicycle.
bizikletaldi *n.* bicycle race.
bizikletari *n.* bicyclist, cyclist.
bizikor *adj.* stimulating, exciting. *adj.* long-living, long-lived.
bizikortasun *n.* liveliness, stimulation.
bizikostu *n.* cost of living.
bizilagun *n.* life companion; spouse. *n.* inhabitant, dweller, resident.
bizilaguntza *n.* living together,

cohabitation.
bizileku *n.* residence, home, dwelling, domicile.
biziluze *n.* longevity.
biziluzeko *adj.* long-lived, having a long life.
bizimodu *n.* job, profession; way of life, life.
bizimolde *n.* way of life.
bizinahi *n.* desire to live. *adj.* wanting life, desiring to live.
bizindar *n.* strength of life, vitality, vigor.
bizinguru *n.* environment.
bizio *n.* vice. *n.(zool.)* intestinal worm.
bizion *n.* good life, pleasant life.
biziopari *n.* sacrifice, immolation.
biziopatzaile *n.* sacrificer, immolator.
biziotsu *adj.* having intestinal worms. *adj.* vicious.
bizipen *n.* life experience.
biziraupen *n.* life span.
bizirako *adj.* for life, lifelong, lasting for life.
bizirik *adv.* alive.
biziro *adv.* lively, expressively, emotionally.
bizitasun *n.* liveliness, vitality, vivacity, activity, expressiveness. *n.* readiness, promptness.
bizitegi *n.* dwelling place, home, residence.
biziterri *n.* village of residence, home town.
bizitetxe *n.* residence, dwelling, home.
bizitiar *adj.* alive; resident.
bizitu *v.t./v.i.* to revive, to grow lively, to light up, to stoke (fires).
bizitza *n.* flat, apartment; floor. *n.* life, existence.
bizitzaile *adj.* vivifying, reviving. *n.* inhabitant, resident, dweller.
bizitzalari *n.* biologist.
bizitzaldi *n.* life, period of life, life span.
bizitzaro *n.* life span.
bizitze *n.* act of living, life. *n.* dwelling, residence, home.
bizizale *adj.* fond of life.
bizizaletasun *n.* love of life.
bizizko *adj.* animating, life-giving.
bizizkotasun *n.* quality of being alive.
Bizkaia *n.* Biscay. One of the four provinces of the southern Basque Country. Its capital is Bilbao. In former times, this name denoted the entire Basque country.
bizkaiera *n.* Biscayan dialect of the Basque language.
bizkaitar *adj./n.* Biscayan.
bizkar *n.(anat.)* back. *n.* small hill, slope. *n.* highest point. *n.* back of a chair.
bizkarbesta *n.* feast when the structure of a building is finished.
bizkargain *n.* ridge of a roof. *n.(anat.)* shoulder(s).

bizkargaineko *adj.* dorsal.
bizkargune *n.* elevation, rise. *n.* small hill, slope.
bizkarkari *n.* loader, porter.
bizkarkatu *v.t.* to load on one's shoulders.
bizkarketa *n.* act of loading on one's shoulders.
bizkarkonkor *n.(anat.)* hump, hunchback.
bizkarmakur *adj.* humpbacked, hunchbacked.
bizkarmin *n.(med.)* backache.
bizkarmuin *n.(anat.)* spinal medulla.
bizkarralde *n.(anat.)* back. *n.* back of a chair.
bizkarraldeko *adj.* dorsal, back.
bizkarrandi *adj.(augm.)* large-backed.
bizkarrantzeko *adj.* similar to the curve in the back, arched.
bizkarraulki *n.* chair with a large back, recliner.
bizkarreko *adj.* dorsal, back. *n.* blow on the back.
bizkarreratu *v.t.* to load onto one's back, to lift onto one's back. *v.t.(fig.)* to blame.
bizkarrezur *n.(anat.)* backbone, spine.
bizkarrezurdun *adj.* vertebrate.
bizkarrezurmin *n.(med.)* pain of the back bone.
bizkarrezurmindun *adj.* having back pain.
bizkarrezurmuin *n.(anat.)* spinal medulla.
bizkarroi *adj.* sponging, cadging, parasitic, living off of others.
bizkarroikeria *n.* act of living at another's expense.
bizkartontor *n.* hill, mound, knoll, hillock.
bizkartsu *adj.* hilly.
bizkarzabal *adj.* having a broad back.
bizkarzorro *n.* backpack.
bizkitartean *adv.* meanwhile.
bizkor *adj.* active, diligent, energetic. *adj.* clever, intelligent. *adj.* fast, quick. *adv.* quickly, fast.
bizkordura *n.* revival, reanimation, restoration.
bizkorgarri *adj.* exciting, fortifying, strengthening. *n.* tonic.
bizkorki *adv.* fast, quickly. *adv.* vividly.
bizkorraldi *n.* spurt of energy. *n.* revival, reanimation.
bizkorrerazi *v.t.* to revive, to reanimate, to strengthen, to fortify.
bizkortasun *n.* vitality, vigor, vivacity, energy. *n.* nimbleness, agility. *n.* quickness.
bizkortu *v.t./v.i.* to revive, to reanimate. *v.i.* to recover (from a disease). *v.i.* to walk faster, to hurry up.
bizkortzaile *adj.* stimulating, animating, invigorating, energizing.
bizkotxo *n.* ladyfinger; cake.
bizkunde *n.* revival, restoration. *n.*

resurrection.

bizpahiru adj. two or three, a few.

biztandu v.i. to inhabit, to dwell, to reside, to live.

biztanle n. inhabitant, dweller, resident.

biztanlegabeko adj. uninhabited, unpopulated.

biztanlego n. population.

biztanle-lerrokada n. census.

biztanleria n. population.

bizte n. act of turning on (a light); lighting (a fire); reviving.

biztu v.t. to light, to turn on. v.t./v.i. to reanimate, to revive. v.t./v.i. to resuscitate, to rise (from the dead).

biztuberri adj. resuscitated, risen (from the dead), resurrected.

biztuera n. act of lighting.

biztuerazi v.t. to vivify, to give life.

biztugarri adj. reviving, vivifying, exciting, strengthening. n. fuel, fuel oil, lamp oil. n. stimulant, stimulation, incentive.

biztukor adj. vivifying, life-giving.

blai adv./adj. soaking, wet, soaked, soaking wet.

blaialdi n. soaking.

blai egon v.i. to be soaked, to be thoroughly wet.

blast n.(onomat.) splash! Sound caused by an object falling into the water. n.(onomat.) smack! Sound of a slap.

blaust n.(onomat.) smack! pow! Sound of a blow.

blaustada n. slap, blow in the face. n.(onomat.) crash! Sound of a falling object.

blink n.(onomat.) gulp.

blist-blast n.(onomat.) sound of several slaps.

boasuge n.(zool.) boa constrictor.

bobina n. bobbin, reel, coil.

bobinatu v.t. to wind.

boga n. act of rowing.

bogalari n. rower.

boikot n. boycott.

bokale n.(gram.) vowel.

bola n. bowling.

bolada n. group of people. n. gust. n. occasion, time.

bolagile n. maker of bowling balls.

bolajoko n. bowling (game).

bolaka adv. bowling.

bolakada n. blow with a bowling ball.

bolaketa n. bowling (game).

bolaleku n. bowling alley.

bolandera n. fireworks.

bolari n bowler.

bolategi n. bowling alley.

bolatoki n. bowling alley.

bolatxo n.(dim.) small ball, little ball.

boli n. ivory.

boligrafo n. ball-point pen.

bolina n. mill.

bolinaga n. place of mills.

bolizko adj. ivory, made of ivory.

bolo n. coins thrown by the godfather to the children after baptism.

bolo-bolo adv.(onomat.) way of scattering something by throwing it into the air; spreading like wildfire; publicized.

boltsa n. handbag; woman's purse.

bolu n. old mill.

boludun n. miller.

bolueta n. place of mills.

bolukari n. miller.

bolumen n.(phys.) volume.

bolusari n. price of milling.

bonba n.(phys.) bomb.

bonbakada n. explosion of a bomb, blast.

bonbakari n. bomber.

bonbakatu v.t. to bomb.

bonbaketa n. bombing.

bonbaleherketa n. explosion of a bomb, blast.

bonbardin n.(mus.) saxhorn.

bonbaztapen n. bombing.

bonbaztatu v.t. to bomb.

bonbil n. bottle. n. net float, buoy.

bonbileratu v.t. to bottle.

bonbilgile n. bottlemaker.

bonbon n. lavish spending.

bonbonka adv. lavishly, prodigally, excessively.

bonbonkada n. lavish spending, prodigality.

bonbonkeria n. lavishness, mismanagement.

bonbontzaile n. waster, squanderer. adj. lavish, wasteful, prodigal.

boneta n. bonnet.

bor-bor n.(onomat.) noise of a boiling liquid.

borborka adv. boiling, boilingly.

borborka egin v.t. to bubble, to boil.

borborkada n. bubbling, gushing up of water.

borborkatu v.i. to bubble, to gush up, to boil.

borda n. cottage, cabin, hut. n. stable.

bordaberri n. new farmhouse.

bordaketa n. embroidery.

bordalde n. area surrounding the farmhouse; farmland, field.

bordari n. farmer; colonist, settler.

bordategi n. place of farmhouses.

bordatu v.t. to embroider.

bordatxo n.(dim.) small cottage, little farmhouse.

bordatzaile n. embroiderer.

bordazain n. farmer, colonist, granger.

borla n. tassel.

borobil adj. round.

borondate n. will.

borondatetsu adj. willful.

borondatez adv. voluntarily, willfully.

borondatezko adj. non-coactive, non-compulsory, non-forcing, voluntary.

borrero n. executioner, hangman,

headsman.

borrerotza *n.* job of an executioner.

borroka *n.* battle, fight, combat, struggle, quarrel.

borroka egin *v.t.* to fight, to combat, to struggle, to contend, to battle.

borrokagile *adj.* belligerent, bellicose, warlike, hostile. *n.* fighter, combatant, struggler.

borrokagorri *n.* bloody fight.

borrokagrina *n.* quarrelsomeness, pugnacity.

borrokakor *adj.* belligerent.

borrokakortasun *n.* belligerence, belligerency.

borrokalari *adj.* feisty, belligerent. *n.* fighter, warrior, disputant, litigant, struggler, combatant.

borrokaldi *n.* fight, quarrel, combat. *n.* match, contest.

borrokan *adv.* fighting.

borrokan egin *v.t.* to fight, to contend, to quarrel, to battle, to combat, to struggle, to dispute.

borrokari *n.* fighter, boxer. *adj.* belligerent, feisty, disputing, quarrelling.

borrokategi *n.* place to fight, boxing arena.

borrokatoki *n.* place to fight, boxing arena.

borrokatu *v.i.* to fight, to box, to struggle, to combat, to dispute, to contend, to battle.

borrokazale *adj.* bellicose, warlike, belligerent, quarrelsome.

bort *adj.* bastard, illegitimate (child).

bortitz *adj.* hard, severe, strict, tough, cruel, harsh.

bortizkeria *n.* violence, cruelty, harshness.

bortizki *adv.* loudly; violently; vigorously.

bortiztasun *n.* violence, cruelty. *n.* rudeness, roughness, toughness.

bortiztu *v.i.* to become violent. *v.t.* to fortify, to harden.

bortu *n.* mountain pass. *n.* desert, arid place.

bortxa *n.* violence, coercion.

bortxagarri *adj.* coercive, forcing, compulsory.

bortxakeria *n.* cruelty, violence, coercion.

bortxaketa *n.* constraint, compulsion, coercion. *n.* rape.

bortxaldi *n.* coercion, compulsion, constraint.

bortxapen *n.* act of violence, coercion. *n.* rape.

bortxari *adj.* violent, bellicose, belligerent, coercive.

bortxatu *v.t.* to force, to coerce, to compel. *v.t.* to rape.

bortxatzaile *adj.* oppressive, tyrannical, burdensome. *n.* oppressor. *n.* rapist.

bortxaz *adv.* violently, compulsorily, forcibly, by force.

bortxazko *adj.* violent, coactive, coercive, compulsory. *adj.* mandatory, obligatory, unavoidable.

bos- Used in compound words. Derived from *bost*, five. Always followed by a consonant.

boskarren *adj.* fifth.

boskarrendu *v.t./v.i.* to place in the fifth position.

boskarrengo *adj.* fifth.

boski *adj./n.* quintuplet.

boskoitz *adj./n.* five-fold, quintuple; quintuplet.

boskoizte *n.* quintuplication, multiplying five-fold.

boskoiztu *v.t.* to make five-fold, to quintuplicate.

bosna *adj.* five each.

bosnaka *adv.* in groups of five.

bosnakatu *v.t.* to divide in groups of five, to distribute by fives.

bosnako *adj.* consisting of five.

bost *adj./n.* five.

bost- Used in compound words. Derived from *bost*, five. Always followed by a vowel.

bostaldeko *n.(geom.)* pentahedron.

bostehun *adj./n.* five hundred.

bostehungarren *adj.* five hundredth.

bosteko *n.(mus.)* quintet. *n.* hand. *n.* five (of a suit of cards). *adj.* having five parts or members of five; made up of five.

bostekote *n.(mus.)* quintet.

bostetan *adv.* at five o'clock.

bosteterdi *n.* half past five, five thirty.

bostortzeko *n.* five-pronged rake.

bosturte *n.* a five-year period, lustrum.

bosturteko *adj.* quinquennial; lasting five years.

bosturtero *adv.* every five years.

bota *v.t.* to throw, to cast, to throw out. *v.t.* to fire, to lay off, to throw away. *v.t.* to vomit, to throw up. *v.t.* to launch. *n.* boot. *n.* bota bag, leather sack for carrying and drinking wine.

botagale *n.* nausea.

botagarri *adj.* disposable.

botagura *n.* nausea.

botaketa *n.* lay-off, expulsion, firing. *n.* launch, launching.

botakin *n.* residue, leftover. *n.* vomit.

botakor *adj.* disposable.

botalarri *n.* nausea.

botaldi *n.* throwing. *n.* casting (net). *n.* launching.

botanika *n.* botany.

botari *n.* caster, thrower, ejector, launcher.

botatxo *n.(dim.)* small boot. *n.(dim.)* small bota bag.

botatzaile *n.* caster, thrower, ejector, launcher.

botazio *n.* voting.

botere *n.* power.

boteredun *adj.* powerful.
boteretsu *adj.* powerful.
botika *n.* pharmacy, drugstore. *n.* medicine, drug.
botikaedari *n.* potion, syrup (as in cough syrup).
botikagintza *n.* manufacture of medicines, pharmaceutical production.
botikakaxa *n.* first-aid kit.
botikari *n.* pharmacist, druggist, apothecary.
botikategi *n.* pharmacy.
botila *n.* bottle.
botilakada *n.* contents of a bottle, bottleful, bottle (full of something). *n.* blow with a bottle.
botilaketa *n.* bottling.
botilari *n.* bottle maker. *n.* bottler.
botilategi *n.* place where bottles are stored.
botilatu *v.t.* to bottle.
botilatzaile *n.* bottler.
botoi *n.* button.
botoigile *n.* button maker.
botoigintza *n.* button making.
botoizulo *n.* buttonhole.
botu *n.* vote. *n. (eccl.)* vow.
botuazterraldi *n.* counting of votes, tabulation of votes.
botudun *adj.* professed, avowed, having taken vows.
botuemaile *n.* voter.
botu eman *v.t.* to vote.
botuemate *n.* voting.
botuzenbaketa *n.* counting of votes, tabulation of votes.
botxo *n.* hole in the ground. *n.* deep, narrow valley. *n.* familiar nickname of Bilbao.
boxeaketa *n.* boxing, pugilism.
boxealari *n.* boxer.
boxeatu *v.t.* to box, to hit with the fists.
boz *n.* voice. Var. of *botz. n.* vote.
bozaldaketa *n.* change in the tone of voice.
bozaldi *n.* election time.
bozazterketa *n* tabulation of votes.
bozdun *adj.* having a voice, voiced. *n.* person who has the right to express something.
bozemale *n.* voter.
bozeman *v.t.* to vote.
bozeramale *n.* spokesperson.
bozgabe *adj.* voiceless, aphonic.
bozgabezia *n.* voicelessness, aphonia, lack of a voice, loss of voice.
bozgorabehera *n.* modulation of the voice.
bozgorailu *n.* loudspeaker.
bozina *n.* horn (on a vehicle).
bozkario *n.* joy, merriment.
bozkariogarri *adj.* joyful, happy, pleasant.
bozkariotan *adv.* joyfully, happily.
bozkariotasun *n.* joy, merriment.
bozkariotsu *adj.* joyful, merry.

bozkariotu *v.i.* to rejoice, to be happy.
bozkarioz *adv.* joyfully, merrily, for joy.
bozkariozko *adj.* joyful, happy, pleasant.
bozkarioztatu *v.i.* to be or become joyful, to rejoice.
bozketa *n.(pol.)* election.
branka *n.(naut.)* bow, prow.
brankako *adj.* belonging to the prow. *n.* bow hand, bowman, seaman at the prow.
brankalde *n.* area of the prow, fore of a boat.
brankari *n.* seaman at the prow, bowman.
brankaz *adv.* with the prow facing the waves, prow first.
brast *n.(onom.)* sound which represents a sudden blow or snatch.
brastada *n.* sudden blow by a wave or gust of wind.
brastadako *n.* sudden movement in order to catch something.
breka *n.(zool.)* kind of red snapper.
brintza *n.* cleft, crack, fissure, split. *n.* splinter, chip. *n.* spark, ray, beam of light.
brintzatsu *adj.* splintery. *adj.* shining, luminous.
brintzatu *v.t./v.i.* to crack, to splinter.
briska *n.* type of card game.
brisko *n.(bot.)* variety of peach.
briskondo *n.(bot.)* variety of peach tree.
bronkio *n.(anat.)* bronchus, bronchial tube.
brontze *n.* bronze.
brontzegile *n.* bronzesmith.
brontzezko *adj.* bronze, made of bronze.
brontzeztu *v.t.* to cover with bronze, to plate with bronze.
buba *n.* children's expression for sleep.
buhame *n.* gypsy.
bukaera *n.* end, termination, ending.
bukaerako *adj.* final, terminal.
bukaezin *adj.* unending, interminable, endless.
bukagabe *adj.* unfinished. *adj.* defective, imperfect.
bukagaitz *adj.* interminable, endless.
bukagarri *adj.* terminable, finishable.
bukatu *v.t./v.i.* to finish, to end, to terminate.
bukatzaile *adj.* finishing. *n.* finisher.
bular *n.(anat.)* male or female breast, chest.
bular-anaia *n.* male children raised simultaneously by the same mother such as male twins, foster brothers; milk brothers.
bularbabes *n.* bib. *n.* shield.
bularbabeski *n.* shield.
bularkide *n.* child who nurses from the same mother as another child.
bularmin *n.* pain in the chest or breast.

bularmutur *n.(anat.)* nipple.
bularralde *n.(anat.)* thorax.
bularrandi *adj.* having a large breast.
bularreko *n.* infant. *n.* brassiere, bra. *adj.* mammary.
bularremale *n.* wet nurse.
bularreri *n.(med.)* tuberculosis.
bularresne *n.* mother's milk.
bularretako *n.* infant. *n.* brassiere, bra.
bularrezur *n.(anat.)* sternum, breastbone.
bularrikuskin *n.(med.)* stethoscope.
bularrikuspen *n.(med.)* stethoscopy.
bularringuru *n.(anat.)* chest cavity.
bularringuruko *adj.* thoraxic.
bularrondoko *n.* blow to the breast.
bulartsu *adj.* having large breasts, big busted. *adj.(fig.)* brave, courageous.
bulartu *v.t.* to nurse, to breast feed.
bulda *n.(eccl.)* papal bull. *n.(eccl.)* religious document bought by individuals permitting them to skip fasts.
bulego *n.* office.
bulegoburu *n.* office head, office manager, boss.
bulegolari *n.* office clerk.
bulka *n.* shove, push, thrust.
bulkada *n.* shove, push, thrust.
bulkaldi *n.* pushing, shoving.
bulkatu *v.t.* to push, to thrust, to shove, to impel. *v.t.(fig.)* to oblige, to force.
bultz *z* *n.* shove, thrust.
bultzada *n.* shove, push, thrust. *n.(fig.)* help.
bultzadakoi *adj.* vehement, impetuous, impulsive.
bultzadatasun *n.* impulsiveness, impetuousness.
bultzadura *n.* impulse.
bultzagai *n.* incentive.
bultzagailu *n.(mech.)* spring, coil of wire.
bultzagarri *n.* incentive, motive. *adj.* pushable.
bultzagarritasun *n.(phys.)* elasticity.
bultzagile *adj.* pushing, promoting; pushy.
bultzaka *adv.* pushing.
bultzakada *n.* push, thrust.
bultzakari *n.* promoter. *adj.* impulsive, impetuous.
bultzakatu *v.t.* to shove, to push, to thrust.
bultzaketa *n.* act of pushing.
bultzakor *adj.* impulsive, impetuous.
bultzaldi *n.* push, thrust, shove.
bultzapen *n.* push, encouragement.
bultzarazi *v.t.* to cause to push.
bultzarazle *adj.* compulsive, pushing.
bultzatu *v.t.* to push, to shove. *v.t.* to influence, to bias.
bultzatzaile *n.* pusher; promoter. *adj.* pushing, pushy.
bultzegile *adj.* pushing, pushy, compelling. *n.* promoter.

bultz egin *v.t.* to push, to thrust, to shove.
bultzeragile *adj.* compulsive, pushing.
bultzeragin *v.t.* to cause to push, to make (someone) push (something).
bulunba *n.* cattle bell.
bulunbari *adj.* belled, having a bell (sheep, etc.).
bunbada *n.* explosion, blast, shot.
bunpada *n.* blast, explosion.
burbuila *n.* bubble.
burbuilatu *v.i.* to bubble.
burbuileztatu *v.i.* to bubble.
burdin- Used in compound words. Derived from *burdina*, iron.
burdina *n.(chem.)* iron.
burdinaga *n.* iron bar.
burdin aro *n.* Iron Age.
burdinarri *n.(min.)* iron ore.
burdinatsu *adj.* rich in iron.
burdinazko *adj.* made of iron.
burdinaztu *v.t.* to decorate with iron, to cover with iron. *v.t.* to shoe horses.
burdinbide *n.* railroad.
burdinbizi *n.* magnet.
burdindegi *n.* blacksmith's shop, smithy.
burdindenda *n.* hardware store.
burdindendari *n.* hardware store owner.
burdindu *v.t./v.i.* to give or to acquire an iron color, to cover with iron, to plate with iron.
burdinesi *n.* iron fence.
burdineztatu *v.t.* to ornament or to decorate with iron, to cover or plate with iron.
burdingalda *n.* cast iron.
burdingaldaketa *n.* iron smelting, melting of iron.
burdingile *n.* blacksmith, iron worker.
burdingintza *n.* manufacture of iron. *n.* job of a blacksmith, smithery.
burdingorri *n.(chem.)* copper.
burdingune *n.* iron deposit.
burdinkaka *n.* slag, scoria.
burdinkari *n.* iron dealer.
burdinki *n.* piece of iron.
burdinola *n.* forge. *n.* iron foundry, iron manufacturing plant.
burdinori *n.(chem.)* brass.
burdinsare *n.* metallic net.
burdinsaredi *n.* metallic fence.
burdinsaretu *v.t.* to put up a metallic fence.
burdintsu *adj.* containing iron, ferruginous, iron-bearing.
burdinur *n.* iron-bearing water, ferruginous water.
burdinxafla *n.* lamina of iron, thin sheet or plate of iron.
burdinziri *n.* iron bar, iron wedge.
burduntzali *n.* iron ladle (large spoon with handle).
burduntzi *n.* roasting spit.
bureskunde *n.(neol.)* crowning.

burges *adj./n.* bourgeois, middle-class person.

burgesia *n.* bourgeoisie, middle-class.

burgestu *v.i.* to become bourgeois, to become middle-class.

burokrata *n.* bureaucrat.

burokrazia *n.* bureaucracy.

burruka *n.* fight, quarrel, combat, battle, struggle.

burrukaide *adj.* belligerent.

burrukaidetasun *n.* belligerence, belligerency.

burrukalari *n.* fighter, warrior, disputant, litigant, struggler, combatant. *adj.* feisty, belligerent.

burrukaldi *n.* fight, combat, quarrel. *n.* match, contest.

burrukan *adv.* fighting.

burrukan egin *v.t.* to fight, to combat, to quarrel, to contend, to battle, to struggle, to dispute.

burrukari *n.* fighter. *adj.* feisty, belligerent.

burrukatoki *n.* fighting place, boxing arena.

burrukatu *v.i.* to fight, to quarrel, to combat, to struggle.

burrukazale *adj.* quarrelsome, belligerent, warlike, bellicose.

burrunba *n.* loud noise, clatter. *n.* resonating, resonance, echo.

burrunbada *n.* loud noise, clatter.

burrunbaka *adv.* loudly, noisily.

burrunbari *adj.* noisy, resounding, clamoring.

burrunbatsu *adj.* clamorous, loud, deafening.

burrunbatu *v.t.* to make a loud noise.

burrundara *n.* deafening noise, clamor, clatter, racket. *n.* high speed.

buru *n.* head. *n.* top, summit. *n.* tassel (of grain); ear (of corn). *n.* end, conclusion. *n.* boss, leader, chief, superior, chairperson, president. *n.* head (of cattle), unit, person or people. *n.* intelligence. *pron.* self. Used to form reflexive verbs. **Bere burua hil zuen.** He killed himself. a(lit.) He killed his head.

burualde *n.* headboard. *n.* main place, place of importance. *n.(anat.)* cephalic part.

buruan *prep.* after, at the end of.

buruan erabili *v.t.* to think, to think about.

buruan hartu *v.t.* to memorize. *v.t.* to consider, to ponder.

buruan sartu *v.i.* to be or become persuaded or convinced. *v.t.* to persuade, to convince. *v.i.* to desire something suddenly, to have a whim.

buru apaindu *v.t.* to justify oneself, to claim one's innocence.

buruargi *adj.* clever, intelligent, bright, smart.

buruargitasun *n.* brightness,

intelligence, ingeniousness, smartness, ingenuity.

buru argitu *v.i./v.t.* to sharpen the wit or ingenuity, to get smart.

buruargiz *adv.* cleverly, ingeniously, brightly.

buruarin *adj.* foolish.

buruarinkeria *n.* foolishness, simplicity of mind.

buru atera *v.t.* to defend someone.

burubabes *n.* helmet, hard hat.

burubabeskin *n.* helmet, hard hat.

burubatez *adv.* unanimously.

buru behetu *v.t.* to bow one's head, to nod.

buru-belarri *adv.* attentively, intensively, carefully, hard.

burubero *adj.* wild, hot-headed, fanatical.

buruberokeria *n.* fanaticism.

buru berotu *v.i.* to become tired of intellectual work. *v.t.* to cause trouble. *v.t.* to incite, to stimulate; to irritate.

buruberotzaile *adj./n.* troublemaking; troublemaker.

burubide *n.* thought, idea, opinion. *n.* advice, counsel.

burubidetsu *adj.* wise, prudent.

burubidetu *v.t.* to advise, to counsel, to give advice.

burubiko *adj.* having two heads, two-headed.

burubira *n.* giddiness, vertigo, dizziness.

buru bota *v.t.* to kill oneself, to commit suicide.

buru-buruko *adj.* final.

burudun *adj.* having a head (people, wheat, corn, etc.) *adj.* clever, intelligent, thoughtful. *adj.* prudent, cautious, judicious, wise.

buru egin *v.t.* to lead. *v.t.* to face, to resist.

buruemaile *adj.* defiant.

buru eman *v.t.* to face, to confront; to resist, to defy. *v.t.* to finish up, to solve a problem.

burueraile *n.* person who commits suicide, suicide.

buru erakutsi *v.t.* to show off, to brag.

buru erantzi *v.t.* to take off a headdress or hat.

buru estali *v.t.* to cover the head.

buruestalki *n.* mantilla; headcover.

burugabe *adj.* headless, acephalous. *adj.* irresponsible, foolish.

burugabekeria *n.* nonsense, stupidity, folly, foolishness.

burugabeki *adv.* irresponsibly, carelessly, foolishly.

burugabeko *adj.* fool, idiot, foolish.

burugabetu *v.i.* to lose one's mind, to act absurdly. *v.t.* to behead, to decapitate.

burugain *n.(anat.)* top part of the head, crown (of the head).

burugaineko n. hard hat, helmet.

buru galdu v.t. to lose one's head or mind, to become foolish, to go crazy. (lit.) to lose the head.

burugalketa n. deviation; mania, craziness.

buru garbitu v.t. to justify oneself, to claim one's innocence. v.t. to commit suicide.

burugogor adj. stubborn, obstinate, opinionated, thick-headed.

burugogorkeria n. stubbornness, obstinacy, contumacy, pertinacity.

burugogorki adv. stubbornly, obstinately.

burugogortasun n. stubbornness, obstinacy, contumacy, pertinacity.

buru gogortu v.i. to be or become obstinate or stubborn, to be hard-headed.

buruhandi adj. stupid, foolish.

buruhausgarri adj. troublesome, worrisome.

buruhaustailu n. puzzle (toy).

buruhauste n. problem; puzzle; confusion.

buru hautsi v.t. to break one's head, to fracture one's skull.

buruhezur n.(anat.) skull.

buru hil v.t. to commit suicide, to kill oneself.

buruhilketa n. suicide.

buruhiltzaile n. person who commits suicide, suicide.

buruil n. September.

buru izan v.i. to lead, to chair. v.i. to be able to, to be capable of.

burujabe adj. autonomous, emancipating. adj. independent.

burujabetasun n. autonomy. n. independence.

burujabetza n. autonomy. n. independence.

buru jaso v.t. to be or become proud.

buruka n. tassel (of wheat).

burukada n. hit with the head.

burukapen n. self-denial, abnegation.

buru kendu v.t. to behead.

buruko n. cap, hat. n. pillow

burukoi adj. stubborn, obstinate, opinionated.

burukoitu v.i. to become stubborn, to become opinionated, to become obstinate, to be hard-headed.

burukomin n. headache.

burukorratz n. hatpin, hairpin.

burukozahi n. dandruff.

burulan n. intellectual work.

buruluze adj. long-headed.

buru makurtu v.t. to bow one's head, to nod.

burumotz adj. having a short head.

burumozketa n. beheading, decapitation.

burumoztasun n. lack of intelligence.

burumozte n. act of beheading.

buru moztu v.t. to behead. v.t. to cut

someone's hair.

burumuin n.(anat.) brain.

burunahasketa n. delirium, insanity, madness.

burunahastazio n. delirium, madness, insanity.

buruoihal n. turban.

buruoker adj. having the head twisted.

buruorde n. vice-chairperson.

buruorratz n. hairpin

burupeko n. pillow.

burura ekarri v.t. to remind, to bring to mind.

burura etorri v.i. to figure out, to imagine, to occur to, to come to mind.

bururapen n. suggestion. n. thought, idea. n. end.

bururatu v.i. to occur to, to come to mind, to imagine, to figure out, to invent. v.i. to recall, to remember. v.t./v.i. to finish, to end. ·

burusare n. hair net.

buruska n. gleanings. n.(dim.) small head.

burusoil adj. bald.

buru soildu v.i. to become bald, to go bald.

burusoildura n. baldness.

burusoileri n. baldness.

burutaezin adj. inconceivable.

burutapen n. idea, conception, thinking.

burutaratu v.t. to imbue, to inspire with principles, to suggest.

burutasun n. idea, thought. n. quality of being principal, importance, precedence, primacy.

burutazio n. thought, idea.

buruti adj. stubborn, obstinate, opinionated.

burutik egin v.t. to be delirious, to rave, to go crazy, to be crazy.

burutik egon v.i. to be crazy, to be insane, to go crazy.

burutik eragin v.t. to drive someone crazy.

burutik galdu v.i. to lose one's reason, to lose one's mind, to go crazy.

burutik joan v.i. to go out of one's head, to become delirious.

burutik kendu v.t. to change (someone's) mind, to cause (someone) to abandon a plan or idea.

burutsik adv. having the head uncovered.

burutsu adj. ingenious, talented, bright, intelligent. adj. wise, prudent, careful, judicious. adj. having a head (corn, wheat, etc.), having many tassels of grain or ears of corn.

burutu v.i. to plan, to imagine, to figure out. v.i. to finish, to carry out, to perfect, to complete. v.t. to glean. v.i. to succeed, to triumph, to achieve, to get, to obtain.

burutxo n.(dim.) small head.
burutza n. office of a chief, position of importance.
burutzapen n. achievement, realization.
buruz prep. about, concerning, around. It is always used as a preposition for indirect objects. adv. by heart.
buruzabal adj. broad-headed, having a wide head.
buruzagi n. leader, chief.
buruzagigo n. office or job of chief, leadership.
buruzagitasun n. leadership quality.
buruzagitu v.i. to stand out. v.i. to act as a leader, to become leader.
buruzagitza n. leadership.
buruzale adj. selfish, egotistical.
buruzalekeria n. selfishness.
buruzaletasun n. selfishness.
buruzapal adj. flat-headed.
buruz-buru adv. from head to toe. adv. face to face.
buruzgora adv. upside up, face up.
buruz jakin v.t. to know by heart.
buruz ikasi v.t. to memorize, to learn by heart.
buruzko adj. mental, intellectual. adj. concerning, relating to.
buruzolitasun n. genius, extreme intelligence.
buruzoradura n. stupidity. n. craziness, foolishness.
buruzorakeria n. nonsense, stupidity, folly. n. craziness, foolishness.
buruzorrotz adj. having a pointed head.
buruzpide n. way of thinking, opinion.
buruzulaketa n.(med.) trepanation, trepanning, cutting out a section of the skull with a trephine.
buru zulatu v.t. (med.) to trepan, to cut a hole in the skull with a trephine.
buruzuri adj. white-headed, white-haired.
buru zuritu v.t. to justify oneself, to claim one's innocence.
burzako n. pasture.
busti v.t./v.i. to wet, to humidify, to moisten, to dampen; to soak. v.t. to sprinkle, to spray. v.t.(colloq.) to bribe, to suborn. adj. wet, humid, moist.
bustialdi n. soaking, bath. n. sprinkling, watering.
bustibide n. irrigation.
bustidura n. sprinkling, spraying, act of getting wet.
bustiera n. act of wetting.
bustigabe adv. without wetting.
bustigailu n. sprayer, sprinkler, wetting instrument.
bustiketa n. act of getting wet, sprinkling, spraying.
bustitasun n. humidity, wetness, dampness.

bustite n. wet period, rainy season.
bustitzaile adj. wetting, sprinkling. n.(fig.) briber, suborner.
bustiune n. wet area, wet part.
butano n.(chem.) butane.
buxia n.(mech.) spark plug.
buzo n. diver.
buzojantzi n. wetsuit, diving suit.
buztan n. tail. n.(bot.) rootlet, radicle.
buztanbeltz n.(zool.) small gray edible saltwater fish with a black tail.
buztandu v.i. to germinate, to sprout.
buztandun adj. having a tail, with a tail.
buztangabe adj. without a tail, tailless.
buztangorri n.(zool.) redstart.
buztanikara n.(zool.) wagtail.
buztanmotz adj. short-tailed.
buztantxo n.(dim.) small tail, little tail.
buztin n. clay.
buztindu v.t. to cover with clay.
buztindun adj. clayey.
buztinezko adj. clay, made of clay.
buztingintza n. pottery, ceramics.
buztingorritsu adj. containing red clay.
buztinki n. piece of clay.
buztinlari n. potter.
buztinola n. potter's shop.
buztinontzi n. clay pot, ceramic pot.
buztintsu adj. clayey.
buztintza n. abundance of clay, clayey place.

D

d n. letter of the Basque alphabet.
da v.aux. he is (izan, to be).
da- (gram.) Prefix used for verbs. **Dabil.** He walks.
-da- (gram.) Infix which indicates to me, for me. **Ekarri didate.** They have brought it to me.
-da (gram.) Suffix which indicates the past participle. **Hilda dago.** He is dead.
dagokion adj. fitting (for him or her), suitable (for him or her).
dagokionez adv. accordingly, according to, fittingly, suitably; concerning.
-daino (gram.) Suffix used with expressions of time meaning until, up to. **Egundaino.** Until today.
damajoko n. game of checkers, draughts.
damataula n. checker board.
damatxo n.(dim.) young lady.
damu n. repentance, contrition.
damubera adj. sorry, remorseful, repentant.
damubide n. cause for remorse or repentance.
damudun adj. regretful, remorseful, sorry, showing repentance.
damugabe adj. impenitent, obdurate, not sorry.
damugabekeria n. impenitence, obdurateness, lack of remorse.
damugabeko adj. not sorry.

damugabezia *n.* impenitence, obdurateness, lack of remorse.
damugai *n.* reason for repentance.
damugaitz *adj.* slightly sorry.
damugarri *adj.* lamentable, deplorable. *adj.* capable of repenting.
damu izan *v.t.* to repent, to regret.
damukor *adj.* remorseful, sorry.
damutasun *n.* repentance, regret, sorrow.
damutu *v.i.* to repent, to regret.
damuz *adv.* regretfully, sorrowfully.
damuzko *adj.* penitential, penitent.
dan *n.(onomat.)* sound which expresses knocking at the door.
danba *n.* bang. Onomatopoeic sound which represents a shot, an explosion, a collision.
danbada *n.(onomat.)* shot, detonation, explosion. *n.* toll of a bell. *n.* slamming of the door. *n.* collision, crash.
danbadaka *adv.* banging loudly. *adv.* shooting.
danbadako *n.* loud noise, like a shot.
danbadatsu *adj.* loud, clamorous.
danba egin *v.t.* to detonate, to explode.
danbaka *adv.* hitting, knocking loudly, banging.
danbolin *n.(mus.)* drum. *n.* round iron basket used to roast chestnuts.
danbolindari *n.* drummer.
danbor *n.(mus.)* drum.
danborjole *n.* drummer.
danborrada *n.* Basque marching band composed mostly of drums.
danborrari *n.* drummer.
dangada *n.(onomat.)* sound which expresses the tolling of bells. *n.* blow, bang. *n.* gulp, swallow.
dangadatu *v.i.* to toll (a bell), to ring.
-danik *(gram.)* Suffix meaning from, since.
dantza *n.* dance, ball.
dantza egin *v.t.* to dance.
dantzagarri *adj.* danceable.
dantzakide *n.* dance partner.
dantzakorda *n.* line of dancers holding hands.
dantzalagun *n.* dance partner.
dantzaldi *n.* dancing, dance.
dantzaleku *n.* place for dancing, dance floor, dance hall.
dantzan *adv.* dancing.
dantzan egin *v.t.* to dance.
dantzareto *n.* ballroom, dance hall, dance floor.
dantzari *n.* dancer. *adj.* dancing.
dantzaritalde *n.* group of dancers, dance group.
dantzaritxo *n.(dim.)* young dancer.
dantzatoki *n.* place for dancing.
dantzatu *v.i./v.t.* to dance. *v.t.(fig.)* to shake, to make (something) dance or tremble.
dantzazale *adj.* fond of dancing.

dantzazalekeria *n.* excessive fondness for dancing, dance mania.
-dar *(gram.)* Suffix which means native of.
daratulu *n.* drill.
daratulutu *v.t.* to drill.
dardara *n.* trembling, shaking, shivering, quivering.
dardaradun *adj.* convulsive, shaking, trembling, quivering, shivering.
dardaragarri *adj.* vibrating. *adj.* moving, shaking (emotionally).
dardaraka *adv.* trembling, shaking, quivering, shivering.
dardarakoi *adj.* vibrating, shaking.
dardarakor *adj.* vibrant, vibrating, shaking.
dardaraldi *n.* shake, shaking, vibration.
dardarati *adj.* shaking, shivering, trembling, quivering, tremulous.
dardaratsu *adj.* tremulous, vibrating, shaky.
dardaratu *v.t./v.i.* to shake, to shiver, to vibrate, to quiver.
dardaratxo *n.(dim.)* light tremor.
dardaraz *adv.* shakily, tremblingly.
dardarazi *v.t.* to cause to shake, to make (someone or something) shake.
dardarazko *adj.* convulsive, trembling, shaking. *adj.* vibratory, vibrating.
dardarazle *adj.* vibrating. *n.* vibrator.
dardar egin *v.t.* to tremble, to shake, to quiver.
dardar eragin *v.t.* to make (someone or something) shake.
dardargai *adj.* vibrating, capable of vibrating.
dardargarri *adj.* shaking. *adj.* frightening, frightful.
dardarikatu *v.i.* to shake, to tremble, to quiver.
dardariketa *n.* trembling, quivering, shaking, shivering.
dardarka *adv.* shaking, trembling.
dardarketa *n.* vibrating movement, vibration, convulsion, trembling.
dardarneurkin *n.(geol.)* seismometer.
dardarti *adj.* trembling, shivering, tremulous, quivering, shaking.
dardartsu *adj.* trembling, shivering, tremulous, shaky.
dario *v.i.* it springs (*erion*, to spring from). Usually used with indirect objects. **Iturriari ura dario.** Water springs from the fountain.
dart *n.* onomatopoeic sound of a punch or a blow.
dasta *n.* tasting.
dastaezin *adj.* tasteless, unsavory.
dastagarri *adj.* tasteful.
dastaketa *n.* tasting.
dastaleku *n.* tasting place.
dastamen *n.* taste, sense of taste.
dastapen *n.* tasting.
dastari *n.* taster.
dastatu *v.t.* to taste.

dastatzaile n. taster.
datibo n.(gram.) dative.
datil n.(bot.) date.
datilondo n.(bot.) date palm, date tree.
datorren adj. coming, next.
datu n. datum, (pl.) data.
deabru n. devil. adj. naughty, rascally.
deabrudun adj. possessed of an evil spirit.
deabrugurtza n. demonology, the worship of demons.
deabrukeria n. trick, mischief, devilry. n. black magic.
deabrukeriaz adv. devilishly, wickedly.
deabruki adv. devilishly, wickedly.
deabruzko adv. devilishly, wickedly.
deabrukoi adj. devilish.
deabruno n.(dim.) little devil.
deabrutu v.i. to be or become possessed by the devil.
deabrutxo n.(dim.) little devil.
deabruzko adj. devilish, wicked.
debalde adv. free of charge.
debekaezin adj. inalienable.
debekagarri adj. forbiddable, prohibitable.
debekaldi n. closed season (for hunting, fishing, etc.)
debekatu v.t. to prohibit, to forbid.
debekatzaile n. prohibitor. adj. prohibitive.
debeku n. prohibition, obstacle, hindrance, obstruction, ban.
debekuz adv. unduly. adv. fraudulently, deceptively, deceitfully.
debekuzko adj. undue, improper, unsuitable.
deblauki adv. frankly, emphatically.
debozio n. devotion, piety.
deboziozko adj. devotional, of devotion.
dedikapen n. dedication.
dedikatu v.t. to dedicate to.
dedu n. honor, reputation.
deduz adv. honorabily.
deduzko adj. honorable.
defendaezin adj. indefensible.
defendagaitz adj. difficult to defend.
defendagarri adj. defensible, defendable.
defendatu v.t. to defend.
defendatzaile n. defender, protector, supporter.
defenditu v.t./v.i. to defend, to protect, to guard.
defentsa n. defense.
defentsazko adv. defensive.
definigaitz adj. indefinable, difficult to define.
definigarri adj. definable.
definitu v.t. to define.
definizio n. definition.
-degi (gram.) Suffix which indicates abundance; place of. **Arrandegi.** Fish market.
dei n. call; vocation. n. cry, publication by crier, announcement, warning. n.

ringing, toll of a bell. n. marriage banns.
deiadar n. horn used to call (someone). n. shouting, clamor. n. alarm, siren.
deiegile n. crier; town crier.
deiegin v.t. to call, to summon, to convoke. v.t. to invite. v.t. to cry, to shout.
deiera n. call, calling.
deigailu n. megaphone.
deigarri adj. attractive, interesting, attention-getting.
deigintza n. office of a town crier.
deika adv. calling, shouting.
deikunde n. announcement. n. (eccl) Annunciation (March 25).
deilari n. town crier, announcer. n. person who used to wake up the fishermen to go to sea.
deitoragarri adj. deplorable, lamentable, distressing, sorrowful.
deitoratu v.t. sympathize with. v.t. to lament, to complain, to regret.
deitore n. lamentation, complaint, groaning, lament.
deitu v.t. to call. v.t/v.i to name, to be called, to be named. v.t. to summon, to call, to invite. v.t to invite
deitura n. last name, family name.
deitzaile n. invoker, crier, caller, announcer.
deklinabide n. (gram.) declension
deklinaezin adj. indeclinable.
deklinagaitz adj. difficult to decline.
deklinagarri adj. declinable.
deklinatu v.t. to decline (nouns, etc.)
deklinazio n. (gram.) declension.
demagogia n. demagogy.
dematu v.t. to bet, to wager. v.t. to complete
demografia n. demography
demokrata adj.(pol.) democrat.
demokratiko adj. democratic.
demokrazia n. (pol.) democracy.
demonioa! int. shoot!, damn!
dena adj./pron. everything, all.
dena dela adv. anyway, in any case.
denak adj./pron. (pl.) everybody, all.
dena den adv. anyway, in any case.
denbora n. period of time.
denbora eman v.t. to spend time.
denboraldi n. season, period of time.
denborale n. storm.
denda n. shop, store.
dendako n. shopkeeper. adj. belonging to the shop, pertaining to the shop.
dendalagun n. shop assistant.
dendari n. shopkeeper.
dendaritza n. job of a shopkeeper.
dendatxo n. (dim) little shop.
dendorde n. branch shop, branch store. Contr. of denda + orde.
dendoste n. back room of a shop. Contr. of denda + oste.
denen adj. general, common,

universal.

denera adv. in total, totally, in all.

denok pron. everybody, all of us.

dentsitate n. (phys.) dentsity.

derrigor adv. by force, forcibly.

derrigorrean adv. by force, forcibly.

derrigorrez adv. by force, forcibly.

derrigorrezko adj. mandatory, compulsory, obligatory, forced.

derrigortasun n. compulsoriness, obligatoriness.

derrigortu v.t. to force, to oblige, to compel.

desabantaila n. disadvantage.

desabantailatsu adj. disadvantageous.

desadartu v.t./v.i. to dehorn. v.t. to strip of branches, to debranch.

desadostasun n. disagreement, disparity.

desafiatzaile adj. challenging, competing. n. challenger, competitor, rival, defier.

desafio n. challenge, competition, rivalry.

desagarakunde n. desecration.

desagaratu v.t. to desecrate.

desagertu v.i. to disappear.

desamorio n. lack of love.

desamortizatu v.t. to free from mortmain, to destroy the inalienable possession oflands, etc., by a church , corporation, etc.

desamortizazio n. disentailment, freeing from mortmain.

desantolaketa n. disorder, disorganization.

desantolatu v.t. disorganize.

desapaindu v.t. to denude, to lay bare, to divest of ornaments.

desardura n. negligence, lack of worry.

desarduratsu adj. careless, negligent, indifferent, apathetic.

desarduratu v.i. to neglect, to overlook.

desarildu v.t. to unravel.

desarrazoin n. unreason, absurdity, irrationality.

desaserre n. calmness, calm (after anger).

desaserretu v.i. to appease, to conciliate, to pacify, to calm down.

desatxekidura n. loosening of an attachment, unsticking.

desbalioketa n.(econ.) devaluation, depreciation.

desbaliotu v.t./v.i. to devaluate, to diminish the value, to depreciate.

desbalioztapen n.(econ.) devaluation, depreciation.

desbalioztatu v.t. to devaluate, to depreciate.

desberdin adj. different, unequal, uneven.

desberdindu v.t. to make unequal, to make different, to make uneven.

desberdindura n. difference,

inequality, dissimilarity. n. unevenness, gradient, drop.

desberdinki adv. diversely, differentlly.

desberdintasun n. difference, inequality, unevenness.

desberdintzapen n. differentiation, diversification.

desbideketa n. deviation, detour. n. digression.

desbiderapen n. deviation, detour. n. digression.

desbideratu v.t./v.i. to deviate, to turn away, to divert.

desegiketa n. destruction. n. annihilation, abrogation.

desegile adj. destructive.

desegin v.t. to undo, to demolish, to dismantle, to destroy, to take apart, to take to pieces.

desegingarri adj. destructible.

desegite n. destruction, demolition, dissolution.

desegintza n. destruction, dissolution, demolition.

desegoki adj. inadequate, unsuitable, incongruous, inappropriate. adj. unfitted, disarranged, maladjusted. adv. unsuitably, inappropriately.

desegokidura n. maladjustment.

desegokiro adv. inappropriately, unsuitably, incongruently, incorrectly.

desegokitasun n. inappropriateness, inopportuneness, incongruity, unsuitability.

desegokitu v.t./v.i. to misfit, to mismatch.

desehortzi v.t. to dig up, to unearth, to disinter, to exhume.

desehundu v.t. to unweave, to unbraid, to unravel.

desenkusa n. excuse, apology.

desenkusagaitz adj. inexcusable.

desenkusagarri adj. excusable, pardonable.

desenkusatu v.t. to excuse.

deseraketa n. deformation, deformity, disfigurement.

deserakor adj. deforming, disfiguring.

deseratasun n. deformity.

deseratu v.t./v.i. to deform, to malform.

deserazko adj. deformed, malformed.

deserdiratu v.t./v.i. to decentralize.

deserdiratzaile adj. decentralizing.

deserdoildu v.t./v.i. to deoxidize, to remove rust.

deseroso adj. uncomfortable.

deserosotasun n. lack of comfort, uncomfortableness, discomfort.

deserraindu v.t. to eviscerate, to disembowel.

deserri n. exile.

deserritu v.t./v.i. to exile, to go into exile, to be exiled, to expatriate.

deserrodura n. eradication.

deserrogarri adj. eradicable.

deserroketa n. eradication.
deserrotu v.t. to eradicate, to root out, to extirpate, to uproot. v.t. to unhinge.
desertu n. desert.
desesan v.t. to retract, to take back (words).
desestali v.t./v.i. to uncover.
desestalketa n. uncovering.
desezkondu v.i./v.t. to divorce.
desezkontza. n. divorce.
desgarai n. unseasonable time.
desgaraiko adj. unseasonable, untimely.
desgaraitasun n. untimeliness.
desgaraiz adv. untimely, unseasonably.
desgidaketa n. lack of direction, confusion, lack of guidance.
desgiro n. unseasonableness.
desgizondu v.i. to become or to be less human, to become insociable.
desgobernu n. lack of government, anarchy. n. disorganization, mess.
desgogatu v.t./v.i. to discourage, to dishearten; to be discouraged.
desgogo n. discouragement, lack of desire.
desiraunkor adj. unsteady, not constant, inconsistent.
desiraupen n. inconsistency, unsteadiness.
desitxuragarri adj. deformable.
desitxurakor adj. deforming, disfiguring.
desitxurapen n. deformation, deformity, disfigurement.
desitxuratasun n. disfiguredness, hideousness.
desitxuratu v.t./v.i. to deform, to disfigure.
desitxurazko adj. deformed, disfigured, hideous.
desizozketa n. act of defrosting, act of thawing.
desizozte n. defrosting, thawing.
desizoztu v.t./v.i. to defrost, to thaw.
desizurritu v.t. to disinfect, to decontaminate.
desjabeketa n. expropriation, dispossession; transfer of property.
desjabekuntza n. expropriation, dispossession; transfer of property.
desjabetu v.t. to expropriate, to attach property.
desjabetzapen n expropriation, dispossession; transfer of property.
desjostura n. removing seams, taking out seams.
deskateaketa n. unchaining.
deskateatu v.t. to unchain.
deskontatu v.t. to discount, to deduct, to reduce (the price).
deskontu n. discount.
deskorapilatu v.t. to unknot, to loosen, to untie a knot.
deskutsadura n. decontamination, disinfecting.
deskutsakin n. disinfectant, antiseptic.
deskutsatu v.t. to disinfect, to decontaminate.
deskutsatzaile n. one who disinfects.
deslainotu v.i. to clear up.
deslandatu v.t. to uproot.
deslegekuntza n. revocation, annulment, abolition (of a law).
desleial adj. disloyal, unloyal.
desleialkeria n. disloyalty, unloyalty.
desleialki adv. disloyally.
desleialtasun n. disloyalty.
deslekuketa n. dislocation; displacement.
deslekuraketa n. dislodging, displacement.
deslekutu v.t. to displace, to dislodge, to move out.
desloratu v.t. to deflower, to remove flowers.
deslotu v.t./v.i. to loosen, to untie.
deslotura n. untying, loosening.
deslurperaketa n. exhumation, disinterment, digging up.
deslurpetu v.t. to exhume, to disinter, to dig up, to unearth.
desnaturaldu v.i. to pervert, to denature.
desnorabide n. disorientation, deviation, going astray, losing one's way.
desobeditu v.t. to disobey.
desobeditzaile adj. disobedient.
desohitu v.i. to be or become unaccustomed to.
desohore n. dishonor.
desohoregarri adj. denigrating, humiliating, degrading.
desohoregarriki adv. dishonorably.
desohoreki adv. reproachfully, infamously, scurrilously.
desohoretsu adj. scurrilous, disgraceful, reproachful, infamous.
desohoretu v.t./v.i. to denigrate, to degrade, to humiliate.
desohorezko adj. dishonorable, indecent.
desoinordekotu v.t. to disinherit.
desordu n. inconvenient time, unseasonable time, unreasonable time, wrong time.
desorduko adj. unseasonable, untimely.
desorduz adv. unseasonably, untimely.
desoreka n. lack of balance, lack of equilibrium.
desornitu v.t. to leave unprovided with provisions, to leave without supplies or food.
desorridura n. defoliation, loss of leaves.
desorritu v.t. to strip leaves. v.i. to fall off (leaves).
desostoketa n. defoliation, loss of leaves.
desoztopatu v.t. to remove an

impediment.

despopulaketa n. depopulating, depopulation.

despopulatu v.t. to depopulate. v.i. to become deserted.

despuztu v.t. to reduce a swelling, to deflate. v.i. to be deflated, to become deflated.

despuztuketa n. deflating.

destaina n. disdain, contempt, scorn.

destainari n. disdainful person, one who scorns, one who despises.

desterru n. exile.

destolesketa n. unfolding, unfurling.

destolestu v.t. to unfold, to spread open, to unfurl.

desustraidura n. uprooting, eradication, extirpation.

desustraigarri adj. uprootable, eradicable.

desustraiketa n. uprooting, eradication, extirpation.

desustraitu v.t. to uproot, to eradicate, to extirpate.

desustraitzaile n. eradicator. adj. eradicating.

desuztarketa n. unyoking.

desuztartu v.t. to unyoke.

deszamaketa n. unloading.

deszamatu v.t. to unload.

deun n. saint.

deunoro n. All Saints. Used also as a first name.

deus pron./adv. something. pron. nothing, anything.

deuseztagarri adj. destructible, destroyable, annihilatable.

deuseztakor adj. frail, brittle, fragile; annihilatable.

deuseztapen n. annihilation, destruction, dissolution. n.(econ.) liquidation.

deuseztatu v.t./v.i. to annihilate, to destroy, to abolish, to exterminate.

deuseztatzaile n. destroyer. adj. destroying.

deuseztu v.t. to abolish, to extinguish, to annihilate, to destroy. v.t.(econ.) to liquidate.

deusgai adj. useful.

dexente adj. enough.

dezigramo n. decigram. Equivalent to 0.1 gram.

dezilitro n. deciliter. Equivalent to 0.1 liter.

dezimetro n. decimeter. Equivalent to 0.1 meter.

-di (gram.) suffix which indicates: place of, forest. **Elordi.** Place abundant in hawthornes.

diabete n.(med.) diabetes.

diabetiko adj. diabetic.

diakono n.(eccl.) deacon.

diakonotza n.(eccl.) deaconship.

diamante n. diamond.

diamantegile n. diamond cutter.

diamantezko adj. made of diamonds.

diametro n.(geom.) diameter.

diapasoi n.(mus.) pitchpipe.

diapositiba n. slide (film).

dibisa n.(econ.) foreign currency.

dibisio n.(math.) division.

dibortziatu v.i. to get divorced.

dibortzio n. divorce.

dieta n. diet.

digestio n. digestion.

diglosia n. bilingual instruction.

-dik (gram.) suffix which means from (time, place).

-diko (gram.) suffix that indicates origin.

diktadore n. dictator.

diktadura n. dictatorship.

dilin n.(onomat.) ding-dong; sound of a bell.

dilindaka adv. hanging or suspended from. adv. staggering.

dilindaka egon v.i. to be suspended from. v.i.(fig.) to be in doubt.

dilindakatu v.i. to be hung, to be suspended from. v.t. to hang.

dilin-dalan adv. swinging. n.(onomat.) ding-dong, tolling of a bell.

dilindan adv. hanging. adv.(fig.) in doubt.

dilindan egon v.i. to hang, to be suspended from. v.i.(fig.) to be in doubt.

dilindari adj. staggering, swaying.

dilista n.(bot.) lentil.

dina adv. as much as.

dinamita n.(chem.) dynamite.

dinamitari n. dynamiter.

dinamo n.(elec.) dynamo, generator.

dinastia n.(pol.) dynasty.

dinbi-danba int.(onomat.) sound which expresses repeated blows or shots.

din-dan n.(onomat.) ding-dong, sound which indicates the tolling of a bell.

dindan-boleran n.(onomat.) ding-dong.

dindilizka adv. hanging, suspending.

dindirri n.(colloq.) sniffles, mucus.

dinosaurio n.(zool.) dinosaur.

diosale n. greetings, good-bye, hello.

diploma n. diploma.

diplomadun adj. having a diploma.

diplomari n.(pol.) diplomat.

diplomatiko n. diplomat. adj. diplomatic.

diplomatikoki adv. diplomatically.

diplomazia n.(pol.) diplomacy.

diputatu n.(pol.) deputy, representative, delegate.

diputazio n. deputation, governing body of a province (especially for economic interests). n. place where the deputation has meetings.

dirdai n. glow, shine.

dirdaitsu adj. glowing, luminous, gleaming, resplendent, brilliant.

dirdarako n. glimmering, twinkling, shimmering.

dir-dir n.(onomat.) sunbeam, sun ray,

sunshine, glimmer. n.(onomat.) reflection (of the sun).

diru n. money, currency.

diruagiri n. receipt.

dirualdaketa n. money exchange.

diru atera v.t. to draw money (out of a bank).

diru aurreratu v.t. to save money; to advance money, to loan money.

diru batu v.t. to collect money, to make money.

dirubatzaile n. collector, money collection, bill collector.

diru beheratu v.i./v.t. (econ.) to depreciate.

dirubide n. business.

dirubihurkortasun n.(econ.) liquidity.

diru bildu v.t. to make money, to collect money. v.t. to accumulate money.

dirubilketa n. collection of money, fund raising.

dirubiltzaile n. collector, bill collector.

diru bota v.t. to spend lavishly.

dirudi v.i. it seems (3rd pers. sing. pres. ind.) (irudi, iruditu, to seem).

dirudun adj. rich, wealthy. n. cashier.

diruegarri n. greed, great desire for money.

diru egin v.t. to earn money.

dirueske n. collection, fund raising.

diruezarketa n. deposit (money).

diruezarle n. depositor (money).

diruezarpen n. cash deposit.

diru ezarri v.t. to deposit money.

diru galdu v.t. to lose money.

dirugaltzaile n. loser of money.

dirugarbiketa n. final tally, balancing the books, final accounting.

dirugin n. minter, coiner. Contr. of diru + egin. n. money winner, bread winner.

dirugintza n. money creation, minting of money, coining money, printing money.

dirugordailu n. treasury.

diru gorde v.t. save money, to keep money.

dirugose n. cupidity, greediness, avarice.

diruhondaketa n. lavishness, misadministration, waste.

diru hondatu v.t. to spend lavishly, to squander.

diruhondatzaile n. waster, squanderer.

diru itzuli v.t. to reimburse, to refund, repayment.

diruitzulpen n. reimbursement, refund, repayment.

diru jaso v.t. to get money.

dirujasoketa n. act of collecting money.

dirujokalari n. gambler, wagerer, bettor.

dirujoko n. speculating, speculation.

diruketa n. amount of money. n.

wealth, opulence, affluence.

diruketari n. financier.

dirukoi adj. greedy, avaricious.

dirukoikeria n. avarice, usury.

dirukoitasun n. greediness (for money).

dirukontaketa n. counting money.

diru-kopuru n. amount of money.

dirukutxa n. money box, cash box.

dirulaguntza n. subsidy, welfare.

dirulapurketa n. theft, robbery.

diru lapurtu v.t. to steal money.

dirulari n. money broker.

dirumerkatu n. money market.

dirumin n. cupidity, greed, greediness (for money).

dirumolde n. die for coining money.

diru moldetu v.t. to coin, to mint.

dirumoltso n. capital, fortune, pile of money.

dirunahi n. cupidity, greed (for money).

diruontzi n. piggy bank. n. safe deposit box.

diru ostu v.t. to steal money.

dirupaper n. paper money, bill.

dirupilo n. large amount of money.

dirusarketa n. deposit (of money).

diru sartu v.t. to deposit money in the bank.

dirutan adv. cash.

dirutoxa n. wallet or purse.

diru trukatu v.t. to exchange money.

dirutruke n. (econ.) money exchange.

dirutsu adj. very rich, wealthy.

dirutu v.i. to become wealthy.

ditia kendu v.t. to wean.

ditialde n. breast.

ditianaia n. foster brother.

ditiburu n.(anat.) nipple.

ditidun adj. having breasts, mammalian.

ditihaundi adj. having large breasts.

ditiko adj. related with the breast. n. breast baby.

ditimin n.(med.) mastitis.

ditimutur n.(anat.) nipple.

ditiorde n. rubber nipple.

ditipunta n.(anat.) nipple.

dogma n. dogma

dogmakeria n. dogmatism.

dogmatiko adj. dogmatic.

dogmatikoki adv. dogmatically.

dogmatizatu v.t. to dogmatize.

dohain n. gift, grace, favor. adv. gratuitously, freely.

dohaindu v.t. to return a favor.

dohainik adv. gratuitously, freely.

dohakabe adj. unfortunate.

dohakabeki adv. unfortunately.

dohakabetasun n. misfortune, bad luck, disgrace.

dohakabetu v.i./v.t. to become unfortunate; to cause misfortune for others.

dohakaitz n. disgrace, misfortune.

dohakaizdun adj. unlucky,

unfortunate.
dohakaiztu v.t. to become unfortunate.
dohako adj. free, gratuitous.
dohan adv. gratis, freely, free.
dohatasun n. happiness, well-being.
dohatsu adj. happy, blessed,
fortunate.
dohatsuki adv. happily.
dohatsutasun n. happiness.
dohatsutu v.i. to become happy. v.t. to
make someone happy.
doi adj. well-fitting.
doi-doi adv. hardly, barely, scarcely,
just. adv. sharp.
doikuntza n. adjustment.
doilor adj. mean, vile, infamous.
doilorgarri adj. degrading, debasing.
doilorkeria n. vilification, debasement,
degradation.
doilorki adv. meanly, basely, vilely,
abjectly, villainously.
doilortasun n. meanness, villainy,
vileness, baseness.
doilortu v.i. to become vile.
doilortze n. act of becoming vile.
doinu n.(mus.) tune, melody.
doinualdaketa n.(mus.) transposition.
doinu aldatu v.t. to transpose.
doinubakar adj. unison, in unison.
doinu berritu v.t. to transpose.
doinuemale n. person who gives the
note for tuning (voices or
instruments).
doinuera n.(mus.) tone. n.(mus.)
intonation.
doinuerdi n.(mus.) semitone, half tone.
doinugailu n.(mus.) pitch pipe.
doinukidetasun n. tuning in (a radio
station, etc.), tuning up (an
orchestra, etc.)
doinukidetu v.t. to tune in (a radio
station), to tune up (an orchestra).
doinulari n. musician.
doinutasun n. tonality.
doinutu v.t. to intone.
doinuzko adj. tonal.
doitasun n. aptitude, capacity, fitness.
n. adaptation. n. fit, coupling.
doitu v.t. to adjust, to adapt. v.i. to
accommodate, to coincide, to fit.
doitzaile n. fitter. adj. fitting.
doktoradutza n. doctorate, Ph.D.
doktore n. physician, medical doctor.
doktorego n. doctorate, Ph.D.
doktoretu v.i. to earn a Ph.D., to earn a
doctorate, to become a Ph.D.
doktoretza n. status of having a
doctorate.
dokumentu n. document.
dokumentugabe adj. lacking the
documents for identification.
dolamen n. sorrow, affliction. n.
repentance.
dolar n.(econ.) dollar.
dolare n. wine press.
dolaretxe n. house which has a wine
press.

dolmen n. dolmen.
dolore n. pain, emotional suffering.
dolu n. mourning. n. mourning dress,
widow's weeds. n. sorrow, affliction.
n. regret, repentance, contrition.
doludun adj. in mourning, dressed in
mourning clothes.
dolu eman v.t. to express sympathy,
to console, to offer one's
condolences.
dolugarri adj. mournful. adj. pitiable,
worthy of sympathy.
dolujantzi n. mourning clothes.
dolumin n. sympathy, condolence.
dolutalde n. funeral cortege, group of
mourners.
dolutsu adj. sorrowful, sad.
dolutu v.t./v.i. to sadden, to make
(someone) sad, to become sad. v.t.
to deplore; to repent.
doluzko adj. sympathetic, consoling.
domagaitz adj. untamed, difficult to
tame.
domagarri adj. capable of being
tamed.
domaketa n. taming.
domakuntza n. taming.
domatu v.t. to tame.
domatzaile n. tamer, horsebreaker,
animal trainer.
domeka n. Sunday. n. man's first
name.
domina n. medal. n. insignia.
dominikar adj. dominican.
doministiku n. sneeze.
domunsanturu n.(eccl.) All Saints Day
(November 1st). Derived from the
Latin Omnium Sanctorum.
done adj. saint.
donekuntza n. canonization,
sanctification, making holy.
Donostia n. San Sebastian, capital city
of the province of Guipúzcoa.
Donostiar. Native of Donostia.
dontsu adj. saint.
dorpe adj. unskillful, awkward, clumsy.
dorpeki adv. unskillfully, awkwardly,
clumsily.
dorpetasun n. awkwardness,
clumsiness.
dorpetu v.i. to be awkward, to be
clumsy.
dorre n. tower. n. rook (chess).
dorreno n.(dim.) small tower.
dorretxe n. house or manor with
towers.
dorretxo n.(dim.) small tower.
dorretzar n.(aug.) tall tower.
dorrexka n.(dim.) small tower.
dorrezain n. tower guard.
dorreztatu v.t. to fortify with towers or
turrets.
dorronsoro n. field of brambles. Used
as a last name.
dortoka n.(zool.) tortoise.
dote n. dowry.
dote eman v.t. to give a dowry.

dotegabe *adj.* without a dowry.
dotemale *n.* person who gives a dowry.
dotore *adj.* elegant, smart, dressed-up. *adv.* fine, elegantly.
dotoredura *n.* ornamentation, ornament.
dotorekeria *n.* excessive embellishment.
dotoreketa *n.* embellishment, adornment.
dotoreki *adv.* elegantly, finely, resplendently.
dotoretasun *n.* elegance, resplendence, decoration.
dotoretu *v.i.* to ornament, to embellish, to adorn oneself. *v.t.* to ornament, to adorn, to decorate.
dotoretzaile *n.* decorator.
dotoretze *n.* act of decorating, act of ornamenting.
dotorezia *n.* elegance, decoration.
dotrina *n.* Catechism.
dozena *n.* dozen.
dozenaka *adv.* by the dozen.
dozenakatu *v.t.* to classify by the dozen.
dozenerdi *n.* half-dozen.
dra *int.(onomat.)* sound which indicates guessing the right answer. *int.(onomat.)* sound which indicates the sudden appearance of something.
draga *n.* dredge, dredger.
dragatu *v.t.* to dredge, to clean the bottom of a river or port.
dragoi *n.* dragon.
drama *n.* drama.
dramagile *n.* playwright, dramatist.
dramagintza *n.* playwriting.
dramatiko *adj.* dramatic.
dramatizatu *v.t.* to dramatize.
drangada *n.(onomat.)* sound which indicates tolling of a bell. *n.(onomat.)* gulp, swallow.
droga *n.* drug.
drogagile *n.* manufacturer of drugs, pharmacist.
drogalari *n.* pharmacist, druggist.
drogasaltzaile *n.* pusher, seller of illegal drugs.
drogatu *v.i./v.t.* to take drugs, to use drugs.
drogazale *adj.* drug addict, dope addict.
-du *(gram.)* verbal suffix which replaces *-tu* after *l, n.* **Gizondu.** To become a man.
duda *n.* doubt.
dudaezin *adj.* indisputable, indubitable.
dudagabeki *adv.* certainly, undoubtedly.
dudagabeko *adj.* indubitable, certain, indisputable.
dudagabez *adv.* certainly, undoubtedly.
dudagarri *adj.* doubtful, questionable.

dudakor *adj.* skeptical, doubting.
dudarazi *v.t.* to cause to doubt.
dudatu *v.t.* to doubt.
dudazko *adj.* doubtful.
duin *adj.* honorable, worthy.
duindu *v.t./v.i.* to dignify.
duingabe *adj.* unworthy.
duingarri *adj.* dignifiable.
duin izan *v.i.* to deserve, to be worthy of.
duintasun *n.* dignity.
dukat *n.(econ.)* ducat, coin.
duke *n.* duke.
dukego *n.* status of duke.
dukerri *n.* dukedom, duchy.
dukesa *n.* duchess.
dultzaina *n.* kind of Basque musical instrument, an end-blown flute made of wood and iron with nine holes and a wide bell, played especially in Navarra.
dun *v.aux.* you (fam. sing. fem.) have it (*ukan,* to have).
-dun *(gram.)* *Suffix which indicates possession, having. Used to form adjectives which are placed before the noun.* **Dirudun gizona.** Wealthy man.
dunbada *n.(onomat.)* loud noise, shot, detonation, explosion.
dunbadaka *adv.* noisily, obstreperously; banging loudly. *adv.* shooting.
dunbadaldi *n.* crash, violent fall, noisy fall.
dunbadatsu *adj.* noisy, booming, exploding.
duo *n.* abundance of rushes. Used as a last name.
-dura *(gram.)* suffix which indicates action or effect of an action. **Abiadura.** Speed, velocity.
durdu *n.(zool.)* marine fish of medium size which has a yellowish green color.
durduzatu *v.t.* to doubt, to hesitate.
durrunda *n.(onomat.)* loud noise.
durrundatu *v.t.* to make a very loud noise.
durunda *n.* echo, resonance.
durunda egin *v.t.* to resound, to echo.
durundaka *adv.* resounding, echoing.
durundari *adj.* resonant, resounding, echoing.
durundatsu *adj.* resonant, resounding, echoing.
durundatu *v.t.* to resound, to echo.
durundi *n.* echo, resonance.
durundi egin *v.t.* to resound, to echo.
durunditsu *adj.* resonant, resounding, echoing.
durunditu *v.t.* to resound, to echo.
dutxa *n.* shower.
dutxatu *v.i.* to take a shower.
dzanga *n.(onomat.)* dive.
dzanga egin *v.t.* to dive.
dzapart egin *v.t.* to grabe, to seize, to

snatch suddenly and vigorously.

dzartada *n.(onomat.)* snapping of a string. *n.(onomat.)* sound of a slap.

dzastada *n.(onomat.)* puncture (pin, shot, needle, etc.)

dzaust *int.* splash, sound of a sudden dive off a boat into the water.

dzaustada *n.(onomat.)* sudden dive *n.(onomat.)* gulp, swallow.

E

e *n.* letter of the Basque alphabet. *int.* exclamation to call somebody's attention or to ask questions.

ea *int.* word which introduces an indirect question, emphasizing it. The auxiliary verb should end in -*n*. **Esaidazu ea etorri den.** Tell me if he has come. *int.* exclamation which invites somebody to do something. **Ea mutilak!** Come on, boys!

ebadura *n.* cut, dissection, incision, slice.

ebagarri *adj.* cuttable, sliceable. *adj.* operable, removable with surgery.

ebakera *n.* way of cutting.

ebaketa *n.* cut, act of cutting.

ebaketari *n.* surgeon.

ebaki *v.t.* to cut. *v.t.* to amputate.

ebakidura *n.* cut, incision, surgery.

ebakiera *n.* way of cutting. *n.* separation of a word into syllables.

ebakiezin *adj.* not cuttable, not sliceable. *adj.* inoperable.

ebakigarri *adj.* cuttable, sliceable.

ebakile *n.* cutter (harvester, surgeon, etc.).

ebakin *n.* remnant (of a piece of cloth).

ebakitza *n.* act of cutting.

ebakitzaile *adj.* cutting. *n.* amputator, surgeon.

ebakor *adj.* cutting, incisive.

ebakune *n.* point of entry (of a cut), incision, cut.

ebakuntza *n.(med.)* surgery.

ebaluaketa *n.* evaluation, appraisal.

ebaluapen *n.* evaluation, appraisal.

ebaluatu *v.t.* to evaluate, to appraise.

ebaluatzaile *n.* appraiser, evaluator.

ebanjelari *n.* evangelist.

ebanjelio *n.* gospel.

ebanjeliotu *v.t.* to evangelize, to preach.

ehanjeliozko *adj.* evangelical, evangelistic.

ebaska *adv.* secretly, in a hidden manner.

ebaskeria *n.* robbery, swindle, fraud, theft.

ebasketa *n.* theft, plunder, despoliation.

ebaskin *n.* plunder, swag, booty, loot, object of a theft.

ebaskindegi *n.* stash, hideout, place where a robber hides his loot.

ebasle *n.* thief, plunderer, robber.

ebaste *n.* robbery, theft, despoliation.

ebatsi *v.t.* to steal, to rob, to pillage.

ebatura *n.* cut, incision, surgery.

ebatzaile *adj.* cutting, incisive. *n.* surgeon.

eboluzio *n.* evolution; development.

eboluzionatu *v.t.* to develop, to evolve.

eboluzionismo *n.* evolutionism.

eboluziozko *adj.* developing, evolving.

eda- Used in compound words. Derived from *edan*, to drink.

edabe *n.* potion, drink.

edagale *n.* thirst. *adj.* thirsty, very thirsty.

edakera *n.* act of drinking. *n.* way of drinking.

edaketa *n.* drinking.

edakin *n.* leftover drink.

edal- Used in compound words. Derived from *edari*, drink.

edale *n.* drinker.

edalontzi *n.* glass, drinking vessel, drinking glass.

edan *v.t.* to drink *n.* drink. **Edanari eman.** To drink heavily.

edanaldi *n.* drink, portion of liquid drunk or for drinking. *n.* time spent drinking.

edanarazi *v.t.* to force to drink, to make (someone) drink. *v.t.* to water (animals).

edanarazle *n.* one who waters cattle.

edanda *adj.* drunk.

edangai *adj.* drinkable, potable.

edangaitasun *n.* potability, drinkableness.

edangaitz *adj.* undrinkable, nonpotable.

edangarri *adj.* drinkable, potable.

edangarritasun *n.* quality of being drinkable, potability.

edangiro *n.* time suitable for drinking.

edangura *n.* desire to drink.

edanketa *n.* act of drinking.

edantzaile *n.* drinker.

edaratu *v.t.* to water cattle.

edari *n.* beverage, drink.

edaridenda *n.* liquor store.

edarigaizto *n.* poison.

edariketa *n.* collection of beverages.

edaritegi *n.* bar, tavern, cantina.

edaritxar *n.* poison.

edarizale *n.* fond of drinking.

edarizaletu *v.i.* to become fond of drinking.

edate *n.* act of drinking, drinking.

edateko *n.* liquid to drink, drink, something to drink. *adj.* potable, drinkable.

edeki *v.t.* to take from, to remove.

eden *n.* poison, venom.

edendu *v.i./v.t.* to poison oneself, to poison.

edendun *adj.* poisonous, venomous.

edendura *n.* poisoning.

edentsu *adj.* poisonous, venomous.

edentzaile *n.* poisoner.
eder *adj.* beautiful, pretty, marvelous.
n. pleasure, satisfaction. *n.* beauty.
n. appreciation, esteem, value.
ederbera *adj.* sensitive to beauty,
aesthetic, appreciative of beauty.
ederdura *n.* beauty; embellishment,
ornament.
eder egin *v.t.* to give pleasure or
satisfaction. *v.t.* to be in someone's
good graces.
edergai *n.* ornament, decoration.
edergailu *n.* ornament.
edergarri *n.* ornament. *adj.* aesthetic,
decorative, ornamental.
eder izan *v.i.* to be pleased *v.i.* to like,
to appreciate, to esteem.
ederketa *n.* embellishment,
decoration, act of ornamenting.
ederki *adv.* beautifully, very well, great,
brilliantly.
ederlan *n.* work of art.
ederra egin *v.t.* to do well, to do
beautifully (often with the opposite
meaning).
ederrago *adj.(comp.)* prettier.
ederragotu *v.t.* to make more beautiful,
to beautify. *v.i.* to become more
beautiful.
ederrak bota *v.t.* to exaggerate.
ederrak eman *v.t.* to hit, to beat.
ederrak hartu *v.t.* to be defeated. *v.t.*
to be beaten up.
ederra sakatu *v.t.* to exaggerate. *v.t.*
to lie exaggeratedly, to trick, to fool,
to mislead.
ederra sartu *v.t.* to lie; to mislead, to
fool, to trick.
ederren *adj.(superl.)* the most
beautiful.
ederrespen *n.* approval; pleasure,
satisfaction, complacency.
ederretsi *v.t.* to please, to like. *v.t.* to
approve.
ederreztatu *v.t.* to embellish, to
beautify, to adorn, to ornament, to
decorate.
edertasun *n.* beauty, handsomeness.
ederti *n.* fine arts.
edertilari *n.* artist.
ederto *adv.* very well.
edertu *v.t.* to embellish, to beautify, to
make beautiful, to adorn, to
ornament, to decorate. *v.i.* to grow
more beautiful. *v.i.* to justify oneself.
edertzaile *n.* decorator, interior
decorator.
edertzale *adj.* fond of beauty.
edertzapen *n.* embellishment,
adornment.
ederz tadura *n.* ornamentation,
decoration, embellishment.
ederztatu *v.t.* to decorate, to
ornament, to embellish.
edesti *n.(neol.)* history.
ediren *v.t.* to find (after looking).
edo *conj.* or. *adv.* more or less, about,
approximately. *conj.* either. **Edo . . .
edo . . .** Either . . . or . . . *adv.*
probably.
edonoiz *adv.* anytime.
edonoizko *adj.* for all seasons, for any
time.
edonola *adv.* anyway, anyhow. *adv.* in
a disorderly way, in a mess.
edonolako *adj.* common, ordinary.
edonon *adv.* anywhere, wherever,
everywhere.
edonongo *adj.* of anywhere; from
anywhere. *adj.* cosmopolitan, from
many places, from everywhere.
edonongotasun *n.* cosmopolitanism.
edonor *pron.* anybody, whoever.
edonora *adv.* anywhere (direction).
edonorako *adj.* for anywhere.
edoskailu *n.* baby bottle.
edoskaldi *n.* period of suckling.
edosketa *n.* act of sucking.
edoski *v.t.* to suck, to draw milk, to
nurse.
edoskialdi *n.* sucking, nursing.
edoskiarazi *v.t.* to make (a baby)
nurse, to give (a baby) a bottle or
breast.
edoskitzaile *n.* sucker, nursing baby,
one who sucks.
edoskitzaro *n.* lactation; suckling
period, nursing period.
edoskuntza *n.* sucking.
edozein *adj./pron.* anybody, any (at
all), anyone, whichever.
edozela *adv.* anyway, anyhow; any old
way.
edozelako *adj.* vulgar; common,
ordinary.
edozelan *adv.* in any way.
edozenbat *adv.* a lot, much, many, as
much as one wants.
edozer *adv.* anything, whatever.
edozertarako *adj.* useful for
everything, good for everything.
edozertarakotasun *n.* quality of being
useful for everything, aptitude.
eduki *v.t.* to have. *v.t.* to keep, to
maintain, to hold onto. *v.t.* to hold.
v.t. to contain. *n.* contents.
edukiera *n.* capacity.
edukigailu *n.* container.
edukin *n.* contents.
edukitasun *n.* ability to contain,
capacity.
edukitsu *adj.* powerful.
edukitza *n.* ownership, possession.
edukitzaile *adj.* possessing,
containing. *n.* payee.
ee! *int.* exclamation used to call
somebody's attention.
egar- Used in compound words.
Derived from *egarri*, thirst.
egarbera *adj.* thirsty.
egarberatasun *n.* state of being
thirsty, thirstiness.
egarberatu *v.i.* to become thirsty.
egarmin *n.* intense thirst.

egarmindu *v.i.* to become very thirsty.
egarri *n.* thirst. *adj.* thirsty. *n.(fig.)* anxiety, strong desire.
egarrialdi *n.* time of thirst.
egarriarazi *v.t.* to cause thirst, to make (someone) thirsty.
egarri izan *v.i.* to be thirsty.
egarrite *n.* drought.
egarritu *v.i.* to become thirsty. *v.t.* to cause thirst, to make (someone) thirsty.
egarti *n.* thirsty.
egartsu *adj.* very thirsty.
-egi *(gram.)* Suffix used with adj. and adv. indicating excess of quantity, quality and time. **Gehiegi.** Too much.
egia *n.* truth.
egia esan *v.t.* to tell the truth.
egiantz *n.* probability.
egiantzeko *adj.* plausible, probable, likely.
egiantzez *adv.* probably, plausibly, likely.
egiatan *adv.* truly, certainly.
egiati *adj.* truthful, sincere.
egiaz *adv.* truly, certainly.
egiazki *adv.* truly, certainly.
egiazko *adj.* true; real, genuine.
egiazkotasun *n.* authenticity, genuineness.
egiaztagailu *n.* lie detector.
egiaztagarri *adj.* verifiable. *n.* document, certificate.
egiaztagarritasun *n.* verification.
egiaztapen *n.* verification.
egiaztatu *v.t.* to verify, to double check.
egiaztatzaile *n.* verifier.
egiaztu *v.t.* to verify, to double check.
egiberatasun *n.* truthfulness, sincerity, frankness.
egibide *n.* testimony, proof.
egiera *n.* act, moment of execution of an action, moment of happening or doing.
egigabe *adj.* false, untruthful.
egigabezia *n.* untruthfulness.
egikera *n.* way of acting, behavior. *n.* form given to a thing, shape, build.
egiketa *n.* completion, performance, operation.
egikor *adj.* truthful.
egikuntza *n.* proof, verification, testimony.
egile *n.* author. *n.* agent. *n.(gram.)* active subject.
egiletasun *n.* authorship.
egin *v.t.* to create. *v.t.* to make, to do, to perform. *v.t.* Aux. verb used with nouns to make verbal phrases. **Negar egin.** To cry. *v.t.* to die. **Horrenak egin du.** He has died. *v.t.* to suppose, to assume; to seem to. **Egin dezagun egia dela.** Let's suppose it is true. *v.t.* to bet. *v.t.* to be (related with weather). **Bero egiten du.** It is hot. *v.t.* Emphasizes

the main verb in the past tenses. **Jan egin dut.** I have eaten. (lit.)What I have done precisely is to eat.
egina *n.* deed, work, action, act. *adj.* made, done.
eginahal *adj.* possible.
eginahalak egin *v.t.* to try one's best, to do one's best, to do everything possible.
eginahalean *adv.* doing one's best; conscientiously.
eginahalez *adv.* conscientiously.
eginaldi *n.* performance, action, act.
egin arazi *v.t.* to cause to do, to make (someone) do something.
eginbehar *n.* duty, obligation, task, chore.
eginberri *adj.* newly made.
eginbide *n.* procedure, means, way, mode of doing something. *n.* duty, obligation, responsibility, task.
eginbidetsu *adj.* conscientious, responsible.
eginbidezko *adj.* mandatory, obligatory.
egindako *adj.* made, artificial, constructed.
eginerraz *adj.* easy to do, easy to make.
eginezin *adj.* impossible to do, unrealizable.
eginezinezko *adj.* impossible to do, unrealizable.
egingabe *adj.* unfulfilled, not done.
egingai *n.* project, what remains to be done.
egingaitasun *n.* capacity for action, capacity for work.
egingaitz *adj.* difficult to make, difficult to do.
egingarri *adj.* feasible, practicable.
egingarritasun *n.* viability, feasibility.
eginkari *n.* agent, executor, doer.
eginkide *n.* co-author.
eginkizun *n.* obligation, duty, task, occupation, chore, something to do.
eginkor *adj.* feasible. *adj.* efficient, active.
eginkortasun *n.* feasibility.
eginkunde *n.* action, act, effect. *n.* deal, bargain.
eginlari *n.* agent.
eginmolde *n.* way of acting.
egintza *n.* deed, execution, action, undertaking.
egintzaile *n.* agent. *adj.* active, efficient.
egipen *n.* action, act, execution, performance.
egipide *n.* management.
egitaldi *n.* time to act.
egitan *adv.* truly, certainly.
egitar *adj.* fond of the truth.
egitaratu *v.t.* to execute, to carry out, to fulfill, to perform, to act.
egitarau *n.* method, methodology. *n.* project, program.

egitasun *n.* truthfulness, veracity.
egitazko *adj.* truthful, veracious. *adj.* genuine, authentic, true.
egitaztu *v.t.* to double check, to verify, to prove.
egite *n.* action, act, deed, realization, execution (of a plan, etc.), undertaking.
egiteko *n.* task, duty, thing to do, work.
egiterraz *adj.* easy to do.
egitez *adv.* in deed, in fact.
egiti *adj.* truthful, fond of the truth.
egitordu *n.* time for action, time to do something.
egitura *n.* structure; composition. *n.* making, tailoring, creation.
egituratu *v.t.* to structure, to organize.
egiturazko *adj.* structural.
egitxura *n.* probability, likelihood.
egitxurako *adj.* probable, likely, plausible.
egizale *adj.* truthful, sincere, fond of truth.
egizaletasun *n.* love of truth, sincerity.
egiztabide *n.* proof, justification, attesting document; way of proving.
egiztabidezko *adj.* verifying.
egiztadura *n.* verification, act of proving.
egiztaezin *adj.* unverifiable.
egiztagaitz *adj.* difficult to prove.
egiztagarri *adj.* verifiable, provable.
egiztaketa *n.* verification, act of proving, confirmation, corroboration.
egiztalari *n.* verifier, prover.
egiztapen *n.* verification, confirmation, proof, corroboration.
egiztarazle *adj.* convincing, swaying.
egiztatu *v.t.* to verify, to prove, to confirm, to corroborate, to certify.
egiztatzaile *n.* verifier, certifier, corroborator.
egoera *n.* situation, status, state. *n.* attitude; manner of being.
egoeraldaketa *n.* change in attitude.
egoile *n.* inhabitant, dweller.
egoiliar *n.* inhabitant, resident, dweller.
egoite *n.* stay.
egoitza *n.* state, situation. *n.* residence, dwelling, place, home.
egoitzaleku *n.* place of residence.
egoki *adj.* convenient, adequate, apt, appropriate, suitable, fitting. *v.i.* to be concerned, to concern, to be (someone's) concern, to fall in to (duty, obligation, etc.). *v.i.* to suit, to fit. *adv.* adequate, conveniently, properly, appropriately, suitably, well.
egokialdi *n.* good opportunity.
egokidura *n.* adjustment, fit; arrangement.
egokien *adj.(superl.)* the most convenient, optimum, the best.
egokiera *n.* convenience. *n.* fit; adaptation, accommodation. *n.* chance, opportunity.
egokierazi *v.t.* to cause to adapt, to make (something) fit.
egokiezin *adj.* unadaptable, unsuitable.
egokigaitz *adj.* difficult to adapt, unadaptable, unsuitable.
egoki izan *v.i.* to suit, to be convenient. *v.i.* to concern.
egokiro *adv.* adequately, conveniently, properly.
egokitasun *n.* opportunity, convenience. *n.* aptitude. *n.* adaptability. *n.* adequateness, suitability, appropriateness.
egokitu *v.i.* to adapt oneself, to fit, to go together. *v.t.* to arrange, to adjust, to adapt.
egokitzaile *n.* adaptor, arranger. *adj.* adaptive.
egokitzapen *n.* adaptation.
egon *v.i.* to be, to consist of, to stay, to remain. *v.i.* to reside, to dwell, to inhabit, to live. *v.i.* to wait.
egonaldi *n.* stop, intermission, pause.
egonarazi *v.t.* to cause to be still, to cause to stay, to make (someone) stay.
egonbehar *n.* obligation to reside, compulsory residence.
egonean egon *v.i.* to do nothing, to be doing nothing.
egonez *adv.* sedentarily.
egonezin *adj.* restless, anxious, agitated. *n.* restlessness.
egonezintasun *n.* restlessness.
egongaitz *adj.* unstable.
egongaiztasun *n.* instability.
egongela *n.* living-room.
egongura *n.* desire to stay or remain.
egonkoi *adj.* stable, durable, lasting.
egonkor *adj.* stable, durable, lasting.
egonkortasun *n.* stability, durability, firmness.
egonkortu *v.i./v.t.* to stabilize.
egonkortzapen *n.* stabilization.
egonkortzaile *n.* stabilizer.
egonleku *n.* place of residence, dwelling.
egonlekuko *adj.* residential.
egonluze *n.* long waiting period.
egontoki *n.* place of residence, dwelling.
egos- *(gram.)* Used in compound words. Derived from *egosi*, to boil, to digest.
egosaldi *n.* boiling time.
egosarin *adj.* partially cooked, parboiled.
egosbera *adj.* easy to boil. *adj.* digestible.
egosberatasun *n.* quality of being easy to boil.
egosberri *adj.* recently boiled.
egoserraz *adj.* easy to boil. *adj.* easy to digest.
egoserraztasun *n.* quality of being easy to boil.
egosgabe *adj.* uncooked, raw. *adj.*

undigested.

egosgailu n. boiler. n.(anat.) digestive tract.

egosgaitz adj. difficult to boil. adj. indigestible.

egosgaiztasun n. state of being difficult to boil. n. indigestion.

egosgaiztu v.i. to have indigestion.

egosgarri adj. boilable. adj. digestible.

egosgarritasun n. quality of being boilable. n. digestibility.

egosgogor adj. difficult to boil. adj. indomitable, stubborn.

egosi v.t./v.i. to boil. adj. boiled. v.t. to digest.

egoskaitz adj. difficult to boil.

egoskari n. vegetable.

egoskera n. boiling, way of boiling.

egosketa n. boiling. n. digestion.

egoski v.t. to nurse, to suckle.

egoskin n. something boiled.

egoskor adj. easy to boil. adj. easy to digest.

egospen n. boiling.

egostaldi n. boiling time. n. digestion.

egoste n. act of boiling.

egotaldi n. pause, rest, quiet period. n.(eccl.) station of the cross.

egote n. stay, staying.

egotegi n. place to stay; home, residence.

egotetxe n. residential building.

egotoki n. place to stay.

egotzi v.t. to throw, to expel. v.t. to attribute, to impute. v.t. to vomit, to throw up.

egozgale n. nausea. adj. nauseous.

egozkarri adj. expellable, throwable, ejectable. adj. attributable, imputable.

egozkarritasun n. imputability.

egozketa n. expulsion. n. imputation.

egozle n. expeller. n. imputer.

egozpen n. expulsion, elimination. n. imputation.

egozte n. act of expelling, expulsion.

egu- Used in compound words. Derived from egun, day.

eguargi n. daylight. n. clear day.

eguargiz adv. by daylight.

eguberri n. Christmas.

eguberritako adj. Christmas.

eguerdi n. noon, midday.

eguerdialde adv. around midday, around noon.

eguerdian adv. at noon, midday.

eguerdiaurre n. before noon, time before noon, a little before noon.

eguerdiaurreko adj. related to the period of time before noon, antemeridional (a.m.).

eguerdiko adj. related to noon, midday.

eguerdiondoko adj. afternoon, related to the period of time after noon, postmeridional (p.m.).

egun n. day.

egunaldi n. daytime.

egunargi n. daylight. n. clear day.

egunargitako adj. diurnal.

egunargite n. dawn, daybreak.

egunargitu v.t. to dawn.

egunaro n. the day's weather.

egunaurre n. the day before.

egunbete n. full day.

egunbide n. course of a day.

egunbira n. one day's rotation of the earth.

egundaino adv. (not) up until now, never.

egundainoko adj. exceptional, extraordinary. adj. eternal, perpetual, perennial.

egundainotik adv. always in the past.

egundo adv. never.

egundoko adj. extraordinary, great.

egundu v.t. to dawn, to break (the day).

egunean-egunean adv. every day.

eguneko adj. diurnal, daily. adj. modern. n. daily provision, daily bread.

egunekotasun n. modernness, quality of being up to date.

egunerapen n. updating.

eguneratu v.i./v.t. to update, to modernize.

egunero adv. daily, every day.

eguneroko adj. daily, quotidian. n. daily provision, daily bread.

egunetan n. life.

egunetik-egunera adv. day by day.

egunez adv. by day.

egunezko adj. day, daytime, diurnal.

egungiro n. the day's weather.

egungo adj. modern, for today.

egungotasun n. present time, modernity.

egunkari n. newspaper.

egunkaritegi n. library of newspapers and periodicals.

egunlangile n. temporary worker, migrant worker.

egunlangintza n. daily work.

egun on! int. good morning!

egunoro adv. every day.

egunoroko adj. daily, quotidian.

egunsenti n. dawn, daybreak.

egunurratze n. dawn, daybreak.

egur n. wood. n.(fig.) punishment.

eguraldi n. weather.

eguras n. airing.

egurasketa n. act of airing, ventilating, freshening.

eguraste n. act of airing, ventilating, freshening. n. strolling, taking the air.

egurastoki n. place to go for a walk.

egurastu v.t./v.i. to air, to ventilate. v.i. to take a walk, to stroll, to take the air.

egurats n. air, atmosphere.

eguratsaldi n. airing, freshening.

egurbide n. road to transport wood; flume.

egurbrintz *n.* sliver, wood chip.
egur egin *v.t.* to cut firewood.
egurgile *n.* woodcutter.
egurgin *n.* woodcutter.
egurgintza *n.* job of a woodcutter.
egurkada *n.* blow with a stick.
egurkari *n.* woodcutter, wood gatherer.
egurketa *n.* act of transporting wood; load of wood. *n.* pile of wood, woodpile.
egurketari *n.* loader of wood; wood gatherer.
egurki *n.* piece of lumber.
egurkintza *n.* job of a woodcutter; act of cutting wood.
egurmeta *n.* pile of wood, woodpile.
egurmozketa *n.* woodcutting, act of cutting wood.
egurmozte *n.* act of cutting wood, woodcutting.
egurpilo *n.* pile of wood, woodpile.
egurrikatz *n.* charcoal.
egurrola *n.* woodshed.
egursaltzaile *n.* wood seller.
egursorta *n.* bundle of sticks, fagot.
egurtegi *n.* woodshed.
egurtoki *n.* woodshed.
egurtsu *adj.* woody.
egurtu *v.t.* to make (into) firewood. *v.t.(fig.)* to hit, to slap, to beat.
egurtxikitzaile *n.* woodcutter.
egurtza *n.* pile of wood.
egurxehatzaile *n.* woodcutter.
egurzama *n.* load of wood.
egutegi *n.* calendar.
eguzki *n.* sun.
eguzkialde *n.* east, orient.
eguzkialdi *n.* interval of sunlight.
eguzkiargi *n.* sunlight.
eguzkiarte *n.* short interval of sunlight, intermittent sun.
eguzkibegi *n.* sunny place, sun porch.
eguzkibide *n.(astron.)* orbit of the sun.
eguzkierloju *n.* sundial.
eguzkierre *n.* sun's glare; sunburn.
eguzkihaize *n.* east wind.
eguzkigalda *n.* scorcher, very hot sunny day.
eguzki galdatu *v.i.* to sunbathe a lot, to take a lot of sun.
eguzki hartu *v.t.* to sunbathe.
eguzkihurbil *n.(astron.)* perihelion.
eguzki jo *v.t.* to burn, to sunburn, to scorch (the sun).
eguzkilore *n.(bot.)* sunflower.
eguzkilune *n.(astron.)* solar eclipse.
eguzkiordu *n.* standard time, time according to the sun.
eguzkiorratz *n.* sundial.
eguzkipeko *adj.* under the sun, subsolar.
eguzkirtera *n.* sunrise.
eguzkisarrera *n.* sunset.
eguzkisorketa *n.* sunrise.
eguzkitako *n.* parasol.
eguzkitar *adj.* solar, sunny.

eguzkitaratu *v.t.* to sun, to put in the sun.
eguzkitatu *v.t.* to put in the sun.
eguzkitsu *adj.* sunny.
eguzkitzar *n.* very hot sun.
eguzkiztapen *n.* sunbathing.
eguzkiztatu *v.t.* to sun, to put in the sun. *v.i.* to sunbathe.
ehe *n.* bleach.
ehiza *n.* hunting.
ehizaketa *n.* hunting.
ehizaldi *n.* hunt.
ehizan ibili *v.i.* to go hunting.
ehizaro *n.* hunting season.
ehizatoki *n.* place for hunting, hunting ground.
ehizatu *v.t.* to hunt.
ehizatxakur *n.* hunting dog.
ehizazale *adj.* fond of hunting.
ehizi *n.* piece of game (animals, birds, etc.).
ehizibarruti *n.* enclosed ground for hunting, hunting grounds, game farm.
ehizibiltzaile *n.* beater (in hunting).
ehiziketa *n.* hunting.
ehiziko *adj.* venatic, related to hunting.
ehizilarru *n.* hide, pelt, fur.
ehizisare *n.* hunting net.
ehizitoki *n.* blind (used in hunting); hunting ground.
ehiziuxaketa *n.* flushing the game.
ehizi uxatu *v.t.* to flush game.
ehizizakur *n.* hunting dog.
ehizizorro *n.* game bag (hunting).
ehiztari *n.* hunter.
ehiztatu *v.t.* to hunt.
eho *v.t.* to grind. *v.t.* to weave. *v.t.* to digest. *v.t.(fig.)* to beat.
ehoaldi *n.* grinding, time spent milling. *n.(fig.)* beating.
ehoerraz *adj.* easy to grind, easy to mill.
ehogailu *n.* grinder.
ehogaitz *adj.* difficult to grind. *adj.* difficult to digest.
ehogarri *adj.* grindable, crushable.
ehoketa *n.* grinding, milling.
ehortz *n.(anat.)* molar (tooth).
ehortze *n.* burial, interment, act of burying.
ehortzi *v.t.* to bury.
ehorzale *n.* gravedigger, burier, undertaker.
ehorzkabe *adj.* unburied, uninterred.
ehorzketa *n.* interment, burial, burying.
ehorzle *n.* gravedigger, burier, sexton.
ehorzleku *n.* burial place, grave, sepulchre, tomb.
ehorzpen *n.* burial, interment, burying.
ehorztetxe *n.* funeral parlor, funeral home.
ehorztoki *n.* burial place, grave, tomb.
ehosari *n.* money paid for milling (corn, wheat, etc.).
ehotaldi *n.* time spent milling.
ehotarri *n.* grist, millstone.

ehotegi *n.* textile mill, place where weaving is done. *n.* mill, place where corn, wheat, etc. are ground.

ehotu *v.t.* to grind.

ehotza *n.* act of grinding. *n.* act of digesting.

ehotzaile *n.* miller.

ehule *n.* weaver.

ehuletegi *n.* textile mill.

ehun *adj./n.* a hundred. *n.* cloth.

ehunardatz *n.* spindle. *n.* axis of a spinning wheel.

ehunburu *n.* centurion.

ehunburugo *n.* office of a centurion.

ehundaka *adv.* by the hundreds.

ehundar *adj.* hundredth.

ehundegi *n.* factory for weaving, textile mill.

ehundenda *n.* fabric store.

ehundu *v.t.* to weave.

ehundura *n.* weaving.

ehuneko *n.* percentage, percent. *n.* bill of a hundred (francs, dollars, pesetas, etc.). *n.* company of one hundred soldiers. *n.(math.)* one hundred (as a unit).

ehuneko hainbeste *n.* percentage.

ehuneko honenbeste *n.* percentage.

ehungabe *adj.* unwoven, unraveled, unbraided.

ehungabetu *v.i./v.t.* to unweave, to unravel, to unbraid.

ehungailu *n.* weaving machine, loom.

ehungarren *adj.* hundredth.

ehungile *n.* weaver.

ehungin *n.* weaver.

ehungintza *n.* manufacture of textile.

ehunka *adv.* by the hundreds, by hundreds.

ehunkada *n.* a hundred.

ehunkoitz *n.* centuple.

ehunkoizpen *n.* multiplying by a hundred.

ehunkoiztu *v.t.* to multiply by a hundred, to increase 100 times, to centuple.

ehunmetro *n.* hectometer (100 meters).

ehunoindun *n.(zool.)* centipede.

ehunsaltzaile *n.* textile merchant.

ehuntari *n.* centurion.

ehuntaritza *n.* office of a centurion.

ehuntegi *n.* factory for weaving, textile plant.

ehunurte *n.* century.

ehunurteburu *n.* centennial.

ehunurtedun *adj.* centenary, of or pertaining to one hundred years, hundred-year-old.

ehunurteko *adj.* centennial, centenary.

ehunzango *n.(zool.)* centipede.

ehunzangodun *n.(zool.)* centipede.

ei Term used before the verb to express *they say*. **Ez ei dator.** They say that he's not coming.

-ei *(pl. dat.)* Suffix used with nouns and pronouns to indicate plural indirect object. **Gizonei.** To the men.

eihera *n.* mill.

eiheraharri *n.* grist, millstone.

ehieraldi *n.* milling, grinding.

eiherari *n.* miller.

eiherazain *n.* miller.

eiherazaingo *n.* job of a miller.

eiherazaintsa *n.* lady miller.

eiki *adv.* certainly, really.

eite *n.* likeness, resemblance *n.* form, aspect, appearance.

-ek *(gram.)* Suffix used to mark active plural subjects of transitive verbs.

ekai *n.* substance, subject.

ekaina *n.* June.

ekainaldi *n.* solstitial season, time surrounding the summer solstice.

ekaitz *n.* storm.

ekaitzaldi *n.* time of a storm.

ekaiztaro *n.* stormy season.

ekaizte *n.* big storm. *n.* stormy season.

ekaiztsu *adj.* stormy, tempestuous.

ekaiztu *v.i.* to storm.

ekaiztun *adj.* stormy, tempestuous.

ekandu *n.* custom. *v.t./v.i.* to be accustomed to, to be used to, to get used to.

ekargarri *adj.* transportable.

ekarketa *n.* bringing.

ekarkor *adj.* fertile, productive.

ekarkortasun *n.* fertility, fecundity.

ekarle *n./adj.* bringer, carrier. *adj.* fertile, fruitful.

ekarpen *n.* contribution; production.

ekarraldi *n.* carrying, bringing, transportation.

ekarrarazi *v.t.* to cause to bring, to make (someone) bring (something).

ekarrarazle *n.* person who causes someone to bring something.

ekarrera *n.* bringing. *n.* way of bringing.

ekarreraz *adj.* easy to bring, easy to transport.

ekarri *v.t.* to bring, to contribute, to provide with.

ekartzaile *n.* bringer, carrier, transporter.

eki *n.* sun.

ekialde *n.* East, Orient.

ekialdeko *adj.* eastern, oriental, east.

ekialdetu *v.i./v.t.* to easternize, to adopt eastern customs.

ekialdezale *adj.* fond of the east.

ekiera *n.* insistence, perseverance.

ekile *adj.* pushy; insistent, persistent, enterprising.

ekimen *n.* initiative.

ekin *v.t.* to persist, to continue, to keep on (doing); to attempt, to undertake.

ekinaldi *n.* attempt, persistence, perseverance. *n.* attack.

ekinarazi *v.t.* to cause to be persistent, to implant persistence in (someone).

ekinaz *adv.* persistently, by persisting, by persevering.

ekinbide *n.* initiative.

ekinez adv. persistently, by persisting, by persevering.
ekinezko adj. persistent.
ekingabezia n. inactivity.
ekinkide n. militant.
ekinkideria n. militant group.
ekinkidetasun n. militance, quality of being militant.
ekinkor adj. active; persistent.
ekintasun n. persistence, perseverance.
ekintza n. activity, action, undertaking.
ekintzagabe adj. inoperative.
ekintzaile n. activist.
ekintzari n. activist.
ekipo n. team.
ekitaldi n. action over a period of time; shift (of work). n. exercise.
ekoitzi v.t. to produce, to give fruit.
ekoizkin n. product, produce.
ekoizkor adj. productive.
ekoizkortasun n. productivity, productiveness.
ekoizle adj. fertile, producing, productive.
ekoizpen n. production, product, fruitfulness.
ekoiztu v.t. to produce, to be fruitful.
ekologari n. ecologist.
ekologia n. ecology.
ekologista n. ecologist.
ekonomi- adj. Used in compound words. Derived from *ekonomia*, economy.
ekonomia n. economy; economics.
ekonomiko adj. economic.
ekonomikoki adv. economically.
ekonomilari n. economist.
ekonomista n. economist.
ekonomizaketa n. economization.
ekonomizatu v.t. to economize.
ekonomo n. administrator.
ekuadore n.(astron., geog.) equator.
ekuazio n. equation.
ekuru adj. quiet, peaceful.
ekurugaitz adj. uneasy, worried, restless.
ekurugaiztasun n. uneasiness, worry.
ekurutasun n. tranquility, peace of mind.
el- Used in compound words. Derived from *eri*, sickness.
ela- Used in compound words. Derived from *ele*, word, story.
elabergile n. novelist.
elabergintza n. novel writing.
elaberri n. novel. n. news.
elaberritsu adj. talkative. adj. fond of the news.
elastiko adj. elastic, flexible, stretchable. n. sweater.
elastikotasun n. elasticity.
elbarri adj. disabled, crippled, paralytic.
elbarridun adj. paralytic, disabled, crippled.
elbarridura n. disablement, crippled

condition, paralysis.
elbarritasun n. disablement, crippled condition, paralysis.
elbarritu v.i./v.t. to become crippled, to cripple.
elbera adj. sickly.
eldarniagarri adj. delirious.
eldarniatu v.i. to become delirious.
eldarnio n. delirium. n. insomnia.
elder n. slobber, spittle, drool.
elderjario adj. drooling, dribbling, slobbering.
elderti adj. dribbling, drooling, slobbering.
eldertsu adj. dribbling, drooling, slobbering.
eldertu v.i. to drool, to slobber.
elderzapi n. bib, chin-cloth.
ele n. story. n. word; conversation. n. cattle.
elealdi n. conversation.
eleaskodun adj. poliglot, multilingual.
eleberri n. novel.
elebide n. theme of a conversation.
elebidun adj. bilingual.
elebitasun n. bilingualism.
elebitza n. bilingualism.
eleburu n. head of cattle.
eleder adj. eloquent.
ele egin v.t. to talk, to speak.
elefante n.(zool.) elephant.
elegile n. talker, speaker, converser.
elekari n. talker, chatter.
elekatu v.t. to talk, to chat.
elekeria n. long-windedness, gabbiness.
eleketa n. conversation.
eleketari n. talker, speaker. adj. talkative.
elektra- adj. electric. Used in compound words.
elektrabide n. electric circuit.
elektragai n. electrical material.
elektragailu n. electrical apparatus.
elektragarri adj. electrifiable.
elektrahari n. electrical wire.
elektrakorronte n. electric current.
elektraneurketa n.(phys.) electrometry.
elektraneurkin n.(elec.) electrometer.
elektrapen n. electrification.
elektrargi n. electric light.
elektratren n. electric train.
elektratu v.t. to electrify.
elektratzaile n. electrifier. adj. electrifying.
elektretxe n. power station.
elektrika adj. electric.
elektrikari n. electrician.
elektrikazko adj. electric.
elektriko adj. electric.
elektrindar n. electric power.
elektrindarpen n. electrification.
elektrindartu v.t. electrify.
elektrizatu v.t. to electrify.
elektrizitate n. electricity.
elektrizazio n. electrification.

elektronika *n.* electronics.
elektronikailu *n.* electronic apparatus.
elektronikari *n.* electrical engineer, electronics technician.
elektroniko *adj.* electronic.
ele-mele *n.* chatter, gossip.
ele-melezale *adj.* fond of gossip.
elemendu *n.* element.
elerdi *n.* half a word.
elerti *n.* literature.
elertilari *n.* writer, person who writes literature.
elertiz *adv.* literarily, in a literary manner.
eletalde *n.* list of words.
eletari *adj.* talkative.
eletegi *n.* stable, barn.
eletsu *adj.* talkative.
elexurika *adv.* fawningly, flatteringly.
elexurikeria *n.* adulation, false flattery, fawning, brown-nosing.
elexuritu *v.t.* to trick, to deceive; to adulate, to flatter, to fawn, to brown-nose.
elezoro *n.* inanity, nonsense.
eleztatu *v.t.* to converse, to talk.
elezuri *adj.* flattering, fawning, cajoling. *n.* adulation, fawning.
elgar *adj.* mutual, reciprocal. *adv.* each other, mutually.
elgorri *n.(med.)* measles.
elikadura *n.* nutrition, nourishment; food.
elikadurazko *adj.* nutritious.
elikagai *n.* food.
elikagaitz *adj.* difficult to feed.
elikagarri *adj.* nutritive, nourishing.
elikapen *n.* nutrition.
elikatu *v.t.* to feed, to nurse, to nourish. *v.i.* to take nourishment, to feed.
elikatzaile *n.* one who nourishes, feeder, nourisher.
elikera *n.* way of feeding. *n.* food.
eliz- Used in compound words. Derived from *eliza*, church.
eliza *n.* church, temple; Christian assembly.
elizain *n.* sacristan.
elizaingo *n.* office of sacristan.
elizako *adj.* ecclesiastic, church, of the church.
elizakoak *n.(pl.)* Last Rites.
elizalde *n.* church surroundings, area beside the church, churchyard.
elizaratu *v.i.* to go to church.
elizarau *n.(eccl.)* canon.
elizaraudi *n.(eccl.)* canon law.
elizarauz *adv.* according to the laws of a church, ecclesiastically, canonically.
elizarauzko *adj.* canonic, canonical.
elizatari *n.* portico, atrium of a church.
elizataurre *n.* portico, atrium of the church.
elizate *n.* church door.
elizatiar *adj.* pious, devout.

elizatxo *n.(dim.)* small church.
elizaurre *n.* area in front of a church. *n.* facade of a church.
elizaz *adv.* according to the laws of the church, by the church.
elizbarneko *adj.* pertaining to the interior of a church.
elizbarru *n.* interior of a church.
elizbarruti *n.(eccl.)* diocese. *n.* jurisdiction of a parish.
elizbarrutiar *adj./n.* diocesan.
elizbatzar *n.* church meeting; council.
elizbatzarreko *adj.* pertaining to a church council.
elizbira *n.* procession around a church.
elizbirako *adj.* processional.
elizbular *n.(archit.)* apse of a church.
elizburu *n.* head of a church.
elizdebeku *n.(eccl.)* interdict.
elizdei *n.* marriage banns.
elizdiru *n.(eccl.)* oblation.
elizegutegi *n.(eccl.)* liturgical calendar.
elizelkarte *n.* congregation; meeting of parishioners.
elizezkontza *n.* religious marriage, church wedding.
elizgizon *n.* cleric, clergyman.
elizinguru *n.* church surroundings. *n.* procession.
elizinguruak *n.(pl.)* church surroundings, church yard.
elizjantzi *n.(eccl.)* sacred vestment.
elizkide *n.* parishioner.
elizkidetu *v.i.* to become a member of a church.
elizkizun *n.* religious ceremony.
elizkoi *adj.* pious, devout.
elizkoikeria *n.* sanctimony, affected piety.
elizkoitasun *n.* piety, religiousness.
elizkoitu *v.i.* to be religious, to be pious.
elizlege *n.* canon law.
elizlegedi *n.* collection of canon law.
elizlegelari *n.(eccl.)* canonist (an expert in canon law).
elizlegezko *adj.* canonical, related to canon law.
elizliburu *n.* church register.
elizmahai *n.* altar.
elizmutil *n.* altar boy, church assistant.
elizpe *n.* portico. *n.* crypt.
eliztar *adj.* pious, devout. *n.* parishioner.
eliztar egin *v.i.* to be pious, to be religious.
eliztarreria *n.* parish, group of parishioners.
eliztartu *v.i.* to become a parishioner.
elkar *adj.* mutual, reciprocal. *adv.* each other, mutually.
elkar- *(gram.)* Used in compound words. Signifies each other, mutual, inter-, common.
elkarbanakuntza *n.* separation, disintegration.

elkarbatu *v.i.* to join, to meet, to gather together. *v.i.* to mate.
elkarbildu *v.i.* to gather together, to join, to meet.
elkarbizitza *n.* cohabitation, living together, coexistence.
elkardura *n.* tie, bond.
elkar erakarri *v.t.* to attract each other.
elkarfederaketa *n.(pol.)* confederation.
elkarfederatu *v.i.* to confederate, to ally.
elkargaitz *adj.* incompatible, not conciliable; unsociable.
elkargaiztasun *n.* unsociability; incompatibility.
elkarganako *adj.* reciprocal, mutual.
elkarganakotasun *n.* reciprocity, reciprocalness, mutualness.
elkarganatu *v.i.* to join, to meet, to gather together. *v.t.* to gather.
elkargarri *adj.* connectable, unifiable, compatible.
elkargarritasun *n.* connectability, compatibility.
elkargo *n.* association, union. *n.* pact, alliance, covenant, treaty.
elkargune *n.* point of union, juncture, connection.
elkar gorrotatu *v.t.* to hate each other.
elkargotu *v.i.* to associate, to interrelate.
elkar hartu *v.t.* to accept each other, to agree; to gather together. *v.t.* to plot, to scheme.
elkar ikusi *v.t.* to see each other, to interview.
elkarjarrera *n.* juxtaposition.
elkar jo *v.t.* to hit each other, to collide.
elkarjoaldi *n.* collision.
elkarjoketa *n.* collision.
elkarketa *n.* association, union.
elkarki *adv.* jointly, in a group.
elkarkide *n.* associate, fellow member, copartner. *adj.* solidary.
elkarkidego *n.* mutuality, reciprocity, mutualism.
elkarkidetasun *n.* mutualism, mutuality, reciprocity.
elkarkidetu *v.i.* to become an associate, to join.
elkarkizun *n.* connection, correspondence.
elkarkoi *adj.* sociable, associative, gregarious.
elkarkoitasun *n.* sociability; mutual attraction.
elkarkor *adj.* sociable, associative.
elkarkuntza *n.* coordination.
elkarlaguntza *n.* collaboration, cooperation.
elkarlan *n.* mutual work, teamwork, community work.
elkarleihaketa *n.* mutual competition, rivalry.

elkar lotu *v.t.* to tie, to connect, to link, to join, to ligate.
elkarlotura *n.* connection, linking.
elkarmaitasun *n.* mutual love.
elkar maitatu *v.t.* to love each other.
elkarmaiteak *n.(pl.)* lovers.
elkarmenderapen *n.* interdependency.
elkarmenpekotasun *n.* interdependency.
elkarmerkatu *n.* common market.
elkarmeza *n.(R.C.Ch.)* celebration of the mass by more than one priest.
elkarmezemale *n.* cocelebrant.
elkarpen *n.* combining, joining.
elkarpide *n.* connection, juncture, joining.
elkarraditu *v.t.* to come to an agreement.
elkarraldaketa *n.* interchange.
elkarraldatu *v.t.* to interchange.
elkarraldi *n.* date (with a person, often of the opposite sex).
elkarrarteko *adj.* reciprocal, mutual.
elkarrekiko *adj.* reciprocal, mutual.
elkarrekin *adv.* together.
elkarrekin egon *v.i.* to be together.
elkarrekin izan *v.i.* to be together; to coexist.
elkarrekintza *n.* interaction, cooperation, collaboration.
elkarren *adj.* mutual, reciprocal, each other('s).
elkarrenganako *adj.* mutual, reciprocal.
elkarreragin *n.* interaction.
elkar eraman *v.t.* to put up with one another, to endure one another.
elkarretenketa *n.* divergence, disagreement, falling out.
elkarrezin *adj.* incompatible. *n.* incompatibility.
elkarrezko *adj.* mutual, reciprocal.
elkarrikusketa *n.* act of seeing each other, interview.
elkarrikuste *n.* interview, act of seeing each other.
elkarritz *n.(gram.)* conjunction.
elkarrizketa *n.* dialogue, conversation, discussion.
elkarrizketako *adj.* conversational, related to a dialogue.
elkarrizketari *n.* interviewer, one who participates in a dialogue, converser.
elkarrune *n.* joint, splice; mortise.
elkartasun *n.* union, alliance, solidarity.
elkarte *n.* union, society, association.
elkartegi *n.* meeting place.
elkartekide *n.* associate, member.
elkartetu *v.i.* to be affiliated with, to belong to.
elkartezin *adj.* incompatible.
elkartezinezko *adj.* incompatible.
elkartezintasun *n.* incompatibility.
elkartoki *n.* meeting place.
elkartrukaketa *n.* exchange.
elkartrukatu *v.t.* to exchange.
elkartruke *n.* exchange.

elkartu v.i. to meet, to gather together. v.t. to join, to gather.
elkartzaile n./adj. coordinator; coordinating. n.(gram.) relative (pronoun).
elkarziri n.(gram.) hyphen.
elki v.i. to go out, to leave.
elkor adj. dry, sterile, unfertile. adj.(fig.) stingy, miserly.
elkorkeria n. stinginess, miserliness.
elkorrune n. dry area.
elkortasun n. dryness, aridity. n.(fig.) stinginess, avarice.
elkortu v.i. to become dry, to dry up. v.t. to dry up. v.i. to become a miser.
elorri n.(bot.) hawthorn. n. thorn.
elorridun adj. having hawthorns, having thorns.
elorritsu adj. thorny, spiny. adj.(fig.) rough, rugged; difficult; crude.
elorrizko adj. made of thorns.
elorrizuri n.(bot.) hawthorn.
eltxar n.(zool.) flesh fly, bluebottle.
eltxo n.(zool.) mosquito.
eltxosare n. mosquito net.
eltze n. stewpot. n. act of seizing, act of grasping.
eltzegile n. potter.
eltzegin n. potter.
eltzegintegi n. pottery kiln, pottery works.
eltzegintza n. job of pottery making. n. pottery making.
eltzeitsu n. piggy bank.
eltzekada n. contents of the stewpot, potful of something.
eltzekari n. vegetable stew, pot of beans, etc.
eltzeki n. piece of a clay pot.
eltzeko n. stew, pot of beans, etc.
eltzetegi n. pottery shop.
eltzeteria n. number of pots.
eltzetxo n.(dim.) small pot.
eltzetzar n.(augm.) big pot.
eltzezain n. cook; scullion, kitchen boy.
elur n. snow.
elurbasa n. muddy snow, slush.
elurbera adj. snowy (weather, place).
elurbolada n. snow flurry, light snowfall.
elurbusti n. slush, half-melted snow.
elurdun adj. snowy. n. iceman.
elurgabe adj. snowless, cleared of snow.
elurgabetu v.i. to thaw, to melt (snow).
elurgezal n. muddy snow.
elurgiro n. snowy ambience.
elurkengailu n. snowplow.
elurketa n. abundance of snow, heavy snowfall.
elurlauso n. snow flurry.
elurlera n. sled, snow sled.
elurlili n.(bot.) edelweiss.
elurluma n. snowflake.
elurmalo n. snowflake.
elurmaluta n. snowflake.

elurmataza n. snowflake.
elurmeta n. pile of snow.
elurpilota n. snowball.
elurra egin v.t. to snow.
elurra gezaldu v.i. to melt (snow).
elurraldi n. snowfall, snow flurry.
elurreuri n. sleet.
elurrezko adj. snowy.
elurrorein n.(zool.) reindeer.
elurte n. snowfall. n. snow season.
elurtegi n. snowy place, place of snow.
elurtoki n. snowy place, place of snow.
elurtsu adj. snowy.
elurtu v.t./v.i. to freeze.
elurtxori n.(zool.) chaffinch.
elurtza n. snowfall.
elurtze n. act of snowing. n. large snowfall.
elurzulo n. hole made in the snow.
ema- Used in compound words. Derived from eme, female; to calm.
emabakar adj. monogamous (relationship with one woman).
emabide n.(anat.) vagina.
emabideko adj. vaginal.
emabidemin n.(med.) vaginitis.
emagaiso n. disgraced woman.
emagaldu n. prostitute, whore. v.i. to become a prostitute.
emagaldutza n. prostitution.
emagale adj. philandering, fond of women.
emagaletu v.i. to have sexual desire (male for the female).
emagaletxe n. house of prostitution, brothel, bordello.
emagalkeria n. prostitution.
emagarri adj. mitigating, calming, mollifying.
emagile n. pacifier, calmer, appeaser.
emagin n.(med.) midwife, obstetrician.
emagintza n. midwifery, obstetrics.
emagizon n. effeminate man.
emagizondu v.i. to become effeminate.
emagizonkeria n. effeminacy.
emagose n. sexual drive of the male for the female, lust.
emaile n. giver. adj. giving.
emaitza n. gift, present. n.(math.) result, product. n. outcome, result.
emajoera n. sexual drive of the male for the female, lust.
emakeria n. excessive femininity, affected femininity.
emakin n. fertilizer.
emakoi adj. generous. adj. fertile, fecund. adj. philandering, fond of women.
emakoitasun n. philandering.
emakor adj. fertile, fecund.
emakume n. woman, lady.
emakumealdeko adj. feminist.
emakumekeria n. effeminacy.
emakumekoi adj. philandering, fond of women.
emakumetasun n. femininity.

emakumetu *v.i.* to become effeminate.
emakumezko *n.* woman. *adj.* female, womanish.
emaldi *n.* calmness.
emalege *n.* menstruation.
emalizun *n.* prostitute.
emalizunkeria *n.* prostitution.
emamin *n.(med.)* venereal disease.
emamintz *n.(anat.)* hymen.
eman *v.t.* to give. *v.t.* to seem, to look like. *v.i.* to devote oneself. *v.t.* to produce, to render. *v.t.* to transmit. *v.t.* to hit, to beat. *v.t.* to loosen up.
emanagiri *n.* receipt, delivery notice.
emanaldi *n.* act of delivering, delivery; act of giving, giving. *n.* performance; broadcast, transmission, emission. *n.* coat of paint.
eman arazi *v.t.* to cause to deliver; to cause to give, to make (someone) give (something).
emanarazle *n.* person who causes one to give, giver.
emanbide *n.* means of giving, delivering.
emanezin *adj.* intransmissible, not transmittable, not broadcastable.
emangailu *n.* transmitter.
emangaitz *adj.* infertile, not fecund. *adj.* intransmissible, not transmittable, not broadcastable.
emangarri *adj.* transmissible, transmittable, broadcastable.
emangarritasun *n.* quality of being transmittable.
emankizun *n.* broadcast, transmission, emission; performance.
emankor *adj.* generous. *adj.* fertile, fecund, prolific, fruitful. *adj.* productive.
emankorki *adv.* fertilely, fecundly, fruitfully.
emankortasun *n.* generosity. *n.* fertility, fecundity. *n.* productivity.
emankortu *v.t.* to fertilize.
emantzaile *adj.* generous.
emarazi *v.t.* to calm, to calm down, to appease.
emarazle *n.* calmer, appeaser.
emari *n.* donation, present, gift.
emaro *adv.* slowly.
emarrapaketa *n.* abduction, kidnapping of a woman.
emarrapatu *v.t.* to abduct, to kidnap a woman.
emasabel *n.(anat.)* uterus, womb.
ematasun *n.* femininity. *n.* smoothness, softness; gentleness.
emate *n.* act of giving, donation.
ematsu *adj.* temperate, moderate, calm.
ematu *v.t./v.i.* to calm, to calm down, to moderate, to smooth.
ematutu *n.(anat.)* vagina.
ematxar *n.* prostitute.
ematxarkeria *n.* prostitution.
ematzar *n.* prostitute.

emazain *n.* pimp.
emazaintza *n.* pimping.
emazakil *n.(anat.)* clitoris.
emazte *n.* wife.
emaztebakar *adj.* monogamous (relationship with one woman).
emaztebakartza *n.* monogamy (relationship with one woman).
emaztebiko *n.* bigamist. *adj.* bigamous.
emaztebitasun *n.* bigamy (relationship with two women).
emaztedun *adj.* having a wife. *n.* married man, husband.
emaztegabe *n.* bachelor.
emaztegai *n.* fiancee, woman engaged to be married.
emaztehilketa *n.* uxoricide, murder of a wife by her husband.
emaztehiltzaile *n.* uxoricide, one who kills his wife.
emaztekoi *adj.* very fond of one's wife.
emaztetu *v.i.* to become a wife, to get married (woman).
emaztetxo *n.(dim.)* little wife.
emaztorde *n.* mistress, concubine.
eme *adj./n.* female. *adj.* feminine. *adj.* smooth, soft, slow. *adj.* female (screw, joint).
-eme *(gram.)* Suffix meaning female. **Kateme.** Female cat.
emeki *adv.* smoothly, gently, softly, slowly, little by little.
emekiro *adv.* smoothly, gently, softly, slowly, little by little.
emendagarri *adj.* enlargeable, increasable, capable of being augmented or increased.
emendatu *v.t.* to enlarge, to increase, to augment.
emetasun *n.* gentleness, pleasing manner, sweetness of character. *n.* femininity.
emeti *adj.* effeminate.
emetu *v.i./v.t.* to calm, to soften, to smooth. *v.i.* to become effeminate.
emezko *adj.* feminine.
-en *(gram.)* Plural possessive suffix used with animate beings. The rights of men and women. *(gram.)* Verbal suffix used to express the future with infinitives that end in *n.* **Eginen du.** He will do it. *(gram.)* Superlative suffix. **Handien(a).** The biggest.
-(e)na *conj.* that.
enara *n.(zool.)* swallow.
enbarazu *n.* disturbance, difficulty, obstacle.
enbata *n.* seawind preceding a storm. *n.* political group in North Euskadi.
enbataldi *n.* northeaster.
enbaxada *n.* embassy.
enbaxadari *n.* ambassador.
enbaxadarisa *n.* ambassador (female).
enbaxadore *n.* ambassador.
enbaxadorego *n.* ambassadorship, office or post of an ambassador.
enbor *n.* trunk.

enborki n. piece of the trunk.

enbortu v.i. to be related to, to become related to, to settle down, to put down roots.

enbortzar n.(augm.) large tree trunk.

enbragatu v.t. to engage the clutch.

enbrage n.(mech.) clutch.

enda n. race, caste, breed.

endai n. baker's peel.

endaitz n. handle, haft (of a plow).

endalahar n.(bot.) sarsaparrilla plant.

endekagarri adj. degenerating, deteriorating, corrupting.

endekatu v.i. to deteriorate, to degenerate; to pervert, to corrupt.

endekoi adj. sociable, friendly, affable, easy-going.

endelgatu v.t. to understand, to comprehend.

endelgu n. intelligence.

endurtu v.i. to atrophy, to shrink up, to shrivel. v.t. to damage; to cripple.

ene adj. my. int. exclamation which denotes surprise, pain, difficulty, etc.

-enea (gram.) Suffix indicating possession of property (house).

-(e)nean (gram.) Verbal suffix indicating time (when).

eneganatu v.t. to attract to me. v.i. to come to me, to approach me.

-(e)neko (gram.) Verbal suffix which means when, by the time, at the moment when, or similar time-related phrases.

-(e)nerako (gram.) Verbal suffix which indicates the idea of when, before, etc.

-(e)netan (gram.) Verbal suffix meaning always, when, every time, each time.

-(e)netik (gram.) Verbal suffix meaning since, from the time that.

enetxo adj.(dim.) my dear.

enetzat pron.(dat.) for me.

-(e)nez (gram.) Verbal suffix meaning according to.

-(e)nez gero (gram.) Verbal suffix meaning since.

engainagarri adj. deceptive; cheating.

engainakor adj. fraudulent.

engainamendu n. fraud, deception.

engainamenduz adv. falsely, deceptively, fraudulently.

engainari n. cheater, fraud, crook, trickster.

engainatu v.t./v.i. to deceive, to cheat, to defraud, to trick.

engainatzaile n. cheater, imposter, deceiver. adj. cheating.

engainu n. deception, lie, fraud, trick, falseness, guile.

engoitik adv. from now on.

engranaia n.(mech.) gear.

eni pron.(dat.) to me.

enkailatu v.i. to run aground.

enpagu n. repugnance, aversion, repulsion.

enparantza n. plaza or square surrounded by covered walkways.

enperadore n. emperor.

enperadoresa n. empress.

enperadoretza n. office or position of emperor.

enplasto n. plaster, medicinal plaster.

enpresa n. enterprise, business, factory.

enpresari n. manager, boss, man in charge.

enpresaritza n. managerial position, job or office of a boss.

entrenamendu n. training.

entsalada n. salad.

entsaladontzi n. salad bowl.

entsegu n. rehearsal; test.

entsegualdi n. rehearsal time, rehearsal.

entsegulari n. person who rehearses, rehearser.

entsegutegi n. rehearsal hall.

entsegutu v.t. to rehearse; to test, to experiment.

entseguzko adj. experimental.

entseiatu v.t. to rehearse; to test, to try.

entseiu n. rehearsal; testing, essay, test.

entxufatu v.t. to plug in.

entxufe n. electrical outlet; plug.

-entzat (gram.) Suffix meaning intended for, for (destination).

entziklika n.(R.C.Ch.) encyclical letter.

entziklopedia n. encyclopedia.

entzima n.(biol.) enzyme.

entzuera n. fame, reputation. n. means of hearing.

entzukin n. hearing aid, hearing instrument.

entzule n. listener.

entzulego n. audience, group of listeners.

entzuleria n. audience, group of listeners.

entzulesail n. audience, group of listeners.

entzumen n. hearing.

entzumenezko adj. auditive, aural, related to hearing.

entzun v.t. to listen, to hear.

entzunahi n. desire to hear, curiosity. adj. curious, wanting to hear.

entzunaldi n. time of listening, audition.

entzunarazi v.t. to make (someone) listen.

entzunbera adj. being a good listener, attentive.

entzunezin adj. inaudible.

entzungabe adj. unheard of.

entzungailu n. earphone. n. hearing aid.

entzungaitz adj. difficult to hear.

entzungarri adj. audible; worthy of being heard, worth hearing.

entzungogor adj. inattentive.

entzungor adj. deaf, hard-of-hearing.

entzungura *n.* desire to hear. *adj.* anxious to hear.

entzunguraz *adv.* anxiously.

entzunikuskin *n.* audio-visual apparatus.

entzunkor *adj.* attentive.

entzunmin *n.* desire to hear. *adj.* anxious to hear.

entzunminez *adv.* curiously.

entzuntzale *adj.* anxious to hear.

entzupen *n.* hearing, audition.

entzupide *n.* auditive faculty, sense of hearing. *n.* way of hearing.

entzute *n.* hearing, audition. *n.* fame, renown.

entzutedun *adj.* famous, renowned.

entzutetsu *adj.* famous, renowned, celebrated.

enuldu *v.i.* to atrophy, to become atrophied, to become useless.

enulkeria *n.* inertia, debility, weakness.

enulki *adv.* weakly.

enultasun *n.* weakness.

ep *int.* used in difficult or dangerous moments. Be careful!

epai *n.* decision, sentence, judgement. *n.* cut, incision.

epaialdi *n.* trial, duration of a trial. *n.* pruning season.

epaiaro *n.* pruning season.

epaiaulki *n.* tribunal, court.

epaiaurreko *adj.* prejudgmental, pretrial.

epaibide *n.* judicial negotiations.

epaibidez *adv.* judicially.

epaibidezko *adj.* judicial.

epai eman *v.t.* to judge, to hand down a judgment.

epaierabaki *n.* judicial decision, judgment.

epaietxe *n.* courthouse.

epaiezko *adj.* judicial.

epaigarri *adj.* judicable. *adj.* cuttable.

epaikaritza *n.* judgeship, office of a judge.

epaiketa *n.* judgment, arbitration.

epaikunde *n.* judgment, arbitration.

epaikuntza *n.* judgment, arbitration.

epail *n.* March.

epaile *n.* judge.

epaileku *n.* tribunal, court.

epaimahai *n.* tribunal bench. *n.* jury.

epaimahaiko *n.* member of the jury.

epaipeko *adj.* judged, sentenced.

epaipetu *v.t.* to sentence, to judge.

epaisari *n.* fee formerly paid to judges.

epaite *n.* act of cutting, cut, incision.

epaitegi *n.* courthouse.

epaitu *v.t.* to judge, to sentence. *v.t.* to cut.

epe *n.* period of time, term.

epe atzeratu *v.t.* to postpone.

epebete *n.* deadline.

epe bete *v.i.* to be due, to fall due; to finish one's time.

epe eman *v.t.* to give (someone) time (to pay something, etc.).

epegabeki *adv.* indefinitely.

epegabeko *adj.* continuous, incessant, unlimited.

epe galdu *v.t.* to expire (time), to run out (time).

epegarri *adj.* postponable, deferrable.

epeka *adv.* on credit.

epekatu *v.t.* to divide into periods of time.

epel *adj.* lukewarm, warm. *adj.(fig.)* weak, feeble. *adj.* apathetic; indecisive.

epelalde *n.* temperate zone.

epelaldi *n.* warm spell. *n.(fig.)* timidness, shyness.

epeldu *v.t./v.i.* to warm; to be warm. *v.i.(fig.)* to cool, to lessen, to decrease.

epeldura *n.* condition of warmth, state of being warm, warmth.

epelkeria *n.(fig.)* indecisiveness; feebleness.

epelki *adv.* warmly.

epeltasun *n.* warmth.

epelune *n.* warm spell.

epeluzapen *n.* extension of time, prolongation, postponement.

epe luzatu *v.t.* to prolong, to extend time.

epemaile *n.* postponer, one who postpones something.

epemuga *n.* deadline, due date.

eper *n.(zool.)* partridge.

eperki *n.* partridge meat.

eperkume *n.(dim.)* partridge chick.

eperlari *n.* partridge hunter.

epertxakur *n.* partridge hunting dog.

epetan *adv.* on credit.

epetu *v.t.* to set a time limit, to set a date, to set a deadline.

epika *n.* epic.

epokeria *n.* dwarfism.

epotu *v.i.* to become a dwarf; to grow very little.

epotx *n.* dwarf.

epuru *n.(bot.)* juniper.

epuruale *n.* juniper berry.

epurudi *n.* juniper grove.

epuruki *n.* piece of juniper, juniper wood.

era *n.* way, manner, appearance; kind. *n.* occasion, opportunity, chance. *n.* face (of a coin); side (of clothing).

-era *(gram.)* Suffix used with various adjectives to denote size of the body or of physical objects. **Lodiera.** Thickness, fatness. *(gram.)* Verbal suffix which indicates way, manner; action. **Ibilera.** Way of walking. *(gram.)* Suffix for languages. **Euskera.** Basque. **Gaztelera.** Spanish. *(gram.)* Directional suffix. **Parisera.** To Paris.

erabaki *v.t.* to decide, to make a decision, to determine. *n.* decision, resolution. *v.t.* to sentence.

erabakidun *adj.* decisive, resolute.

erabakiezin adj. unsolvable, indeterminable. adj. indecisive, irresolute.

erabakiezintasun n. indecision, irresolution.

erabakigabe adj. indecisive, irresolute.

erabakigaitz adj. difficult to resolve.

erabakigarri adj. solvable.

erabakikor adj. decisive.

erabakikortasun n. decisiveness.

erabakikuntza n. resolution, decision.

erabakitako adj. determined, decided.

erabakitzaile adj. deciding, decisive, determining.

erabakiz adv. decisively, definitively.

erabakizko adj. decisive, deliberate.

erabat adv. entirely, very, altogether, completely, utterly, totally.

erabatasun n. uniformity.

erabateko adj. definite, decisive, conclusive. adj. total, complete. adj. same, equal.

erabatez adv. uniformly.

eraberdineko adj. uniform.

eraberdinez adv. uniformly.

eraberean adv. likewise, in the same manner, as well, also.

erabereko adj. homologous; uniform.

eraberri n. reform. n. new fashion, new style.

eraberritu v.t./v.i. to renovate, to reform, to modernize.

eraberritzaile n. renovator, reorganizer, reformer.

eraberritzapen n. renewal, renovation, reform.

eraberrizale adj. reformist, fond of renewal or renovation.

eraberrizte n. renovation, reformation, modernization.

erabide n. formula; process (of getting something), method. n. education. n. composure, moderation. n. sedateness. n. organization, order.

erabideko adj. attentive, courteous, pleasant, polite, well-mannered.

erabidetasun n. decency, courtesy.

erabidetsu adj. polite, well-mannered, courteous; moderate, sedate.

erabidetu v.i. to control oneself, to moderate oneself.

erabidez adv. politely, courteously, decently. adv. moderately.

erabidezko adj. polite, courteous. adj. moderate, measured.

erabiko adj. biform, biformed.

erabilaldi n. period of use, usage. n. handling, operation.

erabilbide n. use, usage, utilization.

erabilera n. manner of using, managing, use, utilization.

erabilgaitz adj. difficult to use, unusable, inoperable.

erabilgarri adj. usable, available, useful.

erabilgarritasun n. usefulness, availability.

erabili v.t. to manage, to use, to employ, to operate, to manipulate. v.t. to move. v.t. to shake, to stir (liquids).

erabilketa n. management, use, utilization.

erabilkizun n. management, use, utilization.

erabilkontu n.(econ.) checking account.

erabilkor adj. usable, useable, manageable, available.

erabilkortasun n. usefulness, usability, usableness, manageability, availability.

erabilkuntza n. usage, use.

erabilpen n. use, utilization.

erabilterraz adj. manageable, easy to use.

erabiltezin adj. unmanageable, difficult to use.

erabiltzaile n. user.

eradale n. drink server. n. one who waters cattle.

eradan v.t. to cause to drink, to give a drink to, to water (livestock).

eradoski v.t. to suckle.

eragabe adj. irregular, deformed. adj. impolite; immoderate. adj. unorganized.

eragabekeria n. senselessness, nonsense; foolish remark. n. impoliteness, discourtesy. n. inappropriateness.

eragabeki adv. inappropriately, discourteously, impolitely.

eragabeko adj. irregular, deformed. adj. impolite, immoderate. adj. disorganized.

eragabetu v.t. to deform. v.i. to be impolite. v.t. to disorganize, to mess up.

eragabetasun n. deformity. n. impoliteness.

eragabez adv. impolitely; immoderately. adv. in a disorganized way.

eragabezia n. deformity.

eragaitz adj. inopportune, inconvenient.

eragarri adj. formative.

eragidura n. diligence, efficacy.

eragiketa n. exercise, activity, movement, operation. n. incitement, motivation.

eragikor adj. active, motivating.

eragikortasun n. activity. n. efficacy, efficiency.

eragikuntza n. impulsion, motivation, urging.

eragile n. promoter. adj. effective, dynamic.

eragiletasun n. power to promote.

eragimen n. efficacy. n. impulsion, motivation. n. power of persuasion.

eragin v.t. to activate, to cause to do, to stimulate, to promote. v.t. to move;

to wag. *v.t.* to shake. Used with indirect objects. *n.* action, influence. *n.* stimulation, encouragement, agitation, push.
eraginaldi *n.* agitation, period of agitation.
eraginbera *adj.* easily influenced.
eragindar *n.* engine power.
eragindura *n.* activity, movement. *n.* influence.
eraginez *adv.* actively.
eraginezko *adj.* activated, motivated.
eragingailu *n.* handle, crank. *n.(mech.)* button.
eragingarri *n.* motivation, stimulus.
eraginiko *adj.* induced, caused.
eraginkor *adj.* active; efficient, effective.
eraginkortasun *n.* efficiency, effectiveness.
eragintasun *n.* efficiency. *n.* influence.
eragintsu *adj.* effective, efficient.
eragintza *n.* activity. *n.* influence. *n.* stimulant.
eragintzale *n.* activist.
eragipen *n.* influence. *n.* stimulus.
eragitailu *n.* mixer, beater, apparatus for beating or mixing.
eragite *n.* activation, stimulus. *n.* wagging, shaking. *n.* influence.
eragitez *adv.* efficiently. *prep.* by virtue of, because of.
eragotzi *v.t.* to prohibit, to impede. *v.t.* to cause to fall, to knock down, to throw down, to overthrow.
eragozbide *n.* impediment, obstacle, prohibition.
eragozkarri *adj.* troublesome; cumbersome. *adj.* prohibitive. *n.* obstacle, impediment, problem.
eragozketa *n.* prohibition; obstacle, impediment, difficulty.
eragozkor *adj.* hindering, impeding, obstructing.
eragozle *n.* obstructor. *adj.* troublemaking, troublesome.
eragozlege *n.* law which prohibits.
eragozpen *n.* impediment, obstacle, hindrance, difficulty, problem.
eragozpenezko *adj.* difficult. *adj.* prohibitive.
eragozpide *n.* adversity, difficulty, impediment.
eragozpidetu *v.t.* to prohibit, to prevent, to hinder.
eragozte *n.* act of prohibiting, act of impeding; act of overthrowing.
eraiketa *n.* construction, building.
eraiki *v.t.* to build, to construct; to set up, to raise. *v.t.* to found, to establish. *v.t.* to motivate.
eraikidura *n.* building, construction.
eraikiezin *adj.* unbuildable.
eraikikuntza *n.* building, construction.
eraikile *n.* builder.
eraikintza *n.* building, constructing.
eraikitzaile *n.* builder. *n.* founder.

eraikuntza *n.* building, construction.
eraile *n.* murderer, assassin. *adj.* murderous.
erailketa *n.* murder, assassination.
erailkintza *n.* homicide, murder.
erailkor *adj.* fatal, mortal.
eraisketa *n.* milking.
eraistailu *n.* milking machine.
eraitsi *v.t.* to lower, to take down, to demolish, to knock down. *v.t.* to milk. *v.t.* to knock down.
erakaitz *adj.* inopportune, inconvenient.
erakaizki *adv.* inconveniently.
erakargarri *adj.* attractive.
erakargarritasun *n.* attraction, attractiveness.
erakarketa *n.* attraction. *n.* contribution.
erakarkor *adj.* attractive, attracting.
erakarle *n.* bringer, carrier *adj.* attracting, attractive.
erakarmen *n.* attraction.
erakarpen *n.* attraction, attracting, force.
erakarri *v.t.* to attract; to captivate. *v.t.* to transport, to bring, to carry. *v.t.* to cause, to occasion, to give rise to.
erakartasun *n.* attraction. *n.* gravity.
eraketa *n.* adaptation, arrangement. *n.* formation, systematization.
erakide *adj.* uniform, same.
erakidetasun *n.* uniformity, sameness.
erakidetu *v.t.* to adjust (to), to conform (to).
erako *adj.* convenient, appropriate. *adj.* like, similar to.
erakor *adj.* accommodating, adaptable.
erakunde *n.* institution, organization.
erakundetu *v.t.* to institutionalize.
erakundezko *adj.* institutional.
erakuntza *n.* organization.
erakus- Used in compound words. Derived from *erakutsi*, to show.
erakusaldi *n.* explanation.
erakusbide *n.* method, pedagogical method. *n.* example.
erakusbidezko *adj.* explanatory.
erakusgaitz *adj.* difficult to show, inexplicable, unexplainable.
erakusgarri *adj.* demonstrable. *n.* sample.
erakuskari *n.* sample, display item.
erakuskariketa *n.* sampling.
erakuskeria *n.* exhibitionism.
erakusketa *n.* instruction; training. *n.* exhibition, exposition. *n.* parade.
erakuskin *n.* piece of a sample.
erakuskor *adj.* demonstrative.
erakusle *n.* guide, demonstrator, exhibitor, presenter. *adj.(gram.)* demonstrative; revealing.
erakusleiho *n.* display window.
erakusleku *n.* showcase, framework for exhibiting something.
erakusmahai *n.* counter.
erakusmen *n.* manifestation.

erakusnahi *n.* ostentation, desire to show.

erakuspen *n.* manifestation. *n.* example, model, sample.

erakuspide *n.* example, proof. *n.* advice, moral (of a story).

erakustaldi *n.* exposition, exhibit. *n.* parade.

erakustapal *n.* showcase, display shelves.

erakustari *n.* exhibitor, shower. *adj.* showing, exhibiting.

erakustazoka *n.* fair pavilion.

erakuste *n.* demonstration, manifestation. *n.* instruction, education.

erakustegi *n.* showcase. *n.* place of exhibition.

erakusten eman *v.t.* to explain, to cause to understand.

erakustetxe *n.* teaching center, school. *n.* place of exhibition, museum.

erakustoki *n.* place of exhibition, (art) gallery, exhibition hall. *n.* showcase, display window.

erakutsaulki *n.* professorial chair.

erakutsi *v.t.* to show, to exhibit, to reveal. *v.t.* to teach, to show. *n.* expression.

eraldagarri *adj.* transformable, renewable, reformable.

eraldaketa *n.* transformation, renewal, reform.

eraldakor *adj.* transforming, renewing, reforming.

eraldakuntza *n.* transformation, renewal, renovation, reform.

eraldapen *n.* transformation, renewal, renovation, reform.

eraldatu *v.t.* to transform, to renew, to reform, to redo.

eraldatzaile *adj.* transforming, renewing.

eramale *n.* carrier, bearer, conductor. *n.* sufferer, one who bears suffering.

eraman *v.t.* to carry, to transport, to take (to a place), to lead. *v.t.* to bear, to endure, to suffer, to tolerate. *v.t.* to guide, to conduct. *v.t.* to return a serve (in a ball game). *n.* patience.

eraman-ekarle *n.* carrier, transporter.

eramanerrez *n.* portable, easy to transport.

eramanez *adv.* patiently.

eramanezin *adj.* not transportable, not carriable, not portable. *adj.* intolerable, insufferable, unbearable.

eramangaitz *adj.* difficult to carry or transport. *adj.* difficult to tolerate or to bear; insufferable.

eramangaiztasun *n.* quality of being not portable. *n.* intolerance, intransigence.

eramangarri *adj.* transportable, conveyable, conductible. *adj.* tolerable, bearable.

eramankizun *n.* patience, tolerance. *n.* something to be carried or transported, load, cargo. *n.* suffering.

eramankor *adj.* transportable, carriable. *adj.* patient, tolerant, enduring.

eramankortasun *n.* quality of being transportable or carriable. *n.* patience, tolerance, endurance.

eramanpen *n.* tolerance, patience.

eramantzaile *n.* bearer, carrier.

eramate *n.* act of transporting, transportation, carrying.

eransgarri *adj.* sticky, adhesive.

eranskailu *n.* sticker.

eransketa *n.* adhesion, sticking, agglutination.

eranskin *n.* appendix, addition, supplement. *n.* sticker.

eranskor *adj.* sticky, adhesive *adj.* contagious.

eransle *adj.* sticky, adhesive.

eranspen *n.* addition, appendix, supplement.

eranste *n.* act of adding to.

erantsi *v.i.* to adhere, to stick. *v.t.* to aggregate, to add to. *v.t./v.i.* to contaminate, to infect, to catch, to contract (an illness).

erantzi *v.t.* to undress, to strip, to take off.

erantzuki *n.* reprimand, reproach.

erantzukizun *n.* responsibility.

erantzukoi *adj.* fond of answering. *adj.* pert, saucy, impudent.

erantzule *n.* answerer, respondent.

erantzun *v.t.* to answer, to respond, to reply; to pay. *n.* answer, response, reply. *v.t.* to fulfill, to accomplish.

erantzunbide *n.* way of answering, answer.

erantzunezin *adj.* unanswerable, irrefutable.

erantzunezinezko *adj.* unanswerable, irrefutable.

erantzungabe *adj.* unanswered.

erantzungarri *adj.* answerable.

erantzunkizun *n.* responsibility, obligation.

erantzunkor *adj.* fond of answering, responsive.

erantzunzale *adj.* fond of answering, responsive.

erantzute *n.* act of answering.

eraoneko *adj.* courteous, polite, correct. *adj.(fig.)* honest.

eraonez *adv.* courteously, with moderation. *adv.* honestly.

erara *prep.* in the way of, like, way.

erasan *v.t.* to cause to say, to make (someone) say. *v.t.* to attack, to assail, to charge. *v.t.* to influence, to affect.

erasgarri *adj.* adhesive; addable.

erasketa *n.* adhesion; sticking. *n.* addition, supplement.

eraskor *adj.* sticky, adhesive. *adj.* contagious.

eraso *v.t.* to attack, to rush on, to assault, to charge. *n.* attack. *v.t.* to serve the mass.

erasoaldi *n.* attack, assault, offensive, aggression. **Bigarren erasoaldian hil zuten.** They killed him in the second attack.

erasoera *n.* order of attack, way of attacking.

erasoezin *adj.* inexpugnable, resistant, impregnable.

erasogaitz *adj.* impregnable, unconquerable, difficult to attack, inexpugnable.

erasogarri *adj.* vulnerable, conquerable.

erasoka *adv.* attacking, rushing (on).

erasoketa *n.* attack, assault, offensive, aggression.

erasokor *adj.* aggressive, attacking, vehement, impetuous.

erasotasun *n.* aggressiveness, impulsiveness, impetuousness.

erasotzaile *n.* attacker, assailant. *adj.* aggressive, offensive.

erasoz *adv.* offensively, aggressively.

eraspen *n.* inclination, tendency. *n.* affection, fondness, attachment. *n.* addition, aggregation.

eratasun *n.* moderation, composure.

eratorkin *n.* derivative.

eratorle *adj.* derived (from).

eratormen *n.* derivation, deduction.

eratorpen *n.* derivation, deduction.

eratorri *v.t.* to make (someone) come. *v.i.* to derive, to deduce.

eratsu *adj.* moderate, composed, polite.

eratu *v.t.* to prepare. *v.t.* to organize, to put in order.

eratzaile *n.* organizer. *adj.* component.

eratzan *v.t.* to lay (something or someone) down; to knock over, to overthrow.

erauntsi *n.* torrential rain, violent storm. *v.i.* to be doing (something), to be occupied with. *v.i.* to talk a lot. *v.t.* to slam (a door). *v.t.* to knock down (fruit from trees).

erauntsitsu *adj.* stormy.

erausi *v.t.* to chat, to murmur; to gossip. *n.* murmuring. *v.t.* to bark; to low (cattle). *n.* barking; lowing (cattle).

erausle *n.* murmurer, chatter, gossiper. *adj.* murmuring; talkative, gossipy.

erauste *n.* act of murmuring, gossiping, talking.

erauzgailu *n.* extractor.

erauzgarri *adj.* eradicable.

erauzi *v.t.* to seize, to take, to extract. *v.t.* to shake down the fruit; to remove the grain from.

erauzketa *n.* extraction, removal,

eradication. *n.* demolition.

erauzle *n.* remover, extractor.

erauzpen *n.* extraction, removal, eradication.

erauztaldi *n.* extraction, eradication.

erauzte *n.* extraction, removal.

erauztezin *adj.* ineradicable.

eraz *prep.* according to, like. *adv.* properly, formally, adequately, appropriately. *adv.* right side out.

erazagutu *v.t.* to reveal, to make known.

-erazi *(gram.)* Suffix which signifies to make (someone) do (something), to cause (someone) to do (something). **Edanerazi.** To make (someone) drink.

erazketa *n.* act of undressing.

erazko *adj.* convenient, appropriate, opportune.

eraztun *n.* ring.

eraztunbegi *n.* interior part of a ring.

eraztundu *v.t.* to put on a ring.

eraztuneztatu *v.t.* to form into rings.

eraztuntsu *adj.* made of rings.

eraztuntxo *n.(dim.)* little ring.

erbatz *n.* wood chip, sliver.

erbestaldi *n.* time of exile, exile, expatriation.

erbeste *n.* foreign country. *n.* exile.

erbesteko *n.* foreigner, immigrant. *adj.* exiled, expatriated.

erbesteraketa *n.* exile, expatriation.

erbesterapen *n.* expatriation, exile.

erbesteratu *v.t.* to exile, to expatriate. *v.i.* to emigrate, to go abroad. *v.i.* to go into exile.

erbestetar *adj.* foreign, exotic.

erbestetasun *n.* alienation, foreignness.

erbestetu *v.i.* to go into exile. *v.t.* to expatriate, to exile.

erbi *n.(zool.)* hare.

erbikari *adj.* hare.

erbiki *n.* meat of the hare, piece of hare meat.

erbikume *n.(dim.)* baby hare.

erbinude *n.(zool.)* weasel.

erbioin *n.* hare track(s).

erbitalari *n.* hunter of hares.

erbitan ibili *v.i.* to hunt hares, to go hare hunting.

erbitara joan *v.i.* to go hare hunting.

erbiti *n.* place of hares.

erbitzar *n.(augm.)* large hare.

erbizakur *n.* hare-hunting dog.

erbizale *adj.* hare-hunting.

erbiztatu *v.t.* to restock with hares.

erdaindu *v.t.* to circumcise.

erdaingabe *adj.* uncircumcised.

erdainketa *n.* circumcision.

erdainkuntza *n.* circumcision.

erdal *adj.* foreign.

erdal- Used in compound words. Var. of *erdara*.

erdaldun *n.* non-Basque speaker. *adj.* non-Basque speaking. *n.* Spanish or

French person, foreigner.

erdaldundu *v.i./v.t.* to become alienated from Basque culture, to become estranged from Basque culture.

erdalduntzaile *adj.* fond of foreign culture.

erdalerri *n.* foreign country, country where Spanish or French is spoken.

erdalerriko *adj.* belonging to a foreign country, especially France or Spain.

erdal herri *n.* non-Basque-speaking country, foreign country (especially France or Spain).

erdalkeria *n.* excessive fondness of foreign things, xenomania.

erdaltzale *adj.* fond of the foreign, xenophile.

erdaltzalekeria *n.* excessive fondness of the foreign.

erdaltzaletasun *n.* fondness for foreign things, state of being fond of the foreign.

erdara *n.* foreign language, language other than Basque. *n.* Spanish or French language.

erdarakada *n.* foreign expression, barbarism.

erdaratu *v.t.* to translate into a non-Basque language (usually into Spanish or French).

erdaratzaile *n.* translator of Basque into a foreign language.

erdaraz *adv.* in a foreign language (especially Spanish or French).

erdarazko *adj.* foreign (especially Spanish or French).

erdein *n.* disdain, contempt.

erdeinagarri *adj.* disdainable, contemptible, despicable.

erdeinagarritu *v.t.* to disdain, to hold in contempt.

erdeinari *n.* despiser, scorner, contemner.

erdeinatu *v.t.* to disdain, to scorn, to despise. *v.t.* to bore.

erdeinatzaile *adj.* disdainful, scornful.

erdeinu *n.* scorn, contempt, disdain.

erdeinu egin *v.t.* to despise, to scorn, to disdain.

erdeinuz *adv.* disdainfully, scornfully.

erdera *n.* foreign language; Spanish; French.

erdera-merdera *n.* poorly spoken Spanish or French.

erderamordoilo *n.* jargon, gibberish in a non-Basque language.

erdi *n.* center, middle. *adj.* semi, half, central. *adv.* almost.

erdi- Used in compound words.

erdiageri *v.i.* to half-appear, to appear in part.

erdialde *n.* central part, midsection.

erdialdeko *adj.* central, of the center.

erdialdi *n.* time of birth.

erdian *prep.* in the middle of, in the center.

erdiarazi *v.t.* to cause to give birth.

Erdi Aro *n.* Middle Age(s).

erdiarteko *adj.* intermediate.

erdiazal *n.(anat.)* mesoderm.

erdibana *adv.* in half.

erdibanatu *v.t.* to divide, to cut in half.

erdibeltz *adj.* mulatto.

erdiberdin *adv.* similarly, almost in the same way. *adj.* similar, almost equal.

erdiberotu *v.i.* to be warm, to be almost warm.

erdiberri *adj.* (woman) who recently gave birth. *adj.* half-new, almost new.

erdibete *adj.* half full.

erdibide *n.* middle road, middle ground; compromise.

erdibideko *adj.* intermediate. *n.* median.

erdibi egin *v.t.* to divide in two, to halve. *v.i.* to split in two.

erdibigarri *adj.* divisible into two.

erdibiketa *n.* partition, division in two.

erdibildu *v.t.* to centralize.

erdibiribil *adj.* semicircular.

erdibitu *v.t.* to cut in two. *v.i.* to split in two. *v.t.* to divide (something) between two (people, etc.). *v.i.(fig.)* to be emotionally upset, to break (heart).

erdibitzaile *n.* cutter, divider in two. *n.* bisector.

erdibizi *adj.* barely alive.

erdibokale *n.* semivowel.

erdibusti *adj.* half wet, damp.

erdiedan *adj.* half-drunk.

erdiegin *v.t.* to do partially (to build, to bake, to boil, etc.). *adj.* half-done (half-baked, half-built, partially boiled, etc.), unfinished.

erdiegosi *v.i./v.t.* to half-boil, to parboil. *adj.* half-boiled.

erdi-erdiko *adj.* central, perfectly centered.

erdiero *adj.* half-crazy.

erdierotu *v.i.* to be half-crazy, to go half-crazy.

erdieskor *adj.* acquisitive.

erdiesna *adv.* half-awake, sleepy.

erdiespen *n.* attainment, acquisition.

erdiespide *n.* way of obtaining.

erdiestali *v.t.* to half-cover. *adj.* half-covered.

erdietan *adv.* half of the time(s). *adv.* half past.

erdietsi *v.t.* to obtain, to get, to acquire.

erdigor *adj.* half-deaf, hard-of-hearing.

erdigordin *adj.* half-raw.

erdigune *n.* center, central point.

erdihil *adj.* half-dead. *v.t.* to almost kill. *v.i.* to almost die. *v.t./v.i. (fig.)* to deaden.

erdika *n.* half. *adv.* half.

erdikara *n.* labor pain, contraction.

erdikari *n.(geom.)* bisector.

erdikatu *v.t.* to cut in two. *v.i.* to reduce to half, to reduce by half.

erdiki *n.* half.

erdikide *n.* participant, sharer, partner.

erdikin *n.* half, almost half. *n.* fragment.

erdiko *adj.* central, centric. *adj.* intermediate. *n.* intermediary. *n.* center (sport). *n.(geom.)* median.

erdikoi *adj.* centralist, fond of the center.

erdikoitasun *n.* centrality, centralism.

erdikusi *v.t.* to see imperfectly, to see vaguely, to catch a glimpse of.

erdilari *n.* centrist, centralist. *n.* center (sports).

erdilo *adj./adv.* half-asleep.

erdilokartu *v.t.* to fall half-asleep.

erdilotan *adv.* half-asleep.

erdimaila *n.* average, mean.

erdi-merdi *adv.* in a mediocre manner.

erdimin *n.* labor pain.

erdimintzatu *v.i.* to stutter, to stammer, to babble.

erdimintzo *n.* stuttering, stammering, babbling.

erdimozkor *adj.* half-drunk.

erdimozkortu *v.i.* to become half-drunk.

erdimuin *n.* nucleus, core.

erdineurri *n.* average.

erdioharmen *n.* semiconsciousness.

erdiohartu *adj.* half-conscious, semiconscious.

erdiondo *n.* time after giving birth.

erdiondoko *adj.* near the center. *adj.* having recently given birth.

erdiondore *n.* time after giving birth.

erdioso *adj.* half-complete, incomplete.

erdipurdi *adj.* mediocre. *adv.* in a mediocre manner.

erdipurdika *adv.* in a mediocre manner, so-so, not very well. *adv.* hardly.

erdipurdiko *adj.* mediocre, rather bad.

erdipurdizka *adv.* in a mediocre manner.

erdiragarri *adj.* heartrending, tearing; blood-curdling (fear).

erdiraketa *n.* centralization.

erdirakoi *adj.* centralist.

erdirakoitasun *n.* centralism.

erdirakor *adj.* concentric. *adj.* moving, emotional.

erdirapen *n.* centralization. *n.* pain, sorrow, affliction.

erdiratu *v.i.* to come to the middle, to go to the middle. *v.t.* to bring (something) to the middle, to put in the middle. *v.i.* to cut in half; to break (one's heart).

erdiratzaile *n.* centralizer. *adj.* centralizing.

erdirazale *adj.* centralizing.

erdireki *v.t./v.i.* to partially open, to be ajar, to be partially open.

erdisendatu *v.i./v.t.* to heal partially. *adj.* partially healed.

erditaldi *n.* time of giving birth, labor.

erditik *adv.* through, from the middle,

through the middle, in the middle, of the middle.

erditoki *n.* center. *n.* place to give birth.

erditsu *adj.* half-blind.

erditu *v.i./v.t.* to give birth.

erditxo *adj.(dim.)* half.

erditzaile *n.* midwife.

erditzal *n.* half-darkness, penumbra.

erditzali *v.i./v.t.* to partially turn off, to dim (lights), to turn down (an appliance).

erditzapen *n.* childbirth, labor.

erdiz *adv.* partially.

erdizabaldu *v.t./v.i.* to open part way; to be partially open, to be ajar.

erdizabalik *adv.* partially open, ajar.

erdizka *adv.* in two equal parts, in half, partially.

erdizkako *adj.* half and half.

erdizkatu *v.t.* to cut in half.

erdizoratu *v.i.* to be half-crazy.

erdizoro *adj.* half-crazy.

erdutu *v.i.* to come. Defective verb usually used in the imperative. **Erdu hona!** Come here!

ere *conj.* too, as well, also, even. Always follows the word it refers to. **Ni ere bai.** Me, too. *conj.* neither, not even; either. **Zu ere ez zara gelditu.** Not even you have remained. *conj.* though, although. **Ahalegin guztiak eginda ere ez dut lortuko.** Although I did my best, I have not succeeded.

eredu *n.* model, ideal, example.

eredugarri *adj.* typical, representative, exemplary. *n.* model, ideal.

eredugile *n.* modeler.

eredulan *n.* model, sculpture, statue.

eredura *prep.* according to.

eredutasun *n.* exemplariness, outstanding quality.

ereduz *prep.* according to, like.

ereduzko *adj.* exemplary, ideal.

ereduztatu *v.t.* to mold, to model, to fashion; to fit, to adapt.

ereile *n.* sower.

erein *v.t.* to sow.

ereinaro *n.* time for sowing.

ereindako *adj.* sowed.

ereindura *n.* sowing, planting.

ereingailu *n.* machine for sowing.

ereingarri *adj.* ready for sowing.

ereingiro *n.* time for sowing.

ereinketa *n.* sowing.

ereinlur *n.* land prepared for sowing.

ereinmakina *n.* machine for sowing.

ereinotz *n.(bot.)* laurel.

ereinotzar *n.(bot.)* laurel.

ereinozko *adj.* lauraceous.

ereinoztatu *v.t.* to crown with a laurel wreath.

ereinoztu *v.t.* to crown with a laurel wreath.

ereintza *n.* sowing, seeding.

ereintzale *n.* sower, seeder. *adj.*

sowing.

ereite n. act of sowing, seeding.

eremu n. wasteland, wilderness, desert; moor, heath. n. piece of land, tract of land. n. area, space, zone, sector.

eremueta n. wilderness area.

eremutar n. hermit.

eremutoki n. place with one or more hermitages.

eremutu v.i. to turn into wasteland, to become depopulated.

eremuzale adj. fond of deserts, fond of wastelands.

ereserki n. hymn; anthem.

eresi n. elegy.

eresiazko adj. elegiac.

eresmintz n. record, phonograph record.

ereti n. occasion, moment.

ergel adj. imbecilic, idiotic, foolish.

ergelaldi n. stupidity.

ergeldu v.i. to become senile, to go crazy, to become foolish.

ergeldura n. senility.

ergelkeria n. foolishness, stupidity, nonsense, folly.

ergelkerizko adj. foolish, silly, stupid.

ergelki adv. foolishly, stupidly.

ergeltasun n. foolishness, stupidity, imbecility.

ergi n. bull calf.

ergizko n.(dim.) small bull calf.

eri- n. sickness, illness. adj. sick, ill. n.(anat.) finger.

eri- Used in compound words. Derived from eri, illness; finger.

erialdi n. period of illness, bout of illness.

eriarazi v.t. to make (someone) ill.

eriatal n. phalanx, finger bone.

eriauto n. ambulance.

eriazterketa n. dactyloscopy, study of fingerprints.

eriazterpen n.(med.) diagnosis.

eribeila n. vigil, night vigil with a sick person.

eribeilatu v.t. to maintain a vigil over a sick person.

eribera adj. sickly, ailing.

eribizkar n. knuckle, finger joint.

eriekarle adj. pathogenic, causing disease.

erietxe n. hospital.

erigarri adj. unhealthy, noxious, pathogenic.

erihezur n.(anat.) bone of the finger.

erikoi adj. sickly, ailing.

erikoitu v.i. to become sickly.

erikor adj. noxious, unhealthy, ailing.

erikortasun n. morbidity, sickness, disease.

erikortu v.i. to be sickly, to be ailing.

erimami n. fingertip, pad of the finger.

erimoko n. fingertip, extremity of the finger.

erion v.i. to spill, to pour, to leak. n.

spill, leak.

eriongarri adj. pourable, flowable.

eripunta n. fingertip, extremity of the finger.

erisortzaile adj. pathogenic, causing disease.

eritasun n. sickness, state of being sick.

eritegi n. infirmary, sanitarium, hospital.

eritegizai n. hospital administrator. n. nurse.

eritsu adj. sick, ill, sickly.

eritu v.i. to become sick, to fall ill, to get sick.

eritxiki n.(anat.) little finger, pinky.

eritzale adj. pathogenic, causing disease.

eritzi n. opinion. v.t. to think, to have an opinion. v.t. to call, to name.

erixka adj. sick, ill.

erizahar adj. chronically sick, invalid.

erizahartasun n. quality of being chronically ill.

erizain n. nurse, intern, medical assistant.

erizaindegi n. infirmary, sanitarium, hospital.

erizaintza n. nursing profession, nursing career.

erizaintzaile n. nurse.

erizgarri adj. opinionable, thought-provoking.

erizkide n. person of the same opinion. adj. unanimous.

erizkidetasun n. unanimity.

erizkidetu v.i. to agree with someone, to be of the same opinion.

erizle n. one who thinks, one who has an opinion.

erizpen n. opinion, judgment.

erizpide n. criterion, criteria.

erkaezin adj. incomparable.

erkaketa n. comparison.

erkatu v.t. to compare, to parallel.

erki n.(bot.) linden tree.

erkide n. associate, comrade, partner. Contr. of erdi + kide. adj. common, general. adj. comparable to.

erkidego n. partnership, association; community.

erkidetasun n. partnership; relationship, communication.

erkidetu v.i. to associate, to become partners.

erkidetza n. partnership, consortium.

erkin adj. slender, frail, wasted away, gaunt, emaciated.

erkinaldi n. slenderness, frailness, gauntness, emaciation.

erkintasun n. gauntness, emaciation.

erkitu v.i. to weaken, to grow tired, to become emaciated. adj. weak, weakened, emaciated, frail.

erla- Used in compound words. Derived from erle, bee.

erlaberritu v.i. to swarm (bees).

erlabio n.(zool.) wasp.
erladun n. beekeeper, apiarist.
erlaitz n.(archit.) cornice.
erlaizketa n. entablature.
erlaizpe n.(archit.) architrave.
erlajaun n. beekeeper, apiarist.
erlakume n.(zool.) young bee.
erlalfer n.(zool.) drone bee.
erlama n.(zool.) queen bee.
erlamando n.(zool.) bumblebee, drone (bee). n.(coll.) idler, loafer.
erlamordo n. swarm of bees.
erlantz n. shine, glare, glow.
erlategi n. beehive, apiary.
erlateria n. group of bees, swarm of bees.
erlatibitate n.(phys.) relativity.
erlatibo adj.(gram.) relative.
erlatiboki adv. relatively.
erlatibotasun n. relativity.
erlatoki n. apiary.
erlatxori n.(zool.) bee-eater.
erlatxorta n. swarm of bees.
erlauntza n. hive, beehive.
erlazain n. beekeeper, apiculturist, apiarist.
erlazaintza n. beekeeping.
erlazale adj. fond of bees.
erlazio n. relationship.
erlaziokera n. way of relating to others.
erlazionatu v.i. to be related. v.t. to connect, to relate.
erlazulo n. cell of the honeycomb.
erlaztu v.i. to become hoarse.
erle n.(zool.) bee.
erlepilo n. swarm of bees.
erletalde n. group of bees, swarm of bees.
erletxe n. hive, beehive.
erletxo n.(dim.) little bee.
erlijio n. religion.
erlijioetsai n. enemy of religion. adj. antireligious.
erlijiogabe adj. irreligious.
erlijiogabekeria n. irreligiousness, impiety.
erlijiogabeko adj. irreligious.
erlijiogabetasun n. irreligiousness, impiety.
erlijiogabez adv. irreligiously.
erlijiogabezia n. irreligion, impiety.
erlijiokeria n. false religiosity, false piety.
erlijiokide n. person of the same religion.
erlijiokoi adj. very religious.
erlijiokontrako adj. antireligious.
erlijiosgo n. religious state.
erlijioski adv. religiously.
erlijioso n. friar.
erlijiotasun n. religiousness, religiosity.
erlijioz adv. religiously.
erlijiozale adj. pious, fond of religion.
erlijiozaletasun n. religiousness, piety.
erlijiozko adj. religious.
erliki n. relic.

erlikikutxa n. shrine, reliquary.
erlikiontzi n. reliquary, shrine.
erlikitegi n. shrine, reliquary.
erlojari n. watchmaker, clockmaker.
erlojorratz n. hand of a clock, hand of a watch.
erloju n. watch, clock.
erlojudenda n. watchmaker's shop, clockmaker's shop.
erlojugile n. watchmaker, clockmaker.
erlojugin n. watchmaker, clockmaker.
erlojugintza n. clockmaking, watchmaking. n. manufacture of clocks or watches.
erlojukutxa n. watchcase.
erlojusaltzaile n. clock seller, watch seller.
erlojutegi n. clock shop, watch shop.
ermita n. hermitage.
ermitari n. hermit.
ermitaritza n. life of a hermit.
erna- Used in compound words. Derived from *erne* meaning reproduction of plants and animals.
ernaberri adj. newborn; newly budded. n.(anat.) embryo, fetus.
ernaberritu v.i. to resprout, to bud again, to regenerate.
ernaberritzaile adj. regenerating, renewing.
ernaberrizko adj. embryonic.
ernaberrizte n. act of regenerating.
ernagailu n. inseminating device.
ernagarri adj. stimulating, exciting. n. stimulant, generator.
ernakor adj. stimulating, invigorating, exciting; germinative.
ernakuntza n. germination, fertility, pregnancy.
ernalarazi v.t. to breed animals.
ernalaro n. mating season, breeding season.
ernalbide n.(anat.) genitalia, sexual organ.
ernaldi n.(med.) gestation, pregnancy. n. germination.
ernaldizko adj. germinal; pertaining to pregnancy.
ernaldu v.t. to breed animals, to impregnate animals. v.i. to become pregnant.
ernaldura n. gestation, pregnancy, procreation.
ernalgai adj. potent, fertile, able to procreate.
ernalgarri adj. fertile, fecund, capable of fecundation.
ernalindar n. capacity for reproduction, fertileness, fecundity.
ernalketa n. mating of animals, fecundation, impregnation.
ernalkin n.(anat.) genitalia, sexual organs.
ernalmen n. fecundity, capacity for breeding.
ernalmin n. labor pains.
ernaltsu adj. fertile, very fecund.

ernaltzaile adj. fertilizing, reproducing.
ernaltzaro n. gestation.
ernaltzulo n.(anat.) genital orifice, vagina.
ernamuin n.(bot.) bud, germ.
ernamuindu v.i. to bud, to put forth shoots.
ernamuindura n. germination, sprouting.
ernamuinezko adj. germinal.
ernamuinkor adj. gemmiparous, producing or reproducing by buds.
ernamuintsu adj. full of buds.
ernamuintxo n.(dim.) gemmule, small bud.
ernani n. (zool.) swallow.
ernarazi v.t. to germinate, to cause to sprout. v.t. to breed animals, to inseminate. v.t. to activate; to excite.
ernarazle n. germinator. adj. fecund, fertile. n.(fig.) animator, enlivener.
ernarazpen n. germination, sprouting. n. excitement, stimulation.
ernari n. pregnant animal.
ernaritu v.i./v.t. to breed, to inseminate, to impregnate animals. v.i. to become pregnant.
ernatu v.t./v.i. to enliven, to excite; to become excited, to become lively. v.i. to germinate, to sprout. v.i. to become pregnant. v.t. to pollinate.
ernatzaile adj. exciting, enlivening, germinating, generating.
erne v.i. to germinate, to sprout. adj. alive, alert, attentive. v.t. to conceive, to engender. n. bud.
ernealdi n. period of germination. n. vigil, period of alertness.
erne egon v.i. to be alert, to stay awake.
ernegagarri adj. bothersome, irksome, annoying.
ernegaldi n. fit of temper.
ernegamendu n. anger, fit of temper.
ernegarazi v.t. to anger, to make angry.
ernegari n. short-tempered person, ill-tempered person. adj. renegade.
ernegarri adj. fructiferous, fruit-bearing; fruitful.
ernegatu v.t. to anger, to make angry. v.i. to become angry, to get angry. v.t. to rebel.
ernegatzaile adj. annoying, vexing.
ernegu n. rage, anger, vexation.
ernejarri v.i. to be alert, to be vigilant. v.t. to alert.
ernekera n. way of budding, way of sprouting.
erneketa n. germination, sprouting, budding.
erneki adv. attentively, actively, diligently.
erneleku n. seedbed, seed plot.
ernerazgarri adj. fertilely, fruitfully.
ernetasun n. liveliness. n. vigilance, alertness.

ero n./adj. crazy, mad, demented.
-ero (gram.) Suffix meaning all, every, periodicity. **Egunero.** Every day.
eroaldi n. period of insanity, craziness.
eroan v.t. to take, to carry, to transport.
eroetxe n. insane asylum, madhouse.
erogarri adj. maddening.
erogo n. craziness, insanity.
erohaize adj. slightly crazy.
erokeria n. dementia, insanity, craziness, foolishness. n. foolish remark.
erokeriazko adj. insane, demented, mad.
eroki adv. insanely, crazily. adv. foolishly.
eromen n. insanity, dementia, craziness.
eroraldi n. decline, fall, drop; depression. n. decadence. n. weakness, prostration, decline. n. ruin, fall (moral).
eror arazi v.t. to cause to fall, to destroy, to demolish.
erorarazle n. one who demolishes, destroyer, overthrower; scandalmonger.
erorbera adj. liable to fall; deciduous. adj. backsliding, relapsing.
erorberri adj. newly fallen.
erorbide n. cause of a fall, occasion of a fall; danger. n. scandal, bad example, bad influence, cause of a (moral) fall.
erorerrez adj. unstable, tending to fall easily.
erorgailu n. parachute.
erorgarri adj. apt to fall; risky, dangerous.
erorgarriki adv. riskily, dangerously.
erori v.i. to fall, to fall out, to fall down, to fall into; to drop. v.i. to grow weak, to succumb, to die. adj. fallen.
eroriko n. fall, act of falling (physically or morally).
eroritasun n. falling; depression. n. prostration.
erorka adv. stumbling, falling, staggering.
erorkaldi n. fall, act of falling.
erorkera n. way of falling; falling.
erorketa n. fall, downfall, collapse, decline.
erorkor adv. liable to fall, likely to fall, decadent; deciduous. adj. weak (morally), liable to fall (into sin, etc.)
erorkortasun n. tendency to fall; fragileness, fragility. n. deciduousness.
erorpen n. ruin, downfall, fall.
erorpide n. cause of a fall, occasion of a fall.
erorte n. act of falling.
erorti adj. liable to fall. adj. backsliding, relapsing.
erortoki n. slide, slippery place,

precipice, cliff.

erortza n. falling.

eros- Used in compound words. Derived from *erosi*, to buy.

eros-ahalmen n. purchasing power.

erosalketa n. sales, purchase and sale.

erosarazi v.t. to cause (someone) to buy, to sell.

erosberri adj. newly bought, newly purchased.

erosendagile n. physician in an asylum, alienist.

erosgai n. merchandise, goods, wares.

erosgarri adj. purchasable. adj.(fig.) bribable.

erosi v.t. to buy, to purchase. v.t. to bribe.

eroska adj. slightly crazy, eccentric, somewhat foolish.

eroskera n. purchase, way of buying.

eroskeria n. bribery.

erosketa n. purchase.

eroskide n. fellow buyer.

eroskin n. purchase.

erosle n. buyer, purchaser, customer.

eroso adj. comfortable. adv. comfortably, easily.

erosokeria n. excess comfort.

erosoki adv. comfortably, easily.

erosotasun n. comfort, comfortableness.

erospen n. purchase, acquisition. n. redemption; rescue.

erosta n. mourning, grieving, complaining, lamenting.

erostari n. mourner, weeper. n. buyer.

erostale adj. complaining, crying, weeping.

erostatu v.i. to lament, to mourn, to complain.

eroste n. act of purchasing.

erostetxe n. store, shop.

erostezin adj. impossible to buy.

erostun n. buyer, purchaser, customer.

erotasun n. insanity, dementia, craziness.

erotegi n. insane asylum, madhouse.

erotiko adj. erotic.

erotismo n. eroticism.

erotu v.i. to go insane, to go crazy. v.t. to drive (someone) crazy.

erozain n. guard or attendant in a lunatic asylum.

erpe n. claw.

erpekada n. blow with a paw or claw, scratch.

erpekatu v.t. to claw, to scratch.

erpetsu adj. having many claws.

erpil adj. weak (people, things).

erpildu v.i. to grow weak, to grow thin.

erpildura n. weakness.

erpilkor adj. weakly, weakling.

erpilkortu v.i. to develop a tendency for weakness.

erpiltasun n. weakness.

erpin n. vertex, summit, top, pinnacle.

erpintsu adj. pointed.

erpuru n.(anat.) thumb.

erraboila n.(bot.) bulb.

erraboiladun adj. bulbous.

erraboilatsu adj. bulbous.

erradikal adj. radical, extreme.

erradikalismo n. radicalism, extremism.

erradikalki adv. radically.

errai n.(anat.) viscera, bowels.

erraietako adj. visceral, abdominal.

erraiki n. entrail(s), piece of viscera or bowel.

errail n. rail, track.

erraildu v.t. to lay rails; to put (a train) back on the rails.

erraile n. speaker, talker.

erraimin n.(med.) abdominal pain, intestinal pain.

errain n. daughter-in-law.

errainazti n. soothsayer, haruspex.

errainaztikeria n. augury using the entrails of birds.

errainu n. sun ray.

errainukada n. sparkle, sunbeam.

errainuketa n. sunlight, radiation.

errainutsu adj. radiant.

errainutu v.i. to shine (sun), to radiate sunshine.

errakuntza n. error, mistake, equivocation.

erralde n. five kilo weight. Used to weigh cattle.

erraldi n. batch of bread, etc. baked at the same time.

erraldoi n. giant, colossus.

erramin n. pain or disease of the teat.

erramu n.(bot.) laurel; palm. n. oar.

erramulari n. rower.

erran v.t. to say, to tell. n. saying, proverb. v.t. to call, to name.

erranak n.(pl.) sayings.

erranarazi v.t. to cause (someone) to say, to make (someone) confess.

erranarazle n. person who makes (someone) confess.

erranbide n. means of saying, telling; cause for gossip.

erranezin adj. unspeakable, inexpressible, unmentionable, unutterable.

errangarri adj. worth saying.

erranka adv. by constantly saying.

erran-merran n. gossiping (usually used in plural).

errantxu n. ranch.

erranzahar n. old refrain.

errape n. udder.

errasti n.(bot.) field of broom, field of furze.

errasumin n. stinging, itching.

erratu v.i. to make a mistake.

erratz n. broom. n.(bot.) Spanish broom.

erratzaga n. land covered with Spanish

broom.
erratzar *n.(augm.)* large broom.
erratz-belar *n.(bot.)* barberry bush.
erratzatu *v.t.* to sweep.
erratzaile *n.* sweeper, street cleaner.
erratzeztu *v.t.* to sweep.
errausgailu *n.* cremation oven, incinerator.
errausketa *n.* cremation, incineration.
errauskolore *adj.* ash-colored.
errauskutxatila *n.* cinerary urn.
errausle *n.* incinerator, cremator. *adj.* destructive, demolishing, pulverizing.
errauspen *n.* incineration, cremation. *n.* devastation.
erraustatu *v.t.* to cover with ashes.
erraustontzi *n.* ashtray.
erraustoki *n.* ash deposit; place where furnace ashes or stove ashes are dumped.
erraustu *v.t.* to incinerate, to burn, to cremate. *v.t.* to destroy, to annihilate.
erraustun *adj.* ashy.
errauts *n.* ash.
errautsezko *adj.* ashy, cinerary.
errautsi *v.t.* to pulverize, to destroy. *v.i.* to become dust, to become pulverized.
errautsontzi *n.* ashtray.
errauztu *v.t.* to pulverize, to destroy.
erraz *adj.* easy. *adv.* easily.
errazionamendu *n.* rationing.
errazkada *n.* blow or swat with a broom.
errazkeria *n.* laxity, negligence.
errazketa *n.* act of sweeping.
errazki *adv.* easily, comfortably.
errazkile *n.* broom maker.
errazoi *n.* reason.
errazola *n.(bot.)* field of broom, field of furze.
errazpide *n.* easiness, facility.
erraztasun *n.* easiness, facility, comfortableness.
erraztatu *v.t.* to sweep.
erraztu *v.t.* to facilitate, to make easy.
erre *v.t.* to burn. *v.t.* to bake, to roast. *v.t.* to smoke. *v.i.* to be burned out.
erreabilitatu *v.t./v.i.* to rehabilitate.
erreabilitazio *n.* rehabilitation.
erreaktore *n.* reactor, atomic reactor.
erreakzio *n.* reaction.
erreakzionari *n.* reactionary.
erreakzionario *adj.* reactionary.
erreakzionatu *v.t.* to react.
erreakziozko *adj.* reactive.
erreal *n.* real (Spanish coin, quarter of a *peseta*).
errealdi *n.* burning, roasting, baking. *n.* batch, bread baked at one time. *n.(fig.)* impatience.
errealismo *n.* realism.
errealista *adj.* realistic.
errealitate *n.* reality.
errealizazio *n.* realization.
errealtasun *n.* realism.
errealtasuneza *n.* unreality.

errearazi *v.t.* to cause (someone) to burn.
errearin *adj.* half-baked.
errearindu *v.i./v.t.* to roast slightly, to toast slightly.
errebelar *n.(bot.)* cuckoopint, arum.
errebelatu *v.t.* to develop (film).
errebera *adj.* burnable. *adj.* irritable.
errebero *n.* milk just taken from the cow, fresh milk.
erreberri *adj.* just cooked; just burned, recently burned.
errebes *n.* backhand shot or throw in pelota. *adj.* gruff, brusque.
errebeska *adv.* inversely, in reverse; backhand (in sports).
errebestasun *n.* brusqueness, gruffness. *n.* ineptness, awkwardness, clumsiness.
errebista *n.* magazine.
erreboil *n.* root, bulb.
erreboilo *n.(zool.)* turbot.
erreboiltsu *adj.* rooty.
errebote *n.* specific play in the game of pelota; the place on the court where this play is made.
errebolber *n.* revolver.
errediza *n.* piece of furniture.
erredizatu *v.t.* to furnish, to supply a house with furniture.
erredola *n.* coat-of-arms, escutcheon. *n.* shield.
erredoleztatu *v.t.* to protect with a shield, to shield.
erredura *n.* burn. *n.(fig.)* restlessness.
erreezin *adj.* not flammable, noncombustible, not burnable.
erreferentzia *n.* reference.
erreformagaitz *adj.* unreformable, difficult to reform.
erreformategi *n.* reformatory, reform school.
erreformista *adj.* reformist. *n.* reformer.
errefrau *n.* proverb, refrain, old saying.
erregai *n.* combustible.
erregailu *n.* burner.
erregaitz *adj.* not flammable, noncombustible.
erregalatu *v.t.* to present with, to give a present to.
erregalia *n.* present, gift.
erregaliz *n.* licorice.
erregalu *n.* present, gift.
erregarri *n.* combustible matter. *adj.* ardent, burnable, combustible, flammable.
erregarriki *adv.* ardently, passionately, burningly.
errege *n.* king.
erregealaba *n.* king's daughter, princess.
erregealdeko *adj.* monarchist, monarchic.
erregealdi *n.* dynastic period, reign.
erregeantzera *adv.* royally, regally.
erregeaulki *n.* throne.

erregebide n. royal road; wide road, highway.

erregegai n. pretender to the throne, heir to the throne.

erregegisa adv. royally, regally.

erregego n. reign, position or office of a king.

erregegun n. Epiphany (January 6), Twelfth-night, Twelfth-day.

erregehilketa n. regicide, murder of a king.

erregehiltzaile n. person who commits regicide.

erregejatorri n. royal lineage, royal dynasty.

erregejauregi n. royal palace.

erregekeria n. misuse of royal power.

erregekide n. coregent.

erregekidetza n. coreign, joint rule.

erregekiro adv. majestically, royally, regally.

erregekontrako adj. antimonarchic, antiroyalist.

erregela n. rule, law.

erregeleinu n. royal lineage.

erregemakila n. royal scepter.

erregeorde n. regent, viceroy.

erregeordego n. regency, office of a viceroy.

erregeordetza n. regency, office of a viceroy.

erregeraile n. person who commits regicide.

erregeseme n. prince, son of the king.

erregetar adj. monarchist, royal.

erregetasun n. royalty, quality of being king, kingliness, regalness.

erregetiar adj. royal, monarchist.

erregetu v.i. to become king. v.t. to make (someone) king.

erregetxo n.(dim.) little king. n.(zool.) kinglet.

erregetza n. royalty, royal power.

erregexka n.(dim.) little king.

erregezale adj. monarchist, fond of the king.

erregezaletasun n. monarchism.

erregezko adj. royal, pertaining to the king.

erregina n. queen. n.(zool.) queen bee. n. queen (chess piece).

erregingai n. heiress to the throne.

erreginorde n. regent for the queen.

erregintasun n. royalty (referring to queen).

erregintza n. power of the queen.

erregio n. region.

erregioarteko adj. interregional.

erregioko adj. regional.

erregionalismo n. regionalism.

erregiozale adj. regionalist.

erregistratu v.t. to register.

erregistro n. register.

erregla n. ruler (measuring device).

erregosi v.t./v.i. to stew.

erregu n. request, petition. n. supplication.

erregugile n. supplicant, one who entreats, impetrator, one seeking a favor.

erreguka adv. by requesting, by praying.

erregukor adj. supplicating.

erregulaketa n. regulation.

erregular adj. regular, normal, average.

erregularizatu v.t. to regularize.

erregularki adv. regularly.

erregulatu v.t. to regulate.

erregulatzaile n. regulator.

erregutu v.t. to pray, to supplicate.

erregutzaile n. prayer, one who prays.

erreguz prep. at (someone's) request.

erreguzko adj. supplicatory, pleading.

erreinu n. kingdom.

erreinutar n. native of a kingdom.

erreka n. creek, brook, stream.

errekabide n. waterway, riverbed.

errekadu n. errand; message.

errekalde n. place next to a stream.

errekaratu v.i. to go to a stream, to get to a stream.

errekargu n. surcharge.

errekarri n. pebble.

errekasto n.(dim.) riverlet.

errekatxo n.(dim.) streamlet, rill, riverlet.

errekeitatu v.t. to care for the sick. v.t. to feed, to provide food for.

erreketa n. burning, fire.

erreketari n. pyromaniac, one who burns things.

erreki n. piece of roasted meat. n. burned item.

errekin n. combustible, fuel.

erreklamatu v.t. to claim, to demand.

erreklamo n. call, inducement.

erreklutaketa n. recruitment, year's draft.

erreklutatu v.t. to recruit.

errekondo n. riverside.

errekontxo! int. gracious! my goodness!

errekor adj. inflaming. adj. corrosive.

errelabe n. crematorium.

errelari n. burner; smoker.

errelebu n. relief, change of (the guard, work shift).

erreleku n. place of cooking or smoking. n. crematorium.

erremediaezinezko adj. irremediable, hopeless, incurable (disease).

erremediagaitz adj. difficult to remedy, hopeless.

erremediagarri adj. remediable.

erremediatu v.t. to remedy.

erremedio n. remedy, cure; solution.

errementaldegi n. blacksmith's shop.

errementari n. blacksmith.

errementeria n. the blacksmith's shop.

erremin n. burning, stinging. n.(fig.) resentment, misgiving.

erremindu v.i. to burn, to sting. v.i. to become resentful.

erremindura *n.* burning, stinging. *n.(fig.)* resentment, misgiving.
erreminez *adv.* excitedly. *adv.* bitingly, satirically.
erremingarri *adj.* biting, satirical. *adj.* irritating, aggressive.
erreminta *n.* tool.
erremintasun *n.* state of being resentful.
erreminteria *n.* collection of tools, set of tools.
erremintetxe *n.* tool box.
erremolatxa *n.(bot.)* beet.
erremolkatu *v.t.* to tow, to haul.
erremolkatzaile *n.* tow truck, tugboat.
erremolke *n.* towing, towage.
erremonte *n.* Basque game similar to jai alai.
erremusina *n.* alms, charity.
erremusinari *n.* almsgiver.
erremuska *n.* grumbling, growl.
erremuskada *n.* grumbling, growl.
erremuska egin *v.t.* to grumble, to growl.
erremuskatu *v.i.* to grumble, to growl.
errenazentista *adj.* Renaissance.
errenazimendu *n.* Renaissance.
errenboltsu *n.(econ.)* refund, repayment, reimbursement.
errenderi *n.* customs house.
errendimendu *n.* rendition, surrendering, yielding. *n.* efficiency.
errenditu *v.i./v.t.* to surrender, to yield.
errenta *n.* rent.
errentabilitate *n.(econ.)* profitability.
errentadore *n.* lessee, tenant, renter.
errentadun *n.* landlord, renter, one who lives off rents or rentals.
errentagabetu *v.t.* to break the lease of.
errentagarri *adj.* leasable, rentable. *adj.* profitable.
errentagarritasun *n.* rentability. *n.* profitability.
errentamendu *n.* leasing, renting.
errentapen *n.* renting, rental.
errentari *n.* renter, landlord or tenant.
errentatu *v.t.* to rent, to rent out.
errentatzaile *n.* renter, landlord.
erreopari *n.* burnt offering, holocaust.
erreparu *n.* objection.
errepide *n.* royal road; wide road, highway.
errepika *n.* repetition. *n.* tolling. *n.* refrain.
errepikagailu *n.* relay station (television or radio).
errepikagaitz *adj.* indisputable.
errepikagarri *adj.* reiterable, repeatable.
errepikakor *adj.* repetitive.
errepikan *adv.* tolling.
errepikari *n.* repeater, one who repeats.
errepikatu *v.t.* to repeat, to reiterate, to say again. *v.t.* to ring (bells).
errepikatzaile *n.* repeater, one who

repeats. *adj.* repetitive.
erreposki *adv.* slowly.
errepostu *n.* replacement, spare part.
errepresentagarri *adj.* representable.
errepresentaketa *n.* representation.
errepresentakor *adj.* representative.
errepresentapen *n.* representation.
errepresentatu *v.t.* to represent.
errepresentatzaile *n.* representative.
errepresentazio *n.* representation.
errepresio *n.* repression.
erreprodukzio *n.* reproduction.
errepublika *n.* republic.
errepublikar *adj.* republican.
erresaka *n.* undertow.
erreserba *n.* reserve.
erresinul *n.(zool.)* nightingale.
erresistentzia *n.* resistance.
erreskada *n.* line, row.
erreskadan *adv.* in line, one after the other, in a row.
errespetagaitz *adj.* difficult to respect.
errespetagarri *adj.* respectable.
errespetagarritasun *n.* respectability.
errespetatu *v.t.* to respect.
errespetu *n.* respect.
errespetugabeko *adj.* disrespectful.
errespetutsu *adj.* respectful.
errespetuz *adv.* respectfully.
errestatu *v.t.* to return (the ball in handball).
erresultatu *n.* result. *n.* score.
erresuma *n.* kingdom.
erresumin *n.* burning, stinging. *n.(fig.)* resentment, misgiving. *n.* constant pain, dull pain.
erresumindu *v.i.* to be irritated, to be inflamed. *v.i.* to become irritated, to be impatient.
erresumindura *n.* irritation, inflammation.
erresumingarri *adj.* irritating.
erreta *adj.* burnt, baked, roasted. *adj.(fig.)* burned out. *adj.* furious, highly irritated.
erretasun *n.* burn. *n.(fig.)* restlessness, impatience, uneasiness, anxiety.
erretaula *n.* altarpiece, retable.
erretegi *n.* spit, roasting jack, barbecue.
erreteila *n.* retiling, roof repairing.
erreteilari *n.* roof repairer.
erreteilatu *v.t.* to retile, to repair a roof.
erreten *n.* trench, drain, gutter. *n.* irrigation ditch.
erretenarri *n.* manhole cover, access to an underground ditch or drainage system.
erretendu *v.t.* to install rain gutters.
erretilu *n.* tray; platter.
erretina *n.(anat.)* retina.
erretiraro *n.* age of retirement.
erretiratu *v.i./v.t.* to retire.
erretiro *n.* retirement.
erretirodun *adj.* receiving a retirement income (person).

erretirosari *n.* retirement pension.
erretoki *n.* place for burning things. *n.* place for smoking.
erretolika *n.* argument. *n.* eloquence, verbosity, talkativeness. *n.* reprimand, scolding.
erretore *n.* main priest in the parish. *n.* head of a university, school or seminary.
erretorego *n.* position of the parish priest.
erretoretxe *n.* rectory.
erretoretza *n.* rector's post.
erretoregela *n.* rector's office (room).
erretorika *n.* rhetoric.
erretoriko *adj.* rhetorical.
erretororde *n.* vice-rector.
erretratari *n.* photographer.
erretratatu *v.t.* to photograph, to take a picture.
erretratatzaile *n.* photographer.
erretratu *n.* picture, photograph.
erretura *n.* burning, combustion.
erretxin *n.* resin. *adj.* burnt, incinerated. *adj.* touchy, fastidious, irritable.
erretxinaldi *n.* tantrum, fit of temper. *n.* season for tapping trees for sap or resin.
erretxinari *n.* resin tapper or extractor.
erretxinbera *adj.* irritable.
erretxindu *v.i.* to become irritated, to become exasperated. *v.t.* to irritate, to vex, to annoy.
erretxindura *n.* irritation, vexation, exasperation.
erretxintsu *adj.* resinous. *adj.* touchy, irritable.
erretzaile *n.* burner; smoker. *adj.* burning; smoking.
erretzapen *n.* burning, combustion.
erreuma *n.(med.)* rheumatism.
erreumadun *adj.* rheumatic.
erreumakontrako *adj.* antirheumatic.
erreumatismo *n.(med.)* rheumatism.
erreune *n.* burned patch.
erreusain *n.* burned smell.
erreusaindu *v.i.* to smell burned.
errezatu *v.t.* to pray, to supplicate.
errezauri *n.* burn (wound), burn injury.
errezelagarri *adj.* suspicious.
errezelatu *v.t.* to suspect, to distrust.
errezelu *n.* distrust, suspicion, misgiving.
errezeta *n.* prescription.
errezetagarri *adj.* prescribable.
errezetari *n.* prescriber.
errezetategi *n.* prescription book.
errezetatu *v.t.* to prescribe.
errezibimendu *n.* welcome, reception.
errezibu *n.* receipt.
errezu *n.* prayer.
erribera *n.* shore, bank.
errifa *n.* raffle; lottery.
errifatu *v.t.* to raffle, to raffle off.
errima *n.* rhyme.
errimatu *v.t.* to rhyme.

errimatzaile *n.* rhymer.
errime *adj.* hard, solid, strong. *adj.* skillful.
errinozero *n.(zool.)* rhinocerous.
erritmo *n.* rhythm, time, tempo; meter (verses).
errito *n.* rite.
erritozale *adj.* ritualist.
erro *n.* root; stem; cause, origin. *n.* tentacle. *n.* teat. *n.* frame jamb (of a door or window).
errodura *n.* settling in a place, taking root.
errogabe *adj.* rootless.
errogatiba *n.(eccl.)* public prayer, rogation.
erroi *n.(zool.)* crow.
erroitz *n.* crack, fissure; precipice.
erroiztu *v.i.* to fall down, to plunge.
errojale *adj.* root-eating.
errokatu *v.i.* to plant roots, to take root. *v.i.* to settle down, to become established in an area.
erroketa *n.* root system, web of roots.
errokimu *n.* rootlet, offshoot of a root.
errokoko *n./adj.* rococo.
errolda *n.* census. *n.* catalog.
erroldaketa *n.* cataloguing.
erroldatu *v.i.* to register, to enlist, to sign up. *v.t.* to catalog.
erroldatzaile *n.* census taker.
erromaneztapen *n.* romanization.
erromaneztatu *v.t./v.i.* to romanize.
erromaniko *adj.(arch.)* Romanesque.
erromantiku *adj.* romantic.
erromantizismo *n.* romanticism.
erromantzari *n.* writer of romances; balladeer, singer of ballads.
erromantze *n.* romance, lyric or narrative poem in octosyllabic meter with alternate lines in assonance.
erromantzegile *n.* writer of romances (poems).
erromantzesorta *n.* collection of romances (poems).
erromantzetegi *n.* collection of romances (poems).
erromantzidazle *n.* writer in a Romance language. *n.* writer of romances (poems).
erromatar. *adj./n.* Roman.
erromatarkuntza *n.* romanization.
erromatartu *v.t./v.i.* to romanize.
erromeria *n.* festival, picnic. *n.* pilgrimage.
erromerizale *adj.* fond of festivals.
erromero *n.(bot.)* rosemary bush.
erromes *n.* pilgrim.
erromesaldi *n.* pilgrimage.
erromeskeria *n.* begging, mendicity.
erromestalde *n.* group of pilgrims.
erromestasun *n.* indigence, extreme poverty.
erromin *n.* soreness or pain in the teat.
erromuskil *n.* small branch, twig, sprig.
erronda *n.* round of drinks. *n.* rounds (usually nocturnal trips from one bar

to another).

errondaila *n.* band of strolling musicians.

errondari *n.* one who makes the rounds of the taverns.

errondo *n.* grapevine stock. *n.* root.

erronka *n.* dispute, quarrel, argument.

erronkariera *n.* dialect of Roncal (has almost completely disappeared).

erronkatu *v.i.* to argue, to dispute.

erronkazale *n.* fond of challenges, fond of disputes.

errono *n.(dim.)* small root.

erropa *n.* clothes; laundry.

erropilo *n.* cluster of roots.

errosario *n.(R.C.Ch.)* rosary.

erroskila *n.* ring shaped pastry especially popular during Holy Week.

errosta *n.(bot.)* gentian.

errota *n.* mill.

errotabegi *n.* hole in the center of the millstone.

errotadi *n.* place where there are mills.

errotagin *n.(anat.)* molar.

errotaldi *n.* milling, grinding. *n.* time spent milling or grinding.

errotari *n.* miller.

errotaritza *n.* miller's job.

errotarri *n.* millstone.

errotasegailu *n.* milling machine.

errotatxo *n.(dim.)* small grinder for coffee, etc.

errotaxka *n.(dim.)* small grinder for coffee, etc.

errotazai *n.* miller.

errotazaintza *n.* miller's job.

errotik *adv.* basically, fundamentally.

errotiko *adj.* essential, basic.

errotsu *adj.* having many roots; having many tentacles. *adj.* robust, solid.

errotu *v.i.* to settle, to take root.

errozko *adj.* fundamental, basic, essential.

erroztapen *n.* taking root.

erroztatu *v.i.* to take root.

erru *n.* guilt, fault; mistake.

erru bota *v.t.* to blame.

errudun *adj.* guilty, culpable.

erru egin *v.t.* to err, to make a mistake.

errugabe *adj.* innocent, blameless.

errugabeki *adv.* innocently.

errugabeko *adj.* innocent, blameless.

errugabetasun *n.* innocence, blamelessness.

errugabetu *v.t.* to forgive, to excuse; to acquit.

erru garbitu *v.t.* to pay one's debt to society.

errukarri *adj.* worthy of compassion, pitiable.

errukarriro *adv.* sadly, sorrowfully.

errukarritu *v.i.* to become worthy of compassion.

erruki *n.* pity, compassion, mercy.

errukibera *adj.* compassionate, merciful.

errukide *n.* accomplice, accessory.

errukidetasun *n.* complicity.

errukidun *adj.* compassionate, merciful.

errukietxe *n.* house of charity (for orphans, poor people, etc.)

errukigabe *adj.* cruel, unmerciful, pitiless.

errukigabekeria *n.* cruelty, mercilessness.

errukigabeki *adv.* cruelly, unmercifully, pitilessly.

errukigabeko *adj.* cruel, unmerciful.

errukigabetu *v.i.* to become cruel, to be unmerciful, to be pitiless.

errukigintza *n.* act of mercy.

erruki izan *v.i.* to be compassionate, to have pity (on).

errukior *adj.* compassionate, merciful.

errukitasun *n.* compassionateness, mercifulness.

errukitsu *adj.* compassionate, merciful.

errukitu *v.i.* to become compassionate, to have pity on.

errukiz *adv.* compassionately, mercifully.

errukizko *adj.* merciful, compassionate, of mercy.

errule *adj.* oviparous, egg producing, laying (hens).

erruleta *n.* roulette.

errulota *n.* trailer.

errumes *n.* beggar.

errumeskeria *n.* mendicity, begging.

errun *v.t.* to lay eggs.

errunaldi *n.* egg laying.

errutaro *n.* egg-laying time, season.

errutasun *n.* culpability.

errutatu *v.t.* to inculpate, to blame, to accuse.

errute *n.* egg laying.

errutoki *n.* egg-laying place.

erruz *prep./adv.* by fault of; guiltily. *adv.* abundantly.

erruztatu *v.t.* to inculpate, to blame, to accuse.

ert- Used in compound words. Derived from *erdi* (half, mid-, center).

Ertafrika *n.(geog.)* Central Africa.

ertaldi *n.* childbirth, parturition.

Ertamerika *n.(geog.)* Central America.

ertaro *n.* season of parturition (animals), lambing or calving season.

Erteuropa *n.(geog.)* Central Europe.

erti *n.(neol.)* art.

ertz *n.* corner, edge, border; shore, bank.

ertzain *n.* police of the Basque government.

ertzaintza *n.* Basque police force.

ertzalde *n.* periphery.

ertzaldeko *adj.* peripheral.

ertzatu *v.t.* to marginalize, to put aside, to corner.

ertzedun *adj.* have corners, having edges, rough.

ertzeko *adj.* lateral, marginal, of the corner. *adj.* extreme, radical.

ertzeratu v.i. to approach the shore, bank or border.

esa- Used in compound words. Derived from *esan*, to say.

esaera n. saying, expression, refrain, maxim, idiom, proverb.

esaerabilduma n. collection of proverbs.

esaerasorta n. collection of proverbs.

esaeratsu adj. full of sayings, witty. adj. wise.

esaeraz adv. proverbially.

esaerazale adj. fond of refrains, fond of proverbs.

esaerazko adj. proverbial, idiomatic.

esaka adv. saying, speaking. n. saying, expression.

esakune n. saying, expression, refrain, maxim, proverb.

esaldi n.(gram.) sentence, phrase.

esalditu v.t. to phrase.

esale n. talker, speaker.

esamesa n. gossip, empty talk; rumor, murmuring.

esamesaka adv. gossiping.

esamolde n. saying, expression.

esan v.t. to say, to tell, to narrate, to relate. n. saying.

esanahi n. meaning; significance.

esanaldi n. sentence, phrase. n. lecture, discourse.

esan arazi v.t. to cause (someone) to say (something), to make (someone) confess.

esanbehar n. desire to say something. n. that which must be said.

esaneko adj. obedient, submissive. adj. loyal to one's word.

esanekotasun n. obedience.

esanera adv. by dictation, from dictation.

esanera etorri v.i. to agree, to acquiesce.

esanetik irten v.i. to disobey.

esaneratu v.i. to obey.

esanezgarri adj. unspeakable, inexpressible, unutterable.

esanezin adj. inexpressible, unspeakable, unutterable, unmentionable.

esanezina n. stuttering, stammering. n. uncommunicativeness.

esanezinezko adj. inexpressible, unspeakable, unutterable.

esangabeko adj. unsaid, unspoken.

esangaitz adj. difficult to say, difficult to express.

esangarri n. expressible, speakable, utterable.

esangura n. meaning, significance.

esangurako adj. meaningful, significant.

esanguratsu adj. significant, meaningful.

esankor adj. expressive, meaningful.

esanondore n. moral of a story.

esanoneko adj. docile, obedient.

esantxarreko adj. disobedient.

esate n. saying, act of saying.

esateko adj. mentionable.

eseka adv. in a zigzag manner, (weaving) to and fro.

eseki v.t. to hang.

esekidura n. hanging.

esentzia n.(phil.) essence.

eseraldi n. sitting, session.

eseri v.i. to sit (down). v.t. to seat.

eserleku n. seat, chair.

esertoki n. seat, place to sit.

esetsaldi n. attack, duration of an attack, battle.

esetsi v.t. to attack. v.t. to object; to argue. n. attack.

esfera n. sphere.

eskabide n. order, petition, request; application; demand.

eskabidezko adj. supplicatory, requesting, demanding.

eskaera n. petition, request. n. manner of solicitation, way of requesting.

eskaerazko adj. requesting, demanding.

eskagarri adj. exigible, requirable.

eskahalmen n. license; power of solicitation, ability to make requests.

eskailera n. stairs (usually used in the plural).

eskain n. offering.

eskainaldi n. time of offering, offering. n.(eccl.) offertory.

eskaingai n. offering.

eskaingarri adj. worthy of offering.

eskaini v.t. to offer. v.i. to offer oneself, to devote oneself. n. offering.

eskainka adv. offering.

eskaintza n. offer, offering; supply.

eskaintzaile n. offerer; supplier.

eskaintzazko adj. related to the offering.

eskaka adv. asking, demanding, requesting.

eskakeria n. impertinent request.

eskaketa n. petition, solicitation, request.

eskakizun n. exigency, requirement, demand. n. object of a demand, request.

eskakizunezko adj. requisitory, required, demanded.

eskakor adj. exigent, demanding.

eskala n.(mus.) scale.

eskalapoin n. heavy wooden shoe.

eskalari n. climber.

eskalatu v.t. to climb.

eskalda n. scale (of a fish).

eskale n. beggar.

eskalego n. beggary, mendicancy.

eskaleria n. group of beggars; pauperism, abject poverty.

eskaletasun n. mendicancy, mendicity, beggary, begging.

eskaletu v.i. to become a mendicant, to become a beggar.

eskaletza *n.* begging, beggary.

eskalo *n.(zool.)* small greenish fresh water fish.

eskama *n.* scale.

eskandalizatu *v.t./v.i.* to scandalize.

eskandalu *n.* scandal.

eskapabide *n.* hole, means of escape, escape route.

eskapatu *v.i.* to escape.

eskarazi *v.t.* to make (someone) ask for, to cause to ask for.

eskari *n.* petition, request, demand. *n.* application.

eskariak *n.(pl.)* prayers.

eskariorri *n.* application form.

eskarizko *adj.* petitionary.

eskarmendu *n.* punishment, severe correction.

eskarmentau *v.i./v.t.* to punish, to correct severely.

eskas *adj./adv.* scarce, scanty, little, not enough. *n.* lack of, decrease.

eskasaldi *n.* scarcity, shortage.

eskasdura *n.* act of diminishing, decreasing.

eskasgo *n.* scarcity, indigence, penury.

eskasia *n.* penury, scarcity, shortage.

eskaskeria *n.* niggardliness, stinginess.

eskasketa *n.* diminution, decrease, lack.

eskaski *adv.* scarcely, barely, hardly.

eskastasun *n.* scarcity, lack; indigence, penury. *n.* mediocrity.

eskaste *n.* time of scarcity, time of need.

eskastu *v.i.* to run out of, to become scarce. *v.t.* to ration; to reduce.

eskatima *n.* quarrel, dispute.

eskatimari *n.* quarreler, arguer, fighter.

eskatimatu *v.i.* to quarrel, to dispute, to argue.

eskatu *v.t.* to ask for. *v.t.* to request, to beg; to pray.

eskatzaile *adj.* solicitous, requesting, complaining. *n.* solicitor, petitioner, applicant.

eske *n.* petition, request, demand, asking for. *n.* mendicity, begging. *adv.* begging.

eskean *adv.* begging.

eskean egin *v.t.* to beg.

eskean ibili *v.i.* to go begging.

eske batu *v.t.* to collect money or goods.

eskebatzaile *n.* collector (of money or goods).

eske bildu *v.t.* to collect money or goods.

eskebilketa *n.* collection for a charitable purpose.

eskebiltzaile *n.* collector (of money)

eskegi *v.t./v.i.* to hang.

eskegile *n.* collector (of money).

eskeko *n.* beggar.

eskekotasun *n.* mendicity, begging.

eskela *n.* obituary notice.

eskeleto *n.(anat.)* skeleton.

eskema *n.* resume, brief, summary, outline.

eskemazko *adj.* schematic, summarized.

eskemaztu *v.t.* to summarize, to abbreviate, to outline.

esker *n.* thanks, gratefulness, gratitude. *n.* favor, mercy, gift. *n.(theol.)* grace.

eskerbeltz *n.* ingratitude, ungratefulness, thanklessness.

eskerbeltzeko *adj.* ungrateful, thankless.

eskerbide *n.* gratitude.

eskerdun *adj.* grateful, thankful, appreciative.

eskerga *adj.* enormous, huge.

eskergabe *adj.* ungrateful, thankless.

eskergabekeria *n.* ingratitude, ungratefulness, thanklessness.

eskergabeki *adv.* ungratefully, thanklessly.

eskergabeko *adj.* ungrateful, thankless.

eskergabetasun *n.* ungratefulness, thanklessness, ingratitude.

eskergabetu *v.i.* to be ungrateful.

eskergaitz *n.* ingratitude, ungratefulness, thanklessness.*adj.* ungrateful, thankless.

eskergaizto *n.* ingratitude, ungratefulness, thanklessness.

eskergaiztoko *adj.* ungrateful, thankless.

eskergaiztotasun *n.* ingratitude, ungratefulness, thanklessness.

eskergaiztoz *adv.* ungratefully, thanklessly.

eskergarri *adj.* estimable, worthy of thanks.

eskerrak *n.(pl.)* many thanks; expression of thanks.

eskerrak eman *v.t.* to thank.

eskerremale *n.* one who thanks.

eskerron *n.* gratitude, gratefulness, thankfulness.

eskerroneko *adj.* grateful, thankful, appreciative.

eskerrontasun *n.* gratitude, gratefulness, thankfulness.

eskerrordain *n.* repayment of a favor.

eskerrordaindu *v.t.* to pay back, to return a favor.

eskertasun *n.* gratitude, gratefulness, thankfulness.

eskertsu *adj.* thankful, grateful, appreciative.

eskertu *v.t.* to thank, to show thanks, to give thanks.

eskertxar *n.* ingratitude, ungratefulness, thanklessness.

eskertxardun *adj.* ungrateful, thankless.

eskertxarreko *adj.* ungrateful, thankless.

eskertxarrez *adv.* ungratefully, thanklessly.

eskertza *n.* gratitude, gratefulness, thankfulness.

eskerztatu *v.t.* to give thanks, to thank.

eskilara *n.* stairs, stairway, staircase. *n.* ladder.

eskilaraburu *n.* stair landing, top of the stairs.

eskilarape *n.* space under the stairway.

eskilaratxo *n.(dim.)* little ladder, step ladder.

esklabu *n.* slave.

esklabutza *n.* slavery.

esklabutzapen *n.* enslavement.

eskoba *n.* broom. *n.* certain card game.

eskobakada *n.* blow with a broom.

eskobaratu *v.t.* to rake.

eskobare *n.* rake.

eskobatu *v.t.* to sweep.

eskola *n.* school. *n.* culture, education, instruction.

eskoladin *n.* school age.

eskoladun *adj.* educated, literate.

eskolaemaile *n.* teacher, instructor.

eskola eman *v.t.* to teach, to instruct.

eskolagabe *adj.* uncultured, ignorant, illiterate.

eskolagabeko *adj.* uncultured, ignorant, illiterate.

eskolaketa *n.* instruction.

eskolakide *n.* classmate, schoolmate.

eskolalagun *n.* classmate, schoolmate.

eskolalanak *n.(pl.)* homework.

eskolaliburu *n.* textbook, school book.

eskolamahai *n.* student's desk.

eskolamaistra *n.* female school teacher.

eskolamaisu *n.* male school teacher.

eskolamutil *n.* schoolboy.

eskolape *n.* school porch; school basement.

eskolapen *n.* instruction.

eskolaro *n.* school age.

eskolastika *n.* scholastics.

eskolastiko *adj.* scholastic.

eskolastikoki *adv.* scholastically.

eskolastizismo *n.(phil.)* scholasticism.

eskolatu *v.t.* to indoctrinate, to teach, to instruct. *v.i.* to instruct oneself. *adj.* instructed, educated, cultivated, learned.

eskolaurre *n.* preschool.

eskolaurreko *adj.* preschool.

eskolazain *n.* school monitor. *n.* school janitor.

eskolegun *n.* school day.

eskolordu *n.* hours spent in school, school hour.

eskolume *n.* school-age child, schoolchild.

eskomunikatu *v.t.(eccl.)* to excommunicate.

eskomunikatzaile *n.* excommunicator.

eskomuniku *n.(eccl.)* excommunication.

eskopeta *n.* shotgun.

eskopetagile *n.* shotgun maker, gunsmith.

eskopetakada *n.* blow with the butt of a shotgun.

eskopetari *n.* gunsmith.

eskopetategi *n.* gun arsenal, gun shop.

eskorbuto *n.(med.)* scurvy.

eskorga *n.* hand truck, dolly.

eskorta *n.* sheepfold, pen for sheep.

eskortaratu *v.t.* to gather sheep into the fold.

eskote *n.* neck, neckline.

eskribau *n.* notary, notary public.

eskribautegi *n.* notary public's office.

eskribautza *n.* job of a notary public.

esku *n.* hand. *n.* power, attribute, right, control. *n.* deal (in cards).

eskuaira *n.* drawing square.

eskuak eman *v.t.* to reconcile.

eskuak ezarri *v.t.* to seize, to put hands on.

eskuak sartu *v.t.* to take part in something.

eskualdagarri *adj.* transferable, transmissible.

eskualdagarritasun *n.* transmissibility, transferability.

eskualdaketa *n.* transmission, transference.

eskualdare *n.* portable altar.

eskualdatu *v.t.* to hand over, to transfer (power), to change hands (ownership).

eskualde *n.* region, area, district, county. *n.* side.

eskualdekapen *n.* zoning, dividing into regions or zones.

eskualdekatu *v.t.* to zone.

eskualdi *n.* hand, round (in a game of cards, sport). *n.* coat (of paint, whitewash). *n.* luck.

eskualdun *n./adj.* Basque.

eskuan egon *v.i.* to depend on, to rely on, to be in one's hands.

eskuantza *n.* dexterity, skill.

eskuara *n.* Basque language.

eskuare *n.* rake.

eskuarekada *n.* raking.

eskuaretu *v.t.* to rake, to gather with a rake, to rake in.

eskuargi *n.* flashlight. *n.* small candlestick.

eskuarki *adv.* usually, commonly, ordinarily, most of the time.

eskuarra *n.* palm's width.

eskuarrantza *n.* act of catching fish by hand.

eskuarte *n.* means of subsistence, recourses.

eskuarteko *adj.* manual; common, ordinary, everyday. *n.* money for everyday necessities.

esku artu *v.t.* to take part, to intervene,

to participate, to interfere. *v.t.* to intrude.

eskuazpikeria *n.* bribe, subornation.

eskuazpiz *adv.* by contraband; secretly.

eskubabes *n.* gauntlet, glove.

eskubahe *n.* sieve.

eskubarne *n.* palm (hand), metacarpus.

eskubarru *n.* palm (hand).

eskubete *n.* handful, content of the hand.

eskubeteka *adv.* by the handful, abundantly.

eskubi *adj./n.* right.

eskubide *n.* right, authorization.

eskubidea eman *v.t.* to authorize, to empower, to delegate.

eskubidea kendu *v.t.* to take away (someone's) authority.

eskubidedun *adj.* authorized, empowered, delegated.

eskubidetasun *n.* state of having rights, jurisdiction.

eskubidetu *v.t.* to empower, to authorize, to delegate.

eskubidetza *n.* jurisdiction.

eskubidez *adv.* authoritatively, with authorization.

eskubidezko *adj.* just, right.

eskubiko *adj.* bimanual, two-handed. *adj.* pertaining to the right side or right hand.

eskubonba *n.* hand grenade.

eskuburdinak *n.(pl.)* handcuffs.

eskubustialdi *n.* hand washing.

eskudantza *n.* Basque dance performed in a circle with dancers holding hands.

eskudel *n.* bannister, rail, stair railing, handrail.

eskudiru *n.* cash; pocket money.

eskudun *adj.* powerful, empowered, authorized.

eskuemale *n.* helper, sponsor, mentor. *n.* promoter.

esku eman *v.t.* to help, to aid, to give a hand, to protect. *v.t.* to give reason, to give cause. *v.t.* to permit, to authorize, to delegate, to empower.

eskuemate *n.* sponsorship, backing.

eskuenbor *n.(anat.)* metacarpus.

eskuera *n.* jurisdiction, domain.

esku eragin *v.t.* to gesticulate, to wave the hands.

eskueragite *n.* hand movement.

eskuerakutsi *n.* gift, present.

eskuerloju *n.* wristwatch.

eskueskilara *n.* stepladder.

eskuetaratu *v.t.* to obtain, to get. *v.i.* to fight, to come to blows. *v.t.* to give to, to turn over to, to put in (someone's) hands.

eskuetari *adj.* quarrelsome, troublemaking.

eskueutsi *adj.* stingy, niggardly, miserly, ungenerous, tight-fisted.

eskuezarketa *n.* laying on of the hands, laying hands on.

eskuezarpen *n.* laying on of the hands, laying one's hands on.

eskuezker *n.* left hand.

eskugain *n.* back of the hand, dorsal part of the hand.

eskugarbi(ko) *adj.* honest (not a thief).

eskugurdi *n.* handcart.

eskuhaga *n.* wooden lever.

eskuharmen *n.* influence, participation, intervention.

eskuharri *n.(min.)* emery stone.

eskuharritu *v.t.* to polish with emery.

esku hartu *v.t.* to participate, to take part, to intervene, to interfere. *v.t.* to appropriate the rights of another, to usurp the rights of another.

eskuhartzaile *n.* participant; interferer. *adj.* participating, participatory, sharing, taking part.

eskuhatz *n.* handprint.

eskuialde *n.* right side.

eskuidazki *n.* manuscript.

eskuidazti *n.* manuscript.

eskuikara *n.* trembling of the hands.

eskuila *n.* brush.

eskuilaketa *n.* brushing.

eskuilatu *v.t.* to brush.

eskuin *adj.* right, right-handed. *n.* right hand. *adj.* rightist, right (in politics, etc.).

eskuinalde *n.* right side. *n.(naut.)* starboard.

eskuindar *adj./n.* rightist (in politics).

eskuindu *v.i.* to go to the right.

eskuineko *adj.* rightist. *adj.* right.

eskuineratu *v.i.* to go to the right, to turn to the right. *v.t.* to put (something) on the right.

eskuitxi *adj.* stingy, niggardly, miserly, tight-fisted, ungenerous.

eskuizkribu *n.* manuscript.

esku jaso *v.t.* to threaten.

eskujokalari *n.* prestidigitator, sleight of hand artist.

eskujoko *n.* sleight of hand.

eskuka *adv.* handling, touching or feeling with the hands.

eskukada *n.* handful, contents of the hand.

eskukadaka *adv.* by handfuls.

eskukaketa *n.* handling, feeling with the hands. *n.* kneading.

eskukatu *v.t.* to knead. *v.t.* to fight, to come to blows. *v.t.* to handle, to manage, to use; to manipulate (with the hands).

eskuketa *n.* gesticulation. *n.* sleight of hand. *n.* fight, battle. *n.* handling, feeling with the hands.

eskuketari *n.* prestidigitator, sleight of hand artist. *n.* gesticulator.

eskuko *n.* staff, stick. *adj.* manual, portable. *adj.* dependent.

eskukoi *adj.* manageable, handleable.

eskuko izan *v.i.* to be the owner of.

eskukotasun n. power, authority.
eskulabe n. small oven.
eskulabur adj. stingy, niggardly.
eskulan n. handicraft.
eskulandu v.t. to manufacture.
eskulanezko adj. manufactured.
eskulangile n. artisan, blue collar worker. n. day laborer, hodman.
eskulangilego n. artisan's guild, group of artisans.
eskulangileria n. group of artisans.
eskulangintza n. arts and crafts. n. job of artisan or day laborer.
eskulari n. handball player.
eskularru n. gauntlet, glove.
eskuleku n. handle. n. plow handle.
eskuliburu n. textbook.
eskulohi n. burglar, thief, robber.
eskultismo n. scouting.
eskultore n. sculptor.
eskultura n. sculpture.
eskulturazko adj. sculptural.
eskulturgintza n. art of sculpture.
esku luzatu v.t. to help, to aid.
eskuluze adj. generous, charitable. n. thief, robber, burglar.
eskuma adj./n. right.
eskumakila n. cane, stick, staff.
eskumako adj. right.
eskumami n. flesh of the hand.
eskumen n. authority, domination, power. n. handful.
eskumende n. sphere of power, dominion.
eskumenpeko adj. subsidiary, subordinate.
eskumenperagaitz adj. indomitable, unruly, untamed.
eskumotz adj. amputated hand.
eskumuin n. greetings.
eskumuinak n.(pl.) greetings.
eskumutur n.(anat.) wrist. n. cuff.
eskumuturreko n. bracelet.
eskuoihal n. towel, rag.
eskuoihaltxo n.(dim.) small towel.
eskuoneko adj. handy, dextrous, skillful.
eskuorga n. handcart, wheelbarrow.
eskuorgari n. wheelbarrow man.
eskuoso n. plenipotence, full powers.
eskuosodun adj. plenipotent, full-powered.
eskuotzara n. hand basket.
eskupe n. subordination, dependence. n. secret.
eskupean adv. subordinately. adv. secretly.
eskupeko n. tip, gratuity. adj. subordinate, submissive, obedient.
eskuperatu v.t. to appropriate. v.t. to subject (someone) to (something or someone). v.t. to tame, to domesticate.
eskupilota n. handball.
eskurabide n. means of obtaining something.
eskura ekarri v.t. to dominate.

eskuraerraz adj. easily obtainable.
eskuraezin adj. unattainable. adj. untamable, indomitable.
eskuragaitz adj. difficult to obtain, unreachable. adj. indomitable, difficult to tame.
eskuragarri adj. accessible, attainable.
eskuraketa n. capture, obtainment.
eskurakoi adj. accessible, manageable, easy to get.
eskurakor adj. acquisitive, obtainable.
eskurakotu v.t. to tame. v.t. to dominate.
eskurantza n. right, appropriation, power, authorization.
eskurapen n. obtainment, acquisition.
eskurapetu v.t. to tame.
eskuratu v.t. to get, to obtain, to reach. v.t. to seize with the hand. v.t. to tame, to domesticate.
eskuratzaile adj. capturing; acquiring.
eskusare n. netted bag.
eskusari n. tip, gratuity; bonus.
eskusarketa n. intervention. n. meddling, manipulating.
esku sartu v.t. to intervene. v.t. to meddle, to manipulate.
eskusaski n. hand basket.
eskutako n. brass knuckles, knuckle-duster.
eskutik-eskura adv. from hand to hand.
eskutitz n. letter.
eskutitzazal n. envelope.
eskutizketa n. written correspondence, letter writing.
eskutoki n. handle.
eskutrapu n. hand cloth.
eskutrebe adj. dextrous, handy.
eskutresna n. hand instrument, hand tool.
eskuts adj. empty-handed.
eskutu n.(econ.) escudo (money).
eskutur n.(anat.) wrist.
eskuturreko n. wristband; bracelet; watch strap, watchband.
eskutxo n.(dim.) little hand.
eskutzar n.(augm.) big hand.
eskuz adv. by hand, manually.
eskuzabal adj. generous, charitable.
eskuzabaleko adj. generous, charitable.
eskuzabalki adv. generously, open-handedly.
eskuzabaltasun n. generosity, magnanimity.
eskuzafla n. applause.
eskuzapi n. hand towel.
eskuzarta n. applause.
eskuzartada n. slap. n. applause.
eskuzartaka n. applauding, clapping.
eskuzartaldi n. ovation, round of applause.
eskuzartatu v.t. to slap. v.t. to applaud.
eskuzatar n. kitchen cloth, rag.
eskuz egin v.t. to manufacture, to

hand-make, to do (something) by hand.

eskuz-esku *adv.* hand in hand, hand to hand.

eskuzikin *adj.* dishonest (thieving).

eskuzko *adj.* handmade. *adj.* manual.

eskuzorro *n.* hand covering, glove.

eskuztatu *v.t.* to handle; to pet. *v.t.* to knead, to squeeze.

eskuztatzaile *adj.* handling, manipulating.

eskuzulo *n.* palm of the hand.

eskuzuri *adj.* lazy.

eskuzuzi *n.* torch, fire brand.

esleitu *v.i.* to separate oneself.

esmalte *n.* enamel paint, nail polish.

esna- Used in compound words. Derived from *esne*, milk and *esnatu*, to awaken.

esna egon *v.i.* to be awake.

esnaerale *n.* awakener.

esnaerazi *v.t.* to cause (someone) to awaken.

esnaerloju *n.* alarm clock.

esnagailu *n.* alarm clock.

esnagarri *adj.* awakening.

esnagin *n.* milk tooth.

esnaldi *n.* vigil, period of wakefulness.

esnaldu *v.i./v.t.* to be supplied with milk, to supply with milk.

esnale *n.* awakener.

esnarazi *v.t.* to waken someone.

esnaro *n.* period of lactation.

esnatu *v.i.* to awaken (oneself), to wake up. *v.t.* to awaken (someone), to wake (someone) up. *v.i.* to become alert. *v.t.* to excite, to stimulate.

esnatzaile *n.* awakener.

esne *n.* milk. *n.* milky juice of plants.

esnealdi *n.* period of lactation.

esnebehi *n.* milk cow.

esnebelar *n.(bot.)* sun spurge.

esnebero *n.* fresh milk.

esnebiltzaile *n.* one who goes from farm to farm collecting milk to sell at market.

esnedenda *n.* dairy.

esnedun *n.* milkman (male or female). *adj.* good milker, giving abundant milk.

esnegabeketa *n.* weaning.

esnegabetu *v.i.* to wean.

esnegain *n.* cream.

esnehortz *n.* milk tooth.

esneketa *n.* lactation.

esneketari *n.* milkman (male or female).

esneki *n.* dairy product.

esneko *adj.* suckling.

esnekor *adj.* milk-giving.

esnekume *n.* suckling animal.

esnemami *n.* milk curd. *n.* cream.

esneontzi *n.* milk can.

esnesaltzaile *n.* milkman, seller of milk.

esnetegi *n.* dairy.

esnetsu *adj.* abundant in milk (animals).

esnetxe *n.* dairy.

esnezale *adj.* fond of milk.

esnezko *adj.* milky, made of milk.

esneztatu *v.t.* to dunk in milk.

Espainia *n.(geog.)* Spain.

espainiamerikar *adj./n.* Hispano-American.

espainiar *adj.* Spanish.

espainiartu *v.i.* to become Spanish (language, culture, citizenship, etc.).

espainiera *n.* Spanish language.

espainikontrako *adj.* anti-Spanish.

espainizale *adj.* devoted to Spanish things.

espainizalekeria *n.* excessive devotion to Spanish things.

espainizaletasun *n.* devotion to Spanish things.

espal *n.* sheaf of grain.

espaldu *v.t.* to sheave.

espalkatu *v.t.* to sheave.

espalmeta *n.* pile of sheaves.

espaloi *n.* pavement; sidewalk. *n.* mortar, cement.

espaloiertz *n.* edge of the sidewalk.

espaloiontzi *n.* cement mixer.

espaloiztatu *v.t.* to make mortar, to mix cement. *v.t.* to cement, to cement with mortar.

espaloiztu *v.t.* to make mortar, to mix cement. *v.t.* to cement with mortar.

espantagarri *adj.* scary, frightening.

esparadrapu *n.* bandage tape.

esparru *n.* scope, area, field. *n.* delimitation. *n.* fenced in field.

espartin *n.* rope-soled shoe with a canvas top.

espartingile *n.* person who makes rope-soled shoes.

espartingintza *n.* manufacture of rope-soled shoes. *n.* job of rope-soled shoemaker.

espartzatu *v.t.* to stuff or fill with esparto.

espartzu *n.(bot.)* hemp, esparto. *n.* dishcloth made of esparto.

espartzudi *n.* field of esparto grass.

espartzugin *n.* person who processes esparto grass.

espartzugintza *n.* manufacture of esparto grass.

espartzutu *v.t.* to cover with esparto grass.

esperanto *n.* Esperanto.

esperantza *n.* hope.

esperantzagabe *adj.* hopeless, without hope.

esperantzagarri *adj.* hopeful.

esperientzia *n.* experience.

esperimentu *n.* experiment.

esperma *n.* sperm.

espero ukan *v.t.* to expect, to hope.

espetxaldi *n.* period of imprisonment, jail term.

espetxe *n.* prison, jail.

espetxeko *adj.* pertaining to the prison.

espetxeragarri *adj.* imprisonable.
espetxeratu *v.t.* to imprison, to jail.
espetxetu *v.t.* to imprison, to put in jail.
espetxezain *n.* jailer, prison guard.
espetxezaingo *n.* job of the jailer.
espezialista *n./adj.* specialist (usually a physician).
espezialitate *n.* speciality, specialty.
espezializapen *n.* specialization.
espezializatu *v.i.* to specialize.
espezializazio *n.* specialization.
espezie *n.* species.
espeziekide *n.* member of the same species.
espezifikatu *v.t.* to specify.
espezifikazio *n.* specification.
espezifiko *adj.* specific.
espinaka *n.(bot.)* spinach.
espioi *n.* spy.
espioitza *n.* espionage.
espiral *n.* spiral.
esponda *n.* side slope.
esposatu *v.i.* to get married.
estabilizatu *v.t./v.i.* to stabilize, to become stable.
estabilizazio *n.(econ.)* stabilization.
estai *n.* floor (second floor, etc.).
estainu *n.(min.)* tin.
estakuru *n.* excuse, pretext.
estalaldi *n.* covering. *n.* breeding animals.
estalarazi *v.t.* to cause to cover. *v.t.* to cause the mating of animals.
estaldu *v.t.* to cover, to cover up. *v.t.* to mate animals. *v.i.* to hide oneself.
estaldura *n.* covering. *n.* copulation, coitus. *n.* hiding.
estalgabe *adj.* uncovered, defenseless.
estalgabetu *v.t.* to uncover.
estalgarri *n.* all objects which cover (blanket, lid, top, etc.). *n.* hideable.
estalgetu *v.t.* to uncover.
estalgune *n.* covered place.
estali *v.t.* to cover. *v.t.* to mate animals. *v.t.* to hide, to cover up. *v.i.* to hide oneself. *adj.* covered.
estalketa *n.* covering. *n.* hiding. *n.* mating.
estalki *n.* cover; roof. *n.* covering (blanket, scarf, dress, etc.). *n.* bookcover; envelope.
estalkidun *adj.* covered.
estalkigabe *adj.* uncovered.
estalpe *n.* shelter, covering. *n.* protection.
estalpen *n.* concealment; covering.
estalpetu *v.t.* to cover. *v.t.* to protect.
estaltoki *n.* hiding place.
estaltzaile *n.* concealer, hider.
estanku *n.* tobacco shop.
estatari *n.* statesman.
estatistika *n.* statistics.
estatu *n.(pol.)* state.
estatuarteko *adj.* interstate.
estatubatuar *adj./n.* American, United States citizen.

estatuburu *n.* head of a state.
estatugizon *n.* statesman.
estatutu *n.(pol.)* statute.
estatutuzko *n.* statutory.
estatuzale *adj.* supportive of the state.
estazio *n.* station.
esteka *n.* tie, fastener.
estekada *n.* satiety, glut, fullness.
estekadura *n.* tying, fastening. *n.* tie, fastener.
estekailu *n.* tying, fastening.
estekaldi *n.* act of tying, fastening.
estekarri *n.* tie, fastener.
estekatu *v.t.* to tie, to fasten.
estereo *n.* stereo.
esterlina *adj.(econ.)* sterling (pound).
estetika *n.* aesthetics.
estetikakontrako *adj.* antiaesthetic.
estetiko *adj.* aesthetic.
estibor *n.(naut.)* starboard.
estima *n.* esteem, appreciation.
estimagaitz *adj.* difficult to be appreciated.
estimagarri *adj.* worthy, appreciable, appreciated.
estimagarritasun *n.* worthiness, appreciation.
estimatu *v.t.* to appreciate, to esteem.
estimatzaile *n.* person who appreciates.
estimu *n.* esteem, appreciation.
estoka *n.(mech.)* lathe.
estokari *n.* lathe operator.
estokatu *v.t.* to turn on a lathe.
estolda *n.* sewer.
estolderia *n.* sewerage system.
estraperlo *n.* black market.
estrapu *n.* oarlock. *n.* stumble.
estratu *n.(geol.)* stratum.
estreinaldi *n.* first performance, inauguration, debut.
estreinari *n./adj.* debutante.
estreinatu *v.t.* to inaugurate, to use for the first time, to debut.
estropada *n.* regatta.
estropadak egin *v.t.* to hold a regatta.
estruktura *n.* structure.
estrukturatu *v.t.* to structure.
estu *adj.* narrow, anxious. *adj.* nervous, anxious, worried. *adj.(fig.)* rigid, rigorous, strict, severe. *adj.* tight (clothing, etc.). *adv.* anxiously, nervously.
estuagotu *v.t.* to fit tighter.
estualdi *n.* strait, scrape, tight spot. *n.* affliction, tribulation, sorrow.
estuasun *n.* anxiety, nervousness; affliction. *n.* difficulty, difficult moment.
estu egon *v.i.* to be nervous; to be uptight.
estuera *n.* tightness; narrowness.
estu-estu *adv.* very tightly. *adv.* very nervously. *adv.* very strictly, very severely.
estugarri *n.* tie, string, rope, something used to tie with.
estugune *n.* narrowness, tightness. *n.*

narrow passage.

estu hartu *v.t.* to be a threat (in competition), to be a challenge, to be competition for (someone).

estukaketa *n.* tight squeezing.

estukaldi *n.* squeezing, pressing.

estukatu *v.t.* to tighten.

estuketa *n.* tightening, narrowing.

estuki *adv.* tightly, narrowly. *adv.(fig.)* anxiously. *adv.* rigidly, strictly.

estukiro *adv.* tightly, narrowly.

estukoi *adj.* easily tightened, compressible.

estukor *adj.* easily tightened. *adj.* astringent.

estun *n.* link.

estune *n.* narrow passage. *n.(geog.)* strait.

estunketa *n.* linking.

estuntsu *adj.* having many links.

estura *n.* strait, scrape. *n.* tightening, narrowing.

estutasun *n.* narrowness, tightness. *n.* anxiety, nervousness; problem. *n.* suffocation.

estutasunez *adv.* anxiously.

estutu *v.t.* to tighten; to press; to grip, to clench. *v.i.* to become narrow. *v.i.* to become worried. *v.t.* to urge, to press on, to herd, to corral.

estutzaile *n.* tightener, presser. *n.* exploiter, oppressor. *adv.* oppressive.

eta *conj.* and. *n.(pol.)* Basque political movement called *Euskadi ta Askatasuna* (Basque Country and Liberty). *conj.* and everybody else. Used after a noun. **Ama eta etorri dira.** Mother and everybody else have come. *conj.* because, since. Used at the end of a sentence. *conj.* and so on, et cetera.

-eta *(gram.)* Suffix used to express abundance, quantity, place of. **Harrieta.** Place of stones. *(gram.)* Suffix used to express action. **Lapurreta.** Robbery.

etabar *n.* et cetera, and so on. **Etab.** Etc.

etako *adj./n.* member of E.T.A.

-etako *(gram.)* Suffix which expresses pertaining to, of.

-etan *(gram.)* Suffix which expresses the idea of the preposition in (pl.).

etapa *n.* stage, step, era, epoch; leg, hop, stretch (of a race).

etar *adj.* belonging to E.T.A.

-etara *(gram.)* Suffix which expresses the idea of the preposition to (pl.)

-etaraino *(gram.)* Suffix which expresses the idea of the preposition up to (pl.)

-etarantz *(gram.)* Suffix which expresses the idea of the preposition towards (pl.)

-etariko *(gram.)* Suffix which expresses one among a group, one

of a group.

-etatik *(gram.)* Suffix which expresses the idea of the preposition from (pl.)

etekin *n.* profit, wages, benefit, earnings (usually related to cattle, fields).

eten *v.t./v.i.* to break, to cut. *v.i.* to become tired. *n.* discontinuity; interruption; break, cut; caesura. *adj.* interrupted, intermittent, not continuous.

etenaldi *n.* interruption, pause, break.

etenbehar *n.* tension, tenseness, tautness, tightness.

etenbera *adj.* breakable.

etenda *adj.* interrupted, broken. *adj.* tired, exhausted.

etendura *n.* interruption, break. *n.* fracture, break.

etenezin *adj.* unbreakable; irrevocable.

etenezinezko *adj.* unbreakable.

etengabe *adj.* incessant, continuous, constant, ceaseless, uninterrupted. *adv.* incessantly, continuously, constantly, uninterruptedly.

etengabeki *adv.* incessantly, continuously.

etengabeko *adj.* incessant, continuous, uninterrupted.

etengabetasun *n.* continuousness, ceaselessness, constantness, perpetualness.

etengabezia *n.* constancy; continuance.

etengailu *n.* switch, breaker.

etengaitz *adj.* uninterruptable, difficult to interrupt.

etengarri *adj.* breakable.

etenka *adv.* brokenly, interruptedly, intermittently.

etenkari *n.* interruptor.

etenkatu *v.t.* to interrupt, to break in.

etenketa *n.* act of breaking. *n.* exhaustion, tiredness.

etenkor *adj.* breakable; fragile.

etenune *n.* breaking point.

etika *n.* ethics.

etiketa *n.* etiquette, formality. *n.* label.

etiketatu *v.t.* to label.

etnia *n.* race.

etniko *adj.* ethnic.

etor *v.i.* come! (*etorri*, to come).

etorberri *adj.* newcomer, recently arrived.

etorbide *n.* origin, beginning. *n.* procedure.

etorburu *n.* origin, source.

etordei *n.* summons. *n.* decoy bird, bird call, decoy whistle.

etorki *n.* origin, source; nature. *n.* caste, lineage, line (of descent). *n.* family.

etorkin *n.* immigrant.

etorkizko *adj.* original, genealogical, innate, inborn.

etorkizun *n.* future.

etorkizuneko *adj.* futuristic, coming,

upcoming, future.

etorkor *adj.* docile, accommodating, conciliatory, affable.

etorkortasun *n.* docility, indulgence, tolerance.

etorle *n.* one who comes, one who arrives.

etorpen *n.* arrival.

etorraldi *n.* arrival; time spent in coming.

etorrarazi *v.t.* to cause (someone) to come, to attract.

etorrera *n.* arrival. *n.* origin, source.

etorri *v.i.* to come. *n.* eloquence; inspiration, talent.

etorrialdi *n.* time of inspiration, visit from the muse.

etsai *n.* enemy, adversary. *n.* demon.

etsaiarazi *v.t.* to make an enemy of.

etsaiezko *adj.* inimical, hostile. *adj.* demoniacal.

etsaigo *n.* hostility, enmity, rivalry.

etsaikeria *n.* hostility, enmity, rivalry.

etsaiki *n.* hostilely, inimically.

etsaitalde *n.* group of enemies.

etsaitasun *n.* enmity, hostility.

etsaitu *v.i.* to become enemies. *v.t.* to make enemies.

etsi *v.t.* to abandon, to desist. *n.* resignation, renouncement. *v.i.* to become desperate. *n.* desperation.

-etsi *(gram.)* Verbal suffix usually accompanying nouns and adjectives, meaning considering as, taking for; appreciating. **Ederretsi.** To admire.

etsialdi *n.* moment of desperation.

etsiarazi *v.t.* to cause (someone) to despair.

etsibide *n.* cause for desperation.

etsigarri *adj.* causing despair, discouraging.

etsigarriki *adv.* despairingly, discouragingly, desperately.

etsimen *n.* desperation, discouragement, disillusionment.

etsimendu *n.* desperation.

etsipen *n.* desperation, hopelessness, despair, discouragement, pessimism, deception. *n.* resignation.

etsipenez *adv.* desperately; deceptively. *adv.* resignedly.

etsipengarri *adj.* causing despair, discouraging.

etsita *adj.* desperate, hopeless. *adj.* resigned.

etsitu *v.i.* to despair, to become desperate. *v.i.* to become resigned.

etxa- Used in compound words. Derived from *etxe*, house.

etxabe *n.* cellar, basement.

etxabere *n.* domestic animal.

etxadi *n.* neighborhood, group of houses.

etxaguntza *n.* rented house usually with land. *n.* primogeniture, exclusive right of firstborn to inherit.

etxalaba *n.* heir (daughter).

etxaldaketa *n.* moving (from a house).

etxaldatu *v.t.* to move (from a house).

etxalde *n.* farmhouse.

etxaleku *n.* location of a house.

etxandre *n.* housewife.

etxarte *n.* space between houses.

etxaseme *n.* heir (son).

etxate *n.* door of a house; doorway.

etxatiar *n.* family member. *adj.* domestic.

etxatze *n.* back of the house.

etxaurre *n.* porch, front part of the house.

etxazpi *n.* basement.

etxe *n.* house, home; building.

etxeagentzia *n.* real estate agency.

etxebarneko *adj.* pertaining to the inner part of a house.

etxebarrigintza *n.* construction of new houses.

etxebarru *adj.* inner part of a new house.

etxebarruti *n.* the lands pertaining to a farmhouse.

etxebazter *n.* corner of the house.

etxeberritu *v.t.* to renew (a house), to renovate, to remodel.

etxebitarte *n.* space between houses.

etxebizitza *n.* apartment; floor.

etxebizkar *n.* main beams of a house; upper part of a house.

etxedun *n.* owner of a house. *adj.* proprietary.

etxegabe *adj.* houseless, homeless.

etxegabetu *v.i.* to become houseless. *v.t.* to take away one's house.

etxegain *n.* upper part of the house; roof.

etxegaltzaile *n.* one who allows a house to become run down; one who wastes the household money.

etxegazti *n.* domestic fowl.

etxegelak *n.(pl.)* rooms of a house.

etxegile *n.* builder, constructor; mason.

etxegin *n.* builder, constructor; mason.

etxegintza *n.* construction of houses, house construction.

etxegite *n.* act of constructing houses.

etxegizon *n.* majordomo, administrator of household funds.

etxeirakasle *n.* governess; tutor.

etxejabe *n.* owner of a house, proprietor.

etxejabetza *n.* homeowner's rights.

etxejale *n.* waster, ruiner, squanderer; one who spends the household funds; one who destroys a household. *adj.* wasteful.

etxejantzi *n.* robe, housecoat.

etxejaun *n.* head of a household.

etxekalte *n.* ruiner, waster, squanderer.

etxekide *n.* co-dweller of a house.

etxeko *adj.* familial; pertaining to a house, of the house, house's.

etxekoak *n.(pl.)* members of a family.
etxekoandre *n.* housewife, lady of the house, female head of household.
etxekoi *adj.* home-loving, homey, devoted to one's family.
etxekojaun *n.* head of a household.
etxekomin *n.* homesickness, nostalgia.
etxekor *adj.* home-loving, homey, devoted to one's family. *adj.* concerned about homey things (finances, repairs, etc.).
etxekotasun *n.* domesticity.
etxekotu *v.i.* to become familiar with. *v.t.* to tame, to domesticate.
etxelan *n.* house construction. *n.* housework, domestic work.
etxeleherketa *n.* house demolition.
etxeleku *n.* place where a house is built, site, location, position.
etxelerro *n.* row of houses.
etxeliar *n.* tenant, renter.
etxemin *n.* homesickness, nostalgia.
etxemordo *n.* group of houses.
etxemutil *n.* servant, houseboy; groom.
etxeno *n.(dim.)* small house.
etxeogasun *n.* heritage of a house, patrimony.
etxeondasun *n.* real property, real estate.
etxeondo *n.* surroundings of a house.
etxeondoko *n.* next door neighbor, neighboring tenant.
etxeorde *n.* outbuilding, toolshed.
etxeorratz *n.* skyscraper.
etxerakoi *adj.* home-loving, devoted to one's family, homey. *adj.* concerned with affairs of the home (finances, etc.).
etxerakotu *v.t.* to receive at home; to lodge. *v.t.* to domesticate, to tame. *v.t.* to intend (something) for home use; to allocate (something) for one's family.
etxeratu *v.i.* to dwell, to live. *v.i.* to go or arrive home, to return home. *v.t.* to take (something) home, to carry (something) home.
etxerraldoi *n.* skyscraper.
etxerrenta *n.* renting of a house. *n.* house rent.
etxesail *n.* group of houses.
etxetiar *adj.* domestic, familiar. *adj.* home-loving. *n.* tenant, renter.
etxetiargo *n.* tenancy, occupancy.
etxetxo *n.(dim.)* small house.
etxetza *n.* multitude of houses.
etxetzar *n.(augm.)* big house.
etxezain *n.* housekeeper, guardian.
etxezaindegi *n.* conciergerie, porter's office.
etxezaingela *n.* conciergerie, porter's office.
etxezaingo *n.* administration of a house. *n.* job of a porter, doorman or concierge.
etxezaintza *n.* administration of a

house. *n.* job of a porter, doorman or concierge.
etxezale *n.* home-loving, homey.
etxezaletu *v.i.* to be fond of home. *v.t.* to domesticate.
etxezeregin *n.* housework.
etxezoko *n.* corner of the house.
etxezulo *adj.* home-loving, homebody.
etxezuriketa *n.* whitewashing.
etxola *n.* hut, cabin.
etxolatxo *n.(dim.)* small hut, cabin.
etxolatzar *n.(augm.)* large cabin, large hut.
etxoste *n.* back of a house.
etzaketa *n.* act of lying down, reclining.
etzaldi *n.* nap, rest, period of time spent lying down.
etzaleku *n.* resting place, reclining place.
etzan *v.i.* to lie down, to rest. *v.t.* to put down.
etzanaldi *n.* act of lying down. *n.* resting period.
etzanarazi *v.t.* to cause to lie down, to rest.
etzankor *adj.* fond of resting, fond of lying down.
etzanordu *n.* naptime, nap, resting hour.
etzauntza *n.* resting place, shelter; bed, couch. *n.* straw bed for cattle.
etzi *adv.* the day after tomorrow.
etzidamu *adv.* three days from today, in three days' time, the day after the day after tomorrow.
etziko *adj.* pertaining to the day after tomorrow.
etzirako *adv.* for the day after tomorrow.
eukaristia *n.* eucharist.
eukalitu *n.(bot.)* cucalyptus, gum tree.
euki *v.t.* to have, to possess, to contain.
eukipen *n.* act of possessing.
euli *n.(zool.)* fly. *adj.* cowardly, shy.
eulikaka *n.* fly excrement.
eulimando *n.(zool.)* black fly.
eulisare *n.* mosquito net.
eulitalde *n.* group of flies.
euliteria *n.* group of flies.
eulitu *v.i.* to become discouraged; to become a coward.
eulitxori *n.(zool.)* flycatcher.
eulitzar *n.(augm.)* big fly.
eulixka *n.* small fly.
eultzi *n.* faggot, bundle. *n.* thresher, instrument for threshing.
eultzigile *n.* thresher.
eultzitu *v.t.* to thrash, to thresh.
eup! *int.* hey! A cry used to call someone or to encourage someone.
eupada *n.* call, cry. *n.* boo, catcall, insult.
eupadaka *adv.* calling out to.
eup egin *v.t.* to call out to, to encourage. *v.t.* to boo, to make fun of, to insult.

euri *n.* rain.
euria egin *v.t.* to rain.
eurialdi *n.* lengthy rainfall, long shower.
euriantz *n.* drizzle.
euribide *n.* rain trench.
euribolada *n.* rainstorm.
euridun *adj.* rain, rainy.
eurihaize *n.* rainy wind.
euriketa *n.* rainstorm.
eurilanbro *n.* drizzle.
eurineurgailu *n.* rain gauge.
eurineurkin *n.* rain gauge.
euriputzu *n.* rain puddle.
euritako *n.* umbrella. *n.* raincoat.
euritakogile *n.* umbrella maker.
euritakontzi *n.* umbrella stand.
euritanta *n.* raindrop, drop of rain.
eurite *n.* rainy season.
euritsu *adj.* rainy.
euriur *n.* rain water.
eurixka *n.* drizzle.
eurizaparrada *n.* downpour.
eurizirin *n.* drizzling, sprinkling.
eurizko *adj.* rain, rainy.
eurizurrunbilo *n.* rain squall, whirlwind of rain.
Europa *n.(geog.)* Europe.
europaorotar *adj.* Pan-European.
europartasun *n.* Europeanness.
europartu *v.i.* to become European. *v.t.* to Europeanize.
Euskadi *n.* Basque Country. (Used as a political entity.)
euskailu *n.* holder, clamp, vise.
euskaitz *adj.* difficult to contain or control, irresistible.
euskal- Used in compound words. Derived from *euskara*, Basque.
euskalari *n.* Bascologist.
euskaldun *n./adj.* Basque.
euskaldunberri *n.* person who learns Basque after his mother tongue, new Basque speaker.
euskaldundu *v.i.* to become Basque (language, culture, etc.), to become a Basque speaker, to learn Basque. *v.t.* to make Basque, to make (someone) familiar with Basque culture.
euskaldunmotz *n.* native who doesn't speak Basque.
euskalduntasun *n.* Basqueness, Basque characteristics.
Euskalerri *n.* historical and traditional name of the Basque Country.
euskalgintza *n.* Basque cultural activity, promotion of Basque culture.
Euskal Herri *n.* historical and traditional name of the Basque Country.
euskalherriratu *v.i.* to immigrate to the Basque Country.
euskalki *n.* Basque dialect.
euskalkiratu *v.t.* to translate into one of the Basque dialects.
Euskal-Lur *n.* Basque homeland.

euskaltegi *n.* Basque school, Basque language center.
euskaltzain *n.* member of the Basque Academy.
Euskaltzainburu *n.* president of the Basque Academy.
euskaltzainburugo *n.* board of directors of the Basque Academy.
Euskaltzaindi *n.* Academy of the Basque Language, Basque Academy.
euskaltzale *adj./n.* Bascophile.
euskaltzaletasun *n.* Bascophilia, love of all things Basque.
euskaltzaletu *v.i.* to devote oneself to Basque.
euskara *n.* Basque language.
euskarakada *n.* Basque expression used in a foreign language.
euskaraketa *n.* translation into Basque.
euskarapen *n.* becoming Basque, making (someone or something) Basque.
euskaratu *v.t.* to translate into Basque.
euskaratzaile *n.* Basque translator.
euskarri *n.* handle. *n.* support, stay.
euskera *n.* Basque language.
eusko- Used in compound words. Derived from *euskara*, Basque.
euskor *adj.* tenacious, perseverant.
euskortasun *n.* tenacity, perseverance.
euskotar *n.* native Basque.
euskozale *adj.* Bascophile.
euskozaletasun *n.* tendency towards Basque culture; fondness for Basque things.
euskozaletu *v.i.* to become fond of Basques or Basque culture.
euslari *n.* holder.
eusle *adj.* holding, sustaining. *n.* holder, sustainer, supporter.
euspen *n.* containment; maintenance; conservation.
eustaga *n.* stick-like brake of a cart.
eustarri *n.* pillar. *n.* retaining wall.
euste *n.* act of containment, act of controlling.
eustezin *adj.* difficult to contain, uncontrollable.
eutsarazi *v.t.* to support, to sustain, to maintain.
eutsarazle *n.* holder, sustainer.
eutsarazpen *n.* retention, containment.
eutsezin *adj.* unsustainable, unsupportable, unfounded.
eutsi *v.t.* to maintain, to sustain, to keep. *v.t.* to hold; to grab, to take.
eutsigaitz *adj.* difficult to sustain, difficult to support (physical objects, ideas, etc.).
Euzkadi *n. (geog.)* Euskadi.
exkomunikatu *v.t.* excommunicate.
exkomunio *n.* excommunication.
exorzismo *n.* exorcism.
exorzista *n.* exorcist.
exorzizatu *v.t.* to exorcise.

exotiko *adj.* exotic.
exotismo *n.* exoticism.
experientzia *n.* experience.
experientzigabe *adj.* inexperienced.
experientzigabezia *n.* inexperience.
experimenduz *adv.* experimentally.
experimental *adj.* experimental.
experimentatu *v.t.* to experiment.
experimentatzaile *n.* experimenter.
experimentazio *n.* experiment.
experimentuzko *adj.* experimental.
explotazio *n.* exploitation.
exportazio *n.* export.
expresio *n.* expression.
expresiobide *n.* means of expression.
expresiokera *n.* form of expression.
express *adj./n.* express.
extradizio *n.* extradition.
exzepzio *n.* exception.
exzepzionalki *adv.* exceptionally.
exzepziozko *adj.* exceptional.
ez *adv.* no; not, don't, do not. *conj.* not . . . nor, neither . . . nor. *prep.* except.
ez- *(gram.)* Prefix indicating negation or exclusion. Not, non-, un-, in-. **Ezberdin.** Different.
eza *n.* lack, deficiency. *n.* negation, no, negative answer. *n.* poverty, indigence, misery.
ezabadura *n.* erasing.
ezabaezin *adj.* indelible, not erasable.
ezabagaitz *adj.* indelible, difficult to erase.
ezabagarri *adj.* erasable.
ezabagoma *n.* eraser.
ezabailu *n.* eraser, wiper, blackboard eraser.
ezabapen *n.* erasure, cancellation, elimination, annulment.
ezabatu *v.t.* to erase, to wipe out *v.t./v.i.* to suppress, to disappear.
ezaguarazi *v.t.* to cause to discover, to indicate, to point out.
ezagubide *n.* indication, mark, signal, clue.
ezaguera *n.* knowledge, acquaintance. *n.* judgement; age of reason. *n.* consciousness.
ezagueradun *adj.* rational, conscious.
ezaguerazi *v.t.* to cause (someone) to discover (something), to point out, to indicate.
ezaguezin *adj.* unknowable.
ezagugailu *n.* signal, distinctive mark.
ezagugaitz *adj.* difficult to know.
ezagugarri *n.* signal, distinctive mark, characteristic, feature. *adj.* knowable, recognizable.
ezagukor *adj.* knowing, cognitive.
ezagule *n.* knower, one who knows.
ezagumen *n.* knowledge. *n.* reason, judgement, reasoning ability, power of reason.
ezagumendu *n.* knowledge, acquaintance.
ezagun *adj.* evident, known,

well-known, obvious. *n.* acquaintance.
ezagungarri *n.* signal, indication, distinctive mark, characteristic, feature.
ezagungarritasun *n.* cognoscibility, knowability.
ezagungarritu *v.t.* to signal, to mark, to indicate. *v.t.* to characterize.
ezagun izan *v.i./v.t.* to be evident, to be obvious, to be clear.
ezagupen *n.* knowledge, acquaintance.
ezagutarazi *v.t.* to advise, to show, to reveal. *v.t.* to cause to know, to explain, to inform, to introduce. *v.t.* to introduce.
ezaguterrez *adj.* easy to know.
ezagutezin *n.* unrecognizable.
ezagutu *v.t.* to know, to be acquainted with, to be familiar with, to get to know, to meet. *v.t.* to discern, to identify, to recognize. *v.t.* to recognize as, to acknowledge as, to treat as.
ezagutza *n.* knowledge, acquaintance.
ezagutzaile *n.* knower, one who knows.
ezain *adj.* ugly.
ezaindu *v.t.* to make ugly, to make disagreeable.
ezaintasun *n.* ugliness.
ezaipaketa *n.* omission, act of not mentioning, lack of a mention.
ezaipatu *v.t.* to silence; to omit, to not mention.
ezakor *adj.* discordant, disagreeing, contrary.
ezan *v.t.* auxiliary verb used only in certain tenses as a variation of *ukan*, *izan* (*v.t.*). **Egin dezagun otoitz.** Let us pray.
ezargarri *adj.* adaptable, accommodating, suitable. *adj.* attributable, imputable, assignable.
ezarkera *n.* way of placing something, way of situating something.
ezarketa *n.* installation, placement.
ezarkunde *n.* foundation.
ezarkuntza *n.* foundation, settlement.
ezarlari *n.* usher; founder; installer, placer.
ezarle *n.* usher; founder; installer, placer.
ezarpen *n.* installation, placement. *n.(econ.)* deposit.
ezarrera *n.* manner of installing, placing.
ezarrerazi *v.t.* to cause to install, put or place, to make (someone) put (something somewhere), to make (someone) place (something somewhere).
ezarri *v.t.* to put, to place, to set up; to deposit. *v.t.* to establish, to found. *v.i.* to perch.
ezartoki *n.* seat; post, station.

ezartzaile *n.* putter, arranger, placer, installer.

ezaugarri *n.* insignia, signal, sign, mark. *n.* characteristic, feature. *adj.* distinctive.

ezaugarritasun *n.* recognizableness, cognoscibility, knowability.

ezaupide *n.* signal, sign, mark; understanding, awareness. *n.* acquaintance, relationship.

ezaxol *adj.* negligent, careless, remiss, indifferent.

ezaxola *n.* indifference, neglect, carelessness.

ezaxolakeria *n.* carelessness, negligence.

ezaxolarazi *v.t.* to cause to neglect.

ezaxolatasun *n.* negligence, carelessness, abandon.

ezaxolati *adj.* negligent, indifferent, carefree, careless.

ezaxolatu *v.i.* to neglect, to ignore, to be careless with.

ezbai *n.* doubt, perplexity, confusion. *n.* discussion.

ezbaialdi *n.* indecision, irresolution, hesitation.

ezbaian egon *v.i.* to be indecisive, to be irresolute, to hesitate.

ezbaidura *n.* indecision, irresolution, hesitation.

ezbaiean *adv.* dubiously, hesitatingly, hesitantly.

ezbaiezin *adj.* indubitable, indisputable.

ezbaiezko *adj.* doubtful, dubious, uncertain.

ezbaigabeko *adj.* unequivocal, certain.

ezbaigabez *adv.* indubitably, without a doubt.

ezbaiko *adj.* doubtful, dubious.

ezbaikor *adj.* sceptical, dubious; indecisive.

ezbaikorkeria *n.* scepticism, doubt.

ezbaitasun *n.* uncertainty, dubiousness.

ezbaiti *adj.* indecisive, irresolute, hesitant.

ezbaliadura *n.* uselessness.

ezbaliagarri *adj.* useless.

ezbaliapen *n.* disability, disablement, incapacitation.

ezbaliatu *v.t.* to incapacitate, to disable.

ezbalio *n.(econ.)* devaluation, depreciation.

ezbaliotu *v.t./v.i.* to devaluate, to depreciate.

ezbehar *n.* disgrace, adversity, misfortune; accident.

ezbeharrez *adv.* disgracefully, adversely, unfortunately.

ezbeharrezko *adj.* unnecessary.

ezbehartu *v.t.* to not force, to not make (someone) do (something).

ezberdin *adj.* different, distinct, dissimilar, unlike, unequal.

ezberdindu *v.t.* to diversify, to make different.

ezberdintasun *n.* difference, inequality, dissimilarity.

ezberdintzaile *n.* differentiator.

ezberdintzapen *n.* differentiation, diversification.

ez beste *prep.* except, but.

ezbide *n.* unreasonableness.

ezdeus *adj.* null, useless. *n.* nothing.

ezdeustu *v.t.* to annihilate, to reduce to nothing.

ezegin *v.t.* to omit, to leave out.

ezeginkor *adj.* impractical, unfeasible.

ezegoki *adj.* inadequate, insufficient, unsatisfactory.

ezegokitasun *n.* inadequateness, insufficiency.

ezegonkor *adj.* unstable, unbalanced.

ezegonkortasun *n.* instability, unstableness.

ezelako *adj.* not any kind, of any kind, at all.

ezemankor *adj.* nonproductive, infertile, unproductive. *adj.* stingy, niggardly.

ezen *conj.* since, given that. *conj.* that.

ezentzun *adj.* unheard of.

ezer *pron./adv.* something, anything. *pron./adv.* nothing, anything.

ezer ere ez *adv.* nothing at all.

ezerez *adv.* nothing, nothing at all.

ezereza *n.* incapacity, nothingness.

ezerezgarri *adj.* nullifying, voiding, able to annul.

ezerezkeria *n.* nothingness, insignificance, void.

ezerezkor *adj.* annihilatable, annullable, voidable; destructible.

ezereztapen *n.* annulment; annihilation, destruction.

ezereztasun *n.* nullity, nothingness. *n.* smallness.

ezereztatu *v.t./v.i.* to annihilate, to destroy, to abolish, to exterminate. *v.t.* to annul, to cancel, to invalidate.

ezereztu *v.t./v.i.* to annihilate, to destroy, to abolish, to extinguish. *v.t.* to annul, to cancel, to invalidate.

ezergabe *adj.* poor, needy, destitute.

ezergabetu *v.i.* to lose everything, to be deprived of everything.

ezertarako *adj.* useful. Usually used with the negative to mean useless, good for nothing. **Ez da ezertarako gauza.** It's a useless thing.

ezertxo *adv.(dim.)* a little something, anything. *adv.(dim.)* nothing at all, anything at all.

ezetz *adv.* emphatic no. Used sometimes to express the English word bet. **Ezetz dio.** He says no. *adv.* betting against (something). Used in wagering.

ezetza *n.* no, negative answer, refusal.

ezetza eman *v.t.* to refuse, to give a

negative answer, to say no.

ezeuskor *adj.* fragile, inconsistent, unsupported.

ezezaguketa *n.* lack of knowing, lack of recognition, unknowingness.

ezezagumen *n.* ignorance, unknowingness.

ezezagun *adj.* unknown. *n.* anonymous person, stranger.

ezezagutu *v.t.* to not recognize, to fail to know; to ignore.

ezezik . . . ere *conj.* not only . . . but also . . .

ezezka *adv.* expresses the idea of saying no, negativeness.

ezezkari *n.* contradictor. *adj.* quarrelsome, contentious, contradictory.

ezezko *adj.* derogatory; negative. *n.* negative response, no.

ezezkoan *conj.* in case it is not, if not, in the negative case.

ezezkoi *adj.* negative, pessimistic, opposite, contrary.

ezezkor *adj.* contrary, contradictory; negative, pessimistic.

ezezkotasun *n.* negativity, pessimism.

ezezle *adj.* reproving, disapproving.

ezezpen *n.* negation, denial, refusal, rejection.

ezeztadura *n.* annihilation, destruction; cancellation, nullification.

ezeztaezin *adj.* undeniable, irrefutable.

ezeztagaitz *adj.* difficult to deny, hard to refute.

ezeztagarri *adj.* deniable, refutable, not provable. *adj.* destructible, destroyable.

ezeztaile *n.* denier, annuller, suppressor, one who denies, prohibits, etc.

ezeztaketa *n.* annulment, suspension, negation.

ezeztakor *adj.* argumentative; annulling.

ezeztaldi *n.* cancellation, annulment.

ezeztapen *n.* annulment, revocation, cancellation, abolition.

ezeztarazi *v.t.* to cause to destroy, to cause to deny.

ezeztatu *v.t.* to annul, to abolish, to destroy. *v.t.* to deny, to negate; to contradict, to refute, to rebut, to revoke, to countermand; to disapprove.

ezeztatzaile *n.* revoker, denier, destroyer. *adj.* revoking, denying, destructive.

ezeztu *v.t.* to deny, to negate. *v.t.* to prohibit, to refuse.

ezgai *adj.* incapable, inept, useless.

ezgaitasun *n.* incapacity, ineptitude, unskillfulness, uselessness.

ezgaitu *v.t.* to invalidate, to annul; to make useless. *v.i.* to become unable, to become incapacitated, to become useless.

ezgarai *n.* inconvenient time, wrong time.

ezgaraitasun *n.* inconvenience, inopportuneness.

ezgauza *n.* trifle, triviality. *adj.* incapable, inept, incompetent; useless.

ezgauzadura *n.* inability, ineptitude.

ezgauzatasun *n.* ineptitude, incompetence.

ezgauzatu *v.t.* to incapacitate, to disable, to make useless.

ezgisako *adj.* unsuited, unfitting, inappropriate.

ezgizakor *adj.* inhuman.

-ezia *(gram.)* suffix which denotes an abstract idea. **Ahulezia.** Weakness.

ezik *prep.* except, save. *conj.* if not, unless, without.

ezikasi *adj.* uneducated, unlearned, illiterate.

ezikusi egin *v.t.* to ignore, to pay no attention to.

ezikuskor. *adj.* invisible.

ezikustaldi *n.* temporary blindness.

ezin *(gram.)* can't. Word preceding the verb and denoting impossibility, inability, incapability. **Ezin jan.** To be unable to eat. *n.* inability, the impossible, impossibility, impotence, incapability. *adj.* impossible.

ezinase *adj.* insatiable, gluttonous.

ezinbeste *n.* great difficulty; unavoidable necessity. *n.* destiny, fate.

ezinbestean *adv.* necessarily, inevitably, with no other choice, out of necessity, as a last resort.

ezinbesteko *adj.* absolutely necessary, inevitable, indispensable, mandatory, obligatory.

ezinbestez *adv.* necessarily, inevitably.

ezindu *v.t./v.i.* to incapacitate, to make impossible, to paralyze. *adj.* incapacitated, paralyzed.

ezindun *adj.* incapacitated; paralyzed.

ezindura *n.* disablement, incapacitation, paralyzation.

ezinegin *n.* impotence, powerlessness, inability.

ezineginezko *adj.* impossible to do, unrealizable.

ezinegon *n.* impatience, uneasiness, nervousness. *adj.* impatient, nervous.

ezinegonezko *adj.* nervous, unsettled, uneasy.

ezinegonik *adv.* nervously, anxiously, uneasily.

ezinelkartuzko *adj.* incompatible.

ezinerabakizko *adj.* undecidable, unsolvable.

ezinerabilizko *adj.* unuseable, useless.

ezineramanezko *adj.* unbearable, unsupportable, insufferable.

ezineramangarri *adj.* unbearable, unsupportable, insufferable.

ezinesana n. speechlessness, inability to speak.

ezinesanaldi n. aphasia, temporary loss of speech.

ezinesandako adj. inexpressible, unutterable.

ezinesanezko adj. indescribable, inexpressible; excellent.

ezinezko adj. impossible.

ezinezkoan adv. in case it's not possible.

ezingehiagoko adj. insuperable, unsurmountable; unsurpassable, supreme.

ezingogortuzko adj. incohesive, incapable of setting, hardening, thickening, etc.

ezingordezko adj. unconcealable, unpreservable, not maintainable.

ezinibilizko adj. impassable (road, street, etc.)

ezinikusi n. grudge, animosity, ill-will, malevolence.

ezin ikusi. v.t. to not be able to see. v.t. to hate.

ezinikusiaz adv. grudgingly, malevolently.

ezinikusizko adj. invisible.

ezinikutuzko adj. untouchable, intangible.

eziniraganezko adj. impassable; unsurmountable. adj. impermeable.

ezinirakurrizko adj. illegible.

eziniritxizko adj. inaccessible, unreachable.

ezinitzalizko adj. unextinguishable, incapable of being turned off or put out, eternal (flame).

ezinitzulizko adj. unexchangeable, unreturnable; untranslatable.

ezin izan v.i. to be impossible.

ezinjasanezko adj. unbearable, insufferable.

ezinkizun n. impossibility (in the future). n. impotence, impotency.

ezinkor adj. impotent, incapable; not realizable.

ezinluzatuzko adj. unextendible, unprolongable.

ezinmoldatuzko adj. inflexible, unbendable; unadaptable.

ezinmugituzko adj. immobile, immovable.

ezinsendatuzko adj. incurable.

ezinsinetzizko adj. incredible, unbelievable.

ezinsinisgarri adj. unbelievable, incredible.

ezintasun n. impossibility, impotence, inability, incapability.

ezin ukan v.t. to be unable to, can't, cannot.

ezinukatuzko adj. undeniable.

ezinulertuzko adj. incomprehensible, unintelligible.

ezinustelduzko adj. incorruptible.

ezinzimelduzko adj. unperishable,

unwithering.

eziraunkor adj. precarious, unstable, unsteady, fleeting, not lasting.

ezizate n. nonexistence; unreality.

ezizen n. nickname.

ezjakin adj. ignorant, uneducated, illiterate; rude. n. ignorance.

ezjakinean adv. ignorantly, unknowingly.

ezjakinez adv. ignorantly, unknowingly.

ezjakintasun n. ignorance, illiteracy, lack of education.

ezjakintza n. ignorance, lack of education, illiteracy.

ezjakite n. ignorance, lack of education, illiteracy.

ezjakitez adv. ignorantly, unknowingly.

ezjakituria n. ignorance, lack of education, illiteracy.

ezkabia n. dandruff. n. mange; ringworm.

ezkabiatsu adj. full of scabs, mangy.

ezkabiatu v.i. to scab, to form a scab.

ezkailu n. (zool.) minnow, small greenish fresh water fish.

ezkal n. splinter, chip.

ezkanda n. chip, splinter.

ezkaratz n. vestibule, entrance, entryway. n. kitchen.

ezkata n. scale.

ezkatadun adj. scaly.

ezkatadura n. scaling (of fish).

ezkatatsu adj. scaly.

ezkel adj. cross-eyed.

ezkeldu v.i. to become cross-eyed. v.t. to squint, to make (someone) squint.

ezkeltasun n. (med.) strabismus, squint.

ezker adj. left-handed. n. left hand. n. left (part); left (turn). adj. leftist.

ezker-eskuin adj. ambidextrous, left and right-handed.

ezkerka adv. with the left hand, left-handed (playing, etc.).

ezkerkada n. left, blow with the left hand.

ezkero conj. once, after. conj. since. conj. in case, in case of, if.

ezkeroz conj. considering that, given that, since, after, in that case.

ezkerralde n. left side. n. (naut.) port, left side of a boat.

ezkerraldeko adj. on the left, of the left side, pertaining to the left.

ezkerreko adj. leftist, left.

ezkerreratu v.i. to go to the left, to incline towards the left, to lean to the left.

ezkerreria n. leftist group.

ezkerreskuindar adj. ambidextrous.

ezkerrindar n. leftist force.

ezkerti adj. left-handed.

ezkertiar n. leftist. adj. leftist, left.

ezkertiartasun n. leftism.

ezkertu v.i. to go to the left.

ezki n. (bot.) linden tree.

ezkila n. small bell.

ezkiladorre n. belfry, bell tower.
ezkilagile n. bell maker.
ezkilajoile n. bellman, bell ringer.
ezkilaldi n. tolling of the bell, ringing of the bell.
ezkilamihi n. bell clapper.
ezkilano n.(dim.) small bell.
ezkilasoinu n. sound of the bell.
ezkilategi n. bell tower.
ezkilatxo n.(dim.) small bell.
ezkilots n. peal, ringing of bells.
ezko n. wax. n. long wax candle.
ezkoargi n. wax candle, taper.
ezkodun adj. waxy.
ezkodura n. waxing.
ezkogile n. candlemaker.
ezkogin n. candlemaker.
ezkogintza n. candlemaking.
ezkon- Used in compound words. Derived from ezkondu, to marry.
ezkonagintza n. engagement, betrothal.
ezkonahaidego n. relationship by marriage.
ezkonahizpa n. sister-in-law (for a female speaker).
ezkonanaia n. brother-in-law (for a male speaker).
ezkonarauz adv. matrimonially, conjugally.
ezkonaro n. marriageable age.
ezkonarreba n. sister-in-law (for a male speaker).
ezkonberri adj. newlywed, just married.
ezkonbiziera n. married life.
ezkondei n. marriage proclamation, banns (usually used in plural).
ezkondu v.i. to get married.
ezkoneragozpen n. matrimonial impediment, obstacle that prevents one from marrying.
ezkoneraile n. person who kills his spouse.
ezkonetsai n. misogamist (person who hates marriage).
ezkonetsaigo n. misogamy, hatred of marriage.
ezkonezin adj. unmarriable.
ezkongabe adj. single, unmarried.
ezkongabetasun n. bachelorhood, spinsterhood, singleness, quality of being unmarried.
ezkongabezia n. bachelorhood, spinsterhood, singleness, quality of being unmarried.
ezkongai n./adj. single, unmarried; fiancé(e).
ezkongaialdi n. period preceding marriage, single days; engagement, courtship.
ezkongaiaro n. period preceding marriage, single days; time of courtship.
ezkongaitasun n. state of being sweethearts.
ezkongaitu v.i. to become engaged.

ezkongarri adj. marriageable, marriable.
ezkongarritasun n. state of being marriageable, state of being eligible for marriage.
ezkonge adj. unmarried, single.
ezkongetasun n. bachelorhood, spinsterhood, quality of being unmarried.
ezkongile n. matchmaker, marriage broker, matrimonial agent.
ezkonkide n. bride, groom. n. best man, maid of honor.
ezkonlagun n. bride, groom, consort, companion. n. best man; person who presents a bride for marriage.
ezkonlaguntasun n. state of being a bride or groom; state of being best man; state of being one who presents a bride for marriage.
ezkonlege n. marriage law, nuptial law.
ezkonlegez adv. matrimonially, conjugally.
ezkonlokarri n. marriage bonds.
ezkonmin n. desire to marry.
ezkontadin n. marriageable age.
ezkontadineko adj. marriageable, marriable.
ezkontarazi v.t. to cause to get married; to marry.
ezkontasun n. state of being married.
ezkontaurreko adj. prenuptial.
ezkontegun n. wedding day.
ezkonteragozpen n. marriage impediment, obstacle preventing one from marrying.
ezkonteraztun n. wedding ring.
ezkontide n. bride, groom. n. best man, maid of honor.
ezkontidetu v.i. to become a spouse, to be a bride, to be a groom.
ezkontitz n. marriage vows; proposal of marriage.
ezkontohe n. marriage bed.
ezkontsari n. dowry.
ezkontza n. marriage, matrimony.
ezkontzagile n. matchmaker, marriage broker, matrimonial agent.
ezkontzagin n. matchmaker, marriage broker, matrimonial agent.
ezkontzagintza n. marriage agency, matchmaking.
ezkontzahaide n. in-law, relative by marriage.
ezkontzahaidetasun n. relationship by marriage.
ezkontzahaidetu v.i. to be related by marriage, to become in-laws.
ezkontzako adj. conjugal, matrimonial, marital.
ezkontzalari n. matchmaker, marriage broker, matrimonial agent.
ezkontzama n. mother-in-law.
ezkontzaurre n. time preceding marriage.
ezkontzaurreko adj. prenuptial, prematrimonial, premarital, before

the wedding.

ezkontzausle n. divorced person, one who instigates a divorce; home wrecker.

ezkontzauste n. divorce

ezkontzazko adj. marital, nuptial, matrimonial.

ezkor adj. negative, pessimistic.

ezkortasun n. negativism, pessimism.

ezkosaltzaile n. candle seller, wax seller.

ezkotzaile n. waxer.

ezkozko adj. made of wax.

ezkoztadura n. waxing, applying wax.

ezkoztatu v.t. to wax.

ezkozuzi n. wax taper.

ezku n.(bot.) linden tree, basswood.

ezkur n.(bot.) acorn.

ezkurdi n. place abundant in acorns.

ezkurdia n. abundance of acorns.

ezkurdun adj. acorn-bearing.

ezkurketa n. acorn harvest.

ezkurrazal n. acorn shell.

ezkutaketa n. hiding, concealment.

ezkutaleku n. hiding place, hideaway, shelter.

ezkutapen n. hiding, concealment.

ezkutarazi v.t. to hide, to conceal.

ezkutari adj. enigmatic, mysterious. n. accomplice, hider, shelterer.

ezkutatu v.t./v.i. to hide, to conceal.

ezkutatzaile n. hider, concealer.

ezkutu n. hiding place. adj. hidden, secret.

ezkutuan adv. secretly, mysteriously.

ezkutuki adv. secretly, furtively. n.(R.C.Ch.) one of fifteen mysteries of the Rosary.

ezkutuko adj. secret, hidden, secretive; latent.

ezkutune n. hidden place, hideaway, shelter, secret part.

ezkutuz adv. secretly, mysteriously.

ezkutuzko adj. secret, mysterious.

ezlegetasun n. illegitimacy.

ezlegetu v.t. to make illegitimate.

ezlegez adv. illegitimately.

ezlegezko adj. illegitimate.

ezleial adj. disloyal, unfaithful, unloyal.

ezleialtasun n. disloyalty, unfaithfulness.

ezmoral adj. immoral.

ezmoraltasun n. immorality.

eznormal adj. abnormal.

eznormalki adv. abnormally.

ezohitu v.i. to become unaccustomed to. adj. inexperienced.

ezohore n. dishonor, disgrace.

ezongi adj./adv. indisposed, unwell.

ezongialdi n. indisposition, passing illness.

ezordainketa n. nonpayment.

ezordu n. inconvenient time, wrong time, unseasonable time, unreasonable time.

ezorduko adj. untimely, inopportune, inconvenient.

ezorduz adv. untimely, inopportunely, inconveniently.

ezoso adj. incomplete, unfinished.

ezosoki adv. incompletely.

ezpain n.(anat.) lip. n.(fig.) edge, border, rim.

ezpainandi adj. large lipped.

ezpaindun adj. labiate (plant).

ezpaineko adj. labial. n. a blow to the lips.

ezpainetako n. blow to the lip, slap on the mouth.

ezpainkatu v.t. to kiss repeatedly.

ezpainketa n. repeated kissing.

ezpainlodi adj. thick-lipped, fat-lipped.

ezpal n. chip, splinter.

ezpaldu v.t. to split wood.

ezpalkatu v.t. to split wood.

ezpalketa n. splitting.

ezpalkor adj. splintery, having splinters; brittle, fragile.

ezpaltsu adj. splintery, having splinters.

ezpanpintura n. lipstick.

ezpare adj. unpaired, unmatched.

ezparetu v.t. to separate a pair. v.t. to break a tie, to make uneven.

ezpata n. sword. n. suit of swords in playing cards.

ezpatabelar n.(bot.) cattail, reed mace.

ezpataburu n. sword hilt.

ezpatada n. blow from a sword.

ezpatadantza n. Basque sword dance.

ezpatadantzari n. dancer in the Basque sword dance.

ezpatagile n. sword maker.

ezpatagin n. sword maker.

ezpatagintza n. sword manufacture.

ezpataho n. cutting edge of a sword.

ezpatajoko n. fencing, sword play, sword fighting.

ezpatakada n. sword stroke, blow with a sword.

ezpataketa n. fencing, sword play, sword fighting.

ezpataketari. n. fencer, sword fighter.

ezpatalari n. swordsman, fencer.

ezpatalore n.(bot.) cattail, reed mace.

ezpatandi n.(augm.) large sword.

ezpatari n. fencer, swordsman.

ezpatarrain n.(zool.) swordfish.

ezpatatu v.t. to fence; to fight with swords.

ezpatatxo n.(dim.) small sword.

ezpatatzar n.(augm.) large sword, broadsword.

ezpatazorro n. scabbard, sheath.

ezpel n.(bot.) box tree.

ezpeldi n.(bot.) forest of box trees.

ezpeldoi n.(bot.) forest of box trees.

ezpelki n. chip of boxwood.

ezpeltsu adj. abundant in box trees.

ezpi n. fish spine. n. snake fang.

ezproin n. spur.

ezproindu v.t. to spur.

ezproineztatu v.t. to spur.

ezproinkada n. spurring.

ezproinketa n. spurring.

ezprointxo n.(dim.) small spur.

ezta conj. neither, not either; not even. v. aux. Var. of ez da, is not. Word used at the end of interrogative sentences. Equivalent of isn't it?, aren't you?, etc. **Zu ere etorriko zara, ezta?** You are coming too, aren't you? int. go on! get out of here! no way! **Ni hirekin ezkondu? Ezta..!** Me, marry you? Go on!

eztabaida n. argument, discussion, dispute. n. doubt, vacillation.

eztabaida egin v.t. to argue, to dispute, to discuss.

eztabaidagarri adj. arguable, disputable, discussible.

eztabaidaka adv. arguing, argumentatively, discussing.

eztabaidako adj. pertaining to a discussion. adj. doubtful, uncertain.

eztabaidakor adj. argumentative, quarrelsome.

eztabaidari n. polemicist, arguer, disputer, discusser.

eztabaidatsu adj. indecisive, hesitant.

eztabaidatu v.t./v.i. to discuss, to debate, to argue.

eztabaidatzaile n. discusser, arguer. adj. argumentative, discussing.

eztabaidazale adj. fond of argument, argumentative.

eztabaidazko adj. doubtful, dubious, uncertain.

ezta ere conj. neither, not either, neither . . . nor, either . . . or.

eztainadura n. tinning, plating or coating with tin.

eztainari n. tinsmith.

eztainatzaile n. tinsmith.

eztainu n. tin.

eztainugile n. tinsmith.

eztainulari n. tinsmith.

eztainutegi n. tin refinery.

eztainutsu adj. tinny.

eztainuzko adj. tin, made of tin.

eztainuztapen n. tinsmithing, act of working with tin.

eztainuztu v.t. to solder with tin.

eztanda n. explosion.

eztanda egin v.t. to explode, to blow up; to burst, to break, to break out (a storm).

eztanda eragin v.t. to make (something) explode, to blow (something) up.

eztandaezin adj. unexplodable.

eztandagailu n. explosive, bomb.

eztandagarri adj. explosive, explodable.

eztandatu v.t./v.i. to explode, to blow up, to blast, to burst.

eztarmin n.(med.) laryngitis.

eztarri n.(anat.) throat.

eztarriko adj. guttural, throaty.

eztarrimozketa n. cutting the throat; beheading.

eztarriz adv. gutturally.

eztarrizulo n.(anat.) trachea.

-eztatu (gram.) Verbal suffix meaning to cover with or to supply with. **Papereztatu.** To cover with wallpaper, to paper.

eztei n. wedding party, wedding celebration, reception, wedding anniversary.

eztei- Used in compound words.

ezteiak n.(pl.) wedding celebration, wedding festivities, wedding anniversary.

ezteibazkari n. wedding banquet.

ezteibidaia n. honeymoon.

ezteibilaldi n. honeymoon.

ezteidei n. wedding invitation.

ezteiegun n. wedding day.

ezteietako adj. nuptial, wedding.

ezteikanta n. nuptial song, epithalamium.

ezteilagun n. wedding guest.

ezteiliar n. wedding guest.

ezten n. awl. n. stinger.

eztendu v.t. to sting; to poke. v.t.(fig.) to stimulate, to incite.

eztendun adj. having a stinger.

eztenka adv. stingingly.

eztenkada n. stinging, sting. n.(fig.) irony, stinging words, satire.

eztenkari n. stinger. adj.(fig.) biting, sarcastic, ironic.

eztenkatu v.t. to sting, to prick. v.t.(fig.) to stimulate, to incite.

eztenkatzaile n./adj. stinger; stinging. n./adj.(fig.) exciter, stimulator; exciting, stimulating.

eztenmakila n. goad, prod.

eztentxo n.(dim.) small stinger. n.(dim.) stiletto.

ezti n. honey. adj. agreeable, sweet, easy, docile, soft, calm, gentle.

eztialdi n. season of abundant honey production. n. calm, smoothness.

eztiarazi v.t. to calm, to pacify.

eztiarazle n. calmer, pacifier.

eztibilaldi n. honeymoon.

eztidun adj. honeyed, mellifluous. n. honey seller.

eztidura n. smoothing, mitigation, pacification; reduction of swelling.

eztiegite n. honey making.

eztigai n. nectar. adj. calming, mitigating.

eztigarri adj. calming, mitigating.

eztigile n. honey producer.

eztigintza n. honey production.

eztijario adj. sweet, mellifluous, honeyed.

eztikeria n. excessive sweetness. n. adulation, flattery.

eztiketa n. search for honey. n. grafting.

eztiki adv. sweetly. adv. calmly, smoothly, slowly.

eztikiro adv. smoothly, calmly, slowly.

eztikoi adj. fond of honey.
eztikoloredun adj. honey-colored.
eztikor adj. softening, mollifying, calming.
eztimargodun adj. honey-colored.
eztiro adv. sweetly. adv. smoothly, softly, agreeably, calmly, slowly.
eztisaltzaile n. honey seller.
eztitasun n. sweetness. n. smoothness, softness; calmness (at sea); meekness.
eztitsu adj. sweet, mellifluous, honeyed. adj. smooth, soft, agreeable; calm; moderate.
eztitu v.i./v.t. to sweeten (with honey), to put honey in. v.t./v.i. to calm (down), to smoothen, to mitigate, to alleviate.
eztitzaile n./adj. sweetener; sweetening. n./adj. mollifier, pacifier; mollifying, pacifying.
eztiur n. honeywater.
eztiurdun adj. honeyed (water).
eztizale adj. fond of honey, honey-loving.
eztizko adj. honey, made of honey.
eztiztatu v.t. to smear with honey, to honey.
eztiztu v.t. to smear with honey, to sweeten with honey.
eztrakzio n. extraction.
eztul n. cough.
eztulak eman v.t. to have a coughing fit, to have an attack of coughing.
eztulaldi n. coughing attack.
eztuldun adj. coughing.
eztul egin v.t. to cough.
eztulka adv. coughing.
eztulkari n. cougher.
eztulkukurruku n. whooping cough.
ezuste n. coincidence, chance, serendipity. n. spontaneity.
ezustean adv. casually, unthinkingly, by chance.
ezusteko adj. surprising, unforeseen.
ezustel adj. not rotten.
ezustelkor adj. incorruptible; unspoilable.
ezustez adv. unexpectedly, accidentally, coincidentally.

F

f n. Letter of the Basque alphabet which occurs in all dialects and also in the earliest literature dating from the sixteenth century. Many Basques have substituted p for f. The current tendency is to use f again. There are not many words in Basque which begin with f.
faboragarri adj. favorable.
fabore n. favor, help, assistance, aid.
faboredun adj. favored, privileged.
faboretu v.t. to help, to aid, to assist.
faboretzaile n. protector, benefactor.
faborez int. please.
fabrika n. factory.

fabrikaketa n. fabrication, manufacture.
fabrikante n. manufacturer.
fabrikapen n. manufacturing.
fabrikatu v.t. to manufacture, to fabricate.
fabrikatzaile n. manufacturer.
fabrikazio n. manufacturing.
fadura n. salt marsh, swamp.
fago n.(bot.) beech tree.
fagoaga n. place or abundance of beech trees. Used as a last name.
fagodi n. forest of beech trees, beech tree grove.
fagoki n. piece of beech wood.
fagondo n. beech tree.
faisai n.(zool.) pheasant.
faktore n. factor.
faktura n. bill, invoice.
fakturaketa n. billing.
fakturapen n. billing.
fakturatu v.t. to bill.
fakturazio n. billing.
fakultate n. faculty.
falta n. error, mistake; sin. n. fault in sports. n. scarcity, lack.
faltadun adj. guilty.
faltagabe adj. innocent, guiltless.
falta izan v.i. to lack, to be missing.
faltatsu adj. faulty, prone to error, full of mistakes.
faltatu v.i. to lack, to miss. v.t. to bother, to insult.
falta ukan v.t. to need.
faltsu adj. false, counterfeit. adj. deceptive. adj. inexact.
faltsukeria n. falsity, duplicity.
faltsuketa n. falsification.
faltsuki adv. falsely.
faltsupen n. falsification.
faltsutasun n. falseness, falsity.
faltsutu v.t. to falsify, to counterfeit.
faltsutzaile n. falsifier, counterfeiter.
faltsuztapen n. falsification, adulteration, counterfeiting, tampering (with a product).
faltsuztatu v.t. to falsify, to adulterate, to counterfeit, to tamper (with).
fama n. fame, reputation.
famadun adj. famous, reputed.
famagabe adj. infamous, base, vile. adj. unknown.
fama kendu v.t. to defame.
famakenketa n. defamation, slander.
famakentzaile n. defamer, slanderer.
famatsu adj. famous, celebrated, renowned.
famatu v.t. to make famous, to bring fame. adj. famous, celebrated, renowned.
famatxar n. infamy, baseness, vileness.
familia n. family.
familiako adj. familial, pertaining to a family.
familiarki adj. familiarly.
familiburu n. head of a family.

fanatiko n./adj. fanatic; fanatical.
fanatismo n. fanaticism.
fanatizatu v.i. to be a fanatic.
fandango n. type of Basque dance; melody for the Basque flute.
faneka n.(zool.) bib, small white-meated fish.
fantasia n. fantasy.
fantasiatsu adj. fantastic, capricious.
fantasioski adv. fantastically, capriciously.
fardel n. knapsack, bag, bundle, package. adj. untidy, slovenly. adj. indolent, lazy.
fardeldu v.t. to pack, to bundle, to package. v.i. to become untidy, to become slovenly.
fardeleria n. luggage, baggage.
fardelkari n. packer, shipper.
fardelkeria n. indolence, laziness.
fardelki adv. carelessly, untidily, in a slovenly manner.
fardeltoki n. place where bundles are kept.
fardeltxo n.(dim.) small bundle.
fardeltzar n.(augm.) large bundle, large suitcase or trunk.
fardo adj. spongy, mushy (wood, fruit). n. rough cloth. n. large bolt of cloth, bale.
fardotasun n. sponginess, mushiness.
fardotu v.i. to become spongy (wood, mushrooms, etc.), to become mushy.
fardoztatu v.t. to pack, to bale, to crate.
fardoztagailu n. machine for packing or crating, baler.
farfaila adj. presumptuous, vain. adj. untidy, slovenly.
farfailadun adj. presumptuous, vain.
farfailtasun n. frivolity.
farfar n. rustling, onomatopoeic sound of moving leaves or branches.
farmazia n. pharmacy, drugstore.
farmaziagintza n. pharmacy, profession of a pharmacist.
faro n. lighthouse.
farol n. lantern.
farolari n. lamplighter.
farolgile n. lantern maker.
farozain n. lighthouse keeper.
farozaintza n. lighthouse keeping.
farra-farra adv. profusely, abundantly.
farranda n. boast, brag, ostentation.
farrasta n. splash, onomatopoeic sound made by spilling liquids.
farrastada n. amount of liquid spilled, sloshed, etc.
farrastaldi n. act of throwing out liquids.
farrastatu v.t. to throw out liquids (with a tub, bucket).
farre n. laugh.
fase n. phase, facet.
faseaskodun adj. polyphase, multiphase.

fasebakar adj. monophase.
fasebiko adj. diphase, diphasic.
fasetsu adj. polyphase.
faun adj. spongy, soft. adj. withered, wilted.
faundu v.i. to wither, to wilt.
faungarri adj. perishable, witherable, wiltable.
faunki adv. softly, gently; weakly.
fauntasun n. softness, lack of vigor.
faxa n. girdle; swaddling.
faxismo n. fascism.
faxista n./adj. fascist.
fede n. faith, belief. n. intention.
fedeaitorle n. confessor, one who proclaims his faith.
fedeaitormen n. profession of faith.
fedeaitortzaile n. believer.
fededun n. believer, faithful. adj. believing, faithful.
fedegabe adj. atheist; incredulous; nonbelieving.
fedegabekeria. n. incredulity; lack of faith; atheism.
fedegabeki adv. incredulously; lacking faith; atheistically.
fedegabeko adj. incredulous; nonbelieving; atheistic.
fedegabetasun n. atheism; disbelief; infidelity.
fedegabetu v.i. to lose faith.
fedegabezia n. unbelief, lack of faith.
fedegaizto n. falseness, perfidy, disloyalty.
fedegaiztoz adv. falsely, disloyally.
fedegalduko adj. apostate; renegade.
fedegutxiko adj. having a little faith; sceptical.
fedehausketa n. heresy; apostasy.
fedehauskor adj. heretic, heretical.
fedehausle n. heretic.
federakor adj. federal, federated.
federakunde n. federation.
federakuntza n. federation.
federal adj. federal.
federalismo n.(pol.) federalism.
federalista adj. federalist.
federatu v.i./v.t. to federate, to federalize.
federazio n. federation.
fedetsu adj. faithful, believing.
fedeukapen n. renunciation of faith, apostasy.
fedeukatzaile n. renouncer of faith.
fedezko adj. faithful, believing.
femenino adj. feminine.
feminismo n. feminism.
feminista adj. feminist.
fereka n. caress; stroke, petting. n. flattery.
ferekaldi n. caressing, petting, rubbing.
ferekari n. flatterer, brown-noser. n. caresser, masseur.
ferekatu v.t. to caress, to stroke gently. v.t. to flatter, to brown-nose, to cajole. v.t. to rub, to stroke.

ferekatzaile n./adj. caresser, masseur; caressing. n./adj. flatterer, fawner; flattering, fawning.
fereku n. caress. n. flattery, fawning.
feria n. fair.
ferialari n. fairgoer.
fermentagarri adj. fermentable.
fermentapen n. fermentation.
fermentatu v.i. to ferment.
ferra n. horseshoe.
ferradura n. horseshoeing.
ferraezarle n. horseshoer, farrier.
ferragabetu v.t. to remove shoes from a horse or cow.
ferratoki n. place for shoeing livestock.
ferratu v.t. to shoe livestock.
ferratzaile n. farrier, horseshoer.
festa n. festival, feast.
festazale adj. party lover, lover of festivals.
festegun n. holiday, festival day.
fetitxe n. fetish.
fetitxismo n. fetishism.
feudal adj. feudal.
feudalismo n. feudalism.
fiantza n.(econ.) bail, security, guarantee, deposit, bond.
fidagaitz adj. untrustworthy. adj. distrustful.
fidagaiztasun n. distrust.
fidagarri adj. trustworthy.
fidagarritasun n. confidence, trust; credibility.
fidakaizkor adj. distrustful.
fidakaizkortasun n. distrustfulness.
fidakaiztu v.i. to distrust.
fidaketa n. confidence, trust.
fidakor adj. confident, trusting.
fidakorki adv. trustingly.
fidantza n. confidence, trust. n.(econ.) deposit, bail, security, guarantee, bond.
fidarazi v.t. to assure, to guarantee.
fidatu v.i. to have faith in, to trust, to rely on, to believe in.
fidatuki adv. faithfully, trustingly.
fideo n. very thin noodle, vermicelli.
fiit! n. toot!, tweet!, onomatopoeic sound of a whistle.
fikzio n. fiction.
fikziozko adj. fictional.
filma n. film, movie.
filma egin v.t. to film, to make a movie.
filmagailu n. movie camera.
filmari n. film maker, movie maker.
filmatu v.t. to film, to make a movie.
filmina n. slide(s).
filologari n. philologist.
filologia n. philology.
filosofari n. philosopher.
filosofatu v.t. to philosophize.
filosofia n. philosophy.
filtrakor adj. filterable.
filtrapen n. filtration, filtering.
filtratu v.i./v.t. to filter.
filtro n. filter.
fin adj. fine. adj. diligent, hard-working.

adj. honest. adj. polite, considerate, well-mannered.
finantzak n.(econ.) finances.
finantzaketa n. financing.
finantzapen n. financing.
finantzari n. financer.
finantzatu v.t. to finance.
finantzatzaile n. financer.
finantzetxe n. house of finance.
findu v.t. to polish, to refine. v.i. to become refined, to be polite, to become educated.
findura n. courtesy, refinement, fineness.
finkadura n. firmness, stability, steadfastness.
finkagabe adj. nomadic, drifting, wandering.
finkagailu n.(mech.) vise, clamp.
finkagarri adj. fixing, fastening, propping, supporting.
finkaketa n. fixation, fixing, consolidation.
finkamendu n. fixation, fixing, consolidation. n. security, guarantee.
finkapen n. fixation, fixing, consolidation. n. security, guarantee.
finkatu v.t. to fix, to stabilize, to fasten. v.i. to settle, to establish.
finkatzaile n. fixer, fastener, stabilizer. adj. fixative.
finkeria n. excessive delicacy, preciosity.
finki adv. firmly. adv. finely, politely.
finko adv. firmly.
finkotasun n. firmness, stability, surety, durability.
fintasun n. fineness; courtesy.
fir-fir n. sound of the wind, sound of the leaves rustling in the wind.
firi-firi n. breeze.
firrinda n. whistling sound (wind, whip, etc.).
fisika n. physics.
fisikari n. physicist.
fisiko adj. physical.
fisikoki adv. physically.
fisiologari n. physiologist.
fisiologia n. physiology.
fiskal n. prosecutor, prosecuting attorney.
fiskalgela n. prosecuting attorney's office.
fiskalgo n. prosecuting attorney's job.
fiskalizagarri adj. inspectable, supervisable.
fiskalizapen n. investigation, inspection; supervision.
fiskalizatu v.t. to investigate, to inspect; to supervise.
fisku n. national treasury.
fisonomia n. physiognomy.
fisonomista n. physiognomist.
fite adv. rapidly, quickly.
fits n. trifle, trinket.
fitsik adv. nothing, anything. Always used in negative sentences.

fitskeria n. futility.
fitxa n. card. n. chip, marker (gambling).
fitxategi n. card file, index file, card catalog.
flamenkera n. Flemish language.
flamenko n. flamenco. n./adj. Flemish.
flauta n. flute.
flautajole n. flautist.
flota n. flotilla.
flotagailu n. life jacket, inner tube.
flotagarri adj. floatable.
flotagarritasun n. floatability.
flotapen n. flotation.
flotatu v.t. to float.
flotatxo n.(dim.) small flotilla.
foku n. electric light socket.
folklore n. folklore.
folklorezko adj. folkloric.
folklorezale adj. folklorist.
folkloriko adj. folkloric.
folklorista n./adj. folklorist.
fonema n. phoneme.
fonetika n. phonetics.
fonologia n. phonology.
forma n. form.
formagabeko adj. formless, shapeless.
formal adj. honest, good, well behaved, nice.
formaldu v.i. to become honest, to become well behaved.
formalismo n. formalism.
formalki adv. formally. adv. honestly, nicely.
formula n. formula.
formulapen n. formulation.
forratu v.t. to line, to cover (clothes, books, etc.).
foru n. name for individual autonomous rights of the Basque people.
foruak n.(pol.) old Basque liberties; compilation of Basque laws.
forukontrako adj. illegal, against the old Basque laws.
forutar adj. statutory, pertaining to the *foruak*.
forutu v.t. to make statutes or old Basque laws.
foruzale adj. devoted to the old Basque laws.
foruzaletasun n. devotion to the old Basque laws.
foruzko adj. pertaining to the old Basque laws.
fosforargi n. phosphorescence.
fosforeztatu v.i./v.t. to phosphoresce.
fosforo n.(chem.) phosphorous.
fosil n. fossil.
fosildu v.i. to fossilize.
fosileztapen n. fossilization.
foto n. photograph, picture.
fraide n. friar.
fraidegai n. novice, preparing to be a friar.
fraidego n. religious state of being a friar.

fraidemotz n. friar, not ordained, sees to domestic matters.
fraidetasun n. quality of being a friar or a monk.
fraidetegi n. convent, monastery.
fraidetu v.i. to become a friar.
fraidetxe n. convent, monastery.
fraile n. friar.
fraka n. pants, trousers (usually used in the plural).
frakadun adj. male. adj.(fig.) valiant, brave. n. man.
frakagile n. pants maker, tailor.
frakajosle n. pants maker, tailor.
frakak n.(pl.) pants, trousers, slacks.
frakamotz n. short pants, shorts.
frakasatu v.t. to fail.
frakasu n. failure.
frakazahar adj. sluggard, slacker, listless.
frakerre adj. nervous, jittery, irritable.
frango adj. many, much, abundant, plenty of. adv. abundantly, much.
frangoki adv. abundantly.
frangotan adv. often.
frangotasun n. abundance.
franko adv. abundantly, a lot. adj. large, great, plenty of.
frankoki adv. abundantly.
frankolin n.(zool.) stone curlew, thick-knee.
frantzes n./adj. French.
frantzesarbi n.(bot.) beet.
frantzeseri n.(med.) syphilis.
frantzeskada n. gallicism.
frantzeskeria n. gallicism.
frantzesporru n.(bot.) asparagus.
frantzestiar adj. fond of French people, etc.
frantzestu v.i. to become French-like or gallicized. v.t. to make French-like, to gallicize.
frantzeszale adj. francophile.
Frantzia n.(geog.) France. **Frantziar.** French.
frantziskotar adj./n. Franciscan.
frantzizale adj. gallicist.
frenaldi n. braking.
frenatu v.t. to brake, to hit the brake.
frenu n. brake.
freskadura n. refreshment, act of refreshing.
freskagarri adj. refreshing. n. refreshment.
freskaketa n. refrigeration.
freskakor adj. refrigerant.
freskatu v.i./v.t. to refresh, to refrigerate, to cool.
freskatzaile adj. refreshing, cooling.
fresku adj. fresh. n. cool, coolness. adj. newly made, fresh.
freskura n. freshness, coolness.
freskutasun n. freshness, coolness.
frijialdi n. fry, dish of anything fried.
frijidura n. frying.
frijigailu n. frying pan.
frijitegi n. frying place.

frijitu *v.t./v.i.* to fry.
frijitzaile *n.* one who fries.
fristi-frasta *adv.* willy-nilly, carelessly.
froga *n.* proof, demonstration, verification.
frogabide *n.* verification, checking, way of proving.
frogaezin *adj.* unprovable, unverifiable.
frogagaitz *adj.* difficult to prove, difficult to verify.
frogagarri *adj.* provable, verifiable.
frogagarritasun *n.* provability, verifiability.
frogagiri *n.* written proof.
frogaketa *n.* proving, verification.
frogakor *adj.* probatory, probative.
frogaldi *n.* trial, test, attempt, proof.
frogaleku *n.* area for oxen weight pulling competition.
frogantza *n.* proving, verification, demonstration.
frogapen *n.* proving, verification.
frogarri *n.* main proof.
frogatu *v.t.* to demonstrate, to prove.
frogatzaile *n.* verifier, prover. *adj.* verifying, proving.
frontoi *n.* jai alai court, handball court, fronton.
fruita *n.* fruit.
fruitadenda *n.* fruitstand.
fruitakor *adj.* fruitful, fruit-bearing.
fruitari *n.* fruit seller.
fruitategi *n.* orchard. *n.* fruit store, place to store fruit.
fruitazain *n.* fruit grower.
fruitazaintza *n.* fruit cultivation.
fruitontzi *n.* fruit container, fruit bowl.
fruitu *n.* fruit, any kind of product of the earth. *n.(fig.)* consequence, result, product.
fruitudun *adj.* fruit-bearing.
fruituekarle *adj.* fruitful, fruit-bearing.
fruituemale *n.* fertilizer. *adj.* fertilizing.
fruitu eman *v.t.* to fructify, to bear fruit. *v.t.* to produce.
fruitugabe *adj.* fruitless, unproductive.
fruitugabetasun *n.* unfruitfulness, unproductiveness.
fruitugabezia *n.* unfruitfulness, unproductiveness.
fruitukor *adj.* fruitful, productive.
fruitukorki *adv.* fruitfully, productively.
fruitupen *n.* fructification.
fruitutsu *adj.* fruitful, productive.
fruitutu *v.i.* to fructify, to bear fruit.
fruituz *adv.* fruitfully.
fundapen *n.* act of laying a foundation, act of pounding.
fundatu *v.t.* to found, to settle, to establish.
fundatzaile *n.* founder.
fundigarri *adj.* meltable, smeltable.
funditu *v.t./v.i.* to smelt, to melt. *v.t.* to annihilate, to destroy, to ruin.
funditzaile *n.* destroyer, annihilator. *adj.* destroying, annihilating.
funikular *n.* funicular railway, ski lift,

tram.
funts *n.* foundation, base, basis. *n.* bottom, foundation, basement. *n.* character. *n.* exactitude.
funtsatu *v.t.* to base, to establish, to found, to settle.
funtsean *adv.* fundamentally, basically; primarily. *adv.* in summary, in brief, in short.
funtsez *adv.* basically, fundamentally.
funtsezko *adj.* essential, basic, elemental, fundamental.
funtsgabe *adj.* groundless, ephemeral, unfounded, unestablished, baseless.
funtsgabekeria *n.* inconstancy; absurdity. *n.* groundlessness.
funtsgabeki *adv.* groundlessly, without any reason, reasonlessly.
funtsgabeko *adj.* unfounded, unestablished, baseless, groundless, ephemeral.
funtsgabetasun *n.* groundlessness.
funtsik ez *adv.* nothing.
funtzio *n.* function (religious or civil).
funtzionalki *adv.* functionally.
funtzionamendu *n.* functioning.
funtzionari *n.* functionary.
funtzionatu *v.t.* to function, to work.
furgoi *n.* wagon, train car.
furra! *int.* here, chick, chick, chick! Onomatopoeic sound used to call chickens.
furrustada *n.* grumbling, growl.
furrustadaka *adv.* grumbling, growling.
furrustatu *v.t.* to reject, to think little of.
furrust egin *v.t.* to grumble, to growl; to snort, to chuckle.
fusil *n.* musket, rifle.
fusilamendu *n.* execution by shooting.
fusilari *n.* rifleman, fusilier.
fusilategi *n.* place of execution by shooting.
fusilatu *v.t.* to execute before a firing squad, to shoot (someone).
fusilkada *n.* blow with the butt of a rifle.
futbol *n.* soccer.
futbolari *n.* soccer player.
futboltzale *n.* soccer fan. *adj.* fond of soccer.
futbol-zelai *n.* soccer field.
futz *n.* blow, puff of air.
futz egin *v.t.* to blow (air on something).

G

g *n.* Letter of the Basque alphabet.
gaban *n.* overcoat.
gabardina *n.* raincoat.
gabarra *n.* barge, freight boat.
gabarrari *n.* bargeman.
gabe *prep.* without. *adj.* needy.
-gabe *(gram.)* Adjective suffix meaning lack of, -less. **Zentzugabe.** Irrational, senseless.
gabealdi *n.* time of need.

gabe izan *v.i.* to lack, to need, to be without.

gabekeria *n.* need, want, lack, privation.

gabeko *adj.* needy.

-gabeko *(gram.)* Suffix used to form adjectives denoting lack, privation.

gabetasun *n.* need, want, lack, scarcity.

gabetu *v.t.* to deprive (of). *v.i.* to be without, to lack.

-gabetu *(gram.)* Suffix used to form verbs denoting lack or privation. **Odolgabetu.** To bleed copiously; to lose a lot of blood.

gabez *prep.* without, for lack of.

gabezia *n.* need, lack, want.

gabezko *n.* lacking, needing.

gabi *n.* blacksmith's mallet.

gabon *int.* good night! *n.* Christmas.

gabon-abesti *n.* Christmas carol.

gabonak *n.(pl.)* Christmas.

gabonaldi *n.* Christmas time.

gabon-egun *n.* Christmas day.

gabonetako *adj.* Christmas, pertaining to Christmas.

gabon-gau *n.* night of Christmas eve.

gabonil *n.* December.

gabonjaiak *n.* Christmas holidays.

gabonkantari *n.* Christmas caroler.

gabonkantu *n.* Christmas carol.

gabonsari *n.* Christmas present, Christmas bonus.

gabonzahar *n.* New Year's Eve.

gai *adj.* apt, deserving, suited, suitable. *n.* material, matter, subject, theme.

-gai *(gram.)* Verbal suffix which denotes material; aptness.

gai egin *v.t.* to enable. *v.i.* to become deserving, to be fitting.

gaiez *adj.* undeserving, unfitting, incapable.

gaieza *n.* inability, ineptitude, incapacity, unsuitability.

gaieztapen *n.* inability, disability, incapacity, unsuitability.

gaieztasun *n.* inability, disability, incapacity, unsuitedness.

gaieztu *v.i.* to incapacitate, to disable, to be unsuited for.

gai izan *v.i.* to be able to, to be capable of, to be apt.

gaiki *n.* material, part, component.

gaikuntza *n.* qualification, capacity.

gailen *adj.* superior, excellent, superb.

gailendu *v.t./v.i.* to triumph, to beat, to overcome, to surpass, to prevail.

gailentasun *n.* excellence, superiority, supremacy.

gaileta *n.* cookie.

gailetontzi *n.* cookie jar, cookie box or package.

gailu *n.* instrument, device.

-gailu *(gram.)* Suffix which denotes instrument. **Haizegailu.** Ventilator, fan.

gailur *n.* top, summit, crest, peak. *n.* ridge of a roof.

gailurdun *adj.* peaked, crested.

gailurreratu *v.i.* to reach the summit, to reach the top.

gailurreria *n.* mountain range; cresting, an ornamental ridging to a wall or roof.

gailurteila *n.* tile of the ridge of a roof.

gailurtu *v.i.* to excel, to be prominent.

gain *n.* top, surface, summit, peak. *prep.* over, above, on, on top of. *n.* cream. *n.* responsibility; on one's own.

gain- *(gram.)* Prefix which denotes on top of, upper; over-, super-. **Gainbalio.** Surplus value.

-gain *(gram.)* Suffix which means over, above, on. Used to form nouns, usually place names and last names. **Ondargain.** On the sand.

gainaginte *n.* predominance, superiority.

gainalde *n.* height, altitude, elevation. *n.* surface. *n.* upper part.

gainalderatu *v.i.* to go towards the top.

gainarin *adj.* half-witted, scatter-brained.

gainarri *n.* key stone, topmost stone. *n.* upper grist stone of a mill.

gainartu *v.t.* to take charge of, to care for. *v.t.* to conquer, to vanquish, to dominate; to excel, to surpass.

gainase *v.i.* to oversaturate. *adj.* supersaturated.

gainasealdi *n.* supersaturation.

gainaseketa *n.* supersaturation.

gainasetasun *n.* supersaturation.

gainazal *n.* extra cover.

gainazpi egin *v.t.* to turn upside down, to subvert; to overthrow.

gainazpika *adv.* turning upside down; overthrowing.

gainazpikaldi *n.* overturning, subversion, upset.

gainazpikatu *v.t.* to turn upside down, to overturn. *v.t.* to dominate. *v.i.* to turn somersaults, to somersault.

gainazpiraketa *n.* inversion, turning upside down, overthrowing.

gainbalio *n.(econ.)* surplus value, increase in value.

gainbegiraketa *n.* supervision.

gainbegiraldi *n.* supervision.

gainbegirari *n.* supervisor, observer, overseer.

gainbegiratu *v.t.* to eye, to supervise. *n.* superficial glance.

gainbegiratzaile *n.* supervisor.

gainbehera *adv.* from head to toe; downhill. *n.* physical decline; decadence.

gainbeheraketa *n.* decadence, decline.

gainbeheraldi *n.* decline, decadence, fall, ruin.

gainbeheratsu *adj.* unlevel, uneven.
gainbeheratu *v.t.* to unlevel, to make uneven. *v.t.* to invert; to subvert. *v.t.* to overturn, to turn upside down, to carry upside down. *v.i.* to disintegrate, to collapse. *v.i.* to decline, to decrease. *v.i.*
gainbete *v.t./v.i.* to overfill; to overflow. *adj.* overflowing.
gainbide *n.* upper road, upper path, high road.
gainbizi *v.i.* to survive.
gainbizidun *adj.* surviving.
gainbizitza *n.* survival.
gainburuzketa *n.* somersault.
gaindi *n.* residue, leftovers, excess.
gaindiarazi *v.t.* to cause to overflow, to go out of the limits.
gaindidura *n.* redundancy, excess, redundance. *n.* spill, overflow.
gaindi egin *v.t.* to overflow.
gaindiezinezko *adj.* insuperable, insurmountable.
gaindigaitz *adj.* unsurpassable, insurmountable, not easily excelled.
gaindigarri *adj.* surpassable, superable, surmountable, able to be overcome.
gaindigarritasun *n.* quality of being surpassable, state of being superable.
gaindik *prep.* from above.
gaindikatu *v.i.* to overflow. *v.t.* to fill to overflowing.
gaindiko *adj.* superior, preponderant, prevailing.
gaindiro *adv.* superficially. *adv.* advantageously.
gainditasun *n.* superiority, preponderance, prevalence.
gainditu *v.t.* to overcome, to top, to surpass, to surmount. *v.i.* to overflow. *v.i.* to transcend, to exceed.
gaindizka *adv.* overflowingly, superabundantly, overabundantly, excessively.
gaindizkako *adj.* excessive, superfluous.
gaindizki *adv.* overflowingly, superabundantly, overabundantly, excessively.
gainean *prep.* on top of, over, on.
gainegaketa *n.* fly over.
gainegatu *v.t./v.i.* to fly over.
gainegitura *n.* superstructure.
gainegiturazko *adj.* superstructural.
gaineko *adj.* top. *adj.* dominant, high, predominant. *n.* overcoat.
gainelikadura *n.* overfeeding.
gainelikatu *v.t./v.i.* to overfeed; to overeat.
gainera *adv./prep.* furthermore, in addition to, other than; besides.
gaineragin *v.t.* to excel, to surpass.
gaineragipen *n.* surpassing, excelling.
gaineraiki *v.t.* to build over, to build on.

gainerako *adj.* secondary, nonessential, accessory, further; residual. *n.* surplus, extra money. *n.* rest, remains.
gainerakoak. *n.(pl.)* leftovers, remains.
gainerakoan *adv.* besides, moreover, furthermore.
gainerantzean *adv.* besides, moreover, furthermore.
gainerantzeko *adj.* secondary, nonessential, residual.
gaineraso *v.t.* to invade, to raid.
gainerasoketa *n.* invasion, raid.
gainerasotzaile *n.* invader, raider.
gaineratiko *adj.* supplementary, additional, secondary, nonessential.
gaineratu *v.t.* to put on top. *v.i.* to come to the surface. *v.t.* to add, to increase, to augment. *v.i.* to get to the top.
gainerazko *n.* residue, excess, leftovers.
gainerein *v.t.* to sow again.
gainerre *v.t./v.i.* to singe, to scorch.
gainestaldura *n.* covering, coating.
gainestalki . cover, overcoat.
gainetik *prep.* from the top, over. *adv.* superficially, lightly.
gainetiko *adj.* superficial, secondary.
gainetorrera *n.* sudden or surprising happening.
gainetorri *v.t.* to take by surprise. *v.i.* to happen suddenly.
gainetsi *v.t.* to overestimate.
gainez *adv.* overflowing, boiling over.
gainezarketa *n.* superposition, act of putting on.
gainezarpen *n.* superposition, act of putting on.
gainezarri *v.t.* to put on, to put over. *v.t.* to impute, to accuse of, to charge with. *v.t.* to add.
gainez egin *v.t.* to overflow, to boil over. *v.t.(fig.)* to irritate, to become irritated.
gainez eragin *v.t.* to cause to overflow. *v.t.(fig.)* to exasperate, to make (someone) lose patience, to irritate (someone).
gainez egon *v.i.* to be overflowing.
gainezka *adv.* excessively, overflowingly.
gainezka egin *v.t.* to overflow, to boil over.
gainezkaldi *n.* overflowing, boiling over. *n.(fig.)* irritation, alienation.
gainezkapen *n.* overflowing, boiling over.
gainezkatu *v.t.* to heap up; to overflow. *v.i.* to be left over, to exceed.
gainezko *adj.* overflowing; superfluous, redundant.
gaineztadura *n.* covering.
gaineztatu *v.t.* to cover.
gaineztu *v.i.* to overflow. *v.t.* to stuff, to fill, to cram.
gain-gain *n.* the highest part

(mountain).
gain-gaineko *adj.* the highest.
gain-gainetik *prep.* from the highest part. *prep.* immediately above. *adv.* lightly, superficially.
gaingari *n.(bot.)* white wheat.
gaingarri *adj.* conquerable.
gaingiroki *adv.* lightly, superficially.
gaingoitiko *adj.* supreme, uppermost, highest.
gaingoititasun *n.* supremacy.
gaingona *n.* overskirt.
gaingune *n.* elevated place.
gain hartu *v.t.* to dominate, to win, to conquer, to vanquish; to excel, to surpass.
gainidatzi *v.t.* to superscribe, to write over.
gainirabazi *v.i.* to profit.
gainirabazpen *n.* profit.
gainjantzi *n.* cape, overcoat, wrap.
gainjarpen *n.* superposition, act of putting on top of.
gainjarri *v.t./v.i.* to put on top, to superimpose.
gainkarga *n.* overload.
gainkargatu *v.t.* to overload, to overburden.
gainkor *adj.* superable, conquerable.
gainlan *n.* overwork.
gainontzeko *n.* rest, leftovers, remains. *adj.* residual, left over, nonessential, accessory, secondary.
gainordain *n.* extra pay.
gainordu *n.* extra hour, overtime.
gainpagu *n.* extra pay.
gainpasatu *v.i./v.t.* to exceed, to surpass.
gainpisu *n.* overweight.
gainpopulaketa *n.* overpopulation.
gainpopulatu *v.i./v.t.* to overpopulate.
gainugaritasun *n.* superabundance.
gainugaritu *v.i.* to overflow, to superabund, to abound in excess.
gainzama *n.* overload.
gainzamatu *v.t.* to overload.
gainzerga *n.* surcharge, extra tax.
gainzergatu *v.t.* to levy a surcharge, to tax.
gainzuri *adj.* false, hypocritical.
gainzurikeria *n.* false and excessive flattery, adulation. *n.* dissimulation, fraud.
gainzuriketa *n.* cajolery, flattery, adulation. *n.* dissimulation.
gainzuritu *v.t.* to whitewash. *v.t.* to cover up, to pretend, to feign. *v.i.* to excuse oneself, to justify oneself.
gaiso *adj.* sick, ill. *n.* sickness, illness.
gaisoaldi *n.* sickness, period of sickness, bout of illness.
gaisobera *adj.* sickly, unhealthy, diseased.
gaisoetxe *n.* hospital.
gaisoka *adj.* sickly, sick, sickish, indisposed, under the weather.
gaisokor *adj.* morbid, harmful, noxious.

adj. sickly, ailing.
gaisondo *n.* convalescence, recovery.
gaisorik *adv.* sick, ill.
gaisotasun *n.* sickness, illness.
gaisotegi *n.* hospital, infirmary, sanitarium.
gaisoti *adj.* sick, unhealthy, sickly.
gaisotsu *adj.* sickly, ill, sick.
gaisotu *v.i.* to become sick, to fall ill.
gaisozain *n.* nurse, intern, medical assistant.
gaisozaintza *n.* nursing profession, nursing career.
gaita *n.* kind of Basque musical instrument similar to the *dultzaina*, played especially in Navarra.
gaitajotzaile *n. gaita* player.
gaitari *n. gaita* player.
gaitasun *n.* ability, capacity, aptitude, competence.
gaitu *v.i.* to become able, to prepare, to be empowered. *v.t.* to enable, to qualify, to prepare. *adj.* capable, qualified.
gaitz *adj.* difficult, hard. *n.* damage, injury, harm; misfortune. *n.* sickness, disease. *adj.* unhealthy, sick. *adj.* perfidious. *n.* fault, lack, imperfection, flaw. *adv.* badly.
-gaitz *(gram.)* Suffix which denotes difficulty or resistance. **Adigaitz.** Unintelligible.
gaitzaldi *n.* passing illness. *n.* time of adversity, time of misfortune.
gaitzarin *n.* minor illness. *n.* minor damage.
gaitzaurreko *adj.* symptomatic.
gaitzaztarna *n.* symptom.
gaitz egin *v.t.* to damage, to injure.
gaitzegingarri *adj.* damaging, harmful, injurious.
gaitzegite *n.* offense, transgression.
gaitzekarle *adj.* morbid, causing disease.
gaitzeragile *n.* instigator, provoker.
gaitzerako *adj.* inclining toward evil.
gaitzeratu *v.t.* to entice to do evil, to tempt (to do evil).
gaitzerazi *v.t.* to bother, to annoy.
gaitzerraiketa *n.* slander, defamation.
gaitzerraile *n.* slanderer, defamer.
gaitzerraite *n.* slander, malicious gossip, defamation.
gaitzerran *v.t.* to slander, to defame.
gaitzesale *n.* slanderer, defamer.
gaitz esan *v.t.* to slander, to defame.
gaitzesbide *n.* demerit, unworthiness.
gaitzesgarri *adj.* despicable, disgusting, detestable, vituperable, condemnable, abominable.
gaitzesgarriki *adv.* detestably, disgustingly, abominably.
gaitzesgarriro *adv.* detestably, disgustingly, abominably.
gaitzesi *v.t.* to condemn, to reprove. *v.t.* to lose hope for (a patient's recovery).

gaitzesko *adj.* condemning, damning.

gaitzesle *n.* condemner, despiser. *adj.* condemning, despising, disapproving.

gaitzespen *n.* condemnation, disapproval, disgust, repulsion, rejection.

gaitzestasun *n.* scorn, contempt, slight.

gaitzestu *v.t.* to condemn, to reprove.

gaitzetsi *v.t.* to condemn, to reprove, to disapprove of, to reject. *v.t.* to blame; to judge to be guilty. *v.t.* to hate, to despise. *v.t.* to consider (something) difficult.

gaitzez egon *v.i.* to be angry (with someone).

gaitzezko *adj.* condemnatory, damnatory.

gaitzezkor *adj.* detestable, abominable.

gaitzezpen *n.* condemnation, refusal, disapproval, rejection.

gaitz hartu *v.t.* to contract a disease, to become ill, to get sick.

gaitzi *n.* resentment, rancor, enmity.

gaitziarazi *v.t.* to vex, to bother, to offend.

gaitziarazle *n.* vexer, offender, botherer. *adj.* vexing, offensive, bothersome.

gaitzidura *n.* indignation.

gaitzigarri *adj.* offensive, annoying.

gaitzigarriki *adv.* offensively, annoyingly.

gaitzi izan *v.i.* to be disagreeable, to be unfriendly, to be hostile.

gaitzikara *n.* fear of illness.

gaitzikor *adj.* damaging, injurious. *adj.* susceptible, sensitive, touchy.

gaitzikortasun *n.* susceptibility; irritability.

gaitzikortu *v.i.* to become susceptible. *v.i.* to become angry.

gaitzitu *v.i.* to get angry, to get mad. *v.t.* to bother, to vex, to annoy, to offend.

gaitz izan *v.i.* to be difficult.

gaitzizen *n.* nickname, pseudonym, alias.

gaitzizendatu *v.t.* to give (someone) a nickname.

gaitzizendu *v.t.* to give (someone) a nickname.

gaitzondo *n.* convalescence, recovery.

gaitzondore *n.* effect of a disease.

gaitzuru *n.* old measure for grain.

gaitzuste *n.* ill will, malice.

gaitzustean *adv.* with ill will, maliciously.

gaitzustegabean *adv.* with good intentions, without malice.

gaitzustez *adv.* with ill will, maliciously.

gaiz- Used in compound words. Derived from *gaitz*, sickness, scandal.

gaizbidekor *adj.* easily scandalized.

gaizdun *adj.* sick, ill.

gaizerrenda *n.* inventory. *n.* agenda.

gaizjatorri *n.* origin or development of illnesses.

gaizkabe *adj.* innocent, guiltless, blameless. *adj.* unhurt, uninjured; harmless.

gaizkabetasun *n.* innocence, guiltlessness, blamelessness.

gaizkabetu *v.i./v.t.* to save, to liberate from evil.

gaizkabide *n.* way of salvation.

gaizkagarri *adj.* savable, redeemable.

gaizkapen *n.* salvation.

gaizkatu *v.t.* to save, to liberate from evil.

gaizkatzaile *n.* savior.

gaizkeria *n.* perversity, evil, malignity, wickedness.

gaizki *adv.* bad, badly. *adv.* not well, gravely ill. *n.* reproach, reprimand.

gaizkiago *adv.(comp.)* worse, more poorly.

gaizkiagotu *v.i.* to aggravate, to worsen.

gaizkialdi *n.* deterioration, worsening.

gaizkiarazle *n.* vexer, harasser.

gaizkide *n.* accomplice, accessory.

gaizkidego *n.* complicity in wrong doing, abetment.

gaizkidetasun *n.* complicity in wrong doing, abetment, abettal.

gaizkidun *adj.* possessed, evil.

gaizki egin *v.t.* to offend, to injure, to insult, to annoy. *v.t.* to reproach, to reprimand.

gaizki erabili *v.t.* to mishandle; to mistreat, to maltreat, to abuse.

gaizkierabiltzaile *n.* abuser, harmer; persecutor.

gaizkierapen *n.* malformation.

gaizkiesaka *adv.* cussing, cursing, damning, grumbling.

gaizkiesale *n.* calumniator, maligner, defamer. *n.* cusser, curser, damner.

gaizki esan *v.t.* to censure, to defame, to execrate, to calumniate, to speak badly of.

gaizkiesate *n.* slander, defamation, calumny.

gaizki etorri *v.i.* to fail to get along; to disagree, to quarrel, to fall out (friends).

gaizkigura *n.* antipathy, ill will, hatred.

gaizki hartu *v.t.* to mistreat, to maltreat, to abuse.

gaizkikasi *adj.* badly educated, uncourteous, ill-mannered.

gaizkile *n.* criminal, wrong-doer, bandit, delinquent. *adj.* criminal, delinquent, bad, perverse, harmful.

gaizkiletasun *n.* criminality, delinquency.

gaizkin *n.* criminal, wrongdoer, bandit, delinquent. *adj.* bad, wicked, evil, perverse, criminal. *n.* devil, demon.

gaizkinahi *n.* hatred, aversion, enmity, ill will.

gaizkinahiezko *adj.* malevolent, evil.

gaizkindu *v.i.* to pervert, to corrupt.

gaizkintasun *n.* criminality, evil, corruption.

gaizkintza *n.* delinquency, perversity, evil.

gaizkitu *v.i.* to worsen, to get worse. *v.i.* to become ill, to get sick. *v.t.* to scold, to berate, to vituperate.

gaizkoadura *n.* act of becoming infected, infection. *n.* growing worse (an illness), declining (one's health).

gaizkoatu *v.i.* to become infected, to fester. *v.i.* to grow worse, to worsen (an illness), to decline (one's health).

gaizkor *adj.* morbid, harmful, injurious, noxious. *adj.* sickly, unhealthy, ailing.

gaizpera *adj.* sickly, unhealthy, diseased.

gaizperatu *v.i.* to be sickly, to be unhealthy.

gaizperrialdi *n.* relapse, recurrence of disease.

gaizperritu *v.i.* to have a relapse, to get sick again.

gaizpide *n.* vice, bad habit. *n.* scandal, sin, action of setting a bad example.

gaizpideratu *v.t.* to scandalize (someone), to lead (someone) into scandal, to set a bad example.

gaizpidetsu *adj.* scandalous, infamous.

gaizpidetu *v.t.* to scandalize, to cause a scandal.

gaizpidez *adv.* scandalously.

gaizpidezko *adj.* scandalous.

gaiztagile *n.* evildoer, malefactor, wrongdoer.

gaiztagin *n.* evildoer, malefactor, wrongdoer, criminal.

gaiztakeria *n.* evil, wrong, perversion.

gaiztakeritu *v.i.* to become a bad person, to go bad.

gaiztarazi *v.t.* to corrupt, to vitiate.

gaiztasun *n.* difficulty.

gaiztatu *v.i.* to become evil, to go bad, to go wrong. *v.t.* to corrupt, to lead astray. *v.i.* to fester, to become infected.

gaiztatzaile *n.* corruptor, perverter. *adj.* corrupting, perverting.

gaiztetsi *v.t.* to cuss, to curse, to condemn. *v.t.* to judge (something) as bad.

gaiztetsigarri *adj.* detestable, abhorrent, hateful.

gaizto *adj.* mischievous, naughty. *adj.* perverse, bad, evil, wicked.

gaiztoago *adj.(comp.)* worse.

gaiztoagotu *v.i.* to become worse, to worsen.

gaiztoarazi *v.t.* to pervert, to corrupt.

gaiztoarazle *adj.* malignant, evil, malicious. *n.* corruptor, perverter, bad influence.

gaiztodura *n.* infection, soreness, inflammation.

gaiztoki *adv.* wickedly, malevolently, perversely. *n.* Hell.

gaiztotasun *n.* evil, wrongness, perversity.

gaiztotu *v.i.* to become evil, to go bad, to become perverted.

gaiztotzaile *n.* corruptor, perverter. *adj.* corrupting, perverting.

gaiztotzar *adj.* very bad, infamous, nefarious, heinous.

gaiztu *v.i.* to become evil, to go bad. *v.i.* to get angry, to become irritated.

gako *n.* key (to a lock); key (music). *n.* hook. *n.* hanger. *n.(fig.)* problem, catch, difficulty.

gakodun *adj.* hooked, curved, bent.

gako-mako *n.* trap, snare, trick, stratagem.

gakopetu *v.t.* to lock.

gakotu *v.i./v.t.* to curve, to bend. *v.t.* to hook, to catch with a hook.

gakotxak *n.(gram.)* quotation marks.

gakotxartetu *v.t.* to put quotation marks around (something).

gal- Used in compound words. Derived from *galdu*, loss. **Galbide.** Lost way, road to ruin, vice. Used in compound words. Derived from *gari*, wheat. **Galondo.** Wheat stubble.

galale *n.* grain of wheat.

galanki *adv.* elegantly, gallantly, beautifully.

galankiro *adv.* elegantly, gallantly, beautifully.

galant *adj.* beautiful, elegant, handsome, good-looking. *adj.* enormous, huge.

galantasun *n.* elegance, beauty. *n.* corpulence, enormity, hugeness.

galanteder *adj.* very handsome, graceful, elegant, gallant.

galantedertasun *n.* handsomeness, beauty, elegance.

galantu *v.i.* to become beautiful, to become elegant. *v.i.* to get fat, to become corpulent, to become large.

galarazi *v.t.* to prohibit, to impede, to hinder.

galarazketa *n.* prohibition, impediment, hindrance, forbiddance.

galarazkor *adj.* obstructive, hindering.

galarazle *n.* impeder, obstructor, hinderer.

galarazpen *n.* prohibition, impediment, hindrance, forbiddance.

galarren *n.* stormy northwest wind.

galarri *n.* grist stone. Contr. of *gari* + *arri*.

galbahaketa *n.* act of sifting, act of sieving.

galbahaldi *n.* sifting, sieving, screening.

galbahe *n.* sieve, screen.

galbahetu *v.t.* to sift, to sieve, to screen (especially wheat).

galbahetxo n.(dim.) small sieve.
galbaneztatu v.t. to galvanize.
galberri adj. newly lost.
galbide n. road to ruin, way of
perdition, temptation. n. danger, risk.
n. bad example, scandal. n. vice.
galbidegarri adj. dangerous, risky.
galbideratu v.i. to be risky, to be
dangerous, to be in danger. v.t. to
risk (something), to place (someone)
in danger; to set a bad example, to
scandalize.
galbidetsu adj. dangerous, risky;
scandalous.
galbidetu v.i. to become dangerous, to
be risky or dangerous. v.t. to set a
bad example for, to exert an evil
influence on.
galbidezko adj. dangerous, risky;
scandalous.
galbihi n. grain of wheat.
galbizar n. beard of the wheat.
galbizardun n. bearded wheat.
galburu n. head of wheat.
galburuketa n. gleaning of wheat.
galburutu v.t. to glean wheat.
galburuxka n.(dim.) small tassle of
wheat; gleanings.
galda n. smelting, casting, melting. n.
smelted metal. n. scorching, very hot
(sunlight).
galdaburni n. cast iron.
galdagarri adj. fusible, smeltable.
galdaketa n. smelting, casting,
melting.
galdaldi n. smelting (of metal). n. burst
of sunlight.
galdara n. semispherical boiler,
caldron.
galdaragin n. boilermaker, caldron
maker.
galdaragintza n. boilermaker's job,
boilermaking, caldron making.
galdaraska n.(dim.) small boiler, small
caldron.
galdaratzar n.(augm.) large boiler,
large caldron.
galdatu v.t. to smelt, to melt, to cast.
v.t. to solder.
galde n. question, interpellation.
galdeagiri n. questionnaire, query.
galdealdi n. interrogation,
cross-examination, questioning.
galdebide n. questionnaire.
galdebidez adv. questioningly,
interrogatively.
galde egin v.t. to question, to ask.
galdegai n.(gram.) focus (of a
question).
galdegarri adj. questioning,
interrogative.
galdegile n. questioner, interrogator,
inquirer.
galdegite n. act of questioning.
galdeikur n.(gram.) question mark.
galdeka adv. questioning,
interrogating.

galdekari n. questioner, interrogator,
inquirer.
galdekatu v.t. to question, to ask, to
inquire, to interrogate.
galdekeria n. impertinent question.
galdeketa n. interrogation,
questioning, inquiry, list of questions,
questioning.
galdeketari n. questioner, interrogator,
inquirer.
galdekizun n. question, interrogation.
n.(gram.) focus (of a question).
galdekuntza n. interrogation, question.
galdeliburu n. questionnaire,
questionary booklet.
galdemarka n.(gram.) question mark.
galdeontzi adj. inquisitive, nosey.
galdera n. question.
galderagile n. questioner, interrogator,
inquirer.
galderakizun n. question,
interrogation.
galderako adj. interrogative,
questioning.
galderantzunak n. questions and
answers.
galderazko adj. interrogative,
questioning.
galdesorta n. booklet of questions,
group of questions, questionary,
questionnaire.
galdetaldi n. time of interrogation.
galdetegi n. information bureau.
galdetoki n. information bureau.
galdetsu adj. inquisitive, nosey.
galdetu v.t. to question, to ask. v.t. to
find out, to inquire into. v.t. to
require, to demand.
galdetzaile n. questioner, inquirer,
interrogator. adj. interrogative.
galdezka adv. questioning, inquiring,
interrogating, asking.
galdezkatu v.t. to request, to
investigate, to examine.
galdezko adj. interrogative,
questioning, inquisitive, rogatory. adj.
requisite, required.
galdu v.t. to lose (money, a war, a bet,
etc.), to mislay, to misplace. v.t. to
waste. v.i. to become corrupt; to
become spoiled (food, people). v.i.
to be shipwrecked, to sink. v.i. to get
lost, to lose one's way, to be lost. v.i.
to disappear. v.i./v.t. to become evil;
to pervert, to corrupt, to spoil.
gale n. desire. adj. avid, anxious.
-gale (gram.) Suffix which means avid,
enthusiastic, desirous of, wishing,
given to. **Logale.** Sleepy, given to
sleep.
galeper n.(zool.) kind of quail
(Cotturnix Cotturnix).
galera n. damage, loss, perdition, ruin,
demise; defeat. n. galley (ship).
galerazi v.t. to cause to lose. v.t. to
forbid to, to prohibit from, to keep
(someone) from (doing something),

to impede.

galerazle adj. prohibitive, prohibiting, forbidding, unpermitting.

galerazpen n. prohibition, forbiddance.

galerazte n. act of prohibiting, act of forbidding.

galerrez adj. easy to get lost.

galetsi v.t. to consider (something) lost, to assume (someone or something) is lost or dying, to lose hope for (recovery of the sick). adj. hopeless.

galezin adj. unlosable.

galga n. brake of a cart. n. level.

galgai n. cause of perdition.

galgaitz adj. difficult to lose.

galgaketa n. act of braking. n. leveling, grading.

galgara n. act of boiling, ebullition.

galgarau n. grain of wheat.

galgarri adj. losable. adj. harmful, detrimental, ruinous, noxious, corrupting. adj. squandering, wasteful.

galgarriro adv. scandalously, shockingly. adv. harmfully, noxiously.

galgarritasun n. harmfulness, noxiousness.

galgarrizko adj. harmful, noxious.

galgatu v.t. to level, to grade, to even out. v.t. to brake, to rein in.

galgatzaile n. leveler. n. leveling.

galgo n.(zool.) greyhound.

galgoe n. west wind.

galipot n. tar.

galipotatu v.t. to pitch, to tar.

galirin n. wheat flour.

galkeria n. perversion, vice, bad habit.

galketa n. loss, damage, perdition, ruin; defeat.

galkor adj. spoilable, given to rot, perishable, fleeting. adj. corrupting, perverting, harmful.

galkortasun n. corruptibility, caducity. n. fugacity, fleetingness, perishableness.

galmen n. loss, perdition, ruin.

galmotz n. kind of low wheat.

galondar n. chaff.

galondo n. wheat stubble.

galpar n. disarranged, loose hair; lock of hair.

galpardun adj. wild-haired, long-maned.

galparsoro n. prairie.

galpartsu adj. disarranged, loose, wild (hair).

galpartu v.t./v.i. to dishevel, to make untidy (hair).

galpen n. loss, perdition, ruin. n. harm, injury.

galsoro n. wheat field.

galtegi n. granary.

galtza n. pants, trousers. (Usually used in plural.)

galtzada n. paved highway; sidewalk.

galtzadun adj. male. adj.(fig.) valiant, brave. n. man.

galtzagorri n.(colloq.) demon, devil. (lit.) red pants.

galtzaile n. loser. n./adj. perverter, corrupter; perverting, corrupting.

galtzairu n. steel.

galtzajario adj.(colloq.) lacking willpower, lackadaisical.

galtzajosle n. one who sews trousers, trouser maker (usually a woman).

galtzamotz n. shorts, short pants.

galtzandi adj.(colloq.) lacking willpower, lackadaisical.

galtzar n.(anat.) part of the body between the armpit and the waist.

galtzarbe n.(anat.) armpit, underarm.

galtzarbegi n. armhole.

galtzarpe n.(anat.) armpit, underarm, axilla.

galtzarperatu v.t. to put (something) under one's arm, to put (something) in one's armpit.

galtzazpiko n. underwear.

galtze n. loss, damage, defeat, act of losing.

galtzerdi n. stockings.

galtzerdigile n. stocking maker.

galtzerdigintza n. stocking manufacture.

galtzerdimotz n. sock.

galtzerdizola n. foot of a stocking.

galtzerdizulo n. hole in a stocking.

galtzontzilo n. underwear (for men).

galtzorratz n. knitting needle.

galtzu n. chaff.

galzori n. risk, danger, hazard.

gamelu n.(zool.) camel.

gameluaire adj. camel-like.

gameluantzeko adj. camel-like.

gameluki n. camel meat.

gamelukume n. baby camel, camel calf.

gamelutegi n. camel stable.

gamelutxo n.(dim.) little camel.

gameluzain n. camel keeper, camel herder.

gameluzaingo n. camel herding.

gameluzaintza n. camel herding.

-gana (gram.) suffix used to denote movement to humans and animals.

ganadu n. cow, ox, steer.

ganadutza n. cattle, livestock. n. cattle raising.

ganbara n. attic, chamber, loft. n.(pol.) chamber, legislative house. n.(colloq.) crazy.

ganbarabiko adj. bicameral, having two legislative houses.

ganbarabikotasun n.(pol.) bicameralism.

ganbaragain n. upper part of the attic.

ganbarari n. valet.

ganbaratu v.t. to store, to put in an attic or a loft.

ganbaratxo n.(dim.) small attic.

ganbela n. crib, rack, manger.

ganbelu n.(zool.) camel.

ganbil adj. convex.
ganbilbiko adj. biconvex.
ganbiltasun n. convexness.
ganbio n.(econ.) exchange, exchange rate.
-gandik (gram.) suffix which denotes from, used with pronouns, nouns (people, animals). **Izena eta izana gurasoengandik hartzen ditugu.** We take our name and our being from our parents.
gando n. germ.
gandor n. crest, tuft of feathers. n. vertex, peak, summit.
gandordun adj. crested.
gandorgabetu v.t. to take off the crest.
gandorreztatu v.t. to adorn with a crest, to decorate with plumes.
gandortu v.i. to stiffen its crest (a bird). v.i.(fig.) to swell with pride, to be arrogant.
gandu n. cataract, eye film. n. mist, low fog; vapor (on glass).
gandutsu adj. misty, foggy, vaporous.
gandutu v.i. to cloud up (vision, window, horizon), to mist over.
ganga n. vault, dome, cupola. n. gain, profit.
gangaila n.(anat.) uvula.
gangar n. crest of birds and fowl. adj. fatuous, pompous, vain. adj. obnoxious. adj. wishy-washy, flighty, irresponsible. n.(gram.) diacritical mark formerly used to indicate rr.
gangarkeria n. fatuity, foolishness, flightiness, vanity.
ganglio n.(anat.) ganglion.
ganguren-manguren ibili v.i. to sway, to stagger, to zig-zag.
ganibet(a) n. knife.
ganibetada n. knifing.
ganora n. diligence, import, importance, substance, aptitude.
ganoradun adj. active, diligent, competent. adj. serious, responsible.
ganoragabekeria n. indolence, sloth, laziness.
ganoragabeki adv. clumsily, awkwardly, ungracefully.
ganoragabe(ko) adj. clumsy, awkward, maladroit, ungraceful. adj. flighty, characterless. adj. lazy, indolent.
ganoragabetu v.i. to lose interest in.
ganoratsu adj. apt, diligent, important, responsible.
ganoraz adv. dependably, responsibly.
ganorazko adj. dependable, responsible.
gantz n. fat, lard.
gantzadun adj. adipose, fatty, obese.
gantzadura n. anointment, anointing, unction.
gantzagi n. lard, fat.
gantzateratzaile n. ripper.
gantzatsu adj. full of lard, fatty.
gantzatu v.t. to anoint, to grease, to oil.

gantzazal n. animal membrane in which lard is wrapped and preserved.
gantzontzi n. lard container.
gantzu n. fat, grease, lard; unguent, ointment.
gantzualdi n. anointing, unction.
gantzudun adj. fatty, lardy; balsamic, balmy.
gantzudura n. unction, anointing; embalming.
gantzuera n. way of anointing; embalming.
gantzugai n. unguent.
gantzugailu n. ointment, balsam, unguent.
gantzugarri n. unguent, ointment; lotion.
gantzuketa n. embalming; unction, anointing, oiling.
gantzuki n. unguent, ointment.
gantzupen n. embalming; anointing.
gantzutasun n. greasiness, oiliness.
gantzutsu adj. unctuous, fatty, greasy, full of lard.
gantzutu v.t. to anoint, to grease, to oil. v.t. to embalm.
gantzutzaile n. embalmer; anointer.
gantzuzko adj. balsamic, balmy.
gapirio n. joist, beam.
gar n. flame. n.(fig.) enthusiasm, exaltation, ardor.
garabi n. crane, hoist.
garagar n.(bot.) barley. n. rolling on its back (burro, horse, etc.).
garagardi n. barley field.
garagardo n. beer.
garagardogile n. brewer.
garagardogintza n. beer brewing.
garagardotegi n. brewery; beer joint.
garagarril n. June.
garagarsoro n. barley field.
garagartza n. barley field.
garagarza n. barley field.
garai adj. high, tall. n. season, time, period, occasion, opportunity. adj. prominent, outstanding, excellent.
garaiago adj.(comp.) higher.
garaiaurreko adj. premature, anticipated.
garaibereko adj. contemporaneous, contemporary.
garaien adj.(superl.) the highest, the uppermost; the most excellent; supreme.
garaiera n. height; altitude.
garaiezin adj. invincible, unconquerable, unbeatable, undefeatable.
garaiezinez adv. invincibly, unconquerably.
garaiezintasun n. invincibility, unconquerability, unbeatableness.
garaigaitz adj. difficult to conquer, difficult to overcome, difficult to surpass.
garaigarri adj. conquerable, beatable.
garaiki adv. superiorly, excellently.

garaikide adj. contemporaneous, contemporary.

garaikunde n. victory, triumph.

garailari n. winner, victor, champion.

garaile adj. triumphant, victorious. n. winner, victor, champion.

garaile izan v.i. to be victorious, to win.

garailiar adj. triumphant, victorious.

garaimen n. victory, triumph.

garaioneko adj. punctual, prompt.

garaionez adv. on time, promptly, punctually; opportunely.

garaipen n. victory, triumph.

garaipenezko adj. victorious, triumphant.

garaipentsu adj. victorious, triumphant.

garaipide n. victory, triumph.

garaisari n. prize, trophy.

garaitar adj./n. inhabitant of the highlands, highlander.

garaitasun n. elevation, altitude, height. n. superiority, supremacy, supereminence, hegemony, dominion.

garaitiar adj. triumphant, victorious.

garaitiko adj. upper, from above. adj. residual, left over.

garaitsu adj. elevated, high. adj. superior, outstanding, eminent.

garaitsuki adv. victoriously, triumphantly.

garaitu v.t. to win, to triumph, to overcome, to prevail, to defeat, to beat, to conquer; to crown with victory.

garaitza n. victory, triumph.

garaitzaile adj. triumphant, victorious. n. winner, victor, champion.

garaitzapen n. victory, triumph.

garaiz adv. in time, early, in season, on time.

garaizko adj. timely, opportune; punctual.

garaje n. garage.

garandu v.t. to shell, to shake out the grain, to remove the seeds.

garantia n. guarantee; security.

garapen n. development.

garastailu n. sprinkler, watering can.

garastaketa n. sprinkling, watering, irrigation.

garastaldi n. watering, irrigating, time spent irrigating.

garastatu v.t. to irrigate, to water, to sprinkle.

garatu v.i. to bloom, to bud, to sprout. v.i./v.t. to develop, to increase.

garatxo n. wart.

garatxotsu adj. warty, full of warts.

garatzaile n. developer.

garau n. seed, grain; fruit.

garautegi n. granary, barn.

garba n. brake, instrument for dressing flax.

garbai n. repentance, contrition.

garbaialdi n. repentance.

garbaiaro n. time of repentance.

garbaibide n. cause for remorse or repentance.

garbaidun adj. repentant, contrite.

garbaigabe adj. impenitent, unrepentant, obdurate.

garbaiketa n. act of repenting.

garbaikide n. condolence.

garbaitasun n. repentance, contrition.

garbaitsu adj. repentant, remorseful.

garbaitu v.i. to repent.

garbal adj. bald. adj. nude, naked, stripped, empty (of leaves).

garbaldu v.i. to become bald. v.i. to clear up.

garbaltasun n. baldness.

garbantzu n.(bot.) garbanzo, chickpea.

garbari n. carder.

garbatu v.t. to dress hemp or flax with a brake; to card wool.

garbi adj. clean, clear. adj. pure, honest. adv. clearly. adj. explicit, clear, obvious. adv.(fig.) dead. adj. net, take-home.

garbiagotu v.t. to clean again.

garbialdi n. cleaning, purification, purge.

garbiarazi v.t. to purify, to cleanse, to refine.

garbiarazle adj. cleansing, purging.

garbiarazpen n. purification, depuration, refinement.

garbibide n. means of cleaning. n. means of exonerating oneself, means of self-justification.

garbidura n. cleaning.

garbiezin adj. unwashable. adj. inexpiable.

garbigai n. cleaning materials. n. laxative, purgative.

garbigailu n. washing machine, washer, cleaning utensil.

garbigarri adj. cleansing, purifying. adj. washable, purifiable.

garbigela n. washroom, cleaning room, bathroom.

garbikari n. detergent, cleaner.

garbikera n. manner of cleaning.

garbikeria n. excessive purism, fanaticism.

garbiketa n. cleaning, washing. n. garbage collection. n. liquidation (of bills), clearing of accounts. n. sale, liquidation (of stock).

garbiki adv. cleanly, clearly. adv. frankly, explicitly, directly.

garbikin n. detergent, cleaner. n. soap residue, soap film; soap water, dirty wash water.

garbikor adj. hygienic, cleanly, sanitary. adj. purgative.

garbikuntza n. purification, cleaning, purge.

garbileku n. laundry, cleaning place.

garbiontzi n. washing basin, bucket,

tub.

garbipen n. purification, cleaning, purge.

garbiro adv. clearly, evidently. adv. fairly, honestly.

garbisoil adj. clear (sky).

garbitasun n. cleanness, pureness, clearness; cleaning. n. account of, accounting of, report on. n. honesty, integrity, purity.

garbitegi n. laundry, cleaning place.

garbitoki n. cleaning place, laundry. n.(eccl.) purgatory.

garbitu v.t. to purify, to clean, to wash, to purge, to filter. v.t. to pay (off), to liquidate, to clear up, to sell off. v.t.(fig.) to kill; to ruin, to destroy. v.t. to self-justify, to exculpate oneself, to vindicate. v.t.(fig.) to steal.

garbitzaile n. cleaner. n.(fig.) exterminator, liquidator.

garbizale adj. puristic. adj. honest.

garbizalekeria n. excessive purism, fanaticism.

garbizaletasun n. purism.

garburagailu n.(mech.) carburetor.

garda n. carding comb, carding instrument.

garda- Used in compound words. Derived from gardatu, to card (wool).

gardabera n.(bot.) thistle.

gardagile n. maker of carding instruments.

gardalatz n.(bot.) cotton thistle.

gardalore n.(bot.) thistle.

gardantxilo n.(zool.) goldfinch.

gardari n. carder, one who cards wool.

gardatu v.t. to card.

garden adj. transparent, clear, limpid, bright.

gardendu v.i. to become transparent, to become clear.

gardenia n.(bot.) gardenia.

gardenketa n. clarification, brightening.

gardenki adv. transparently, clearly.

gardentasun n. transparency, clarity, brightness.

gardinga n. verdigris.

gardingadura n. rancidness, staleness, sourness.

gardingatu v.i. to turn rancid (bacon, etc.), to turn sour (wine).

gardostu v.t./v.i. to singe, to scorch, to sear.

gardots n. prickly husk of the chestnut.

gardu n.(bot.) thistle.

gardun adj. flaming, blazing.

gardura n. act of inflaming.

garesti adj./adv. expensive, costly, dear; at a high price.

garestialdi n. price increase.

garestidura n. rise in price, price increase.

garestigarri adj. inflationary.

garestitasun n. expensiveness.

garestitu v.i. to go up in price, to rise in price. v.t. to raise the price.

garestitzaile adj. inflationary; causing prices to rise.

garestizale adj. fond of expensive things.

garezur n.(anat.) skull, cranium.

garezurbarneko adj. intracranial.

gargail n.(anat.) uvula. adj. weak.

gargailatu v.i. to grow weak, to weaken.

gar-gar n. onomatopeic sound of ebullition, boiling.

gargara n. gargling.

gargar(ak) egin v.t. to gargle.

gari n.(bot.) wheat.

gariale n. grain of wheat.

garialor n. wheat field.

gariazi n. wheat seed.

garibizar n. beard of wheat.

gariebate n. wheat harvesting.

garijo v.t. to thresh wheat. n. wheat field.

garijotzaile n./adj. wheat thresher.

gariketa n. abundance of wheat.

garikolore adj. wheat-colored.

garilur n. land suitable for wheat. n. wheat field.

garimami n. semolina, grits, groats, semola.

garimeta n. shock of wheat sheaves.

garimetatu v.t. to stockpile wheat, to heap up wheat.

garipilo n. pile of wheat.

garisail n. wheat field.

garisoro n. wheat field.

garisorta n. sheaf of grain.

garitsu adj. abundant in wheat.

garitxori n.(zool.) wheat sparrow.

garitza n. wheat field.

garizko adj. pertaining to wheat.

garizuma n.(eccl.) Lent.

garkor adj. inflammable.

garkortasun n. inflammability.

garlopa n. large carpenter's plane.

garmendi n. volcano.

garmeta n. sudden blaze.

garmin n. burned taste and smell.

garmindu v.i. to smell burned, to taste burned.

garnata n. bait.

garo n.(bot.) fern.

garodi n. fern field.

garondo n.(anat.) cervix, nape of the neck.

garondoko n. slap on the back of the neck. adj. occipital.

garrafoi n. decanter, demijohn.

garraiabide n. means of transportation; circulation (blood).

garraiaketa n. transportation, carrying.

garraialari n. carrier, transporter (person).

garraialdi n. transportation, carrying.

garraiari n. carrier, transporter (person).

garraiatu v.t. to carry, to ship, to

transport, to tow.

garraiatzaile *n.* carrier, transporter. *adj.* carrying, transporting.

garraigailu *n.* carrier, transporter (machine).

garraigarri *adj.* transportable, carriable.

garraio *n.* transport, conveyance.

garraiobide *n.* means of transportation.

garraiontzi *n.* transporter (ship).

garraldi *n.* sudden blaze of fire, powder flash, flare up.

garranga *n.* barb of a hook. *n.* spiked collar.

garrantz *n.* rancid bacon.

garrantzatu *v.i.* to turn rancid, to go bad.

garrantzi *n.* importance, significance.

garrantzidun *adj.* important, significant.

garrantzigabe(ko) *adj.* unimportant, of little importance.

garrantzitsu *adj.* important, significant, essential.

garrantzizko *adj.* important, significant.

garrasi *n.* scream, cry.

garrasi egin *v.t.* to scream, to cry shrilly, to yell.

garrasika *adv.* screaming, screeching, shrieking, yelling, shouting.

garratz *adj.* sour, acid, acidic, bitter. *adj.(fig.)* severe, rigorous.

garrauspo *n.* bellows.

garrazkeria *n.* bitterness, sourness, acrimony. *n.(fig.)* severity, rigorousness, roughness.

garrazki *adv.* severely, bitterly, harshly, sharply, cruelly.

garrazkin. *n.(chem.)* acid.

garrazpera *n.* hoarseness, scratchy throat.

garraztasun *n.* acidity. *n.* bitterness, sourness. *n.(fig.)* severity, rigorousness.

garraztsu *adj.* acid, acidic; sour, bitter.

garraztu *v.i.* to sour, to turn sour, to become bitter. *v.i.* to become embittered.

-garren *(gram.)* suffix used to form ordinal numbers. **Bigarren.** Second.

garrezko *adj.* flaming, inflamed.

garreztatu *v.t.* to inflame. *v.i.* to burst into flame, to catch fire. *v.i.(fig.)* to become inflamed, to become stirred up, to be excited.

-garri *(gram.)* Suffix which denotes worthy of, deserving, apt. **Ikusgarri.** Spectacular, worthy of being seen. *(gram.)* Suffix which denotes cause or origin. **Sendagarri.** Healthy; antidote, remedy.

gartegi. *n.* forge.

gartsu *adj.* flaming, fiery. *adj.* ardent, vehement, fiery, fervent, passionate, enthusiastic.

gartsuki *adv.* ardently, passionately,

fervently, enthusiastically, vehemently.

gartu *v.t.* to inflame. *v.i.* to become inflamed. *v.i.* to be enthusiastic, to be passionate, to be vehement.

gartza *n.* link in a chain. *n.(zool.)* heron.

gartzela *n.* jail, prison.

gartzelaratu *v.t.* to jail, to imprison, to put in prison.

gartzelari *n.* jailer, warden, prison guard.

gartzelatu *v.t.* to jail, to imprison.

garun *n.(anat.)* brain.

garuntxo *n.(anat.)* cerebellum.

gas *n.* gas (not gasoline), vapor.

gasbide *n.* gas line, gas pipe.

gasdun *adj.* gaseous, gassy, carbonated.

gasedari *n.* soda water.

gasezko *adj.* gaseous, gassy, carbonated.

gaseztapen *n.* gasification, carbonation.

gaseztatu *v.t./v.i.* to gasify, to carbonate; to be carbonated.

gaseztu *v.t.* to gasify, to carbonate.

gasjario *n.* gas leak.

gaskuntza *n.* carbonation, gasification.

gasneurkin *n.* gasometer.

gasodi *n.* gas pipe.

gasoil *n.* diesel fuel.

gasolina *n.* gasoline, gas.

gasolindegi *n.* gas station, service station.

gasolinontzi *n.* gas can.

gasolinsaltzaile *n.* gas station attendant.

gastaezin *adj.* long-wearing, durable.

gastagaitz *adj.* hard to wear out, longlasting, durable.

gastapen *n.* wear and tear, wearing away, wearing out.

gastatu *v.t.* to spend. *v.i.* to be used up, to be expended, to be gone, to wear out.

gastatzaile *n./adj.* spender, big spender; wasteful, squandering.

gastritis *n.(med.)* gastritis.

gastronomia *n.* gastronomy.

gastu *n.* expense.

gatazka *n.* conflict, argument, dispute, battle, fight, war.

gatazkakor *adj.* conflicting, quarreling, fighting.

gatazkari *n.* fighter, arguer.

gatazkatu *v.t.* to fight, to argue, to battle.

gatibu *n./adj.* captive.

gatibualdi *n.* period of capture, captivity.

gatibutasun *n.* captivity.

gatibutza *n.* state of being in captivity.

-gatik *(gram.)* Prepositional suffix which means for, because of, on account of; although, in spite of.

gatilu *n.* cup.

gatilukada n. cupful.
gatilutxo n.(dim.) small cup.
gatilutzar n.(augm.) big cup.
gatz n. salt.
gatzadura n. curdling (of milk).
gatzaga n. salt mine, salt works.
gatzagaitz adj. difficult to curdle, hard to thicken.
gatzagarri adj. capable of being curdled.
gatzagi n. curd.
gatzaketa n. action of curdling. n. act of salting.
gatzale n. grain of salt.
gatzapen n. salting. n. curdling, coagulation.
gatzari n. salter, person who salts. n. curd, curdling.
gatzarri n. rock salt.
gatzartu n. jerky.
gatzatzaile adj. coagulant, thickening, curdling.
gatzemaile n. salter.
gatz eman v.t. to salt.
gatzeztadura n. salting.
gatzeztatu v.t. to salt.
gatzitu v.t. to salt.
gatzneurgailu n.(chem.) salinometer.
gatzontzi n. salt shaker, salt box.
gatzozpin n. vinegar and salt dressing for salads.
gatzun n. brine, pickle.
gatzunaska n. container for brine or salt; brine deposit.
gatzundu v.t. to salt.
gatzune n. salt flat.
gatzunketa n. act of salting.
gatzur n. saltwater.
gau n. night.
gaualde n. late evening, dusk.
gaualdi n. nighttime, night. n. vigil, night watch.
gauargi n. beacon, lantern, flashlight.
gauargino n.(dim.) small beacon, small lantern, flashlight.
gauaro n. night temperature.
gauaz adv. at night, during the night, by night.
gaubatzar n. night meeting.
gaubeila n. vigil, wake, nightwatch, especially for the dead.
gaubeilari n. person keeping night vigil for the dead.
gaubeilatu v.t. to keep a night vigil for the dead, to hold a wake.
gaubele n. nocturnal person, night owl.
gaubesta n. partying at night.
gaubesta egin v.t. to go partying.
gaubestaldi n. nighttime celebration.
gaubilera n. night meeting.
gau egin v.t. to spend the night. v.t. to grow dark, to get dark, to fall (night).
gaueko adj. nocturnal, night.
gauerdi n. midnight.
gauerditu v.i. to become midnight, to be midnight.
gauero adv. nightly, every night.

gauez adv. at night, during the night.
gaugiro n. night temperature.
gauhontz n.(zool.) horned owl.
gauibilaldi n. night patrol.
gauibilketa n. night patrol.
gauikastaldi n. nocturnal studying.
gauikasketa n. nocturnal studying.
gaujai n. night festival.
gaukanta n. serenade.
gaukari n./adj. night owl, nocturnal person.
gaukotasun n. nocturnalness, quality of being nocturnal.
gaulan n. night work. n. contraband; smuggling operation.
gaulangile n. night worker. n. contrabandist, smuggler.
gaulapur n. night thief.
gaulehen n. night (up until midnight).
gaumahai n. nightstand.
gaumin n. darkest part of night, midnight.
gau on! int. good night!
gaupizti n. nocturnal animal.
gaur adv. today. n. present.
gaurdaino adv. until today.
gaurdanik adv. from now on, from today on.
gaurgero adv. from now on.
gaurgerozko adj. successive, upcoming.
gaurko adj. current, present, pertaining to today. adv. for today.
gaurkoraketa n. modernization.
gaurkoratu v.t./v.i. to modernize.
gaurkotasun n. modernity, modernness, present time. n. applicability, pertinent nature, relevance.
gaurkotu v.t. to modernize, to update. v.i. to be up to date, to be in current usage.
gaurkoz adv. today's, for today.
gaurregun adv. nowadays, currently, at present.
gaurregunean adv. at present, nowadays.
gaurreguneko adj. current, modern.
gautar adj. nocturnal.
gautegun n. night and day.
gautiar adj. nocturnal, night-loving.
gautu v.t. to become night, to grow dark, to get dark.
gautxo n. gaucho.
gautxori n. night bird. n./adj.(colloq.) night owl, nocturnal person.
gauza n. thing, object.
gauzaez adj. useless, worthless, valueless, good-for-nothing. n. uselessness, ineptness, worthlessness.
gauzaeztasun n. incompetence, ineptitude.
gauzain n. night watchman.
gauzaintza n. work of the night watchman.
gauza izan v.i. to be useful, to be able

to, to be of use, to be capable of.
gauzaki n. object, thing.
gauzale adj. nocturnal, fond of the
night.
gauzaletasun n. fondness of the night;
noctambulism, wandering about at
night.
gauzatasun n. aptitude, capacity,
aptness.
gauzatu v.t. to enable, to capacitate.
v.t. to realize, to fulfill, to accomplish,
to attain.
gauzatxo n.(dim.) small thing.
gauzelatari n. night sentinel.
gaz- Used in compound words. Derived
from gatz, salt.
gazberritu v.t. to salt again, to resalt.
gazdun adj. salty, saline. n. salt
merchant. adj.(fig.) humorous, witty.
gazi adj. salty, salt. adj. acidic, bitter.
gazialdi n. salting; curing.
gaziaska n. brine deposit.
gazidura n. act of salting.
gazigozo adj. bittersweet.
gaziketa n. salting.
gaziki n. piece of salted meat. adv.
severely; bitterly. adv. wittily.
gazitasun n. salinity, saltiness. n.
bitterness, sourness. n. harshness,
severity, acrimony.
gazitegi n. brine deposit.
gazitu v.t. to salt, to cure (with salt).
v.i. to become salty.
gazitxo adj.(dim.) a little salty.
gazitzaile n. salter.
gazkabe adj. unsalted. adj.(fig.) dull,
bland, insipid, plain.
gazkabekeria n. nonsense,
foolishness, silliness.
gazkabeki adv. insipidly.
gazkabeko adj. dull, bland, insipid.
gazkabetasun n. unsaltiness.
gazkabetu v.t./v.i. to desalt, to lose
saltiness.
gazkarri adj. saltable.
gazketa n. act of salting, salification.
gazketari n. salt merchant.
gazkile n. salter, salt miner.
gazkin n. salt miner.
gazkosko n. lump of salt.
gazlur n. salt flat, salty place, saline
land.
gazpatxo n. gazpacho.
gazperritu v.t. to salt again, to resalt.
gazpiper n. mixture of salt and pepper.
gazpipertu v.t. to season with salt and
pepper.
gazpiperztatu v.t. to season with salt
and pepper.
gazta n. cheese. n.(colloq.) bald head.
gaztaina n.(bot.) chestnut.
gaztainadi n. grove of chestnut trees.
gaztainantzeko adj. chestnut-like.
gaztainilun adj. dark chestnut color.
gaztainkolore n. chestnut color.
gaztainondo n. chestnut tree.
gaztainsaltzaile n. chestnut seller.

gaztan- Used in compound words.
Derived from gazta, cheese.
gaztanapal n. shelf used to cure
cheeses.
gaztanaska n. storage container where
cheeses are kept or aged.
gaztanbera n. pot cheese, cottage
cheese.
gaztanbide n. road of chestnut trees.
gaztandegi n. place where cheeses
are cured and kept.
gaztangile n. cheesemaker.
gaztangin n. cheesemaker.
gaztangintza n. cheesemaking. n.
cheesemaker's work.
gaztaro n. youth (epoch).
gaztaroko adj. juvenile, young.
gaztasaltzaile n. cheese seller.
gaztasun n. saltiness, salinity.
gazte n. young people, youth. adj.
young.
gazteagotu v.i. to rejuvenate, to
become rejuvenated.
gaztealdi n. youth (epoch).
gazteberritu v.i. to rejuvenate, to
become rejuvenated.
gazteder n. beautiful young person.
gaztedi n. youth, young people.
gaztegi n. salt deposit.
gaztegisa adv. youthfully.
gaztekeria n. youthful prank, mischief.
gaztekeriak egin v.t. to play around, to
fool around.
Gaztela n.(geog.) Castile, region of
Spain.
gaztelania n. Spanish language,
Castilian.
gaztelaniar adj. Castilian, Spanish.
gaztelaniatu v.i./v.t. to hispanicize.
gaztelaniaztapen n. hispanicization.
gaztelaniaztatu v.t. to hispanicize.
gaztelanizale n. hispanist.
gaztelar adj. Castilian, Spanish.
gaztelartu v.t./v.i. to hispanicize.
gaztelazale adj. fond of Castilian.
gazteleku n. place where young
people gather.
gaztelera n. Castilian language,
Spanish.
gazteleratu v.t. to translate into
Spanish.
gaztelu n. castle.
gaztelubegi n. machicolation, opening
in the walls of a castle used for
battle.
gaztelugile n. castle builder.
gazteluratu v.i. to shut oneself up in a
castle.
gaztelutxo n.(dim.) small castle.
gazteluzain n. castle guard.
gazteluztatu v.t. to fortify with castles.
gazteno n./adj.(dim.) youngster.
gazteria n. youth, young people.
gaztesail n. group of young people.
gaztetalde n. group of young people.
gaztetasun n. youth.
gaztetegi n. place where young people

gather.
gazteteria
gaztetto *n./adj.(dim.)* youngster.
gaztetu *v.i./v.t.* to rejuvenate, to become rejuvenated.
gaztetxo *n./adj.(dim.)* youngster.
gaztezahar *adj.* prematurely old.
gaztigar *n.(bot.)* maple tree.
gaztigatu *v.t.* to punish. *v.t.* to notify, to advise.
gaztigatzaile *n.* punisher. *n.* adviser, counselor.
gaztigu *n.* punishment. *n.* advice, message.
gazur *n.* whey.
G.B. *n.* abbreviation for *goian bego*, Rest in Peace.
-ge *(gram.)* Suffix which denotes lack, privation. **Indarge.** Weak, without strength.
gedar *n.* soot.
gedartsu *adj.* sooty, smutty, smudged.
gedartu *v.i.* to become sooty, to cover with soot.
gehi- Used in compound words. Denotes more; superior.
gehiago *adv.* more; else.
gehiagoka *adv.* progressively. *n.* higher bid.
gehiagokari *n.* bidder.
gehiagokatu *v.t.* to bid up, to outbid.
gehiagoko *adj.* superior.
gehiagotan *adv.* more often, more frequently.
gehiagotu *v.t./v.i.* to increase, to increment, to augment, to add to. *v.t.* to exaggerate.
gehiarazi *v.t.* to cause to augment, to increase, to make (someone) add to (something).
gehiarazle *adj.* increasing, augmenting.
gehiegi *adv.* too much, excessively. *adj.* too much, too many.
gehiegikeria *n.* excess, excessiveness; exaggeration.
gehiegikeriaz *adv.* abusively, exaggeratedly.
gehiegitasun *n.* excessiveness, superfluousness.
gehiegitsu *adj.* excessive, inordinate, exhorbitant.
gehiegitu *v.t./v.i.* to augment, to increase; to exceed, to surpass; to exaggerate.
gehiegitxo *adv.* immoderately, a little too much.
gehiegiz *adv.* excessively, exaggeratedly.
gehiegizale *adj.* fond of excess.
gehiegizka *adv.* excessively, exaggeratedly.
gehiegizko *adj.* excessive, exaggerated.
gehien *adj.(superl.)* best, maximum, principal, most important, most.
gehienbat *adv.* generally, usually;

principally, mainly, primarily, especially.
gehienetan *adv.* usually, generally, most of the time.
gehienez *adv.* at the most.
gehienezko *adj.* maximum, highest.
gehiengo *n.* majority. *n.* supremacy, superiority.
gehiengotasun *n.* superiority, superiorness. *n.* majority.
gehienik *adv.* particularly; principally, for the most part, mostly.
gehientasun *n.* generality. *n.* majority. *n.* superiority, supremacy.
gehientsu *adj.* pertaining to or depending on the majority.
gehigarri *adj.* extra, additional; augmentable; additive. *n.* addition, increase, appendix, complement, supplement.
gehigarrizko *adj.* superfluous, nonessential.
gehihazkuntza *n.* excessive growth, overgrowth.
gehiketa *n.* addition, adding.
gehikor *adj.* augmentative, additional.
gehikuntza *n.* increment, increase, augmentation, addition, raise (salary), growth.
gehipen *n.* increase, growth, addition.
gehitu *v.t./v.i.* to grow, to enlarge, to augment, to multiply, to increase, to raise (salary). *v.t.* to exaggerate.
gehitzaile *adj.* adding, increasing. *n.* increaser, augmenter.
gehitzapen *n.* incorporation, increase, addition.
gehizale *adj.* fond of exaggeration.
gehizama *n.* overload, surcharge.
gela *n.* room, cell, chamber.
gelakide *n.* roommate.
gelalagun *n.* roommate. *n.* valet.
gelamutil *n.* valet.
gelaratu *v.t./v.i.* to take into a room, to put into a cell; to go into a room.
gelarazpen *n.* putting into a room.
gelari *n.* valet.
gelatxo *n.(dim.)* small room.
gelaurre *n.* anteroom, antechamber.
gelazain *n.* valet.
gelazaingo *n.* job of a valet.
gelbera *adj.* shy, timid, hesitant, withdrawn.
gelberaki *adv.* timidly, shyly, hesitantly.
gelberatasun *n.* shyness, timidity.
gelberatu *v.i.* to become timid, to become shy, to become intimidated, to become cowed.
geldi *adv.* little by little, slowly. *adj.* still, quiet. *adj.* slow. *int.* stop.
geldiagotu *v.i.* to slow down.
geldialdi *n.* rest; stop, pause. *n.* interruption, suspension.
geldialdizka *adv.* pausing, little by little, by intervals, at intervals.
geldiarazi *v.t.* to immobilize, to cause to stop, to detain. *v.t.* to interrupt, to

suspend.

geldiarazpen n. detention, immobilization; interruption.

geldiarazte n. act of stopping, act of detaining.

geldiarte n. intermittency, interruption, interval. n. intermission, short rest period.

geldiarteka adv. by intervals, intermittently.

geldi egon v.i. to stay quiet, to be still.

geldiegote n. inactivity, immobility, staying put.

geldiera n. slowness, stillness.

geldierazi v.t. to immobilize, to detain, to stop.

geldierazpen n. immobilization, stop, detainment.

geldierazte n. immobilization, stop, detainment, act of stopping or detaining.

geldiezin adj. unstable; hyperactive, unable to stop, ceaseless, unstoppable, incessant.

geldiezinik adv. incessantly, unceasingly.

geldigabeki adv. incessantly, ceaselessly.

geldigabe(ko) adj. incessant, uninterrupted.

geldigailu n. wedge, tire block (used to prevent a car from rolling).

geldigaitz adj. hyperactive, difficult to stop, uneasy, unstable, inconstant.

geldigarri adj. stoppable, detainable.

geldi-geldi adv. very slowly, gradually, little by little.

geldika adv. little by little, slowly, calmly.

geldikeria n. inactivity, inertia, laziness.

geldiki adv. slowly, calmly, little by little.

geldikor adj. stationary, immobile.

geldileku n. stopping place.

geldimen n. pause, cessation.

geldirik adv. calmly, peacefully.

geldiro adv. slowly, gradually, little by little.

gelditasun n. slowness, gradualness. n. calmness, tranquility. n. delay, detaining.

gelditoki n. station, stop (bus, train, etc.).

gelditu v.i. to be left; to stop, to pause, to remain. v.i. to stay, to remain, to remain behind. v.t. to stop, to cease. v.i. to end up, to be.

gelditzaile n. stopper, detainer. adj. stopping, detaining.

geldiune n. station, stop. n. pause, rest period, interruption.

geldizale adj. fond of rest, fond of calmness.

geldo adj. stupid, foolish. adj. naive. adj. lacking willpower or energy. adj. inactive, lazy, slow; useless. n. ash,

burned material.

geldoarazi v.t. to make a fool of (someone).

geldokeria n. naivety, stupidity.

geldoki adv. stupidly, foolishly.

geldotasun n. laziness, inactivity, immobility. n. stupidity, foolishness.

geldotu v.i. to make a fool of oneself. v.i. to be reduced to ashes or cinders.

gelgarri n. obstacle, obstruction, hindrance.

geloste n. back of the room.

geltoki n. station, stop (bus, train, etc.).

geltokiburu n. station master.

geltokizain n. station master.

genealogari n. genealogist.

genealogia n. genealogy

genealogiko adj. genealogical.

genetika n. genetics.

genetiko adj. genetic.

genitibo n.(gram.) genitive

geografari n. geographer.

geografia n. geography.

geografiko adj. geographical.

geologari n. geologist.

geologia n. geology.

geologiko adj. geological.

geometrari n. geometrician.

geometria n. geometry.

geraezin adj. unstoppable, ceaseless.

geragaitz adj. difficult to stop.

geraketa n. act of stopping.

gerakor adj. stationary, immobile.

geraldi n. stop, pause, detention. n. calm, tranquility, calmness. n. immobilization.

geraleku n. station, depot, stop.

geranio n.(bot.) geranium, crane's-bill.

gerarazi v.t. to detain, to cause to stop, to immobilize. v.t. to interrupt.

gerarazle n. stopper, detainer.

gerarazpen n. detention, stop, immobilization. n. interruption.

geratu v.i. to be left; to stop, to pause, to remain. v.i. to make an appointment. v.i. to be left over.

geratzaile n. stopper, detainer. adj. stopping, detaining.

gerba n.(bot.) ament, cattail.

gerente n. manager, director, foreman.

gerentorde n. assistant manager.

gerentzia n. management.

gerezi n.(bot.) cherry.

gerezidi n. grove of cherry trees.

gereziondo n.(bot.) cherry tree.

geriza n. shade; refuge, shelter. n.(fig.) protection, help.

gerizagarri adj. protective. n. defense, refuge, shelter.

gerizagabe adj. unprotected, exposed, unsheltered.

gerizapen n. protection, help.

gerizatu v.t. to cover, to protect, to shelter. v.i. to take refuge.

gerizpe n. shade, shady place. n. protection, shelter. n.(fig.) prison.

gerizpetu v.i. to be shady, to shade oneself. v.t. to shade, to give shade. v.t. to protect, to defend, to shelter.

gerla n. war.

gerlabide n. reason for war, cause for war.

gerla egin v.t. to war, to make war.

gerlagile adj. belligerent, bellicose, warlike. n. warmonger.

gerlagizon n. soldier, man of war.

gerlagorri n. violent disagreement.

gerlakide n. companion in war, fighting companion, war buddy.

gerlako adj. warlike, bellicose, belligerent.

gerlari n. warrior, fighter, soldier.

gerlarte n. truce, armistice, cease-fire.

gerlate n. wartime.

gerlati adj. fond of war, belligerent, bellicose.

gerlatu v.t. to fight, to make war, to battle.

gerlazale adj. fond of war, warlike, belligerent, bellicose.

gerlazalekeria n. belligerence, bellicosity, excessive fondness for war.

gerli n. pus.

gerlitsu adj. full of pus.

gerlitu v.i. to draw out pus, to make purulent.

gerlondo n. postwar period.

gernu n. urine.

gernualdi n. act of urinating, act of pissing.

gernubide n.(anat.) urinary tract, urethra.

gernu egin v.t. to urinate.

gernuki n. urea.

gernuntzi n. urinal, chamber pot, bed pan.

gernupuxika n.(anat.) bladder.

gernuzko adj. urinary.

gero adv. after, later, next. n. future, time to come. adv. gero eta . . . -ago. Used with adjectives and adverbs to form comparatives. **Gero eta txarrago.** Worse. adv. word indicating warning or threat placed at the end of the sentence. **Ez gezurrik esan gero!** Don't tell a lie!

geroago adv.(comp.) later, after.

geroagoko adj. later, following (time), successive.

geroaldi n.(gram.) future (tense). n. future.

geroaldizale adj. fond of the future, futurist.

geroasmatzaile n. guesser, diviner, one who guesses.

geroko adj. coming, future. n. future. adv. for later.

gerokoak n.(pl.) descendants.

gerokoan adv. ahead, in the future, upcoming.

gerokoratu v.t. to adjourn, to postpone. v.t. to save, to keep, to hold on to, to economize (for the future).

gerokotasun n. posterity.

gerokotu v.t. to adjourn, to postpone.

gerokoz adv. at last.

geroraezin adj. undeferable, unpostponable, non-delayable.

gerorako adv. for later.

gerorakotu v.t. to postpone, to defer.

gerorapen n. postponement, deferment, adjournment.

geroratu v.t. to postpone, to defer, to delay, to put off.

gerotan eman v.t. to loan.

gerotan saldu v.t. to sell on credit.

gerotasun n. futurity.

gerotiar adj. procrastinating; tardy.

gerotxoago adv. a little later.

geroz adv. afterward, subsequently, following.

gerozale adj. procrastinating; delaying.

gerozko adj. posterior, ulterior.

gerozkoan adv. from now on, subsequently.

geroztik adv. since then, since that time, since.

geroztikako adj. posterior, subsequent, following.

geroztikan adv. afterward, subsequently, later on.

geroztiko adj. subsequent, following.

gerra n. war.

gerraldi n. wartime.

gerrakontrako adj. antiwar, against the war.

gerraondoko adj. postwar.

gerraondore n. postwar period.

gerraosteko adj. postwar.

gerrari n. soldier, warrior.

gerrate n. wartime, war.

gerraurre n. prewar.

gerrazale adj. bellicose, warlike, belligerent, feisty.

gerrazaletasun n. bellicosity, aggressiveness.

gerri n. waist. n. trunk of a tree. n. middle.

gerrialde n.(anat.) lumbar region of the body; hips and lower back.

gerrialdeko adj. lumbar.

gerrikatu v.t. to gird, to swaddle; to encircle; to tie up.

gerriko n. belt, sash.

gerrikogile n. beltmaker.

gerrikogin n. beltmaker.

gerrikomin n.(med.) lumbago.

gerrikotu v.t. to cinch the waist, to gird, to sash, to belt.

gerrila n. guerrilla.

gerrilari n. guerrilla fighter.

gerrimin n.(med.) lumbago.

gerripeko n. loincloth.

gerrontzi n. warship, battleship.

gertabehar n. fate, destiny, inevitability.

gertaberri adj. recent.

gertabide n. origin, cause. n. process.

gertaera *n.* event, ocurrence, happening.
gertaerazko *adj.* incidental, anecdotal.
gertaezin *adj.* impossible, unrealizable.
gertagabe *adj.* not realized, not occurred, not happened.
gertagaitz *adj.* improbable, unlikely.
gertagaiztasun *n.* improbability.
gertagarri *adj.* possible, eventual; probable.
gertagarritasun *n.* probability; possibility, eventuality.
gertakari *n.* happening, occurrence, event.
gertaketa *n.* happening, event, occurrence.
gertakizun *n.* happening, upcoming event, occurrence.
gertakor *adj.* probable.
gertakortasun *n.* probability.
gertakuntza *n.* happening, event, occurrence.
gertaldi *n.* happening, event, occurrence.
gertapen *n.* adaptation, arrangement, preparation. *n.* happening, event, occurrence.
gertarazi *v.t.* to bring about, to cause.
gertarazle *n.* causer, preparer, instigator.
gertatu *v.i.* to happen, to occur. *v.i.* to find oneself.
gertu *v.i./v.t.* to get ready, to prepare, to dispose, to arrange. *adj.* ready, prepared: *adv.* close, near.
gertualdi *n.* preparation, readying.
gertuera *n.* preparation, arrangement, organization.
gertugabe *adj.* unprepared, improvised.
gertugabetasun *n.* lack of preparation, lack of readiness.
gertugarri *adj.* preparable.
gertuki *adv.* certainly, surely, for sure, for certain.
gertuko *adj.* nearby, close.
gertulan *n.* preparation.
gertumen *n.* preparation.
gerturatu *v.i.* to approach, to draw near.
gertutasun *n.* proximity, closeness.
gertutu *v.t.* to prepare, to get ready, to dispose, to arrange.
gertutzaile *n.* preparer.
gerundio *n.(gram.)* gerund.
geruza *n.* skin. *n.(geol.)* stratum, crust, layer.
geruzapen *n.* stratification.
gesal *n.* melted snow, slush. *n.* salt water, sea) water.
gesaldu *v.t.* to melt, to thaw. *v.i.* to be melted.
gesaldura *n.* melting.
gesalgarri *adj.* meltable, soluble.
gesalketa *n.* melting, thawing.
gesalkor *adj.* melting, liquefying.
gestio *n.* management. *n.* taking steps (toward a goal).
gestionatu *v.t.* to negotiate, to manage, to take steps (toward a goal).
geu *pron.* emphatic form of *gu*, we, we ourselves.
geuk *pron.* emphatic form of *gu*, we, we ourselves.
geure *adj./pron.* emphatic form of *gure*, our.
geureganaketa *n.* act of attracting (someone or something) to us. *v.t.* act of getting or obtaining for us.
geureganatu *v.t.* to appropriate for us.
geuregandu *v.t.* to appropriate for us.
geurekoi *adj.* egotistical, egoistic.
geurtz *adv.* next year.
geza *adj.* saltless; insipid, dull. *adj.* flavorless, bland, mild. *adj.(fig.)* dull, boring, without spark.
gezagozatu *v.i./v.t.* to sweeten.
gezagozo *n.* pippin, type of apple. *adj.* bittersweet.
gezakeria *n.* dullness, flavorlessness.
gezaki *adv.* insipidly.
gezal *n.* salt water, sea water. *n.* slush. *n.* brine.
gezaldu *v.i./v.t.* to desalt. *v.i./v.t.* to melt.
gezamin *adj.* tasteless. *n.* type of apple.
gezatasun *n.* tastelessness, insipidity. *n.(fig.)* nonsense.
gezatu *v.i./v.t.* to desalinate, to desalt, to lose salty flavor.
gezi *n.* arrow, shaft, dart.
gezidun *adj.* having arrows, arrow-shooting.
gezigile *n.* arrow maker.
gezikada *n.* arrow shot.
gezikatu *v.t.* to shoot (an arrow).
gezilari *n.* archer, bowman.
gezileiho *n.* loophole, embrasure.
geziontzi *n.* quiver (for arrows).
gezitari *n.* archer, bowman.
gezitu *v.t.* to shoot or kill with an arrow.
gezitxo *n.(dim.)* small arrow, dart.
gezitzar *n.(augm.)* large arrow, long arrow.
geziztatu *v.t.* to attack or kill with an arrow.
gezur *n.* lie, falsehood, prevarication, untruth.
gezur-asmaketa *n.* fabrication of lies, web of lies.
gezur-asmatzaile *n.* creator of lies, liar.
gezurjario *adj.* liar.
gezurkeria *n.* lie, falsehood.
gezurketa *n.* imposture, fraud.
gezurkiro *adv.* falsely, fraudulently.
gezurlaido *n.* calumny, libel, slander.
gezurlaidozko *adj.* slanderous, calumnious.
gezurra esan *v.t.* to tell a lie.
gezurretan *adv.* lyingly, deceitfully, falsely.

gezurrez *adv.* falsely.
gezurrezko *adj.* false.
gezurreztatu *v.t.* to refute, to prove false, to prove to the contrary.
gezurrizen *n.* alias, false name.
gezurrontzi *adj.* habitual liar.
gezurtabide *n.* rebuttal.
gezurtaezin *adj.* irrefutable, indisputable.
gezurtagaitz *adj.* difficult to refute, hard to dispute.
gezurtagarri *adj.* arguable, disputable, refutable.
gezurtakor *n.* refuting, denying.
gezurtapen *n.* refutation, disproof, denial.
gezurtarazi *v.t.* to disprove, to prove false, to prove to the contrary.
gezurtatu *v.t.* to contradict, to refute, to disprove.
gezurtatzaile *n.* refuter, denier, disprover.
gezurti *adj.* liar; deceitful, deceptive. *n.* cheater, swindler, liar.
gezurtoki *n.* place where people gossip.
gezurtsu *adj.* lying, deceitful, full of lies.
gezurtu *v.t.* to disprove, to prove false, to contradict, to refute.
gezurtxo *n.(dim.)* little white lie.
gezurzale *adj.* fond of lying, deceitful.
gezurzin *n.* false oath.
gibel *n.(anat.)* liver. *prep.* behind, back part of (house, mountain, etc.).
gibel- Used in compound words. Derived from *gibel*, back part.
gibelaitzin *n.* back and front parts. *n.* pros and cons.
gibelalde *n.* back part, rear.
gibelalderatu *v.i.* to fall back, to go back, to back up, to recoil.
gibelaldi *n.* backwards movement.
gibelamendu *n.* setback, delay.
gibelandi *adj.* easygoing, unconcerned, mellow.
gibelarazi *v.t.* to push back, to turn back. *v.t.(fig.)* to dissuade, to change someone's mind.
gibelari *adj.* late, tardy, not punctual. *n.* one who delays.
gibelarri *n.(med.)* gallstone.
gibelasmo *n.* secondary intention, ulterior motive.
gibelatu *v.t.* to delay, to postpone, to set back. *v.i.* to go backward, to back up.
gibelatzaile *n.* postponer, delayer, deferrer.
gibelbeldur *n.* distrust, suspicion.
gibelbeldurti *adj.* distrustful, suspicious, mistrustful.
gibeldu *v.i.* to go back, to go backwards, to back up.
gibelean *prep.* in back of, behind, in the back.
gibelegile *adj.* backing up,

withdrawing. *n.* fugitive, deserter.
gibel egin *v.t.* to go back, to move backwards.
gibeleko *adj.(med.)* hepatic. *n.* liver disease, hepatitis. *adj.* rear, posterior.
gibelerakor *adj.* regressive, backward, moving backwards.
gibeleratu *v.i.* to move into the liver (a disease). *v.i.* to go back, to move backwards. *v.t.* to delay, to postpone.
gibelerazi *v.t.* to cause to go back, to cause to go backwards.
gibelerrai *n.* tripe.
gibeljale *n.* gossiper, slanderer, libeler.
gibeljate *n.* gossip, slander, defamation.
gibeljoko *n.* dirty play, cheating, treason.
gibelka *adv.* backwards, backing up.
gibelkari *adj.* withdrawn, retiring, reclusive, misanthropic.
gibelki *n.* piece of liver.
gibelkoi *adj.* laggard, laggardly, fond of being last, tardy. *adj.* retiring, withdrawn, reclusive.
gibelkoitasun *n.* laggardliness. *n.* reclusiveness, withdrawnness.
gibelkor *adj.* regressive, recessive.
gibelkortasun *n.* tendency to remain stationary; regressiveness.
gibelmin *n.(med.)* liver disease, hepatitis.
gibelso *n.* backwards glance.
gibelurdin *n.(bot.)* type of edible mushroom (*Russula virescens*).
gidabaimen *n.* driver's license.
gidabide *n.* guideline.
gidaerraz *adj.* easily influenced, easily swayed. *adj.* easy to drive.
gidagarri *adj.* manageable, steerable, easily driven.
gidagela *n.* control room.
gidakarnet *n.* driver's license.
gidaketa *n.* transportation, conveyance; guidance.
gidakor *adj.* docile, obedient, sensitive to the rein (horse).
gidaliburu *n.* guidebook.
gidari *n.* guide. *n.* conductor, driver.
gidaritza *n.* manager's position, directorship; guidance.
gidaritzape *n.* protection, guidance, direction.
gidatu *v.t.* to guide, to direct, to conduct.
gidatzaile *n.* guide, director. *adj.* guiding, directing.
gider *n.* handle.
giderdun *adj.* having a handle.
giderreztatu *v.t.* to put a new handle on.
gidoi *n.* script (of a film, etc.), screenplay.
gidoigile *n.* script writer.

giharbarneko adj. intramuscular.
gihardun adj. muscular.
giharmin n.(med.) myalgia, muscular pain.
giharrarteko adj. intramuscular.
giharre n.(anat.) muscle. n. lean part of the meat.
giharreko adj. muscular.
giharreria n.(anat.) musculature.
giharrestura n. muscle contraction.
gihartasun adj. thinness, leanness.
gihartsu adj. muscular, brawny.
gihartu v.i. to become lean. v.i.(fig.) to get in shape.
gihartza n. muscular system.
gilbera adj. ticklish, touchy.
-gile (gram.) suffix which denotes agent or doer. **Sendagile.** Doctor, physician.
giltza n. key. n.(anat.) joint. n.(mus.) clef. n.(archit.) keystone. n. key, solution, thing that explains or solves something else. n. electrical switch.
giltzadura n.(anat.) articulation, joint.
giltzain n. concierge, doorkeeper.
giltzape n. jail, prison.
giltzapeko n. prisoner, convict.
giltzaperatu v.t. to imprison, to incarcerate, to put in jail.
giltzapetu v.t. to imprison, to incarcerate, to put in jail.
giltzari n. concierge, doorkeeper.
giltzarri n.(archit.) keystone. n.(fig.) key, solution.
giltzatako n. keyring, keychain.
giltzatu v.t. to lock. v.t. to place a keystone.
giltzatxo n.(dim.) small key.
giltzazain n. concierge.
giltzezur n.(anat.) clavicle, collar bone.
giltz-hitz n key word.
giltzots n. sound of jingling keys.
giltzurrin n.(anat.) kidney.
giltzurrinbarneko adj. intrarenal.
giltzurrineko adj. renal, pertaining to the kidney.
giltzurrineri n.(med.) nephritis.
giltzurrinetako adj. renal, pertaining to the kidneys. n.(med.) attack of nephritis.
giltzurrinezko adj. related to the kidney.
giltzurringaineko adj. suprarenal.
giltzurrinzorro n.(anat.) renal capsule or gland.
giltzurrun n.(anat.) kidney.
giltzuztai n. keyring, keychain.
gimnasia n. gymnastics.
-gin (gram.) suffix which denotes agent, doer, maker.
ginbail n. hat.
ginbailandi n. large hat.
ginbaildegi n. hat shop, millinery shop.
ginbailgako n. hat rack.
ginbailgile n. hat maker, milliner.
ginbailgintza n. manufacture of hats.
ginbelet n.(dim.) small drill, auger.

ginbeletatu v.t. to bore, to drill.
ginbeletatzaile n. driller.
ginda n.(bot.) type of cherry.
gindondo n.(bot.) cherry tree.
gingila n.(anat.) lobe.
-gintza (gram.) suffix which denotes manufacture, fabrication; profession. **Zilargintza.** Silversmithing.
ginol n. marionette, puppet.
gioi n.(gram.) hyphen. n. libretto, screenplay.
gioilari n. librettist, script writer.
gipuzkera n. Guipuzcoan dialect.
Gipuzkoa n. Guipúzcoa. One of the four provinces of the southern Basque Country. Its capital is San Sebastian.
gipuzkoar n. Guipuzcoan, native of Guipúzcoa.
girgilari n. peddler.
girgileria n. valueless jewel, trinket, bauble, superfluous ornament.
girgileztatu v.t. to dress up elaborately, to dress to the nines.
girgiltruke n. exchange of little value; exchange of trinkets or baubles.
girgilu n. shackle, fetter; handcuffs.
girgiluztu v.t. to shackle, to fetter; to handcuff.
giri n. heat, rut, mating period for animals (mares, jennies, etc.) n. nickname used by Carlists in the Basque Country to describe liberalists or centralists during the nineteenth century.
giristino adj./n. Christian. n. supporter of Queen Cristina (liberalist) during the Carlist War in Spain.
giristinotasun n. Christianity.
giristinotu v.t. to Christianize.
giritu v.i. to come into heat (mare, jenny, etc.).
girla n. bowling ball.
girlanda n. garland, wreath.
giro n. weather. n. atmosphere, ambience, environment. n. disposition, temper, mood.
giroaldaketa n. change in the weather. n. change of mood.
giroasmatzaile n. weatherman, meteorologist.
giroezagupen n. weather report, forecast.
girogailu n. air conditioner.
girogogortasun n. severity of the weather.
girogorri n. bad weather.
giroiragarle n. weather forecaster.
giroiragarpen n. weather report, forecast.
gironeurkin n. weather predicting apparatus, barometer, etc.
girorapen n. atmosphere, ambience.
girosendabide n. climatotherapy.
girotu v.i. to acclimatize, to acclimate. v.i. to be in season. v.i. to improve (weather).

girotxar *n.* bad weather.
giroztapen *n.* acclimatization.
girten *n.* handle. *adj.(fig.)* slow, imbecilic, dim-witted.
girtenkeria *n.* stupidity, foolishness, dullness, torpor.
gisa *adv.* in the manner of, in the way of, as, for, like. *n.* manner, mode, style, way.
gisa-berean. *adv.* in the same way, in the same manner, likewise.
gisagabe *adj.* discourteous, impolite. *adj.* meaningless, irregular.
gisagabekeria *n.* discourtesy, impoliteness. *n.* incongruity, illogic.
gisako *adj.* having a pleasant appearance; affable, easy to get along with. *adj.* similar, alike, having a resemblance.
gisakotu *v.i.* to become affable. *v.i.* to be similar, to resemble.
gisaonez *adv.* orderly, in order.
gisara *adv.* in imitation of, like, in the same manner as.
gisu *n.* lime.
gisubizi *n.* quicklime.
gisugile *n.* limemaker.
gisugintza *n.* limemaker's work.
gisuharri *n.(min.)* limestone.
gisuharrobi *n.* limestone quarry.
gisulabe *n.* lime burner, limekiln.
gisuzko *adj.* made with lime, made of limestone.
gisuztatu *v.t.* to sprinkle lime.
gitargile *n.* guitarmaker.
gitarra *n.* guitar.
gitarrari *n.* guitarist.
giza- Used in compound words. Signifies human or virile. Derived from *gizon*, man.
gizabakarka *adv.* individually.
gizabakartasun *n.* individuality.
gizabanako *n.* human being.
gizabide *n.* conduct, behavior. *n.* courtesy, good manners, consideration, respect.
gizabidegabe *adj.* discourteous, ill-bred, impolite, ill-mannered.
gizabideratu *v.i.* to become civilized. *v.t.* to civilize (someone).
gizabidetasun *n.* courtesy, civility.
gizabidetsu *adj.* civilized, well-bred, well-mannered, courteous.
gizabidez *adv.* courteously, politely, humanely.
gizabidezko *adj.* courteous, polite; humanitarian.
gizaeraile *n.* murderer, assassin, killer.
gizaerazko *adj.* human.
gizagabetasun *n.* inhumanity, barbarism.
gizagabetu *v.i./v.t.* to dehumanize.
gizagaineko *adj.* superhuman.
gizagaixo *adj.* poor, unfortunate. *adj.* naive.
gizagaiztatu *v.i.* to become a rascal.
gizagaizto *adj.* perverse, vile, bad.

gizagaldu *v.i.* to become perverted.
gizagintza *n.* humanization. *n.* philanthropy, love for one's fellow man, brotherly love.
gizagoitiko *adj.* superhuman.
gizahilketa *n.* assassination, homicide, murder.
gizahiltzaile *n.* murderer, assassin, killer, homicide.
gizaigel *n.* frogman.
gizairudi *n.* statue of a person, figure, image.
gizaitxurako *adj.* anthropoid, anthropomorphous.
gizajale *adj.* cannibal, anthropophagous.
gizajalekeria *n.* cannibalism, anthropophagy.
gizajo *adj.* unfortunate, wretched (male).
gizakeria *n.* human debility, human weakness.
gizaketa *n.* crowd, multitude.
gizaki *n.* person, human being, individual.
gizakide *n.* fellowman.
gizakoi *adj.* philanthropic, humane, humanistic. *adj.* fond of men, man-crazy.
gizakoitasun *n.* philanthropy, humanism.
gizakontrako *adj.* antihuman, inhumane.
gizakortasun *n.* humanitarianism, philanthropy, altruism.
gizakote *n.* corpulent man, big man.
gizakozkor *adj.* small (man).
gizakume *n.* man, male.
gizakunde *n.* virility. *n.(theol.)* Incarnation. *n.* incarnation.
gizakuntza *n.* humanization.
gizalan *n.* man's work, human labor.
gizaldeko *adj.* humanitarian, humane, altruistic.
gizaldi *n.* century; generation.
gizalege *n.* behavior, conduct, deportment; justice.
gizalegez *adv.* humanely, courteously, politely.
gizalegezko *adj.* humane, humanitarian, courteous, polite.
gizapeko *adj.* subhuman.
gizaragi *n.* human flesh.
gizaragiki *n.* piece of human flesh.
gizaro *n.* maturity, adulthood.
gizarte *n.* human society.
gizarteko *adj.* social, societal.
gizartekoi *adj.* courteous, sociable.
gizartemaila *n.* social class.
gizartetsai *adj.* antisocial.
gizartetu *v.t./v.i.* to socialize; to be social.
gizartezko *adj.* social.
gizaseme *n.* man, male.
gizatalde *n.* group of people, crowd, multitude.
gizatar *adj.* humane, humanistic.

gizatarkuntza n. humanization.
gizatartu v.i. to humanize.
gizatasun n. humanity, mankind. n. manliness, virility.
gizateria n. crowd, group of men.
gizatiar adj. humane, philanthropic, humanistic.
gizatsu adj. courteous, social, polite, humanistic.
gizatu v.i. to humanize, to socialize. v.i. to become man, to incarnate, to appear on Earth as a mortal.
gizatxar adj. despicable, corrupt. n. evil man, scoundrel, rogue.
gizatxarkeria n. knavery, roguery, cunning.
gizatxartu v.i. to become roguish, to be despicable.
gizatzar n.(augm.) husky man, large man. n. rabble, riffraff.
gizaxka n.(dim.) small man.
gizazale adj. philanthropic, humanistic.
gizazi n. human semen.
gizazko adj. human.
gizebasle n. kidnapper.
gizen adj. fat, obese. n. fatty part of meat. adj. abundant, rich, fertile.
gizenaldi n. fattening up, getting fat.
gizenarazi v.t. to fatten, to cause to get fat.
gizenarazle n. one who fattens animals.
gizendu v.t. to fatten up; to graze (an animal somewhere). v.i. to become fat, to get fat.
gizendun adj. fatty, greasy.
gizengai n. special feed for fattening animals.
gizengarri n. special feed for fattening animals.
gizengihar n. meat with fat.
gizengiro n. fattening up period.
gizenkeria n. obesity, fatness, quality of being grossly overweight.
gizenketa n. fattening, gaining of weight.
gizenki n. piece of fatty meat. adv. thickly, richly, abundantly.
gizenkor adj. prone to obesity. adj. nutritive, nourishing, nutritious.
gizenkortasun n. tendency to get fat.
gizenkote adj. chubby, plump, fatty, fat.
gizentasun n. obesity, fatness, plumpness.
gizentsu adj. fat, obese. adj. greasy, fatty.
gizentzaile n./adj. fattener; fattening.
gizeraile n. murderer, assassin, homicide.
gizerailketa n. homicide, murder, crime.
gizon n. man, human being. n. husband.
gizonadin n. age of a mature man, prime of life.
gizonantzeko adj. manlike, anthropoid.

gizondu v.i. to become a man, to incarnate. v.t./v.i. to mature (as a person), to grow up. v.i. to get married (man).
gizonerdi n. eunuch.
gizonezko n. man, male. adj. masculine, pertaining to man.
gizonezkotasun n. masculinity, maleness.
gizongai n. boyfriend, fiance; bachelor.
gizongisa adv. in a manly way; humanely. adv. honorably, honestly.
gizongisako adj. manly.
gizonkada n. manly gesture, macho behavior. n. boast, brag.
gizonkeria n. macho behavior.
gizonketa n. group of men, multitude, crowd.
gizonki adv. humanly, with dignity. adv. bravely, courageously, in a courageous way, in a manly way, virilely.
gizonkiro adv. bravely, courageously, in a courageous way.
gizonkoi adj. fond of men.
gizonorde n. mannequin; puppet.
gizontasun n. human nature, humanity. n. virility, manhood, manliness. n. gentlemanliness, courtesy.
gizonteria n. group of men.
gizontsu adj. virile, manly, masculine. adj. brave, courageous, valiant.
gizontto n.(dim.) little man. n. despicable man.
gizontxo n.(dim.) little man.
gizontzar n.(augm.) big man, corpulent man.
gizonxka n.(dim.) little man.
gizonzale adj. philanthropic. adj. fond of men.
gizurde n.(zool.) dolphin.
glandula n.(anat.) gland.
glandulatsu adj. glandular, full of glands.
glandulazko adj. glandular.
globu n. globe, sphere; planet. n. balloon.
globulu n.(anat.) globule, blood cell.
gloria n. glory.
glukosa n. glucose.
-go (gram.) Suffix which indicates position, job, work, office. **Erregego.** Office of the King. (gram.) Suffix which indicates group, collectivity, relationship. **Senidego.** Kinship, relationship. (gram.) Var. of the future suffix -ko, used following the consonants n and l. **Joango gara.** We will go. (gram.) Var. of the possessive -ko. **Irungo.** Of Irun.
goardia n. guard; policeman.
goardia egin v.t. to guard, to watch over, to hold a vigil, to keep a vigil.
goarditoki n. military barracks, quarters.
gobernadore n. governor.

gobernaezin *adj.* ungovernable.
gobernagailu *n.* handle of an apparatus, steering wheel, controls (of a plane).
gobernagaitz *adj.* ungovernable, uncontrollable.
gobernagarri *adj.* governable, controllable.
gobernamendu *n.* governing, controlling.
gobernapen *n.* governing, controlling.
gobernari *n.* governor.
gobernariorde *n.* lieutenant governor, vice-governor.
gobernaritza *n.* governorship.
gobernatu *v.t.* to rule, to govern. *v.t.* to feed cattle or livestock.
gobernu *n.(pol.)* government, governing body. *n.* government building. *n.* management, direction.
gobernuburu *n.* head of government.
gobernuetxe *n.* government building.
gobernugabezia *n.* anarchy.
gobernugizon *n.* statesman.
gobernukontrako *adj.* antigovernmental.
gobernutza *n.* governing.
godo *n.* Goth.
goga- Used in compound words. Derived from *gogo*, mind, thought, etc.
gogagarri *adj.* desirable, appealing; appetizing. *adj.* intelligible, understandable, comprehensible.
gogai *n.* idea, concept, opinion.
gogaide *n.* person of the same opinion or idea.
gogaidegarri *adj.* reconcilable, agreeable.
gogaide izan *v.i.* to be compatible or congenial.
gogaidego *n.* agreement, harmony, concord, conformity, compatibility.
gogaidetasun *n.* agreement, harmony, concord, conformity, compatibility. *n.* unanimity.
gogaidetu *v.i.* to agree (with), to become reconciled, to be compatible (with).
gogaidura *n.* tedium, boredom, ennui.
gogaikarri *adj.* boring, dull, annoying, tedious.
gogaikarriro *adv.* tediously, bothersomely, boringly, fastidiously, inopportunely.
gogaikarritasun *n.* tediousness, boredom.
gogaikarritu *v.i.* to be bothered, to be annoyed. *v.i.* to be bored.
gogaiketa *n.* tedium, boredom, ennui.
gogait *n.* tedium, boredom, ennui.
gogaitaldi *n.* period of boredom, annoyance, nuisance.
gogaitarazi *v.t.* to bore; to annoy, to disturb.
gogaitarazle *n.* vexer, annoyer, botherer.

gogaitasun *n.* tedium, boredom, ennui.
gogait egin *v.t.* to bore; to annoy, to disturb.
gogait eragin *v.t.* to bore; to bother, to annoy, to vex.
gogaitsu *adj.* boring; bothersome, irksome, annoying.
gogaitu *v.t.* to bore; to annoy, to disgust, to vex, to bother. *v.i.* to become bored, to grow weary.
gogaitza *n.* boredom. *n.* sloth, laziness, indolence.
gogaldi *n.* humor.
gogamen *n.* thought, idea, consideration. *n.* intelligence.
goganbehar *n.* suspicion, misgiving, mistrust, fear.
goganbeharrez *adv.* suspiciously, mistrustfully.
goganbehartsu *adj.* distrustful, mistrustful, suspicious.
goganbehartu *v.i.* to be worried, to worry. *v.i.* to suspect.
gogangarri *adj.* memorable.
gogapen *n.* thought, idea, consideration, reflection.
gogara *adv.* in one's manner, style or way.
gogaragarri *adj.* agreeable, pleasant, satisfactory.
gogarazi *v.t.* to remind (someone of something), to cause to remember, to evoke.
gogarazle *n.* reminder (person). *adj.* suggestive, evocative.
gogarazpen *n.* memory, evocation, remembrance.
gogargai *n.* subject for thought, matter for reflection.
gogarketa *n.* reflection, consideration, meditation, thought.
gogarpen *n.* meditation, reflection, thought.
gogarte *n.* meditation, consideration, thought, reflection.
gogartetsu *adj.* thoughtful, pensive, meditative.
gogartu *v.i.* to think, to reflect, to ponder, to consider, to meditate.
gogartuz *adv.* reflectively, pensively, thoughtfully.
gogartzaile *adj.* pensive, thoughtful, meditating, thinking.
gogatsu *adj.* eager, anxious, enthusiastic, active; diligent.
gogo *n.* thought, mind; spirit. *n.* wish, desire, appetite. *n.* memory, recall. *n.* will, purpose, intention.
gogoa berotu *v.t./v.i.* to animate, to stimulate, to enliven, to encourage.
gogoa bete *v.t./v.i.* to satisfy, to fulfill.
gogoa galdu *v.t.* to become discouraged, to become disinterested.
gogoahuleko *adj.* lacking willpower, abulic.
gogoak eman *v.t.* to occur to, to think

of. *v.t.* to feel like, to want to.
gogoalai *adj.* jovial, cheerful.
gogoalaitasun *n.* joviality,
cheerfulness.
gogo aldatu *v.t.* to change one's mind.
gogoan erabili *v.t.* to consider, to
reflect upon, to think about.
gogoangarri *adj.* memorable. *n.*
memorial.
gogoangarriro *adv.* memorably.
gogoan gorde *v.t.* to remember, to
keep in mind.
gogoan hartu *v.t.* to take notice of, to
remember.
gogoan ukan *v.t.* to remember, to
recall, to think about, to think of, to
have on (one's) mind.
gogoargi *adj.* shrewd, clever,
intelligent, wise, keen-minded. *adj.*
happy, joyous, cheerful.
gogoargitasun *n.* perspicacity, clarity,
keenness, shrewdness.
gogoarin *adj.* feather-brained.
gogoarrangura *n.* moral restlessness,
moral uneasiness.
gogobatasun *n.* unanimity.
gogobateko *adj.* unanimous.
gogo batez *adv.* unanimously, by
common consent.
gogobehera *adj.* discouraged,
despondent.
gogoberdin *adj.* equable, impartial.
gogoberdintasun *n.* equanimity,
impartiality.
gogobero *n.* enthusiasm, vehemence,
strong desire. *adj.* vehement,
impetuous, ardent, passionate.
gogoberotsu *adj.* anxious, animated,
desirous; impetuous.
gogoberotu *v.t./v.i.* to animate, to
inflame, to fire with passion; to be
animated, to be impetuous.
gogoberotzaile *n./adj.* animator,
inciter, enlivener, exciter; exciting.
gogoberoz *adv.* enthusiastically,
vigorously.
gogoberozko *adj.* enthusiastic,
vigorous.
gogobete *v.t.* to sicken, to bore. *n.*
loathing. *v.t.* to please, to satisfy.
gogobetegarri *adj.* agreeable,
pleasing. *adj.* disgusting, annoying.
gogobeteko *adj.* pleasant, pleasing,
satisfying.
gogobetez *adv.* satisfactorily.
gogobidez *adv.* spiritually.
gogoernetasun *n.* perspicacity,
shrewdness, sagacity.
gogoernez *adv.* perspicaciously,
acutely, alertly.
gogoeta *n.* reflection, meditation,
thought, consideration.
gogoetagarri *adj.* thought provoking.
adj. disquieting, preoccupying,
disturbing.
gogoetak egin *v.t.* to meditate, to
ponder, to think over, to consider.

gogoetaldi *n.* consideration, reflection,
thought.
gogoetari *n.* thinker, meditator. *adj.*
speculative.
gogoetatu *v.i.* to become thoughtful, to
become pensive. *v.t.* to speculate, to
theorize, to reflect.
gogoetazale *adj.* pensive, thoughtful,
fond of speculation, fond of theory.
gogoetazko *adj.* reflexive, theoretical.
gogoetsi *v.t./v.i.* to bore, to annoy; to
be boring, to be annoying.
gogoeza *n.* lack of desire, lack of
appetite.
gogogabe *adj.* unwilling, reluctant,
indifferent; discouraged.
gogogabekeria *n.* apathy, lack of
desire.
gogogabeko *adj.* abulic, lacking
willpower, apathetic.
gogogabetasun *n.* lack of willpower,
loss of energy, apathy.
gogogabetu *v.t./v.i.* to dishearten, to
discourage, to dismay; to become
discouraged.
gogogabezia *n.* lack of willpower, loss
of energy, apathy.
gogogaizto *n.* ill will, hatred,
malevolence.
gogo galdu *v.t.* to become
discouraged, to lose one's interest
or desire.
gogogalgarri *adj.* discouraging,
disheartening.
gogohandi(ko) *adj.* magnanimous,
generous.
gogohanditasun *n.*
magnanimousness, generosity.
gogoilun *adj.* unhappy, sad,
melancholy, gloomy.
gogojardun(ak) *n.(pl.)* spiritual retreat.
gogoketa *n.* mental exercise;
meditation.
gogokidetasun *n.* unanimousness,
unanimity.
gogoko *adj.* preferred, predilect,
favorite; agreeable, sympathetic. *adj.*
spiritual.
gogoko izan *v.i./v.t.* to be pleasing; to
please; to like.
gogomin *n.* ardent desire, passion,
yearning.
gogoneko *adj.* well-meaning, having
good intentions.
gogonez *adv.* with good will, with good
intentions. *adv.* with a good appetite.
gogor *adj.* hard, difficult. *adj.* rigid,
stubborn. *adj.* violent, authoritarian,
severe, cruel, merciless. *adj.*
durable, solid. *adj.* tenacious,
persevering, constant, patient, long-
suffering. *adv.* despotically.
gogora ekarri *v.t.* to bring to mind, to
remember, to recall.
gogora etorri *v.i.* to remember, to
come to mind.
gogoraezin *adj.* not memorable,

unrememberable, immemorial.

gogoragarri *adj.* memorable, evocative.

gogoramen *n.* consideration, thought, idea. *n.* memory.

gogorapen *n.* memory; souvenir. *n.* thought, idea, conception, consideration.

gogoratu *v.i./v.t.* to remember, to recall; to think of, to occur to.

gogorazi *v.t.* to cause to remember, to make (someone) recall, to suggest (something),to bring to mind.

gogorazio *n.* memory, recollection. *n.* thought, idea.

gogordura *n.* hardness, harshness, severity, cruelty, unfeelingness. *n.* rigidity, hardening, stiffening, inflexibility.

gogor egin *v.t.* to struggle, to strive; to resist, to oppose, to face. *v.t.* to reprimand, to scold, to chastise.

gogor egon *v.i.* to resist, to be obstinate, to persevere.

gogorgarri *adj.* strengthening, fortifying.

gogor hartu *v.t.* to treat harshly, to reprimand, to scold, to chastise.

gogorkeria *n.* cruelty, violence, hardness, inhumanity, coercion, hardness.

gogorki *adv.* harshly, cruelly, severely, rigorously. *adv.* strongly, hard.

gogorkiro *adv.* harshly, cruelly, severely.

gogorpen *n.* hardening.

gogorraldi *n.* bad treatment, severe treatment.

gogorrarazi *v.t.* to harden, to make hard.

gogorrean *adv.* forcefully, by force, violently.

gogorregile *n.* one who treats (someone) harshly, hard-hearted person.

gogorrezko *adj.* hard, harsh, cruel, violent. *adj.* forced, not voluntary, not spontaneous.

gogortada *n.* severity, harshness, cruelty.

gogortasun *n.* hardness, strength, firmness. *n.* rigidity, severity, harshness. *n.* consistency; durability, solidity, firmness.

gogortu *v.i./v.t.* to harden, to become hard, to become rigid. *v.t.* to strengthen, to fortify; to harden. *v.i.* to become insensitive, to become irritable. *v.i.* to become crusty; to coagulate, to thicken.

gogotan erabili *v.t.* to make plans, to project, to design, to devise a plan.

gogotan hartu *v.t.* to consider, to take into account, to take into consideration.

gogotik *adv.* with pleasure, desirously, from the heart.

gogotsu *adj.* ardent, desirous. *adj.* tenacious, persistent, persevering, constant, diligent.

gogotxarreko *adj.* malevolent, evil, having bad intentions.

gogotxarrez *adv.* by force, unwillingly. *adv.* malevolently, with bad intentions.

gogo ukan *v.t.* to like, to desire.

gogoz *adv.* voluntarily, desirously, willingly, with pleasure. *adv.* mentally, spiritually.

gogozko *adj.* agreeable, pleasurable. *adj.* voluntary, willfull. *adj.* mental; spiritual.

gogozkoen(a) *adj.* preferred, favorite, predilect.

gogozkontra *adv.* against one's will, by force.

gogozkontrako *adj.* violent, forced, contrary to one's will, obligatory.

gogozkotasun *n.* willingness, voluntariness.

goi *adj.* high, tall, top, superior. *n.* height, top, summit. *n.* ceiling. *n.* sky, heaven.

goiaginte *n.* great power, influence.

goiagintedun *adj.* powerful, influential, predominant.

goiahalmen *n.* great power, powerful influence.

goiaingeru *n.(theol.)* archangel.

goialde *n.* top, summit, height, upper part, area close to the top.

goialdeko *adj.* nordic, northern.

goian *adv.* above; in heaven, on high; upstairs.

goiargi *n.* clear sky. *n.* brightness, extreme intelligence, smartness. *n.* divine inspiration, illumination, revelation.

goiargitsu *adj.* resplendent, bright, brilliant; very intelligent.

goiargitu *v.t.* to clear up (sky). *v.t./v.i.* to get inspiration.

goiargiz *adv.* by inspiration.

goiarin *adj.(colloq.)* feather-brained, scatterbrained.

goiarnas *n.* inspiration.

goibegirale *n.* watcher, observer.

goibegiratoki *n.* watchtower, vantage point.

goibegiratu *v.t.* to observe from on high, to watch over.

goibehera *n.* downhill slope; ups and downs, rising and falling.

goibeheraldi *n.* depression.

goibeheratu *v.t.* to defeat, to prostrate, to humiliate.

goibel *adj.* cloudy. *adj.* dark, shady. *adj.(fig.)* sad, depressed.

goibelaldi *n.* time of clouding (up). *n.* darkening, shading, growing dark. *n.(fig.)* sadness, sorrow, affliction, melancholy.

goibelarazi *v.t.* to make (someone) sad, to make (someone) unhappy, to afflict.

goibeldu *v.i.* to become cloudy, to cloud up. *v.i.* to become dark, to be shady. *v.t./v.i.* to make sad; to become sad.

goibeldura *n.* darkening, blackening, obscuring. *n.(fig.)* sadness, affliction, melancholy.

goibelgarri *adj.* saddening, sorrowful, melancholy.

goibelki *adv.* gloomily, sadly, melancholically. *adv.* vaguely, confusedly.

goibeltasun *n.* cloudiness, darkness. *n.(fig.)* sadness, affliction, melancholy. *n.* vagueness, imprecision.

goibeltsu *adj.* dark, tenebrous, gloomy, cloudy. *adj.* sad, melancholy.

goiburu *n.* upper part, top, head, heading. *n.* high goal. *n.* symbol, slogan.

goiburutu *v.t.* to write the headline, to title.

goidun *adj.* high, elevated. *adj.* eminent, outstanding, prominent.

goidura *n.* prominence.

goien *adj.(superl.)* highest, superior, superlative, supreme. *n.* upper extreme, vertex, apex, peak.

goieneko *adj.* sublime, supreme, uppermost.

goienez *adv.* at most.

goiengo *adj.* supreme, highest, uppermost.

goienkale *n.* upper street, high street.

goiensari *n.* first prize.

goientasun *n.* excellence.

goiera *n.* height, elevation, altitude.

goieragin *n.* enthusiasm, inspiration.

goieratu *v.i.* to reach the top.

goiesgarri *adj.* praiseworthy, laudable.

goieskar *n.(theol.)* grace.

goietsi *v.t.* to praise, to commend, to eulogize, to extol, to laud.

goiezarketa *n.* superposition, placing (something) on top of (something).

goigain *n.* peak, summit, top.

goigarbi *n.* clear sky.

goigela *n.* upstairs room.

goigizon *n.* superman.

goi-goi *adj.* supreme, highest.

goi-goian *adv./prep.* supremely, in the highest place.

goi-goiko *adj.* very high, supreme, highest, sublime.

goigoren *adj.* supreme, highest, most eminent.

goigorri *n.* red sky, red clouds.

goihabe *n.* chief supporting beam.

goijatorri *n.* noble lineage.

goiko *adj.* superior, upper, upstairs. *adj.* eminent, sublime, supreme.

goikozbehera *adv.* upside down.

goilare *n.* spoon.

goilarekada *n.* spoonful.

goilaretxo *n.(dim.)* small spoon.

goimaila *n.* height. *n.* apogee, highest point.

goimailako *adj.* superior, excellent, superb.

goimaitasun *n.* charity.

goimerkatu *n.* supermarket.

goimin *n.* altitude sickness.

goimintzo *n.* grandiloquence, bombast, pompous eloquence.

goinatura *n.(theol.)* supernatural.

goinaturaz *adv.* supernaturally. .

goinaturazko *adj.* supernatural.

goisentibera *adj.* hypersensitive.

goitar *adj.* superior; elevated, high. *n.* inhabitant of the highlands.

goitasun *n.* height, altitude. *n.* excellence, supereminence.

goiti *adv.* on high, above.

goitibehera *n.* scooter, go-cart.

goiti egin *v.t.* to vomit.

goitigale *n.* nausea, need to vomit.

goitik *adv.* from above, from the top.

goitika *n.* vomit. *adv.* vomiting, throwing up.

goitikagarri *adv.* nauseating.

goitikatu *v.i.* to vomit, to throw up.

goitiko *adj.* superior, excellent. *n.* nausea. *adj.(fig.)* ambitious.

goitinahi *n.* nausea. *adj.* ambitious.

goititu *v.t.* to raise, to lift; to build, to erect. *v.t.* to overcome, to defeat, to win. *v.i.* to be left over; to exceed. *v.i.* to be stuffed (with food).

goitizen *n.* nickname, pseudonym, alias.

goitsu *adj.* excellent, highest, superior.

goitu *v.t.* to raise, to lift. *v.t.* to defeat, to overcome, to win.

goiz *n.* morning. *adv.* early.

goiz- Used in compound words. Derived from *goize*, early; precocity.

goizago *adv.(comp.)* earlier.

goizalde *n.* dawn, daybreak.

goizaldeko *adj.* pertaining to early morning, matinal.

goizaldi *n.* morning time (until noon).

goizale *adj.* fond of heights (mountains). *adj.(fig.)* ambitious.

goizargi *n.* light of dawn.

goizargitu *v.t.* to dawn.

goizaro *n.* morning temperature.

goizean *adv.* in the morning, this morning.

goizegi *adv.* too early, too soon; precociously.

goizeko *adj.* pertaining to morning, matinal.

goizerdi *n.* midmorning.

goizerdiko *adj.* pertaining to midmorning.

goizero *adv.* every morning.

goizetik *adv.* from morning. *adv.* early.

goizetiko *adj.* morning, pertaining to the morning.

goiz-goizean *adv.* very early in the morning.

goiz-goizeko *adj.* pertaining to early morning.
goizgorri *n.* red dawn.
goizik *adv.* early, prematurely.
goizizar *n.* morning star; Venus.
goizkorri *n.* red morning sky.
goiznabar *n.* dawn, sunrise.
goizoilanda *adj.* coquettish, flirtatious (woman).
goizoilasko *adj.* precocious, flirtatious, presumptuous (man).
goizondo *n.* morning (from about 8 a.m. til 11 a.m.).
goiztar *n.* early riser. *adj.* premature, early, advanced.
goiztartasun *n.* precociousness, prematurity.
goiztartu *v.t.* to get up early.
goiztiar *n.* early riser. *adj.* premature, early, precocious.
goiztiarki *adv.* early.
goiztiri *n.* early morning hours, dawn.
goiztizar *n.(astron.)* morning star, Venus.
gol *n.* soccer goal (point).
golda- Used in compound words. Derived from *golde*, plow.
goldagider *n.* handle of a plow.
goldaketa *n.* plowing, act of plowing.
goldaketan *adv.* plowing.
goldalan *n.* plowing, tillage work.
goldalari *n.* plowman, tiller.
goldaldi *n.* time of plowing.
goldalur *n.* arable land, plowable land.
goldamutur *n.* plowshare.
goldatu *v.t.* to plow, to till, to break up the ground.
goldatzaile *n.* plowman, tiller.
golde *n.* plow.
goldegile *n.* maker of plows.
golf *n.* golf.
golko *n.* breast, bosom, space between shirt and chest. *n.* bay, gulf.
golkokada *n.* bosom full of, shirtfront full of.
golkoratu *v.t.* to hide in one's bosom.
goma *n.* gum, rubber.
gomadun *adj.* rubber, rubbery.
gomatsu *adj.* gummy, rubbery.
gomatu *v.t.* to glue, to gum.
gomazko *adj.* made of gum, elastic, rubber.
gomaztatu *v.t.* to line, face or cover with rubber.
gomendagarri *adj.* recommendable.
gomendari *n.* recommender.
gomendatu *v.t.* to recommend. *adj.* recommended.
gomendio *n.* recommendation.
gomendiozko *adj.* recommendatory, recommending.
gomit *n.* guest.
gomita *n.* invitation.
gomitatu *v.t.* to invite.
gomitolarri *n.* nausea, desire to vomit.
gona *n.* skirt.
gonabarren *n.* ruffle, flounce of a skirt.

n. underskirt, slip.
gonadun *adj.* skirtwearing. *n.* woman.
gonazale *adj.* fond of women, philandering.
gonazpiko *n.* slip, petticoat.
gonbarabide *n.* comparison.
gonbaraezin *adj.* incomparable.
gonbaragarri *adj.* comparable.
gonbaraketa *n.* comparison.
gonbaratu *v.t.* to compare, to parallel.
gonbarazio *n.* comparison.
gonbaraziozko *adj.* comparative.
gonbidaketa *n.* invitation.
gonbidapen *n.* invitation.
gonbidatu *v.t.* to invite.
gonbidatzaile *n.* host, inviter.
gonbite *n.* invitation (to dinner, for a drink, etc.).
gonbite egin *v.t.* to invite.
gonbitolarri *n.* being about to vomit, nausea.
gondola *n.* gondola.
gondolari *n.* gondolier.
gongeta *n.* asphodel field.
gopor *n.* goblet or large glass or cup made of wood or clay.
gor *adj.* deaf. *adj.* stubborn, deaf to reason.
gora *int.* long live, up with. *adv.* upward, above, up, upstairs. *adv.* loudly, strongly. *adj.* high.
gorabehera *n.* ups and downs, rising and falling. *n.* problem.
gorabeheraka *adv.* up and down.
gorabeherako *n.* diarrhea. *adj.* approximate.
gorabeherakor *adj.* fluctuating.
gorabeheratsu *adj.* craggy.
gorabeheratu *v.i.* to climb and descend, to go up and down.
gorabide *n.* appeal (law). *n.* ascent, upward progress.
goragale *n.* nausea, being about to vomit, need to vomit.
goragalegarri *adj.* nauseating.
goragaletu *v.i.* to be nauseous, to become nauseous, to vomit.
goragarri *adj.* praiseworthy, glorious, esteemed, applaudable, commendable.
goragarriki *adv.* gloriously, laudibly.
goragarriro *adv.* gloriously, laudibly.
goragile *n.* vomiter, one who vomits.
gorago *adv.* higher.
goragoko *adj.(comp.)* higher.
gora-goraka *adv.* out of control, losing control.
goragotasun *n.* superiority; quality of being higher.
goragotu *v.t./v.i.* to elevate further, to raise higher; to go higher, to rise higher. *v.t.* to exalt, to praise. *v.t.* to put in a higher place.
goragune *n.* elevated place, upper part.
goraino *adv.* up to the top.
gorainotu *v.i.* to reach the top.

goraintzi(ak) n. regards, greetings.
goraipaketa n. exaltation, praise, eulogy.
goraipamen n. praise, exaltation, eulogy.
goraipatu v.t. to praise, to exalt, to eulogize, to honor, to glorify.
goraipatzaile n./adj. eulogist, praiser; eulogizing, praising.
goraipu n. eulogy, praise.
gora jo v.t. to appeal (to a higher authority).
gorajole n./adj. appellant; appealing.
goraka adv. forcefully, powerfully.
gorakada n. rise, increase. n. burp, belch. n. growth, expansion.
gorakaldi n. rising, rise, ascension. n. rising tide, high tide.
gorakatu v.t. to applaud, to cheer, to acclaim.
gorakeria n. exaggerated praise.
goraketa n. praising. n. promotion; raising, elevating. n. progress.
goraki adv. highly, praisingly. adv. outloud, aloud, loudly.
gorako adj. preeminent; over. n. nausea, vomiting.
gorakoi n. vomitive, emetic.
gorakor adj. raising, lifting, capable of being raised or lifted; rising.
goralarri n. nausea.
goraldi n. praise, exaltation, glory. n. high tide. n. apogee. n. recovery of a sick person. n. period of prosperity, boom.
goraldu v.t. to praise, to exalt, to eulogize.
goralgarri adj. praiseworthy, exalted, estimable.
goralketa n. praise, eulogy.
goralpen n. praise, eulogy.
goramen n. eulogy, praise.
goranahi n. ambition. n. desire to vomit, nausea.
goranahi(ko) adj. ambitious.
gorantz adv. toward the top, upward.
gorantza n. praise, eulogy. adv. toward the top, upward.
goranzko adj. ascending, ascendant, rising.
gorapen n. praise, exaltation. n. increasing, raising.
goratasun n. praise, excellence. n. height. n. superiority, supremacy.
gorati adj. haughty, arrogant, lofty, uppity.
goratu v.t. to praise, to exalt, to eulogize. v.t. to raise, to elevate. v.i. to go up, to rise; to take off (airplane).
goratzaile adj./n. praising, flattering; praiser, eulogizer, flatterer. adj./n. raising, elevating; raiser, elevator.
goratzapen n. increase, growth; prosperity. n. praise, eulogy.
goratzarre n. homage, tribute. n. panegyric. n. hymn, anthem.

goratzartu v.t. to pay homage to, to eulogize, to praise.
gorazale adj. fond of praise. adj. fond of altitude.
gorazarre n. homage, praise, eulogy, tribute, honor.
gorbata n. tie, necktie.
gordailu n. cache, stash, depository, secret hiding place.
gordailuzain n. depository.
gorde v.t. to keep, to store. v.t./v.i. to hide, to conceal. v.t. to guard, to protect, to save. v.t. to keep, to accomplish, to observe. adj. hidden, secret, concealed.
gordean adv. secretly, in hiding.
gordegai n. preserves, canned food.
gordegarri adj. preservable, keepable, protectable. adj. hideable, secretable, concealable.
gordegela n. store room.
gordeka adv. secretly, in hiding, clandestinely.
gordekeria n. excessive secrecy.
gordeketa n. conservation; guarding, keeping, preserving.
gordekin n. ticket stub.
gordelari n. guardian.
gordeleku n. hiding place, refuge, retreat, sanctuary, fortress, stronghold.
gordetegi n. depository, hiding place.
gordetoki n. depository, hiding place.
gordetzaile adj./n. guarding, caretaking; guard, custodian, watchman. adj./n. accomplice, complier. adj./n. hiding, concealing; hider, concealer.
gordin adj. raw, uncooked. adj. strong, robust, vigorous. adj.(fig.) obscene, indecent, offensive. adj. cruel, ruthless. adj. unprepared, unrefined. adj. bad (weather).
gordindu v.i. to get worse, to worsen.
gordinik adv. crudely, rawly, in a raw state. adv. severely.
gordinkeria n. obscenity (word or action), immorality, lasciviousness, lustfulness, shameless act.
gordinki adv. roughly, crudely. adv. obscenely, immorally, lasciviously, licentiously.
gordinkiro adv. crudely, roughly. adv. obscenely.
gordinska adj. partly raw, somewhat rare, medium rare.
gordintasun n. crudity, crudeness. n. vigor, freshness. n. rigorousness, severity.
gordintzale adj. shameless, impudent, obscene.
goregi adv. too high.
gor egin v.t. to not listen to, to ignore, to turn a deaf ear to.
goren adj. (superl.) highest, excellent, outstanding, supreme.
gorenaldi n. apogee.

gorendu v.t. to raise, to place in the highest position.

goreneko adj.(superl.) supreme, highest, greatest.

gorengo adj.(superl.) highest, greatest, supreme.

gorengotasun n. supremacy, superiority.

gorentasun n. height, culmination, supremacy, superiority.

goresgarri adj. praiseworthy, glorious, estimable, applaudable, commendable.

goresketa n. praising, eulogizing.

goreskunde n. praising, eulogizing.

goresle n. praiser, eulogizer, glorifier.

goresmen n. eulogy, praise, exaltation.

goresmenezko adj. praising, eulogistic, complimentary.

gorespen n. praise, eulogy, exaltation.

goretsi v.t. to praise, to eulogize, to exalt.

gorgarri adj. deafening.

gorgoil n.(anat.) Adam's apple.

gorgoilo n. double chin.

gori adj. molten, incandescent, glowing, ardent, burning. adj.(fig.) ardent, burning, vehement.

gori-gori adv. glowingly, ardently, incandescently, moltenly.

gori-goritu v.i. to become molten, to be red hot.

goriketa n. act of melting, act of becoming red hot.

goriki adv. moltenly, glowingly, incandescently. adv.(fig.) vehemently, enthusiastically, ardently.

goritasun n. incandescence, moltenness. n.(fig.) ardor, enthusiasm.

goritu v.t./v.i. to heat, to melt, to weld, to warm; to heat up, to get warm. v.i.(fig.) to become enthusiastic, to kindle passion, anger, etc.

gormutu adj. deaf and dumb.

gormututasun n. deaf-mutism.

goroldio n.(bot.) moss. n.(bot.) marine algae.

goroldiotsu adj. mossy.

goroldiotu v.i. to become covered with moss, to gather moss.

goroldiozko adj. mossy, made of moss.

goroldioztatu v.i. to gather moss, to be covered with moss.

gorosti n.(bot.) holly tree (Ilex aquifolium).

gorostieta n. holly grove.

gorostiki n. wood of the holly tree.

gorotz n. manure, dung, animal excrement.

gorotz egin v.t. to defecate (animals).

gorotzezko adj. manure-like, dung-like.

gorozjale adj. habitually feeding on manure or dung, scatophogous, coprophagous.

gorozketa n. act of defecating (animals).

gorozki n. manure, dung, excrement.

goroztegi n. manure pile, dung heap.

goroztsu adj. full of dung, full of excrement.

goroztu v.t. to fertilize with manure.

gorpu n. cadaver, corpse.

gorpuaire adj. cadaverous, corpse-like.

gorpuazterketa. n. autopsy.

gorpuebaketa n.(med.) autopsy.

gorpugela n. morgue.

gorpuno n.(dim.) little body. n.(anat.) corpuscle.

gorputegi n. morgue.

gorputz n. body.

gorputzalde n. part of the body.

gorputzaldi n. condition of the body, physical state.

gorputzar n.(aug.) large body.

gorputzatal n. part of the body.

gorputzatalketa n. dissection of the body.

gorputzatiketa n. dissection of the body.

gorputzeko adj. corporal, bodily, physical, pertaining to the body.

gorputzenbor n.(anat.) trunk of the body.

gorputzeratu v.t. to incorporate, to embody.

gorputzez adv. corporally, bodily, physically, carnally.

gorputzezko adj. corporal, physical, bodily.

gorputzikara n. convulsion, shiver, tremble.

gorpuzdun adj. having a body.

gorpuzgintza n. development of the body.

gorpuzkabe(ko) adj. bodiless, incorporeal.

gorpuzkera n. size of the body, physical constitution, physical makeup. n. physical appearance.

gorpuzketa n. physical exercise.

gorpuzki n. part of the body. n.(anat.) corpuscle.

gorpuzkide n. Siamese twins.

gorpuzkin n. mortal remains.

gorpuztasun n. corporality, quality or state of being or having a body, materiality.

gorpuzti n.(eccl.) Corpus Christi.

gorpuztu v.t./v.i. to compact, to solidify.

gorrail adj. rubicund, reddish (with a yellow tinge).

gorrailtasun n. rubicundity, reddishness (with a tinge of yellow).

gorraire adj. reddish, ruddy.

gorraize n. slight deafness.

gorraldi n. temporary deafness.

gorreri n. deafness.

gorri adj. red. adj. rosé (wine). adj. naked, nude, stripped, peeled, skinned. *n.(pol.)* communist. *adj.(fig.)* terrible, awful, extreme, intense. *n.* school of fish.

gorriak ikusi *v.t.* to suffer a lot.

gorrialdi *n.* period of blushing; blush.

gorriantz *adj.* reddish.

gorriantzeko *adj.* reddish.

gorriargi *adj.* light red, pink.

gorribizi *adj.* bright red.

gorridura *n.* ruddiness, redness, rosiness.

gorrigai *n.* red dye.

gorri-gorri *adj.* very, very red, scarlet.

gorrilun *adj.* dark red.

gorrimin *adj.* bright red.

gorrimotel *adj.* pale red, light red, pink.

gorrina *n.* rust, mildew, plant rot, red blight.

gorrindu *v.i.* to contract red blight.

gorringo *n.* egg yolk.

gorrino *n.(dim.)* purple, purple-colored, purplish.

gorriska *adj.* reddish, ruddy, rosy.

gorriskatu *v.t./v.i.* to dye red.

gorritasun *n.* reddening, redness; blush, flush.

gorritu *v.i.* to redden. *v.t.* to make red, to dye red. *v.i.* to blush, to be embarrassed.

gorriune *n.* red spot, rash.

gorriztatu *v.i.* to redden, to blush. *v.t.* to dye (something) red, to paint (something) red.

gorriztu *v.t.* to paint red, to dye red.

gorro *n.* phlegm, spit.

gorroaldi *n.* expectoration, spitting out of phlegm.

gorrota- Used in compound words. Derived from *gorroto*, hatred.

gorrotabera *adj.* hateful, despising.

gorrotadura *n.* hatred, hate.

gorrotagarri *adj.* odious, detestable, hateful, worthy of hatred.

gorrotagarriro *adv.* hatefully, odiously, detestably.

gorrotagarritasun *n.* odiousness, hatefulness.

gorrotagarriz *adv.* hatefully, odiously, detestably.

gorrotakor *adj.* detestable, odious, hateful.

gorrotarazi *v.t.* to irritate, to inspire hatred in (someone).

gorrotatu *v.t.* to hate, to despise, to detest.

gorrotatzaile *n.* hater, detester.

gorroti *adj.* continually spitting, expectorating or hawking.

gorroto *n.* hatred, rancor, ire, animosity.

gorrotodun *adj.* rancorous, hateful, despising.

gorrotolari *n.* detester, despiser, hater.

gorrototsu *adj.* rancorous, hateful, despising.

gorroto ukan *v.t.* to hate, to detest, to despise.

gorrotoz *adv.* hatefully, odiously.

gorrotozko *adj.* hated, despised, odious.

gorrotsu *adj.* continually expectorating, spitting or hawking.

gorta *n.* stable, stall.

gortamorroin *n.* stable boy.

gortamutil *n.* stable boy.

gortaoste *n.* back part of the stable.

gortaratu *v.t.* to put in a stable, to stable.

gortasun *n.* deafness.

gortatze *n.* barnyard.

gorte *n.* court, palace.

gortelari *n.* courtesan.

gortu *v.i.* to become deaf, to go deaf. *v.t.* to deafen, to make deaf.

gortugarri *adj.* deafening.

goru *n.* distaff, staff for holding wool in spinning.

gorueta *n.* act of spinning.

goruetan *adv.* spinning thread.

goruetan egin *v.t.* to spin thread.

gorulari *n.* spinner; weaver.

gorunzko *adj.* ascendant, rising, uphill.

gosal- Used in compound words. Derived from *gosari*, breakfast.

gosalaurre *n.* time before breakfast.

gosaldu *v.t.* to have breakfast.

gosalgarai *n.* breakfast time.

gosalketa *n.* breakfasting.

gosalondo *n.* time after breakfast.

gosalordu *n.* breakfast hour, breakfast time.

gosaltiar *n.* breakfast guest, breakfast companion.

gosari *n.* breakfast.

gose *n.* hunger. *adj.* hungry. *n.(fig.)* appetite; desire, ambition, hunger.

-gose hungry. Used in compound words. **Edergose.** Hungry for beauty, lover of beauty.

gosealdi *n.* period of hunger, famine.

gosebera *adj.* hungry.

gosedun *adj.* hungry, having hunger.

gosegabe *adj.* not hungry, having no appetite.

gosegabezia *n.* lack of appetite.

gosegarri *adj.* causing hunger.

gosegorri *n.* starvation.

gose izan *v.i.* to be hungry.

gosekil *adj.* very hungry.

gosete *n.* famine, period of hunger.

goseti *adj.* hungry, famished, starving.

gosetu *v.i.* to be hungry, to have an appetite, to get hungry.

gosexka *n.* light hunger.

gosez *adv.* hungry, hungrily.

gosezto *adj.* hungry, famished, starving.

gostu *n.* taste.

gostudun *adj.* tasty, pleasant.

gostuko *adj.* tasty, agreeable.

gostura *adv.* agreeably, pleasurably, pleasantly, enjoyably.

gostuz *adv.* enjoyably, pleasantly.

goteun n.(neol.) Holy Spirit.
gotiko adj. gothic.
gotor adj. inflexible, solid; hardcovered; strong, robust.
gotorgarri adj. inflexible, firm, solidifying, strengthening.
gotorki adv. firmly, solidly.
gotorleku n. stronghold, fortified castle.
gotorrezin adj. unfortifiable.
gotortasun n. firmness, solidness, solidity.
gotortu v.t. to make solid, to give solidity to. v.i. to become solid, to solidify.
gotzai(n) n.(eccl.) bishop.
gotzainagiri n. episcopal document.
gotzainaldi n. period of time one is a bishop.
gotzainaulki n. episcopal see, bishop's chair.
gotzainburu n.(eccl.) archbishop.
gotzainburugo n. bishopric.
gotzaindegi n. episcopal residence.
gotzaingo n. office or position of the bishop.
gotzainmakila n.(eccl.) bishop's crosier.
gotzon n.(neol.) angel.
goxo n. sweets, candy, treats.
goza- Used in compound words. Derived from *gozo*, sweet.
gozadura n. moderation, mitigation, softening, calming. n. sweetening.
gozagabe adj. tasteless, unsweet. adj. disagreeable, rough, intemperate, brusque, unpleasant, hard to get along with.
gozagabekeria n. tastelessness, unpleasantness, disagreeableness.
gozagabetasun n. state of being unsweet or disagreeable.
gozagabetu v.i. to lose all sweetness.
gozagai n. sweetener. n. sedative; liniment.
gozagailu n. sweetener. n. sedative; liniment.
gozagaitz adj. rough, disagreeable, unpleasant, brusque, unsociable, rude, crude. adj. out of tune, dissonant.
gozagaizkeria n. roughness, rudeness, disagreeableness, unsociableness, unpleasantness.
gozagaizki adv. rudely, disagreeably, unsociably.
gozagaiztasun n. harshness, disagreeableness, rudeness.
gozagaiztu v.i. to be rude, to be brusque, to be harsh, to be disagreeable. v.i. to become annoyed, to become irritated, to become upset.
gozagarri n. consolation, comfort. adj. soothing, consoling, comforting. n. condiment, seasoning.
gozagarritasun n. sweetness,

tastiness, flavorfulness. n. sweetness of temperament, calmness, sensitivity.
gozagarritu v.t. to sweeten. v.t. to season, to make tasty.
gozakeria n. excessive sweetness, false sweetness.
gozaketa n. act of sweetening. n. act of comforting, soothing, relieving.
gozakin n. sweetener.
gozakitu v.t. to sweeten.
gozakor adj. sweetening.
gozakuntza n. sweetening.
gozaldi n. rest, relaxation, break.
gozalditu v.i. to take a break, to have fun, to enjoy oneself.
gozamen n. enjoyment, pleasure. n. sense of taste. n. use, enjoyment, profit, usufruct.
gozamendari n. usufructuary, one having the use or enjoyment of something.
gozamendun adj. using or profiting from something.
gozarazi v.t. to cause to enjoy, to make (someone) enjoy.
gozaro adv. sweetly, pleasantly, agreeably; smoothly, tranquilly, calmly.
gozarotu v.t. to delight, to please, to give pleasure.
gozartu v.t. to enjoy, to delight in, to take pleasure in.
gozatasun n. flavor, tastiness. n. calmness, smoothness, tranquility. n. sweetness (flavor or temperament).
gozategi n. pastry shop, sweet shop, candy store. n. place of relaxation.
gozatsu adj. savory, tasty, flavorful; agreeable, delightful. adj. affectionate, mild-mannered. adj. fertile, fruitful.
gozatu v.t. to sweeten. v.i. to mitigate, to smooth, to calm, to ease, to alleviate. v.t. to savor, to taste, to enjoy. v.t. to fertilize with manure. v.t. to tune (a musical instrument). v.t. to usufruct, to use, to enjoy, to profit from.
gozatzaile adj. flavoring. adj. tranquilizing, calming, softening, soothing. n. enjoyer, taster.
gozo adj. sweet. adj. tasty, savory, delicious. adj. calming, sweet, gentle, soft, mild. n. sweet, candy.
gozodenda n. candy store.
gozoegi adj. too sweet.
gozoemale adj. flavoring.
gozogarratz adj. sweet-and-sour.
gozogile n. candy maker, pastry maker.
gozogin n. candy maker, pastry maker.
gozogintza n. candy making.
gozo-gozo adj. very sweet, exquisite.
gozokari n. confection, candy, sweet.
gozokatu v.i. to nibble at tidbits, to be constantly nibbling, to have a sweet

snack.
gozokeria *n.* false pleasure.
gozoki *n.* candy, sweet, confection.
adv. sweetly, softly, smoothly,
agreeably, pleasantly.
gozontzi *n.* candy jar, sugar bowl.
gozotasun *n.* sweetness (taste and
personality), pleasantness,
agreeableness. *n.* calmness,
smoothness, tranquility, placidity.
gozoteria *n.* an amount of pastry or
candy.
gozozale *adj.* having a sweet tooth,
fond of sweets.
gozozalekeria *n.* excessive fondness
for sweets.
grabagailu *n.* tape recorder.
grabaketa *n.* recording.
grabapen *n.* recording.
grabatu *v.t.* to record.
grabatzaile *n.* one who records with a
tape recorder.
grabitapen *n.(phys.)* gravitation.
grabitate *n.(phys.)* gravity.
grabitazio *n.(phys.)* gravitation.
gradu *n.* degree, grade, class.
graduagarri *adj.* adjustable, regulated.
graduapen *n.* adjustment, regulation,
graduation.
graduatu *v.i.* to graduate. *v.t.* to adjust,
to regulate.
graduazio *n.* graduation.
gradudun *adj.* adjusted, regulated,
gradated, having different levels.
gramatika *n.* grammar.
gramatikako *adj.* grammatical.
gramatikalki *adv.* grammatically.
gramatikari *n.* grammarian.
gramo *n.* gram (unit of weight in the
metric system).
gramofono *n.* gramophone.
granada *n.(bot.)* pomegranate. *n.*
projectile, grenade.
granadari *n.* grenadier.
granito *n.(min.)* granite.
granitozko *adj.* granite.
granpoi *n.* eyebolt, screw eye, staple.
grapa *n.* staple, clamp, clasp.
grapagailu *n.* stapler.
grapatu *v.t.* to staple, to clamp, to
clasp.
gratis *adv.* free, gratis.
grausk *int.(onomat.)* sound of biting.
grauska *adv.* biting, bitingly.
grauskada *n.(onomat.)* bite.
grazi *n.* wit, humor, charm, grace,
gracefulness. *n.* taste, flavor.
grazia *n.(theol.)* grace.
grazidun *adj.* gracious, charming,
pleasing; funny, witty.
grazigabeko *adj.* boring, dull,
graciousless.
grazigabezia *n.* lack of charm.
grazios *adj.* funny, witty.
greba *n.* strike, walkout.
grebalari *n.* striker.
grebari *n.* striker.

grebausle *n.* strikebreaker, scab,
blackleg.
gregoriano *n.* Gregorian music,
Gregorian chant.
gregoriar *adj.* Gregorian.
grekolari *n.* Hellenist.
grekozale *adj.* Hellenist, Hellenistic,
fond of Greek culture.
greziera *n.* Greek language.
grezi-erromatar *adj.* Greco-Roman.
grina *n.* passion, strong feeling, habit,
tendency, inclination. *n.* worry, care.
grinadun *adj.* impassioned,
passionate.
grinagabe(ko) *adj.* dispassionate,
uninterested, listless.
grinagabetu *v.i.* to become
dispassionate, to be uninterested.
grinagarri *adj.* exciting, stimulating,
passionate, inciting.
grinaldi *n.* period of passion or
excitement.
grinarazi *v.t.* to cause passion, to
make (someone) passionate or
excited.
grinati *adj.* passionate. *adj.* diligent,
hard-working. *adj.* worrisome.
grinatsu *adj.* passionate, excited. *adj.*
worried, upset, nervous.
grinatu *v.i.* to become impassioned, to
get excited. *v.i.* to worry, to be
worried.
grinaz *adv.* passionately, excitedly.
grinazko *adj.* passionate.
gripe *n.* flu, influenza.
gris *n./adj.* gray.
grua *n.* crane.
gu *pron.* we; us.
guda- Used in compound words.
Derived from *gudu*, war.
gudadei *n.* call to war, bugle call.
gudagile *n./adj.* warmonger;
belligerent, bellicose, warlike.
gudagisaz *adv.* martially, bellicosely, in
a warlike manner.
gudagrina *n.* bellicosity.
gudagurdi *n.* tank.
gudakatu *v.i.* to fight, to battle, to make
war.
gudaketa *n.* fight, combat, battle.
gudakide *n.* war buddy, fighting
companion, comrade in arms,
companion in war.
gudakin *n.* war booty, spoils of war.
gudakoi *adj.* fond of war, belligerent,
bellicose.
gudakortasun *n.* belligerence,
bellicosity.
gudalan *n.* military maneuver.
gudalburu *n.* military chief.
gudaldi *n.* wartime. *n.* attack, battle.
gudaleku *n.* battlefield.
gudaletxe *n.* military barracks.
gudaletxeratu *v.t.* to quarter in
barracks.
gudalsail *n.* troop of soldiers.
gudaltalde *n.* troop of soldiers.

gudamutil n. soldier, fighter, warrior.
gudandere n. female soldier.
gudantz n. war games.
gudari n. soldier, warrior, fighter. n. Basque soldier.
gudariburu n. military chief.
gudarijantzi n. military uniform.
gudari-matxinada n. military rebellion, military uprising.
gudarisail n. troop of soldiers.
gudaritalde n. troop or platoon of soldiers.
gudaritaldetxo n.(dim.) squad, patrol.
gudaritu v.i. to enter the military, to enlist.
gudaritza n. military service, soldiering.
gudarontzi n. warship, battleship.
gudaroste n. army.
gudarte n. truce, armistice.
gudartetu v.t. to make a truce, to declare a truce.
gudate n. wartime.
gudategi n. battlefield.
gudatiar adj. fond of war, belligerent, bellicose.
gudatoki n. battlefield.
gudatsu adj. bellicose, belligerent, martial.
gudatu v.i. to fight a war, to make war, to battle.
gudatzaile n. soldier, fighter, warrior. adj. fighting, warlike, belligerent, troublesome.
gudazale adj. bellicose, belligerent, fond of war, feisty.
gudazalekeria n. excessive fondness for war, belligerence, bellicosity.
gudazaletasun n. bellicosity, belligerence, pugnaciousness.
gudondo n. postwar period.
gudontzi n. warship, battleship.
gudontzitalde n. naval fleet.
gudu n. war.
guduka n. battle, fight, war. adv. fighting, warring.
gudukaldi n. fight, battle.
gudukari adj. warlike, bellicose, belligerent.
gudukatu v.i. to fight, to war, to make war.
guduketa n. combat, fight, battle.
gudukontrako adj. antiwar.
gudulari n. warrior, fighter, soldier.
guduxka n.(dim.) skirmish, dispute, fray, scuffle.
guduxkatu v.i. to skirmish, to have small battles.
guduztatu v.i. to fight, to battle, to make war, to war.
guk pron. we (used with transitive verbs).
gune n. plot, place, space, point.
-gune (gram.) Suffix meaning space, place, point.
gupida n. pity, mercy.
gupidagabe adj. unmerciful, pitiless, severe, cruel, merciless.
gupidagabekeria n. mercilessness, pitilessness.
gupidagabeki adv. unmercifully, mercilessly.
gupidagaitz adj. merciless, unmerciful, pitiless.
gupidagarri adj. pitiful, worthy of compassion.
gupidatsu adj. compassionate, merciful.
gupidatu v.i. to be merciful, to be compassionate.
gur n. greeting.
gura n. want, desire.
-gura (gram.) Suffix which indicates wanting, desiring, wishing. **Ikusgura.** Desiring to see.
guraeza n. unwillingness.
guraezezko adj. involuntary.
guragarri adj. desirable, pleasant.
gura izan v.t. to want, to desire.
guraize(ak) n. scissor(s) (usually used in the plural).
guraizetu v.t. to cut with scissors.
guraizkatu v.t. to cut with scissors.
guraizketa n. act of cutting with scissors.
gurari n. will, want, desire.
guraso n. parent (usually used in plural), progenitor, father or mother.
gurasoak n.(pl.) parents.
gurasoengandiko adj. patrimonial, from the parents.
gurasoeraile n. one who commits patricide or matricide, parent killer.
gurasoerailtza n. patricide, matricide.
gurasohilketa n. patricide, matricide.
gurasokeria n. excessive paternalism.
gurasorde n. foster parent.
gurasordetasun n. guardianship.
gurasotasun n. paternity, maternity, quality of being parents.
gurasotu v.i. to become a parent.
guratsu adj. desirous, wishful, wishing.
gurazko adj. voluntary.
gurbil adj. prudent, careful, sensible, judicious. n. small barrel, ten liter barrel.
gurbildu v.i. to become careful, to become prudent.
gurbilki adv. prudently, carefully.
gurbiltasun n. carefulness, prudence.
gurbiltegi n. place where barrels are made.
gurbitz n.(bot.) madrone tree (Arbutus unedo).
gurdi n. cart, wagon.
gurdiabere n. animal used for pulling a cart.
gurdiardatz n. axle of a cart.
gurdibete n. cartful, cartload.
gurdibide n. trail for carts, cart road, wagon trail.
gurdigile n. cart maker, blacksmith.
gurdigin n. cart maker, blacksmith.
gurdihaga n. shaft, thill (of an

ox-drawn vehicle). *n.* pole in a cart against which hay is stacked.

gurdikada *n.* cartload, cartful.

gurdikatu *v.t.* to cart.

gurdiketa *n.* act of carting, act of transporting in carts.

gurdikintza *n.* job of a cart maker.

gurdilanga *n.* transom, crosspiece (of a cart frame).

gurdilantegi *n.* place where carts are made.

gurdilari *n.* cart driver.

gurdino *n.(dim.)* small cart.

gurdiraulketa *n.* overturning of a cart.

gurditegi *n.* carriage house, coach house.

gurditoki *n.* coach house, carriage house.

gurditxo *n.(dim.)* small cart.

gurditzar *n.(augm.)* big cart.

gurdixka *n.(dim.)* small cart.

gurdiz *adv.* by cart.

gurdizain *n.* cart driver, coachman.

gurdizkatu *v.t.* to cart, to convey by wagon or cart.

gure *adj.* our.

gureak egin *v.t.* to be lost, to be done for, to lose all hope; to die.

gureganaketa *n.* appropriation (for us, by us).

gureganako *adj.* pertaining to us.

gureganatu *v.t.* to appropriate (for us); to attract (to us); to assimilate.

gur egin *v.t.* to revere, to venerate, to honor.

Gurejaun *n.(eccl.)* the Lord Christ in the eucharist, communion.

gurekiko *adj.* pertaining to us.

guren *n.* limit, edge, bank. *adj.* preferred, favorite. *adj.* good, holy, sainted. *adj.* healthy, robust, hefty; lush, luxuriant (vegetation).

-guren Used in compound words to express limit, edge in place names. **Mendiguren.** Edge of the mountain.

gurendu *v.i.* to augment, to increase, to grow, to prosper. *v.t.* to sanctify, to consecrate, to canonize.

gurendura *n.* growth, increase, development.

gurentasun *n.* sanctity. *n.* growth, increase, development.

guretar *adj.* supporting us, in favor of us.

guretu *v.t.* to appropriate (for us).

guretzakotu *v.t.* to appropriate (for us), to prepare (for us), to intend (for us).

gurgarri *adj.* adorable, venerable, honorable.

gurgale *adj.* haughty, arrogant.

gurgarriro *adv.* reverently, sacredly, respectly.

gurguilu *n.* bubble.

gurguilutsu *adj.* full of bubbles.

gur-gur *n.(onomat.)* gurgling sound of the stomach. **Gur-gur egin.** To growl (the stomach).

gurgurio *n.(zool.)* grub, weevil.

gurgurkatu *v.i.* to gurgle, to gargle.

gurgurketa *n.* gurgling, gargling.

gurgurlari *n.* one who gargles.

guri *adj.* hefty, robust; luxuriant. *pron.(dat.)* to us, for us. *adj.* smooth, soft. *adj.* tender.

gurialdi *n.* period of vigor or exuberance.

guriarazi *v.t.* to make soft, to soften.

guridura *n.* softening, smoothing.

gurikeria *n.* excessive laxness; excessive ease.

guriketa *n.* softening, smoothing.

guriki *adv.* softly, smoothly, easily; indulgently.

gurin *n.* butter; grease, animal fat.

gurindegi *n.* dairy, dairyshop, place where butter is made or sold.

gurinezko *adj.* buttery, buttered.

guringile *n.* buttermaker.

guringintza *n.* butter making.

gurinontzi *n.* butter dish.

gurinsaltzaile *n.* butter seller.

gurintsu *adj.* creamy, buttery, greasy.

guriro *adv.* softly, smoothly; indulgently.

guritasun *n.* smoothness, softness.

guritu *v.i./v.t.* to soften, to become smooth; to smooth out, to fluff up. *v.i./v.t.* to get fat, to fatten, to fatten up. *v.i.(fig.)* to become tender, to soften up.

guritzaile *adj.* softening.

gurkada *n.* cartload, cartfull.

gurkari *n.* greeter, one who greets. *n.* adorer, venerator, praiser.

gurkatu *v.t.* to venerate, to revere.

gurkera *n.* reverence, veneration.

gurkeria *n.* excessive reverence.

gurketa *n.* adoration, reverence.

gurma *n.* mist, fog.

gurmen *n.* reverence, adoration.

gurpegi *n.* place of firewood, kindling.

gurpide *n.* cart road, trail for carts.

gurpil *n.* tire, wheel.

gurpilbakar *n.* unicycle.

gurpilbiko *n.* bicycle.

gurpildu *v.i.* to move on wheels, to roll.

gurpildun *adj.* having wheels, wheeled.

gurpilgile *n.* tire maker.

gurpilketa *n.* wheels, set of wheels.

gurt- Used in compound words. Derived from *gurdi*, cart.

gurtabere *n.* animal used for pulling a cart.

gurtaket *n.* hay press (wooden pole used to secure a load of hay on a cart).

gurtardatz *n.* axle of a cart.

gurtarrasto *n.* cartwheel rut or track.

gurtasun *n.* veneration, adoration, reverence.

gurtede *n.* leather straps that attach the yoke to the shaft of a cart.

gurtestalki *n.* cover for a wagon or

cart.

gurtohol *n.* wooden sides of a wagon or cart.

gurtu *v.t.* to adore, to worship, to venerate, to revere; to bow down.

gurtza *n.* adoration, worship, veneration.

gurtzaile *n.* worshiper, one who adores.

gurtzain *n.* cart driver, coachman.

gurtzaldi *n.* adoration, worship, veneration.

gurtzapen *n.* adoration, worship, veneration.

guruin *n.(anat.)* gland.

gurutzada *n.* crusade.

gurutzadura *n.* interweaving, intercrossing.

gurutzagune *n.* intersection, crossroads.

gurutzaire *adj.* cross-shaped.

gurutzaketa *n.* crossing.

gurutzamendu *n.* crossing.

gurutzantzeko *adj.* cross-like, cross-shaped.

gurutzargi *n.* dims, dim headlights.

gurutzatu *v.t.* to cross. *v.t.* to crucify.

gurutze *n.* cross, crucifix. *n.(archit.)* cross vault. *n.(fig.)* pain, suffering, cross to bear.

gurutzean josi *v.t.* to crucify, to nail to the cross.

gurutzebeso *n.* arm of the cross.

gurutzebide *n.(eccl.)* Stations of the Cross. *n.* crossroads.

gurutzedun *adj.* bearing a cross.

gurutzedura *n.* crossing, intersecting.

gurutzegrama *n.* crossword puzzle.

gurutzekarle *n.* one who bears or carries a cross.

gurutzelkardura *n.* crossing, intersecting.

gurutzelkartu *v.t.* to intercross, to interweave.

gurutzeramale *n.* cross bearer.

gurutzeratu *v.t./v.i.* to carry someone to the cross; to approach the cross.

gurutzerazle *n.* crucifier.

gurutzeria *n.(archit.)* transept.

gurutzeta *n.* place of a cross.

gurutzetu *v.i.* to cross, to intersect.

gurutzgudaldi *n.* Crusade, war against the Moors.

gurutzgudari *n.* crusader.

gurutziltzapen *n.* crucifixion.

gurutziltzatu *v.t.* to crucify, to nail to the cross.

gurutzirudi *n.* crucifix.

gurutzune *n.* intersection, crossroads.

guruzki *n.* piece of the cross.

guruzpide *n.(eccl.)* Stations of the Cross.

gustagaitz *adj.* unpleasing, unpleasant.

gustagarri *adj.* pleasant, pleasing, pleasurable; tasty.

gustaketa *n.* tasting.

gustatu *v.i.* to like. *v.t.* to taste.

gustatzaile *n.* taster.

gustodun *adj.* tasty (food); having good taste (people).

gustoko *adj.* pleasant, agreeable. *adj.* favorite.

gustora *adv.* pleasantly, happily, gladly.

gustu *n.* taste; sense of taste. *n.* flavor, taste. *n.(fig.)* pleasure.

gutar *n./adj.* one of us, member of our group.

guti *adv./adj.* little, few, little bit, not much, not many.

gutiezia *n.* scarcity, lack, decrease.

gutigarri *adj.* decreasable, reducible, diminishable.

gutigorabeherako *adj.* approximate.

gutika *adv.* little by little, in pieces, by lots, gradually.

gutikasaltzaile *n.* retail seller, retailer, one who sells things little by little.

gutiketa *n.* decrease, reduction.

gutiko *adj.* having little (of something).

gutikor *adj.* decreasing, waning, lessening, languishing.

gutimen(du) *n.* diminution, decrease, reduction. *n.* contempt, scorn.

gutino *adv.* little bit, few.

gutitan *adv.* rarely, seldom, once in a while.

gutitasun *n.* smallness, littleness. *n.* reduction, insufficiency, scarcity.

gutitu *v.t./v.i.* to decrease, to diminish, to wane, to lessen.

gutitzaile *n.* reducer.

gutizia *n.* desire, longing, yearning.

gutiziagarri *adj.* covetous, envious, desirous. *adj.* enviable, desirable.

gutiziamendu *n.* covetousness, envy, desire.

gutiziatsu *adj.* covetous, envious, desirous.

gutiziatu *v.t.* to covet, to desire.

gutizios *adj.* covetous, envious, desirous.

gutiziDski *adv.* covetously.

gutti *adv./adj.* little, few, little bit.

gutun *n.* letter, missive, card. *n.(eccl.)* scapular.

gutunazal *n.* envelope.

gutunketa *n.* written correspondence.

gutunohar *n.* P.S., postscript.

gutunontzi *n.* mailbox.

gutunsorta *n.* epistolary, collection of letters.

gutxi *adv./adj.* little, few, little bit, not much, not many.

gutxiago *adv.(comp.)* less. *adj.(comp.)* fewer, less.

gutxiagotan *adv.* fewer times.

gutxiagotasun *n.* inferiority, quality of being least or fewest, disadvantage.

gutxiagotu *v.t./v.i.* to reduce, to decrease, to diminish, to lessen.

gutxialdi *n.* reduction, diminution, lessening.

gutxiegi adv. too little. adj. too little, too few, insufficient.

gutxien adv.(superl.) least.

gutxienez conj./adv. at least.

gutxienezko adj. minimum, minimal, least, lowest.

gutxiengo n. minority (party, group, etc.).

gutxiespen n. underestimation, underrating; contempt.

gutxietsi v.t. to underrate, to underestimate, to undervalue, to despise.

gutxigarri adj. lessening, diminishing, reducing.

gutxika adv. little by little, in pieces, by lots, gradually.

gutxiketa n. reduction, decrease.

gutxikor adj. decreasing, lessening, waning, languishing.

gutximen n. diminution, decrease, reduction.

gutxitan adv. rarely, seldom, once in a while.

gutxitasun n. smallness, littleness. n. reduction, insufficiency, scarcity.

gutxitu v.t./v.i. to diminish, to lessen, to decrease, to reduce, to wane.

guzti adj. all, every, whole, entire.

guztia n.(econ.) total, sum, amount, all.

guztiahaldun adj. omnipotent, all-powerful.

guztiahaltsu adj. omnipotent, all-powerful.

guztiekiko adj. collective, collected.

guztien adj. general, common.

guztijakintza n. omniscience.

guztijakitun adj. omniscient.

guztijale adj. omnivorous.

guztikotasun n. totality, totalness, completeness.

guztira adv. in total, totally, in sum, in all.

guztiratu v.t./v.i. to total, to sum up.

guztiro adv. completely, entirely, totally, absolutely.

guztitara adv. in total, in sum, in all.

guztitariko adj. general, generic, common.

guztitasun n. totality.

guztiz adv. completely, perfectly, totally, very, utterly.

guztizko adj. total, very, all.

guztizkotasun n. totality, comprehensiveness.

H

h n. letter of the Basque alphabet.

habaila n. sling.

habailari n. slinger, one armed with a sling.

habarrots n. noise, sound.

habarrotsu adj. noisy.

habe n. beam. n. column, pillar. n. cross.

habetu v.t. to put up beams, to raise beams (in a house, etc.).

habetxo n. small beam.

habia n. nest.

habia egin v.t. to nest.

haboro adv. more.

habuin n. foam.

haga n. long pole, stick. n. rod, unit of measurement.

hagaka adv. hitting with a stick, beating with a cane.

hagakada n. blow with a stick.

hagakaldi n. act of beating with a stick.

hagakatu v.t. to lash, to whip, to beat.

hagaketa n. beating or knocking with a pole.

haganeurketa n. act of measuring with a rod.

hagatu v.t. to knock down fruit from a tree, to beat, to hit with a rod or staff.

hagatxo n.(dim.) small pole.

hagatzar n. long thick pole.

hagaxka n.(dim.) small pole.

hagin n. tooth. n.(bot.) yew.

haginateratzaile n. dentist.

haginazketa n. teething, cutting of teeth, dentition.

hagindun adj. having teeth, with teeth.

hagineko adj. tooth, dental, molar.

haginerro n. tooth root.

hagingabe adj. toothless.

hagingaizto n. bad tooth, rotten tooth, decayed tooth.

haginka adv. bitingly, biting.

haginka egin v.t. to bite.

haginkada n. bite, gnashing of teeth, grinding of molars.

haginkari n. biter.

haginkatu v.t. to bite with the teeth.

haginlari n. dentist.

haginmin n. toothache.

haginoi n. gum (of the teeth).

hagoan adv. balancing, in balance.

hagorandu v.i. to suffer, to be afflicted, to agonize. v.t. to torture, to torment.

hagorikatu v.i. to be exhausted, to be worn out, to be dying.

haia-haia adv. quickly, rapidly (walking).

haiek adj./pron. those; those ones; they.

haien adj./pron. (genit. pl.) their, of those, of those ones; theirs.

hain adv. so, so much; such.

haina conj. as much . . . as.

hainbana adj./adv. equally or proportionately (divided). n. tie (score).

hainbanaketa n. action of prorating, act of dividing proportionately, apportionment.

hainbanapen n. tie (score), equal division.

hainbanatu v.t. to divide into equal parts, to apportion, to prorate.

hainbat adv./conj. so much, so many. adj. so much, so many, much, many.

hainbatasun n. equivalency, equality.

hainbateko *adj.* equal, identical.
hainbatu *v.t.* to guess, to calculate, to estimate.
hainbatzaile *n.* guesser, estimator.
hainbeste *adv./adj.* so much, very much, so many.
hainbesteko *adj.* of medium quality, mediocre.
hainbestetan *adv.* so many times.
hainbestetasun *n.* equalness, equality, equivalence, proportionateness.
hain zuzen *adv.* precisely.
haitada *n.* time, turn.
haitz *n.* rock, stone.
haitzaki *n.* rock, stone, boulder, stone outcropping.
haitzarte *n.* space between rocks, narrow passage between two rocks.
haitzeta *n.* rocky hill or mountain. *n.* rock, stone, boulder (in the sea).
haitzetako *adj.* rocky, stony, rupestrian.
haitzlerro *n.* row or file of rocks.
haitzondo *n.* bottom of a rock, underside of a boulder.
haitzulo *n.* cave, cavern.
haitzurdin *n.* marble.
haiza- Used in compound words. Derived from *haize*, wind.
haizababes *n.* place sheltered from the wind, windbreak.
haizaberrizte *n.* ventilation, aeration, air conditioning.
haizabide *n.* windy pass, place through which a constant wind blows.
haizagailu *n.* fan, ventilator.
haizageldi *n.* calm, very little wind.
haizagordeleku *n.* wind shelter, windbreak.
haizaketa *n.* ventilation, air conditioning.
haizakor *adj.* windy, gusty. *adj.(fig.)* voluble, fickle, changeable.
haizakortasun *n.* windiness. *n.(fig.)* volubility, fickleness.
haizalde *n.* windward side, side on which the wind blows.
haizaldi *n.* gust of wind.
haizaputz *adj.(fig.)* arrogant, haughty.
haizarrosa *n.(naut.)* rose of a mariner's compass.
haizatu *v.t./v.i.* to blow (wind), to ventilate, to air. *v.t.* to winnow. *v.t.* to frighten away (animals), to shoo.
haizatzaile *n.* one who blows. *n.(fig.)* annoyer, harasser.
haize *n.* wind. *n.* bodily gasses, fart. *int.* out! get out!
haizea hartu *v.t.* to walk.
haizebeltz *n.* north wind.
haizebihur *n.* whirlwind.
haizebolada *n.* gust of wind, violent wind.
haizeburrunba *n.* gust of wind.
haizeburrunda *n.* gust of wind.
haizedun *adj.* windy. *adj.(fig.)* scatterbrained.
haizegailu *n.* ventilator, air conditioner.
haizegeriza *n.* wind shelter, windbreak.
haizegile *n.* blower, one who blows.
haizegorri *n.* very cold wind.
haizelaster *n.* current of air.
haizeleku *n.* windy place.
haizemaile *n.* fan, ventilator.
haizeneurketa *n.* anemometry, measurement of the wind.
haizeneurkin *n.(phys.)* anemometer, wind meter.
haizeno *n.(dim.)* small gust of wind, breeze, light wind.
haizepuzkeria *n.(fig.)* arrogance, vanity, boastfulness, haughtiness, pomp, conceit.
haizerauntsi *n.* storm, tempest, squall.
haizerre *n.* warm wind.
haizerrota *n.* windmill.
haizetako *n.* windshield (of a car).
haizetasun *n.* windiness.
haizete *n.* windy season.
haizeti *adj.* windy. *adj.(fig.)* farting, farter.
haizetsu *adj.* windy. *adj.(fig.)* boastful, vainglorious.
haizetu *v.t.* to ventilate, to aerate.
haizetxo *n.(dim.)* breeze, light wind, small gust of wind.
haizexka *n.(dim.)* breeze, small gust of wind, light wind.
haizeztaketa *n.* ventilation, aeration.
haizeztatu *v.t.* to ventilate, to aerate, to air, to blow (wind). *v.i.* to be arrogant, to be inflated with self-importance.
haizeztitu *v.i.* to die down, to calm down (wind).
haizoihal *n.* sail.
haizontzi *n.* balloon, dirigible, airship.
haizorratz *n.* weathercock, weathervane.
haizorro *n.* roar of the wind.
haizpe *n.* cave, cavern.
haizu *adj.* permitted, allowed.
haizutu *v.t.* to authorize, to permit, to allow.
hala *adv.* in that way, so, like that, like so, thus.
halabaina *conj.* although, nevertheless.
halabedi *int.* amen, let it be so.
halabehar *n.* fate, destiny.
hala ere *conj.* however, even so, although, nevertheless, nonetheless.
hala hola *adv.* so-so, not very well; more or less, vaguely, sort of.
halaholako *adj.* not very good, mediocre, wishy-washy.
halakatu *v.t.* to change, to make (someone) like that.
halako *adj.* anything like that, such a thing, that kind of, like that.
halakoxe *adj.* just like that, similar, exactly like that.
halatsu *adv.* like that, more or less like

that.

halaxe *adv.* just like that, in that way, in that manner.

halda-maldaka *adv.* suddenly, precipitously, in confusion.

halere *conj.* nevertheless, however, even so, although.

haltsar(rak) *n.(pl.)* entrails, guts, intestines.

haltsarki *n.* tripe.

haltza *n.(bot.)* alder tree.

haltzadi *n.* forest of alder trees, grove of alder trees.

haltzaga *n.* grove of alder trees, group of alder trees.

haltzari *n.* furniture, piece of furniture.

haltzarigile *n.* furniture maker.

haltzaridenda *n.* furniture shop.

haltzarigintza *n.* furniture making.

haltzaritegi *n.* furniture store.

haltzaritu *v.t.* to furnish, to supply a house with furniture.

haltzatsu *n.* place abundant in alder trees.

haltzeta *n.* grove of alder trees.

hamabi *adj./n.* twelve.

hamabiak *n.* twelve o'clock (noon or midnight).

hamabigarren *adj.* twelfth.

hamabika *adv.* by the dozen, by dozens.

hamabikatu *v.t.* to distribute by dozens.

hamabiko *n.* dozen.

hamabina *adv.* twelve (to each person), twelve apiece.

hamabiren *adj.* twelfth, one-twelfth.

hamabisilabadun *adj.* dodecasyllabic.

hamaboskari *n.* biweekly publication, periodical issued at two-week intervals, fortnightly.

hamaboskarren *adj.* fifteenth.

hamabost *adj./n.* fifteen.

hamabostaldi *n.* two weeks, fortnight.

hamabostaldiko *adj.* biweekly, fortnightly.

hamabostero *adv.* fortnightly, every two weeks.

hamabosteroko *adj.* biweekly, fortnightly. *n.* biweekly publication, something published every two weeks.

hamahiru *adj./n.* thirteen.

hamahirugarren *adj.* thirteenth.

hamaika *adj./n.* eleven. *adv.(fig.)* many, many times.

hamaikagarren *adj.* eleventh.

hamaikasilabadun *adj.* hendecasyllabic.

hamaikatxo *adj./adv.* much, a lot, many, many times.

hamaiketako *n.* snack at eleven a.m.

hamalau *adj./n.* fourteen.

hamalaugarren *adj.* fourteenth.

hamalauko *n.* sonnet.

hamar *adj./n.* ten.

hamarbiltzaile *n.* tithe collector.

hamargarren *adj.* tenth.

hamarkatu *v.t.* to decimate.

hamarkera *n.(arith.)* metric system, decimal system.

hamarnakotu *v.t.* to choose one from a group of ten. *v.t.* to decimate. *v.t.* to count by tens.

hamarnatu *v.t.* to divide by ten, to divide into groups of ten.

hamarraldeko *adj.* having ten sides. *n.(geom.)* decagon, decahedron.

hamarratz *n.(zool.)* sea crab. *n.(zool.)* octopus.

hamarreko *n.* decade. *n.(arith.)* ten, group of ten. *adj.* tenth.

hamarremale *n.* tithe payer.

hamarren *adj.* tenth. *n.* tithe.

hamarrendun *n.* tither, tithe collector, one who receives tithes.

hamarretako *n.* snack at ten a.m.

hamarrurte *n.* decade, ten years.

hamarrurteko *adj.* decennial, ten-year-old.

hamarsilabadun *adj.* decasyllabic, having ten syllables.

hamasei *adj./n.* sixteen.

hamaseigarren *adj.* sixteenth.

hamazazpi *adj./n.* seventeen.

hamazazpigarren *adj.* seventeenth.

hamazortzi *adj./n.* eighteen.

hamazortzigarren *adj.* eighteenth.

han *adv.* over there, there.

handi *adj.* big, large, enormous, great. *adv.* much, a lot. For passions, liquids and gases sometimes *handi* is used instead of *asko*. **Ur handia.** Open sea. *adj.* tall. *adj.* famous, important, great.

handiago *adj.(comp.)* bigger, larger.

handiagotu *v.t./v.i.* to enlarge, to expand, to magnify.

handiairezko *adj.* grandiose, majestic, having airs.

handiarazi *v.t.* to enlarge, to cause to grow, to make larger.

handidura *n.(med.)* inflammation, swelling. *n.(fig.)* arrogance, conceit.

handiegi *adj.* too big, too large.

handien(a) *adj.(superl.)* the largest, the biggest, the greatest.

handiera *n.* greatness, largeness, extension. *n.* height.

handiesgarri *n.* praiseworthy.

handiesle *n.* glorifier, praiser, exalter.

handiespen *n.* exaltation, glorification, praise. *n.* eulogy, panegyric.

handietsi *v.t.* to praise, to exalt, to glorify.

handigai *adj.* tending to grow.

handigailu *n.* amplifier.

handigaitasun *n.* tendency to grow.

handigarri *adj.* growing, increasing, amplifying, augmentative.

handik *adv.* from there (remote time or place).

handika *adv.* in bulk, in large quantities.

handikari *adj.* fond of being around important people. *n.(gram.)* augmentative.

handikeria *n.* arrogance, vanity, conceit, pomp, boastfulness.

handikeriaz *adv.* arrogantly, insolently, vainly, haughtily.

handiki *adv.* magnificently, grandiosely, majestically, ostentatiously. *n.* aristocrat, magnate, rich man.

handikiro *adv.* majestically, magnificently, grandiosely, grandly.

handiko *adj.* distant, remote; from the other side.

handikoi *adj.* tending to grow.

handikoitasun *n.* tendency to grow. *n.* tendency to be arrogant.

handikor *adj.* tending to grow. *adj.* arrogant, ostentatious, self-important.

handikote *adj.(augm.)* bulky, gigantic.

handikotetu *v.i.* to grow very large.

handikuntza *n.* increase, enlargement.

handi-mandi *adj.* ostentatious, pompous, vain, self-important.

handi-mandiak *n.(pl.)* aristocrats, magnates.

handi-mandikeria *n.* vanity, ostentation, pomposity.

handi-mandiko *adj.* ostentatious, pompous, vain.

handi-manditu *v.i.* to be ostentatious, to be pompous, to be vain.

handimin *n.* ambition.

handinahi *n.* ambition. *adj.* ambitious, arrogant, ostentatious, vain.

handinahikeria *n.* megalomania, arrogance.

handinahiko *adj.* arrogant, ambitious, ostentatious, vain.

handiputz *adj.* arrogant, insolent, pretentious, vain, pompous.

handipuzkeria *n.* vanity, ostentation, boastfulness.

handipuztu *v.i.* to be overly vain.

handiro *adv.* greatly, magnificently, grandly.

handisamar *adj.* fairly large.

handitasun *n.* greatness, bigness. *n.* growth, increase.

handitsu *adj.* huge, gigantic. *n.(med.)* tumor.

handitu *v.i./v.t.* to increase, to develop, to grow, to enlarge, to become big; to make larger. *v.i.* to swell (up), to inflate, to puff up. *v.t.* to amplify.

handitzaile *n.* increaser. *adj.* increasing.

handitzar *adj.(aug.)* huge, enormous, gigantic.

handiuste *n.* vanity, presumptuousness. *adj.* arrogant, vain, presumptuous.

handiustekeria *n.* presumptuousness, vanity.

handiusteko *adj.* arrogant, bold, presumptuous.

handixka *adj.* fairly large.

handizale *adj.* ambitious, greedy. *adj.* ostentatious, sumptuous.

handizaletasun *n.* ambition; vanity, arrogance.

handizaletu *v.i.* to become ambitious.

handizkari *n.* wholesaler.

handizki *adv.* majestically, grandly, magnificently, grandiosely, ostentatiously. *n.* magnate, aristocrat.

handiztatu *v.t./v.i.* to increase, to enlarge, to augment.

hango *adj.* from there, native of that place.

hangoxe *adj.* from right there, native of that precise location.

hanka *n.(anat.)* leg; foot; paw (of an animal). *int.* get out!

hankabakar *adj.* one-legged.

hankabidun *adj.* biped, two-legged.

hankabihur *adj.* bandy-legged, knock-kneed, crippled.

hankabiko *adj.* biped, two-legged.

hankadun *adj.* having legs; having feet.

hanka egin *v.t.* to run away, to go away, to escape.

hankagabe *adj.* legless, without legs.

hankagain *n.(anat.)* instep. *n.(anat.)* hip.

hankagiltza *n.(anat.)* hip joint.

hankaluze *adj.* long-legged.

hankamin *n.* pain in the leg, leg ache, pain in the feet.

hankamotz *adj.* short-legged.

hankandi *adj.* long-legged.

hankapetu *v.t.* to trample underfoot, to tread down, to crush, to step on.

hankapilota *n.* soccer.

hankapilotari *n.* soccer player.

hankapuntako *n.* kick.

hankarin *adj.(fig.)* fast moving (person).

hankarte *n.* crotch, the place where the legs fork from the human body.

hankarteka *adv.* spraddled, straddling.

hankazabal *adj.* bandy-legged, bow-legged.

hankazgora *adv.* feet up, upside down.

hankezur *n.(anat.)* shinbone, tibia.

hankoker *adj.* bandy-legged, knock-kneed, crippled.

hankokertu *v.t./v.i.* to sprain one's leg, to have a sprained leg or foot, to become crippled.

hankots *n.* act of stamping the foot. *n.* sound of footsteps.

hankuts *adj.* barefooted.

hankutsik *adv.* barefoot.

hanpa *n.* gang, group of criminals, band (of thieves).

hanpatu *v.t./v.i.* to inflate, to swell.

hanpatune *n.* contusion, lump, bruise.

hanpuru *n.* tumor, growth, swelling.
hanpurudun *adj.* swollen.
hanpuruskeria *n.* arrogance, boasting, bragging.
hanpuruski *adv.* boastingly, arrogantly.
hanpurustu *v.i.* to be arrogant, to be boastful, to be vain.
hanpurutasun *n.* arrogance, arrogant character.
hanpurutsu *adj.* vain, presumptuous, arrogant, boasting, boastful, conceited, show-off.
hanpurutu *v.i.* to swell with pride, to become arrogant.
hantu *v.t./v.i.* to inflate, to swell, to puff up.
hantuskeria *n.* arrogance, presumption.
hantuski *adv.* arrogantly, presumptuously.
hantuste *n.* boastfulness, presumptuousness, vanity, arrogance.
hantustedun *adj.* presumptuous, vain, arrogant.
hantustu *v.i.* to boast, to brag.
hantxe *adv.* right there.
har *n.* worm. *n.(fig.)* remorse, regret.
har- Used in compound words. Derived from *harri*, stone.
hara *adv.* there (indicating direction towards). *int.* look! there! Exclamation to call someone's attention.
haragi *n.* meat, flesh. *n.* concupiscence, sexual desire.
haragiantzeko *adj.* meaty, meat-like.
haragiatsegin *n.* sexual pleasure, sensual pleasure.
haragibizi *adj.* scraped to the bone, skinned.
haragidun *adj.* meaty, fleshy.
haragidura *n.* healing properties.
haragigorri *adj.* scraped.
haragigrina *n.* lust, lasciviousness.
haragijale *adj.* carnivorous.
haragikeria *n.* lust, lasciviousness, lewdness; fornication.
haragikeria egin *v.t.* to fornicate.
haragiki *adv.* sexually. *n.* piece of meat.
haragikoi *adj.* lustful, lascivious, carnal, licentious. *adj.* carnivorous.
haragikoitasun *n.* sexual desire, sexual appetite.
haragikoitu *v.i.* to become lustful, to develop a sexual appetite.
haragikor *adj.* lustful, lascivious. *adj.* carnivorous.
haragikortu *v.i.* to become lustful.
haragikuntza *n.* healing process. *n.* incarnation.
haragimami *n.* soft or tender portion of meat.
haragipen *n.* incarnation.
haragirrits *n.* carnal desire, sexual desire, lust.

haragisaltzaile *n.* butcher.
haragitegi *n.* butcher shop, meat shop.
haragitsu *adj.* fleshy, meaty.
haragitu *v.i.* to incarnate, to become a man, to take on human form. *v.i.* to begin healing, to flesh over. *v.t.(fig.)* to assimilate.
haragiustel *n.* rotten meat.
haragiuzle *n.* one who abstains from eating meat.
haragiuzte *n.* abstinence from eating meat.
haragixerra *n.* slice of meat.
haragiz *adv.* lustfully, sexually, carnally.
haragizale *adj.* fond of meat.
haragizalekeria *n.* licentiousness, lasciviousness.
haragizko *adj.* meaty, fleshy. *adj.* carnal, sexual, lusty.
haragiztatu *v.i.* to be lustful. *v.i.* to incarnate, to become man, to take on human form.
harago *adv.* farther, over there.
haraino *adv.* as far as (that place), up to (a place).
harakaitz *n.* rotten meat.
harakin *n.* butcher.
harakintegi *n.* butcher shop, meat shop.
harakintza *n.* butcher's job. *n.* butchery, massacre, slaughtering.
harako *adv.* for there. *adj.* above-mentioned, former, like that.
haran *n.* valley.
harantz *adv.* toward there.
hara-hona ibili *v.i.* to wander.
harat- Used in compound words. Derived from *haragi*, meat.
harategi *n.* butcher shop, meat market.
harategun *n.* days to eat meat.
haratu *v.i.* to go there.
haratustel *n.* rotten meat. *n.* gangrene.
haratusteldu *v.i.* to spoil, to rot, to corrupt, to decay. *v.i.* to become gangrenous.
haratutzi *v.t.* to abstain from eating meat.
haratuzte *n.* third day of carnival (day preceding Lent) when people celebrate with parties.
harbera *adj.* wormy, worm-ridden. *adj.* receptive, open.
harbete *v.i.* to be filled with worms.
harbide *n.* road, path, cobblestone road, stone path.
harbiribil *n.* round pebble.
harburu *n.* outcrop of stone or rock.
hardun *adj.* verminous, wormy, worm-ridden.
hardundu *v.i.* to become wormy, to rot, to become worm-eaten.
harea *n.* sand.
hareaga *n.* beach; sandy ground.
hareatsu *adj.* sandy.
hareatza *n.* sandy ground; beach.

haredun *adj.* sandy.
harehaitz *n.* sandstone.
hareharri *n.* sandstone.
harekatu *v.t.* to sand, to polish; to cover with sand.
haren *adj.(genit.)* his, her, its. *pron.(genit.)* his, hers.
haretsu *adj.* sandy.
hareztatu *v.t.* to cover with sand.
hargailu *n.* receiver, receiving apparatus.
hargaitz *adj.* unacceptable.
hargarri *adj.* acceptable, admissible.
hargarritasun *n.* acceptability, admissibility.
hargatik *pron.* because of him or her, because of that, for that reason.
hargin *n.* stonecutter. *n.* bricklayer, mason.
hargindegi *n.* stonecutting workshop.
hargingo *n.* stonecutting job.
harginlan *n.* stonecutter's work, masonry.
harginmailu *n.* stonecutter's hammer.
harginmutil *n.* stonecutter's apprentice.
hargintza *n.* stonecutter's profession, stonecutting.
hari *n.* thread, linen. *n.(fig.)* thread, theme, topic. *pron.(dat.)* to him, to her, to it, to that. *n.* string, filament, wire.
hari(a) sartu *v.t.* to thread a needle.
haridun *adj.* threaded, having thread, thready.
harigabe(ko) *adj.* wireless.
harigrama *n.* cablegram, telegram.
haril *n.* skein of thread, hank of thread, ball of yarn.
harilardatz *n.* axle in a winding frame.
harildu *v.t.* to wind a ball of thread, to ball yarn, to reel.
harilgailu *n.* reel, spool, bobbin.
harilkari *n.* winding frame.
harilkatu *v.t.* to wind a bobbin, to reel, to ball yarn.
harilkatzaile *n.* reeler, winder.
harilketa *n.* action of winding a bobbin.
harilketari *n.* one who winds bobbins.
hariltegi *n.* winding frame; bobbin, spool.
hariltoki *n.* winding frame.
harira etorri *v.i.* to be appropriate (for the conversation), to get to the point, to return to the topic of conversation.
hariteria *n.* collection of threads.
haritsu *adj.* thready, stringy, wiry. *adj.* fibrous.
haritu *v.t.* to thread, to make thread, to spin, to make wire or string.
haritz *n.(bot.)* oak.
harizketa *n.* group of oak trees.
harizki *n.* oak (wood), piece of oak.
harizko *adj.* (made) of thread, linen.
harizpi *n.* filament.
hariztatu *v.t.* to thread. *v.t.* to unravel, to remove threads from a garment.

hariztegi *n.* grove of oak trees.
harizti *n.* forest of oak trees.
hariztoki *n.* place of oaks.
harjale *adj.* vermivorous, worm-eating.
harjo *v.i./v.t.* to rot, to be eaten away by worms, to be worm-eaten. *adj.* worm-eaten.
harjodura *n.* rottenness, decay, putrefaction.
hark *pron.* he, she, that one. Used as subject of transitive verbs.
harkaitsu *adj.* rocky, stony.
harkaitz *n.* rock.
harkaitzeta *n.* rocky place, group of rocks.
harkaizkabra *n.(zool.)* small red fish with large head, sharp dorsal spines and tasty flesh found on rocky coasts.
harkaizperatu *v.i.* to find shelter under rocks, to go under rocks for shelter.
harkaizpuru *n.* reef.
harkaiztegi *n.* place of rocks, rocky place.
harkaiztsu *adj.* rocky, stony.
harkaskar *n.* pebble.
harketa *n.* conquest, capture, seizure, act of taking.
harkor *adj.* clinging, grasping, capable of taking hold. *adj.* hospitable.
harkortasun *n.* acceptance. *n.* hospitality.
harlan *n.* stonecutter's work, masonry work.
harlanabes *n.* tool made of stone.
harlandu *v.t.* to work stone, to hew stone, to carve stone. *n.* hewn stone, cut stone.
harlanduketa *n.* stonecutter's work.
harlandutu *v.t.* to work stone, to cut stone, to hew stone.
harlangile *n.* stonecutter, mason.
harlangintza *n.* stonecutter's job, masonry.
harlatz *n.* whetting stone, stone used for sharpening things. *n.* emery.
harlauza *n.* stone blocks, large stone squares or tiles.
harlosa *n.* large flat paving stone.
harmaila *n.* stone step.
harmailu *n.* hammer made of stone. *n.* stonecutter's hammer or pick.
harmailutu *v.t.* to hew stone, to cut stone with a hammer.
harmen *n.* receptiveness, receptivity.
harmeta *n.* pile of rocks, mountain of rocks, rock pile.
harmonia *n.* harmony.
harmutur *n.* rock with a projection, rock outcropping.
harpa *n.(mus.)* harp.
harpajole *n.* harpist.
harpe *n.* cave, cavern.
harpelaritza *n.* spelunking, speleology.
harpide *n.* subscription.
harpidetu *v.i./v.t.* to subscribe, to take

a subscription.
harpidetza n. subscription.
harpiko n. rock chisel.
harpilo n. pile of worms. n. pile of rocks.
harrapaezin adj. uncatchable, inapprehensible, unapprehendable.
harrapagailu n. trap, snare.
harrapagaitz adj. hard to catch, difficult to apprehend.
harrapagarri adj. catchable, apprehensible, apprehendable.
harrapaka adv. tumultuously, disorderly, confusedly.
harrapakari n. thief, robber, pillager, looter, depredator.
harrapakatu v.t. to pillage, to sack, to loot, to rob.
harrapakeria n. robbery, theft, looting, pillage.
harrapaketa n. pillage, plunder, looting. n. capture, apprehension.
harrapakin n. catch, prey; booty, loot.
harrapaldi n. capture, seizure, detainment, apprehension.
harraparazi v.t. to cause to trap, to make (someone) catch (something or someone).
harrapari adj. voracious, rapacious, ravenous. n. bird of prey.
harrapatu v.t. to trap, to grab, to catch, to seize. v.t. to kidnap, to steal, to rob. v.t. to surprise in the act, to catch red-handed.
harrapatzaile n. robber, seizer, trapper, kidnapper, catcher, capturer, abductor.
harrarte n. opening among rocks, opening between two rocks. n. stony ground.
harraska n. stone sink, manger.
harrate n. ancient stone door. n. narrow mountain pass between two rocks.
harreman. n. relationship. n.(econ.) transaction.
harreman izan v.t. to have a relationship, to relate to, to have relations (with).
harremankor adj. sociable, gregarious.
harrera n. welcome, reception.
harrera egin v.t. to welcome, to receive, to accept.
harreragabe adj. inhospitable; unwelcome.
harreragabezia n. inhospitableness, lack of hospitality.
harreragile n. receptionist; welcomer, receiver.
harrerakor adj. kind, amiable, gentle, affable, pleasant, accepting.
harreratasun n. kindness, gentleness, amiability, affability.
harreratsu adj. kind, gentle, amiable, affable, pleasant.
harrerazi v.t. to cause to take, to make (someone) take (something).

harrerazko adj. hospitable.
harresi n. rock wall, stone fence.
harresibarneko adj. within the ancient walls of a city.
harresidun adj. walled, fenced (with stone walls), fortified.
harresitu v.t. to wall up, to fortify, to fence in (with a stone wall).
harresitzar n.(augm.) large wall.
harrespil n. cromlech.
harretxe n. stone house, rock house.
harrezin adj. unacceptable.
harri n. rock, stone. n. hail. n.(med.) kidney stone, gallstone. int. exclamation used to encourage donkeys to move forward. n. laundry sink, kitchen sink, sink.
harria bota v.t.(med.) to pass stones. v.t. to blame, to cast blame (on someone).
harrialdaketa n. petrification. n. act of moving stones from one place to another.
harriapal n.(archit.) cornice. (lit.) flat rock.
harriarazi v.t. to frighten, to make (someone) afraid, to petrify with fear.
harri aro n.(geol.) Stone Age.
harriaska n. stone sink, manger.
harribitxi n. gem, precious stone, jewel.
harribizi n. gem, jewel, precious stone. n. shiny stone.
harridi n. pile of rocks.
harridura n. astonishment, amazement, surprise. n. bewilderment, confusion.
harrierorketa n. rock slide, landslide.
harrigarriro adv. extraordinarily, marvelously.
harrigarri adj. amazing, astonishing, surprising, astounding, great, fantastic, marvelous, admirable, stupendous.
harrigarritasun n. admiration, surprise, wonder.
harrigarritu v.i. to be astonished. v.t. to marvel, to admire.
harrigarritza n. prodigy, wonder, marvel, portent.
harrigarrizko adj. surprising, amazing. adj. terrible, awful, shocking.
harrigeldo n. pumice stone.
harrigile n. stonecutter, mason.
harrigiltza n. keystone.
harrihorma n. stone wall.
harrihormagile n. mason, builder of stone walls.
harri jaso v.t. to lift stone(s).
harrijasoketa n. lifting of stones, stone lifting.
harrijasotzaile n. stone lifter (popular rural sport in the Basque Country).
harrijaurtailu n. catapult.
harrika adv. (by) throwing stones.
harrikada n. act of hitting with a stone, act of stoning, throwing of a stone,

casting of stones.
harrika egin *v.t.* to stone.
harrikaketa *n.* stoning, lapidation.
harrikaldi *n.* blow from a stone. *n.* season of hail storms.
harrikari *n.* thrower of stones.
harrikaskar *n.(dim.)* pebble, gravel.
harrikatu *v.t.* to stone, to lapidate.
harrikatz *n.* coal.
harrikatzaile *n.* thrower of stones.
harrikaztegi *n.* coal yard, coal bin.
harriketa *n.* stoning. *n.* transporting of stones, delivery of stones.
harriko *n.* dirty dishes, dishes to be cleaned.
harrikoa egin *v.t.* to do the dishes.
harrikoskor *n.(dim.)* pebble, gravel.
harrikoxkor *n.(dim.)* pebble, gravel.
harrikuntza *n.* petrification, turning to stone.
harrilan *n.* stone carving, worked stone.
harriloza *n.* large flat paving stone or rock.
harrimen *n.* surprise.
harrimeta *n.* pile of rocks.
harrimin *n.(med.)* pain caused by kidney stones or gall stones.
harrimuga *n.* milestone, landmark.
harripilo *n.* pile of rocks, pile of stones.
harritasun *n.* surprise, amazement, astonishment.
harrite *n.* season of hail stones. *n.* act of carrying stone.
harritsu *adj.* rocky, stony.
harritu *v.i.* to be or become petrified, to turn to stone. *v.i.(fig.)* to be surprised, to be amazed, to be astonished, to be frightened. *v.t.(fig.)* to marvel at, to amaze, to surprise.
harritxo *n.(dim.)* small stone.
harritza *n.* stony place, stony ground.
harritzapen *n.* astonishment, fright, amazement.
harritzar *n.(augm.)* block of stone, large stone.
harritzeko *adj.* terrible, shocking, surprising, awful. *adj.* marvelous, extraordinary, fantastic.
harrixka *n.(dim.)* small stone, pebble, gravel.
harrizabal *n.* flagstone, slab of stone.
harrizko *adj.* of stone, made of stone.
harriztaketa *n.* petrification, turning to stone. *n.* paving with stone.
harriztatu *v.t.* to pave (with flagstones).
harriztatzaile *n.* paver, one who paves (roads, etc.).
harriztu *v.t.* to pave (with flagstones).
harro *adj./adv.* proud, arrogant; arrogantly. *adj.* spongy, soft.
harroaldi *n.* moment of pride. *n.* shaking, fluffing up.
harrobi *n.* quarry, rock quarry, stone quarry.

harrodura *n.* arrogance, conceit.
harro-harrotu *v.t.* to rise (bread), to fluff up, to soften. *v.i.* to be very arrogant.
harroin *n.* base, foundation.
harrokeria *n.* arrogance, vanity, conceit.
harrokeriaz *adv.* arrogantly, conceitedly, vainly.
harrokeriazko *adj.* arrogant, pedantic, conceited.
harroketa *n.* fluffing up (bed or pillow), softening, rising (bread).
harroki *adv.* arrogantly, vainly, boastfully, conceitedly, pedantically, ostentatiously.
harroputz *adj.* arrogant, boastful, vain, presumptuous, conceited, show-off.
harropuzkada *n.* boast, brag.
harropuzkeria *n.* arrogance, boastfulness, vanity, conceit, pomp.
harropuzkeriaz *adv.* arrogantly, boastfully, conceitedly.
harropuztu *v.i.* to be arrogant, to boast, to be conceited, to be vain.
harrotasun *n.* arrogance, vanity, boastfulness, conceit; pride. *n.(fig.)* fluffiness, softness.
harrotsu *adj.* arrogant, vain, conceited; proud. *adj.* fluffy, soft.
harrotu *v.i./v.t.* to be arrogant, to be conceited, to be proud; to make (someone) arrogant, proud or conceited. *v.t./v.i.* to soften, to fluff up; to break up.
harrotzaile *n.* one who fluffs up, one who softens, one who breaks up (soil).
harroxka *adj.(dim.)* presumptuous, proud.
hartarako *adj.* apt, appropriate, adequate.
hartarakotu *v.t./v.i.* to adapt, to modify, to make adequate or appropriate, to equip for.
hartaratu *v.i.* to conform to. *v.i.* to get there, to take there. *v.i.* to naturalize.
hartaz *adj./pron.* about that.
hartezin *adj.* uncatchable, not receivable, untouchable, not apprehendable.
hartoki *n.* place of worms.
hartsu *adj.* wormy, full of worms.
hartu *v.t.* to take. *v.t.* to receive, to accept. *v.t.* to conquer, to take over. *v.t.* to shrink.
hartxirri *n.* pebble, gravel.
hartxo *n.(dim.)* small worm.
hartz *n.(zool.)* bear.
hartzaile *n.* receiver, collector, taker; creditor; conqueror. *n.* addressee.
hartzeko *n.* credit balance, credit, assets.
hartzekodun *n.(econ.)* creditor.
hartzeme *n.(zool.)* female bear.
hartzi *n.* leavening. *adj.* disheveled, unkempt.

hartzidura *n.* fermentation.
hartzigarri *n.* ferment. *adj.* fermentable.
hartzitu *v.i.* to ferment.
hartzulo *n.* cave, cavern.
hartzuloratu *v.i./v.t.* to go into a cave; to put into a cave.
hartzuri *n.* alabaster.
haruntz *adv.* toward there.
haruntz-honuntzak *n.(pl.)* back and forth movements. *n.(pl.)* round trips.
haruntz-honuntz ibili *v.i.* to rove, to wander, to go back and forth.
hasberri *n.* beginner, novice, initiator. *adj.* newly begun, just started.
haserraldi *n.* dispute, fight, quarrel, period of anger.
haserre *n.* anger, rage, fury. *adj.* angry, furious, mad, bad-tempered. *adj.(fig.)* stormy, squalling.
haserrebide *n.* cause for anger, reason for anger, grounds for anger.
haserredun *adj.* choleric, angry, furious, mad.
haserredura *n.* fury, rage, anger.
haserre egon *v.i.* to be angry; to be rough (sea).
haserregaitz *adj.* slow to anger, easygoing.
haserregarri *adj.* irritating, exasperating, bothersome.
haserregorri *n.* extreme anger, fury, rage.
haserregorritan *adv.* furiously, in a great rage.
haserregorritu *v.i.* to become furious, to fly into a rage.
haserre izan *v.i.* to be angry, to be mad.
haserrekeria *n.* anger, rage, fury.
haserrekoi *adj.* furious, irascible, choleric.
haserrekoitasun *n.* irascibility, anger, wrath, rage.
haserrekor *adj.* angry, having a temper, infuriating, irascible, enraging.
haserrekortasun *n.* irascibility, wrath, anger, irritability.
haserrekortu *v.i.* to become irascible, to become angry.
haserrerazi *v.t.* to irritate, to infuriate, to make someone angry, to anger, to exasperate.
haserrerazle *n.* enrager, irritator.
haserreti *adj.* angry, mad, furious, bad-tempered, ill-humored.
haserretsu *adj.* angry, furious, mad, choleric, bad-tempered, ill-humored.
haserretu *v.i.* to be angry, to become angry, to get mad. *v.t.* to anger, to make angry, to make mad.
haserretzaile *n.* one who causes anger, exasperator, provoker.
haserrez *adv.* angrily, furiously.
hasgarri *adj.* incipient, preliminary, related to the beginning.

hasi *v.i./v.t.* to begin, to start, to commence.
hasiera *n.* beginning, start; beginnings, origins.
hasierako *adj.* initial, elementary, of the beginning.
hasikin *n.* first fruit.
hasimasiak *n.(pl.)* rudiments, basic principles.
hasimasizko *adj.* elementary, rudimentary.
haskunde *n.* inception, beginning, founding.
hasle *n.* beginner, initiator, founder.
hasperen *n.* sigh, panting, groan, moan.
hasperen egin *v.t.* to sigh.
hasperenka *adv.* sighing, with a sigh.
hastan *adj.* distant, far away.
hastandu *v.i./v.t.* to move away, to leave.
hastandura *n.* repulsion, pushing away, moving away from.
hastangarri *adj.* repulsive, repugnant, disgusting, abominable, detestable, loathsome.
hastapen *n.* beginning, start, initial stage.
hastapeneko *adj.* initial, of the beginning, elementary.
hastari *n.* reel, spool, bobbin.
haste *n.* act of beginning, act of starting, act of initiating.
hastiatu *v.t.* to hate, to find repugnant, to find disgusting, to detest.
hastio *n.* nausea, repugnance, disgust.
hastura *n.* young pig.
hats *n.* breath. *n.* odor, bad smell, stench, stink.
hatsaldi *n.* breathing, respiration.
hatsartu *v.t.* to breathe. *v.t.* to rest, to take a breather.
hats egin *v.t.* to breathe.
hatu *n.* trousseau, dowry.
hatxe *n.* h, aitch, letter in the Basque alphabet.
hatz *n.(anat.)* finger, thumb. *n.* inch. *n.* track, sign, trail, imprint, mark.
hatzamar *n.(anat.)* finger.
hatzamarka *adv.* scratching.
hatzamarkada *n.* scratch.
hatzamarkatu *v.t.* to scratch.
hatzamarketa *n.* scratching.
hatzamartu *v.t.* to scratch.
hatzazal *n.(anat.)* fingernail, claw.
hatzazaljale *n.* fingernail chewer, nail biter.
hatzazalmin *n.* pain in the fingernail.
hatz egin *v.t.* to scratch oneself, to scrape.
hau *adj./pron.* this, this one.
hau da *adv.* that is, in other words, that is to say.
hauek *adj./pron.* these, these ones.
haupa! *int.* exclamation used for cheering. *int.* sound used when

lifting weights.
haur n. baby, infant, child.
haurberri n. newborn infant.
haurberridun adj. having just had a child.
haurbide n. pregnancy.
haurbidezko adj. pertaining to pregnancy.
haurdun adj. pregnant.
haurdunaldi n. period of pregnancy, gestation.
haurdundu v.i. to get pregnant. v.t. to impregnate, to make pregnant, to get someone pregnant.
haurdun egon v.i. to be pregnant.
haurdun gelditu v.i. to get pregnant.
haurdun gertatu v.i. to get pregnant.
haur egin v.t. to give birth, to have a baby.
haurgabe adj. childless, sterile, barren.
haurgabetu v.i. to be sterile, to be childless, to become sterile.
haurgaitz adj. difficult delivery (childbirth). n. naughty child, mischievous child.
haurgaizto n. difficult childbirth. n. mischievous child, naughty child.
haurgaldu n. fetus.
haurgin n. woman in labor.
haurgintza n. childbirth, labor. n. pediatrics.
haurgisa adv. childishly, puerilely.
haurjale n. ogre.
haurkada n. childish action, childishness.
haurkeria n. childish action, childishness.
haurketa n. group of children. n. infancy, childhood.
haurkide n. contemporary, one born at or about the same time.
haurkoi adj. fond of children.
haurlilitegi n. kindergarten, preschool, nursery school.
haurmin n. labor pain, labor.
haurraire adj. child-like, childish.
haurraldi n. gestation, pregnancy.
haurraldiko adj. pertaining to pregnancy.
haurrantzeko adj. childish, child-like.
haurrantzera adv. childishly, in a childish way.
haurrazkuntza n. child care.
haurrazle n. one who cares for children, babysitter.
haurregoizte n. miscarriage, abortion.
haurreraile n. person who commits infanticide.
haurreria n. group of children.
haurretsi v.t. to consider (someone) a child.
haurretxe n. orphanage.
haurride n. child of the same family, brother or sister, sibling. n. brethren, brother or sister in a religious sense.
haurridetasun n. brotherhood.

haurrilketa n. infanticide.
haurriltzaile n. person who commits infanticide.
haurroihal n. diaper.
haurrondore n. time after giving birth, post-partum period.
haurrorde n. foster child, adopted child.
haurseme n. male child.
haursendagile n. pediatrician.
haursendagintza n. pediatrics, science of childhood diseases.
haurtalde n. group of children.
haurtasun n. childhood.
haurtegi n. kindergarten, nursery, childcare center.
haurtoki n.(anat.) womb, uterus.
haurtokiko adj. uterine, pertaining to the womb.
haurtsu adj. having many children, having given birth to many.
haurtu v.i. to behave childishly.
haurtxar n. naughty child, brat.
haurtxo n.(dim.) baby, infant.
haurtzain n. babysitter.
haurtzaindegi n. nursery, childcare center.
haurtzaintza n. childcare.
haurtzale adj. fond of children. n. nanny, nurse, babysitter.
haurtzaro n. infancy, childhood.
haurtzaroko adj. infantile, childish, pertaining to childhood.
haur ukan v.t. to have a baby, to give birth.
haurzapi n. diaper.
hausbero n. hot ash.
hauskabetu v.t. to dust, to dust off, to remove dust.
hauskailu n. duster, dust mop, dust rag.
hauskaitz adj. difficult to break.
hauskaiztasun n. unbreakableness.
hauskarri adj. breakable.
hausketa n. breakage, break, rupture. n. pulverization. n. pile of ashes.
hauskor adj. fragile, brittle, breakable.
hauskortasun n. fragility, brittleness, breakableness.
hauskortu v.i. to become brittle, to become fragile.
hausle n. breaker, violator, transgressor.
hausnar n. rumination, chewing of one's cud.
hausnar egin v.t. to chew one's cud, to ruminate. v.t.(fig.) to muse, to reflect, to think over.
hausnarkari n. ruminant, cud-chewing animal.
hausnarketa n. rumination, chewing the cud. n.(fig.) reflection, consideration, thinking over, meditation.
hausnartu v.t. to ruminate, to chew the cud. v.t.(fig.) to think over, to ponder, to meditate.

hausnartzaile n. ruminant, cud chewer.

hausno n.(dim.) fine ash, fine dust.

hauspen n. break, rupture. n. infraction, violation.

hauspo n. bellows, blower.

hauspoeragile n. one who pumps the bellows.

hauspohaga n. handle of the bellows, bellows pole.

hauspokada n. blast of air from a bellows, single pump of the bellows.

hauspoketa n. blowing with a bellows.

hauspotu v.t. to pump the bellows, to work the bellows, to blow with the bellows.

hauste n. fracture, breaking, breakage, break. n. infraction, violation.

hausterre n. ash.

hausterregun n.(eccl.) Ash Wednesday.

haustezin(ezko) adj. unbreakable, indissoluble, undissolvable.

haustezintasun n. indissolubility, undissolvability.

haustsu adj. dusty, powdery.

haustu v.t./v.i. to grind, to pulverize.

haustun adj. dusty, powdery.

haustura n. breakage, break, fracture.

hauta n. selection, option, choice, election.

hautabide n. option, choice, alternative. n. vote, ballot. n. power to choose or elect.

hautabidezko adj. alternative.

hautaera n. option, selection, choice, election.

hautagai n. candidate.

hautagailu n. apparatus for selecting (voting machine, harvester, etc.).

hautagarri adj. eligible, selectable, choosable; electable.

hautagarritasun n. elegibility.

hautakeria n. arbitrariness.

hautaketa n. selection, choice; election.

hautakizun n. upcoming election.

hautaldi n. election time; time of choosing.

hautalege n. electoral law.

hautamahai n. table at which the jury sits.

hautamen n. election. n. option, alternative, faculty to choose.

hautapen n. election; selection, option.

hautapenezko adj. optional, elective.

hautarazi v.t. to cause to elect; to make (someone) choose.

hautari n. elector, voter; chooser.

hautatu v.t. to choose, to select; to elect.

hautatzaile n. chooser; voter, elector.

hautatzaileria n. electorate.

hautemale adj. perceptive, observant.

hauteman v.t. to perceive, to observe, to note, to investigate. v.t. to elect, to choose.

hautemangarri adj. perceptible, observable, perceivable. adj. electable, eligible.

hautemate n. act of perceiving, act of observing.

hauteskunde n. election; selection, choice.

hautesle n. elector, voter.

hautesleria n. electorate.

hautestontzi n. voting box.

hautespen n. selection; election.

hautespenezko adj. selective; elective.

hautespide n. selectivity.

hautetsi v.t. to elect. v.t. to observe, to perceive. v.t.(eccl.) to predestine, to predestinate.

hauts n. dust, powder; ash.

hautsaga n. long pole used to remove ashes.

hautsaldi n. dusting.

hautsantzeko adj. dust-like, ash-colored.

hautsarazi v.t. to cause to break.

hautsastinketa n. act of hitting.

hautsedaketa n. sprinkling dust, dusting, powdering.

hauts egin v.t. to grind, to pulverize, to powder, to turn to dust. v.t.(fig.) to destroy, to annihilate.

hautsezin adj. unbreakable, indestructible.

hautsezko adj. dusty, ashy, ashen.

hautseztaketa n. covering with dust, dusting.

hautseztapen n. covering with dust, dusting.

hautseztatu v.t. to cover with dust. adj. dusty, powdery.

hautseztu v.t./v.i. to cover with dust, to be covered with dust.

hautsi v.t. to break, to fracture. v.t. to tear, to rip. v.t. to win, to defeat; to break (records).

hautsontzi n. ashtray.

hautsu adj. dusty, powdery.

hautu n. election, choice, selection. v.t. to choose, to select.

hauxe adj./pron. this; this one.

hazaldi n. growth, period of growth.

hazama n. foster mother.

hazarazi v.t. to raise, to make (something) grow.

hazaro n. season to sow, planting season.

hazbete n. full inch.

hazbide n. way of raising, method of growing.

hazgale n. itch, tickle, desire to scratch.

hazgarri adj. growable, growing, capable of growing.

hazi v.t. to raise, to bring up. v.i. to grow, to grow up. v.t. to cultivate, to grow. v.i. to swell, to inflate. n. seed.

n.(anat.) semen, sperm.

hazibanaketa *n.* seeding, sowing, spreading seed.

hazibanatzaile *n.* sower.

hazidun *adj.* having a seed, semniferous.

hazienda *n.(econ.)* public treasury.

haziera *n.* growth.

hazila *n.* November.

hazinahi *n.* desire to grow, desire to grow up.

hazirin *n.* pollen.

hazitarako *n.* seed grain. *n.* stud, breeding animal.

hazitegi *n.* seedbed.

hazka *adv.* scratching.

hazka egin *v.t.* to scratch oneself, to scrape.

hazkatu *v.t./v.i.* to scratch.

hazkera *n.* way of growing, method of raising.

hazketa *n.* growing, raising, bringing up, rearing.

hazkor *adj.* tending to grow, fast growing.

hazkunde *n.* growth, development.

hazkuntza *n.* growth, development, increase. *n.* breeding, rearing, raising, upbringing.

hazkura *n.* itch, tickle.

hazkuratsu *adj.* itchy, itching.

hazkuratu *v.i.* to scratch oneself.

hazkurri *n.* food; nourishment, nutrition.

hazle *n.* grower, cultivator.

hazleku *n.* nursery.

haznahi *n.* itch, tickle.

hazta *n.* weight of an object. *n.* touch.

haztadura *n.* touching.

haztaka *adv.* touching, groping.

haztakatu *v.t.* to touch. *v.t.* to paw, to handle, to manhandle.

haztamu *n.* touching.

haztamuka *adv.* touching, by touching, by feeling.

haztatu *v.t.* to touch, to grope, to feel.

haztegi *n.* nursery.

haztura *n.* growing up, growth.

hebain *adj.* weak, exhausted. *n.* cripple, paralytic.

hebaindu *v.i.* to be exhausted, to be overcome with fatigue. *v.t.* to weaken, to make weak.

hebaindura *n.* tiredness, exhaustion. *n.* dismay, depression.

hebaintasun *n.* state of exhaustion. *n.* paralysis, state of temporary or partial paralysis.

hebraiera *n.* Hebrew language.

hebraitar *adj./n.* Hebrew.

hebreotar *adj./n.* Hebrew.

hedabanatu *v.t.* to extend, to expand, to spread, to propagate.

hedabide *n.* means of diffusing, method of spreading.

hedadura *n.* extension, expanse, length.

hedaezin *adj.* unexpandable, nonextendible.

hedagailu *n.* machine for spreading (fertilizer, seeds, etc.)

hedagaitz *adj.* nonextendible, unexpandable.

hedagarri *adj.* extendible, expandable, prolongable.

hedagarritasun *n.* extensibility, extendibleness, spreadability.

hedagune *n.* place for hanging clothing.

hedaketa *n.* extension, prolongation, expansion.

hedakor *adj.* expandable, spreadable.

hedakortasun *n.* expandableness, spreadability.

hedakunde *n.* expansion, extension, prolongation, length.

hedakuntza *n.* expansion, extension, prolongation, length

hedamen *n.* expansion, spread, extension, diffusion.

hedapen *n.* expansion, spread, extension, diffusion.

hedatasun *n.* extension, expansion, diffusion.

hedatoki *n.* place where clothes are hung to dry.

hedatsu *adj.* expansive, extensive, ample.

hedatu *v.t.* to extend, to expand.

hedatzaile *n.* extender, expander, prolonger.

hede *n.* strip of leather, strap, tether, leash. *n.* bridle.

hederia *n.* tack, stable gear; bunch of strips of leather, tethers, etc.

hedonismo *n.* hedonism.

hedonista *adj.* hedonistic.

hega- Used in compound words. Derived from *hego*, wing.

hegabera *n.(zool.)* lapwing (*Vanellus vanellus*).

hegabiko *n.* glider. (lit.) two wings.

hegabiraketa *n.* act of hovering.

hegabiratu *v.i.* to hover.

hegada *n.* flight.

hegadun *adj.* winged, having wings.

hegagailu *n.* anything that flies, flying object.

hegagile *adj.* flying.

hegaka *adv.* flying.

hegakada *n.* fluttering or flapping of wings.

hegakaldi *n.* flight time.

hegakari *n.* flyer. *adj.* flying.

hegakatu *v.i.* to fly across, to fly.

hegakera *n.* way of flying.

hegaketa *n.* flight, flying, act of flying.

hegakor *adj.* capable of flying.

hegakortasun *n.(chem.)* volatility.

hegal *n.* wing. *n.* edge, side; eaves (roof). *n.* compass point; corner.

hegalada *n.* flight.

hegalaldi *n.* flight time, flight.

hegalari *adj.* flying. *n.* flyer.

hegaldaka *adv.* flying, in flight.
hegaldakatu *v.i.* to flutter, to fly around.
hegaldaketa *n.* fluttering, act of flying around.
hegaldatu *v.i.* to fly, to take flight.
hegaldi *n.* flight, flight time.
hegaldu *v.t.* to put aside, to put in a corner.
hegaldun *adj.* winged, having wings. *adj.* having sides, having edges.
hegalezkatadun *adj.* lepidopterous. *n.(zool.)* Lepidoptera.
hegalfer *n.(zool.)* ostrich.
hegalgabe *adj.* wingless, having no wings. *adj.* having no sides, edgeless.
hegalkolpe *n.* blow with a wing.
hegalpe *n.* region under the wing. *n.(fig.)* protection.
hegan *adv.* flying, in flight.
hegandi *n.* having large wings.
hegan egin *v.t.* to fly. *v.t.(fig.)* to escape, to run away.
hegape *n.* space under the wing.
hegapetu *v.t.* to protect under the wings, to shelter under the wings. *v.t.* to protect, to favor.
hegarrain *n.(zool.)* flying fish.
hegaskada *n.* movement of the fins, wiggling of the fins.
hegats *n.* fin of a fish (tuna, etc.).
hegatsu *adj.* finned, having large fins.
hegatu *v.i.* to fly.
hegaz *adv.* flying, in flight.
hegazabal *adj.* having broad wings, broad-winged.
hegaz egin *v.t.* to fly.
hegazkari *n.* pilot, flyer, aviator.
hegazkatu *v.t.* to flutter, to flap the wings.
hegazkilari *n.* aviator, pilot, flyer.
hegazkin *n.* plane, airplane.
hegazkinontzi *n.* aircraft carrier.
hegazkintxo *n.(dim.)* small plane.
hegazkintza *n.* aviation, aeronautics, manufacture of aircraft.
hegazkor *adj.* tending to fly, capable of flying; volatile.
hegazkortasun *n.(chem.)* volatility.
hegazkortu *v.i.* to volatize, to become volatile.
hegazpi *n.* part under the wing, underside of the wing.
hegazpiko *adj.* axillar, pertaining to the part under the wing.
hegaztaldi *n.* flight, period of flight.
hegazti *n.* fowl.
hegaztiazti *n.* augurer, fortuneteller, predictor.
hegaztiaztikeria *n.* augury, fortunetelling.
hegaztidenda *n.* poultry shop.
hegaztihazkuntza *n.* aviculture, bird raising, bird keeping.
hegaztihazle *n.* aviculturist, bird fancier.

hegaztilari *n.* ornithologist.
hegaztimordo *n.* flock of birds, group of fowl.
hegaztino *n.(dim.)* small fowl, small bird.
hegaztipasaia *n.* bird migration.
hegaztisail *n.* flock of birds, group of fowl.
hegaztitxo *n.(dim.)* small fowl.
hegaztizain *n.* aviculturist, bird keeper.
hegaztizaintza *n.* aviculture, bird keeping.
hegi *n.* border, corner edge. *n.* top, ridge, summit, long narrow summit with two slopes.
hegidun *adj.* ridged, edged, cornered, bordered, having edges, etc.
hegigo *n.* hatred, rancor, aversion.
hego *n.* wing.
hego- Used in compound words, meaning southern.
hegoalde *n.(geog.)* South.
hegoaldeko *adj.* southern, meridional.
Hegoamerika *n.(geog.)* South America, Latin America.
hegoamerikar *n.* South American, Latin American.
hegoar *n.* southerner.
hegoburu *n.* South Pole.
hegoekialde *n.(geog.)* Southeast.
hegogabe(ko) *adj.* wingless.
hegogabetu *v.t.* to remove the wings.
hegogalgoe *n.* southwesterly wind.
hegohaize *n.* southerly wind, south wind.
hegokada *n.* blow with a wing. *n.* flight.
hegoko *adj.* southern, south, meridional, southerly.
hegomendebal *n.* southwesterly wind, southwest wind.
hegomendebalde *n.(geog.)* Southwest.
hegosartalde *n.(geog.)* Southwest.
hegosortalde *n.(goeg.)* Southeast.
hein *n.* measure, proportion, extent.
hektarea *n.* hectare.
hektogramo *n.* hectogram.
hektolitro *n.* hectoliter.
hektometro *n.* hectometer.
hel- Used in compound words. Derived from *heldu*, to arrive.
helarazi *v.t.* to cause to arrive, to deliver, to transmit.
helberri *adj.* newly arrived.
helbide *n.* access. *n.* way, means, recourse. *n.* address, direction; destination.
helburu *n.* goal, aim, destination, objective, target; intention.
heldu *v.i.* to arrive, to reach. *v.t.* to grab, to grasp, to catch. *v.i.* to ripen, to mature. *v.i* to become, to come to be. *v.t.* to bite (fish), to nibble, to take the bait. *v.i.(fig.)* to maturate, to supperate, to come to a head (wound). *adj.(fig.)* mature, grown; ripe.

heldugabe adj. immature; green, unripe.

heldugabezia n. immaturity; unripe state.

heldu-heldu adj. very ripe, very mature.

helduleku n. handle.

heldura n. maturation, ripening.

heldutasun n. maturity, ripeness.

hel egin v.t. to call (someone), to shout (at someone).

helgabe adj. immature; unripe, green.

helgabezia n. immaturity; unripe state.

helgaitz adj. difficult to ripen. adj. inaccessible, unapproachable.

helgarri adj. attainable, accessible.

helikoptero n. helicopter.

helmuga n. goal.

heltasun n. maturity; ripeness.

heltoki n. handle.

heltzaile n. catcher, grabber, seizer.

heltzaro n. maturity.

heme- Used in compound words. Derived from *hamar*, ten.

hemen adv. here.

hemendik adv. from here; from now.

hemengo adj. from here, of here.

hementxe adv. right here.

hemeretzi adj./n. nineteen.

hemeretzigarren adj. nineteenth.

hemezortzi adj./n. eighteen.

hemezortzigarren adj. eighteenth.

hemisferio n.(geog.) hemisphere.

hera n. fowl droppings, entrails of a fowl, stomach of a bird.

herabe adj. shy, timid, fearful. adj. indolent, lazy. n. shyness, timidity. n. repugnance, resistance.

herabe izan v.i. to be shy, to be timid.

herabekeria n. indolence, laziness.

herabeki adv. timidly, shyly.

herabetasun n. timidness, shyness. n. repugnance.

herabeti adj. shy, bashful, timid.

herabetu v.i. to become timid or shy.

herabez adv. timidly, shyly, embarrassedly.

heraldika n. heraldry.

herbal adj. weak, exhausted. adj. sick, sickly, invalid.

herbaldu v.i. to weaken, to become debilitated, to become weak.

herbaldura n. weakness, feebleness, frailty, debilitation.

herbalgarri adj. debilitating, weakening.

herbalkeria n. weakness.

herbalki adv. weakly, feebly, frailly.

herbalkiro adv. weakly, feebly, frailly.

herbaltasun n. weakness, feebleness, debility.

herdoil n. rust, oxidation. n. blight.

herdoildu v.i. to rust, to oxidize. v.i. to contract blight, to be blighted.

herdoildun adj. rusty, oxidized.

herdoildura n. rusting, oxidation.

herdoilgabetu v.t./v.i. to deoxidize, to remove rust.

herdoilgaitz adj. rustproof, nonrusting.

herdoilgarri adj. oxidizable, capable of rusting.

herdoilketa n. oxidation, rusting.

herdoilkoi adj. oxidizable, capable of rusting.

herdoilkontrako n./adj. anticorrosive, antirust (agent).

herdoiltsu adj. rusty, full of rust.

herdoiltzaile adj. oxidizing.

heredatu v.t. to inherit.

heren adj./n. third; one-third, third part.

herenaitona n. great great grandfather.

herenamona n. great great grandmother.

herenegun adv. day before yesterday.

hereniloba n. great great grandchild.

herensuge n.(zool.) dragon.

herensugeme n. female dragon.

herentzia n. heredity; inheritance.

herentziazko adj. hereditary.

herexe n. heretic.

herexia n. heresy.

herio n. Death (personified), death.

herioaldi n. death throes, agony.

herioekarle adj. death-dealing, fatal, mortal, lethal.

heriogaitz n. fatal illness.

heriogarri adj. fatal, mortal, lethal.

heriogile n. assassin, murderer.

heriotze n. death, demise.

heriotzekarle adj. death-dealing, fatal, mortal.

heriotzemale adj. fatal, death-dealing, mortal. n. executioner.

heriotzepai n. death sentence.

heriotzerakotu v.t. to sentence to death, to send to death.

heriotzondo n. beyond the grave, life after death, hereafter.

herkide n. compatriot, fellow countryman.

herkidetasun n. state of being compatriots; quality of belonging to the same village or town.

herkidetu v.i. to be compatriots, to become compatriots.

heroe n. hero.

heroesa n. heroine.

heroiko adj. heroic.

heroina n. heroin.

heroizitate n. heroism.

herots n. loud noise, clamor. n. fame, reputation, renown.

herra n. hate, rancor, hatred.

herradun adj. hateful, odious, rancorous, despising.

herragarri adj. odious, hateful, abominable.

herrakor adj. hateful, odious.

herrakunde n. hatred, rancor.

herratsu adj. rancorous, hateful, despising.

herratu v.t. to hate, to despise, to detest.

herrausketa *n.* demolition, destruction.
herrausle *n.* destroyer, demolisher.
herraustu *v.t.* to demolish, to pulverize, to destroy.
herrautsi *v.t.* to raze, to demolish, to destroy.
herren *n.* cripple.
herrenbel *adj.* defective, imperfect.
herrenbeldu *v.i.* to be useless, to lose value, to become worthless or useless.
herrenbeltasun *n.* uselessness; lack of ability.
herrendu *v.i.* to be crippled, to become a cripple, to be handicapped. *v.t.* to cripple, to make lame.
herren egin *v.t.* to limp.
herrenka *adv.* limping, hobbling.
herrenkatu *v.i.* to limp.
herrenketa *n.* lameness, limp.
herrenkura *n.* lameness, limp.
herrentasun *n.* quality or state of being crippled, lameness.
herresa *n.* guarantee.
herresta *adj.* dragging. *adj.(fig.)* slow, inactive.
herrestadura *n.* anguish, distress, anxiety, haste.
herrestaka *adv.* dragging, by dragging (a foot, etc.).
herrestaketa *n.* act of crawling, act of moving along by dragging oneself.
herrestan *adv.* dragging.
herrestarazi *v.t.* to drag, to drag along.
herrestari *n.(zool.)* reptile, snake, serpent.
herrestatu *v.i.* to drag oneself, to creep up, to slither. *v.t.* to drag, to haul.
herrestatzaile *n.* dragger. *adj.* creeping, dragging, slithering.
herri *n.* town, village. *n.* people, population, public. *n.* country, nation. *adj.* popular, regional, public, folk.
herrialdaketa *n.* emigration; transmigration. *n.* move from one town to another.
herrialde *n.* region, district, territory, country.
herrialdearteko *adj.* interregional. *adj.* international.
herrialdeko *adj.* popular, local. *adj.* regional.
herrialdezale *adj.* regionalist.
herrialdezaletasun *n.* regionalism.
herriartekotasun *n.* internationalness, quality of being international.
herribarru *n.* downtown, center of town.
herribarruti *n.* municipal district.
herribaso *n.* communal forest.
herribatza *n.* commonwealth, union of towns.
herribazter *n.* outskirts. *n.* distant town.
herribide *n.* local road, town street.

herridirutza *n.* town funds, town treasury.
herrietxe *n.* city hall, town hall.
herrigabe(ko) *adj.* without a country, nationless.
herrigizon *n.* public man, public figure.
herrijai *n.* popular festival, village festival.
herrijakintza *n.* popular culture.
herrikide *n.* fellow villager.
herrikidego *n.* state of being compatriots or co-villagers.
herrikidetasun *n.* quality of belonging to the same village or town.
herriko *adj.* popular, public; communal, municipal. *adj.* national. *adj.* local, indigenous, native.
herrikoetxe *n.* city hall, town hall.
herrikoi *adj.* popular, local. *adj.* patriotic.
herrikoikeria *n.* excessive patriotism.
herrikoitasun *n.* popularity. *n.* patriotism.
herrikoitu *v.i.* to be popular, to become popular. *v.t.* to popularize, to make popular.
herrikomin *n.* homesickness.
herrikomutil *n.* kind of sheriff in charge of public order in towns and villages, constable.
herrikontrako *adj.* unpopular.
herrikontseilu *n.* municipal council, town council.
herrikotu *v.i.* to become acclimated, to grow accustomed to, to get familiar with a town. *v.i.* to become naturalized.
herrilan *n.* municipal work; public works.
herrilur *n.* municipal property, city property.
herrimin *n.* homesickness.
herriminaldi *n.* homesickness.
herrimindu *v.i.* to be homesick, to become homesick, to get homesick.
herrimutil *n.* constable, municipal employee.
herriondasun *n.* public treasury.
herriratu *v.i.* to immigrate. *v.i./v.t.* to come home, to return to a town or country, to repatriate.
herrisail *n.* city property, municipal land.
herrisendagile *n.* local doctor, town doctor.
herritar *adj.* local, popular. *n.* inhabitant, fellow villager.
herritargo *n.* state of belonging to a town; citizenship, nationality.
herritarketa *n.* naturalization.
herritartu *v.i.* to become accustomed to a village. *v.i.* to become naturalized.
herritiar *adj.* popular.
herritxo *n.(dim.)* small village, hamlet.
herrixka *n.(dim.)* small village, small town, hamlet.

herrizain *n.* constable.

herrizale *adj.* fond of one's village. *adj.* patriotic.

herrizaletasun *n.* fondness for one's village. *n.* patriotism.

herrizaletu *v.i.* to become fond of one's village. *v.i.* to become patriotic.

herrizkera *n.* common language, vulgar tongue, vernacular.

herrizkeratu *v.t.* to translate into the vernacular.

herronka *n.* line, file, row.

herronkatu *v.i.* to align, to get in line, to line up.

herskailu *n.* clamp, vise.

herskari *adj.* squeezing, compressing, clamping.

hersketa *n.* compression, squeezing, pressure.

herskin *n.* press (machine).

herstu *adj.* difficult, tight, stressful, nervewracking. *adj.* strict, anxious.

herstuki *adv.* tightly, strictly, narrowly. *adv.(fig.)* severely, harshly.

herstura *n.* anguish, strait, distress; anxiety, tension, apprehension.

hersturadun *adj.* distressed, anxious, nervous, troubled.

hertsadura *n.* pressure, distress, tension, straits, difficulties.

hertsagarri *adj.* distressing, nervewracking, constricting, tense.

hertsaketa *n.* distress, anxiety, pressure, tension.

hertsakor *adj.* distressing, constricting, nervewracking, tense.

hertsaldi *n.* period of squeezing, tightening, narrowing.

hertsapen *n.* tightening, squeezing. *n.* compulsion, coercion, constraint.

hertsarazi *v.t.* to repress, to tighten, to squeeze, to compress.

hertsatu *v.t.* to repress, to tighten, to squeeze, to compress. *v.t.* to oblige, to obligate, to require.

hertsatzaile *n.* repressor, one who obligates someone to do something.

hertsi *v.t.* to shut, to close. *adj.* tight, tight-fitting, narrow. *v.t.* to bind, to tie tightly. *adj.(fig.)* strict, scrupulous, rigid, severe. *v.t.* to restrict, to limit.

hertsidura *n.* tightening, squeezing, enclosing, encircling.

hertsigarri *adj.* tightening, squeezing, encircling, enclosing.

hertsikeria *n.* moral strictness, rigidity, tightness, severity.

hertsiki *adv.* strictly, tightly, narrowly.

hertsikor *adj.* restricting.

hertsiro *adj.* strictly, narrowly, tightly.

hertsitasun *n.* tightness, strictness, narrowness.

hertsitu *v.t.* to tighten, to squeeze, to constrict, to narrow.

hesi *n.* fence, enclosure, wall.

hesigabe *adj.* fenceless, unfenced.

hesigabetu *v.t.* to take down a fence.

hesiketa *n.* blockade, siege.

hesinguraketa *n.* act of fencing in.

hesinguratu *v.t.* to besiege, to block, to surround, to hem in, to fence in.

hesitu *v.t.* to fence in, to surround, to close in.

hesitzaile *n.* attacker, besieger, surrounder.

hesiztatu *v.t.* to surround, to enclose, to fence in.

hesohol *n.* fence post, pole, stake.

hesoholdu *v.t.* to enclose with stakes, to enclose with a picket fence.

heste *n.(anat.)* intestine.

hestebete *n.* satiety, glut, gorge.

hestegorri *n.(anat.)* esophagus.

hesteki *n.* tripe; piece of the intestine.

hesteko *n.* intestinal.

hestelodi *n.(anat.)* large intestine.

hesteluze *n.(anat.)* small intestine.

hestemehe *n.(anat.)* duodenum.

hestemin *n.* intestinal pain.

hestemutur *n.(anat.)* appendix.

heterodoxia *n.* heterodoxy.

heterodoxo *adj.* heterodox.

hetika *n.(med.)* tuberculosis.

hetikatu *v.i.* to become tubercular, to get tuberculosis.

hetsi *v.t.* to close, to shut.

heu *pron.* you yourself (fam., used with intransitive verbs).

heuk *pron.* you yourself (fam., used with transitive verbs).

heure *adj./pron.* yours, your own (fam.).

heurekoi *adj.* egotistical (you fam.).

hexaedro *n.(geom.)* hexahedron.

hexagonal *adj.* hexagonal.

hez- Used in compound words.

hezbide *n.* education, educative process, way of raising, upbringing (of a child). Contr. of *hezi* + *bide*.

heze *adj.* damp, moist, humid; green.

hezedura *n.* humidity, moistness, dampness. *n.* state of being green or unseasoned (usually refers to wood).

hezegabetu *v.t.* to dry, to become seasoned (wood).

hezetasun *n.* dampness, humidity, moistness; greenness (wood).

hezete *n.* wet season, humid season.

hezetsu *adj.* humid, wet, moist, damp.

hezetu *v.i.* to be damp, to get damp, to be moist.

hezgabe *adj.* uneducated, uncivilized. *adj.* untamed, wild, savage.

hezgabeki *adv.* uncivilly, rudely.

hezgaitz *adj.* uneducable, untamable, untrainable, indomitable.

hezi *v.t.* to educate, to train, to raise, to bring up. *v.t.* to domesticate, to tame. *v.t.* to dominate, to control.

heziera *n.* education, manner of bringing up or raising.

heziezin *adj.* untamable, untrainable, indomitable, ineducable.

hezigarri *adj.* tamable, domitable,

trainable. *adj.* raiseable.

hezikaitz *adj.* difficult to tame, difficult to raise, uneducable, indomitable.

hezikera *n.* way of educating, way of raising.

heziketa *n.* education, raising, upbringing, training.

hezikor *adj.* educational, instructive, formative.

hezilari *n.* educator, raiser, teacher. *n.* tamer, trainer, domesticator.

hezitzaile *n.* raiser, educator, teacher. *n.* tamer, trainer, domesticator.

hezkunde *n.* education, training. *n.* domestication, taming.

hezkuntza *n.* education, training, formation. *n.* domestication, taming.

hezle *n.* educator, raiser, teacher. *n.* trainer, tamer, domesticator.

hezueri *n.(med.)* gout.

hezur *n.* bone.

hezurbihurketa *n.* sprain, twist (ankle).

hezurdun *adj.* bony; vertebrate.

hezurdura *n.(anat.)* skeleton.

hezurgabe(ko) *adj.* invertebrate; boneless.

hezurgabetu *v.t.* to debone, to bone.

hezurgiltza *n.(anat.)* joint.

hezurgiltzadura *n.(anat.)* joint.

hezurketa *n.* ossification.

hezurki *n.* piece of bone.

hezurlari *n.(med.)* orthopedist.

hezurlaritza *n.(med.)* orthopedics.

hezurlokadura *n.* dislocation (of a joint).

hezurlokarri *n.(anat.)* cartilage.

hezurmin *n.(med.)* ostalgia, pain in the bones.

hezurmuin *n.* bone marrow.

hezurreri *n.(med.)* ostalgia, pain in the bones.

hezurreria *n.* bone structure, skeletal structure.

hezurrezko *adj.* osseus, bony, made of bone, out of bone.

hezurruts *n.* skeleton, carcass. *n.* very skinny person.

hezurtegi *n.* ossuary, bone deposit.

hezurtoki *n.* ossuary, bone deposit.

hezurtsu *adj.* very bony.

hezurtto *n.(dim.)* little bone.

hezurtu *v.i.* to ossify, to turn to bone.

hezurtza *n.* large quantity of bones.

hezurtzapen *n.* ossification.

hi *pron.* you (fam.).

hidrato *n.(chem.)* hydrate.

hidrogeno *n.(chem.)* hydrogen.

higadura *n.* waste, using up, deterioration, erosion.

higatu *v.i.* to wear out, to deteriorate, to wear away, to corrode, to abrade. *v.t.* to wear (something) out, to deteriorate, to waste away.

higiarazi *v.t.* to move, to run, to power.

higidura *n.* movement, motion.

higiera *n.* way of moving.

higierazle *adj.* motor, moving, motive.

higiezin *adj.* immovable, unmovable, immobile.

higigailu *n.* machine which causes motion.

higigaitz *adj.* difficult to move, immovable.

higigaiztu *v.i.* to become immovable, to be immobilized.

higigarri *adj.* movable, mobile.

higigune *n.* movement, motion.

higiketa *n.* mobilization, act of moving.

higikor *adj.* mobile, movable.

higikortasun *n.* mobility, movableness.

higitsu *adj.* agitated, shaken, stirred up.

higitu *v.t./v.i.* to move, to stir, to agitate.

higitzaile *n./adj.* mover; moving.

higuin *n.* loathing, repugnance, disgust, hate, revulsion. *adj.* disgusting, revolting, loathsome.

higuinaldi *n.* period of repugnance, disgust, revulsion.

higuinbera *adj.* disgusting, loathsome, detestable, repugnant.

higuindu *v.t.* to hate, to despise, to detest, to repulse. *v.i.* to be disgusted with, to feel repugnance for, to be repulsed by. *v.t.* to wean a child.

higuindura *n.* disgust, loathing, abhorrence, repugnance, detestation.

higuingarri *adj.* repugnant, disgusting, abominable, detestable, loathsome, repulsive. *adj.* annoying, bothersome.

higuingarriki *adv.* disgustingly, repugnantly, abominably, detestably, loathsomely. *adv.* fastidiously, annoyingly.

higuingarriro *adv.* disgustingly, repugnantly, abominably, detestably, loathsomely. *adv.* fastidiously, annoyingly.

higuingarritasun *n.* repugnance, loathsomeness, detestableness.

higuin izan *v.i.* to be repugnant, to be disgusting, to be detestable. *v.t.* to hate, to detest, to abhor, to abominate.

higuinkeria *n.* detestable act, atrocity, abomination.

higuinkor *adj.* repulsive, repugnant, abhorrent, abominable, disgusting.

higuintasun *n.* tediousness, boringness, bothersomeness.

higuintza *n.* repugnance. *n.* aversion, antipathy.

higuintzaile *n.* abominator, detester, one who abhors or hates.

hik *pron.* you (fam.). Used with transitive verbs.

hika *adv.* using the second person familiar form, familiar usage among friends.

hika egin *v.t.* to talk in the familiar

manner, to speak using the familiar form.

hikatu *v.t.* to speak using the second person familiar form.

hiketa *n.* use of the familiar form (you).

hil *v.i.* to die. *v.t.* to kill. *n.* corpse, dead (person). *adj.* death, mortal. *n.* month. *adj.(fig.)* dead, extinguished, exhausted, lifeless, stagnant.

hilabete *n.* month, full month.

hilabeteka *adv.* monthly, by the month.

hilabetekari *n.* bulletin, monthly periodical, magazine.

hilabeteko *adj.* one month's, monthly, mensual, of one month. *n.* monthly salary.

hilabetero *adv.* monthly, every month.

hilabetesari *n.* monthly pay, salary.

hilaldi *n.* mortality. *n.* coma.

hilarazi *v.t.* to assassinate, to kill, to murder.

hilarri *n.* gravestone, tombstone, grave marker, headstone.

hilazti *n.* necromancer.

hilaztikeria *n.* necromancy.

hilbehar *adj.* mortal. *n.* mortality.

hilbeila *n.* vigil for the dead.

hilbera *adj.* likely to die.

hilberri *n./adj.* recently deceased, newly dead. *n.* new moon. *n.* death notice, obituary.

hilbizi *n.* gravely ill person.

hilburuko *n.* last will and testament.

hilburukogile *n.* testator, testatrix (female), a person who leaves a will.

hilburuzain *n.* executor, executrix.

hildako *adj.* dead, deceased. *n.* dead person.

hildantza *n.* death dance.

hildegi *n.* funeral home, mortuary; tomb, sepulchre.

hildei *n.* funeral announcement, death notice, obituary.

hildeitore *n.* death knell.

hildura *n.* mortification, flagellation.

hilduraketa *n.* flagellation, whipping.

hilduratu *v.t.* to flagellate, to scourge, to whip.

hile *n.* month.

hilebiko *adj.* bimonthly.

hilegun *n.* dying day, day a person dies.

hileko *n.* salary for the month. *n.* menstruation. *adj.* monthly, mensual.

hilen *adj.* necrological, of the dead.

hilenegun *n.* All Soul's Day (November 2).

hil erazi *v.t.* to order (someone) to kill, to cause (someone) to kill.

hilerdi *n.* half a month.

hilero *adv.* monthly, every month.

hileroko *adj.* monthly, mensual. *n.* monthly publication. *n.* menstruation.

hilerri *n.* graveyard, cemetery.

hileta *n.* funeral. *n.* lament for the dead. *n.* complaint.

hiletadun *adj.* mourning, in mourning.

hiletajantzi *n.* mourning clothes.

hiletajazki *n.* mourning clothes.

hileta jo *v.t.* to complain.

hiletajole *n.* mourner.

hiletari *n.* mourner, professional or paid mourner. *adj.* complaining, whining.

hiletasoineko *n.* mourning clothes.

hiletasoinu *n.* death dirge; elegy.

hiletsi *v.t.* to give (someone) up for dead.

hilezin *adj.* immortal, everlasting, enduring.

hilezintasun *n.* immortality.

hilezkila *n.* death knell.

hilezko *adj.* funereal, mournful, sad.

hilezkor *adj.* immortal, everlasting, enduring.

hilezkorreztatu *v.t./v.i.* to immortalize.

hilezkortasun *n.* immortality.

hilgai *adj.* sacrificial, destined for death. *n.* victim.

hilgarri *adj.* lethal, mortal. *adj.* deserving to die. *adj.(fig.)* very tiring, fatiguing.

hilgogor *n.* corpse, stiff, dead body.

hilgurdi *n.* hearse, funeral coach.

hiliki *n.* carrion, putrid flesh.

hiljale *adj.* necrophagous, carrion-eating.

hiljantzi *n.* mourning clothes. *n.* shroud.

hiljazki *n.* shroud, winding sheet, clothing the dead are buried in.

hiljazle *n.* undertaker, mortician.

hiljoaldi *n.* death toll, death knell.

hilkanpai *n.* death toll, death knell.

hilkantu *n.* funeral dirge; elegy.

hilkantuzko *adj.* pertaining to the funeral dirge.

hilketa *n.* murder, assassination, killing.

hilki *n.* mortal remains.

hilkintza *n.* massacre, murder.

hilkoi *adj.* likely to die.

hilkor *adj.* mortal, likely to die. *adj.(fig.)* grave, lethal, deadly, mortal. *adj.* dying, dying out.

hilkortasun *n.* mortality.

hilkuntza *n.* killing.

hilkutxa *n.* coffin, casket.

hilmahai *n.* catafalque, tumulus, platform for the dead.

hilmeza *n.* requiem mass.

hilmihise *n.* shroud, winding sheet.

hilnahi *n.* desire to die, death wish.

hilobi *n.* tomb, grave, sepulchre.

hilobiko *adj.* sepulchral, pertaining to the grave.

hilobiratu *v.t.* to bury, to inter, to entomb.

hilohe *n.* death bed.

hilohore *n.* funeral honors.

hiloihal *n.* shroud, clothes the dead are buried in.

hilondo *n.* mourning period, period of mourning.

hilondoko *adj.* posthumous. *n.* mortal remains.

hilordu *n.* hour of death, death throes.

hiloren *n.* hour of death.

hilosteko *adj.* posthumous.

hilotoitz *n.(eccl.)* responsory for the dead.

hilotoitz egin *v.t.* to repeat the responses in a responsory for the dead, to recite the funeral prayer.

hilots *n.* death toll, death knell.

hilotz *n.* corpse, body, cadaver.

hilsari *n.* monthly salary.

hiltasun *n.* mortality. *n.* apathy, insensibility. *n.* weakness.

hiltegi *n.* cemetery. *n.* slaughterhouse.

hiltoki *n.* cemetery, graveyard. *n.* place of one's death, place where someone died. *n.* slaughterhouse.

hiltronu *n.* catafalque, tumulus, platform for the dead.

hiltxartel *n.* obituary notice.

hiltzaile *n.* killer, murderer, assassin.

hiltzarre *n.* killing, bloody murder, assassination.

hilurre *adj.* dying, in the death agony. *n.* agony, death agony.

hilurren *adj.* moribund, at the point of dying, on the verge of dying.

hilzori *n.* death throes, agony, point of death.

hilzorian *adv.* about to die, at the point of death.

hilzorian egon *v.i.* to be dying, to be at the point of death, to be in the throes of death.

hilzoriaz *adv.* mortally.

hilzorizko *adj.* pertaining to the death throes.

hindu *n./adj.* Hindu.

hipa *n.* sob.

hipertentsio *n.(med.)* hypertension.

hipopotamo *n.(zool.)* hippopotamus.

hire *adj./pron.* your, yours (fam.).

hireganatu *v.i.* to get to you, to approach you, to reach you, to come to you. *v.t.* to bring (someone) to you.

hiri *n.* town, city. *pron.(dat.)* to you (fam.).

hiriarteko *adj.* interurban.

hiribarren *n.* lower part of the city; lower part of the fern field.

hiribide *n.* avenue.

hiriburutasun *n.* quality of being a capital.

hirietxe *n.* city hall, town hall.

hirigin *n.* developer, city planner.

hirigintza *n.* urbanism, urbanization, city planning.

hirikide *n.* fellow city dweller.

hiriko *adj.* urban, civic.

hiringuru *n.* suburb, outskirts of a city.

hirino *n.(dim.)* small city.

hiriska *n.(dim.)* small city.

hiritar *n.* city dweller, town dweller. *adj.* urban.

hiritargo *n.* citizenship, rights of citizenship.

hiritarpen *n.* urbanization.

hiritartasun *n.* citizenship, quality of being a citizen. *n.* quality of being a city dweller.

hiritartu *v.i.* to get used to the city, to become accustomed to the city.

hirizain *n.* city policeman, city police, local police.

hirizerga *n.* city taxes.

hirrikadura *n.* crack, fissure.

hirrikatu *v.i.* to crack, to crack open.

hiru *adj./n.* three.

hiruadardun *adj.* three-cornered.

hiruadarreko *adj.* three-cornered; having three branches.

hirualderdiko *adj.* three-sided.

hirualdiko *adj.* three-sided.

hiruangelu *n.(geom.)* triangle.

hiruatz *n.* tridactyl.

hirubide *n.* three-way crossing.

hirubideko *adj.* pertaining to a three-way crossing, three-way.

hiruburudun *adj.* three-headed.

hiruburuko *adj.* three-headed.

hiruerako *adj.* triform.

hirugarren *adj.* third.

hirugurpileko *adj.* three-wheeled. *n.* tricycle.

hiruhariko *adj.* three-threaded, having three threads, three-wired (plug).

hiruhegodun *adj.* three-winged.

hiruhilabete *n.* trimester, three month period.

hiruhilabetekari *n.* trimestral magazine, trimestral bulletin.

hiruhilabeteko *adj.* trimestral, having three months, lasting three months, three months old, three-month-old, three month.

hiruhilabetero *adv.* every three months, trimestrally.

hiruhileko *adj.* trimestral; three months long, three month long, three month.

hiruhortzeko *n.* trident, three-pronged fork or pitchfork.

hiruki *adj./n.* member of a trio, triplet(s). *n.(geom.)* triangle.

hiruko *n.* trio; triplet(s). *n.* tray (cards). *n.(mus.)* triplet; triad. *n.* trilogy.

hirukoitz *adj.* triple. *n.* member of a trio; triplet.

hirukoiztu *v.t.* to triple, to triplicate, to multiply by three.

hirukoloreko *adj.* tricolored, three-colored.

hirukote *n.* triplets. *n.* trio, group of three.

hiruloreko *adj.* three-flowered.

hirumargodun *adj.* tricolor, tricolored, three-colored.

hirumargoko *adj.* tricolor, tricolored, three-colored.

hiruna *adv.* three to each one.

hirunaka *adv.* three by three, by threes, in groups of three, in threes.

hirunako adj. ternary, consisting of three parts.

hirunan adv. three by three, by threes, in threes, in groups of three.

hiruoineko adj. tripod, three-footed.

hiruorriko adj. having three leaves, three-leaved, trefoil.

hirurehun adj./n. three hundred.

hirurehungarren adj. three hundredth.

hiruren adj./n. third; one third.

hirurendu v.t. to divide in three parts.

hirurenketa n. tripartition, division into three parts.

hirurogei adj./n. sixty.

hirurogeigarren adj. sixtieth.

hirurogeiko adj. sixtieth; sexagenarian, sixty-year-old, sixty years old.

hirurogeitamar adj./n. seventy.

hirurogeitamargarren adj. seventieth.

hirurren n.(eccl.) devotional exercise (usually prayer) lasting for three days.

hirurte n. triennium, term of three years.

hirurteko adj. three-year-old, three years old, triennial.

hirusilabadun adj. trisyllabic, having three syllables.

hirusta n.(bot.) trefoil, clover, shamrock.

hirutariko adj. of three kinds, of three types.

hirutasun n. trinity.

hirutu v.t. to triple, to triplicate, to multiply by three.

hiruzatidun adj. having three parts, three part.

hiruzatiketa n. division into three parts or categories, tripartition.

hiruzatiko adj. having three parts, three part.

hiruzpalau adj. some, a few.

hisdura n. paleness, pallor, fadedness.

hisi n. spite, grudge, resentment, despair, hate. n. tenacity, obstinance.

hisialdi n. period of stubbornness, obstinacy.

hisiatu v.i. to be obstinate, to be stubborn.

hisigogor adj. stubborn, obstinate.

hisikatu v.i. to be stubborn, to be obstinate, to be persistent.

hisikor adj. obstinate, stubborn, opinionated, thick-headed.

hisikortasun n. stubbornness, obstinacy, contumacy, pertinacity.

hispaniar adj. Hispanic.

hispanizale n. hispanist, fond of hispanic culture, language, etc.

historia n. history.

historialari n. historian.

historiaurre n. prehistory.

historiaurreko adj. prehistoric, prehistorical.

historigile n. historian.

historiko adj. historical.

historitasun n. historicalness, quality of being historic.

hitano n. use of second person (fam.) when speaking (usually referring to women).

hitano egin v.t. to speak using second person (fam.).

hitanoka adv. using second person (fam.).

hits adj. pale, matte. adj. mediocre, undistinguished.

hitz n. word. n. promise, word.

hitzaldaketa n. twisting of words, distortion of a statement, mixing up of words.

hitzaldi n. sermon, speech, talk, lecture; conference, discussion.

hitzaldioste n. end of the speech, conclusion.

hitzalfer n. redundant word, redundancy, pleonasm.

hitzamai n.(gram.) desinence, ending, termination of a word.

hitzandidura n. grandiloquence, lofty and pompous eloquence.

hitzandiko adj. grandiloquent, pompously eloquent.

hitzarmen n. verbal agreement, accord, pact, deal, treaty.

hitzarmenezko adj. agreed, agreed upon.

hitzarrokeria n. empty talk, bragging.

hitzarrotasun n. verbosity, pomposity.

hitzartu v.t. to take (someone's) word for (something), to believe (someone). v.t. to agree with.

hitzasperen n.(gram.) interjection.

hitzaspertu n. idle conversation, chatter.

hitzatze n. epilogue, afterword.

hitzaurre n. prologue, foreword, introduction.

hitzaurreko adj. introductory.

hitzeder adj. eloquent.

hitzegile n. speaker, orator.

hitz egin v.t. to speak, to talk.

hitzeko adj. honest, true to one's word.

hitzelkarketa n. joining of two words to make a single word, making of compound words.

hitzelkartu n. compound word.

hitzemaile n. promiser, one who promises (and keeps the promise).

hitz eman v.t. to promise, to give your word.

hitzerdi n. allusion, hint, reference.

hitzerdika adv. ambiguously, vaguely, indirectly. adv. in a few words.

hitzerraztasun n. fluency, language facility, speaking ability.

hitzerrepika n.(gram.) alliteration.

hitzerro n.(gram.) etymology.

hitzerroz adv. etymologically.

hitzerrozko adj. etymological.

hitzeten n. word broken into parts or syllables.

hitzetik hortzera adv. suddenly, immediately.

hitzetorri n. eloquence, facility for speaking, fluency.

hitzez adv. verbally, orally.

hitzez-hitz adv. word by word, literally, to the letter.

hitzezko adj. verbal, oral.

hitzezti n./adj. sweet talk, smooth talk; sweet talking, smooth talking.

hitzgabe(ko) adj. mute, deprived of speech; speechless. adj. disloyal in the sense of not keeping one's word.

hitzgurutzaketa n. crucigram, crossword puzzle.

hitzgutxiko adj. quiet, reserved, silent.

hitzinguru n. context. n. paraphrase, circumlocution.

hitzinguruko adj. periphrastic, using a longer phrase in place of a shorter, clearer one.

hitzingurukatu v.t. to paraphrase.

hitzisil n. secret.

hitzjario adj. loquacious, talkative, chatterbox. n. talkativeness, wordiness, verbosity.

hitzjariokeria n. chattiness, excessive talkativeness.

hitzjariotasun n. talkativeness, loquaciousness, loquacity.

hitz lau n. prose.

hitz-mitz n. chatter, frivolous conversation.

hitzontzi adj. chatterbox, loquacious, talkative.

hitzontzikeria n. excessive talkativeness, excessive verbosity, wordiness.

hitzots n. sound of voices, murmur of voices.

hitzurri adj. taciturn, quiet, of few words.

hitzustel adj. disloyal, traitorous.

hitzuts n. meaningless word.

hiz- Used in compound words. Derived from hitz, word.

hizdun adj. loquacious, talkative.

hizjoko n. pun, play on words.

hizkabe adj. speechless, deprived of speech.

hizkabetu v.i. to be speechless. v.i. to become a mute.

hizkabezia n. aphasia, muteness.

hizkelgi n. dialect.

hizkenketa n.(gram.) elision.

hizkera n. language, way of speaking.

hizkeramordoilo n. speaking a language poorly, speaking a language using too many foreign words.

hizketa n. chat, talk, conversation.

hizketakide n. fellow talker, converser, interlocutor.

hizketalagun n. fellow talker, converser, interlocutor.

hizketaldi n. chat, period of conversation, talk.

hizketari n. converser, talker, speaker.

hizketatu v.i. to talk, to converse, to chat, to speak.

hizki n. letter of the alphabet. n.(gram.) affix.

hizki-mizki n. gossip, chatter.

hizki-mizkizale adj. gossipy, gossiping, fond of gossip.

hizkirimiri n. gossip.

hizkuntz- Used in compound words. Derived from hizkuntza, language.

hizkuntza n. language, tongue, idiom.

hizkuntzakide n. cospeaker of a language, person who speaks the same language.

hizkuntzalari n. linguist, philologist.

hizkuntzalaritza n. linguistics, philology.

hizkuntzaskodun adj. multilingual. n. polyglot.

hizlabur n. abbreviation.

hizlaburpen n.(gram.) syncope, loss of one or more sounds or letters in the interior of a word.

hizlaburtu v.t. to shorten a word, to omit part of a word, to syncopate.

hizlari n. orator, preacher, speaker.

hizlaritza n. rhetoric, art of public speaking.

hizlohi n. obscene word, obscenity.

hizmoteldura n. stuttering, act of stuttering.

hizmoteltasun n. stuttering.

hiznahasketa n. speaking in a confused manner, confusion of speech.

hizneurketa n. versification.

hizneurri n. meter of verses.

hizneurtu v.t. to versify, to write verses.

hizneurtzaile n. versifier.

hiztegi n. dictionary, vocabulary.

hiztegigile n. lexicographer.

hiztegigintza n. lexicography.

hiztegilari n. lexicographer.

hiztegitxo n.(dim.) small dictionary.

hiztun adj. loquacious, talkative. n. chatterbox; speaker.

hobari n. advantage, benefit, bonus.

hobaritu v.t. to improve.

hobe adj. better, preferable, advantageous. Comparative of on. adv. better. Comparative of ongi.

hobeagotu v.i./v.t. to improve, to get better; to make better.

hobealdi n. improvement, betterment.

hobe-beharrez adv. with all the best intentions, well-meaning.

hobegarri adj. improvable, ameliorable, perfectable.

hobegarritasun n. perfectability, improvability.

hobe izan v.i./v.t. to be better, to be preferable.

hobeki adv. better. Comparative of ongi.

hobekiago adv. better.

hobekien adv.(sup.) best, the best.
hobekuntza n. betterment, improvement.
hoben n. fault, blame, culpability. n. sin.
hobendun adj. guilty, culpable, blamable; sinful.
hobendura n. culpability, guiltiness.
hobenezko adj. sinful.
hobengabe adj. blameless, innocent, sinless.
hobengabetasun n. lack of guilt, innocence, sinlessness.
hobentsu adj. guilty, culpable. adj. sinful.
hoberen adj.(superl.) the best, optimum. Superlative of on.
hoberentsu adj. almost the best.
hobespen n. preference, priority.
hobeto adv. better. Comparative of ondo, well.
hobeto beharrean adv. with all the best intentions, in good faith.
hobetsi v.t. to prefer.
hobetu v.i./v.t. to improve, to get better; to perfect, to make better.
hobezale adj. fond of improvement.
hobezin adj. optimum, perfect, outstanding.
hobezintasun n. perfection, perfectness.
hobi n. grave, sepulchre, tomb.
hobiharri n. gravestone, headstone.
hobiragabe adj. unburied.
hobiratu v.t. to bury, to inter.
hobiratzaile n. burier, gravedigger, undertaker.
hobitegi n. cemetery, graveyard, burial ground.
hodei n. cloud.
hodeiarte n. partial cloudiness.
hodeidun adj. cloudy.
hodeidura n. clouding over, clouding.
hodeiertz n. horizon.
hodeieztatu v.i. to cloud over, to be covered with clouds.
hodeimordo n. large cloud.
hodeimordotu v.i. to cloud up, to cloud over.
hodeitasun n. cloudiness.
hodeite n. clouds, a lot of clouds.
hodeitsu adj. cloudy, overcast.
hodeitu v.t. to cloud up, to cloud over, to get cloudy, to be cloudy.
hodeitxo n.(dim.) little cloud.
hodeitzar n.(aug.) large cloud.
hodeiztatu v.i. to get cloudy, to cloud up, to cloud over, to be cloudy.
hodi n. tube, pipe. n.(anat.) alimentary canal.
hodiantzeko adj. tubular, pipe-like, vascular.
hodibarneko adj. intravascular.
hodibide n.(anat.) vascular system.
hodieria n. conduit, pipeline. n.(anat.) visceral system conduit.
hodigile n. pipe maker, pipe fitter.

hodigintza n. pipe making, tube manufacture.
hodino n.(dim.) small tube, small pipe.
hodiratu v.t. to conduct through tubes or pipes, to pipe (in).
hoditxo n.(dim.) small tube, small pipe.
hodixka n.(dim.) small tube, small pipe.
hoditza n. net of tubing or piping.
hodizko adj. tubular, vascular.
hodiztapen n. inserting a tube (into someone or something); connecting pipe, laying pipe.
hodiztatu v.t. to insert a tube (into someone or something); to connect pipe, to lay pipe.
hogei adj./n. twenty.
hogeigarren adj. twentieth.
hogeiko n.(econ.) bill worth one hundred pesetas or twenty duros.
hogeina adv. twenty each.
hogeinaka adv. twenty by twenty, by twenties, in groups of twenty, by the score.
hogeinakatu v.t. to divide into groups of twenty.
hogeinako adj. twentieth.
hogeiren adj. one-twentieth.
hogeitabost adj./n. twenty-five.
hogeitamar adj./n. thirty.
hogeiurtedun adj. twenty years old, twenty-year-old.
hogeiurteko adj. twenty years old, twenty-year-old.
hogerleko n.(econ.) currency (bill) worth five pesetas.
hoiek adj./pron. those; those ones.
hola adv. like so, like this, like that, so, in this manner.
holako adj. that kind of.
holakoxe adj. like, similar.
holaxe adj. just like this, just so, in this very way.
homologo adj. homologous.
hona adv. here (in this direction). adv. here (it is), here (you have).
hona hemen adv. here is, right here.
honaino adv. up to here.
hondabide n. road to ruin, path to perdition, scandalous path, temptation.
hondaezin adj. unsinkable, indestructible.
hondagarri adj. disastrous, devastating, destructive, ruinous, harmful, noxious. adj. sinkable.
hondagarriro adv. disastrously, destructively, ruinously.
hondagarritasun n. destructiveness, disastrousness.
hondaketa n. razing, demolition, destruction. n. ruin, damage, disaster.
hondakin n. rest, remains, residue, sediment, leftovers.
hondakinbilketa n. salvaging, scavenging.
hondakindegi n. garbage can,

garbage bin, trash bin, dumpster.
hondakinezko adj. leftover, residual.
hondakintsu adj. residual, fecal.
hondalan n. excavation.
hondalangile n. digger, excavator.
hondamen n. ruin, havoc, destruction, disaster, damage, harm.
hondamendi n. ruin, perdition, destruction, damage, disaster, havoc.
hondamenezko adj. ruinous, disastrous, destructive.
hondapen n. waste, squandering. n. ruin, destruction.
hondar n. sand, beach. n. residue, remains, sediment, grounds (coffee), leftovers. n.(math.) rest, remainder.
hondardun adj. sandy, having sand. adj. having leftovers, having residue or sediment.
hondarmeta n. pile of sand, sand dune.
hondar-mondarrak n.(pl.) residue, remains, leftovers.
hondarmuino n. dune, sand dune.
hondarmuinotsu adj. full of dunes, dune covered.
hondarpeko n.(zool.) sand scorpion.
hondarpilo n. pile of sand.
hondarraldi n. running aground, stranding, beaching.
hondarrerloju n. hourglass.
hondarreta n. beach, sandy ground.
hondarrezko adj. sandy, sand, of sand. adj. residual, left over.
hondarreztatu v.t. to cover with sand.
hondarreztu v.t./v.i. to sand, to cover with sand; to become covered with sand.
hondartegi n. beach, sandy ground.
hondartsu adj. sandy. adj. cloudy, having sediment.
hondartu v.i. to run aground, to be stranded, to beach.
hondartza n. beach; sand dune.
hondatu v.t. to ruin, to destroy. v.t. to go bankrupt, to squander, to waste. v.i./v.t. to sink, to dive, to submerge.
hondatzaile adj. destructive, ruinous. n./adj. spendthrift, wasteful person; wasteful, squandering.
hondeagailu n. digging machine, excavating machine.
hondeaketa n. digging, excavating.
hondealan n. excavation work, digging.
hondeatu v.t. to excavate, to dig.
hondeatzaile n. excavator, digger.
hondo n. base, foundation, bottom. n. root, base, foot (of a tree). n. bottom of the sea, depths of the sea.
hondodun adj. profound, deep.
hondogabe adj. bottomless, endless, immense.
hondo(a) jo v.t. to run aground, to be stranded, to beach (a boat).
hondoragarri adj. sinkable, submergible.
hondoraketa n. shipwreck, wreck, sinking.
hondorapen n. shipwreck, wreck, sinking.
hondoratu v.i./v.t. to sink, to shipwreck. v.i. to go to the bottom.
honek adj./pron. this; this one (active subject).
honela adv. in this way, so, like this, thus.
honelako adj. like this, this kind of, such, so.
honelaxe adv. just like this, in this very way.
honen adj./pron. (genit.) of this, of this one. adv. so, such. adv. at such and such a time.
honenbeste adv. so much, as much as this.
honenbesteko n. remuneration, reward.
honeratu v.i. to come here.
honetara adv. in this way, thus, like this, so.
honez gero adv. by now, right now.
honi adj./pron. (dat.) to this; to this one.
hontaz adj./pron. about this.
hontza n.(zool.) barn owl.
hontzuri n.(zool.) owl.
honuntz adv. towards here, in this direction.
hor adv. there (nearby).
hordago int. term used in card games to challenge another player.
hordi adj./n. drunk, inebriated, intoxicated, drunken; drunkard, drunk.
hordialdi n. drunkenness, tipsiness; period of time spent drunk, a drunk.
hordiarazi v.t. to make (someone) get drunk.
hordigarri adj. intoxicating, alcoholic, inebriating.
hordikeria n. drunkenness, inebriation, alcoholism.
hordiputz n./adj. drunkard, alcoholic, boozer; drunk.
horditasun n. drunkenness, inebriation, intoxication.
horditu v.t. to get (someone) drunk, to make (someone) drunk. v.i. to become drunk, to get drunk.
hordizale adj. drunken, fond of getting drunk.
hori adj./pron. that. adj. yellow, pale.
horiaire adj. yellowish.
horibizi adj. deep yellow, gold colored.
horidura n. yellowness, paleness.
horigorri adj. golden yellow.
horimin adj. bright yellow.
horiska adj. yellowish, yellow.
horiskatu v.i. to yellow, to turn yellow.
horitasun n. yellowness; paleness, pallor.
horitu v.i. to turn yellow, to yellow. v.i.

to grow pale, to turn pale. *v.t.* to make yellow, to turn (something) yellow.

horixe *pron.* that one (and no other), just that.

horiztatu *v.i./v.t.* to yellow, to turn yellow; to turn (something) yellow, to paint (something) yellow.

hor konpon *int.* what's it to me?

horma *n.* wall. *n.* ice.

hormagarri *adj.* glacial.

hormate *n.* cold snap, period of cold weather.

hormatu *v.t.* to wall up, to wall in, to build a wall. *v.i.* to freeze.

hormaztatu *v.t.* to make walls, to put up walls, to build walls, to wall up, to encircle with walls.

hormona *n.* hormone.

horni *n.* provision, supply.

hornialdi *n.* supplying food, provisioning food, laying in provisions, shopping for food.

hornidenda *n.* grocery store.

hornidura *n.* providing provisions, supplying food, stocking up on food.

hornigabetu *v.i.* to be without provisions or food.

hornigabezia *n.* lack of provisions, lack of supplies.

hornigai *n.* supply, supplies, provisions, stock.

hornigarri *adj.* suppliable, provisionable.

hornigintza *n.* supplying food, provisioning.

horniketa *n.* supplying, provisioning.

hornikuntza *n.* supplying (food).

hornilari *n.* provider, supplier.

hornilaritza *n.* post or office of supplier or purveyor.

hornimendu *n.* supplying, provisioning.

hornitegi *n.* grocery store, place for purchasing provisions.

hornitu *v.i./v.t.* to be supplied, to be stocked with, to supply, to provide, to stock, to furnish.

hornitzaile *n.* grocer, provider, supplier, purveyor.

hornitzailetza *n.* grocery store, office or post of supplier or purveyor.

horoskopo *n.* horoscope.

horra *adv.* there (directional), to there, to that place.

horra hor *adv.* right there.

horraino *adv.* there, as far as there, up to that point, to there.

horregatik *adv./conj.* because of that, for that, for that reason, that's why.

horregatio *conj.* nevertheless.

horrek *adj./pron.* that; that one. Used as subject of transitive verbs.

horrela *adv.* like so, like that, in that way, so, thus, that way.

horrelako *adj.* like that.

horrelaxe *adv.* just like that.

horren *adj./pron.(genit.)* of that, pertaining to that, that . . . 's; that one's. *adv.* so.

horrenbeste *adv.* that much, as much as that, so many, that many.

horri *adj./pron.(dat.)* to that (one).

hortaz *conj.* therefore, consequently.

hortik *adv.* from there (nearby).

hortxe *adv.* right there.

hortz *n.* tooth. *n.* tooth (of a machine, gear, etc.).

hortzagin(ak) *n.(pl.)* molars and teeth.

hortzaro *n.* teething, teething age.

hortzateratzaile *n.* dentist.

hortzatto *n.(dim.)* baby tooth.

hortzazketa *n.* teething, dentition.

hortzeko *adj.* dental.

hortzeria *n.* set of natural teeth.

hortzerro *n.* root of a tooth.

hortzeskuila *n.* toothbrush.

hortzikada *n.* gnawing.

hortzikadura *n.* act of gnawing.

hortzikari *n.* gnawer.

hortzikatu *v.t.* to gnaw.

hortzikatzaile *adj.* gnawing.

hortzorde *n.* false tooth.

hortzordeko *n.* set of false teeth, dentures.

hortzore *n.* toothpaste.

hortzulo *n.* cavity (in a tooth).

horzdun *adj.* having teeth.

horzka *adv.* with the teeth, by the teeth.

horzkabe *adj.* toothless.

horzkabetu *v.t.* to knock out a tooth, to remove a tooth, to pull a tooth. *v.i.* to lose one's teeth.

horzkada *n.* bite, gnawing of teeth.

horzkadura *n.* biting, notching, grooving, making a cut in, making an incision in.

horzka egin *v.t.* to bite.

horzkaketa *n.* biting, notching, grooving, making a cut in, making an incision in.

horzkalari *n.* biter, notcher, groover.

horzkari *n.* biter, notcher, groover.

horzkarraska *n.* grinding of teeth, gnashing of teeth.

horzkarraskatu *v.t.* to grind one's teeth, to gnash one's teeth.

horzkatu *v.t.* to bite.

horzki *n.* unpleasing tingling or pain in the teeth.

horzkidura *n.* act of having pain in the teeth, act of having sensitive teeth, toothache.

horzkitu *v.t./v.i.* to hurt one's teeth, to hurt a sensitive tooth.

hoska *adv.* noisily.

hoskabe *adj.* soundless, silent.

hosketa *n.* vociferation, shouting.

hoslari *n.* shouter, yeller.

hosta- Used in compound words. Derived from *hosto*, leaf.

hostadura *n.* foliation.

hostagabetu *v.i.* to lose leaves (trees,

hostail *n.* foliage.

hostatu *v.i.* to sprout leaves, to be covered with leaves, to have leaves.

hostia *n.(eccl.)* host.

hostiontzi *n.(eccl.)* ciborium, pyx, box in which the holy host is kept.

hosto *n.* leaf.

hostoaskodun *adj.* having many leaves, leafy, full of leaves.

hostodun *adj.* leafy, having leaves.

hostogabe *adj.* leafless.

hostogabetu *v.i.* to lose leaves, to fall (leaves).

hostoka *adv.* leaf by leaf.

hostokatu *v.t./v.i.* to remove leaves; to lose leaves.

hostokide *adj.* foliaceous, of a leaf, relating to a leaf.

hostope *n.* shade, shadow.

hostotasun *n.* leafiness.

hostotsu *adj.* leafy, frondy, frondose.

hostotu *v.i.* to be leafy, to have leaves, to be covered with leaves.

hostotza *n.* foliage, leafage.

hotel *n.* hotel.

hotelari *n.* hotelkeeper, innkeeper.

hots *n.* noise, sound. *adv.* that is, in other words.

hotsandiko *adj.* resonant, loud. *adj.* pompous.

hotsegile *n.* convoker, convener, caller, announcer. *n.* town crier, street crier.

hots egin *v.t.* to call, to shout, to make a noise, to make a sound.

hotsemaile *n.* one who shoos away animals. *n.* cheerleader, one who cheers or applauds, one who encourages. *n.* driver of oxen.

hots eman *v.t.* to drive cattle. *v.t.* to shoo away (animals); to flush (game).

hotsizen *n.* onomatopoeic word.

hotz *n.* cold. *adj.* cold, frigid, cool, stand-offish, aloof.

hotzagotu *v.i.* to cool off, to cool down.

hotzalde *n.* place with a cold climate.

hotzaldi *n.* cold season, cold snap. *n.* cold chill.

hotzarazi *v.t.* to chill, to make cold.

hotzarazle *adj.* cooling, refrigerating.

hotzaro *n.* cold season, cold snap.

hotz egin *v.t.* to be cold (weather).

hotzepel *adj.* warm, tepid, lukewarm.

hotzikara *n.* chill, shiver.

hotzil *adj.* almost cold.

hotzildu *v.i.* to let up (cold weather), to lessen (cold temperatures).

hotzitu *v.i./v.t.* to get cold; to make cold. *v.i.* to catch a cold.

hotz izan *v.i.* to be cold, to feel the cold, to be chilly.

hoxalata *n.* tin, tinplate.

hoxalatari *n.* tinsmith.

hozberokatu *v.t.* to cool down (something hot), to cool off.

hozdun *adj.* feeling the cold, cold.

hozdura *n.* cold, coldness (physical and emotional).

hozgarri *adj.* refrigerating, chilling.

hozgiro *n.* cold season, cold snap, period of cold weather.

hozi *n.* germ, bud, seed; spring, source.

hozidura *n.* germination.

hozitu *v.i.* to germinate, to sprout, to bud.

hozka *n.* bite. *n.* notch, groove, chip, nick.

hozkada *n.* biting. *n.* notching, chipping, grooving.

hozkadura *n.* bite, wound from a bite. *n.* notch, nick, groove, indentation.

hozka egin *v.t.* to bite, to sink one's teeth into.

hozkailu *n.* refrigerator, cooler.

hozkari *n.* biter. *adj.* biting.

hozkarri *adj.* refreshing, cooling.

hozkatu *v.t.* to bite, to sink one's teeth into. *v.t.* to nick, to notch, to groove, to indent.

hozkeria *n.* emotional coldness, estrangement, frigidity.

hozketa *n.* cold, cooling, chill, becoming cold.

hozki *adv.* coolly, coldly.

hozkidura *n.* unpleasant tingling in the teeth.

hozkirri *adj.* chilly, cold, cool. *n.* chill, shiver.

hozkirri izan *v.i.* to be chilly, to feel chilly.

hozkirritu *v.t./v.i.* to cool down, to cool off, to grow cool (weather).

hozkor *adj.* susceptible to cold. *adj.* chilling, cooling, refrigerating.

hozkura *n.* coolness, cold, chill.

hozmin *n.* penetrating cold.

hozmindu *v.i.* to get very cold, to become very cold, to feel the cold intensely.

hozmindura *n.* getting very cold, freezing, feeling intense cold.

hozpera *adj.* sensitive to the cold.

hozperatasun *n.* sensitivity to cold.

hozperatu *v.i.* to become sensitive to the cold.

hoztaile *adj.* refrigerating, cooling.

hoztasun *n.* coldness, chilliness, frigidness (physical or emotional).

hozte *n.* cold snap, cold period.

hoztegi *n.* cooler, refrigerated place, refrigerator.

hoztoki *n.* cooler, cool place.

hoztu *v.i.* to get cold. *v.t.* to chill, to make cold. *v.i.* to grow cold (affection), to lose affection (for someone).

hoztura *n.* cooling, refrigerating. *n.* frigidness, coolness, frigidity.

humanismo *n.* humanism.

humanista *n.* humanist.

hunki *n.* touching, feeling, touch, feel.

hunkialdi *n.* touching, feeling.
hunkibera *adj.* emotional, sensitive.
hunkiberatasun *n.* emotionalness, sensitivity.
hunkigarri *adj.* moving, emotional, touching.
hunkigarriro *adv.* emotionally, touchingly, sensitively.
hunkikor *adj.* emotional, sensitive.
hunkipen *n.* emotion, feeling, sensation, sensitivity.
hunkipenezko *adj.* emotional, sensitive.
hunkitu *v.t.* to touch, to feel, to palpate. *v.t.* to move, to touch, to affect (emotionally). *v.i.* to be moved, to be touched, to show emotion.
hunkitzaile *adj.* emotional.
huntz *n.(bot.)* ivy.
huntzadar *n.(bot.)* ivy vine.
huntzorri *n.* leaf of ivy.
huntzosto *n.* leaf of ivy.
hur *adv.* close, near. *adj.* close, nearby.
hura *pron./adj.* he, she, it, that one; him, her; that.
huraxe *pron.* that very one, just that one.
hurbil *adv.* near, nearby, close. *adj.* close, nearby. *prep.* close to, near.
hurbildu *v.i.* to approach, to draw near, to come close.
hurbilbide *n.* shortcut.
hurbildura *n.* nearing, approaching.
hurbilegi *adj.* too close, too near.
hurbileko *adj.* near, close, nearby.
hurbilgo *adj.* nearby, close. *n.* proximity, nearness.
hurbilketa *n.* approaching, drawing near, nearing; merging.
hurbilkor *adj.* converging, convergent.
hurbilpen *n.* approximation; approach, convergence.
hurbiltasun *n.* proximity, closeness, nearness, contiguousness.
hur eman *v.t.* to guess, to approximate.
hurko *adj.* nearby, close, proximate.
hurkotasun *n.* proximity, closeness, nearness, contiguousness.
hurre *adv.* close, nearby.
hurrean *adv.* close, near, nearby.
hurreko *adj.* next, close, nearby.
hurren *adj.* next, following. *adj.(super.)* the closest.
hurrendu *v.i.* to approach, to draw near, to come close.
hurrengo *adj.* next, following.
hurrengoan *adv.* next time, on another occasion.
hurrenondoko *adj.* subsequent, succeeding, following, next.
hurrentasun *n.* proximity, nearness, contiguousness, closeness. *n.* subsequentness, quality of being next.
hurrera *adv.* close, near.

hurreraketa *n.* approach, nearing, act of drawing closer.
hurreratu *v.i.* to approach, to draw near, to come close.
hurretasun *n.* subsequentness, quality of being next, immediacy, nearness, closeness.
hurretu *v.i.* to approach, to draw near.
hurrupa *n.* drink, swallow, slug, sip.
hurrupada *n.* swallow, drink, sip, slug, gulp.
hurrupa egin *v.t.* to sip, to gulp, to take a drink.
hurrupagarri *adj.* swallowable, drinkable, sippable, gulpable.
hurrupaka *adv.* sipping, in sips, by sips, gulping.
hurrupaketa *n.* act of swallowing, act of sipping, act of gulping. *n.(fig.)* pillage.
hurrupako *n.* gulp, swallow.
hurrupakuntza *n.* sipping, gulping, swallowing. *n.(fig.)* pillage, plundering.
hurrupari *n.* sipper, swallower, gulper.
hurrupatu *v.t.* to sip, to gulp, to take a drink.
hurrupatzaile *n.* sipper, gulper, drinker. *n.* pillager, exploiter, spoiler.
hus- Used in compound words. Derived from *huts*, empty.
husgune *n.* empty space.
huskabe *adj.* perfect, excellent, flawless, unimprovable.
huskailu *n.* hollower, hollowing tool.
huskeria *n.* trifle, triviality, insignificant thing, pettiness.
husketa *n.* emptiness, vacuum. *n.* evacuation.
huskor *adj.* fallible, capable of making a mistake.
huskortasun *n.* fallibility. *n.* defectiveness.
huskune *n.* hole, space, cavity.
hustasun *n.* emptiness, vacuum.
hustu *v.i./v.t.* to empty, to vacate; to deflate.
hustura *n.* emptying, vacating, evacuating.
hustzaile *n.* hollower; one who empties, emptier, evacuator. *adj.* hollowing; emptying, evacuating.
huts *n.* fault, lack, mistake, error, defect, absence. *adj.* pure, just, mere, net. *n./adj.* zero, nought. *n.* miss, fault, error (in sports). *n.* vacuum, nothingness.
hutsal *adj.* transient, ephemeral, trifling.
hutsalarazi *v.t.* to weaken, to devalue, to lose consistency. *v.t.* to make (someone) empty (something).
hutsaldi *n.* error, mistake. *n.* act of emptying. *n.* vacant period, vacancy.
hutsaldu *v.i.* to weaken, to grow weak or discouraged, to become discouraged.

hutsalkeria n. vanity, fickleness, shallowness.

hutsalketa n. lessening of value.

hutsalki adv. vainly.

hutsaltasun n. nullity, nothingness.

hutsarazi v.t. to make (someone) empty (something), to evict, to dislodge, to dispossess.

hutsarte n. space.

hutsarteka adv. in one's free time, in one's spare time, now and then.

hutsean adv. free, gratis, freely.

hutsegile n. one who makes mistakes.

huts egin v.t. to make a mistake, to make an error, to fail. v.t. to not attend, to miss (school, a target, a point, etc.), to skip, to be absent.

hutseginez adv. mistakenly.

hutsegingarri adj. defective, faulty, capable of making a mistake.

hutseginkor adj. fault inducing, error producing.

hutsemaile n. fraud, cheater; one who disappoints or lets (someone) down.

huts eman v.t. to defraud, to cheat; to disappoint, to let (someone) down.

hutsezin(ezko) adj. infallible.

hutsezintasun n. infallibility.

hutsezko adj. free, free of charge, gratuitous.

hutsune n. hollow, hole, empty space, gap, cavity, lack.

I

i n. Letter of the Basque alphabet which is pronounced in a manner similar to the long e of English see.

-i (gram.) Dative suffix most often expressed in English by the preposition to.

ia adv. nearly, almost; hardly, barely. int. let's see.

iadanik adv. already.

iaio adj. jovial, cheerful, good-humored. adj. able, dextrous, expert.

iaiotasun n. expertise, dexterity.

ibai n. river.

ibaiadar n. branch of the river.

ibaiaho n. mouth of the river.

ibaialde n. lowland (near a river).

ibaibeso n. branch of a river.

ibaibide n. riverbed, course of a river.

ibaibiltoki n. confluence (of rivers).

ibaibira n. bend, riverbend.

ibaiburu n. source of the river.

ibaiertz n. bank, riverside.

ibaigurutze n. confluence (of rivers).

ibaiondo n. riverbank, shore. n. riverbed, bottom.

ibaiontzi n. barge, ferry, riverboat.

ibairatu v.i. to flow into the river.

ibaizaldi n.(zool.) hippopotamus.

ibaizoko n. bend, riverbend.

ibar n. valley; lowlands. n. riverbank.

ibarbide n. valley road.

iberiar adj. Iberian.

iberiera n. Iberian language.

ibi n. ford of a river.

ibide n. ford of a river.

ibiezin adj. uncrossable, incapable of being forded.

ibigarri adj. fordable.

ibilaldi n. trip; excursion, walk, march.

ibilalditxo n.(dim.) short trip, short walk, excursion.

ibilarazi v.t. to cause to move, to put into motion. v.t. to tow away.

ibilari n. walker.

ibilbide n. road, way, route, path; trajectory. n. road map. n. visa, passport; authorization to travel.

ibilera n. walking, act of walking.

ibilezin adj. unable to walk. adj. impassable, unwalkable.

ibilgailu n. vehicle.

ibilgaitz adj. impassable, uncrossable.

ibilgaiztasun n. immobility.

ibilgarri adj. walkable, transitable.

ibilgiro n. good weather for walking.

ibilgune n. place to walk, pass, way.

ibilgura n. desire to walk.

ibili v.i. to walk, to move, to pass, to go, to go along. v.i. to be, to stay.

ibilkari n. walker, runner. adj. nomadic, errant, wandering, vagabond.

ibilkera n. way of walking.

ibilketa n. route, way, movement.

ibilkide n. walking companion, traveling companion.

ibilkizun n. travel plan, itinerary. adj. passable, walkable.

ibilkor adj. fond of walking, fond of traveling.

ibilkortasun n. mobility.

ibilkuntza n. walk.

ibilmolde n. way of walking.

ibilpen n. walk, march, trip, journey.

ibilpide n. process.

ibiltaldi n. walk, trip, journey.

ibiltari adj. walking. n. traveler, walker, pedestrian.

ibiltegi n. walking place, hiking trail.

ibiltoki n. walking place, hiking trail; sidewalk.

ibiltresna n. vehicle.

ibiltxartel n. ticket, pass.

ibiltzaile adj. walking. n. walker.

ibilzale adj. fond of walking, fond of traveling.

ibiragankor adj. fordable, wadeable, crossable (river).

ibitsu adj. having fords, shallow.

ibitu v.t. to ford. v.i. to recede, to go down (river level).

ibitzaile n. forder, wader.

iceberg n. iceberg.

idabur n. threshing flail.

idaburlari n. thresher, flailer.

idar n.(bot.) pea.

idatzaldaketa n. transcription.

idatzaldatu v.t. to transcribe.

idatzarau(ak) n.(pl.) rules of orthography.

idatzaurre n. prologue, foreword.
idatzi v.t. to write, to annotate, to edit.
n. document; application, petition.
idatzinguru n. context.
idaz- Used in compound words.
Derived from *idatzi*, to write.
idazbilduma n. anthology, collection of
writings.
idazikerle n. graphologist, one who
interprets handwriting.
idazkai n. content, subject (of writing).
idazkailu n. typewriter.
idazkari n. secretary.
idazkarigela n. secretary's office.
idazkariorde n. assistant secretary.
idazkariordegela n. assistant
secretary's office.
idazkariordetza n. position of assistant
secretary.
idazkaritza n. position of secretary.
idazkera n. writing, style of writing;
penmanship, handwriting.
idazketa n. writing, composition;
editing.
idazkide n. co-writer.
idazkikutxa n. mailbox.
idazkino n.(dim.) brief writing or written
work.
idazkitxo n.(dim.) brief writing or
written work.
idazkizun n. scholarly composition or
writing.
idazkortz n. pen.
idazkuntza n. composition; editing.
idazlan n. writing, composition, article,
literary work.
idazlari n. writer; editor. n. secretary.
idazlaritza n. editing.
idazle n. writer.
idazlerro n. line (on writing paper).
idazluma n. pen, fountain pen,
ballpoint.
idazmahai n. desk.
idazmakina n. typewriter.
idazpaper n. paper, writing paper,
stationery.
idazpeko n. underlining.
idazpen n. writing, editing.
idazpuru n. title, heading.
idazpurutu v.t. to title, to put a heading
on.
idaz-sariketa n. literary contest.
idaz-sorta n. literary collection,
anthology.
idaztaldi n. duration of writing.
idaztegi n. writing desk; office.
idazti n. writing, scripture.
idaztino n.(dim.) pamphlet, brief
written work.
-ide (gram.) Suffix which denotes a
companion, a person who is of the
same group as another. **Ezkontide.**
Spouse, marriage partner.
ideia n. idea.
ideiadura n. ideology, system of ideas
and principles.
ideializatu v.t. to idealize.

ideialki adv. ideally.
ideialtzale n. idealist.
ideiatu v.t. to plan, to invent.
identifikagarri adj. identifiable.
identifikapen n. identification.
identifikatu v.t. to identify.
identifikazio n. identification.
identitate n. identity.
ideologari n. ideologist.
ideologia n. ideology.
idi n.(zool.) ox.
idiaska n. ox manger, crib.
ididema n. competition to see whose
oxen can pull a large stone the
greatest distance. n. betting on the
outcome of the competition.
idiestalki n. ox blanket.
idigai n. bull calf.
idiki n. oxmeat.
idikide n.(zool.) bovid.
idiko n.(dim.) ox calf.
idimihi n.(bot.) bugloss, oxtongue.
(lit.) ox tongue.
idiprobak n.(pl.) competition to see
whose oxen can pull a large stone
the greatest distance.
idirin n.(bot.) clump of rushes.
idisko n.(dim.) ox calf.
idiskotu v.i. to mate, to breed (cattle).
iditalde n. herd of oxen.
iditegi n. stable for oxen or cattle. n.
herd of oxen.
iditxo n.(dim.) small ox.
iditza n. herd of oxen.
iditzar n.(augm.) large ox.
idiuztarri n. yoke. n. yoked team of
oxen.
idizain n. ox keeper, ox herder.
idizil n. club made from the umbilical
cord of the ox, billy club.
idizko adj. bovine.
idolgurtzaile n. idolater.
idolo n. idol.
idolokeria n. idolatry.
idor adj. arid, dry. adj. sterile, infertile.
idordura n. state of dryness.
idorgarri n. that which produces
dryness, drying agent. adj.
astringent.
idorgiro n. time for drying things; dry
season.
idorgune n. dryness, drought.
idorketa n. dry spell, drought. n.
constipation.
idorki adv. drily, unfeelingly.
idorreri n. constipation.
idorreritu v.i. to be constipated.
idortasun n. dryness, aridness. n.
dessication. n. infertility, sterility.
idorte n. dryness, aridness. n. penury,
poverty, lack.
idortegi n. dryer, clothesline.
idortoki n. dryer, clothesline.
idortu v.t. to dry. v.i. to harden (earth).
ifernu n. hell.
ifernuratu v.i. to be damned to hell, to
go to hell. v.t. to send to hell.

igali n. fruit.
igande n. Sunday.
igandeko adj. dominical, Sunday.
igandero adv. every Sunday.
igargarri n. signal, sign, mark.
igarkizun n. riddle, brainteaser.
igarle n. guesser.
igaro v.t. to pass, to cross, to travel through. v.i. to pass (time); to pass by.
igaroagiri n. pass, ticket.
igaroaldi n. passage of time. n. transition.
igarobide n. pass, crossing.
igarogarri adj. tolerable, bearable, supportable.
igaroketa n. act of passing, act of crossing, act of traveling through.
igarokor adj. ephemeral, transitory, passing.
igarokortasun n. transitoriness, fleetingness, impermanence.
igaroleku n. pass, crossing.
igarotxartel n. pass, ticket.
igarotzaile n. passer, one who passes.
igarpen n. guess, prediction, prophecy.
igarrezin adj. unpredictable; indecipherable.
igarri v.t. to guess, to ascertain, to divine. v.t. to notice, to realize, to become aware of, to perceive.
igarterraz adj. easy to guess, predictable.
igartzapen n. adivination, guessing, foretelling, prophesying, predicting.
igel n.(zool.) frog.
igelkide adj. batrachian.
igeltoki n. place of frogs.
igeltsari n. mason, wall plasterer.
igeltsaritza n. masonry, wall plastering.
igeltsero n. mason, wall plasterer.
igeltserotza n. masonry, wall plastering.
igeltsobi n. chalk pit, gypsum mine.
igeltsu n. gypsum, chalk, plaster.
igeltsudura n. plastering.
igeltsugin n. maker of plaster.
igeltsugintza n. plasterwork, trade of the plasterer.
igeltsuharri n. gypsum.
igeltsulabe n. gypsum forge, plaster furnace.
igeltsutegi n. gypsum plant, plaster factory.
igeltsuztatu v.t. to plaster, to cover with plaster.
igergailu n. life preserver, lifesaver, inner tube.
igeri adv. swimmingly, swimming. n. swimming.
igerialdi n. time spent swimming.
igerian adv. swimming, swimmingly.
igeri egin v.t. to swim.
igerigailu n. lifesaver, life preserver, inner tube.

igerigile n. swimmer.
igerika adv. swimmingly, swimming.
igerikai n. lifesaver, life preserver, inner tube.
igerikakortasun n. flotation, floating, buoyancy.
igerikapen n. flotation, floating, buoyancy.
igerikari n. swimmer.
igerikatu v.i. to swim, to float.
igeriketa n. swimming.
igerilari n. swimmer.
igerileku n. swimming pool, place for swimming.
igeritako n. lifesaver, life preserver, inner tube.
igeriz adv. swimming, swimmingly.
igerizko adj. swimming, natatorial.
igerkizun n. riddle, conundrum, brain teaser.
igerleku n. swimming pool, place for swimming.
igertoki n. swimming pool, place for swimming.
igita n. harvest.
igitagailu n. harvesting machine, reaper.
igitagarri adj. reapable, mowable, harvestable.
igitai n. sickle.
igitaialdi n. harvest time (with a sickle).
igitaiari n. harvester (with a sickle).
igitaiaro n. harvest time.
igitaiketa n. act of harvesting with a sickle.
igitaite n. act of harvesting with a sickle.
igitaitu v.t. to harvest with a sickle, to reap with a sickle.
igitandu v.t. to harvest with a sickle.
igitari n. harvester (with a sickle).
igo v.i. to ascend, to rise, to go up, to climb.
igoaldi n. ascent, rise, escalation.
igo arazi v.t. to lift, to help a person get up, to raise.
igonaldi n. ascension, climb, rise.
igoera n. ascent, ascension, rise, climb.
igogailu n. lift, elevator.
igokada n. ascent, ascension, rise, climb.
igokari n. climber.
igokunde n. ascension.
igon v.i. to ascend, to rise, to go up, to climb.
igorgarri adj. transmittable, transmissible, sendable.
igorgarritasun n. transmittability.
igorketa n. sending, shipping, shipment, remittance, transportation.
igorkor adj. regularly sent.
igorle n. agent, shipper, sender, transmitter.
igorpen n. sending, shipping.
igorraldi n. act of sending.
igorri v.t. to transmit, to emit. v.t. to

send, to dispatch, to forward.

igortzaile *n.* sender, transmitter.

igotzaile *n.* climber.

igurika *adv.* waiting, expecting.

igurika egon *v.i.* to be waiting.

igurikaldi *n.* wait.

igurikapen *n.* expectation.

igurikarazi *v.t.* to cause to wait, to make (someone) wait.

igurikatu *v.t.* to wait for, to await, to watch for.

iguriki *v.t.* to await, to wait for, to watch for.

igurikigabeko *adj.* unexpected, unforeseen.

igurikitza *n.* wait. *n.* patience, tolerance.

igurikitzaile *n./adj.* waiter, one who waits; waiting.

igurikor *adj.* patient, long-suffering.

iguripen *n.* act of waiting; expectation.

igurtzaile *n.* rubber, masseur, masseuse. *adj.* rubbing. *adj.(gram.)* fricative.

igurtzi *v.t.* to rub. *v.t.* to anoint. *n.* friction, rubbing, rubdown, massage. *n.* anointing.

igurtzialdi *n.* massage, rubdown, rubbing.

igurtzikera *n.* rubbing, way of rubbing, means of friction.

igurtziketa *n.* rubbing, rubdown, massage.

igurtzimendu *n.* massage, rubbing; friction.

igurzkatu *v.t.* to massage, to give a massage, to rub.

igurzketa *n.* act of rubbing, act of massaging.

igurzki *n.* scrub brush, grooming brush.

igurzpaper *n.* cylinder of rolled paper with conical ends used for shadingcrayon or pencil strokes.

igurzpen *n.* friction; rubbing.

igurztailu *n.(mech.)* rubber, scraper, sander.

igurztoki *n.* massage parlor.

ihalozkatu *v.i.* to wallow, to roll on one's back.

ihar *adj.* dry, arid.

ihardesgarri *adj.* answerable.

ihardesle *n.* answerer, responder.

ihardespen *n.* answer.

ihardetsi *v.t.* to answer, to respond, to reply.

iharduera *n.* activity.

iharduki *v.t.* to argue, to dispute, to fight; to resist, to face (a problem).

ihardukigarri *adj.* arguable, questionable.

ihardun *v.t.* to spend time, to keep busy, to occupy oneself with. *n.* activity.

ihardunaldi *n.* period of activity.

ihargarri *adj.* perishable, liable to wilt. *adj.* wilting, drying, with a drying

effect.

iharketa *n.* act of drying, drying up.

iharki *n.* dry part of a tree.

iharrausaldi *n.* shake, jerk, shaking.

iharrausi *v.t./v.i.* to shake, to shake out.

iharrausle *n.* shaker, sifter, winnower.

iharrauspen *n.* sifting, shaking,winnowing.

ihartasun *n.* state of dryness, desiccation.

ihartu *v.i.* to dry up, to wither. *v.t.* to parch, to dry up, to shrivel.

ihaurkin *n.* cattle bed.

ihaurri *v.t.* to spread, to scatter, to disperse. *adv.* plenty, in abundance, very full.

ihauska *adv.* rolling over, rolling about, wallowing.

ihauskaldi *n.* wallowing, rolling over.

ihauskatu *v.i.* to roll over, to roll about, to wallow.

ihauteriak *n.(pl.)* carnival.

ihes *n.* flight, escape.

ihesaldi *n.* escape, flight, evasion.

ihesarazi *v.t.* to cause to escape, to run away.

ihesari eman *v.t.* to escape.

ihesbide *n.* evasion, escape route, means of escape. *n.* pretext, way out.

ihesbidezko *adj.* evasive, fugitive.

ihesean *adv.* by escaping, in flight, fleeing.

ihes egin *v.i.* to evade, to escape, to run away.

ihesezin *adj.* inevitable.

ihesgile *n.* escapee, one who flees.

ihesi *adj.* escaped, evaded.

ihes ibili *v.i.* to escape.

ihesi joan *v.i.* to escape, to flee.

ihesindar *n.* centrifugal force.

iheska *adv.* escaping, fleeing.

iheskari *n.* fugitive, deserter.

ihesketa *n.* evasion, escape, flight.

iheskoi *adj.* fugitive.

iheskor *adj.* evasive, fugitive, escaping.

iheskorki *adv.* fleetingly, briefly.

iheskortasun *n.* fugacity, brevity.

iheslari *n.* fugitive, escapee. *adj.* fugitive, escaping.

ihesle *n.* fugitive, deserter.

ihesleku *n.* refuge, shelter, safety zone.

ihespide *n.* evasion, escape. *n.* means of escape.

ihestoki *n.* safety zone, shelter, refuge.

ihi *n.(bot.)* rush.

ihiaga *n.* place of rushes.

ihintz *n.* dew.

ihintzaldi *n.* dewfall; sprinkling (of water).

ihinztadura *n.* sprinkling.

ihinztailu *n.* sprinkler, sprayer.

ihinztaldi *n.* dewfall; sprinkling

(duration).

ihinztatu *v.t.* to sprinkle, to cover with dew.

ihinztontzi *n.* watering pot, irrigation ditch.

ihitegi *n.* place of rushes.

ihitoki *n.* place of rushes.

ihitsu *adj.* abundant in rushes.

ihitu *v.i./v.t.* to become covered with rushes; to cover with rushes.

ihitza *n.* place of rushes.

ihitzaga *n.* place of rushes.

ihortziri *n.* thunder.

ijiteria *n.* band of gypsies.

ijito *n.* gypsy.

ijitoera *n.* gypsy language.

ijitohizkera *n.* gypsy language.

ijitokada *n.* gypsy mischief, trick.

ijitokeria *n.* gypsy mischief, trick.

ijitotalde *n.* band of gypsies.

ijitozko *adj.* gypsy, gypsylike.

-ik Suffix used in negative, interrogative, partitive and superlative sentences.

ikara *n.* fear, fright, anxiety, terror. *n.* shivering, quaking, trembling.

ikaradun *adj.* fearful, frightened, afraid.

ikara egin *v.t.* to frighten, to terrify.

ikaraezin *adj.* fearless, intrepid, dauntless, imperturbable.

ikaragabe *adj.* fearless, intrepid, dauntless, imperturbable.

ikaragaitz *adj.* fearless, intrepid, dauntless.

ikaragarri *adj.* horrible, frightening, terrible, terrifying. *adj.(fig.)* tremendous, large, enormous.

ikaragarriki *adv.* horribly, terribly, frightfully.

ikaragarrikoi *adj.* fearful, timid.

ikaragarrikortasun *n.* fearfulness, frightfulness.

ikaragarriro *adv.* horribly, terribly, frightfully.

ikaragarritasun *n.* terribleness.

ikaragarritu *v.i.* to become terrible, to become horrible.

ikaragarrizko *adj.* terrible, horrible.

ikara izan *v.t.* to tremble (with fear), to be afraid.

ikaraketa *n.* intimidation.

ikarakor *adj.* fearful, timid.

ikarakortu *v.i.* to be fearful, to be afraid.

ikaraldi *n.* shock, fright, fear, scare.

ikararazi *v.t.* to terrorize, to frighten, to intimidate.

ikarati *adj.* fearful, timid.

ikaratsu *adj.* fearful.

ikaratu *v.i.* to be scared, to be frightened. *v.t.* to intimidate, to terrorize, to scare, to frighten.

ikaratzaile *n./adj.* terrorist.

ikaraz *adv.* fearfully, timidly, timorously.

ikarazle *adj.* frightful, terrifying.

ikarazpen *n.* intimidation, fright, fear.

ikasareto *n.* classroom, room for studying.

ikasberri *n.* apprentice. *n.* recent knowledge, something recently learned.

ikasbide *n.* teaching method, means of learning. *n.* doctrine, teachings. *n.* example, model.

ikasezin *adj.* not learnable, impossible to learn.

ikasgabe *adj.* uneducated, unlearned, illiterate.

ikasgai *n.* lesson, learning material.

ikasgale *adj.* studious, anxious to learn. *n.* desire to learn.

ikasgarri *adj.* learnable.

ikasgela *n.* classroom, room for studying.

ikasgintza *n.* learning.

ikasgiro *n.* study time; learning environment.

ikasgo *n.* occupation of student. *n.* instruction, learning.

ikasgura *n.* desire to learn.

ikasi *v.t.* to learn. *adj.* educated, cultivated, instructed, learned, skilled.

ikaskai *n.* lesson, learning material, assignment.

ikaskaitz *adj.* difficult to learn.

ikaskari *n.* assignment, learning material.

ikaskera *n.* study method, learning method.

ikasketa *n.* study, apprenticeship.

ikaskide *n.* schoolmate, fellow student.

ikaskintza *n.* instruction, study, apprenticeship.

ikaskizun *n.* lesson to be learned, study material, learning material.

ikaskor *adj.* studious, scholarly, fond of studying.

ikaskuntza *n.* studies, learning, course of studies, major.

ikaslagun *n.* schoolmate, fellow student.

ikaslari *n.* student.

ikaslaritza *n.* occupation of student.

ikasle *n.* student, pupil, disciple.

ikaslego *n.* occupation of student. *n.* class, group of students.

ikasleku *n.* school, learning center.

ikasleria *n.* group of students.

ikasletalde *n.* group of students.

ikasletza *n.* occupation of student, discipleship.

ikasmahai *n.* study table, desk.

ikasmen *n.* capacity for learning.

ikasmin *n.* desire to study. *adj.* anxious to learn.

ikasnahai *n.* studiousness, desire to study.

ikaspen *n.* study, apprenticeship, instruction.

ikastalde *n.* group of students, class.

ikastaldi *n.* study time (semester, school year or any unit of time).

ikastaro *n.* school year; course. *n.*

apprenticeship period.

ikaste *n.* act of learning, studying.

ikastegi *n.* school, learning center.

ikasterraz *adj.* easy to learn.

ikastetxe *n.* school, college.

ikastetxebarneko *adj.* intramural (schools).

ikastetxeko *adj.* pertaining to school, collegiate.

ikastezin(ezko) *adj.* impossible to learn, unlearnable.

ikastezintasun *n.* impossibility of learning something.

ikastola *n.* Basque school.

ikastolaurreko *n.* preschool.

ikastun *n.* student, scholar. *adj.* wise, erudite, learned.

ikasturte *n.* school year, academic course.

ikatz *n.* coal, charcoal.

ikatz egin *v.t.* to make charcoal.

ikatzegurmeta *n.* pile of wood used in making charcoal.

ikatzerrauts *n.* small piece of coal, piece of coal which has been almost totally consumed.

ikatzulo *n.* coal bin.

ikazbizi *n.* glowing ember, red hot coal.

ikazgela *n.* coal bin.

ikazkai *n.* material used to make charcoal.

ikazketa *n.* charcoal making. *n.* pile of charcoal.

ikazketari *n.* charcoal carrier; coal carrier.

ikazki *n.(chem.)* carbon.

ikazkin *n.* charcoal maker.

ikazkintza *n.* occupation of charcoal maker.

ikazpaper *n.* carbon paper.

ikazsaltzaile *n.* charcoal seller.

ikaztegi *n.* coal yard, charcoal shop.

ikaztobi *n.* hole in the forest where charcoal is made.

ikaztoki *n.* coal yard, charcoal shed.

ikaztu *v.t./v.i.* to carbonize, to char.

ikaztun *n.* coal seller, charcoal seller. *adj.* carboniferous.

ikerbide *n.* experimentation, exploration, investigation.

ikergabe *adj.* unexplored.

ikergai *n.* research subject, topic for investigation.

ikergaitz *adj.* difficult to investigate, inscrutable.

ikergarri *adj.* explorable, investigable, researchable.

ikergarritasun *n.* quality of being researchable, quality of being investigable.

ikerketa *n.* research, investigation. *n.* inspection, scrutiny.

ikerketari *n.* investigator, researcher.

ikerkor *adj.* exploratory, investigative.

ikerkunde *n.* inspection, investigation. *n.(eccl.)* Feast of the Visitation.

ikerkuntza *n.* research, investigation.

ikerlan *n.* research (work).

ikerlari *n.* investigator, researcher. *n.* examiner, inspector; visitor.

ikerle *n.* investigator, researcher. *n.* examiner, inspector; visitor.

ikermen *n.* investigation, research. *n.* inspection, examination. *n.* experiment.

ikerpen *n.* investigation, research. *n.* inspection, examination.

ikerraldi *n.* exploring, inspecting, checking.

ikertaldi *n.* visit.

ikertezin(ezko) *adj.* uninvestigable, unexplorable, unresearchable.

ikertoki *n.* research center.

ikertu *v.t.* to research, to investigate, to explore. *v.t.* to visit.

ikertzaile *n.* investigator, researcher.

ikertzapen *n.* investigation, study, research.

ikerzale *adj.* fond of investigation, fond of research.

-iko *(gram.)* Suffix used to form verbal adjectives. **Nik ekarririko liburua.** The book that I brought.

ikuilu *n.* stable.

ikur *n.* symbol, sign.

ikurrin *n.* flag. *n.(pol.)* Basque flag.

ikurrindun *n./adj.* flag bearer.

ikurrineztu *v.t.* to cover with flags.

ikurrinmakila *n.* flagpole.

ikurrinpetu *v.t.* to register a ship under a flag, to sail under a flag.

ikurrintxo *n.(dim.)* small Basque flag.

ikurritz *n.* motto, maxim, slogan.

ikurton *n.* sacrament.

ikusbera *adj.* curious, watchful.

ikusbide *n.* vision, sight; view, scenery.

ikusentzungailu *n.* audio-visual machine.

ikusentzuteko *adj.* audio-visual.

ikuserazpen *n.* persuasion.

ikusezin *adj.* invisible. *n.* invisibility. *n.* animosity, hostility, enmity, aversion.

ikusezintasun *n.* invisibility.

ikusgai *adj.* visible.

ikusgailu *n.* visual apparatus.

ikusgaitasun *n.* visibility.

ikusgale *adj.* curious. *n.* curiosity.

ikusgarri *adj.* visible. *adj.* worthy of being seen, scenic, spectacular. *adj.* marvelous, magnificent, admirable.

ikusgarriki *adv.* visibly, scenically.

ikusgarriro *adv.* visibly, scenically. *adv.* admirably.

ikusgarritasun *n.* visibility; scenicness.

ikusgela *n.* visitor's room, consulting room, examination room.

ikusgelaurre *n.* anteroom, vestibule, waiting room.

ikusgune *n.* lookout point, place from which the view can be seen. *n.* view, that which can be seen.

ikusgura n. desire to see, curiosity. adj. curious.

ikusi v.t. to see, to view, to look. v.t. to visit. v.t. to notice, to realize. n. look, glance.

ikusiarte int. good-bye, until we see each other again (usually a long separation).

ikusi-makusi n. children's guessing game in which one player gives the clues (usually the first and last letter of an object) and the other players try to guess the name of the object.

ikuska adv. seeing, looking; spying.

ikuska egon v.i. to spy on, to keep a vigil.

ikuskai n. spectacle, sight, vision.

ikuskailu n. binoculars.

ikuskaitz adj. invisible, difficult to see.

ikuskapen n. inspection, examination.

ikuskari n. vision, spectacle, sight.

ikuskaseta n. videocassette.

ikuskatu v.t. to explore, to investigate, to search. v.t. to watch (over), to spy on, to supervise. v.t. to visit.

ikuskatzaile n. inspector. n. visitor. n. searcher, explorer.

ikuskera n. means of seeing, vision, sight.

ikusketa n. act of seeing, vision, sight. n. visit.

ikusketari n. visitor.

ikuskizun n. spectacle, panorama; vision, sight.

ikuskor adj. curious. adj. visible.

ikuslari n. spectator, viewer. n. eyewitness.

ikuslaritza n. inspector's job.

ikusle n. spectator, viewer. n. eyewitness.

ikusleku n. lookout point, place from which view can be seen; mirador, balcony.

ikusleria n. group of spectators.

ikusliar n. visitor.

ikusmen n. sense of sight, vision, sight.

ikusmenezko adj. visual.

ikusmin n. curiosity. adj. curious.

ikusminez adv. curiously.

ikusmira n. observation point; viewpoint.

ikusmiraketa n. act of scrutinizing, act of investigating, act of examining.

ikusmiratu v.t. to scrutinize, to inspect, to search; to pry.

ikusmiratzaile n. scrutinizer, examiner.

ikusmolde n. perspective.

ikusmuga n. horizon.

ikusnahi n. desire to see, curiosity.

ikuspegi n. panorama, scenery. n. perspective, viewpoint.

ikuspegizko adj. panoramic, scenic.

ikuspen n. vision, seeing. n. consideration.

ikuspuntu n. point of view, viewpoint, perspective.

ikustaile n. eyewitness. n. spectator, viewer.

ikustaldi n. visit, visiting time.

ikustapen n. vision, sight, act of seeing. n. visit.

ikustari n. visitor, explorer.

ikustatu v.t. to visit, to make frequent visits. v.t. to inspect, to explore.

ikuste n. act of seeing.

ikusteko adj. worthy of being seen; beautiful, spectacular, admirable. n. optic instrument (glasses, etc.).

ikustezin adj. invisible.

ikustezin(ezko) adj. invisible.

ikustezintasun n. invisibility.

ikustoki n. balcony, spectator's gallery.

ikustordu n. visiting hour, office hour, appointment.

ikuzaldi n. act of washing, cleaning.

ikuzdura n. act of washing, cleaning.

ikuzgai n. laundry. n. cleaning substance, laundry soap, detergent.

ikuzgailu n. washer, dishwasher, (clothes) washing machine.

ikuzgaitz adj. unwashable.

ikuzgarri adj. washable, purifiable.

ikuzi v.t. to wash, to clean.

ikuzketa n. act of washing, wash, purification, cleaning. n. pile of laundry.

ikuzkin n. residue of washing (lint, dirty water).

ikuzkizun n. laundry, dirty laundry.

ikuzle n. cleaner, washer, washerwoman, laundryman.

ikuzleku n. laundry room, washing place; sink.

ikuzpen n. act of washing.

ikuztailu n. washer, dishwasher, (clothes) washing machine.

ikuztaldi n. act of washing. n. time spent washing or cleaning.

ikuztarri n. washing stone.

ikuztegi n. laundry room, washing place.

ikuztezin n. unwashable, uncleanable.

ikuztohol n. washboard.

ikuztoki n. laundry room, washing place.

ikuztontzi n. wash tub, bucket, washing basin.

ilar n. (bot.) pea.

ilara n. line, row.

ilaran adv. in a row.

ilargi n. moon.

ilargialdi n. lunar cycle.

ilargiberri n. new moon.

ilargibete n. full moon.

ilargibide n. lunar orbit.

ilargierdi n. half moon.

ilargijo n. lunatic.

ilargiko adj. lunar, of the moon.

ilargiraketa n. lunar landing, act of landing on the moon.

ilargiratu v.i. to land on the moon.

ilargitan *adv.* by moonlight.

ilargitar *n.* supposed inhabitant of the moon.

ilargiurbil *n.(astron.)* perigee.

ilaun *n.* whitish ash. *adj.* ephemeral, transient.

ilaundu *v.i./v.t.* to reduce to ash; to destroy. *v.i.* to lose flavor, to weaken (flavor, etc.).

ilbeltz *n.* January.

ildo *n.* rut, furrow. *n.(fig.)* road, direction, way.

ildokatu *v.t.* to plow, to furrow, to till.

ildoki *n.* part of a branch, chunk of wood, club.

ile *n.* hair; fur.

ile(a) apaindu *v.t.* to fix the hair, to comb or brush the hair.

ileadats *n.* long hair, head of hair, lock of hair.

ilealdatze *n.* change in the condition of the hair.

ile(a) moztu *v.t.* to cut hair, to get a haircut; to shear sheep.

ileapaindegi *n.* hairdresser's shop, beauty parlor.

ileapainketa *n.* hairdo, hair style.

ileapaintzaile *n.* barber, hairdresser.

ile(a) zuritu *v.i.* to turn white, to go gray.

iledi *n.* head of hair, lock of hair.

iledun *adj.* hairy.

ilegabezia *n.* baldness, lack of hair.

ilegorri *n.* red hair. *adj.* red-haired, redheaded.

ilehodi *n.* capillary, blood vessel.

ilekorda *n.* hair braid.

ilekordatu *v.t.* to braid the hair.

ilelokarri *n.* hair tie, hair clasp, ribbon.

ilemataza *n.* lock of hair, hank of hair.

ilemotots *n.* hair braid.

ilemozketa *n.* act of cutting hair.

ilemozkin *n.* hairdresser, barber, haircutter.

ilemozkintza *n.* occupation of barber or hairdresser.

ilemozle *n.* barber, hairdresser, haircutter.

ilemoztaile *n.* barber, hairdresser; sheep clipper, sheepshearer.

ilemoztailu *n.* hair clippers, shears.

ilemozte *n.* haircut.

ilemoztegi *n.* hairdresser's shop, barber shop.

ilenahasi *n.* messy hair, unkempt hair.

ileorde *n.* wig, postiche, toupee.

ilepilo *n.* thick hair, mop of hair.

ilesare *n.* hair net.

iletsu *adj.* hairy, woolly.

iletxo *n.(dim.)* small hair.

iletxorta *n.* hair braid.

ileurdin *adj.* grey-haired.

ileurdindu *v.i.* to become gray-haired, to go gray.

ileurdinketa *n.* grayness, graying of the hair.

ileurdintasun *n.* gray-headedness.

ileurkula *n.* hairpin.

ilezuri *adj.* white-haired.

ilezuridun *adj.* white-haired.

ilezuriketa *n.* act of going gray, act of turning white (hair).

ilezuritasun *n.* white-hairedness, grayness.

ilezutidura *n.* messiness of the hair, disarray, disheveling of the hair.

ilinti *n.* half-burned stick, burning wood, firebrand.

ilintikada *n.* blow with a burning stick.

ilintitegi *n.* heap or pile of half-burned wood.

ilintitu *v.t.* to stir up a fire.

ilintitxo *n.(dim.)* small half-burned stick.

ilintxa *n.* wheat smut. *n.* half-burnt wood or tree.

ilki *v.i.* to leave, to go out.

ilkialdi *n.* time to leave, time to go.

ilkibide *n.* exit. *n.* way out, means of escape.

ilkipen *n.* going out, leaving.

iloba *n.* nephew, niece.

ilobahidego *n.* state of being a nephew or a niece.

ilobatasun *n.* state of being a nephew or a niece.

ilobatxo *n.(dim.)* little nephew, little niece.

iltzatu *v.t.* to nail.

iltze *n.* nail. *n.* hangover. *n.(fig.)* difficulty, problem.

iltze(a) atera *v.t.* to take out a nail.

iltzeburu *n.* head of a nail.

iltzedun *adj.* full of nails.

iltzegile *n.* maker of nails.

iltzegin *n.* maker of nails.

iltzegintza *n.* nail manufacturing.

iltzemotz *n.* short nail, tack.

iltzeria *n.* bunch of nails.

iltzetegi *n.* nail store, hardware store.

iltzeztatu *v.t.* to nail.

ilun *n.* darkness, dark. *adj.* dark, shady. *adj.* obscure, difficult to understand, vague. *adj.* sad.

ilunabar *n.* sunset, sundown, twilight.

ilunabarreko *adj.* sunset, twilight, crepuscular.

ilunabartu *v.t.* to grow dark, to become evening.

ilunalde *n.* evening, twilight, sunset.

ilunaldi *n.* darkening, obscuring, blackening. *n.(astron.)* eclipse. *n.(fig.)* obscured reason, confusion. *n.(fig.)* sadness, melancholy, affliction.

ilunarazi *v.t.* to darken, to dim. *v.t.(fig.)* to make sad, to make melancholy.

ilunbe *n.* darkness, obscurity.

ilunbeko *adj.* dark, shadowy, shady.

ilunbeltz *adj.* very dark, gloomy, darkly shadowed. *adj.(fig.)* sad, gloomy, depressed.

ilunbera *adj.* lugubrious, mournful, sad.

ilunbetsu *adj.* dark, cloudy, obscure. *adj.* gloomy, sad, funereal, lugubrious.

ilunbetu *v.t.* to get dark, to grow dim, to darken.

ilunbezko *adj.* dark, gloomy, obscure.

ilundu *v.t.* to darken, to get dark; to eclipse; to turn out the light. *v.t.* to dye. *v.i./v.t.(fig.)* to get angry, to anger, to worry, to sadden. *v.i.* to tan, to become dark.

ilundura *n.* darkening. *n.* sadness, melancholy.

ilungarri *adj.* somber, lugubrious, depressing, saddening.

ilungune *n.* dark spot.

ilunkeria *n.* obscurantism, opposition to the spreading of knowledge among the people.

ilunki *adv.* obscurely, vaguely, confusedly.

ilun-milun *adj.* having a sad face, sad-looking.

ilun-milunka *adv.* at twilight, in the last light of the day.

ilunpe *n.* darkness, obscurity. *n.(fig.)* jail.

ilunpean *adv.* darkly, obscurely.

ilunpeko *adj.* dark, shaded, shadowy. *adj.* secret, occult, hidden.

ilunpetu *v.t.* to darken, to get dark; to eclipse; to turn out the light.

ilunsenti *n.* sunset, twilight, dusk.

ilunska *adj.* darkish, somewhat dark.

iluntasun *n.* darkness, state of being dark, obscurity. *n.(fig.)* sadness.

iluntsu *adj.* shady, dark, darkened. *adj.* sad, melancholic.

iluntze *n.* sunset, evening, twilight; act of getting dark.

iluntzean *adv.* in the evening, at dark, at dusk, at sunset.

iluntzero *adv.* every evening at dusk.

ilunzale *adj.* fond of darkness.

imajina *n.* statue, image.

iman *n.* magnet

imanburdina *n.* magnetized iron.

imanburu *n.* magnetic pole.

imandu *v.t.* to magnetize, to make magnetic.

imandura *n.* magnetization.

imanezpen *n.* magnetization.

imaneztatu *v.t.* to magnetize, to make magnetic.

imangarri *adj.* magnetizable.

imanketa *n.* magnetization.

imanorratz *n.* magnetic needle.

imitaezin *adj.* inimitable.

imitagarri *adj.* worthy of being imitated, imitable, exemplary.

imitapen *n.* imitation.

imitatu *v.t.* to imitate.

imitatzaile *n.* imitator.

imitazio *n.* imitation, reproduction.

imurtxi *n.* pinch, pinching.

imurtxi egin *v.t.* to pinch.

imurtxika *adv.* pinching.

imurtxikada *n.* pinch, act of pinching.

inarrosi *v.t.* to shake, to agitate.

inarroska *adv.* shaking.

inarroskatu *v.t.* to shake, to stir, to agitate.

inarrosketa *n.* agitation, shaking.

inarrospen *n.* shake, shaking, agitation.

inauguratu *v.t.* to inaugurate, to open (buildings, etc.).

inaurkin *n.* dead branches and leaves; underbrush.

inbasio *n.* invasion.

inbertitu *v.t.(econ.)* to invest.

inbertitzaile *n.* investor.

inbertsio *n.(econ.)* investment.

inbitazio *n.* invitation.

indaba *n.(bot.)* bean.

indar *n.* strength, vitality, vigor, force. *n.* authority, influence, prestige. *n.* impetus, vigor; courage. *n.* vitality. *n.* power, electricity.

indarberritu *v.i./v.t.* to recover strength, to recuperate, to renew vigor, to invigorate. *v.i./v.t.* to renovate, to renew, to rejuvenate.

indarbide *n.* remedy, cure.

indardun *adj.* strong, powerful, robust, vigorous. *adj.* in force, valid.

indardura *n.* fortification, strengthening.

indar egin *v.t.* to try, to make an effort, to force.

indar eman *v.t.* to fortify, to strengthen.

indargabe *adj.* weak, exhausted; flat (carbonation). *adj.* null, revoked, void.

indargabetasun *n.* weakness, debility. *n.* ineffectiveness.

indargabetu *v.t./v.i.* to weaken, to debilitate. *v.t./v.i.* to invalidate, to become invalid, to nullify, to annul.

indargabezia *n.* weakness, lack of vigor.

indargarri *adj.* strengthening, fortifying; healthy, nutritious.

indargegailu *n.(mech.)* shock absorber.

indargetasun *n.* weakness, lack of vigor.

indargetu *v.i./v.t.* to weaken; to become weak; to go flat (people and beverages); to cushion (a blow). *v.t.* to annul, to invalidate.

indargetzaile *adj.* muffling, softening, absorbing, cushioning. *n.* cushion, damper, muffler.

indarka *adv.* forcedly, by force, involuntarily, violently.

indarkaldi *n.* struggle, strife.

indarkatu *v.t.* to struggle, to strive. *v.t.* to force, to coerce, to oblige to do.

indarkeria *n.* violence, coercion, cruelty.

indarketa *n.* struggle, strife. *n.* contest of strength. *n.* reinforcing,

strengthening.
indarkor *adj.* strengthening, fortifying.
indarneurkin *n.(mech.)* dynamometer.
indarperatu *v.t.* to conquer by force.
indarraldi *n.* force, courage, vigor.
indarremale *adj./n.* reinforcing,
　strengthening; helper, supporter.
indarrez *adv.* strongly, with strength,
　by power, under power. *adv.*
　violently, by force.
indarrezko *adj.* violent, strong,
　forceful. *adj.* in force, standing, valid.
indarrikara *n.* terrorism.
indartasun *n.* energy, vitality, vigor,
　strength.
indarti *v.t.* strong, robust.
indartsu *adj.* strong, robust. *adj.*
　powerful, potent.
indartu *v.t./v.i.* to strengthen, to
　reinforce; to invigorate; to become
　strong. *v.t.* to confirm, to
　consolidate.
indartzaile *adj.* strengthening,
　reinforcing, fortifying.
indarztatu *v.t.* to fortify, to invigorate,
　to strengthen.
indemnizapen *n.* compensation,
　indemnity.
indemnizatu *v.t.* to compensate
　(someone for something), to
　indemnify.
indemnizazio *n.(econ.)* compensation,
　indemnity.
independentzia *n.* independence.
indi- Used in compound words to
　indicate that the product or object is
　from America. Derived from India.
India *n.(geog.)* India.
Indiak *n.(geog.)* America, the
　Americas.
indiano *n.* Basque who has made
　money in America and returned to the
　Basque Country.
indiar *n.* bean. *adj.* American Indian;
　East Indian.
indioilanda *n.(zool.)* young turkey.
indioilar *n.(zool.)* turkey; peacock.
indioilasko *n.(zool.)* young turkey.
indioilo *n.(zool.)* turkey (hen).
indizio *n.* shot, injection.
indoeuropar *adj.* Indo-European.
induska *adv.* rooting up, digging with
　the snout.
induskada *n.* act of rooting up or
　digging with the snout.
induskari *n.* rooter, one that digs with
　the snout.
induskatu *v.t.* to root up, to dig with
　the snout.
indusketa *n.* act of uprooting or
　digging with the snout; excavation.
induspen *n.* act of uprooting or digging
　with the snout; excavation.
industri *adj.* industrial.
industria *n.* industry.
industrialeztapen *n.* industrialization.
industrialeztatu *v.t.* to industrialize.

industrialki *adv.* industrially.
industriari *n.* industrialist.
industrigintza *n.* industrialization.
industrigintzako *adj.* industrial.
inertzia *n.(phys.)* inertia.
infekzio *n.* infection.
infernu *n.* hell.
inflazio *n.(econ.)* inflation.
inflazio-joera *n.* inflationary tendency.
inflazio-neurriak *n.* inflationary
　measures.
informaketa *n.* act of informing.
informatu *v.t.* to inform.
informatzaile *n./adj.* informer;
　informative.
informazio *n.* information.
ingeles *n.* Englishman, Britisher. *n.*
　English language. *adj.* English.
ingeles-amerikar *adj.* Anglo-American.
ingeleste *n.* Anglicization.
ingelesesaera *n.* Anglicism.
ingelesetsai *n.* Anglophobe.
ingelesgorroto *n.* Anglophobia.
ingeleskada *n.* Anglicism.
ingeleskeria *n.* Anglicism (pejorative).
ingeleszale *adj.* Anglophile.
ingeleszaletasun *n.* Anglophilia.
ingira *n.* disposition. *n.* repugnance.
ingiratu *v.t.* to prepare, to make ready.
　v.i. to be disgusted.
ingude *n.* anvil.
ingudeaulki *n.* anvil stand.
ingudetxo *n.(dim.)* small anvil.
inguma *n.* butterfly.
ingumar *n.(zool.)* silkworm.
ingurakatu *v.t.* to situate, to surround.
inguraketa *n.* siege, blockade.
inguralde *n.* surroundings, vicinity,
　environs.
inguraldeko *adj.* peripheral.
inguraldi *n.* surrounding,
　encirclement.
inguramendu *n.* environment.
ingurapen *n.* fencing, enclosing.
inguratu *v.t.* to corral, to surround, to
　encircle. *v.t.* to wrap, to gird, to belt.
　v.i. to approach, to come close, to
　draw near.
inguratzaile *n.* besieger.
ingurikatu *v.t.* to besiege, to blockade.
ingurrazti *n.* notebook.
inguru *n.* surroundings, vicinity,
　outskirts, environs, environment.
inguru`aldi *n.* round, circular trip or
　path.
inguruan *adv./prep.* around, by, in the
　area of, near.
ingurubide *n.* ring road.
ingurubilka *adv.* in a spiral, spiraling.
ingurubilkatu *v.t.* to spiral.
ingurubilketa *n.* act of spiraling.
ingurubira *n.* circle, circling.
ingurugiro *n.* atmosphere,
　environment.
inguruka *adv.* circling, spiraling. *adv.*
　using circumlocution, periphrasing.
ingurukari *n.* surrounder, one who

circles.

ingurukatu v.t. to circle, to surround. v.t. to besiege, to maraud.

ingurukeria n. evasiveness, evasion, subterfuge.

inguruketa n. encircling, surrounding.

inguruko adj. near, neighboring, next to, proximate. adj. encircling, surrounding, around.

ingurumari n. surroundings, environs.

ingurumariak n.(pl.) surroundings, environs.

ingurumen n. environment, outskirts, surroundings.

ingurumendu n. encircled area.

inguru-minguru n. meander, curve, bend (of a river). n. subterfuge, evasion, roundabout way of talking, circumlocution.

inguru-minguruak n. curves, bends, meanderings (of a river, etc.).

ingurune n. surroundings, environs, environment.

ingurupen n. surrounding, encircling.

ingurutren n. local train.

injineru n. engineer.

injinerutza n. profession of engineer, engineering.

injustizia n. injustice.

inkesta n. inquest, investigation, inquiry, poll, study, survey.

inkestagarri adj. investigable.

inkestalari n. researcher, pollster, inquirer.

inkestatu v.t. to make an inquest, to inquire, to poll.

inkestatzaile n. inquirer, investigator, pollster.

inmigraketa n. immigration.

inmigraketazko adj. immigratory.

inmigratu v.i. to immigrate.

inmigratzaile n. immigrant.

inoiz adv. ever. adv. never (in negative sentences).

inoiz edo behin adv. from time to time, at one time or another.

inoiz ere ez adv. never, ever.

inoiz ez adv. never.

inoizka adv. from time to time, sometimes.

inoizkako adj. occasional.

inola adv. in some way, somehow. adv. in any way, anyhow, in no way, not at all (used usually in negative sentences).

inola ere ez adv. in any manner, at all, in no way, no way.

inolako adj. not any kind, at all, whatsoever, of any kind.

inolaz adv. in some way, somehow (in affirmative and interrogative sentences). adv. in no way, not in any way, absolutely note (in negative sentences).

inon adv. somewhere, anywhere, someplace, anyplace. adv. no place, nowhere, anywhere (usually in negative sentences).

inondik inora adv. absolutely not.

inon ere ez adv. nowhere, in no place, not . . . anywhere.

inon ez adv. nowhere, not anywhere.

inongo adj. from anywhere.

inor pron. someone, anyone, anybody (in affirmative or interrogative sentences). pron. no one, nobody, anyone (in negative sentences).

inora adv. (to) some place, somewhere, anywhere. adv. (to) no place, nowhere, anywhere (in negative sentences).

inora ere ez adv. (to) any place, anywhere, no place, nowhere.

inoren pron.(genit.) someone's, someone else's, anyone's (in affirmative and interrogative sentences). pron.(genit.) no one's, anyone's (in negative sentences with ez).

inorendu v.i. to become alienated, to become estranged.

inorenganatu v.t./v.i. to alienate, to estrange, to make someone lose his self control; to become alienated. v.t. to transmit (something) to another person.

inor ere ez pron. no one, nobody, not anyone.

inorgabe adj. vacant, uninhabited, deserted.

inorgabeko adj. vacant, uninhabited, deserted.

inork pron. somebody, someone (active subject of transitive verb in affirmative and interrogative sentences). pron. nobody, no one (active subject of transitive verb in negative sentences).

inozo adj. naive, gullible. adj. stupid, foolish, silly.

inozokeria n. stupidity, foolishness, foolish things.

inozoketa n. naive or foolish speech or action.

inozoki adv. stupidly, foolishly.

inozotasun n. naivety, foolishness, stupidity.

inozotu v.i. to become naive, to become foolish or stupid. v.i. to be cowed, to be intimidated.

inperialismo n. imperialism.

inportazio n.(econ.) import.

inposaketa n. act of imposing, imposition.

inposatu v.t. to impose.

inpresio n. impression.

inpresionismo n. impressionism.

inprimagintza n. printing.

inprimaketa n. printing, act of printing.

inprimailu n. printing press.

inprimategi n. printshop, press.

inprimatu v.t. to print, to publish. v.t. to imprint.

inprimatzaile n. printer.

inskribatu *v.t./v.i.* to register, to sign up.
inskripzio *n.* registration.
inspektore *n.* inspector.
inspekzio *n.* inspection.
instalazio *n.* installation, plant, factory. *n.* installation, setting up.
institutu *n.* institute.
instituzio *n.* institution.
integragarri *adj.* integrable.
integrakuntza *n.* integration.
integratu *v.t./v.i.* to integrate.
integratzaile *adj.* integrative.
integrazio *n.* integration.
interbentore *n.* controller.
interbentzio *n.* intervention.
interes *n.(econ.)* interest.
interesatu *v.i.* to become interested.
interesdun *adj.* interested.
interesgabe *adj.* disinterested.
interesgabetu *v.i.* to become disinterested, to lose interest.
interesgabezia *n.* disinterest.
interesgarri *adj.* interesting.
intereskide *n.* person with the same interests.
internazionalismo *n.* internationalism.
interpretazio *n.* interpretation.
intsektu *n.* insect.
intsentsaketa *n.* act of spreading incense.
intsentsaldi *n.* incensing.
intsentsari *n.* censer-bearer.
intsentsatu *v.t.* to incense.
intsentsatzaile *n.* censer-bearer, incenser.
intsentsontzi *n.* censer, thurible.
intsentsu *n.* incense.
intsentsualdi *n.* incensing.
intsentsudun *adj.* incense-bearing.
intsentsuontzi *n.(eccl.)* navicula (metal incense holder shaped like a boat).
intsulina *n.(med.)* insulin.
intsusa *n.(bot.)* elder tree, elderberry.
intsusadi *n.* grove of elder trees.
intsusondo *n.(bot.)* elder tree.
intxarri *n.* baby's rattle.
intxarrots *n.* charivari, tin-pan serenade, shivaree.
intxaur *n.(bot.)* walnut.
intxaur arbola *n.(bot.)* walnut tree.
intxaurdi *n.* grove of walnut trees.
intxaurdun *adj.* walnut-bearing, nutty.
intxaurki *n.* meat of the walnut. *n.* walnut wood.
intxaurkolore *adj.* walnut-colored.
intxaurmami *n.* walnut meat.
intxaurmargo *n.* walnut brown color.
intxaurrazal *n.* walnut shell.
intxaurrondo *n.(bot.)* walnut tree.
intxaurroskol *n.* walnut shell.
intxaursaltsa *n.* walnut sauce.
intxaurtinta *n.* walnut brown color.
intxaurtza *n.* grove of walnut trees.
intzigar *n.* frost.
intzigarra egin *v.t.* to freeze, to frost.
intziri *n.* groan, moan, sigh. *n.* wail,

howl.
intziri egin *v.t.* to groan, to moan, to sigh. *v.t.* to wail, to howl.
intzirika *adv.* screaming, wailing.
intzirikari *n.* screamer, shouter, crier.
intzirikatu *v.i.* to groan, to moan.
inude *n.* wet nurse.
inudetu *v.t.* to wet nurse, to nurse another's child.
inudetza *n.* job or position of a wet nurse.
inular *n.* sunset, evening, twilight.
inurria *n.* heath.
inurritegi *n.* ant hill.
inurritu *v.i.* to feel prickly, to tingle.
inuzente *adj.* stupid, foolish, gullible. *n.* idiot, fool, mental defective.
inuzentekeria *n.* foolishness, stupidity, idiocy.
inza *n.* heath.
iodo *n.(chem.)* iodine.
ipar *adj.* north, northern. *n.* north wind (however, used by Basque fishermen for east wind).
iparbeltz *n.* cold, strong north wind.
iparburu *n.(geog.)* North Pole.
iparburuko *adj.* polar.
ipargorri *n.* cold north wind.
iparmendebal *n.* northwesterly wind.
iparmendebalde *n.* northwest.
iparmendebaleratu *v.i.* to go in a northwesterly direction.
iparraize *n.* north wind (however, used by Basque fishermen for east wind).
iparraizete *n.* time of northeasterly wind, northeaster.
iparralde *n.* North; the northern Basque country; northern region.
iparraldeko *adj.* northern, nordic; from the north of the Basque country.
Iparramerika *n.(geog.)* North America.
iparrekialde *n.* northeast.
iparreko *adj.* northern, nordic.
iparreratu *v.i.* to go north.
iparrizar *n.(astron.)* North Star.
iparrorratz *n.* compass.
iparsartalde *n.(geog.)* northwest.
iparsartalderatu *v.i.* to go northwest.
iparsortalde *n.* northeast.
iparsortalderatu *v.i.* to go northeast.
ipartar *adj.* north, northern. *n.* northerner.
ipingarri *adj.* placeable, capable of being put or placed somewhere.
ipingi *n.* patch.
ipini *v.t.* to place, to put; to put on (clothing).
ipintzaile *n.* installer, placer.
ipuin *n.* story, tale, legend.
ipuin(a) kontatu *v.t.* to tell stories.
ipuinezko *adj.* legendary, fable-like. *adj.* pretended, feigned, imaginary.
ipuingile *n.* fabulist, writer of fables.
ipuingintza *n.* narrative.
ipuinlari *n.* story teller.
ipuinsorta *n.* collection of stories, anthology of stories, short story

collection.

ipuintxo n.(dim.) little story, short story.

ipuintzale adj. story-loving.

ipurdi n.(anat.) buttocks, bottom, butt, bum, ass. n. bottom.

ipurdika adv. bouncing or sliding on the buttocks, by scooting, by bouncing on one's bottom.

ipurdikada n. blow to the buttocks (received in a fall).

ipurdikatu v.t. to turn upside down.

ipurdiko n. slap on the buttocks, spanking.

ipurditsu adj. having large buttocks.

ipurgarbitzaile adj./n. brown-nosing, fawning, adulating; brown-noser, fawner, adulator, sycophant.

ipurkada n. blow to the buttocks.

ipurkonkor n.(anat.) coccyx, tailbone.

ipurmasail n.(anat.) buttocks.

ipurpeko n. seat cushion; bicycle seat.

ipurt- Used in compound words. Derived from *ipurdi*, buttocks, bottom.

ipurtalde n. buttocks, rear.

ipurtandi adj. having large buttocks.

ipurtargi n.(zool.) glowworm (*Lampyris noctiluca*).

ipurtats n.(zool.) polecat (*Mustela putorius*).

ipurterre adj. impatient, restless, fretful, bad tempered.

ipurteste n.(anat.) rectal-intestine.

ipurtezur n.(anat.) coccyx, tailbone.

ipurtikara n.(anat.) white wagtail.

ipurtmami n. buttock(s), rump, flesh of the buttocks, cheek of the buttocks.

ipuroihal n. diaper.

ipurtxuntxur n.(anat.) coccyx, tailbone.

ipurtzapi n. diaper.

ipurtzulo n.(anat.) anus.

ipurtzuloko adj. anal.

ipuru n.(bot.) juniper tree.

ipuruki n. juniper wood, piece of juniper.

ipuruko n. yoke pad.

ipurzabal adj. having large buttocks.

ira n.(bot.) fern.

irabazbide n. profession, job, means of making a living, work, source of income.

irabazezin adj. difficult to win, hard to earn.

irabazgaitz adj. difficult to win, hard to earn.

irabazgarri adj. profitable.

irabazgarritasun n. profitableness.

irabazi v.t. to earn, to gain, to win, to win over, to triumph (over), to conquer. v.t. to grow, to grow up.

irabazidun adj. making a profit, profiting.

irabazitako adj. pertaining to earnings or profit, earned; profitable, lucrative.

irabazizko adj. pertaining to earnings

or profit, earned, profitable, lucrative.

irabazketa n. earnings, profit. n. victory.

irabazkin n. winnings, earnings, benefits, interest.

irabazkizun n. prospective earnings, that which will be earned.

irabazkoi adj. fond of wealth, money hungry.

irabazkor adj. lucrative, profitable.

irabazle adj. victorious, triumphant. n. winner, victor, champion.

irabazpen n. gain, profit. n. victory, triumph.

irabazpide n. job, work, occupation, business, source of income.

irabazpidezko adj. remunerative, paying.

irabazte n. act of profiting, act of gaining. n. earnings, profits, benefits.

irabazteko adj. lucrative, profitable, beneficial.

irabaztun n. winner, earner.

irabelar n.(bot.) wolfsbane, aconite, monkshood.

irabiagailu n. beater, mixer.

irabiaka adv. tumbling.

irabiamen n. beating (eggs, etc.). n. turning over.

irabiatu v.t. to beat, to mix. v.t. to turn over.

irabio n. beating, mixing, shaking.

irabiratu v.i./v.t. to turn over, to tip over, to upset (a boat).

iradi n. fern field.

iradoki v.t. to make (someone or something) leave, to entice away. v.t. to get out of, to wheedle (out of), to elicit.

iradokitzaile n. enticer, wheedler, one who draws out information.

iradokizun n. suggestion, enticement.

iradokor adj. suggestive, suggesting, enticing.

iragabide n. hallway, corridor.

iragaile n. passer, crosser; bargeman. n. pedestrian. adj. transitory, passing, migratory.

iragaite n. passage, passing; transition, transit; migration.

iragaiteko adj. passable, crossable.

iragaitza n. passage, crossing.

iragaitzaz adv. in passing, superficially.

iragaitzazko adj. transitory, passing, fleeting, migratory.

iragan v.t./v.i. to pass, to cross. v.i./v.t. to spend (time). n. past. v.t./v.i. to pass through, to put through.

iraganaldi n. past. n. transition, migration.

iraganaldiko adj. transitory, passing.

iraganarazi v.t. to cause to pass.

iraganbide n. pass, passage, crossing.

iraganez adv. in passing, transitorially.

iraganezin adj. impassable. adj.

untransferable.

iragangai adj. passable, crossable.

iragangaitz adj. impassable, difficult to pass. adj. durable, lasting, constant, permanent. adj.(gram.) intransitive.

iragangaiztasun n. quality of being impassable. n. endurance, durability.

iragangarri adj. passable, crossable.

iragangarritasun n. quality of being passable or crossable.

iraganketa n. passing, crossing.

iragankor adj. ephemeral, passing, transitory. adj.(gram.) transitive. adj. extinguishable, perishable.

iragankorki adv. transitorially, ephemerally, in passing.

iragankortasun n. ephemeralness, fleetingness, transitoriness.

iraganleku n. crossing, passage.

iragansari n. bridge toll, ferry toll.

iragantasun n. quality of being passable.

iragantxartel n. pass, safe-conduct.

iragarbide n. announcement, publicity.

iragarketa n. propaganda, publicity.

iragarki n. advertisement, ad, announcement, program.

iragarkizun n. forecast, guess, prediction.

iragarlari n. advertiser, announcer.

iragarle n. advertiser, announcer. n. forecaster; prophet.

iragarlesa n. prophetess, female prophet.

iragarmen n. prediction, forecast. n. gift of prophecy.

iragarpen n. announcement, warning, advertisement. n. prediction, forecast; prophecy.

iragarpentsu adj. prophetic, predicting, foretelling, foreboding.

iragarri v.t. to announce, to communicate, to advertise, to notify, to explain, to inform. v.t. to guess, to predict, to foretell, to forecast, to foresee.

iragazdura n. filtering, filtration.

iragazezin adj. impermeable, impenetrable.

iragazgailu n. filter, strainer, colander.

iragazi v.t./v.i. to filter, to strain. v.t./v.i. to penetrate, to soak, to drench; to get drenched.

iragazkaitz adj. impermeable, impenetrable.

iragazkaiztasun n. impermeability, the quality of being waterproof.

iragazkaiztu v.i./v.t. to be waterproof; to waterproof, to make waterproof.

iragazkarri adj. permeable, penetrable. adj. distillable, filterable.

iragazketa n. filtering, straining.

iragazki n. filter, colander, strainer.

iragazkin n. filter, strainer, colander.

iragazkor adj. filterable, permeable.

iragazkortasun n. permeability.

iragazle n. colander, filter, strainer.

iragazpaper n. filter paper.

iragazpen n. filtering, soaking, drenching.

iragaztegi n. refinery.

iragaztezin adj. impermeable, waterproof. adj. not filterable.

iragaztezintasun n. impermeability.

iragaztontzi n. strainer, colander, filter.

iraila n. September.

irain n. offense, injury, insult, infamy.

iraindu v.t. to insult, to offend, to injure.

iraingaizto n. invective, verbal abuse, denunciatory speech.

iraingarri adj. insulting, offensive, injurious, outrageous.

iraingile n. injurer, offender, insulter.

irainketa n. offending or insulting act.

irainkor adj. offensive, insulting.

irainordain n. vindication, reparation, satisfaction.

irainordaindu v.t. to right a wrong, to apologize, to compensate, to make compensation.

irainordainle n. apologizer, compensator, righter of wrongs, vindicator.

irainorde n. vindication, compensation, satisfaction.

iraintsu adj. injurious, offensive.

iraintzaile n. offender, insulter, defamer. adj. offensive, insulting, outrageous.

iraitzarazi v.t. to cause to throw, to make (someone) cast (something), to cause to eject.

iraitzi v.t. to throw, to hurl, to cast. v.t. to empty, to evacuate (the bowels), to leave. v.t. to reject, to dismiss; to repel; to dispossess. n. throw, cast, toss.

iraizgarri adj. rejectable, reproachable, condemnable.

iraizketa n. excretion. n. projection, throwing, ejection.

iraizkin n. excretory system or apparatus. n. projectile, missile.

iraizkor adj. evacuative, purgative, excretory.

iraizpen n. excretion; extraction; eradication. n. shot, blast. n. dismissal.

iraizpide n. excretory canal.

iraiztaile n. thrower, hurler, flinger.

iraiztaldi n. throwing, launching, casting, hurling, flinging, tossing.

iraizte n. act of casting or throwing. n. act of evacuating or emptying. n. act of shooting (a gun), act of firing (a weapon). n. act of rejecting or repelling.

iraka n.(bot.) darnel, weed.

irakasbide n. teaching method, pedagogy.

irakasgela n. classroom.

irakaskai n. educational matter.

irakasgarri adj. teachable; instructive,

educational.
irakaskera n. teaching method.
irakasketa n. teaching, education.
irakaskintza n. education, instruction; teaching profession.
irakaskizun n. teaching material, instructional matter.
irakaskoi adj. easily taught, tractable.
irakaskor adj. didactic, educational, instructive.
irakaskuntza n. teaching, education.
irakaslaritza n. teaching profession, education.
irakasle n. teacher, instructor, professor.
irakaslego n. faculty, group of professors. n. teaching, instruction.
irakasleria n. teaching faculty, group of professors.
irakaslesa n. female teacher, instructor, professor.
irakasletu v.i. to graduate, to become a teacher.
irakasletza n. teaching profession; teaching, education.
irakasmaila n. grade, level of education.
irakaspen n. instruction, teaching, education.
irakastaldi n. period of instruction.
irakaste n. act of teaching, instruction.
irakastegi n. teaching center, classroom, lecture hall.
irakasteko adj. didactic, pedagogical, instructive.
irakastetxe n. teaching center, school.
irakastoki n. teaching center, school. n. podium, lectern, place where one teaches.
irakatsi v.t. to teach, to instruct, to educate. v.t. to preach, to give a sermon. n. instruction, teaching.
irakidura n. act of boiling, bubbling, ebullition. n.(fig.) fervor, fire, vigor.
irakin v.t. to boil. v.t.(fig.) to fire with passion, to inflame, to become enraged. n.(fig.) fervor, fire, vigor.
irakinaldi n. boiling, ebullition.
irakinarazi v.t. to cause to boil.
irakindura n. boiling, ebullition. n.(fig.) anger, fervor, fire.
irakingai n. effervescent liquid, bubbly liquid. adj. effervescent, bubbly.
irakingarri adj. boilable. adj.(fig.) agitating, irritating, enraging.
irakinontzi n. pot for boiling water; barber's water pitcher for boiling water; chafing dish.
irakinots n. sound of boiling liquid.
irakintsu adj. boiling.
irakite n. boiling, bubbling, ebullition.
irakurgai n. reading, reading material.
irakurgaitz adj. difficult to read; illegible, undecipherable.
irakurgarri adj. readable, legible.
irakurgarritasun n. legibility, readability.

irakurgela n. reading room.
irakurketa n. reading.
irakurkizun n. reading material.
irakurlari n. reader, one who reads.
irakurlaritza n. office of lector, reader's job.
irakurle n. reader.
irakurlego n. group of readers. n. office of lector, reader's job.
irakurleria n. group of readers.
irakurpen n. act of reading.
irakurraldi n. reading, time of reading.
irakurri v.t. to read.
irakurterraz adj. easy to read.
irakurtezin adj. impossible to read, illegible.
irakurtu v.t. to read.
irakurtzaile n. reader, one who reads.
irameta n. tall cone shaped pile of ferns, fern heap.
irarketa n. printing, impression.
irarkola n. print shop, press.
irarri v.t. to print.
irasagar n.(bot.) quince.
irasagarrondo n.(bot.) quince tree.
irati n. fern field.
iratsi v.i. to adhere, to stick.
iratxeki v.t./v.i. to join, to put together, to weld, to solder; to adhere (to), to stick (to).
iratxekidura n. welding, soldering, joining; annexation.
iratxo n. elf, goblin, fairy; ghost.
iratzargailu n. alarm clock.
iratzargarri n. alarm clock. adj. stimulating, exciting, alarming, awakening.
iratzarle n. awakener, one who awakens. adj. stimulating, exciting, alarming.
iratzarmendu n. warning, exhortation, admonition.
iratzarpen n. awakening.
iratzarri v.i. to wake up, to awaken. v.t. to wake (up), to awaken. v.t.(fig.) to stimulate, to goad, to incite.
iratzi v.t. to filter, to strain. n. colander, strainer.
iraulaldi n. somersault, tumble, turning over, rolling, wallowing. n. plowing, overturning of the soil.
iraulgailu n. tipcart, dumpcart, tilt truck.
iraulgarri adj. capable of being overturned, tippable. adj. arable, plowable, tillable.
iraulgurdi n. tipcart, dumpcart, tilt truck.
irauli v.t. to turn over, to overturn; to alter, to change, to upset. v.t. to cultivate, to till, to plow.
iraulikatu v.i. to buck.
iraulka adv. throwing off, turning around. adv. rolling, wallowing.
iraulkalari n. acrobat.
iraulkatu v.t. to upset, to overturn, to tilt.

iraulketa *n.* inversion, overturning, upset. *n.* plowing, tilling. *n.* somersault, tumble.

iraulkor *adj.* rollable, slideable. *adj.* subversive, overturning.

iraulkortasun *n.* subversion, changeability, variability.

iraulpen *n.* overturning; whirling, revolving. *n.* plowing, tilling, working the soil.

iraultoki *n.* wallowing place for animals.

iraultza *n.* revolution, overthrow, subversion.

iraultzaile *n.(pol.)* overthrower, revolutionary. *adj.* revolutionary.

iraultzatu *v.t.* to revolt, to overthrow.

iraun *v.t.* to last, to endure, to persist, to continue, to be consistent; to survive. *v.t.* to suffer, to bear, to endure (pain, suffering).

iraunaldi *n.* duration, permanence. *n.* persistence, assiduousness.

iraunarazi *v.t.* to cause to last, to perpetuate, to maintain, to preserve, to conserve.

iraunarazle *n.* perpetuator, maintainer, preserver, conserver.

iraunarazte *n.* conservation, maintenance, preservation, perpetuation.

iraundura *n.* duration, conservation. *n.* firmness, stability, durability.

iraungabe(ko) *adj.* insubstantial, ephemeral, transient, discontinuous.

iraungarri *adj.* durable, lasting, permanent, constant. *adj.* tolerable, bearable, supportable.

iraungarriro *adv.* permanently, stably, lastingly.

iraungi *v.t.* to extinguish, to turn off, to put out. *v.i.* to debilitate, to weaken, to lessen.

iraungiera *n.* extinction, extinguishing, putting out, switching off, turning off.

iraungiezin *adj.* inextinguishable.

iraungigaitz *adj.* inextinguishable, undying.

iraungigaiztasun *n.* inextinguishableness, quality of being inextinguishable or undying.

iraungigarri *adj.* extinguishable, perishable.

iraungikor *adj.* extinguishable, perishable, expendable.

iraungikortasun *n.* perishability, transient quality, quality of being extinguishable.

iraungipen *n.* extinguishing.

iraungitu *v.i.* to extinguish, to go out, to finish, to end.

iraungitzaile *adj.* extinguishing, dying, going out.

iraunketa *adj.* endurance, permanence, constancy, perseverance.

iraunki *adv.* permanently, durably, for a long time.

iraunkiro *adv.* permanently, durably, for a long time.

iraunkor *adj.* durable, lasting, permanent, constant.

iraunkorki *adv.* durably, lastingly, stably, permanently, constantly.

iraunkortasun *n.* endurance, durability.

iraunkortu *v.i.* to become stable, to become permanent.

iraupen *n.* constancy, perseverance, persistence, subsistence. *n.* patience. *n.* firmness, fortitude, integrity.

iraupeneko *adj.* durable, lasting, permanent.

iraupengabe *adj.* inconstant, fleeting, perishable, inconsistent.

iraupengabeki *adv.* inconsistently.

iraupengabetasun *n.* inconstancy, inconsistency.

iraupentsu *adj.* constant, stable. *adj.* patient, long-suffering.

iraute *n.* permanence, durability, lastingness. *n.* fortitude, firmness.

irauteko *adj.* durable, persevering, constant, abiding, lasting.

irauti *adj.* tenacious, persistent, constant. *adj.* lasting, durable.

irazeki *v.t.* to light, to ignite, to fire, to set fire to.

irazgaitz *adj.* impermeable, impenetrable.

irazgaiztasun *n.* impermeability, impenetrability.

irazgaiztu *v.i.* to become impermeable, to become impenetrable.

irazgarri *n.* penetrable, permeable.

irazi *v.t./v.i.* to filter, to strain. *v.t.* to warp (yarn).

irazki *v.t.* to warp (yarn). *n.* warp, warping (of yarn).

irazkidura *n.* warping (of yarn).

irazkitu *v.t.* to weave; to warp.

irazpen *n.* filtration, act of refining, filtering or straining.

iraztontzi *n.* colander, filter, strainer.

ireki *v.t.* to open.

irekidura *n.* opening, gap, hole, crack.

irekiera *n.* opening, aperture, gap, hole; way of opening.

irekigailu *n.* opener, can opener, corkscrew.

irekigarri *adj.* openable, capable of being opened.

irekigune *n.* hole, aperture, opening.

irekitasun *n.* openness, quality of being open.

irekitzaile *n.* opener. *adj.* opening.

irekiune *n.* crack, narrow opening.

iren *adj.* castrated.

irenaldi *n.* castration, time of castration.

irendu *v.t.* to castrate, to geld, to fix (dogs, etc.). *adj.* castrated, fixed, gelded.

irenketa *n.* castration, act of

castrating.
irensbide n.(anat.) pharynx.
irensgarri adj. absorbent; absorbable; swallowable.
irenskor adj. voracious, devouring. adj.(fig.) destructive, destroying.
irenskortasun n. voracity, insatiability, insatiableness.
irensle n. devourer. adj. devouring, swallowing, voracious, engulfing.
irenste n. act of devouring, swallowing, deglutition.
irenstura n. absorption; swallowing.
irenstezin n. dysphagia, difficulty in swallowing.
irentsi v.t. to swallow, to gobble, to devour, to gulp down. v.t. to absorb, to suck. v.t.(fig.) to destroy, to ruin.
irentzaile n. castrator.
irin n. flour.
irindatu v.t. to flour, to cover or dust with flour, to powder (with flour).
irindegi n. flour mill. n. bread board.
irindu v.t. to grind, to mill, to make flour. v.t.(fig.) to pulverize.
irindun adj. floured, floury.
irineztadura n. act of flouring.
irineztatu v.i./v.t. to be covered with flour; to flour, to dip in flour, to cover with batter.
iringela n. sifting room (for flour).
irinkari n. flour carrier.
irinketari n. flour merchant.
irinkutxa n. flour bin, flour box.
irinore n. dough.
irintsu adj. floury, floured.
iriole n./adj. wasteful person, spendthrift; wasteful, squandering.
irion v.t. to waste, to squander.
irispen n. achievement, success, acquisition.
irispide n. way of getting, achieving or reaching something.
iriste n. act of getting, acquiring.
iritsi v.i. to arrive. v.t. to obtain, to reach, to get.
iritzezin adj. indisputable, inconceivable.
irla n. island, isle.
irlako adj. insular, pertaining to an island.
irlatar n. islander.
irlategi n. archipelago, group of islands.
irlatxo n.(dim.) islet, isle, small island.
irme adj. firm, solid, definite, stable.
irmo adj. firm, solid, definite, stable.
irmoki adv. firmly, solidly, definitely, surely.
irmotu v.t./v.i. to secure, to guarantee, to assure.
irmotasun n. firmness, strength.
iroi n. reproach, reproof.
iroiztatu v.t. to reproach, to reproof.
ironia n. irony.
ironiatsu adj. ironic.
ironizatu v.t. to ironize.

irradiaketa n. radiating, spreading.
irradiapen n. radiating, spreading.
irradiatu v.t. to radiate, to spread.
irrat- Used in compound words. Derived from irrati, radio.
irratailu n. radio, radio apparatus.
irratargailu n. radio, radio apparatus.
irratartegi n. radio station.
irratemandegi n. radio transmitter.
irratentzukin n. radio receiver, radio.
irratentzule n. radio listener.
irratetxe n. radio station.
irrati n. radio.
irratialdi n. radio broadcast.
irratidazki n. telegram.
irratigailu n. radio, radio apparatus.
irratigorpen n. radio transmission.
irratimezu n. radio message, announcement.
irratitelegrafari n. wireless operator.
irratitelegrafia n. wireless, radiotelegraphy.
irratitelegraflatu v.t. to send a message by wireless or radiotelegraphy, to send a wire.
irratitelegrafiko adj. wireless, radiotelegraphic.
irratitelegrama n. telegram.
irratitzaldi n. radio message, announcement.
irratizabalkunde n. radio transmission.
irratizain n. custodian of the radio station.
irratizko adj. pertaining to the radio.
irratsaio n. radio program, radio broadcast.
irratsaiotu v.t. to broadcast, to transmit.
irri n. malignant smile, laugh. n. joke, ridicule, jest; mockery.
irriantzerki n. theatrical farce.
irribarre n. smile.
irribarre egin v.t. to smile.
irribarreka adv. smilingly, with a smile.
irribartsu adj. smiley, full of smiles.
irribera adj. smiling.
irribide n. reason for smiling.
irribidez adv. smilingly.
irribidezko adj. laughable, ridiculous, ludicrous.
irri egin v.t. to joke, to make fun of, to ridicule.
irrieragile adj. funny, jovial, jocular.
irrigaizto n. derision, ridicule.
irrigarri adj. ridiculous, laughable, grotesque, derisive.
irrigarriro adv. jokingly, jestingly, ridiculously, laughably.
irrigarritasun n. laughableness, funniness.
irrigarritu v.t. to ridicule, to make ridiculous.
irrigile n. joker, jester, mocker, scoffer.
irrigura n. desire to laugh adj. wanting to laugh, jolly, good natured.
irrika n. desire, ambition. adv.

mockingly, jestingly.

irrikagarri *adj.* desirable, appealing.

irrikan *adv.* desiring.

irrikatsu *adj.* desirous, anxious.

irrikatu *v.t.* to desire vehemently.

irrikitasun *n.* desire, yearning.

irrikitu *v.i.* to desire, to yearn for, to be anxious.

irrikor *adj.* smiling, having a tendency to smile.

irrikortasun *n.* jocularity, humor, funniness.

irrilari *n.* joker, ridiculer, mocker.

irrintzi *n.* popular yodel-like cry of happiness. *n.* screech, creak (of a cartwheel). *n.* neigh, whinny.

irrintzi egin *v.t.* to give a yodel-like shout of joy.

irrintzilari *n.* person giving yodel-like shouts of joy, person giving the Basque yell.

irrintzika *adv.* giving yodel-like shouts of joy, giving the Basque yell.

irrintzina *n.* yodel-like shout of joy. *n.* whinny, neigh.

irrintzina egin *v.t.* to give a yodel-like shout of joy. *v.t.* to whinny, to neigh.

irrintzinari *n.* person giving a yodel-like shout of joy, person giving the Basque yell.

irrino *n.(dim.)* small smile.

irriskatu *v.t.* to risk, to endanger, to put in danger.

irrist *n.(onomat.)* sound of slipping or sliding.

irristabera *adj.* slipping, sliding, having a tendency to slip.

irristabide *n.* slide, slippery road.

irristada *n.* sliding, slipping.

irristadura *n.* slipping, sliding, act of sliding.

irristagarri *adj.* slippable, slippery, slidable.

irristailu *n.* skate.

irristaka *adv.* sliding, slipping.

irristakatu *v.i.* to slip, to slide, to skid.

irristaketa *n.* skating. *n.* sliding, slipping.

irristakor *adj.* slippery, slick.

irristaldi *n.* slip, slide, slipping, sliding.

irristaleku *n.* slide, toboggan, sled.

irristapen *n.* slipping, sliding, skidding.

irristari *n.* skater.

irristategi *n.* toboggan, sled, slide.

irristatoki *n.* toboggan, sled, slide.

irristatu *v.i.* to slip, to slide, to skid.

irristatzaile *n.* slipper, slider, skidder.

irrist egin *v.t.* to slip, to slide, to skid.

irristoki *n.* slippery place, slide.

irrits *n.* ardent desire, passion, lust. *n.* ambition.

irritsatu *v.t.* to desire, to yearn for, to covet.

irritsu *adj.* joking, tricky, funny.

irriz *adv.* laughing, smilingly.

irrizale *adj.* fond of tricks, teasing or jokes.

irriz egon *v.i.* to be laughing.

irteera *n.* exit, departure, leaving. *n.* solution, way out, arrangement.

irten *v.i.* to leave, to go, to depart, to exit. *v.i.* to get lucky, to win (gambling).

irtenaldi *n.* departure time, moment of leaving.

irtenarazi *v.t.* to cause to leave, to make (someone) leave.

irtenbide *n.* fire escape, escape route, exit. *n.* evasiveness, evasive speech. *n.* solution, recourse, arrangement.

irtenegun *n.* departure day, day of departure.

irtenezin *n.* cul-de-sac, dead-end road. *n.(fig.)* dead end, problem without a solution.

irtenleku *n.* exit.

irtentoki *n.* point of departure. *n.* exit.

irtenune *n.* projection, promontory, point (of land).

irtirin *adj.* coquettish, flirtatious.

irudi *n.* image, picture, likeness, statue. *v.t.* to seem, to look like, to resemble, to be apparent. *n.* allegory, symbol.

irudialdaketa *n.* transfiguration.

irudibide *n.* allegory.

irudibidetu *v.t.* to allegorize, to speak in allegories.

irudibidez *adv.* allegorically, figuratively.

irudibidezko *adj.* allegoric, figurative.

irudidun *adj.* illustrated.

irudiezin *adj.* unimaginable.

irudigaitz *adj.* difficult to imagine.

irudigarri *adj.* imaginable, conceivable.

irudigile *n.* sculptor.

irudigin *n.* sculptor.

irudigintza *n.* carving or painting of images.

irudigurkeria *n.* idolatry.

irudigurtza *n.* worship of icons.

irudihausle *n.* iconoclast.

irudikagaitz *adj.* inimitable.

irudikagarri *adj.* imitable.

irudikakor *adj.* imitable, copiable.

irudikapen *n.* representation, imitation, copy.

irudikatu *v.t.* to imagine, to seem like. *v.t.* to imitate, to simulate.

irudikeria *n.* illusion, hallucination, false belief, chimera.

irudiketa *n.* fantasy, imagining. *n.* imitation.

irudiko *adj.* similar, alike, resembling.

irudikor *adj.* imaginative.

irudimen *n.* imagination.

irudimenezko *adj.* imaginary, fantastic, illusory.

irudimentsu *adj.* imaginative.

irudipen *n.* imagination, imagining.

irudipentsu *adj.* imaginative.

irudipetu *v.t.* to represent, to symbolize.

iruditu *v.i.* to seem like, to appear, to

resemble, to look like. *v.t.* to
represent, to symbolize.
iruditxo *n.(dim.)* small image or figure,
icon.
iruditzaile *n.* painter or sculptor of
religious images.
iruditzar *n.(augm.)* large statue.
irudiz *adv.* symbolically,
metaphorically.
irudiz aldatu *v.i.* to transfigure.
irudizko *adj.* symbolic, metaphoric,
figurative.
irudiztatu *v.t.* to illustrate.
irule *n.* weaver; spinner.
irundegi *n.* weaving factory, textile mill.
irungai *n.* weavable material.
irunkintza *n.* weaver's job.
irunkor *adj.* weavable, easily woven.
iruzur *n.* fraud, trick, falseness,
deception, guile, lie.
iruzurbide *n.* deceit, fraudulent
manner, trickery.
iruzur egin *v.t.* to defraud, to deceive,
to trick.
iruzurgile *n.* imposter, cheater, fraud,
deceiver.
iruzurkeria *n.* fraud, cheat, deception,
guile.
iruzurkeriazko *adj.* fraudulent,
cheating, deceitful.
iruzurketa *n.* fraudulent act, cheating,
deceit.
iruzurlari *n.* imposter, cheater, fraud,
deceiver.
iruzurle *n.* cheater, fraud, deceiver,
imposter.
iruzurrez *adv.* falsely, deceptively,
fraudulently.
iruzurrezko *adj.* false, fraudulent,
deceptive.
iruzurti *adj.* false, fraudulent,
deceptive.
iruzurtsu *adj.* tricky, deceitful,
fraudulent.
iruzurtu *v.t.* to cheat, to deceive, to
trick.
iruzurtzaile *n.* cheater, swindler,
crook.
isaskada *n.* blow with a broom.
isats *n.(bot.)* broom plant. *n.* broom
made of furze. *n.* tail (animals, fish,
etc.).
iseka *n.* joke, jest, jeer; mockery.
iseka egin *v.t.* to joke, to make fun of,
to ridicule.
isekagarri *adj.* mocking, derisive.
isekagile *n.* ridiculer, mocker, joker.
adj. joking, mocking.
isekaldi *n.* time of mockery, ridicule,
teasing.
isekari *n.* joker, jokester, mocker. *adj.*
joking, mocking.
isekatu *v.t.* to ridicule, to make fun of,
to mock; to satirize.
isekatzaile *n.* mocker, joker, satiricist.
adj. mocking, joking.
isekaz *adv.* mockingly, jokingly, with

ridicule.
isi! *int.* be quiet!
isil *adj.* quiet, calm, reserved; modest,
humble. *adj.* secret, occult,
clandestine. *adv.* quietly.
isilaldi *n.* period of silence.
isilalditxo *n.(dim.)* short period of
silence.
isilarazi *v.t.* to quiet, to calm
(someone).
isilarazle *n.* silencer, quieter.
isilarte *n.* period of silence.
isilate *n.* secret door, false door.
isilbatzar *n.* secret meeting,
clandestine meeting.
isilbidez *adv.* quietly; implicitly,
virtually.
isilbidezko *adj.* implicit, tacit.
isildu *v.i.* to be quiet, to shut up. *v.t.* to
quiet, to shut (someone) up.
isildu eragin *v.t.* to quiet down, to
make (someone) be quiet.
isilean *adv.* silently, in a low voice. *adv.*
secretly, hiddenly.
isileko *adj.* silent, clandestine, secret.
n. bastard child.
isilerazi *v.t.* to cause to be quiet.
isilezko *adj.* secret, occult,
clandestine.
isilgailu *n.* silencer (apparatus).
isilgarri *adj.* silenceable. *adj.*
irrefutable. *adj.* unmentionable,
unspeakable.
isilgune *n.* silence, period of silence.
isilik *adv.* quietly, secretly. *int.* quiet!
be quiet!
isilikako *adj.* secret, occult, hidden.
isilik egon *v.i.* to be quiet, to shut up.
isiljoko *n.* plot, secret plan, scheme.
isilka *adv.* confidentially, secretly; in a
low voice, in a whisper, quietly.
isilka-misilka *adv.* whispering, in a
whisper.
isilkari *n.* secretmonger. *adj.*
secretive, mysterious, clandestine.
isilkatu *v.i.* to speak in private.
isilkeria *n.* dissimulation, cover-up.
isilketa *n.* secretiveness. *n.*
whispering, murmuring.
isilki *adv.* silently, quietly.
isilkide *n.* co-conspirator, fellow
keeper of a secret.
isilkoi *adj.* quiet, taciturn, reserved,
silent.
isilkoitasun *n.* quietness, silentness,
taciturnity.
isilkor *adj.* taciturn, quiet, silent.
isilmandatari *n.* secret messenger,
confidante, go-between.
isilmandatu *n.* secret, confidence,
secret message.
isil-misilka *adv.* whisperingly, in a
whisper.
isil-misilka ari *v.i.* to whisper.
isilotoitz *n.(eccl.)* secret (prayer) of
the mass.
isilpe *n.* secret, clandestinity, secrecy.

isilpean adv. whispering, muttering, silently, clandestinely, secretly.
isilpeko n. secret. adj. secret, hidden, clandestine.
isilpetasun n. secrecy, clandestineness.
isilpetu v.t. to silence, to hide, to quiet.
isilpolizia n. secret police.
isilsari n. hush money, payoff for being silent.
isiltarte n. period of silence.
isiltasun n. silence, taciturnity. n. clandestineness, secretiveness. n. reserve, discretion.
isiltoki n. secret place, hiding place.
isiltsu adj. silent, quiet, clandestine, reserved.
isiltzaile n./adj. silencer; silencing.
isilume n. bastard, illegitimate child.
isilune n. period of silence, silence, silent moment, pause.
iskanbila n. riot, tumult, disorder, confusion, trouble, mess. n. crash, din, deafening noise.
iskanbilari n. agitator, disturber, rioter.
iskanbilatsu adj. agitating, disturbing, riotous, noisy.
iskanbilka adv. noisily, turbulently, tumultuously.
iskilo n. weapon.
iskilotegi n. armory, depository for arms or weapons.
iskiloztatu v.t. to provide arms, to supply weapons.
isla n. reflection.
islada n. reflection, reverberation.
islada egin v.t. to reflect, to reverberate.
isladaketa n. reflection, act of reflecting (light), act of reverberating.
isladakor adj. reflecting, reflective.
isladapen n. reflection of light, reverberation of light.
isladatsu adj. reflective, reflecting, reverberating.
isladatu v.i./v.t. to reflect; to reverberate.
isladatzaile adj. reflective, reflecting, reverberating.
islam n. Islam. **Islamiar.** Islamic.
iso! int. whoa!
isolagarri adj. isolatable.
isolamendu n. isolation.
isolatu v.t./v.i. to isolate, to insulate.
isolatzaile n./adj. isolator; isolating.
ispilu n. mirror.
ispilugile n. mirror maker.
ispilutegi n. place of mirrors.
istil n. puddle. n. drop of water. n. mud.
istildu v.i. to pool, to puddle. v.i. to turn to mud.
istiltsu adj. muddy, miry.
istilu n. disturbance, uprising, trouble, riot, confusion, disorder, mess. n. anxiety, difficulty, bad times.

istiluzale adj. quarrelsome, troublesome.
istimu n. esteem, respect.
istinga n. marsh, swamp, mire, bog.
istingadi n. swamp ground, marsh ground.
istingapen n. wallowing in mud.
istingatu v.i. to wallow in mud, to get muddy.
istingor n.(zool.) snipe (Gallinago gallinago).
istorio n. story, narration, tale, anecdote.
istribor n.(naut.) starboard.
istripu n. accident.
isun n. fine.
isundu v.t. to fine.
isurbera adj. flowing, running, effusive.
isurbide n. drainage ditch, canal.
isurdura n. flow, spill, effusion.
isurezin adj. unspillable.
isurgabe adj. unflowing, still (water).
isurgaitz n. unspillable, difficult to spill.
isurgarri adj. fluid, flowing.
isuri v.t. to flow, to spill. v.t. to inspire. n. flowing, spilling.
isurialdi n. spilling, overflow, leakage.
isurigaitz adj. unspillable.
isurika adv. spilling, shedding.
isurikatu v.i./v.t. to flow; to spill, to shed (blood).
isurkai adj. fluid, liquid.
isurketa n. spill, spilling; ejaculation.
isurki adj. fluid, liquid.
isurkin n. residue of a spill.
isurkitasun n. liquidness, liquidity.
isurkor adj. effusive, flowing.
isurkortasun n. liquidity, liquidness.
isurle adj. flowing, spilling, overflowing. n. one who spills.
isurodi n. drainpipe.
isurpen n. spilling, effusion.
isurtasun n. fluidness, fluidity.
isurtegi n. spillway, mouth of a drain.
isurtoki n. spillway, dumping place.
isurtzulo n. drain, outlet.
isusi n. place where furze grows.
it- Used in compound words. Derived from idi, ox. **Itegi.** Oxen's stable.
-it- (gram.) Infix indicating a plural object, used in the auxiliary verb accompanying a transitive verb. **Lau liburu erosi ditut eta bat galdu dut.** I have bought four books and I have lost one.
itaizur n. leak, leakage, drip.
italiera n. Italian language.
italieratu v.t. to translate into Italian.
itaska n. ox manger.
itaun n. question.
itaundu v.t. to ask, to question.
itegi n. oxen's stable.
itegun n. work performed by one team of oxen in one day.
ito v.i./v.t. to drown, to suffocate, to asphyxiate, to smother, to choke. v.i.(fig.) to laugh a lot.

itoaldi n. suffocation, drowning, asphyxiation. n.(fig.) period of disgrace, shame, embarrassment, worry, etc.

ito arazi v.t. to suffocate, to drown, to asphyxiate, to smother, to strangle.

itoarazle n. strangler, asphyxiator.

itobehar n. drowning, asphyxiation, suffocation. n.(fig.) anxiety, strait, difficulty, jam.

itobeharrean adv. quickly, hastily, hurriedly.

itobeharrez adv. quickly, hastily, hurriedly.

itodura n. drowning, asphyxiation, strangulation.

itogarri adj. suffocating, asphyxiating, drowning.

itogin n. leak, leakage, drip.

itoi n. pigpen, pigsty, filthy place. n. muddy place.

itoka adv. quickly, hastily, hurriedly.

itoketa n. drowning, suffocation, strangulation.

itomen n. drowning, suffocation. n.(fig.) anguish, difficulty.

itotasun n. drowning, suffocation, asphyxiation. n.(fig.) anguish, difficulty.

itotzaile n. strangler, murderer, one who drowns (someone else).

itsas- Used in compound words. Derived from *itsaso*, sea.
Itsas-legetza. Maritime law.

itsasadar n. branch of the sea, mouth of a river.

itsasaingira n.(zool.) conger eel, sea eel.

itsasalde n. coast, coastal region, bank, shore.

itsasaldeko adj. coastal.

itsasalderatu v.i. to approach the coast.

itsasaldi n. tide. n. navigation, sea travel, ocean voyage.

itsasandi n. ocean. n. high tide. n. rough sea.

itsasandiarteko adj. interoceanic.

itsasandiko adj. oceanic.

itsasapar n. sea foam.

itsasapo n.(zool.) angler.

itsasarkakuso n.(zool.) sand flea.

itsasarmada n. maritime war fleet.

itsasaro n. condition of the sea.

itsasarrain n. sea fish, salt water fish.

itsasarrano n.(zool.) marine eagle, sea eagle.

itsasarrantza n. ocean fishing, salt water fishing.

itsasarrapakin n. pirate's booty.

itsasarte n. cove, inlet, bay. n.(geog.) strait.

itsasarteko adj. interoceanic.

itsasarunzko adj. ultramarine, oversea.

itsasazpialde n. bottom of the sea.

itsasazpiko adj. undersea.

itsasbare n.(zool.) blenny (*Blennius pavo*). n.(zool.) sea slug.

itsasbarne n. deep sea, depths of the sea. n. high sea.

itsasbarneratu v.i. to sail on the open sea, to sail on the high seas.

itsasbarraskilo n.(zool.) sea snail.

itsasbarren n. high sea; deep sea.

itsasbarrendu v.i. to go to sea.

itsasbazter n. coast, seacoast, shore.

itsasbazterkatu v.i. to border the coast.

itsasbazterreko adj. coastal.

itsasbehera n. low tide, ebb tide.

itsasbelar n.(bot.) seaweed, marine algae.

itsasbeso n.(geog.) branch of the sea, inlet, bay.

itsasbide n. sea route, sea lane, shipping lane.

itsasbidetu v.i. to sail the shipping lane, to sail the sea route.

itsasbiraketa n. circumnavigation.

itsasbiratu v.t. to circumnavigate.

itsasdura n. act of adhering.

itsasekaitz n. sea storm, tempest, squall.

itsaserri n. coastal village.

itsasertz n. seacoast, shore.

itsasertzeko adj. coastal.

itsaserzketa n. coastal sailing.

itsasgain n. surface of the sea.

itsasgaitz n. seasick.

itsasgarri adj. adhering, adhesive, adherible.

itsasgeltoki n. seaport, port of call.

itsasgintza n. merchant marine.

itsasgizon n. sailor; fisherman; seaman.

itsasgolko n.(geog.) bay, gulf.

itsasgora n. high tide.

itsasgorabehera n. tides (high and low).

itsasgorena n. high tide.

itsasgorenaldi n. time of high tide.

itsasibilaldi n. sea journey.

itsasibilezin n. unnavigable.

itsasibilgaitz adj. difficult to navigate.

itsasibilketa n. navigation.

itsasikara n. seaquake.

itsasirtera n. act of going to sea, weighing anchor.

itsasitzulbira n. circumnavigation.

itsasizar n.(zool.) starfish.

itsasjakintza n. art of navigation, seamanship.

itsasjira n. sea crossing.

itsaskabra n.(zool.) small red fish with a large head, sharp dorsal spines and tasty flesh found on rocky coasts.

itsaskatu n.(zool.) catfish.

itsasketa n. navigation n. sticking, adhesion, attachment.

itsaski n. part that adheres or sticks on; addition. n. shellfish. n. poultice, plaster.

itsaskintza n. art of navigation.

itsaskirol n. sea sport.

itsaskoi adj. sticky, adhesive.
itsaskolpe n. huge wave, crash of a huge wave.
itsaskor adj. sticky, adhesive. adj. contagious, pestilent, noxious.
itsaskortasun n. stickiness, adhesiveness. n. contagiousness.
itsaskuntza n. navigation, art of navigating.
itsaskurkuilo n.(zool.) sea shell.
itsaslakatz n.(zool.) sea urchin.
itsaslamia n. sea nymph.
itsaslapur n. pirate, sea thief.
itsaslapurreta n. piracy.
itsaslapurtza n. piracy.
itsaslore n.(zool.) sea anemone, actinia, polyp.
itsasmaila n. sea level, level of the sea.
itsasmalda n. steep coast, craggy coast.
itsasmin n. seasickness. n. nostalgia for the sea.
itsasmindu v.i. to get seasick.
itsasmugida n. coming and going of the tide.
itsasmutil n. cabinboy.
itsasneska n. siren, mermaid.
itsaso n. sea.
itsasoko adj. nautical, maritime.
itsasondar n. sea sand. n. bottom of the sea, sea bottom.
itsasondo n. sea bottom, depths of the sea. n. sea coast, sea shore.
itsasondoko adj. pelagic, oceanic, pertaining to the bottom of the sea. adj. coastal.
itsasondoratu v.i. to dive.
itsasontzi n. ship, boat.
itsasontzisail n. fleet of ships.
itsasontzitegi n. harbor, port.
itsasontzitxo n.(dim.) small ship, boat, launch.
itsasoraketa n. departure, going out to sea. n. sea landing, splashdown.
itsasorapen n. departure, going out to sea.
itsasoratu v.i. to go out to sea.
itsasorratz n. compass, magnetic needle.
itsasoste n. high sea(s).
itsasosteko adj. transoceanic.
itsasote n. departure, going out to sea to fish.
itsasotso n.(zool.) walrus, sea lion.
itsaspe n. bottom of the sea.
itsaspekari n. frogman, underwater diver, deep-sea diver.
itsaspeko adj. submarine, underwater. n. submarine.
itsaspen n. grasping, sticking, adhering.
itsasperatu v.i./v.t. to sink, to submerge, to dive.
itsasportu n. harbor, seaport.
itsastar adj. maritime, nautical, marine, sea.
itsastatu v.i. to navigate.

itsasuge n.(zool.) moray (Muraena helena).
itsasuntzi n. ship.
itsasur n. sea water, salt water.
itsaszaldi n.(zool.) seahorse.
itsaszintzur n. narrow sea passage.
itsaszoko n.(geog.) inlet, bay, cove.
itsaszokoratu v.i. to enter a harbor, to put into a cove or bay.
itsaszurrunbilo n. roar of the sea.
itsatsi v.i. to adhere (to), to stick (to). v.i./v.t. to root, to take root, to grab, to grasp.
itsu n. blind man, blind person. adj. blind.
itsualdi n. period of blindness, blindness. n. time of passion, obfuscation.
itsuargi n. blind person's guide.
itsuaurreko n. blind person's guide.
itsudura n. blindness n. stubbornness.
itsuerazi v.t. to blind. v.t. to obscure reason, to blind (someone) to the truth.
itsueri n. blindness.
itsugarri adj. blinding.
itsuidazkera n. Braille, method of writing used by the blind.
itsu-itsuka adv. gropingly, blindly. n. blind man's bluff (children's game).
itsuka adv. gropingly, blindly.
itsukeria n. blindness, stubbornness, obstinacy.
itsuketa n. confusion, obfuscation.
itsuki adv. blindly, obsessively, fanatically.
itsulagun n. guide to the blind.
itsulapiko n. piggy bank.
itsumaitakeria n. excessive affection, blind love.
itsumakila n. blind man's cane, white cane.
itsumen n. blindness. n. obsession, obfuscation.
itsumendu n. obstinance, stubbornness, obsession.
itsumustu n. blinding, obfuscation.
itsumustuan adv. blindly, gropingly. adv. in a hurry.
itsumustu egin v.t. to meet, to encounter, to bump into, to run into.
itsumustuka adv. blindly, gropingly.
itsumustuko adj. quick, sudden.
itsumutil n. guide to the blind.
itsusdura n. ugliness, disfiguration.
itsusgarri adj. causing ugliness, deforming.
itsusi adj. ugly. adj. crude, obscene.
itsusitasun n. ugliness.
itsusitu v.t. to make ugly, to disfigure, to deface, to mar. v.t. to denigrate, to defame, to dishonor, to disgrace.
itsuskeria n. ugliness, vileness, meanness, lowliness. n. crudity, obscenity.
itsusketa n. making ugly, defacing, deformation.

itsuski *adv.* in an ugly way. *adv.* vilely, crudely, grossly, cruelly. *adv.* obscenely.

itsusko *adj.* near-sighted, short-sighted.

itsustasun *n.* ugliness; crudeness.

itsustu *v.t.* to deform, to deface, to disfigure, to make ugly, to ruin. *v.i.* to become ugly, to become disfigured.

itsutasun *n.* blindness.

itsutu *v.i.* to go blind. *v.i./v.t.* to be blinded (by), to be obsessed with; to blind (someone). *v.i./v.t.* to obfuscate, to confuse, to puzzle, to blind.

itsutuki *adv.* blindly, passionately.

itun *n.* agreement, pact, accord, testament, covenant, deal, treaty. *adj.* sad, melancholic, depressed.

itundu *v.i./v.t.* to agree, to come to an agreement; to make a pact. *v.i.* to be advised, to be counseled. *v.i.* to be sad, to become sad.

itungile *n.* agreer, one who makes a deal.

itunketa *n.* pact, agreement, contract.

itur- Used in compound words. Derived from *iturri*, fountain.

iturbegi *n.* spring, fountain.

iturbide *n.* road to the fountain.

iturburu *n.* source of the fountain, fountainhead. *n.* source, origin, beginning.

iturgin *n.* plumber, fountain builder, pipe layer.

iturgintza *n.* profession of plumber.

iturri *n.* fountain. *n.* source, origin, beginning.

iturriberri *n.* new fountain.

iturrigorri *n.* rusty fountain.

iturrikari *n.* plumber, pipe-layer.

iturriketari *n.* plumber.

iturriratu *v.i.* to go to the fountain.

iturritxo *n.(dim.)* small fountain.

iturrizulo *n.* fountain, spring.

iturtxo *n.(dim.)* small fountain.

itxaro *v.t.* to hope, to trust. *n.* hope. *v.t.* to wait, to await, to wait for.

itxaroaldi *n.* wait, time spent waiting.

itxarobide *n.* reason for hope, reason for trust.

itxaroezin *adj.* hopeless.

itxarogabe *adj.* hopeless, without hope.

itxarogabetu *v.i.* to lose hope, to be without hope, to despair.

itxarogabez *adv.* hopelessly.

itxarogarri *adj.* hopeful.

itxarogune *n.* waiting period, interval of waiting.

itxarokizun *n.* hope, faith in achieving something.

itxarokor *adj.* hopeful.

itxaron *v.t.* to wait.

itxarongela *n.* waiting room.

itxaropen *n.* hope; expectation.

itxaropenez *adv.* hopefully, with hope.

itxaso *n.* sea.

itxi *v.t.* to close; to enclose; to cloister; to stop up, to plug (a sink).

itxialdi *n.* closure, closing, shutting.

itxiarazi *v.t.* to shut in, to close up.

itxiera *n.* closing, closure, shutting.

itxiezin *adj.* unclosable.

itxigarri *adj.* closable.

itxita *adj.* closed, shut.

itxitzaile *n.* closer.

itxura *n.* aspect, appearance, image, look, resemblance; shape, condition.

itxuradun *adj.* similar. *adj.* apparent, feigned. *adj.* probable, likely.

itxura egin *v.t.* to simulate, to act like, to seem.

itxuragabe(ko) *adj.* formless, shapeless, disfigured, deformed, misshapen, irregular. *adj.* absurd; senseless; unrealistic; improbable.

itxuragabekeria *n.* absurdity.

itxuragabeki *adv.* unrealistically, improbably.

itxuragabetasun *n.* deformity, shapelessness, formlessness. *n.* improbability; absurdity; lack of realism.

itxuragabetu *v.i./v.t.* to be disfigured, to be deformed; to disfigure, to deform.

itxuragaitz *n.* bad appearance.

itxuragaiztoko *adj.* having a bad appearance, ugly, unsightly.

itxuragile *n.* imitator. *n.* pretender, fraud.

itxurakeria *n.* affectation; hypocrisy, falseness; pretense.

itxurako *adj.* similar, seeming the same, alike, resembling. *adj.* apparent, feigned.

itxuraldagarri *adj.* transfigurable, transformable.

itxuraldaketa *n.* transfiguration, transformation, metamorphosis.

itxuraldapen *n.* transfiguration, transformation, metamorphosis.

itxuraldatu *v.t./v.i.* to transfigure, to transform, to change.

itxuramendu *n.* feigning, pretense.

itxurapaindu *v.t.* to apply make-up, to apply cosmetics.

itxurapainketa *n.* making up, applying cosmetics, putting on one's make-up.

itxurapen *n.* appearance, pretense, representation. *n.* similarity, resemblance, likeness.

itxurapenezko *adj.* apparent. *adj.* having a false appearance, fictitious, deceptive, simulated.

itxurati *adj.* hypocritical; feigned; apparent.

itxuratu *v.t.* to imitate, to simulate. *v.t.* to make presentable; to form, to shape. *v.t.* to feign, to appear.

itxuraz *adv.* apparently, in appearance. *adv.* feignedly, seemingly, in a dissembling manner.

itxurazale adj. hypocritical, pretending, feigning, fake.

itxurazko adj. decent, honest, well-mannered. adj. apparent, seeming. adj. false, fake, unreal, fictitious, simulated.

itzain n. ox tender, herder of oxen.

itzaingo n. work of the ox tender.

itzaintza n. work of the ox tender.

itzal n. shadow, shade. n. respect, prestige. n. protection. adj. sad, somber, morose.

itzalaldi n. time of darkness, lights out. n. eclipse.

itzaldu v.t./v.i. to eclipse, to cover in shadows, to shade. v.t. to turn off, to turn out, to extinguish. v.t. to darken, to get dark.

itzaldun adj. shady, shade-giving. adj. honorable, respectable, influential.

itzaldura n. diminution of light, dimming of light.

itzal egin v.t. to cast a shadow.

itzaleko adj. hidden, secret. adj. prestigious, respected; majestic.

itzalezin adj. inextinguishable, incapable of being put out.

itzalezko adj. shady. adj. prestigious, respected; majestic. adj. tremendous.

itzaleztatu v.t./v.i. to darken (colors).

itzalgabekeria n. irreverence, disrespect, disregard.

itzalgabe(ko) adj. unrespected, having lost respect. adj. unprotected. adj. perfect, impeccable.

itzalgabetasun n. disrespectfulness.

itzalgabetu v.i. to lose respect, to fall into disgrace.

itzalgailu n. fire extinguisher; candle snuffer.

itzalgaitz adj. difficult to extinguish, hard to put out.

itzalgarri adj. extinguishable. adj. shady. adj. venerable, respectable.

itzalgarriro adv. respectfully.

itzalgarritasun n. respectableness, venerableness.

itzalgile adj. shading, casting a shadow.

itzalgune n. shady place.

itzali v.t./v.i. to turn off, to turn out, to put out, to extinguish; to go out (a light); to turn off. v.i. to disappear from sight, to fade away, to die away.

itzalka adv. furtively, secretly, in secret.

itzalkatu v.t. to cast a shadow, to shade (something).

itzalkeria n. bad influence.

itzalketa n. act of turning off or putting out; extinction.

itzalkor adj. extinguishing (flame), dying out; capable of being turned out or off.

itzalpe n. shadow, shade, shady place.

n.(fig.) refuge, protection, relief, comfort.

itzalpekari adj. mysterious, secretive, furtive.

itzalpeko adj. secret, hidden. adj.(fig.) protected.

itzalperatu v.i. to go into the shade. v.i. to hide oneself, to disappear. v.t.(fig.) to jail, to imprison.

itzalpetu v.t. to hide, to conceal. v.t. to obscure, to shade, to darken. v.t. to protect, to guard.

itzalpetzaile adj. protecting, protective. adj. darkening.

itzaltegi n. shady place, place of shadows.

itzaltsu adj. shady, shadowy, dark, shade. adj. lugubrious, sad. adj. respectful.

itzaltzaile adj. extinguishing. n. extinguisher.

itzalzale adj. fond of shade, fond of darkness.

itzarri v.i./v.t. to wake, to wake up, to awaken.

itzulaldi n. return. n. change, turn. n. translation.

itzulbide n. route of return trip.

itzulbira n. turn, gyration, revolution.

itzulera n. return. n. devolution, restitution, exchange. n. form of translation.

itzulerakor adj. regressive, returning.

itzulerazi v.t. to cause to return or go back, to expel, to repel.

itzulerraz adj. easy to turn. adj. easy to translate. adj. versatile, changeable.

itzulerraztasun n. versatility, changeability.

itzulezin adj. irreversible, unchangeable. adj. untranslatable.

itzulezin(ezko) adj. untranslatable.

itzulezintasun n. irreversibility, unchangeableness. n. quality of being untranslatable.

itzulgai n. subject of translation, material for translation.

itzulgaitz adj. difficult to change, difficult to turn. adj. difficult to translate.

itzulgarri adj. reversible, restorable, returnable. adj. translatable. adj. arable, workable, turnable (land).

itzulgarritasun n. reversibility, restorability.

itzuli v.t. to return, to reinstate. v.i. to return, to go back. v.t. to translate. v.t. to turn, to turn over. v.t. to return, to send back, to remit, to resend.

itzuliberri adj. recently returned. adj. recently translated.

itzulika adv. circling, turning about, revolving.

itzulikaldi n. turn, revolution, winding. n. return.

itzulikari n. revolver, turner, one who

circles. *adj.* versatile.

itzulikatu *v.i./v.t.* to turn, to rotate, to revolve. *v.t.* to invert, to turn over, to upset. *v.i.* to convert, to return (to God).

itzulinguratu *v.i.* to turn around, to go in circles.

itzulinguru *n.* bend, turn. *n.(fig.)* circumlocution, periphrasis, beating about the bush.

itzulinguruka *adv.(fig.)* furtively, ambiguously, in a round about way, evasively.

itzulingurukatu *v.t.* to turn, to revolve, to rotate.

itzulipurdi *n.* tumble, somersault.

itzulipurdika *adv.* tumblingly, with somersaults.

itzulipurdikari *n.* acrobat, tumbler.

itzulipurdikatu *v.i.* to somersault, to tumble. *v.i.(fig.)* to change.

itzulkari *adj.* rotary, rotative.

itzulkor *adj.* changeable, versatile.

itzulkortasun *n.* versatility, changeableness, volubility.

itzulpen *n.* return, restitution, devolution. *n.* return (from a trip). *n.* translation, translated version.

itzulterraz *adj.* easy to translate.

itzultzaile *n.* one who returns (property or objects). *n.* translator.

itzuri *v.i.* to flee, to escape.

itzurkoi *adj.* fleeting, escaping, elusive.

itzurkor *adj.* fleeting, escaping, elusive.

itzurpen *n.* evasion, escape, flight.

itzurpide *n.* escape, flight. *n.* way out, excuse, subterfuge, loophole.

itzurti *adj.* fugitive, elusive.

ixarradatu *v.t.* to prune, to trim.

ixartu *v.i./v.t.* to wake, to wake up, to awaken.

ixo *int.* quiet!

izadi *n.* nature, creation.

izaera *n.* character, personality, nature, way of being.

izaeraldaketa *n.* character change, personality change.

izaeratu *v.t.* to characterize.

izain *n.(zool.)* leech.

izakera *n.* character, personality, nature.

izaki *n.* being, creature, entity.

izakide *adj.* coexistent.

izakidego *n.* coexistence.

izakidetasun *n.* coexistence.

izan *aux. v.i.* to be, to exist. *aux. v.t.* to have. *n.* realness, reality, existence. *n.* being, entity, identity, nature.

izan ere *adv.* in fact, in effect, in reality.

izanez *adv.* in reality; by nature.

izan ezik *prep.* except, excepting, save.

izangaitasun *n.* possibility of existence.

izangaitz *adj.* impossible, hard to be.

izankide *adj.* coexistent.

izankidego *n.* coexistence.

izankidetasun *n.* coexistence.

izapide *n.* procedure, steps of a plan or project.

izar *n.* star. *n.(fig.)* star, celebrity.

izara *n.* sheet.

izardun *adj.* starry.

izari *n.* measure, dimension, size. *n.(fig.)* moderation, prudence.

izaridun *adj.* proportionate, having the proper measurements.

izarigabeko *adj.* disproportionate.

izariko *adj.* proportionate, having the proper measurements; size.

izarketa *n.* constellation, group of stars.

izarmoltzo *n.* constellation.

izarniadura *n.* twinkle of the stars, starlight.

izarniatu *v.t.* to twinkle, to shine (stars).

izarno *n.(dim.)* small star.

izarraide *n.(astron.)* asteroid.

izarrarri *n.(min.)* crystalline quartz.

izarrarte *n.* starry sky, starry space.

izarrarteko *adj.* interstellar.

izarratu *n.* starry sky. *adj.* starry, star-studded.

izarreria *n.* abundance of stars.

izarreztatu *v.i.* to be covered with stars.

izarrontzi *n.* spaceship, starship, skylab.

izartalde *n.* constellation, group of stars.

izartegi *n.* starry sky, firmament.

izarti *adj.* starry.

izartsu *adj.* starry.

izartu *v.i.* to cover with stars, to be covered with stars.

izartxo *n.(dim.)* asterisk.

izartza *n.* constellation, group of stars.

izate *n.* nature, identity, existence. *n.* being, life.

izeba *n.* aunt.

izebatipi *n.* second aunt, distant aunt.

izeki *v.i./v.t.* to burn.

izekidura *n.* burn.

izekiezin *adj.* not flammable, noncombustible.

izen *n.* name, noun. *n.* fame.

izena eman *v.t.* to give (one's) name.

izenbereko *adj.* homonymic, having the same name.

izenburu *n.* title (of a work), heading, inscription.

izendaezin *adj.* unnameable, unmentionable; indescribable.

izendagaitz *adj.* unnameable, unmentionable.

izendagarri *adj.* mentionable.

izendapen *n.* designation, naming, mention, assignment.

izendatu *v.t.* to name, to designate, to appoint; to mention. *v.t.* to elect. *v.t.* to assign.

izendatzaile *n.* denominator, namer, designator.

izendegi *n.* catalog, list of names, glossary.

izen-deiturak *n.* first and last names, complete name.

izendun *adj.* named, called. *adj.* illustrious, celebrated, famous.

izenegun *n.* saint's day, day of one's namesake.

izeneko *adj.* designated, named, called, by the name of.

izenemaile *n.* subscriber.

izeneman *v.t.* to list (your own name), to register yourself.

izenemate *n.* registration, giving your name to be registered.

izenez *adv.* nominally, by name.

izenezko *adj.* nominal. *adj.* onomastic, pertaining to names.

izeneztapen *n.* designation, naming, indicating by name.

izeneztatu *v.t.* to name, to indicate by name, to designate.

izengabe *adj.* anonymous, nameless. *adj.* not famous, unknown.

izengabeki *adv.* anonymously.

izengabetu *v.t./v.i.* to discredit, to defame, to disgrace, to denigrate.

izengoiti *n.* nickname, pseudonym, alias.

izengoititu *v.t.* to nickname.

izenjoko *n.* declension of nouns.

izenkide *adj./n.* homonym, having the same name, of the same name, namesake.

izenkidetasun *n.* homonymy.

izenlagun *n.* adjective.

izenlaguntza *n.* conversion into an adjective, use as an adjective.

izenorde *n.* pseudonym, alias, nickname. *n.(gram.)* pronoun.

izenpe *n.* signature.

izenpedun *adj.* having a signature, signed.

izenpeko *n.* signature, flourish (of a signature).

izenpetu *v.t.* to sign.

izenpetzaile *n.* signer.

izenzerrenda *n.* list of names.

izer- Used in compound words. Derived from *izerdi*, sweat.

izerbera *adj.* sweaty, tending to sweat.

izerdi *n.* sweat, perspiration. *n.(fig.)* difficulty, affliction.

izerdialdi *n.* period of sweating.

izerdidura *n.* sweating, perspiring.

izerdigabetu *v.i.* to wipe off sweat; to be dehydrated.

izerdigarri *adj.* sweaty, perspiring.

izerdikatu *v.i.* to sweat, to perspire.

izerdikoi *adj.* tending to sweat, sweaty.

izerdikor *adj.* sweaty, causing sweat.

izrdilaino *n.* sweaty film, fog of sweat.

izerdi pats *n.* copious or profuse sweat.

izerditan *adv.* sweating.

izerditanta *n.* drop of sweat, bead of perspiration.

izerditsu *adj.* sweaty, tending to sweat.

izerditu *v.i.* to sweat.

izerditxorta *n.* drop of sweat.

izerdixka *n.* light sweat.

izerdixkatu *v.i.* to sweat lightly.

izergarri *adj.* sweaty.

izerketa *n.* perspiration, sweating.

izerkoi *adj.* sweaty, tending to sweat.

izerkoitasun *n.* sweatiness, tendency to sweat.

izerpera *adj.* sweaty, tending to sweat.

izerperatasun *n.* tendency to sweat.

izerperatu *v.i.* to become sweaty.

izertaldi *n.* period of sweating, sweat.

izertarazi *v.t.* to make (someone) sweat, to cause to sweat.

izertarazle *adj.* sweaty, causing to sweat.

izerteragile *adj.* sweaty, causing sweat.

izerterraz *adj.* sweaty, tending to sweat.

izertxukaldi *n.* wiping off sweat.

izkira *n.(zool.)* shrimp.

izkiriatu *v.t.* to write.

izkribau *n.* notary, court clerk, secretary.

izkribu *n.* written work, written word.

izokin *n.(zool.)* salmon.

izokinantzeko *adj.* salmon-like.

izokinki *n.* salmon meat.

izokinkide *n.* salmonoid.

izokinkume *n.* salmon fry.

izor *adj.* pregnant.

izorraldi *n.* gestation, pregnancy.

izorrandi *n.* advanced stage of pregnancy, late stage of pregnancy.

izorratu *v.i.* to get pregnant. *v.t.* to impregnate. *v.t.(colloq.)* to bother, to annoy.

izotz *n.* ice, frost.

izotz(a) egin *v.t.* to freeze, to make ice.

izotzaldi *n.* frozen period, frozen season; Ice Age.

izotzauskailu *n.* icebreaker, snow removal equipment.

izotzezko *adj.* glacial, icy, frozen.

izozkailu *n.* refrigerator, freezer.

izozkarri *adj.* glacial, icy, frozen.

izozketa *n.* freezing. *n.* frost season, frozen period.

izozki *n.* ice cream; iced drink. *adv.* glacially, icily.

izozkidenda *n.* ice cream shop.

izozkidun *n.* ice cream vendor.

izozkigile *n.* ice cream maker (person).

izozkisaltzaile *n.* ice cream vendor.

izozkitegi *n.* ice cream shop.

izozkor *adj.* easily frozen.

izozmendi *n.* iceberg.

izozpilo *n.* glacier, pile of ice.

izozte *n.* freezing. *n.* cold season, frost season, period of cold weather. *n.* glaciation.

izoztealdi *n.* series of frosts.
izoztegi *n.* place of ice; freezer.
izozti *adj.* glacial.
izoztontzi *n.* freezer; ice cube tray.
izoztu *v.t./v.i.* to freeze, to make ice.
izoztura *n.* freezing, act of freezing.
izpi *n.* fragment, chip, or splinter of wood. *n.* filament, frayed thread. *n.* little piece, little bit. *n.* light ray, luminous ray. *adj.* small, little, minute, insignificant. *adv.* a little bit, a little; at all, any.
izpidun *adj.* fibrous, prickly, stickly.
izpikatu *v.t.* to mince, to splinter, to chip, to chop, to divide into small pieces.
izpiketa *n.* radiation (of light).
izpil *n.* spot, mark, dot.
izpildun *adj.* spotted, marked, dotted.
izpiritu *n.* spirit, noncorporeal entity.
izpiritualeztapen *n.* spiritualization.
izpiritualeztatu *v.t.* to spiritualize, to make spiritual.
izpiritualitate *n.* spirituality.
izpiritualki *adv.* spiritually.
izpiritutasun *n.* spiritualness, spirituality.
izpirituzko *adj.* spiritual.
izpitsu *adj.* fibrous, thready; chipped, fragmented, splintered. *adj.* resplendent, shining, brilliant.
izpitu *v.t.* to mince, to splinter, to cut into little pieces; to unravel, to undo threads. *v.t.* to divide into tiny bits.
izter *n.(anat.)* thigh.
izterbabes *n.* protection (pads, armor) for the thighs.
izterbegi *n.* enemy; disagreeable person.
izterbegiko *adj.* disagreeable, unpleasant.
iztermami *n.* fleshy part of the thigh.
iztermin *n.(med.)* sciatica.
izterralde *n.* thigh region.
izterrarte *n.* inner thigh, inside of thigh.
izterreko *adj.* pertaining to the thigh.
izterrezur *n.(anat.)* femur.
izterrondo *n.(anat.)* groin.
izterzabal *adj.* spraddle-legged, wide-legged, bow-legged.
iztil *n.* falling drop of liquid. *n.* puddle, pool.
iztingor *n.(zool.)* kind of woodcock which prefers marshland to forest.
iztripu *n.* mop.
iztupa *n.* rough hemp; oakum; tow.
iztupalari *n.* caulker, one who caulks.
iztupatu *v.t.* to caulk.
iztupazko *n.* pertaining to tow (maritime term).
izu *n.* panic, horror, fright, scare.
izualdi *n.* scare, fright, fear.
izuarazi *v.t.* to terrify, to scare, to frighten, to intimidate.
izuarazkor *adj.* intimidating, frightening.
izuarazle *n.* terrorist, frightener,

scarer.
izuarazpen *n.* fright, fear, terror, intimidation.
izubera *adj.* fearful, frightened.
izuberatasun *n.* timidness, timidity, fearfulness.
izubide *n.* reason for fright, motive for terror.
izudura *n.* fear, fright, terror.
izuerraz *adj.* timid, fearful, frightened.
izuezin *adj.* fearless, imperturbable.
izugabe *adj.* fearless, imperturbable.
izugaitz *adj.* difficult to frighten, daring, audacious.
izugarri *adj.* terrible, frightful, horrible, atrocious, scary. *adj.(fig.)* tremendous, big, huge, enormous. *adj.* surprising, shocking. *adv.* terribly, very.
izugarrikeria *n.* atrocity, monstrosity, terrible thing.
izugarriki *adv.* atrociously, terribly, horribly, frightfully.
izugarriro *adv.* atrociously, terribly, horribly.
izugarritasun *n.* enormity, hugeness; monstrousness.
izugarrizko *adj.* horrendous, atrocious. *adj.* enormous, tremendous.
izugile *adj.* easily frightened, jumpy.
izu izan *v.t.* to be afraid, to be terrified.
izukaitz *adj.* daring, audacious, difficult to frighten.
izukaiztasun *n.* imperturbability, audacity.
izukeria *n.* barbarity, ferocity, cruelty.
izukor *adj.* surprised, shocked, spooked, spooky.
izukortasun *n.* timidity, fearfulness.
-izun *(gram.)* Suffix which indicates in-law; false, pseudo. **Arrebaizun.** Sister-in-law.
izur *n.* fold, pleat. *n.* curl (of hair).
izurde *n.(zool.)* type of marine mammal, kind of dolphin.
izurdun *adj.* wavy, waved, curled, undulating.
izurdura *n.* curliness. *n.* wrinkledness.
izurgabetu *v.t.* to remove wrinkles from.
izurkatu *v.t.* to curl (hair). *v.i.* to wave, to ripple, to undulate.
izurreztatu *v.i./v.t.* to infect, to contaminate, to catch (a disease).
izurri *n.* plague, epidemic, contagious disease.
izurrialdi *n.* time of plague, epidemic.
izurridun *adj.* infected, infested.
izurridura *n.* infestation, contagion.
izurrigarri *adj.* contagious.
izurrikeria *n.* speech or doctrine which corrupts people.
izurrikor *adj.* contagious.
izurrite *n.* time of plague, epidemic.
izurritsu *adj.* contagious, infested.
izurritu *v.t./v.i.* to infect, to contaminate, to catch (a disease).

adj. infected, infested, contaminated, contagious.

izurriz *adv.* contagiously.

izurrizko *adj.* contagious, pestilent, pestiferous.

izurriztatu *v.t./v.i.* to spread a disease, to contract a disease.

izurtsu *adj.* wavy, waved, undulating.

izurtu *v.t.* to double, to bend, to fold, to pleat. *adj.* wrinkled, pleated, folded, puckered.

izuti *adj.* surprised, shocked, spooked, spooky; fearful.

izutu *v.i.* to be frightened, to get scared, to be terrified. *v.t.* to frighten, to scare, to terrify. *adj.* upset, anguished.

izutzaile *n.* terrifier, frightener. *adj.* terrifying, frightening.

J

j *n.* Letter of the Basque alphabet, usually pronounced like English *h* as in house, but in some parts of the Basque Country it is pronounced like *y* in yellow. The latter pronunciation is now recommended in Unified Basque.

jabal *adj.* calm (sea). *adj.* lazy. *adj.* weak, cowardly.

jabalaldi *n.* moment of calm (on the sea), period of calm seas.

jabalarazi *v.t.* to calm, to make calm.

jabaldu *v.i.* to slow down, to calm down, to die down. *v.i.* to pacify, to calm.

jabaldura *n.* pacification, calming, cessation (wind).

jabalgarri *adj.* calmable; mitigant, calmative, calming.

jabalpen *n.* calmness, tranquility.

jabe *n.* owner, proprietor.

jabedun *adj.* propertied, having property.

jabe egin *v.i.* to become the owner of. *v.t.* to make (someone) the owner of.

jabegabe *adj.* vacant. (lit.) without an owner.

jabegabe(ko) *adj.* vacant. (lit.) without an owner.

jabegai *n.* heir, prime heir, heir apparent.

jabegaitasun *n.* quality of being an heir, position as heir, status as heir.

jabego *n.* right of property, ownership, dominion.

jabe izan *v.i.* to possess, to own, to be in control of, to dispose of.

jabekeria *n.* authoritarianism.

jabeketa *n.* appropriation, domination.

jabekide *n.* co-owner.

jabekidego *n.* joint ownership.

jabekidetasun *n.* joint ownership.

jabekidetu *v.i.* to buy jointly.

jabekidetza *n.* partnership, joint acquisition, co-ownership, co-tenancy.

jabekor *adj.* possessive, acquiring.

jabekunde *n.* appropriation, taking, possession.

jabekuntza *n.* acquisition, appropriation.

jabetasun *n.* ownership, domination, proprietorship. *n.* self-determination, autonomy; independence.

jabetu *v.i.* to appropriate, to acquire, to own; to dominate. *v.i.* to capture, to seize. *v.i.(fig.)* to realize, to become aware of.

jabetza *n.* ownership, dominion, proprietorship.

jabetzaile *adj.* appropriating.

jabetzapen *n.* appropriation.

jaboi *n.* soap.

jadaneko *adv.* already, by now. *adj.* in force, in vogue, present.

jadanik *adv.* already.

jadetsi *v.t.* to obtain, to get, to acquire.

jagi *v.i.* to get up, to rise.

jagole *n.* custodian, guardian, watchman.

jagon *v.t.* to take care of, to care for, to guard.

jai *n.* celebration, festival, day off, holiday.

jaialai *n.* handball game played with a basket-like glove. (lit.) happy festival.

jaialdi *n.* festival, festivity. Usually a period of music and dancing.

jaialditxo *n.(dim.)* small festival.

jaiaurre *n.* eve of a festival.

jaibezpera *n.* eve of a festival or holiday.

jaiburu *n.* most important day of a festival or celebration. *n.* president of the festival.

jaidura *n.* tendency, inclination.

jai egin *v.t.* to take a day off. *v.t.* to celebrate.

jaiegun *n.* holiday, festival day.

jaierdi *n.* half-day off, afternoon off, half-day holiday.

jaietxe *n.* recreation hall, activities building.

jaigela *n.* recreation room.

jaihondatzaile *n.* wet blanket, party pooper.

jai izan *v.t.* to have a vacation. *v.t.(fig.)* to be lost, to have nothing to do.

jaijantzi *n.* party clothes.

jaiki *v.i.* to get up, to rise. *v.i.* to rise up, to rebel, to be insubordinate. *v.i.* to rise (bread dough).

jaikiarazi *v.t.* to make (someone) get up.

jaikiera *n.* rising, levitation, getting up.

jaikiezin *adj.* unable to rise. *adj.* unleavenable (bread), unleavened.

jaikigarri *adj.* leavened, risen. *adj.* fermentable.

Jainko *n.* God.

jainkoantzeko *adj.* God-like.

jainkoarren *int.* by God!, my God!

jainkogabe *adj.* godless, atheist.

jainkogabetasun n. atheism.
jainkogisako adj. God-like.
jainkojakintza n. theology.
jainkojale adj. affectedly devout or pious.
jainkoki adv. divinely.
jainkorde n. idol, fetish.
jainkosa n. goddess.
jainkotar adj. divine. adj. devout, pious.
jainkotasun n. divinity, godliness.
jainkotiar adj. devout, pious.
jainkotiartasun n. piety, piousness, devotion.
jainkotu v.t. to deify, to make a god of.
jainkozale adj. devout, pious.
jainkozaletasun n. piety, piousness, devotion.
jainkozko adj. divine.
jaio v.i. to be born. adj. born.
jaioaurreko adj. prenatal.
jaioberri n./adj. newborn.
jaioera n. birth.
jaiogabe adj. unborn. adj. born by means of a Caesarian operation.
jaiokunde n. nativity, birth.
jaiokuntza n. nativity, birth.
jaioleku n. cradle, crib. n. place of birth.
jaiotegun n. birthday.
jaioterri n. native land, native country; home town, native village.
jaioterro n. origin, family tree, genealogy.
jaiotetxe n. house where one was born.
jaiotizkera n. native tongue, vernacular.
jaiotizkuntza n. native tongue, vernacular.
jaiotza n. birth. n. nativity, nativity scene.
jaiotzaile adj. born, rising (sun).
jaiotzako adj. congenital, inborn, innate.
jaitarte n. day between holidays often treated as a holiday or day off.
jaitoki n. place for festivals or celebrations.
jaitsi v.i. to descend, to go down, to get down, to come down. v.t. to lower, to take down.
jaitsialdi n. decadence, decay.
jaitsiarazi v.t. to make (someone) get down or descend.
jaitsiarazle n. person who helps another get down or out (of a bus, etc.), or to dismount.
jaitsiera n. lowering, descending.
jaitsu adj. festive.
jaitu v.t. to celebrate, to commemorate.
jaizale adj. fond of festivals, celebrations, or holidays.
jaizubi n. day between holidays which is often treated as a holiday or day off.

jaka n. jacket.
jakan adj. picky (eater), having little or no appetite.
jakandu v.i. to lose one's appetite.
jakera n. act of eating.
jaki n. snack, provisions, food.
jakile n. person who knows, knowledgeable person.
jakimen n. learning faculty, mental faculty.
jakin v.t. to know, to be familiar with, to be informed, to find out, to discover. adj. manifest, evident, known, notorious, obvious.
jakina adv. of course, certainly.
jakinarazi v.t. to notify, to inform, to cause to know, to let (someone) know, to communicate.
jakinarazle n. informer.
jakinarazpen n. communication, advice, notification.
jakinbide n. teaching method, means of knowing.
jakinduria n. knowledge, education, wisdom.
jakinean adv. knowingly, in the know, aware.
jakineko adj. aforesaid, said, mentioned above.
jakinez adv. deliberately, consciously.
jakinez(a) n. ignorance, lack of knowledge or education.
jakinezin adj. unknowable.
jakingabe adj. ignorant.
jakingabetasun n. ignorance.
jakingabez adv. ignorantly.
jakingabezia n. ignorance.
jakingale n. curiosity, desire to know. adj. curious, desirous of knowing.
jakingarri adj. worthy of being known. n. object of knowing.
jakingura adj. curious. n. curiosity.
jakinguraz adv. curiously.
jakiniturri n. source of knowledge, fountain of information.
jakinmin n. curiosity. adj. curious.
jakinnahi n. curiosity, desire for knowledge. adj. curious.
jakintasun n. knowledge, wisdom.
jakintsu adj. wise, clever; knowledgeable, erudite.
jakintsuki adv. knowingly, in a scholarly manner, eruditely.
jakintza n. knowledge, wisdom; education.
jakintzale adj. studious, diligent (in study).
jakinzale adj. curious.
jakitate n. knowledge, wisdom.
jakite n. knowing, knowledge.
jakitegi n. pantry; grocery store.
jakitoki n. pantry.
jakitun adj. aware, informed, in the know.
jakitun egon v.i. to be aware of.
jakituria n. knowledge, wisdom.
jakitxartel n. menu.

jale adj./n. having a good appetite; a good eater.

-jale Used in compound words. Derived from *jale*, eater. **Belarjale.** Herbivorous.

jaletasun n. gluttony, voracity (of appetite).

jalgi v.i. to go outside, to go out.

jalgiarazi v.t. to make (someone) go out or leave.

jalgigune n. point of departure.

jalgitza n. departure.

jalki v.i. to sediment, to settle (liquid).

jalkiera n. sedimentation, settling.

jan v.t. to eat. n. feast, feed, meal. v.t.(fig.) to corrode, to decay.

janaldi n. banquet. n. dinner hour, time to eat.

janarau n. diet, regimen.

janarazi v.t. to make (someone) eat; to feed, to nourish.

janari n. food.

janaridenda n. grocery store.

janarigela n. pantry.

janaritegi n. grocery store; pantry.

janaritoki n. pantry.

janaritu v.i. to feed oneself, to nourish oneself, to eat. v.t. to feed, to nourish.

janbehar n. gluttony, voracious appetite.

janbera adj. flavorful, tasty, appetizing.

jandei n. dinner invitation.

janedan n. food and drink, feasting, banquet.

jan-edariak n.(pl.) provisions, groceries, food and drink.

janerazi v.t. to make (someone) eat, to stuff with food.

janeurri n. diet.

janeurritu v.t. to diet.

janeza n. fast, abstinence from food.

janezin adj. inedible. n. loss of appetite.

jangai n. food, nourishment.

jangaiak n.(pl.) provisions, groceries, food.

jangaitz adj. inedible.

jangarri adj. edible.

jangiro n. weather that invites eating.

jangura n. appetite.

jankide n. dinner companion, dinner guest, companion in eating.

jankor adj. having a voracious appetite.

janleku n. dining room.

janondo n. after dinner hour, period after eating.

janordu n. eating hour, dinner hour.

janornitu v.i./v.t. to provide food.

janornitzaile n. supplier or provider of food.

jantoki n. dining room.

jantsenismo n. Jansenism.

jantsenista n./adj. Jansenist.

jantxakur n.(colloq.) mooch, a person who lives off of other people.

jantxakur izan v.i. to be a mooch, to sponge off people.

jantxakurkeria n. mooching, sponging off someone.

jantzale adj./n. having a good appetite; big eater.

jantzi v.t./v.i. to dress, to put on (clothing); to get dressed. v.t.(fig.) to furnish.

jantziaraza n. clothes closet.

jantzidenda n. clothing store, dress shop.

jantzi-erantzi n. change of clothes, old clothes.

jantzigain n. cape, overcoat.

jantzigaineko n. coat, overcoat.

jantzigarri adj. wearable.

jantzigela n. dressing room, fitting room.

jantzigile n. seamstress, dress designer, tailor.

jantzigin n. seamstress, dress designer, tailor.

jantzigintza n. tailoring, clothes making.

jantzikutxa n. trunk, clothes chest, chest of drawers.

jantzileku n. dressing room; cloakroom, coat room.

jantzitegi n. dressing room; cloakroom, coat room.

jantziteria n. wardrobe, group of clothes.

jantzitoki n. dressing room.

jantzitxo n.(dim.) small dress.

jantzizain n. valet, coat (or hat) check person, cloak room attendant.

jantzizaintza n. job of the coat (or hat) checker, job of cloak room attendant.

janzale adj. having a good appetite; gluttonous.

janzkera n. fashion, manner of dress.

janzki n. clothing, article of clothing.

japoniera n. Japanese language.

jaramon n. attention, notice.

jaramon egin v.t. to pay attention, to notice, to listen to.

jaramongarri adj. noticeable, worthy of attention.

jaraunsgarri adj. inheritable.

jaraunskide n. co-heir, co-inheritor.

jaraunskin n. patrimony, inheritance.

jaraunsle n. heir.

jaraunspen n. act of inheriting, inheritance.

jarauntsi v.t. to inherit.

jarauntsi-ondasunak n. inherited goods.

jardun v.t. to spend time.

jaregin v.t. to free, to liberate, to let loose.

jareitasun n. liberation.

jario n. spill, secretion, drip, emanation. v.i. to spill, to drip, to ooze, to flow.

jarioaldi n. spill, flow, drip.

jariodura n. act of spilling, flowing, oozing, emanating, outpouring.

jariogarri adj. flowable, oozable, spillable.
jariokor adj. fluid.
jariokortasun n. fluidity.
jariokin n. secretion, flow, spill.
jariotasun n. fluidity, fluidness.
jariotu v.i. to spill, to secrete.
jaritxi v.t. to obtain, to get, to acquire.
jarkera n. way of positioning, way of placing. n. attitude.
jarki v.t. to face, to confront.
jarkiezin adj. irresistible.
jarkigarri adj. resistible, opposable.
jarkipen n. rebuttal, refutation.
jarkitzaile adj. opposite, opposing, adverse, resisting, argumentative. n. opponent, adversary, arguer.
jarle n. one who places or puts; usher (in a theater).
jarleku n. seat, place to sit down.
jarpen n. installation, placement, putting.
jarralaldi n. continuation, continuance, sequel.
jarraibide n. example, norm; way of continuing.
jarraibidezko adj. imitative.
jarraidun adj. consecutive, continuing.
jarraiera n. continuity, continuation.
jarraigabe adj. discontinuous, interrupted.
jarraigarri adj. exemplary, imitable.
jarraigarritasun n. exemplariness.
jarraika adv. uninterruptedly, continuously.
jarraikarazi v.t. to make (someone) continue, to cause to continue.
jarraikera n. succession, order, continuation.
jarraiketa n. pursuit, following, continuation.
jarraiki v.i. to follow, to go behind, to trail. v.i. to persecute, to attack, to go after. adj. assiduous, tenacious, constant, diligent.
jarraikiro adv. continuously, diligently, constantly, tenaciously, assiduously.
jarraikitasun n. continuity. n. persistence, assiduousness, regularity.
jarraikor adj. persistent, continuous, diligent, assiduous.
jarraikuntza n. continuity.
jarraile n. imitator, follower. n. successor, continuer. adj. hard-working, assiduous, diligent.
jarraipen n. continuation. n. imitation.
jarraipenezko adj. imitative, copying.
jarraipide n. continuation, continuance.
jarraitasun n. continuity.
jarraitu v.t./v.i. to follow, to continue, to persevere. v.t. to persecute. v.t. to imitate.
jarraitza n. act of following, imitating; constancy.
jarraitzaile adj. following, continuing.

n. follower, disciple.
jarrera n. attitude, behavior. n. position, posture.
jarrerazi v.t. to seat (someone). v.t. to place, to put.
jarri v.i. to sit down. v.t. to put, to place; to put on (clothes).
jarrialdi n. sitting, time spent sitting.
jarritako adj. placed, put.
jartoki n. seat.
jartzaile n. one who puts or places; putter, placer.
jasa n. torrential rain, storm.
jasale adj.(gram.) passive (subject or verb, etc.). n. sufferer.
jasamen n. tolerance, patience.
jasan v.t. to uphold, to support, to bear, to carry (a weight or burden), to put up with. v.t. to suffer, to bear, to tolerate.
jasanarazi v.t. to make (someone) suffer or bear. v.t. to make (someone) carry or support.
jasanbehar n. suffering. n. passivity, passiveness.
jasanbera adj. patient, tolerant, suffering, forebearing.
jasanbidez adv. passively; patiently.
jasanerraz adj. bearable, tolerable, sufferable.
jasanezin adj. intolerable, unbearable, insufferable.
jasanezinez adv. insufferably, unbearably.
jasanezin(ezko) adj. intolerable, unbearable, insufferable.
jasangabe adj. intolerant, unbearable, insufferable. adj. intransigent, uncompromising.
jasangaitz adj. unbearable, intolerable.
jasangaizkeria n. impatience.
jasangaiztasun n. intolerance, impatience.
jasangarri adj. tolerable, bearable, supportable.
jasangarriro adv. tolerably, bearably.
jasankizun n. that which must be born or suffered.
jasankor adj. patient, tolerant, longsuffering, forebearing.
jasankortasun n. tolerance, patience.
jasapen n. tolerance, patience.
jasate n. act of tolerating, suffering, bearing.
jaso v.t. to lift, to raise, to pick up. v.t. to construct, to build, to raise (a barn, etc.). v.t. to get, to collect, to receive. v.t. to found, to institute, to establish. v.t. to endure, to undergo, to bear. v.t. to improve, to get better (weather).
jasoagiri n. receipt.
jasoaldi n. lift, action of lifting, time spent lifting.
jasoarazi v.t. to raise, to lift, to make (someone) lift (something).
jasoera n. hoisting, raising, lifting.

jasogailu n. crane, freight elevator, dumbwaiter.

jasogune n. raised place, high place.

jasoketa n. raising, lifting.

jasokor adj. liftable, raisable.

jasokunde n. lifting, raising. n.(R.C.Ch.) Assumption of the Virgin (August 15).

jasokuntza n. lifting, raising.

jasotzaile n./adj. lifter, raiser; lifting, raising.

jataldi n. meal, mealtime, time to eat.

jatarbi n. radish.

jataurre n. time before a meal.

jate n. eating.

jateko n. food.

jatekoak n.(pl.) food, provisions.

jaten eman v.t. to nourish, to feed, to give (someone something) to eat.

jatetxe n. restaurant.

jatondo n. after-dinner hour, time after a meal.

jatontzi n. plate, dish, platter.

jator adj. authentic, typical, original, native, pure. adj. real, true, sincere. adj. correct, good; nice. adj. fertile.

jatorburu n. beginning, origin, source.

jatordu n. mealtime, time to eat.

jatorkeria n. excessive purity (of language, customs, etc.).

jatorki adv. purely, correctly.

jatorri n. origin, source, beginning.

jatorriko adj. native, originated, derived.

jatorriz adv. originally.

jatorrizko adj. original, primitive.

jatortasun n. originality, authenticity, genuineness, pureness.

jatoste n. time after eating, after-dinner hour.

jatots n. sound of chewing.

jats n.(bot.) sorghum.

jatun adj./n. having a good appetite; good eater.

jauki n. attack, assault, violent attack.

jaukimendu n. attack, assault.

jaukitu v.t. to attack, to assault.

jaulki v.i. to fall from a tree (ripe fruit). v.i. to narrate, to report, to refer, to relate.

jaulkigarri adj. narratable, describable.

jaulkitzaile n. narrator, relator, teller.

jaun n. mister, sir, lord; sometimes used for God. Used especially as an honorary title.

jaun(a) eman v.t. to give communion.

jaun-andreak n. Mr. and Mrs., ladies and gentlemen.

jaunartu v.t. to take communion, to receive communion.

jaunartze n. act of receiving communion, communion.

jaunartzeondore n.(eccl.) Post-Communion; time after communion.

jaundu v.i. to dominate, to rule, to lord it over (someone). v.i. to become lord and master.

jauneria n. group of gentlemen, group of noblemen.

jaunetxe n. house of the master. n. city hall.

jaungo n. seigniorial authority.

Jaungoiko n. God.

jaungoikotasun n. divinity, divine nature, godliness.

jaungoikotu v.t. to deify, to make a god of. v.i. to become god-like.

jaungoikozale adj. devout, pious.

jaungoikozko adj. divine.

jauntasun n. dominion, authority. n. quality of being a gentleman, boss, or person in control.

jauntxo n.(dim.) lord, master. n. boss, despot, little dictator.

jauntxogo n. authority or power of a boss.

jauntxokeria n. domination by petty chiefs or political bosses.

jauntzapen n. seizure, taking possession.

jauntzar n. despot, tyrant, dictator.

jaur- Used in certain compounds and derived from jaun, lord.

jauregitxo n.(dim.) small palace.

jauregizain n. guardian of the palace.

jauregizaintza n. job of the guardian of the palace.

jaurerri n. seignory, domain of the lord of the manor.

jauresgarri adj. venerable, respectable, worthy of worship or adoration.

jauresle n. worshiper, adorer.

jauresketa n. worship, adoration.

jaurespen n. worship, adoration.

jauretsi v.t. to adore, to worship.

jauretxe n. manor, ancestral home.

jaurgo n. dominion, authority.

jaurkera n. way of governing.

jaurketa n. act of governing.

jaurlari n. governor.

jaurlaritza n. government.

jaurtaldi n. cast, throw, toss.

jaurti v.t. to throw.

jaurtierraz adj. easily thrown.

jaurtigai adj. easily thrown. n. projectile (bomb, arrow, anything thrown).

jaurtigailu n. apparatus used to hurl a projectile (catapult, bow, etc.).

jaurtigarri adj. throwable.

jaurtika adv. throwing, launching.

jaurtiketa n. act of throwing.

jaurtiki v.t. to throw, to launch, to toss.

jaurtikor adj. throwable.

jaurtilari n. thrower, launcher.

jaurtitzaile adj./n. throwing; thrower, launcher.

jausgailu n. parachute.

jausi v.i. to fall.

jausialdi n. fall. n. decline, depression, prostration.

jausiarazi v.t. to make (something) fall,

to let fall, to destroy, to demolish.

jauskera *n.* fall, way of falling.

jausketa *n.* fall, falling, downfall, collapse, decline.

jauskor *adj.* likely to fall, deciduous, decadent, liable to fall.

jauskortasun *n.* tendency to fall.

jausleku *n.* precipice, cliff, ravine, chasm, gorge.

jauspen *n.* fall, act of falling, downfall, ruin.

jaustasun *n.* decline, prostration.

jaustegi *n.* precipice, chasm, gorge, abyss.

jaustoki *n.* precipice, cliff; slippery place.

jautsaldi *n.* descending.

jauzi *v.i.* to jump, to leap. *n.* jump, leap.

jauziarazi *v.t.* to make (someone) jump.

jauzi egin *v.t.* to jump.

jauzika *adv.* jumping.

jauzikari *n.* jumper, skydiver, parachutist, leaper.

jauzilari *adj.* jumping, frisky, frolicsome. *n.* jumper, leaper.

jauzketa *n.* action of jumping.

jauzkor *adj.* jumpy, lively.

jauzleku *n.* trampoline, diving board.

jazar *n.* combat, fight, quarrel, struggle.

jazargo *n.* opposition, contradiction. *n.* quarrel, dispute.

jazarketa *n.* persecution.

jazarkunde *n.* persecution.

jazarle *n.* persecutor.

jazarpen *n.* persecution. *n.* attack.

jazarraldi *n.* period of persecution. *n.* attack.

jazarri *v.t./v.i.* to persecute. *v.t.* to attack. *v.i./v.t.* to scold, to reprimand.

jazartzaile *adj./n.* persecuting; persecutor.

jazkarri *adj.* dressable, wearable.

jazkera *n.* way of dressing.

jazo *v.i.* to occur, to happen, to come to pass.

jazobehar *n.* fate, destiny.

jazoera *n.* happening, event, occurrence.

jazokuntza *n.* occurrence, happening, incident.

jazte *n.* act of getting dressed, act of wearing.

jaztegi *n.* dressing room.

jaztoki *n.* dressing room.

jeinu *n.* genius, talent, skill.

jeinudun *adj.* genius, talented, skillful.

jeinutasun *n.* ingeniousness, talent, skillfulness.

jeinutsu *adj.* skillful, talented, dextrous, ingenious.

jeinutsuki *adv.* skillfully, ingeniously.

jeinuz *adv.* ingeniously, skillfully.

JEL *n.(pol.)* Initials of the motto of the PNV (Basque Nationalist Party). The motto is *Jaungoikoa eta lege zarra*, God and the old law.

jela *n.* ice, especially artificially made.

jelagailu *n.* freezer.

jelate *n.* frost season, period of cold weather, cold snap.

jelatsu *adj.* icy, frosty.

jelatu *v.i.* to freeze.

jelkide *n.(pol.)* member of the PNV, the Basque Nationalist Party.

jelos *adj.* jealous.

jelosia *n.* envy, jealousy.

jeloskor *adj.* jealous.

jeloskortasun *n.* tendency for being jealous.

jelostu *v.i.* to become jealous. *v.i.* to not trust, to distrust, to suspect.

jendaila *n.* rabble, riff-raff, mob.

jendalde *n.* multitude, masses, crowd.

jendarte *n.* people, public.

jendarteko *adj.* public.

jendaurreko *adj.* public.

jende *n.* people (usually singular in Basque).

jendegabe *adj.* unpopulated, uninhabited.

jendegabetu *v.i.* to depopulate; to become depopulated or uninhabited.

jendeketa *n.* group of people, gathering, crowd.

jendeki *adv.* courteously, politely.

jendekiko *adj.* courteous, affable, polite.

jendekin *adj.* sociable, gregarious.

jendekintasun *n.* sociableness, gregariousness.

jendekoi *adj.* sociable, gregarious.

jendekoitasun *n.* sociability, gregariousness.

jendelerro *n.* line of people, row of people.

jendemultzo *n.* group, crowd, multitude.

jendepilo *n.* group, crowd, multitude.

jendetalde *n.* crowd, multitude.

jendetasun *n.* courtesy, politeness.

jendeteria *n.* crowd, multitude, masses.

jendetsu *adj.* populous, populated, crowded.

jendetza *n.* crowd, multitude, people.

jendexka *n.* common people, simple people.

jendeztatu *v.t.* to repopulate, to inhabit again.

jeneral *n.(mil.)* general. *adj.* general, common.

jeneralgo *n.(mil.)* generalship.

jeneralizapen *n.* generalization.

jeneralizatu *v.t./v.i.* to generalize.

jeneralizazio *n.* generalization.

jeneraltasun *n.* generality.

jenero *n.* gender. *n.* food.

jentil *n./adj.* pagan.

jentilarri *n.* dolmen, menhir.

jentildu *v.i.* to become a pagan.

jentileria *n.* group of pagans.

jentiltasun *n.* paganism.

jerez *n.* sherry, Andalusian wine made near the city of Jerez.

jertse *n.* sweater.

jin *v.i.* to come.

Jinko *n.* God.

jipoi *n.* beating, blow, swat.

jipoialdi *n.* beating, blow, time such a beating lasts.

jipoiemale *n.* beater, hitter.

jipoindu *v.t.* to hit, to strike, to beat.

jipoitu *v.t.* to hit, to strike, to beat.

jipoitzaile *adj.* bruising, contusive.

jira *n.* turn, return, gyration.

jirabide *n.* circuit.

jirabira *n.* turn, rotation, gyration, turning.

jirabiraka *adv.* turning, rotating, gyrating.

jirabiratu *v.i.* to gyrate, to whirl, to rotate, to turn. *v.t.* to turn, to whirl, to rotate.

jirafa *n.(zool.)* giraffe.

jiragarri *adj.* turnable, rotatable.

jiraka *adv.* spinning, whirling, turning, rotating.

jiratu *v.i./v.t.* to gyrate, to spin, to whirl, to turn.

jite *n.* instinct, nature, character.

jitez *adv.* instinctively, by nature.

jitezko *adj.* instinctive, innate, natural, inborn.

jo *v.t.* to hit, to strike, to beat. *v.t.* to run into, to bump into, to collide. *v.t.* to play (music or an instrument). *v.t.* to head for, to aim for, to go. *v.t.* to strike (the hour). *v.t.* to appeal (legally). *v.t.* to knock. *v.t.* to act, to proceed, to do. *adj.* crazy; sick; bankrupt.

joaldi *n.* continuous striking, repeated hitting, beating. *n.* sound, tune, click, ring, knock.

joale *n.* emigrant, one who is leaving.

joan *v.i.* to go, to leave. *v.i.* to pass (time). *v.i.* to fit, to suit, to look good on. *n.* departure, going, leaving.

joanaldi *n.* departure, leaving, going. *n.* past, past time. *n.* trip, journey.

joanarazi *v.t.* to make (someone) go.

joandako *n.* past, preterite.

joan-etorri *n.* round trip, going and coming.

joangai *adj.* ready to go.

joan-itzuli *n.* round trip.

joan-jin *n.* round trip.

joan-jinka *adv.* going back and forth, going to and from.

joankor *adj.* transitory, ephemeral, passing.

joankortasun *n.* caducity, perishableness, transitoriness.

joanordu *n.* hour of departure.

joare *n.* cow bell, bell on an animal.

joate *n.* act of going, departure.

jo egin *v.t.* to hit, to collide with, to run into.

joera *n.* inclination, tendency, disposition, trend. *n.* behavior, conduct.

joera izan *v.t.* to have a tendency.

joerakor *adj.* inclined, having a propensity for.

joeraldatu *v.t.* to change direction.

joeratsu *adj.* inclined, disposed.

joeratu *v.i.* to become fond of, to become attached to.

joezin(a) *n.* impotence (sometimes sexual).

jogailu *n.* mallet, hammer.

joka *adv.* hitting, striking, by blows, beating.

jokabide *n.* behavior, conduct, comportment.

jokaera *n.* behavior, conduct.

jokaezin *adj.* not able to be conjugated; uncombinable.

jokagarri *adj.* playable. *adj.* able to be conjugated.

jokalari *n.* player. *adj./n.* gambler.

jokaldi *n.* turn (in a game), game, playing time, contest.

jokalege *n.* rule(s) of the game.

jokaleku *n.* playing field, recreational park.

jokamolde *n.* behavior, conduct; orientation.

jokatu *v.t.* to play. *v.t./v.i.* to behave, to act like. *v.t.* to conjugate. *v.t.* to bet.

jokatzaile *n.* player.

jokazain *n.* referee, umpire (baseball).

jokera *n.* hitting, striking. *n.* tendency, inclination, trend. *n.* behavior, comportment, conduct.

joketa *n.* repeated and frequent touching.

joketaldi *n.* pounding, pommeling, hammering.

joko *n.* sport, recreation, diversion, game. *n.(fig.)* trick, practical joke.

jokoetxe *n.* casino.

jokozale *adj.* fond of games; gambling.

jolas *n.* game, diversion, recreation, sport.

jolasalde *n.* recreational area.

jolasaldi *n.* period of recreation, play, action of playing.

jolasbide *n.* means of playing.

jolas egin *v.t.* to play.

jolas eragin *v.t.* to entertain, to make (people) have fun.

jolaseta *n.* recreation place, club.

jolasgarri *adj.* recreational, entertaining.

jolasketa *n.* diversion, entertainment. *n.* play, action of playing, period of recreation.

jolaskide *n.* player, participant, teammate.

jolasleku *n.* recreational park, amusement park, playing field.

jolastoki *n.* playing field, recreational park.

jolastordu *n.* recreational time,

playtime, recess.
jolastu *v.i.* to play, to entertain oneself.
jolaszale *adj.* sporty, athletic, fond of sports.
jolaszaletasun *n.* fondness for sports.
jole *n.* hitter, attacker. *n.* player (of a musical instrument).
jomuga *n.* objective, goal, end.
jopu *n.* servant, slave, captive.
jopukeria *n.* slavery.
jopulan *n.* servile work, work of servants.
joputasun *n.* servitude; slavery.
joran *n.* anxiety, worry, desire, ardor, enthusiasm.
jorantsu *adj.* anxious, worried, desirous.
jori *adj.* prodigious, copious, abundant. *adj.* fecund, fertile; rich. *adv.* copiously, abundantly.
joridura *n.* prosperity.
jorigarri *adj.* fertilizable.
jori izan *v.i.* to abound, to be abundant.
joriki *adv.* abundantly.
joritasun *n.* abundance, fertility, copiousness; richness, eloquence.
joritsu *adj.* abundant, copious, prodigious, rich, eloquent.
joritu *v.t.* to enrich, to improve, to make abundant. *v.i.* to become enriched, to become richer, to prosper. *v.t.* to fertilize.
joritzaile *adj.* fertilizing.
jorra *n.* weeding with a hoe.
jorrai *n.* small hoe.
jorraiko *n.* small hoe.
jorraila *n.* April.
jorraketa *n.* hoeing, weeding with a hoe.
jorraldi *n.* weeding, time spent weeding.
jorrale *n.* weeder, hoer.
jorran *adv.* weeding.
jorraro *n.* weeding, time of weeding.
jorratu *v.t.* to weed, to hoe.
jorratzaile *n.* weeder, hoer.
josgabe *adj.* seamless, unsewn.
josi *v.t.* to sew. *v.t.* to nail.
joskera *n.* way of sewing. *n.(gram.)* syntax.
josketa *n.* act of sewing.
joskile *n.* seamstress, tailor, dressmaker.
joskin *n.* seamstress, tailor, dressmaker.
joskintza *n.* profession of seamstress or tailor.
joskura *n.* seam, stitch; suture.
josle *n.* tailor, seamstress, dressmaker.
josmakina *n.* sewing machine.
josta *n.* recreation, diversion, game, entertainment.
jostabide *n.* recreation, way of having fun, play.
jostadura *n.* amusement, diversion.

jostagarri *adj.* fun, recreational, entertaining. *adj.* joking, funny, teasing.
jostailu *n.* toy, plaything.
jostailudenda *n.* toy store.
jostailugintza *n.* toy making, manufacturing of toys.
jostailusaltzaile *n.* toy seller.
jostakatu *v.i.* to play, to have fun, to entertain oneself.
jostakeria *n.* dirty trick.
jostaketa *n.* recreation, diversion, entertainment. *n.* sport. *n.* competition, contest.
jostakin *adj.* funny, joking, jesting, amusing.
jostakor *adj.* playful, frisky, frolicsome.
jostalari *n.* player, entertainer, amuser, frolicker. *adj.* playful, frolicsome; fun, entertaining, enjoyable; funny, humorous, amusing.
jostaldi *n.* recreation period, play time.
jostaleku *n.* recreation area, playing field.
jostarazi *v.t.* to entertain.
jostarazle *n.* entertainer.
jostari *adj.* playful, frolicsome, funny, joking. *n.* sewing thread.
jostatu *v.i.* to play, to have fun, to entertain oneself.
jostazale *adj.* fond of diversions; humorous, jovial, funny, entertaining.
josteta *n.* play, diversion.
jostorratz *n.* sewing needle.
jostotzara *n.* sewing basket.
jostun *n.* seamstress, dressmaker, tailor.
jostundegi *n.* dressmaker's shop.
jostungela *n.* sewing room.
jostura *n.* seam, stitch; suture.
josulagun *n.* Jesuit.
jota *n.* kind of dance. *adj.* sunk, exhausted, broke, crazy.
jo ta ke *adv.* ardently, anxiously, fervently, earnestly.
jotari *n.* dancer of the *jota*.
jo ta su *adv.* ardently, fervently, anxiously.
jotera egin *v.t.* to make like one is going to hit or strike, to pretend to hit.
jotzaile *n.* hitter, striker. *n.* player (of a musical instrument).
jubilatu *v.i.* to retire, to receive a pension, to be on retirement.
jubilazio *n.* retirement.
judas *n.* traitor. *adj.* traitorous, disloyal.
judaskeria *n.* treason, treachery, disloyalty.
judeobatzar *n.* Sanhedrin; religious Jewish assembly.
judu *adj.* Jewish.
juduetsai *n.* antisemite.
juduetsaikeria *n.* antisemitism.
judukeria *n.* trick, nasty prank.
judulege *n.* Jewish law.
judutalde *n.* group of Jews.

judutar *adj.* Jewish.
judutegi *n.* Jewish ghetto.
juduteria *n.* group of Jews.
judutu *v.i.* to become Jewish, to convert to Judaism.
judutza *n.* group of Jews.
jujamendu *n.* judgment.
jujatu *v.t.* to judge.
juje *n.* judge.
jukutria *n.* cunning, slyness, shrewdness.
juntetxe *n.* meeting hall.
juramendu *n.* oath. *n.* swear word, blasphemy.
juramendu egin *v.t.* to take an oath, to swear. *v.t.* to cuss, to blaspheme.
justizia *n.* justice.
justu *adj.* exact, precise, just.
justutasun *n.* exactness, preciseness.
juzgatu *v.t.* to judge.
juzgu *n.* judgment. *n.* suspicion.

K

k *n.* Letter of the Basque alphabet.
-k *(gram.)* Suffix which indicates one agent. *(gram.)* Suffix of the aux. *ukan* (2nd person singular, masculine familiar form). **Jon, bukatu al duk lan hau?** John, have you finished this work?
-ka *(gram.)* Suffix which denotes continuous action, added to verbs and nouns to form modal adverbs. **Harrika.** Throwing stones.
kabal *n.* any domestic animal (especially cattle).
kabaret *n.* cabaret.
-kabe *(gram.)* Suffix meaning without, or indicating lack or deprivation.
kabia *n.* nest.
kabiar *n.* caviar.
kabiezin *adj.* uncontainable.
kabila *n.* pole; mast. *n.* wooden brake on a cart. *n.(anat.)* ankle.
kabilara *n.(zool.)* sparrow hawk.
kabitu *v.i.* to fit.
kable *n.* cable. *n.* cablegram, telegram.
kablegrama *n.* cablegram, telegram.
kabu *n.(mil.)* corporal *n.* calculation, evaluation; initiative.
-kada *(gram.)* Suffix which indicates a hit or blow. **Harrikada.** Blow with a stone. *(gram.)* Suffix which indicates a measure. **Eskukada.** Handful.
kadira *n.* seat, chair.
kafe *n.* coffee.
kafegailu *n.* coffeemaker, coffee pot.
kafegarau *n.* coffee bean.
kaferrota *n.* coffee grinder.
kafesne *n.* coffee with milk.
kafesoro *n.* coffee plantation.
kafetegi *n.* coffee shop.
kafetondo *n.(bot.)* coffee tree, coffee plant.
kafetontzi *n.* coffee pot.
kafetxe *n.* coffee house.
kai *n.* dock, pier. *n.* port, harbor.

-kai *(gram.)* Suffix denoting material designated for something. Used instead of *-gai* after *z* and *s*.
kaiar *n.(zool.)* large seagull.
kaiargi *n.* lighthouse.
kaiku *n.* wooden bowl (used for milking sheep). *adj.(colloq.)* imbecile, idiot, stupid. *n.* special jacket (in blue, green or red) used by Basque mountaineers.
kaikukeria *n.* stupidity, idiocy, imbecility.
kaikuki *adv.* foolishly, stupidly, idiotically.
kaikuontzi *adj.* idiot, fool.
kaikutu *v.i.* to become stupid, to become an idiot or a fool.
kaiman *n.(zool.)* alligator.
kainabera *n.(bot.)* cane, reed.
kainaberadi *n.* cane field.
kainaberatu *v.t.* to stake up plants for support using pieces of cane.
kainamo *n.(bot.)* hemp.
kainoi *n.* cannon.
kainoialdi *n.* cannonading, shelling.
kainoigile *n.* cannon maker.
kainoigintza *n.* cannon making.
kainoikada *n.* cannon shot.
kainoikatu *v.t.* to cannonade, to shell with a cannon, to fire a cannon.
kainoiketa *n.* cannonade, shelling, bombardment with a cannon.
kainoilari *n.* gunner, artilleryman.
kainoilaritza *n.* job of the artilleryman.
kainu *n.* drain, drain pipe, sewer drain.
kainuzulo *n.* drain.
kaio *n.(zool.)* seagull.
kaiola *n.* cage. *n.(fig.)* jail, prison.
kaiolaratu *v.t.* to cage, to put in a cage. *v.i.* to enter a cage, to approach a cage.
kaiolatu *v.t.* to cage, to put in a cage.
kaixa *n.* trunk, chest.
kaixo! *int.* hello! hi!
kaka *n.* excrement, feces, crap, shit. *n.(colloq.)* filth, nastiness, vile thing, dirt.
kaka egin *v.t.* to defecate, to have a bowel movement, to go to the bathroom, to shit.
kakagale *n.* need to defecate, desire to defecate. *adj.* having the desire to defecate.
kakagale izan *v.i.* to want to defecate.
kakagaletu *v.i.* to want to got to the bathroom.
kakagura *n.* need or desire to defecate.
kakagura izan *v.t.* to want to go to the bathroom.
kakajario *adj.* afflicted with diarrhea. *n.* dysentery, diarrhea.
kakalardo *n.(zool.)* large black beetle.
kakalarri *n.* diarrhea. *adj.* needing to defecate. *adj.(fam.)* nervous, impatient, fretful.
kakalarri izan *v.i.* to need to defecate,

to need to go to the bathroom.

kakalarritu *v.i.* to have to go to the bathroom, to need to defecate.

kakaldi *n.* act of defecating, having a bowel movement, evacuation of the bowels.

kakamerke *adj.(colloq.)* worthless (person).

kakamokordo *n.* turd.

kakanarru *adj./n.(colloq.)* short legged (person); short person.

kakao *n.(bot.)* cocoa.

kakapirri *n.(colloq.)* diarrhea. *adj.(colloq.)* bad tempered (person).

kakara *n.* cackling, cackle.

kakaraka *adv.* cackling. *n.* cackle.

kakaraka egin *v.t.* to cackle.

kakarakatu *v.i.* to cackle, to cluck.

kakategi *n.* toilet, bathroom, latrine, restroom.

kakati *adj.* one who defecates a lot. *adj.(fig.)* cowardly, fearful, coward.

kakatoki *n.* toilet, bathroom, restroom.

kakats *n.* odor of excrement.

kakatsu *adj.* full of excrement. *adj.(fig.)* dirty, unpleasant, disgusting.

kakatza *n.* pile of dung or manure. *n.(fig.)* pile of garbage.

kakazto *adj.* filthy, dirty, disgusting.

kakaztu *v.t./v.i.* to dirty, to soil, to ruin, to tarnish, to spoil, to discredit.

kakegite *n.* evacuation of the bowels.

kakeri *n.* dysentery, diarrhea.

kakerre *adj.* irritable, irascible.

kakeuli *n.* kind of large fly.

kako *n.* hook. *n.* two-pronged hoe. *n.* hanger, hook, clotheshanger. *n.(fig.)* key, solution.

kakontzi *n.* toilet, urinal. *adj.(fig.)* vile, disgusting (person).

kakotegi *n.* closet, cloakroom; pole on which clotheshangers hang.

kaktus *n.(bot.)* cactus.

kakume *n.(dim.)* baby still in diapers.

kakusain *n.* odor of excrement.

kala *n.* fishing ground, place for casting fish nets or fishing.

kalaka *n.* bolt, latch, catch. *adj.* chattering, jabbering, talkative, loquacious. *n.* long conversation, chat.

kalakari *adj.* chattering, talkative, loquacious.

kalakatu *v.i.* to chatter, to gossip.

kalaketa *n.* act of rattling with wooden clappers.

kalamatrika *n.* jibberish, babble, unintelligible language. *n.* trick, ruse, stratagem.

kalamu *n.(bot.)* hemp.

kalamudi *n.* hemp field.

kalanbre *n.* shock, cramp.

kalanbretu *v.t./v.i.* to shock, to receive a shock (from an electric wire).

kalapita *n.* argument, quarrel; cacophony of voices.

kalapitari *n.* arguer, quarreler. *adj.*

quarrelsome; noisy.

kalapitatsu *adj.* noisy.

kalatxori *n.(zool.)* seagull.

kale *n.* street.

kalearte *n.* intersection (street), crossroads.

kalebazter *n.* street corner. *n.* sidewalk.

kaleburu *n.* end of a street. *n.* intersection, place where one street meets another.

kale egin *v.t.(colloq.)* to fall, to flunk; to fault, to miss (a shot or play), to lose (in sports); to miss (a day of school).

kalegarbitzaile *n.* street cleaner, street sweeper.

kalegurutze *n.* crossroad, intersection.

kalejira *n.* musical stroll, parade.

kalekoi *adj.* fond of going out, fond of roaming the streets.

kalemutur *n.* street corner.

kalenagusi *n.* main street.

kaleratu *v.t.* to expell, to dismiss, to throw out in the street. *v.i.* to go out (into the street).

kalerdi *n.* center of the street.

kalertz *n.* sidewalk; edge of the street, shoulder of the road.

kaletar *n.* town dweller, city dweller, city boy. *adj.* urban.

kaletarte *n.* alley.

kaletartu *v.i.* to urbanize, to become acclimated to the city life. *v.t.* to take into the streets, to put on the streets.

kaletxo *n.(dim.)* small street.

kalezale *adj.* fond of going out or roaming the streets.

kalifa *n.* caliph.

kalifaldi *n.* period of a caliph's reign.

kaliferri *n.* caliphate.

kalifikaezin *adj.* unclassifiable. *adj.* unnamable, unmentionable, indescribable.

kalifikagarri *adj.* classifiable. *adj.* mentionable, describable, notable.

kalifikapen *n.* classification.

kalifikatu *v.t.* to classify.

kalifikatzaile *n./adj.* classifier; classifying. *adj.(gram.)* qualifying.

kalitate *n.* quality.

kaliza *n.(eccl.)* chalice.

kalkagailu *n.* tracer, instrument for tracing.

kalkatu *v.t.* to trace. *v.t.* to step on, to trample.

kalkatzaile *n./adj.* tracer; tracing.

kalko *n.* tracing.

kalkulagailu *n.* calculator, computer.

kalkulagaitz *adj.* incalculable.

kalkulagarri *adj.* calculable.

kalkulatu *v.t.* to calculate.

kalkulatzaile *adj.* calculating (person).

kalkulezin *adj.* incalculable, immeasurable.

kalkulu *n.(arith.)* calculus.

kalonje *n.* canon, priest qualified to

hold a special office in the cathedral.

kalonjego n. canonry, office of a canon.

kalonjetza n. canonry, office of a canon.

kaloria n. calorie.

kalostra n. balustrade, railing, bannister.

kalpar n. wild, unmanageable hair. n. bald spot on top of the head.

kalte n. harm, hurt, damage, loss.

kaltedun adj. damaged, hurt, harmed.

kalte egin v.t. to hurt, to harm, to damage, to bother.

kaltegabe adj. harmless. adj. unhurt, undamaged, safe and sound.

kaltegabeko adj. inoffensive. adj. unharmed, safe and sound.

kaltegabetasun n. harmlessness, innocuousness.

kaltegabezia n. harmlessness, innocuousness.

kaltegarri adj. harmful, damaging.

kaltegarriro adv. perniciously, harmfully.

kaltegarritasun n. harmfulness.

kaltegarrizko adj. harmful, damaging.

kaltegile n. offender, damager, one who harms. adj. harmful, damaging.

kaltegite n. damage, harm.

kaltekeria n. damage, harm, loss.

kalteko adj. calamitous, regrettable, damaging.

kaltekor adj. damaging, harmful.

kaltekortasun n. harmfulness.

kalteordain n. indemnification, compensation, reparation.

kalteordaindu v.t. to make reparations, to compensate, to make up for.

kalteordaingarri adj. worthy of compensation.

kalteordaintzaile n./adj. compensator; compensatory.

kalterako adj. counterproductive, harmful, damaging.

kaltetsu adj. harmful, damaging.

kaltetu v.t. to hurt, to harm.

kaltzio n.(chem.) calcium.

kamaina n. bunk, cot, poor miserable bed.

kamalehoi n.(zool.) chameleon.

kamamila n.(bot.) camomile.

kamelia n.(bot.) camellia.

kamelu n.(zool.) camel.

kamioi n. truck.

kamioiari n. truck driver.

kamioikada n. truckload.

kamioiketa n. truck convoy.

kamioixka n.(dim.) pickup truck.

kamisoi n. nightgown.

kamusdura n. blunting, dulling.

kamusketa n. blunting, dulling.

kamustasun n. bluntness, dullness.

kamustu v.t./v.i. to dull, to blunt.

kamuts adj. blunt, dull. adj.(geom.) obtuse.

kana n. unit of measurement used for

measuring cloth.

kanabete n. full measurement of one kana.

kanale n. canal.

kanaleztapen n. canalization, building canals.

kanaleztatu v.t. to channel.

kanario n.(zool.) canary.

kanbio n. change. n.(econ.) money exchange.

kanbor n. live coal, red-hot coal.

kandela n. candle.

kandelagile n. candlemaker.

kandelario n.(R.C.Ch.) Candlemas, liturgical feast, February 2, during which the candles are blessed.

kandidatu n. candidate.

kandidatura n. candidacy.

kanela n.(bot.) cinnamon.

kanelondo n.(bot.) cinnamon tree.

kanguru n.(zool.) kangaroo.

kanika n. marble (toy).

kankailatu v.i. to become large and awkward, to become large and possibly misshapen.

kankailu adj. big, tall and awkward, possibly slightly misshapen.

kankailukeria n. clumsiness, awkwardness.

kankal adj. scatterbrained, featherbrained.

kankarreko n. blow to the head.

kankarro n. big earthen jug.

kanoa n. canoe.

kanore n. aptitude; diligence.

kanpadenda n. camping tent.

kanpai n. bell.

kanpai(a) jo v.t. to ring the bell.

kanpaialdi n. bell toll, ringing of the bell.

kanpaiantzeko adj. bell-shaped, bell-like.

kanpaigile n. bell maker.

kanpaihots n. bell toll, knell, ringing of bells, tolling of the bell.

kanpaijoaldi n. tolling of the bell, ringing of the bell.

kanpaijole n. bell ringer.

kanpailore n.(bot.) bell-shaped flower.

kanpaina n. campaign.

kanpaitxo n.(dim.) small bell.

kanpaize n. north wind.

kanpamendu n. camp (military), encampment, boot camp.

kanpandorre n. bell tower.

kanping n. camping.

kanpo n. outside, outdoors. prep. except, but. prep. out of, off (of).

kanpo- Used in compound words. Derived from kanpo, outside.

kanpoalde n. outside place, outdoors.

kanpoaldi n. absence, period of absence, time spent outdoors.

kanpoan adv. outside, outdoors.

kanpoeder adj. affable with strangers (but not at home).

kanpokeria n. absenteeism.

kanpoko *adj.* outside, exterior, foreign. *n.* outsider, foreigner.

kanpokotasun *n.* quality of being an outsider.

kanpokotza *n.* state of being an outsider, foreigner.

kanpolan *n.* outside work, outdoor work.

kanpora *int.* get out, out! *adv.* outside.

kanporagarri *adj.* exportable.

kanporaketa *n.* exportation, exporting, export. *n.* disposal, elimination.

kanporakoi *adj.* extrovert, extroverted, out-going.

kanporakoitasun *n.* extroversion, quality of being out-going.

kanporaldaketa *n.* migration.

kanporaldi *n.* absence, time away. *n.* flight, escape.

kanporatu *v.i.* to go outside, to remove oneself, to absent oneself. *v.t.* to expel, to deport, to expatriate, to dismiss, to fire (from a job). *v.t.* to export.

kanporatzaile *n.* exporter.

kanposantu *n.* cemetery.

kanpotar *n.* stranger, outsider, foreigner. *adj.* strange, outside, foreign.

kanpotiko *adj.* exterior, external, outside.

kanta *n.* song. *n.* term used in the card game *mus.*

Kantabriar Itsaso *n. (geog.)* Cantabrian Sea.

kantaera *n.* way of singing.

kantaezin *adj.* unsingable.

kantagarri *adj.* singable, worthy of being sung.

kantagile *n.* songwriter.

kantajaialdi *n.* song festival, music festival.

kantaketa *n.* act of singing.

kantalari *n.* announcer of scores in pelota.

kantaldi *n.* musical recital, musical performance.

kantarazi *v.t.* to make (someone) sing.

kantari *n.* singer.

kantaritalde *n.* chorus, choir, choral group.

kanta-sorta *n.* collection of songs, song book.

kantatu *v.t.* to sing.

kantatzaile *n.* singer.

kantika *n.* canticle, song.

kantin *n.* metal milk jug, milk can.

kantiniersa *n.* character in a Zuberoan dance, a man dressed as a woman.

kantitate *n.* quantity.

kantitatezko *adj.* quantitative.

kantoi(n) *n.* edge, border, corner.

kantore *n.* song.

kantu *n.* song.

kantubide *n.* theme of a song.

kantutegi *n.* song book, collection of songs.

kantuzale *adj.* fond of songs.

kantzer *n. (med.)* cancer.

kaoba *n. (bot.)* mahogany.

kaobazur *n.* mahogany wood.

kaobondo *n. (bot.)* mahogany tree.

kapa *n.* cape. *n.* coarse woolen cloth.

kapar *n. (zool.)* sheep and cattle tick. *n. (bot.)* bramble bush.

kapaz izan *v.i.* to be able to, to be capable of, to be of use.

kapazu *n.* straw bag.

kapela *n.* hat.

kapelagin *n.* hat maker, hatter, milliner.

kapelari *n.* hat maker, hatter, milliner.

kapelu *n.* cap.

kapera *n.* chapel.

kaperau *n.* chaplain.

kaperautza *n.* chaplaincy.

kapitain *n. (mil.)* captain. *n.* skipper.

kapitaintza *n.* captaincy, captainship.

kapital *n. (econ.)* capital. *n.* capital (city).

kapitaldu *v.t.* to capitalize.

kapitaleztapen *n.* capitalization, investing.

kapitaleztatu *v.t.* to capitalize, to convert into capital.

kapitalgarri *n.* capitalizable.

kapitalismo *n.* capitalism.

kapitalista *n.* capitalist.

kapitalizagarri *adj.* capitalizable.

kapitalizatu *v.t.* to capitalize, to convert into capital.

kapitalizazio *n. (econ.)* capitalization.

kapitulu *n.* chapter of a book.

kapoi(n) *n. (zool.)* capon.

kapusai *n.* parka, jacket with hood.

kaputxino *n.* Capuchin friar.

-kara Used in compound words. Signifies oestrus, heat (in mammals). **Ahunzkara.** Goat's oestrus.

karabilkatsu *adj.* torturous, twisting.

karabilkatu *v.i.* to zigzag, to twist and turn (river, etc.), to slither, to undulate (snakes).

karabina *n.* carbine (rifle).

karabinari *n.* rifleman.

karaitz *n.* limestone.

karakari *adj.* cackling.

karakoildu *v.i.* to wind around, to entwine.

karamelu *n.* candy.

kararri *n.* limestone.

karate *n.* karate.

karbonato *n. (chem.)* carbonate.

karbono *n. (chem.)* carbon.

karburagai *n.* fuel.

karburagailu *n. (mech.)* carburator.

karburaketa *n.* carburetion.

karburatu *v.t.* to carburate, to carburet, to carburize.

karburo *n. (chem.)* carbide.

karda *n.* card, carder, instrument for carding wool, etc.

kardatu *v.t.* to card (wool, etc.).

kardenal *n.* cardinal.

kardenalgo *n.* cardinalship,

cardinalate.
kardenaltza n. cardinalship,
cardinalate.
kardinal n.(gram.) cardinal (numbers).
kardiologia n. cardiology.
kardiologari n. cardiologist.
kare n. lime.
kareaketa n. calcination.
karealdi n. whitewashing with lime,
lime covering.
karebizi n. quicklime.
karehaitz n. calcareous rock,
limestone.
kareharri n. calcareous rock,
limestone.
kareharritsu adj. limy, calcareous.
karehil n. slaked or hydrated lime.
karel n. edge, rim of boat.
karelur n. calcareous earth, ground
containing lime.
karesne n. whitewash.
karetsu adj. calcareous, limy.
karetza n. lime deposit.
karezko adj. calcareous, limy.
kareztadura n. whitewashing.
kareztaldi n. whitewashing.
kareztatu v.t. to whitewash, to cover
with lime.
karga n. load, burden.
kargagorailu n. freight elevator.
kargakenketa n. unloading.
kargakentoki n. wharf, pier, unloading
place.
kargakentzaile n. seaman on a lighter
or barge used to unload other
vessels.
kargaketa n. loading cargo. n. cargo,
load.
kargamendu n. loading cargo.
kargari n. loader, stevedore, dock
worker.
kargatu v.t. to load.
kargatzaile n. loader, stevedore, dock
worker.
kargu n. job. n. care, charge,
responsibility.
kargudun n. person in charge,
manager. adj. responsible, careful.
kargu hartu v.t. to be responsible for,
to take care of, to take charge of.
kargutu v.i. to realize, to become
aware of, to notice.
kari n. motive, cause, reason.
-kari (gram.) Noun suffix meaning
enthusiast or agent.
karikatura n. caricature.
kario adj. expensive, dear, costly. adv.
expensively, dearly.
kariotasun n. scarcity, lack, shortage.
n. rise in price, price increase.
kariotu v.t./v.i. to raise the price; to
rise in price, to become more
expensive.
karitate n. charity.
karitatezko adj. charitable.
karka adj. pejorative nickname meaning
reactionary, applied to the carlists by

the Liberals during the Carlist Wars of
the 19th century.
karkaba n. septic tank.
karkail adj. tough, rough, crude.
karkaila n. uproarious laughing,
guffawing.
karkaildu v.i. to shrink, to shrivel, to
fade away.
karkaisa n. phlegm, spit.
karkaisaldi n. expectoration, spitting
out of phlegm.
karlismo n.(pol.) Carlism, 19th century
political movement which supported
Carlos in the Bourbon struggle for
the throne of Spain.
karlista n./adj. Carlist.
karlistada n. Carlist war.
karmeldar n./adj. Carmelite.
karmin adj. sour, bitter.
karmindu v.i. to sour, to turn bitter.
karmindura n. bitterness, sourness.
karnet n. card, driver's license.
karnetagiri n. identification papers,
I.D.
karobi n. limeburner, lime oven.
karpanta adj. bold, outspoken, brazen
(woman).
karpeta n. portfolio, letter file.
karpetaratu v.t. to file away, to put in a
file or portfolio, to put in a letter file.
karraka n. wooden rattle, noisemaker.
n. scraping, scratching.
karrakada n. creak, crackle, crackling,
rustle. n. grating, noise. n. act of
making noise or racket with a rattle.
karrakadura n. crack, cracking,
crackling, rustling. n. grating or
scraping noise.
karraka egin v.t. to caw, to cackle. v.t.
to scrape, to grate, to crack.
karrakagailu n. scraper, grater, rasp,
file. n. noisemaker.
karraka jo v.t. to shake a rattle, to
make noise with a noisemaker.
karrakaldi n. scraping, grating,
rasping.
karrakari n. one who makes noise with
a wooden noisemaker.
karrakatu v.t. to make noise with a
noisemaker. v.t. to scratch, to rasp,
to grate.
karrakela n.(zool.) small sea snail.
karramarro n.(zool.) crab. n. dredge.
n. Cancer, sign of the zodiac.
karramarrozale adj. crab lover, fond of
crabs.
karramarroztu v.t. to dredge.
karranka n. noise. n. caw, croak,
cackle. n. creaking, squeaking. n.
snoring, hoarseness. n. water
turbine.
karrankari n./adj. shouter, screecher;
shouting, screeching, strident, shrill.
n./adj. snorer; snoring.
karrankatu v.i. to squeak, to creak. v.i.
to grind (teeth). v.i. to snore.
karrask n.(onomat.) sound of cracking,

crackling, splitting.

karraska n. creaking, squeaking. n. grinding of the teeth.

karraskada n. creaking, crackling, squeaking. n. caw, cackling, croak.

karraskailu n. scraper, rasp, grater, file.

karraskaldi n. scraping, grating, rasping. n. grinding of teeth.

karraskari n./adj. gnawer; gnawing. n./adj. cawer, cackler; cawing, cackling.

karraskatu v.t. to gnaw, to chew on.

karrask egin v.t./v.i. to crack, to split.

karrasketa n. cracking, splitting. n. grinding of teeth.

karraskila n.(bot.) buckthorn.

karraskots n. sound of cracking, splitting. n. sound of teeth grinding.

karraskots egin v.t. to grind (teeth), to chatter, to clack.

karraspio n.(zool.) small brown saltwater fish.

karrera n. university career, higher learning. n. race.

karretila n. wheelbarrow.

karrika n. street.

karrikaburu n. street intersection, end of a street.

karrile n. rail, track (train).

karrilerapen n. act of putting on the right track.

karrileratu v.t. to put on rails, to put on tracks.

karrilgalketa n. derailment, derailing.

karroza n. float (parade).

karrozari n. driver of a float.

karta n. playing card.

kartaboi n. drawing triangle, set square.

kartajoko n. card game.

kartakutxa n. mailbox.

kartazal n. envelope.

kartel n. poster. n. sign; roadsign.

karteldegi n. billboard; bulletin board.

kartera n. purse, wallet, billfold. n. bookbag, briefcase.

kartoi n. cardboard.

kartoigile n. cardboard manufacturer.

kartoigintza n. cardboard making.

kartoipanpina n. cardboard doll, paper doll.

kartoitegi n. cardboard factory.

kartoiztatu v.t. to cover with cardboard.

kartoiztu v.t. to cover with cardboard, to bind with cardboard.

kartola n. mule chair, frame harness for mules used for carrying loads (baskets, etc.); vertical sideboards on the bed of a truck.

kartutxo n. cartridge (for rifles).

kartutxontzi n. cartridge belt.

kartzela n. prison, jail.

karu adj. expensive.

karutasun n. rise in price, price increase.

karutu v.t./v.i. to raise the price; to rise in price, to go up in price.

kasik adv. almost, nearly.

kasino n. casino.

kaska n. skull, cranium. n. layer(s) of badly cut hair. n. onomatopoeic sound of a blow.

kaska- Used in compound words, derived from kasko, skull, head.

kaskabeltz n.(zool.) greater titmouse.

kaskagain n. crown of the head.

kaskagogor adj. stubborn, obstinate, hard-headed. (lit.) hard skull.

kaskagogorkeria n. stubbornness, hard-headedness, obstinacy, contumacy, pertinacity.

kaskagorri adj. red-headed. adj. tonsured, shorn, shaved (head).

kaskailu adj. stubborn, obstinate, hard-headed. n.(zool.) bitterling. n. pebble.

kaskaineta n. clicking sound of castanets. n. castanet.

kaskamotz adj. tonsured, shorn, shaved (head).

kaskamoztu v.t. to tonsure, to shave the head.

kaskar adj. insignificant, futile, mediocre, of little value. n. skull, cranium, head.

kaskarin adj. foolish.

kaskarinkeria n. frivolity; indiscretion, tactlessness, nonsense, foolishness.

kaskarraldi n. period of obstinacy, stubbornness.

kaskarreko n. blow to the head.

kaskarrondoko n. blow to the head.

kaskartu v.i. to diminish, to decrease; to ruin oneself, to be vile. v.i. to be in a bad mood, to become irritable.

kaskasoil adj. bald.

kaska soildu v.i. to go bald, to become bald.

kaskasoildura n. baldness.

kaskasoilune n. bald spot.

kaskazuri adj. white-haired, white-headed.

kasket n. skull, cranium; head.

kasketa n. stubbornness, obstinacy, contumacy.

kasketaldi n. stubbornness, obstinacy.

kasketatsu adj. stubborn, obstinate.

kasketatu v.i. to be obstinate, to be stubborn.

kaskezur n.(anat.) cranium, skull.

kasko n.(colloq.) head. n. top, peak, summit.

kaskotik egon v.i. to be crazy, to be out of one's mind, to be insane.

kaskomurritz adj. tonsured, shorn, shaved (head).

kaskuts adj. foolish.

kasta n. breed, lineage, caste.

kastitate n. chastity.

kasu n. attention, care. n.(gram.) case. n. case, circumstance.

kasual adj. accidental, unexpected.

kasualitate *n.* coincidence.
kasualki *adv.* accidentally, unexpectedly.
kasu egin *v.t.* to notice, to listen to, to pay attention to.
kata- Used in compound words. Derived from *katu*, cat.
katabuta *n.* coffin.
katakara *n.* mating period of female cat, heat, oestrus.
katakume *n.(dim.)* kitten.
katakunba *n.* catacomb.
katalan *n./adj.* Catalan.
katalanera *n.* Catalan language.
katalantzale *adj.* fond of Catalan language, culture, etc.
katalantzaletasun *n.* fondness for things Catalan.
katalarru *n.* cat skin.
katalogatu *v.t.* to catalog.
katalogo *n.* catalog.
Katalunia *n.(geog.)* Catalonia.
katamotz *n.(zool.)* lynx.
katamuturluze *n.(zool.)* genet.
katanar *n.(zool.)* blue titmouse.
katar *n.* male cat.
katarrain *n.(zool.)* catfish.
katarro *n.* cold (illness).
kate *n.* chain.
kateadura *n.* chaining.
kateaketa *n.* chaining; linking.
kateapen *n.* chaining; linking.
kateatu *v.t.* to chain, to chain up. *v.t.* to link, to chain together.
katebegi *n.* link of a chain.
kateburu *n.* end link (of a chain).
katedra *n.* professorship, (professorial) chair.
katedrale *n.* cathedral.
kategile *n.* chain maker.
kategoria *n.* category.
katekesi *n.* catechism.
katekista *n.* catechist, catechism teacher.
katekizatu *v.t.* to teach catechism.
kateme *n.* female cat.
katetxo *n.(dim.)* small chain.
katexima *n.* catechism.
kateztatu *v.t.* to chain, to enchain, to fasten with chains.
katezulo *n.* hole in hull through which the anchor chain passes.
katilu *n.* bowl.
katilukada *n.* bowlful, cupful.
katoi *n.* child's primer, first reader.
katoliko *adj./n.* Catholic.
katolikoki *adv.* in a Catholic manner.
katolikotasun *n.* catholicness.
katolikotu *v.i./v.t.* to catholicize.
katolikutza *n.* Catholicism.
katramila *n.* task, problem, difficulty; puzzle, perplexity, dilemma, entanglement.
katramildu *v.t.* to complicate, to entangle.
katu *n.(zool.)* cat. *n.* trigger of a gun. *n.(colloq.)* drunkenness.

katu- Used in compound words. Derived from *katu*, cat.
-katu *(gram.)* Verbal suffix indicating action. **Harrikatu.** To stone.
katuka *adv.* on all fours, quietly, catlike.
katukeria *n.(fig.)* wheedling.
katuki *n.* cat meat.
katukide *adj.* feline, felid.
katutzar *n.(augm.)* large cat.
katuzale *adj.* cat lover, cat loving.
kaudimen *n.(econ.)* solvency.
kaudimengabe *n.* insolvent.
kaudimengabezia *n.* insolvency.
kaukasiar *n./adj.* Caucasian.
kaukezia *n.* poverty, misery, penury.
kausitu *v.t.* to find. *v.i.* to find oneself, to meet.
kausk *n.* crunch! onomatopoeic sound of biting.
kauskada *n.* bite.
kauta *n.* charge, responsibility, obligation.
kautxu *n.* rubber.
kautxuztatu *v.t.* to cover with rubber.
kaxa *n.* box, chest, case, trunk.
kaxako *adj./n.* abandoned; foundling, abandoned child.
kaxari *n.* cashier.
kaxarranka *n.* traditional Basque dance from Lekeitio (Biscay) in which one man dances on top of a trunk carried by four other men.
kaxatxo *n.(dim.)* small box.
kaxkar *adj.* insignificant, mediocre, of little value.
kaxkarkeria *n.* mediocrity, meanness, baseness.
kaxkartu *v.i.* to degrade oneself, to become vile, base, mean.
kaxoi *n.* drawer.
-kaz *(gram.)* Suffix derived from *gaz* meaning with (pl.).
kazeta *n.* magazine, journal, newspaper.
kazetalgo *n.* journalism.
kazetari *n.* journalist, reporter.
kazetaritza *n.* journalism.
kazetarizko *adj.* journalistic.
kazkabar *n.* hail.
kazkabarraldi *n.* hailstorm.
kazola *n.* casserole dish.
kazolakada *n.* casserole (food prepared in a casserole dish).
ke *n.* smoke.
keadar *n.* column of smoke.
kealdi *n.* period of smokiness, length of time the smoke lasts.
kebide *n.* smokestack, chimney.
kedura *n.* fumigation.
keinatu *v.t.* to menace, to threaten.
keinu *n.* wink. *n.* gesture.
keinu egin *v.t.* to wink.
keinugile *n./adj.* one who winks, gestures, or grimaces, winker; winking.
keinuka *adv.* gesturing, winking.

keinukada n. gesture, wink, grin.
keinukari n./adj. gesturer, gesticulator; gesturing.
keinukatu v.i. to gesture, to gesticulate, to wink.
keinuketa n. gesticulation, gesturing.
keinulari adj. gesturing, grimacing.
keinutsu adj. grimacing, gesturing.
keltar adj. Celtic.
kemen n. force, energy, vigor, strength. n. valor, courage.
kemendu v.i. to be brave, to have courage. v.t./v.i. to strengthen, to vitalize; to be strong.
kemendun adj. energetic, strong, forceful; brave, courageous, valiant.
kemendura n. strength, vigor; courage, valor.
kemengabe adj. weak, without energy; without courage.
kemengabetu v.i. to lose strength, to lose energy, to become weak.
kemengarri adj. animating, enlivening, encouraging.
kementsu adj. vigorous, strong, energetic. adj. valiant, courageous, brave.
kemeta n. column of smoke.
kemin n. smoky flavor (of cheese, smoke-cured meat, fish, etc.).
kemindu v.t. to give a smoky flavor to foods, to smoke (meat, fish or cheese). v.i. to smell burnt.
ken n.(arith.) minus sign, minus, less, take away.
kenarazi v.t. to depose, to overthrow, to dethrone.
kenarazle n. deposer, dethroner, expropriator.
kendu v.t. to take away, to take from, to take off, to depose, to remove, to abolish, to dispossess. v.t. to subtract. v.i. to get away, to leave, to withdraw, to get out, to remove oneself. v.t. to charge, to get (for something). v.t. to annul; to exclude.
kenezin adj. unmovable, immobile. adj. indelible, unerasable, unremovable.
kengai n.(arith.) minuend.
kengaitz adj. difficult to remove, difficult to take away.
kengarri adj. annullable, rescindable, revocable. adj. deductible, discountable, allowable.
kengarritasun n. revocability.
kenka n. critical moment or situation, problem, critical point.
kenkari n.(arith.) subtrahend.
kenketa n. privation, suppression, deletion, removal. n.(arith.) subtraction.
kentzaile adj. subtractive, expropriative, depriving. n. subtractor, expropriator, depriver, remover, nullifier.
kera n. likeness, resemblance; adaptation.

-kera (gram.) Modal suffix used with infinitives to express manner, way of, act of. **Edakera.** Way of drinking. (gram.) Noun suffix meaning oestrus, mating season, heat (animals). **Katakera.** Mating season of the cat.
-keria (gram.) Suffix used with nouns and adjectives. Denotes abstract quality with pejorative meaning. **Azalkeria.** Shallowness; hypocrisy.
keru n. stench, stink, putrid odor.
-keta (gram.) suffix denoting action, act of. **Orrazketa.** Combing. (gram.) Suffix denoting a search. **Urketa.** Search for water. (gram.) Suffix denoting quantity, amount. **Arrainketa.** Quantity of fish.
ketan adv. smoking, fuming.
-ketari (gram.) Suffix denoting agent, seeker.
ketsu adj. smoky; steaming, fuming.
kexadura n. anxiousness, preoccupation, uneasiness, worry, restlessness. n. complaint.
kexagarri adj. disquieting, worrying, troubling, perturbing.
kexagarriki adv. worriedly, disquietingly, in a troubled manner.
kexakor adj. worrying, worried, preoccupied.
kexakunde n. worry, anguish, anxiety, uneasiness.
kexaldi n. period of worry, anxiety, uneasiness.
kexarazi v.t. to make (someone) worry, to make (someone) anxious.
kexati adj. complaining, whining, whiny, plaintive. adj. worried, worrying, preoccupied, uneasy.
kexatiar adj. anxious, very worried.
kexatu v.i. to complain. v.i. to become distressed.
kexu adj. worried, preoccupied, uneasy, nervous, distressed, anguished. n. worry.
kexu izan v.i. to be preoccupied, to be worried, to be uneasy, to be anxious.
kexuki adv. uneasy, uneasily, anxiously.
kexukoi adj. worried, preoccupied; tending to complain, whiny, cranky, fretful.
kezka n. worry, care, anxiety, problem, preoccupation, uneasiness.
kezkagabe adj. unconcerned, unworried. adj. careless, negligent.
kezkagabetu v.i. to forget one's worries. v.i. to become careless or negligent.
kezkagabezia n. carelessness, negligence.
kezkagarri adj. worrisome, worrying, troubling, perturbing, annoying, troublesome.
kezkaldi n. uneasiness, anxiety, worry, obsession, preoccupation.
kezkarazi v.t. to cause anxiety (in

others), to worry (someone), to perturb, to bother.

kezkarazle n./adj. troublemaker, one who causes anxiety or worry; worrisome, troublesome.

kezkati adj. worried, preoccupied, disturbed, uneasy. adj. scrupulous.

kezkatsu adj. worried, preoccupied, disturbed, uneasy. adj. scrupulous.

kezkatu v.i./v.t. to be preoccupied, to be worried; to preoccupy (someone), to worry (someone).

kezulo n. chimney.

-ki (gram.) modal adverbial suffix. **Poliki.** Slowly. (gram.) Noun suffix signifying material, made of. **Adarki.** Piece of horn, piece of branch. (gram.) Noun suffix signifying meat of. **Idiki.** Ox meat.

kide n. member, colleague, fellow, associate.

-kide (gram.) Noun suffix signifying interrelation or companionship. **Aberkide.** Countryman, compatriot.

kidego n. affinity, equality, parity.

kidegarri adj. similar, comparable. adj. sociable, communicative.

kidekadura n. classification, grouping.

kidekapen n. classification, grouping.

kidekatu v.t. to classify, to group together.

kidekatzaile n. classifier, one who classifies.

kideko n. companion, fellow. adj. similar, like, (of) the same age.

kidetasun n. affinity, similarity.

kidetu v.i. to be similar, to be alike, to resemble. v.t./v.i. to pair (up), to match up.

kidetza n. affiliation, association, relation.

kidetzaile adj. equalizing, evening.

kikara n. small cup.

kikil adj. timid, shy, cowed, intimidated.

kikildu v.i. to be frightened, to be timid, to be cowed. v.t. to frighten, to cow, to intimidate.

kikildura n. shrinking (in fear), wincing. n. timidity, irresolution.

kikilgarri adj. intimidating, discouraging, demoralizing.

kikimako n. curve, bend, angle, twist.

kikindera n.(zool.) tiger beetle.

kikiriki n. cockle-doodle-doo, sound of a young rooster.

kilate n. carat.

kilika n. tickling, tickle, prickle.

kilikabera adj. ticklish, sensitive to tickling.

kilikaberatasun n. ticklishness, touchiness.

kilikadun adj. ticklish.

kilikadura n. tickle, tickling; prickling.

kilikagarri adj. ticklish. adj. exciting, stimulating.

kilikaldi n. period of tickling.

kilikari n. tickler, teaser, tantalizer. n.

one who excites, stimulator.

kilikatsu adj. ticklish, sensitive to tickling.

kilikatu v.t. to tickle. v.t. to excite, to stimulate.

kilikatzaile adj. tickling. adj. exciting, stimulating.

kili-kili n. tickling.

kili-kili egin v.t. to tickle (someone).

kili-kolo adv. unstably, wobbly, loosely, uncertainly, not well.

kili-kolo egin v.t. to tip, to wobble, to move slightly, to lean.

kilikor adj. ticklish, sensitive to tickling.

kilikortasun n. excitability, ticklishness.

kilima n. tickling, tickle.

kilimaka adv. tickling, by tickling.

kilimakari n. tickler. n.(fig.) teaser, tempter.

kilimakatu v.t. to tickle.

kilimakor adj. ticklish, sensitive to tickling.

kilimakortasun n. ticklishness, excitability.

kilimatsu adj. sensitive to tickling.

kilimatu v.t. to tickle. v.t.(fig.) to tempt, to tease.

kilimusi n. bow, curtsy.

kilkir n.(zool.) cricket.

kilo n. kilogram.

kilometro n. kilometer.

kilometrokontagailu n.(mech.) odometer, mileage recorder.

kima n. shoot, sprout, bud (on a branch). n. mane (of a horse).

kimaketa n. twig trimming, pruning.

kimatsu adj. full of sprouts, shoots or buds.

kimatu v.t. to prune, to trim (twigs, branches). v.i. to bud, to sprout, to germinate.

kimetz n. bud, germ, sprout, shoot.

kimika n. chemistry.

kimikagaiak n.(pl.) chemicals.

kimikari n. chemist.

kimiko adj. chemical.

kimikoki adv. chemically.

kimono n. kimono.

kimu n. bud, sprout, shoot.

kimuketa n. germination, sprouting, budding.

-kin (gram.) Suffix, with. **Aitarekin.** With father. (gram.) Suffix, agent, doer, maker. **Gaizkin.** Wrongdoer. (gram.) Suffix, residue, remainder. **Ebakin.** Scraps, clippings (tree, cloth, etc.).

kinada n. stimulus, provocation, instigation.

kiniela n. kind of wager, quiniela. In the Basque Country quiniela tickets are filled out for soccer. In the U. S. quiniela refers to a type of race track betting. Also in U. S., a form of wagering on jai-alai.

kinina n.(chem.) quinine.

kinka *n.* critical moment or situation, problem, critical point.

kinkail *n.* small hardware.

kinkaldi *n.* critical moment or period.

kinkan *adv.* on the point of, nearly, on the verge of, almost. *adv.* with great longing, with great desire.

kinkiladenda *n.* dry-goods store, notions store.

kinkilari *n.* dry-goods merchant.

kintal *n.(arith.)* 100 pounds.

-kintza *(gram.)* Suffix denoting job or profession.

kina *n.* stirring up, rousing (something or someone with a stick), agitating.

kinatu *v.t.* to incite, to stir up, to rouse, to agitate.

kiosko *n.* kiosk, sidewalk stand, booth.

kipula *n.* onion.

kiraskarri *adj.* miasmic, miasmatic, fetid, stinking.

kirastasun *n.* fetidness, stench, stink.

klraste *n.* act of rotting, stinking, becoming fetid.

kirastsu *adj.* pestilent, stinking, fetid, foul.

kirastu *v.i.* to rot, to spoil, to putrify, to stink.

kirastun *adj.* putrid, stinking, rotten.

kirastura *n.* rottenness, stench, fetidness.

kirats *n.* stench, fetidness, rotten smell.

kiribil *n.* thread (of a screw). *n.* spiral, coil. *adj.* spiraling, coiled, twisted.

kiribilapen *n.* curling (of hair, etc.), coiling, twisting, screwing.

kiribilatu *v.i.* to coil, to twist, to spiral, to curl.

kiribildu *v.i.* to curl (up), to coil, to spiral, to twist.

kiribildura *n.* curling, twisting, coiling, screwing.

kiribilka *adv.* spiraling, twistedly, curlingly.

kirik *n.* child's expression used in game of hide-and-seek to attract the attention of the seeker.

kirika *adv.* hide-and-seek.

kirikalari *n.* watcher, observer; child who is the seeker in hide-and-seek.

kirikaldi *n.* period of vigilance, watching, observing.

kirikari *n.* watcher, observer; child who is the seeker in hide-and-seek, it (hide and seek).

kirikatu *v.t.* to observe, to watch, to spy (on).

kirikatzaile *n./adj.* observer, watcher, seeker; watchful, observant.

kirik egin *v.t.* to peep, to spy on.

kiriketa *n.* hide-and-seek, child's game. *n.* sudden appearance.

kiriketan *adv.* playing hide and seek.

kirikino *n.(zool.)* hedgehog.

kirio *n.(anat.)* nerve.

kirkileria *n.* excessive luxuriousness, extravagant ostentation.

-kiro *(gram.)* Adverbial suffix formed by *ki* and *ro*. **Maitekiro.** Nicely, courteously.

kirofano *n.* operating room. *n.(fig.)* form of torture.

kirol(a) *n.* sport, game.

kirolanda *n.* playing field.

kirolari *n.* athlete, sportsman.

kiroldegi *n.* sports pavilion, sports complex, stadium.

kiroltoki *n.* sports arena, complex, pavilion.

kiroltza *n.* sportiveness, athletic quality.

kirolzale *adj.* athletic, sportive, sports-loving.

kirolzelai *n.* playing field.

kirri *n.* sound or sensation of grinding teeth.

kirrika *n.* grinding of teeth.

kirrika egin *v.t.* to grate, to grind, to gnash.

kirrikatsu *adj.* grating, grinding, gnashing, scraping.

kirrikatu *v.i.* to crack, to split, to burst, to break.

kirrinka *n.* squeak, squeaking (of a door, cartwheel, etc.).

kirrinkada *n.* squeaking, creaking.

kirrinka egin *v.t.* to squeak, to creak.

kirrinkaldi *n.* grinding of teeth.

kirrinkari *adj.* squeaking, creaking.

kirrinkatu *v.i.* to squeak, to creak.

kirrizka *n.* squeaking, creaking.

kirrizkada *n.* grinding of teeth, gnashing of teeth.

kirrizka egin *v.t.* to grind the teeth.

kirriz-karraz *n.* onomatopoeic sound of grinding teeth. *n.* sound of dragging feet.

kirru *adj.* curled, kinky. *adj.* blonde. *n.* rough hemp; oakum; tow.

kirten *n.* handle. *n.(fig.)* stupid, idiot, imbecilic.

kirtenkeria *n.* stupidity, foolishness, nonsense, dullness.

kiskal *adj.* burned, scorched, charred.

kiskaldu *v.t.* to burn, to scorch, to toast; to tan. *v.i.* to burn, to be scorched.

kiskalgarri *adj.* burning, scorching.

kiskali *v.i.* to be scorched, to burn, to char.

kiskalketa *n.* burning, scorching, charring.

kiskalpen *n.* burning, scorching, charring.

kiskaltoki *n.* place of intense heat.

kiskaltzaile *adj.* burning, scorching.

kisket *n.* latch, lock, sliding bolt; doorknob. *n.* knocker.

kisketada *n.* knocking.

kisketots *n.* sound of knocking; sound of bolting or throwing the latch.

kiskil *adj.* mean, stingy.

kiskildu *v.i.(fig.)* to grow stingy, to be

mean and stingy.

kiskilkeria *n.* meanness, stinginess, miserliness.

kisu *n.* lime, gypsum, plaster.

kisualdi *n.* light coat of plaster.

kisudura *n.* plastering, plasterwork.

kisugile *n.* lime maker.

kisugin *n.* lime maker.

kisuharri *n.* limestone.

kisulabe *n.* lime oven, lime furnace, lime burner.

kisutsu *adj.* limy, calcareous; plastery.

kisutu *v.i.* to convert into lime. *v.t.* to plaster, to whitewash.

kisuzko *adj.* limy; plastery.

kisuztadura *n.* whitewashing.

kisuztaldi *n.* whitewashing.

kisuztatu *v.t.* to whitewash; to sprinkle lime.

kisuztatzaile *n.* whitewasher.

kitagarri *adj.* liquidatable (debts, etc.). *n.* payment, compensation.

kitaketa *n.(econ.)* liquidation, clearing of accounts, payment of debts.

kitapen *n.(econ.)* liquidation, amortization, clearing of accounts.

kitatu *v.t.* to pay debts, to liquidate debts, to settle debts. *v.t.* to compensate, to indemnify, to pay.

kitatzaile *n.* payer of debts, one who liquidates debts.

kito *adj.* finished, over, terminated; out of debt. *int.* that's that, that's all, that's it.

kito egon *v.i.* to be out of debt, to be at peace (without debts or obligations).

kitzika *n.* excitement. *n.* provocation, stimulation. *adv.* stirring up, rousing, agitating, inciting.

kitzikabera *adj.* excitable.

kitzikaberatasun *n.* excitability.

kitzikadura *n.* stimulation, agitation, incitation, instigation.

kitzikagarri *adj.* exciting, stimulating, rousing, provoking, instigating.

kitzikapen *n.* provocation, stimulation. *n.* tickling.

kitzikari *adj.* agitator, rouser, stimulator, exciter.

kitzikatu *v.t.* to stir up (ashes), to rouse (bees). *v.t.* to excite; to tickle, to tease. *v.t.(fig.)* to provoke, to incite.

kitzikatzaile *adj.* exciting, tantalizing. *n./adj.(fig.)* provoker, exciter; provocative.

Kixote *n.* Quixote. **Kixote Jauna.** Don Quixote.

kixotekada *n.* quixotism, quixotic act or deed.

kixotekeria *n.* quixotism, quixotic behavior.

kizkur *adj.* curly, kinky.

kizkurbera *adj.* curly, wavy.

kizkurberatasun *n.* curliness, waviness.

kizkurdura *n.* curling, waving (hair).

kizkurgailu *n.* curler, curling iron.

kizkurgarri *adj.* curlable, wavable.

kizkurketa *n.* curling, waving.

kizkurpen *n.* curling, waving.

kizkurtasun *n.* curliness, waviness.

kizkurtsu *adj.* curly, wavy.

kizkurtu *v.i.* to curl, to wave. *v.i.* to contract, to shrink (up), to shrivel (up).

kizkurtzapen *n.* curling, contracting.

-kizun *(gram.)* Verbal suffix which indicates possible action in the future. **Eginkizun.** Obligation, task.

klak *n.* glug, onomatopoeic sound of drinking or chewing noisily.

klakada *n.* bite; swallow, gulp.

klakatu *v.t.* to drink or eat noisily.

klarintxo *n.(mus.)* clarinet.

klase *n.* course, class.

klasekide *n.* classmate.

klasifikagarri *adj.* classifiable.

klasifikapen *n.* classification.

klasifikari *n.* classifier.

klasifikatu *v.t.* to classify, to catalogue.

klasiko *adj.* classic, classical.

klasikoki *adv.* classically.

klasizismo *n.* classicism.

klask *n.* onomatopoeic sound of tearing, cracking, snapping.

klaskada *n.* sound of cracking, snapping, breaking. *n.* bite.

klaska egin *v.t.* to bite.

klaskatu *v.t.* to devour, to swallow, to gulp down.

klera *n.* chalk.

kleratsu *adj.* chalky.

klerazko *adj.* chalky.

klerikal *adj.* clerical.

klerikalismo *n.* clericalism.

klerikalki *adv.* clerically.

klikatu *v.t.* to swallow, to gulp (down).

klinika *n.* clinic.

klink *n.* clink, clinking sound. *n.* onomatopoeic sound of swallowing liquid.

klinkada *n.* drink, gulp, swallow.

klink egin *v.t.* to have a drink.

klitxe *n.* cliché.

kloro *n.(chem.)* chlorine.

klorotsu *adj.* chlorinated.

kloruro *n.(chem.)* chloride.

klub *n.* club (organization).

-ko *(gram.)* Verbal suffix indicating the future. Becomes *-go* after *-n.* **Ikusiko dut.** I will see it. **Jakingo du.** He will know. *(gram.)* Noun suffix indicating made of, material. **Egurrezko.** Wooden, made of wood. *(gram.)* Suffix indicating origin, place; time; possession. **Bilboko alkate jauna.** The mayor of Bilbao. *(gram.)* Diminutive suffix. **Idiko.** Small ox. *(gram.)* Adverbial suffix indicating for, of. **Atzoko.** Of yesterday, yesterday's. *(gram.)* Suffix indicating a blow. **Kaskarreko.** Blow to the head. *(gram.)* Suffix used with numbers meaning consisting of, made up of (a number of parts, etc. **Biko.** Consisting of two.

koadratu *adj.* squared, square.

koadro *n.* picture.

koartza *n.(zool.)* heron.

koba *n.* cave, cavern.

kobalto *n.(chem.)* cobalt.

kobazulo *n.* cave opening, cave, cavern.

kobla *n.* old Basque sung verse.

koblakari *n.* troubadour, minstrel.

koblakaritza *n.* minstrelsy, troubadourism.

koblari *n.* balladeer, minstrel, bard.

koblatu *v.t.* to sing verses, to improvise verses.

kobraezin *adj.* uncollectable, unrecoverable, irretrievable.

kobragarri *adj.* collectable.

kobraketa *n.* collection (of money).

kobrantza *n.* collection (of money).

kobratu *v.t.* to collect (money), to receive money, to get money.

kobratzaile *n.* collector, one who gets money, ticket taker, collector of fares, conductor.

kobre *n.(min.)* copper.

kobretsu *adj.* copper, coppery, abundant in copper.

kobrezko *adj.* copper, made of copper.

kobreztatu *v.t.* to cover with copper.

kodaina *n.* scythe.

koefiziente *n.* coefficient, measure, degree.

-koi *(gram.)* Suffix which forms adjectives and indicates propensity, tendency, fondness. **Berekoi.** Self-centered.

koinak *n.* cognac, brandy.

koinata *n.* sister-in-law.

koinatu *n.* brother-in-law.

koiote *n.(zool.)* coyote.

koipe *n.* grease, animal fat. *n.(fig.)* filth, dirt, grime. *n.(fig.)* flattery.

koipealdi *n.* spattering with grease, grease stain.

koipedun *adj.* greasy, fatty, lardy.

koipegabetu *v.i./v.t.* to degrease, to clean grease off.

koipejario *adj.* greasy, fatty. *adj.(fig.)* flattering, fawning.

koipekeria *n.(fig.)* false flattery, fawning, brown-nosing, adulation.

koipeketa *n.* greasing, oiling, larding.

koipemale *n.* greaser.

koipeontzi *n.* grease container, grease can.

koipetasun *n.* greasiness, oiliness.

koipetsu *adj.* greasy, fatty, full of lard. *adj.* fawning, flattering, servile.

koipetu *v.t./v.i.* to grease, to oil. *v.t./v.i.(fig.)* to flatter, to fawn.

koipetzaile *n./adj.* greaser; greasing. *n./adj.(fig.)* flatterer, fawner; flattering, fawning.

koipeztadura *n.* greasing, act of greasing.

koipeztailu *n.* oil can, grease gun.

koipeztaketa *n.* greasing, act of greasing.

koipeztapen *n.* greasing, larding.

koipeztatu *v.t.* to grease, to oil.

koipeztatzaile *n.* lubricator, oiler, greaser.

koipezto *adj.* greasy, filthy, dirty.

koipeztu *v.t.* to grease, to smear with grease or fat.

koitadu *adj.* poor, unfortunate.

-koitz *(gram.)* Suffix used with numbers. Signifies multiplicity, -fold. **Bikoitz.** Double; twin(s).

kok *n.* fill, bellyful.

kokada *n.* burp, belch, eructation.

kokada egin *v.t.* to burp, to belch.

kokadura *n.* pausing, perching. *n.* mounting, fitting, joining.

kokaina *n.(chem.)* cocaine.

kokaketa *n.* inserting, enclosing.

kokaldi *n.* fill, bellyful, satiety, overeating. *n.* perching, pausing.

kokarazi *v.t.* to insert, to enclose.

kokatu *v.i.* to perch, to pause. *v.t.* to put, to place. *v.t.* to enclose, to insert. *v.t.* to hang.

kok egin *v.t.* to choke (on food).

koko *n.(zool.)* mealy bug, small insect. *n.(bot.)* coconut.

kokodrilo *n.(zool.)* crocodile.

kokolo *adj.(colloq.)* foolish, stupid, idiotic. *adj.(fam.)* chocolate. Used by and for children.

kokoloaldi *n.* foolishness, stupidity.

kokolokeria *n.* stupidity, foolishness.

kokolotu *v.i.* to become stupid or foolish, to be stupid or foolish.

kokondo *n.(bot.)* coconut tree.

kokor *n.(anat.)* throat, pharynx.

kokorika *adv.* squatting, crouching, curled up.

kokorikatu *v.i.* to crouch, to squat, to curl up.

kokorro *adj.(colloq.)* stupid, dull, idiotic; drowsy, sleepy.

kokorrotu *v.i.* to be stupid, to be dull, to be an idiot.

kokospe *n.* dewlap, double chin.

kokospeko *n.* blow to the chin or dewlap. *n.* bib.

kokot *n.(anat.)* nape of the neck, back of the neck.

kokoteko *n.* blow to the back of the neck.

kokotezur *n.(anat.)* occipital bone.

kokotondo *n.* dewlap, double chin; throat.

kokots *n.(anat.)* chin.

kokotsazpi *n.* dewlap, double chin, area under the chin.

kokotxa *n.* fleshy underchin of the hake.

kola *n.* glue.

kolaio *n.(zool.)* brown, scaleless,

saltwater fish with a rough skin, resembling an eel.

kolaka *n.(zool.)* shad.

kolapen *n.* gluing.

kolatu *v.t.* to glue.

koldar *adj.* cowardly, timid, shy.

koldarkeria *n.* cowardice, timidity.

koldarki *adv.* timidly, cowardly.

koldarti *adj.* cowardly.

koldartu *v.i.* to become a coward, to become intimidated, to turn chicken. *v.t.* to intimidate, to make cowardly.

kolitxa *n.* bell tower, campanile.

koloka *adj.* unstable, wobbly. *adj.(fig.)* wavering, indecisive, perplexed. *adv.* inconsistently.

kolokadura *n.* vacillation, inconsistency, doubt. *n.* dislocation.

kolokaldi *n.* wobbling, teetering, vacillation.

koloka(n) egon *v.i.* to be unstable, to be wobbly, to be loose. *v.i.* to vacillate, to waver, to be indecisive, to be inconsistent.

kolokarazi *v.t.* to astound, to astonish, to shock, to baffle.

kolokari *adj.* oscillating, swinging, teetering, wobbling.

kolokati *adj.* indecisive, wishy-washy.

kolokatu *v.i.* to vacillate, to wobble, to fluctuate, to waver, to teeter. *v.i./v.t.* to displace, to dislocate (joints). *v.i.* to cluck, to cackle.

kolonia *n.* cologne.

koloniakuntza *n.* colonization.

kolonialismo *n.* colonialism.

koloniar *adj.* colonial.

kolonigile *n.* colonizer.

kolonitar *n.* colonist.

kolonizagarri *adj.* colonizable.

kolonizaketa *n.* colonization.

kolonizatu *v.t.* to colonize.

kolonizatzaile *n.* colonizer.

koloragailu *n.* coloring matter, dye, tint.

koloragarri *adj.* capable of being colored, tintable.

koloraketa *n.* coloring, coloration.

kolorapen *n.* coloring, coloration.

koloratzaile *adj.* coloring, dye. *n.* dye, coloring agent.

kolorazio *n.* coloration, coloring.

kolore *n.* color.

koloreanitz *adj.* multicolor, of many colors, many-colored, polychrome.

koloreaskodun *adj.* multicolor, of many colors, many-colored, polychrome.

kolorebakar *adj.* monochromatic.

kolorebakarreko *adj.* monochromatic, of one color, all one color.

kolorebidun *adj.* of two colors, two-colored, having two colors. *adj.(phys.)* dichroic.

kolorebiko *adj.* of two colors, having two colors, two-colored.

koloregabe *adj.* colorless, faded, discolored.

koloregabetu *v.i.* to pale, to fade, to lose color.

koloregai *n.* dye, coloring, coloring agent.

koloretasun *n.* coloration, coloring.

koloretsu *adj.* colored, colorful.

kolorezko *adj.* chromatic, colored, colorful.

koloreztatu *v.t.* to color, to paint.

kolorge *adj.* colorless, faded, discolored.

kolpaketa *n.* beating, clubbing.

kolpatu *v.t.* to hit, to strike, to deal a blow, to beat. *v.t.(fig.)* to offend (someone).

kolpe *n.* blow.

kolpe egin *v.t.* to grab, to catch.

kolpeka *adv.* hitting, striking, beating, by blows.

kolpekatu *v.t.* to hit one another, to exchange blows.

kolpeko *adj.* sudden, quick, immediate, instantaneous.

kolpetxo *n.* small blow, tap.

koltxoi *n.* mattress, cushion.

koltxoitegi *n.* mattress store.

koltxoitu *v.t.* to make a mattress.

koltxoixka *n.* bunk mattress, light mattress; air mattress.

koma *n.(gram.)* comma. *n.(med.)* coma, comatose state.

komandante *n.(mil.)* commander, commandant.

komandantzia *n.* headquarters.

komedia *n.* comedy, play.

komedidazle *n.* playwright, one who writes plays.

komedilari *n.* comedian, comic actor.

komeni *v.i.* to be convenient, to be helpful, to be advantageous, to be advisable, to be good for, to suit.

komenientzia *n.* convenience, advantage, benefit, advisability.

komenigarri *adj.* useful, advantageous, beneficial.

komeni izan *v.i.* to be convenient, to be helpful, to be advantageous, to be advisable, to be good for, to suit.

komentu *n.* convent, monastery.

komenturaketa *n.* entering a convent.

komenturatu *v.i.* to enter a convent, to be cloistered.

komeria *n.* joke, fun, jest.

komertzial *adj.* commercial.

komertzialdu *v.t.* to commercialize.

komertzialpen *n.* marketing, commercialization.

kometa *n.(astron.)* comet.

komiki *n.* comic(s), comic book.

komiko *adj.* comic, comical.

komikoki *adv.* comically.

komisari *n.* commissar.

komisartegi *n.* commissariat.

komoda *n.* chest of drawers, bureau.

komun *n.* toilet, lavatory, bathroom, restroom.

komunikabide *n.* means of

communication, media.
komunikaezin adj. incommunicable.
komunikaezintasun n.
incommunicability.
komunikagaitz adj. difficult to
communicate (message, telegram).
komunikagarri adj. communicable,
transmittable.
komunikagarritasun n.
communicability, quality of being
transmittable.
komunikakor adj. communicative.
komunikapen n. communication.
komunikatu v.i./v.t. to communicate.
komunikatzaile n./adj. communicator;
communicative.
komunikazio n. communication.
komunio n.(eccl.) communion.
komunione n. communion.
komunismo n.(pol.) communism.
komunista n.(pol.) communist.
komunistazale adj. fond of
communism, pinko.
komunitate n. community.
komun-paper(a) n. toilet paper.
konbenio n. labor agreement,
contract.
konbentzigaitz adj. difficult to
convince.
konbentzigarri adj. convincing,
persuasive; convincible,
persuadable.
konbentzimendu n. conviction,
convincing.
konbentzitu v.t./v.i. to convince.
konbertzio n. conversion.
konbexu adj.(geom.) convex.
konbinaketa n. combination.
konbinapen n. combination.
konboi n. convoy.
kondaira n. history.
kondairagile n. historian.
kondairaurre n. prehistory.
kondairaurreko adj. prehistoric.
kondar n. leftovers, remains, residue.
Almost always used in the plural. adj.
ultimate, final.
kondari n. narrator.
kondarrezko adj. residual, remaining,
leftover.
kondartsu adj. having residue.
kondartu v.i. to leave dregs, to leave a
residue.
konde n. count (nobleman).
kondego n. earldom, countship.
kondekorapen n. decoration (military).
kondekoratu v.t. to decorate (military),
to honor.
kondenagarri adj. condemnable.
kondenamendu n. condemnation,
damnation.
kondenatu v.i. to be condemned, to be
damned. v.t. to condemn, to damn,
to convict, to sentence.
kondenatzaile n./adj. condemner,
damner, sentencer, one who passes
judgment; condemning, damning.

kondentsagailu n. condenser.
kondentsagarri adj. condensable.
kondentsagarritasun n.
condensability.
kondentsapen n. condensation.
kondentsatu v.i. to condense.
kondentsazio n. condensation.
kondeorde n. viscount.
kondeordetza n. viscountship.
konderri n. county.
kondesa n. countess.
kondesaorde n. viscountess.
kondetza n. earldom, countship.
kondizio n. condition, circumstance.
kondiziogabe adj. unconditional.
kondiziogabeki adv. unconditionally.
kondizionamendu n. conditioning.
kondizionatu v.t. to condition.
kondiziozko adj. conditional,
dependent on.
koneju n. rabbit.
konexio n. connection.
konfederazio n. confederation.
konfidantza n. confidence, trust,
reliance, faith.
konformagaitz adj. nonconformist.
konformatu v.i. to conform, to comply
with, to be satisfied with.
konforme adj. satisfied, in agreement,
conforming.
konforme egon v.i. to agree.
kongregazione n. religious
congregation.
kongresu n. meeting, conference,
congress.
konketa n. washbasin, sink, washtub.
konkil n. wooden soup bowl.
konkor n. bump, lump. n. hump,
hunchback.
konkordatu n.(eccl.) concordat,
agreement between the Pope and a
government with regard to their
mutual interests.
konkordun adj. humped, humpbacked,
hunchbacked.
konkordura n. swelling, prominence.
konkortasun n. bending of the back,
hunching over, curvature.
konkortu v.i. to hunch over, to become
hunchbacked. v.i. to swell, to
increase in size.
konkretatu v.t. to specify, to make
precise.
konkretu adj. concrete, specific,
precise, exact.
konkretuki adv. concretely,
specifically, precisely, exactly.
kono n.(geom.) cone.
konorte n. consciousness, awareness.
konparagai adj. comparable.
konparagaitz adj. difficult to compare,
incomparable.
konparatu v.t. to compare.
konparazio n. comparison.
konpas(a) n. compass. n.(mus.)
tempo, time signature, rhythm.
konpetizio n. competition.

konplitu v.t. to complete, to finish, to carry out.

konponbide n. compromise, solution, settlement.

konpondu v.t. to arrange, to settle, to solve, to fix, to repair. v.i. to get along (with). v.i. to manage (to do something).

konpondura n. adjustment, readjustment, repair.

konponezin adj. irreparable; unsolvable.

konpongabe adj. not arranged, unrepaired, unsolved.

konpongarri adj. repairable, solvable, surmountable.

konponkeria n. unsatisfactory settlement or solution, haphazard repair; dishonest or immoral solution or arrangement.

konponketa n. repair, solution, arrangement, agreement.

konpontzaile n. fixer, mender, repairer, repairman; compromiser, solver. adj. repairing, solving.

konposaketa n. composition.

konposatu v.t. to compose, to constitute, to make up, to form. adj. composite, compound.

konposatzaile n. composer.

konpota n. compote.

konprimagailu n.(mech.) compressor.

konpromisu n. involvement; engagement, social obligation, commitment.

konputagailu n. computer.

konputagarri adj. computable.

konputagarritasun n. computability.

konstituzio n.(pol.) constitution.

konstituzioaurkako adj. unconstitutional.

konstituziogai n. draft of the constitution.

konstituziogile n. writer of the constitution, member of the Cortes convened to reform the Spanish constitution.

konstituziogintza n. process of writing a constitution.

konstituziogintzaldi n. period of writing the constitution.

konstituzionalki adv. constitutionally.

konstituzionaltasun n. constitutionality.

konstituziozko adj. constitutional.

konstruzio n. construction.

kontabilitate n. accounting, bookkeeping.

kontadore n. meter (water meter, light meter, etc.), regulator.

kontaera n. way of speaking, recounting, relating. n. mention.

kontaezin adj. countless, innumerable, immeasurable. adj. unnarratable, impossible to narrate.

kontaezinbesteko adj. innumerable.

kontaezinez adv. countlessly, endlessly. adv. indescribably.

kontaezintasun n. innumerability, uncountability.

kontagailu n. calculator.

kontagaitz adj. innumerable, difficult to count.

kontagaiztasun n. difficulty in counting, countlessness.

kontagarri adj. countable. adj. narratable, expressible, describable.

kontagela n. accountant's office.

kontaketa n. enumeration, computation, counting. n. narration, report, account.

kontakizun n. narration, story.

kontaktu n. contact.

kontalari n. narrator, storyteller, relator.

kontari n. counter. n. narrator, storyteller.

kontatu v.t. to count, to compute, to calculate. v.t. to narrate, to report, to refer, to relate, to tell (a story).

kontatzaile n. counter, one who counts, tallyman. n. narrator, storyteller, relator, teller.

kontentagaitz adj. hard to please.

kontentagaiztasun n. quality of being hard to please, pickiness.

kontentakor adj. easily pleased, easygoing.

kontentatu v.i. to become content, to become satisfied; to be pleasing. v.t. to please.

kontenterraz adj. easily satisfied, easily pleased, easy to please.

konterri n. county.

kontinentar adj. continental, of the continent.

kontinentarteko adj. transcontinental, intercontinental.

kontinente n.(geog.) continent.

kontra adv./prep. against. prep. next to, against.

kontra- (gram.) Prefix which indicates opposition, against, counter-, anti-.

kontrabalio n.(econ.) countervalue, equivalent.

kontrabandista n. smuggler, contrabandist.

kontrabandu n. contraband, smuggled item, smuggling.

kontrabaxu n.(mus.) bass viol, bass fiddle.

kontrabideko adj. inadequate, inappropriate, unfitting.

kontradikzio n. contradiction.

kontra egin v.t. to go against, to oppose, to resist.

kontra egon v.i. to be against.

kontraekintza n. opposition, resistance.

kontraeragin v.t. to oppose, to resist.

kontraerantzun n. retort, rejoinder, comeback.

kontraeraso n. counteroffensive.

kontraerasoaldi n. counterattack.

kontraesale n. contradictor.
kontraesan n. contradiction.
kontraesanezko adj. contradictory.
kontraesankor adj. contradictory, contrary.
kontraeskaintza n. counteroffer.
kontraespioi n. counterspy.
kontraespionaia n. counterespionage.
kontraeutsi v.t. to resist, to go against.
kontraezaugarri n. countersign, secret signal, password.
kontraezin adj. irresistible, unopposable, impossible to oppose.
kontraeztarri n.(anat.) trachea, windpipe.
kontraeztarriratu v.i. to choke.
kontragindu n. counter order.
kontraibilaldi n. countermarch.
kontrairaultza n. counterrevolution.
kontrairaultzaile n. counter-revolutionary, counterrevolutionist.
kontrajardun v.t. to oppose, to go against.
kontrajarketa n. confrontation, altercation, affront.
kontrajarle adj. adverse, opposing, contrary.
kontrajarrera n. opposition.
kontrajarri v.i./v.t. to oppose, to pit oneself against.
kontrajoera n. opposition, resistance.
kontrakari n. opponent, refuter, challenger.
kontrako n. adversary, enemy, opponent. adj. contrary, opposite, opposing, unfavorable, antagonistic.
kontrakotasun n. antagonism, opposition.
kontrakzio n. contraction. n. abbreviation.
kontramaisu n. foreman, overseer, supervisor.
kontrapisu n. counterweight, counterbalance.
kontrapozoi n. antidote.
kontrapuntu n.(mus.) counterpoint.
kontrara adv. backwards, over, around.
kontraste n. contrast.
kontrata n. contract.
kontratapen n. hiring, contracting.
kontratari n. employer, one who offers a contract.
kontratatu v.t. to hire, to contract (someone) to do something, to give a contract.
kontratatzaile n. contractor, hirer, employer; contracting party.
kontratista n. contractor, building contractor.
kontratu n. contract.
kontratugile n. contractor, employer, hirer.
kontrazko adj. contrary, against, opposed, antagonistic.
kontrezarketa n. opposition, resistance, contraposition.

kontrezarle n. opponent.
kontrezarri v.t. to oppose, to resist, to pit oneself against.
kontribuzio n.(econ.) tax.
kontrokots n. double chin, dewlap.
kontrol n. control.
kontrolaezin adj. uncontrollable.
kontrolagaitz adj. difficult to control, hard to control.
kontrolagarri adj. controllable.
kontrolatu v.t. to control, to check (on), to regulate, to govern, to inspect.
kontrolatzaile n. controller.
kontrolgabe adj. uncontrolled.
kontrolgailu n. control, control panel, controlling device.
kontseilagarri adj. advisable.
kontseilaketa n. counseling, giving advice.
kontseilari n. counselor, adviser. n.(pol.) councillor, alderman, councilman.
kontseilariorde n. substitute adviser, vice-counselor.
kontseilaritza n. job of adviser or counselor.
kontseilatu v.t. to advise, to counsel, to give advice.
kontseilu n. advice, counsel. n. board of advisers, council.
kontserba n. canned food, preserved fish.
kontserbadore adj. conservative.
kontserbagile n. person who preserves food, canner.
kontserbaketa n. preserving, canning.
kontserbakor adj. conservative.
kontserbari n. fish canner, person who cans food.
kontserbatorio n. conservatory.
kontserbatu v.t./v.i. to conserve, to preserve.
kontserbazio n. conservation, preservation.
kontsolabide n. consolation, relief.
kontsolaezin adj. inconsolable.
kontsolagaitz adj. hard to console.
kontsolagarri adj. comforting, consoling.
kontsolamendu n. consolation, comfort.
kontsolatu v.t./v.i. to console, to comfort.
kontsolatzaile n. consoler, sympathizer.
kontsolazio n. consolation.
kontsonante n. consonant.
kontsul n. consul.
kontsulaldi n. consulship.
kontsuletxe n. consulate.
kontsulgo n. job of a consul, consulship.
kontsulorde n. vice-consul.
kontsulordego n. office of vice-consul.
kontsulta n. doctor's office, consulting room, professional office. n.

counseling, advice.

kontsultagela *n.* doctor's office, consulting room.

kontsultari *n.* consultant.

kontsultategi *n.* consulting room, doctor's office.

kontsultatu *v.t.* to consult, to ask for advice.

kontsumo *n.* consumption.

kontsumogai *n.* consumer good(s).

kontu *n.* charge, responsibility, care, caution, precaution. *n.* account; bill, check (in a restaurant or hotel). *n.* story.

kontu(a) ireki *v.t.* to open an account.

kontu(a) itxi *v.t.* to close an account.

kontu(ak) atera *v.t.* to calculate, to do the accounts, to balance the accounts. *v.t.* to think over; to be careful.

kontu(ak) egin *v.t.* to do the accounts, to balance the accounts, to calculate.

kontu(ak) garbitu *v.t.* to pay debts, to clear the account, to adjust the accounts.

kontu(ak) hartu *v.t.* to ask for an accounting, to ask for information or a report.

kontuan eduki *v.t.* to keep in mind, to remember.

kontuan hartu *v.t.* to consider.

kontuan jausi *v.t.* to realize.

kontuan sartu *v.t.* to put money into one's account, to deposit, to make a deposit.

kontu eduki *v.t.* to take care, to be careful.

kontu egin *v.t.* to pay attention, to care for, to watch out.

kontu eman *v.t.* to account for, to give an account of, to report.

kontugabeki *adj.* uncautiously, carelessly, unwarily, not carefully.

kontugarbialdi *n.* payment of debts, clearing of accounts.

kontugarbiketa *n.* settling of accounts, paying debts, liquidation, closing an account.

kontugile *n.* bookkeeper, accountant.

kontugintza *n.* accounting, bookkeeping.

kontulari *n.* bookkeeper, accountant. *n.* narrator, storyteller.

kontularitza *n.* accounting, bookkeeping.

kontuliburu *n.* ledger, account book.

konturagabe(ko) *adj.* inadvertent, unintentional, thoughtless.

konturatu *v.i.* to become aware of, to realize, to notice, to perceive.

kontutxo *n.(dim.)* short story, little story.

kontuz *adv.* carefully, attentively. *int.* careful!

kontuzuriketa *n.* liquidation, settling of accounts, paying bills.

kontxo *int.* exclamation of surprise, wow!, gosh!

kontzejal *n.* councillor, alderman, councilman.

kontzentratu *v.t./v.i.* to concentrate.

kontzentrazio *n.* concentration.

kontzertu *n.* concert.

kontzertulari *n.* concert artist, concert performer.

kontzientzia *n.* conscience. *n.* consciousness.

kontzientziapen *n.* conscientiousness.

kontzientziatsu *adj.* conscientious, responsible.

kontzientziatu *v.t./v.i.* to make aware, to make (someone) conscious of (something); to be aware of, to be conscious of.

kontzilio *n.* council.

kooperatiba *n.* co-op, cooperative.

koordinaketa *n.* coordination.

koordinapen *n.* coordination.

koordinatu *v.t.* to coordinate.

koordinatzaile *n.* coordinator.

koordinazio *n.* coordination.

kopa *n.* cup, goblet, brandy glass; drink; winner's cup, trophy. *n.* one of four suits in Basque playing cards.

kopakada *n.* cupful, glassful, gobletful, drink.

kopalet *n.* shallow basket with handles used for carrying fish, etc.

kopari *n.* wine server, wine steward, cupbearer.

kopau *n.* bite, mouthful, morsel of food. *n.* snack.

kopeta *n.(anat.)* forehead.

kopetadun *adj.* audacious, daring, bold, valiant. *adj.* shameless, brazen.

kopetako *n.* yoke pad (of an ox).

kopetatu *v.i.* to be impudent, to be brazen. *adj.(fig.)* audacious, bold, brazen.

kopetile *n.* bang, lock of hair falling over the forehead.

kopetilun *adj.* angry, frowning, scowling. *adj.* sad, unhappy, gloomy.

kopetilundu *v.i.* to frown, to scowl, to glower. *v.i.(fig.)* to become sad.

kopia *n.* copy.

kopiaketa *n.* plagiarism; copying.

kopiatu *v.t.* to copy, to rewrite.

kopiatzaile *n.* copier, transcriber.

kopidazle *n.* transcriber, copier.

kopla *n.* old Basque sung verse.

koplari *n.* troubadour, minstrel.

koplakeria *n.* stupid act, foolishness, folly.

kopoi *n.(eccl.)* ciborium.

kopuratu *v.t.* to sum up, to add.

kopuratzaile *n./adj.* adder; adding.

kopuru *n.* quantity, amount. *n.(arith.)* sum, total.

kopurutsu *adj.* numerous, considerable.

kopuruzko *adj.* numeric, numerical, composed of numbers.

-kor *(gram.)* Suffix of verbal adjectives, which indicates propensity for, tendency toward (something). **Aldakor.** Changeable.

korain *n.* kind of fish hook used for catching squid.

koral *n.(zool.)* coral.

koraltsu *adj.* coralline, coral.

koran *n.(rel.)* Koran.

korapilaketa *n.* knotting.

korapilatu *v.t.* to knot, to tie in a knot. *v.i.(fig.)* to become complicated, involved. *v.i.(fig.)* to become tongue-tied.

korapilo *n.* knot, lump. *n.(fig.)* complication, trouble, difficulty, muddle, tangle, problem.

korapilotsu *adj.* knotty. *adj.(fig.)* complicated, complex, difficult, troublesome.

korapiltasun *n.* knottiness.

korda *n.* string, cord, or rope (of garlic, onions, etc.).

kordaketa *n.* stringing (onions, etc.).

kordatu *v.t.* to string (onions, garlic, etc.).

kordaztu *v.t.* to bind with a cord, to put string on (something).

kordel *n.* shoelace, shoestring. *n.* cord, rope. *n.* fishing line.

kordeldegi *n.* rope or cord maker's shop.

kordeleria *n.* pile of cord or rope.

kordeleztatu *v.t.* to tie or bind with cord.

kordoi *n.* cord, shoelace.

kordoka *n.* tottering, wobbling, swaying, wavering. *n.(fig.)* vacillation, irresolution, doubt. *adj.* vacillating, hesitant, irresolute.

kordokadura *n.* wobbling, tottering, swaying, wavering, shaking.

kordokaldi *n.* shake.

kordokan *adv.* indecisively, vacillatingly.

kordokari *adj.* teetering, wobbling, swaying; vacillating, indecisive.

kordokarazi *v.t.* to make (something) wobble or shake. *v.t.(fig.)* to cause (someone) to vacillate or doubt.

kordokatu *v.i.* to vacillate, to be uncertain, to be insecure. *v.t.* to sway, to rock, to swing, to balance, to wobble, to totter, to waver.

korkoin *n.(zool.)* mullet.

korkoitz *n.* hunchback, hump.

korkoizdun *adj.* hunchbacked, humpbacked, humped.

korkoiztu *v.i.* to become hunchbacked.

koroa *n.* crown. *n.(econ.)* money, type of currency. *n.* tonsure.

koroaketa *n.* coronation.

koroapen *n.* coronation.

koroatu *v.t.* to crown.

koroatzaile *n.* crowner.

koronel *n.(mil.)* colonel.

koronelgo *n.* colonelship.

koroneltza *n.* colonelship.

korribide *n.* race track.

korrika *n.* race, run. *adv.* running, hurriedly.

korrika egin *v.t.* to run, to race.

korrikaldi *n.* race, foot race.

korriketa *n.* race, foot race.

korritu *v.t.* to run, to race. *n.(econ.)* interest.

korrok *n.* onomatopoeic sound of a belch.

korroka *adv.* belching, burping. *n.* sound of stomach rumbling. *n.* snoring.

korrokada *n.* burp, belch.

korrok egin *v.t.* to burp, to belch.

korronte *n.* current (electric, water).

korru *n.* circle, ring, group (of talkers).

kortse *n.* corset.

kortsetegi *n.* corset factory or shop.

kortxel *n.* roof of a church.

kortxo *n.* cork.

kortxogintza *n.* cork making.

kortxoztatu *v.t.* to cork (a bottle), to cover with cork (a wall, etc.).

koru *n.* choir loft, place for the choir. *n.* choir, group of singers, choral group.

koruatze *n.* place in back of the choir.

koruoste *n.* place in back of the choir.

korupe *n.* space under the choir.

kosk *n.* crunch, munch, onomatopoeic sound of biting.

koska *n.* edge, ledge, nick, crack. *n.(geol.)* fault, crack. *n.(fig.)* hair badly layered or cut. *n.(fig.)* difficulty.

koskadun *adj.* layered. *adj.* toothed, serrated.

koskadura *n.* striation, groove, flute.

koskagabetu *v.t.* to break off the edges or corners, to chip off.

koskamaila *n.* fault, crack.

koskatu *v.t./v.i.* to nick, to notch, to chip; to be nicked, notched, chipped. *v.t./v.i.* to groove, to striate; to be grooved, to be striated.

kosk egin *v.t.* to bite, to chew, to gnaw.

koskor *adj.* small, reduced, little, limited. *n.* piece, bit. *n.* bump, swelling (on the head). *n.* crust of bread.

koskordun *adj.* bumpy, lumpy.

koskorreko *n.* blow to the head.

koskortu *v.i.* to grow up, to develop.

kosmetiko *n.* cosmetics, make-up.

kosmiko *adj.* cosmic.

kosmo *n.* cosmos.

kosmolari *n.* cosmologist.

kosmologia *n.* cosmology.

kosmopolita *adj.* cosmopolitan.

kosta *n.* coast.

kostal *n.* big sack.

kostalde *n.* littoral, coast, coastline, shore, bank.

kostalderatu *v.i.* to approach the coast, to near the coast, to come into shore, to border the coast.

kostaratu *v.i.* to reach the shore.
kostatu *v.i.* to cost. *v.i.* to have difficulty, to find it a lot of trouble (to do something).
kostazain *n.* coast guard.
kostontzi *n.* coastal sailing or trading boat.
kostu *n.(econ.)* cost, price.
-kote *(gram.)* Adjectival suffix used with numbers signifying multiplicity.
Laukote. Four-fold. *(gram.)* Adjectival suffix signifying very.
Handikote Very big, huge, gigantic.
kotoi *n.(bot.)* cotton.
kotoindegi *n.* cottonfield.
kotoinondo *n.(bot.)* cotton plant.
kotoinsoro *n.* cotton field.
kotorro *n.(zool.)* kind of black gull which dives beneath the water to fish.
kotxe *n.* car.
kotxegain *n.* baggage rack (on a car), roof of a car.
kotxetegi *n.* garage.
kotxorro *n.(zool.)* grub, weevil.
koxka *n.(dim.)* small fissure, fault, crack. *adj.(fig.)* crazy, nuts.
koxkor *adj.* small, little.
-koz *(gram.)* Adverbial suffix signifying for, intended for (a time period).
Gaurkoz. For today.
krabelin *n.(bot.)* carnation.
krak *n.* onomatopoeic sound of breaking, cracking, splitting.
krakada *n.* creak, crackle, cracking. *n.* snack (especially in the afternoon).
krakada egin *v.t.* to creak, to crackle. *v.t.* to snack, to have a snack.
krak egin *v.t.* to crash, to crack, to break.
krask *n.* onomatopoeic sound of breaking, cracking, splitting.
kraskadura *n.* break, split, crack, interstice.
kraskagailu *n.* nutcracker.
kraskaldi *n.* cracking, breaking, rupturing.
kraskari *adj.* crunchy, crunching, crushing, cracking.
kraskatu *v.t.* to break, to crack, to split. *v.i.* to grow weak, to weaken (physically or morally).
kraskatzaile *adj.* breaking, cracking, splitting.
kraskots *n.* sound of crunching, crushing, cracking.
krater *n.(geol.)* crater.
kreagabe *adj.* uncreated.
kreagarri *adj.* creatable.
kreamen *n.* creativity.
kreapen *n.* creating, creation.
kreatu *v.t.* to create.
kreatzaile *n.* creator, God.
kreazio *n.* creation.
kreditu *n.(econ.)* credit.
kredo *n.(rel.)* creed, credo, beliefs.
kremailera *n.* zipper.

kresal *n.* salt water, seawater.
kriket *adj.* well-groomed, spruced up; foppish, dandy.
kriketasun *n.* quality of being well-groomed; foppishness, pulchritude.
kriketu *v.i.* to be well-groomed, to be spruced up; to be foppish.
kriseilu *n.* oil lamp; large candle.
kriseilugin *n.* candlemaker, oil lamp maker.
kriseilugintza *n.* candlemaking, manufacture of oil lamps.
kriseilutegi *n.* candle shop, oil lamp shop.
kriseilutxo *n.(dim.)* small candle, small oil lamp.
kriseilutzar *n.(augm.)* large beacon or lamp.
krisis *n.* crisis.
krisisaldi *n.* critical period, time of crisis.
krisket *n.* latch, bolt (of a door). *n.* castanet.
krisketatu *v.t.* to bolt, to lock with a bolt.
kriskitin *n.* castanet.
kriskitinketa *n.* action of playing or clacking castanets.
kriskitin-kraskitin *n.* sound produced by castanets; snapping of fingers.
kriskitinots *n.* sound of castanets.
kriskitinsuge *n.(zool.)* rattlesnake.
krisma *n.(eccl.)* chrism, consecrated oil.
krismontzi *n.(eccl.)* small vessel where the chrism is kept.
kristal *n.* crystal. *n.* glass.
kristalari *n.* crystal maker. *n.* glass maker, glass blower.
kristaldegi *n.* crystal shop; glass shop.
kristaldu *v.i.* to vitrify.
kristaldura *n.* crystallization.
kristalezko *adj.* glassy, made of glass, vitreous, crystalline.
kristalgaitz *adj.* uncrystallizable.
kristalgin *n.* glass maker, crystal maker.
kristalgintza *n.* manufacture of glass or crystal, glassware making.
kristalki *n.* piece of glass.
kristau *adj.* Christian. *n.* person, human being, people; anyone, no one (in the negative).
kristau aro *n.* Christian era.
kristauberri *n.* new Christian, converted Christian; newly baptized baby.
kristaugai *n./adj.* catechumen, convert to Christianity receiving instruction to prepare for baptism.
kristaugaialdi *n.* period of religious instruction for Christian converts in preparation for baptism.
kristau ikasbide *n.* catechism.
kristaujarduera *n.* Christian behavior.
kristauki *adv.* as a Christian, in a

Christian manner, Christianly.
kristaukiro adv. Christianly.
kristaukontrako adj. antichristian.
kristaupen n. Christianization.
kristautasun n. Christianity.
kristauteria n. group of Christians, Christianity.
kristautu v.t. to Christianize, to baptize as a Christian. v.i. to become a Christian.
Kristo n. Christ.
kritika n. criticism.
kritikagarri adj. criticizable.
kritikalari n. critic.
kritikari n. critic.
kritikatu v.t. to criticize.
kritikatzaile n. critic, criticizer. adj. gossipy.
kritiko adj. critical.
kroa egin v.t. to croak.
kroaka n. croaking (of a frog).
kromlech n. cromlech.
kromo n.(chem.) chrome.
kromosoma n.(biol.) chromosome.
kronika n. chronicle.
kronikari n. chronicler.
kronologia n. chronology.
kronologiko adj. chronological.
kronologikoki adv. chronologically.
kronometraketa n. timekeeping.
kronometro n. chronometer.
krudel adj. cruel, pitiless, merciless.
krudeldu v.i. to grow cruel, to become mean.
krudelkeria n. cruelty, meanness, savageness, mercilessness.
krudelki adv. cruelly, meanly, mercilessly.
krudeltasun n. cruelty, meanness.
kuaderno n. notebook.
kualitate n. quality.
kubiko adj. cubic.
kubismo n. cubism.
kubo n.(geom.) cube.
kudeatu v.t. to manage, to supervise, to be an agent (for someone).
kudeatzaile n. manager, agent, administrator, supervisor.
kui n.(zool.) Indian rabbit; rabbit.
kuia n.(bot.) pumpkin; cucumber.
kuiondo n.(bot.) cucumber plant.
kukaina n. greased pole or competition in which players navigate a greased pole extended over the water to retrieve a flag.
kuku n.(zool.) cuckoo. n. sound of the cuckoo.
kukubelar n.(bot.) digitalis, foxglove.
kukubilka adv. squatting, crouching.
kukubilkatu v.i. to squat, to crouch, to curl up.
kuku egin v.t. to cuckoo. v.t. to play hide-and-seek.
kukufraka n.(bot.) digitalis, foxglove.
kukuka adv. playing hide-and-seek; spying, peeking.
kukukari n. player of hide-and-seek.

kukuka ibili v.i. to be secretive, to be mysterious.
kukukeria n. mystery, concealment, secrecy.
kukula n. rooster's crest, cockscomb. n. summit, peak. n. crest or top of a tree.
kukulu n.(bot.) calyx.
kukurruku n. cockle-doodle-doo, sound of a rooster crowing.
kukurruku egin v.t. to crow (rooster).
kukurruku jo v.t. to crow (rooster). v.t.(fig.) to proclaim a victory.
kukuso n. flea.
kukutu v.i. to stoop, to crouch, to stalk, to ambush.
kulatz n.(neol.) period.
kuliska n.(zool.) golden plover, gray plover.
kulpa n. fault, blame.
kulpitu n.(rel.) pulpit.
kultur adj. cultural.
kultura n. culture, education, acquired knowledge.
kulturadun adj. cultured, sophisticated, educated.
kulturagabetasun n. lack of culture, lack of education.
kulturagabetu v.i. to lose one's culture, to lose one's education. v.t. to cause someone to lose his culture.
kulturagabezia n. lack of culture or education.
kulturapen n. act of acquiring or spreading culture or education.
kulturgabe adj. illiterate, uneducated.
kulturgabetasun n. illiteracy, lack of education.
kulturgiro n. cultural atmosphere.
kulturtzale adj. fond of culture.
kulubiz n. bob, float, cork used for fishing. n. cork lifesaver.
kulunka n. swing; teeter-totter.
kulunkada n. balancing, bobbing, teetering, rocking, swinging.
kulunkadura n. rocking, bobbing, balancing, swinging.
kulunkaketa n. rocking, swinging, swaying, bobbing.
kulunkarazi v.t. to rock, to sway, to swing, to teeter-totter.
kulunkari n. rocker, swinger, swayer (person).
kulunkatsu adj. rocking, swinging, or swaying a lot.
kulunkatu v.t. to rock, to sway, to swing. v.i. to rock, to bob.
kulunkatzaile n. rocker, swinger (person).
kuluska n. short nap, nodding off. n. rocking.
kuluskada n. rocking.
kuluskatu v.i. to nod off, to drop off, to fall asleep.
kuma n. cradle.
-kume (gram.) Suffix signifying offspring of an animal. **Arkume.**

Lamb.

-kunde *(gram.)* Suffix signifying an act or action. **Igokunde.** Ascent. *(gram.)* Suffix meaning faculty, capacity, personal power. **Nahikunde.** Will. *(gram.)* Suffix meaning state of being or social class. **Apezkunde.** Priesthood.

kunplitu *v.t.* to carry out, to perform, to complete. *v.t.* to fulfill, to keep (a promise, etc.).

-kuntza *(gram.)* Verbal suffix signifying an abstract act or action.

kuntzurrun *n. (anat.)* kidney.

kupoi *n.* coupon.

kuraia *n.* courage.

kurbi *n.* large carpenter's plane.

kurkuildu *v.i.* to become numb with cold.

kurkuilo *n.(zool.)* shell (especially seashell).

kurlinka *n.(zool.)* gray plover.

kurloi *n.(zool.)* sparrow.

kurrika *n.* large pinchers or tongs.

kurrilo *n.(zool.)* crane.

kurrinka *n.* creaking, squeaking. *n.* groaning, squealing.

kurrinkada *n.* grunt (of a pig), squeal.

kurrinka egin *v.t.* to creak, to squeak. *v.t.* to squeal, to groan.

kurrinkari *adj.* creaking, squealing, groaning.

kurrinkatsu *adj.* squealing, squeaking, creaking, groaning.

kurrinkatu *v.t.* to grunt, to groan, to squeal.

kurruka *adv.* cooing.

kurrusku *n.* heel of a loaf of bread, end crust.

kurubilkatu *v.i.* to curl (up), to twist, to roll (up), to spiral.

kurubilketa *n.* curling up (around), twisting, spiraling.

kusku *n.* eggshell. *n.(zool.)* nymph, pupa, immature, life stage of insects. *n.(bot.)* shell (of peas), outer covering of vegetables.

kuso *n.* scarecrow.

kutsadura *n.* pollution, contamination.

kutsaezin *adj.* unpollutable, incapable of being contaminated.

kutsagabe(ko) *adj.* uncontaminated, unpolluted.

kutsagaitz *adj.* difficult to contaminate, difficult to pollute.

kutsagaiztasun *n.* immunity (to disease or to pollution).

kutsagarri *adj.* contagious, contaminant, contaminating.

kutsaketa *n.* contamination, pollution. *n.(fig.)* violation, profanity, profanation.

kutsakoi *adj.* easily stained, soiled, contaminable.

kutsakor *adj.* contaminating, contagious.

kutsakortasun *n.* contagiousness.

kutsapen *n.* contagion, contamination, infection.

kutsarazi *v.t.* to contaminate, to make contagious.

kutsarazle *adj.* polluting, contaminating.

kutsatu *v.i./v.t.* to be polluted, to be contaminated; to pollute, to contaminate.

kutsatzaile *adj.* polluting, contaminating.

kutsu *n.* contagion, contamination. *n.* aftertaste, flavor. *n.* stain, spot.

kutsudun *adj.* contaminated. *adj.* stained, spotted.

kutsugabe *adj.* unpolluted, uncontaminated. *adj.* immaculate, spotless.

kutsugabetu *v.t.* to disinfect.

kutsugalgarri *adj.* antiseptic.

kutsugarri *adj.* contagious.

kutsukor *adj.* contagious, pestilent.

kuttun *adj.* beloved, favorite, dear.

kuttundu *v.i.* to be intimate, to become close to someone.

kuttunen *adj.(superl.)* beloved, dearest, favorite.

kuttunki *adv.* intimately.

kuttuntasun *n.* intimacy, familiarity. *n.* prediliction, favoring.

kutun *adj.* cherished, beloved, dear, darling. *n.(eccl.)* scapulary. *n.* amulet. *n.* pincushion.

kutunkeria *n.* favoritism, spoiling, excessive or unfair partiality.

kutxa *n.* chest, trunk.

kutxagile *n.* chest maker, trunk maker.

kutxarapen *n.* act of boxing (something) up, putting (something) in a trunk.

kutxaratu *v.t.* to box (up), to put in a trunk.

kutxatila *n.* case, box, casket.

kutxatto *n.(dim.)* small box, case.

kutxatzar *n.(augm.)* large chest, large trunk.

kutxazain *n.* teller, cashier.

kutxontzi *n.* large box.

kuzkur *adj.* shrinking, shriveling, retiring, constricting. *n.* stalk of some vegetables and fruits (cabbage, etc.).

kuzkurdura *n.* shrinking, contracting, shriveling.

kuzkurkor *adj.* shrinking, shriveling, contracting, cowering.

kuzkurtu *v.i.* to shrink, to shrivel, to cower, to curl up.

L

l *n.* letter of the Basque alphabet.

-la *(gram.)* Modal suffix used to form adverbs. **Bestela.** Otherwise, in another way. *(gram.)* Verbal suffix appended to the verb of a subordinate clause. Used as the conjunction *that.* **Aita etorri dela**

esan diot. I have told him that father has come.
labaho n. mouth of the oven, opening to the oven.
labain adj. slippery, slick, sliding. adj. smooth, soft, even.
labaina n. razor, switchblade, shaver. n. knife.
labainada n. gash, slash (with a razor or switchblade).
labainbera adj. slick, slippery.
labainbide n. slide, slippery place, slippery road.
labaindu v.i. to slip, to slide. v.t. to polish, to burnish; to smooth out.
labaindura n. polish, shine; smoothness. n. lubrication.
labain egin v.t. to slip, to slide.
labaingai n. lubricant, lubricating material.
labaingarri adj. polishable, shinable. adj. lubricating. adj. slippery.
labaingarritasun n. slipperiness.
labainkeria n. false flattery.
labainketa n. sliding, slipping, skidding. n. lubrication.
labainki adv. smoothly, evenly, slickly.
labainkor adj. slippery, slick, sliding. adj. lubricating.
labainkortasun n. slipperiness, slickness.
labaintasun n. smoothness, slipperiness, lubricity. n. state of being polished, shininess.
labaintoki n. slippery place.
labaintzaile adj. slippery, slick.
labaintzeko adj. lubricating.
labaki n. field plowed and ready for planting.
labakitu v.t. to clear and break up land.
labalde n. place where the oven is.
labaldi n. baking time; batch (of bread, cookies, etc.) baked at the same time.
laban adj. slippery, slick.
labar n. edge of the precipice.
labari n. baker. n. one who stokes the oven or furnace.
labate n. oven door.
labazomorro n.(zool.) cockroach.
labe n. oven.
labehaga n. baker's peel.
labehauspo n. bellows.
labekada n. baking time, ovenful, batch (of bread, bricks, etc., baked at the same time).
labekari n. baker, one who operates an oven.
labeleiho n. vent of a furnace or oven.
laberatu v.t. to put in the oven.
labetxe n. oven house.
labetxo n.(dim.) small furnace; kitchen oven.
labexka n.(dim.) small oven, small furnace, small portable stove.
laboragaitz adj. difficult to cultivate.
laboragarri adj. arable, cultivatable.

laborantza n. agriculture, farming.
laborari n. farmer, peasant.
laborarigo n. agriculture.
laboraritza n. agriculture.
laborategi n. laboratory.
labore n. harvest, grain harvest.
labur adj. short, brief.
laburbide n. shortcut.
laburdura n. abbreviation, summary.
labur egin v.t. to shorten, to summarize, to abridge, to condense.
laburgarri adj. capable of being shortened, abbreviated or reduced; reducible; restricting.
laburkeria n. timidity, shyness; irresolution. n.(fig.) vile or mean act, despicable act.
laburketa n. abbreviation, shortening, reduction; diminution, decrease.
laburki adv. briefly, shortly, in short.
laburkor adj. restrictive, abbreviating.
laburlari n. summarizer, person who makes a synopsis.
laburpen n. summary, abbreviation, condensation, reduction, synopsis.
laburrarazi v.t. to shorten.
laburrera n. brevity, shortness, conciseness. n. summary, compendium.
laburritz n. abbreviation by initials, e.g. USA.
laburtasun n. brevity, shortness, conciseness.
laburtezin(ezko) adj. irreducible, unshortenable.
laburtu v.t. to shorten, to abbreviate, to summarize. v.i. to shrink, to shrivel, to contract. v.t.(gram.) to syncopate, to omit a sound or letter from the interior of a word.
laburtza n. reduction, abbreviation, summary, condensation.
laburtzaile n./adj. abbreviator; abbreviating.
laburtzapen n. contraction, abbreviation, reduction.
laga v.t. to abandon, to leave, to desert. v.t. to permit, to allow, to tolerate, to authorize. v.t. to resign, to give up, to relinquish.
lagaezin adj. not refusable, not abandonable.
lagagarri adj. permissible, authorized.
lagapen n. concession, permission, authorization. n.(econ.) transfer (of funds).
lagi n. law.
lagun n. friend. n. colleague, comrade, companion, member. n. person, individual, people. n. inhabitant, resident. n. pair, match, mate.
-lagun Used in compound words. Signifies colleague, companion. **Ikaslagun.** Schoolmate.
lagunabar n. crowd, multitude, group.
lagunarte n. company of friends, group of friends, friends.

lagunarteko *adj.* friendly, sociable, affable. *n.* member, associate.
lagunartekor *adj.* sociable, friendly, amiable, affable.
lagunartetasun *n.* friendship, companionship, sociability.
lagunartetu *v.i.* to join a club, to form a group, to associate with.
lagunbatz *n.* company, society, association, club.
lagunbera *adj.* easygoing, sociable, tractable, friendly, amiable.
lagundu *v.t.* to accompany, to sympathize. Can be used with direct or indirect objects.
lagun egin *v.t.* to accompany; to help.
lagungabe *adj.* alone, solitary.
lagungarri *n.* help, aid, assistance, relief. *adj.* helpful, propitious.
lagungisa *adv.* amiably, in a friendly way.
lagungo *n.* accompaniment, companionship; entourage.
lagunkari *adj.* sociable, amiable, friendly.
lagunketa *n.* help, aid, assistance. *n.* crowd, multitude.
lagunkide *n.* companion, associate, collaborator, colleague.
lagunkidetasun *n.* quality of being a member of a society.
lagunkidetza *n.* companionship.
lagunkoi *adj.* sociable, friendly, amiable.
lagunkoitasun *n.* sociability, amiableness, friendliness.
lagunkor *adj.* sociable, friendly, amiable, affable.
lagunorde *n.* stand-in, temporary helper.
laguntalde *n.* group of friends; crowd, group of people.
laguntari *adj.* helpful, obliging.
laguntasun *n.* help, aid, assistance, protection. *n.* company, companionship. *n.* friendship.
lagunteria *n.* group of friends.
laguntsa *n.* female friend.
laguntsu *adj.* having many friends.
laguntxo *n.(dim.)* little friend, buddy, pal.
laguntza *n.* help, aid, assistance, protection.
laguntzabide *n.* means of aid, help, assistance.
laguntzagabe *adj.* defenseless, helpless, unprotected.
laguntzaile *n.* partner, companion. *n.* helper, assistant. *adj.* auxiliary, helping, helpful.
laguntzale *adj.* sociable, communicative, helpful, friendly.
laguntzaletasun *n.* sociability, amiableness, affability.
lagunurko *n.* fellowman, neighbor.
lahar *n.(bot.)* bramble.
lahardi *n.* uncultivated brushland, place of brambles.
laharraga *n.* uncultivated brushland, place of brambles.
laharreta *n.* brambly place.
lahartsu *adj.* brambly, full of brambles.
lahartu *v.i.* to be covered with brambles.
lai *n.(bot.)* vine shoot.
laia *n.* two-handed double-pointed spade used for turning over earth.
laiaberri *n.* newly plowed field.
laiagarri *adj.* plowable, workable (with a *laia*).
laiaketa *n.* act of spading, act of turning over earth.
laiaketan *adv.* spading, turning over with a spade.
laiari *n.* spader, one who spades.
laiatu *v.t.* to spade; to plow (with a *laia*).
laido *n.* affront, insult, ignominy, infamy.
laidogarri *adj.* insulting, infamous, ignominious, deprecatory, dishonorable, offensive.
laidogarrikeria *n.* dishonor, disgrace, affront, ignominy, infamy.
laidogarriki *adv.* dishonorably, ignominiously, infamously.
laidogarriro *adv.* dishonorably, infamously, insultingly, ignominiously.
laidogarritasun *n.* infamy, ignominy, disgrace.
laidotsu *adj.* dishonorable, infamous, defamatory, insulting, injurious, offensive.
laidozko *adj.* insulting, offensive, vile.
laidoztatu *v.t.* to insult, to defame, to offend.
laidoztatzaile *n.* defamer, insulter, deprecator. *adj.* defamatory, insulting, deprecatory.
laiko *adj.* lay, laic, secular.
laikotasun *n.* secularity, the quality of laicism.
laina- Used in compound words. Derived from *laino*, fog.
lainaize *n.* cold and foggy wind.
laino *n.* fog, mist. *adj.* amiable, affable.
lainoaldi *n.* foggy season.
lainodura *n.* damage to crops from mist.
lainokeria *n.* simpleness, ingenuousness, naivety.
lainoki *adv.* simply; affably. *adv.* vaguely, mysteriously.
lainotasun *n.* fogginess. *n.(fig.)* ambiguity, vagueness. *n.* affability.
lainotsu *adj.* foggy. *adj.(fig.)* ambiguous, vague.
lainotu *v.t./v.i.* to become cloudy, to cloud up, to get foggy; to cloud up, to fog up (windows, glasses). *v.t.* to get dark. *v.i.(fig.)* to be confused. *v.i.* to become affable, to become honest, open, frank.
lainoztatu *v.i.* to fog up, to cloud up

(windows, glasses).

laiotz n. shady place, patch of shade.

laka n. price of milling, cost of milling. n. unit of measure for grain. n.(bot.) bramble. Used as a last name.

lakar n. knot of a tree. adj. rough, rugged.

lakari n. old unit of measure for grain.

lakartasun n. roughness, ruggedness.

lakartsu adj. rough.

lakasta n.(zool.) cricket.

lakatu v.t. price paid for having grain milled into flour. v.t. to collect (money), to get money.

lakatz n. burr (of chestnuts, etc.). n. section, slice (of an orange); small bunch of grapes, part of a bunch of grapes. adj. rough, tough, coarse.

laket n. pleasure. adj. pleasant, agreeable, appetizing.

laketasun n. satisfaction, complacency.

laketetsi v.t. to cause pleasure, to please.

laketgarri adj. delightful, pleasant. n. pleasant place, pleasant thing.

laketgura adj. wanting to have fun.

laket izan v.i. to please, to like, to be pleased.

laketkuntza n. pleasure, enjoyment.

laketu v.i. to be pleased, to be delighted, to be content. v.i. to adjust, to become accustomed (to a place).

lakio n. trap, cord or string used for trapping animals. n.(fig.) trick, trap, ruse.

lakiolari n. trapper, one who sets traps.

lakiotu v.t. to trap, to entrap, to catch with a cord.

lako n. wine press.

-lako (gram.) Causal suffix meaning because. (gram.) Adjectival suffix denoting quality, like, how, what kind. Variation of bezalako.

-lakoan (gram.) Verbal suffix expressing a certain amount of belief that something has happened or will happen. Variation of lako. **Irakaslea etorri delakoan nago.** I believe that the teacher has come.

lakotegi n. place where the wine press is located.

lakotu v.t. to press (grapes, apples, etc.).

laku n. lake.

lakunza n. bramble.

lamia n. elf, gnome, brownie, troll; mythological character in Basque folklore which incorporates the characteristics of these creatures.

lamikari adj. fond of sweets, having a sweet tooth.

lamikatu v.t. to lick.

lamizkatu v.t. to take a lick, to taste.

lamiztu v.t. to take a lick, to lick.

lamizulo n. witches' cave, gnome's cave, troll's cave, etc. Cave of the lamia.

lan n. work, labor, activity, occupation, job.

lanabes n. tool, instrument for work.

lan(a) eman v.t. to give work to, to hire.

lanagiri n. job report.

lanaldi n. occupation. n. workday.

lanarte n. break, rest from work.

lanbas n. kind of mop or swab made with a stick and pieces of cloth used for removing water from boat decks.

lanbasaldi n. swabbing or mopping the decks.

lanbasketa n. swabbing, mopping.

lanberritu v.t. to plow land, to till land.

lanbide n. job, work, occupation, profession.

lanbro n. dense fog. n.(med.) cataract.

lanbroaldi n. season of dense fog.

lanbrodun adj. very foggy.

lanbrodura n. light mist.

lanbrotasun n. fogginess, mistiness.

lanbrotsu adj. foggy, misty.

lanbrotu v.t. to be foggy, to become foggy. v.i. to cloud the vision.

landa n. field, prairie, plain, terrain.

landagarri adj. transplantable, plantable.

landaketa n. planting.

landako adj. rural, country, pastoral.

landare n. plant.

landaretegi n. greenery, place of plants.

landaretxo n.(dim.) small plant.

landaretza n. vegetation, flora, plant kingdom.

landarezain n. plant keeper, gardener, nurseryman.

landareztatu v.t. to plant.

landatu v.t. to plant, to transplant.

landatzaile n. planter.

landazain n. groundskeeper.

lander adj. miserable, despicable. adj. poor, indigent, destitute. adj. untidy, slovenly.

landerki adv. miserably, vilely, despicably, villainously. n. mop, rag mop, dish rag.

landerreria n. indigence, destitution.

landertasun n. state of indigence, misery.

landertu v.i. to degrade oneself, to become villainous. v.i. to become poor, to be destitute.

landeski n. mop, rag mop, dish rag.

landetxe n. country house, farmhouse.

landu v.t. to cultivate, to work the fields. v.t. to work (at a craft), to work on (a problem). v.t. to elaborate (on). adj. cultivated, elaborate, crafted, worked.

landuberri adj. newly plowed, tilled.

landugabe adj. uncultivated, untilled.

landugarri adj. tillable, cultivatable,

arable.
landuketa n. tilling, cultivating.
lan egin v.t. to work.
lanegun n. work day, weekday.
laneko adj. pertaining to work or labor.
laneratu v.i. to go to work.
langa n. fence, barrier. n. crossbar.
langabe adj. unemployed, out of work.
langabealdi n. period of being unemployed, unemployment.
langabetu v.i. to be out of work.
langabezia n. unemployment, idleness.
langai n. material to be worked (wood, marble, etc.).
langailu n. tool; instrument of work.
langar n. dense fog, condensation from dense fog; mist; drizzle.
langarri adj. arable, cultivable, cultivatable, tillable.
langela n. office, workroom.
langeldiketa n. break (from work), work stoppage.
langeraldi n. work stoppage.
langile n. worker, laborer.
langile-alderdi n.(pol.) labor party.
langilego n. working class, proletariat.
langileria n. proletariat, working class.
langiletalde n. group of workers.
langiletu v.i. to become hard-working, to become a hard worker. v.i. to become a worker, to become a laborer.
langilezain n. foreman, overseer, supervisor.
langintza n. job, work, occupation.
langose n. industriousness, eagerness to work. adj. industrious, eager to work.
lanjeros adj. dangerous, risky, hazardous.
lanketa n. work, act of working.
lankide n. fellow worker, work mate.
lankidego n. cooperation, collaboration, work done collectively. n. co-op, cooperative.
lankidetasun n. cooperation, collaboration.
lankidetu v.i. to collaborate, to cooperate.
lankidetza n. cooperation, collaboration.
lankor adj. industrious, diligent, hard-working.
lankortasun n. industriousness, diligence.
lanmaisu n. master builder, construction foreman.
lanmaisutza n. job of a master builder.
lanordu n. time to go to work. n. working hour(s).
lanpara n. lamp.
lanparaburu n.(elec.) socket, bulb socket.
lanparagin n. lamp maker.
lanparagintza n. lamp making.
lanperna n.(zool.) barnacle.

lanpetasun n. tiredness, fatigue, state of being tired.
lanpetu v.i. to be busy, to be overworked.
lanpostu n. occupation, job, work, position, post, employment.
lanpustu v.t./v.i. to blunt, to dull.
lanputs adj. blunt, dull. adj. rude, vulgar.
lansari n. daily wage, salary, pay; compensation.
lansaritu v.t. to compensate (for work), to pay (wages or salary).
lantegi n. factory; workshop (with chimneys, etc.).
lantegiburu n. foreman.
lantegizain n. watchman, guard of a factory.
lantoki n. shop, workshop; factory. n. office, place of work.
lantresna n. tool, instrument for work.
lantsu adj. occupied, busy; overworked.
lantza n. lance.
lantzada n. blow with a lance.
lantzakada n. blow with a lance.
lantzakatu v.t. to wound with a lance, to lance.
lantzari n. lancer, pikeman.
lantzean behin adv. sometimes, every so often, every now and then, from time to time.
lantzoi n.(zool.) kind of fish, larger than a sardine, blue and white with a pointed mouth.
lantzurda n. frost, hoarfrost. n. mist, fine rain.
lanuzte n. strike; quitting work.
lanzale adj. industrious, diligent, hard-working, fond of work.
lanzaletasun n. industriousness.
lapa n.(zool.) limpet.
lapabelar n.(bot.) burdock.
lapastu v.i. to turn (milk), to sour, to curdle.
lapats n. curd.
lapazorri n.(zool.) tick, chigger.
lapiko n. pot. adj.(colloq.) stupid, foolish.
lapikogin n. pot maker, potter.
lapikoko n. stew, cooked pot of meat and/or vegetables.
lapikotxo n.(dim.) small pot.
lapitz n. pencil. n.(min.) slate.
laprasketa n. slip, slide, sliding, slipping.
laprast n. slip, slide, skid.
laprastada n. slipping, sliding.
laprast egin v.t. to slip, to slide, to skid.
lapur adj./n. thief, robber.
Lapurdi n.(geog.) Labourd, one of the northern Basque provinces. **Lapurtar.** Labourdin, native of Labourd. **Lapurtera.** Labourdin, Labourd dialect.
lapurkeria n. vandalism, robbery, theft.

lapurketa n. robbery, theft, pillage.
lapurketari n. one who seeks out thieves, bounty-hunter.
lapurleize n. hide-out of thieves.
lapurreria n. thievishness, rapaciousness; robbery, thievery.
lapurreta n. robbery, theft, thievery.
lapurretan egin v.t. to steal, to rob.
lapurtalde n. band of thieves.
lapurteria n. band of thieves.
lapurtu v.t. to rob, to steal; to sack, to pillage. v.i. to become a thief.
lapurtxo n.(dim.) pickpocket, petty thief.
lapurzulo n. cave where thieves hide out.
larako n.(anat.) clavicle. n. peg, dowel pin.
laranja n.(bot.) orange.
laranjadi n. orange grove.
laranjedari n. orange juice.
laranjondo n.(bot.) orange tree.
laranjur n. orange juice.
laratz n. pothanger, pothook (in a fireplace).
larazkako n. pothook, pothanger.
larbalio v.t. to cost too much. n. appreciation, increased value.
larberotu v.i./v.t. to overheat.
larbete v.t./v.i. to overfill.
larda n. rustic sled or sleigh.
lardabide n. path for a rustic sled.
lardai n. perch, main shaft connecting front and rear axles of a cart.
lardakatu v.t. to squeeze, to press, to crush. v.t. to complicate, to entangle, to confound.
lardaska n. disorder, confusion, entanglement.
lardaskatsu adj. disordered, confused, tangled.
lardaskatu v.t. to disorder, to confuse, to complicate, to mix.
lardaskatzaile adj. shoddy, slipshod.
lardaskeria n. shoddiness, shoddy work.
lardasketa n. smearing, daubing. n. confusion, embroglio, mess.
lardaskontzi adj. sloppy, bungling, careless (worker or person).
lardatu v.t. to grease, to anoint.
larde adj. fearful, pusillanimous.
larde izan v.i. to be afraid, to be timid, to be apprehensive, to fear.
larderia n. intimidation, excessive severity. n. stiffness, rigor, inflexibility.
larderiadun adj. despotic, severe, authoritarian.
larderialdi n. imposition, authoritarian act, despotism.
larderiatsu adj. authoritarian, dictatorial, despotic. adj. severe, austere, rigid.
larderiatsuki adv. menacingly, threateningly, with intimidation.
larderiatu v.t. to threaten, to menace.

v.t. to order imperiously, to dictate (to), to dominate.
larderiatzaile adj. rebuking, scolding, reprimanding.
-lari (gram.) Suffix which indicates fond of, fan, enthusiast; occupation, job. **Abeslari.** Singer.
-larik (gram.) Suffix used with conjugated verbs to form gerunds.
laritz n.(bot.) larch tree.
larjan v.t. to overeat, to gorge on food.
larnekatu v.i. to become overly tired, to become exhausted.
larneke n. exhaustion, state of being overly tired.
larogei adj./n. eighty. Contr. of lau + ogei.
larogeigarren adj. eightieth; octogenarian.
larogeitamar adj./n. ninety.
larogeitamargarren adj. ninetieth.
larr- (gram.) Prefix signifying wild, uncultivated, undomesticated.
larrabehi n.(zool.) wild cow.
larrabere n. wild cattle.
larrain n. threshing floor, threshing stone.
larraindu v.t. to extend the harvest to allow grain to dry; to lay out a garden patch.
larraineratu v.t. to extend the harvest to allow grain to dry.
larraintxo n.(dim.) small threshing floor, threshing stone.
larraki n. fallow land, barren land.
larraldaketa n. transhumance, nomadism.
larraldatu v.t. to migrate seasonally in search of pasture.
larraldatzaile adj. transhumant, nomadic.
larralde n. next to the pasture, beside the pasture.
larrapote n.(zool.) grasshopper.
larratu v.t./v.i. to graze, to pasture, to put out to graze.
larratz n. uncultivated land.
larre n. pastureland, meadowland, prairie.
larregi adv. too much, to many, excessively.
larregi izan v.i. to exceed, to be left over, to be too much.
larregikeria n. excess, abuse.
larregizko adj. excessive.
larreko adj. rustic, country, rural.
larreratu v.t. to pasture, to take out to pasture, to graze. v.i. to graze, to go out to pasture.
larresari n. fee paid to use pasture, grazing fee; toll for moving cattle through a pasture.
larri adv./adj. worriedly, anxiously, nervously, in a state of anxiety; worried, anxious. adj. important, critical, urgent, serious; sick. n.

anxiety. adj. big, large, voluminous. n. critical moment, urgency, crisis.

-larri Used in compound words. Desirous of, wanting to.

larrialdi n. dizziness, nausea; anxiety, worry, embarrassment. n. critical moment.

larridura n. anxiety, restlessness, worry, embarrassment.

larri egon v.i. to be indisposed, to be anxious, to be upset, to be preoccupied.

larrigabe adj. unworried, free from anxiety.

larrigabetu v.i. to not worry.

larrigarri adj. distressing, worrisome, anguishing, upsetting.

larri ibili v.i. to be nervous, to be worried.

larri izan v.i. to be afraid, to be nervous, to be worried.

larriki adv. uneasily, anxiously. adv. severely.

larrikor n. perturbing, disturbing, disquieting.

larriordu n. anxious moment, critical point.

larritasun n. annoyance, vexation, irritation, worry, anxiety. n. indisposition, nausea.

larritsu adj. full of anguish, distressed; anguishing, distressing, worrisome.

larritu v.i./v.t. to be nauseated, to nauseate. v.t. to bother, to disturb, to distress. v.i. to worry, to be worried.

larriune n. emergency, critical moment.

larru n. leather, hide, skin, pelt.

larruapaindegi n. tannery.

larruapaindu v.t. to tan hides, to tan leather.

larruapainketa n. tanning leather, tanning hides.

larruapaintzaile n. tanner, leather tanner.

larruarte n.(anat.) dermis, inner layer of the skin.

larruarteko adj. intercutaneous, subcutaneous.

larruazpiko adj. subcutaneous, intercutaneous.

larrubarneko adj. intracutaneous, intercutaneous.

larrubarru n. inner layer of skin.

larrudenda n. leather shop.

larrudun adj. covered with leather.

larrudura n. peeling off skin, skinning.

larrueri n.(med.) pellagra, skin disease.

larruerizain n. dermatologist.

larrugain n. complexion, surface of the skin.

larrugin n. tanner, leather worker, leather maker; furrier.

larrugintza n. manufacture of leather; leather tanning craft.

larrugorri adj. naked, nude; skinned.

larrugorrian adv. nakedly, naked, in the nude.

larrugorrikeria n. nudity, nudism, nakedness (pejorative).

larrugorritasun n. nudity, nudism, nakedness. n. (fig.) extreme misery.

larrugorritu v.t. to undress, to strip. v.i.(fig.) to be stripped of one's goods.

larru jo v.t.(colloq.) to have sex; to fornicate.

larrujole n. one who has sex; fornicator.

larrukentzaile n. skinner. n.(fig.) skinner, one who charges high prices.

larruketa n. skinning, flaying, fleecing. n.(fig.) stripping, robbing, plundering, sacking. n. group or quantity of hides; dealing in hides. n. trapping (animals for their hides); transporting hides.

larruketari n. dealer in hides, dealer in pelts, fur trader.

larruki n. piece of leather.

larrulantzaile n. furrier, dealer in hides, tanner.

larrumin n.(med.) skin neuralgia.

larrumintz n.(anat.) epidermis, surface layer of skin.

larruondegi n. leather tanning shop or factory.

larruondu v.t. to tan hides, to tan leather.

larruonketa n. tanning hides, dressing hides.

larruontzaile n. furrier, dealer in hides, leather tanner.

larrupeko adj. intercutaneous, subcutaneous.

larrusaltzaile n. dealer in hides, seller of hides or leather.

larrusendagile n.(med.) dermatologist.

larrutegi n. fur trade or business, leather shop.

larruteria n. group of hides or skins.

larruts adj. nude, naked.

larrutsik adv. nude, naked, nakedly.

larrutu v.t. to skin, to flay, to fleece. v.t.(fig.) to ruin, to despoil, to pillage, to sack, to plunder, to fleece (monetarily). v.t.(fig.) to discredit, to defame, to slander, to speak against (someone).

larrutxo n.(dim.) small hide or skin.

larrutza n. group of skins, group of hides.

llarrutzaile n. skinner, tanner of hides. n.(fig.) usurer, profiteer.

larruzko adj. leather.

larruztatu v.t. to cover with leather, to bind with leather (books).

lartasun n. excessiveness, quality of being or doing too much.

laru adj. pale yellow

larumin n.(med.) jaundice.

larunbat n. Saturday.

lasai adj./adv. relaxed, calm, easygoing; comfortable, loose-fitting; comfortably.

lasaialdi n. rest period, repose. n. loosening.

lasaibide n. tranquility, relaxation.

lasaidura n. tranquility, relaxation, rest, alleviation, calm.

lasaiegi adj./adv. too relaxed, lax.

lasai egon v.i. to be calm, to be relaxed.

lasaiera n. looseness.

lasaigarri adj. sedating, sedative, tranquilizing, relaxing, calming. n. sedative. adj. tranquilizable, calmable.

lasaikeria n. unruliness, abandon, wantonness.

lasaiki adv. tranquilly, easily, relaxedly. adv. wantonly, licentiously.

lasaipen n. tranquility, relaxation.

lasaitasun n. tranquility, rest, relaxation, alleviation, relief, calm.

lasaitu v.i. to relax, to calm down, to take it easy. v.t./v.i. to loosen, to loosen up.

lasaitzaile adj. calming, relaxing, tranquilizing.

laser n./adj.(phys.) laser.

laso adj. satisfied, comfortable.

lasotasun n. relief, alleviation; satisfaction.

lasotu v.i. to unburden oneself, to let go, to make oneself comfortable, to take it easy.

lasta- Used in compound words. Derived from lasto, straw.

lastai n. straw mat, rush matting.

lastaki n. corn stalk.

lastamarraga n. straw mattress.

lastameta n. pile of straw.

lastardatz n. stabilizing pole used in the stacking of straw.

lastargi n. straw torch.

lastategi n. hayloft, straw loft.

lastatsu adj. full of straw, covered with straw. adj. full of stalks, covered with stalks.

lastatu v.t. to cover with straw, to fill with straw. v.t. to remove the last grains from the straw.

lastatxo n.(dim.) small stalk of straw.

lastatza n. pile of straw.

laster adv. soon. adv. quickly, fast. adj. active, industrious, quick, fast, hasty.

lasterbide n. shortcut.

lasterdura n. haste, hastiness, hurry.

laster egin v.t. to do (something) quickly. v.t. to hurry, to rush, to run.

lasterka adv. hurriedly, in a rush. n. race, run.

lasterka egin v.t. to run, to race.

lasterkaldi n. race, period of running, galloping.

lasterkari n. racer, runner. adj. quick, fast, agile.

lasterkatu v.t./v.i. to hurry, to rush, to run, to race.

lasterketa n. race, run.

lasterraldi n. race.

lasterrari n. runner, racer.

lasterreri n. diarrhea, disentery.

lastertasun n. quickness, promptness, speed.

lastertu v.i. to rush, to hurry, to run.

lasto n.(bot.) straw.

lastoztatu v.t. to cover with straw, to fill with straw, to weave with straw (chairs, etc.).

lastoztu v.t. to fill with straw, to stuff with straw, to cover with straw.

lasun n. mullet, small black and white freshwater fish.

lata n. can.

latagailu n. can opener.

latin n. Latin.

latindar adj. Latin, of Latin origin.

latindu v.t./v.i. to Latinize, to Romanize.

latinera n. Latin language.

latineratu v.t. to translate into Latin.

latinetiko adj. Romance.

latinez adv. in Latin.

latinezko adj. Latin, written in Latin.

latinitzuli n. translation into Latin.

latinkeria n. dog Latin, bad Latin.

latinmordoilo n. dog Latin, bad Latin.

latoi n. brass.

latoigile n. brass worker, one who works with or in brass.

latoigintza n. brass working, brass manufacture, making (something) in brass.

latontzi n. can, tin can.

latsa n. streamlet, riverlet.

latsari n. laundress, laundrywoman, washerwoman.

latsarri n. washing stone, scrubbing stone.

latsatu v.t. to do laundry in the river.

latsazur n. scrubbing board, washboard.

latz adj. rough, crude. adj.(fig.) bad, horrible, unpleasant.

lau adj./n. four. adj. smooth, flat.

laualdeko adj. four-sided, quadrilateral.

laubide n. crossroads, crossing of four roads.

lauburu n. Basque cross or swastika.

lauburuko adj. four-headed, quadricipital.

laudabide n. reason for praise.

laudagarri adj. praiseworthy, laudable, applaudable, commendable.

laudagarriki adv. laudably, honorably.

laudamen n. agreement, consent.

laudatu v.t. to praise, to laud, to glorify, to honor.

laudatzaile n./adj. praiser; praising.

laudorio n. praise, exaltation, commendation, eulogy.

laudoriotsu adj. praising, laudatory. adj. flattering, adulating.

laudoriotu v.t. to praise, to laud. v.t. to

flatter, to adulate, to compliment.
laudorioztatu *v.t.* to praise, to exalt, to glorify, to honor. *v.t.* to flatter, to adulate.
laufraka *n.(bot.)* columbine.
laugarren *adj.* fourth.
laugarrenaro *n.(geol.)* quaternary age.
lauhankadun *adj.* quadruped(al), four-legged.
lauhankaka *adv.* on all fours, creeping, crawling, galloping.
lauhankaka ibili *v.i.* to crawl, to crawl on all fours, to creep.
lauhankako *adj.* four-legged, quadrupedal.
lauhilabete *n.* period of four months.
lauhilabeteko *adj.* four-month, four months.
lauhortz *n.* four-pronged rake.
lauhortzeko *n.* fork.
lauka *adv.* crawling, on all fours.
laukatu *v.t.* to distribute by fours, to distribute in fours. *v.i.* to crawl.
lauki *adj.* square, four-sided. *n.* frame. *adv.* flatly, smoothly.
laukidura *n.* squaring.
laukigailu *n.* T-square (carpenter's tool).
laukitasun *n.* squareness.
laukitu *v.t.* to square, to make (something) square. *v.t.* to frame, to put into a frame.
laukitxo *n.(dim.)* small frame.
laukizko *adj.* squared.
laukizuzen *n.(geom.)* rectangle.
lauko *adj.* made of four elements (song, choir, etc.). *n.* four (in cards).
laukoitz *adj.* quadruple, having four.
laukoiztu *v.i./v.t.* to quadruple.
laukoloreko *adj.* four-colored.
laukote *n.* quartet, group of four. *adj.* quadruple.
laukotu *v.t.* to square. *adj.* squared, square.
laumargoko *adj.* four-colored.
launa *adj.* four to each one.
launaka *adv.* four by four, in groups of four, by fours.
launakatu *v.t.* to arrange by fours, to put in groups of four.
launako *n.* original Basque dance. *adj.* having four parts or members.
lauoineko *adj.* quadruped(al), four-legged.
lauoinka *adv.* galloping; on all fours.
lauoinkada *n.* galloping.
lauoinkaldi *n.* galloping.
lauoinkari *n./adj.* galloper; galloping.
lauoinkatu *v.i.* to gallop.
lauorri *adj.(bot.)* quadrifoliate, four-leafed.
laurden *n./adj.* quarter, one-fourth.
laurdendu *v.t.* to divide into four, to quarter.
laurdenka *adv.* in fourths, by fours.
laurdenkagarri *adj.* divisible by four, capable of being divided into four

parts.
laurdenkatu *v.t.* to divide into four, to quarter. *v.t.* to divide into pieces.
laurehun *adj./n.* four hundred.
lauremin *n.(med.)* jaundice, icterus.
lauremindu *v.i.* to become jaundiced, to contract jaundice.
lauremindun *adj.* jaundiced, sick with jaundice.
lauretan *adv.* at four o'clock.
laurleko *n.(econ.)* peseta, Spanish currency.
lausengaldi *n.* praise, adulation, flattery.
lausengari *adj.* praising, adulating, flattering (person).
lausengarri *adj.* flattering, praising, adulating, cajoling.
lausengatu *v.t.* to praise, to laud. *v.t.* to adulate, to flatter.
lausengatzaile *adj.* flattering, praising, adulating (person).
lausengu *n.* flattery, cajolery, adulation.
lausenguka *adv.* in a flattering way.
lausengukeria *n.* excessive praise, excessive adulation, false flattery, cajolery.
lausenguketa *n.* quest for glory, search for flattery or praise.
lausengukoi *adj.* given to being praised.
lausengutsu *adj.* honored, praised, lauded, flattered.
lauskidura *n.* twisting, squeezing.
lauskigailu *n.* juicer, fruit squeezer.
lauskitu *v.t.* to squeeze, to press, to remove juice.
lauskitzaile *adj.* squeezing, crushing.
lauso *n.* cataract. *n.* spot. *n.* fog, mist. *n.* windy and snowy weather.
lausogarri *adj.* blinding, obfuscating.
lausotasun *n.* quality of being blinding.
lausotu *v.i.* to be blinded, to cloud over (eyes), to have clouded vision.
lautada *n.* plain; prairie.
lautariko *adj.* of four kinds.
lautasun *n.* simplicity, frankness, ingenuousness.
lautu *v.t.* to level, to smooth out.
lauza *n.* slab, large stone, flagstone.
lauzadura *n.* laying flagstones.
lauzangodun *adj.* quadruped(al), four-legged.
lauzangoko *adj.* quadruped(al), four-legged.
lauzari *n.* tiler, tile layer, paver.
lauzatu *v.t.* to smooth out, to level, to even out, to lay flagstones.
lauzatzaile *n.* tiler, tile layer, paver.
lauzkatu *v.i.* to climb, to mount, to scale, to clamber. *v.t.* to yoke (animals) together in fours, to harness (animals) together in fours.
lauzkitu *v.t.* to cut into pieces, to ruin, to wreck.
lauzpabost *adj./n.* four or five.

lazdura n. crudeness, roughness. n. slight fear.

lazeria n. lack, scarcity, paucity, penury.

lazeriatu v.t. to afflict, to make (someone) suffer (need or poverty, etc.).

lazgarri adj. terrible, horrible.

lazgarrikeria n. terrible action, horrible act, atrocity.

lazgarriki adv. horribly, terribly, atrociously.

lazgarritasun n. horribleness, terribleness, atrociousness.

lazgarritu v.i. to be horrible, to become terrible.

lazkeria n. roughness, brusqueness, harshness.

lazki adv. roughly, harshly.

lazo adj. loose, loose-fitting. adj. unkempt, negligent.

lazokeria n. laxness. n. negligence.

lazoki adv. loosely. adv. carelessly, laxly, negligently.

lazotasun n. looseness. n. negligence, abandon.

laztan n. kiss. adj. beloved, dear, darling, cherished. n. affection, caress, endearment. adj. tidy, neat.

laztanbera adj. caressing, tender, loving.

laztandu v.t. to kiss, to caress, to show affection (for someone).

laztangarri adj. kissable, lovable.

laztan egin v.t. to kiss, to caress.

laztanka adv. kissing, caressing.

laztankeria n. excessive affection, exaggerated affection.

laztanketa n. caressing, show of affection.

laztanki adv. lovingly, affectionately; caressingly. adv. neatly.

laztankor adj. loving, friendly, affectionate. adj. caressing, petting.

laztankortasun n. friendliness, affability.

laztantasun n. tenderness, lovingness. n. neatness, tidiness.

laztasun n. roughness, harshness, severity. n.(fig.) brusqueness, crudeness. n. hardship.

laztu v.i. to stand on end (hair). v.t. to raise one's hackles, to make one's hair stand up.

-le (gram.) Verbal suffix indicating the agent of an action. **Ekarle.** Carrier, transporter.

legamia n. yeast, leavening.

legamiatu v.t./v.i. to add yeast, to add leavening; to leaven.

legamibera adj. leavenable, capable of rising (bread).

legamidura n. fermentation with yeast, leavening, rising (bread).

legamiezin adj. unfermentable, incapable of being fermented, unleavenable.

legamigabe adj. unleavened (bread).

legamin n. yeast, leavening (baking powder, baking soda).

legar n. small stone, pebble, gravel. n. tax, toll.

legarbide n. gravel road.

legardi n. gravelly place, pebbled place.

legarketa n. gravel pile.

legarno n.(dim.) fine gravel.

legarri n. small rock, pebble, gravel.

legartegi n. gravel pit. n. toll booth, small house where tolls or taxes are paid.

legartsu n. gravelly place, pebbly place.

legartu v.t. to gravel, to fill with gravel, to cover with gravel.

legarztatu v.t. to gravel, to fill with gravel, to cover with gravel.

legatz n.(zool.) hake (fish).

legatzerdino n.(zool.) medium-sized hake.

legazki n. flesh of a hake (fish).

lege n. law, rule, regulation.

legealdeko adj. law-abiding.

legeaurkako adj. criminal, illegal, against the law.

legeaurre n. preamble to a law.

legebidezko adj. legitimate, lawful.

legebilduma n. code of laws.

legebilketa n. codification.

legebiltzar n. legislative assembly.

legegabe adj. lawless, libertine, undisciplined.

legegabekeria n. debauchery, libertinism.

legegabetu v.i. to be undisciplined, to be lawless, to be unruly.

legegabezia n. lack of discipline, lawlessness.

legegai n. bill, proposed law.

legegarri adj. subject to legislation.

legegile n. legislator, lawmaker.

legegin n. legislator, lawmaker.

legegintza n. legislation, lawmaking.

legegintzaldi n. session of the legislature, legislative session.

legegizon n. lawyer.

legehausketa n. legal transgression, breaking of the law, infraction of the law.

legehausle n. violator of the law, lawbreaker, infringer of the law.

legehauste n. infraction of the law, breaking of the law, legal transgression.

legejakintza n. Jurisprudence, Law.

legejakitun n. legal expert, legal consultant.

legekenketa n. abolition, revocation of a law, repeal.

legeketa n. legalization.

legekontrako adj. illegal.

legelari n. legislator, jurist.

legeliburu n. code book of laws, statute book.

legemale *n.* administrator of laws, lawgiver.
legen *n.(med.)* leprosy.
legenar *n.(med.)* leprosy.
legenardun *adj.* leprous.
legenarti *adj.* leprous.
legendun *adj.* leprous.
legendundegi *n.* hospital for lepers.
legentsu *adj.* leprous, covered with leprosy.
legenzauri *n.(med.)* leprous sore, leprous ulcer.
legepeko *adj.* subject to the law.
legeperatu *v.t.* to regulate, to rule.
legepetu *v.t.* to regulate, to rule.
legeria *n.* code of laws.
legesorta *n.* code of laws, body of laws.
legetasun *n.* legality.
legetiar *adj.* law abiding. *n.* one who is in favor of the law.
legetsai *n.* lawbreaker, outlaw.
legetsu *adj.* authoritarian.
legetxe *n.* legislature (place).
legetza *n.* jurisprudence, study of law.
legetzaile *n.* law giver.
legez *adv.* legally, lawfully. *conj.* as, in the way of, by way of, by means of.
legezahar *n.(pol.)* traditional Basque liberties revoked as a result of the Carlist wars in the 19th century.
legezaharreko *adj.* pertaining to the old Basque liberties.
legezaharzale *adj.* specializing in or defending the old Basque liberties.
legezale *adj.* legalistic, fond of law, sticking to the letter of the law.
legezkanpo *adv.* illegally, outside of the law.
legezkanpoko *adj.* illegal.
legezko *adj.* legal, judicial, lawful. *adj.* like, similar.
legezkotasun *n.* legitimacy.
legezkotu *v.t.* to legalize, to legitimate.
legeztapen *n.* legalization.
legeztasun *n.* legality.
legeztatu *v.t.* to legalize, to legitimize.
legeztu *v.t.* to legalize, to legitimize.
legio *n.(mil.)* legion.
legionari *n.(mil.)* legionnaire.
lehartu *v.t.* to stamp on, to tread on.
lehen *adj.* first, primary. *adv.* before. *n.* past.
lehenago *adv.* before, previously, formerly.
lehenagoko *adj.* previous, before, antecedent, preceding. *adj.* preferred.
lehenagotasun *n.* preference. *n.* preeminence.
lehenagotu *v.t.* to put before; to prefer, to give preference to.
lehenaldi *n.* beginning, debut. *n.* past, past time. *n.(gram.)* past tense.
lehenaro *n.(geol.)* primary age.
lehenaroko *adj.* ancient, antique. *adj.(geol.)* belonging to the primary age.
lehenarri *n.* foundation stone, cornerstone.
lehenbailehen *adv.* as soon as possible.
lehenbizi *adv.* first, at first, initially; previously.
lehenbizian *adv.* first, at first.
lehenbiziko *adj.* first, initial, primary.
lehenbizidun *n./adj.(biol.)* protozoan.
lehendabizi *adv.* first, at first, initially.
lehendabiziko *adj.* original, first, initial, primary.
lehendakari *n.* president.
lehendakariorde *n.* vice-president, vice-chairman.
lehendakariordetza *n.* vice-presidency.
lehendakarisa *n.* female president.
lehendakaritza *n.* presidency.
lehendanik *adv.* previously, from the beginning, originally.
lehendik *adv.* beforehand, before, already.
lehendu *v.i.* to precede, to come before; to anticipate.
leheneko *adj.* past, former, previous.
lehenengo *adj.* first, primary.
lehenengotasun *n.* priority, preference.
lehenengoz *adv.* primarily, at first.
leheneraketa *n.* rehabilitation, replacement.
leheneratu *v.t.* to restore, to renew, to renovate. *v.t.* to rehabilitate, to replace.
lehenespen *n.* priority, preference.
leheneuskara *n.* proto-Basque (language).
lehenezarle *n.* settler, founder, establisher.
lehengai *n.* raw material.
lehengizon *n.* primitive man, first man, prehistoric man.
lehengo *adj.* first, primary. *adv.* at first, primarily. *adj.* past, previous, former.
lehengoraketa *n.* restoration, renovation, renewal, remodeling.
lehengoratu *v.t.* to restore, to renovate, to renew, to remodel.
lehengotasun *n.* priority, preference, preeminence. *n.* previousness.
lehengusina *n.* female first cousin.
lehengusintipi *n.* female second cousin.
lehengusu *n.* male first cousin.
lehengusu-lehengusinak *n.(pl.)* male and female cousins.
lehengusutipi *n.* male second cousin.
lehengusutza *n.* cousinship.
lehenik *adv.* first, first of all.
lehen izan *v.i.* to be first, to precede, to pre-exist.
lehenizkuntza *n.* protolanguage, first language; native tongue.
lehenmartiri *n.* first martyr, protomartyr.

lehenseme *n.* first-born son.
lehensemego *n.* primogeniture.
lehensemetza *n.* primogeniture.
lehentasun *n.* priority, preference, preeminence. *n.* primogeniture.
lehentsu *adj.* early, almost the first.
lehenumedun *adj.* giving birth for the first time, primiparous.
leherdura *n.* explosion. *n.* exhaustion, fatigue, extreme weariness.
leher egin *v.t.* to explode, to blow up. *v.t.* to exhaust.
lehergai *n.* explosive, bomb, detonating device.
lehergailu *n.* explosive, bomb, detonating device.
lehergaitz *adj.* unexplodable, difficult to explode.
lehergarri *adj.* explodable, explosive. *adj.* exhausting, crushing.
lehergarritasun *n.* explosiveness.
leherketa *n.* explosion.
leherkin *n.* explosive, bomb.
leherkor *adj.* explosive, tending to explode.
leherpen *n.* explosion. *n.* exhaustion; ruin, disaster.
leherrarazi *v.t.* to make (something) explode, to blow up.
lehertu *v.t./v.i.* to explode, to blast, to blow up, to burst. *v.i.* to be exhausted, to get very tired, to break down, to be overcome.
lehertzaile *n.* bomber, exploder, one who blows things up.
lehertzapen *n.* explosion, eruption.
leher zorian *adv.* on the point of exploding, on the verge of erupting. *adv.* on the verge of exhaustion.
lehia *n.* laboriousness, diligence.
lehiadun *adj.* insistent, intent, diligent.
lehiadura *n.* persistence, insistence.
lehiagarri *adj.* competitive, rivalrous. *adj.* insistent, persistent, diligent.
lehiaka *adv.* persistently, insistently; competitively.
lehiakatu *v.t.* to compete, to rival. *v.i.* to persist, to be diligent.
lehiaketa *n.* competition, contest.
lehiaketari *n.* competitor.
lehiakide *n.* rival, competitor.
lehiakidetasun *n.* rivalry, competition.
lehiakor *adj.* competitive, insistent, diligent.
lehiakortasun *n.* competitiveness, rivalry.
lehiarazi *v.t.* to incite, to provoke competition.
lehiarazle *n.* promoter, inciter. *adj.* inciting, aggravating, promoting.
lehiati *adj.* hardworking, laborious, persistent, constant, persevering.
lehiatoki *n.* place of competition, place where a contest is held.
lehiatsu *adj.* eager, zealous, hardworking, studious.
lehiatsuki *adv.* tenaciously, insistently,

persistently, obstinately, eagerly, zealously.
lehiatu *v.i.* to be diligent, to persist, to compete.
lehiatuki *adv.* hurriedly, hastily.
lehiatzaile *n.* competitor. *n.* persistent one, insister.
lehiaz *adv.* insistently, persistently.
lehoi *n.(zool.)* lion.
lehoieme *n.(zool.)* lioness.
lehoikume *n.(zool.)* lion cub.
lehoinabar *n.(zool.)* leopard.
lehor *adj.* arid, dry; hard. *adj.* sterile. *n.* land, dry land, mainland.
lehorbera *adj.* tending to be dry.
lehorgailu *n.* drier.
lehorgaitz *adj.* difficult to dry, undryable.
lehorgarri *adj.* capable of being dried, dryable.
lehorgiro *n.* temperature appropriate for drying, drought, dry weather.
lehorketa *n.* drying. *n.* desiccation.
lehorketari *n.* drier.
lehorki *n.* drying agent. *adv.* dryly.
lehorpe *n.* awning, porch, covering, pent roof.
lehorraldi *n.* drought, dry season.
lehorregi *adj.* too dry.
lehorreraketa *n.* landing, approaching land, docking.
lehorrerapen *n.* landing, docking.
lehorreratu *v.i.* to dock, to land, to arrive at a port.
lehorrezin *adj.* undryable, incapable of drying.
lehortar *n.* landsman, landlubber. *adj.* pertaining to the land, terrestrial.
lehortasun *n.* aridness, dryness.
lehorte *n.* dryness, drought.
lehortegi *n.* drying place, place where things are hung to dry.
lehortoki *n.* drying place, place where things are hung to dry.
lehortu *v.i./v.t.* to dry up, to dry.
lehortzaile *n.* drier, one who dries.
leial *adj.* loyal, faithful.
leialdu *v.i.* to become loyal, to become faithful.
leialki *adv.* loyally, faithfully, honestly.
leialkiro *adv.* loyally, faithfully.
leialtasun *n.* faith, faithfulness, loyalty, honesty. *n.* sincerity; frankness.
leihatila *n.(dim.)* little window. *n.* ticket window, counter.
leiho *n.* window.
leihoratu *v.i.* to go to the window.
leihotxo *n.(dim.)* little window.
leihotzar *n.(augm.)* large window.
leinu *n.* lineage, genealogical line, generation.
leinukide *n.* member of a family tree.
leitu *v.i.* to freeze.
leize *n.* chasm, abyss, gorge, ravine.
leizeikerle *n.* spelunker, speleologist.
leizeratu *v.i.* to descend into an abyss.
leizetsu *adj.* cavernous, full of caverns.

leizezulo n. cave, cavern.
leka n.(bot.) bean pod.
lekadun adj. leguminous, having pods.
lekaide n.(neol.) friar, monk.
lekaidego n. religious order, state of being a monk.
lekaidetu v.i. to join a religious order.
lekaidetxe n. monastery, convent.
lekaidetza n. religious order.
lekaime n.(neol.) nun, sister.
lekaimegai n. postulant, candidate for joining a religious order.
lekaimego n. religious order, state of being a nun.
lekaimetxe n. convent, nunnery.
lekaketa n. shelling, husking.
lekaratu v.t. to sheathe.
lekari n.(bot.) legume, vegetable. adj. leguminous.
lekat prep. except, but.
lekatsu adj. full of pods, covered with pods.
lekatu v.t. to leave out, to exclude, to exempt. v.t. to shell. v.i. to grow (a pod), to form (a pod). v.t. to lick.
lekatxo n.(dim.) small shell, small pod.
lekazi n. legume.
lekore n. outside, outdoors. **Lekorean.** Except.
lekoreko adj. exterior, outside, outdoor.
lekoreratu v.t. to put (something) outside. v.i. to go outside.
leku n. place, location, site. n. position, post, job. n. consent, approval.
-leku (gram.) Suffix signifying place of, place for (an activity). **Sorleku.** Place of origin.
lekualdagarri adj. movable, transportable, portable.
lekualdaketa n. moving, transfer, displacement.
lekualdakor adj. migratory, nomadic.
lekualdatzaile adj. moving, transferring.
lekuan prep. instead of, in (someone's) place, in place of.
leku egin v.t. to make room (for), to make a place.
leku eman v.t. to give one's consent, to approve. v.t. to welcome.
lekuko n. local, pertaining to a place; vernacular. adj. sedentary. n. substitute, replacement. n. witness.
lekukotasun n. testimony, affidavit.
lekukotu v.i. to become accustomed to a place. v.t. to testify, to bear witness.
lekune n. place, site, location, position.
lekuratu v.i. to arrive at a place.
lekutako adj. very distant, far.
lekutan adv. far away, very far.
lekutan egon v.i. to be far away.
lekutara adv. (to) so far away, (to) such a distant place.
lekutasun n. place, location, situation, position.
lekutatik adv. from very far away.
lekutu v.t. to localize, to situate, to place, to put. v.i. to be absent.
lekutxo n.(dim.) small place; favorite place.
lelo n. refrain, chorus. adj. idiot, foolish, dunce. n. fame, renown.
leloaldi n. period of foolishness.
lelokeria n. stupidity, foolishness, tomfoolery.
lelotasun n. foolishness, imbecility.
lelotu v.i. to become foolish, to become silly, to be silly, to act foolish.
lema n. rudder.
lemadun n. helmsman.
lemari n. helmsman.
lemaritza n. piloting, art of piloting a boat.
lematu v.t. to pilot a boat.
lemazain n. pilot of a boat.
lemazaintza n. job of piloting a boat.
lenteja n.(bot.) lentil.
lepa- Used in compound words. Derived from lepo, neck, back.
lepagain n.(anat.) nape (of the neck).
lepagiltzadura n. neck joint.
lepagogordura n.(med.) torticollis, wryneck, stiff neck.
lepagorri n.(zool.) red-necked bird.
lepahori n.(zool.) pine marten.
lepakari n. loader, carrier, transporter (person).
lepaketa n. loading onto a man's back; cargo, load.
lepamin n.(med.) torticollis, wryneck, stiff neck.
lepamozketa n. beheading, decapitation.
lepamozte n. decapitation, beheading.
lepamoztu v.t. to behead, to decapitate.
lepandi adj. big-necked, thick-necked.
lepazain n.(anat.) jugular, cervical tendon.
lepazaztada n. killing of the bull with one thrust of the sword in the neck.
lepo n. neck.
lepoa eman v.t. to disdain.
lepokada n. cargo carried on one's back.
lepoker adj. humpbacked, hunchbacked.
lepoko n. neck scarf, muffler, neckerchief. n. blow on the back.
lepokomin n. torticollis, wryneck, stiff neck.
lepondo n.(anat.) cervix, back of the neck, nape.
lepondoko n. blow to the back of the neck.
leporaketa n. loading cargo onto a person's back.
leporatu v.t. to load onto a person's back. v.t.(fig.) to put on (someone's) shoulders, to give (someone)

responsibility for (something), to
attribute, to impute.
lepotik *prep.* at the expense of, off of.
lera *n.* rustic sled, sledge.
lerdakatu *v.t.* to step on, to stomp on,
to trample.
lerde *n.* spit, spittle, drool, saliva.
lerdejario *n.* drooling, dribbling. *adj.*
drooling, dribbling, spitting.
lerdeketa *n.* abundance of spittle,
drool.
lerden *adj.* svelte, lithe, graceful.
lerdendu *v.i.* to become svelte, to
become graceful.
lerdenki *adv.* sveltely, lithely,
gracefully, airily, prettily.
lerdentasun *n.* litheness,
gracefulness.
lerderia *n.* spittle, drool.
lerdetsu *adj.* dribbling, drooling.
lerdezapi *n.* bib, chin-cloth.
lerdezkatu *v.t.* to dribble, to drool.
lerdo *adj.* foolish, silly.
lerra *n.* slip, slide, skid.
lerrabide *n.* slippery road, slide. *n.(fig.)*
temptation, danger, path of perdition.
lerrada *n.* slipping, sliding, skidding.
lerradura *n.* slipping, sliding, skidding.
lerragarri *adj.* slippery, slick.
lerragune *n.* slippery place. *n.*
toboggan.
lerraketa *n.* slipping, sliding, skidding.
lerrakor *adj.* slippery, slick.
lerrakortasun *n.* slipperiness,
slickness.
lerrakortu *v.i.* to become slippery, to
get slick.
lerraldi *n.* slip, slipping, sliding,
skidding.
lerraleku *n.* slippery place.
lerrati *adj.* excessively
condescending. *adj.* slippery;
sneaky (person).
lerratu *v.i.* to slip, to slide, to skid.
lerro *n.* line (on a page, on the ground,
etc.). *n.* line, file, row, succession of
things or people.
lerroalde *n.* paragraph.
lerroaldi *n.* paragraph.
lerroan *adv.* in line, in a line, single file,
in a row.
lerroarte *n.* space between lines.
lerroarteko *adj.* between the lines,
interlinear.
lerrodun *adj.* lined, striped.
lerrodura *n.* lining up, putting in rows
or lines.
lerroeta *n.* ruling, ruled lines (on
paper).
lerrogailu *n.* compass (apparatus for
holding a pen and assisting in
drawing lines of different shapes).
lerroka *adv.* in line, in a line, single file.
n. row, file.
lerrokada *n.* line, row, file; list.
lerrokatu *v.t.* to align, to put in a line, to
put in rows. *v.t./v.i.* to enlist, to

recruit, to inscribe.
lerroketa *n.* lining up, putting in rows or
lines.
lerrotu *v.t.* to delineate, to align, to line
up, to put into line.
lerroztatu *v.t.* to put in lines, to arrange
in rows, to line up.
lerrun *n.* rank, status.
lertxun *n.(bot.)* aspen tree.
lertxundi *n.* aspen grove.
letagin *n.(anat.)* canine tooth,
eyetooth; fang. *n.* boar tusk.
letaginkada *n.* wound or bite caused
by a fang or tusk.
letania *n.(eccl.)* litany.
letari-egunak *n.(pl.)* days of rogation,
days of public prayer.
letra *n.* letter. *n.(econ.)* installment,
monthly payment; bill of exchange.
letrakatu *v.t.* to spell.
letxu *n.(bot.)* lettuce.
leun *adj.* soft, fluffy. *adj.* smooth, even.
leunaldi *n.* smoothing, evening out.
leundu *v.i./v.t.* to soften, to soften up.
v.t. to polish, to smooth (out).
leundura *n.* smoothing out, polishing.
n. softening.
leungailu *n.* polisher, polishing
machine.
leungarri *adj.* polishable, smoothable.
adj. smoothing, softening.
leunkari *n.* polisher, smoother;
softener. *n.* praiser. *adj.* praising,
adulatory, flattering.
leunkeria *n.* excessive praise,
adulation, flattery, smooth talk.
leunketa *n.* polishing, smoothing,
softening. *n.(fig.)* praising, adulating.
n. attenuation.
leunki *adv.* smoothly, evenly, in a
polished manner.
leunkiro *adv.* smoothly, evenly, in a
polished manner.
leunkor *adj.* lenient, lenitive.
leuntasun *n.* smoothness, softness,
evenness. *n.* polish.
leuntzaile *n./adj.* softener, smoother,
polisher; polishing, softening.
adj.(fig.) adulatory, flattering.
leuzemia *n.(med.)* leukemia.
-liar *(gram.)* suffix indicating guest,
invited to a function. **Ezteiliar.**
Wedding guest.
libera *n.(arith.)* pound, unit of measure
equal to .45 kilo. *n.* franc, French
monetary unit.
liberal *adj.* liberal.
liberaldu *v.i.* to become liberal.
liberalismo *n.(pol.)* liberalism.
liberalki *adv.* liberally.
liberdi *n.(arith.)* half a pound.
liberlaun *n.(arith.)* quarter of a pound.
libertate *n.* liberty, freedom.
libra *n.(arith.)* pound, unit of measure
equal to .45 kilo.
libragailu *n.* instrument used to free a
blockage (crane, plunger, etc.).

libragarri n./adj. laxative, purgative.
libraketa n. freeing, deliverance, liberating.
librantza n. act of setting free, liberation.
libratu v.t. to set free, to liberate, to release. v.i. to free, to be free, to be liberated. v.i. to purge, to defecate.
libreta n.(econ.) savings book, deposit book.
liburu n. book.
liburuazal n. book cover, book binding.
liburudenda n. bookstore.
liburudun n. bookseller. adj. having a book.
liburugile n. publisher, printer, bookmaker. n. author, writer.
liburugintza n. publishing, printing.
liburujoskura n. bookbinding.
liburujosle n. bookbinder.
liburujospen n. bookbinding.
liburujostura n. bookbinding.
liburuketa n. set of books, collection of books.
liburuki n. volume (of a set of books).
liburukote n.(augm.) large book.
liburulari n. bibliographer.
liburuno n.(dim.) small book.
liburusaltzaile n. bookseller.
liburutegi n. library.
liburutxo n.(dim.) small book, booklet, brochure.
liburutza n. collection of books.
liburuxka n.(dim.) small book, brochure, booklet.
liburuzain n. librarian.
liburuzale n./adj. fond of books; book lover, bibliophile, bookworm.
liburuzorro n. book bag, sack.
lider n. leader.
lidertasun n. leadership.
liga n. garter. n. competitive league (sports).
liho n.(bot.) flax, linen.
lihohazi n. flaxseed.
lihotegi n. place where flax is kept.
lihotu v.t. to break (flax), to swingle (flax), to crush (flax).
lika n. kind of glue used to trap birds.
likaketa n. sticking, gluing, affixing.
likatasun n. stickiness, viscosity.
likatsu adj. sticky, viscous.
likatu v.t. to glue, to stick, to paste. v.i. to become sticky.
likido n./adj. liquid. n.(econ.) net amount.
likidotu v.t./v.i. to liquefy, to make liquid; to become liquid.
likin adj. sticky, viscous. n. viscosity. adj.(fig.) lascivious, dirty.
likinkeria n. stickiness, viscosity. n.(fig.) lasciviousness, dirtiness.
likintasun n. stickiness, viscosity.
likisdura n. lasciviousness, lechery, lust.
likisgarri adj. soiling, dirtying.

likiskeria n. dirtiness. n. lasciviousness, obscenity.
likiski adv. dirtily, filthily. adv. lasciviously, obscenely, sordidly.
likiskor adj. sticky. adj. dirtying, staining.
likistasun n. dirtiness, filthiness, dirt, filth. n. lasciviousness, lustfulness.
likistatu v.i. to dirty, to soil, to stain, to get (something) dirty.
likistu v.i. to get dirty. v.i. to become obscene, to be lascivious. v.t. to dirty, to soil, to stain. v.t. to fornicate.
likits adj. dirty, filthy. adj. impure, corrupt, lustful, lascivious. n. stickiness, viscosity.
likitsu adj. sticky, viscous. adj. lascivious, lustful.
likore n. liquor, liqueur.
likortegi n. liquor store.
lili n.(bot.) lily.
lilikatu v.t. to decorate with flowers.
liliketa n. bunch of flowers, abundance of flowers.
lilipa n.(bot.) narcissus, daffodil.
lilitegi n. flower garden. n.(fig.) kindergarten.
lilitxo n.(dim.) small flower. n.(fig.) prostitute, whore.
lilura n. rapture, fascination, enchantment. n.(fig.) delirium. n. faint, dizziness.
liluradura n. rapture, fascination, enchantment.
liluragarri adj. fascinating, enchanting.
liluragarriki adv. fascinatingly, enchantingly.
lilurakeria n. seduction.
liluraketa n. attraction, seduction, allurement, enchantment.
lilurakor adj. seductive, alluring, attractive, fascinating.
liluraldi n. moment of enchantment, fascination.
liluramendu n. fascination, attraction.
lilurapen n. fascination, attraction.
liluratu v.t. to dazzle. v.t./v.i. to fascinate, to seduce; to be fascinated by.
liluratzaile adj. fascinating, seductive, attractive.
lilurazko adj. attractive, seductive.
lima n. file, rasp.
limadura n. file mark, rasp mark.
limagarri adj. capable of being filed or rasped.
limatu v.t. to file, to rasp.
limatzaile n. filer, one who uses a file or rasp.
limoi n.(bot.) lemon.
limoiedari n. lemonade, lemon juice.
limoiondo n.(bot.) lemon tree.
limoiur n. lemon juice.
limoixerra n. lemon slice, lemon wedge.
limonada n. lemonade.
limosna n. alms, charity, handout.

limosnari *n.* almsgiver.
limosnatxo *n.(dim.)* small handout, alms.
limuri *n.* slipping, sliding, skid. *adj.* libertine, lustful, lascivious.
limuritu *v.i.* to slip, to slide, to skid.
limurkari *n.* adulator, flatterer, praiser. *adj.* adulating, flattering.
limurkeria *n.* seduction, false flattery, fawning, adulation.
limurketa *n.* flattery, fawning, cajolery.
limurki *adv.* seductively, voluptuously.
limurkoi *adj.* voluptuous, seductive, flattering.
limurkor *adj.* slippery, slick. *adj.* voluptuous, seductive, flattering.
limurkortasun *n.* voluptuousness, seductiveness.
limurtasun *n.* slipperiness, slickness. *n.* smoothness, glossiness.
limurtu *v.i.* to slip, to slide, to skid. *v.t.* to persuade, to convince.
linazi *n.* flaxseed, linseed.
linbu *n.(eccl.)* limbo.
linburkeria *n.* lasciviousness, obscenity, lustfulness.
linburketa *n.* sliding, slipping.
linburkoi *adj.* licentious, lascivious.
linburkoikeria *n.* lasciviousness, obscenity, lustfulness.
linburkoitasun *n.* lasciviousness, lecherousness.
linburkor *adj.* slippery, slick. *adj.* lustful, lascivious, obscene.
linburkortasun *n.* slipperiness. *n.* obsceneness, lasciviousness.
linburtegi *n.* slide, sled, toboggan.
linburtoki *n.* slippery place.
linburtu *v.i.* to slip, to slide, to skid. *v.t.(fig.)* to woo, to court, to cajole, to flatter.
lingirda *n.* slime. *n.* viscosity.
lingirdatsu *adj.* slimy, viscous.
linterna *n.* lantern, flashlight.
linu *n.(bot.)* flax, linen.
lipar *n.* moment, instant, second. *n.* bit, little bit, smidgen.
lipu *n.(med.)* anthrax, carbuncle, malignant boil.
lira *n.(mus.)* lyre. *n.(econ.)* lira, Italian monetary unit.
lirain *adj.* svelte, graceful, lithe, agile.
liraindu *v.t.* to beautify, to adorn, to embellish. *v.i.* to be beautiful, to become graceful, to become svelte.
liraindura *n.* prettiness, loveliness.
lirainki *adv.* elegantly, prettily, neatly, gracefully.
liraintasun *n.* neatness, prettiness. *n.* svelteness, litheness, gracefulness.
lirika *n.* lyric.
liriku *adj.* lyrical, lyric.
lirin *adj.* mature, ripe, grown.
lirio *n.(bot.)* iris, lily.
lirismo *n.* lyricism.
lisaketa *n.* ironing.
lisakin *n.* iron, flatiron.

lisaldi *n.* ironing, time spent ironing.
lisatu *v.t.* to iron, to press.
lisatzaile *n.* ironer, one who irons.
liserigaitz *adj.* difficult to digest, undigestible.
liseriketa *n.* digestion.
liseritu *v.t.* to digest.
lisiba *n.* clothes washing, the wash, laundry. *n.* bleach, detergent.
lisibaketa *n.* bleaching.
lisibatu *v.t.* to bleach clothes.
liska *n.* pond scum; moss or algae on rocks, water surfaces, etc.
liskar *n.* argument, quarrel, dispute, squabble.
liskarbide *n.* subject for dispute, object or reason for arguing.
liskardura *n.* dispute, quarrel, argument.
liskar egin *v.t.* to dispute, to quarrel, to argue.
liskargile *n.* arguer, quarreler.
liskarkeria *n.* dispute, quarrel, argument.
liskarkide *n.* arguer, quarreler.
liskarraldi *n.* duration of a quarrel or dispute; quarrel, dispute.
liskarrari *n.* arguer, quarreler. *adj.* disputing, argumentative, quarrelsome.
liskarremaile *n.* arguer, quarreler, litigator. *adj.* argumentative, quarrelsome.
liskarti *adj.* quarrelsome, belligerent, argumentative.
liskartsu *adj.* argumentative, belligerent, quarrelsome.
liskartu *v.i.* to argue, to quarrel, to dispute.
liskarzale *adj.* argumentative, quarrelsome, belligerent, pugnacious.
liskatasun *n.* viscosity, stickiness.
liskatsu *adj.* viscous, sticky.
liskatu *v.i.* to get sticky, to be viscous.
listoi *n.* strip of wood, lath, cleat.
listoitu *v.t.* to make with laths or strips of wood.
listu *n.* saliva, spit, spittle.
listubera *adj.* salivating excessively, spitting excessively.
listubide *n.(anat.)* saliva duct.
listu bota *v.t.* to spit, to expectorate.
listu egin *v.t.* to spit, to expectorate.
listujario *n.* salivation, spitting.
listuka *adv.* spitting, salivating.
listukada *n.* salivating, spitting.
listukaketa *n.* spitting, expectoration.
listukari *n.* spitter, salivator. *adj.* spitting, expectorating.
listukatu *v.t.* to salivate, to spit, to expectorate.
listuketa *n.* spitting, expectoration.
listuontzi *n.* cuspidor, spittoon.
listutu *v.t.* to insalivate, to mix with saliva.
listuzko *adj.* salivary.

listuztu *v.t.* to insalivate, to mix with saliva.
literal *adj.* literal.
literalki *adv.* literally.
literato *n.* writer (of literature).
literatur *adj.* literary.
literatura *n.* literature.
literaturzale *adj.* fond of literature.
litro *n.* liter.
lits *n.* thread, strand.
liturgia *n.* liturgy.
liturgia egin *v.t.* to give the liturgy.
liturgigile *n.* celebrant, officiating priest.
liturgijazki *n.* liturgical robe.
liturgikizun *n.* liturgical celebration.
liturgilari *n.* officiating priest.
litxar *adj.* sweet-toothed, having a sweet tooth. *n.* petty thief, pickpocket.
litxarkeria *n.* excessive fondness for sweets. *n.* petty thievery, rapaciousness.
litxarketa *n.* taking a liking to, growing fond of (something).
litxarki *adv.* with relish, greedily.
litxarreria *n.* petty theft, larceny. *n.* sweets.
litxarrero *adj.* sweet-toothed, having a sweet tooth. *n.* petty thief, pickpocket.
lixiba *n.* bleach, detergent. *n.* laundry, wash.
lixibaketa *n.* wash, laundry, bleaching laundry.
lixibaldi *n.* bleaching.
lixibatu *v.t.* to bleach clothes.
lixibontzi *n.* washtub.
lizar *n.(bot.)* ash tree.
lizardi *n.* ash tree grove.
lizarki *n.* piece of ash wood.
lizarrezko *adj.* pertaining to ash trees.
lizentzia *n.* degree.
lizentziamendu *n.* graduation; discharge (from service).
lizentziapen *n.* graduation; discharge (from service).
lizentziatu *v.i./v.t.* to earn a master's degree; to confer a master's degree. *v.i.* to be discharged from the service.
lizentziatura *n.* master's degree.
liztor *n.(zool.)* wasp.
liztorkabia *n.* wasp's nest.
liztortalde *n.* swarm of wasps.
liztortxo *n.(dim.)* small wasp.
liztortzar *n.(augm.)* hornet, large wasp.
lizun *n.* mold, mildew. *adj.(fig.)* obscene, lewd, lascivious.
lizunarazi *v.t.* to corrupt (sexually), to prostitute (someone).
lizunarazle *adj.* voluptuous; lustful, lascivious.
lizunbera *adj.* lustful, lascivious, lewd.
lizundu *v.i.* to grow moldy, to mildew. *v.t.* to make moldy. *v.i.(fig.)* to become immoral, to become

lascivious.
lizundura *n.* molding, mildewing.
lizungarri *adj.* susceptible to mold or mildew.
lizunkeria *n.* moldiness. *n.* pornography; lasciviousness, obscenity, lustfulness, immoral act.
lizunkerizale *adj.* obscene, lascivious, lustful.
lizunki *adv.* immorally, obscenely, lasciviously, licentiously.
lizunkoi *adj.* lascivious, licentious, immoral, lustful.
lizunkoikeria *n.* voluptuousness, lasciviousness.
lizunkor *adj.* lustful, immoral.
lizuntasun *n.* moldiness. *n.(fig.)* dirtiness.
lizuntsu *adj.* moldy.
lizuntzaile *adj.* corrupting, perverting.
lizunzalekeria *n.* lasciviousness, lustfulness; obscenity.
lo *n.* sleep, act of sleeping.
loak hartu *v.t.* to fall asleep, to go to sleep.
loaldi *n.* nap, short period of sleep.
loalditxo *n.(dim.)* short nap.
loarazi *v.t.* to put to sleep, to cause to sleep.
loba *n.* nephew, niece.
lobelar *n.(bot.)* herb used for falling asleep; opium poppy.
lodi *adj.* fat, corpulent, obese, overweight. *adj.* thick. *adj.* low, deep, bass (voice).
lodiegi *adj.* too fat, obese, overweight.
lodiera *n.* obesity; thickness, bulk.
lodikor *adj.* susceptible to getting fat.
lodikortasun *n.* propensity for getting fat.
lodikote *adj.* very fat; chubby, plump.
loditasun *n.* fatness; thickness.
loditu *v.i.* to get fat; to get thick. *v.i./v.t.* to thicken, to coagulate. *v.i.(phys.)* to condensate (liquid).
loditzaile *adj.* fattening; thickening.
lodiune *n.* fattening period.
lo egin *v.t.* to sleep, to snooze.
loegite *n.* sleeping, act of sleeping.
lo egon *v.i.* to be asleep, to sleep.
loeragile *n.* sleeping pill, narcotic, soporific. *n.* hypnotist.
lo eragin *v.t.* to cause to sleep, to put to sleep, to make (someone) sleep.
loeragingarri *adj.* soporific, narcotic, sleeping aid.
loerazle *n.* narcotic. *adj.* soporific, causing sleep, sleep-inducing.
loeri *n.* sleeping sickness. *n.* sleepiness, drowsiness, lethargy.
loeuli *n.(zool.)* tsetse fly.
loezin *n.* insomnia, lack of sleep, inability to sleep.
logabe *adj.* unsleeping, sleepless.
logabetasun *n.* insomnia, sleeplessness, lack of sleep.
logabetu *v.t./v.i.* to keep someone

awake at night; to stay awake.

logabezia *n.* insomnia, lack of sleep.

logaitz *n.* difficult sleep.

logale *n.* sleepiness. *adj.* sleepy.

logale izan *v.i.* to be sleepy, to fall asleep.

logaletasun *n.* sleepiness, somnolence.

logaletu *v.i.* to fall asleep. *v.t.* to put one to sleep.

logarri *adj.* sleep-inducing, soporific. *n.* sleeping aid, sleeping pill.

logela *n.* bedroom, sleeping room.

logika *n.* logic.

logiko *adj.* logical.

logikoki *adv.* logically.

logiro *n.* time for sleeping.

logose *n.* sleepiness.

logura *n.* sleepiness. *adj.* sleepy.

logura izan *v.i.* to be sleepy.

lo hartu *v.t.* to fall asleep, to go to sleep.

lohi *adj.* dirty. *adj.(fig.)* immoral, indecent. *n.* mud.

lohidura *n.* dirtiness, muddiness, staining.

lohiestalki *n.* fender.

lohigarri *adj.* dirtying, spotting, staining.

lohikengarri *n.* spot remover, stain remover.

lohikeria *n.* dirtiness, filth. *n.(fig.)* immorality, lust, licentiousness, impurity, lasciviousness.

lohiki *adv.* dirtily, filthily. *adv.(fig.)* sordidly, impurely, dirtily, dirty.

lohikor *adj.* spotting, staining, dirtying. *adj.* easily soiled.

lohikortasun *n.* quality of being easily soiled.

lohitasun *n.* muddiness, sliminess, dirtiness, filth. *n.(fig.)* impurity, immorality.

lohitsu *adj.* muddy, dirty. *adj.(fig.)* immoral, sordid.

lohitu *v.i./v.t.* to get muddy; to muddy, to spot, to stain, to soil, to get dirty.

lohitzaile *n./adj.* dirtier, soiler, stainer; dirtying, soiling, staining.

lohiune *n.* spot, stain.

lohiztapen *n.* wallowing in mud. *n.(fig.)* wallowing in vice.

lohiztatu *v.i./v.t.* to get muddy, to muddy, to splatter with mud. *v.t.(fig.)* to defame, to slander, to muddy (someone's) name.

loka *n.* clucking. *n.(fig.)* female lust, sensuality.

lokadura *n.(med.)* luxation, dislocation.

lokaldi *n.* incubation period (eggs). *n.(fig.)* lust or sexual excitement in a woman.

lokantu *n.* lullaby, cradle song.

lokarri *n.* cord, rope, tie, lace. *n.* grommet, becket. *n.* bond, link, tie.

lokarrimendu *n.* tie, knot, tying.

lokarritu *v.t.* to tie with rope or cord, to join together, to bind, to link.

lokarritxo *n.(dim.)* small cord, slender cord.

lokarriztatu *v.t.* to tie, to attach.

lokartu *v.t.* to fall asleep. *v.i.* to be asleep, to be numb (legs, extremities).

lokatu *v.i.* to become broody (said of an incubating hen). *v.t./v.i.* to dislocate, to become dislocated (joints).

lokatz *n.* mud, clay.

lokazketa *n.* wallowing in mud.

lokazpen *n.* muddying.

lokaztadura *n.* muddying.

lokaztu *v.i./v.t.* to get muddy, to become muddy.

loki *n.(anat.)* temple.

lokomotore *n.* locomotive.

lokuluxka *n.* light sleep, nap.

lolo *n.(fam.)* sleep, beddy-bye, night-night. Children's expression.

lolo egin *v.t.* to go to sleep, to go beddy-bye, to go night-night. Children's expression.

lor *n.* transportation, cartage, freight. *n.* beam which is transported by dragging or towing. *n.(fig.)* tribulation, suffering, vexation, annoyance.

lora- Used in compound words. Derived from *lore*, flower.

loraburu *n.* flower bud.

loradenda *n.* flower shop.

loradi *n.* flora.

loragile *n.* florist.

loragintza *n.* floriculture, flower gardening.

lorail *n.* May.

loraketa *n.* flowering, abundance of flowers.

lorakuntza *n.* flowering.

loraldi *n.* flowering, blossoming, blooming. *n.(fig.)* renaissance. **Euskal literaturaren loraldia.** The renaissance of Basque literature. *n.* period of flowering or blossoming.

lorasaltzaile *n.* florist, flower vendor.

loraskodun *adj.* multifloral, having many flowers.

lorasorta *n.* bouquet, bunch of flowers.

lorate *n.* period of flowers, blooming season.

lorategi *n.* flower garden. *n.* anthology, selection.

lorateria *n.* multitude of flowers.

loratsu *adj.* flowering, blossoming, flowery, full of blossoms.

loratu *v.i.* to flower, to bloom, to blossom.

lorazain *n.* gardener.

lorazaintza *n.* gardening, floriculture.

lore *n.* flower, blossom.

loredun *adj.* flowering, blooming, having flowers.

loregabetu *v.i.* to lose flowers, to lose blossoms, to deflower.

loreirin n.(bot.) pollen. (lit.) flower's flour.

lorejaiak n.(pl.) Floral Games, poetry competition for Basque troubadours and poets.

lorekadura n. embroidered flowers, embroidery of flowers.

lorekatu v.t. to embroider flowers (on something), to paint flowers (on something).

loretxo n.(dim.) small flower.

lorezko adj. floral.

loreztatu v.t. to decorate with flowers.

lorbide n. freight route, transportation route. n. means of getting something.

lorgaitz adj. unobtainable, hard to get.

lorgarri adj. obtainable.

loria n. glory. n. joy, jubilation.

loriatu v.i. to praise, to glorify. v.t. to cause great joy.

lorketa n. obtaining, obtainment, getting. n. transportation, carrying.

lorketari n. carrier, transporter (person).

lormen n. purchasing power, power of acquisition, power to obtain things.

loro n.(zool.) parrot. n. fine wire used in fishing.

lorontzi n. flower vase, bud vase, flower pot.

lorontzitegi n. plant stand, flower pot stand.

lorosto n.(bot.) flower petal.

lorpen n. achievement, attainment.

lorratz n. track, trace, footprint.

lorreta n. hauling, transportation, cartage, carrying.

lorrin n. piece of overturned earth. adj. rainy.

lorrinaldi n. breakage, spoilage, waste. n. rolling, wallowing, turning over, tumbling.

lorrindu v.t./v.i. to worsen; to waste, to ruin, to spoil. v.i. to wallow, to roll, to turn over.

lortezin adj. unobtainable, unachievable, hard to get.

lortu v.t. to get, to obtain, to acquire, to achieve.

lortzaile n./adj. acquirer; acquiring.

losa n. slab, stone, flagstone, tile.

losin n. caress. n. flattery, adulation, cajolery.

losindu v.t. to caress, to treat affectionately. v.t. to flatter, to adulate.

losintxa n. compliment, flattery, cajolery, adulation.

losintxari adj. flattering, praising, cajoling, adulating.

losintxatu v.t. to compliment, to flatter, to adulate.

losintzaile adj. flattering, praising, adulating.

lotan egon v.i. to be asleep, to be sleeping, to sleep.

lotara joan v.i. to go to sleep.

lotaratu v.i. to go to sleep, to fall asleep.

lotaro n. pleasant sleeping temperature.

lotazil n. December.

loteria n. lottery.

loterisaltzaile n. lottery ticket seller.

lotezin adj. unconnectable, unlinkable, difficult to tie. adj. incoherent, disconnected.

loti adj. sleepyhead, sleepy, one who sleeps a lot. ·

lotoki n. place for sleeping, place to sleep.

lotsa n. disgrace, shame, shyness, embarrassment; modesty. n. fear. n. respect.

lotsabako adj. shameless.

lotsabera adj. sensitive to shame, sensitive to scandal, honorable.

lotsadun adj. ashamed, embarrassed.

lotsa eman v.t. to fill with respect, to earn respect, to make (someone) respect (someone).

lotsagabe adj. shameless, brazen; immoral.

lotsagabekeria n. shamelessness, shameless act, immorality, indecency; insolence.

lotsagabeki adv. shamelessly, brazenly, irreverently, impudently.

lotsagabetasun n. shamelessness, immodesty.

lotsagabetu v.i. to become shameless, to become a shameless person, to behave shamelessly.

lotsagabezia n. shamelessness, lack of respect.

lotsagaizto n. insult, affront. n. cynicism.

lotsagaiztoko adj. shameless, insulting.

lotsagaldu v.t. to become shameless, to lose respect. adj. shameless; cynical.

lotsagalduko adj. shameless, brazen; immoral.

lotsagarri adj. shameful, immodest, indecent, disgraceful, outrageous.

lotsagarrikeria n. shamelessness, indecency. n. dullness, slowness.

lotsagarriki adv. shamelessly; disrespectfully.

lotsagarriro adv. shamelessly, shamefully; disrespectfully.

lotsagarritasun n. shamefulness. n. clumsiness, awkwardness, dullness.

lotsagarritu v.t. to ridicule, to make fun of, to humiliate, to embarrass.

lotsagarrizko adj. shameful, embarrassing.

lotsa izan v.i. to be ashamed, to feel shame, to be embarrassed. v.t. to respect. v.i. to fear, to be afraid of.

lotsakizun n. dishonor, ignominy. n. modesty, shyness, bashfulness.

lotsakor adj. timid, shy, bashful, embarrassed. adj. fearful.

lotsakortasun n. timidness, shyness, bashfulness.

lotsakortu v.i. to be timid, to be shy. v.i. to become timid, to become fearful.

lotsaldi n. period of embarrassment, period of shame. n. blushing. n. moment of fear.

lotsarazi v.t. to blush, to be embarrassed. v.t. to cause fear, to inspire fear.

lotsarazle adj. humiliating, debasing, embarrassing, degrading.

lotsari n. shame, disgrace.

lotsati adj. shy, timid; ashamed.

lotsatu v.i. to be embarrassed, to be ashamed. v.t. to embarrass, to shame. v.t. to intimidate.

lotsor adj. timid, shy, embarrassed.

lotu v.t. to tie, to attach, to connect, to knot. v.i. to grab, to grasp.

lotugabe adj. loose, free.

lotugarri adj. linkable, connectible, capable of being tied, joinable.

lotune n. tie, link, joining, coupling, place where one thing joins another.

lotura n. tie, liaison, connection, bond, nexus, link, union. n. relationship, bond. n. bandages, dressing (on a wound).

loturagabe adj. disconnected, unconnected; incoherent.

lotza n.(zool.) loach, kind of salt water fish.

lotzaile n. packer, wrapper, boxer.

lozaku n. sleeping bag. adj.(colloq.) sleepy, sleepy head.

lozorro n. lethargy, stupor, drowsiness.

lozorroaldi n. period of lethargy, period of drowsiness.

lozorroan egon v.i. to be lethargic, to be in a stupor.

lozorrotu v.i. to become drowsy, to get sleepy.

lozurrunga n. snoring.

lozurrungatu v.i. to snore.

lu- Derived from lur, earth. Used in some compound words.

lubeltz n. humus, organic soil.

luberri n. tilled earth, newly plowed land.

luberrigarri adj. arable, tillable.

luberriketa n. tilling, plowing.

luberritu v.t. to plow, to till, to break up the ground.

lubeta n. embankment.

lubizi n. landslide, mudslide.

ludi n. world, earth.

luebaki n. long trench.

luebakitu v.t. to dig trenches.

lugin n. worker, laborer; farmer.

luginketa n. plowing, tilling.

lugintza n. agriculture, farmer's profession, laborer's work.

lugorri n. tilled land, cultivated land.

luhartz n.(zool.) scorpion. n.(zool.) mole cricket.

luhesi n. earthen fence, barrier, banks of earth and branches used to channel irrigation water.

lukainka n. chorizo, spicy Basque pork sausage. n.(colloq.) idiot, simpleton. n.(colloq.) lie, trick, deception.

luki n.(zool.) fox. adj.(fig.) astute, foxy, shrewd, mischievous.

lukieme n. female fox.

lukikeria n. foxiness, cleverness, cunning.

lukikume n.(dim.) small fox, fox kit.

luku n. cluster, bunch. n. forest.

lukur adj. avaricious, usurious, miserly. n. usurer, scrooge, miser.

lukurantza n. usury, profiteering.

lukurari n. usurer, scrooge, miser.

lukurreria n. usury, profiteering.

lukuru n. usury, profiteering.

luma n. feather. n. pen.

lumaberritu v.i. to molt, to change feathers.

lumaberrizte n. molting of birds.

lumabizi n. pin feathers, first feathers.

lumadun adj. feathered, plumed.

lumagabe adj. featherless.

lumaia n. plumage.

lumaizto n. penknife.

lumaketa n. plucking (feathers off a bird).

lumapilo n. feathers, bunch of plumes.

lumatsu adj. feathered, feathery.

lumatu v.t. to pluck (the feathers from). v.i. to grow feathers, to sprout feathers. v.t./v.i.(fig.) to rob; to be robbed.

lumatxa n. down. n. down mattress, feather mattress.

lumatxo n.(dim.) small feather, pin feather.

lumatza n. pile of feathers, bunch of feathers. n. pillow.

lumaztatu v.t. to feather, to cover with feathers. v.i. to be feathered, to be covered with feathers.

lupa n. magnifying glass.

lupe n. subway, underground. n. cave, cavern.

lupeme n. female procurer, female pimp.

luperia n. landslide, mudslide.

lupetsu adj. muddy, mirey.

lupetu v.t. to bury, to inter. v.i. to bury oneself, to be buried.

lupetza n. mire, bog, marsh.

lupeztu v.i. to get muddy, to get mired down, to bog down (in mud).

lupina n.(zool.) sea bass.

lupu n. scorpion. n.(colloq.) pimp, procurer. n. poison.

lupubelar n.(bot.) black hellebore, Christmas rose, used to cure carbuncles.

lupu egin v.t. to procure, to pimp, to

pander.

lupukeria *n.* pimping.

lur *n.* land, ground, earth, soil, dirt. *n.* floor, ground. *n.* country; territory.

lurbeso *n.(geog.)* peninsula.

lurbira *n.* world, earth, terrestrial sphere. *n.* rotation of the earth.

lurdun *adj.* earthy; soiled. *n.* landowner.

lurgain *n.(geol.)* surface of the earth, crust of the earth.

lurgaineko *adj.* pertaining to the earth's surface.

lurgile *n.* potter.

lurgin *n.* laborer.

lurgintza *n.* agriculture; plowing, cultivation of the earth.

lurgoratu *v.t.* to turn over the earth, to plow the land.

lurgorri *n.* tilled land, cultivated land. (lit.) red earth.

lurgorritu *v.t.* to till the land.

lurjabe *n.* landowner.

lurjabetu *v.i.* to acquire land, to own land.

lurjabetza *n.* ownership of land.

lurjale *adj.* geophagous, earth-eating.

lurjausi *n.* landslide, mudslide.

lur jo *v.t.* to fall down, to tumble, to hit the ground. *v.t.(fig.)* to be broke, to be ruined, to go bankrupt. *v.t.(fig.)* to get discouraged, to be discouraged, to be depressed.

lurjoaldi *n.* defeat, dejection.

lurjota *adj.* discouraged, dejected, defeated.

lurkenketa *n.* digging up, exhuming, removing from the earth.

lurkentzaile *n.* exhumer, one who digs up or disinters.

lurketa *n.* pile of dirt. *n.* load of dirt.

lurkoi *adj.* mundane, worldly, earthly.

lurkoskor *n.* clod of dirt.

lurlan *n.* cultivation of the soil.

lurlandu *v.t.* to cultivate the soil.

lurlangile *n.* laborer.

lurlantza *n.* agriculture, cultivation, tillage of the earth.

lurlantzaile *n.* laborer, farmer.

lurmen *n.* land from which the snow has melted, land cleared of snow.

lurmendu *v.t.* to remove the snow, to clear away snow.

lurmengailu *n.* snow remover, snowplow.

lurmeta *n.* pile of dirt.

lurmugatu *n.* fenced land, demarcated land.

lurmutur *n.* cape, promontory, point, headland. *n.* mound of dirt, clod of dirt.

lurneurketa *n.* land surveying.

lurneurkin *n.* surveyor's tool.

lurneurkintza *n.* land surveying.

lurneurlari *n.* land surveyor.

lurpe *n.* underground. *n.* catacomb.

lurpeko *adj.* subterranean, underground.

lurpelan *n.* drilling underground, digging underground. *n.(fig.)* defaming.

lurperagabe *adj.* unburied, uninterred.

lurperaketa *n.* interment, burial, burying.

lurperaldi *n.* burying, burial, interment.

lurperatu *v.t.* to bury, to inter. *v.i.* to be underground.

lurperatzaile *n.* one who buries, gravedigger.

lurpetu *v.t.* to inter, to bury, to place underground.

lurpoto *n.* earthenware jar, jug, pot.

lurra eman *v.t.* to bury, to inter.

lurra hartu *v.t.* to land.

lurrak hartu *v.t.* to acclimatize, to get used to a place.

lurraldatu *v.t.* to transplant.

lurralde *n.* territory, region.

lurraldearteko *adj.* interterritorial.

lurraldeko *adj.* territorial, regional.

lurraldetasun *n.* territoriality.

lurrandi *n.(geog.)* continent.

lurrandiarteko *adj.* intercontinental.

lurrandiko *adj.* continental.

lurrazpi *n.* subsoil; underground.

lurrazpiko *adj.* underground, subterranean.

lurreko *adj.* terrestrial, worldly, earthly.

lurremaile *n.* gravedigger, burier; sexton.

lurremate *n.* interment, burying, burial.

lurrematzaile *n.* gravedigger, undertaker, burier.

lurreraketa *n.* landing. *n.* demolition.

lurreratu *v.i.* to fall on the ground, to cave in. *v.t.* to demolish, to tear down. *v.i.* to land. *v.i.* to approach land, to dock, to land.

lurreten *n.* landslide, mudslide.

lurrez *adv.* by land. *adv.* territorially, civilly.

lurrezko *adj.* earthen, made of earth, earthenware.

lurreztadura *n.* hilling plants; reinforcing (foundations with dirt).

lurreztapen *n.* covering with dirt.

lurreztatu *v.t.* to cover with dirt.

lurrikara *n.* earthquake.

lurrin *n.* steam, vapor.

lurrindatu *v.t./v.i.* to evaporate, to vaporize. *v.t.* to perfume, to scent, to aromatize.

lurrindegi *n.* perfumery, perfumer's shop.

lurrindun *adj.* vaporous, vaporized, evaporated, steamy.

lurrindura *n.* evaporation, vaporization.

lurrineztapen *n.* evaporation. *n.* aromatization, scenting.

lurrineztatu *v.t.* to evaporate, to vaporize. *v.t.* to scent, to perfume, to aromatize. *v.i.* to cloud up, to mist over, to become steamed or misty.

lurringailu *n.* vaporizer, atomizer,

perfumer.

lurringintza n. perfume making.

lurrinkatu v.t. to perfume, to scent, to perfume with incense.

lurrinketa n. vaporization, evaporation.

lurrinkor adj. easily evaporated.

lurrinkortasun n. evaporation; volatility.

lurrinontzi n. steamboat.

lurrintsu adj. vaporous, steamy, steamed. adj. perfumed, scented, aromatic.

lurrontzi n. clay pot or jar, earthenware jar.

lurrontzigin n. potter, maker of clay vessels.

lurrontzigintza n. pottery (craft), potmaking.

lurrun n. steam, vapor.

lurrundu v.i. to vaporize, to turn to steam, to evaporate.

lurrundun adj. vaporous, vaporized, evaporated, steamy.

lurrunketa n. vaporization, evaporation.

lurrunkor adj. easily evaporated.

lurruntsu adj. vaporous, steamy, steamed. adj. perfumed, scented, aromatic.

lursagar n. potato.

lursail n. tract of land.

lurtar n. earthling, inhabitant of earth, earth dweller, earth man. adj. earth, land, pertaining to the earth, earthly.

lurte n. landslide, mudslide.

lurtiar adj. worldly, earthly, tied to the land.

lurtontor n. knoll, hillock, mound.

lurtsu adj. earthy, abundant in soil.

lurtu v.i. to turn into earth or soil. v.t./v.i. to till; to be tilled.

lurtupin n. earthenware pot or jar, earthenware casserole.

lurzatitu v.t. to parcel land, to divide land.

lutu n. mourning, period of mourning.

lutxo n.(zool.) pike, freshwater fish.

luxo n. luxury.

luza- Derived from luze, long. Used in compound words.

luzabide n. delay, prolongation, extension (of time).

luzadura n. prolongation, delay.

luzaezin adj. undeferable, unpostponable, nondelayable, nonextendable.

luzagaitz adj. difficult to defer, difficult to postpone, difficult to put off.

luzagarri adj. extendable, prolongable, deferable. adj. deferred, delaying. n. procrastinating excuse, procrastination.

luzakari n. delayer, procrastinator.

luzakeria n. slowness, tardiness, delay, delinquency.

luzaketa n. lengthening, prolongation, delay, extension. n. adjournment,

prorogation, extension.

luzakin n. prolongation, extension.

luzakizun n. prolongation, delay; postponement. adj. deferable, postponable.

luzakor adj. prolonging, procrastinating, dilatory, prorogative.

luzakortasun n. prolongation, procrastination, delay.

luzaldi n. prolongation, delay, extension.

luzamen n. delay, postponement.

luzamendu n. extension, prolongation, moratorium, postponement.

luzanga adj. lanky, gangly, tall and thin.

luzapen n. lengthening, extension. n. delay, prolongation, postponement.

luzapide n. delay, prolongation, extension (of time).

luzaro adv. for a long time, extensively, at great length. n. long period of time, a long time.

luzaroan adv. at great length, extensively, prolongedly, for a long time.

luzaroko adj. durable, lasting; old.

luzarotu v.i. to last a long time.

luzatu v.i. to get longer, to stretch out, to lengthen. v.t. to lengthen, to make longer, to extend, to prolong. v.t. to delay, to postpone.

luzatzaile n. lengthener, stretcher; postponer, delayer, prolonger. adj. postponing, delaying, prolonging; lengthening, stretching.

luzaz adv. for a long time, long, at length.

luze adj. long (time or things).

luze izan v.i. to last a long time, to endure.

luzeka adv. in length, longitudinally, lengthwise.

luzeki adv. for a long time, extensively, at great length; lengthwise.

luzera n. length, duration.

luzeraz adv. along, longitudinally, lengthwise.

luzetara adv. lengthwise, longitudinally.

luzetasun n. length; duration.

luzetsi v.t. to seem like a long time, to seem long.

luzetsu adj. lengthy, very long.

luzexka adj. tall and slim; elongated.

M

m n. letter of the Basque alphabet. M never occurs at the end of a Basque word.

ma n.(fam.) kiss (children's language).

madari n.(bot.) pear.

madaridi n. pear orchard.

madarikagarri adj. accursed, damnable, damned.

madarikatu v.t. to curse, to cuss, to swear, to damn. adj. darned, damned, accursed, goddamn.

madarikatzaile *adj.* damning, blasphemous. *n.* curser, blasphemer. *n.* slanderer, defamer.
madarikazio *n.* curse, swear word, imprecation.
madariondo *n.(bot.)* pear tree.
madarisagar *n.(bot.)* variety of apple which resembles a pear in shape and flavor.
madaritxo *n.(dim.)* small pear.
ma egin *v.t.* to kiss (children's language).
magal *n.* lap; breast. *n.(fig.)* protection.
magalpe *n.* protection, defense, asylum.
magalpeko *n./adj.* baby; youngest in the family, favorite, beloved.
magalperatu *v.t.* to favor; to protect, to shelter.
magnesio *n.(chem.)* magnesium.
magnetindar *n.* magnetic force.
magnetofono *n.* tape recorder.
magurio *n.(zool.)* small sea snail.
mahai *n.* table.
mahaiburu *n.* head of the table, position of honor at the table. *n.* person presiding at a table or a meeting, chairman, chairperson.
mahaiburuko *n.* person at the head of the table, person presiding (at a table or meeting).
mahaiburutza *n.* presidency, head (of the board), chief of staff, chairmanship.
mahaieratu *v.i.* to approach the table. *v.i.* to sit down at the table. *v.t.* to take (someone or something) to the table.
mahaiestalki *n.* tablecloth.
mahaigaineko *n.* tablecloth.
mahaikide *n.* table companion.
mahaikidego *n.* table companionship.
mahaikidetasun *n.* table companionship.
mahaikidetu *v.i.* to be a table companion.
mahaikidetza *n.* table companionship.
mahaiko *n.* guest at table, dinner guest. *n.* member of a tribunal, panel, or committee, etc.
mahailagun *n.* table companion.
mahaimutil *n.* busboy, table servant, waiter.
mahaioihal *n.* tablecloth.
mahaiondo *n.* time spent at table after eating.
mahairakotu *v.t.* to invite.
mahairatu *v.i.* to go to the table, to sit down at the table.
mahaitxo *n.(dim.)* small table.
mahaizain *n.* waiter, head waiter.
mahaizango *n.* table leg.
mahasbildu *v.t.* to harvest grapes, to gather grapes.
mahasbilketa *n.* grape harvest, grape crop, vintage.
mahasbiltzaile *n.* grape harvester,

grape picker.
mahasgiro *n.* good weather for grapes.
mahaskintza *n.* viticulture, grape growing.
mahasmordo *n.* bunch of grapes, cluster of grapes.
mahasparra *n.* grapevine.
mahaspasa *n.* raisin.
mahastegi *n.* vineyard.
mahasti *n.* vineyard.
mahastiratu *v.i.* to go to the vineyard.
mahastitsu *adj.* abundant in vineyards, having many grapevines.
mahastizain *n.* vineyard keeper.
mahastizaintza *n.* viticulture, grape growing.
mahats *n.(bot.)* grape, bunch of grapes.
mahatsaihen *n.* vine shoot.
mahatsardo *n.* grape wine.
mahatsaro *n.* grape harvesting season.
mahatsondar *n.* grapes left over in the vineyard, gleanings after the grape harvest.
mahatsondo *n.(bot.)* grapevine.
mahatsosto *n.* grape leaf.
mahel *n.* stagnant water, still water.
mahoi *n.* sturdy blue fabric.
mahomatar *n./adj.* Mohammedan, Muslim.
mahuka *n.* sleeve.
mahukaburu *n.* cuff, wristband (of a shirt).
mai *n.* table.
maia *n.* Maya.
maiatza *n.* May.
maila *n.* level, step, grade (school). *n.* degree, category. *n.* mesh (of a net).
mailadi *n.* steps, tiered seats (in a stadium, etc.).
mailadiburu *n.* landing (of a staircase).
mailadun *adj.* tiered, stacked, having steps.
mailagune *n.* projection, ledge, ridge.
mailaka *adv.* gradually, by degrees, in stages, step by step.
mailakatu *v.t.* to do (something) in stages; to classify, to grade (in different levels).
mailaketa *n.* gradation, doing (something) in stages.
mailarte *n.* landing (of a staircase).
mailasto *n.* corn stalk.
mailatu *v.i.* to bruise, to be dented (fruit). *v.t.* to gradate, to do in stages, to arrange in tiers or levels.
mailatune *n.* bruise.
mailaz-maila *adv.* gradually, step by step.
mailegari *n.* borrower.
mailegatu *v.t.* to borrow.
mailegatzaile *n.* borrower.
mailegu *n.(econ.)* loan.
maileguz *adv.* by loan, on loan, as a loan.

mailu n. hammer. adj.(fig.) bothersome, importune, vexing.
mailuarrain n.(zool.) hammerhead.
mailuhots n. sound of a striking hammer.
mailujoka adv. firmly, solidly.
mailuka adv. by hitting with a hammer, with blows from a hammer, with a hammer. n.(dim.) small hammer.
mailukada n. blow from a hammer.
mailuka egin v.t. to hammer.
mailukaketa n. hammering.
mailukaldi n. hammer blow.
mailukari n. hammerer.
mailukatu v.t. to hammer, to forge.
mailukatzaile n. hammerer, forger (of metal).
mailuketa n. hammering, forging.
mailuskatu v.t. to crush, to pound, to beat.
mailutzar n.(augm.) large hammer, sledge hammer.
mailuxka n.(dim.) small hammer, mallet.
maina n. fondling, pampering. n. whining, whimpering, complaining. n. skill, knack, ability, dexterity.
mainada n. family.
mainati adj. spoiled, pampered; whining.
mainatsu adj. pampered, indulged, spoiled. adj. ingenious, sharp, clever, skillful.
mainatu v.t. to spoil, to pamper, to coddle. v.i. to be spoiled, to be pampered.
mainaz adv. ingeniously, skillfully, dextrously.
maindire n. sheet, bed sheet.
maingu adj. one-armed. adj. lame, crippled.
maingudura n. lameness, crippledness.
maingu egin v.t. to be a cripple, to be lame, to walk with a limp, to become a cripple.
maingueri n. lameness, state of being lame or crippled.
mainguka adv. lamely, limpingly, hobbling.
maingutasun n. lameness, state of being lame or crippled. n. state of having only one arm.
maingutu v.i. to become crippled, to go lame, to limp.
maionesa n. mayonnaise.
mairu n. Moor.
mairuantzeko adj. Moorish, Moor-like.
mairudorre n. minaret, tower of a Moorish mosque.
mairutalde n. group of Moors.
mairutar adj. Moorish, Moor.
mairutegi n. Moorish neighborhood.
mairuteria n. group of Moors.
mairutza n. multitude of Moors.
maiseabide n. subject of gossip, topic of conversation.

maiseagarri adj. criticizable, worthy of gossip, slanderous.
maiseaketa n. criticism, gossip, slander.
maiseatari n. critic, gossip, criticizer.
maiseatu v.t. to censure, to criticize, to gossip, to slander.
maiseatzaile n. gossip, critic, one who gossips.
maistra n. female teacher in a Spanish school.
maisu n. male teacher in a Spanish school.
maisugo n. teaching, teaching profession.
maisukeria n. pedantry, parading of knowledge or learning.
maisukeriazko adj. pedantic.
maisukeritu v.i. to be pedantic, to boast of being scholarly, to parade one's learning.
maisuki adv. masterfully, skillfully.
maisukide n. co-teacher; fellow teacher or professor.
maisukintza n. teaching, teaching profession.
maisukiro adv. masterfully, skillfully.
maisulan n. masterpiece.
maisuorde n. substitute teacher.
maisuordetza n. assistantship.
maisutalde n. faculty, group of teachers.
maisutasun n. teaching ability.
maisuteria n. faculty, group of professors or teachers.
maisutu v.i. to become a teacher, to get a teaching certificate.
maisutza n. job or profession of teaching.
maita- Used in compound words.
maitabera adj. affectionate, lovable, susceptible to falling in love.
maitadamu n.(eccl.) perfect contrition, repentance.
maitagarri adj. lovable, darling, beloved, dear.
maitagarriro adv. lovingly, dearly.
maitagarritasun n. lovableness.
maitagarritu v.i. to become lovable.
maitagrina n. amorous inclination, passion.
maitajoko n. flirt.
maitakeria n. false love, exaggerated affection; illicit love.
maitakor adj. lovable, affectionate, loving.
maitakortasun n. lovableness.
maitaldi n. being in love, period of loving.
maitale n. lover.
maita-maitati adj. very much in love.
maitarazi v.t. to make (someone) love (someone), to make (someone) fall in love.
maitarazle n. lover, flirter, person who inspires love in another, lovable person.

maitasun *n.* love, affection.
maitasunez *adv.* amorously, affectionately, lovingly.
maitasunezko *adj.* amatory, for love, based on love.
maitati *adj.* beloved.
maitatu *v.t.* to love. *adj.* loved, beloved, dear.
maitatzaile *n.* lover. *adj.* loving, amorous.
maite *adj.* beloved, dear.
maiteago *adj.(comp.)* preferred, favorite.
maiteago izan *v.t.* to prefer.
maiteagotasun *n.* predilection.
maitealdi *n.* love affair, period of love.
maiteen(a) *adj.(superl.)* favorite, preferred, best loved.
maite izan *v.t.* to love.
maiteki *adv.* affectionately, lovingly.
maitekide *n.* lover.
maitekiro *adv.* warmly, amorously, lovingly, affectionately.
maitekoi *adj.* tending to fall in love.
maitelagun *n.* lover.
maitemin *n.* love affair, fling, crush.
maiteminaldi *n.* love affair.
maitemindu *v.i.* to fall in love. *adj.* in love, loving.
maitemindura *n.* love affair, fling, crush.
maiteminez *adv.* lovingly, passionately.
maiteno *adj.* dear, beloved, darling.
maitetasun *n.* love, affection.
maitetxo *adj.(dim.)* dear, darling, beloved.
maite ukan *v.t.* to love.
maiz *adv.* often, frequently. *n.* clump of rushes.
maiztapen *n.* frequency, habitualness.
maiztasun *n.* frequency, habitualness.
maiztatu *v.i./v.t.* to repeat often.
maizter *n.* tenant, renter, lessee.
maiztergo *n.* tenancy, occupancy.
maizterketa *n.* renting, leasing, letting.
maiztertasun *n.* tenancy, occupancy.
maiztertu *v.t.* to rent, to rent out, to let.
maiztertza *n.* renting, letting, hiring.
maiztu *v.t./v.i.* to frequent, to become frequent.
makailo *n.(zool.)* codfish.
makailontzi *n.* boat for catching codfish.
makal *adj.* weak, sick. *n.(bot.)* poplar.
makalaldi *n.* depression, period of depression, weakness, illness.
makaldi *n.* grove of poplars.
makaldu *v.i./v.t.* to get sick, to weaken, to become debilitated. *v.i.* to be a coward, to become a coward.
makaldura *n.* weakness, depression, decline, discouragement.
makalgarri *adj.* debilitating, weakening.
makalkeria *n.* weakness, debilitated state, feebleness.
makalki *adv.* weakly, feebly.

makalkor *adj.* weakening, exhausting, extenuating.
makaltasun *n.* weakness, languor, feebleness, debility.
makar *n.* sleep (secretion of the eyes). *adj.* thin, slender.
makarroi *n.* spaghetti, macaroni, pasta.
makartsu *adj.* sleepy, having sleep in one's eyes.
makatz *adj.* wild (used with fruits and trees). *n.(bot.)* wild pear.
makera *n.* uncastrated pig. *n.* sow with piglets.
maketa *n.* model, maquette.
maketo *n./adj.* pejorative word once used to refer to non-Basque immigrants to the Basque Country.
makila *n.* cane, stick, baton of authority.
makilada *n.* blow with a stick or a cane.
makilaka *adv.* hitting with a stick, beating with a cane.
makilakada *n.* blow with a cane or stick.
makilakari *n.* one who beats with a stick.
makilaldi *n.* beating with a stick, thrashing.
makilatu *v.t.* to beat with a stick or cane, to thrash.
makildantza *n.* Basque dance in which sticks are used by dancers.
makiltxo *n.(dim.)* small stick.
makina *n.* machine.
makina bat *adj./pron.* a lot of, many, much. *adv.* many, a lot, a great deal.
makinagela *n.* engine room, room of machinery.
makinagintza *n.* machine making.
makinari *n.* mechanic, machinist.
makinazain *n.* keeper of machines, mechanic, engineer.
makineria *n.* group of machines, machinery.
makinidazkera *n.* typewriting, typing.
makinidazle *n.* typist, typer.
mako *n.* hook. *adj.* curved, hooked. *n.(gram.)* parenthesis (usually used in the plural, parentheses).
makotu *v.i.* to be bent (over), to be hunchbacked.
makulu *n.* cane, walking stick.
makur *adj.* curved, twisted, bent, hunched, crooked. *adj.(fig.)* bad, perverted, false, wrong. *n.* error, mistake, fault, imperfection. *n.* evil, harm, harmful actions, bad actions. *adv.* badly, incorrectly, wrongly.
makurbide *n.* sinful path, opportunity for sin.
makurdura *n.* twisting, bending, curving.
makur egin *v.t.* to be wrong, to make a mistake.
makurgarri *adj.* bendable, twistable,

curvable.

makurgune n. curve, twist, bend.

makurgunetsu adj. twisting, bending, curving, curved, twisted.

makurka adv. staggering, weaving, zig-zag fashion. adv. unjustly, unfairly.

makurkatu v.t. to twist, to bend, to curve.

makurkeria n. evil, injustice, bad action, perversity. n. dissension, quarrel.

makurketa n. bending, twisting, curving.

makurki adv. curvily, twistingly, in a bent fashion. adv. badly, evilly, perversely.

makurraldi n. decline, decadence; discouragement. n. setback, mishap, inconvenience, hard time.

makurrarazi v.t. to make (someone) bend over. v.t. to pervert, to corrupt, to make (someone) do evil.

makurrarazle adj./n. corrupting, perverting; corruptor, perverter, one who sways another from the right path.

makurtasun n. quality of being curved, twisted, bent or hunched over; curviness, twistedness. n. tendency to be evil, inclination to do evil. n. injustice.

makurtezin adj. unbending, unbendable, unswaying, unswayable.

makurtu v.i./v.t. to bend, to tilt, to incline. v.i. to tend to. v.i. to make a mistake, to be wrong. v.i./v.t. to submit, to surrender, to capitulate.

makurtzaile adj. bending, curving.

malakita n. malachite.

malardatz n. kind of spinning wheel.

malaria n.(med.) malaria.

malda n. slope.

maldabehera n. downhill slope, incline.

maldagora n. uphill slope, incline.

maldagune n. slope, grade.

maldatsu adj. steep, sloping.

maldatu v.i./v.t. to take refuge. v.t. to protect, to shelter.

maldizio n. curse.

malerus adj. unhappy, unfortunate.

malerusia n. misfortune, unhappiness.

maleruski adv. unhappily, unfortunately.

maleta n. suitcase.

maletari n. porter.

maletatxo n.(dim.) small suitcase.

maletatzar n.(augm.) big suitcase.

maletegi n. baggage check, baggage counter, luggage counter, luggage compartment.

malgor adj. swollen.

malgortu v.i. to swell, to be swollen.

malgu adj. flexible, springy, elastic, expandable; soft. adj.(fig.) docile, manageable.

malgudura n. flexibility, elasticity, softness.

malguezin adj. inflexible, nonelastic.

malgugailu n.(mech.) spring, elastic or expandable object.

malgugaitz adj. inflexible.

malgugarri adj. flexible, bendable, foldable, malleable.

malguki adv. flexibly. adj. softly.

malgukor adj. flexible, bendable, malleable.

malgutasun n. flexibility, malleability; softness.

malgutu v.i./v.t. to be flexible, to become flexible. v.i.(fig.) to become meek, to become docile.

malizia n. evil, perversity.

malkar adj. rough, rugged, craggy (terrain). n. steep rough slope.

malkargune n. pothole, depression or hole in the ground or terrain.

malkarki adv. roughly, ruggedly, craggily, harshly.

malkartegi n. rough terrain, rugged place.

malkartsu adj. rough, rugged, craggy, full of potholes, uneven, irregular.

malko n. tear.

malkor n. precipice, cliff. adj. sterile.

malkortegi n. precipice, cliff, chasm, ravine.

malkortsu adj. rocky, craggy, rough.

malkortu v.i. to fall off a cliff, to fall down a ravine.

malmutz adj. fat, obese. adj. shrewd, tricky.

malmuzkatu v.t. to cheat, to trick.

malmuzkeria n. trick, shrewdness, trickery.

malmuzki adv. shrewdly, fraudulently, deceitfully, cunningly.

malo n. fright, scare.

maloka n. dried rotten tree bark.

malokatu v.i. to dry up, to dry out, to rot (trees).

maltzur adj. mischievous, shrewd.

maltzurkeria n. trickiness, trickery, mischief, fraud, deceit.

maltzurkeriazko adj. malicious, tricky, deceitful.

maltzurki adv. maliciously, trickily, shrewdly, deceitfully.

maltzurtasun n. maliciousness, deceit, trickery.

maltzurtu v.i. to become mischievous, to become malicious.

malura n. misfortune, bad luck, adversity. n. rottenness.

maluskatu v.t. to chew. v.t. to squeeze, to crush, to wring.

maluskatzaile n. chewer.

malusketa n. chewing. n. squeezing, wringing.

maluta n. corn husk. n. flake.

mama n. juice recently extracted from grapes.

mamala *adj.(colloq.)* idiot, stupid (used with women).

mamarro *n.* caterpillar, insect, bug. *n.(fam.)* bogey man. *n.(fig.)* lazy person.

mami *n.* crumb. *n.(anat.)* marrow. *n.(fig.)* essence, point, meaning. *n.* milk curd. *adj.* dear.

mamidun *adj.* meaty, substantial, well-bodied, full-bodied.

mamiezin *adj.* unclottable, unthickenable.

mamigarri *adj.* clottable, coagulable, thickenable.

mamijario *adj.* fat, chunky, stout, portly.

mamiki *adv.* intimately, dearly, with all one's heart.

mamitasun *n.* fleshiness, meatiness. *n.(fig.)* intimacy.

mamitsu *adj.* fleshy, meaty. *adj.* being soft inside, soft (usually said of bread). *adj.(fig.)* substantial, meaty.

mamitu *v.i.* to thicken, to coagulate.

mamu *n.* ghost, bogey man (children's language).

mamuka *n.* peekaboo, children's game in which the face is covered and uncovered to mildly frighten someone.

mamukeria *n.* ghostly action; monstrosity.

mamurtu *v.t.* to chew, to masticate, to ruminate.

mamurtzaile *n./adj.* chewer.

mamutu *v.i.* to put on a mask, to put on a costume.

mamutz *n.* insect, worm. *adj.* fat, huge.

mamutzar *n.(augm.)* monster, phantasm, ghost.

managaitz *adj.* disobedient, unmanageable, insubordinate.

managaiztasun *n.* insubordination, disobedience.

managaiztu *v.i.* to be insubordinate, to be disobedient.

manakor *adj.* docile, obedient.

manamendu *n.* demand, order.

manatu *v.t.* to command, to order.

manatzaile *n.* commander, giver of orders.

manda- Used in compound words. Derived from *mando*, mule.

mandabelar *n.(bot.)* knapweed, tough wiry grass.

mandabide *n.* mule path, mule road.

mandaguraizak *n.(pl.)* clippers, large scissors for clipping mules.

mandagurdi *n.* large mule cart.

mandakeria *n.* bestiality, mule-like behavior. *n.(fig.)* stupid action, foolishness.

mandaketa *n.* herd of mules. *n.* search for mules. *n.* brutishness.

mandaketari *n.* muleteer, mule driver.

mandako *n.(dim.)* young or little mule.

mandamozle *n.* gypsy.

mandamutil *n.* young muleteer.

mandar *n.(zool.)* male mule.

mandarina *n.(bot.)* mandarin orange.

mandarinondo *n.(bot.)* mandarin orange tree.

mandarran *n.* large mule bell.

mandartazi *n.* clippers, scissors for grooming mules.

mandasaki *n.* large baskets carried by mules.

mandaska *n.* mule manger.

mandatalde *n.* herd of mules.

mandatari *n.* messenger, emissary.

mandataritza *n.* delegation, commission.

mandategi *n.* mule stable.

mandatresna *n.* mule tack.

mandatu *n.* errand, job, task, commission. *v.i.(fig.)* to become a brute.

mandatu egin *v.t.* to propose marriage.

mandatugile *n.* messenger, runner of errands.

mandatzar *n.(augm.)* large mule.

mandazain *n.* muleteer.

mandazaingo *n.* job of the muleteer.

mandazaintza *n.* job of the muleteer.

mandeme *n.(zool.)* female mule.

mandeuli *n.(zool.)* horse fly, mule fly.

mandio *n.* granary, barn loft, grain attic.

mandioka *n.(bot.)* manioc, bitter cassava.

mando *n.(zool.)* mule. *adj.(colloq.)* large, bulky.

mandotar *adj.* mulish, mule, mule-like.

mandotu *v.i.* to become brutish, to become insensitive.

mandoxka *n.(dim.)* little mule.

maneaketa *n.* trick, intrigue, device. *n.* dressing food, spicing food.

maneatu *v.i.* to prepare, to get ready. *v.t.* to dress (food), to fix (food). *v.t.* to prepare (the earth), to work (the soil), to plow.

maneatzaile *n.* operator, doer, handler; political intriguer. *n.* cook, preparer of food.

mangera *n.* water spout (caused by a tornado), typhoon. *n.* water hose.

mangerdi *n.* short sleeve, half a sleeve.

mango *n.(bot.)* mango (tropical fruit).

mangolino *n.(zool.)* sea snail.

mangondo *n.(bot.)* mango tree.

mangu *adj.* numb.

mangutasun *n.* numbness.

mangutu *v.i.* to go numb, to become numb, to numb.

manifestaldi *n.* demonstration, protest march.

manifestapen *n.* demonstration, protest march.

manifestari *n.* demonstrator, protester.

manifestazio *n.* demonstration, protest

march.

manikeismo *n.* Manicheanism.

manikeo *n.* Manichean.

maniki *n.* mannequin.

mankatu *v.t./v.i.* to bump, to bump into, to give or receive a blow.

mantal(a) *n.* apron.

mantaltxo *n.(dim.)* small apron.

mantar *n.* blouse, woman's shirt. *n.* laundry. *n.* medicinal plaster. *n.* filth, grime, dirt (especially on clothing).

mantartsu *adj.* filthy, dirty, greasy (clothing).

mantartu *v.t.* to plaster, to apply a medicinal plaster. *v.i.* to be covered with filth. *v.i.* to deteriorate.

mantendu *v.t.* to feed, to nourish. *v.t./v.i.* to maintain, to keep, to remain.

mantenketa *n.* conservation, maintenance.

mantentzaile *n.* feeder, nourisher; maintainer.

mantso *adj.* calm, meek, tame.

mantsogarri *adj.* placating, calming; calmable, quietable.

mantsoketa *n.* calming, placating, pacification, taming.

mantsoki *adv.* meekly, tamely, calmly.

mantsotasun *n.* meekness, tameness, calmness.

mantsotu *v.t./v.i.* to tame, to calm down, to quiet (usually animals).

mantxu *adj.* amputated, missing, lacking.

manu *n.* decree, commandment, order; rule, precept, prescription.

manugaitz *adj.* rebellious, disobedient.

manugarri *adj.* orderable, commandable.

manuko *adj.* submissive, subject to, obedient.

manukor *adj.* obedient, submissive, docile.

manukortasun *n.* obedience, submissiveness, docility.

manukortu *v.t.* to dominate, to make (someone) obey.

manupe *n.* domination; submission, subjection.

manupeko *adj.* subject to, submissive. *n.* subject, vassal.

manupekotasun *n.* submission, subjection, servitude.

mapa *n.(geog.)* map.

mapagile *n.* cartographer, map maker.

mapagintza *n.* cartography, map making.

mapamundi *n.(geog.)* world map, world globe.

mapaneurketa *n.* cartometry, map measuring.

mara-mara *adv.* softly, silently, copiously; onomatopoeic word describing silent but continuous movement.

marasma *n.* spider.

marasmasare *n.* spider web, cobweb.

maratila *n.* catch, latch (to fasten doors).

maratz *adj.* diligent, hardworking.

mardo *adj.* luxuriant, leafy, frondose, vigorous.

mardotasun *n.* luxuriousness, luxuriance, robustness, healthiness, strength (usually used with trees). *n.* softness.

mardotu *v.i.* to be luxuriant, to be robust (usually used with trees).

mardul *adj.* robust, healthy, strong.

marduldu *v.i./v.t.* to be strong, to be robust, to be healthy.

mardulki *adj.* exuberantly, vigorously, luxuriantly (used with plants).

mardultasun *n.* luxuriance, vigor, robustness.

mareatu *v.i.* to faint, to pass out. *v.i.* to get sick (seasick or car sick).

marebehera *n.* low tide, ebb tide.

maregora *n.* high tide.

marfil *n.* ivory.

marfilezko *adj.* ivory, made of ivory.

margarina *n.* margarine.

margo *n.* color.

margoaldi *n.* coat (of paint).

margoaskodun *adj.* multicolor, many colored.

margobakar *adj.* unicolor, single colored.

margodun *adj.* colored.

margogabe *adj.* colorless.

margoki *n.* painting, picture.

margola *n.* dye. *n.* paint factory.

margolari *n.* painter.

margotu *v.t.* to paint, to color; to dye, to tint.

margozko *adj.* colored.

margoztatu *v.t.* to paint, to color.

margul *adj.* faded, discolored, colorless.

marguldu *v.i.* to fade.

marguldura *n.* fading, discoloration.

maribidetako *n.* prostitute.

marigaizto *n.* bad woman.

marigizon *n.* masculine woman.

marigorringo *n.(zool.)* ladybug (*Coccinella septempunctata*).

marihuana *n.(bot.)* marihuana.

marikoi *adj.* effeminate (man), homosexual.

marimaistra *n.* know-it-all woman.

marimatraka *n.* loud or boisterous woman.

marimutil *n.* tomboy.

marina *n.* navy (branch of military service).

marinel *n.* fisherman; mariner.

marineleria *n.* group of fishermen, fishermen (as a group).

marinelgo *n.* profession or job of the fisherman or mariner.

marineltalde *n.* group of fishermen or mariners.

marineltxo *n.(dim.)* young errand boy

on a boat, cabin boy.

marineltza n. job or profession of mariners or fishermen.

marioneta n. marionette, puppet with strings.

maripulis n. vest.

maripurtzil n. prostitute. adj. dirty, filthy (woman).

mariskal n.(mil.) marshal, field marshal.

mariskalgo n. position of a field marshal.

marisorgin n.(zool.) praying mantis.

maritsusi n. ugly woman.

maritxu adj.(colloq.) effeminate (man), homosexual.

maritxukeria n.(colloq.) effeminacy, homosexuality.

maritxutu v.i. to be effeminate, to be homosexual.

marizikin n. dirty woman, pig.

marka n. mark, trademark, sign, signal. n. record.

markagailu n. apparatus for marking (something), scoreboard, marquee.

markaketa n. marking, painting lines (traffic, etc.).

markatu v.t. to signal, to mark.

markatzaile n. signaller, marker.

markes n. marquis.

markesa n. wife of the marquis, marquise.

markeserri n. territory ruled by a marquis.

markesgo n. marquisate (title).

markets adj. imperfect, defective, malformed.

marko n.(econ.) German mark. n. frame, framework.

marmar n. murmur, whisper. n. mewing or meowing of a cat. n. growling, grumbling.

marmara n. whisper, murmur, muttering.

marmaraka adv. in a whisper, murmuring.

marmaraldi n. whispering, muttering.

marmar ari v.i. to criticize.

marmarati adj. complaining, grumbling.

marmar egin v.t. to whisper, to murmur. v.t. to growl, to grumble.

marmario n. whispering, murmuring, rumor.

marmarka adv. whispering, murmuring, groaning, grumbling.

marmarra n. rumor, murmur, whisper.

marmarraldi n. whispering, murmuring.

marmarti adj. gossipy, murmuring.

marmitako n. typical Basque meal of tuna, potatoes, tomatoes, etc.

marmoka n.(zool.) jelly fish.

marmol n. marble.

marmolari n. sculptor, one who works with marble.

marmoldegi n. marble quarry.

marmoleria n. quantity of marble.

marmolezko adj. made of marble.

marmolgin n. sculptor who works with marble.

marmolgintza n. working with marble.

marra n. line, mark, ray, stripe. n. part (in one's hair).

marradura n. striping, lining.

marraga n. coarse woolen cloth.

marragailu n. drawing pen, ruling pen.

marragarri adj. linable, stripable.

marraka n. bleat of a goat, meow of a cat, lowing of a cow, etc.

marrakari adj. tearful, teary, cry-baby.

marrakatu v.t. to draw lines, to line.

marraketa n. drawing lines, lining.

marralari n. tracer, designer, liner.

marranta n. congestion, chest congestion. adj. congested, having a cold.

marrantatu v.i. to catch cold, to be congested.

marrao n. meow, mew, yowl.

marrao egin v.t. to meow, to yowl.

marraolari adj. meowing, yowling.

marraska n. cry, groan, grunt.

marraska egin v.t. to grunt, to moo, to bray. v.t. to scratch, to gnaw.

marraskari adj. gnawing, scratching.

marraskatu v.t. to gnaw, to grate one's teeth. v.t. to bleat (goats), to shout, to cry (people).

marratu v.t. to draw lines, to line, to mark.

marratxo n.(gram.) hyphen.

marratzaile n. draftsman, tracer.

marraxo n.(zool.) shark. **Marraxo zuri.** White shark.

marrazain n. judge (in jai alai), referee.

marrazki n. drawing, design.

marrazkigile n. drawer, designer.

marrazkilari n. drawer, designer.

marraztu v.t. to draw, to draft.

marro n. trick, deception, wrong. n.(zool.) ram.

marro egin v.t. to play a trick, to trick, to deceive.

marroi n. brown.

marrokeria n. wrong, deception, fallacy.

marru n. mooring, lowing; meowing; mewing; roar of the ocean or sea.

marrubi n.(bot.) strawberry. n. mooing, lowing.

marrubidi n. strawberry patch.

marruma n. lowing, mooing, roar, sound of animals.

marrumaka adv. lowing, mooing, roaring.

marrumalari adj. mooing, braying, grunting.

marruskadura n. friction, rubbing.

marruskaketa n. filing (metal). n. restraining, holding onto.

marruskaldi n. filing (metal). n. restraining, holding onto.

marruskari adj. mushy, pawing, given to excessive fondling.

marruskatu v.t. to file, to scrape. v.t.

to paw, to fondle excessively.
marruskatzaile n. filer, scraper. adj. fondling, pawing.
marrusketa n. filing, scraping (with a carpenter's plane). n. fondling, pawing.
marrusketatu v.t. to file, to scrape with a carpenter's plane.
marti n. March.
martinarrantzale n.(zool.) kingfisher.
martiri n. martyr.
martiri egin v.t. to martyr, to martyrize.
martiriliburu n. martyrology, historical account of the lives of religious martyrs.
martiritza n. martyrdom.
Martitz n. Mars (mythological god). n.(astron.) Mars (planet).
martitzen n. Tuesday.
martiztar adj./n. Martian.
martxoa n. March.
marxismo n. Marxism.
marxista n./adj. Marxist.
masaiari n. masseur, masseuse.
masaiatu v.t. to give a massage.
masaila n.(anat.) cheek, jaw.
masailako n. blow to the jaw.
masailalbo n.(anat.) cheekbone.
masaileko n. blow to the jaw. adj. maxillary.
masailekotu v.t. to box, to hit in the face.
masailezur n.(anat.) mandible, jawbone.
masailezurreko adj. maxillary, mandibular, pertaining to the jawbone.
maskal adj. weak, poor.
maskar adj. weak, feeble, frail.
maskara n. mask.
maskarada n. masquerade.
maskaradun adj. masked.
maskaratu v.t./v.i. to mask, to be masked.
maskaratzaile adj./n. concealing, masking; concealer; wearer of a mask.
maskartu v.i. to weaken, to grow feeble or frail.
maskor n. shell, sea shell.
maskulino adj. masculine.
maskur n. callus.
maskurdura n. callosity, callousness.
maskuri n.(anat.) bladder.
maskurlari n. pedicurist, chiropodist.
maskurtsu adj. calloused.
maskurtu v.i. to get hard, to grow callouses.
masoi n. Mason, Freemason.
masoibiltzar n. meeting of Freemasons.
maspil(a) n.(bot.) azarole.
maspilale n. grain of the azarole.
maspildu v.t./v.i. to dent, to chip; to bruise; to wilt. v.t.(lit.) to fondle excessively, to paw.
maspildura n. denting, chipping;

bruising; wilting.
maspilondo n.(bot.) hawthorn.
masta n.(naut.) mast.
mastekatu v.t. to chew.
mastika n. putty, mastic.
mastikaketa n. puttying windows, caulking windows with putty.
mastikatu v.t. to putty, to caulk with putty.
masusta n.(bot.) blackberry.
masustadi n. blackberry bush.
masustegi n. place of blackberries.
masustondo n.(bot.) blackberry bush.
mataza n. skein of thread, hank, tangle.
matazari n. thread of the skein.
matazatu v.t. to make skeins (of thread). v.t.(fig.) to mess up, to confuse, to quarrel.
matela n. jaw.
matelako n. blow to the jaw.
mateleko adj. maxillary, pertaining to the jaw.
matelezur n. mandible, jawbone.
matematika n. mathematics.
matematikari n. mathematician.
matematiko adj. mathematic.
matematikoki adv. mathematically.
materia n. pus.
materiale n. material.
materialeztatu v.t./v.i. to materialize.
materialismo n. materialism.
materialista adj. materialist.
materialitate n. materiality.
materialki adv. materially.
materialkuntza n. materialization.
materiatsu adj. full of pus.
materiatu v.i. to fill with pus.
materigabe adj. immaterial.
materigabetasun n. immateriality.
matraila n. (anat.) check, jaw.
matraka n. quarrel, dispute, fight. n. rattle, noise maker (child's toy).
matrakalari n. altercator, fighter, quarreler.
matrikula n. registration, matriculation, enrollment. n. license plate.
matrikulatu v.t./v.i. to matriculate, to register, to enroll.
matxinada n. conspiracy, rebellion, revolt, war.
matxinatu v.i. to revolt, to rebel, to be in a conspiracy.
matxino adj. rebellious, conspiratorial.
matxinsalto n.(zool.) grasshopper.
matxura n. mechanical breakdown.
matxuratu v.i. to break down (mechanically).
mau egin v.t. to bite.
maugurio n.(zool.) tiny sea snail.
mauka-mauka adv. gluttonously, like a pig.
mazal adj. good, decent, of noble character.
mazapan n. marzipan, almond paste.
mazela n. side of the mountain.
mazi n. large quantity of bait.

mazi egin *v.t.* to cast bait, to throw bait.

mazitu *v.t.* to throw bait.

mazopa *n.(zool.)* porpoise.

mazpildu *v.t.* to slit chestnuts (in preparation for roasting).

me *n.* baa, onomatopoeic sound of sheep.

mea *n.* mine. *n.* mineral.

meabide *n.* mine tunnel, shaft, corridor of a mine.

meagintza *n.* mining.

meaiturri *n.* mineral spring or fountain.

meategi *n.* mine.

meatoki *n.* mine, mineral deposit.

meatzari *n.* miner, mine worker.

meazulo *n.* mine shaft, mine cavity.

medikaezin *adj.* incurable, untreatable.

medikagaitz *adj.* difficult to treat.

medikamendu *n.* medication.

medikapen *n.* medical treatment.

mediku *n.* doctor, physician.

medikuntza *n.* medicine, medical science.

medio *prep.* by means of, through; because.

meditazio *n.* meditation.

meha- Used in compound words. Derived from *mehe*, thin.

mehagune *n.* narrow section, narrow part (of an object or place).

mehar *adj.* narrow, tight. *adj.* thin, slender.

mehardura *n.* narrowing, narrowness, thinness. *n.* thinning, slimming down.

mehargune *n.* strait; narrow passage.

meharketa *n.* thinness.

meharreri *n.* thinness, narrowness. *n.* dysentery (in animals).

mehartasun *n.* narrowness, thinness.

mehartu *v.i./v.t.* to be narrow, to narrow. *v.i.* to thin, to be thin, to slim down.

mehatxagarri *adj.* menacing.

mehatxakor *adj.* menacing, threatening.

mehatxatu *v.t.* to menace, to threaten.

mehatxatzaile *adj.* menacing, threatening.

mehatxu *n.* menace, threat.

mehatxuka *adv.* menacingly, threateningly.

mehatxuz *adv.* menacingly, threateningly.

mehatxuzko *adj.* menacing, threatening.

mehe *adj.* thin (objects or liquids), light, attenuated, weak.

meheki *adv.* thinly, finely, weakly.

mehekor *adj.* easily thinned, capable of thinning easily.

mehetasun *n.* thinness, slenderness. *n.* subtlety, tenuousness.

mehetu *v.t.* to thin down, to slim down.

mekanika *n.* mechanic.

mekanikaketa *n.* mechanization.

mekanikakuntza *n.* mechanization.

mekanikamutil *n.* apprentice mechanic, mechanic's helper.

mekanikari *n.* mechanic.

mekanikapen *n.* mechanization.

mekanikategi *n.* parts house, shop that sells mechanical parts.

mekanikatu *v.t.* to mechanize.

mekaniko *adj.* mechanical. *n.* mechanic.

mekanikoki *adv.* mechanically.

mekanismo *n.* mechanism.

mekanografari *n.* typist.

mekanografia *n.* typing, typewriting.

mekanografiatu *v.t.* to type.

melodi(a) *n.* melody.

meloditsu *adj.* melodic, tuneful.

melodioski *adv.* melodically, tunefully.

meloi *n.(bot.)* melon.

meloisaltzaile *n.* melon seller.

meloitxo *n.(dim.)* small melon.

memela *adj.(colloq.)* foolish, scatterbrained, hairbrained (women).

memelo *adj.(colloq.)* foolish, stupid, scatterbrained, hairbrained (men).

memelokeria *n.* foolishness.

memelotu *v.i.* to become silly, to become foolish.

memento *n.* moment.

mementoan *adv.* immediately, in a moment, instantaneously.

mementoko *adj.* momentary, fleeting, provisional.

men *n.* power, capacity. *adj.* docile, obedient.

-men *(gram.)* Used in compound words. Suffix meaning faculty, ability, action. **Aipamen.** Mention.

menaz *adv.* seriously, really.

menda *n.(bot.)* mint.

mende *n.* power, authority, dominion. *n.* century.

mendebal *n.* gusty west wind which comes from the northwest in the Basque Country. *n.* west.

mendebalaize *n.* west wind.

mendebaldar *adj.* western, west. *n.* westerner.

mendebalde *n.* west, western area.

mendebaldu *v.i.* to westernize.

mendebaleko *adj.* western, of the west.

mende eduki *v.t.* to have under one's power, to have authority over, to be in charge of.

mende egon *v.i.* to depend on, to be dependent on.

mendeetako *adj.* secular, worldly.

mendekakor *adj.* vindictive, vengeful.

mendekaldi *n.* revenge, act of vengeance.

mendekari *n.* avenger, one who takes revenge.

mendekati *adj.* vengeful, vindictive.

mendekatu *v.i./v.t.* to avenge (oneself), to take revenge.

mendekatzaile *n.* avenger. *adj.* avenging.

mendekide *n.* contemporary of the same century.

mendekidetasun *n.* contemporaneity.

mendeko *adj.* submissive, subject to, subjected. *n.* subject, employee, dependent.

mendeko izan *v.i.* to depend on, to be dependent on.

mendekoste *n.* Pentecost.

mendekotasun *n.* subordination, inferiority, dependence.

mendeku *n.* revenge, vengeance.

mendel *n.* lapel, edge (of a shirt, cloth, etc.).

mendemuga *n.* centennial, centenary, hundredth anniversary.

menderaezin *adj.* invincible, unconquerable, difficult to dominate.

menderagaitz *adj.* difficult to dominate, difficult to conquer, difficult to subject.

menderagarri *adj.* conquerable, subject to domination, controllable.

menderaketa *n.* taking by storm, conquering, subjugation, domination.

menderapen *n.* domination, subjugation, overcoming.

menderatu *v.t.* to overcome, to conquer, to dominate, to subjugate, to subdue.

menderatzaile *n.* conqueror, dominator, vanquisher. *adj.* conquering, dominating.

mendetasun *n.* authority, power. *n.* docility, submissiveness, subordination, dependence.

mendi *n.* mountain.

mendialde *n.* mountain region. *n.* side of the mountain, incline.

mendigain *n.* summit, top of the mountain.

mendigoizale *n.* mountaineer, alpinist, mountain climber.

mendikate *n.* mountain range, chain of mountains, sierra.

mendiketa *n.* mountain range, chain of mountains, sierra.

mendiko *adj.* mountain, pertaining to the mountains. *adj.(fig.)* rustic, wild.

mendikume *n.(dim.)* hill.

mendilepo *n.* slope of the mountain.

mendilerro *n.* sierra, mountain range, chain of mountains.

mendimultzo *n.* mountain range, sierra.

mendino *n.(dim.)* small mountain.

mendioste *n.* place beyond the mountain.

mendipe *n.* place at the foot of the mountain.

mendirakoi *adj.* backwoodsy, fond of the mountains.

mendiratu *v.i.* to go to the mountain. *v.t.* to take to the mountain.

mendiska *n.(dim.)* little mountain, hill.

mendiskatsu *adj.* mountainous.

menditar *n.* mountaineer, highlander, mountain dweller.

menditartu *v.i.* to become a mountain dweller, to accustom oneself to mountain ways.

menditontor *n.* summit, top of the mountain peak.

menditsu *adj.* mountainous.

menditsutasun *n.* hilliness.

menditxo *n.(dim.)* little mountain.

menditza *n.* mountain range, chain of mountains.

mendiur *n.* water from the mountains.

mendiuso *n.(zool.)* ringdove, woodpigeon.

mendizain *n.* ranger, forest ranger.

mendizaingo *n.* ranger's job.

mendizale *adj./n.* fond of the mountains; mountaineer, mountain climber.

mendizaletasun *n.* fondness for the mountains, mountaineering.

mendizerra *n.* sierra, chain of mountains, mountain range.

mendizintzur *n.* mountain pass.

mendizorrotz *n.* peaked mountain.

mendizulo *n.* cave, grotto.

mendoitz *n.* side slope, incline.

mendre *adj.* weak.

mendretasun *n.* weakness, thinness, lack of strength.

mendretu *v.i.* to grow thin or emaciated, to weaken, to become weak.

mendrezka *n.* lower forepart of a tuna.

mendu *n.* graft. *v.t.* to graft, to join. *n.* character, personality, temperament.

-mendu *(gram.)* Suffix which means act. **Kontsolamendu.** Consolation.

men egin *v.t.* to obey.

meneko *adj.* obedient, submissive. *n.* subordinate. *adj.* dependent, subject to.

menekotasun *n.* submission, subordination, obedience.

menekotu *v.i.* to be subordinate (to). *v.t.* to dominate, to force (someone) to submit.

menerabide *n.* means of domination.

meneraezin *adj.* indomitable, unconquerable.

meneragarri *adj.* submissive.

menerakor *adj.* subordinate, submissive.

menerapen *n.* domination, subordination.

meneratu *v.t.* to dominate, to overcome, to subjugate, to conquer. *v.i.* to submit to, to obey.

meneratzaile *n.* dominator, conqueror. *adj.* dominant, conquering.

menestra *n.* stew (of meat and vegetables).

mengel *adj.* weak, inconsistent, feeble, frail. *adj.* fleeting, ephemeral.

mengeldu *v.i.* to weaken, to be inconsistent, to be feeble, to be frail.

mengeltasun *n.* feebleness.

mengo *n.* necessity, need.
mengoatu *v.t.* to oblige, to force. *v.i.* to decrease.
menpe *n.* subordination, domination, dependence.
menpean egon *v.i.* to be subordinate to, to be under (someone's) control or domination.
menpegabe *adj.* emancipated, undominated, uncontrolled.
menpeko *adj.* subordinate to, dependent on, dominated by, controlled by. *n.* subordinate, domestic servant.
menpeko izan *v.i.* to be dependent on, to be subordinate to, to be dominated by.
menpekotasun *n.* dependence, subordination, domination; obedience.
menpekotu *v.i.* to be subordinate to, to obey, to submit to. *v.t.* to dominate, to subordinate.
menpekotza *n.* servitude, dependence.
menperaezin *adj.* indomitabe, unconquerable, not submissive.
menperagaitz *adj.* indomitable, unconquerable, difficult to dominate, not submissive.
menperagarri *adj.* conquerable, dominatable, controllable.
menperaketa *n.* domination, servitude, subjection, vassalage.
menperakoi *adj.* submissive, docile, easily controlled.
menperatu *v.t.* to conquer, to make (someone) submit, to subject, to subjugate, to overcome. *v.t.(fig.)* to master (material), to learn perfectly.
menperatzaile *n.* conqueror, subjugator, dominator, vanquisher. *adj.* conquering, dominating.
menpetasun *n.* dependence, servitude, subordination, submissiveness.
menta *n.* sale. *n.* fashion.
mentadun *adj.* fashionable, in vogue.
mentasun *n.* docility, obedience.
mentatsu *adj.* fashionable, in vogue.
mentura *n.* luck, chance, fortune, opportunity, possibility.
menturatu *v.i.* to risk.
menturaz *adv.* perhaps, maybe, by chance.
merezi *v.t.* to deserve.
merezigabe(ko) *adj.* undeserving, unworthy.
merezigarri *adj.* deserving, worthy, meritorious.
merezi izan *v.t.* to deserve, to be worthwhile, to be worth (doing).
mereziki *adv.* deservedly, worthily.
merezimendu *n.* merit, value, quality.
merezitako *adj.* merited, deserved.
merezi ukan *v.t.* to deserve, to have merit, to be worthwhile, to be worth (doing).

merienda *n.* midafternoon snack.
meriendatoki *n.* snack bar, place for having a snack.
meritu *n.* value, merit, worth.
meritudun *adj.* meritorious, worthy, deserving.
merkagai *n.* merchandise, goods.
merkagaitz *adj.* unnegotiable, uncommercial.
merkagarri *adj.* negotiable, commercial.
merkaldi *n.(econ.)* devaluation, depreciation.
merkantzia *n.* merchandise, goods.
merkantzigintza *n.* production of merchandise.
merkatal *adj.* commercial, mercantile, business.
merkatalbide *n.* commercial route.
merkataldegi *n.* business center, commercial center.
merkataldu *v.t.* to trade, to traffic, to do business.
merkataletxe *n.* firm, house of business, company.
merkatalgai *n.* piece of merchandise, article, commodity.
merkatalgarri *adj.* marketable.
merkatalgo *n.* business profession. *n.* commerce, business.
merkatalki *adv.* commercially.
merkatari *n.* businessman, merchant, dealer, tradesman.
merkataritza *n.* commerce. *n.* business profession.
merkatu *n.* market, supermarket.
merkatuegun *n.* market day.
merkatulari *adj.* fond of markets.
merkaturatu *v.t./v.i.* to commercialize; to become commercialized.
merkatuzale *adj.* fond of markets.
merke *adj.* cheap, inexpensive.
merkeago *adj.(comp.)* cheaper, more inexpensive.
merkeagotu *v.t.* to lower the price.
merkealdi *n.* sale, liquidation.
merkedura *n.* cheapness, inexpensiveness.
merkeegi *adv.* too cheaply.
merkekeriak *n.(pl.)* trinkets, baubles, notions.
merkeketa *n.* lowering of prices, slashing prices.
merketasun *n.* cheapness, inexpensiveness.
merketu *v.i./v.t.* to lower the price, to cut the price.
merkurio *n.(astron.)* Mercury. *n.(chem.)* mercury.
merlenka *n.(zool.)* variety of hake.
mermelada *n.* marmalade, jam.
mertxika *n.(bot.)* variety of peach.
mertxikondo *n.(bot.)* variety of peach tree.
mertzenari *n.* mercenary.
mertzeria *n.* notions store, dry-goods

store, fabric shop.
meru n.(zool.) grouper, sea bass.
mesede n. favor, advantage, good.
mesede egin v.t. to do a favor. v.t. to do (something) good, to be good for.
mesedegarri adj. beneficial.
mesedetu v.t. to do (someone) a favor, to help.
mesedez int. please.
mesfidakor adj. distrustful, not trusting.
mesfidantza n. distrust, suspicion.
mesfidatu v.i. to distrust, to not trust.
mesprezagarri adj. disparageable, disdainful.
mesprezakor adj. disdainful, disrespectful, disparaging.
mesprezatu v.t. to disparage, to disdain, to scorn, to hold in contempt.
mesprezatzaile n. disparager, one who shows disdain or disrespect, despiser, scorner.
mesprezu n. disdain, disrespect, contempt, scorn.
mesprezuz adv. disdainfully, disrespectfully.
mesprezuzko adj. disdainful, disrespectful.
meta n. pile, heap.
-meta Used in compound words to denote pile, heap. **Garimeta.** Pile of wheat.
metadura n. piling up, putting in a pile.
metafisika n. metaphysics.
metafisikari n. metaphysicist.
metafisikaz adv. metaphysically.
metafisiko adj. metaphysical.
metafora n. metaphor.
metaforaz adv. metaphorically.
metaforazko adj. metaphoric.
metaforizatu v.t. to use metaphors.
metaga n. support pole for a haystack.
metagai adj. accumulatable, pilable, heapable.
metagarri adj. cumulable, pilable, heapable.
metaka adv. by piles, in heaps.
metakatu v.t. to pile up, to heap, to put into piles.
metaketa n. piling up, heaping, accumulation.
metakor adj. cumulative.
metal- Used in compound words to denote metal, mineral.
metalantegi n. metal working factory.
metalari n. metal worker.
Metal Aro n. Metal Age.
metaldu v.t./v.i. to convert into metal, to be converted into metal.
metaldun adj. metallic, made of metal.
metale n. metal.
metalezko adj. metal, made of metal.
metalgin n. metallurgist.
metalgintza n. metallurgy.
metalketa n. metalization, converting into metal.

metalki n. piece of metal.
metalkuntza n. metalization, converting into metal.
metalondar n. mineral residue.
metalpuska n. piece of metal, metal scrap.
metalur n. mineral water.
metatu v.t. to accumulate, to pile up.
metatxo n.(dim.) small pile.
metatzaile n./adj. piler, one who piles or heaps, accumulator; piling, accumulating.
meteorito n.(astron.) meteorite.
meteoro n.(astron.) meteor.
meteorologari n. meteorologist.
meteorologia n. meteorology.
metileno n.(chem.) methylene.
metodiko adj. methodical.
metodo n. method, system, way.
metodologia n. methodology.
metodoz adv. methodically.
metodozko adj. methodical.
metraila n. shrapnel.
metrailadore n. machine gun.
metrailatu v.t. to machine gun.
metraileta n. submachine gun, tommy gun.
metrailkada n. discharge of grapeshot or shrapnel.
metro n. meter.
metro-neurkera n. metric system.
metxa n. wick.
metxero n. cigarrete lighter.
meza n. mass.
mezaberri n. first mass of a new priest.
mezadiru n. money received by a priest for celebrating a mass, stipend.
mezajantziak n.(pl.) vestments worn by a priest while officiating at the mass.
mezaliburu n. missal.
mezamutil n. acolyte, altar boy.
mezanagusi n. Solemn Mass, usually sung.
mezaotoitz n.(eccl.) collect, prayer of the mass.
mezasari n. money given to the priest for officiating at a special mass, stipend.
mezemale n. celebrant (of the mass).
mezeman v.t. to celebrate the mass.
mezemate n. act of celebrating the mass.
mezentzule n. person attending mass.
mezkita n. mosque.
mezontzi n. chalice.
mezordu n. hour of the mass.
mezu n. message, advice, warning.
mezudun n./adj. emissary, messenger.
mezu egin v.t. to send a message, to warn, to inform.
mezu igorri v.t. to send a message.
mezulari n. emissary, messenger. adj. messenger.
mezularitza n. job or duty of a messenger.

mezutu *v.t.* to send a message.
mezutzaile *adj./n.* messenger, one who gives a message or warning.
mi *n.(mus.)* mi, E (on the musical scale).
miau *n.* meow.
miau egin *v.t.* to meow, to mew.
miauka *adv.* meowing.
miauka ari *v.i.* to meow, to be meowing.
miaukatu *v.t.* to meow.
miaulari *adj.* meowing, mewing.
miazkaldi *n.* licking.
miazkatu *v.t.* to lick.
miazkatzaile *adj./n.* licking; licker.
miazketa *n.* lick.
miaztu *v.t.* to lick.
mielga *n.(zool.)* selachian, cartilagenous phosphorescent fish; dogfish.
miga *n.* young female cow.
migrakuntza *n.* migration.
migrapen *n.* migration.
migrari *n.* emigrant.
migratu *v.i.* to emigrate.
migrazio *n.* migration.
mihi *n.(anat.)* tongue. *n.* clapper (in a bell). *n.* bolt (of a lock).
mihiarrain *n.(zool.)* sole, flounder.
mihiazpiko *n.(anat.)* frenum, underside of the tongue.
mihidun *adj.* having a tongue, tongued. *adj./n.(fig.)* chatterbox.
mihigain *n.* top of the tongue.
mihigaizto *adj.* talkative, gossipy.
mihihari *n.* frenum, underside of the tongue.
mihiluze *adj.* indiscrete, critical, criticizing, gossipy.
mihiluzekeria *n.* indiscretion, gossiping.
mihimen *n.(bot.)* willow, osier willow, wicker.
mihimenezko *adj.* made of wicker.
mihimentsu *adj.* wicker.
mihimentza *n.* land planted with willows.
mihimotz *adj.* babbling, stammering.
mihipeko *adj.* hypoglossal, under the tongue. *n.* frenum, underside of the tongue.
mihipunta *n.* tip of the tongue.
mihise *n.* sheet, cloth.
mihizkatu *v.t.* to lick.
mihizketa *n.* licking, act of licking.
mihizko *adj.* pertaining to the tongue.
mihizorrotz *adj.* sharp-tongued, gossiping, bad-mouthing.
mihiztadura *n.* joining, assembling, coupling, connecting.
mihiztaketa *n.* joining, coupling, connecting, assembling.
mihiztapen *n.* joining, coupling, connecting, assembling.
mihiztatu *v.t.* to engage, to connect, to link, to join. *v.t.* to taste. *v.t.* to put a clapper in a bell.

mihiztatzaile *adj.* joining, connecting. *adj.* licking.
mihura *n.(bot.)* moss.
mihuri *n.* kernel of corn, piece of fruit, nut meat, etc.
mika *n.(zool.)* magpie.
mikatz *adj.* acid, acidic, sour; bitter.
mikaztasun *n.* acidity, sourness.
mikaztsu *adj.* acid, sour, tart.
mikaztu *v.i.* to sour, to turn sour.
mikelete *n.* member of the Basque militia which used to control economic matters, etc.
miko *n.* crumb, breadcrumb. *adv.* little bit; anything, nothing (in negative sentences).
mikrobio *n.* microbe.
mikrobus *n.* small bus.
mikrofilme *n.* microfilm.
mikrofono *n.* microphone.
mikrokosmo *n.* microcosm.
mikroskopo *n.* microscope.
mila *adj./n.* thousand, one thousand.
milagarren *adj.* thousandth.
milaka *adv.* by the thousands, in the thousands, for thousands.
milakada *n.* thousand.
milako *adj.* thousand. *n.* thousand peseta bill.
milaren *adj.* thousandth.
milarri *n.* milliary, stone marking one thousand paces on the road.
milatan *adv.* many times, a thousand times.
miligramu *n.* milligram.
milika *adj.* picky, spoiled. *adv.* tasting. *n.* licking.
milikaldi *n.* licking.
milikaketa *n.* licking.
milikari *adj.* picky, spoiled. *adj.* licking. *adj.* flattering, sycophantic.
milikatu *v.i.* to become spoiled, to become picky. *v.t.* to lick.
milikatuz *adv.* licking, by licking.
milikatzaile *adj.* spoiling, pampering. *adj.* licking.
milikeria *n.* pickiness, spoiledness, impertinence.
miliki *adj.* picky, choosy, meticulous, particular.
mililitro *n.* milliliter.
milimetro *n.* millimeter.
milioi *adj./n.* million.
milioiaskodun *adj.* multimillionaire.
milioidun *adj.* millionaire.
milioigarren *adj.* millionth, one-millionth.
militar *adj./n.* military.
militarburu *n.* military chief, military leader.
militarkeria *n.* militarism, military dictatorship.
militarki *adv.* militarily.
militartu *v.t./v.i.* to militarize, to be militarized.
milizkatu *v.t.* to eat pickily, to taste.
milurte *n.* millenium.

milurteburu *n.* thousandth anniversary, millenium.

milurteko *adj.* millenary, pertaining to a thousand years.

mimen *n. (bot.)* willow, wicker.

mimika *n.* mimic.

min *n.* pain, physical pain. *adj.* intense, deep, intimate; in the midst of. *adj.* bitter, acidic, acid.

-min Used in compound words. Derived from *min*, pain. **Burukomin.** Headache. Used in compound words. Signifies nostalgia, longing, desire. **Aberrimin.** Homesickness (for one's country).

mina *n.* mine, submarine mine, explosive device.

minabiltzaile *n.* mine sweeper.

minaezarle *n.* mine layer.

minaldi *n.* intermittent pain, momentary pain.

minarazi *v.t.* to torment, to torture.

minatu *v.t.* to lay mines, to mine.

minbera *adj.* painful, sore, aching. *adj.* sensitive, sentimental; susceptible. *n.(bot.)* sensitive plant.

minberadura *n.* sensitivity, touchiness, susceptibility.

minberakeria *n.* sentimentalism, maudlinism.

minberakor *adj.* very sensitive, sentimental; susceptible.

minberatasun *n.* sensitiveness, sentimentality, impressionableness; susceptibility.

minberati *adj.* sensitive, susceptible.

minberatsu *adj.* painful, sore, aching. *adj.* sensitive, susceptible.

minberatu *v.i.* to get sore, to become painful. *v.t.* to hurt, to harm, to make (something) hurt. *v.i.* to become sensitive, to grow sensitive.

minbizi *n.(med.)* cancer. (lit.) living pain.

minbizidun *adj.* cancerous.

minbizikontrako *adj.* anticancer, anticancerous.

minbizitu *v.i.* to become cancerous, to get cancer.

minbizizko *adj.* cancerous.

mindegi *n.* greenhouse, hothouse, seedbed, nursery. *n.* seminar, investigation.

mindegizain *n.* tree surgeon, gardener, arborist, nursery owner, caretaker of a greenhouse.

mindegizaingo *n.* job of tree surgeon.

mindu *v.i.* to sour, to get bitter, to go bitter. *v.t.* to offend, to bother, to molest, to annoy. *v.i.* to feel pain, to be hurt.

mindun *adj.* in pain, sore, out of sorts.

mindura *n.* affliction, anguish, bitterness, resentment. *n.* sourness, bitterness.

minduri *n.* weeper, hired mourner.

mindurikari *adj.* whining, complaining.

mindurikatu *v.i.* to mourn, to weep, to grieve.

minduz *adv.* offensively, offending.

min egin *v.t.* to hurt, to cause pain; to harm. *v.t.* to offend.

minemale *n./adj.* torturer, tormentor; torturing, tormenting.

min eman *v.t.* to hurt, to cause (someone) pain. *v.t.* to offend.

mineral *adj.* mineral.

minerale *n.* mineral.

mineralki *n.* piece of mineral.

mineralogia *n.* mineralogy.

minez *adv.* in pain, with pain, painfully.

mingabe *adj.* without pain, not hurt, unhurt, safe and sound.

mingabeki *adv.* without suffering.

mingabe(ko) *adj.* unhurt, without pain, safe and sound.

mingabetasun *n.* lack of pain, painlessness.

mingabezia *n.* lack of pain, painlessness.

mingar *adj.* sour; bitter.

mingarki *adv.* bitterly.

mingarratz *adj.* sour, bitter. *n.(bot.)* sorrel.

mingarri *adj.* painful, offensive, biting, sharp.

mingarriki *adv.* caustically, bitingly.

mingarriro *adv.* caustically, bitingly.

mingarritasun *n.* bitingness, sharpness, sarcasm, mordacity.

mingor *adj.* sour, bitter, acid, tart. *adj.* painful, sore, aching. *n.(zool.)* snipe (*Gallinago Gallinago*).

mingordun *adj.* sore, slightly painful.

mingordura *n.* becoming rancid, souring.

mingorki *n.* snipe meat.

mingorri *n.* strong pain. *n.* measles.

mingortasun *n.* sourness; sourness.

mingortu *v.i.* to grow rancid, to sour.

mingoski *adv.* bitterly.

mingostasun *n.* bitterness; sourness.

mingostu *v.i.* to sour, to become rancid, to get stale.

mingots *adj.* sour, bitter. *adj.(fig.)* bitter.

mingrana *n.(bot.)* pomegranate.

mingranondo *n.(bot.)* pomegranate tree.

min hartu *v.t.* to hurt oneself, to harm, to do (oneself) harm.

miniatura *n.* miniature.

minio *n.(chem.)* minium.

ministergo *n.* ministry.

ministeriarteko *adj.* interministerial.

ministeritza *n.* office or job of a minister (politics), ministry (political or religious).

ministral *adj.* ministerial.

ministrari *n.* minister, chaplain.

ministraritza *n.* ministry (religious or political).

ministro *n.(pol.)* minister (of

agriculture, education, etc.). *n.* minister, chaplain.

ministrotza *n.* office or job of a minister (politics).

min izan *v.t.* to hurt, to feel pain.

minki *adv.* offensively, bitterly. *adv.* intimately, affectionately.

minkide *n.* one who shares the same pain, co-sufferer. *adj.* compassionate, merciful.

minkor *adj.* sour, bitter, acid, tart. *adj.* painful. *adj.* offensive, biting, caustic.

minkun *adj.* whining, complaining, oversensitive.

minkunkeria *n.* whininess, quality of complaining too much.

minkunki *adv.* sentimentally, mawkishly.

minondo *n.* base of the tongue. *n.* convalescence, recovery.

minontzi *adj.* sickly, unhealthy.

minoria *n.* minority (party, group, etc.).

minsor *n.* slight nagging pain.

minsortu *v.i.* to go numb, to fall asleep (part of the body).

mintasun *n.* bitterness, sourness. *n.* sarcasm, mordacity.

mintegi *n.* greenhouse.

mintsu *adj.* sickly, in pain. *adj.* painful.

mintz *n.* membrane, epidermis, skin. *n.* film (photographic).

mintza- Used in compound words. Derived from *mintzo*, language, talk.

mintzabide *n.* way of speaking, method of speaking, language system.

mintzaera *n.* expression, idiom. *n.* language, speech.

mintzaerraz *adj.* sociable, affable.

mintzaerraztasun *n.* sociableness, affability.

mintzagai *n.* subject of the conversation, subject of the speech, topic.

mintzagarri *adj.* discussible, suitable for discussion.

mintzagela *n.* locutory (in a convent or monastery), visiting room, meeting room.

mintzagura *n.* desire to speak.

mintzaia *n.* language, speech.

mintzaide *n.* speaker, converser, interlocutor.

mintzaile *n.* talker, speaker.

mintzaira *n.* language, speech.

mintzaketa *n.* talk, conversation.

mintzakide *n.* person who speaks the same language.

mintzakidetasun *n.* quality of sharing a language, quality of speaking the same language.

mintzakizun *n.* topic of a speech (to be given in the future), projected topic.

mintzalari *n.* talker, speaker. *adj.* talkative, loquacious.

mintzaldi *n.* speech, conversation, talk, discourse.

mintzaleku *n.* speaking platform, podium; locutory, visiting room.

mintzamen *n.* faculty of speech.

mintzapide *n.* way of speaking. *n.* topic of the conversation.

mintzarazi *v.t.* to make (someone) talk.

mintzatoki *n.* locutory, meeting room, visiting room.

mintzatsu *adj.* membranous.

mintzatu *v.i.* to speak, to tell.

mintzatzaile *n.* speaker, talker. *adj.* talkative, loquacious.

mintzo *n.* speech, language, faculty of speech. *n.* conversation, chat.

mintzodun *adj.* eloquent.

mintzogabe *adj.* mute, speechless.

mintzogabetu *v.i.* to become mute; to be left speechless.

mintzo izan *v.i.* to say, to be speaking, to be talking.

mintzoz *adv.* orally, out loud.

mintzozko *adj.* verbal, oral, spoken.

mintzura *n.* speech, discourse, talk, lecture.

min ukan *v.t.* to hurt, to feel pain.

minutari *n.* minute hand (on a watch).

minutorratz *n.* minute hand (of a watch).

minutu *n.* minute.

miopia *n.(med.)* myopia, near-sightedness.

mirabe *n.* serf. *n.* servant.

mirabealdi *n.* duration of indentured servitude, duration of service.

mirabekeria *n.* vile submission.

mirabetasun *n.* servitude, slavery.

mirabetu *v.t.* to subjugate, to enslave.

mirabetza *n.* servitude, slavery.

miragarri *adj.* marvelous, wonderful. *n.* wonder.

miragarriki *adv.* marvelously, admirably.

miragarriro *adv.* marvelously, admirably.

miragarritasun *n.* marvelousness, admirableness.

miragarritsu *adj.* marvelous.

miragarrizko *adj.* marvelous.

mirail *n.* mirror.

mirakulu *n.* miracle.

mirari *n.* religious miracle. *n.* marvel, marvelous thing, miracle.

mirarigile *n.* miracle worker, thaumaturge.

mirarigintza *n.* miracle working, thaumaturgy.

miraritsu *adj.* miraculous.

miraritu *v.i.* to wonder.

mirariz *adv.* miraculously.

miresgarri *adj.* marvelous, wonderful.

miresgarriki *adv.* marvelously, wonderfully.

miresgarriro *adv.* marvelously, wonderfully.

miresgarritasun *n.* marvelousness, wonderfulness.

mireskor *adj.* admiring.
mireskunde *n.* admiration.
miresle *n.* admirer.
mirespen *adj.* admiration.
mirestu *v.t.* to admire, to wonder at.
miretsi *v.i./v.t.* to be marvelous, to be wonderful; to marvel at, to admire. *v.i.* to be surprised, to be startled.
mirgitsu *adj.* finicky, fastidious, affected.
mirra *n.* myrrh.
mirrin *adj.* shriveled, scraggly; thin, feeble, frail.
mirrindu *v.i.* to get thin.
mirrintasun *n.* frailty, feebleness.
mirrizka *adj.* fine, thin, frail.
mirrizkatu *v.t.* to gnaw.
miru *n.(zool.)* goshawk, kite.
mirumotz *n.(zool.)* kestrel, sparrow hawk.
miseria *n.* misery, poverty.
misio *n.* mission (place). *n.* special series of sermons.
misio eman *v.t.* to preach a special series of sermons.
misiolari *n.* missionary.
misiolur *n.* territory of a mission.
mistela *n.* kind of sweet wine, flavored brandy.
misterio *n.* mystery.
misteriotsu *adj.* mysterious.
mistika *n.* mystic.
mistiko *n.* mystic. *adj.* mystic, mystical.
mistikoki *adv.* mystically.
mistizismo *n.* mysticism.
misto *n.* match.
mitiko *adj.* mythic, mythical.
mitin *n.(pol.)* meeting.
mito *n.* myth.
mitologari *n.* mythologist.
mitologia *n.* mythology.
mitozko *adj.* mythic, mythical.
mitra *n.(eccl.)* mitre.
mitxoleta *n.(bot.)* poppy, field poppy.
mixitxu *n.* cat (children's language).
miz *int.* sound used to call a cat; kitty, kitty!
mizkatu *v.i.* to be spoiled, to become pampered, to be choosy (about food).
mizki *n.* trifle, trinket.
mizkin *adj.* spoiled, pampered, choosy (about food), picky (about food).
mizkindu *v.i.* to become picky or choosy (about food).
mizkinkeria *n.* finickiness, pickiness, choosiness.
mizkino *adj.* finicky, picky, choosy (about food).
mizpira *n.(bot.)* medlar.
mizpiradi *n.* medlar orchard.
mizpiraki *n.* medlar wood, piece of medlar wood.
mizpirondo *n.(bot.)* medlar tree.
mizto *n.* sting, bite, snakebite.
moda *n.* fashion, mode.

modagintza *n.* dressmaking, dress designing, fashion designing.
modazale *adj.* fond of fashion.
modazalekeria *n.* snobbishness, slavery to fashion.
modelo *n.* fashion model.
modernismo *n.* modernism.
moderno *adj.* modern.
modernoki *adv.* modernly.
modernotasun *n.* modernness.
modu *n.* way, manner, style.
moduan *conj.* as, like.
moduko *adj.* similar, alike, resembling.
moduoneko *adj.* well-mannered, polite.
modutsu *adj.* capable, able, apt.
moduz *adv.* ably, skillfully, aptly. *adv.* how.
moduzko *adj.* able, capable. *adj.* well-mannered, polite.
moduztatu *v.i.* to get ready, to prepare oneself.
moeta *n.* type, kind.
moja *n.* nun.
mojaberri *n.* novice nun.
mojaburu *n.* mother superior.
mojasarketa *n.* entering a convent, becoming a nun.
mojetxe *n.* convent, nunnery.
moketa *n.* strong pile cloth used for carpeting.
moketatu *v.t.* to carpet, to lay carpet.
mokil *n.* clod of dirt.
moko *n.* point. *n.* beak, bill.
mokobelar *n.(bot.)* geranium.
mokodun *adj.* beaked, billed, having a beak or bill.
mokogabe *adj.* beakless, without a beak or bill.
mokoka *adv.* pecking. *adv.* arguing, disputing, squabbling.
mokokada *n.* peck, blow with a beak.
mokoka egon *v.i.* to be fighting constantly, to be quarrelsome.
mokokaldi *n.* pecking. *n.(fig.)* argument, dispute, squabble.
mokokari *n./adj.* pecker; pecking (bird). *n.* arguer, quarreler.
mokokatu *v.i.* to peck. *v.i.(fig.)* to argue, to discuss, to dispute. *v.t.* to scold, to reprimand.
mokokatzaile *adj.* pecking, pecker. *adj.* arguing, argumentative.
mokoketa *n.* argument, quarrel, squabble, dispute.
mokolo *n.* chocolate (children's language).
mokoloi *n.* ink spot.
mokoluze *adj.* long-beaked.
mokor *n.* dry clod of earth. *n.* bottom, buttocks. *n.* protuberance, protrusion, point.
mokordo *n.(colloq.)* turd. *adj.(fig.)* imbecilic, stupid.
mokorka *adv.* on one's bottom.
mokorkada *n.* landing on one's bottom.
mokorkatu *v.i.* to bounce on one's bottom. *v.i.* to form (clods of earth).

mokorkeria *n.* brutality, cruelty.
mokorki *adv.* brutally, cruelly, ferociously.
mokorraldi *n.* fit of temper, fit of rage.
mokortasun *n.* brusqueness, asperity, hardness of character.
mokortsu *adj.* full of dirt clods.
mokortu *v.i.* to form (clods of dirt), to dry out (earth or dirt clods). *v.t./v.i.(fig.)* to shrink, to shrink up.
mokote *adj.* having a long beak. *adj.* bad tempered, irascible.
mokoti *adj.* snotty, having mucous. *adj.* roguish, devilish, villainous, scoundrelly.
mokoz-moko *adv.* head on.
mokozorrotz *adj.* cursing, having a nasty mouth; speaking badly of others. *adj.* bad tempered, irascible.
mokozuri *adj.* picky, choosy, finicky.
mokozurikeria *n.* pickiness, choosiness, finickiness (about food).
molda Used in compound words. Derived from *molde*, adaptation, means, way.
moldabide *n.* adaptation, means, way.
moldadura *n.* casting (from a mold).
moldaera *n.* adaptation, adjustment.
moldaerraz *adv.* adaptable, adjustable.
moldagabe *adj.* maladjusted; badly formed.
moldagabezia *n.* maladjustment.
moldagaitz *adj.* inept, clumsy, dense, unsuited, unskillful.
moldagaizkeria *n.* ineptitude, unsuitability.
moldagaizki *adv.* ineptly, unsuitably.
moldagaiztasun *n.* ineptitude, unsuitability.
moldagaiztu *v.i.* to become inept, to be unsuited for.
moldagarri *adj.* adaptable, adjustable.
moldagarritasun *n.* adaptability.
moldaketa *n.* arrangement, adjustment, adaptation.
moldakoi *adj.* accommodating, obliging, flexible.
moldakoitasun *n.* accommodation, quality of being obliging, flexibility.
moldakor *adj.* flexible, adaptable, accommodating, easygoing.
moldakortasun *n.* quality of being easygoing, flexibility.
moldamen *n.* adaptability, flexibility.
moldapen *n.* adaptation, arrangement, preparation.
moldatsu *adj.* capable, able, apt, skillful.
moldatu *v.i.* to adapt oneself, to manage, to get along, to get oneself out of a situation. *v.t.* to prepare, to get (something) ready, to arrange, to form, to formulate.
moldatzaile *n.* adapter. *adj.* adaptive.
molde *n.* structure, form. *n.* manner, way, style. *n.* expertness. *n.* mold.
moldedun *adj.* capable, skilled, able.

molde egin *v.t.* to mold, to model (clay, clothes, etc.), to make a model.
moldegabe *adj.* inept, unskilled; unformed, badly formed.
moldegabekeria *n.* ineptitude.
moldegabeki *adv.* ineptly.
moldegabetasun *n.* lack of skill, ineptness. *n.* shapelessness.
moldegabetu *v.t.* to not adapt, to fail to manage.
moldegaitz *adj.* inept, clumsy, unskilled, unsuited. *adj.* incapable.
moldekari *n.* molder, cast maker.
moldekatu *v.t.* to mold, to cast in a mold.
moldelan *n.* molding, casting.
molderrez *adj.* docile, manageable (people). *adj.* manageable, portable (things).
molderreztasun *n.* docility.
moldetsu *adj.* skilled, capable, able.
moldez *adv.* skillfully, with dexterity.
moldezko *adj.* skillful, dextrous.
moldeztatu *v.t.* to cast in a mold, to stamp in a die; to coin, to mint.
molditz *n.* printed letter, block letter.
moldizkin *n.* printer.
moldiztegi *n.* printing press, printshop, press.
moldura *n.* form, shape, structure.
molekula *n.* molecule.
molekular *adj.* molecular.
molko *n.* bunch of grapes.
molkodun *adj.* bunchy, having bunches of grapes.
molkotsu *adj.* having many bunches of grapes.
molkotu *v.i.* to form bunches of grapes, to sprout bunches of grapes.
molokot *n.* failure.
molokot egin *v.t.* to fail, to go bankrupt, to squander.
moltso *n.* pile, heap.
moltsoka *adv.* in groups, in piles.
moltsokatu *v.t.* to put in piles or groups, to classify into groups.
moltsotu *v.t.* to put into piles or groups, to group together.
momentu *n.* moment.
momia *n.* mummy.
momorro *n.* insect, bug. *adj.(colloq.)* silly, foolish.
momorrotu *v.i.* to become foolish, to become silly.
monarkia *n.* monarchy, royal power.
monarkiko *adj.* monarchic.
monastegi *n.* monastery.
mondongo *n.* large sausage.
monografia *n.* monograph.
monografiko *adj.* monographic.
monolito *n.* monolith.
monopolio *n.* monopoly.
monopolizatu *v.t.* to monopolize.
montzoi *n.* monsoon.
monumendu *n.* monument.
moñoño *adj.(dim.)* funny, amusing, charming. *adj.* dear, darling, beloved.

moral *n.* morality, moral. *adj.* moral.
moralezko *adj.* moral.
moralgabe *adj.* amoral, immoral.
moralgabekeria *n.* immorality.
moralgabetasun *n.* immorality.
moralista *n./adj.* moralist.
moralizatu *v.t.* to moralize.
moralizatzaile *adj.* moralizing.
moral-jakintza *n.(eccl.)* moral theology.
moralki *adv.* morally.
moraltasun *n.* morality.
moralzale *adj.* moralist, fond of morals.
mordo *n.* bunch of grapes. *n.* group, bunch, abundance.
mordoilatu *v.t./v.i.* to complicate, to tangle; to become complicated.
mordoildu *v.t./v.i.* to tangle, to involve, to complicate; to get involved, to become complicated.
mordoilo *n.* confusion, mess. *adj.* impure, broken (language), macaronic.
mordoiloka *adv.* confusedly, messily.
mordoilokada *n.* solecism, minor blunder in speech.
mordoilokeria *n.* blunder in speech, solecism, error in language.
mordoiloki *adv.* tangledly, confusedly, messily, macaronically.
mordoilotu *v.i.* to get mixed up (in), to mess up.
mordoilozale *adj.* fond of solecisms.
mordoka *adv.* by the bunch (grapes).
mordokatu *v.i.* to sprout bunches of grapes.
mordoketa *n.* growing vineyards.
mordoska *n.(dim.)* small bunch, small group.
mordoskada *n.* bunch, group (of people).
mordoskatu *v.t.* to pile (up), to accumulate.
mordotsu *adj.* having bunches of grapes.
mordotu *v.i.* to form bunches of grapes, to sprout bunches of grapes.
mordotxo *n.(dim.)* small bunch, small group.
mordoxka *n.(dim.)* small bunch, small group, small pile.
more *n.* purple.
moredura *n.* purple; turning purple.
moregorri *adj.* violet, violaceous, violet-like.
moretasun *n.* purpleness.
moretu *v.i.* to become purple, to turn purple.
moreztatu *v.t.* to dye (something) purple.
morfema *n.(gram.)* morpheme.
morfina *n.* morphine.
morfinazale *adj.* addicted to morphine.
morfinazalekeria *n.* morphine addiction.
morfologia *n.(gram.)* morphology.
morfologiko *adj.* morphological.

morkots *n.(bot.)* chestnut burr.
mormoi *n./adj.(rel.)* Mormon.
morokil *n.* porridge made of corn flour.
morrale *n.* muzzle.
morroi *n.* boy servant, servant.
morroialdi *n.* time of service, servitude, indenture (of a boy servant).
morroigisa *adv.* subserviently.
morroi izan *v.i.* to be in service (domestic), to be a servant (always boys or men).
morroikeria *n.* vile submission, subservience, servility.
morroiketa *n.* service, domestic service, act of serving.
morroikide *n.* fellow servant.
morroikintza *n.* position of a servant (male).
morroikuntza *n.* servitude (male).
morroilan *n.* work of a servant, domestic work (performed by males).
morroildu *v.t.* to bolt (the door), to lock.
morroilo *n.* bolt.
morroilokada *n.* locking up.
morroilope *n.* jail, prison.
morroilopetu *v.t.* to lock up, to imprison, to jail.
morrosko *adj./n.* healthy young (boy).
morroskote *n.* healthy young boy.
morteiru *n.* mortar.
mortifikapen *n.* mortification, suffering.
mortifikatu *v.i.* to suffer.
mortifikagarri *adj.* suffering.
mortifikarazi *v.t.* to cause suffering.
mortsa *n.(zool.)* walrus.
mortuliar *adj.* solitary, hermit-like.
mosaiko *n.* mosaic.
moskan *n.* dark spot or stain on hands, lips, etc. (from nuts, apples, etc.).
moskatel *n.(bot.)* muscat. *n.* muscatel wine.
mosketoi *n.* short musket.
mota *n.* kind, type, class, caste.
motagarri *adj.* classifying, classifiable.
motaka *adv.* by types, by kind.
motatu *v.t.* to classify, to type.
motel *n.* stutterer. *adj.* dull, flat, tasteless, weak, faded (light, drink, food, etc.). *adj.* insipid, inexpressive (voice). *adj.* dead, lacking bounce (ball).
motelaldi *n.* stuttering. *n.* slump, physical lapse, dullness.
moteldu *v.i.* to become a stutterer. *v.i.* to weaken, to fade, to grow dull, to become tasteless, to lose flavor or strenght; to decrease.
moteldura *n.* stuttering, babbling. flatness, dullness, blandness, lack of spirit (wine, people, etc.).
motelgailu *n.* silencer, silencing apparatus, mute (for an instrument).
motelgarri *adj.* weakening.
motelkeria *n.* dullness, insipidness,

flatness.

motelki adv. dully, flatly, without spirit.

moteltasun n. stuttering. n. dullness, flatness, tastelessness, weakness, fadedness. n. insipidness, inexpressiveness. n. slowness, lateness, tardiness.

moto n. motorcycle.

motoi n. pulley.

motolari n. motorcyclist.

motor n. motorcycle.

motore n. engine, motor.

motorebakar n. single engine.

motorebiko n./adj. bimotor, two-engined (plane).

motorlari n. mechanic.

motorzale adj. fond of motorcycles; fond of engines.

motorzikleta n. motorcycle.

motots n. plume, crest, tuft (of hair).

motxila n. backpack.

motz adj. short, cut, cut-off. adj. blunt, dull. adj. bald, shaven.

-motz Used in compound words. Derived from motz, short. **Belarrimotz.** Spaniard.

motzaile n. gypsy.

motzailekeria n. gypsy mischief.

motzaldi n. clipping, shearing.

motzondo n. stump (of a tree).

moxal n.(zool.) colt, young horse.

moxalarre n. grazing ground for horses.

moxaltalde n. group of colts.

moxaltzain n. one who cares for colts, groom, wrangler.

moxkor adj. a little drunk.

moxkortu v.i./v.t. to get a little drunk, to get tipsy.

mozketa n. clipping, cutting, shearing, shaving. n. amputation, mutilation.

mozki adv. briefly, shortly.

mozkin n. wood chip, clippings. n. gathering the harvest. n. profit, earnings.

mozkindu v.t. to cut down (a tree), to fell. v.t. to save, to economize.

mozkor adj. drunk, drunken, inebriated. n. drunk, drunkard. n. drunkenness; period of time spent drunk.

mozkorgarri adj. alcoholic, inebriating.

mozkorraldi n. drunkenness, tipsiness; drunk, period of time spent drunk.

mozkorrarazi v.t. to make (someone) get drunk.

mozkorreria n. alcoholism.

mozkorrondo n. hangover.

mozkorsalda n. soup made with garlic, pepper and cheese.

mozkortarazi v.t. to get (someone) drunk, to make (someone) get drunk.

mozkorti adj./n. drunk, inebriated, drunken.

mozkortu v.i. to get drunk. v.t. to get (someone) drunk, to make (someone) drunk.

mozkortzale adj. drunken, fond of getting drunk.

mozkorzuku n. soup made with garlic, pepper and cheese.

mozkote adj. stocky, short and thick of build.

mozkotetu v.i. to be stocky, to be short and thick of build.

mozolo n.(zool.) owl. adj.(fig.) surly, rude, churlish.

mozolokeria n. surly action, rude behavior.

mozorro n. mask. n. scarecrow.

mozorrodun adj. masked, disguised.

mozorrotalde n. masked and/or costumed group (usually at carnival time).

mozorrotu v.i./v.t. to wear a mask; to put a mask on (someone).

moztaldi n. shearing time, clipping time.

moztasun n. shortness. n. timidity, shyness, bashfulness. n. ugliness.

mozte n. clipping, cutting, shearing (trees, animals, etc.). n. mutilation, amputation.

moztoki n. place where shearing is done.

moztu v.i./v.t. to cut, to trim; to shave. v.i./v.t. to dull (an edge), to blunt; to get dull. v.t. to amputate. v.t. to summarize, to abbreviate.

moztuezin adj. difficult to cut, uncuttable; difficult to shorten.

moztura n. cut, incision.

moztutzaile n./adj. cutter, amputator; cutting.

mu n. lowing, mooing, moo. n. cow (children's language). adv. nothing, anything.

muga n. limit, border, frontier, boundary. n. period (of time), limit. n. limit, extreme, extremity.

mugabizkar n. top part of a fence or wall (sometimes marking a border).

mugadura n. setting limits, marking boundaries.

muga egin v.t. to border (on), to be adjacent (to).

mugaezin adj. incapable of being delimited or bounded by borders, unlimitable.

mugagabe adj. borderless, without boundaries, unlimited. adj.(gram.) indefinite.

mugagabeki n. unlimitedly, immensely, infinitely, indefinitely.

mugagabeko adj. unlimited, without borders or boundaries.

mugagabetasun n. unlimitedness, immenseness.

mugagarri adj. limitable, capable of being bound by borders.

mugaketa n. limiting, marking, bordering.

mugakide adj. neighboring, bordering on, contingent.

mugakidetasun *n.* quality of neighboring on, quality of bordering on.

mugakidetu *v.i.* to border on, to share a common border.

mugako izan *v.i.* to border on, to share the same border.

mugalde *n.* border area, region near the border.

mugaldeko *adj.* bordering, conterminous, limiting, frontier, border.

mugaldi *n.* epoch, season, occasion.

mugapen *n.* delimitation, staking out, marking boundaries.

mugarri *n.* boundary marker, landmark.

mugarrieta *n.* boundary stones, line of boundary stones, landmark.

mugarriketa *n.* delimitation, marking of boundaries.

mugarritu *v.t.* to place landmarks, to set boundary markers.

mugarritzaile *n.* demarcator, boundary maker, one who fixes boundaries. *adj.* demarcating, dividing.

mugarriztatu *v.t.* to delimit, to set boundaries.

mugatar *n.* border resident, native of the border region.

mugatasun *n.* delimitation, demarcation.

mugatu *v.t.* to limit, to set the boundaries, to determine, to define, to restrict. *adj.* delimited, limited, marked (border). *adj.(gram.)* definite.

mugatxartel *n.* passport.

mugatzaile *n.* one who sets boundaries. *adj.* limiting, delimiting.

mugazain *n.* border guard.

muger *adj.* craggy, rugged, steep. *n.* silica.

mugerreri *n.(med.)* silicosis.

mugertsu *adj.* siliceous, abundant in silica.

mugi- Used in compound words. Implies movement.

mugialdi *n.* mobilization.

mugiarazi *v.t.* to activate, to set in motion, to start (a car, etc.).

mugida *n.* motion, movement.

mugiezin *adj.* immobile, unmovable.

mugiezintasun *n.* immobility.

mugigabe *adj.* stationary, immobile, unmoving.

mugigabeki *adv.* sedentarily, unmovingly, immobily.

mugigabeko *adj.* immobile, unmoving, stationary.

mugigaitasun *n.* mobility.

mugigaitz *adj.* stationary, immobile, difficult to move.

mugigarri *adj.* movable, mobile.

mugiketa *n.* mobilization.

mugikor *adj.* mobile, moving, movable.

mugikortasun *n.* mobility, movableness.

mugimendu *n.* activity, circulation, movement, move.

mugitu *v.t.* to move. *v.t.* to activate.

mugitzaile *n./adj.* mover, starter, activator; moving, starting, activating.

muilo *n.* yarn, knitting wool. *n.* rag, burlap, old cloth.

muin *n.* substance, inner part. *n.(fig.)* essential point or part.

muino *n.* hill, slope, rise.

muker *adj.* hard, difficult to break. *adj.(fig.)* unsociable, unfriendly, aloof.

mukerkeria *n.* aloofness, unfriendliness, unsociability.

mukerki *adv.* unsociably, aloofly.

mukerraldi *n.* act of being aloof or unfriendly.

mukertasun *n.* aloofness, unfriendliness, unsociableness.

mukertu *v.i.* to get hard, to harden. *v.i.* to become aloof, to become unfriendly. *v.i.* to oppose (someone).

muki *n.* mucus, nasal mucus. *n.* resin, gum (trees).

mukidun *adj.* mucous, slimy.

mukieri *n.* cold in the nose, nasal congestion.

mukigai *n.* nasal mucus.

mukijario *adj.* slimy.

mukitsu *adj.* runny-nosed, snotty. *adj.(colloq.)* very young.

mukitxo *n.(dim.)* small amount of mucus.

mukizapi *n.* handkerchief.

muku *n.* mucus, nasal mucus.

mukueri *n.* cold in the nose, nasal congestion.

mukueritu *v.i.* to be congested.

mukuru *n.* top, limit.

mukuruka *adv.* completely, entirely, abundantly.

mukurutu *v.t.* to fill completely.

mula *n.* ferrule, metal cap (on a cane, umbrella, etc.).

mulko *n.* bunch. *n.* pile, group.

mulkoka *adv.* in bunches, in groups, by the bunch.

mulkokatu *v.t.* to gather bunches. *v.i.* to cluster in groups.

mulkotsu *adj.* bunchy, having bunches, bunched.

mulkotu *v.t.* to gather bunches. *v.i.* to cluster in groups.

multa *n.* fine, fee.

multatu *v.t.* to impose a fine.

multiplikatzaile *n./adj.* multiplier.

multiplikazio *n.(arith.)* multiplication. *n.* reproduction; abundance.

multzo *n.* quantity, pile, abundance, set; group.

multzogarri *adj.* gatherable, groupable, pilable.

multzoka *adv.* in groups, in piles, in bunches.

multzokatu *v.t.* to pile (up), to bunch (together), to gather, to group.

multzoketa *n.* accumulation,

conglomeration, act of putting in groups.

multzotasun *n.* multitude, quantity.

multzotu *v.t.* to accumulate, to conglomerate, to put into groups or bunches.

multzozko *adj.* collective, group.

mulu *n.* shrub.

mulutsu *adj.* bushy, having shrubs.

mundrun *n.* tar, pitch.

mundrunadura *n.* tarring, covering with pitch.

mundrunaldi *n.* paving, tarring.

mundrunatu *v.t.* to tar, to cover with pitch.

mundu *n.* world, globe, earth.

munduikustera *n.* world view, a conception of the world from a specific viewpoint.

mundukeria *n.* worldly vanity.

munduko *adj.* mundane. *adj.* of the world, world. *adj.* excellent, magnificent.

mundukoi *adj.* mundane, worldly.

mundukoitu *v.i.* to become worldly, to become profane.

mundulerkuntza *n.* world view, comprehension of the world.

munduratu *v.i.* to come into the world, to be born. *v.t.* to bring into the world.

mundutar *adj.* mundane, worldly. *n.* inhabitant of the world, earth dweller earthman.

mundutasun *n.* mundaneness, worldliness.

mundutiar *adj.* mundane, worldly, terrestrial.

mundutxo *n.(dim.)* microcosm.

mundutzar *n.(augm.)* macrocosm.

munduzale *adj.* fond of the world; worldly.

munduzalekeria *n.* worldliness.

munduzaletasun *n.* worldliness.

munduzaletu *v.i.* to become worldly, to become a layman.

mun egin *v.t.* to kiss (not on the face, usually the hand or a religious image).

munizio *n.* ammunition.

munizioztatu *v.t.* to load with ammunition, to provide with ammunition.

munizipal *adj.* municipal.

munstro *n.* monster.

munta *n.* importance.

muntadura *n.* act or way of assembling (something), way of installing (something).

muntaia *n.* fitting, set up, installation, assembly.

muntaketa *n.* setting up, assembly, installation.

muntatu *v.t.* to set up, to assemble, to organize.

muntatzaile *n.* fitter, assembler, installer, organizer.

murgil *n.* dive, plunge. *n.* somersault.

murgilaldi *n.* dive, act of diving, submerging.

murgilarazi *v.t.* to drown; to dunk; to flood, to inundate.

murgilari *adj.* diver.

murgildu *v.i./v.t.* to dive; to duck, to dunk. *v.i.(fig.)* to submerge (oneself), to dive (into). *v.i.* to get wet.

murgildura *n.* diving; ducking, dunking. *n.(fig.)* becoming involved in, involvement, submersion in.

murgilean *adv.* diving; ducking, dunking.

murgilgarri *adj.* submergible, sinkable.

murgilketa *n.* diving, submerging.

murmu *n.* glanders, contagious and destructive disease in horses, cats and dogs.

murmur *n.* murmur, whisper.

murmurika *n.* murmur, whisper.

murmurikari *n.* slanderer, one who speaks evilly of another. *n.* murmurer, whisperer.

murmurikatu *v.t.* to whisper, to murmur.

murmurio *n.* murmuring, whispering, murmur, whisper.

murmurrots *n.* murmur, whispering sound.

murrika *n.* mocking laugh, mocking smile, sneer.

murrikaldi *n.* period of mocking laughter, ridicule.

murrikari *n.* mocker, ridiculer.

murrikatu *v.i.* to mock, to ridicule, to make fun of.

murrikatzaile *adj.* mocking, ridiculing.

murritu *v.t.* to deprive (of), to strip. *v.i.(fig.)* to be ruined, to go broke, to be destroyed.

murritz *adj.* lacking something, short. *adj.* bare, barren, naked. *adj.(fig.)* stingy.

murritzaile *adj.* restricting, restrictive, limiting.

murrizgarri *adj.* reducible; restricting.

murrizkeria *n.* unsociable act, brusque action.

murrizketa *n.* pruning, trimming, cutting back. *n.* reduction, restriction.

murrizki *adv.* very short, very close. *adv.(fig.)* briefly.

murrizkin *n.* cutting, clipping, paring, piece that has been cut away.

murriztaile *n.* trimmer, pruner. *adj.* restrictive, specifying, limiting, restraining.

murriztapen *n.* reduction, trimming, pruning, cutting down or back.

murriztasun *n.* brevity, shortness, conciseness. *n.* bareness, barrenness.

murriztu *v.t./v.i.* to reduce, to trim, to prune, to diminish, to cut back (or down). *v.t.* to cut very close, to cut very short. *v.t.* to limit, to restrict, to restrain.

murru *n.* wall.

murrunga *n.* scolding, reprimand; grumbling.

murrungari *n./adj.* one who scolds or reprimands; grumbler; scolding, grumbling.

murrungatu *v.t./v.i.* to scold, to reprimand; to grumble.

murruskada *n.* grumbling; growling.

murruskaldi *n.* rubbing.

murruskatu *v.t.* to scrub, to scrape, to rub with force.

murruskatzaile *n.* rubber, one who rubs.

murrutu *v.t.* to build a wall, to wall up, to wall in.

murrutzar *n.(augm.)* sea wall, dike.

murruzkari *adj./n.* jabberer, grumbler.

murruzkatu *v.t.* to speak a language badly.

murtxikapen *n.* chewing, mastication.

murtxikatu *v.t.* to chew, to masticate.

mus *n.* kind of Basque card game.

musean *adv.* playing *mus* (a Basque card game). *adv.* swimming underwater.

musean egin *v.t.* to play *mus*. *v.t.* to swim underwater.

mus egin *v.t.* to swim underwater.

museo *n.* museum.

musika *n.* music, melody.

musikagile *n.* musician; composer.

musikalari *n.* musician.

musikaldi *n.* concert; time spent playing music.

musikalki *adv.* musically.

musikaltasun *n.* musicalness, musicality.

musikari *n.* musician.

musikaste *n.* music(al) week, week of concerts.

musikategi *n.* place for storing music (furniture).

musikatresna *n.* musical instrument.

musikatu *v.t.* to put to music.

musikaz *adv.* musically.

musikazale *adj.* melomaniac, fond of music.

musikazalekeria *n.* excessive melomania, excessive love of music.

musikazaletasun *n.* love of music, fondness for music, melomania.

musikeskola *n.* conservatory of music.

muskar *n.(zool.)* lizard.

musker *n.(zool.)* lizard. *n./adj.* green (color).

muskerkume *n.(dim.)* baby lizard.

muskil *n.* bud, sprout, shoot, sucker. *n.* nasal mucus, snot. *n.* core (apple, pear, etc.).

muskilaldi *n.* pruning season; time for trimming or pruning.

muskilaro *n.* pruning season, trimming season.

muskildu *v.t.* to prune, to trim. *v.i.* to

bloom, to blossom, to bud, to sprout. *v.i.* to go numb with cold. *v.t.* to leave (something) half eaten.

muskildura *n.* budding, sprouting, blooming.

muskiltsu *adj.* having many buds or sprouts.

muskiltxo *n.(dim.)* tiny bud, tiny sprout.

muskiltzaile *adj.* budding, sprouting. *adj.* clipping, paring, cutting.

muskuilu *n.(zool.)* mussel.

muslari *n. mus* player.

mustu *n.(zool.)* tiny dark brown inedible sea fish.

mustuka *n.* dust mop, feather duster; dishcloth.

mustukatu *v.t.* to dust, to remove dust.

mustur *n.* corner, edge, extremity.

musturka *adv.* nuzzling; rooting up (with one's snout).

musturkatu *v.t.* to nuzzle; to root up (with one's snout).

musturrak apurtu *v.t.* to break one's snout, to break one's face (more than the nose). *v.t.(fig.)* to work intensely, to work with one's nose to the grindstone.

musturrandi *adj.* large-muzzled, having a big snout.

musturreko *n.* blow, sock, hit (in the face or snout). *n.* muzzle (device used on dogs).

musturtu *v.i.* to get angry, to become unfriendly.

musu *n.* kiss. *n.* face.

musu eman *v.t.* to kiss.

musuemaile *n.* kisser.

musuestalki *n.* masking, covering the face (with a cape), muzzling.

musuka *adv.* kissing.

musukari *n./adj.* kisser.

musukatu *v.t.* to kiss repeatedly, to cover with kisses, to lavish kisses on.

musukatzaile *adj.* kissing repeatedly, lavishing kisses on.

musuketa *n.* act of giving many kisses.

musukitarra *n.(mus.)* harmonica.

musuko *n.* face, facial, pertaining to the lower half of the face. *n.* muzzle, covering for the mouth of an animal to prevent biting.

musulman *n./adj.* Moslem, Arab.

musurika *n.* nuzzling; rooting out (with the snout).

musuritu *v.t.* to nuzzle; to root out or dig out with the snout.

musutxo *n.(dim.)* little kiss.

musuzabal *adj.* having a wide face.

musuzapi *n.* handkerchief.

musuz-musu *adv.* face to face.

musuzulo *n.(anat.)* nostril.

mutiko *n.(dim.)* small boy, little boy.

mutikokeria *n.* childish prank.

mutikotalde *n.* gang of small boys.

mutikotasun *n.* childhood, quality of being a little boy.

mutikoteria n. group of little boys.
mutikotxo n.(dim.) little boy.
mutil n. boy, lad; fellow, guy. n. servant, errand boy.
-mutil Used in compound words. Signifies apprentice.
mutildu v.i. to become a young boy.
mutilgo n. domestic service (for boys).
mutilki adv. boyishly, childishly.
mutilkoskor n. boy, average-sized boy, youth, lad.
mutiltasun n. boyhood, quality of being a boy.
mutiltxo n.(dim.) little boy.
mutiltzar n.(augm.) big boy.
mutilzahar n. old bachelor, confirmed bachelor.
mutilzale adj. fond of boys, boy crazy.
mutiri adj. strong, violent. adj. insolent, bold, petulant.
mutirialdi n. period of excessive violence.
mutirikeria n. insolence, impudence.
mutiriki adv. insolently, shamelessly, impudently.
mutirikor adj. insolent, impudent.
mutiritasun n. insolence, impudence, shamelessness.
mutiritu v.i. to become insolent, to become impudent.
mutu n. mute. adj. quiet, taciturn, reserved, silent, speechless.
mutualdi n. period of muteness.
mutuarazi v.t. to quiet, to calm (someone) down, to silence.
mutukeria n. mutism, dumbness, inability to speak.
mutur n. snout, muzzle, mouth. n. corner, extreme, edge. n. point of an instrument or tool.
muturdun adj. thick-lipped, blubber-lipped. adj. pointed.
muturka adv. face down.
muturka egon v.i. to be angry, to be frowning, to be unfriendly or unsociable.
muturka ibili v.i. to be angry, to be miffed, to be peeved.
muturkari n. boxer. n. animal that roots out or digs with the snout.
muturkatu v.i. to get mad, to get angry. v.i. to fall face down. v.t. to dig out or root out with the snout.
muturkeria n. anger, aversion.
muturketa n. quarrel, fracas, squabble.
mututasun n. mutism, dumbness. n. stuttering.
mututu v.i. to become mute, to fall silent, to quiet down. v.i. to lose the sound. v.t. to quiet (someone), to shut (someone) up, to silence.
mutxikin n. core.
mutxurdin n. old maid, old unmarried woman.
mutxurdintasun n. state of being an old unmarried woman.

mutxurdintu v.i. to become an old maid.
muxar n.(zool.) mojarra.
muxikadi n. peach orchard.
muxikondo n.(bot.) peach tree.
muxin n. whining, whimpering. n. grimace, facial contortion.
muxindu v.i. to whine, to whimper.
muxinka adv. whiningly, whimperingly. adv. grimacingly.
muxinkada n. whining, whimpering.
muxinkari n./adj. whiner, whimperer; whining, whimpering.
muxinkatu v.i. to whine, to whimper.
muzin n. facial gesture of disgust, grimace. adj. unfriendly, unsociable, aloof.
muzinaldi n. being unfriendly, period of unsociability.
muzin egin v.t. to be unfriendly, to be unsociable, to be disdainful, to disdain.
muzinka adv. with gestures of disgust, grimacing.
muzinkeinu n. grimace, expression of disgust.
muzinkeria n. unsociability, unfriendliness.
muztio n. must, unfermented grape juice.

N

n Letter of the Basque alphabet.
-n pron. relative pronoun meaning who, whom, that, which. Attached to auxiliary verb. **Etorri den gizona zure aita da.** The man who has come is your father. prep. in. **Bilbon.** In Bilbao.
-na (gram.) Used with numbers to mean distribution into groups. **Launa.** Four each.
nabar adj. multicolored, pertaining to badly mixed or clashing colors. adj. gray, drab.
nabardun adj. having many colors, multicolored, many colored, pertaining to clashing colors.
nabardura n. variety of colors, confusion of colors.
nabari adj. obvious, evident, manifest.
nabarigarri adj. noticeable, notable, remarkable.
nabarigarritasun n. notableness, noticeableness.
nabari izan v.i. to be obvious, to be evident.
nabariki adv. notoriously, patently, ostentatiously, obviously.
nabarikor adj. perceptive.
nabariro adv. patently, notoriously, ostentatiously, obviously.
nabaritasun n. obviousness, notoriousness, ostentatiousness.
nabaritu v.t. to realize, to notice, to perceive.
nabaritza n. fame, notoriety.

nabarkeria n. underhandedness, duplicity, trickery, double-dealing.

nabarmen adj. manifest, evident, obvious. adj. shocking, dirty, immoral.

nabarmenarazi v.t. to make (something) obvious, to make (something) evident.

nabarmendu v.i. to stand out, to excel, to be outstanding. v.t. to show, to show off, to exhibit, to display.

nabarmendura n. showing, displaying.

nabarmengarri adj. noticeable, remarkable, notable.

nabarmenkeria n. exhibitionism, ostentation; extravagance, eccentricity.

nabarmenki adv. notoriously, patently, ostentatiously, obviously. adv. discourteously, impolitely, inappropriately.

nabarmenkiro adv. notoriously, patently, ostentatiously, obviously. adv. discourteously, impolitely.

nabarmenkor adj. ostentatious, extravagant.

nabarmentasun n. obviousness. n. rudeness, impoliteness.

nabartasun n. dark gray; shades of gray in combination. n. indiscretion; rudeness; hypocrisy.

nabartu v.t. to paint with many colors.

nabo n. turnip. n. N.A.B.O., North American Basque Organizations, Inc.

nafar adj. Navarrese.

nafarrera n. Navarrese dialect.

nafarreri n.(med.) smallpox.

Nafarroa n.(geog.) Navarra. One of the four provinces of the southern Basque Country. Its capital is Pamplona. **Nafarroa Beherea.** Low Navarra. **Nafarroa Garaia.** High Navarra. **Nafarroako Erresuma.** The Kingdom of Navarra.

nafartar n./adj. native of Navarra.

nagi adj. lazy, idle. n. laziness. n.(zool.) sloth.

nagialdi n. passing laziness, temporary laziness, slump, period of laziness.

nagidura n. abandon, idleness, temporary laziness.

nagigarri adj. causing idleness, causing laziness.

nagi izan v.i. to be lazy.

nagikeria n. laziness, idleness, sloth, indolence, slowness.

nagiki adv. lazily, languidly, indolently, slowly.

nagitasun n. laziness, indolence, slowness, languidness; negligence.

nagitsu adj. lazy, indolent, slow; negligent.

nagitu v.i. to become lazy, to become indolent, to become slow.

nagusi n. boss, owner, head, chief. adj. main, chief, principal, supreme; oldest, eldest.

nagusien adj.(superl.) principal, main; oldest, eldest.

nagusigo n. command, responsibility, leadership.

nagusikeria n. despotism, authoritarianism, abuse of power, tyranny.

nagusikeritu v.t. to tyranize, to abuse authority.

nagusiki adv. despotically, tyranically. adv. primarily, mainly, principally.

nagusiorde n. foreman, overseer, supervisor, assistant to the boss, number two man (or woman).

nagusiro adv. principally, mainly, primarily.

nagusitasun n. power, dominance, dominion, supremacy, rule, command, primacy.

nagusiteria n. group of bosses, group of owners.

nagusitu v.t./v.i. to conquer, to take over, to take power, to dominate. v.i. to prevail, to surpass. v.i. to grow up, to develop.

nagusitza n. command, responsibility, dominion, leadership. n. boss's job.

naharo adj. abundant, rich, prolific. adv. abundantly.

naharoki adv. abundantly, copiously, prolificly.

naharotasun n. abundance, copiousness, fertility, prolificness.

naharotsu adj. abundant, copious.

naharotu v.i. to become fertile, to become abundant, to be copious.

nahasbide n. mess, confusion.

nahasezin adj. unmixable; unmistakable.

nahasgabe adj. unmixed, pure; unconfused, not mistaken. adj.(fig.) sincere.

nahasgabeki adv. unmistakably; purely, simply.

nahasgailu n. mixer, mixing apparatus.

nahasgaitz adj. difficult to mix; difficult to confuse or mistake (for something else).

nahasgarri adj. mixing, mixable. adj. confusing.

nahasgarriki adv. confusedly, in confusion.

nahasi v.t. to mix (up), to confuse; to mess up. adj. mixed, disorganized, rough, uncalm (water). v.i.(fig.) to get mixed up (with), to get involved (with). v.i. to be mixed up, to be confused, to be mistaken.

nahasiki adv. confusedly, in a muddled manner, messily.

nahasitako adj. mixed (up), confused, muddled.

nahaskeria n. mess, confusion, mix-up.

nahasketa n. mixture, mix. n. disorder, confusion, mess.

nahasketari n. quarreler, busybody,

troublemaker.

nahaski adv. mixed up, confusedly.

nahaskiro adv. confusedly, mixed-up.

nahaskor adj. mixable, miscible.

nahaskortasun n. mixableness, quality of being mixable.

nahasle n./adj. mixer, one who mixes. adj. troublemaking.

nahas-mahas n. confusion, mess, disorganization. adv. confusedly, mixed in, scattered (in confusion).

nahas-mahasi n. confusion, mess, disorganization.

nahas-mahaska adv. confusedly, in a muddled manner, confusing.

nahas-mahastu v.i./v.t. to mix up, to disorganize, to confuse, to be confused.

nahasmen n. mixture. n. confusion, mess, problem.

nahasmendu n. disorder, mess, confusion.

nahaspila n. mess, confusion, problem, involvement, jam.

nahaspilari adj. troublesome, bothersome, troublemaking.

nahaspilatsu adj. confusing, disorganized.

nahaspilatu v.t. to confuse, to mess up, to disorganize, to turn upside down.

nahaspilatzaile n./adj. troublemaker, agitator, busybody, one who causes jams or messes; troublesome, troublemaking.

nahastagarri adj. mixable, confusable. adj.(fig.) troublesome, messy.

nahastaile n./adj. troublemaker, busybody; troublemaking.

nahastakeria n. confusion, mess, tangle, muddle, jam.

nahastaldi n. upset, upheaval, disturbance, confusion.

nahastale n./adj. troublemaker, busybody; troublemaking.

nahastapen n. mixture, mix-up, act of mixing or mixing up.

nahastari n./adj. agitator, troublemaker; troublemaking, troublesome.

nahastatu v.t. to mix up, to confuse. v.t. to mix.

nahastatzaile n./adj. troublemaker, one who gets mixed up in something, busybody, agitator; troublemaking.

nahaste n. mixture, mixing. n. disorder, confusion.

nahaste-borraste n. mixture. n. mess, jam; confusion.

nahasteka n. mixture, mess, confusion, muddle. adv. confusedly, in a muddled manner.

nahastekari n./adj. troublemaker, agitator; troublesome, troublemaking.

nahastekatu v.t. to confuse (things), to mess up, to make a mess.

nahastekamendu n. mess, mix-up, confusion, muddle.

nahaste-mahaste n. mixture, blend.

nahastero n. troublemaker, busybody, agitator. adj. troublemaking, meddling.

nahastezin adj. unmixable, immiscible.

nahastezinezko adj. unmixable, impossible to mix or blend. adj. unmistakable, unconfusable.

nahastu v.t. to mix, to blend; to confuse, to mess up.

nahastura n. mixture. n. mess, confusion.

nahi n. desire, will, wish.

-nahi (gram.) Suffix used with nouns and adjectives, meaning desire, desirous. **Jakinnahi.** Studious.

nahiago adj. preferable, preferred, favorite.

nahiago izan v.t. to prefer.

nahiagotu v.t. to prefer.

nahiago ukan n. to prefer.

nahiera n. free will. n. satisfaction.

nahiez n. apathy, indecision. n. annoyance, vexation.

nahigabe n. sorrow, suffering, affliction.

nahigabedun adj. sorrowful, afflicted, suffering.

nahigabeki adv. sufferingly, afflictedly.

nahigabeko adj. involuntary.

nahigabetasun n. lack of willpower, apathy.

nahigabetsu adj. anguished, suffering, afflicted.

nahigabetu v.t./v.i. to hurt, to cause pain, to inflict suffering; to suffer, to become sad or depressed.

nahigabetzaile adj. distressing, depressing, afflicting.

nahigabez adv. painfully, sorrowfully.

nahigarri adj. desirable; estimable.

nahi izan v.t. to want, to want to, to desire.

nahikara n. desire, satisfaction.

nahikari n. whim, caprice, desire.

nahikeria n. greed, cupidity, covetousness. n. arbitrariness.

nahikeriazko adj. arbitrary.

nahikide n. rival, competitor.

nahiko adv. enough, quite.

nahiko izan v.i. to be enough, to be sufficient.

nahikor adj. constant, persistent, tenacious.

nahikotan adv. enough, enough times.

nahikotasun n. sufficiency, quality of being enough.

nahikotu v.i. to have enough; to have had enough of, to be fed up with.

nahikunde n. volition, will.

nahimen n. volition, will.

nahita adv. deliberately, intentionally, expressly.

nahitaez adv. inevitably, necessarily.

nahitaezko adj. inevitable, absolutely

necessary, mandatory, obligatory, compulsory.

nahitanahiez *adv.* necessarily, inevitably.

nahitanahiezko *adj.* necessary, obligatory, inevitable.

nahitasun *n.* voluntariness, willfulness.

nahitezko *adj.* obligatory, mandatory.

nahi ukan *v.t.* to want, to like.

nahiz *conj.* although. *conj.* either . . . or, whether . . . or, or. *adv.* willingly, voluntarily.

nahiz eta *conj.* although, even though, in spite of.

nai *n.* desire, will, wish.

-naka *(gram.)* Suffix signifying distribution, in groups of, at a time. **Binaka.** Two at a time.

nakaitz *n.* aversion, repugnance, disgust, revulsion.

nakaizgarri *adj.* disgusting, repulsive, repugnant.

nakaizgo *n.* aversion, repulsion, repugnance, disgust.

nakaizki *adv.* disgustingly, repugnantly, detestably.

nakaiztasun *n.* aversion, repulsion, repugnance, disgust.

nakaiztu *v.t.* to disgust, to repulse, to despise.

nakar *adj.* unwilling, indifferent. *n.* mother-of-pearl, nacre.

nakare *n.* mother-of-pearl, nacre.

nakareztatu *v.t.* to decorate with mother-of-pearl.

narda *n.* aversion, repugnance, revulsion, disgust.

nardabera *adj.* inclined to nausea, easily disgusted.

nardaberakatu *v.t.* to disgust, to repulse.

narda egin *v.t.* to cause disgust, to disgust (someone).

nardagarri *adj.* disgusting, abominable, repugnant, repulsive, detestable, loathsome.

nardagarrikeria *n.* repugnant act, disgusting act, atrocity.

nardagarriki *adv.* disgustingly, repugnantly.

nardagarriro *adv.* disgustingly, repugnantly.

nardagarritasun *n.* loathsomeness, repulsiveness.

nardagarritu *v.i.* to be disgusting, to become repulsive, to be loathsome.

nardaka *n.* filth, dirt, dirtiness.

nardakatu *v.t.* to cause disgust, to disgust (someone).

nardakeria *n.* repugnant action, disgusting action.

nardakor *adj.* repulsive, disgusting, loathsome.

nardatasun *n.* quality of being disgusting, repulsiveness, loathsomeness.

nardatsu *adj.* repugnant, disgusting.

nardatu *v.t.* to disgust, to repulse.

nardatzaile *n./adj.* disguster, one who causes disgust; disgusting.

narda ukan *v.t.* to disgust, to incite loathing, to repulse.

nare *adj.* calm, easy-going.

naretasun *n.* tranquility, quietness, calm.

naretu *v.i.* to become calm, to calm down.

narga *n.* aversion, repugnance, revulsion, disgust.

nargatu *v.t.* to disgust, to repulse.

narkotiko *n.* narcotic.

narkotizapen *n.* narcotization, act of treating with narcotics.

narkotizatu *v.t.* to narcotize, to treat with narcotics, to subject to a narcotic.

narra *n.* dragging. *n.* drag, dray, sledge, sled.

narrabide *n.* sledge path, drag path.

narra egin *v.t.* to drag, to haul. *v.t.* to slip, to tilt (foundation of a house, etc.).

narra eragin *v.t.* to make (something) move.

narraketa *n.* dragging, hauling.

narraz *adv.* dragging, by dragging.

narraz ibili *v.i.* to drag oneself, to slither, to move along the ground.

narrazio *n.* narration, story, report.

narrazka *adv.* dragging, by dragging.

narrazkari *n.* crawler, one who slithers along the ground.

narrazketa *n.* act of slithering, crawling, moving along the ground, dragging oneself along the ground.

narraztari *adj.* slithery; dragging, trailing, creeping. *n.(zool.)* snake, reptile.

narrazti *n.(zool.)* snake, serpent, reptile.

narraztu *v.i.* to slither, to drag oneself along the ground. *v.t.* to drag, to haul.

narriadura *n.* damage, harm, deterioration.

narriapen *n.* damage, harm, deterioration.

narriatu *v.t.* to deteriorate, to worsen. *v.i.* to have a relapse, to suffer a setback (in illness).

narrio *n.* illness, infirmity, indisposition. *n.* deterioration.

narriodun *adj.* defective, deteriorated, imperfect.

narriogabe *adj.* spotless, immaculate.

narriotasun *n.* defectiveness, imperfection.

narriotsu *adj.* defective; spotted.

narriotu *v.t.* to spot, to stain, to dirty. *v.t.* to profane.

narrita *n.* instigation, provocation.

narritadura *n.* provocation, instigation.

narritagarri *adj.* provocative, instigative.

narritaldi n. instigating, provoking.
narritamendu n. provocation, instigation.
narritari n. instigator, provoker.
narritatu v.t. to instigate, to provoke.
narritatzaile n./adj. instigator, provoker, inciter; provoking, instigating.
narru n. leather, hide, skin.
nartziso n.(bot.) narcissus.
nasa n. dock, pier.
natur- Used in compound words. Derived from natura, nature.
natura n. nature.
naturagaindiko adj. supernatural.
natural adj. natural, innate.
naturalizapen n. naturalization.
naturalizatu v.i./v.t. to naturalize.
naturalki adv. naturally.
naturaltasun n. naturalness.
naturazko adj. natural, innate.
naturgaineko adj. supernatural.
naturkontrako adj. against nature.
naturlege n. natural law.
naturtzale adj. fond of nature.
nazi n./adj.(pol.) Nazi.
nazio n. nation.
nazioarteko adj. international.
nazioartekotasun n. quality of being international.
nazioartekotu v.t./v.i. to internationalize, to become or make international.
nazioaskodun adj. multinational.
nazioaskotako adj. multinational, of many nations.
naziogaindiko adj. supranational.
nazional adj. national.
nazionaldu v.t. to nationalize.
nazionalismo n. nationalism.
nazionalista n./adj. nationalist.
nazionalitate n. nationality.
nazionalizatu v.t. to nationalize.
nazionalizazio n. nationalization.
nazionalki adv. nationally.
nazionalkuntza n. nationalization.
nazionalpen n. nationalization.
naziotasun n. nationality (abstract idea).
nazismo n. Nazism.
nazka n. aversion, revulsion, repugnance, disgust.
nazkabera. adj. easily disgusted, easily repulsed.
nazkadura n. aversion, disgust, repugnance, revulsion, detestation.
nazka eman v.t. to disgust, to repulse, to detest.
nazkagarri adj. disgusting, repulsive, repugnant. adj. annoying, obnoxious, bothersome.
nazkagarrikeria n. disgusting act, repugnant deed.
nazkagarriro adv. disgustingly, repugnantly, detestably.
nazkakor adj. repulsive, fastidious, disgusting, repugnant, abhorrent,
abominable.
nazkaldi n. repugnance, revulsion.
nazkarazi v.t. to annoy, to bother, to disgust.
nazkatu v.t./v.i. to disgust, to repulse, to despise; to be disgusted. v.t. to bother, to annoy.
neba n. brother (word used by females only, in Biscayan dialect).
negar n. cry, crying, tear. n. candle drippings.
negarbera adj. weepy, teary.
negarbide n.(anat.) tear duct. n. reason for crying, motivation for weeping.
negar egin v.t. to cry, to weep.
negargale n. desire to cry. adj. wanting to cry.
negargarri adj. sad, woeful, regrettable, lamentable.
negargile adj. crybaby, crying a lot.
negargura n. desire to cry.
negarjario n. weeping, shedding of tears. adj. crybaby.
negarkantari n. hired mourner.
negarkantu n. elegy, dirge, mournful song.
negarmalko n. tear, teardrop.
negarmin n. weeping, crying.
negarraldi n. weeping, crying, crying jag.
negarranpula n. large tear, crocodile tear.
negarrarazi v.t. to make (someone) cry.
negarrarazle n. one who makes (someone) cry. adj. sad, mournful, tear-jerking.
negarreria n. mass weeping.
negarrez adv. crying, weepingly.
negarreztatu v.t. to feel great sorrow or grief, to grieve, to mourn.
negarriturri adj. crybaby.
negarrontzi adj. crybaby.
negarti adj. crybaby. adj.(fig.) complaining.
negarzorro n.(anat.) tear sac.
negarzotin n. sob, sobbing.
negarzotinka adv. sobbing.
negarzotinkari adj. sobbing.
negarzotinkatu v.i. to sob.
negatibo adj. negative.
negoziaezin adj. not negotiable, non-negotiable.
negoziagaitz adj. difficult to negotiate.
negoziagarri adj. negotiable.
negoziaketa n. negotiation, transaction.
negoziapen n. business negotiation, transaction.
negoziari n. negotiator.
negoziatu v.t. to negotiate.
negoziatzaile adj./n. negotiating; negotiator.
negoziazio n. negotiation.
negozio n. business, trade.
negu n. winter.

negua igaro v.t. to spend the winter.
negualdi n. winter (season).
neguaurren n. beginning of winter, onset of winter.
neguazken n. end of winter, late in the winter. n. spring.
negubihotz n. middle of winter, heart of winter.
neguburu n. winter solstice.
negugiro n. winter weather.
negugorri n. hard winter, harsh winter, cold winter.
negukari n. person who likes winter.
neguko adj. winter, pertaining to winter.
negulehen n. beginning of winter, onset of winter.
negumin n. very hard winter, extremely harsh winter.
negumuga n. winter solstice.
neguri n. winter residence.
neguta n.(zool.) chaffinch (Fringilla coelebs).
negutar adj. winter, hibernal, wintry.
negute n. long winter, harsh winter, bad winter.
negutegi n. winter quarters.
negutoki n. special place to spend the winter, winter resort area, winter quarters.
negutsu adj. wintery.
negutu v.t. to set in, to arrive, to come (all used with winter).
neguzale adj. fond of winter.
nehoiz adv. never.
nehola adv. not at all, in no way.
nehon adv. nowhere, not anywhere.
nehor pron. no one, anyone.
neka- Used in compound words. Derived from neke, pain, affliction, suffering.
nekabide n. annoyance, bother.
nekadura n. tiredness, fatigue.
nekaezin adj. tireless.
nekaezintasun n. tirelessness.
nekagaitz adj. tireless.
nekagarri adj. tiring, fatiguing, exhausting. adj. tiresome, annoying.
nekagarriro adv. tiringly.
nekaketa n. fatigue, tiredness.
nekakor adj. getting tired, tending to be tired.
nekaldi n. exhaustion, fatigue, tiredness. n. passion. n. annoyance, nuisance, bother.
nekaldu v.i. to suffer. v.t. to martyr, to martyrize.
nekarazi v.t. to tire (someone) out, to make (someone) tired. v.t. to annoy, to bother.
nekarazle adj. annoying, impertinent, bothersome. adj. tiring, draining, exhausting.
nekatu v.i. to get tired, to be tired. adj. tired.
nekatzaile n./adj. one who makes (someone) tired; tiring, tiresome.

nekazal adj. rural, country, agricultural farming.
nekazale adj. rural, agricultural, rustic.
nekazaleria n. peasantry.
nekazalgo n. peasantry; peasant's work, agricultural labor.
nekazari n. farmer, peasant.
nekazarisa n. peasant woman, female farmer.
nekazaritza n. farming, agriculture. n. peasantry.
neke n. tiredness, fatigue. n. difficulty, problem. n. suffering, pain.
nekebide n. cause of suffering.
nekedun adj. suffering, experiencing pain or sorrow.
nekegabe adj. not tired.
nekegaitz adj. not tired.
neketsu adj. painful, tiring, fatiguing, difficult, hard (life).
nekez adv. tiringly. adv. with difficulty. adj. difficult.
nekezka adv. with great difficulty.
nekezko adj. difficult, tiring. adj. bothering, annoying.
-neko (gram.) Verbal suffix meaning when, at the moment when, by the time, or similar time-related phrases. **Konturatu nintzeneko, lapurrek ihes egin zuten.** By the time I realized it, the thieves escaped.
nekrologia n. necrology.
nekrologiko adj. necrological.
neoklasiko adj. neoclassical.
neologia n. neology.
neologiko adj. neological.
neologismo n. neologism.
neon n.(chem.) neon.
nerabe n. teenager, adolescent. n. servant.
nerabetasun n. quality of being a teenager, pubescence, adolescence.
nerabetu v.i. to enter puberty, to become a teenager.
nerabetza n. adolescence, puberty.
nerabezaro n. adolescence, puberty.
nerau pron. I myself.
nerbio n.(anat.) nerve.
nerbioaldi n. fit of nerves, attack of nerves, nervous breakdown.
nerbiobera adj. nervous, jittery.
nerbioeri n.(med.) neuritis.
nerbiomin n.(med.) neuralgia.
nere pron./adj. my, mine.
neronek pron.(nom.) I myself. Used with transitive verbs.
neska n. girl, unmarried young woman.
neskabeharketa n. sexual abuse (against a female). Sexual relations obtained by trickery, deceit or without the woman's consent.
neskabehartu v.t. to abuse (a woman) sexually, to rape.
neskabehartzaile n./adj. sexual abuser of women, rapist.

neskafe n. instant coffee.

neskagaldu n. prostitute, fallen woman.

neskagaltzaile n./adj. rapist.

neskakoi adj. fond of girls, girl crazy.

neskakoitasun n. quality of being fond of girls.

neskakoitu v.i. to become fond of girls.

neskalagun n. girl friend, female friend. n. sweetheart, fiancée (female).

neska lagundu v.t. to take one's girl friend home, to accompany one's fiancée home.

neskame n. maid, female servant.

neskametza n. service, job of being a maid.

neskaso n. virgin, maiden, maid.

neska-mutil adj./n. mannish; tomboy, masculine woman.

neskatasun n. quality of being a lady, young womanhood.

neskateria n. large group of young ladies.

neskatila n.(dim.) little girl, young girl.

neskatilakari adj. fond of girls, girl crazy.

neskato n.(dim.) little girl, young girl, young lady.

neskatxa n.(dim.) little girl, young girl.

neskatzar n. bad girl.

neskazahar n. spinster, old unmarried woman. n.(zool.) reddish fish similar to sea bream but having larger eyes.

neskazale adj. fond of girls, girl crazy.

-netan (gram.) Verbal suffix meaning when, each time, every time, always.

-netik (gram.) Verbal suffix meaning since, from the time that. **Etxeratu nintzenetik ongi aurkitzen naiz.** I am fine since I came home.

neu pron.(nom.) I myself, I (emphatic).

neuk pron.(nom.) I myself, I (emphatic). Used with transitive verbs.

neur- Used in compound words. Derived from neurri, measure.

neuralgia n.(med.) neuralgia.

neurastenia n.(med.) neurasthenia, nervous prostration.

neurbide n. metrics.

neure adj./pron. my (emphatic); myself; mine.

neureganaketa n. taking for myself.

neureganatu v.t. to attract to myself, to take for myself.

neuretu v.i. to take for myself.

neurgabe adj. unlimited, excessive, without measure.

neurgabekeria n. lack of moderation, limitlessness, excessiveness.

neurgabetasun n. immensity.

neurgailu n. measuring instrument, ruler, yardstick, etc.

neurgaitz adj. immeasurable, unmeasurable.

neurgarri adj. measurable.

neurgarritasun n. quality of being measurable.

neurkari n. regulator.

neurkatu v.t. to measure with a compass or metronome.

neurkera n. symmetry, rhythm, movement with conductor's arm marking tempo.

neurketa n. measurement.

neurkin n. instrument for measuring, metric gauge, yardstick, etc. n. motion of conductor's arm marking rhythm, tempo.

neurlari n. measurer, one who measures.

neurle n. measurer, one who measures.

neurpen n. measuring, measurement.

neurraldi n. measurement, time spent measuring.

neurrarazi v.t. to make (someone) measure (something).

neurrera n. measurement.

neurri n. measure, measurement, extent, degree, size. n. meter (verse), rhythm, tempo. n. moderation.

neurriak hartu v.t. to take measurements. v.t. to take precautions, to take steps, to take measures. v.t. to control.

neurribide n. measurement.

neurridun adj. moderate, balanced.

neurriemale n. moderator, regulator.

neurrigabe adj. unlimited, enormous.

neurrigabekeria n. excess, excessiveness, exhorbitance; exaggeration.

neurrigabeki adv. excessively, to excess.

neurrigabeko adj. excessive, unlimited.

neurrigabetasun n. unlimitedness, excessiveness.

neurrigabetu v.i. to be asymmetrical, to be unlimited, to be without limit or measure.

neurrigaitzeko adj. difficult to measure, excessive.

neurrigarri adj. measurable, limited.

neurritasun n. moderation, prudence.

neurritzaile n./adj. measurer, one who measures.

neurrizgain adv. excessively, exhorbitantly.

neurrizgaineko adj. immoderate, excessive.

neurrizko adj. measured, proportionate. adj. sober, sombre, serious.

neurtarazi v.t. to make (someone) measure (something).

neurterraz adj. easy to measure.

neurtezin adj. immeasurable, impossible to measure.

neurtezinezko adj. immeasurable.

neurtitz n. line (of verse, etc.).

neurtizkera n. way of versifying.
neurtizketa n. versification.
neurtizlari n. one who creates verses, versifier.
neurtresna n. measuring instrument.
neurtu v.t. to measure, to calculate. v.t. to compete. v.t. to dose, to measure out the doses.
neurtzaile n. measurer; appraiser, assessor.
neutral adj. neutral.
neutraldu v.t./v.i. to neutralize.
neutralgarri adj. neutralizable.
neutralki adv. neutrally.
neutralpen n. neutralization.
neutraltasun n. neutrality.
neutraltzaile adj. neutralizing.
neutro adj. neutral.
neutroi n. neutron.
-nez (gram.) Verbal suffix meaning according to. **Diotenez euskara oso zaharra da.** According to what they say, Basque is very old.
ni pron.(nom.) I (subj. with intransitive verbs). pron.(acc.) me (dir. obj. with transitive verbs).
nibel n. level.
nibelbide n. railroad crossing.
nibeldu v.t. to level.
nibelgailu n. level (instrument).
nigar n. cry, tear.
nihaur pron. I myself.
nik pron.(nom.) I, me (with transitive verbs).
nikel n.(chem.) nickel.
nikeldura n. nickel-plated, nickel-plating.
nikeleztatu v.t. to nickel-plate.
nikeleztatzaile n./adj. nickel-plater.
nikeltsu adj. containing nickel, nickeliferous.
niki n. polo shirt, short-sleeved sport shirt.
nikotina n.(chem.) nicotine.
nini n. pupil (of the eye). n. baby. n. doll.
ninika n.(bot.) bud, shoot, sprout.
ninikadura n. budding, sprouting.
ninikatu v.i. to bud, to sprout, to germinate.
ninikeria n. puerility, childishness.
ninitu v.i. to be a baby. v.i. to become childlike.
nire adj./pron. my; mine.
nirnir n. shimmering light, reflecting light.
nitrato n.(chem.) nitrate.
nitrogeno n.(chem.) nitrogen.
no int. hey, you! Word used to call a woman or attract her attention. **No, garbi ezan txapel hau!** Hey, clean this beret!
nobela n. novel.
nobelari n. novelist.
nobelatu v.t. to write novels.
nobelazale adj. fond of novels.
nobelazalekeria n. excessive

fondness for novels.
nobiziago n. novitiate, state of being a novice.
nobiziatu n. novitiate.
nobizio n. novice.
noble n./adj. nobleman, noble.
noharroin n. beggar.
noharroindu v.i. to become a beggar.
noharrointasun n. begging, mendicity, beggary.
noiz adv. when (interrogative). conj. at times, sometimes. n. date, specific day or time.
noiz arte adv. until when, how long.
noizbait adv. sometime, at some time, at a given moment.
noizbaiteko adj. for a long time. adj. uncertain, indeterminate.
noizbehingo adj. sporadic, periodic, infrequent.
noizbehinka adv. from time to time, every now and then.
noizbehinkako adj. sporadic, infrequent, occasional.
noizdaino adv. until when, how long.
noizdanik adv. since when, how long, for how long?
noizean behin adv. from time to time, occasionally, every now and then.
noiz edo behin adv. from time to time, every now and then.
noiz edo noiz adv. every now and then, from time to time, occasionally.
noizero adv. how often.
noizetik noizera adv. from time to time, occasionally, every so often.
noizgailu n. date stamper, time puncher, machine for marking orrecording the date.
noizik behin adv. every now and then, from time to time, occasionally.
noizko adj. how old. adv. when, for when.
noizkotasun n. dating (something), fixing a date to.
noizkotu v.t. to date, to set a date.
noiznahi adv. any time, frequently.
noiznahiko adj. frequent, common.
noiztik adv. since when, how long.
noka adv. speaking familiarly (to women).
nokatu v.t. to speak familiarly (to women), to address women in afamiliar fashion.
noketa n. speaking familiarly to women, using familiar you with women.
nola adv. how.
nolabait adv. in some way, somehow (in affirmative phrases).
nolabaiteko adj. some kind, some type. adj. mediocre.
nola edo hala adv. in some way, one way or another (in affirmative phrases).
nola eta adv. Used at the beginning of a sentence to express surprise,disbelief, or the illogical

content of the sentence.
nolako *adj.* what kind of?
nolakotasun *n.* characteristic, feature, quality, attribute.
nolakotu *v.i.* to change. Used usually in exclamations.
nolakoxe *adj.* how exactly.
nolanahi *adv.* anyhow, anyway, any old way.
nolanahi ere *adv.* anyway.
nolanahika *adv.* arbitrarily.
nolanahiko *adj.* common, ordinary.
nolatsu *adv.* how (more or less, no specific answer required).
nomada *n./adj.* nomad.
nomadismo *n.* nomadism.
non *adv.* where.
nonbait *adv.* somewhere. *adv.* apparently, seemingly.
nonbaitetik *adv.* from somewhere.
nondik *adv.* where . . . from, (from) where.
nondik edo handik *adv.* from somewhere. *adv.* one way or another.
nondik nora *adv.* from where to where, what distance, how far. *adv.* how.
non edo non *adv.* somewhere.
non eta *adv.* of all places! Used at the beginning of a sentence to express surprise, disbelief or the illogical content of the sentence. **Non eta Siberian elkartu ginen.** We met in Siberia, of all places!
nongo *adv.* where . . . from, from where.
nongotasun *n.* location, situation, position.
nonnahi *adv.* wherever, anywhere, everywhere.
nonnahiko *adj.* common, ordinary.
nor *pron.* who. *pron.* the one. *adj.* deserving, worthy of.
nora *adv.* (to) where.
norabait *adv.* somewhere (with verbs of movement in affirmative sentences).
norabide *n.* orientation, direction; address.
norabideratu *v.t.* to direct (someone).
norabidetu *v.i.* to direct oneself to a point, to orient oneself, to aimoneself.
norabidetzaile *n./adj.* orienter, one who directs himself to a point.
norabidezko *adj.* directional.
nora edo hara *adv.* somewhere.
nora eta *adv.* of all places! Used at the beginning of a sentence to express surprise, disbelief or the illogical content of the sentence.
noraezean *adv.* aimlessly, without direction.
noraezeko *adj.* inevitable, unavoidable.
noragabe *adv.* without direction, aimlessly. *adj.* wandering, roving,

vagabond, vagrant.
noragabe ibili *v.i.* to wander aimlessly, to be without direction.
noragabetu *v.i.* to wander, to roam, to rove.
noragabezia *n.* deviation.
noragiri *n.* identification card, I.D.
noraino *adv.* how far, up to what point.
norako *n.* destination.
noranahi *adv.* anywhere, somewhere, to any place.
noranahiko *adj.* suited to a place, good for anywhere.
norantz *adv.* to where, toward where.
norbait *pron.* someone, somebody. Used in affirmative sentences. *n.* someone, important person.
norbera *pron.* oneself, himself, herself.
norberaganatu *v.t.* to attract to oneself.
norberagandu *v.t.* to attract to oneself.
norberakiko *adj.* subjective, personal.
norberaldi *n.* absorption in thought, thinking only about oneself.
norberatasun *n.* individuality.
norbere *pron.* oneself. *adj.* one's own.
norbereganaketa *n.* attraction, captivation.
norbereganako *adj.* self, personal.
norbereganatu *v.t.* to attract to oneself.
norberekeria *n.* egotism, self-centeredness.
norberekiko *adj.* reflexive.
norberekikotasun *n.* subjectivity.
norberekikozale *adj.* subjective, fond of oneself.
norberekoi *adj.* individualist.
norberekoikeria *n.* egotism.
norberekoitasun *n.* self love, egotism.
norberekor *adj.* individual.
norberetasun *n.* individuality.
norberetu *v.i.* to be lost in oneself, to think only of oneself.
norberezagutza *n.* self-knowledge.
nor edo nor *pron.* someone.
norgabe *adj.* impersonal.
norgabeki *adv.* impersonally.
norgabeko *adj.* impersonal.
norgabetasun *n.* impersonalness.
norgabetu *v.i.* to impersonalize.
norgehiagoka *adv.* competitively, in contention. *n.* competition, contest.
norgehiagoketa *n.* competition, contest.
nork *pron.(nom.)* who. Used with transitive verbs.
normal *adj.* normal.
normaldu *v.i.* to become normal. *v.t.* to normalize, to standardize.
normalean *adv.* normally.
normaleztapen *n.* normalization, standardization.
normalizazio *n.* normalization, standardization.
normalki *adv.* normally.
normaltasun *n.* normality.

nornahi *pron.* whoever, everyone, anybody.
nortasun *n.* personality.
nortu *v.t.* to personalize, to individualize; to personify.
nortzapen *n.* personalization; personification.
nortzu *pron.(nom.)* who. Used with intransitive verbs.
nortzuk *pron.* who. Usually used with transitive verbs.
noruntz *adv.* to where, toward where.
noski *adv.* of course, undoubtedly.
nota *n.* grade.
notari *n.* notary public.
notarimutil *n.* scribe, clerk.
notaritza *n.* profession of notary.
notin *n.* person.
nozio *n.* notion.
nozitu *v.t.* to suffer, to bear.
-ntzako *(gram.)* Nominal suffix designating destination, for.
-ntzat *(gram.)* Nominal suffix designating destination, for.
nuklear *adj.* nuclear.
nuntziatura *n.(eccl.)* office of papal ambassador; residence of papal ambassador; nunciate.
nuntzio *n.(eccl.)* papal ambassador, nuncio.
nuntzio-etxe *n.* residence of papal ambassador.
nuntziogo *n.* office (profession) of the nuncio.
nuntziorde *n.* substitute for the nuncio.
nuntziotza *n.* office (profession) of the nuncio.
nylon *n.(chem.)* nylon.

Ñ

ñ Letter of the Basque alphabet. Palatization of *n*, used in diminutives and words of affection.
ñimiño *adj.* small, miniscule, very tiny.
ñimiñoño *adj.* very tiny, very small.
ñimiñotu *v.i.* to become tiny.
ñir-ñir *n.* reflecting light.
ñirñir egin *v.t.* to sparkle, to twinkle, to flicker, to glimmer.
ñirñirkada *n.* sparkle, twinkle, flicker, glimmer.
ñirñirkari *adj.* sparkling, twinkling, flickering, glimmering.
ñirñirketa *n.* sparkling, twinkling. *n.(fig.)* blinking.
ñirñirlari *adj.* sparkling, twinkling, flickering, glimmering.
ñirñira *n.* blinking; flickering; sparkle, shimmer, twinkle. **Begien ñirñira.** Blinking of the eyes.
-ño *(gram.)* diminutive suffix.

O

o *n.* Letter of the Basque alphabet. Changes to *a* in cases of derived words when followed by a

consonant. **Beso. Besape.** Arm. Armpit. *int.* oh! Expresses admiration. **O, zein polita den zure baserria!** Oh, how pretty your farm is! *int.* whoa! Used to stop beasts of burden. *(gram.)* Verbal infix, 3rd person sing.; to him, to her, for him, for her. **Liburu bat eman diot.** I have given him a book.
oasis *n.* oasis.
obedientzia *n.* obedience.
obedigarri *adj.* obeyable.
obeditu *v.t./v.i.* to obey.
oboe *n.(mus.)* oboe.
obra *n.* building, construction. *n.* action, act.
odol *n.* blood.
odolahaide *n.* blood relative.
odolahaidego *n.* blood relationship.
odolahaidetasun *n.* blood relationship, quality of being related by blood.
odolahul *adj.* anemic.
odolahuldura *n.(med.)* anemia.
odolaire *adj.* blood-like.
odolaitortza *n.* martyrdom.
odolaldaketa *n.* blood transfusion.
odolaldatu *v.t.* to transfuse blood.
odolaldi *n.(med.)* hemorrhage.
odolantzeko *adj.* blood-like.
odolbateko *adj.* agnate, of the same blood, consanguineous.
odolbatu *n.* coagulated blood.
odolbero *adj.* hot-blooded, violent, aggressive.
odolberoaldi *n.* fit of rage.
odolberoko *adj.* hot-blooded, impulsive, brave, daring.
odolberotasun *n.* impulsiveness, vehemence, impetuousness.
odolberotu *v.i.* to get overexcited, to get angry.
odolberri *n.(anat.)* arterial blood.
odolberritu *v.i.* to purify blood, to renew.
odolberritze *n.* hematosis, conversion of dark blood into arterial blood by replenishing oxygen supply.
odolbide *n.(anat.)* vascular system, blood stream.
odolbildu *n.* coagulated blood.
odolbizi *adj.* nervous, jumpy.
ododdu *v.t./v.i.* to bleed, to cover with blood, to be covered with blood, to be bloody.
odoldun *adj.* bloody, having blood. *adj.* vehement, lively, energetic, brave.
odoldura *n.* covering with blood.
odoledale *n.(zool.)* leech.
odoleko *adj.* pertaining to blood. *n./adj.* blood relative.
odolemate *n.(med.)* blood transfusion.
odoleri *n.* disease of the blood.
odolestu *adj.* nervous, jittery, upset.
odoletan *adv.* bleeding.
odolez *adv.* bloodily, savagely, cruelly. *adv.* hereditarily.
odolezko *adj.* bloody, bleeding.

odoleztatu *v.t./v.i.* to bleed, to cover with blood, to be covered with blood, to stain with blood.

odolgabe *adj.* bloodless, anemic, exsanguine. *adj.* apathetic, listless.

odolgabeko *adj.* bloodless, exsanguine, anemic. *adj.(fig.)* coward; apathetic, listless.

odolgabetasun *n.* indolence, apathy, listlessness; cowardice.

odolgabetu *v.i./v.t.* to bleed, to let all the blood out of. *v.i.(fig.)* to become apathetic.

odolgaitz *adj.* cruel, hard, violent.

odolgaizto *adj.* violent, ferocious, cruel.

odolgaltze *n.* loss of blood, act of losing blood.

odolgarbiko *adj.* noble, high born, of noble descent. (lit.) of clean blood.

odolgarbitasun *n.* nobility of lineage.

odolgeldimen *n.* menopause.

odolgernu *n.(med.)* uremia, hematuria.

odolgetu *v.i.* to bleed, to lose blood.

odolgogortu *v.i.* to coagulate (blood).

odolgoritu *v.i.* to become very angry.

odolgorritu *v.t.* to bleed, to be covered with blood, to cover with blood.

odolguri *n.* blood clot, coagulation.

odolguritsu *adj.* clotted, coagulated.

odolguritu *v.i.* to coagulate, to clot (blood).

odolibilketa *n.* blood circulation.

odolisuri *n.(med.)* hemorrhage, flow of blood, bleeding.

odolisuriz *adv.* bloodily, with bloodshed.

odolisurketa *n.(med.)* hemorrhage, flow of blood, bleeding.

odolisurle *adj.* bloody, stained with blood. *adj.* ferocious, cruel.

odoljale *adj.* hematophagous, feeding on blood.

odoljario *n.(med.)* hemorrhage, blood loss, flow of blood, bleeding.

odoljariodun *adj.* suffering from a loss of blood.

odoljariotasun *n.* quality of being hemophiliac.

odoljarioz *adv.* bloodily, with bloodshed.

odoljatorri *n.* lineage, family origin, bloodline.

odolkeria *n.* butchering. *n.* cruelty, ferocity.

odolketa *n.* slaughter, butchery, mass murder, beheading. *n.* effusion of blood, a lot of blood.

odolki *n.* black pudding, blood sausage.

odolkide *n.* blood relative. *adj.* consanguineous.

odolkidego *n.* kinship, blood relationship, consanguinity.

odolkidetasun *n.* kinship, blood relationship, consanguinity.

odolkigile *n.* blood sausage maker.

odolkigintza *n.* blood sausage making.

odolkoi *adj.* cruel, ferocious, vicious.

odolkolpe *n.(med.)* apoplexy.

odolmamitu *n.* clotted blood, coagulated blood.

odolnahasdura *n.* crossing of blood, mixing of blood (one race to another). *n.* transfusion.

odolodi *n.(anat.)* blood vessel.

odoloste *n.* blood sausage.

odolotz *adj.* calm, tranquil, non-violent.

odoloztu *v.i.* to become calm.

odoltsu *adj.* bloody, blood-filled.

odoltza *n.* great quantity of blood.

odoltzale *adj.* cruel, ferocious, vicious.

odoltzalekeria *n.* cruelty, ferocity.

odoluri *n.* blood clot.

odoluritsu *adj.* varicose.

odoluritu *v.i.* to clot, to coagulate (blood).

odolusketa *n.* bleeding, flow of blood.

odolustailu *n.* lancet for bloodletting.

odolustel *n.* corrupted blood. (lit.) rotten blood.

odolusteldura *n.(med.)* septicemia.

odolustu *v.t./v.i.* to let (someone's) blood, to bleed. *adj.* bloodless, anemic, exsanguine.

odolustzaile *n.* bloodletter.

odoluzki *n.(med.)* hemorrhoid.

odolzalekeria *n.* cruelty, viciousness, ferocity.

ofizial *adj.* official.

ofiziale *n.* official, officer.

ofizialeria *n.* group of officials, group of officers.

ofizialki *adv.* officially.

ofizialorde *n.* vice-official.

ofizialtasun *n.* officialness.

ofizio *n.* job, living, profession.

ogasun *n.* property, estate, wealth, goods.

ogi *n.* bread. *n.* wheat.

ogiapur *n.* bread crumb.

ogiazal *n.* crust, crust of bread.

ogibegi *n.* hole in the bread.

ogibide *n.* job, living, profession.

ogibihi *n.* grain of wheat.

ogiburu *n.* spike of wheat.

ogidun *n.* baker.

ogierre *n.* toast, toasted bread.

ogigarri *adj.* capable of being made into bread.

ogigazta *n.(zool.)* weasel.

ogigile *n.* baker, bread maker.

ogigintza *n.* baking, bread making.

ogijale *adj.* fond of bread.

ogijatun *adj.* fond of bread.

ogijoaldi *n.* threshing (of wheat).

ogijorra *n.* weeding the wheat.

ogijotze *n.* threshing of wheat.

ogiketa *n.* act of furnishing bread, supplying bread. *n.* large quantity of wheat. *n.* harvesting wheat.

ogiketari *n.* one who delivers bread.

ogikosko *n.* end crust of bread.

ogikoskor *n.* end crust of bread, crumb

of bread.

ogimami *n.* soft inner part of bread.
ogimeta *n.* pile of wheat.
ogipeko *n.* servant, maid, domestic.
ogipuska *n.* piece of bread. *adj.(fig.)* good-natured, easygoing.
ogisaltzaile *n.* bread seller, baker.
ogitarteko *n.* sandwich filling.
ogitartetu *v.t.* to make a sandwich of, to put between slices of bread; to dip in breadcrumbs.
ogite *n.* season for harvesting wheat. *n.* wheat harvest.
ogitegi *n.* bakery, bake shop.
ogitsu *adj.* abundant in bread. *adj.* abundant in wheat.
ogitu *v.t.* to make bread.
ogitxo *n.(dim.)* small loaf of bread.
ogixerra *n.* slice of bread.
ogizale *adj.* fond of bread.
ogizatiketa *n.* slicing bread.
oguzi *v.t.* to pronounce, to articulate, to say out loud.
oha- Used in compound words. Derived from *ohe*, bed.
ohaide *n.* concubine, mistress.
ohaidego *n.* concubinage.
ohaidetasun *n.* concubinage, state of being a concubine.
ohaidetu *v.i.* to become a concubine, to be a concubine.
ohaidetza *n.* concubinage.
ohantze *n.* nest. *n.* cot, crudely made bed.
ohar *n.* advice, warning, remark, comment, observation. *n.* caution, care.
ohara *n.* oestrus, mating time, heat (cats, dogs, etc.).
oharatu *v.i.* to go into heat, to become receptive to mating, to enter oestrus (dogs, cats, etc.).
oharbide *n.* advice, warning.
ohardun *adj.* thoughtful, pensive.
ohargailu *n.* attention getting signal, sign (road signs, etc.).
oharkabe *adj.* inadvertent, spontaneous, unintentional, distracted, unthinking. *n.* carelessness, lack of caution.
oharkabekeria *n.* thoughtlessness, rashness, impetuousness, impulsiveness.
oharkabeki *adv.* carelessly, rashly, unthinkingly.
oharkabeko *adj.* inadvertent, unintentional, rash, impetuous, thoughtless, impulsive, spontaneous, unthinking, automatic.
oharkabetasun *n.* carefree state, state of innocence, lack of awareness.
oharkabetu *v.i.* to be distracted, to be careless.
oharkabez *adv.* carelessly, distractedly, unthinkingly, negligently.
oharkaitz *adj.* unnoticeable, difficult to perceive.
oharkarazi *v.t.* to give advice, to warn.
oharkari *n.* adviser; monitor.
oharkarri *adj.* observable, notable, noticeable, remarkable, perceptible.
oharkarritasun *n.* perceptibility, noticeability.
oharkatu *v.i.* to observe, to perceive, to notice.
oharkera *n.* perception, notice, attention.
oharketa *n.* observation, note.
oharki *adv.* perceptibly, noticeably.
oharkor *adj.* vigilant, cautious, careful.
oharkortasun *n.* vigilance, precaution, cautiousness.
oharkortu *v.i.* to become cautious, to become vigilant.
oharkuntza *n.* consideration, reflection, thought; attention, vigilance.
oharleku *n.* lookout point, guard post.
oharliburu *n.* guidebook, information booklet; agenda, date book, address book.
oharmen *n.* perception, attention.
oharpen *n.* observation, perception, note, consideration.
oharpide *n.* observation, perception.
oharrarazi *v.t.* to advise, to warn, to observe.
oharrarazle *n.* adviser, observer, warner.
oharraurre *n.* premonition, forewarning, presentiment.
oharrez *adv.* consciously, perceptively, thoughtfully, carefully.
oharrezin *adj.* imperceptible, unnoticeable.
oharrezko *adj.* admonishing, warning.
ohart- Used in compound words. Derived from *ohartu*, to warn, to notice, to observe.
ohartarazi *v.t.* to make (someone) realize (something), to make (someone) aware of.
ohartarazle *n.* one who makes (someone) aware.
ohartasun *n.* vigilance, attention, sagacity, alertness.
ohartezin *adj.* imperceptible, unnoticeable.
oharti *adj.* observant, penetrating, thoughtful, reflective.
ohartoki *n.* observatory, lookout point, guardpost.
ohartu *v.i.* to realize, to become aware of. *v.t.* to observe, to perceive, to note. *v.t.* to warn, to admonish.
ohartuaz *adv.* cautiously, with awareness.
ohartuki *adv.* deliberately, consciously, intentionally.
ohartxo *n.(dim.)* brief explanation, footnote.
ohartzaile *n.* adviser, warner, observer.

ohartzailetza n. counseling, advising.

ohatze n. den, lair (animals), hollow or place used by animals.

ohazal n. bedspread.

ohe n. bed.

oheburu n. head of the bed, headboard.

oheburuko n. pillow.

ohegaineko n. bedspread.

ohekada n. litter, brood (of animals).

ohekide n. concubine, mistress.

ohekidetza n. concubinage.

ohekoi adj. sleepyhead, tending to sleep a lot.

ohelagun n. concubine, mistress.

oheratu v.i./v.t. to go to bed; to put to bed.

ohestalki n. bedspread.

ohetoki n. bedroom, sleeping room.

ohetxo n.(dim.) small bed, cot.

ohexka n.(dim.) small bed, cot.

ohi n. habit, custom. adv. usually, usual.

ohi bezala adv. as usual.

ohi denez adv. as usual.

ohigabe adj. unusual, unaccustomed, uncustomary.

ohigabeko adj. unusual, uncustomary.

ohigabetu v.i. to lose the habit or custom, to get out of the habit.

ohigaitz adj. difficult to adjust, difficult to become accustomed to.

ohi izan v.i./v.t. to be in the habit of, to be accustomed to; usually (+ verb).

ohiko adj. customary, usual, habitual.

ohikunde n. custom, habit.

ohikuntza n. custom, habit.

ohil adj. savage, ferocious.

ohildu v.t. to chase away, to stampede, to drive away, to shoo away.

ohitasun n. custom, habit.

ohitu v.i./v.t. to be used to, to become accustomed to, to get used to.

ohituarazi v.t. to get (someone else) used to (something), to accustom (someone else) to (something).

ohitura n. habit, custom.

ohiturari adj. adherer to routine.

ohituratu v.i. to get used to, to be used to, to become accustomed to.

ohituraz adv. habitually, usually, customarily.

ohiturazko adj. habitual, accustomed, usual, customary, common.

ohituzko n. habitual, routine, usual, customary.

ohizko adj. usual, ordinary, habitual, customary, common.

ohoin n. thief.

ohoindu v.i. to become a thief.

ohoingo n. profession of thief.

ohoinkeria n. robbery, theft, swindle, fraud.

ohoinkide n. accomplice in theft.

ohoinkidetasun n. complicity (in a theft).

ohointegi n. thieves den, hideout, place of thieves.

ohointza n. robbery, thievery.

ohol n. wood.

oholbeltz n. blackboard, chalkboard.

oholdegi n. lumberyard, timber yard.

oholdu v.t. to cut lumber into boards or planks.

oholdura n. boarding up, putting boards or planks on or over something.

oholeria n. boarding, planking, lumber, boards, planks.

oholesi n. wooden fence, board fence.

oholeztatu v.t. to board up, to cover with boards or planks; to lay a floor.

oholeztu v.t. to board up, to cover with planks or boards.

oholgintza n. cutting boards or planks from lulber.

oholketari n. wood dealer, timber dealer; lumberjack; woodworker.

oholtxo n.(dim.) small plank or board.

oholtza n. pile of lumber. n. scaffold, scaffolding.

oholtzar n. large board or plank.

ohondikari adj. kicking.

ohondikatu v.t. to kick.

ohora- Used in compound words. Derived from ohore, honor.

ohoragarri adj. honorable, laudable.

ohorarazi v.t. to honor.

ohoratu v.t. to honor, to praise, to exalt, to glorify.

ohore n. honor, respect, esteem.

ohoredun adj. famous, celebrated, honorable.

ohore eman v.t. to honor, to praise, to exalt, to glorify.

ohoregabe adj. dishonored, without honor.

ohoretsu adj. honorable, famous, celebrated.

ohorezale adj. seeking honors, desirous of honor.

ohorezki adv. honorably.

ohorezko adj. honorable.

ohorgo n. robbery, theft.

ohosketa n. robbery, theft.

ohostu v.t. to steal, to rob.

oi int. exclamation of surprise and pain.

oihal n. cloth, fabric, material.

oihalarte n. interlining, interior lining (of clothing).

oihalatz n. coarse woolen cloth, rough cloth.

oihaldegi n. place of cloth or fabric.

oihaldenda n. fabric store.

oihaldu v.t. to weave, to knit. v.t. to wrap in swaddling clothes.

oihaleria n. quantity of cloth.

oihalertz n. selvage (of cloth).

oihaleztatu v.t. to cover with cloth.

oihaleztu v.t. to cover with cloth; to wrap in swaddling clothes.

oihalgile n. weaver, cloth maker,

textile manufacturer.

oihalgin *n.* weaver, cloth maker, textile manufacturer.

oihalgintza *n.* weaving, cloth making, textile industry.

oihalki *n.* remnant, piece, clipping, scrap (of cloth).

oihalontzi *n.* sailboat.

oihalsakratu *n.(eccl.)* corporal, white cloth used in the Eucharist.

oihalsaltzaile *n.* cloth seller, dealer in textiles.

oihaltxo *n.(dim.)* small piece of fabric, cloth.

oihan *n.* forest, wood(s).

oihanarte *n.* denseness of foliage or trees.

oihanazkuntza *n.* forestry.

oihanbide *n.* forest road, path caused by cutting of trees, provisional road in the forest; fire road.

oihanburu *n.* upper part of the forest.

oihandar *n.* forest dweller. *adj.* rustic, forest, of the woods.

oihandu *v.i.* to be covered with trees, to be forested. *v.t.* to plant trees.

oihaneder *n.* beautiful forest.

oihaneko *adj.* forestal, forest.

oihaneratu *v.i.* to go to the woods, to go into the forest.

oihaneztaketa *n.* reforestation.

oihaneztapen *n.* reforestation.

oihaneztatu *v.t.* to reforest, to replant a forest.

oihangintza *n.* forestry.

oihanguren *n.* edge of the wood or forest.

oihanlangile *n.* forester, forest ranger; lumberjack.

oihanperatu *v.i.* to go deep into the forest.

oihantoki *n.* forested place, woodsy place.

oihantsu *adj.* forested, wooded.

oihar- Used in compound words. Derived from *oihan,* forest.

oiharbide *n.* forest road.

oihartzaingo *n.* job of a forest ranger, ranger's post.

oihartzaintza *n.* job of a forest ranger, ranger's post.

oihartzun *n.* echo.

oihartzundu *v.i.* to echo.

oihartzuntsu *adj.* echo, (place) producing echoes.

oiharzabal *n.* wide forest.

oiher *adj.* twisted, winding, tortuous. *adj.(fig.)* evil, bad, mischievous.

oihertu *v.i.* to curve, to wind, to twist, to bend.

oihes *adj.* crude, rustic.

oiheskeria *n.* vulgarity, coarseness, uncouthness, bad manners.

oiheski *adv.* vulgarly, coarsely, uncouthly, in an ill-mannered way.

oihestasun *n.* slantedness; curviness.

n.(fig.) crudeness, coarseness, vulgarity.

oihestu *v.i.* to slant; to curve, to wind. *v.i.* to become crude, to go bad.

oihu *n.* scream, cry, yell, groan.

oihualdi *n.* clamoring, yelling, screaming, crying out, groaning.

oihugile *n.* town crier, town caller.

oihu egin *v.t.* to shout, to yell, to scream, to cry out, to groan.

oihuka *adv.* shouting, screaming, yelling.

oihukari *n.* crier, screamer, shouter, yeller. *adj.* shrieking, screaming, strident, harsh, shrill.

oihukatu *v.i./v.t.* to cry, to shout, to scream, to yell, to call out; to chase away (animals by shouting).

oihuketa *n.* shouting, screaming, yelling.

oihulari *n.* shouter, screamer, yeller, crier. *n.* town crier.

oihularitza *n.* office of town crier.

oihuteria *n.* shouting, clamoring, yelling, shrieking.

oihuz *adv.* screaming, shouting, crying, by shouting.

oila- Used in compound words. Derived from *oilo,* hen, chicken.

oiladenda *n.* poultry store, butcher shop.

oilagor *n.(zool.)* woodcock (*Gallinago gallinago*).

oilagorki *n.* meat of a woodcock.

oilakeria *n.* timidity, vacillation, cowardice.

oilaki *n.* chicken (meat), poultry.

oilakide *adj.* gallinaceous, chicken-like.

oilaloka *n.* brooding hen.

oilanda *n.(zool.)* pullet, young hen. *n.(fig.)* precocious young girl.

oilandaki *n.* pullet meat, chicken.

oilandatzar *n.(zool.)* large chicken.

oilantzeko *adj.* gallinaceous, chicken-like.

oilar *n.(zool.)* cock. *adj.(fig.)* arrogant, presumptuous, precocious. *n.(zool.)* sand dab.

oilargatu *n.* cockfight arena.

oilargudutoki *n.* cockfight arena.

oilarite *n.* dawn. (lit.) time of the cock's crow.

oilarjoko *n.* cockfight.

oilarkeria *n.(fig.)* pride, vanity, arrogance.

oilarki *n.* meat of a cock, chicken.

oilarmeza *n.* midnight mass.

oilartu *v.i.* to become vain, to become proud.

oilasaltzaile *n.* chicken seller, poultry dealer.

oilasko *n.(zool.)* chicken.

oilaskoki *n.* poultry, chicken (meat).

oilategi *n.* hen yard, chicken coop.

oilateria *n.* flock of hens or chickens.

oilatu *v.i.(fig.)* to become afraid, to turn chicken.

oilo n.(zool.) hen. adj.(fig.) afraid, chicken, cowardly.

oilobusti adj. cowardly, chicken.

oilojale n.(zool.) goshawk, kite.

oilokaka n. chicken excrement.

oiloluma n. chicken feather.

oilosalda n. chicken broth, chicken bouillon.

oilozale adj. fond of chicken (hens).

oimin n.(med.) gingivitis.

oin n.(anat.) foot; leg. n. foot, unit of measurement. n. rhyme. n. motive, occasion, reason.

oinarrasto n. footprint.

oinarri n. base, basis, foundation, cornerstone.

oinarrigabe adj. unfounded, without basis.

oinarriko adj. basic, fundamental, essential, rudimentary.

oinarritu v.i./v.t. to be based on; to base (something) on. adj. based (on).

oinarriz adv. basically, essentially, fundamentally.

oinarrizko adj. basic, elementary, essential, rudimentary.

oinatz n. footprint, track.

oinaulki n. footstool.

oinaze n. physical pain, suffering. n. moral suffering, pain.

oinazedun adj. tormented, suffering, afflicted.

oinazegailu n. instrument of torture.

oinazegarri adj. painful, tormenting.

oinazemale n. torturer, one who inflicts pain.

oinazetsu adj. tortured, tormented, pained.

oinazetu v.i. to torment, to torture.

oinaze-txirringa n. rack (instrument of torture.

oinazez adv. painfully, tormentedly.

oinaze-zaldi n. rack (instrument of torture).

oinazezko adj. painful.

oinazeztatu v.t. to torment, to torture.

oinazpi n. sole, bottom of the foot

oinazpiko n. base, pedestal; altar step. n. carpet.

oinazpitu v.t. to step on, to trample, to crush underfoot. v.t. to subjugate, to subject, to reign over. v.t. to despise, to disdain, to look down on.

oinaztargi n. lightning, flash of lightning.

oinaztarri n. bolt of lightning.

oinaztu v.t. to leave footprints. n. lightning.

oinbabes n. spat, gaiter.

oinbakar adj. one-legged, one-footed, having one foot.

oinberogailu n. foot warmer.

oinbide n. crosswalk, pedestrian crossing.

oinbihurketa n. sprain of the foot, twisting of the foot.

oinbiko adj. bipedal, having two feet.

oinbular n. instep of the foot.

oinburdin n. stirrup. n. shackle.

oinburdineztu v.t. to shackle, to put shackles on (someone).

oindardara n. trembling of the feet, involuntary movement of the feet.

oindun adj. having feet.

oinegitura n. infrastructure, substructure.

oineko adj. foot, pertaining to the foot. adj. fundamental, basic.

oinenbor n.(anat.) metatarsus.

oinetako(ak) n. shoe (usually used in plural).

oinetakodenda n. shoe store.

oinetakogile n. shoemaker, cobbler.

oinetakogintza n. shoemaking, cobbling.

oinetakotegi n. shoe store.

oinetxe n. ancestral home.

oinetxeko adj. ancestral, pertaining to the ancestral home.

oineurkin n. shoemaker's size stick.

oinez adv. on foot, by foot.

oinezaldi n. walk, stroll, promenade.

oinezko adj. walking. n. walker, pedestrian.

oinezkoak n.(pl.) infantry, foot soldiers.

oineztari n. pedestrian, walker.

oineztatu v.t. to put on shoes. v.t. to stand on, to trample.

oingabeko adj. apodal, having no feet, footless.

oingain n. top of the foot, instep.

oingarbiketa n. washing the feet.

oingurpil n. potter's wheel.

oinkada n. step, length of a step.

oinkapen n. stepping, footstep.

oinkari n. walker; infantry soldier

oinkatu v.t. to stomp, to trample, to stamp the ground with the feet.

oinkatzaile n. stomper, trampler.

oinketa n. tapping with the foot.

oinlasterketa n. pedestrian race, walking race.

oinlege n.(pol.) constitutional law, fundamental law

oinlegedi n.(pol.) constitution.

oinlegez adv. constitutionally.

oinlepo n.(anat.) instep, top of the foot.

oinmin n. pain in the foot, ache in the foot.

oinmindu v.i./v.t. to injure one's feet by excessive walking.

oinmuturreko n. toe cap (of a shoe).

oinoihal n. carpet.

oinoihaldu v.t. to carpet, to cover with carpet, to lay carpet.

oinoihaltxo n.(dim.) small carpet, rug.

oinoker adj. club footed, having a twisted foot.

oinorde n. inheritance. n. heir, successor, descendant (receiving inheritance).

oinordegabe adj. disinherited.

oinordekide n. co-heir.

oinordeko n. heir, first-born, successor.

oinordeko izan v.i. to be an heir, to inherit.

oinordekotasun n. quality of being an heir.

oinordekotza n. succession, primogeniture.

oinordetu v.t. to inherit.

oinordetza n. primogeniture, succession.

oinots n. footsteps, sound of footsteps, footfalls.

oinpasabide n. crosswalk, pedestrian crossing.

oinpeko n. base, pedestal, stand. n./adj. subordinate.

oinperaketa n. stamping, stomping, trampling.

oinperatu v.t. to stomp on, to trample. v.t. to oppress, to subjugate, to disdain.

oinperatzaile n. oppressor, subjugator, repressor, dictator.

oinpuntako n. toe cap (on a shoe).

oinsendagile n. podiatrist; chiropodist.

ointoki n. step, footboard, runningboard.

oinustu v.i./v.t. to take off shoes, to take one's shoes off.

oinuts adj. barefoot.

oinutsik adv. barefoot.

oinzapi n. rug, carpet.

oinzola n. sole (of the foot).

ok n. satiety, surfeit, fullness. n. vomiting.

-ok (gram.) Suffix used with articles and nouns to express the idea of being part of a group or to denote a nearby group.

oka n. surfeit, satiety, fullness. n. vomiting.

okada n. overfullness, satiety. n. nausea.

oka egin v.t. to oversatiate, to eat too much. v.t. to vomit, to throw up.

okagarri adj. overly full, stuffed, overly satiated. adj. vomitive, emetic, causing nausea.

okagile adj. nauseous, vomiting, throwing up.

okaka adv. desiring to vomit, nauseously, nauseatingly.

okaldi n. surfeit, fill, bellyful.

okanahi n. nausea, desire to vomit.

okaran n. plum, prune.

okarazi v.t. to make (someone) eat too much. v.t. to make (someone) vomit, to make (someone) throw up.

okarazle adj. vomitive, emetic, nauseating.

okasio n. occasion.

okasionalki adv. occasionally.

okasiozko adj. occasional.

okatu v.t. to eat one's fill, to get a bellyful, to satiate. v.t. to vomit, to throw up.

okaztadura n. repugnance, repulsion, disgust, abhorrence, detestation.

okaztagarri adj. repulsive, repugnant, disgusting.

okaztatu v.t. to repulse, to cause repugnance, to despise, to disgust.

okela n. meat.

okeladun n. deliverer of meat.

okelategi n. butcher shop.

okelatu v.t. to slice meat, to cut meat.

okelazale adj. fond of meat.

okelerre n. roasted meat, broiled meat.

oker adj. twisted, curvy, tortuous, sinuous. adv. mistakenly, erroneously, wrongly. adj. bad, perverted, evil. n. harm, offense, injury. adv. unfairly, unjustly. n. error, mistake; fault. adj. rascal, brat. n. wild ball, bad ball, unplayable ball (in handball).

okerbehar n. misfortune. n. obstacle, impediment, hindrance, setback.

okerbera adj. harmful, damaging.

okerbide n. perdition, going astray, misconduct.

okerbidetu v.i. to go astray.

okerbidez adv. unfairly, unjustly, unduly.

okerdun adj. defective.

okerdura n. twisting, turning, curving. n. going astray.

oker egin v.t. to make a mistake, to do something wrong.

oker egon v.i. to be wrong, to be mistaken.

okergabe adj. uninjured, unharmed. adj. innocent, blameless.

okergaitz adj. difficult to be mistaken.

okergarri adj. twistable (words or things). adj. pervertable, changeable for the worse.

okergile n. one who harms. adj. harmful.

okergune n. curve, twist.

okerka adv. obliquely, slantingly, out of the corner of one's eye. adv. backwards, in reverse.

okerkeria n. injury, injustice, harm, bad action, evil.

okerki adv. badly, mistakenly, erroneously. adv. twistedly.

okerkor adj. easily mistaken.

okerrago adj./adv.(comp.) worse.

okerragotu v.i. to get worse, to become aggravated (a condition).

okerraldi n. detour; going astray. n. adversity, misfortune, setback.

okerrarazi v.t. to twist, to curve, to detour. v.t. to corrupt, to pervert. v.t. to falsify.

okerrarazle n./adj. corruptor, perverter; perverting.

okerreko adj. wrong, erroneous, mistaken.

okerren(a) adj.(superl.) the worst; the curviest, the twistiest.

okerreratu v.t. to make (someone) make a mistake, to cause (someone) to be mistaken. v.t. to corrupt, to pervert, to lead astray.

okerreria n. prank, mischief, knavery.

okerretara adv. obliquely, slantingly, out of the corner of one's eye. adv. erroneously, mistakenly. adv. twistedly, crookedly.

okerrez adv. erroneously, mistakenly. adv. obliquely, slantingly.

okerrezin adj. infallible, unmistakable.

okerrezinezko adj. infallible, unmistakable.

okerrune n. curve, twist, bend.

okertasun n. twistedness, curviness. n. iniquity, fault, blame, culpability.

okerterraz adj. easily mistaken.

okertezintasun n. infallibility.

okertsu adj. curvy, winding, twisting. adj. full of errors.

okertu v.i./v.t. to curve, to twist, to bend. v.i. to go wrong, to become corrupted, to become evil, to go bad. v.t. to falsify.

okertzaile n./adj. twister (of ideas or objects); bender; twisting, bending. n./adj. perverter, corruptor; perverting, corrupting.

okidura n. satiety, quality of being gorged.

okil n.(zool.) woodpecker.

okin n. baker, bread maker.

okindegi n. bakery, bread store.

okintza n. baking, breadmaking (profession).

okitu v.i./v.t. to become bored; to bore (others). adj. full, very, complete, total.

okolu n. stable. n. pasture next to the house.

okotz n. chin.

okozpe n. double chin; dewlap.

okuntza n. fertile field ready for sowing.

ola n. factory, foundry. n. wood, wooden plank. n. cabin, hut.

ola (gram.) Suffix denoting location, place of.

olabahe n. sieve or screen for separating oats from chaff.

olagarro n.(zool.) octopus.

olagintza n. metal working industry.

olagizon n. iron worker, metal worker, foundry worker.

olajaun n. owner of the foundry.

olana n. awning, canopy.

olanaztapen n. covering with an awning.

olanaztatu v.t. to cover with an awning.

olatu n. wave.

olatualdi n. big wave.

olatugain n. crest of a wave.

oldar n. instant, moment. n. impetus, momentum, attack. n. bravery, valor, courage.

oldargune n. assault, attack.

oldarka adv. impetuously, impulsively, vehemently.

oldarkeria n. impetuousness, impulsiveness.

oldarketa n. attack, assault.

oldarki adv. audaciously, impulsively, impetuously, vehemently.

oldarkoi adj. audacious, bold. adj. impetuous, impulsive.

oldarkoitasun n. audaciousness, boldness, daring.

oldarkor adj. impetuous, impulsive, vehement, aggressive, attacking. adj. audacious, bold.

oldarkortasun n. impulsiveness, impetuousness, aggressiveness.

oldarpen n. impetus, attack.

oldarraldi n. attack, assault; charge, offensive, aggression. n. rebellion, uprising.

oldarrez adv. vehemently, impetuously, impulsively.

oldarrezko adj. sudden, instantaneous.

oldartasun n. vehemence, impetuousness.

oldarti adj. impulsive, impetuous, vehement.

oldartsu adj. impetuous, impulsive, vehement.

oldartsuki adv. impetuously, impulsively, vehemently.

oldartu v.i. to attack, to assault, to charge. v.i. to throw oneself, to launch, to begin. v.i. to rebel, to desert (army), to mutiny (navy).

oldartzaile adj. aggressive, attacking, offensive.

olde n. free will. n. spontaneity.

oldei n.(bot.) moss. n. compost.

oldez adv. spontaneously.

oldezko adj. spontaneous, voluntary.

oleazio n.(eccl.) last rites, extreme unction.

oleazioa eman v.t. to give extreme unction, to administer the last rites.

olerkari n. poet.

olerkarisa n. poetess

olerki n. poem, poetry.

olerkiro adv. poetically.

olerti n.(neol.) poetry, poetic art.

oles n. summons, call used at the door to summon someone; invocation.

oles egin v.t. to invoke, to call upon.

olgau v.i./v.t. to play, to have fun.

olgeta n. game, diversion, fun, entertainment.

olgura n. amusement, recreation, fun.

oliba n.(bot.) olive.

olibabiltzaile n. olive picker.

olibadi n. olive grove.

olibadun adj. rich in olives.

olibatsu adj. rich in olives.

olibolio n. olive oil.

olibondo n.(bot.) olive tree.

oligarkia n.(pol.) oligarchy.

olinpiada n. Olympic games,

Olympics.

olinpiar *adj.* olympic.

olio *n.* oil.

oliobide *n.* oil pipeline.

oliodun *adj.* oily. *n.* oil vendor.

oliodura *n.* annointing, oiling.

oliogile *n.* oil maker, oil producer.

oliogintza *n.* oil making.

olioketa *n.* supply of oil.

oliokriseilu *n.* oil lamp.

oliontzi *n.* oil container.

oliosaindu *n.(eccl.)* holy oils.

oliotasun *n.* oiliness.

oliotsu *adj.* oily.

oliotu *v.t.* to annoint with oil.

oliozko *adj.* oily.

oliozopa *n.* soup made with oil.

oliozpinontzi *n.* cruet.

olioztadura *n.* annointing, oiling.

olioztatu *v.t.* to season with oil.

olioztu *v.t.* to season with oil.

olo *n.(bot.)* oats.

oloale *n.* oat grain.

olodun *adj.* having oats.

olohazi *n.* oat seed.

olotsu *adj.* rich in oats.

oloztatu *v.t.* to feed with oats, to feed oats to.

omen *n.* honor, fame. *(gram.)* Expression meaning it is said, they say. Used with verbs. Placed before the auxiliary verb when present or before the synthetic verb. **Hil omen dira.** They say they have died.

omenaldi *n.* homage, tribute.

omendatu *v.t.* to praise, to honor, to pay homage, to pay tribute.

omendu *v.t.* to pay homage to (someone), to honor.

omendun *adj.* famous.

omen egin *v.t.* to honor, to pay homage to, to pay tribute to.

omenezko *adj.* honorable.

omengabeko *adj.* discredited, dishonored.

omengabetu *v.i.* to discredit, to dishonor.

omengarri *adj.* honorable, praiseworthy.

omengarritasun *n.* honorableness.

omenka *adv.* according to others, referring to others.

omentsu *adj.* famous, illustrious, celebrated.

on *adj.* good, nice. *adj.* able, capable. *n.* benefit, good, profit.

on- Used in compound words. Derived from *on*, good. **Onetsi.** To bless.

onaldi *n.* prosperity. *n.* recovery (from an illness).

onargaitz *adj.* difficult to accept, unacceptable.

onargarri *adj.* acceptable, admissible.

onargarritasun *n.* acceptability, admissibility.

onarketa *n.* acceptance, approval, recognition. *n.* welcome.

onaro *n.* period of prosperity.

onarpen *n.* recognition, acceptance, approval, admission.

onartezin *adj.* unacceptable, inadmissible.

onartezintasun *n.* unacceptability, inadmissibility.

onartu *v.t.* to approve, to admit, to authorize, to permit, to accept.

onartuezin *adj.* unacceptable, inadmissible.

onartzaile *n.* acceptor, approver, authorizer, one who accepts.

onbegirada *n.* sympathetic look.

onbehar *adj.* indigent, poor, needy. *n.* poverty, misery.

onbera *adj.* kind, sympathetic.

onberatasun *n.* goodness, niceness.

onberatu *v.i.* to favor, to do a favor for.

onbide *n.* good example. *n.* conversion. *n.* virtue.

onbidegarri *adj.* edifying, setting a good example.

onbiderako *adj.* edifying, exemplary.

onbideratu *v.i./v.t.* to change for the better, to become good. *v.t.* to set a good example.

onbidetsu *adj.* virtuous. *adj.* edifying, exemplary.

onbidezko *adj.* edifying, exemplary.

onbihurketa *n.* change in one's life for the better.

onbihurtu *v.i.* to change for the better.

ondamuz *adv.* enviously.

ondasun *n.* goods, property, wealth (usually used in the plural), possession(s), asset(s), resource(s). *n.* goodness.

ondasundun *adj.* landed, owning real estate, rich in property.

ondasunezko *adj.* patrimonial, pertaining to inherited goods or money.

ondasunketa *n.* treasure, quantity of wealth.

ondasuntsu *adj.* rich, landed, owning lots of property.

onddo *n.(bot.)* toadstool, fungus.

onddojakintza *n.* mycology, the study of fungi.

ondiko *n.* misery, misfortune.

ondikotsu *adj.* unfortunate, miserable.

ondikotz *adv.* unfortunately.

ondikozki *adv.* unfortunately.

ondikozko *adj.* unfortunate.

ondina *n.* mermaid.

ondo *n.* side. *n.* bottom, base, foundation. *adv.* well. *adv.* very. *n.* root, base, foot (of a tree). *n.* residue, rest, remains, leftovers. *n.* proximity, closeness.

-ondo *(gram.)* Noun suffix meaning tree, used with flowers and plants. **Pikondo.** Fig tree.

ondoan *prep.* next to, beside, close to, near. *adv.* after.

ondoegi *adv.* too well.

ondoez *n.* malaise, minor illness, indisposition.

ondoezaldi *n.* illness, period of minor illness.

ondoezik *adj./adv.* sick, ill.

ondoezik egon *v.i.* to be sick, to be ill, to not be well.

ondoezik ibili *v.i.* to be sick, to not be well.

ondoezik jarri *v.i.* to get sick.

ondoeztu *v.i.* to fall ill, to get sick.

ondo hartu *v.t.* to get along well, to treat well, to take well.

ondoko *adj.* close, nearby, next to. *adj.* secondary, posterior, following, next. *n.* successor, descendant, heir. *n.* assistant, deputy.

ondoko izan *v.i.* to be close to.

ondokotasun *n.* proximity, closeness, nearness.

ondonahi *n.* affection, love, fondness.

ondoragarri *adj.* sinkable, submergible.

ondoraketa *n.* shipwreck, sinking.

ondorapen *n.* sinking, shipwreck.

ondoratu *v.i./v.t.* to approach, to draw near. *v.i./v.t.* to sink, to shipwreck. *v.i.* to go to the bottom.

ondore *n.* result, consequence. *n.* future. *n.* succession, quality of coming after. *n.* inheritance *n.* successor, descendant.

ondoregabe *adj.* disinherited.

ondoregabetu *v.t.* to disinherit.

ondoregabezia *n.* inefficiency.

ondore izan *v.t.* to have an effect, to bring about a consequence.

ondorekide *n.* co-heir.

ondorekidego *n.* common inheritance.

ondoreko *n.* result, consequence. *adj.* following, last.

ondoren *n.* consequence, result, conclusion. *conj./prep.* after.

ondorengo *n.* successor, descendant. *adj.* following, next.

ondorengoak *n.(pl.)* descendants, progeny, offspring.

ondorengotasun *n.* succession (of a family line).

ondorengotza *n.* succession (of a family line).

ondoretasun *n.* succession, lineage, continuity.

ondoretu *v.i.* to deduce, to infer, to conclude. *v.t.* to inherit, to become an heir.

ondorezko *adj.* deductive, inferred. *adj.* hereditary.

ondorio *n.* result, consequence, conclusion, repercussion, effect, outcome.

ondoriogabe *adj.* inconsequential, ineffectual.

ondoriokunde *n.* deduction.

ondoriotsu *adj.* efficient, effective.

ondorioz *adv.* consequently, as a result.

ondoriozko *adj.* consequential; consecutive.

ondorioztatu *v.t.* to deduct, to infer.

ondotik *prep.* next to. *adv.* immediately.

ondotxo *adv.* very well, beautifully, quite well.

ondra *n.* honor.

ondradu *adj.* honorable.

ondu *v.i./v.t.* to improve, to get better, to make better, to correct. *v.t.* to cure (hides, cheese, meat). *v.i.* to get well, to recover. *v.t.* to break a record. *v.t.* to mature, to ripen.

onduezin *adj.* incorrigible.

ondugabe *adj.* unripe, not ripe.

ondugabetasun *n.* immaturity, lack of ripeness.

ondugabezia *n.* immaturity, lack of ripeness.

ondun *adj.* rich, wealthy, landed.

onean *adv.* kindly, gently.

onegi *adj.* too good.

onegikeria *n.* excessive benignity, extreme kindness.

onegile *n.* benefactor, do-gooder.

on egin *v.t.* to benefit, to enjoy, to treat well.

onegitasun *n.* extreme patience, excessive kindness or benignity.

onegite *n.* act of benefitting, favor, doing good.

onen *adj.(superl.)* the best. *adj./pron.(genit.)* of this; of this one.

onera egin *v.t.* to improve, to recover.

oneragile *adv.* edifying, exemplary.

onera hartu *v.t.* to take (something) well, to accept.

onerako *adj.* beneficial, providential.

oneratsu *adj.* beneficial, advantageous.

oneratu *v.i./v.t.* to improve, to change for the better, to correct oneself. *v.i.* to come here. *v.t.* to bring (something) here.

onerazko *n.* recovery, convalescence.

oneritzi *v.i.* to accept, to take (something) well (emotionally). *n.* acceptance, approval.

oneritzia eman *v.t.* to approve of, to accept.

onerizgarri *adj.* acceptable, appreciable.

onerizpen *n.* acceptance, approval.

onerizte *n.* esteem, respect, appreciation.

on esan *v.t.* to praise, to speak well of.

oneskaitz *adj.* unacceptable, inadmissible.

oneskarri *adj.* acceptable, admissible. *adj.* worthy of respect, esteemed.

oneskarriki *adv.* acceptably.

oneski *adv.* decently, chastely, modestly.

oneskor *adj.* acceptable, admissible, approvable.

oneskuntza *n.* acceptance, approval.

onesle *adj.* accepting, tolerant, approving.

onesmen *n.* approval, acceptance.

onespen *n.* approval, acceptance. *n.* blessing.

onespena eman *v.t.* to approve (of), to accept.

onestasun *n.* rectitude, honesty, decency.

oneste *n.* act of accepting, approving. *n.* act of blessing.

onetsi *v.t.* to accept, to approve, to admit. *v.t.* to appreciate, to esteem. *v.t.* to bless.

onez *adv.* for better; peacefully; voluntarily.

onezia *n.* goodness, beneficence.

onezkero *adv.* by now, right now.

onezko *adj.* favorable, propitious. *adj.* beneficial, useful.

onezkoak *n.(pl.)* reconciliation, making up, settling differences, restoring friendship.

ongabe *adj.* immature, unripe. *adj.* indigent.

ongabetasun *n.* indigence, poverty, need.

ongai *n.* condiment, seasoning. *adj.* beneficial, useful.

ongailu *n.* condiment, seasoning.

ongaitasun *n.* usefulness.

ongaitzak *n.(pl.)* good and bad (things), pros and cons.

ongaizkatu *v.t.* to mix good and bad.

ongarri *n.* fertilizer, manure. *adj.* beneficial, useful. *n.* condiment, seasoning, flavoring, dressing.

ongarridun *adj.* fertilized.

ongarriketa *n.* spreading fertilizer.

ongarritegi *n.* place where manure is stored.

ongarritsu *adj.* full of manure, covered with manure, excremental.

ongarritu *v.t.* to fertilize.

ongarriztadura *n.* fertilization.

ongarriztatu *v.t.* to fertilize, to spread fertilizer on.

ongarriztatzaile *n.* one who fertilizes.

ongi *adv.* well. *n.* good, the good.

ongialdi *n.* recovery, period of recovery.

ongiegi *adv.* too well.

ongiegile *n.* benefactor.

ongi egin *v.t.* to do good, to treat well.

ongiegite *n.* charity, beneficence.

ongi egon *v.i.* to be well, to be okay.

ongietorri *v.i.* to welcome. *adj.* welcome, welcomed.

ongi-etorri *n.* welcome.

ongi-etorria eman *v.t.* to welcome, to give a warm welcome to.

ongi izan *v.i.* to be well.

ongile *n.* benefactor. *adj.* beneficial.

onginahi *n.* affection, love, fondness. *n.* good will, kindness, benignity. *n.* respect, appreciation.

ongintza *n.* beneficence, goodness.

ongiro *n.* prosperity. *n.* calm (at sea), fair weather.

ongiroz *adv.* prosperously. *adv.* seasonably.

onibar *n.* real estate (land, house, etc.).

onibardun *n./adj.* landowner, property owner, homeowner; owning real estate.

onibilera *n.* success, good fortune, luck; prosperity.

onik *adj./adv.* safe and sound, unharmed.

onil *n.* funnel.

oniraun *v.t.* to remain good, to be constantly good.

oniritzi *n.* consent, approval.

onirizgarri *adj.* acceptable, approvable.

onirizgarriro *adv.* acceptably.

onirizte *n.* approval, acceptance.

on izan *v.i.* to be good, to be useful.

onkide *n.* companion in doing good works.

onkote *adj.* easygoing, good-natured (and naive).

on-on *adj.(superl.)* very good, exquisite.

ontarazi *v.t.* to season, to flavor.

ontarazle *n.* one who seasons or flavors food.

ontasun *n.* property, wealth. *n.* goodness.

onto *n.(bot.)* kind of mushroom.

ontologia *n.* ontology.

ontologiko *adj.* ontological.

ontologilari *n.* ontologist.

ontsa *adv.* well, fine.

ontsaldi *n.* recovery (from an illness).

ontsu *adj.* kind, good.

ontza *n.(zool.)* barn owl.

ontza eman *v.t.* to approve (of), to confirm, to admit, to authorize, to accept.

ontzat hartu *v.t.* to accept, to approve (of).

ontzerdi *n.* half an ounce.

ontzi *n.* container. *n.* boat, ship.

ontzia galdu *v.i.* to shipwreck, to sink, to be lost at sea.

ontzialdaketa *n.* changing from one ship to another. *n.* changing from one pot to another.

ontzialdatzaile *n.* one who decants, one who pours from one vessel to another.

ontziarrastari *n.* trawler, boat used for trawler fishing.

ontziaurre *n.* prow.

ontzibidazti *n.* ship's passenger.

ontzibizkar *n.* bridge of a ship.

ontziburu *n.* skipper, captain.

ontzidesgite *n.* dismantling of a ship.

ontzidi *n.* armada, fleet of ships.

ontzidun *n./adj.* ship owner; having a ship.

ontziestalki *n.* canvas cover.

ontzigain n. deck.
ontzigalera n. shipwreck, wreck, sinking.
ontzigarbigailu n. dishwasher.
ontzigarraio n. transportation by boat, ferrying, shipping.
ontzigela n. cabin (on a ship).
ontzigidari n. skipper, ship's captain.
ontzigidatu v.t. to pilot a ship, to captain a vessel.
ontzigile n. shipbuilder. n. potter, maker of pots.
ontzigin n. shipbuilder. n. potter.
ontzigindegi n. shipyard, dockyard.
ontzigintza n. shipbuilding, ship construction, naval construction. n. pottery.
ontzigizon n. sailor, merchant marine.
ontzigudu n. naval battle.
ontzihaga n. mast.
ontzijabe n. ship owner.
ontzikada n. cargo, shipload. n. contents of a vessel or container.
ontzikarga n. cargo.
ontzikari n. boatman, crewman.
ontziketa n. convoy of ships. n. navigation.
ontziko adj. pertaining to a boat or ship, of the boat. n. navigator, member of a ship's crew.
ontzilagun n. crew member (of a boat or ship).
ontzilaguntalde n. crew (of a boat or ship).
ontzilangintza n. naval industry, shipbuilding.
ontzilari n. crewman, navigator, member of a ship's crew. n. boatman.
ontzilerro n. convoy of ships, naval convoy.
ontzimutiko. n. cabinboy, shipboy.
ontzimutil n. cabinboy, shipboy.
ontzimutur n. cutwater.
ontzineurketa n. gauging, surveying of ships.
ontzineurtzaile n. gauger, surveyor of ships.
ontzioihal n. sail.
ontziragailu n. machine for canning, bottling, etc.
ontziraketa n. act of canning, bottling, etc. n. act of loading cargo on a ship. n. act of embarking, getting on a ship.
ontziraldi n. act of embarking, getting on a ship. n. act of loading cargo.
ontziratu v.t./v.i. to put (someone) on a ship; to embark, to get on a ship. v.t. to can, to bottle.
ontziratzaile n. canner, bottler.
ontziraulketa n. act of capsizing.
ontzisaihets n. broadside of a boat.
ontzisail n. fleet, convoy of ships.
ontzitantai n. mast.
ontzitalde n. fleet, convoy.
ontzitegi n. shipyard, dockyard. n.

cupboard, closet, cabinet.
ontziteria n. group of ships. n. dishes.
ontzitxo n.(dim.) small boat, little ship.
ontzitza n. fleet, convoy.
ontzitzar n. barge, freight boat, tanker.
ontzixka n.(dim.) little boat.
ontzixukategi n. dish drainer.
ontzizain n. skipper, pilot. (lit.) ship keeper.
ontzizama n. cargo.
ontzizerga n. freight charge.
ontzizubi n. bridge of a ship. n. pontoon bridge.
onura n. profit, earning, benefit.
onuradun adj. receiving profits on benefits; beneficiary.
onuragabeko adj. useless, fruitless, not beneficial.
onuragabetasun n. uselessness, fruitlessness.
onuragarri adj. beneficial, useful, profitable, advantageous.
onurakor adj. useful, beneficial, fruitful.
onuratsu adj. useful, beneficial, advantageous.
onuratu v.i. to be useful.
onuraz adv. usefully, beneficially.
onurazko adj. useful, beneficial.
onuste n. good faith.
onustez adv. in good faith, well-intentioned.
onuts adj. very good, very nice, very kind. adj. perfect, excellent.
onzale adj. fond of goodness, kind, nice, good.
onzaletasun n. goodness, kindness.
opa n. desire. n. offering.
opaezin adj. undesirable.
opagai n. offering, sacrificial victim.
opagarri adj. desirable. adj. worthy of being offered.
opa izan v.t. to desire (for), to wish (for). v.t. to offer.
opakor adj. offering.
opakuntza n. offering.
opari n. offering, sacrifice. n. gift.
opari egin v.t. to give, to present with. v.t. to offer, to sacrifice.
oparigai n. offering, sacrifice, sacrificial victim.
oparitxo n.(dim.) small gift, present.
oparizko adj. offering.
oparo adj. rich, abundant. adv. prodigiously, profusely.
oparoaldi n. prosperity.
oparo izan v.i. to be overabundant, to be very rich.
oparotasun n. abundance, copiousness, great quantity, profusion.
oparotasunez adv. abundantly, profusely.
oparotasunezko adj. abundant, profuse.
oparotsu adj. abundant, profuse, copious.
opatsu adj. copious, profuse,

abundant.

opatu v.t. to desire (for), to wish (for). v.t. to offer.

opatzaile n. desirer, one who desires. n. offerer. adj. offering.

opa ukan v.t. to desire (for), to wish (for). v.t. to offer.

opera n. opera.

operagarri adj. operable.

operagile n. composer of operas.

operatu v.t. to operate (on), to perform surgery (on).

operatxo n. operetta.

operatzaile n.(med.) surgeon.

operaxka n.(dim.) operetta.

operazale n. opera fan.

operazio n. surgical operation.

opil n. bun, roll.

opildu v.i. to flatten out. v.i. to ball up (usually food in the stomach).

opilgile n. baker, maker of buns and rolls.

opilgozo n. sweet roll.

opilsaltzaile n. seller of buns, baker.

opilsaski n. basket for carrying buns or rolls.

opiltxo n.(dim.) small bun, small roll.

opio n.(bot.) opium.

opiozale adj. fond of opium.

opor n. vacation, time off (usually used in the plural). n. glove for playing handball or pelota, gauntlet.

opor egin v.t. to take a vacation. v.t. to not arrive on time. v.t. to fail to keep one's word. v.t. to go on strike; to lose a day of work. v.t. to not finish the job.

opor egon v.i. to be doing nothing.

opor gelditu v.i. to be off work, to be free from work.

oporketa n. vacation time.

oporkide n. traveling companion, co-vacationer.

oporraldi n. vacation, time off.

oporregun n. day off, day of vacation.

oporretan adv. on vacation.

oporrez adv. lazily.

oposaketa n. opposition, antagonism.

oposatu v.t. to oppose, to pit oneself against, to go against.

oposizio n. competitive examination. n. opposition.

opots n. wooden pouch attached to a mower's belt, used for carrying a whetting stone and water.

or n. dog.

ora- Used in compound words. Derived from ore, dough, and or, dog.

oradura n. kneading. n. puttying, filling with putty, filling a tooth.

oragailu n. kneader, machine for kneading dough.

orain adv. now, presently, at present; ago. n. present.

orainaldi n. present. n.(gram.) present tense.

orainaldian adv. at present.

orainaldiko adj. modern, current, up-to-date.

orainaro n. contemporary age.

orainarte adv. until now.

oraindaino adv. until now.

oraindanik adv. from now on.

oraindik adv. still, yet.

oraindino adv. still.

oraingo adj. current, modern, present-day. adv. by now.

oraingoan adv. this time, on this occasion.

oraingoera n. modernization, updating.

oraingoratu v.t./v.i. to modernize, to become modern, to update.

oraingotasun n. modernness.

oraingotu v.i./v.t. to become modern, to modernize, to update.

oraingoz adv. for now, for the moment; as yet. adv. provisionally, temporarily, for now.

oraino adv. still, yet.

oraintsu adv. recently, a short time ago.

oraintsuko adj. modern, current, present, up-to-date.

oraintxe adv. right now.

orakada n. catching, grasping, seizing.

orakarri n. handle.

oraketa n. act of kneading dough. n. act of filling a tooth.

orakume n.(zool.) puppy, small dog.

oraldi n. kneading dough.

orangutan n.(zool.) orangutan.

orantza n. yeast, leaven.

orapilo n. knot.

orataldi n. kneading dough.

oratasun n. doughiness, pastiness.

orategi n. doghouse.

oratu v.t. to knead dough. v.t. to seize, to grab.

oratzaile n. one who kneads bread. n. one who grabs, one who seizes.

oratzar n.(augm.) large dog. n.(augm.) dough, large lump of dough.

orazain n. keeper of the dogs, kennel keeper.

orbain n. spot. n. scar.

orbaindu v.t. to spot. v.i. to scar.

orbaindun adj. spotted. adj. scarred.

orbaindura n. spot, act of spotting. n. scar, act of scarring.

orbaingabe adj. spotless, immaculate, clean, pure.

orbaingaitz adj. incapable of being spotted or stained. adj. unable to scar.

orbaingarri adj. spottable, capable of spotting. adj. capable of forming a scar.

orbaintsu adj. spotted, full of spots. adj. scarred, full of scars.

orbaizeta n. field of oats. Used as a last name.

orbel n. fallen leaves, dead foliage.

ordago exclam. there it is! Used in the card game mus when challenging another player.

ordain n. retribution, revenge, satisfaction. n. compensation, remuneration. n. substitute, equivalent.

ordainagindu n.(econ.) promissory note, I.O.U., receipt.

ordainagiri n.(econ.) receipt, promissory note, I.O.U.

ordainbehar n. debt, payment.

ordainbide n. compensation, reparation, satisfaction. n. way of paying, means of payment, method of payment. n.(econ.) I.O.U., promissory note.

ordainbidezko adj. satisfactory.

ordaindiru n. indemnity, compensation.

ordaindu v.t. to pay, to compensate for, to remunerate, to reward. v.t. to indemnify, to compensate.

ordaindugabeko adj. unpaid.

ordaineko adj. substituted, temporary, provisional.

ordainepe n. number of installments, period of time in which to pay back a loan.

ordainetan adv. in exchange (for), in trade.

ordainez adv./prep. in exchange (for), as compensation for.

ordainezin adj. unpayable, not compensable.

ordainezintasun n.(econ.) insolvency.

ordaingabe adj. behind in the payments, late with a payment.

ordaingaitasun n.(econ.) solvency.

ordaingaitz adj. difficult to pay. adj. difficult to substitute for.

ordaingarri adj. payable, reparable. adj. substitutable.

ordainkatu v.t. to compensate.

ordainketa n. payment, remuneration, compensation. n. retribution.

ordainkizun n. retaliation, revenge; compensation.

ordainkor adj. remunerative, rewarding, paying.

ordainkunde n. compensation, indemnification.

ordainlari n. payer, one who compensates, paymaster.

ordainlaritza n. job or office of paymaster.

ordainorde n.(econ.) compensation, indemnification.

ordainordetu v.t. to compensate (someone) for (something). v.t. to indemnify.

ordainpide n. payment, compensation.

ordainsari n. payment, remuneration, reparation, fee, reward.

ordaintasun n. reciprocity.

ordaintoki n. paymaster's office, cashier's office.

ordaintxartel n. I.O.U., promissory note, due-bill.

ordaintza n. reparation, compensation, remuneration.

ordaintzaile n. one who pays, payer. adj. remunerative.

ordaintzapen n. compensation, indemnification.

ordaintzeko adj. payable. n. due-bill, promissory note.

ordainzka adv. mutually, reciprocally, in exchange (for).

ordainzkatu v.t. to pay, to pay back in kind, to indemnify, to compensate.

orde n. compensation, remuneration. prep. in place of, instead of.

-orde (gram.) Suffix which indicates substitution, step-, vice-, etc. **Aitorde.** Stepfather.

ordea conj. but, however.

ordealdi n. temporary employment.

ordegarri adj. substitutable, replaceable.

ordeinatu v.t. to make a will.

ordeinatzaile n. maker of a will.

ordeinu n. will and testament.

ordeka n. plain.

ordeko n. substitute, replacement. adj. false, artificial.

ordenamendu n. putting in order, organizing.

ordenadore n. computer.

ordenketa n.(eccl.) ordination.

ordez prep. instead of, in place of, on behalf of.

ordezgarri adj. exchangeable, substitutable.

ordezkaezin adj. irreplaceable, unexchangeable.

ordezkagaitz adj. difficult to exchange.

ordezkagarri adj. exchangeable, replaceable.

ordezkagarritasun n. quality of being replaceable.

ordezkakor adj. supplementary, replaceable.

ordezkapen n. substitution, replacement.

ordezkari n. substitute, representative, delegate.

ordezkariorde n. subdelegate.

ordezkaritasun n. representativeness.

ordezkaritza n. delegation, representation.

ordezkatu v.t. to substitute, to replace, to relieve. v.t. to represent.

ordezkatzaile n. substitute, replacement. adj. replacing, substitutional.

ordezketa n. substitution, replacement.

ordezko adj. supplementary, substitutional. n. substitute, replacement.

ordezkotasun n. delegation, substitution.

ordezkotu v.t. to deputize, to delegate, to name a delegate or substitute.

ordezkotza n. substitution,

replacement.

ordezpen n. substitution, delegation.

ordeztagarri adj. substitutable, exchangeable, replaceable.

ordeztagarritasun n. exchangeability.

ordeztapen n. substitution, replacement, exchange.

ordeztatu v.t. to substitute (for), to exchange (for), to replace.

ordeztatzaile n. substitute, replacement. adj. substituting, replacing.

ordeztezin adj. irreplaceable.

ordeztu v.t. to replace, to substitute (for).

ordeztuezin adj. irreplaceability, incapable of being substituted for.

ordoki n. plain.

ordotz n. male pig. adj. pig. Disrespectful term of address.

ordozki n. meat of a male pig.

ordu n. hour; o'clock (used only with one and two).

orduan adv. then.

orduantxe adv. at that very moment, right then.

orduberean adv. at the same time, at the same hour.

ordubete n. one hour, full hour.

ordudanik adv. since then.

ordudun adj. punctual, on time. adj. knowing the time.

orduerdi n. half an hour.

orduka adv. by hours, by the hour.

ordukide adj. simultaneous.

orduko adj. of that time. adv. for then, at that time. conj./adv. as soon as. adj. punctual. conj. before. adv. per hour, by the hour.

ordukotasun n. punctuality.

ordulari n. clock, wall clock; watch.

ordulaurden n. quarter of an hour.

orduoneko adj. opportune; punctual.

orduonez adv. opportunely; on time, punctually.

orduraoko adv. for then, at that time.

ordurarte adv. until then.

ordutegi n. schedule, timetable.

orduterdi n. hour and a half.

ordutiar adj. waiting for the right time (a person).

ordutik adv. since then, since that time, from that point on.

ordutsu adj. punctual, exact.

ordutxar n. inconvenient time, bad time, inopportune time.

ordutxarreko adj. untimely, inopportune, inconvenient.

orduz adv. punctually, on time.

orduzkanpo adv. untimely.

orduzkanpoko adj. untimely, inopportune, inconvenient.

orduzko adj. punctual.

orduzkotasun n. punctuality.

ore n. dough, paste n. putty; filling for teeth.

orein n.(zool.) deer, stag, hart. n.

mole, beauty mark.

oreinandi n.(zool.) elk, moose.

oreinki n. elk meat, moose meat.

oreinkume n. elk calf, moose calf.

oreinlarru n. deerskin.

oreintzar n.(aug.) large moose, large elk.

oreka n. balance, equilibrium.

orekagabe adj. unbalanced.

orekan adv. keeping one's balance, balancing.

orekari n. tightrope walker, equilibrist, aerialist.

orekatasun n. equilibrium, balance; equanimity.

orekatu v.t./v.i. to balance, to keep one's balance, to be balanced.

orekatzaile adj. balancing.

oren n. hour; o'clock.

orenerdi n. half an hour.

orenka adv. by the hour.

orenlari n. watch, clock.

orenorratz n. hour hand (of a clock).

oretsu adj. pasty, doughy.

oretsutasun n. pastiness, doughiness.

oretu v.t. to knead dough.

oretzar n.(aug.) large ball of dough.

oreztari n. filling (in a tooth).

oreztari n. dentist.

oreztatu v.t. to fill a tooth.

oreztu v.t. to fill (teeth), to fill (holes before painting), to size.

orfeoi n. choral ensemble.

orfeoiko n. member of a choral ensemble.

orga n. cart.

orgabide n. cart track, cart path, wagon trail.

orgada n. cartload, cart full.

orgagile n. cartwright, cart maker, blacksmith.

orgagin n. cart maker.

orgagintza n. cart making.

orgahaga n. pole used in a cart to support the load.

organista n. organist.

organizazio n. organization.

organo n.(mus.) organ.

organogile n. organ maker.

organojole n. organist.

organoxka n.(dim.) small organ.

orgari n. cart driver.

ortategi n. carriage house.

orgatila n.(dim.) small cart.

orgato n. small cart. n. baby walker, handcart.

orgazain n. cart driver.

orizta n. freckle.

orka n.(zool.) killer whale.

orkatila n.(anat.) ankle.

orkatz n.(zool.) chamois, deer.

orkatzeme n.(zool.) female chamois, female deer.

orkazki n. chamois meat, deer meat.

orkazkume n.(dim.) young or small deer.

orkesta n.(mus.) orchestra.

orkestapen n. orchestration.
orkestatu v.t. to orchestrate.
orkestazko adj. orchestral.
orkoi n. form, mold, shoe block.
orlegi adj. green.
orlegitu v.i. to turn green.
orno n.(anat.) vertebra.
ornodun adj. vertebrate.
ornogabe adj. invertebrate.
ornomuin n.(anat.) spinal cord.
oro adj./pron. all. adv. every, everything.
-oro (gram.) Nominal suffix meaning all, every.
orobat adv. also, as well, in addition, likewise, in the same manner.
orobatasun n. totality.
orobateko adj. similar, identical, alike.
orobatsu adv. very similar, almost equal.
orobatu v.i./v.t. to become equal, to be similar. v.t. to unify, to pull together. v.t. to monopolize.
orobildu v.t. to buy up, to hoard, to corner the market, to monopolize.
orobiltzaile n. monopolizer, one who corners the market.
oroegile n. factotum, jack of all trades, person who can (and does) do everything. n. the Creator, Maker, God.
oroialdi n. memorial, time spent remembering.
oroiarazi v.t. to remind.
oroigailu n. memorial, monument; souvenir, reminder, memento.
oroikarri adj. memorable. n. memorial, monument; souvenir, reminder, memento.
oroikarriki adv. memorably.
oroikarrizko adj. commemorative.
oroimen n. memory.
oroimengarri adj. memorable.
oroimentsu adj. having a good or retentive memory.
oroipen n. memory.
oroipengarri n. memory.
oroit- Used in compound words. Derived from oroitu, to remember.
oroitagiri n. written reminder.
oroitaldi n. memorial, time spent remembering.
oroitarazi v.t. to commemorate. v.t. to remind (someone of something), to bring to mind.
oroitarazle n. one who reminds (someone of something). adj. reminiscent.
oroitarazpen n. reminding.
oroitarazte n. act of reminding.
oroitarri n. monument, memorial plaque or stone.
oroitaurreko adj. immemorial.
oroitegun n. day of commemoration.
oroitezin n.(med.) amnesia adj. not memorable.
oroitu v.i. to remember, to recall.

oroitza n. memory.
oroitzaile n. one who remembers.
oroitzaldi n. commemoration.
oroitzapen n. memory, reminiscence.
orojakin adj. omniscient, all-knowing.
orojakitun adj. omniscient, all-knowing.
orojale adj. omnivorous.
orokor adj. universal, general.
orokorki adv. universally, generally.
orokorpen n. generalization.
orokortasun n. universality, generality.
orokortu v.t. to generalize.
ororen adj. universal, common, general.
orotan adv. everywhere.
orotar adj. universal, common, general.
orotara adv. all together, in total.
orotasun n. universality, totality; integrity.
orots adj. male (animal).
orotu v.t. to universalize, to make common. v.t. to total, to add up, to sum up.
oroz adv. completely, absolutely, totally.
orozale adj. ambitious.
orozgaintasun n.(phil.) transcendence.
orpa- Used in compound words. Derived from orpo, heel.
orpagain n. upper part of the heel.
orpahezur n.(anat.) heel, heel bone.
orpaketa n. tapping with the heels.
orpo n.(anat.) heel. n. hinge.
orpokada n. blow with a heel.
orpoketa n. tapping with the heels.
orpoketan adv. tapping with the heels.
orporatu v.t. to put (a door) on hinges, to put (a window) in a frame.
orpozko adj. pertaining to the heel.
orpoz-orpo adv. closely, on one's heels.
orratio int. gosh! gracious! expression of surprise, dismay, anger, etc.
orratz n. pin, needle. n.(zool.) pipefish.
orratzain n. switchman, pointsman.
orratzontzi n. pin cushion.
orratzulo n. eye of a needle.
orrazi n. comb.
orrazigile n. comb maker.
orrazigintza n. comb making.
orraziluze n. large toothed comb.
orraziontzi n. box for combs.
orrazisaltzaile n. seller of combs.
orrazitxo n.(dim.) little comb.
orrazkera n. hairdo, hair style.
orrazketa n. combing, dressing the hair. n.(fig.) editing, correcting a written work, finishing touch.
orrazkile n. maker of combs.
orrazlan n. sewing, needlework.
orrazle n. one who combs, comber.
orrazsaltzaile n. seller of needles.
orraztaile n. one who combs, comber.
orraztaldi n. combing.
orraztari n. one who combs, comber. n.(fig.) corrector, editor.

orraztatu *v.t.* to comb.

orrazte *n.* act of combing.

orraztegi *n.* place where one combs one's hair. *n.* pin cushion, place for keeping needles.

orraztoki *n.* pin cushion.

orraztontzi *n.* box for holding straight pins or needles.

orraztu *v.t.* to comb. *v.t.(fig.)* to strip, to rob, to despoil, to deprive, to dispossess. *v.t.* to edit, to correct or change a written work.

orraztxo *n.(dim.)* little needle.

orre *n.(bot.)* juniper tree.

orredi *n.* grove of juniper trees.

orri *n.* leaf (of a tree), sheet (of paper, etc.); folio, slip.

orrialde *n.* page.

orrialdeztapen *n.* pagination, act of numbering the pages.

orrialdeztatu *v.t.* to paginate, to number the pages.

orrialdi *n.* foliation, numbering the leaves of a book.

orribakar *adj.* monophyllous, having only one leaf.

orridun *adj.* leafy, having leaves; having pages.

orridura *n.* foliage.

orrierorketa *n.* exfoliation, falling of leaves.

orrigabe *adj.* leafless.

orrigabetu *v.t./v.i.* to exfoliate, to lose leaves; to remove pages from a book.

orrika *adv.* leaf by leaf. *adv.* page by page.

orrikara *n.(bot.)* aspen tree.

orrikatu *v.t.* to turn pages. *v.i.* to lose leaves.

orrilaurden *n.* one-fourth of a page; small sheet of paper.

orrino *n.(dim.)* little leaf. *n.(dim.)* small page, leaflet.

orriska *n.(dim.)* little leaf. *n.(dim.)* leaflet, small page.

orrisorta *n.* series of pages, group of pages.

orritasun *n.* leafiness.

orritsu *adj.* leafy, full of leaves, frondy, frondose.

orritu *v.i.* to have leaves, to be covered with leaves.

orritxo *n.(dim.)* small leaf. *n.(dim.)* leaflet, small page.

orritza *n.* foliage, leafage.

orroaka *adv.* roaring.

orroaldi *n.* continual roar.

orroe *n.* roar. *n.* mooing, lowing (of a cow). *n.* roar of the ocean, sound of the sea.

orroe egin *v.t.* to roar.

orroegile *adj.* roaring.

orrokatu *v.i.* to shout, to scream, to roar.

orrolari *adj./n.* roaring, screaming; one who roars, screamer.

ortodoxia *n.* orthodoxy.

ortodoxo *adj.* orthodox.

ortografia *n.* orthography.

ortopedia *n.(med.)* orthopedics.

ortopedigailu *n.* orthopedic instrument.

ortozik *adv./adj.* barefoot.

ortu *n.* garden, orchard.

ortuari *n.* vegetable.

ortz *n.* heavens, sky.

ortzadar *n.* rainbow.

ortzaldeak *n.(pl.)* points of the compass.

ortze *n.* heavens, sky, firmament.

ortzeko *adj.* dental. *adj.* celestial, heavenly.

ortzeontzi *n.* spaceship, space shuttle.

ortzeune *n.* heavenly space, outer space.

ortzi *n.* mythological character, ancient name of the sky god. *n.* heavens, sky, firmament.

ortzune *n.* outer space, cosmic region.

osa *n.* grama grass. Used as a last name.

osaba *n.* uncle.

osaba-ilobak *n.* uncle and nephew(s).

osabelar *n.* medicinal herb.

osabide *n.* medical treatment, healing method, cure, therapy.

osabidetasun *n.* complementariness.

osabidezko *adj.* complementary.

osaera *n.* composition.

osaezin *adj.* incurable. *adj.* which cannot be completed.

osagabe *adj.* incomplete, unfinished, imperfect.

osagabetasun *n.* incompleteness.

osagai *n.* component, element.

osagaitz *adj.* incurable, difficult to heal. *adj.* difficult to complete.

osagarri *n.(gram.)* complement. *adj.* complementary. *n.* cure, remedy. *adj.* curable. *n.* health.

osagarridun *adj.* healthy, having good health.

osagarritsu *adj.* beneficial, healthy.

osagarrizko *adj.* complementary.

osagile *n.* doctor.

osakera *n.* medical treatment, cure.

osaketa *n.* cure, healing.

osakin *n.* complement, addition.

osakizun *n.* complement, addition. *n.* cure, remedy, medication.

osakor *adj.* complementary. *adj.* healing, healthy.

osalari *n.* doctor, physician.

osasun *n.* health.

osasunbelar *n.* medicinal herb.

osasunbide *n.* medication, therapy.

osasundu *v.i.* to get well.

osasundun *adj.* healthy.

osasunezko *adj.* healthy, hygienic, medicinal.

osasungabe *adj.* unhealthy, sick, ill.

osasungaitz *adj.* incurable, difficult to cure.

osasungarri *adj.* healthy, medicinal,

curative.

osasungarriro adv. hygienically, healthily.

osasungarritasun n. healthiness.

osasungarritu v.t. to make hygienic, to sanitize.

osasungiro n. state of health.

osasunketa n. sanitizing, making hygienic or healthy.

osasunkoi adj. hygienic.

osasunkor adj. hygienic, medicinal, healthy.

osasuntsu adj. healthy.

osatasun n. completeness, integrity, complementariness, perfection.

osategi n. hospital, clinic.

osatetxe n. hospital, clinic, sanitarium.

osatu v.t. to complete, to perfect, to unify, to make complete. v.i./v.t. to get well, to cure.

osatzaile adj. complementary, integral.

osin n. pit; well, hole; moat. n. abyss, depths.

osintsu adj. bottomless, very deep.

osintxo n.(dim.) small pit.

oskarbi n. clear sky.

oskarbiarte n. clearing, period of clear sky.

oskarbitu v.i. to clear, to clear up (sky, weather).

oskarbiune n. period of clear sky, patch of clear sky.

oskol n. shell. n. armor.

oskoldun adj. crustacean, having a shell.

oskoleztatu v.i. to wear armor, to be covered with armor.

oskoltsu adj. multivalve (shellfish).

oskorri n. reddish dawn, first light of day, daybreak.

oskorritu v.i. to dawn, to break (day).

oso adj. total, global, whole, complete, entire. adj. sincere, ingenuous; simple. adv. very, entirely, completely, totally.

osoki adv. thoroughly, totally, completely, absolutely. adv. perfectly.

oso ondo adv. very well, perfectly.

oso ongi adv. very well, perfectly.

osorik adv. completely, totally, entirely. adj. entire, intact, whole, in one piece.

osoro adv. completely, absolutely, totally, thoroughly. adv. perfectly.

osotasun n. integrity, wholeness, totality, entirety. n. sincerity, ingenuousness.

osotoro adv. completely, absolutely, totally.

osotu v.t. to complete, to complement, to make whole.

ospa int. get out! get away!

ospa- Used in compound words. Derived from ospe, fame.

ospabide n. means of becoming famous, road to fame.

ospa egin v.t. to escape, to run away, to get away.

ospagarri adj. praiseworthy, glorifiable, laudable; emeritus.

ospagarritasun n. magnificence, praiseworthiness.

ospaketa n. celebration.

ospakizun n. celebration.

ospakuntza n. celebration.

ospatsu adj. illustrious, famous, renowned, celebrated; emeritus.

ospatu v.t. to celebrate, to commemorate. v.t. to glorify, to honor, to pay homage to, to praise.

ospatzaile adj./n. praising, eulogizing; eulogizer.

ospe n. fame, glory, honor, renown.

ospedun adj. glorious, famous, celebrated.

ospegabe adj. dishonored, defamed.

ospegabeko adj. without fame, unknown, dishonored.

ospegabetu v.i. to dishonor, to discredit.

ospegarri adj. praiseworthy, honorable, emeritus. n. decoration (for valor, etc.).

ospel n. chilblain, goosebump (usually on the feet).

ospeldu v.i. to be covered with chilblains.

ospetasun n. majesty, stateliness.

ospetsu adj. famous, renowned.

ospetsuki adv. majestically, solemnly, in a stately manner.

ospez adv. gloriously, famously, celebratedly.

ospitale n. hospital.

ospitaleratu v.t. to take (someone) to the hospital, to hospitalize. v.i. to go to the hospital.

ost- Used in compound words. Derived from ortze, heavens, sky.

ostadar n. rainbow.

ostadarketa n. iridescence.

ostalari n. innkeeper, hotelkeeper.

ostalaritza n. innkeeping.

ostaler n. innkeeper.

ostalersa n. female innkeeper.

ostaletxe n. inn.

ostalgintza n. innkeeping.

ostargi n. clearness of the sky.

ostargitu v.i. to clear (sky).

ostarte n. clearing, partial clearing, sun peeking through the clouds.

ostatari n. innkeeper.

ostatatu v.i./v.t. to lodge, to stay; to put (someone) up.

ostatetxe n. inn.

ostatu n. inn, hotel.

ostatukari n. lodger, guest (at an inn).

ostatuketa n. lodging.

ostatuko n. innkeeper.

ostaturaketa n. lodging.

ostaturatu v.i. to stay (at an inn), to lodge (at an inn).

ostatutu v.i./v.t. to stay (at an inn), to

lodge; to put (someone) up, to give lodging.

ostatutza n. lodging.

ostatuxka n.(dim.) small inn.

ostatuzain n. innkeeper.

oste n. multitude, large number of people. n. back part. n. hangover.

-oste Suffix meaning after. **Bazkaloste.** After lunch.

ostean prep. behind.

ostegun n. Thursday.

ostendu v.t. to hide, to conceal.

ostera conj. however, but. adv. again. n. trip, round trip, going and coming.

ostera egin v.t. to take a trip, to travel. v.t. to do again, to redo.

osterantzean conj. otherwise, if not, or else.

osterantzeko adj. further, remaining, all the rest.

osteratu v.t. to repeat, to reiterate.

ostikada n. kick.

ostikadura n. stamping of feet.

ostikalari n. kicker, stamper. n. soccer player.

ostikaldi n. kicking or stamping the feet.

ostikari n./adj. kicker, stamper; kicking.

ostikatu v.t. to kick, to stamp the feet, to tread underfoot.

ostikatzaile n. kicker. adj. infringing, trampling, violating.

ostiketa n. soccer.

ostiko n.(anat.) heel. n. kick.

ostikojolas n. soccer.

ostikoka adv. kicking.

ostikokada n. kick.

ostikokari n. one who kicks, kicker.

ostikokatu v.t. to stamp, to trample, to kick.

ostikoketa n. kicking, stamping.

ostikope n. sole of the foot, heel.

ostikopetu v.t. to trample, to stomp on.

ostiral n. Friday.

ostosketa n. rolling of thunder, thunder clap, thundering, thunderpeal.

ostoskile adj. thundering, thunderous.

ostostsu adj. thundering, thunderous.

ostots n. thunder.

ostotsaldi n. thunderclap, roll of thunder.

ostots egin v.t. to thunder.

ostra n.(zool.) oyster.

ostrahazkuntza n. oyster breeding.

ostrahazle n. oyster breeder.

ostraleku n. oyster bed.

ostrari n. oyster breeder, oysterman.

ostrasaltzaile n. oyster selling.

ostrategi n. oyster bed; oyster shop.

ostratsu adj. full of oysters.

ostrazale adj. fond of oysters.

ostruka n.(zool.) ostrich.

ot- Used in compound words. Derived from ogi, bread.

ota- Used in compound words. Derived from ote, gorse, furze.

otabar n. stubble of furze or gorse.

otabaso n. field of furze or gorse.

otadi n. field of furze or gorse.

otaleku n. furze field.

otalore n.(bot.) flower of the furze plant.

otalur n. land covered with furze.

otalurmendiak n.(pl.) uncultivated mountains, mountains covered with furze.

otamen n. mouthful, bite; light snack.

otapur n. crumb

otar n. hard furze. n. basket.

otargile n. basket maker, basket weaver.

otargin n. basket maker, basket weaver.

otargintza n. basket making, basket weaving.

otarrain n.(zool.) lobster.

otarrainska n.(zool.) prawn.

otarraintxo n.(zool.) prawn.

otarre n. basket.

otarsaltzaile n. basket seller.

otarteko n. mouthful, bite; sandwich filling.

otartxo n.(dim.) little basket.

otatxori n.(zool.) flycatcher.

otatze n. gorse thicket.

ote adv. perhaps, might, maybe. Expresses doubt or questionableness. Placed between interrogative and verb. **Ba ote dakizu nor etorri den?** Might you know who has come? n.(bot.) furze, gorse.

oteme n. kind of furze without stickers or spines.

oterre n. burned gorse thicket.

otetsu adj. full of furze.

oti n.(zool.) grasshopper.

otoi n. prayer, supplication, request. int. please.

otoi egin v.t. to pray, to supplicate.

otoigile adj. praying, entreating, supplicating, pleading, requesting.

otoikatu v.t. to pray, to plead, to beg, to request.

otoikera n. way of praying, way of requesting.

otoiketa n. prayer, supplication, request.

otoitu v.t. to pray, to supplicate.

otoitz n. prayer.

otoitz egin v.t. to pray, to supplicate.

otoitzera n. way of praying.

otoitzeragile adj. inviting prayer, inspiring prayer (in others).

otoitzezko adj. pertaining to prayer, prayer; begging, pleading, supplicating.

otoizbera adj. devout.

otoizka adv. through prayer, praying, in a prayer, pleading, requesting.

otoizkatu v.t. to pray.

otoizketa n. rogation, public prayer.

otoizkile adj. devout, prayerful.

otoizko adj. supplicating, begging,

imploring, pleading.

otoizle adj. devout, prayerful, requesting, entreating.

otoizliburu n. prayer book.

otoizte n. act of praying.

otoiztegi n. oratory, small private chapel, place to pray.

otoiztiar adj. devout.

otoiztoki n. oratory, small private chapel, place to pray.

otoiztu v.t. to pray.

otondu n.(bot.) furze plant.

otordu n. mealtime, meal, time to eat.

otorduero adv. at every meal.

otorduondo n. time after dinner.

otsa- Used in compound words. Derived from otso, wolf.

otsahien n.(bot.) hop vine, hops.

otsaila n. February.

otsakume n.(dim.) wolf cub.

otsalar n.(bot.) eglantine, sweetbriar.

otsamendi n. mountain where wolves abound.

otsanda n. she-wolf.

otsantzeko adj. wolf-like.

otsar n. male wolf.

otsategi n. place where wolves abound.

otsazulo n. wolf's den.

otsein n. servant, domestic (male).

otseindu v.t. to serve.

otseingo n. servant's job.

otseinketa n. service, domestic service.

otseinkide n. fellow servant, co-servant.

otseintalde n. group of servants.

otseintasun n. domestic servitude, condition of being a servant.

otseintza n. service, domestic service, servitude.

otseme n. she-wolf, female wolf.

otserri n. wolf country.

otso n.(zool.) wolf (Canis lupus).

otsokeria n.(fig.) atrocity, act of brutality.

otsoko n.(dim.) wolf cub.

otsotzar n.(augm.) big wolf.

otu v.i. to occur to (someone)

oturuntza n. meal, mealtime.

otzan adj. docile, meek, calm.

otzandu v.t./v.i. to calm, to placate, to calm (someone) down; to tame, to domesticate.

otzandura n. taming, domestication, breaking (horses).

otzangaitz adj. difficult to tame.

otzangarri adj. tamable; calmable.

otzanketa n. taming, domesticating; breaking (horses).

otzanki adv. meekly, docilely, tamely.

otzankor adj. calming, placatory, placating.

otzankortasun n. tamableness; placability, calmableness.

otzantasun n. calmness, meekness, docility.

otzantzaile adj. taming, calming, domesticating.

otzaragile n. basket maker, basket weaver.

otzaragin n. basket maker.

otzarakada n. basketful.

otzaratu v.t. to carry in a basket, to put in a basket.

otzaratxo n.(dim.) little basket.

oxido n.(chem.) oxide.

oxigenatu v.t./v.i. to oxygenate; to become oxygenated.

oxigeno n. oxygen.

ozar adj.(fig.) insolent, impertinent, haughty, arrogant.

ozarkeria n. insolence, arrogance, impertinence.

ozarki adv. insolently, arrogantly, impertinently.

ozartasun n. insolence, impertinence.

ozartu v.i. to be insolent, to be impertinent.

ozeaniko adj. oceanic, ocean, of the ocean.

ozeanoarteko adj. interoceanic.

ozen adj. sharp, penetrating; sonorous voiced.

ozendu v.i. to resound, to boom. v.t. to make (one's voice, etc.) resound.

ozendura n. resonance, resounding.

ozengailu n. loudspeaker, speaker.

ozenketa n. resounding, booming, voicing, sounding.

ozenki adv. out loud, loudly, aloud.

ozentasun n. sonority, quality of being voiced. **Txistuaren ozentasuna.** The sonority of the Basque flute.

ozentsu adj. sonorous voiced.

ozpin n. vinegar. adj. irritating, obnoxious, nervous, caustic, sarcastic.

ozpinandel n. vinegar container, cruet.

ozpindu v.t./v.i. to season with vinegar; to turn to vinegar. v.t./v.i. to irritate, to annoy; to be irritated.

ozpindun n. vinegar merchant. adj. vinegary, sour.

ozpinezko adj. vinegary, sour.

ozpineztatu v.t. to season with vinegar, to soak in vinegar.

ozpineztu v.t. to pickle in vinegar, to soak in vinegar, to season with vinegar.

ozpingarri adj. souring, producing sourness.

ozpingile n. vinegar maker.

ozpinkeria n.(fig.) causticness, bitingness, sharpness (personality), bitterness, sarcasticness.

ozpinkor adj. quick to sour. adj. quick to anger.

ozpinontzi n. vinegar cruet.

ozpintasun n. acetosity, acidity.

ozpintsu adj. seasoned with vinegar. adj.(fig.) caustic, sarcastic.

ozta adv. scarcely, barely.

ozte n. multitude, crowd.

oztopabide n. stumbling place.
oztopagarri adj. impeding, obstructing.
oztopaketa n. obstruction, impediment, difficulty.
oztopaldi n. stumble, trip, stumbling.
oztopaleku n. stumbling place.
oztoparazi v.t. to trip (someone), to trip up, to make someone stumble, to cause to stumble.
oztoparri n. stone on which one stumbles or trips; stumbling block.
oztopatsu adj. difficult, obstructing, impeding, hindering.
oztopatu v.i./v.t. to trip, to stumble; to impede, to obstruct, to be obstructed.
oztopatzaile n./adj. obstructor, one who impedes; obstructing, impeding.
oztopo n. stumble, trip. n. difficulty, obstruction, impediment.
oztopo egin v.t. to stumble, to trip.

P

p Letter of the Basque alphabet.
pa n. kiss (child's language).
padera n. frying pan.
padura n. salt marsh, swamp.
padurako adj. marshy.
paduratsu adj. swampy, marshy, boggy, mirey.
paduretxe n. palafitte, lake dwelling.
paella n. dish made of rice, chicken, saffron, and often seafood.
pa eman n. to kiss (child's language).
pagadi n.(bot.) beech tree grove, forest of beech trees.
pagagarri adj. payable.
pagamendu n. retribution, payment.
pagarazi v.t. to make (someone) pay.
pagatu v.t. to pay.
pagatzaile n. payer.
pagazi n.(bot.) beechnut.
pago n.(bot.) beech.
pagondo n.(bot.) beech tree.
pagotxa n.(bot.) trefoil, clover.
pagotxeta n. clover field.
pagu n. payment, retribution.
paguso n.(zool.) ringdove, wood pigeon.
pailaso n. clown.
pailaskokeria n. clown's antics; something bad, foolishness, stupidity.
pairabide n. reason for suffering.
pairadura n. suffering.
pairaezin adj. insufferable, intolerable, unbearable.
pairagaitz adj. insufferable, intolerable, unbearable.
pairagarri adj. sufferable, bearable.
pairago n. suffering, bearing.
pairakor adj. patient, long-suffering, tolerant.
pairakortasun n. patience, tolerance, endurance.
pairakortu v.i. to become painful, to recur (pain).

pairamen n. suffering, tolerating, bearing.
pairamendu n. suffering, bearing.
pairatsu adj. patient, suffering.
pairatu v.t. to suffer, to bear.
pairatzaile n. sufferer, one who suffers. adj. suffering, patient.
pairu n. suffering, bearing.
pairugabe adj. impatient, fretful, nervous.
pairugabekeria n. impatient act, impatience.
pairugabeki adv. impatiently.
pairugabeko adj. impatient.
pairugabetasun n. impatience. n. impassivity, unfeelingness.
pairutsu adj. patient, long-suffering.
paita n. duck.
pake n. peace.
paketaketa n. packaging, packing.
paketapen n. packaging, packing.
paketari n. packer.
paketatu v.t. to package, to wrap a package, to put in a package.
paketatzaile n. packer.
pakete n. package.
paketegile n. package maker, packer.
pala n. paddle, playing stick, pelota bat.
palada n. one stroke of the oar, one pull of the oar. n. swimming stroke.
palagu n. praise, flattery, adulation.
palakada n. shovelful, spadeful.
palakari n. pelota player (who uses a pelota bat). n. one who uses a shovel.
paladi n. shovelful.
palanka n. lever, crowbar, pole. n. iron bar thrown in sport. n.(zool.) bib, a kind of fish.
palankari n. one who throws an iron bar (in sport).
palankatu v.t. to use a crowbar, to use a lever.
palari n. pelota player who uses a pelota bat.
palatxo n.(dim.) small pelota bat; small shovel or spade.
paleolitiko n. Paleolithic times.
paletakada n. blow with a bat.
palio n.(eccl.) baldachin, cloth canopy carried over a sacred object.
palku n. theater box, raised stand for spectators, grandstand.
palma n.(bot.) palm.
palmadar n. palm frond, branch of a palm tree.
palmadi n. grove of palm trees.
palmadun adj. palm-bearing, abounding in palms.
palmantzeko adj. palmy, palm-like.
palmazko adj. of or pertaining to palms.
palmondo n.(bot.) palm tree.
palmorri n. palm leaf.
paludismo n.(med.) malaria.
panamerikar adj. Pan-American.

pandero n. Basque tambourine.
panderogile n. maker of Basque tambourines.
panderojole n. Basque tambourine player.
panderots n. sound of the Basque tambourine.
panderotxo n.(dim.) small Basque tambourine.
panel n. removable planks used as a low deck in a small boat.
pankarta n. placard, protest sign, poster on a stick.
panpakada n. slamming of the door; slam, bang of a door.
panpakatu v.t./v.i. to slam the door, to bang a door or window.
panpatu v.t. to beat, to hit with heavy blows. v.i. to slam.
panpina n. doll. adj. dolled up.
panpinatu v.t./v.i. to dress up, to spruce up, to dress in style, to doll up.
panpindu v.i./v.t. to dress up, to spruce up, to doll up.
panpoxa adj. pretty, beautiful, handsome, gracious, charming.
panpoxtu v.i. to dress up, to spruce up, to doll up.
pantaila n. screen, movie screen, television screen.
pantaloi n. panties.
panteoi n. pantheon.
pantera n.(zool.) panther.
pantxo n.(zool.) very small spawn or young of a red sea bream.
papagai n.(zool.) parrot.
papaia n.(bot.) papaya.
papaiondo n.(bot.) papaya tree.
papao adj.(colloq.) idiotic, stupid.
papar n. chest, upper part of the chest. n. shirtfront, collar.
papardo n.(zool.) ray's bream, gray comestible saltwater fish (about the size of a rock cod) usually caught in the winter.
papargorri n.(zool.) robin, robin redbreast.
paparralde n. upper part of the chest.
paparreko n. emblem, brooch, pin, decoration worn on the chest. n. blow to the chest. n. bib, baby's bib.
paper n. paper.
paperdenda n. stationery shop.
paperdiru n. paper money, bill.
paperegile n. paper manufacturer.
papereztaile n. wallpaper hanger.
papereztatu v.t. to wallpaper.
papereztatzaile n. paper-hanger.
papergabe adj. without papers, without identification.
papergaineko n. paperweight.
papergintza n. paper industry.
paperketa n. quantity of paper, pile of paper, ream of paper.
paperki n. piece of paper, piece of wallpaper.

paperlatz n. sandpaper.
paperlodi n. untrimmed paper.
papernahaste n. mess of paper.
paperola n. paper factory.
paperontzi n. wastepaper basket.
paperpilo n. mountain of paper, large pile of paper or papers.
paperpisu n. paperweight.
papersaltzaile n. stationery seller.
papersaski n. wastepaper basket.
papersorta n. bundle of papers.
papertegi n. paper warehouse.
papertxo n.(dim.) small piece of paper.
papertxori n. paper bird, origami bird.
papertza n. abundance of paper.
papertzar n.(aug.) useless document; big sheet of paper.
paperzorro n. folder, paper folder.
papo n. crop, craw, maw. n. upper part of the chest.
parabola n. parable.
paradisu n. paradise. n. heaven.
paradisutar adj. paradisal, paradisiacal.
paradoxa n. paradox.
paralelo n. parallel.
paraleloki adv. parallel.
paralisi n.(med.) paralysis.
pare n. couple, pair. adj. equal, compared to.
parean prep./adv. beside, at the side of, by (your, his, etc.) side, on (your, his, etc.) side; next door, across the street; in front of.
parebide n. equality, equalness, comparableness.
paregabe adj. unique, exceptional, unequaled, without equal, extraordinary.
paregabeki adv. incomparably, in an unequaled fashion.
paregabeko adj. exceptional, extraordinary, unique, excellent, incomparable.
paregabetasun n. disparity, dissimilarity, quality of being unequal.
paregabetu v.i./v.t. to be unmatched; to break up a pair; to make unequal.
paregaitz adj. inimitable, incomparable.
paregarri adj. comparable, equal, similar.
pareiatu v.t./v.i. to pair up, to match up, to put in pairs.
parekatu v.t. to compare, to parallel. v.i. to mate, to pair off.
parekatzaile n. matcher, fitter, coupler.
parekide adj. parallel, comparable, matchable.
parekidetasun n. affinity, similarity.
pareko adj. similar, equal; comparable.
parekotasun n. parity.
parentesi n. parenthesis, curved bracket.
pareta n. wall.
paretasun n. parity, equality.
paretsu adj. very similar.

paretu *v.i./v.t.* to be paired up, to pair up, to match up. *v.i.* to mate, to pair off.

paretza *n.* parity, equality.

paretzaile *n.* equalizer. *adj.* equalizing.

paria *adj.* indigent, poverty-stricken. *n.* indigent, poor person.

parlamentari *n.* member of parliament.

parlamentu *n.(pol.)* parliament.

parlamentuko *adj.* parliamentary.

parodia *n.* parody.

parodiatu *v.t.* to parody, to make fun of, to imitate.

parranda *n.* spree, party, revelry, binge.

parranda egin *v.t.* to spree, to go on a spree, to go on a binge, to party.

parrandari *n./adj.* partier, binger, reveler, one who goes on a spree; partying.

parra-parra *adv.* profusely, copiously; lavishly, extravagantly.

parrasta *n.* profusion, abundance. *n.* troop.

parrastada *n.* abundance, profusion. *n.* drenching, dousing (with liquid). *n.* extravagance, squandering, waste.

parrastaka *adv.* profusely, extravagantly, abundantly, copiously; in a large group.

parrastari *n./adj.* spendthrift, wasteful person.

parrastatsu *adj.* extravagant, wasteful; profuse, abundant.

parrastatu *v.t.* to waste, to spend extravagantly.

parrastatzaile *adj.* wasteful, extravagant.

parrokia *n.(eccl.)* parish.

parrokiar *n.* parishioner.

parrokiko *adj.* parochial, pertaining to a parish.

parroko *n.(eccl.)* principal parish priest, rector of a parish.

parrokotza *n.* office or position of parish priest.

partaide *n.* partner, member; participant, co-participant.

partaide izan *v.i.* to take part, to participate.

partaidetasun *n.* co-participation, mutual participation.

partaidetu *v.i.* to become a member, to become a partner.

partaliergo *n.* partnership, co-participation, mutual participation.

partaliertasun *n.* participation, co-participation, mutual participation.

partaliertu *v.i.* to become a member, to become a partner.

parte *n.* part, share, portion.

partedun *n.* participant.

parteharmen *n.* participation.

parte hartu *v.t.* to take part, to participate.

partehartzaile *n.* participant.

parte izan *v.t.* to participate, to take part.

partekatu *v.t.* to share. *v.t.* to cut into pieces.

partekide *n.* participant.

parte ukan *v.t.* to participate, to take part.

partez *prep.* on behalf of, on (someone's) behalf, instead of, in place of.

partidu *n.* match, game. *n.(pol.)* party, political party. Usually used for the PNV (Basque Nationalist Party).

partidukide *n.* party member, member of a political party.

partigarri *adj.* divisible, apportionable, breakable.

partiketa *n.* division, parceling, distribution.

partimen *n.* division, distribution.

partitu *v.t.* to distribute, to deliver. *v.i.* to leave.

partitzaile *n.* deliverer, distributor.

partizipio *n.* participle.

partxe *n.* patch (on a tire).

partzuergo *n.* partnership, mutual participation. *n.* consortium.

partzuergotasun *n.* quality of being a member.

partzuertu *v.i.* to become a member, to join, to associate; to be a partner.

pasabide *n.* passage, means of passing or crossing.

pasadizu *n.* anecdote, adventure, event, tale, story.

pasaera *n.* passing.

pasaezin *adj.* impassable; nontransferable.

pasagaitz *adj.* impassable. *adj.(phys.)* refractory, heat-resistant.

pasagarri *adj.* passable, fair.

pasagarriki *adv.* passably, fairly, so-so.

pasagiri *n.* passport. *n.* visitor's permit, border permit.

pasagune *n.* pass, passage.

pasaia *n.* passageway. *n.* passage, money paid for boat passage. *n.* migration of birds.

pasaiako *adj.* migratory.

pasaiari *n.* passenger.

pasaiestu *n.* narrow strait, narrow passage.

pasaihegazti *n.* migratory bird.

pasakor *adj.* passing, transitory, ephemeral.

pasaldi *n.* passing, passage.

pasaleku *n.* pass, place of passing, passage.

pasaporte *n.* passport.

pasarazi *v.t.* to make (someone) pass or enter.

pasarte *n.* passage, piece of text.

pasasari *n.* toll.

pasatoki *n.* place of passing, passage.

pasatu *v.t./v.i.* to spend (time), to pass (time). *v.t.* to cross, to cross over. *v.i.* to happen.

pasatxartel *n.* border pass, travel permit.
pasatzaile *n.* crosser, passer.
paseko *adj.* migratory.
pasibitate *n.* passivity.
pasibo *adj.* passive.
pasiboki *adv.* passively.
pasibotasun *n.* passivity, passiveness.
pasio *n.* passion of Christ.
pasione *n.* suffering, bearing.
pasiotar *n./adj.* member of a male religious order.
pasmatu *v.i.* to become infected, to become gangrenous.
pasmo *n.* pus. *n.* gangrene.
pasodoble *n.(mus.)* pasodoble.
pastaka *n.* messy desk, messy table.
pastana *n.(bot.)* carrot.
pastel *n.* cake.
pastila *n.* pill.
pastoral *n.* kind of rustic theater. *n.(eccl.)* letter from a bishop to his diocese, etc.
pastoralgintza *n.(eccl.)* work of the bishop in conjunction with the priests of the diocese.
pastoralki *adv.* pastorally.
patar *n.* slope.
patartasun *n.* roughness; steepness.
patartsu *adj.* rough, rugged; steep.
patata *n.* potato.
patatadi *n.* potato field.
patatari *n.* potato seller.
patena *n.(eccl.)* paten.
patentagarri *adj.* patentable.
patentatu *v.t.* to patent.
patente *n.* patent.
patina *n.* skate.
patinaketa *n.* skating.
patinari *n.* skater.
patinatoki *n.* skating rink, place for skating.
patintxo *n.(dim.)* little skate.
patio *n.* patio.
patologia *n.* pathology.
patologiko *adj.* pathological.
patrikara *n.* pocket.
patroi *n.* skipper (of a boat). *n.* patron (saint).
patroindu *v.t.* to patronize.
patrointza *n.* patronage.
pats *n.* sweat. *n.* apple pulp, grape pulp (left after crushing).
pattar *n.* rotgut; low quality brandy.
patu *n.* destiny, fate.
patukoi *adj.* fatalist.
patuzko *adj.* destined, fated.
patxada *n.* slowness, sluggishness. *n.* tranquility, calm, relief.
patxadaldi *n.* rest period, repose.
patxadan *adv.* tranquilly, calmly, relaxed.
patxadatsu *adj.* slow, sluggish.
patxadatu *v.i.* to stretch out, to kick back.
patxadaz *adv.* calmly, without hurrying, unhurriedly, slowly.

patxadazale *adj.* comfort-loving.
patxadazko *adj.* relaxed, calm; comfortable.
patxaran *n.(bot.)* sloe, blackthorn. *n.* sweet liquor made of sloe in Navarra.
pausa *n.* rest, repose.
pausagabe *adj.* nervous, upset, restless.
pausagarri *adj.* resting, reposing.
pausaldi *n.* rest, rest period.
pausaleku *n.* place to rest, rest area.
pausarazi *v.t.* to make (someone) rest.
pausarte *n.* intermission, pause.
pausatu *v.i.* to rest, to repose. *v.i.* to come to rest, to pause, to perch, to light.
pausatuki *adv.* calmly, tranquilly, slowly.
pauso *n.* step, length of a step. *n.* footstep, track.
pausoka *adv.* step by step.
pausokada *n.* large stride, long step. oil press.
pausots *n.* sound of footsteps, footfalls.
pazientzia *n.* patience, tolerance, endurance.
pazko *n.* Easter.
pazkoaldi *n.* Easter time.
pazkoaldiko *adj.* Easter, paschal.
pazkoaro *n.* Easter time.
pazkobildots *n.* paschal lamb.
pazkoz *adv.* on Easter, during Easter.
paztanga *n.(zool.)* fish similar to a ray or skate.
-pe Suffix which indicates lower part. **Elizpe.** Church portico or colonnade.
peaia *n.* toll (paid for passage).
-pean Suffix meaning under, below, beneath. Used with verbs of non-motion.
pedagogari *n.* pedagogue.
pedagogia *n.* pedagogy.
pedagogiaurkako *adj.* antipedagogical.
pedagogiaz *adv.* pedagogically.
pedagogiko *adj.* pedagogical.
pedagogikoki *adv.* pedagogically.
pedal *n.* pedal.
pegar *n.* jug, pitcher, jar.
pegargile *n.* jug maker, pitcher maker.
pegarka *adv.* by the jugful, by the pitcherful.
pegarketari *n.* one who carries (something) in a jar or jug (usuallywater), water carrier.
pegarkintza *n.* job of a water carrier.
pegartegi *n.* place where pitchers or jugs are stored in the kitchen.
pegarxka *n.(dim.)* small jar or jug, small pitcher.
peitu *n.* need, lack, want.
peitutasun *n.* scarcity, lack, paucity.
peitutu *v.i.* to become scarce, to be lacking.
peka *n.* freckle.
pekatari *n.* sinner.

pekatsu adj. freckled.
pekatu n. sin.
pekatzaile n./adj. victim, suffering at the hands of others.
pekazto adj. freckled.
-peko Suffix which denotes subordinate to, under.
pelikano n.(zool.) pelican.
pelikula n. movie, film.
pellokeria n. nonsense, silliness.
pellotu v.i. to become foolish or silly.
pelota n. ball.
pelotaka adv. playing ball, volleying (the handball).
pelotaleku n. fronton, handball court.
pelotari n. handball player, ball player.
pelotatoki n. fronton, handball court.
-pen Suffix indicating action.
pena n. pain, suffering, sorrow, grief.
penadun adj. suffering.
penagarri adj. sad, lamentable, sorrowful. adj. painful, difficult.
penagarriro adv. sadly, lamentably.
penatu v.t./v.i. to torment, to inflict pain upon (someone), to make (someone) sad; to suffer pain, to be sad.
penatzaile adj. painful, tormenting.
pena ukan v.t. to suffer, to have pain.
penintsula n.(geog.) peninsula.
penintsulako adj. peninsular.
penintsular adj. peninsular.
penintsulartasun n. peninsularity.
pendiz n. steep slope.
penitentzia n.(eccl.) sacrament of confession. n.(eccl.) penance.
penitentzia egin v.t. to do penance.
penitentzigile n. penitent.
penizilina n.(med.) penicillin.
pentagono n.(geom.) pentagon.
pentagrama n.(mus.) pentagram.
pentekoste n.(eccl.) pentecost.
pentsabide n. matter for thought, topic of thought.
pentsaera n. mentality, way of thinking, ideology, thought patterns.
pentsaezin adj. inconceivable, unthinkable.
pentsagai n. matter for thought, topic of thought.
pentsagarri adj. thinkable, conceivable.
pentsakera n. mentality, way of thinking, ideology, thought patterns.
pentsaketa n. reflection, meditation, consideration, thought.
pentsakizun n. thought, reflection, meditation, consideration.
pentsakor adj. thoughtful, pensive, reflexive, meditative.
pentsalari n. philosopher, thinker.
pentsamen n. intelligence.
pentsamentu n. thought, idea.
pentsamolde n. way of thinking, ideology, thought patterns.
pentsarazi v.t. to make (someone) think.
pentsatu v.t. to think.

pentsatzaile n./adj. thinker; thinking.
pentsio n. pension fund, retirement money, annuity.
pentsiodun n. pensioner, person living on retirement allowance.
pentsiordain n. pension payment.
pentsu n. feed, cattle feed, fodder. n. thought, deep thinking, pondering.
peoi n. manual laborer. n. pawn (in chess).
peoieria n. gang of laborers.
peoitza n. work or position of a manual laborer.
peontza n. work or position of manual laborer, manual labor.
pepino n.(bot.) cucumber.
perdigoi n. pellet, bird shot, buckshot.
perdigoikada n. blast of a shotgun.
perdigoizorro n. shot pouch, shot bag.
perfume n. perfume.
perito n. expert. n. one holding a special government degree in engineering.
peritolan n. work of an engineer holding a special government degree.
peritotza n. work or career of an expert (engineering, etc.).
perkal n. percale.
perla n. pearl.
perlama n. mother-of-pearl.
perlesi n.(med.) paralysis.
perloi n.(zool.) gurnard; medium-sized comestible salt water fish with a white underbelly, brownish back and spines.
pernil n. ham.
perpaus(a) n. sentence.
perretxiko n.(bot.) mushroom.
perretxikolari n. one who looks for mushrooms, mushroom hunter.
perretxikozale adj. fond of mushrooms.
perrezil n.(bot.) parsley.
pertika n. shaft, pole (of a cart). n. pole (used in pole vaulting).
pertsiana n. Venetian blind.
pertsiera n. Farsi, Iranian.
pertsona n. person, people (pl.)
pertsonaia n. character, personage.
pertsonal adj. personal. n. personnel, staff, employees.
pertsonalki adv. personally.
pertsonaltasun n. personality.
pertsonarteko adj. interpersonal.
pertsu n. verse.
pertxa n. hanger.
pertxenta adj. svelte, lithe.
peskiza n. care.
petaka n. tobacco pouch.
peto adj. similar, like.
petral n. cinch, belly strap. adj. rascally, villainous, dastardly. n. spattering of mud, splashing with mud.
petraldu v.t. to cinch, to cinch up, to girth (a horse, burro, etc.).

petralkeria n. meanness, villainy, low despicable act.

petralki adv. meanly, villainously, mischievously.

petrikilo n.(colloq.) quack, bad doctor.

petrolio n.(chem.) oil, petroleum.

patroliodun adj. oil, petroleum, pertaining to oil.

petroliogune n. oil zone.

petroliontzi n. oil tanker.

petroliotsu adj. oily.

petroliozko adj. oily, oil, pertaining to oil.

petxa n.(econ.) tax, duty.

pezeta n.(econ.) peseta, Spanish currency.

pezoin n. trench, ditch.

piaia n. trip, voyage.

piaiatu v.t. to travel, to take a trip.

piano n.(mus.) piano.

pianogile n. piano maker.

pianojole n. pianist, piano player.

pierola n. fern field.

pigmeo n. pygmy.

pijo adj. skillful, capable.

pika n. pick (tool). n. tar; pitch.

pikada n. peck, bite, sting.

pikadura n. pruning, cutting (wood).

pikaldi n. reaping, mowing, harvesting, cutting.

pikaro adj. rascally, villainous.

pikaroki adv. rascally, roguishly, impishly, mischievously.

pikatu v.t. to cut. v.t. to sting, to bite.

pikatxa n. giblets, tripes, offal.

pikatzaile n. cutter, woodcutter.

pike n. tar; pitch. n. very steep slope.

piko n. fig. n. mason's hammer.

pikodi n. place of fig trees, plantation of fig trees.

pikoka adv. quarreling. adv.(fig.) caustically, bitingly, mordantly.

pikokada n. peck.

pikokari adj. biting, caustic, mordant.

pikokatu v.t. to peck.

pikoketa n. pecking. n.(fig.) biting, causticness.

pikoki n. wood of a fig tree.

pikoluze adj. long-beaked. adj.(fig.) talkative.

pikondo n. fig tree.

pikorkadura n. curdling, lumping.

pikorkatu v.i. to curdle (milk), to form lumps.

pikort n. snowflake. n. pimple, blackhead.

pikortsu adj. curdled, lumpy, granulous.

pikortu v.i. to curdle.

pikotx n. (mason's) hammer.

pikoxtu v.t. to claw with a mason's hammer, to mine with a mason's hammer.

piku n. fig.

pikutara bidali v.t. to tell (someone) to go to hell.

pikutara bota v.t. to tell (someone) to

go to hell, to tell (someone) to get lost.

pikutara joan v.i. to go bankrupt, to fail.

pila n. pile, heap.

pilagarri adj. pilable, heapable.

pilaka adv. in piles.

pilakatu v.t. to pile (up), to heap (up), to accumulate, to bunch (together).

pilaketa n. piling (up), heaping (up), accumulating, accumulation, conglomeration.

pilakor adj. cumulative.

pilatu v.t. to pile (up), to heap (up), to accumulate, to conglomerate.

pilatxo n.(dim.) little pile.

pilatzaile n./adj. piler, accumulator; piling, accumulating.

pilo n. pile.

piloka adv. in piles, in heaps.

pilota n. ball.

pilotada n. blow with a ball, blow to the ball.

pilotagile n. ball maker.

pilotajoko n. handball game, pelota game or match.

pilotaka adv. volleying (the handball), playing ball.

pilotakada n. blow from a ball.

pilotaketa n. play (of the handball), volley (of the handball).

pilotakolpe n. blow from a ball.

pilotalarru n. skin of the ball, surface or covering of the ball.

pilotaldi n. handball game, handball match.

pilotaleku n. fronton, handball court.

pilotan ari v.i. to be playing handball or pelota.

pilota-partida n. handball match, pelota match.

pilotari n. handball player, pelota player, ball player.

pilotatoki n. fronton, handball or pelota court.

pilotazale adj. fan of handball.

pilotsu adj. abundant, copious.

pilotu n. pilot, skipper.

pilotugela n. pilot's cabin, skipper's cabin.

pilotutza n. profession of a pilot (on a boat or plane).

pil-pil n. onomatopoetic sound of boiling. n. onomatopoetic sound of heart beats, lub-dub.

pilpilada n. sauce, gravy.

pilpil egin v.t. to boil. v.t. to beat (heart).

pilpilka adv. boiling.

pilpira n. beating of the heart.

pilpiragarri adj. moving, emotional. adj. beating, throbbing.

pilpiraka adv. beating, palpitating, throbbing.

pilpiramendu n. palpitation, beating of the heart.

pilpiratu v.i. to beat (heart), to

palpitate.

piltxikada *n.* pinch.

piltxikatu *v.t.* to pinch.

piltzarbiltzaile *n.* ragpicker.

piltzarkari *n.* ragpicker.

piltzarkeria *n.(fig.)* roguery, wickedness, meanness.

piltzarketari *n.* ragpicker.

piltzarki *n.* rag.

piltzarreria *n.* bunch of rags.

piltzarsaltzaile *n.* rag seller.

piltzartegi *n.* second hand shop, old clothes store, place where rags are found.

piltzartsu *adj.* ragged, tattered.

piltzartu *v.i.* to become ragged, to be unkempt.

pilula *n.* pill, medicinal capsule.

pinaburu *n.(bot.)* pinecone. *n.(bot.)* pineapple.

pinadi *n.* pine tree grove.

pinazi *n.* pine tree seed.

pindar *n.* sparkle, twinkle.

pindartu *v.i.* to sparkle, to twinkle, to scintillate.

pinguino *n.(zool.)* penguin.

pinpilinpauxa *n.(zool.)* butterfly.

pinpilinpauxatu *v.i.(fig.)* to flit about.

pinpirin *adj.* elegant, svelte. *adj.* boasting, bragging, pretentious.

pinta *n.* pint. *n.* spot.

pintagarri *adj.* paintable.

pintatu *v.t.* to paint.

pinterdi *n.* half pint.

pintore *n.* painter.

pintta *n.(dim.)* small spot.

pintura *n.* paint. *n.* painting, picture.

pintxo *n.* appetizer, tidbit usually broiled and served on skewers in restaurants and bars before lunch.

pintza *n.* clothespin. *n.* tweezers; pincers; clamp, forceps. Usually used in plural.

pintzel *n.* brush, small paintbrush.

pintzelgile *n.* paintbrush maker.

pintzelkada *n.* brush stroke.

pintzelkaxa *n.* paint box.

pinu *n.(bot.)* pine tree (*Pinus insignis*).

pinudi *n.* pine tree grove.

pinugorri *n.(bot.)* redwood; red pine.

pinuhazi *n.* pine nut.

pinuorri *n.* pine branch.

pinutsu *adj.* piny, full of pines.

pinutxo *n.(dim.)* little pine tree.

pinuztatu *v.i./v.t.* to be planted in pines; to plant pine trees.

pinuzuri *n.(bot.)* Austrian pine.

pio *n.* tweet, cheep, chirp. Sound made by birds or chicks.

pio egin *v.t.* to cheep, to tweet, to chirp.

pioka *adv.* cheeping, chirping, tweeting.

piokari *n./adj.* cheeper, chirper, tweeter; cheeping, chirping, tweeting.

piokatu *v.t.* to cheep, to tweet, to chirp.

pipa *n.* pipe (for smoking). *n.* cask, barrel.

pipabelar *n.* pipe tobacco.

pipaldi *n.* smoke, time spent smoking a pipe.

pipari *n.* pipe smoker.

pipatu *v.t.* to smoke a pipe.

pipatzaile *n.* pipe smoker.

piper *n.(bot.)* pepper, red or green pepper.

piperbeltz *n.* black pepper.

piper egin *v.t.* to play hooky.

pipergorri *n.(bot.)* red pepper.

piperlandare *n.(bot.)* pepper plant.

pipermin *n.* hot pepper, chili pepper. *n.(fig.)* quick-tempered person.

piperrada *n.* fried peppers.

piperrandi *n.(bot.)* bonnet pepper.

piperrauts *n.* any ground pepper. *n.* paprika.

piperrezko *adj.* peppery, having the taste of pepper.

piperrontzi *n.* pepperbox, pepper shaker.

pipertu *v.i.* to be nervous, to be jittery, to be tense.

piperzale *adj.* fond of peppers.

piperztatu *v.t.* to season with pepper, to pepper.

pipi *n.(zool.)* moth; wood-borer. *n.* pee-pee, urine (children's language).

pipil *n.(bot.)* bud, bloom.

pipildu *v.i.* to bud, to bloom.

pipita *n.* roup (disease of chickens). *n.* seeds.

pipitatsu *adj.* having many seeds.

pipizulo *n.* moth hole.

pipontzi *n.* pipe stand, humidor (for pipe tobacco).

piragua *n.* canoe.

piramide *n.* pyramid.

pirata *n.* pirate.

piratakeria *n.* piracy, pirating.

Pirenemendiak *n.(geog.)* Pyrenees.

pirri *adj.(colloq.)* nervous, jumpy, jittery, bad tempered (person).

pirri-parra *adv.* profusely, wastefully, hand over fist.

pirripio *n.(zool.)* woodlark, lark.

pirrist *n.* swoosh, splash. Sound of water running forcefully.

pirrist egin *v.t.* to shoot up, to spray (water).

pirrita *n.* rolling, tumbling downhill.

pirritaka *adv.* rolling (downhill).

pirritatu *v.i.* to roll, to roll over; to slide.

pirtxil *adj.* wrinkled, shriveled.

pirtxildu *v.i.* to dry up, to shrivel, to wrinkle.

piru *n.* fiber, strand, thread.

pirudun *adj.* fibrous, having strands, thready.

pirukatu *v.t.* to unravel.

pirutsu *adj.* full of threads, stringy.

pisagarri *adj.* weighable.

pisaketa *n.* weighing.

pisaldi *n.* weighing.
pisaleku *n.* scales, place for weighing.
pisatu *v.t.* to weigh.
pisatzaile *n.* weigher, one who weighs.
pistoi *n.(mech.)* piston.
pistola *n.* pistol.
pistolakada *n.* pistol shot.
pistolari *n.* gunfighter.
pistolatxo *n.(dim.)* small pistol.
pisu *n.* weight. *n.* scale. *n.* lead weight. *n.(fig.)* prudence, caution.
pisualdi *n.* weighing.
pisudun *adj.* heavy.
pisugabe *adj.* not heavy, light.
pisugabetu *v.i.* to lighten, to lessen the weight.
pisugabezia *n.* lightness, lack of weight.
pisugain *n.* overweight.
pisugarbi *n.* net weight.
pisugarri *adj.* weighable.
pisuhil *n.* tare weight.
pisuketa *n.* weighing.
pisuki *adv.* heavily, weightily.
pisutasun *n.* heaviness, weightiness.
pisutsu *adj.* heavy. *adj.* undigested, heavy on the stomach.
pisutu *v.i./v.t.* to increase the weight.
pisuzain *n.* inspector of scales.
pisuzaintza *n.* office of the inspector of weights and measures.
pisuzko *adj.(fig.)* important; prudent. (lit.) heavy.
pita *n.* fishing line.
pitar *n.* watery cider.
pitilin *n.(anat.)* small penis (children's language).
pitin *adv.* little, little bit.
pitinka *adv.* little by little, in pieces, etc.
pittin *n.(dim.)* little bit.
pito *n.(colloq.)* penis.
pitxer *n.* jar, pitcher, jug.
pitxerkada *n.* jarful, pitcherful.
pitzadura *n.* cracking, crack, flaw, fissure.
pitzagarri *adi.* crackable, breakable.
pitzaketa *n.* cracking.
pitzakor *adj.* crackable, breakable.
pitzatu *v.i.* to crack.
pix *n.* urine, pee.
pixabide *n.(anat.)* urethra.
pixagale *n.* desire to urinate. *adj.* wanting to urinate.
pixagale izan *v.i.* to want to urinate.
pixagaletu *v.i.* to want to urinate.
pixagorri *n.(med.)* hematuria, presence of blood in the urine.
pixagura *n.* desire to urinate.
pixaguratu *v.i.* to want to urinate.
pixajario *n.* polyuria, excessive secretion of urine. *adj.* wanting to urinate.
pixakatu *v.i.* to urinate frequently (passing small amounts of urine).
pixaketa *n.* urination.
pixalarri *n.* desire to urinate. *adj.*

wanting to urinate.
pixaldi *n.* urinating.
pixama *n.* pyjama.
pixarri *n.(med.)* calculus, stone, gallstones.
pixategi *n.* restroom, bathroom.
pixati *adj.* wanting to urinate, pissy.
pixatoki *n.* restroom, bathroom.
pixazko *adj.* urinary.
pixegile *adj.* urinating frequently.
pix egin *v.t.* to urinate, to pee.
pixeragile *adj.* diuretic.
pix eragin *v.t.* to make (someone) urinate.
pixka *adv.* little bit, little. *n.* little piece, crumb.
pixka bat *adv.* little bit.
pixkat *adv.* a little bit.
pixodi *n.(anat.)* urethra.
pixoihal *n.* diaper.
pixontzi *n.* urinal, chamber pot, bed pot. *adj.(fig.)* bedwetting, urinating.
pixontzitegi *n.* commode, stand for holding chamber pot.
pixtoki *n.* restroom, bathroom, toilet.
pixusain *n.* odor of urine.
pixusainzto *adj.* smelling of urine (a person).
pizgailu *n.* lighter, cigarette lighter.
pizgarri *n.* incentive.
pizka *adv.* little bit. *n.* little piece, little thing.
pizkana *adv.* a little each.
pizkanaka *adv.* little by little, gradually, slowly, bit by bit.
pizta *n.* sleep (secretion of the eyes).
piztaile *n.* one who lights, lamplighter. *n./adj.* stimulation, animator; stimulating, animating.
piztia *n.* beast, animal (usually wild and ferocious).
piztitasun *n.* ferocity, wildness.
piztitsu *adj.* wild, ferocious.
piztitxo *n.(dim.)* small wild animal.
piztitzar *n.(augm.)* big wild animal.
piztizulo *n.* wild animal's den, cave of beasts
piztu *v.t.* to light, to turn on a light.
piztugarri *adj.* exciting, strengthening, reviving, vivifying.
pla *n.* whack! Sound of a blow with the palm of the hand.
plagiatu *v.t.* to plagiarize.
plagiatzaile *n.* plagiarist, plagiarizer.
plagio *n.* plagiary.
plan *n.* plan, structure.
plan egin *v.t.* to plan, to make plans.
planeta *n.* planet.
planetarteko *adj.* interplanetary.
plangile *n.* planner.
plangintzatu *v.t.* to plan, to make plans.
planifikapen *n.* planning.
planifikatu *v.t.* to plan, to make plans.
planifikatzaile *n.* planner.
planta *n.* appearance, aspect. *n.* pretending; simulation.

plantak egin *v.t.* to pretend, to simulate.

plantati *adj.* pretending, faking; feigned; apparent.

planteamendu *n.* statement, exposition, outlining, posing (of a problem).

planteatu *v.t.* to pose (a problem), to outline, to set forth.

planto *(exclam.)* Word used to stop a game of cards.

planto egin *v.t.* to stop, to pause.

plantxa *n.* iron, flatiron.

plantxaldi *n.* ironing, time spent ironing.

plantxatu *v.t.* to iron, to do the ironing.

plantxatzaile *n.* one who irons, ironer.

plast *n.* smack! Sound of a slap. *n.* splash! Sound of falling into water.

plastada *n.* slap in the face, blow.

plastadako *n.* slap.

plastika *n.* plastic explosive.

plastikalari *n.* terrorist (who uses plastic explosives).

plastiko *n.* plastic.

plastikotasun *n.* plasticity.

plastikozko *adj.* plastic.

platanadi *n.* grove of banana trees.

platanakide *adj.* platanaceous.

platano *n.(bot.)* banana.

platanondo *n.(bot.)* banana tree.

plater *n.* plate, dish, platter.

platergailu *n.* dishwasher (machine).

platergorailu *n.* dumbwaiter.

platerikuztailu *n.* dishwasher (machine).

platerkada *n.* plateful.

platertxo *n.(dim.)* little plate.

platino *n.(min.)* platinum.

platoniar *adj.* platonic.

platonikoki *adv.* platonically.

platonismo *n.(phil.)* Platonism.

platuxa *n.(zool.)* plaice, European flounder.

plaust *n.* splat! Sound of an object falling.

plausta *adv.* gobblingly, noisily.

plaust egin *v.t.* to fall.

plaza *n.* plaza, square, town square. *n.* market, supermarket.

plazagizon *n.* popular man, well-known man, man who is good with an audience.

plazaratu *v.i.* to go to the square; to go to the market. *v.t.* to show.

plazasari *n.* sales tax.

plazatxo *n.(dim.)* little square or plaza; little market.

plazer *n.* pleasure; caprice, whim.

plazer egin *v.t.* to please, to delight.

plazeretsu *adj.* capricious, fickle.

plazerki *adv.* with pleasure.

plazerez *adv.* capriciously.

plazer ukan *v.t.* to please.

plisti-plasta *n.* Onomatopoeic sound of slapping the face. *n.* splish-splash. Onomatopoeic sound of splashing

water.

plomatu *v.t.* to plumb (a wall), to make or build vertically.

plomu *n.(chem.)* lead.

plural *adj.* plural.

pluralismo *n.* pluralism.

pluralista *adj.* pluralist.

pluralitate *n.* pluralism.

pluraltasun *n.* plurality.

plusbalio *n.(econ.)* increased value, appreciation, surplus value.

plutonio *n.(min.)* plutonium.

pobre *n./adj.* poor, needy.

pobreki *adv.* poorly, in poverty.

pobretasun *n.* poverty.

pobretu *v.i.* to become poor.

pobretxe *n.* poorhouse.

pobrezia *n.* poverty.

podere *n.* power.

poema *n.* poem.

poemagintza *n.* poem writing.

poesia *n.* poetry; poem.

poesia egin *v.t.* to write poetry.

poesiarnas *n.* poetic inspiration.

poesiaz *adv.* poetically.

poesietorri *n.* poetic inspiration.

poesizko *adj.* poetical, poetic.

poeta *n.* poet.

poetiko *adj.* poetic, poetical.

poetikoki *adv.* poetically.

poetisa *n.* poetess.

poker *n.* burp, belch.

poker egin *v.t.* to belch, to burp.

pokerka *adv.* burping, belching, wanting to vomit.

pokerlari *adj.* burping or belching frequently.

pokertsu *adj.* sickening, nauseating.

polbora *n.* powder, gunpowder.

polborategi *n.* magazine, arsenal, place where gunpowder is kept.

polea *n.* pulley.

polen *n.* pollen.

poleneztapen *n.* pollenization.

poliki *adv.* beautifully, prettily. *adv.* slowly, gradually, little by little.

polikiroldegi *n.* sports center, recreational center.

polit *adj.* beautiful, pretty.

politasun *n.* beauty, prettiness.

politen(a) *adj.(superl.)* prettiest.

politika *n.* politics.

politikagabe *adj.* apolitical.

politikagintza *n.* political activity.

politikakeria *n.* political maneuvering, political scheming.

politikakontrako *adj.* antipolitical.

politikari *n.* politician.

politikaurkako *adj.* antipolitical.

politikaz *adv.* politically.

politikazale *adj.* fond of politics.

politikeria *n.* political maneuvering, political scheming.

politiko *adj.* political. *n.* politician.

politikoki *adv.* politically.

politizapen *n.* act of getting involved in politics, act of becoming political, making (someone) political.

politizatu *v.i./v.t.* to be involved in politics, to get involved in politics; to get (someone) involved in politics.

polito *adv.* slowly.

politu *v.i./v.t.* to embellish, to adorn, to pretty up, to make beautiful.

poliza *n.* policy (insurance, etc.); tax stamps.

polizia *n.* police.

poliziburu *n.* chief of police.

polizietxe *n.* police station.

polizitalde *n.* group of policemen.

polo *n.(geog.)* pole. *n.* polo.

poloalde *n.(geog.)* polar region.

poloarteko *adj.* interpolar.

poloinguru *n.* polar cap.

polokari *n.* polo player.

poltsiko *n.* pocket.

poluzio *n.* pollution.

pomada *n.* pomade, lotion.

pomelo *n.(bot.)* grapefruit.

pomezarri *n.(geol.)* pumice rock.

pondu *n.* subject, theme, point. *n.* point (in a game). *n.* rhythm, beat.

pontoi *n.* old ship tied to the dock and used as a warehouse.

pontxe *n.* drink made of egg yolk, sugar, milk and brandy. Used for treating colds.

pontxo *n.* poncho.

popa *n.* poop, stern. *n.(colloq.)* bottom, fanny.

popandi *adj.(augm.)* broad in the beam, big-bottomed.

populaketa *n.* populating.

popularki *adv.* popularly.

populatu *v.t.* to populate.

populatzaile *n.* settler, colonist.

populazio *n.* people, population.

populu *n.* people.

populukeria *n.* cheap popularity.

porlan *n.* cement.

porlaneztatu *v.t.* to cement, to cover with cement.

porra *n.* sledgehammer.

porroi *n.* wine carafe with long side spout for communal drinking.

porrokada *n.* failure, destruction, collapse.

porrokaezin *adj.* indestructible.

porrokaketa *n.* destruction, devastation.

porrokaldi *n.* collapse, ruin, failure, destruction. *n.* beating.

porrokarazi *v.t.* to exhaust (someone), to overwork (someone).

porrokatu *v.t.* to destroy, to devastate. *v.i.* to be exhausted. *adj.* exhaustive; fanatical, compulsive.

porrokatzaile *n./adj.* devastator, destroyer; devastating, destroying.

porrot *n.* failure, bankruptcy.

porrotaldi *n.* failure, collapse, bankruptcy.

porrot egin *v.t.* to fail, to collapse, to go bankrupt. *v.t.* to collapse

(buildings, etc.), to cave in.

porrotketa *n.* collapse, downfall, failure.

porru *n.(bot.)* leek.

porrulandare *n.* leek plant.

porruondo *n.(bot.)* leek plant.

porrusalda *n.* leek soup. *n.* lively dance, lively rhythm.

portaera *n.* conduct, behavior.

portale *n.* creche, nativity scene.

portatu *v.i.* to behave.

portu *n.* harbor, port. *n.* mountain pass.

portupilotu *n.* harbor pilot.

porturaketa *n.* entering the harbor.

porturatu *v.i.* to go to port, to enter the harbor.

portutxo *n.(dim.)* cove, bay, small harbor.

portuxka *n.(dim.)* cove, bay, small harbor.

portzelana *n.* porcelain.

portzentaia *n.* percentage.

posibilitate *n.* possibility.

posible *adj.* possible.

positibismo *n.(phil.)* positivism.

positibista *adj.* positivist.

positibo *adj.* positive.

positiboki *adv.* positively.

pospolin *n.(zool.)* kind of quail. *adj.* charming. *n.* top (toy), teetotum (top used in gambling).

pospolo *n.* match (to light a fire).

posta *n.* postal service.

postabide *n.* postal address.

postal(e) *n.* post card.

postalgo *n.* postal service.

postari *n.* postman.

postatren *n.* postal train.

poste *n.* post, pole.

postetxe *n.* post office.

postontzi *n.* mailbox.

postordain *n.* cash on delivery, C.O.D.

postre *n.* dessert.

postura *n.* bet, wager.

postura egin *v.t.* to bet, to wager.

pot *n.* failure. *n.* fatigue, tiredness, exhaustion. *n.* kiss.

pota *n.(zool.)* cuttlefish.

potari *n./adj.* kisser.

potasa *n.(chem.)* potash.

potasiko *adj.* potassic.

potasio *n.(chem.)* potassium.

potasiosko *adj.* potassic.

pot egin *v.t.* to get tired, to tire out, to exhaust. *v.t.* to fail. *v.t.* to kiss.

pot eman *v.t.* to kiss, to hug.

potera *n.* small grappling hook for catching squid and cuttlefish.

potin *n.* small row boat.

poto *n.* can, container. *n.* pouch for carrying whetting stone. *n.* bad rhyme, repetition of a rhyme (a word) in Basque troubadourism.

poto egin *v.t.* to fail, to make a mistake. *v.t.* to make a bad rhyme, to repeat a rhyme (a word) in a verse.

potokada n. canful.
potolo adj. round, chubby; obese.
potolotu v.i. to become chubby.
potoratu v.t. to can, to preserve in cans, to put (something) in a can.
potorro n.(zool.) cormorant. n. vulva, cunt.
potro n.(colloq.) testicle, balls.
potrodun adj.(colloq.) courageous, brave, valiant, strong.
potta n.(zool.) cuttlefish.
pottoka n.(zool.) colt.
pottolo adj.(dim.) chubby. adj. dearest, dear, darling, beloved.
potzolo n. small and chubby.
potzolotu v.i. to be small and chubby.
poxelu n. obstacle.
poxpolo n. match (for lighting fires).
poz n. joy, happiness.
pozagur n. congratulation(s), congratulatory remark.
pozagurtu v.t. to congratulate.
pozaldi n. moment of joy, jubilation.
pozarazi v.t. to make (someone) happy, to cheer (someone) up.
pozarazle n./adj. one who makes others happy; amusing, cheerful.
pozarren adv. happily.
pozemale n. giver of joy.
poz eman v.t. to give joy, to make happy.
pozeragile n./adj. maker of happiness.
pozez adv. happily, joyfully, gladly.
pozezko adj. jubilant.
pozgabe adj. unhappy, sad.
pozgabetasun n. unhappiness, sadness.
pozgabetu v.i./v.t. to become sad, to be unhappy; to make unhappy.
pozgarri adj. happy, cheerful, pleasant. n. happiness, consolation. n. incentive, inducement, stimulus.
pozgarriro adv. joyfully, merrily, happily, gladly.
pozgarrizko adj. consoling, cheering.
pozgile n./adj. bringer of happiness, maker of joy.
poz hartu v.t. to be or become happy, to enjoy.
pozik adv. happily, joyfully, pleasantly, gladly.
pozkide n. companions in happiness.
pozkiro adv. happily.
pozkor adj. joyful, cheerful, happy, merry.
pozoi n. poison, venom, toxin.
pozoiaurkako adj. antitoxic.
pozoidun adj. poisonous.
pozoigabe adj. non-toxic, not poisonous.
pozoigabetu v.i./v.t. to detoxify, to detoxicate.
pozoigai n. toxin.
pozoiki n. toxin, poisonous substance.
pozoikontrako adj. anti-toxic.
pozoin n. poison.
pozoindatu v.t. to poison.

pozoitasun n. poisonousness, poisonous quality.
pozoitsu adj. poisonous, toxic.
pozoitu v.i. to be poisoned. v.t. to poison.
pozoitzaile n. poisoner. adj. poisoning.
poz-pozez egon v.i. to be very happy.
poztarazi v.t. to make happy.
poztasun n. happiness.
poztu v.i./v.t. to be joyful, to be glad, to get happy, to be happy; to make (someone) happy.
poztzaile n./adj. consoler, bringer of happiness.
praile n. friar.
praka n. pants, trousers (usually used in plural).
prakabarren n. cuff of trousers, hem of trousers.
prakadun adj. valiant, courageous, brave. n. man.
prakagin n. trouser maker, tailor.
prakagorri n.(colloq.) devil. n. miquelet, member of the Guipuzcoan foral militia (before the Spanish Civil War).
prakamotz n. shorts.
prakanasai adj. indifferent, lackadaisical.
prakerre adj.(fam.) ill-tempered, impatient, fretful.
prakestu adj. ill-tempered.
praktika n. practice.
praktikari n. first aid practitioner.
praktikatu v.t. to practice.
praktikatzaile adj. practicing.
praktiko adj. practical.
praktikoki adv. practically.
praktikotasun n. practicality, practicalness.
predikagarri adj. preachable.
predikaldi n. sermon.
predikaleku n.(eccl.) place where preaching is done; pulpit.
predikari n. preacher.
predikatu v.t. to preach, to give a sermon.
predikatzaile n. preacher, sermonizer.
predikazio n. sermon.
prediku n. sermon.
prediku egin v.t. to preach.
predikugai n. subject of a sermon.
pregoi n. public proclamation or announcement.
pregoiari n. town crier.
pregoigile n. town crier.
premia n. need, necessity.
premiadun adj. needy.
premiadura n. need, poverty.
premiagabeko adj. unnecessary, superfluous.
premia izan v.t. to need.
premiatasun n. need, urgency.
premiatsu adj. necessary, indispensable.
premiatu v.t. to urge.
premia ukan v.t. to need.

premiaz adv. necessarily, compulsorily, obligatorily, by force.

premiazko adj. urgent, necessary, indispensable.

prentsa n. press, clamp, vise. n. press.

prentsagentzia n. press agency.

prentsaketa n. pressing, printing.

prentsatu v.t. to press, to squeeze, to crush.

prentsatzaile n. presser, one who presses.

prentsaurreko n. press conference.

preposizio n.(gram.) preposition.

presa n. hurry, rush. n. reservoir; dam.

presadun adj. hurried, rushed.

presa eman v.t. to urge.

presa izan v.t. to be in a hurry.

presaka adv. hurriedly, in a hurry.

presakatu v.i. to hurry, to rush.

presatsu adj. urgent, rush. adj. hurrying.

presatu v.i. to hurry, to rush.

presaz adv. hurriedly, in a hurry.

presazko adj. urgent.

presentagarri adj. presentable, worthy of being offered.

presentapen n. presentation.

presentatu v.i./v.t. to introduce (someone), to present. v.t. to offer, to present (something).

presentatzaile n. presenter.

presentazio n. presentation, personal introduction.

presentzia n. presence.

preseski adv. precisely.

presio n. pressure.

preso n. prisoner, convict.

presondegi n. prison, jail.

presondegiko n./adj. prisoner; pertaining to prison.

presondegizain n. jailer, prison guard.

presozain n. jailer, prison guard.

prest adv. ready.

prestaera n. readiness, preparation, disposition.

prestagabe adj. unprepared, not ready.

prestagarri adj. preparatory. adj. loanable.

prestaketa n. preparation, readying.

prestakizun n. preparation.

prestakuntza n. preparation, organization, arrangement.

prestamen n. disposition, readiness, preparedness.

prestametxe n. savings and loan.

prestamo n.(econ.) loan.

prestamoz adv. on loan.

prestapen n. preparation, readiness, arrangement, adaptation.

prestasun n. honesty, integrity, probity.

prestatu v.t. to prepare, to get ready, to ready, to arrange. v.i. to be prepared, to be ready. v.t. to loan.

prestatzaile n. preparer. n. one who

loans money, moneylender, pawnbroker.

prest eduki v.t. to get ready.

prest egon v.i. to be ready, to be prepared.

prestu adj. honest, nice, good, upright, noble.

prestuarazi v.t. to make (someone) honest, to make (someone) be nice.

prestuki adv. honestly, honorably.

prestutasun n. honesty, integrity, probity, rectitude.

prestutu v.i. to become honest.

presupostu n.(econ.) budget.

preziagarri adj. worthy of esteem, esteemable, respected.

preziagarritasun n. valuableness, quality of being worthy of esteem.

preziamendu n. appreciation, esteem.

preziatsu adj. esteemed, appreciated. adj. precious.

preziatu v.t. to esteem, to hold in esteem. adj. esteemed, appreciated. adj. precious.

preziatzaile n. one who appreciates, appreciative person.

prezio n. price.

pribatu adj. private.

pribatuki adv. privately.

prima n. female heir, heiress.

primantza n. right of the first born, right of inheritance.

primeran adv. fantastically, stupendously.

primu n. heir.

primukide n. co-heir, co-inheritor.

primugo n. right of inheritance.

primutasun n. primogeniture, right of inheritance.

primutza n. inheritance.

printz n. ray (of light). n. splinter.

printzagarri adj. splittable, crackable.

printzatsu adj. splintery. adj. shining, luminous.

printzatu v.i. to splinter, to crack. adj. splintered, cracked.

printze n. prince.

printzaoaldi n. roign of a prince, time during which a prince reigns.

printzego n. princehood.

printzerri n. princedom, principate.

printzesa n. princess.

printzetar adj. princely, regal, noble.

printzezki adv. regally, in a princely manner.

proba n. proof, test. n. competition. n. check, proofing, verification.

probabilitate n. probability.

probaketa n. testing, sampling.

probalari n. competitor; ox driver in oxen competitions.

probaldi n. trial period, probation, period of proof.

probaleku n. special stone-paved location for oxen weight pulling competitions. n. fittingroom.

probarri n. stone pulled by oxen during

competition.

probatu *v.t.* to taste. *v.t.* to test. *v.t.* to try (on).

probatzaile *n.* tester, taster, sampler, trier.

probetxatu *v.i.* to do (someone) good. *v.t.* to take advantage of.

probetxu *n.* profit, benefit.

probetxugabe *adj.* unprofitable.

probetxugarri *adj.* profitable, beneficial.

probetxuzko *adj.* profitable.

probintzia *n.* province.

probintziako *adj.* provincial.

probintziar *adj.* provincial, from the province.

probintziarteko *adj.* interprovincial.

probintzikeria *n.* excessive love of one's province.

problema *n.* problem.

produkzio *n.* production.

profanatu *v.t.* to profane.

profanatzaile *n.* profaner.

profanazio *n.* profanation, desecration.

profesional *adj.* professional.

profesionalki *adv.* professionally.

profesionaltasun *n.* professionalism.

profeta *n.* prophet.

programa *n.* program, schedule.

programailu *n.* computer.

programaketa *n.* programming, scheduling, planning.

programakuntza *n.* programming, scheduling, planning.

proletalgo *n.* proletariat.

proletari *n.* proletarian.

promes *n.* promise.

promesari *n.* promiser, one who promises.

promes egin *v.t.* to promise, to make a promise.

promozio *n.* promotion.

propaganda *n.* propaganda.

propioki *adv.* properly, correctly, fittingly.

proportzio *n.* proportion.

proportziogabe *adj.* disproportionate.

proportzionalitate *n.* proportionality.

proportzionalki *adv.* proportionally.

proposamen *n.* proposition, proposal.

proposamendu *n.* proposition, proposal.

proposapen *n.* proposition, proposal.

proposatu *v.t.* to propose.

prosa *n.* prose.

prosalari *n.* prose writer.

prostata *n.(anat.)* prostate.

proteina *n.(chem.)* protein.

protesta *n.* protest.

protesta egin *v.t.* to protest.

protestante *n./adj.(rel.)* protestant.

protestatu *v.t.* to protest.

protestatzaile *n.* protester.

protokolo *n.* protocol.

prozedura *n.* procedure, process.

prozesio *n.(eccl.)* procession.

psikiatra *n.(med.)* psychiatrist.

psikiatria *n.(med.)* psychiatry.

psikiko *adj.* psychic.

psikoanalisi *n.(med.)* psychoanalysis.

psikologari *n.* psychologist.

psikologia *n.* psychology.

psikologiko *adj.* psychological.

psikosi *n.(med.)* psychosis.

psikoterapia *n.(med.)* psychotherapy.

publiko *n.* public, people. *adj.* public.

publikoki *adv.* publicly.

puda *n.* sickle, scythe.

pufa! *int.* whew!

pufada *n.* heavy breathing, puffing.

pufa egin *v.t.* to breathe heavily, to puff.

pufatu *v.t.* to breathe heavily, to puff.

pulpitu *n.(eccl.)* pulpit.

pultsu *n.* pulse.

pultsu hartu *v.t.* to take one's pulse.

pultsulari *n.* arm wrestler.

pultsuneurkin *n.* pulsimeter, instrument for measuring the pulse.

pulunpa *n.* diving.

pulunpada *n.* dive, diving.

pulunpaka *adv.* diving, by diving.

pulunpaldi *n.* submersion, dive, act of diving.

pulunparazi *v.t.* to make (someone) dive or submerge.

pulunpatu *v.i.* to dive.

pulunpatzaile *n.* diver.

puma *n.(zool.)* puma.

punpa *n.* crash, bang. Sound of something falling.

punpada *n.* bang, sound of a gunshot.

punpuila *n.* soap bubble.

punta *n.* end, extreme, point. *n.* summit.

puntada *n.* stitch.

puntadun *adj.* pointed.

puntako *adj.* outstanding, excellent, superior.

puntu *n.(gram.)* period, dot, point. *n.* point (in a game). *n.* rhyme in Basque troubadourism. *n.* stitch (surgical).

puntuaketa *n.* scoring, making points.

puntual *adj.* punctual.

puntualitate *n.* punctuality.

puntualki *adv.* punctually.

puntuatu *v.t.* to score.

puntuazio *n.* score.

puntu egin *v.t.* to knit.

puntuerdi *n.* half a point.

puntutxo *n.(mus.)* dot, point of augmentation.

puntzet *n.* sword.

puntzoi *n.* punch, awl, boring tool, ice pick.

pupu *n.* boo-boo, hurt, pain (children's language).

pupu egin *v.t.* to hurt (children's language).

pupurri *n.* potpourri, mixture.

pure *n.* purée.

puregailu *n.* potato ricer.

purga *n.* purge.

purgagarri *n.* emetic; laxative. *adj.*

purging.
purgapen n. purging.
purgatorio n. (eccl.) purgatory.
purgatu v.t. to purge.
purgatzaile adj. purging.
purpurika adv. abundantly (used when talking about fruit-producing trees).
purpurikatu v.i. to give abundant fruit, to give lots of fruit (trees).
purpurina n. purpurin, white metal powder.
purra! int. onomatopoeic sound of throwing seeds or sowing seeds by hand. int. here, chick-chick-chick. Sound used to call hens to dinner.
purraka erein v.t. to sow by throwing seeds.
purroi n. hazel tree grove.
purrust n. mocking, making fun of, satirizing. n. onomatopoeic sound of throwing seeds. n. mumbling, grumbling.
purrustada n. mumbling, grumbling. n. throwing seeds by the handful.
purrustadaka adv. mumblingly, grumblingly.
purrustaka adv. grumblingly, mumblingly. adv. by handfuls, abundantly.
purrustaldi n. act of throwing seeds.
purrustari n./adj. grumbler, grumpy person; grumbling, grumpy.
purrustatu v.t. to grumble, to mumble. v.t. to scatter, to spread, to disseminate.
purrust egin v.t. to grumble, to mumble, to complain.
purtxileria n. trinket, bauble, notion.
purtxilero n. seller of trinkets.
purtzil adj. insignificant, trifling. adj. despicable, vulgar.
purtzildu v.i. to be vulgar.
purtzilkeria n. vulgarity, lowness, bad behavior.
puska n. piece, portion.
puskaera n. portioning, parceling.
puskagarri adj. crushable, breakable, fragile.
puskakatu v.t./v.i. to break.
puskaketa n. breakage.
puskaketari n. messenger, delivery person.
puskatu v.t. to break, to destroy, to crush.
puskatzaile n. breaker, destroyer, crusher. adj. breaking, destroying, crushing.
pusketa n. fragment, small piece.
pusketatu v.t. to fracture, to break into pieces.
puspulu n. bubble.
puta n. prostitute.
putakeria n. prostitution; bad behavior or action.
putakume n./adj. bastard, son of a bitch.
putalaba n. prostitute.

putaseme n.(colloq.) son of a bitch.
putazain n. pimp.
putazale n./adj. one who frequents whores, trick, john; whoring, libertine, debauched.
putetxe n. brothel, bordello.
putre n.(zool.) vulture.
putretegi n. vulture trap.
putz n. blow, puff of air.
putzaldi n. blow.
putzarro adj. arrogant, presumptuous.
putzarrotu v.i. to be arrogant, to swell with pride.
putzegile n. blower, puffer.
putz egin v.t. to blow, to puff.
putzeragile adj. windy, blowy, full of wind.
putzontzi adj. proud, arrogant, vain, conceited, show-off, presumptuous, boastful. adj.(colloq.) breaking wind frequently, farting often.
putzu n. well, pit, hole. n. puddle.
putzuertz n. edge of a pit.
putzugarbitzaile n. well digger, cesspool cleaner.
putzuratu v.t./v.i. to put in a pit or hole; to enter a pit or a hole.
putzuzulo n. mouth of the pit.
puxika n.(anat.) bladder.
puzela n. difficulty, obstacle, impediment, obstruction.
puzgarri adj. inflatable.
puzka adv. blowing.
puzkailu n. bellows.
puzkari n. one who works the bellows.
puzketa n. swelling.
puzkor adj.(fig.) arrogant, presumptuous.
puztasun n. pomposity, bombast, arrogance.
puztu v.t./v.i. to inflate. v.i. to boast, to be arrogant.

S

s Letter of the Basque alphabet.
-sa Suffix for feminine form.
sabai n. attic, loft. n. roof, ceiling. n. vault, vaulted chamber, dome.
sabaigain n. roof terrace, widow's walk.
sabaileiho n. skylight.
sabairatu v.t. to store (grain, hay, etc.) in the loft.
sabaizulo n. trap door of a loft, door through which hay is pitched.
sabel n.(anat.) stomach, belly. n. cavity, hole.
sabelaize n. intestinal gas, fart.
sabelalde n. abdominal region.
sabelaldi n. litter. n. pregnancy. n. fullness, overeating.
sabelandi adj. big-bellied, pot-bellied. adj. gluttonous.
sabelbera adj. tending to have diarrhea.
sabelbete n. bellyful, large heavy meal.
sabelbetekada n. bellyful, large heavy

meal, overeating, satiety.
sabeldario *n.* diarrhea.
sabeldarraio *adj.* gluttonous, insatiable.
sabeldarraiotasun *n.* gluttony.
sabeldu *v.i.* to become convex, to sag.
sabeldura *n.* diarrhea.
sabelehortasun *n.* constipation.
sabeleko *adj.* abdominal, pertaining to the abdomen; uterine. *n.* diarrhea, colic.
sabeleri *n.* diarrhea.
sabelerori *adj.* having a fallen or sagging stomach (animals).
sabelidor *adj.* constipated.
sabelidortasun *n.* constipation.
sabeliztun *n.* ventriloquist.
sabeliztuntasun *n.* ventriloquism.
sabeljario *n.* diarrhea. *n.* bleeding from the stomach or the womb.
sabelkada *n.* bellyful, large heavy meal. *n.* litter (of animals).
sabelkeria *n.* gluttony.
sabelketa *n.* hollowing.
sabelki *n.* meat from the belly (of a cow, etc.).
sabelkide *adj.* of the same womb; twin.
sabelkoi *adj.* gluttonous, insatiable.
sabelkoikeria *n.* gluttony.
sabelkoitu *v.i.* to become gluttonous.
sabelkorroka *n.* stomach rumbling.
sabelmin *n.(med.)* abdominal pain, stomach ache.
sabelmintzari *n.* ventriloquist.
sabelmintzo *n.* ventriloquism.
sabelondo *n.* puerperium, time directly following childbirth. *n.* overeating.
sabelongarri *n.* manure.
sabelorro *n.* stomach rumbling.
sabelpe *n.(anat.)* pubes, pubis.
sabelpeko *adj.* pubic.
sabelsare *n.(anat.)* peritoneum, membrane that lines the cavity of the abdomen.
sabelsareko *adj.* peritoneal.
sabelsaremin *n.(med.)* peritonitis.
sabeltxo *n.(dim.)* tummy.
sabeltzar *n.(augm.)* big belly.
sabelune *n.* pothole.
sabelzorri *n.(colloq.)* hunger.
sabelzorro *n.(anat.)* stomach, belly, paunch.
sabelustu *v.t.* to rip open the belly of. *v.t.* to defecate, to have a bowel movement.
sabi *n.* clump of slender tree roots. *n.* nursery (plants). *n.(bot.)* amaranth.
sable *n.* saber.
sablekari *n.* saber expert.
sablekatu *v.t.* to fight with a saber.
sabotaia *n.* sabotage.
sabotaiari *n.* saboteur.
saboteiatu *v.t.* to sabotage.
sabuka *n.(bot.)* elder tree.
sadiko *adj.* sadistic.
sadismo *n.* sadism.
safari *n.* safari.

safiro *n.(min.)* sapphire.
sagar *n.(bot.)* apple.
sagara *n.(eccl.)* middle part of the mass.
sagaraketa *n.(eccl.)* consecration.
sagaraldi *n.* time of consecration of the bread and wine in the middle of the mass.
sagarapen *n.(eccl.)* consecration of the bread and wine in the middle of the mass; consecration.
sagaratu *v.t.* to consecrate (in the mass).
sagardi *n.* grove of apple trees, apple orchard.
sagardo *n.* cider.
sagardogile *n.* cidermaker.
sagardotegi *n.* cider shop.
sagarketa *n.* quantity of apples, lot of apples. *n.* shipping of apples.
sagarmin *n.* sour apple.
sagarrondo *n.(bot.)* apple tree.
sagarsabi *n.* nursery, seedbed (for apple trees).
sagartegi *n.* fruitstand, apple stand. *n.* place for storing apples.
sagartsu *adj.* full of apples.
sagartxo *n.(dim.)* little apple.
sagartza *n.* apple orchard.
sagasti *n.* apple orchard.
sagu *n.(zool.)* mouse.
sagukari *adj.* rat terrier; mouser (cat).
sagutegi *n.* place of mice.
sagutxakur *n.* rat terrier.
sagutxo *n.(dim.)* little mouse.
sagutxori *n.(zool.)* blue titmouse.
saguzar *n.(zool.)* bat.
sahaski *n.* wood of the willow tree, piece of willow.
sahasti *n.* willow grove.
sahats *n.(bot.)* willow.
sai *n.(zool.)* vulture.
saia- Used in compound words. Derived from *saio*, session, rehearsal, experiment, attempt.
saiagintza *n.* experiment, experimental activity.
saiakera *n.* essay; try, attempt; rehearsal.
saiaketa *n.* trial run, attempt.
saiaketari *n.* coach, trainer.
saiakuntza *n.* test, experiment, trial.
saialdi *n.* attempt, trial, try. *n.* session.
saiamen *n.* competition, attempt, trial.
saiapen *n.* application, dedication.
saiatsu *adj.* diligent, enterprising, hard-working, active.
saiatu *v.i.* to attempt, to try. *adj.* diligent, dedicated.
saiatzale *n./adj.* one who tries, attempter; trying. *n./adj.* taster; tasting.
saiheska *adv.* sideways, broadside.
saiheskeria *n.* transgression, fault.
saiheski *n.* rib, meat of the rib.
saihespeko *adj.* subcostal.
saiheste *n.* turning off, separating

(from traffic).

saihestu v.i. to turn to one side, to go to one side, to move sideways. v.i. to go astray, to get lost. v.t. to avoid, to elude, to not face.

saihets n. rib. n. side.

saihetsalde n. hillside, slope, side (of a mountain).

saihetsarteko adj. intercostal.

saihetsezur n.(anat.) rib (bone).

saihetsezurreria n. ribcage.

saikume n.(dim.) vulture chick.

sail n. group. n. section, sector, department, branch; series, set. n. parcel, piece of land, tract of land, lot. n. task.

sailburu n. head of a section.

sailburutu v.t. to command (a group).

saildu v.t. to distribute by groups, to put in groups, to group. v.i. to form groups, to meet in groups, to group.

saileko adj. common, ordinary.

sailka adv. by groups, in groups.

sailkagarri adj. classifiable, divisible, partitionable.

sailkaketa n. classification.

sailkapen n. classification.

sailkatu v.t. to classify, to catalogue. v.t. to parcel (out), to divide into parcels.

sailkatzaile n. classifier, cataloguer.

sailketa n. classification, grouping.

sailtxo n.(dim.) small group.

sain n. fat (of a fish).

saindu adj. sainted, holy. n.(eccl.) saint.

sainduarazi v.t. to sanctify, to make holy, to hallow.

sainduarazle n. sanctifier.

sainduetsi v.t. to sanctify; to canonize (a saint).

saindugarri adj. sanctifiable.

saindujale adj. affectedly devout or pious, sanctimonious.

saindukeria n. affected devotion or piety.

sainduki adv. piously.

saindulari n. pilgrim, religious traveler.

sainduoro n. All Saint's Day, November 1.

saindurale n. pilgrim, religious traveler.

sainduralerio n. pilgrimage.

saindutasun n. sanctity, holiness.

saindutegi n. sanctuary.

saindutu v.i. to be holy, to be sanctified. v.t. to make holy; to canonize (a saint).

saindutzaile n./adj. sanctifier; sanctifying, hallowing.

saio n. attempt, try, experiment. n. session, performance.

saioaldi n. attempt, try, essay.

saio eragin v.t. to make (someone) try, to make (someone) practice or rehearse.

saioidazle n. essayist, writer of essays.

saioka adv. trying, attempting, experimenting.

saiokuntza n. experiment.

saiolari n. experimenter, attempter, one who tries. n. essayist.

saiotutu n. test tube.

saioz adv. experimentally.

saiozko adj. experimental.

saitegi n. vulture trap.

saizulo n. vulture's nest. n. animal's den or burrow.

saka n. push, shove. n. large sack. n. anklebone (of a lamb). n. knapsack. n. eaves.

sakabanaketa n. dispersion, dissemination.

sakabanapen n. dispersion, dissemination.

sakabanatu v.i./v.t. to spread, to disseminate, to scatter, to disperse.

sakabanatzaile n./adj. one who scatters, one who spreads or disperses.

sakada n. push, shove.

saka egin v.t. to push, to shove, to thrust.

sakaila n. injury, wound; incision. n. destruction, ruin; extermination, massacre.

sakailakatu v.t. to make an incision, to cut. v.t. to destroy, to ruin; to exterminate, to massacre.

sakailatu v.t. to devastate, to destroy.

sakailatzaile adj. exterminating, destroying.

sakaildura n. cut, incision.

sakalari n. one who puts the ball in action, server.

sakaldi n. push, shove, thrust.

sakan n. ravine, deep hollow, gorge, gully. adj. deep.

sakarina n.(chem.) saccharin.

sakarri n. stone from which the serve was made in Basque handball (before painted courts).

sakats adj. eccentric, extravagant, strange. adj. knotty (tree).

sakatu v.t. to press (a button, etc.), to push, to shove. v.t. to fool (someone), to make (someone) believe a lie.

sake n. serve (in pelota).

sakegile n. server, one who serves (the ball in a game).

sakela n. pocket.

sakeldun adj. marsupial, didelphian.

sakeleratu v.t. to pocket, to put in a pocket.

saki n. incision, lesion, wound. n. large tear in clothing.

sakil n.(anat.) penis.

sakitu v.t. to cut, to make an incision.

sakon adj. deep, penetrating.

sakonagotu v.t. to make deeper, to make more profound.

sakonalde n. depression in the earth.

sakondu v.t. to go deeper, to make

more profound.

sakonera *n.* depth.

sakongune *n.* dip (in a road).

sakonketa *n.* deepening.

sakonki *adv.* deeply, profoundly.

sakontasun *n.* depth.

sakontzaile *n./adj.* one who goes deeper, one who makes (something) deeper.

sakonune *n.* depression, hollow, cavity.

sakotontzi *n.* lunch pail, lunch box.

sakramendu *n.(eccl.)* sacrament.

sakramentalki *adv.* sacramentally.

sakramentu *n.(eccl.)* sacrament.

sakratu *adj.* sacred.

sakratuki *adv.* sacredly.

sakrifikatu *v.i.* to deny oneself (something), to sacrifice, to make a sacrifice.

sakrifikatzaile *n./adj.* sacrificer; sacrificing.

sakrifizio *n.* sacrifice.

sakristau *n.* sacristan.

sakristautza *n.* job of the sacristan.

sakristi *n.* sacristy.

salabardo *n.* fishing net with handle, dip net, scoop net.

salagarri *adj.* denouncible, accusable.

salakeria *n.* treason, informing (on).

salaketa *n.* denunciation, accusation.

salakor *adj.* accusatory, accusing.

salatari *n.* denouncer, accuser. *adj.* accusing, denouncing.

salatu *v.t.* to accuse, to denounce. *adj.* accused, denounced.

salatzaile *n.* accuser, denouncer, informer.

salaurre *n.* anteroom, antechamber.

salbabide *n.* salvation, road to salvation.

salbagarri *adj.* salvageable, savable.

salbagile *n.* saviour.

salbamen *n.* rescue, lifesaving. *n.* salvation.

salbario *n.(zool.)* small edible salt-water fish with poisonous spine on the back of the head.

salbatore *n.* saviour.

salbatu *v.t./v.i.* to save (souls), to be saved. *v.t./v.i.* to save (a life).

salbatzaile *n.* saviour.

salbazio *n.* salvation.

salbea *n.(eccl.)* prayer to the Virgin.

salbide *n.* way of selling.

salbu *prep.* except.

salbuespen *n.* exception, exemption.

salbuespenezko *adj.* exceptional.

salbuetsi *v.t.* to exclude, to except.

salda *n.* soup; hot water and oil.

saldar *n.* boil, furuncle.

saldatsu *adj.* soupy, watery.

saldo *n.* group (of people), herd (of animals).

saldu *v.t.* to sell. *v.t.* to betray.

salduagiri *n.* certificate of sale, sales slip.

saldukeria *n.* treason, disloyalty, treachery.

saldun *n.* merchant, businessman.

salera *n.* sale.

salerazi *v.t.* to make (someone) sell (something).

salerosgarri *adj.* marketable.

salerosgo *n.* marketing, business, buying and selling, commerce, trading.

salerosi *n.* business, commerce, trade.

saleroseta *n.* trading, commerce, business.

salerosketari *n.* businessman, merchant.

saleroski *n.* merchandise.

salerosle *n.* merchant, businessman, dealer, tradesman.

salerospen *n.* trading, commerce, business.

salgai *n.* merchandise. *adj.* on sale, for sale.

salgai egon *v.i.* to be for sale.

salgaitz *adj.* unsellable, unmarketable, difficult to sell.

salgarri *adj.* marketable, sellable.

salgarritasun *n.* marketableness.

salkeria *n.* disloyalty, treason, treachery.

salketa *n.* sale. *n.* treason.

salkoi *adj.* marketable. *adj.* corruptible, capable of being bribed, venal.

salkoitasun *n.* marketableness. *n.* corruptibility, venality, quality of being capable of taking a bribe.

salkor *adj.* marketable. *adj.* corruptible, venal.

salkortasun *n.* venality, corruptibility.

salmenta *n.* sale.

salmo *n.* psalm.

salmogile *n.* psalmist, writer of psalms.

salmokantu *n.* psalm.

salmotegi *n.* Psalter, Book of Psalms.

salneurri *n.* sale price, price.

salo *adj.* gluttonous, insatiable.

salobre *adj.* gluttonous, insatiable.

salokeria *n.* gluttony. *n.* ambition.

salpen *n.* sale, act of selling.

saltagailu *n.* diving board, trampoline.

saltaketa *n.* jump, leap.

saltakor *adj.* lively, jumpy. *adj.* irascible, violent, ill-tempered.

saltalari *n.* jumper, leaper.

saltaleku *n.* loading place (for boats), boat ramp. *n.* trampoline.

saltamatxino *n.(zool.)* grasshopper.

saltarazi *v.t.* to make (someone) jump.

saltari *adj.* lively, jumpy, frolicsome, playful, frisky. *n.* jumper, leaper.

saltatu *v.t.* to jump, to leap.

saltegi *n.* store, market.

salto *n.* jump, leap.

salto egin *v.t.* to jump, to leap, to make a jump.

saltoka *adv.* in jumps, jumping, leaping.

saltokari *adj.* frisky, lively, frolicsome,

jumping. *n.* jumper, leaper.

saltokatu *v.i.* to jump, to frolic, to frisk about.

saltoki *n.* store, market, place of business.

saltsa *n.* sauce. *n.(fig.)* mess.

saltsati *adj.(fig.)* gossiping.

saltsatu *v.t.* to put in sauce. *v.t.(fig.)* to get mixed up in, to get in a jam.

saltsera *adj.(colloq.)* gossiping (woman).

saltsero *adj.(colloq.)* gossiping (man).

saltsontzi *n.* gravy boat, sauce container. *adj.(fig.)* interfering, gossiping.

saltxitxa *n.* small sausage.

saltxitxari *n.* sausage maker.

saltxitxoi *n.* salami.

saltzaile *n.* merchant, salesman, seller. *n.* traitor.

sama *n.* throat, neck.

samalda *n.* large group.

samaldaka *adv.* by groups, in groups.

samaldatu *v.i.* to gather, to crowd together, to form groups.

samar *n.* sliver, chip, tiny piece. *adv.* somewhat, a bit, quite, rather, pretty.

samats *n.* straw bedding (for livestock); straw that is mixed with manure for fertilizer.

samin *n.* pain, suffering, affliction. *adj.* bitter, sour. *adj.* painful, offensive, bitter, angry.

saminaldi *n.* bitterness, suffering.

samindu *v.i.* to become bitter, to turn sour; to ferment. *v.i.* to be irritated, to suffer. *v.i./v.t.* to pain, to afflict, to bother.

samindura *n.* bitterness, affliction, sorrow.

samingarri *adj.* painful.

saminkeria *n.* resentment, irritation.

saminki *adv.* bitterly, sharply.

saminkor *adj.* irritating.

saminkortasun *n.* irritability, irritableness. *n.* acescence, acetic fermentation.

saminkortu *v.i.* to become angry, to become irritated.

samintasun *n.* acidity. *n.* bitterness.

samur *adj.* tender, soft. *adj.(fig.)* tender, affectionate, sensitive. *adj.* irascible, angry.

samurbera *adj.* affectionate, tender, compassionate, sentimental. *adj.* irascible, angry.

samurgarri *adj.* touching, moving.

samurkeria *n.* excessive sentimentalism, maudlinism. *n.* resentment, anger, hate.

samurki *adv.* tenderly, softly, gently.

samurkoi *adj.* sentimental, tender, affectionate.

samurkoitasun *n.* tenderness, affection, gentleness.

samurkor *adj.* moving, touching. *adj.* easily moved, touched. *adj.* irritable, irascible; enraging.

samurkortasun *n.* tenderness, quality of being touching. *n.* irascibility.

samurkortu *v.i.* to become angry, to become irritable.

samurraldi *n.* period of tenderness. *n.* fit of rage.

samurrarazi *v.t.* to irritate, to anger, to make (someone) angry.

samurrarazle *n.* irritant, irritator.

samurtasun *n.* softness, tenderness.

samurterraz *adj.* easily moved (emotionally).

samurtu *v.i.* to be moved, to be compassionate. *v.i.* to be tender, to be soft. *v.i.* to get angry.

sandalia *n.* sandal.

sandia *n.* so-and-so. *n.(bot.)* watermelon.

sandwich *n.* sandwich.

saneaketa *n.* sanitation.

saneamendu *n.* sanitation. *n.* drain pipe; sewer.

sanga *n.(zool.)* pelican.

sano *adj.* healthy, strong, hale, sound. *adj.* sane.

sanoki *adv.* healthily, strongly.

sanotasun *n.* healthiness, heartiness.

sanotu *v.i.* to get well, to become healthy.

santu *adj.* sainted, holy. *n.* saint.

santu egin *v.t.* to sanctify, to canonize (a saint).

santutasun *n.* sanctity, holiness.

santutegi *n.* sanctuary.

santutu *v.i.* to be holy, to be sanctified. *v.t.* to make holy; to canonize (a saint).

sapa *n.(zool.)* small black inedible saltwater fish.

sapalda *n.* plateau, tableland.

sapar *n.* dirty honeycomb. *n.* thicket, underbrush; brambly ground.

sapazto *adj.* unkempt, disheveled.

sarale *n.* livestock feed.

sarberri *adj.* novice, newly entered.

sarbide *n.* entrance.

sarda *n.* pitchfork. *n.* school of fish.

sardakatu *v.t.* to winnow with a pitchfork.

sardanko *adj.* bandy-legged, knock-kneed, crippled.

sarde *n.* winnowing fork, pitchfork.

sardeska *n.* fork.

sardexka *n.(dim.)* fork, table fork.

sardeztatu *v.t.* to prop up with forks (tree branches, etc.).

sardina *n.(zool.)* sardine.

sardinketari *n.* sardine fisherman, sardine dealer.

sardinzahar *n.* crudely preserved sardines, usually stored in barrels.

sare *n.* net, network, web. *n.(fig.)* trap, trick, seduction.

sarebotaketa *n.* throwing a net, casting a net.

saregile *n.* net maker, repairer of nets.

saregintza *n.* net making; making of chain-link fencing.

sarehausketa *n.* breaking of a net, undoing or cutting of the mesh of a net.

sarehun *n.* reticular tissue.

sarekada *n.* netful.

saremaila *n.* mesh (of a net).

sareno *n.(dim.)* little net.

sareratu *v.t.* to net, to trap in a net.

sar erazi *v.t.* to make (someone) enter; to insist (on something). *v.t.* to put or place (in), to insert.

saresakel *n.* sack of a net.

sarestatu *v.t.* to sew nets, to make nets, to mend nets.

saretsu *adj.* reticulate.

saretto *n.(anat.)* reticulum.

saretu *v.i.* to unravel, to come unraveled. *v.t.* to sew a mesh (for a net).

saretxo *n.(dim.)* little net.

sarexka *n.(dim.)* little net.

sareztadura *n.* mending of a net.

sareztari *n.* darner, mender of a net.

sareztatu *v.t.* to make a net, to mend a net.

sargaitz *adj.* impenetrable.

sargarri *adj.* accessible, penetrable.

sargori *n.* suffocating heat, muggy weather.

sargoritsu *adj.* suffocating, very hot.

sari *n.* reward, prize, bonus, premium. *n.* punishment, just reward. *n.* tax, toll.

saria eman *v.t.* to give a prize, to reward.

saribanaketa *n.* distribution of prizes.

saridun *adj.* rewarded.

sariemaile *n.* rewarder, awarder of a prize.

sarigabeko *adj.* unrewarded.

sarigai *adj.* worthy of reward, remunerable, meritorious, prize-winning.

sarigarri *adj.* meritorious, remunerable, prize-winning. *n.* something given as a prize, reward, gratification.

sariketa *n.* competition, contest.

sariketari *n.* competitor, contestant.

saripeko *n.* one who works by the hour. *n.* mercenary (soldier).

saripen *n.* reward, remuneration.

saritu *v.t.* to reward, to give a prize.

saritxo *n.(dim.)* second prize, little prize.

saritzaile *n./adj.* rewarder; rewarding.

sarizale *adj.* fond of rewards, fond of entering contests for the prizes.

sariztagarri *adj.* rewardable, remunerable.

sariztatu *v.t.* to reward, to remunerate, to give a bonus or a prize.

sariztatzaile *n./adj.* rewarder; rewarding.

sarjentu *n.* sergeant.

sarkari *adj.* penetrating, incisive.

sarkeria *n.* interference.

sarketa *n.* act of entering; act of interfering.

sarkin *adj.* interfering, meddlesome, intruding.

sarkoi *adj.* interfering, meddlesome, intruding.

sarkoikeria *n.* meddling, intruding, interfering.

sarkor *adj.* persuasive, incisive, penetrating, sharp, moving.

sarkorki *adv.* incisively, persuasively, sharply, movingly.

sarkortasun *n.* incisiveness, persuasiveness, sharpness.

sarleku *n.* entrance, entry way.

sarmen *n.* power of intervention, influence.

sarna *n.(med.)* mange, scabies.

sarnazto *adj.* mangy.

sarpen *n.* penetration, entering.

sarraila *n.* lock.

sarrailari *n.* locksmith.

sarrailgin *n.* locksmith.

sarrailgintza *n.* locksmithing, lock making.

sarrailtegi *n.* locksmith's shop, hardware store.

sarrailtzulo *n.* keyhole.

sarrakio *n.* fright, terror.

sarrakiotu *v.t.* to frighten, to startle.

sarraldi *n.* entrance, moment of entering.

sarramuska *n.* grumbling, mumbling.

sarramuskada *n.* grumbling, mumbling.

sarramuskari *adj.* grumbling.

sarramuskatu *v.t.* to grumble, to scold, to complain.

sarrarazi *v.t.* to make (someone) enter.

sarrazle *n.* introducer.

sarraski *n.* murder, bloody murder, assassination. *n.* corpse, cadaver. *n.* destruction, ruin.

sarraskiarazi *v.t.* to cause (someone's) death; to make (someone) kill.

sarraskiarazle *n.* instigator of a massacre, one who makes (someone) massacre (others).

sarraskitu *v.t.* to devastate, to destroy. *v.t.* to assassinate, to kill.

sarraskitzaile *n.* exterminator, murderer, killer, butcher.

sarrera *n.* entrance, entry, entry way. *n.* entrance, insertion, introduction. *n.* ticket (to enter). *n.* prologue, introduction, foreword.

sarreraldi *n.* entrance, entering.

sarrerako *adj.* introductory, preliminary.

sarrerazle *n.* introducer.

sarrerraz *adv.* easily accessible.

sarri *adv.* often, frequently. *adv.* soon, immediately.

sarrialdi *n.* frequent repetition.

sarri-askotan *adv.* very often,

frequently.
sarriera n. frequency.
sarriro adv. frequently, often.
sarritako adj. frequent, usual, habitual, repeated.
sarritan adv. often, frequently.
sarritasun n. frequency.
sarritsu adj. habitual, common, frequent.
sarritu v.t./v.i. to repeat, to do (something) frequently, to increase the frequency of; to become frequent.
sartalde n.(geog.) west.
sartaldeko adj. western.
sartezin adj. impenetrable.
sartezintasun n. impenetrability.
sartu v.i. to enter, to come in, to go in. v.t. to insert, to put in, to include.
sartu-irtenka adv. back and forth, in and out.
sartune n. entry(way), entrance.
sartzaile n. one who inserts, one who puts in, one who makes others enter. adj. introducing.
sasi n. bramble bush.
sasi- (gram.) Prefix which indicates wild, pseudo, false. **Sasirakasle.** Bad teacher.
sasiabertzale n. bad patriot.
sasiarrosa n. wild rose.
sasiarte n. bramble thicket.
sasiburduntzi n. picnic, food eaten out of doors (usually in the country).
sasieskola n. playing hooky.
sasieskola egin v.t. to play hooky, to not go to school.
sasieuskaldun n. pseudo-Basque (person).
sasiezkontza n. concubinage, illicit cohabitation; illegal wedding.
sasijainko n. idol, false god.
sasijakintsu adj. pedantic.
sasijakintza n. pedantry, affected knowledge.
sasiketa n. group of bramble bushes.
sasiko n./adj. bastard, illegitimate (child).
sasikume n. bastard, illegitimate child.
sasimahats n. wild grape.
sasimaistra n. pseudo-teacher (female), bad (female) teacher.
sasimaisu n. pseudoteacher (male), bad (male) teacher, wild teacher.
sasisendagile n. quack, inferior doctor.
sasitegi n. bramble bush.
sasitsu adj. brambly, overgrown.
sasitu v.i. to be covered with brambles or weeds.
sasitza n. underbrush, brambly undergrowth.
saskar adj. crude, gross, boorish.
saskarkeria n. crudity, boorishness.
saskarki adv. crudely, boorishly.
saski n. basket.
saskibaloi n. basketball (game).

saskigile n. basket maker, basket weaver.
saskigintza n. basket making, basket weaving.
saskikada n. basketful.
saskilo n.(dim.) little basket.
saski-nahaski n. basket with mixed or jumbled contents. n. illogical or incoherent work.
saskiratu v.t. to put in a basket.
saskitegi n. basket shop.
saskitxo n.(dim.) little basket.
saskitzar n.(augm.) two-handled basket; large basket.
sasoal adj. healthy, healthful. adj. ripe.
sasoaldu v.i. to get well. v.i. to ripen (fruit).
sasoaltasun n. health, healthiness.
sasoi n. time, period, season. n. good health.
sasoiko adj. seasonal, of the time or season; prime.
sasoin n. season, epoch, time. n. good health.
sasoindu v.i. to ripen, to get ripe.
sasoinezko adj. seasonal. adj. vigorous.
sasoitu v.i. to become healthy, to become vigorous. v.i. to become fertile (land).
sasoiz adv. on time.
sastada n. prick, stab, jab.
sastadaka adv. pricking, stabbing.
sastaka adv. by jabbing, by pricking.
sastakari n. stabber, knifer.
sastakatu v.t. to stab, to prick.
sastaketa n. stabbing, knifing; knife fight.
sastako n. jab, stab, prick.
sastar n. garbage, debris. n. bramble bush.
sastatu v.t. to pierce (with a lance), to stab, to prick.
sastraka n. dense undergrowth, dense thicket or bramble, brushwood.
sastre n. tailor, dressmaker (always male).
satelite n. satellite.
satira n. satire.
satirizatu v.t. to satirize.
sator n.(zool.) mole (Talpa europea). n.(fig.) traitor, betrayer.
satorkeria n. conspiracy, treason.
satorlan n.(fig.) conspiracy, intrigue. (lit.) work of the mole.
satorlur n. molehill.
satorzulo n. mole hole.
sats n. manure, fertilizer.
satsadura n. pollution.
sats egin v.t. to defecate (animals).
satsu adj. dirty, filthy.
satsudura n. pollution, contamination.
satsugarri adj. soiling, dirtying.
satsukari n. pollution, polluting substance.
satsukeria n. dirtiness, filth.
satsuri n.(zool.) field mouse.

satsutasun n. dirtiness, filthiness.
satsutu v.t. to get (something) dirty.
sauna n. sauna.
sautrela n. refrain, chorus.
scout n. scout, boy scout.
scoutismo n. scouting.
seda n. silk.
sedazko adj. silk, made of silk.
sega n. scythe.
segagailu n. cutting machine, harvesting machine.
segagarri adj. harvestable, cuttable (with a scythe).
segaharri n. stone used for sharpening a scythe.
segalari n. cutter, harvester, mower, reaper.
segaldi n. season for cutting (hay, grass, etc.).
segamakina n. cutting machine, harvesting machine, mowing machine.
segari n. cutter, mower, harvester.
segatu v.t. to cut, to harvest.
segida n. continuation, succession.
segida eman v.t. to give continuity (to something).
segilari n. follower.
segitu v.t. to continue, to follow, to persevere.
seglar n./adj. lay (person).
segundari n. second hand (on a watch).
segundu n. second.
segur adj./adv. sure, certain; surely, certainly.
seguragaitz adj. insecure, unsure, uncertain.
segurantza n. certainty, assuredness.
seguraski adv. certainly, assuredly.
seguratu v.t. to assure, to make certain, to confirm.
seguratzaile n./adj. assurer, one who assures.
segur izan v.i. to be sure, to be certain.
segurki adv. surely, certainly, undoubtedly, for sure.
segurtatu v.t./v.i. to assure, to confirm; to be secure.
seguru adj. sure, certain.
sehaska n. cradle.
sehaskaketa n. act of putting the child in the cradle, cradling.
sehaskatu v.t. to put a baby in a cradle. v.t. to rock a cradle.
sehaskatxo n.(dim.) little cradle.
sehasketxe n. babysitter's house.
sehi n. domestic servant (male or female), domestic.
sehigo n. servitude, domestic service.
sehikide n. co-servant, fellow servant.
sehikintza n. state of being a servant, domestic servitude.
sei adj./n. six.
seigarren adj. sixth.
seihilabete n. semester.

seihilabetekari n. biannual publication, magazine (etc.) published twice a year.
seihilabeteko adj. biannual (twice a year), semestral. n. publication which appears twice a year.
seihilabetero adv. every semester, twice a year, biannually.
seihileko adj. biannual, semestral.
seiko adj. sextet, comprised of six. n. six (in cards).
seikoitz adj. sextuple.
seikoiztu v.t. to sextuple.
seikote n. sextet, group of six.
seilatu v.t. to stamp.
seilu n. postal stamp.
sein n. child.
seina n. tied at six points. adv. six each, six to each one.
seinaka adv. in groups of six.
seinakatu v.t. to divide or distribute in groups of six.
seinako n. sextet, group of six.
seinalari n. signaller.
seinalatu v.t. to signal, to mark.
seinale n. signal, sign, mark.
seinaleztatu v.t. to signal, to mark.
sein egin v.t. to give birth.
seinu n. gesture, physical signal.
seirehun adj./n. six hundred.
seirehungarren adj. six hundredth.
seiren n. one sixth.
seitu v.t. to sextuple.
sekretalgo n. position of secretary.
sekretari n. secretary.
sekretarigela n. secretary's office.
sekretariorde n. assistant secretary, vice-secretary.
sekretariordetza n. position of assistant secretary.
sekretaritza n. secretarial work, job of a secretary.
sekretu n. secret. adj. secret.
sekretuan adv. secretly, confidentially.
sekretuki adv. secretly, confidentially.
sekretuzko adj. confidential, secret.
sekula adv. never, ever.
sekulabelar n.(bot.) trefoil, clover.
sekulako adj. terrible, outrageous, horrible. adj. fantastic, great. adj. eternal, forever. adv. eternally, for good.
sekulakoz adv. perpetually, eternally, for good, forever.
sekulan adv. for good, forever, eternally. adv. never, ever (in negative sentences).
sekular adj. secular.
sekulargintza n. secularization.
sekularketa n. act of becoming secular.
sekularki adv. secularly, worldly.
sekularpen n. secularization.
sekulartasun n. secular state.
sekulartu v.i. to become a layman, to become secular.
sekulatasun n. eternity, perpetuity.

sekuoia n.(bot.) sequoia tree, redwood tree.

selenio n.(chem.) selenium.

seltza n. seltzer water.

semaforo n. street light, traffic light.

seme n. son; native son.

seme-alaba(k) n. children, sons and daughters.

semebakar n. only son.

semebitxi n. godson.

semenagusitasun n. primogeniture.

semeorde n. stepson.

semeordeko n. stepson.

semeordekotu v.t. to adopt.

semeordekotza n. adoption.

semeponteko n. godson. **semetasun** n. filiation, relationship of child to parent.

semeteria n. large number of offspring.

semetsu adj. prolific.

semetu v.t. to adopt. v.i. to be adopted, to become someone's child.

semetxo n.(dim.) small son, very young son.

semetza n. filiation, filial relationship between a son and his father.

semetzat hartu v.t. to adopt a child.

semezko adj. filial, relating to a son or daughter.

seminario n. seminary.

semitar adj. semitic.

sen n. common sense, mind, senses, sanity. n. instinct.

senadore n.(pol.) senator.

senar n. husband.

senardun adj. married, having a husband.

senar-emazteak n.(plur.) husband and wife.

senargabe adj. unmarried (woman), single.

senargai n. fiancé. adj. single.

senargaiak n.(pl.) engaged couple.

senartu v.i. to get married (man), to become a husband.

senatu n.(pol.) senate.

sendabelar n. medicinal herb.

sendabide n. cure, therapy, medical treatment, healing method.

sendadura n. act of healing, getting well.

sendaerraz adj. easily cured.

sendaezin adj. incurable.

sendagai n. medicine, medication, remedy, prescription.

sendagailu n. medical remedy, medicine, medication.

sendagaitz adj. incurable, difficult to cure.

sendagarri adj. curable, healable. n. antidote, tonic, pill, remedy. adj. strengthening, fortifying, healthful.

sendagile n. physician, doctor, healer.

sendagiletza n. medical profession.

sendagintza n. healing, science of medicine, medical profession.

sendagiri n. health certificate.

sendaketa n. recovery, convalescence.

sendakor adj. curative, healing, medicinal.

sendapen n. cure, healing.

sendar adj. solid (not liquid).

sendarazi v.t. to cure, to heal, to make (someone) get well.

sendartu v.i. to solidify.

sendategi n. hospital, clinic, sanatorium.

sendatu v.i./v.t. to get well, to cure, to heal.

sendatxartel n. prescription.

sendatzaile n. doctor, healer.

sendazterketa n. medical examination.

sendi n. family.

sendo adj. strong, vigorous, robust, sturdy. adj. firm, solid.

sendoagotu v.i./v.t. to become stronger; to make stronger.

sendoketa n. strengthening, fortifying, consolidation.

sendoki adv. strongly, vigorously, solidly.

sendokor adj. strengthening, reinforcing.

sendokote adj. robust, vigorous, strong, hale and hearty.

sendor adj. fat, stout, thick, heavy.

sendotasun n. strength, vitality, vigor. n. firmness, fortitude, courage, integrity.

sendotu v.t. to confirm, to corroborate.

sendotzaile n. reinforcer, strengthener. adj. fortifying, strengthening.

sendotza n.(eccl.) sacrament of confirmation.

senean egon v.i. to be in one's right mind.

sengabe adj. crazy, insensible, senseless.

sengabekeria n. senselessness, foolishness.

sengabeki adv. senselessly, foolishly.

sengabetu v.i. to lose one's common sense, to become foolish.

senide(ak) n. relative.

senidetasun n. brotherhood, relationship by blood. n. fraternity, brotherhood (not by blood).

senidetu v.i. to be related (by blood), to become related (by blood or marriage).

seniparte n. inheritance, patrimony.

senitarte n. family, relatives related by blood, relations, kinfolk.

senitarteko n. relative.

senitasun n. relationship.

seniteskontza n. marriage between relatives, double marriage between the siblings of one family and those of another.

senper n. great pain, great suffering.

sentiarazi v.t. to make (someone) feel.

sentibera adj. sensitive, emotional, touchy.

sentiberatasun n. sensitiveness, sensitivity, emotionalness, impressionableness.

sentiberatu v.i. to be sensitive, to become emotional, to be touchy.

sentigarri adj. moving, emotional.

sentikizun n. feeling.

sentikor adj. emotional, sensitive, touchy.

sentikortasun n. touchiness, sensitiveness.

sentikortu v.i. to become sensitive, to be touchy, to become emotional.

sentimen n. sense (of touching, etc.).

sentimendu n. sentiment, feeling.

sentipen n. feeling, emotion, sensation, affection.

sentipenez adv. emotionally, with feeling, affectionately.

sentipenezko adj. related to affection, emotional, sensitive.

sentitu v.t. to regret, to feel.

sentsazio n. sensation.

sentsual adj. sensual.

sentsualitate n. sensuality.

separatismo n.(pol.) separatism.

separatista n./adj.(pol.) separatist.

serios adj. serious.

serioski adv. seriously.

seriotasun n. seriousness.

sermoi n. sermon. n.(colloq.) reprimand, rebuke.

sermoi egin v.t. to preach, to give a sermon.

sermoigarri adj. preachable.

sermoigintza n. preaching, sermonizing.

sermoilari n. preacher.

serora n. female sacristan. n. nun, sister.

serorategi n. abode of a female sacristan; place where the female sacristan houses her tools. n. convent, monastery (for nuns).

serorego n. position of the female sacristan. n. state of being a nun or religious.

serotetxe n. house of the female sacristan. n. convent, nunnery.

seska n.(bot.) cane.

seskadi n. cane thicket.

seta n. stubbornness, obstinacy.

setakeria n. pigheadedness, stubbornness, obstinacy, contumacy, pertinacity.

setati adj. hard-headed, pigheaded, stubborn.

setatsu adj. enduring, persistent, stubborn.

setatu v.i. to be stubborn, to be obstinate.

sexu n. sex. adj. sexual.

sexual adj. sexual.

sexualki adv. sexually.

sexualtasun n. sexiness, sexuality.

sexubakar adj. unisexual.

sexuberekoi adj. homosexual, lesbian.

sexubiko adj. bisexual.

sexuegarri n. sexual desire, sexual appetite.

sexuezintasun n. sexual impotence.

sexugabe(ko) adj. asexual.

sexugaitz n. venereal disease, sexual illness.

sexugose n. sexual appetite.

sexuhotz adj. frigid.

sexujoketa n. coitus.

sexuketa n. coitus, sexual activity.

sexutasun n. sexuality, sexiness.

sifilidun adj. syphilitic.

sifilis n.(med.) syphilis.

sifoi n. seltzer water; seltzer bottle.

sikate n. dryness.

sikatu v.i./v.t. to dry (up).

siku adj. dry.

sikune n. dry place.

silaba n. syllable.

silbote n.(mus.) kind of large txistu which is played as an accompaniment for the smaller instruments.

silex n.(chem.) silex.

silikosis n.(med.) silicosis.

silo n. silo.

siloraketa n. storing in silos.

siloratu v.t. to store in silos.

simaur n. manure.

simaurgarri adj. fertilizable.

simaurketa n. transport of manure.

simaurki n. manure, material used to make manure (dirty straw, etc.).

simaurtegi n. manure pile, manure pit.

simaurtoki n. manure pile, manure pit.

simaurtu v.t. to fertilize with manure.

sinagoga n. synagogue.

sinboliko n. symbolic.

sinbolo n. symbol.

sindikal adj. of the trade or labor union.

sindikalari n. member of the labor union.

sindikaldu v.i. to belong to a labor union.

sindikalgintza n. (labor) unionism.

sindikapen n. syndication, unionism.

sindikato n. labor union.

sindikatu v.i. to join a union, to go union, to unionize.

sindikatzaile n. unionizer, union organizer.

sinesbera adj. credulous, gullible.

sinesberatasun n. credulity, gullibility.

sinesberatu v.i. to become credulous, to be gullible.

sinesbide n. proof, reason to believe.

sinesgabe adj. incredulous, not gullible, unbelieving.

sinesgabekeria n. lack of faith, lack of belief; disbelief.

sinesgai n.(eccl.) dogma.

sinesgaitz adj. incredible, difficult to believe; incredulous.

sinesgaiztasun *n.* untrustworthiness; unlikelihood, improbability.

sinesgarri *adj.* believable, credible; trustworthy. *n.* proof, testimony.

sinesgarritasun *n.* credibility.

sinesgogor *adj.* incredulous, unbelievable, obstinate.

sinesgogortasun *n.* incredulity; unbelievableness.

sinesgogortu *v.i.* to become incredulous.

sineskera *n.* belief.

sineskeria *n.* false belief, superstition, fanaticism.

sineskeritsu *adj.* superstitious.

sineskide *n.* member of the same religion.

sineskizun *n.* belief, article of faith.

sineskor *adj.* believing, trusting, credulous, ingenuous.

sineskorki *adv.* credulously, believingly, trustingly.

sineskortasun *n.* credulity, credulousness.

sinesle *n.* believer.

sinesmen *n.* belief, faith.

sinespide *n.* proof, reason to believe.

sinestagarri *adj.* credible, plausible.

sinestarazi *v.t.* to persuade, to make (someone) believe.

sinestarazpen *n.* persuasion.

sineste *n.* faith, belief, credence. *n.* belief, conviction.

sinestedun *adj.* believing, faithful, having faith.

sinesterraz *adj.* easy to believe.

sinestezin *adj.* incredible, unbelievable.

sinestezinezko *adj.* incredible, unbelievable.

sinestezintasun *n.* incredibility.

sinetsi *v.t.* to believe, to believe in.

sinfonia *n.(mus.)* symphony.

sinistu *v.t.* to believe.

sinkronizatu *v.t.* to synchronize.

sino *n.* facial expression, gesture. *n.* strangeness, craziness, queerness.

sinoka *adv.* grimacingly, making faces.

sinolari *adj.* exaggerating, gesticulating, animated.

sinoti *adj.* crazy, strange, queer.

sinotsu *adj.* crazy, strange, queer.

sinple *adj.* simple.

sinplekeria *n.* simplemindedness.

sinpleki *adv.* simply.

sinpletasun *n.* simplicity, plainness.

sinpletu *v.i.* to become simple or humble.

sintaxi *n.* syntax.

sintesi *n.* synthesis, summary.

sintetiko *adj.* synthetic.

sintonizapen *n.* tuning, syntonization.

sintonizatu *v.t.* to tune, to syntonize.

sionismo *n.* Zionism.

sionista *adj.* Zionist.

sirena *n.* siren, horn, air-raid signal. *n.* siren, vamp, mermaid, seductive woman.

sirenots *n.* wail of a siren.

sirimiri *n.* light mist, light but steady rain, drizzle.

sirimiri egin *v.t.* to drizzle, to mist.

siroko *n.* sirocco, Mediterranean wind that blows from the southeast.

sisipasa *n.(colloq.)* lisp.

sistima *n.* system.

sistrin *adj.* skinny, thin, puny, emaciated.

sits *n.(zool.)* moth.

sitsadun *adj.* motheaten, having moths.

-ska *(gram.)* diminutive suffix. **Mendiska.** Little mountain.

ski *n.* ski.

skialari *n.* skier.

skiatu *v.t.* to ski.

skiatzaile *n.* skier.

-skila *(gram.)* Diminutive suffix, usually pejorative. **Jaunskila.** Little dictator.

-sko *(gram.)* Diminutive suffix. **Idisko.** Calf.

so *n.* look, glance, gaze. *int.* whoa!

soaldi *n.* act of looking.

sobera *adv./adj.* too much, too many, overly, excessively.

soberakin *n.* leftovers, remains, residue.

soberatu *v.i.* to be left over, to be extra.

soberetsi *v.t.* to overestimate.

sobornatu *v.t.* to bribe.

soborno *n.* bribe.

soda *n.* soda water.

sodio *n.(chem.)* sodium.

soegile *n.* observer, watcher; inspector.

so egin *v.t.* to observe, to watch, to look at.

so egon *v.i.* to be watching, to watch, to pay attention.

sofrikario *n.* suffering.

sogor *adj.* deaf. *adj.* inflexible, hard-hearted.

sogordura *n.* deafness.

sogorkeria *n.* hard-heartedness, insensitivity, lack of sensitiveness.

sogorraldi *n.* temporary deafness.

sogortasun *n.* ankylosis, stiffening, or rigidness of a joint.

sogortu *v.i.* to become stiff, to be rigid or hardened.

soil *adj.* mere, lone, alone. *adj.* bare, barren. *adj.* common, simple. *adj.* net.

soildu *v.t.* to raze, to cut down; to destroy. *v.t.* to crop (hair), to shave (the head).

soileri *n.* baldness.

soilik *adv.* merely, simply, only; exclusively.

soilketa *n.* destruction, devastation, leveling, razing. *n.* simplification.

soilki *adv.* merely, only, simply.

soiltasun *n.* simplicity, plainness.

soilune n. treeless place or clearing, bare patch.

soin n.(anat.) torso, upper part of the body, shoulder, bust. n. body.

soineko n. dress, clothing. adj. corporeal, physical, somatic.

soinenbor n.(anat.) human torso.

soineratu v.t. to put on one's shoulder, to carry on one's shoulder.

soingain n.(anat.) shoulder.

soingaineko n. cape, overcoat. n. epaulet, pauldron, shoulder piece on armor.

soingiltza n.(anat.) shoulder (joint).

soinkari n. carrier, person who carries a burden on the shoulder.

soinu n. sound. n. tune, music, melody.

soinualdi n. musical interlude, period of music, time spent playing music.

soinubakarreko adj. unisonous.

soinuegile n. composer, musician.

soinu egin v.t. to compose. v.t. to make a sound.

soinugabe adj. atonal, soundless.

soinugabetasun n. soundlessness, atonality.

soinugailu n. musical instrument.

soinugaitz adj. dissonant.

soinugaiztasun n. dissonance.

soinugaizto n. dissonance, quality of being off-key.

soinugaiztu v.t. to be, play or sing out of tune or off-key.

soinugarri adj. sonorous, tuneful, pleasant sounding.

soinujole n. musician, player of a musical instrument.

soinulari n. musician, instrumentalist.

soinutasun n. sonority, musicality.

soinutresna n. musical instrument.

soinuztaketa n. sounding.

soinuztatu v.t. to sound, to make a sound, to voice.

soka n. rope, string, cord, line. adv. watching, observing, looking. n.(fig.) line of people dancing.

sokaburu n. end of a rope.

sokadantza n. high wire walking. n. line dance. n. jumping rope.

sokadantzari n. high wire walker, acrobat.

sokagainkari n. acrobat, high wire walker.

sokagile n. rope maker.

sokagintza n. rope making.

sokale n. long line to which shorter hooked fishing lines are attached.

sokamuturra n. game in which participants try to catch the trailing rope of a young bull.

sokasalto n. jumprope.

sokatira n. tug-of-war.

sokatu v.t. to tie with rope.

sokatzar n.(augm.) thick rope.

solairu n. wooden floor.

solas n. conversation, talk. n. game, diversion.

solasaldi n. conversation, talking. n. recreation, fun, period of recreation.

solasbide n. subject of the conversation.

solasegile n. talker, converser, speaker.

solas egin v.t. to talk, to converse.

solaseria n. chat, long conversation.

solasgai n. subject of a conversation.

solasgarri adj. discussible.

solasketa n. talk, conversation, chat.

solaskide n. fellow talker, converser, interlocutor.

solastatu v.i. to talk to, to talk with, to converse with.

solastegi n. place for conversing, conversation pit, locutory.

solastoki n. place for conversation, locutory.

solastun adj. talkative, chattering, loquacious.

soldadu n. soldier.

soldadugo n. military service, army.

soldaduketa n. military draft.

soldadukide n. companion in military service.

soldadusail n. picket, small squad of soldiers.

soldadutalde n. troop of soldiers.

soldaduteria n. group of soldiers.

soldadutu v.i. to enlist, to become a soldier.

soldadutza n. military service, army.

soldaezin adj. unsolderable, unweldable.

soldagailu n. soldering iron.

soldagaitz adj. difficult to solder, difficult to weld.

soldagarri adj. solderable, weldable.

soldaketa n. soldering, welding.

soldata n. salary, wage.

soldatadun adj. salaried.

soldatari n. day laborer.

soldatu v.t. to solder, to weld, to braze.

soldatzaile n. welder, one who solders.

solfeatu v.t. to read music, to sight read music, to sing the scale.

solfeo n. music.

solomo n. loin cut, loin (of the pig).

solte adj./adv. loose, untied.

soluzio n. solution.

soluzionatu v.t. to solve.

somagarri adj. observable, perceptible. adj. foreseeable, divinable, guessable.

somakari n. perceiver, observer.

somaketa n. perception, attention.

somakor adj. perceptive.

somari adj. perspicacious, shrewd, keen-sighted.

somatu v.t. to suspect, to suppose.

sonata n.(mus.) sonata.

sonatatxo n.(dim.) sonatina.

sonatu adj. famous, celebrated.

sonbrero n. hat.
sonbrerogile n. hat maker, hatter.
sondagailu n. sounding line, sounding lead, plummet, sound.
sondagarri adj. soundable, fathomable, penetrable.
sondaketa n. sounding, fathoming. n. inquiry, questioning.
sondalari n. driller, borer.
sondaldi n. sounding, fathoming, drilling.
sondatu v.t. to sound, to fathom, to drill.
sondatzaile n. driller, sounder.
soneto n.(lit.) sonnet.
soprano n.(mus.) soprano.
sor adj. stiff, unbending. adj. dull, throbbing. adj.(fig.) apathetic, unfeeling.
sora- Used in compound words. Derived from soro, field.
soraio adj. impassive, unfeeling, indolent. n. leprous. n. kind of leprosy found in pigs, caused by bladder-worms.
soraiokeria n. indolence, impassivity, lack of feeling.
soraioki adv. unfeelingly, impassively, indolently.
soraiotasun n. insensitivity, indolence.
soraiotegi n. leprosy hospital.
soraiotu v.i. to be unfeeling, to be insensitive, to be indolent. v.i. to be a leper, to become leprous.
sorbalda n.(anat.) shoulder.
sorberri adj. newborn.
sorberritu v.i. to come to life, to appear again, to resurge.
sorbide n. cause, origin.
sorburu n. origin, cause. n.(anat.) shoulder.
sorgabe adj. unborn.
sorgaitz adj. incapable of being engendered or begotten.
sorgarri adj. deafening. n. calmative, sedative.
sorgin n. witch.
sorginbelar n.(bot.) dandelion, lion's tooth.
sorgindu v.t. to bewitch, to cast a spell (on someone). v.i. to become a witch.
sorgindura n. bewitching, act of casting a spell, witchcraft.
sorgingo n. witchcraft, sorcery.
sorginkeria n. witchcraft, sorcery.
sorginorratz n.(zool.) dragonfly.
sorgintza n. witchcraft.
sorgintzaile n. bewitcher, caster of spells, sorcerer.
sorgor adj. insensitive, impassive. adj. disoriented; ecstatic, rapturous.
sorgorkeria n. insensitivity, insensibility, hard-heartedness.
sorgorraldi n. enchantment, ecstasy.
sorgortasun n. insensitivity, insensibility, hard-heartedness.

sorgortu v.t. to stun, to daze. v.i. to be bewildered, to be stunned, to be dazed; to become ecstatic or enraptured.
sori adj. allowed, permitted, legal.
sori izan v.i. to be permitted, to be allowed.
soriki adv. permissibly, with permission, licitly.
sorjes adj. impudent, insolent, bold, shameless.
sorjeskeria n. insolence, impudence, shamelessness.
sorjestu v.i. to become impudent, to become shameless.
sorka adv. pressing, pushing, shoving.
sorkailu n. generator.
sorkari n. creature, entity.
sorkatu v.i. to push, to press.
sorketa n. creative action, action of creating. n. conception.
sorki n. cloth pad (worn on head under heavy loads).
sorkunde n. conception; birth. n. woman's proper name.
sorkura n. birth, origin.
sorleku n. native land, native country; home town, native village.
sormen n. procreation, creativity.
sormin n. dull pain, ache. n. labor pain.
sormindu v.i. to stiffen, to lose feeling.
soro n. field, cultivated land.
sorrera n. origin, source, conception; genesis, beginning; birth. n. numbness of a limb.
sorreri n.(med.) deafness. n.(med.) apoplexy, stroke.
sorrezin adj. incapable of being engendered or begotten.
sorta n. bunch (of flowers, kindling, etc.). n. collection.
sortaketa n. act of bundling, packaging.
sortalde n.(geog.) East.
sortaldeko adj. east, eastern.
sortasun n. stiffness, numbness, lack of feeling. n. apathy, indolence; hard-heartedness.
sortatu v.t. to load. v.t. to bunch, to gather in bunches.
sortatxo n.(dim.) little bunch.
sorterazi v.t. to cause to be born, to bring into the world. v.t. to originate, to suggest, to promote.
sorterri n. native land, native country; native village, home town.
sorterrigabeko adj. without a country.
sorterriratu v.i./v.t. to return to one's country, to repatriate.
sorterro n. origin, ancestry, lineage, family.
sorexe n. house of one's birth.
sortiri n. home town, natal city or town.
sortoki n. place of birth.
sortu v.i. to be born. v.t. to conceive, to engender, to beget, to procreate, to generate. v.t./v.i. to originate, to

cause, to create; to proceed from, to originate in, to break out. *v.i.* to arise.

sortzaile *n.* creator, procreator, one who engenders; founder. *adj.* creative, generative.

sortzain *n.* midwife, obstetrician.

sortzapen *n.* conception, creation.

sortzaro *n.* time of birth.

sortze *n.* conception, act of conceiving. *n.* act of being born, birth, origin.

sos *n.* money.

sosa *n.(chem.)* soda, caustic soda.

sosagile *n.* producer or manufacturer of caustic soda.

sosbilgailu *n.* slot machine.

sosdun *adj.* wealthy, having money, monied.

sosegamendu *n.* tranquility, calm, quiet.

sosegatu *v.i.* to be calm, to be tranquil. *v.t.* to calm (someone) down.

sosegu *n.* calm, tranquility.

soseguz *adv.* calmly, slowly.

soska *adv.* coin by coin.

sostengu *n.* support.

sotana *n.(eccl.)* cassock, soutane.

sotil *adj.* discreet, prudent. *adj.* calm, meek, peaceful, docile. *adj.* robust, strong.

sotildu *v.i.* to be fine, to be elegant. *v.i.* to be discreet, to be prudent. *v.i.* to be calm, to be meek.

sotildura *n.* physical or moral fineness.

sotilki *adv.* docilely, meekly, discreetly.

sotiltasun *n.* courtesy, discretion. *n.* meekness, docility.

soto *n.* cellar, wine cellar.

soviet *n.(pol.)* soviet.

sovietar *adj.* soviet.

sovietarzale *adj.* pro-soviet.

sozial *adj.* social.

sozialdemokrata *adj./n.(pol.)* Social Democrat.

sozialdemokrazia *n.(pol.)* Social Democracy.

sozialdu *v.i.* to socialize.

sozialeztatu *v.t.* to socialize.

sozialismo *n.(pol.)* socialism.

sozialista *adj./n.(pol.)* socialist.

sozialistazale *adj.* pro-socialist.

sozializaketa *n.* socialization.

sozializazio *n.* socialization.

soziologia *n.* sociology.

soziologo *n.* sociologist.

stop *n.* stop.

su *n.* fire. *n.(fig.)* ardor, fervor, enthusiasm, strong desire. *n.(fig.)* rage, fury. *n.* match, light. *n.* heat.

sualdi *n.* fire (emotional or physical), conflagration, fury, burst of rage, exasperation.

suargi *n.* light.

subasta *n.* auction.

subastari *n.* auctioneer.

subastatu *v.t.* to auction off.

subazter *n.* hearth, fireside.

subera *adj.* sensitive to fire, flammable. *adj.* inflammatory, excitable.

suberatu *v.t.* to lose heat (metal), to cool down.

suberri *n.(eccl.)* new fire created in church on Easter Saturday.

subil *n.* log for fire. *n.* fine fishing line that hangs from thicker common line.

subiloste *n.* kitchen wood box.

subjetibismo *n.* subjectivism.

subjetibo *adj.* subjective.

subjetiboki *adv.* subjectively.

subjetibotasun *n.* subjectiveness, subjectivity.

suburdina *n.* fire poker.

suburu *n.* lower sloped part of the chimney.

sudun *adj.* ardent, heated. *(lit.)* having fire.

sudur *n.(anat.)* nose.

sudurbarneko *adj.* intranasal.

sudurgain *n.* upper part of the nose, top of the nose.

sudurjario *n.* cold in the nose.

sudurkari *adj.* nasal.

sudurkatu *v.t.* to nasalize.

sudurluze *adj.* long-nosed, aquiline (nose), sharp-nosed. *adj.(colloq.)* nosy, prying, meddlesome, interfering.

sudurmakur *n.* hooked nose.

sudurmintz *n.(anat.)* nasal cartilage.

sudurmintzo *n.* nasalization, talking through one's nose.

sudurmotz *adj.* flat-nosed, pug-nosed.

sudurpeko *adj.* under the nose, subnasal. *n.(colloq.)* moustache.

sudurpunta *n.* point of the nose, end of the nose.

sudurrandi *adj.* long-nosed, big-nosed.

sudurreko *adj.* nasal. *n.* blow to the nose.

sudurrez *adv.* nasally.

sudurtxo *n.(dim.)* little nose, button nose.

sudurzabal *adj.* platyrrhine, having a wide, flat nose (monkeys, etc.).

sudurzapal *adj.* flat-nosed, pug-nosed.

sudurzapi *n.* handkerchief.

sudurzulo *n.(anat.)* nostril.

suemaile *n.* pyromaniac. *n./adj.(fig.)* troublemaker, busybody.

su eman *v.t.* to set fire to, to set a fire, to burn. *v.t.(fig.)* to cause trouble, to incite anger.

suero *n.(med.)* serum. *n.(med.)* intravenous feeding.

suertatu *v.i.* to run into (someone), to meet accidentally. *v.i.* to happen, to occur.

suerte *n.* luck.

sufre *n.(chem.)* sulfur.

sufreztapen *n.* sulfur treatment.

sufreztatu *v.t.* to spray with sulfur, to treat with sulfur.

sufreztatzaile *n.* one who sprays

(something) with sulfur.
sufrimendu *n.* suffering.
sufritu *v.t.* to suffer.
suga- Used in compound words. Derived from *suge*, snake.
sugai *n.* combustible.
sugandila *n.(zool.)* wall lizard.
sugar *n.* flame. *n.* ardor, fervor. *adj.* impatient.
sugarastatu *v.i./v.t.* to be singed, to be scorched; to singe, to scorch, to sear.
sugarraldi *n.* sudden blaze, flare, flash fire; outburst.
sugarri *adj.* flammable, combustible. *n.* flammable object or matter.
sugartasun *n.* vehemence, ardor.
sugartu *v.i.* to burst into flames.
sugatilu *n.* vessel for melting metals.
suge *n.(zool.)* snake, serpent.
sugebelar *n.(bot.)* green dragon.
sugedun *adj.* bearing or containing serpents.
sugegorri *n.(zool.)* asp, viper.
sugeitsu *n.(zool.)* glass snake.
sugekume *n.(zool.)* small snake.
sugeldo *n.* embers of a fire.
sugestio *n.* suggestion.
sugestionagarri *adj.* suggestible.
sugestionatu *v.i./v.t.* to be influenced by the power of suggestion; to influence by the power of suggestion, to hypnotize.
sugetzar *n.(zool.)* boa constrictor.
sugile *n.* stoker, fireman.
sugiltz *n.* trigger (of a gun).
sugin *n.* stoker, fireman.
suhar *adj.* ardent, fiery, enthusiastic, fervent, passionate, vehement; impetuous.
suhardura *n.* enthusiasm, fervor, passion.
suhargarri *adj.* exciting, empassioning, empassionate.
suharri *n.(min.)* flint.
suhartasun *n.* vehemence, passion, ardor, enthusiasm.
su hartu *v.t.* to catch fire; to get angry.
suhatz *n.* fire tongs.
suhi *n.* son-in-law.
suhil *n.* dying fire, slow fire.
suhiltzaile *n.* fireman.
suil *n.* wooden bucket.
sujetu *n.(gram.)* subject.
sukalaurre *n.* pantry.
sukaldari *n.* cook.
sukaldaritza *n.* cooking, art of cooking.
sukalde *n.* kitchen.
sukalgintza *n.* art of cooking.
sukalmutil *n.* scullion, kitchen boy.
sukaloste *n.* pantry; back kitchen.
sukar *n.* fever. *n.* flame.
sukardun *adj.* feverish, hot, having a fever, fevered.
sukargiro *n.* fever, pyrexia, abnormally high body temperature.

sukarki *adv.* ardently, vehemently.
sukarkontrako *adj.* mitigating or removing fever.
sukarraldi *n.* high fever.
sukarremale *adj.* fever inducing, causing fever.
sukarri *n.(min.)* flint.
sukartsu *adj.* feverish, fevered.
sukartu *v.i.* to have a fever, to be feverish. *v.i.(fig.)* to get angry, to be angry.
suketa *n.* fire, conflagration, burning.
sukoi *adj.* burnable, flammable. *adj.* fond of fire. *adj.* irascible, irate, having a temper.
sukoitasun *n.* flammability.
sukor *adj.* flammable, burnable. *adj.* irate, irascible, having a temper.
sukortasun *n.* irascibility, short-temperedness.
suldar *n.(med.)* pimple; pustule.
suldartsu *adj.* pimply, having pustules.
sulfatailu *n.* sulfur sprayer.
sulfatapen *n.* spraying with sulfur.
sulfatatu *v.t.* to spray with sulfur.
sulfato *n.(chem.)* sulfate.
sulfatontzi *n.* sulfur sprayer.
sulfuriko *adj.* sulfuric.
sulfuro *n.(chem.)* sulfide.
sultan *n.* sultan.
sultanerri *n.* sultanate, territory ruled by a sultan.
suma *n.* smell, sense of smell.
sumaezin *adj.* imperceptible.
sumaezinez *adv.* imperceptibly.
sumagai *n.* sensory input.
sumagailu *n.* detector.
sumagaitz *adj.* imperceptible, difficult to perceive.
sumagarri *adj.* perceptible, observable. *adj.* discoverable, divinable, guessable.
sumaketa *n.* perception, attention.
sumakizun *n.* perception.
sumakor *adj.* perceptive.
sumatu *v.t.* to perceive, to notice, to become aware of, to realize. *v.t.* to smell.
sumatzaile *adj.* detecting, perceiving.
sumendi *n.(geol.)* volcano.
sumendiaho *n.(geol.)* crater.
sumenditsu *adj.* volcanic.
sumendizulo *n.* crater.
sumeta *n.* pyre, bonfire.
sumin *n.* anger, ire, fury. *n.(fig.)* resentment. *adj.* furious, angry.
suminaldi *n.* fury, burst of rage, exasperation.
suminarazi *v.t.* to irritate, to make (someone) happy.
suminbera *adj.* irritable, irascible.
sumindu *v.i.* to get angry, to be furious. *v.i.* to burn up, to be consumed by heat.
sumindura *n.* anger, irritation, fury. *n.* burn, inflammation. *n.(fig.)* resentment, indignation.

sumingarri *adj.* irritating, producing anger, maddening, infuriating.

suminki *adv.* furiously, ardently.

suminkoi *adj.* irascible, easy to anger, quick-tempered.

suminkor *adj.* short-tempered, irascible.

suminkortasun *n.* irritability, irascibility, anger, wrath.

suminkortu *v.i.* to be irritable, to get angry.

sumintasun *n.* irritability, causticness, sharpness, irascibility.

suntsidura *n.* destruction, annihilation.

suntsiezin *adj.* indestructible.

suntsiezintasun *n.* indestructibility.

suntsigaitz *adj.* difficult to destroy, indelible.

suntsigarri *adj.* destructible, destructive, ruinous, devastating, disastrous.

suntsigarritasun *n.* destructiveness, devastation.

suntsiketa *n.* destruction, devastation, ruin.

suntsikor *adj.* destructive, devastating, ruinous. *adj.* destructible, corruptible.

suntsitu *v.t.* to destroy, to defeat. *v.i.* to disappear.

suntsitzaile *adj.* destructive, devastating, defeating, ruinous.

suntsun *adj.* foolish, idiotic. *adj.* meddlesome.

suontzi *n.* brazier, fire-pan.

supazter *n.* hearth, fireplace, chimney corner.

superlatibo *adj.* superlative.

supermerkatu *n.* supermarket.

superstizio *n.* superstition.

suponpa *n.* fire hose.

suponpari *n.* fireman.

suposaketa *n.* supposition.

suposamendu *n.* supposition.

suposatu *v.t.* to suppose.

susal- Used in compound words. Derived from *susara*, heat or rut (of animals).

susalbero *adj.* quick to come into heat (cow).

susaldi *n.* duration of a cow's heat.

susalgori *adj.* quick to come into heat (cow).

susalketa *n.* coming into heat (of a cow).

susara *n.* heat, rut (cows).

susaratu *v.i.* to come into heat (cows).

susmabera *adj.* suspicious, distrustful.

susmaezin *adj.* unpredictable; unsuspected.

susmagabeko *adj.* unsuspected, unexpected.

susmagaitz *adj.* unsuspected.

susmagarri *adj.* suspected; presumable, predictable.

susmaketa *n.* suspicion, hint.

susmakor *adj.* suspicious, distrustful.

susmatu *v.t.* to suspect.

susmatzaile *n.* one who suspects, suspicious person.

susmo *n.* suspicion. *n.* conjecture, indication.

sustatu *v.t./v.i.* to stimulate, to incite, to excite, to promote, to encourage.

sustrai *n.(bot.)* root. *n.* origin, basis, foundation.

sustraidura *n.* taking root.

sustraigabe *adj.* uprooted, rootless.

sustraigabetu *v.i.* to uproot, to become uprooted.

sustraipen *n.* taking root, rooting.

sustraitu *v.i.* to take root, to root, to set down roots.

sustraitxo *n.(dim.)* little root.

sutaldi *n.* sudden blaze, flash of fire.

sutan egon *v.i.* to be on fire, to be burning. *v.i.* to be furious.

sutarazi *v.t.* to set fire to, to set on fire. *v.t.* to enthuse, to enliven, to make (someone) enthusiastic.

sutarazle *adj.* setting on fire. *adj.* enthusing.

sutargi *n.* light of a fire or stove.

sutasun *n.* igniting, ignition.

sutauslari *n.* pyrotechnist, firework maker.

sutaustegi *n.* powder magazine, powder bag.

sutauts *n.* gunpowder.

sute *n.* fire.

sutegi *n.* stove, range; fireplace. *n.* forge, furnace, blacksmith's hearth.

sutondo *n.* kitchen.

sutontzi *n.* brazier, heater.

sutopil *n.* bread baked under ashes.

sutsu *adj.* enthusiastic, passionate, ardent, fiery, fervent.

sutsuki *adv.* fervently, ardently, passionately, enthusiastically.

sutu *v.t.* to light a fire, to set on fire, to set fire to. *v.i.* to get angry. *v.i.* to be enthusiastic, to be passionate.

sutzar *n.* fire, bonfire, forest fire, large fire.

suzaln *n.* fireman.

suzaintoki *n.* fire station, fire house.

suzale *adj.* pyromaniacal.

suzalekeria *n.* pyromania.

suziri *n.* firework (usually in plural).

suzirigile *n.* firework maker.

suzirigintza *n.* pyrotechnics, making of fireworks.

suzko *adj.* igneous, pertaining to fire or fireworks.

suztagarri *adj.* flammable.

suztatu *v.t.* to light a fire. *v.t.* to revive, to liven up. *v.i.* to get furious, to be furious.

suztatzaile *adj.* fomenting, agitating, enlivening, enthusing.

T

t Letter of the Basque alphabet.

-t *(gram.)* Suffix used in the northern

dialects meaning toward. **Etxerat.**
Toward the house. *(gram.)* Verbal
suffix which indicates first
person singular. **Egin dut.** I have
done.
ta *conj.* and. *n.* slap (children's
language).
-ta *(gram.)* Verbal suffix used with
infinitives meaning after. **Bostak jota
heldu zen.** He arrived after it struck
five.
tabakadi *n.* tobacco shop.
tabakari *n.* tobacconist, salesperson in
a tobacco shop.
tabako *n.* tobacco.
tabakobelar *n.* tobacco leaf; tobacco
plant.
tabakodenda *n.* tobacco shop.
tabakogile *n.* tobacco grower.
tabakogintza *n.* tobacco industry.
tabakontzi *n.* tobacco pouch, cigarette
case.
tabakosaltzaile *n.* tobacco seller,
tobacconist.
tabakotegi *n.* tobacco shop.
taberna *n.* tavern, bar.
tabernandre *n.* female tavern keeper,
female bartender.
tabernari *n.* barman, bartender, tavern
keeper, barmaid.
tabernaritza *n.* job of a tavern keeper.
tabu *n.* taboo.
-tada *(gram.)* Suffix meaning act or
action; sometimes means blow.
Egitada. Action.
ta egin *v.t.* to slap, to hit (children's
language).
taiadura *n.* tailoring, fitting.
taiaketa *n.* tailoring, fitting.
taiatu *v.t.* to tailor, to fit, to adjust (a
garment).
taila *n.* size. *n.* tally stick.
taiu *n.* looks, appearance, mien,
aspect. *n.* size. *n.* ability, capability.
taiuera *n.* looks, appearance. *n.* size.
taiulari *n.* appraiser, assessor, one
who assigns values.
taiutu *v.t.* to organize, to put in order,
to put (something) in its place, to tidy
up.
taiuzko *adj.* flattering, well fitting.
tak *n.* onomatopoeic representation of
several sounds (tick-tock, lub-dub,
etc.).
takada *n.* gentle shove, little slap.
taka egin *n.* to hit (a target).
taka-taka *adv.* toddling.
taka-taka ibili *v.i.* to take one's first
steps (child), to toddle.
taket *n.* stake. *adj.* stupid. *n.* wedge,
block, chock, stopper.
taketada *n.* blow with a stake.
taketzar *n.(augm.)* large stake.
takigrafari *n.* stenographer.
takigrafia *n.* stenography.
takigrafiatu *v.t.* to take shorthand.
takigrafiko *adj.* stenographic.

takigrafikoki *adv.* stenographically.
tako *n.* wedge, block, chock, stopper.
-tako *(gram.)* Verbal suffix which
creates a past participle. **Erositako
sagarrak.** The purchased apples.
-takoan *(gram.)* Verbal suffix meaning
after. **Aita etorritakoan bazkalduko
dugu.** We will have lunch after father
comes.
takoi *n.* heel (of a shoe).
takoidun *adj.* with heels.
takoikada *n.* blow with the heel of a
shoe. *n.* noise of shoe heels on floor
or pavement.
takoikatu *v.t.* to tap one's heels, to
stamp the feet.
takoiketa *n.* heel tapping.
taktika *n.* tactics.
taktiko *adj.* tactical.
tala *n.* lookout, vantage point, watch
tower (on the sea).
talaia *n.* lookout, vantage point,
watchtower (on the sea).
talaiari *n.* lookout, observer, watcher.
talaiero *n.* lookout, observer, watcher.
talamazoka *n.(zool.)* gudgeon (*Gobio
gobio*).
talde *n.* group, legion.
-talde Used in compound words.
Derived from *talde*, group.
Gizontalde. Group of men.
taldeareko *adj.* intergroup.
taldebilketa *n.* grouping.
taldeburu *n.* leader of a group, group
leader.
taldeka *adv.* in groups, by groups.
taldekapen *n.* grouping, gathering in
groups.
taldekatu *v.t./v.i.* to form a group, to
group; to join a group.
taldekide *n.* group member, member
(of an organization).
taldekidetza *n.* group membership.
taldeko *adj.* collective.
taldekoi *adj.* gregarious, sociable,
clubbish.
taldekotu *v.i.* to become gregarious, to
be sociable.
taldelan *n.* teamwork, community
work, working in a group.
taldetxo *n.(dim.)* little group.
talentu *n.* intelligence.
talka *n.* collision resulting from the
butting of ram's horns. *n.* collision,
blow, shock.
talka egin *v.t.* to run into (something)
head on, to collide.
talkan *adv.* butting, colliding, ramming
(head on).
talkan ari *v.i.* to butt head on, to
collide, to fight like rams.
talkari *adj.* ramming, butting.
talkatu *v.i.* to ram, to collide, to hit.
talko *n.* talc, talcum.
talkotsu *adj.* talcous, talcose.
talo *n.* large flat corn cake, similar to a
Mexican tortilla.

taloburdin n. long-handled pan for cooking corn cakes.

taloi n.(econ.) check, bank check.

taloisail n. check book, stub book.

taloitegi n.(econ.) check book.

tamainu n. size, measurement.

tamal n. misfortune, bad luck.

tamalez adv. unfortunately.

tamalgarri adj. pitiful, unfortunate, lamentable.

tamalgarriro adv. pitifully, unfortunately.

-tan (gram.) Suffix used with numbers (except the number one) to express times, repetition. **Bitan.** Twice.

tango n.(mus.) tango.

tanke n.(mil.) tank.

tankera n. aspect, form, style.

tankera eman v.t. to guess, to estimate, to make out, to understand, to decipher.

tanpoi n. rubber stamp.

tanta n. drop.

tantai n. large thick log. n. thick branch. n. mast of a ship. n.(fig.) very tall person.

tantaka adv. drop by drop.

tantakada n. series of drops.

tantakatu v.i. to drop, to drip, to fall in drops.

tantakontagailu n. eyedropper, medicine dropper.

tanto n. point (sports score).

tantokari n. scorekeeper.

tantokatu v.t. to keep score.

tantza n. nylon fishing line.

tapa n. onomatopoeic sound of the heartbeat. n. cover, lid.

tapagailu n. cover, lid.

tapa-tapa adv. onomatopoeic sound of walking, slow marching.

tapoi n. stopper, bottle stopper, plug, cap, cork.

tapoigintza n. making of corks, plugs, caps, or stoppers.

tapoikada n. pop (of a cork).

tapoiketa n. stopping (a bottle), corking.

tapoindu v.t. to cork, to stop (a bottle).

tapoiteria n. group or quantity of corks, caps, stoppers, or plugs.

tapoitu v.t. to cork, to stop (a bottle).

tapoiztapen n. plugging, stopping up, capping.

-tar (gram.) Suffix which means native of. **Bilbotar.** Native of Bilbao. (gram.) Suffix meaning follower, member, supporter. **Gutar.** Our supporter.

tarifa n. tariff.

tarifatu v.t. to impose a tariff.

-tariko (gram.) Suffix used with pronouns to indicate of, from, among. **Zuetariko batek salduko nau.** One of you will betray me.

tarin n.(zool.) small yellow and green bird.

tarranta n. old car.

tarrapata n. continuous noise, tumult. n. drum roll.

tarrapata egin v.t. to beat the drum, to do a drum roll.

tarrapataka adv. hurriedly, quickly.

tarrapatan adv. hurriedly, quickly.

tarrapatari adj. unruly, mischievous; hyperactive.

tarrat n. rip. Onomatopoeic sound of clothing being torn.

tarratada n. rip, tear, hole.

tarratatu v.i. to tear, to rip (clothing).

tarrat egin v.t. to rip, to tear (clothing).

tarta n. cake.

tartail adj. raggedy.

tartamutu n. stutterer.

tartar n./adj. blabbermouth, chatterbox; talkative, chatty. Onomatopoeic sound expressing talkativeness.

tartariar adj. Tartar.

tarte n. interval, intermission, break; gap, distance, space.

tartegabeko adj. uninterrupted, incessant.

tart egin v.t. to break (a rope), to snap (a rope).

tartegune n. space, gap, distance; interval, intermission, break.

tarteka adv. at various locations. adv. at intervals, in spare time, occasionally.

tartekapen n. insertion.

tartekatu v.t./v.i. to interpose, to place between, to intervene, to intercalate, to come between.

tarteketa n. placing between, interposing, interposition.

tarteko adj. intermediate.

tartekotasun n. quality of being intermediate.

tarteratu v.t. to insert. v.i. to intervene, to interfere.

tartetxo n.(dim.) very small distance.

tarteune n. space.

tasa n.(econ.) appraisal.

tasaketa n.(econ.) appraisal.

tasatu v.t. to appraise, to evaluate, to assess.

tasatzaile n. appraiser, assessor.

-tasun (gram.) Suffix added to nouns and adjectives to form abstract nouns. Usually corresponds to English -ness, -ity. **Aberastasun.** Wealth.

tata n. nanny, nurse (children's language).

tatarrez adv. dragging.

tatuaia n. tattoo.

tatuatu v.t. to tattoo.

tatxet n. tack (nail).

taula n. table (multiplication, etc.), chart; floorboard.

tauladura n. boarding up; putting boards or planks together.

taulatu v.t. to board up; to cover with floorboards.

taulatzaile *n.* one who lays floorboards.

taup *n.* Onomatopoeic sound denoting a strong heartbeat.

taupada *n.(onomat.)* beating of the heart.

taupadaka *adv.* beating, palpitating, throbbing, pounding (of one's heart).

taupadatu *v.i.* to palpitate, to beat (heart).

taupakari *adj.* palpitating, beating.

tautik *adv.* nothing at all, anything at all.

taxi *n.* taxi.

taximetro *n.* taxi meter.

taxista *n.* taxi driver.

taxu *n.* aspect, appearance, image, look(s). *n.* ability, capability, dexterity. *n.* adjustment, adaptation.

taxugabe *adj.* clumsy, awkward, incapable.

taxugabekeria *n.* clumsiness, awkwardness.

taxugabetu *v.t.* to mess (something) up.

taxugabezia *n.* clumsiness, awkwardness.

taxugarri *adj.* adjustable, adaptable.

taxuketa *n.* adaptation, adjustment.

taxukor *adj.* adaptable, adjustable.

taxutu *v.t.* to adapt, to adjust; to arrange, to organize, to put in order, to tidy up.

-taz *(gram.)* Suffix meaning about. Used especially with pronouns. **Nitaz hitz egin dute.** They have talked about me.

te *n.(bot.)* tea.

-te *(gram.)* Suffix indicating season of the year. **Negute.** Winter season. *(gram.)* Suffix indicating duration. **Gerrate.** Wartime. *(gram.)* Verbal suffix added to the infinitive and used to create action nouns. **Izate.** Being.

-tean *(gram.)* Verbal suffix meaning upon, the moment, at the moment. **Jakitean.** Upon realizing.

teatro *n.* theater (building). *n.* play, stage play.

tegi *n.* stable, corral, pen, enclosed space for livestock.

-tegi *(gram.)* Suffix meaning place of. **Liburutegi.** Library.

teila *n.* roof tile.

teilaberritu *v.t.* to replace the roof, to repair the roof.

teiladura *n.* act of repairing a roof.

teilaetxe *n.* tile works.

teilagain *n.* top of a tile.

teilagile *n.* person who makes tiles.

teilagin *n.* person who makes tiles.

teilagintza *n.* tile making.

teilakada *n.* blow dealt with a tile.

teilape *n.* tiled shed.

teilari *n.* one who makes roofing tiles.

teilarte *n.* opening or break between roofing tiles or shingles.

teilategi *n.* tile works, place where roofing tiles are stored.

teilatu *n.* roof.

teilaxka *n.(dim.)* small roof tile.

teilaztu *v.t.* to tile (a roof).

teileria *n.* tile works, tile kiln.

teinkada *n.* pull, yank.

teinkadura *n.* tension, tenseness (physical quality).

teinkari *n.* puller, yanker.

teinkatasun *n.* tautness, tightness.

teinkatu *v.t.* to pull (on), to yank, to tighten, to stretch, to tauten.

teink egin *v.t.* to pull (on), to yank, to stretch, to tighten, to tauten.

teka *n.(bot.)* pod, husk.

teknika *n.* technique, technology.

teknikari *n.* technician, technologist.

teknikazko *adj.* technical, technological.

tekniko *n.* technician. *adj.* technical, technological.

teknikoki *adv.* technically, technologically.

teknologia *n.* technology.

tele- Used in compound words. Derived from *telebista*, television.

telealbistari *n.* television newscaster.

teleberri *n.* television news, newscast.

telebisatu *v.t.* to televise.

telebista *n.* television, television set, TV.

telebistaldi *n.* period of watching television, viewing time.

telebistari *n.* television watcher, TV viewer.

telebistetxe *n.* television station.

teleferiko *n.* tram, aerial tram, fenicular railway.

telefilm *n.* movie made for TV, movie on television.

telefonari *n.* telephone operator.

telefonatu *v.t.* to call (on the phone), to phone, to telephone.

telefonetxe *n.* telephone company.

telefongela *n.* phone booth.

telefoniko *adj.* pertaining to the telephone.

telefono *n.* telephone, phone.

telefonoz *adv.* by telephone.

telegrafari *n.* telegraph operator.

telegrafetxe *n.* telegraph office.

telegrafia *n.* telegraphy.

telegrafiatu *v.t.* to telegraph, to send a message by telegraph.

telegrafiko *adj.* pertaining to a telegraph.

telegrafikoki *adv.* telegraphically.

telegrafista *n.* telegraph operator.

telegrafo *n.* telegraph.

telegrafoz *adv.* by telegraph.

telegrama *n.* telegram.

teleguneko *n.* daily television news.

telegunkari *n.* daily television newscast.

teleikuskin *n.* television set, TV, television.

teleikusle *n.* television watcher, TV

viewer.

teleirrati *n.* television-radio console.

telekamara *n.* television camera.

telekomunikabide *n.* tele-communication.

telemanaldi *n.* television broadcast, television program.

telentzule *n.* television viewer.

telepatia *n.* telepathy.

telesail *n.* television series.

telesaio *n.* television broadcast, TV program.

tema *n.* stubbornness, obstinacy.

tema egin *v.t.* to be contrary, to take the opposite side, to be obstinate.

temagarri *adj.* obsessive.

temakeria *n.* stubbornness, obstinacy.

temako *adj.* competitive, lively, emotional.

temakor *adj.* obstinate, stubborn, opinionated, thick-headed.

temati *adj.* obstinate, stubborn, opinionated, thick-headed.

tematsu *adj.* obstinate, stubborn, opinionated, thick-headed.

tematu *v.i.* to be obstinate, to be persistent, to be stubborn.

temoso *adj.* obstinate, enduring, persistent, stubborn.

-ten *(gram.)* Verbal suffix used to form gerunds or express habitual action. **Jaten.** Eating.

tenedore *n.* fork, table fork.

ten egin *v.t.* to pull (on), to yank, to stretch taut.

teniente *n.(mil.)* lieutenant.

tenientetza *n.(mil.)* lieutenancy.

tenis *n.* tennis.

tenislari *n.* tennis player.

tenkagailu *n.* turnbuckle.

tenkari *n.* puller, yanker.

tenkatu *v.t.* to tauten, to tighten, to pull, to yank.

tenkor *adj.* firm, having integrity.

tenkortasun *n.* integrity, firmness, fortitude.

tenore *n.* time; hour; occasion. *n.(mus.)* tenor.

tenoretasun *n.* punctuality.

tenoretsu *adj.* punctual.

tenorez *adv.* on time.

tenperamendu *n.* temperament.

tenperatura *n.* temperature.

tentabide *n.* temptation.

tentagarri *adj.* tempting.

tentakari *n.* tempter, temptress. *adj.* tempting.

tentaldi *n.* moment of temptation.

tentatu *v.t.* to tempt, to entice.

tentatzaile *n./adj.* tempter, temptress; tempting.

tentazio *n.* temptation.

tente *adv.* erect, upright, standing.

tentekor *adj.* erect, upright, standing.

tentekortasun *n.* erectness, uprightness, quality of standing up.

tentel *adj.* foolish, fatuous, silly.

tenteldu *v.i.* to be foolish, to be silly.

tentelkeria *n.* stupidity, foolishness.

tentelki *adv.* stupidly, foolishly.

tenteltasun *n.* stupidity, foolishness, imbecility.

tenterazle *n.* erector, one who sets (things) upright.

tentetu *v.i.* to stand up, to be erect, to get erect. *v.t.* to stand (something) up.

tentsio *n.* tension, pressure, stress. *n. (elec.)* voltage.

tentu *n.* caution, care, sense.

tentugabezia *n.* carelessness, senselessness.

tentuz *adv.* carefully, cautiously.

teokratiko *adj.* theocratic.

teokrazia *n.* theocracy.

teologari *n.* theologian.

teologia *n.* theology.

teontzi *n.* tea pot.

teordu *n.* tea time.

teorema *n.* theorem.

teoria *n.* theory.

teoriko *adj.* theoretical.

teorilari *n.* theoretician, theorist.

teorizatu *v.t.* to theorize.

teorizazio *n.* theorization.

-tera *(gram.)* Verbal suffix meaning to. **Hura ikustera joan naiz.** I have gone to see him.

terapeutika *n.* therapeutics.

terapeutiko *adj.* therapeutic.

tergal *n.* synthetic fabric.

-teria *(gram.)* Suffix used with nouns meaning group of (people, animals, etc.). **Umeteria.** A group of children.

termiko *adj.* thermic, thermal.

termita *n.(zool.)* termite.

termitegi *n.* nest of termites.

termodinamika *n.* thermodynamics.

termodinamiko *adj.* thermodynamic.

termometria *n.* thermometry.

termometro *n.* thermometer.

termostato *n.* thermostat.

terraza *n.* terrace.

terreina *n.* earthenware tub.

terrorismo *n.* terrorism.

terrorista *n./adj.* terrorist.

tesina *n.* small thesis (usually written for completion of a Master's degree).

tesi *n.* thesis, dissertation.

testamendu *n.* will, testament.

testamenduzain *n.* executor, executrix.

testatu *v.t.* to make a will or testament.

testatzaile *n.* testator, testatrix, one who makes a will.

testigantza *n.* testimony.

testigu *n.* witness.

testigutza *n.* testimony, deposition, attestation.

testiguzko *adj.* testimonial.

tetano *n.(med.)* tetanus, lockjaw.

tetanoaurkako *adj.* antitetanus.

textu *n.* text.

textugintza *n.* preparation of text.

textuinguru *n.* context.

-ti *(gram.)* Nominal suffix indicating habit, tendency, frequency. **Maitati.** Loving. *(gram.)* Nominal suffix meaning abundant in. **Sagasti.** Apple orchard.

-tiar *(gram.)* Suffix meaning member of, supporter of. **Ezkertiar.** Leftist. *(gram.)* Suffix meaning guest, invited. **Afaltiar.** Dinner guest.

tiburoi *n.(zool.)* shark.

tifoi *n.* typhoon, hurricane.

tifus *n.(med.)* typhus.

tifuskontrako *adj.* antityphoid.

tigre *n.(zool.)* tiger.

tigreme *n.(zool.)* female tiger.

-tik *(gram.)* Suffix meaning from. Used with words of time and place. **Etxetik.** From the house. **Geroztik.** Since then.

tiki-taka *adv.* step by step, slowly, little by little.

-tiko *(gram.)* Nominal suffix meaning originating with, emanating from, coming from. **Zerutiko argia.** The celestial light.

-tila *(gram.)* Diminutive suffix. **Lehiatila.** Small window.

tilin *n.(onomat.)* ringing of a bell, ding-dong.

tilin egin *v.t.* to ring, to ding.

tilinkatu *v.t.* to ring, to ding.

tilinketa *n.* ringing, dinging.

tilin-tilin *n.(onomat.)* ring! ring!, ding-dong.

tina *n.* wooden barrel; large earthen jar.

tinagile *n.* maker of wooden barrels; maker of earthen jars.

tinako *n.(dim.)* little earthen jar.

tinategi *n.* stand or shelf for earthenware jars.

tinatzar *n.(augm.)* large earthen jar.

tinbre *n.* bell. *n.* stamp.

tindadura *n.* dyeing.

tindagai *n.* dye.

tindagintza *n.* dye making, job of dye maker.

tindaketa *n.* dyeing, tinting.

tindalari *n.* dyer, one who tints or dyes.

tindaldi *n.* dyeing, tinting.

tindategi *n.* dye shop, place where dyes are used or stored.

tindatu *v.t./v.i.* to dye, to tint, to color.

tindatzaile *n.* dyer.

tindu *n.* dye.

tindugabetu *v.i./v.t.* to fade, to discolor.

tindugai *n.* material to be dyed.

tindura *n.* dyeing.

tinduztatu *v.t.* to dye, to tint.

tinkadura *n.* thrust, driving or pushing (something) into (something else).

tinkaketa *n.* thrusting or driving (something) into (something else). *n.* crushing, smashing, pressing, squashing.

tinkatu *v.t.* to settle, to settle down. *v.t.* to fix (in something), to push or drive (something) into (something else). *v.t.* to crush, to smash, to press, to squash.

tinkatzaile *n.* one who pushes (something) into (something else).

tink egon *v.i.* to be firm, to be set, to be fixed.

tinkili-tankala *adv.* sluggishly.

tinko *adj.* firm, set, fixed. *adv.* firmly.

tinko egon *v.i.* to be firm, to be set (in one's ways).

tinkogabe *adj.* not firm, not set, inconsistent, unstable.

tinkogabetu *v.i.* to destabilize, to become unsettled.

tinkogabezia *n.* instability.

tinkoki *adv.* firmly, solidly.

tinkotasun *n.* solidity, firmness.

tinkotu *v.t.* to secure, to make firm, to steady.

tinta *n.* ink.

tintin *n.(onomat.)* ringing of a bell, ding-dong.

tintontzi *n.* inkstand, inkwell.

tiobibo *n.* merry-go-round; any amusement park ride.

tipi *adj.* little, small.

tiple *n.* second soprano.

tipula *n.(bot.)* onion.

tipulaburu *n.(bot.)* onion, head of an onion.

tipulakorda *n.* string of onions.

tipulasaltza *n.* onion sauce, onion gravy.

tipulatxo *n.(dim.)* little onion.

tipulatz *n.(bot.)* shallot.

tipulazi *n.* shallot seed, onion seed.

tipulin *n.(bot.)* first shoots of a green onion or small onion; chives.

tira *int.* hey.

tirabira *n.* somersault, tumble. *n.* capsizing, overturning of a boat.

tirabira egin *v.t.* to capsize.

tirabiratu *v.i.* to capsize.

tiradura *n.* tension, tautness, pull.

tiragailu *n.* tension (sewing machine), turnbuckle.

tiragale *n.* stretching.

tiragaletu *v.i.* to stretch.

tiragoma *n.* slingshot.

tiraka *adv.* pulling.

tirakada *n.* pull, yank.

tirakatu *v.t.* to pull, to yank, to stretch, to tauten.

tiraketa *n.* pulling, stretching, yanking.

tirakin *n.* suspenders; brace.

tiraldi *n.* pulling movement, pull, yank.

tiraleku *n.* target shooting range, firing range.

tiratu *v.t.* to pull, to yank.

tiratzaile *n.* puller, yanker.

tiro *n.* shot.

tiroaldi *n.* shooting.

tirobide *n.* trajectory of a bullet.

tiro egin *v.t.* to shoot, to fire.
tiro eman *v.t.* to shoot, to fire, to gun down.
tirogailu *n.* shooter, firer.
tiroka *adv.* shooting.
tirokada *n.* shot, firing of a gun.
tirokaldi *n.* shooting.
tirokatu *v.t.* to shoot, to gun down, to fire.
tiroketa *n.* shot, round of shots, shooting.
tirots *n.* report (of a pistol), bang, explosion (of gunfire).
tirria *n.* ardent desire, burning desire. *n.* ill-will, grudge, rancor, animosity.
tirriagarri *adj.* desirable, yearned for. *adj.* attractive, appealing.
tirriatu *v.i.* to desire, to yearn for, to be anxious. *v.t./v.i.* to urge, to prod, to sic (a dog on someone); to be urged.
tirriki-tarraka *adv.* sluggishly, dragging one's feet.
tirrin *n.(onomat.)* ring, ringing (of a bell); doorbell. *n.* train of a dress.
tirrina *n.* large barrel; large casserole (platter or dish).
tirri-tarra *n.(colloq.)* onomatopoeic sound of a fart.
tirritatu *v.t.* to provoke, to incite desire (in someone).
tirriteri *n.* diarrhea.
tisiko *adj.(med.)* tubercular, consumptive.
tisis *n.(med.)* tuberculosis, consumption.
tita *n.(zool.)* little chick.
titulaketa *n.* giving a title to, giving a degree to.
titulatu *v.t./v.i.* to give a title to, to give a degree to.
titulu *n.* title, degree. *n.* heading, inscription.
tituludun *adj.* titled, having a title or degree, with a title or degree.
titulugabe *adj.* without a degree, without a title.
tiuta *n.* cheeping, tweeting, peeping.
tiutari *adj.* chirping, tweeting.
tiutatu *v.t.* to peep, to tweet, to cheep.
to *int.* hey! ho! Used with men. **To! hemen habil?** Hey! You, here?
-to *(gram.)* Modal suffix used with adjectives to form adverbs. **Polito.** Prettily. *(gram.)* Diminutive suffix. **Neskato.** Little girl.
tobera *n.* noisy serenade of bells, horns, etc. on a widower's second wedding night.
toberakanta *n.* song used in the noisy serenade on a widower's second wedding night.
toga *n.* toga.
toil *n.(zool.)* smooth gray dogfish.
toka *adv.* addressing each other with the familiar form of you (men).
tokata *n.(mus.)* toccata.
toki *n.* place.

tokialdaketa *n.* moving.
toki egin *v.t.* to make room for, to make a place for, to find a seat for.
tokiko *adj.* local.
tokiratu *v.i.* to arrive at a definite destination.
tokitasun *n.* location.
tokizen *n.* place name, toponymic name.
tokizendegi *n.* list of place names, gazetteer.
tokologari *n.* obstetrician, tocologist.
tokologia *n.* obstetrics, tocology.
tolderia *n.* group of awnings, group of canopies.
toldo *n.* canopy, awning. *n.* stooge, fool.
toldodenda *n.* place where awnings and canopies are sold.
toldogabetu *v.t.* to strip the awnings off, to remove the awning from.
toldotasun *n.* foolishness, stupidity.
toles *n.* fold, pleat. *n.(fig.)* insincerity, falseness.
tolesdura *n.* folding, pleating.
tolesgabe *adj.* sincere.
tolesgabeki *adv.* candidly, sincerely.
tolesgabetasun *n.* sincerity, candidness.
tolesgabetu *v.t.* to unfold, to unpleat.
tolesgaitz *adj.* difficult to fold.
tolesgarri *adj.* foldable, pleatable. *adj.* folding.
tolesketa *n.* folding.
toleskor *adj.* flexible, foldable, pleatable.
toleskuntza *n.* folding, pleating.
tolestasun *n.* fold, crease. *n.(fig.)* hypocrisy, insincerity.
tolestatu *v.t.* to fold, to crease, to pleat.
tolestatzaile *n.* one who folds.
tolestezin *adj.* not foldable.
tolestu *v.t.* to fold, to crease, to pleat.
tolestura *n.* fold, crease. *n.(fig.)* lack of sincerity.
tolet *n.(naut.)* rowlock, oarlock, tholepin.
tomate *n.(bot.)* tomato.
tonbola *n.* tombola, charity raffle, fair.
tonelada *n.* ton.
tonelaia *n.* tonnage.
tongo *n.* bribe, dive (in boxing), fix (in sports), put-up job.
tongolari *n.* one who fixes a sporting event.
tonika *n.* tonic water.
tontakeria *n.* stupidity, foolishness.
tonto *adj.* idiot, stupid, foolish.
tontoki *adv.* foolishly, stupidly.
tontolapiko *adj.* idiotic, foolish.
tontor *n.* summit, top. *n.* protruberance; bump, lump. *n.* plume, crest, tuft of feathers.
tontordun *adj.* crested, plumed.
tontortu *v.i.* to crest, to plume, to rise high over the forehead.

tontotasun n. foolishness, stupidity.
tontotu v.i. to become foolish, to become silly.
tonu n.(mus.) tone.
tonuera n. intonation; tonality.
tonuerdi n.(mus.) half tone.
topaketa n. assembly, meeting, reunion.
topaldi n. blow, collision. n. encounter, meeting.
topaleku n. meeting place.
topasari n. reward for finding something.
topatu v.t./v.i. to meet, to encounter, to run into.
topatzaile n. finder, one who finds something.
tope n. collision, blow, crash.
tope egin v.t. to run into, to collide (with something).
topeka adv. hitting head on, colliding, fighting (rams). n. fight (animals).
topekada n. blow with the head, butt, head-on collision.
topo n. encounter, unexpected meeting.
topo egin v.t. to meet unexpectedly, to run into. v.t. to collide with, to run into head on.
topografari n. topographer.
topografia n. topography.
toreaketa n. bullfighting.
toreatu v.t. to fight bulls.
toreatzaile n. bullfighter, toreador, matador.
tori exclam. take this, here, here it is, take it. (Imperative form of the verb which is used as an exclamation.)
Hemen duk hire liburua. Tori! Here is your book. Take it!
torlojo n. screw, wood screw, bolt.
torlojogintza n. manufacture of screws and bolts.
torlojoteria n. screws and bolts.
torlojotu v.t. to screw, to screw in, to bolt.
tornu n. lathe; potter's wheel. n. revolving dumbwaiter (passing things through wall). n. turn, chance.
tornugile n. maker of lathes.
tornulari n. lathe worker, lathe turner.
tornularitza n. job of a lathe worker.
tornuzain n. doorkeeper of a nunnery.
torpedo n. torpedo.
torpedontzi n. torpedo boat.
torpedoztatu v.t. to torpedo.
tortika n. filth, grime, dirt, greasy dirt.
tortikatsu adj. filthy, greasy, grimy.
tortikatu v.i. to become filthy, to become covered with grease and grime.
tortila n. omelette.
tortolo adj. silly, foolish, stupid, idiotic.
tortolos n. jacks (played with tiny sheep bones and a ball).
tortotx n.(bot.) cork.
tortotxondo n.(bot.) cork oak.

toska n. kaolin, china clay, fine white clay.
tosta n. bench in a boat, rower's bench.
total adv. completely.
totalitarismo n. totalitarianism.
totalki adv. totally, completely.
totalkuntza n. totalization.
totaltasun n. totality.
totel n. stutterer. adj. babbling; stuttering.
totelaldi n. stuttering.
toteldu v.i. to stutter, to stammer.
toteldura n. stuttering.
totelka adv. stuttering.
totelkeria n. foolishness, stupidity.
totelki adv. tumbling, confusedly, stutteringly.
totel-motel adv. by stuttering, stammering.
toteltasun n. stuttering.
totolo adj. fat, obese; round, chubby.
totolotu v.i. to get fat, to become chubby.
totxo n. ingot.
toxa n. tobacco pouch.
toxiko adj. toxic.
toxina n. toxin.
traba n. obstacle, impediment, difficulty.
trabagarri adj. annoying, troublesome, embarrassing, bothersome.
trabaketa n. act of obstructing, impeding.
trabakor adj. embarrassing, obstructing.
trabarazi v.t. to be troublesome, to cause difficulty.
trabatu v.t. to impede, to make difficult, to pose obstacles, to cause trouble. v.i. to get stuck.
trabatzaile adj. obstructing, impeding.
trabes(a) n. bet, wager.
trabesa egin v.t. to bet.
trabeska adv. obliquely, slanted.
tradizio n. tradition.
tradizionalismo n. traditionalism.
tradizionalki adv. traditionally.
tradiziozale adj. traditionalist.
tradiziozko adj. traditional.
trafiko n. traffic.
trafikozain n. traffic cop.
traganarru n. typhoon.
tragedia n. tragedy.
tragu n. gulp.
tragu egin v.t. to gulp.
traidore n./adj. traitor.
trailu n. threshing flail.
trailukari n. thresher.
trailukatu v.t. to thresh the grain with a flail.
traineru n. fourteen-man row boat (used in races).
traizio n. treason, disloyalty, treachery.
trakeskeria n. sluggishness, sluggish action, sluggish way.
trakeski adv. clumsily, sluggishly.

trakestasun n. sluggishness, clumsiness, awkwardness.

trakestu v.i. to become sluggish, to be clumsy. v.i. to become crude, to become oafish.

trakets adj. clumsy, unskilled; careless; crude, oafish.

traktorari n. driver of heavy machinery, heavy machinery operator.

traktore n. tractor.

traktorelari n. tractor driver, heavy equipment operator.

tramana n.(zool.) kind of stingray, usually forty or more inches in length.

tramankulu n. roughly made furniture, crude tool.

tranbala n. swinging, swaying, rocking.

tranbalaldi n. swinging, swaying, rocking.

tranbalatu v.i. to swing, to sway, to rock.

tranbia n. streetcar, tram.

tranbiari n. streetcar conductor.

tranga n. crossbar (for securing a door). n. hemp or flax scutcher.

trangaketa n. barring the door (with a crossbar).

trangatu v.t. to bar the door (with a crossbar).

trankil adj. calm, peaceful.

trankildu v.i./v.t. to take it easy, to calm down, to become calm; to calm (someone) down.

trankildura n. calmness, tranquility, peacefulness.

trankilgarri adj. calming, tranquilizing, relaxing.

trankilki adv. calmly, tranquilly.

trankiltasuntratalari n. tranquility, calm, calmness.

trankiltzaile adj. calming, tranquilizing.

tranpa n. trick, deceit. n. trap.

tranpari adj. tricky, deceitful.

tranpolin n. diving board.

transformadore n.(phys.) transformer.

transformismo n.(biol.) transformism.

transformista adj. transformist.

transmisio n. transmission, broadcast. n. drive shaft, transmission.

transporte n. transportation.

trapalote adj. chubby, plump, pudgy.

trapezio n.(geom.) trapezoid.

trapu n. cloth, rag.

trapuketari n. ragpicker.

trapusaltzaile n. ragpicker, seller of rags.

traputzar n.(augm.) swab, mop.

traskil adj. ragged, poorly dressed, torn and tattered. adj. negligent, apathetic, indolent.

traskildu v.i. to be ragged, to dress in rags.

traskilki adv. indolently; raggedly.

trasteria n. household goods, belongings, furnishings, etc.

trataera n. way of treating people, social behavior.

tratagaitz adj. intractable, hard to get along with, grouchy, rude, unsociable.

tratagarri adj. kind, easygoing, easy to get along with.

tratalaritza n. job of a livestock dealer.

tratamendu n. treatment.

tratatu n. treaty, agreement, accord. v.t. to treat.

tratu n. relationship. n. deal, bargain, accord, pact, commercial traffic.

tratu egin v.t. to make a deal.

tratugarri adj. negotiable.

tratuhausketa n. breaking of a deal, breaking of a contract.

tratulari n. bargainer, dealer, businessman.

tratuzale adj. fond of bargaining.

trauma n. trauma.

traumatismo n. traumatism.

traumazko adj. traumatic.

trauskil adj. rough, crude, brusque; ragged, torn and tattered.

trauskildu v.i. to become crude; to be ragged.

trauskilkeria n. crudeness, roughness; raggedness.

trauskiltasun n. crudeness, roughness.

trebaketa n. capability, experience; training.

trebatu v.t./v.i. to enable, to equip, to qualify. v.i. to be familiar with.

trebe adj. apt, capable, experienced, dextrous, expert.

trebegabezia n. inexperience, incapability, ineptness.

trebeki adv. capably, ably, with experience, expertly.

trebera n. tripod, trivet, cook's tripod.

trebetasun n. skill, skillfulness, dexterity.

tren n. train. n. change of trains, transfer from one train to another.

trenbide n. railroad, railway, railroad track.

trenbideko adj. railroad, railway.

trenbideratu v.i. to board a train. v.t. to put a train back on the track.

trenbidesare n. system of railroads, railway network.

trenbidetu v.t. to lay rails, to lay railroad track.

trenbidezain n. trackwalker, switchman.

trengela n. train compartment.

trengidari n. engineer (on a train).

trengizon n. railroad employee.

trengurdi n. railroad car.

trenkadura n. cut, rupture.

trenkarazi v.t. to make (someone) split or rupture (something).

trenkatu v.t. to cut, to split, to rupture.

trenkatzaile adj. cutting, rupturing.

trenlaster n. express, fast train.

trenlerro n. train, engine followed by any number of cars.

trenmakina n. locomotive.

trenzain n. conductor (of a train).

tresna n. tool, instrument, implement, appliance, utensil (usually used in plural).

tresnagabetu v.t. to remove tools.

tresnagile n. toolmaker.

tresnategi n. place where tools are kept (closet, tool shed, etc.).

tresnatu v.t. to equip, to provide with tools; to harness, to put trappings on.

tresnatzar n. roughly made tool.

tresneria n. hardware, collection of tools.

tretza n. trawl line (fishing line with several hooks attached), boulter.

tribu n. tribe.

trigonometria n. trigonometry.

trikaldi n. stop, pause, detention.

trikarazi v.t. to make (someone) stop, to detain, to cause to stop.

trikatu v.i. to stop, to pause.

trikimailu n. trick, ruse, deception.

trikimaina n. arrangement.

trikimako n. crutch.

trikina n. trichina.

trikinosis n.(med.) trichinosis.

trikitilari n. accordion player, accordionist.

trikitixa n. accordion.

trikota n. knitting; knit.

trikotatu v.t. to knit.

trikuharri n. dolmen.

trinitate n.(theol.) Trinity.

trinkaketa n. pressing, crushing, squeezing.

trinkakor adj. crushing, pressing, squeezing. adj. thickening.

trinkaldi n. crushing, pressing, squeezing.

trinkatu v.t./v.i. to crush, to press, to squeeze; to be crushed, to be pressed. v.t. to toast, to make a toast (drinking).

trinkatzaile adj. pressing, crushing, pushing.

trinket n. pelota played in a covered court.

trinko adj. firm, set, fixed, solid, compact. adj.(gram.) synthetic.

trinkotasun n. solidity, compactness, firmness, quality of being set.

trinkotu v.t. to compress, to squeeze, to make more compact.

trintxa n. chisel.

tripa n.(anat.) stomach, belly.

tripabarru n. hake tripe, fish tripe.

tripajale n. ripper, criminal who rips open his victims.

tripakada n. bellyful, satiety, overeating. n. belly flop (swimming).

tripakailu(ak) n.(pl.) tripe (from cows).

tripaki(ak) n.(pl.) tripe(s), giblet(s).

tripakigile n. one who prepares tripe.

tripakitegi n. tripe shop.

tripakoi adj. gluttonous.

tripakomin n. stomach ache, bellyache.

tripaldi n. hearty eating, overeating.

tripandi adj. glutton, gluttonous, having a big belly, being a big eater.

tripaorroe n. stomach rumbling.

tripazain adj. gluttonous. (lit.) keeper of the stomach.

tripazainkeria n. gluttony.

tripazale adj. gluttonous, insatiable.

tripazalekeria n. gluttony.

tripazorri n.(colloq.) hunger, great hunger.

tripazorro adj. voratious, gluttonous. n. belly, stomach.

tripontzi adj. glutton, gluttonous, voracious.

tripontzikeria n. gluttony.

tripotx n. tripe.

tripulazio n. crew (of a ship).

triskantza n. destruction, ruin.

triskatu v.t. to destroy, to devastate.

triskatzaile adj. destructive, devastating.

tristadura n. sadness.

tristagarri adj. saddening, sad.

tristatu v.i./v.t. to become sad, to sadden.

triste adj. sad, unhappy. adv. sad, sadly.

tristeki adv. sadly.

tristetu v.t. to become sad. v.t. to sadden, to afflict, to cause sorrow.

tristezia n. sadness, melancholy.

tristura n. sadness, affliction, melancholy.

trobalari n. troubadour.

trofeo n. trophy.

troka n. gorge, ravine, chasm, abyss. n. truck, pickup truck (U.S.A.).

trokaketa n. sprain, twist (ankle, etc.).

trokatsu adj. having many gorges or ravines.

trokatu v.i./v.t. to sprain, to dislocate.

trolebus n. trolley.

tronadura n. ceiling. n. pavement.

tronatu v.t. to pave.

tronboi n.(mus.) trombone.

tronboilari n. trombone player.

trongil n. bump, swelling (on the head).

tronpa n. trunk (of an elephant). n.(mus.) jew's-harp. n. top, spinning top (toy).

tronpadun adj. proboscidean, having a trunk, belonging to the elephant family.

tronpeta n.(mus.) trumpet.

tronpetajole n. trumpet player.

tronpetaldi n. playing the trumpet.

tronpetari n. trumpet player.

tronpetots n. sound of a trumpet.

tronu n. throne.

tronugabetu v.t. to dethrone.

tronukide n. royal consort, prince.

tronuraketa n. enthroning.

tronuratu *v.t.* to enthrone.
tropiko *n.(geog.)* the Tropics.
tropikoarteko *adj.* intertropical.
tropikoko *adj.* tropical.
troskote *adj.* clumsy, awkward, sluggish.
troxa *n.* swaddling clothes; diaper.
troxadura *n.* swaddling, act of wrapping a child in swaddling clothes.
troxatu *v.t.* to wrap in swaddling clothes.
trufa *n.* joke, jest.
trufa egin *v.t.* to joke, to jest.
trufagailu *n.* object which provokes laughter, sight gag.
trufagarri *adj.* joking, jesting.
trufagile *adj.* joking.
trufaka *adv.* joking, jokingly, in a jesting manner.
trufakeria *n.* joke, bad joke.
trufari *n./adj.* joker; joking.
trufatu *v.i.* to joke, to jest.
trufatzaile *adj./n.* joking; joker.
truk *n.* trade, exchange.
trukaera *n.* trade, exchange.
trukaezin *adj.* not exchangeable, not tradable.
trukagaitz *adj.* not tradable, difficult to exchange.
trukagarri *adj.* interchangeable, exchangeable.
trukagarritasun *n.* exchangeability.
trukaketa *n.* exchange, trade.
trukakor *adj.* exchangeable.
trukalari *n.* money broker, dealer on the exchange.
trukatu *v.t.* to exchange (money), to swap, to interchange.
trukatzaile *n.* money broker, money changer.
truke *n.* exchange, barter, trade; in exchange for.
trukean *prep./adv.* in exchange for.
truk(e) egin *v.t.* to exchange, to trade.
trukemodu *n.* way of exchanging.
trukesagile *n.* maker of pliers, pincers or tongs.
trukesagintza *n.* making of pliers, pincers or tongs.
trukesak *n.(pl.)* pliers, pincers, tongs.
trukesari *n.* user of pliers, pincers or tongs.
trukesatu *v.t.* to grip with pliers, to pull with pliers, pincers or tongs.
trumilka *adv.* rolling, tumbling. *adv.* in a group, in large numbers, in groups.
trumilkako *n.* fall, downfall.
trumilkatu *v.i.* to fall. *v.t.* to overturn.
trumoi *n.* thunder.
trumoialdi *n.* thunderclap, roll of thunder.
trumoiburrunba *n.* roll of thunder.
trumoihots *n.* thunderclap, sound of thunder.
trumoitsu *adj.* thunderous, thundering.
trumoitu *v.t.* to thunder.

truxu *n.* torrential rain.
ts Letter of the Basque alphabet. Sometimes used as a suffix or as an infix in auxiliary verbs to mean *have* (Biscayan dialect). Never used at the beginning of a word. **Euritsu.** Rainy. **Zer ekarri deutso?** What has he brought to him?
-tsu *(gram.)* Suffix used to form adjectives. Expresses abundance. **Argitsu.** Bright.
tt Used to form diminutives, especially in northern dialects and Unified Basque. Replaces *t*. **Pottolo.** Chubby.
ttaka-ttaka *adv.* with baby steps, step by step.
ttantta *n.* tiny drop. *adv.* little bit (of a liquid).
ttattar *adj.* insignificant, tiny (with a bad connotation).
ttiki *adj.* small, little.
ttintta *n.* tiny drop.
ttipi *adj.* tiny, very small.
tto Var. of *to*.
-tto *(gram.)* Diminutive suffix. **Gizontto.** Little man.
ttonttor *n.(dim.)* little bump (on the head). *n.(dim.)* small hunchback.
ttu *n.* spit, saliva.
tu *n.* saliva, spit.
-tu Verbal suffix for infinitives. Becomes *-du* after *l* and *n*.
tualdi *n.* spitting.
tuegile *adj.* expectorant.
tu egin *v.t.* to spit.
tuegite *n.* act of spitting, act of expectorating.
tuka *adv.* spitting, expectorating.
tulipa *n.(bot.)* tulip.
tulunbio *n.* hurricane. *n.* abyss; pit.
-tun *(gram.)* Noun suffix expressing the agent of an action. **Jatun.** Eater.
tunel *n.* tunnel.
tuntun *n.* Basque drum. *adj.* stupid, foolish (woman).
tuontzi *n.* spitoon.
tuparri *n.(min.)* chalk.
tupiki *n.* copper container. *n.(min.)* cast iron; copper.
tupikiaire *adj.* copper colored, copper-like.
tupin(a) *n.* pot.
tupinagile *n.* pot maker, tinker.
tupinategi *n.* place for pots.
tupust *n.* crash, bang, bam. Sound of a collision.
tupustean *adv.* suddenly.
tupust egin *v.t.* to collide (with), to run (into), to crash (into).
-turia *(gram.)* Noun suffix indicating an abstract quality. **Jakituria.** Wisdom.
turismo *n.* tourism.
turista *n./adj.* tourist.
turroi *n.* kind of nougat made with almonds, especially in Alicante, Spain.

turroigile *n.* nougat maker.
turroigintza *n.* nougat making.
turroipilo *n.* pile of nougat.
turrustagarri *adj.* transferrable (liquid) from one vessel to another.
turrustatu *v.t.* to transfer liquid from one vessel to another, to decant.
turrut *n.* joke, jest. *n.* noise.
turrut egin *v.t.* to make fun of, to joke. *v.t.* to fail, to go bankrupt.
turuta *n.* cornet, trumpet, bugle. *n.* siren, whistle.
turutajole *n.* bugler, trumpet player.
turutaldi *n.* blow on the trumpet, bugle call.
turutari *n.* trumpet player, cornet player, bugler.
turuteria *n.* trumpets.
turutu *n.* horn (auto). *n.(mus.)* cornet.
tut *adv.* nothing, anything, hoot.
tute *n.* kind of card game.
tutore *n.* tutor.
tutorego *n.* job of a tutor, tutorship.
tutorkide *n.* co-tutor.
tutu *n.* horn. *n.* tube, roll, pipe, duct. *n.(anat.)* vulva.
tutueria *n.* conduit, pipeline.
tutugile *n.* pipe maker, pipe fitter.
tutugintza *n.* pipe making, making of tubes, pipes, rolls, etc.
tutuhots *n.* beep, toot, sound of a horn.
tutukatu *v.t.* to connect pipes, to pipe in.
tutulu *n.* cane, piece of cane; tube, tubular container. *adj.(colloq.)* stupid, foolish.
tutulualdi *n.* foolishness, silliness.
tutulukatu *v.i.* to become foolish, to be an idiot.
tutulukeria *n.* foolishness, idiocy.
tutulutu *v.i.* to become foolish, to be an idiot.
tutuztapen *n.* inserting a tube; connecting pipe.
tutuztatu *v.t.* to insert a tube; to connect pipe.
tx Letter of the Basque alphabet, representing a sound similar to English *ch*, as in chocolate.
-txa *(gram.)* Diminutive suffix.
 Neskatxa. Little girl.
txabeta *n.* axle.
txabola *n.* cabin, hut, shack.
txabolari *n.* person who lives in a cabin, hut or shack.
txabolatxo *n.(dim.)* small cabin, small hut.
txabolzain *n.* cabin caretaker.
txahal *n.(dim.)* calf.
txahalki *n.* veal.
txahalkor *adj.* capable of dropping many calves (said of a cow).
txahaltxo *n.(dim.)* very small calf.
txairo *adj.* airy, light (on one's feet), graceful, lithe, svelte.
txairoki *adv.* airily, gracefully, lithely.

txairotasun *n.* gracefulness, litheness.
txairotu *v.i.* to become graceful, to become svelte.
txakal *n.(zool.)* jackal. *adj.* weak, exhausted.
txakolin *n.* bitter Basque wine.
txakolindegi *n.* place where Basque wine is served.
txakur *n.(zool.)* dog.
txakurkeria *n.* vile act, treachery, mischief.
txakurkume *n.(dim.)* puppy.
txakurrandi *n.(econ.)* ten cents, one-tenth of a *peseta*.
txakurreme *n.(zool.)* bitch, female dog.
txakurretxe *n.* doghouse.
txakurreztul *n.(med.)* harsh cough.
txakurtoki *n.* doghouse, kennel.
txakurtu *v.i.* to become vile, to turn treacherous.
txakurtxiki *n.(econ.)* five cents, one-twentieth of a *peseta*.
txakurtxo *n.(dim.)* little dog.
txakurzain *n.* dog breeder, kennel keeper.
txakurzale *adj.* fond of dogs, dog loving.
txalaparta *n.(mus.)* rustic wooden instrument which is beaten like a drum, consisting of a trunklinke body and two sticks.
txalapartari *n.* one who plays the *txalaparta*.
txaldan *adj.* foolish, stupid, idiotic.
txaldanaldi *n.* foolish action, stupid action.
txaldandu *v.i.* to become stupid, to become foolish, to be silly.
txaldankeria *n.* stupidity, foolishness.
txaldanki *adv.* stupidly, foolishly.
txaldantasun *n.* stupidity, foolishness, imbecility.
txalet *n.* chalet.
txalin *n.* small wooden dish.
txalma *n.* packsaddle, saddle.
txalmagile *n.* packsaddle maker, saddle maker.
txalmatu *v.t.* to saddle, to put a packsaddle on (an animal).
txalo *n.* applause.
txaloaldi *n.* applause, sustained applause, ovation, round of applause.
txalo egin *v.t.* to applaud.
txalogarri *adj.* praiseworthy, esteemed, applaudable, commendable.
txalogarritasun *n.* commendableness.
txalogose *n.* strong desire for applause.
txalojole *n.* applauder.
txaloka *adv.* applauding.
txalokada *n.* ovation, sustained applause.
txalokari *n.* applauder.
txalokatu *v.t.* to applaud, to clap.

txaloketa n. round of applause, ovation.

txalo pin txalo n. game for small children, version of patty-cake.

txalotu v.t. to applaud.

txalotzaile adj. clapping, applauding.

txalupa n. launch, small boat.

txalupari n. boatman.

txalupazain n. boatman, caretaker of a launch.

txamarra n. type of leather jacket with a zipper closing; any kind of jacket.

txanbela n. kind of small Basque end-blown flute played especially in Zuberoa.

txanbelin adj. graceful, airy, pleasing, pleasant.

txanda n. turn, shift, appointment; place.

txandaka adv. in shifts, in turns, by turns.

txandakatu v.i. to take turns, to alternate.

txandaketa n. alternation, taking turns.

txandako adj. alternate, alternative.

txandatu v.i. to take turns, to alternate.

txanel n. flat-bottomed boat or canoe.

txango n. trip, excursion.

txangolari n. traveler, voyager.

txangurro n.(zool.) spiny spider crab.

txanka n. jack, knave (in cards). n. crutch.

txankal n. field, section, division of farmland.

txankaldu v.t. to divide land into fields, sections, etc.

txankalketa n. dividing land into plots.

txankarranka n. kind of Basque folkdance.

txankeri n. lameness, crippledness.

txanket adj. lame, limping, cripple.

txankil adj. wimpy, weak, feeble.

txano n. hood, cowl; sleeping cap, nightcap. n. coffee filter (cloth).

txanogintza n. manufacture of hoods or nightcaps.

txanotzar n.(augm.) large hood.

txanpa n. final sprint in a rowing competition.

txanpinoin n.(bot.) mushroom.

txanpon n. coined money, change.

txanpondu v.t. to mint a coin, to coin. v.i. to get rich, to become wealthy.

txanponeztatu v.t. to mint (a coin), to coin.

txanpongile n. minter, coiner.

txanpongintza n. minting, coining.

txanponjale n. slot machine.

txanponzorro n. coin purse, change purse.

txanpu n. shampoo.

txantol n. wooden plug, wooden stopper.

txantoldu v.t. to plug, to stop up, to cork.

txantxa n. joke, fun, jest.

txantxangorri n.(zool.) robin redbreast

(Erithacus rubecula).

txantxar n.(med.) cavity (in a tooth).

txantxari n. joker, teaser.

txantxatu v.i. to joke, to tease.

txantxetako adj. joking matter, amusing, funny.

txantxetan adv. playfully, joking, teasing, kidding around.

txantxetazko adj. joking, amusing, sham.

txantxiku n.(zool.) toad.

txantxil n. jug.

txantxo n. mask.

txantxotu v.i./v.t. to wear a mask; to put a mask on (someone), to disguise (someone) with a mask.

txapar n. brush, shrub. adj. very small, short.

txapardi n. chaparral, brush, shrub-covered area; grove of dwarf oaks.

txapartsu adj. shrubby, covered with bushes or shrub trees.

txapel n. Basque beret.

txapeldun n. champion.

txapelgile n. maker of Basque berets.

txapelgin n. maker of Basque berets.

txapelgintza n. making of Basque berets.

txapelkada n. Basque beret full of something. n. blow with a Basque beret.

txapelketa n. championship competition.

txapeloker n. three-cornered hat, tricorn.

txaplata n. patch.

txapligu n. fireworks.

txar adj. bad.

txara n.(bot.) rockrose.

txaramel n. latch (to fasten doors).

txaranga n. brass band.

txarbide n. vice, path of destruction.

txarkeria n. wrong, evil action.

txarketa n. deterioration.

txarki adv. badly. **Txarkiago.** Worse.

txarkitu v.i. to deteriorate, to get worse.

txarol n. patent leather.

txaroldu v.t. to varnish, to lacquer.

txarolezko adj. varnished, lacquered, polished.

txarrago adv./adj.(comp.) worse.

txarraldi n. indisposition, illness, sickness.

txarrantxa n. brake of a cart. n. rein(s). n. card, teasel (instrument for carding wool).

txarrantxatu v.t. to card (wool).

txarrean adv. hard way, with difficulty, with punishment.

txarren adj.(superl.) the worst.

txarretsi v.t. to disapprove of, to censure, to condemn, to consider (something) bad. v.t. to disdain.

txarrez adv. forcibly, against one's will.

txartasun n. evilness, badness.

txartel *n.* card, bill, ticket; ballot.
txarteldegi *n.* ticket booth.
txarteleiho *n.* ticket window.
txartelketari *n.* conductor, ticket puncher on a train.
txartelsaltzaile *n.* ticket seller.
txarto *adv.* badly.
txartu *v.i./v.t.* to go bad, to turn bad, to become bad.
txartzat hartu *v.t.* to take (something) the wrong way, to take (something) in a bad way.
txatal *n.* patch.
txatar *n.* piece of scrap metal.
txatarbiltzaile *n.* junk collector, scrap iron collector.
txatarrari *n.* junk dealer, scrap iron dealer.
txatarsaltzaile *n.* junk seller, scrap iron seller.
txatartegi *n.* junk shop, junk yard.
txatxala *adj.* foolish, stupid, simple (female).
txatxandu *v.i.* to flirt. *v.i.* to fall in love (with).
txatxankeria *n.* coquetry, flirtatiousness.
txatxar *adj.* insignificant, trifling, mediocre.
txatxarkeria *n.* villainy, base action, mediocrity.
txatxartu *v.i.* to get smaller, to shrink, to shrivel. *v.i.(fig.)* to degrade oneself, to become vile.
txatxu *adj.* foolish, stupid, idiotic.
txatxukeria *n.* foolishness, idiocy, stupidity.
-txe *(gram.)* Suffix used with adverbs of location to provide emphasis. Used after consonants. **Hortxe.** Right there.
txeke *n.(econ.)* check.
txepel *adj.* cowardly, timid, shy; mediocre, average.
txepeldu *v.i.* to be shy, to be intimidated, to be a coward. *v.t.* to make (someone) weak or dull.
txepeldura *n.* cowardice; shyness, timidity.
txepelkeria *n.* cowardice.
txepelki *adv.* cowardly, in a cowardly manner; timidly, shyly.
txepeltasun *n.* cowardice, cowardliness; timidness, shyness.
txepetx *n.(zool.)* wren, kind of kinglet (*Troglodytes troglodytes*).
txera *n.* intelligence, cleverness. *n.* welcome. *n.* affection, kindness.
txerakeria *n.* excessive pampering, excessive spoiling.
txerati *adj.* affectionate, kind, amiable.
txeratsu *adj.* affectionate.
txerkagarri *adj.* researchable, investigable.
txerkaketa *n.* examination, investigation, research.
txerkatu *v.t.* to examine, to investigate.

txerkatzaile *n.* examiner, investigator.
txerpolari *n.* pedlar.
txerrama *n.* mother pig, sow.
txerri *n. (zool.)* pig.
txertagarri *adj.* injectable. *adj.* graftable.
txertakera *n.* way of grafting.
txertaketa *n.* grafting; imbedding.
txertapen *n.* grafting; imbedding. *n.* vaccination.
txertatu *v.t.* to graft; to insert, to imbed. *v.t.* to vaccinate, to give an injection.
txertatzaile *n./adj.* grafter; grafting.
txerto *n.* graft; insertion. *n.* vaccination, injection. *n.* bud, germ, sprout.
txertore *n.* putty, mastic.
txibia *n.(zool.)* squid.
txibierro *n.* squid tentacle.
txibikorain *n.* small grappling hook for fishing for squid.
txigor *n.* food dipped in batter and fried. *adj.* toasted.
txigordura *n.* toasting.
txigorketa *n.* toasting.
txigorpen *n.* toasting.
txigorraldi *n.* toasting.
txigortu *v.t.* to toast.
txikano *n./adj.* Chicano.
txiki *adj.* small, little.
txikiago *adj.(comp.)* smaller, inferior.
txikiagotasun *n.* inferiority; quality of being smaller.
txikiagotu *v.i./v.t.* to become smaller; to reduce, to make smaller.
txikien *adj.(superl.)* the smallest, minimum.
txikietsi *v.t.* to undervalue, to underestimate.
txikiezin(ezko) *adj.* irreducible, unshortenable.
txikigarri *adj.* reducible; restricting, diminishing, decreasing.
txikikeria *n.* pettiness, lowness, smallness, insignificance; trifle, triviality; meanness.
txikitan *adv.* in childhood, as a child.
txikitasun *n.* smallness.
txikitatik *adv.* since childhood, from childhood on.
txikito *n.* small amount of wine, sip of wine in a glass.
txikitozale *adj.* fond of bar hopping.
txikitu *v.t.* to make small, to reduce; to cut into pieces. *v.i.* to shrink, to shrivel.
txikitxo *adj.(dim.)* little, very little, itsy-bitsy.
txikitzaile *adj.* diminishing, reducing; cutting.
txikle *n.* (chewing) gum.
txikot *n.* thick rope.
txil *n.* surrender.
txilar *n.(bot.)* heather.
txilardi *n.* heath.
txil egin *v.t.* to defeat; to make

(someone) surrender.

txilibitu *n.* flute; whistle.

txilibituhots *n.* sound of a flute; whistling, whistle.

txilibitulari *n.* flautist; whistler.

txilina *n.* little bell.

txilinaldi *n.* ringing of a small bell.

txilinbelar *n.(bot.)* bellflower, campanilla.

txilindron *n.* lamb stew.

txilingile *n.* maker of small bells.

txilinjole *n.* bell ringer (of a hand bell).

txilinkada *n.* loud ringing of a hand bell.

txilinkari *n.* bell ringer (of a hand bell).

txilinkatu *v.t./v.i.* to ring (bells).

txilinketa *n.* ringing (bells).

txilinlore *n.(bot.)* bellflower, campanilla.

txilinots *n.* ringing of a bell.

txilio *n.* scream, shout.

txilio egin *v.t.* to scream, to yell.

txilioka *adv.* screaming, yelling, shouting.

txima *n.* long tangled hair.

tximadun *adj.* disheveled, unkempt.

tximajario *adj.* disheveled, rumpled, unkempt (usually hair).

tximatu *v.i.* to become disheveled.

tximeleta *n.(zool.)* butterfly.

tximeletatxo *n.(dim.)* little butterfly.

tximinia *n.* chimney, smokestack.

tximinigarbitzaile *n.* chimneysweep.

tximino *n.(zool.)* monkey, simian.

tximinokeria *n.* crazy action, foolishness, monkey business.

tximist *n.* lightning.

tximista bota *v.t.* to strike (lightning), to lightning.

tximista egin *v.t.* to strike (lightning), to lightning.

tximistaketa *n.* lightning, bolt of lightning, flash of lightning.

tximistaldi *n.* flash of lightning, lightning.

tximistargi *n.* flash of lightning.

tximistarri *n.(min.)* flint.

tximistorratz *n.* lightning rod.

tximitxa *n.(zool.)* bedbug.

tximur *n.* wrinkle (skin), fold, pleat (fabric).

tximurdura *n.* wrinkle (skin), fold, pleat (fabric).

tximurtsu *adj.* wrinkled.

txin *n.(colloq.)* coined money; sound of coined money, clinking of coins.

txinbo *n.(zool.)* whitethroat (*Sylvia*).

txindor *n.(med.)* sty. *n.(zool.)* nightingale (*Luscinia megarhyncha*).

txingar *n.* live coal, red-hot coal, ember(s).

txingartu *v.i.* to spark, to crackle (fire).

txingor *n.* hail, hailstorm.

txingor egin *v.t.* to hail.

txingorrada *n.* hailstorm.

txingorraldi *n.* hailstorm.

txinpart *n.* spark.

txinpartaketa *n.* spluttering of a fire, sparking of a fire.

txinpartatu *v.i.* to crackle, to splutter, to spark (a fire).

txinpartatzaile *adj.* crackling.

txinta *n.* chirping, singing (of birds).

txinta egin *v.t.* to warble, to trill, to sing (birds).

txintari *adj.* warbling, trilling.

txintxarri *n.* cowbell, sheep bell. *adj.(fig.)* talkative, loquacious.

txintxeta *n.* thumbtack.

txintxileria *n.* group of trinkets; group of people.

txintxin *n.(colloq.)* coined money; sound of coined money, clinking of coins.

txintxirrin *n.* baby's rattle.

txintxor *n.* small rock, small stone, pebble.

txintxorta *n.* cracklings, fried pork rind.

txio *n.* chirping, cheeping, tweeting (of birds).

txio egin *v.t.* to chirp, to cheep, to tweet.

txioka *adv.* chirping, tweeting.

txiokari *adj.* chirping, cheeping, tweeting, singing (birds).

txiokatu *v.t.* to chirp, to tweet, to sing (birds).

txioketa *n.* chirping, tweeting, singing, warbling.

txiolari *adj.* chirping, tweeting, singing, warbling.

txipa *n.(zool.)* bitterling.

txipiroi *n.(zool.)* squid.

txipli-txapla *n.* splish-splash. Onomatopoeic sound of splashing water.

txipristin *n.* splashing, dousing, spattering, splash.

txipristindu *v.t.* to splash, to spatter, to splatter.

txiri egin *v.t.* to evade, to elude.

txirikorda *n.* string (of onions or garlic). *n.* plait, braid.

txirikordatu *v.t.* to string (onions or garlic).

txirinbol *n.* disk, wheel; slice.

txiringa *n.* syringe, gun (for grease or oil).

txirla *n.(zool.)* clam.

txirlarri *n.(zool.)* pearl oyster.

txirlategi *n.* oyster bed.

txirlatsu *adj.* full of oysters.

txirlora *n.* wood shaving.

txirpil *adj.* wilted, withered.

txirpildu *v.i.* to wilt, to wither.

txirpilgarri *adj.* perishable, liable to wilt.

txirpilketa *n.* wilting, withering.

txirri *n.(zool.)* golden plover.

txirrika *n.* pulley; bobbin, spool. *n.* spinning wheel.

txirrin *n.* doorbell; bicycle bell. *n.* rebec, ancient stringed instrument used by shepherds. *n.(zool.)* small seagull.

txirrindola n. metal ring used as a hitching post or mooring.

txirrindolaketa n. fastening with rings, fastening to a ring.

txirrindolatu v.t. to form into rings, to shape like a ring, to fasten with rings.

txirrindu n. bicycle, bike.

txirrindula n. bicycle, bike.

txirrindulari n. cyclist, biker.

txirringa n. wheel.

txirrinots n. ringing of a bell.

txirrist n.(onomat.) sound of a slip or fall.

txirrista n. slide, sled, toboggan.

txirristada n. slipping, sliding.

txirristaka adv. slipping, sliding, skidding.

txirristatu v.i. to slip, to slide.

txirrist egin v.t. to slip, to slide.

txirrita n. pulley. n.(zool.) cicada, grasshopper.

txirri-txirri n. chirping of a cricket, sound made by crickets.

txirritxori n.(zool.) swift, martin.

txirritxorro n. chirping, cheeping (of birds).

txirta n. scoria, slag, metal shavings.

txirula n.(mus.) small Basque end-blown flute played in the province of Zuberoa.

txirulagile n. flute maker.

txirulari n. flautist, flute player.

txirulatxo n.(dim.) little flute, small Basque flute.

txiruliru n. chirping, warbling, trilling.

txiruliru egin v.t. to sing (birds).

txispa n. harquebus, old type of firearm.

txispoi n. paintbrush; shaving brush.

txistada n. hiss, hissing.

txist egin v.t. to say a word, to speak (usually used in the negative).

txisten n. rag, tatter, piece of clothing or rag; any part of clothing that streams down or behind (train of a wedding dress, etc.).

txistera n. top hat. n. jai alai scoop or basket-like glove.

txistor n. pork sausage.

txistorgile n. sausage maker.

txistorsaltzaile n. butcher, seller of sausages.

txistu n.(mus.) Basque wind instrument similar to the flute or recorder. n. whistle. n. saliva, spit. n.(zool.) small multicolored edible saltwater fish.

txistua bota v.t. to spit.

txistualdi n. whistling, whistle.

txistu egin v.t. to whistle. v.t. to spit.

txistugale n. desire to spit. adj. desirous of spitting, wanting to spit.

txistugile n. whistler. n. maker of Basque flutes.

txistuhots n. whistle, sound of a whistle.

txistujario n./adj. salivating, drooling.

txistu jo v.t. to whistle. v.t. to play the txistu.

txistuka adv. whistling. adv. spitting.

txistukada n. whistling, whistle.

txistukari adj. sibilant.

txistukatu v.t. to jeer, to hiss.

txistuketa n. spitting, salivating. n. jeering, hissing.

txistulari n. txistu player.

txistularri n. desire to spit. adj. wanting to spit, desirous of spitting.

txistumutur n. mouthpiece of the Basque recorder or flute called txistu.

txistuontzi n. spittoon.

txit adv. very.

txita n.(zool.) chick.

txitadun n. chicken breeder, chicken dealer.

txitagailu n. incubator.

txitaldi n. brooding, setting (chicken on eggs).

txitatalde n. brood of chicks.

txitatu v.t. to incubate, to set (on eggs).

txitean-pitean adv. constantly.

txito n. chick.

txitxar n.(zool.) grasshopper, cicada.

txitxardin n.(zool.) baby eel, elver.

txitxarro n.(zool.) horse mackerel.

txitxi n. fleshiness, meatiness. n. meat (children's language).

txitxiburduntzi n.(zool.) dragonfly.

txitxiezpata n.(zool.) swordfish.

txitxirio n.(bot.) garbanzo, chickpea.

txiz n. word used by a mother to coax a child to urinate.

txiza n. urine, pee.

txiza egin v.t. to urinate, to pee.

txizagale n. desire to urinate.

txizagura n. desire to urinate.

txizalarri n. desire to urinate.

txizalarri izan v.i. to want to urinate, to have to go (to the bathroom).

txizaleku n. urinal, place for urinating, restroom, toilet.

txizati adj. pissy, wanting to urinate.

txizatoki n. restroom, bathroom, toilet.

txizestu n. extreme need or desire to urinate.

txizontzi n. urinal, chamber pot, bed pan.

txiztil n. drop.

txo (inter.) hey! Used for calling boys.

-txo (gram.) Diminutive suffix.

txobinismo n. chauvinism.

txobinista n./adj. chauvinist.

txofer n. driver, chauffeur.

txoka n.(zool.) linnet.

txokartu v.i./v.t. to burn (excessively), to char.

txoke n. bump, collision, run-in.

txoko n. corner. n. gastronomical society.

txokokari adj. withdrawn, antisocial.

txokokeria n. local characteristic or

peculiarity. Usually used in a pejorative sense.

txokolatari n. chocolate maker.

txokolate n. chocolate, hot chocolate.

txokolatedenda n. chocolate shop.

txokolategi n. chocolate shop, place for drinking hot chocolate.

txokolategintza n. chocolate making.

txokolatezale adj. fond of chocolate.

txokolatontzi n. chocolate pot.

txokor n.(bot.) cigar rolled in corn husk. n.(neol.) cigar.

txokorreria n. jumble, mess, confusion, mix-up.

txola n.(neol.) cup of brandy.

txolarre n.(zool.) sparrow.

txolarte n. free time.

txolin adj. tipsy. adj. scatterbrained.

txolindu v.i. to be scatterbrained, to become featherbrained.

txolinkeria n. frivolousness, quality of being scatterbrained.

txolintasun n. frivolousness, quality of being scatterbrained.

txominbelar n.(bot.) kind of clover.

txomorro n.(zool.) insect.

txonbo n. dive, act of diving.

txonbo egin v.t. to dive (in).

txondor n. vertex of a pile of wood being made into charcoal.

txongil n. earthen jar with handle and two spouts.

txonta n.(zool.) chaffinch (Fringilla coelebs).

txopa n. poop deck, stern.

txorabiatu v.i. to get dizzy, to become giddy or dizzy.

txorabildu v.i. to feel dizzy.

txorabio n. vertigo, dizziness.

txorabioaldi n. attack of vertigo, dizziness.

txoradura n. vertigo, dizziness.

txorakeria n. insanity, craziness, foolishness.

txorakilo adj.(dim.) slightly crazy.

txoratu v.i. to be crazy with pleasure, to be fascinated.

txoraxka adj.(dim.) slightly crazy.

txori n.(zool.) bird.

txoriarrain n.(zool.) flying fish.

txoribelar n.(bot.) canary grass; birdseed. n.(bot.) small thistle.

txoriburu adj. foolish, irresponsible, featherbrained.

txoriburukeria n. foolishness, irresponsibility.

txoridenda n. bird shop.

txorieme n. female bird.

txorierrege n.(zool.) kinglet.

txorierri n. area of Biscay in the Asua valley.

txorigaizto adj.(colloq.) rascal, crafty (person).

txorigaldu adj.(colloq.) rascally.

txorigardu n.(bot.) thistle.

txoriketa n. abundance of birds.

txoriki n. bird flesh, bird meat.

txorikume n. baby bird.

txorimalo n. scarecrow.

txorimalotu v.t./v.i. to put on a mask, to wear a mask.

txorimordo n. flock of birds.

txoritalde n. flock of birds.

txoritegi n. bird shop.

txoriteria n. flock of birds.

txoritoki n. bird cage. n. aviary.

txoritxo n.(dim.) little bird.

txoritzar n.(augm.) big bird.

txorizain n. aviculturist, bird keeper.

txorizaintza n. aviculture, bird raising.

txorizale adj. fond of birds.

txorizo n. chorizo, spicy Basque pork sausage.

txorizogile n. maker of chorizo sausage.

txoro adj.(dim.) foolish.

txorromorro n. leapfrog.

txorrota n. tap, faucet.

txorrotxio n. chirping, warbling, singing (of birds).

txorrotxio egin v.t. to chirp, to warble, to sing (birds).

txosna n. improvised tavern where drinks are sold during fiestas.

txosten n. report, briefing.

txostenemaile n. lecturer, giver of a report.

txoto n. hood, cowl.

txotor n. sty (in one's eye).

txotxakeria n. foolishness, simpleness.

txotxatu v.i. to become senile, to become childlike, to enter one's second childhood.

txotxin adj. light-headed, featherbrained.

txotxindu v.i. to be featherbrained.

txotxo exclam. hey! Used for calling little boys. n.(fam.) little boy.

txotxola adj. silly, foolish (woman).

txotxolo adj. silly, foolish (man).

txotxolokeria n. silliness, foolishness, nonsense.

txotxolotu v.i. to be foolish, to be silly.

txotxongilo n. marionette, puppet with strings.

txualdi n. spitting.

txu egin v.t. to spit.

txugale n. desire to spit. adj. desiring to spit.

txukun adj. neat, tidy, clean. adv. carefully.

txukundu v.t./v.i. to tidy up, to clean. v.t. to touch up, to retouch.

txukungai n. cleaning product.

txukunkeria n. excessive tidiness.

txukunketa n. cleaning, tidying up.

txukunki adv. tidily, cleanly.

txukuntasun n. cleanliness, tidiness.

txuleta n. chop.

txuliagarri adj. avoidable.

txuliaketa n. avoiding.

txulialdi n. avoiding.

txuliatu v.t. to avoid (something), to

elude, to weather a storm, to make passes with a cape at bulls.

txuliatzaile *adj.* avoiding, eluding.

txundidura *n.* surprise, astonishment, amazement.

txundigarri *adj.* surprising, astonishing, amazing, astounding.

txundiketa *n.* surprise, astonishment.

txundikor *adj.* stupefying, astounding.

txunditu *v.i./v.t.* to be surprised, to be astounded; to surprise, to astound.

txuntxur *n.* summit, promontory, outcropping.

txuri *adj./n.* white.

txurro *n.* fritter, cruller, type of pastry deep-fried in oil and rolled in powdered sugar.

txurrogile *n.* txurro maker, maker of crullers.

txurrontzi *n.* pot for deep frying crullers.

txurrosaltzaile *n.* seller of crullers.

txurrotegi *n.* place where crullers are made or sold.

txurru *n.* faucet, tap.

txurrut *n.* gulp, swallow.

txurrut egin *v.t.* to drink gulpingly, to gulp.

txutxumutxu *n.* whispering. *n.* pretext, unjustified action.

txutxumutxu egin *v.t.* to whisper.

txutxumutxuka *adv.* whispering.

tz Letter of the Basque alphabet. Generally used as a suffix or infix.

-tza *(gram.)* Noun suffix indicating large quantity. **Dirutza.** A lot of money. *(gram.)* Suffix indicating job or profession. **Nekazaritza.** Farming profession. *(gram.)* Suffix indicating action. **Jaiotza.** Birth.

-tzaile *(gram.)* Suffix which forms agent nouns from verbs. **Saltzaile.** Seller.

-tzain *(gram.)* Suffix indicating keeper, caretaker. Var. of - *zain*. **Artzain.** Shepherd.

-tzale *(gram.)* Suffix indicating agent.

-tzapen *(gram.)* Suffix indicating act or action, result or consequence. Usually used with verbs.

-tzar *(gram.)* Augmentative suffix which sometimes has a pejorative connotation.

-tzat *(gram.)* Suffix meaning considered (as), taken for. **Semetzat daukat.** I consider him my son. *prep.(dat.)* for. Used with animate beings. **Aitarentzat.** For father.

-tze *(gram.)* Verbal suffix indicating verbal action. **Gizentze.** Fattening.

-tzean *(gram.)* Verbal suffix indicating time (when, upon). **Etortzean.** Upon coming.

-tzeko *(gram.)* Verbal suffix meaning in order to, to. **Zapaltzeko.** In order to crush.

-tzen *(gram.)* Verbal suffix which forms a gerund or which indicates habitual action.

-tzera *(gram.)* Verbal suffix meaning to. **Irakurtzera noa.** I am going to read.

-tzerakoan *(gram.)* Verbal suffix indicating at the moment (an action is performed).

-tzu *(gram.)* Suffix indicating several. **Batzu.** Some.

U

u Letter of the Basque alphabet.

u! *int.* shoo! Used to scatter small animals.

ubarroi *n.(zool.)* cormorant, shag.

ubehera *n.* ford of a river.

ubel *adj.* purple, blue, livid. *n.* welt, weal.

ubelaire *adj.* purplish.

ubeldu *v.i.* to turn purple.

ubeldura *n.* welt, weal.

ubelilun *adj.* dark purple, blackish (bruise).

ubeltasun *n.* lividness, purplishness.

ubelune *n.* purpling, bruise.

ubelurdin *adj.* bluish purple (bruise).

ubidegintza *n.* canal building, drainage.

ubideketa *n.* drainage.

ubideratu *v.t.* to drain, to conduct (water) through pipes, etc.

ubidetu *v.t.* to drain, to conduct through pipes.

ubidexka *n.(dim.)* small canal, small water pipe.

ubidezain *n.* one who regulates the flow of water in ditches, canals, etc.

ubidohe *n.* canal bed.

ubieta *n.* place of fords, shallow place for fording (a river).

ubil *n.* whirlpool.

uda *n.* summer.

udaberri *n.* spring.

udaberriburu *n.* spring equinox.

udaberriburuko *adj.* equinoctial.

udaberriko *adj.* spring, of spring, pertaining to spring.

udaberritiar *adj.* spring, pertaining to spring.

udaberritu *v.i.* to become spring, to come (spring).

udabihotz *n.* dog days, hottest days of summer.

udaburu *n.* summer solstice.

udagiro *n.* summer weather.

udagoien *n.* fall, autumn.

udako *adj.* summer, of summer, pertaining to summer.

udal *n.* city hall; city council.

udalatx *n.(bot.)* sorb apple, serviceberry.

udalatxondo *n.(bot.)* service tree, sorb tree.

udalbarruti *n.* city limits, municipality, area pertaining to a village or township.

udalbatzar *n.* town meeting, municipal assembly, city council meeting.

udalbatze n. municipal corporation, town council.

udaldi n. summertime, summer.

udaleko adj. municipal, pertaining to the village or town hall.

udaleku n. summer resort.

udalerri n. municipal territory or area.

udaletxe n. town hall, city hall.

udaltzain n. member of the city police force.

udamin n. dog days, hottest days of summer.

udamineko adj. summertime, pertaining to the hottest days of summer.

udamuga n. summer solstice.

udaraldi n. summertime, summer.

udare n.(bot.) pear.

udareardo n. pear nectar, pear juice.

udaredi n. pear tree grove, pear orchard.

udareondo n.(bot.) pear tree.

udaretxo n.(dim.) little pear.

udaro n. summertime, summer.

udate n. summertime, summer.

udatiar n./adj. summer resident, summer vacationer.

udazale adj. fond of summer. n. summer vacationer, summer resident.

udazken n. fall, autumn.

udazkenaldi n. autumn, fall.

udazkenburu n. autumn equinox.

udazkenburuko adj. equinoctial.

udazkendu v.i. to begin (autumn), to turn fall.

udazkeneko adj. autumnal, fall, pertaining to fall.

udetxe n. summer house.

uf! int. whew! Used to express tiredness, boredom, heat.

ufaka adv. panting, puffing.

ufakada n. pant, puff (of air).

ufakari adj. disdainful, scornful, contemptuous.

ufako n. exhalation, air expelled by puffing or panting.

ufaldi n. puffing, panting, sighing, blowing.

ufatu v.t. to blow.

ufaztu v.t. to stink, to smell bad.

ugabere n.(zool.) otter (Lutra lutra).

ugal- Used in compound words. Derived from ugari, abundant.

ugaldu v.i./v.t. to reproduce, to multiply.u, ugaritu.

ugalgarri adj. reproducible, multipliable, increasable, augmentable.

ugalketa n. reproduction; abundance.

ugalkor adj. fertile, fecund, prolific, fruitful.

ugalkorki adv. fertilely, prolifically.

ugalkortasun n. fecundity, fruitfulness, prolificness.

ugalmen n. reproductivity, reproductiveness, capacity for reproduction.

ugalpen n. reproduction.

ugaltasun n. reproductiveness, quality of being reproductive or prolific.

ugaltsu adj. fecund, fertile.

ugari adj. abundant, copious, a lot of. adv. abundantly, copiously.

ugari izan v.i. to be abundant, to abound.

ugariki adv. abundantly, copiously, profusely.

ugarikor adj. fruitful, fecund, fertile.

ugarikortasun n. fertility, fruitfulness, fecundity.

ugariro adv. abundantly, copiously, profusely.

ugaritasun n. abundance, fruitfulness, copiousness.

ugaritsu adj. abundant, profuse, copious.

ugaritu v.i./v.t. to abound, to proliferate, to multiply.

ugatz n. breast, teat.

ugatzeko adj. mammary.

ugazaba n. employer, boss; master, owner.

ugazabandre n. boss's wife.

ugazabatasun n. quality of being the boss, ownership, proprietorship.

ugazaberia n. group of employers, group of bosses, group of owners.

ugazahizpa n. stepsister.

ugazaita n. stepfather.

ugazalaba n. stepdaughter.

ugazama n. stepmother.

ugazanaia n. stepbrother.

ugazarreba n. stepsister.

ugazeme n. stepson.

ugaztun adj. mammiferous, mammalian.

uger n. oxide, rust; blight. n. swimming.

ugerdo adj. filthy, dirty; greasy.

uger egin v.t. to swim.

ugerlari n. swimmer.

ugerraldi n. time spent swimming.

ugertsu adj. filthy, grimy, scabby. adj. rusty.

ugertu v.i. to rust, to oxidize.

uhal n. belt. n. leather lead (for horses or cattle), strap.

uhaldarri n. pebble.

uhalde n. bank of a river; coast, shore. n. flood, inundation, deluge.

uhaldu v.t. to fasten (cattle) with straps.

uhaldun adj. having leather straps.

uhaleztatu v.t. to tie with a lead, to fasten (cattle) with straps.

uhaleztu v.t. to tie with a lead, to fasten with straps.

uharka n. cistern, water tower, water container. n. riverbed.

uharre n. turbulent waters, muddy waters.

uharri n. pebble.

uhartasun n. turbidity, muddiness.

uharte n. island, isle.
uhartedi n.(geog.) archipelago.
uharteko adj. island, pertaining to an island.
uharteta n.(geog.) archipelago.
uhartu v.i. to turn yellowish; to turn bay-colored.
uhaska n. cistern, tank, reservoir.
uhate n. floodgate, tide gate.
uhaza n.(bot.) lettuce.
uher adj. gray. adj. turbid, muddy.
uherdura n. turbidness, muddiness. n.(fig.) turbulence, uproar, confusion.
uhertasun n. muddiness, turbidness. n.(fig.) confusion, turbulence.
uhertu v.i. to turn muddy, to become turbid.
uhin n. wave.
uhindu v.i. to wave, to ripple, to undulate.
uhindura n. undulation, rippling, waving.
uhinkada n. wave, ripple.
uhinkari adj. rippling, undulating.
uhinketa n. undulating movement, rippling.
uhinkor adj. waving, undulating.
uhintsu adj. wavy, ripply, undulating.
uhinurrategi n. breakwater, jetty.
uhol n. flood, inundation.
uholde n. flood, inundation, deluge.
uholdeaurreko adj. antediluvian.
uholdebide n. gully, ravine made by a torrent.
uholdelur n. alluvial deposit, mud carried by floodwaters.
uholdetar adj. diluvian, pertaining to a flood.
uholdetu v.i./v.t. to flood.
uholdezko adj. torrential, deluvial.
uhuka adv. hooting.
uhukada n. hooting.
uhukaketa n. hooting.
uhukaldi n. hooting.
uhukatu v.t. to hoot.
ujuju exclam. aha! Shout of joy.
uka- Used in compound words. Derived from uko, negation.
ukabil n.(anat.) fist.
ukabilka adv. with fists.
ukabilkada n. sock, jab, blow with a fist.
ukabilkaldi n. series of blows with the fists.
ukabilkari n. boxer, pugilist.
ukabilkatu v.t. to box, to hit with the fists.
ukabilketa n. boxing, pugilism.
ukadura n. negation.
ukaezin n. undeniable, not refusable.
ukagaitz adj. undeniable, indisputable, not refusable.
ukagarri adj. deniable, refusable.
ukai n.(anat.) forearm.
ukakor adj. negative, pessimistic.
ukaldi n. blow, sock, jab.

ukaldika adv. with blows, by blows.
ukaldikari n. hitter, one who socks or hits.
ukaldikatu v.t. to pummel, to beat.
ukamen n. negation, denial, refusal.
ukan v.t. to have. Used as an auxiliary verb with transitive verbs.
ukapen n. negation, renunciation, refusal, denial.
ukarai n.(anat.) wrist.
ukatu v.t. to deny, to refuse, to negate.
ukatzaile adj. denying, refusing, negative, revoking.
uki n. touch, touching.
ukialdi n. touching, act of touching.
ukiera n. touching, way of touching.
ukiezin(ezko) adj. untouchable, intangible.
ukiezintasun n. untouchableness, intangibleness.
ukigabe adj. intact, untouched, inviolate.
ukigai adj. tangible, touchable.
ukigaitz adj. untouchable, intangible.
ukigarri adj. tangible, touchable.
ukigune n. point of contact.
ukiketa n. contact, touch.
ukikor adj. tactile, touching.
ukimen n. sense of touch.
ukimenezko adj. tactile.
ukipen n. touch, contact.
ukipuntu n. point of contact.
ukitu v.t. to touch; to affect. v.t.(fig.) to mention, to touch on, to refer to. n. touch.
ukituz adv. tangentially.
ukitzaile n. toucher. n.(geom.) tangent.
ukiune n. point of contact.
uko n. renouncement, refusal, denial.
ukoegile adj. negative, denying, renouncing. n. one who renounces his faith, apostate.
uko egin v.t. to renounce, to deny, to refuse.
ukondo n.(anat.) elbow.
ukondohezur n.(anat.) elbow, bone of the elbow.
ukondoka adv. elbowing.
ukondokada n. blow or jab with the elbow.
ukondokatu v.t. to lean on one's elbow.
ukondoko n. elbow patch.
ukoz adv. negatively.
ukozko adj. negative.
ulerbide n. comprehension, understanding. n. example.
ulergarri adj. intelligible, comprehensible, understandable.
ulergarritasun n. comprehensibility, understandableness, intelligibility.
ulerkaitz adj. incomprehensible, unintelligible.
ulerkaiztasun n. unintelligibility, incomprehensibleness.
ulerketa n. understanding,

comprehension.

ulerkor *adj.* understandable, intelligible, comprehendible.

ulerkuntza *n.* comprehension, understanding.

ulermen *n.* understanding (faculty), intelligence.

ulerterazi *v.t.* to make (someone) understand.

ulerterraz *adj.* intelligible, comprehendible, easy to understand.

ulertezin *adj.* unintelligible, impossible to understand.

ulertezintasun *n.* unintelligibleness, incomprehensibleness.

ulertu *v.t.* to understand, to comprehend.

ulertzaile *adj.* understanding, comprehending.

ultzera *n.(med.)* ulcer.

ultzeraketa *n.* ulceration.

ultzerapen *n.* ulceration.

ultzeratsu *adj.* ulcerous.

ultzeratu *v.i.* to ulcerate, to develop an ulcer.

ulu *n.* wail, howl.

uluka *adv.* howling, wailing; barking.

ululari *n.* howler, wailer.

uma- Used in compound words. Derived from *ume*, child.

umadun *adj.* pregnant, with child, expecting.

umagin *n.* female which produces many children (usually used for animals).

umaketa *n.* reproduction, procreation.

umakor *adj.* fertile, prolific.

umaldi *n.* birth, birthing, giving birth.

umamin *n.* labor pains.

umategi *n.* place where fruit is kept to ripen.

umatu *v.i.* to have children, to reproduce, to procreate. *v.i.* to mature, to ripen, to get ripe.

ume *n.* young, offspring, child. Used in northern dialects exclusively for animals. **Umetan.** In childhood.

ume(a) egin *v.t.* to give birth, to have a baby.

umealdi *n.* giving birth (animals), dropping (a litter or foal). *n.* time of giving birth.

umealdiko *adj.* gestational, pertaining to pregnancy.

umeaskodun *adj.* having many young, multiparous.

umedun *adj.* pregnant.

umegai *n.(anat.)* fetus.

umegaltzaile *n.* corruptor of children.

umegile *adj.* producing many children or young, prolific.

umegintza *n.* procreation, reproduction.

ume izan *v.t.* to give birth, to have a child, to bear young.

umekada *n.* childish action.

umekai *n.(anat.)* fetus.

umekari *adj.* fond of children.

umekeria *n.* childish action, childishness.

umeketa *n.* procreation, reproduction.

umeki *adv.* childishly, puerilely. *n.(anat.)* fetus.

umekoi *adj.* fond of children. *adj.* prolific, having many young.

umekor *adj.* producing many young, prolific (animals).

umekoskor *n.* small child (at least a few months old).

umel *adj.* overripe, overly ripe. *adj.* sultry, muggy, humid.

umeldu *v.i.* to become overly ripe. *v.i.* to be muggy, to be sultry.

umemin *n.* labor pain. *n.* desire for children.

umemoko *n.* small child.

umeondore *n.* time directly after childbirth, post-partum period.

umeorde *n.* adopted child.

umetalde *n.* group of children.

umetasun *n.* childhood.

umetegi *n.* nursery, childcare center, kindergarten.

umeteria *n.* group of children.

umeti *adj.* fond of children.

umetoki *n.(anat.)* uterus, womb.

umetsu *adj.* prolific, multiparous, having many children.

umetu *v.i.* to be pregnant, to get pregnant. *v.i.* to become senile; to enter one's second childhood, to become childlike.

umetxo *n.(dim.)* baby, infant.

umetza *n.* childhood, infancy.

umetzakotu *v.t.* to adopt (a son or a daughter).

umezain *n.* babysitter.

umezaintzaile *n.* babysitter.

umezale *adj.* fond of children.

umezaro *n.* childhood, infancy.

umezorro *n.(anat.)* placenta.

umezurtz *n.* orphan.

umezurtza *n.* orphanhood.

umezurtzetxe *n.* orphanage.

umezurztasun *n.* quality of being an orphan.

umezurztegi *n.* orphanage.

umil *adj.* humble.

umildade *n.* humility.

umildu *v.i./v.t.* to be humble; to humble (someone).

umildura *n.* humiliation.

umilgarri *adj.* humiliating.

umilkeria *n.* false humility.

umilki *adv.* humbly.

umiltasun *n.* humbleness, humility.

umo *adj.* ripe, mature. *adj.* prudent, sensible; experienced.

umodura *n.* maturation, ripening.

umoegi *adj.* too ripe, overly ripe.

umogabe *adj.* unripe, not mature.

umogarri *adj.* ripening, maturing, serving to ripen (something).

umoki *adv.* prudently, sensibly.
umokor *adj.* ripening, maturing.
umontzi *n.(anat.)* uterus, womb.
umontziko *adj.* uterine.
umore *n.* humor, sense of humor, wit.
umorealdi *n.* mood.
umoredun *adj.* good humored.
umoretsu *adj.* funny, humorous, fun.
umoretxar *n.* moody, bad tempered.
umorezko *adj.* humorous, funny.
umotasun *n.* ripeness, maturity. *n.* sensibleness, prudence.
unadura *n.* tedium, boredom; annoyance.
unagarri *adj.* annoying, boring, dull, tedious.
unagarriki *adv.* annoyingly, tediously, boringly, fastidiously.
unaigo *n.* job of a cowherd.
unatasun *n.* boredom, fatigue, tediousness.
unatu *v.i./v.t.* to get tired, to become bored; to tire, to bore.
une *n.* moment. *n.* place, point, part, spot, location.
-une *(gram.)* Noun suffix denoting place, space; time. **Hutsune.** Blank space, hollow.
unean *adv.* instantly.
unebereko *adj.* simultaneous.
uneko *adj.* instantaneous.
unetxo *n.(dim.)* short distance; short period of time.
unibertsal *adj.* universal, general.
unibertsaldu *v.i.* to become universal.
unibertsalki *adv.* universally.
unibertsaltasun *n.* universality, universalness.
unibertsitalgo *n.* group of university members, student body of a university.
unibertsitari *n.* university student.
unibertsitate *n.* university.
unibertsitateaurreko *adj.* pre-university.
untxi *n.(zool.)* rabbit.
untxikume *n.(dim.)* little rabbit, young rabbit.
untxitegi *n.* rabbit hutch.
untxizulo *n.* rabbit warren.
untzi *n.* boat, ship.
untzialdaketa *n.* transfer from one ship to another.
untzidun *n./adj.* shipowner; having a ship.
untzigidari *n.* ship's captain, skipper.
untzigile *n.* shipbuilder.
untzigintza *n.* shipbuilding, ship construction, naval construction.
untzigudu *n.* naval battle.
untzijabe *n.* shipowner.
untzikari *n.* boatman, crewman.
untziko *n.* member of a ship's crew, navigator. *adj.* pertaining to a boat.
untzimutil *n.* cabinboy, shipboy.
untzirapen *n.* embarcation, getting on a ship; loading or putting on a ship.

untziratu *v.i./v.t.* to get on a ship, to embark (on a ship), to go aboard; to put (someone or something) aboard.
untzitegi *n.* anchoring ground, dockyard, shipyard. *n.* cupboard, hutch, cabinet.
untziteria *n.* group of ships. *n.* dishes.
untzixka *n.(dim.)* small boat, launch.
upa *n.* vat, barrel, small cask.
upagile *n.* cooper, cask or barrel maker.
upagin *n.* cooper, cask or barrel maker.
upagintza *n.* cooper's trade, job of cask maker, barrel making, cask making.
uparatu *v.t.* to store in vats, to put wine in barrels or casks.
upategi *n.* warehouse for barrels of wine, wine storehouse, wine cellar.
upateria *n.* group of barrels or casks.
upats *n.* smell of old barrels, odor of the vats.
upatxo *n.(dim.)* small cask, small barrel.
upazotz *n.* spigot on a cask or barrel, tap on a cask or barrel.
upel(a) *n.* small cask or barrel.
upeleratu *v.t.* to put (wine, cider, etc.) in large casks.
upelgile *n.* cooper, cask or barrel maker.
upelgintza *n.* barrel making, cask making, job of cask maker.
upelondo *n.* bottom of the cask or barrel.
upeltegi *n.* wine cellar, warehouse for casks or barrels (of wine, etc.).
upelteria *n.* group of casks or barrels.
upeltxo *n.(dim.)* small cask, small barrel.
upohol *n.* stave of a cask or barrel.
ur *n.* water; juice. *n.(bot.)* hazel nut. *adv.* close.
uraldi *n.* flood, inundation, deluge.
uraldixtu *v.i./v.t.* to flood.
uramil *n.* flood, inundation, rising of water.
urandi *n.* ocean.
urandiko *adj.* oceanic, pertaining to the deep sea.
uranio *n.(chem.)* uranium.
urantzeko *adj.* water-like.
urardo *n.* watered wine.
urardotu *v.t.* to mix water and wine, to put wine in the water.
urarrieta *n.* place of pebbles.
urasetu *v.t./v.i.* to soak in water.
urate *n.* gate of a canal, lock.
urazal *n.* surface of the water.
urazaleratu *v.t.* to float (something). *v.i.* to float, to rise to the surface, to surface.
urazpil *n.* washbasin.
urazukre *n.* sugar water.
urazukretsu *adj.* sugared, sugary (water).

urbazter n. bank of a river; coast, shore.

urbegi n. spring, fountain.

urbelar n.(bot.) pond scum.

urbera adj. liquefying.

urberaketa n. soaking.

urberatoki n. soaking tub, soaking tank.

urberatu v.i./v.t. to soak, to steep.

urbero n. hot water.

urbetaurrekoak n.(pl.) goggles, diving mask.

urbide n. canal, aqueduct, millrace, flume.

urbideketa n. draining, piping water.

urbidetu v.t. to drain, to empty of water, to draw off water.

urbizi n. high sea, rough sea. n. high tide.

urbonba n. water pump.

urburu n. fountain.

urdai n. bacon fat.

urdaiaska n. place for salting bacon fat.

urdaiazpiko n. ham.

urdaidun n. bacon and pork dealer.

urdaigantz n. fat, grease.

urdaigizen n. lean part of the bacon.

urdaiki n. bacon, piece of bacon.

urdail n.(anat.) stomach.

urdailate n.(anat.) pylorus, opening from the stomach into the intestine.

urdaileko n.(med.) gastritis, stomach ailment. adj. gastric, pertaining to the stomach.

urdailekomin n.(med.) stomach ache, abdominal pain, gastric pain.

urdaileri n.(med.) stomach ailment, gastritis.

urdailmin n.(med.) stomach ache, stomach pain.

urdaiztatu v.t. to lard.

urdakeria n.(fig.) filthy action, obscene action, obscenity, lustfulness.

urdalde n. herd (of swine).

urdama n. sow, mother pig.

urdan- Used in compound words. Derived from urde, pig.

urdandegi n. pigpen, pigsty.

urdanga n. female pig, sow. n.(fig.) prostitute, whore.

urdaska n. prostitute. adj. dirty (woman).

urde n.(zool.) male pig. adj.(fig.) dirty.

urdegantz n. pork fat, grease.

urdekeria n. filth, obscenity.

urdeki n. pork. adv. dirtily, filthily.

urdekume n.(dim.) piglet.

urdetalde n. herd (of swine).

urdetu v.i. to become filthy, to get dirty.

urdetzar n.(augm.) big pig, hog.

urdezain n. swineherd, pig keeper.

urdin adj. blue.

urdinargi adj. light blue, sky blue.

urdinbeltz adj. dark blue.

urdinberde adj. turquoise.

urdinbizi adj. bright blue.

urdindu v.t./v.i. to dye blue, to tint blue; to be dyed blue. v.i. to go gray (hair).

urdineztu v.t. to dye blue, to blue.

urdinilun adj. indigo, dark blue.

urdinilundu v.t. to dye dark blue, to color (something) dark blue.

urdinska adj. bluish.

urdinskatu v.t. to color blue, to dye blue or a bluish color.

urdintasun n. blueness.

urdintsu adj. blue.

urdintxa n.(bot.) kind of edible mushroom (Psalliota campestris).

urdin-urdin adj. bright blue, very blue.

urdinzuri adj. bluish, light bluish (usually used to describe eye color).

urdun adj. watery.

urdura n. liquefaction.

urduri adj./adv. jittery, uptight, nervous; nervously, anxiously.

urdurigarri adj. nervewracking, upsetting, worrisome, anguishing.

urdurikeria n. nervousness, jitteriness, quality of being upset.

urduriki adv. nervously, anxiously, worriedly.

urduritasun n. nervousness, jitteriness, quality of being upset, jumpiness.

urduritsu adj. very nervous, very upset, very jittery.

urduritu v.i. to get nervous, to become jumpy.

urea n. urea.

uregazkin n. hydroplane, seaplane.

uregazti n. water fowl.

uregosi n. boiled water.

urekarle n. water carrier, water boy, one who brings water.

urelektrika n. hydroelectricity.

uremia n.(med.) uremia.

urentasun n. nobility, nobleness.

urepel n. warm water, tepid water.

urerdoil n.(chem.) hydroxide.

ureri n. runny nose. n.(med.) dropsy, hydropsy.

ureridun adj. hydropathic, having dropsy.

urerreten n. irrigation ditch.

uresne n. watered down milk.

ureta n. quantity of water.

uretako adj. aquatic, water, appropriate for water.

uretaratu v.t. to launch, to put in the water. v.i. to enter the water, to go in the water.

ureter n.(anat.) ureter.

uretorri n. large quantity of water.

uretxe n. beach resort, spa, building pertaining to or housing a spa.

urez adv. with water, of water. adv. by sea.

urezi n. dike, dam.

urezko adj. watery, aqueous.

urezpata n.(bot.) gladiolus.

urezponda n. high water level, water line, the highest point water reaches in a dam, etc.

ureztabide n. irrigation system.

ureztadura n. irrigating, irrigation.

ureztagarri adj. irrigatable.

ureztailu n. watering can.

ureztaketa n. watering, irrigation.

ureztapen n. irrigating, irrigation, watering.

ureztatu v.t. to water, to irrigate.

ureztatzaile n. irrigator, waterer.

urezti n. honeyed water, water mixed with honey.

ureztodi n. water hose.

ureztontzi n. watering can.

ureztu v.t./v.i. to dilute, to water down.

urgabe adj. dry. (lit.) without water.

urgabetu v.i. to dry out, to dehydrate.

urgain n. surface of the water.

urgainalde n. part of a boat or other object that is visible above the water.

urgaindu v.i. to float, to come to the surface.

urgaindura n. floating.

urgaineko adj. floating.

urgaineratu v.i. to float, to come to the surface. v.t. to float (something) on the water.

urgaineztatu v.i. to flood, to overflow, to run over.

urgainezte n. overflowing, flooding, running over.

urgargara n. gargling.

urgarraio n. transporting water.

urgarri adj. water soluble.

urgarritasun n. solubility.

urgatzi v.t. to help, to protect.

urgazi n. salt water.

urgazle adj. associate (member), helping, auxiliary. n. helper, supporter, protector.

urgazte n. act of helping.

urgeldi n. still water, stagnant water.

urgeza n. fresh water.

urgora n. high tide.

urgoraldi n. high tide, high water.

urgorapen n. high tide, rising of the tide.

urgori n. boiling water.

urgoritu v.i. to boil water, to scald.

urgune n. watery place, marshy place. n. fountain.

uril n. stagnant water. n. low tide.

urindar n. hydroelectric power.

urjasogailu n. irrigation water wheel.

urkabe n. scaffold, gallows.

urkagai adj. condemned to death on the gallows.

urkagarri adj. hanging, hangable.

urkamendi n. gallows, scaffold.

urkamendu n. execution (on the gallows).

urkarazi v.t. to order (someone) to be hung, to sentence to hang.

urkari n. hangman. n. water carrier.

urkasoka n. hangman's noose.

urkatoki n. place of the gallows, scaffold.

urkatu v.t. to hang, to execute.

urkatzaile n. hangman.

urketa n. quantity of water; search for water. n. melting, liquefying.

urketari n. one who searches for water; water carrier.

urki n.(bot.) birch tree (Betula pendula).

urkila n. hairpin.

urkilatu v.t. to pin up one's hair, to pin back one's hair (with hairpins).

urkirol n. water sport.

urkoi adj. liquefying, melting.

urkor adj. meltable, liquefiable.

urkuilu n. forked pole, support for tree branches.

urlamia n. water nymph.

urlandare n. water plant.

urlaster n. running water, fast water, moving water.

urlehortar adj. amphibious.

urlia n. what's-his-name, such and such, so and so; and so on.

urlili n.(bot.) calla lily.

urlurrin n. steam, water vapor.

urmahel n. stagnant water, still water.

urmargo n. watercolor.

urmargolan n. watercolor (painting).

urmargolari n. watercolor artist.

urmin n. dropsy, hydropsy.

urmindu v.i. to go bad (water), to stagnate (water).

urmindun adj. dropsical, hydropic.

urnegar n. steady drip or trickle of water over stones.

urodi n. irrigation canal.

uroditeria n. water conduit, water pipe.

uroditza n. water conduit, water pipe.

uroilanda n.(zool.) marsh hen (female).

uroilo n.(zool.) marsh hen (male).

urologari n. urologist.

urontzi n. cistern, tank, reservoir. n. water container.

urotz n. cold water.

urpe n. under water (space).

urpebide n. submarine route, underwater route.

urpekari n. diver, frogman.

urpeko adj. underwater, subaqueous.

urpekoi adj. subject to flooding, liable to flood.

urpeontzi n. submarine.

urperagarri adj. submergible, sinkable.

urperaketa n. sinking (of a boat, etc.); diving (under water), submerging.

urperakoi adj. submergible.

urperakor adj. subject to flooding, liable to flood.

urperaldi n. immersion, submersion, diving, sinking.

urperatu v.i./v.t. to sink, to submerge, to dive.

urpetu v.t./v.i. to flood. v.i. to dive, to sink, to submerge.

urpintura n. gouache painting.

urputzu n. puddle (of water).
urra n.(bot.) the hazelnut.
urra- Used in compound words. Derived from *urre*, gold.
urradi n. grove of hazel trees.
urradura n. scratching. n. break, crack (in a wall, etc.).
urraezin adj. unscratchable.
urragailu n. jackhammer.
urragarri adj. breakable, fragile. adj. touching, moving.
urrakada n. scratch.
urraketa n. scratching, clawing. n. breakage, rupture.
urrakor adj. easily scratched.
urrantzeko adj. hazel (colored).
urrapen n. scratching, clawing.
urraska-urraska adv. step by step.
urrategi n. grove of hazel trees.
urrats n. step, footstep, track, stride. n. footprint, track.
urratu v.i./v.t. to scratch; to tear, to break; to work (the land), to plow.
urratzaile n. scratcher; breaker.
urratzapen n. scratching, breaking.
urraza n.(bot.) lettuce.
urre n.(min.) gold. n. gold, suit of Basque playing cards.
urreaire adj. gold-like, golden.
urreantz n. glitter, substance resembling gold.
urreantzeko adj. golden, gold-like.
urrebits n. gold plate.
urrebitxi n. gold jewelry.
urrebitxitu v.t. to make gold into jewelry.
urrebotoi n.(bot.) buttercup.
urrediru n. gold coin.
urredun adj. auriferous, gold-bearing.
urregabetu v.i. to ungild, to tarnish.
urregile n. goldsmith.
urregin n. goldsmith.
urregintza n. goldsmithing.
urregorri n.(min.) gold.
urregorrizko adj. golden.
urreketa n. large quantity of gold, gold treasure.
urreketari n. gold prospector.
urreko adj. next, close, nearby, near.
urrelan n. goldsmithing, work of art or jewelry wrought in gold.
urrelanketa n. gold engraving.
urrelili n.(bot.) chrysanthemum.
urrelur n. auriferous earth, gold-bearing earth.
urremakil n. golden sceptre.
urremendi n. mountain of gold.
-urren (gram.) Suffix indicating a period of days, used only with numbers to specify how many.
urrenaldi n. next time.
urreria n. collection of gold jewelry.
urretegi n. jewelry store, goldsmith's shop.
urretsu adj. auriferous, gold-bearing.
urretu v.t. to plate with gold.
urretxa n. hazel tree. n.(bot.) kind of edible mushroom.
urretxindor n.(zool.) nightingale (*Luscinia megarhyncha*).
urretxori n.(zool.) golden oriole.
urretza n. quantity of gold.
urrexafla n. gold plate.
urrezale adj. fond of gold, gold hungry.
urrezalekeria n. lust for gold, gold fever.
urrezko adj. golden.
urreztadura n. gilding.
urreztaldi n. gold filling.
urreztatu v.t. to set (a jewel) in gold; to gold plate.
urreztatzaile n. gilder.
urreztu v.t. to gild, to plate with gold, to set in gold.
urri adj. scarce, rare, little; defective. adj. poor, miserable. adj. slow (in one's work).
urria n. October.
urriagotu v.t./v.i. to decrease, to diminish, to reduce, to dwindle.
urrialdi n. scarcity, lack, penury.
urridura n. diminishing, growing scarce, decreasing, dwindling.
urrigarri adj. reducible, diminishable.
urri izan v.i. to be scarce.
urrikaldu v.i. to be merciful, to be compassionate, to sympathize with, to have pity on, to have mercy on.
urrikalgarri adj. pitiable, pitiful, worthy of compassion.
urrikal izan v.i. to sympathize with, to have pity on, to have mercy on.
urrikalkor adj. merciful, compassionate.
urrikalmendu n. compassion, mercy, pity.
urrikalpen n. mercy, pity.
urrikaltasun n. compassion, mercy, pity.
urrikaltsu adj. merciful, compassionate.
urrikari n. mercy, pity, compassion.
urriketa n. reduction, diminution.
urriki adv. scarcely, barely, in small quantities.
urrilo n.(bot.) mandrake, mandragora.
urrimendu n. reduction, decrease.
urringa n. plane (carpenter's tool).
urringatu v.t. to plane, to smooth with a plane (carpenter's tool).
urripen n. decrease, diminution, reduction.
urritasun n. scarcity, lack, shortage.
urritu v.i. to be scarce, to dwindle.
urritz n.(bot.) hazel tree.
urritzaile adj. decreasing, diminishing, reducing, dwindling.
urritz-perretxiko n.(bot.) kind of edible mushroom (*Russula cyanoxantha*).
urrixa adj. female (animal).
urrizti n. grove of hazel trees.
urrondo n.(bot.) hazel tree.
urruma n. cooing of a dove.
urrumaka n. cooing.

urrumakatu *v.t.* to coo. *v.t.* to sing a lullaby, to comfort a child.

urrun *adj.* far, distant. *adv.* far, far away.

urrunalde *n.* distance, farness.

urrundanik *adv.* from far away.

urrundik *adv.* from far away, far from, from a distance.

urrundu *v.i./v.t.* to move away, to leave, to go away from; to move (something) away.

urruneko *adj.* distant, far (from).

urruneratu *v.i.* to leave, to absent oneself, to go away.

urrunketa *n.* leaving, moving away.

urrunkide *adj.* equidistant.

urrunkidetasun *n.* equidistance.

urrunkor *adj.* divergent, diverging.

urruntasun *n.* distance.

urrunterazi *v.t.* to move (something) away, to take (something) away, to put far away.

urruti *adj.* far, distant. *adv.* far from, far, far away.

urrutiko *adj.* distant, far, far away.

urrutikuskin *n.* binoculars.

urrutimin *n.* nostalgia, homesickness.

urrutiraketa *n.* moving away, distancing oneself from.

urrutiratu *v.i.* to go away from, to distance oneself from.

urrutizkin *n.(neol.)* telephone, phone.

urtabe *n.* good year, year of abundance, profitable year.

urtar *adj.* aqueous, water, fond of water.

urtarazi *v.t.* to melt, to make (something) melt.

urtarazle *adj.* liquefying, melting.

urtaro *n.* season of the year.

urtarrila *n.* January.

urtasun *n.* wateriness, liquidity, aqueousness.

urtatu *v.t./v.i.* to soak, to steep.

urtatzaile *n./adj.* soaker; soaking.

urte *n.* year.

urtealdi *n.* passage of a year, a year's time.

urteazken *n.* end of the year.

urteberri *n.* New Year.

urtebete *n.* full year, year. *n.* anniversary.

urtebetegun *n.* birthday.

urtebeteko *adj.* one-year-old, of one year.

urtebetetze *n.* birthday, anniversary.

urtebira *n.* rotation, yearly rotation around the sun.

urteburu *n.* anniversary.

urtediru *n.* pension, yearly retirement benefit.

urtedun *adj.* yearling, one-year-old.

urtegi *n.* tank of water, cistern.

urtegiro *n.* season of the year.

urtegun *n.* birthday, birth date.

urteka *adv.* yearly, every year, annually.

urtekari *n.* annual publication.

urtekide *adj.* contemporary, born in the same year.

urteko *adj.* annual, yearly. *n.* annual pension, annuity.

urtekotasun *n.* annuity; quality of being annual.

urtelaurden *n.* trimester, one fourth of a year.

urtelaurdeneko *adj.* trimestral.

urtelaurdenka *adv.* trimestrally.

urtemeza *n.* anniversary mass, yearly funeral mass.

urtemin *n.(med.)* tinea, scalp ringworm.

urtemuga *n.* anniversary.

urteordain *n.* annual rent, annual payment.

urterdi *n.* semester.

urterdiko *adj.* semestral.

urtero *adv.* yearly, every year, annually.

urteroko *adj.* yearly.

urterokotasun *n.* annualness.

urtesari *n.* annual rent, annual payment, annuity.

urtesasoin *n.* season of the year.

urtetsu *adj.* very old, long-lived.

urtetu *v.i.* to get old, to grow older.

urteurren *n.* anniversary.

urtezahar *n.* end of the year, old year, New Year's Eve.

urtezin *adj.* impossible to melt, not meltable; indissoluble.

urtezintasun *n.* quality of not being meltable.

urtoki *n.* water place. *n.* swamp, marsh.

urtsu *adj.* watery, juicy.

urtsutasun *n.* wateriness, juiciness.

urtsutu *v.t.* to water down, to mix water with other liquids.

urtu *v.i./v.t.* to melt. *v.i.(fig.)* to disappear. *v.t.* to smelt (metals).

urtubera *adj.* liquefying, melting, smelting.

urtuezin *adj.* insoluble, unmeltable.

urtuezintasun *n.* insolubility, quality of not being meltable.

urtugaitz *adj.* insoluble, unmeltable.

urtugarri *adj.* meltable, liquefiable, dissolvable, smeltable.

urtume *n.* one-year-old (child or animal), yearling.

urtxakur *n.(zool.)* water spaniel, water dog.

urtxintxa *n.(zool.)* squirrel. *(Sciurus vulgaris)*

urtxori *n.(zool.)* white wagtail.

urtza *n.* fen, bog, marsh.

urtzagintza *n.* smelting, founding; casting.

urtzaile *n.* foundryman, smelter; caster.

urtzale *adj.* fond of water.

usa- Used in compound words. Derived from *uso*, dove.

usadio *n.* custom, tradition.

usaia n. usage.
usaiako adj. habitual, usual, ordinary, customary.
usaian adv. usually.
usaiatu v.i. to be used to, to get used to, to become accustomed to.
usaimen n. sense of smell.
usain n. smell, odor, aroma. n. sense of smell. n.(fig.) suspicion, investigation.
usaindu v.t. to smell, to sniff (at). v.t.(fig.) to suspect, to guess, to surmise. v.t. to stink, to smell bad (because of putrefaction).
usaindun adj. smelly, aromatic.
usain egin v.t. to smell. v.t.(fig.) to guess, to suspect.
usainemaile adj. aromatic, fragrant, odorous.
usaingabe(ko) adj. odorless.
usaingarri adj. aromatic, fragrant, odorous. n. aroma, perfume.
usaingozo n. perfume, aroma.
usaingozodun adj. aromatic, perfumed.
usain hartu v.t. to smell. v.t.(fig.) to guess right, to suspect.
usainka adv. smelling, sniffing. adj.(fig.) verifying, guessing, suspecting.
usainkari n. smeller, sniffer.
usainkatu v.t. to smell, to sniff (at).
usainketa n. smelling.
usaintsu adj. aromatic.
usainztatu v.t. to perfume, to scent.
usakaka n. dove droppings, pigeon droppings.
usakide adj. columbine, dovelike.
usakume n.(dim.) little dove, pigeon.
usantza n. custom, habit.
usapal n.(zool.) turtledove. (Streptopelia turtur)
usapalkume n. young turtledove.
usapaltegi n. dovecote, pigeon house.
usar n.(zool.) male dove.
usario n. custom, tradition.
usatar adj./n. native of the United States of America.
usategi n. dovecote, pigeon coop.
usatortola n.(zool.) turtledove.
usazain n. dove keeper, pigeon trainer or breeder.
usazale adj. fond of doves, fond of pigeons.
usma n. sense of smell. n. guess, conjecture.
usmakari adj. sniffing, smelling; tracking (dogs).
usmatu v.t. to sniff, to smell, to catch a scent. v.t. to guess, to suspect, to surmise.
usmatzaile n. sniffer, smeller; tracker (by scent). adj. sniffing, smelling, tracking (by scent).
usmo n. guess, conjecture. n. suspicion.
usna n. sense of smell.

usnadura n. smelling, olfaction.
usnagarri adj. guessable, surmisable.
usnakari adj. sniffing, smelling, having a good sense of smell. adj.(fig.) busybody, interfering, meddlesome.
usnaketa n. smelling. n. interfering, interference, meddling, snooping.
usnamen n. sense of smell.
usnan adv. sniffing, smelling (animals).
usnari n. sniffer, smeller. adj. sniffing, smelling; tracking (dogs).
usnatu v.t. to sniff (at), to smell. v.t. to suspect, to surmise, to guess. v.t.(fig.) to interfere, to meddle, to snoop, to butt in.
usnatzaile n. sniffer, smeller; tracker (by scent). adj. sniffing, smelling; tracking (by scent). adj.(fig.) interfering, meddling.
uso n.(zool.) dove.
usokari n. dove hunter.
usopasa n. migration of doves.
usta n. whip, scourge, lash.
uste n. opinion, belief, idea; plan. n. trust, confidence, faith. n. hope.
ustebereko adj. unanimous, of the same opinion.
ustebide n. cause for trust, reason for confidence.
ustekabe n. surprise, accident. adj. unexpected, unforeseen, accidental. adv. accidentally, without thinking, unexpectedly.
ustekabean adv. unexpectedly, fortuitously, accidentally, inadvertently.
ustekabeko adj. unexpected, unforeseen, fortuitous.
ustekaberik adv. by surprise, unexpectedly, accidentally.
ustekabetu v.i. to surprise, to take by surprise, to happen unexpectedly.
ustekabez adv. by surprise, unexpectedly, accidentally.
ustekabezia n. inadvertence, quality of being unforeseen, unexpectedness.
ustekabezko adj. unforeseen, unexpected, fortuitous.
ustekeria n. false belief, prejudice.
usteko adj. supposed, reputed.
ustel adj. rotten, spoiled; corrupted; gangrenous. adj.(fig.) false, traitorous.
ustelarazi v.t. to make (something) rot, to cause (something) to spoil.
ustelarazle adj. spoiling, corruptive, rotting.
ustelbera adj. spoilable, perishable, corruptible.
usteldegi n. compost heap; garbage dump.
usteldu v.i./v.t. to rot, to spoil; to decompose, to putrify.
usteldura n. rotting, spoiling; decomposing.
ustelerraz adj. perishable, spoilable.
ustelezin adj. unspoilable, not

corruptible.

ustelgabe *adj.* incorrupt, not rotten, not spoiled.

ustelgabetasun *n.* unspoilableness, incorruptibility.

ustelgaitz *adj.* difficult to spoil, not perishable.

ustelgaiztasun *n.* corruptibleness, rottenness, quality of being spoilable.

ustelgarri *adj.* spoilable, perishable, corruptible.

ustelgarritasun *n.* corruptibility, rottenness, quality of being spoilable, perishableness.

ustelkeria *n.* moral corruption.

ustelketa *n.* putrefaction, rot, corruption.

ustelki *adv.* rottenly, spoiledly. *n.* manure, fertilizer.

ustelkor *adj.* putrefactive, putrescent, capable of decomposing, corruptible.

ustelkortasun *n.* corruptibility.

usteltasun *n.* rottenness.

usteltzaile *adj.* corrupting.

ustelune *n.* rotten spot.

usteoneko *adj.* trusted.

usteragikor *adj.* persuasive.

usteragile *adj.* persuasive. *n.* persuader.

ustetsu *adj.* ingenious, creative, having many good ideas.

uste ukan *v.t.* to think, to believe, to suppose. *v.t.* to trust, to have faith in (somebody); to hope.

ustez *adv.* in one's opinion.

ustezin *adj.* unthinkable.

ustezko *adj.* imaginary, supposed, presumed.

usu *adv.* often, frequently.

usutasun *n.* frequency, habitualness.

usutu *v.i./v.t.* to become frequent; to frequent, to increase the frequency of.

utikan *int.* go away! get out!

utopia *n.* utopia.

utopiko *adj.* utopian.

utopizale *adj.* utopianist.

utzarazi *v.t.* to make (someone) abandon or leave (something).

utzi *v.t.* to abandon, to leave. *v.t.* to permit, to let, to allow, to authorize. *v.t.* to omit, to leave out.

utziera *n.* abandon, negligence; way of leaving.

utziezin(ezko) *adj.* unavoidable.

utzikeria *n.* negligence, abandon, omission.

utziketa *n.* omission.

utzitasun *n.* abandonment, negligence.

ux *int.* shoo!

uxada *n.* provoking (animals).

uxagarri *adj.* chaseable, scatterable, shooable.

uxaketa *n.* shooing away; beating for game.

uxatu *v.t.* to shoo away; to beat for game.

uxatzaile *n./adj.* one who shoos (something) away; one who beats for game.

uzkali *v.i./v.t.* to overturn, to knock over. *v.t.* to conquer, to overthrow (a government), to vanquish.

uzkarri *adj.* permissible, allowable, authorizable. *adj.* abandonable, leavable.

uzker *n.* fart, gas, wind, flatulence.

uzkerti *adj.* flatulent, gassy, farting a lot.

uzketa *n.* abandon, abandonment. *n.* ommission.

uzki *n.(anat.)* anus.

uzkiko *adj.* anal.

uzkin *n.* rest, leftovers, remains, residue.

uzkorno *n.(anat.)* coccyx.

uzkur *adj.* shriveled, shrunken; timid, shy, retiring, frightened, misanthropic.

uzkurdura *n.* contracting, curling, contraction, retiring, pulling back.

uzkurgarri *adj.* contracting, shrinking.

uzkurkeria *n.* cowardice, reticence, pusilanimity.

uzkurki *adv.* timidly, retiringly.

uzkurtasun *n.* timidness, reserve.

uzkurtu *v.i.* to curl up, to shrink, to shrivel. *v.i.* to become frightened, to be timid, to be shy.

uzle *adj.* retiring, abstinent, shy, withdrawn.

uzta *n.* harvest.

uztabelar *n.* harvesting grass, harvesting hay.

uztabilgailu *n.* harvester, harvesting machine.

uztabilketa *n.* gathering of the harvest, harvesting.

uztabiltzaile *n.* harvester (person).

uztai *n.* rim (of a barrel or basket); band, hoop, ring (holding barrel staves in place); yoke (for cattle). *n.* arch. *n.* rainbow.

uztaigailu *n.* clamp, band, clasp, brace.

uztaigile *n.* hoopmaker, cooper.

uztaila *n.* July.

uztaile *adj.* retiring, withdrawn, timid, shy, abstinent.

uztaitu *v.t.* to bend, to curve, to arc. *v.t.* to fasten with a band or hoop.

uztamakina *n.* harvester (machine).

uztameta *n.* pile of something harvested.

uztar *n.* yoke.

uztardura *n.* yoking (oxen together).

uztargarri *adj.* dominatable, subjugable, conquerable.

uztargile *n.* yoke maker.

uztargin *n.* yoke maker.

uztarkide *n.* either of two oxen yoked to each other.

uztaro *n.* harvest season.

uztarpe *n.* slavery, captivity.

uztarpeko *n.* slave, captive, prisoner.

uztarpekotasun *n.* slavery, captivity.

uztarpetu *v.t.* to yoke. *v.t.(fig.)* to subjugate, to enslave.

uztarri *n.* yoke. *n.* pair of oxen. *n.(fig.)* dictatorship, domination.

uztartu *v.t.* to yoke.

uztasun *n.* abandonment, negligence, carelessness.

uztatu *v.t.* to harvest.

uztatzaile *n.* harvester.

uzte *n.* act of leaving (out), omission.

X

x Letter of the Basque alphabet. Pronounced like English *sh*. Often indicates diminutive.

xabal *adj.* somewhat wide, a little wide.

xabalo *n.(zool.)* plaice, European flounder.

xaboi *n.* soap.

xaboi(a) eman *v.t.(colloq.)* to flatter, to toady, to soft soap (someone).

xaboialdi *n.* soaping, lathering (up).

xaboidun *adj.* soapy.

xaboidura *n.* soaping.

xaboigarri *adj.* soapable, latherable.

xaboigile *n.* soap maker.

xaboiketa *n.* soaping up, lathering up.

xaboiontzi *n.* soap dish, soapbox.

xaboitsu *adj.* soapy, full of soap.

xaboitu *v.t.* to soap, to lather up, to soap up (something).

xabonadura *n.* laundry.

xafarraldi *n.* rinsing, act of rinsing out.

xafarratu *v.t.* to rinse, to rinse out.

xafla *n.* small slice. *n.* iron slab, iron shingle, iron sheeting, iron plate.

xafladura *n.* lamination, iron plating.

xaflagarri *adj.* laminable.

xaflagile *n.* laminator.

xaflaketa *n.* lamination, iron plating.

xaflalan *n.* lamination, iron plating (work).

xaflatu *v.t.* to laminate, to cover with iron plate.

xafradura *n.* rubbing, scrubbing.

xafraldi *n.* rubbing, scrubbing.

xafratu *v.t.* to rub, to scrub.

xagu *n.(zool.)* small mouse.

xaguxahar *n.(zool.)* small bat.

xahar *adj.* little and old.

xahu *adj.* clean.

xahudura *n.* cleaning.

xahuketa *n.* cleaning.

xahuki *adv.* cleanly.

xahupen *n.* destruction, loss.

xahutasun *n.* cleanliness, cleanness.

xahutegi *n.* washing place.

xahutu *v.t.* to clean, to purify. *v.t.* to spend lavishly, to squander; to destroy.

xahutzaile *n./adj.* squanderer, waster; squandering, wasteful. *n./adj.* cleaner; cleaning.

xake *n.* chess.

xakejoko *n.* game of chess, chess match.

xakelari *n.* chess player, chess master.

xaketaula *n.* chess board.

xalo *adj.* candid, open, affable, simple, honest, frank.

xalokeria *n.* naivety, ingenuousness.

xaloki *adv.* candidly, openly, frankly, honestly.

xalotasun *n.* candor, simplicity, openness, frankness, honesty.

xamar *adv.* quite, rather, pretty.

xamur *adj.* tender, soft.

xamurtasun *n.* tenderness, charm.

xantiobide *n.* Milky Way.

xapi *int.* shoo! Used only for cats.

xarma *n.* charm, enchantment.

xarmadura *n.* enchantment, fascination.

xarmagarri *adj.* charming, enchanting, fascinating.

xarmagarritasun *n.* quality of being charming, charm.

xarmakeria *n.* flirting.

xarmaketa *n.* enchantment, fascination.

xarmakor *adj.* seductive, charming, fascinating.

xarmaldi *n.* enchantment, fascination, captivation, enthrallment.

xarmanki *adv.* charmingly; attractively.

xarmant *adj.* charming, pleasing.

xarmantasun *n.* charm, enchantment.

xarmapetu *v.t.* to seduce, to fascinate (someone) with one's charm.

xarmarazi *v.t.* to seduce, to fascinate (someone) with one's charm.

xarmatu *v.t.* to seduce, to enchant, to fascinate.

xarmatzaile *adj.* seductive, fascinating.

xarmaz *adv.* charmingly; attractively.

xaxa *n.* siccing (a dog on someone); encouraging a hunting dog to follow its prey. *n.* boundary line, foot fault marker (on a pelota court).

xaxaketa *n.* siccing (dogs on someone), act of siccing a dog (on someone).

xaxalari *n.* one who sics a dog on (someone).

xaxatu *v.t.* to sic (dogs on someone).

-xe *(gram.)* Suffix used with demonstrative pronouns and adverbs of location to add emphasis or to indicate immediacy. **Hauxe.** This one (and no other one).

xedaketa *n.* delimitation, marking boundaries.

xedatsu *adj.* full of good (or bad) intentions.

xedatu *v.t.* to mark, to delimit, to delineate. *v.t.* to decide, to dispose, to make a decision.

xede *n.* goal, aim, objective, purpose.

n. limit, border, boundary.

xederatu *v.t.* to reach one's goal, to realize one's goal.

xeha- Used in compound words. Derived from *xehe*, little.

xehadura *n.* smallness, minuteness.

xehakatu *v.t.* to cut into pieces, to chop up, to shred, to break into pieces, to crumble into pieces.

xehakin *n.* wood chip.

xehakor *adj.* choppable.

xehatu *v.t.* to chop up, to break into pieces, to crumble into pieces, to shred.

xehe *adj.* small, minute, diminutive, little. *adj.* simple, common.

xehean *adv.* in small quantities, in small amounts, retail.

xehegailu *n.* grinding machine, chopping machine, shredding machine.

xehegarri *adj.* grindable, choppable.

xeheka *adv.* at retail.

xehekari *n.* retailer, retail merchant.

xehekatu *v.t.* to chop, to grind, to pulverize. *v.t.* to get change, to make change, to exchange a bill for coins.

xehekeria *n.* trifle, triviality, pettiness.

xeheketa *n.* grinding, chopping.

xeheki *adv.* minutely, in great detail, exactly, precisely.

xeherosketa *n.* buying at retail prices.

xehesalketa *n.* selling at retail prices.

xehesaltzaile *n.* retailer, retail merchant.

xehetasun *n.* detail, detailedness, preciseness, exactness.

xeheteria *n.* mixture of things without value, collection of trinkets or trifles.

xehetzaile *n.* one who grinds, one who chops.

xehezale *adj.* punctilious, nit-picking, fond of details, meticulous.

xehezaletasun *n.* meticulousness.

xelebre *adj.* funny.

xelebrekeria *n.* funny story, joke, anecdote.

xelebrekiro *adv.* funny.

xentimo *n.(econ.)* one hundredth of a *peseta*; cent, penny.

xera *n.* affection; caress.

xeragarri *adj.* caressing, affectionate.

xera(k) egin *v.t.* to caress.

xeratsu *adj.* affectionate, kind.

xeratu *v.t.* to caress.

xeraz *adv.* affectionately.

xerra *n.* small slice.

xerraka *adv.* in small pieces.

xerrakatu *v.t.* to cut in small slices.

ximino *n.(zool.)* small monkey.

ximinokeria *n.* crazy action, foolishness, monkey face, funny face.

xinaurri *n.* ant.

xingar *n.* ham.

xingil *n.(bot.)* carob.

xingilondo *n.(bot.)* carob tree.

xingola *n.* ribbon.

xingolagile *n.* ribbon maker.

xingolakintza *n.* job of ribbon making.

xingolatu *v.t.* to beribbon, to adorn with ribbons, to tie with ribbons.

xingolaztatu *v.t.* to adorn with ribbons.

xingoleria *n.* bunch of ribbons, collection of ribbons.

xinple *adj.* ordinary, common. *adj.* simple, naïve.

xirafa *n.(zool.)* giraffe.

xiribista *n.(elec.)* plug.

xiribistatu *v.t.* to plug in (to an electric outlet).

xiringa *n.* syringe.

xiringada *n.* injection, shot.

xiringarri *adj.* injectable.

xiringatu *v.t.* to inject.

xirrika *n.* small pulley.

xirrintola *n.* small pulley.

xirula *n.(mus.)* small Basque end-blown flute played in the province of Zuberoa.

xirulari *n.* flautist, flute player.

xistera *n.* basket used in jai alai.

xisteragile *n.* one who makes baskets used in jai alai.

xixkaketa *n.* stealing, filching, lifting, swiping.

xixkari *n.* filcher, swiper, petty thief.

xixkatu *v.t.* to filch, to swipe, to steal, to lift.

xixketa *n.* petty theft, filching, swiping, swindle.

-xka *(gram.)* diminutive suffix. **Bidexka.**

xo *int.* sh! shush! quiet!

xora- Used in compound words. Derived from *xoro*, enchantment, fascination.

xori *n.* bird.

xorta *n.* drop. *n.(dim.)* bunch, bouquet.

xortaka *adv.* drop by drop.

xortakatu *v.t.* to drip, to sprinkle, drop by drop.

xortatto *n.(dim.)* tiny drop.

xortatu *v.t.* to dispense drop by drop, to cause (something) to drip.

xoxo *n.(zool.)* blackbird. *adj.* idiotic, foolish.

xuhurkeria *n.* stinginess, miserliness, niggardliness.

xuhurki *adv.* stingily, miserly.

xuhurtasun *n.* economic scarcity; miserliness, stinginess.

xuhurtu *v.i.* to become scarce, to be stingy, to be miserly, to be avaricious.

xukabide *n.* drainage ditch.

xukadera *n.* towel. *n.* place for drying things (clothesline, etc.).

xukagailu *n.* drainer, dryer, instrument for removing water.

xukaketa *n.* draining, drying, removing water.

xukaldi *n.* draining, drying, removing water.

xukaleku *n.* place for drying things

(drainboard, dry dock, etc.).
xukapaper *n.* blotting paper.
xukategi *n.* place for drying things (drainboard, dry dock, etc.).
xukatu *v.t.* to drain, to dry, to dry (something) off, to remove water from, to mop up, to sop up.
xukatzaile *n.* one who drains or dries (something).
xularme *n.(anat.)* pore.
xularmetsu *adj.* porous.
xume *adj.* short, small (in stature). *adj.* common, simple, humble.
xumedura *n.* smallness, petiteness. *n.* humility.
xumetasun *n.* smallness. *n.* humbleness; simplicity.
xumetu *v.i.* to humble oneself.
xurgagarri *adj.* suckable, absorbable.
xurgakari *adj.* absorbent.
xurgaketa *n.* suction, absorption.
xurgapaper *n.* blotter, blotting paper.
xurgapen *n.* suction, absorption.
xurgari *n.* sucker, one who sucks.
xurgatu *v.t.* to suck.
xurgatzaile *n.* sucker, one who sucks, gulper.
xurrut *n.* sip, small swallow, gulp.
xurrutada *n.* small swallow, sip, gulp.
xuxurla *n.* whisper, whispering.
xuxurlatu *v.t.* to whisper.

Z

z Letter of the Basque alphabet.
-z *(gram.)* Adverbial suffix indicating manner, way, by means of; according to. **Zaldiz heldu zen.** He arrived by horse. *(gram.)* Verbal suffix used to make the plural. **Dago. Dagoz.** He is. They are.
zabal *adj.* wide, broad. *adj./adv.* open. *adj.* sincere, frank, honest; open. *adj.* generous. *adv.* openly, clearly.
zabalagotu *v.t.* to widen, to extend, to dilate, to open wider.
zabalaldi *n.* opening. *n.* extension, extending.
zabalarazi *v.t.* to make (something) wider.
zabalarazle *n.* one who widens, one who extends.
zabaldi *n.* plain, wide place.
zabaldu *v.t.* to widen, to broaden, to expand, to enlarge. *v.t.* to spread, to scatter, to spread out. *v.t./v.i.* to announce, to disperse, to spread (news). *v.t.* to inaugurate, to open (a house, building, etc.). *v.t.* to open up (emotionally), to declare (one's feelings).
zabaldura *n.* widening, broadening, extension; opening.
zabalera *n.* width, breadth, scope, extent. *adv.* extensively, widely.
zabalerazi *v.t.* to make (someone) open (something). *v.t.* to make (someone) extend or expand

(something), to make (someone) widen (something). *v.t.* to divulge, to spread (the news, etc.).
zabalezin *adj.* inextendible; unwidenable; unopenable.
zabalgailu *n.* transmitter; machine for scattering or spreading (something).
zabalgarri *adj.* extendible, widenable, expandable. *adj.* spreadable, divulgeable.
zabalgo *n.* width, wideness, broadness.
zabalgune *n.* space, wide spot.
zabalik *adv./adj.* open.
zabalketa *n.* opening. *n.* widening, broadening, extending.
zabalki *adv.* spaciously, widely; openly, frankly, clearly.
zabalkiro *adv.* widely, spaciously; openly, frankly.
zabalkor *adj.* diffusive, expansive, expandable, spreadable.
zabalkortasun *n.* expansiveness, diffusiveness, extendedness, quality of being scattered.
zabalkote *adj.* very broad.
zabalkunde *n.* diffusion, dispersion, distribution, divulgation. *n.* opening, inauguration.
zabalkuntza *n.* increase, expansion, enlargement, dilation, widening.
zabalote *adj.* very broad.
zabalpen *n.* widening, opening, dilation, enlargement, expansion, spread.
zabaltasun *n.* wideness, broadness, width, breadth. *n.* openness. *n.* sincerity, frankness, honesty. *n.* generousness, generosity.
zabaltegi *n.* drying place, place where things are hung to dry.
zabaltoki *n.* plain, wide open space.
zabaltsu *adj.* wide, spacious.
zabaltzaile *n.* opener; widener; extender, expander. *adj.* opening; widening; extending, expanding. *n.* spreader of news, town crier.
zabalune *n.* flat land, wide open space.
zabar *adj.* lazy, slow. *adj.* careless, abandoned, messy. *adj.* libertine, immoral, corrupt, dishonest. *n.* scoria, slag, scum, dross (of molten metal); leftovers. Usually used in plural.
zabardura *n.* abandon.
zabarkeria *n.* negligence, abandon, omission, neglect.
zabarki *adv.* negligently, carelessly, thoughtlessly.
zabarkiro *adv.* negligently, carelessly, thoughtlessly.
zabarrarazi *v.t.* to corrupt (someone).
zabartasun *n.* indolence, carelessness, negligence.
zabartu *v.i.* to become lazy, to become negligent, to become careless. *v.i.* to

become corrupted, to become perverted.

zabor *n.* garbage, scum, dregs, trash, rubbish. *n.* rubble.

zaborbiltzaile *n.* garbage man, garbage collector.

zaborgabetu *v.t.* to clear of rubble; to remove rubbish from.

zaborkenketa *n.* removing rubbish, collecting trash, picking up garbage, clearing away rubble.

zaborketa *n.* dumping garbage, dumping trash.

zaborreria *n.* rubbish, garbage; rubble.

zaborreztatu *v.t.* to fill with rubble.

zaborrontzi *n.* garbage can, dumpster.

zabortegi *n.* garbage dump, garbage fill.

zabortsu *adj.* rubbishy, rubbly, filled with garbage.

zabu *n.* staggering, teetering. *n.* swing (child's play equipment).

zabu egin *v.t.* to stagger, to teeter, to weave back and forth. *v.t.(fig.)* to doubt, to vacillate.

zabuka *adv.* staggering, teetering, weaving back and forth. *adv.* swinging.

zabukada *n.* staggering, teetering, weaving back and forth.

zabukatu *v.i.* to teeter, to totter, to balance, to stagger; to oscillate, to swing.

zabun *n.* staggering, tottering, reeling.

zabu-zabuka *adv.* staggering, teetering, weaving back and forth.

zafarda *n.* bruise, contusion.

zafardatu *v.i.* to bruise, to bump (oneself).

zafiro *n.* sapphire.

zafla *n.* slice. *n.*

zaflada *n.* slap, spanking, smack, blow with the open hand.

zafladako *n.* slap, spanking.

zaflaka *adv.* slapping, spanking, hitting.

zaflakatu *v.t.* to hit, to slap, to spank.

zaflaketa *n.* cutting (metal) into plates, slicing.

zaflaldi *n.* spanking, thrashing, beating, drubbing.

zaflatu *v.t.* to hit, to beat, to slap, to spank.

zafraldi *n.* beating, thrashing, drubbing (people, trees, etc.).

zafrarazi *v.t.* to make (someone) hit (someone else).

zafratu *v.t.* to beat, to thrash, to drub, to spank, to slap.

zafratzaile *n.* spanker, hitter, beater.

zahagi *n.* wineskin, large bottle or container made of leather.

zahagingintza *n.* manufacture of wineskins.

zahagikada *n.* contents of a wineskin, wineskinful.

zahar *adj.* old, aged. *n.* old person, old man, senior citizen.

zaharberritu *v.t./v.i.* to renovate, to remodel, to modernize.

zaharberritzaile *n.* remodeler, renovator, modernizer.

zaharberrizte *n.* renovation, modernization, remodeling.

zaharbiltzaile *n.* antique collector.

zahardura *n.* aging, growing old.

zahargarri *adj.* aging, producing age.

zahar-gazteak *n.(pl.)* young and old people.

zaharkeria *n.* behavior of the old, comportment of elderly people.

zaharketa *n.* aging, becoming senile.

zaharki *adv.* like an old person. *n.* antique, old thing.

zaharkin *n.* old thing, anything old.

zaharkindegi *n.* attic, storage room, place where old things are kept.

zaharkitasun *n.* antiquity, old age; senility.

zaharkitu *v.i.* to grow old, to get old, to age.

zaharkoi *adj.* long-lived.

zaharkote *adj.* ancient, decrepit, old. *adj.* young but having the mannerisms of the elderly.

zaharmin *n.* senility, feebleness of old age. *n.* sourness (of wine).

zaharmindu *v.i.* to spoil, to sour (wine).

zaharmindura *n.* rancidness, sourness (wine).

zaharreri *n.* senility, illness of old age, decrepitude.

zaharreria *n.* group of old people.

zaharretxe *n.* old folk's home.

zaharritz *n.* proverb, refrain.

zaharsari *n.* retirement pension.

zaharskila *adj.* very old.

zaharsendagile *n.* physician specializing in geriatrics.

zaharsendagintza *n.* geriatrics.

zahartasun *n.* old age; antiquity.

zahartegi *n.* old folk's home. *n.* place where old things are stored.

zahartu *v.i./v.t.* to grow old, to get old, to age.

zahartza *n.* old age.

zahartzaile *adj.* aging, producing age.

zahartzale *n.* antique dealer. *adj.* fond of old things.

zahartzapen *n.* aging, growing old.

zahartzaro *n.* old age.

zahartzaroko *adj.* pertaining to old age.

zahato *n.* bota bag, small wineskin.

zahatogile *n.* maker of bota bags.

zahatokada *n.* contents of a bota bag (usually wine).

zahi *n.* bran.

zahitsu *adj.* branny, full of bran.

zahitu *v.i.* to ripen excessively, to become overly ripe. *v.t.* to keep, to protect.

zail *adj.* hard, tough, difficult. *adj.* resistant, tenacious, persistent.

zaildu v.i./v.t. to be difficult; to make (something) difficult. v.i. to be obstinate, to be persistent.

zaildura n. tenacity, persistence.

zailki adv. difficultly. adv. persistently, tenaciously.

zailtasun n. difficulty. n. tenacity, persistence.

zailtsu adj. difficult, hard, laborious.

zain n.(anat.) vein, artery. n.(anat.) tendon. n. keeper, custodian. adv. waiting, expecting. n.(anat.) nerve.

-zain (gram.) Suffix which means person who takes care of (something). **Diruzain.** Treasurer.

zainaldi n. waiting period.

zainbarneko adj. intravenous.

zainbelar n.(bot.) plantain.

zainbide n. means of keeping, way of taking care of.

zainbihurketa n. sprain, muscle pull.

zaindari n. caretaker, keeper, patron (saint), protector. adj. guardian, protecting.

zaindarikide n. co-guardian.

zaindaritza n. guardianship, patronage, protection.

zaindegi n. storehouse, warehouse.

zaindu v.t. to keep, to take care of, to look after, to protect, to watch.

zainebaketa n. cutting a vein.

zainebaki n. cut or incision in a vein; bloodletting.

zain egon v.i. to wait, to be waiting (for).

zaineri n.(med.) phlebitis.

zainetako adj. vein, arterial, pertaining to the vein.

zainetxola n. sentry box, porter's lodge.

zaingabe(ko) adj. weak, listless.

zaingabetu v.i. to be listless, to be weak.

zaingarri adj. storable, keepable, preservable.

zaingela n. sentry box, porter's lodge.

zaingo n. sentry's job, porter's job, guardian's job, protector's job.

-zaingo (gram.) Suffix used to indicate job, office of. **Atezaingo.** Doorman's job.

zaingorri n.(anat.) artery. n.(bot.) dodder.

zaingorriko adj. arterial.

zaingorritxo n.(dim.) arteriole, small artery.

zainkor adj. protective, preservative.

zainpeko adj. protected, protective, kept, guarded, tutelar. adj. intravenous.

zainpen n. vigilance, guardianship, protection.

zainpetu v.t. to protect, to patronize, to guard.

zainsormindura n.(med.) arteriosclerosis, hardening of the arteries.

zaintiraketa n. twist, sprain.

zaintiratu n. twist, sprain.

zaintsu adj. veinous, veiny, full of veins. adj. full of tendons. adj. full of nerves. adj. full of rootlets.

zaintxuri n.(anat.) tendon.

zaintza n. protection, care, vigilance, custody.

-zaintza (gram.) Suffix indicating job, office of. **Atezaintza.** Doorman's job.

zaintzaile n./adj. keeper, guardian, protector, custodian.

zainzuri n.(anat.) tendon. n.(bot.) asparagus.

zakar adj. rough, coarse, harsh. n.(med.) pustule, scab, crust.

zakardura n. crudeness, coarseness, roughness. n. pustule, scab, crust.

zakarkeria n. roughness, crudeness, coarseness, rough language. n. garbage, trash, filth.

zakarki adv. roughly, crudely, brusquely, brutally.

zakarraldi n. brusqueness, anger, roughness, crudeness.

zakarreria n. trash, garbage, filth, yard clippings.

zakarrodi n. sewer drain.

zakarrontzi n. trash receptacle, garbage can. adj.(fig.) crude (person), pig, trash.

zakarrote adj. gross, crude, rough, disagreeable, rude, sharp, gruff, surly.

zakartasun n. gruffness, rudeness, surliness, crudeness, roughness.

zakartegi n. dump, rubble heap.

zakartoki n. dump, rubble heap.

zakartsu adj. trashy, covered with garbage. adj. scabby, crusty.

zakartu v.i. to be rough, to become rude, to become gruff. v.i. to be covered with pustules.

zakatz n. gill, branchia.

zakatzeko adj. branchial, pertaining to gills.

zakil n.(anat.) penis. adj.(colloq.) foolish, idiotic.

zakilantzeko adj. phallic.

zakilmoko n. end of the penis, head of the penis.

zaku n. sack. n.(fig.) belly, stomach.

zakubetekada n. act of filling the stomach, stuffing oneself. (lit.) sackful.

zakugile n. sack maker.

zakugintza n. sack making.

zakukada n. bagful, sackful.

zakur n. dog, big dog. adj.(fig.) despicable, base, vile.

zakurapen n. sacking, pillaging. n. act of putting in a sack, bagging.

zakuratu v.t. to sack, to pillage, to plunder. v.t. to put in a sack, to bag.

zakuratzaile n. one who sacks and pillages.

zakurgorotz n. dog feces.

zakurkeria n. vile act, treachery, mischief.

zakurketa n. pack of dogs.

zakurki adv. vilely, despicably, basely, treacherously.

zakurkide adj. canine, dog-like.

zakurkume n.(dim.) puppy.

zakurlokarri n. dog leash.

zakurraire adj. dog-like.

zakurrantzeko adj. dog-like.

zakurrar n.(zool.) male dog.

zakurreme n.(zool.) bitch, female dog.

zakurretxola n. dog house, kennel.

zakurrezko adj. canine, of or pertaining to dogs.

zakurreztul n.(med.) harsh cough, barking cough.

zakurtalde n. pack of dogs.

zakurtegi n. dog house, kennel.

zakurteria n. pack of dogs.

zakurtoki n. dog house, kennel.

zakurtu v.i. to become vile, to turn treacherous.

zakurtzar n.(augm.) large dog.

zakurzain n. dog breeder, kennel keeper.

zakurzale adj. dog-loving, fond of dogs.

zakuteria n. pile of sacks or bags.

zakuto n.(dim.) little sack.

zakutzar n.(augm.) large sack or bag.

zalantza n. uncertainty, doubt.

zalantzadun adj. vacillating, dubious, indecisive, doubtful.

zalantzaezin adj. unquestionable, indubitable, certain.

zalantzagabeko adj. unquestionable, indubitable, certain.

zalantzagarri adj. doubtful, uncertain, questionable, ambiguous.

zalantzagarritasun n. ambiguity, doubtfulness, uncertainty.

zalantzako adj. irresolute, perplexed, uncertain, doubtful.

zalantzakor adj. doubting, uncertain.

zalantzan adv. doubtfully, dubiously.

zalantzan egon v.i. to be in doubt, to be doubtful, to be uncertain, to be insecure.

zalantzarazi v.t. to cause doubt. v.t. to swing back and forth.

zalantzari adj. rocking, swinging, moving to and fro.

zalantzatsu adj. doubtful, indecisive.

zalantzatu v.i. to doubt, to be in doubt. v.t./v.i. to rock, to swing back and forth.

zalantzaz adv. doubtfully, dubiously.

zalantzako adj. uncertain, doubtful, dubious.

zalaparta n. mess, ruckus, noise, confusion, disturbance.

zalapartada n. mess, ruckus, confusion, noise, fuss.

zalaparta egin v.t. to cause a ruckus, to raise a ruckus, to cause confusion.

zalapartaka adv. messily, disorderly, in a ruckus, in confusion, precipitously.

zalapartakatu v.t. to argue violently, to quarrel.

zalapartan adv. disorderly, messily, precipitously.

zalapartari n./adj. agitator, rabble-rouser; agitating, trouble-making.

zalapartatsu adj. noisy, tumultuous.

zalapartatu v.t. to raise a ruckus, to make noise, to cause confusion.

zalapartaz adv. turbulently, noisily, rowdily.

zalbide n. horses' road.

zalburdi n. horse-drawn carriage.

zaldar n.(med.) boil, furuncle.

zaldi n.(zool.) horse.

zaldiarrain n.(zool.) seahorse.

zaldiaulki n. saddle.

zaldibide n. bridle path, cattle path or trail.

zaldibuztan n. horse's tail.

zaldidun n./adj. jockey, rider, horseman; equestrian.

zaldiedergailu n. harness, trappings.

zaldieria n. herd of horses.

zaldiestalki n. horse blanket.

zaldigaineko n. horseback rider, jockey. n. horse blanket.

zaldigorotz n. horse manure.

zaldigorri n.(zool.) sorrel (horse), chestnut (horse).

zaldigurdi n. horse-drawn carriage or cart.

zaldigurzki n. rolled mop of rush or esparto for grooming horses.

zaldihazkuntza n. horse breeding.

zaldika adv. on horseback.

zaldikari n. jockey, rider.

zaldikatu v.t. to go horseback riding, to ride horseback.

zaldiketa n. equitation, horseback riding. n. herd of horses.

zaldiketari n. horse trader.

zaldiki n. horsemeat.

zaldikide adj. equine.

zaldiko n.(dim.) pony, colt, foal, filly.

zaldiko-maldiko n. person in Basque dances who portrays a jockey or horseback rider.

zaldikote n.(augm.) percheron.

zaldikume n.(dim.) pony, colt, foal, filly.

zaldilaster n. horse race.

zaldilasterkari n. jockey.

zaldilasterketa n. horse race.

zaldilasterleku n. racetrack, racecourse, hippodrome.

zaldi-maldiko(ak) n. merry-go-round, carousel.

zaldimutil n. groom, hostler, stable boy.

zaldindar n.(elec.) horsepower.

zaldino n.(dim.) pony, colt, foal, filly.

zaldiongarri n. horse manure.

zalditalde n. herd of horses.

zalditegi n. stable for horses.
zalditegizain n. groom, stable hand.
zalditeria n. herd of horses.
zalditresna n. harness, trappings.
zalditxo n.(dim.) pony, colt, foal, filly.
zalditzar n.(aug.) percheron.
zaldixka n. pony, foal, colt, filly.
zaldiz adv. on horseback.
zaldizain n. groom, stable boy, hostler.
zaldizaintza n. groom's job, stable boy's job.
zaldizale adj. horse-loving, fond of horses.
zaldizko adj. equestrian, horse; mounted. n. jockey.
zaldun n. gentleman, knight. n. playing card bearing a picture of a horse.
zaldunbide n. gentleman's road.
zaldunborroka n. jousting.
zaldundu v.t./v.i. to knight (someone); to be knighted.
zaldun-elkargo n. knightly order, order of knighthood or chivalry.
zalduneria n. group of knights.
zaldungisa adv. nobly, gentlemanly.
zaldungudu n. jousting.
zaldunirudi n. mounted statue.
zaldunki adv. nobly, gentlemanly.
zaldunkiro adv. nobly, gentlemanly.
zaldunmutil n. running footman.
zalduntalde n. mounted squadron, mounted cavalry.
zalduntasun n. noble character, nobility.
zalduntsa n. female jockey, female rider.
zale adj. fond of. Usually used as a suffix.
-zale (gram.) Suffix used to indicate fond of (something). **Mendizale.** Fond of the mountains.
zalegarri adj. covetable, desirable, valuable.
zalegitu v.i. to be overly fond of, to be a fan of.
zalekeria n. avarice, greed; excessive desire for or devotion to (something).
zalekoi adj. excessively fond of.
zalekoitasun n. excessive desire for (something).
zalekor adj. fond of, inclined to.
zalerazi v.t. to become fond of, to become a fan of.
zaletasun n. inclination, fondness.
zaletsu adj. longing, desirous, yearning.
zaletu v.i. to become fond of, to begin liking (something).
zalgi n. dandruff.
zalgudari n. horse soldier, member of the cavalry.
zalgurdi n. horse-drawn cart or carriage.
zalgurditxo n.(dim.) small horse-drawn cart or carriage.
zali n. large spoon, ladle.
zalixka n. spoon.

zalpurdi n. horse-drawn coach or carriage.
zalt- Used in some compound words. Derived from zaldi, horse.
zaltegi n. stable for horses.
zaltegizain n. groom, stable boy.
zaltoki n. stable for horses.
zaltzain n. groom, stable boy, hostler.
zalu adj. flexible, bendable, pliable, foldable. adj. graceful, elegant. adv. quickly, fast.
zaluki adv. gracefully; flexibly.
zalutasun n. agility, gracefulness.
zalutu v.i. to become graceful, to become agile.
zama n. load, burden (physical or spiritual); charge.
zamabere n. beast of burden.
zamaberritu v.t. to reload, to load again.
zamabide n. truck route.
zamadun adj. onerous, burdensome, heavy.
zamagabetu v.t. to unload.
zamagain n. overweight.
zamagarri adj. burdensome, heavy; taxing, grievous.
zamagorailu n. freight lift, freight elevator.
zamakari n. loader.
zamakentoki n. loading dock.
zamaketa n. loading, placement of a load or burden.
zamaketari n. carrier, loader, porter, stevedore.
zamal Used in compound words. Derived from zamari, beast of burden.
zamalde n. herd of horses.
zamaldi n. herd of horses.
zamaldun n. gentleman, nobleman, knight. n. jockey, rider.
zamaleuli n. horse fly.
zamalgorotz n. horse manure.
zamalongarri n. horse manure.
zamaltegi n. stable.
zamaltzain n. groom, stable boy. n. Zuberoan dancer who wears a costume which represents a horse.
zamaltzaingo n. job or business of caring for horses.
zamar n. garbage, trash. n. fleece, tuft of wool.
zamarbiltzaile n. garbage collector. n. person who gathers shorn wool.
zamari n. beast of burden.
zamarikatu v.i./v.t. to ride horseback, to mount (a horse).
zamarrote n. parka, jacket with hood.
zamartxo n.(dim.) small tuft of wool.
zamatoki n. loading dock.
zamatu v.t. to load, to place a burden on, to charge (with a responsibility).
zamatzaile n. loader, porter, stevedore.
zamau n. tablecloth.
zamazain n. stevedore.

zamontzi n. freighter, freight ship.

zanbro n. stinging, itching, smarting, burning. n. lash, black and blue mark from a lash or whip.

zanbrotu v.t./v.i. to lash, to flay; to be marked by the lash.

zanbulu n. teeter-totter; swing (child's toy). n. swinging, swaying, teetering.

zanbuluka adv. swinging, swaying.

zanbulukada n. swinging, to and fro movement.

zanbulukatu v.i. to swing (on a swing). v.i.(fig.) to be in danger (a ship); to sink, to founder, to capsize.

zanga- Used in compound words. Derived from zango, leg.

zangabizkar n. instep.

zangalatraba adv. astride, astraddle.

zangaluze n.(zool.) avocet. adj. long-legged.

zangar adj. valiant, brave, energetic, vigorous. n.(anat.) tibia.

zangartasun n. courage, bravery, valor.

zangarzola n. sole (of the foot).

zango n.(anat.) leg. n. leg (of furniture). n.(anat.) foot.

zangoaztal n.(anat.) calf of the leg.

zangobakar adj. one-legged.

zangobiko adj. biped, bipedal.

zangodun adj. having legs.

zangogabeko adj. legless.

zangohatz n. footprint, track.

zangoka adv. striding, leaping.

zangokada n. kick, blow with the leg.

zangokari n. pedestrian, hiker, walker.

zangokatu v.t. to trip (with the leg), to block (with the leg), to trample, to step on.

zangoker adj. knock-kneed; bowlegged.

zangokertu v.i. to walk in a bowlegged manner; to walk knock-kneed.

zangolodi adj. thick-legged.

zangoluze adj. long-legged.

zangomakila n. leg bone.

zangomakur adj. knock-kneed; bowlegged.

zangomehe adj. having skinny legs.

zangomin n. foot-and-mouth disease.

zangomotz adj. short-legged.

zangopetu v.t. to trample, to step on.

zangosagar n.(anat.) calf of the leg.

zangotzar n.(augm.) big leg.

zangozabal adj. bowlegged.

zangozola n. sole, bottom of the foot.

zangu-mangu adv. ungainly, awkward, inelegant.

zankaluze adj. long-legged. n.(zool.) black-winged stilt (Himantopus himantopus).

zankamotz adj. short-legged.

zankarroi n.(anat.) heel.

zanpa n. crash, bang, splat, boom. Onomatopoeic sound of a blow, collision, fall, etc.

zanpagailu n. crusher (machine).

zanpaka adv. with repeated blows, stamping.

zanpakatu v.t. to beat, to batter, to stomp, to stamp.

zanpaketa n. bruise, contusion. n. stamping, tramping, packing (down with the feet).

zanpako n. blow, hit.

zanpaldi n. beating.

zanpantzar n. Mardi Gras. n. large stuffed figure destroyed on Fat Tuesday to mark the end of Mardi Gras and the beginning of Lent.

zanpatu v.t. to beat, to batter, to bruise, to oppress. v.t. to stamp, to tamp, to pack.

zanpatzaile n./adj. beater, batterer, stomper; beating, battering, stomping.

zanpa-zanpa adv. like pigs, gluttonously.

zantar adj. licentious, obscene, libertine, lusty, lustful. adj. bad, defective.

zantarkeria n. immorality, obscenity, lasciviousness, lustfulness.

zantarki adv. obscenely, lasciviously, lewdly.

zantzolari n. person giving yodel-like shouts of joy.

zantzu n. symptom, sign, characteristic; track, trace, mark.

zantzubilaketa n. tracking, trailing.

zantzuzko adj. symptomatic, characteristic, indicative.

zapaburu n.(zool.) tadpole.

zapadura n. stomping, compressing, squashing.

zapagarri adj. squeezable, squashable.

zapagarritasun n. quality of being squeezable or squashable.

zapaketa n. pressing, compression, squeezing.

zapal adj. flat.

zapalaldi n. pressing, compressing, squeezing. n. beating, drubbing.

zapalbide n. means of repression.

zapaldi n. flattening, crushing. n. stomping.

zapaldu v.t. to crush, to flatten, to stomp. v.t.(fig.) to oppress, to repress, to destroy, to crush.

zapaldura n. stomping, crushing, flattening. n. oppressing, destroying.

zapalgailu n. crusher (machine), steam roller.

zapalgarri adj. crushing, squashing, flattening.

zapalgune n. flattening, crushing. n. depression in the earth. n. flat part of an object.

zapalketa n. crushing, squashing, flattening. n. oppression.

zapalkor adj. oppressive, repressive.

zapalkuntza n. oppression, repression.

zapaltzaile n. oppressor, repressor, dictator.

zapalune n. flattening, crushing.

zapar n. onomatopoeic sound of a strong rain.

zaparrada n. heavy rain, downpour.

zapart n. explosion, blowout (tire, etc.).

zapartatu v.i. to explode, to blow out (a tire), to erupt (a volcano).

zapata n. shoe.

zapatagarbitzaile n. bootblack, shoe shiner.

zapatagile n. shoemaker, cobbler.

zapatagin n. shoemaker, cobbler.

zapatagintza n. cobbling, shoemaking.

zapatari n. shoemaker, cobbler. n.(zool.) threadfish, cobbler fish.

zapataritza n. job of a shoemaker.

zapatasaltzaile n. shoe merchant, shoe salesman.

zapatatxo n.(dim.) little shoe, booty.

zapataundi n.(augm.) large clumsy shoe. adj. clodhopper.

zapatazola n. sole of a shoe.

zapategi n. shoe store.

zapatots n. footstep, sound of shoes on pavement, etc.

zapa-zapa n. onomatopoeic sound indicating abundance. n. onomatopoeic sound indicating continuous marching or movement.

zapelaitz n.(zool.) sparrow hawk.

zapi n. cloth. n. diaper.

zapigarbitzaile n. washerwoman (or man).

zapisorta n. bunch of rags.

zapiztatu v.t. to wrap with cloth or rags.

zaplada n. slap, sock, blow.

zapladaka adv. slapping, socking, hitting.

zaplazta n. slap, sock, blow (especially to the face).

zaplaztaka adv. slapping, socking, hitting.

zaplaztako n. slap, sock, blow, hit.

zaplaztakotu v.t. to slap, to box (one's ears), to sock, to hit.

zaplaztatu v.t. to slap, to box (one's ears), to sock, to hit.

zaplazteko n. sock, slap, blow, hit.

zapo n.(zool.) toad. n.(fig.) traitor. n.(zool.) angler.

zapoeuskera n. bad Basque, poorly spoken Basque.

zapokeria n. villainy, mischief, vile action.

zaporagarri adj. flavoring, flavorful, adding flavor.

zapore n. flavor, taste.

zaporedun adj. flavorful, tasty.

zaporegabe adj. insipid, tasteless.

zaporegabetasun n. tastelessness, flavorlessness.

zaporetsu adj. tasty, flavorful.

zaporeztatu v.t. to give (something) flavor.

zaputz adj. unsocial, unsociable, unfriendly, aloof.

zaputzaldi n. aloofness, unsociability, unfriendliness, disdain.

zapuzkarri adj. disdainful, unsociable, unfriendly, aloof.

zapuzkeria n. aloofness, unsociability, unfriendliness.

zapuzketa n. rejection, repulsion.

zapuzki adv. disdainfully, aloofly, unsociably.

zapuzkor adj. unfriendly, aloof, unsociable.

zapuzti adj. aloof, unfriendly, unsociable.

zapuztu v.t. to abandon, to repudiate, to reject, to disdain, to despise. v.i. to wither, to wilt.

zarabanda n. swing; teeter-totter.

zarabandatu v.i./v.t. to swing in a swing, to rock in a rocker, to ride a see- saw or teeter-totter.

zaragar n.(med.) tinea, scalp ringworm.

zaragardun adj. scabby.

zarama n. garbage, trash, refuse, rubble.

zarata n. noise.

zarata egin v.t. to make noise.

zarataka adv. noisily, clamorously, uproariously.

zarataldi n. uproar, clamor, hubbub.

zaratandiko adj. bombastic, noisy.

zaratari adj. noisy, tumultuous, rowdy, boisterous.

zaratatsu adj. noisy, rowdy, boisterous.

zaratatu v.t. to make noise, to raise a ruckus, to cause an uproar.

zarataz adv. noisily, boisterously, rowdily.

zaratots n. noise, clamor, uproar.

zarba n. leafy branch. n. rustic broom made of branches used by charcoal makers.

zarbaildu v.i. to crumble, to decay, to fall to pieces, to collapse.

zarbatsu adj. leafy.

zarbo n.(zool.) barbel. adj.(fig.) tricky, foxy, wily.

zarbokeria n. trickiness, foxiness, wiliness.

zardai n. flexible wand or stick. adj. svelte, slender.

zardaitasun n. svelteness, slenderness.

zardaitu v.i. to become svelte.

zare n. large basket.

zaregile n. basket maker.

zareta n. basketful.

zaretaka adv. by the basketful.

zaretara n. basketful.

zareteria n. pile of baskets.

zareto n.(dim.) little basket.

zargasta adj./n. mannish; mannish woman.

zarpail adj. rough, rustic. n. old rag.

zarpaildegi n. place of old rags.

zarpaildu v.i. to wear out (clothing), to turn to rags. v.i. to become rowdy, to become a roughneck.

zarpailkeria n. coarseness, grossness, uncouthness, bad manners.

zarpailki adv. roughly, rowdily, noisily, crudely.

zarpailtasun n. uncouthness, grossness, coarseness.

zarpailtsu adj. rowdy, coarse, rough, uncouth.

zarparatu v.t. to pocket, to put in a pocket.

zarpatsu adj. rough, rowdy, crude, gross, uncouth. adj. ragged.

zarrada n. trembling, shaking, emotional upset.

zarrakatu v.i. to crack, to crack open.

zarramar n. ruckus, tumult, clamor, noise.

zarra-marra n. residue, trash, refuse, rubbish.

zarramazka n. scratch.

zarramazkatu v.t. to scratch.

zarraparra n. ruckus, tumult, clamor, noise.

zarrapastada n. hurried action, precipitate action.

zarrapastaka adv. precipitately, hastily, impetuously, confusedly.

zarrapastatu v.i. to hurry excessively, to be in too much of a hurry.

zarrast n. onomatopoeic sound of scratching.

zarrasta n. incision, cut. n. large tear, rip or split.

zarrastada n. cut, incision. n. emotional upset.

zarrastaka adv. scratching.

zarrastaldi n. brusqueness, abrupt change.

zarrastatu v.t. to scratch, to rip. v.t. to tear to shreds, to tatter.

zarratada n. large tear, rip or split.

zarratatu v.t. to tear, to rip, to split.

zarratu adj. dense, thick (forest), heavy (rain). v.i./v.t. to get blocked or stopped up.

zart n. bang, boom. Onomatopoeic sound of an explosion. n. snap, crack. Onomatopoeic sound of a rope snapping or branch breaking. n. Onomatopoeic sound of a blow.

zarta n. stick. n. blow, hit, slap. n. string (of onions or garlic).

zartada n. blow with a stick. n. cracking, snapping. n. slap, sock, hit, blow.

zartadaka adv. by blows, slapping.

zartadako n. strong blow, sharp slap. adj. decisive, resolved.

zartadura n. cracking, splitting open.

zartagailu n. whip, lash.

zartagarri adj. crackable, splittable.

zartagina n. frying pan.

zartaginaldi n. frying panful.

zartagingile n. maker of frying pans.

zartaginkada n. blow with a frying pan.

zartagintxo n.(dim.) little frying pan.

zartaka adv. slapping, hitting.

zartakada n. whipping, hitting, lashing.

zartakatu v.t. to hit, to whip, to lash.

zartako n. slap, blow with a stick.

zartaldi n. beating, whipping.

zartarazi v.t. to make (something) explode.

zartatsu adj. cracked, full of cracks.

zartatu v.i. to crack, to split open. v.t. to whip, to scourge, to beat with a whip. v.i. to explode, to blow up.

zart egin v.t. to crack, to split open.

zartzuela n.(mus.) zarzuela, Spanish musical comedy.

zastada n. slash, cut, blow with a knife, stab. n. putting, inserting, jabbing, stabbing.

zata n.(zool.) goatsucker, nightjar.

zatar n. rag, old cloth. adj. ugly, rough, crude, deformed. adj. obscene, immoral, vile.

zatarbiltzaile n. garbage collector.

zatardun adj. ragged, tattered.

zatarkeria n. vileness, gross action, grossness, crude language. n. crudity, obscenity.

zatarketari n. ragpicker, rag collector.

zatarki n. rag, piece of a cloth. adv. in an ugly way, grossly, crudely.

zatarreria n. garbage, trash, rubbish. n. pile of rags.

zatarreztu v.t. to scrub.

zatartegi n. rag pile, old clothes or second-hand shop.

zatartsu adj. ragged, tattered.

zatartu v.i./v.t. to grow ugly, to become ruined; to ruin, to spoil, to tarnish, to deform.

zati n. part, piece.

zatiarazi v.t. to divide into parts, to cut into pieces, to parcel out (fields).

zatiaskodun adj. having many parts or pieces.

zatibiketa n. division in two, bipartition.

zatibiko adj. two-part, having two parts.

zatidura n. division, break, partition.

zatiezin adj. indivisible, whole, not distributable.

zatiezintasun n. indivisibility.

zatigabe adj. indivisible, whole.

zatigabeki adv. indivisibly.

zatigabeko adj. indivisible, unbroken, whole, undivided.

zatigabetasun n. unbrokenness, undividedness.

zatigai adj. divisible, separable, apportionable. n.(math.) dividend, numerator.

zatigaitasun n. divisibility, separableness.

zatigaitz adj. difficult to divide,

inseparable, not apportionable.

zatigaiztasun *n.* indivisibility.

zatigarri *adj.* divisible, apportionable, breakable.

zatigarrizko *adj.* dividing, separating.

zatika *adv.* in pieces, piece by piece.

zatikagarri *adj.* divisible, sectionable.

zatikako *adj.* fragmentary, partial.

zatikapen *n.* breaking up, taking to pieces, dismantling.

zatikatu *v.t.* to break up, to take to pieces, to dismantle, to split up, to divide.

zatikatzaile *adj.* dismantling, breaking up; divisive.

zatikazko *adj.* fragmentary.

zatikeria *n.* dissidence.

zatiketa *n.* division, fragmentation, partition, parceling.

zatiki *n.* particle, piece. *n.(math.)* fraction.

zatikoi *adj.* fragile, breakable.

zatikor *adj.* fragile, breakable; dividing, breaking.

zatikortasun *n.* fragility, breakableness.

zatitan *adv.* in pieces, in parts.

zatitu *v.t.* to divide, to parcel out, to separate, to cut. *v.t./v.i.(math.)* to divide, to do long division; to be divided (by, into).

zatitxo *n.(dim.)* little piece, bit.

zatitzaile *adj./n.* dividing; divider. *n.(math.)* divisor; factor.

zatiko *n.* part, fragment.

zatixka *n.(dim.)* small part, little piece, bit.

zati-zati egin *v.t./v.i.* to chop into bits, to shatter into pieces, to blow to bits.

zatizko *adj.* fragmentary, fractionary.

zaunka *n.* barking, bark. *adv.* barking.

zaunka egin *v.t.* to bark.

zaunkaka *adv.* barking.

zaunkakera *n.* way of barking.

zaunkalari *adj.* barking.

zaunkari *adj.* barking.

zaunkatu *v.t.* to bark.

zauri *n.* wound, incision, cut.

zauribelar *n.(bot.)* clary.

zauridun *adj.* wounded.

zauridura *n.* lesion, traumatism.

zaurietxe *n.* first-aid station.

zauriezin *adj.* invulnerable.

zaurigabe *adj.* unhurt, uninjured.

zaurigaitz *adj.* difficult to hurt.

zaurigarri *adj.* vulnerable, woundable. *adj.(fig.)* moving, saddening.

zaurigile *adj.* harmful.

zauriketa *n.* wounding, injuring.

zaurikoi *adj.* ulcerous, tending to heal slowly.

zaurimarka *n.* scar.

zauritsu *adj.* wounded, injured, ulcerated.

zauritu *v.i.* to be wounded, to be ulcerated, to be hurt. *v.t.* to harm, to injure (physically or emotionally), to

offend.

zauritzaile *adj.* offensive, injuring, harmful.

zauriztatu *v.i.* to be severely injured, to be covered with wounds. *v.t.* to hurt, to wound, to injure, to offend.

zauzkada *n.* commotion, emotion, emotional upset, sensation.

zazpi *adj./n.* seven.

zazpigarren *adj.* seventh.

zazpihostoko *n.(bot.)* tormentil.

zazpika *adv.* seven by seven.

zazpikatu *v.t.* to place in groups of seven.

zazpiki *adj.* born in seven months, premature. *adj.(fig.)* hyperactive, nervous, impatient, fretful.

zazpiko *adj.* septenary, having seven. *n.* seven (in cards).

zazpikoitz *adj.* septuple, sevenfold.

zazpikoiztu *v.t.* to multiply by seven.

zazpina *adv.* seven each.

zazpinaka *adv.* by sevens, in groups of seven.

zazpinatu *v.t.* to divide into groups of seven, to divide by seven.

zazpiorriko *n.(bot.)* tormentil.

zazpirehun *adj./n.* seven hundred.

zazpirehungarren *adj.* seven hundredth.

zazpiren *adj.* seventh.

zazpisilabadun *adj.* heptasyllabic.

zazpitan *adv.* seven times.

zazpiurren *n.* seven days.

zazpiurtedun *adj.* seven-year-old.

zazpiurteko *adj.* seven-year-old.

zaztagin *n.* drill, auger, borer, gimlet.

zaztakada *n.* killing of an animal with one thrust of a sword to the neck.

zaztakatu *v.t.* to stab, to kill (an animal) with one thrust of a sword to the neck.

zebadura *n.* domestication, taming. *n.* repression.

zebagaitz *adj.* untamable, not domesticable.

zebakor *adj.* domesticable, tamable.

zebatu *v.t.* to domesticate, to tame. *v.i.* to get used to, to be used to.

zebra *n.(zool.)* zebra.

zebrabide *n.* crosswalk, pedestrian crossing.

zebrapasagune *n.* crosswalk, pedestrian crossing.

zedarri *n.* boundary, marker, landmark.

zedarriketa *n.* marking boundaries, bordering, delimitation, limiting, constraint.

zedarritu *v.t.* to mark a boundary, to delimit, to limit, to constrain.

zedarriztatu *v.t.* to limit by boundaries, to mark a boundary.

zedatu *v.t.* to mark a boundary, to make a boundary.

zede *n.* limit, boundary, marker.

zeden *n.(zool.)* moth, wood borer. *n.(zool.)* grub, mite, weevil.

zedendu v.i. to become wormy (meat).
zedro n.(bot.) cedar.
zedula n. document, card, certificate.
zehar prep. across, through, throughout. adj. backward, askew.
zeharbide n. curving road, windy road. n. detour.
zeharbidez adv. slantingly, askance, sideways.
zeharbidezko adj. indirect.
zehardura n. detour. n. obliqueness, bias, slant.
zehargaldera n. indirect question.
zeharka adv. indirectly, sideways, askance, zig-zag, obliquely.
zeharkako adj. zig-zag, twisted, sinuous, curvy, winding, tortuous; indirect.
zeharka-meharka adv. zig-zagging, indirectly, evasively.
zeharkatu v.t. to put (something) crosswise, to put (something) slantwise. v.t. to cross, to traverse, to pass through. v.i. to zig-zag, to move from side to side. v.i. to detour, to leave the road.
zeharketa n. deviation, detour.
zeharki adv. obliquely, sideways, askance.
zeharkor adj. refractory. adj. unwilling, obstinate.
zehar-mehar adv. zig-zagging.
zehar-meharkatu v.i. to zig-zag, to wander aimlessly.
zehar-meharrak n.(pl.) zig-zagging, aimless wandering.
zeharo adv. minutely, in great detail, completely.
zeharradar n. lateral branch.
zeharraize n. west wind.
zeharrargi n. reflected light.
zeharrargitsu adj. translucent.
zeharreko adj. transverse, cross, sideways, askance, zig-zag, side.
zeharresan n. allusion, indirect statement.
zeharretara adv. sideways, askance.
zeharritz n. allusion, vague word, indirect word.
zehartasun n. detour; obliqueness.
zehartu v.t./v.i. to twist (away), to evade, to avoid, to dodge. v.t. to cross, to pass through.
zehatz adj. exact, exacting, strict, detailed, minute. adv. completely, in great detail, minutely.
zehatzale adj. perfectionist, detailed.
zehatzezin adj. indeterminable.
zehatzezko adj. detailed, precise, exact.
zehatz-mehatz adv. clearly, precisely, exactly, concretely, specifically.
zehazkabe adj. indefinite, undetermined, inexact, not specific, imprecise.
zehazkabetasun n. vagueness, inexactness, impreciseness.

zehazkabezia n. imprecision, inexactness.
zehazketa n. precision, exactness.
zehazki adv. exactly, precisely, concretely, specifically.
zehazkiro adv. precisely, exactly.
zehazkizun n. detail.
zehaztagarri adj. capable of being explained in detail, itemizable.
zehaztapen n. specification, determination.
zehaztasun n. exactness, detailedness, preciseness, accuracy, precision.
zehaztu v.t. to specify, to determine, to make precise.
zehe n.(anat.) palm, hand's breadth, span of a hand. adj. ground, chopped.
zeheki adv. minutely, in great detail, exactly, precisely.
zehero adv. at retail (sales); in great detail.
zehetasun n. detailedness, preciseness, exactness.
zehetu v.t. to chop to bits, to grind up, to cut into pieces.
zein adj./pron. which, which one.
zeinadura n. act of crossing oneself.
zeinatu v.t. to make the sign of the cross.
zeinek pron. which one. Used as active subject with transitive verbs.
zein eta Exclamation used to express surprise. English equivalent is an exclamation point or special tone of voice.
zeingehiagoka adv. competitively.
zeinnahi adj./pron. anyone, whichever, anybody.
zeintzu adj./pron. which ones.
zeintzuk adj./pron. which; which ones.
zeinu n. gesture. n. signal, sign.
zeinuka adv. gesturing, making signs.
zeinuketa n. gesticulation, gesturing.
zeinuti adj. gesticulative, gesturing.
zekale n.(bot.) rye.
zeken adj. stingy, niggardly, miserly; greedy.
zekendu v.i. to become stingy.
zekenkeria n. avarice, meanness, stinginess, miserliness.
zekenki adv. stingily, miserly.
zekentasun n. avarice.
zekor n.(zool.) young bull, bull calf.
zekorkari n. herdsman who looks after young bulls or cows; bullfighter.
zekorketa n. drove of young bulls.
zekorki n. veal.
zekortalde n. herd of calves.
zekortegi n. calf pen, corral for calves.
zekortu v.i. to breed (cattle), to mate.
zekortxo n.(dim.) small calf.
zekortzain n. herdsman of calves.
zela n. saddle.
zeladura n. saddling.
zelai n. meadow, plain, field, prairie.

adj. flat.

zelaialde *n.* plain, prairie.

zelaigarri *adj.* flattenable.

zelaigune *n.* plain, flat field.

zelaiketa *n.* flattening.

zelaineurketa *n.* planimetry, measuring a plane surface.

zelaitasun *n.* flatness (of terrain).

zelaitsu *adj.* prairie-like, having large plains.

zelaitu *v.t.* to level off, to flatten.

zelaitzaile *adj.* flattening, leveling.

zelaixka *n.(dim.)* small flat area of land.

zelan *adv.* how.

zelango *adj.* what kind of?

zelanik *adv.* how.

zelata *n.* watching, observing, spying on, lying in wait (for).

zelatada *n.* trap, snare, ambush.

zelatadura *n.* ambush, trap, snare.

zelataka *adv.* spying, watching, observing, laying in wait (for).

zelatakeria *n.* constant prying.

zelatakuntza *n.* espionage.

zelataldi *n.* spying, moment of observation; ambush, trap.

zelataleku *n.* place for an ambush, observation post, spy's lookout.

zelatan *adv.* spying, observing, watching.

zelatan egon *v.i.* to observe, to watch, to spy on.

zelatari *n.* sentinel, guard; spy, watcher. *adj.* curious, watchful.

zelatarte *n.* ambush, trap.

zelatatu *v.t.* to spy on, to watch, to observe, to lie in wait (for).

zelatatzaile *n.* spy; sentinel, guard, watcher.

zelatu *v.t.* to saddle (horses). *v.t.* to spy on, to observe, to watch, to lie in wait (for).

zelatxo *n.(dim.)* small saddle.

zelibato *n.* celibacy.

zelta *adj.* Celtic.

zeltera *n.* Celtic language, Keltic.

zelula *n.(biol.)* cell.

zelulabakar *adj.* unicellular.

zelulabakarreko *adj.* unicellular.

zelulabarneko *adj.* intracellular.

zeluladun *adj.* celled, having cells.

zelularteko *adj.* intracellular.

zelulaskodun *adj.* multicellular.

zelulatsu *adj.* multicellular, cellulated, having many cells.

zelulosa *n.(chem.)* cellulose.

zemaika *adv.* menacingly, threateningly.

zemaitu *v.t.* to threaten, to menace.

zematzaile *adj.* threatening, menacing.

zementu *n.* cement.

zen *adj.* dead, late, defunct.

zenbait *pron./adj.* some, certain, few, several.

zenbakailu *n.* calculator, adding machine.

zenbakarren *adj.* what, which.

Question word requiring an ordinal number in the answer.

zenbakarri *adj.* countable, numberable.

zenbakenketa *n.(arith.)* subtraction.

zenbakera *n.* system of numerals, counting system.

zenbaketa *n.* counting, enumeration, computation.

zenbaki *n.(math.)* number, numeral.

zenbakide *adj.* equivalent.

zenbakiro *adv.* numerically.

zenbakiz *adv.* numerically.

zenbakizko *adj.* numerical, numeral.

zenbakiztu *v.t.* to number (something).

zenbakizun *adj./n.* countable.

zenbakor *adj.* enumerative, countable.

zenbakuntza *n.* countability, enumeration.

zenbalari *n.* counter, one who counts.

zenbalaritza *n.* accountancy, accountant's office or post.

zenbana *adj./pron.* how many . . . each.

zenbanako *adj.* quantitative.

zenbat *adj./pron.* how much, how many. Used in interrogative sentences. *adv.* how much! how many! what a lot! Used in exclamations.

zenbat aldiz *adv.* how many times.

zenbatasun *n.* quantity, amount.

zenbatean *adv.* at what price, how much . . . for.

zenbateko *adj.* how expensive, how valuable. *n.* quantity, amount.

zenbatetan *adv.* how many times. Used in interrogative sentences.

zenbatezin *adj.* noncountable, uncountable.

zenbatezintasun *n.* quality of being noncountable.

zenbatezinezko *adj.* not countable.

zenbatgarren *adj.* what, which.

zenbatnahi *adv.* a lot, as much as one wants.

zenbatsu *adj.* many, numerous. *adj.* about how many.

zenbatu *v.t.* to number (something), to count.

zenbatuezin *adj.* incalculable, uncountable, numerous.

zenbatzaile *n.* counter, tallyman.

zendor *n.* wooden pyre for making charcoal.

zendu *v.i.* to die, to pass away. Used in the indicative mood.

zentilitro *n.* centiliter.

zentimetro *n.* centimeter.

zentimo *n.* cent (of a *peseta*).

zentraldu *v.t.* to centralize.

zentralismo *n.* centralism.

zentralizaketa *n.* centralization.

zentralizapen *n.* centralization.

zentru *n.* center.

zentsura *n.* censorship.

zentsuragarri *adj.* censorable.

zentsuratu v.t. to censor.
zentsuzko adj. censual, pertaining to a census.
zentza- Used in compound words. Derived from zentzu, sense, discretion.
zentzabide n. form of correcting.
zentzadura n. return to one's senses, coming to one's senses. n. correction, rectification.
zentzagaitz adj. difficult to correct, hard to handle, indomitable.
zentzagarri adj. corrective.
zentzarazi v.t. to bring (someone) to his senses.
zentzarazle adj. corrective, correcting.
zentzatu v.i. to come to one's senses, to behave prudently, to be discreet. v.t. to correct, to bring (someone) to justice.
zentzatzaile adj. correcting, dispensing of correction (penal, etc.).
zentzazio n. sensation.
zentzu n. sense, common sense, reason, judgment, right mind. n. consciousness. n. meaning.
zentzuatsegin n. sensual pleasure.
zentzubakar adj. having one meaning, univocal.
zentzubakarreko adj. univocal, having one meaning.
zentzubakartasun n. univocalness, quality of having one meaning.
zentzubatez adv. univocally.
zentzubereko adj. synonymous, homologous.
zentzubizgarri adj. stimulating, exciting (to the senses).
zentzudun adj. wise, reasonable, sensible, discreet, prudent.
zentzugabe adj. imprudent, absurd, illogical, not sensible, insensible, unreasoning.
zentzugabekeria n. absurdity, foolishness; senselessness.
zentzugabeki adv. insensibly, indiscreetly, imprudently.
zentzugabeko adj. indiscreet, imprudent, careless. adj. irrational, absurd, illogical.
zentzugabetasun n. loss of one's senses, irrationality.
zentzugabetu v.i. to lose one's senses, to lose one's reason; to be out of one's mind (with ecstasy, etc.).
zentzugabetze n. act of losing one's reason, act of being irrational.
zentzuko adj. rational, wise, sensible.
zentzukoi adj. sensual.
zentzukoitasun n. sensuality.
zentzukor adj. sensual.
zentzumen n. sense, faculty of sensation.
zentzuratu v.i. to come to one's senses, to recover one's reason.

zentzutasun n. prudence, discretion, reasonableness.
zentzutu v.i. to become serious or earnest.
zentzuz adv. reasonably, prudently, judiciously.
zentzuzki adv. reasonably, prudently, judiciously.
zentzuzko adj. sensory, sensorial, pertaining to the senses. adj. rational, logical.
zepa n. slag, scoria; cement clinker.
zepadun adj. slaggy, containing slag or scoria.
zepatsu adj. slaggy, containing slag or scoria.
zepelin n. dirigible, zeppelin, airship.
zepilaketa n. brushing.
zepilatu v.t. to brush.
zepilu n. brush (clothes brush, etc.).
zer pron./adj. what. n. something, what.
zeramika n. ceramic.
zerba n.(bot.) chard, Swiss chard.
zerbait pron./adv. something.
zerbitu v.t. to serve.
zerbitzari n. servant.
zerbitzarikide n. fellow servant, co-servant.
zerbitzatu v.t. to serve.
zerbitzu n. service.
zerbitzualdi n. period of service.
zerbitzune n. service station.
zerebru n.(anat.) brain, cerebrum.
zer edo zer pron./adv. something.
zeregin n. task, occupation, work, duty, something (or nothing) to do.
zeregin eman v.t. to assign homework, to give (someone) a job to do.
zeregingabe adj. unoccupied, unemployed, having nothing to do.
zeregintsu adj. busy, having lots to do.
zeregintxo n.(dim.) trivial task, small chore.
zeremonia n. ceremony.
zeremonizale adj. fond of ceremony.
zeren conj. because, since. Usually placed at the beginning of a sentence. Also sometimes verb carries the relative -n or the prefix bait-.
zeresan n. gossip.
zerezko adj. what kind, made of what?
zerga n.(econ.) tax, duty.
zergabanatu v.t. to assess (property) for taxes, to tax, to impose taxes on.
zergabildegi n. customs booth, customs office, tax office.
zergabilketa n. tax collection.
zergabiltzaile n. tax collector.
zergadun n. taxpayer.
zergaemale n. taxpayer.
zergaetxe n. customs office, tax office, customs booth.
zergagabe adj. tax free.
zergagabetu v.t. to exempt from

taxes.

zergagabezia n. tax exemption.

zergagarri n. taxable, assessable.

zergagiri n. tax bill.

zerga(k) eman v.t. to pay taxes.

zergakera n. way of paying taxes.

zergaketa n. paying taxes.

zergakide n. co-taxpayer.

zergalari n. tax collector.

zergalege n. tax law(s), tariff regulation(s).

zergalegezko adj. tax, tariff.

zergaordaintzaile n. taxpayer.

zergapeko n. taxpayer.

zergapen n. paying of taxes.

zergapetu v.t. to tax, to impose taxes on.

zergari n. tax collector.

zergaritza n. tax collector's job, post of customs officer.

zergati n. motive, reason.

zergatik conj. why.

zergatiko n. reason, cause, motive.

zergatu v.t. to tax, to impose taxes on.

zerikusi n. influence, impact, connection, repercussion, consequence.

zerketa n. definition.

zernahi pron./adj. whatever, anything, everything.

zero adj./n. zero.

zeroi n.(zool.) sperm whale.

zerori pron. you yourself.

zerorrek pron. you yourself (active subject used with transitive verbs).

zerra n. saw. n. slice.

zerragarri adj. capable of being sawed.

zerragin n. tooth of a saw.

zerrakatu v.t. to slice, to cut into pieces.

zerraketa n. sawing.

zerralari n. one who saws, sawyer.

zerraldo n. coffin. adv. face down. adv./adj. dead.

zerraldotegi n. funeral home.

zerrama n.(zool.) sow, female pig.

zerramagai n. young breeding sow.

zerramakina n. power saw, chain saw.

zerrantzeko adj. saw-like.

zerrari n. one who saws, sawyer.

zerrarrain n.(zool.) sawfish, sierra.

zerraska n. pig trough, hog trough.

zerrategi n. sawmill.

zerratoki n. sawmill.

zerratu v.t. to saw.

zerratzaile n. one who saws, sawyer.

zerrauts n. sawdust.

zerrenda n. list, printout. n. border (of earth, etc.), margin, edge; stripe, strip, band; fringe. n. vein, seam, lode.

zerrendadun adj. striped. adj. veined, seamed, having a lode (mines).

zerrendaketa n. listing, making a list, registering.

zerrendatu v.t. to list. v.t. to tear off (pieces of a sheet, etc.).

zerrendatzaile n. one who makes a list, registrar.

zerrepel adj. warm, lukewarm.

zerrepeldu v.i./v.t. to warm up, to get warm; to warm, to heat up.

zerri n.(zool.) pig (both sexes). n.(fig.) pig, filthy person, person without morals.

zerriantzeko adj. pig-like.

zerrieme n.(zool.) sow, female pig.

zerrigiharre n. lean part of the bacon.

zerrijan n. slop, swill, inedible food, pigslop, pigswill.

zerrikeria n. dirty behavior, pig-like behavior. n.(fig.) immorality (usually sexual). n.(fig.) dirty trick.

zerriki n. pork, pig's meat.

zerrikote n.(augm.) large pig, hog. adj.(fig.) filthy (person).

zerrikume n.(dim.) piglet.

zerrilketa n. killing of a pig, pig butchering.

zerrilketaro n. time for butchering pigs (usually in December).

zerritalde n. herd (of swine).

zerritegi n. pigsty, pigpen.

zerritoki n. pigsty, pigpen.

zerritzar n.(augm.) large pig, hog.

zerriurrixa n.(zool.) sow, female pig.

zerrizain n. swineherd, pig keeper.

zerrote n. handsaw.

zertako conj. for what, for what purpose, what . . . for. conj. why.

zertan conj. what, in what.

zertara conj. for what.

zertarako conj. what . . . for.

zertaz pron./conj. what . . . of, of what; about what, what . . . about.

zertifikapen n. certification.

zertifikatu v.t. to certify. n. certificate.

zertu v.t. to define, to determine, to specify.

zertxobait pron./adv. something, a little bit.

zertzelada n. detail.

zertzeta n.(zool.) garganey.

zertzu(k) adj./pron.(pl.) what.

zeru n. heaven. n. sky.

zerubide n. path to heaven.

zeruertz n. horizon.

zeruetako adj. celestial, heavenly.

zerugain n. sky.

zeruko adj. celestial, heavenly, of heaven.

zerukoi adj. celestial, heavenly.

zeru-lurrak n. heaven and earth.

zerumuga n. horizon.

zerurako adj. predestined, intended for heaven.

zeruratu v.i. to go to heaven, to be saved (in a Christian sense); to go to the sky.

zerusabai n. firmament, heaven.

zerutar adj. celestial.

zerutiar adj. celestial.

zeta n. zed, z. n. silk.

zetabe n. sieve, sifter, screen, riddle.

zetaka *n.* spot, blotch.
zetakatu *v.t.* to spot, to blotch.
zetar *n.(zool.)* silkworm.
zetatsu *adj.* silky.
zetazko *adj.* silk, made of silk.
zetaztatu *v.t.* to cover with silk.
zeu *pron.* you yourself. Used as a subject with intransitive verbs and as a direct object with transitive verbs.
zeuk *pron.* you yourself (used always as a subject with transitive verbs).
zeuek *pron.(pl.)* you yourselves.
zeugandu *v.t.* to appropriate for yourself, to attract to yourself.
zeure *adj./pron.* your, your own; yours.
zeureganaketa *n.* act of appropriating for yourself.
zeureganatu *v.t.* to appropriate for yourself, to make something yours.
zeurekoi *adj.* egoist, egotistic (used with second person singular, you).
zeuretu *v.t.* to appropriate for yourself, to make (something) yours.
zezekari *n.* lisper, one who pronounces *s* like *th*.
zezel *adj./n.* stuttering, stammering; stutterer, stammerer.
zezeldu *v.i.* to become a stutterer.
zezen *n.(zool.)* bull.
zezenaga *n.(astron.)* Taurus.
zezenaldi *n.* bullfight.
zezendari *n.* bullfighter, matador.
zezendegi *n.* bull pen.
zezendu *v.i.* to become furious, to get angry.
zezeneztenkari *n.* banderillero, one who participates in a bullfight by placing barbed darts near the bull's neck (not a matador).
zezeneztenkatu *v.t.* to place barbed darts on the bull.
zezengai *n.(zool.)* young bull.
zezengudu *n.* bullfight.
zezenjai *n.* bullfight. (lit.) bull feast.
zezenka *adv.* bullfighting. *n.* bullfight.
zezenkagarri *adj.* capable of bullfighting.
zezenkari *n.* bullfighter, matador.
zezenkatu *v.t.* to fight bulls in the ring.
zezenketa *n.* bullfight.
zezenketari *n.* bullfighter, matador.
zezenki *n.* meat of the bull.
zezenko *n.(zool.)* bullock, young bull.
zezenlari *n.* bullfighter, matador.
zezenlaritalde *n.* group of bullfighters.
zezenlarru *n.* hide of a bull.
zezenlaster *n.* bullfight.
zezenplaza *n.* bullfighting ring.
zezensari *n.* stud fee.
zezensuzko *n.* bull of fire (kind of fireworks).
zezentalde *n.* herd of bulls.
zezentoki *n.* bull pen.
zezentokiraketa *n.* enclosing bulls in a bull pen.
zezentokiratu *v.t.* to enclose bulls in a bull pen.

zezentxo *n.(dim.)* bullock, young bull.
zezentzain *n.* tender or keeper of bulls.
zezentzale *adj.* bullfighting fan.
zezentzaletasun *n.* fondness for bullfighting.
zezenziri *n.* banderilla, barbed dart used in bullfighting.
zezin *n.* cured meat (corned, dried, smoked or hung); jerky.
zezinatu *v.t.* to cure meat.
zezio *n.* quarrel, dispute, argument, discussion.
zezioti *adj.* quarrelsome, argumentative, belligerent.
zeziozale *adj.* quarrelsome, argumentative.
zezta *n.* jai-alai basket.
ziabelar *n.(bot.)* bedstraw.
ziaboga *n.* putting about (of a rowboat, steamer), turning.
zia egin *v.t.* to row backwards.
zianuro *n.(chem.)* cyanide.
ziape *n.* mustard.
ziba *n.* spinning top.
zibagile *n.* top maker.
zibaka ari *v.i.* to play with a top.
zibilizatu *v.t./v.i.* to civilize; to become civilized.
zibilizazio *n.* civilization; culture.
zibilki *adv.* civilly.
zibiltasun *n.* civility.
zibo *n.* swing.
zidor *n.* narrow path or trail. Usually preceded by *bide*, road.
zidortu *v.t.* to break trail.
zientzia *n.* science.
zientzigizon *n.* scientist.
zientzilari *n.* scientist.
zientzizen *n.* scientific name.
zifra *n.* figure, number, numerical character.
zigala *n.(zool.)* kind of edible marine crustacean with a hard shell and two long claws.
zigarreta *n.* cigarette.
zigarro *n.* cigarette.
zigarrodenda *n.* tobacco shop.
zigarrokin *n.* cigarette butt.
zigarrontzi *n.* cigarette case.
zigarropuru *n.* cigar.
zigarrotxo *n.(dim.)* small cigarette.
zigiladura *n.* stamping (with a rubber stamp).
zigilari *n.* stamper, one who stamps (something) with a rubber stamp.
zigilatu *v.t.* to stamp (with a rubber stamp).
zigilu *n.* stamp, rubber stamp.
zigor *n.* punishment. *n.* whip.
zigordura *n.* punishment.
zigorgabe *adj.* unpunished.
zigorgabekeria *n.* impunity.
zigorgabetasun *n.* impunity.
zigorgabetu *v.t.* to not punish, to pardon.
zigorgabezia *n.* impunity.

zigorgarri adj. punishable, actionable, sanctionable.

zigorkada n. punishment.

zigorkari n. punisher; whipper, lasher.

zigorkatu v.t. to punish, to castigate; to oppress. v.t. to torture, to whip.

zigorketa n. punishment. n. whipping.

zigorkor adj. punitive.

zigorlari n. punisher, castigator.

zigorlege n. punitive law, penal code.

zigorlegelari n. criminal lawyer.

zigorpetu v.t. to punish, to chastise, to penalize.

zigorrada n. blow from a whip, lash.

zigorraldi n. repression, punishment.

zigorrarazi v.t. to torture, to punish, to whip.

zigorrezko adj. pertaining to punishment, penal.

zigortu v.t. to punish, to castigate; to oppress. v.t. to torture, to whip.

zigortzaile n./adj. punisher, torturer; punishing, torturing.

ziho n. tallow, fat, grease.

zihotsu adj. tallowy, greasy, fatty.

zikin adj. dirty, filthy. n. spot, filth, dirt.

zikindu v.i./v.t. to get dirty, to become soiled; to get (something) dirty, to soil (something).

zikindura n. dirtying, soiling, staining.

zikinean egin v.t. to write a rough draft.

zikingarri adj. stainable, capable of getting dirty. adj. staining, dirtying. n. spot remover.

zikinkentzaile n./adj. spot remover; cleansing.

zikinkeria n. disgusting act, atrocious act. n.(fig.) licentiousness, lustfulness, sexual misbehavior.

zikinki adv. sordidly, dirtily, nastily. adv.(fig.) dishonestly.

zikinkiro adv. sordidly, dirtily, filthily. adv.(fig.) dishonestly.

zikinkor adj. soiling, staining.

zikinodi n. sewer; culvert, drain.

zikinontzi n. garbage can. adj. filthy, slimy.

zikintasun n. dirtiness, filthiness, sordidness.

zikintsu adj. dirty, filthy, stained, spotted.

zikintza n. place where dirty clothes are kept. n. mudhole, bog, quagmire.

zikintzaile adj. dirtying, staining.

zikinzulo n. quagmire, mudhole.

zikiraketa n. castration, neutering, fixing (animals).

zikirapen n. castration, neutering, fixing (animals).

zikiratu v.t. to castrate, to neuter, to fix.

zikiratzaile n. castrator, gelder.

zikirio n.(bot.) rye.

zikiro n.(zool.) neutered ram, castrated ram. adj. castrated, neutered.

zikiroki n. ram meat.

zikirotzaile n. castrator, gelder.

ziklismo n. cycling, bicycling.

ziklista n. cyclist, bicycler.

ziklo n. cycle.

zikloi n. cyclone.

zikoina n.(zool.) stork.

zikoinatxo n.(dim.) small stork.

zikoitz adj. stingy, miserly; greedy.

zikoizdura n. avarice, greediness; stinginess, miserliness.

zikoizkeria n. miserliness, stinginess, avarice.

zikoizki adv. miserly, stingily, avariciously.

zikoizkiro adv. stingily, miserly, avariciously.

zikoiztasun n. miserliness, avarice, stinginess.

zikoizte n. act of being stingy, act of being miserly.

zikoiztu v.i. to be stingy, to be miserly, to be avaricious.

zil n.(anat.) bellybutton.

zilar n.(min.) silver.

zilarbistu v.t. to silverplate, to plate or coat with silver.

zilarbits n. silver plate.

zilarbitxi n. silver jewelry.

zilarbitxitu v.t. to adorn with silver.

zilarbizi n.(min.) mercury, quicksilver.

zilarbizitu v.t. to quicksilver, to coat with quicksilver.

zilardenda n. silver shop.

zilardun adj. made of silver, containing silver.

zilargile n. silversmith.

zilargin n. silversmith.

zilargindegi n. silversmith's workshop.

zilargintza n. silversmith's trade, silversmithing.

zilargune n. silver part of an object.

zilarki n. piece of silver.

zilarlan n. piece of worked silver, silver made into something.

zilarlanketa n. silversmithing.

zilarrantzeko adj. silvery, silver-like.

zilarrari n. silver thread.

zilarrariztu v.t. to filligree (with silver thread).

zilarreria n. silver (dishes, jewelry, etc.).

zilarrezko adj. made of silver.

zilarreztadura n. silver plating.

zilarreztari n. silver plater.

zilarreztatu v.t. to silver-plate, to cover with silver.

zilarreztu v.t. to silver-plate, to cover with silver.

zilarrontziteria n. silver (dishes, tea service, etc.).

zilarrorratz n. silver needle.

zilartegi n. silverware shop.

zilarteria n. silver (dishes, jewelry, etc.).

zilartsu adj. silvery, silver.

zilartu v.t. to plate with silver. v.t. to exchange paper money for silver coins.

zilatu *v.t./v.i.* to make a hole, to drill, to bore, to perforate, to puncture; to develop a hole.

zilbor *n.(anat.)* bellybutton, navel.

zilbormin *n.* inflammation of the bellybutton.

zilborrandi *adj.* fat, obese. (lit.) big belly.

zilborreko *adj.* umbilical.

zilborreste *n.(anat.)* umbilical cord.

zilbot *n.(colloq.)* belly, paunch.

zildu *v.i.* to grow shoots, to sprout.

zilegi *adj.* permitted, allowed; lawful.

zilegidura *n.* authorization, permission.

zilegigo *n.* authorization, permission.

zilegi izan *v.i./v.t.* to be allowed, to be permitted; to allow, to permit.

zilegiki *adv.* licitly, lawfully.

zilegitasun *n.* permission, authorization; lawfulness.

zilegitu *v.t.* to permit, to authorize.

zilegitzaile *adj.* authorizing, permitting.

zileko *adj.* umbilical.

zileste *n.(anat.)* umbilical cord.

zilindro *n.(geom.)* cylinder. *n.(mech.)* cylinder (in an automobile engine).

ziliporta *n.* splashing.

ziliportatu *v.t.* to splash.

zilipurdi *n.* tumble, somersault.

zilipurdika *adv.* tumbling, somersaulting.

zilipurdika ari *v.i.* to tumble, to somersault, to turn a somersault.

zilipurdikatu *v.i.* to tumble, to somersault, to turn a somersault.

zilo *n.* hole, orifice. *n.* grave.

zima *n.* character, temperament, temper.

zimardika *adj.* ambiguous, having a double meaning.

zimardikatu *v.t.* to deceive, to cheat, to trick.

zimarku *n.* plot, conspiracy.

zimarkun *adj.* fraudulent, deceptive, tricky.

zimarroi *n.(zool.)* kind of short-finned tuna.

zimartsu *adj.* fraudulent, tricky, deceptive.

zimel *adj.* withered, wilted.

zimeldu *v.i.* to wither, to wilt.

zimeldura *n.* withering, wilting.

zimelezin *adj.* perennial, eternal.

zimelgaitz *adj.* long-lasting, enduring.

zimelgarri *adj.* perishable, capable of withering or wilting.

zimeltasun *n.* witheredness, wiltedness.

zimendapen *n.* laying the foundations of (a building, etc.).

zimendatu *v.t.* to lay the foundations of (a building, society).

zimendatzaile *n.* founder; one who lays the foundations of (a building, etc.).

zimendu *n.* base, basis, foundation.

zimentarri *n.* cornerstone, base, basis, foundation.

zimiko *n.* pinch. *n.* upset, uneasiness.

zimiko egin *v.t.* to pinch.

zimikoka *adv.* pinching.

zimikokari *adj./n.* pinching; pincher.

zimikokatu *v.t.* to pinch.

zimitz *n.(zool.)* bedbug.

zimur *n.* wrinkle, fold, crease, pleat. *adj.* wrinkled. *adj.(fig.)* stingy, miserly.

zimurdura *n.* wrinkle. *n.* frowning, wrinkling (of the forehead).

zimurgabetu *v.i./v.t.* to be unwrinkled; to remove wrinkles.

zimur izan *v.i.(fig.)* to be a miser.

zimurkatu *v.t./v.i.* to wrinkle, to frown; to be wrinkled, to be frowning.

zimurkeria *n.* stinginess, miserliness.

zimurki *adv.* stingily, miserly.

zimurtasun *n.* wrinkled condition, rugosity. *n.* quality of being folded or pleated.

zimurtsu *adj.* wrinkled; folded, pleated.

zimurtu *v.i./v.t.* to wrinkle, to frown. *v.i.(fig.)* to be stingy.

zin *n.* oath.

zinaide *n.* conspirator, plotter.

zinaldi *n.* swearing, taking an oath.

zinaurri *n.(zool.)* ant.

zinausle *n.* one who breaks an oath.

zinauspen *n.* breaking an oath.

zinauste *n.* act of breaking an oath.

zinautsi *v.t.* to break an oath.

zinbel *adj.* flexible, pliant, supple, swaying.

zindo *adj.* fresh. *adj.* solid, firm.

zindotasun *n.* firmness, solidity.

zine *n.* movies; cinema, movie theater.

zinegailu *n.* movie camera.

zinegile *n.* one who takes an oath, one who swears to (something). *n.* movie maker, film maker.

zin egin *v.t.* to swear, to take an oath.

zinegintza *n.* movie making, cinema.

zin egotzi *v.t.* to swear, to take an oath.

zinegotzi *n.* councillor, alderman, councilman.

zinegotzigo *n.* councillorship.

zinema *n.* movie, film.

zinemagela *n.* movie theater.

zinemagile *n.* film producer or maker.

zinemaldi *n.* film festival.

zinemaleku *n.* movie theater.

zinemaratu *v.i.* to go to the movies.

zinemareto *n.* movie theater.

zinemari *n.* movie star.

zinematoki *n.* movie theater.

zinemazale *adj.* fond of movies, movie fan.

zinez *adv.* really, seriously, honestly. *adv.* under oath.

zinezko *adj.* honest, true, sincere, real. *adj.* pertaining to an oath.

zineztagarri *adj.* certifiable, sworn.

zineztatu *v.t.* to swear, to take an oath,

to affirm under oath.

zineztu *v.t.* to swear to, to affirm under oath.

zingezur *n.* perjury.

zingezurti *adj.* perjured, perjurious.

zingila *n.* girth, cinch.

zingilatu *v.t.* to cinch (up).

zingira *n.* swamp, marsh; lake.

zingiradi *n.* swampy ground, marshland.

zingirako *adj.* marshy, boggy, swampy.

zingiratsu *adj.* swampy, marshy, boggy.

zingiratu *v.t./v.i.* to swamp, to flood.

zingle *adj.* ephemeral, fragile, inconsistent.

zinitz *n.* oath, sworn statement. *n.(rel.)* religious vow.

zinitz egin *v.t.* to swear to God, to swear on the Bible.

zink *n.(chem.)* zinc.

zinki *adv.* really, seriously.

zinkun *n.(zool.)* stork.

zinkurin *n.* sigh, groan, moan, sob.

zinkurinaldi *n.* sighing, lamenting.

zinkurinari *adj.* sighing, sobbing, moaning.

zinkurinati *adj.* complaining, lamenting.

zinkurinatsu *adj.* complaining, lamenting.

zinkurinatu *v.i.* to sob, to lament, to sigh.

zinkurinka *adv.* complaining, lamenting.

zinkurinzale *adj.* complaining, moaning, lamenting.

zinta *n.* ribbon, tape, band.

zintabelar *n.(bot.)* cattail.

zintadantza *n.* folkloric Basque dance performed with ribbons attached to a pole.

zintasun *n.* loyalty, fidelity. *n.* sincerity, frankness.

zintz *n.(onomat.)* sound made by blowing one's nose. *n.* nasal mucus, snot.

zintzaldi *n.* blowing the nose.

zintzarri *n.* cattle bell.

zintzarrots *n.* ringing of a cattle bell.

zintzatu *v.i.* to blow one's nose.

zintz egin *v.t.* to blow one's nose.

zintzeragin *v.t.* to make (someone) blow one's nose.

zintzil *adj.* hanging, suspended. *n.* rag, tatter.

zintzilgailu *n.* hanger, clothes hanger, clothes hook.

zintzilik *adv.* hanging, suspending.

zintzilika *adv.* hanging.

zintzilikari *n.* hanging; something hanging from clothing, etc. *n.* pendulum (of a clock).

zintzilikario *n.* earring; hanging object.

zintzilikatu *v.t./v.i.* to hang, to hang out, to hang up.

zintzilipurdi *n.* somersault.

zintzilzubi *n.* suspension bridge.

zintzo *adj.* nice, honest, reliable, faithful, loyal. *adv.* honestly, loyally, faithfully.

zintzoera *n.* honesty, fidelity, loyalty.

zintzogabetasun *n.* dishonesty, disloyalty, infidelity.

zintzoki *adv.* honestly, loyally, faithfully.

zintzotasun *n.* loyalty, honesty, upright character.

zintzotu *v.i.* to be well-behaved, to be reasonable.

zintzur *n.(anat.)* Adam's apple; throat; trachea. *n.* neck (of a bottle).

zintzurkeria *n.* gluttony.

zintzurketa *n.* choking.

zintzurkoi *adj.* gluttonous, voracious.

zintzurkoikeria *n.* gluttony, voraciousness.

zintzurkoitasun *n.* gluttony, voraciousness.

zintzurkoitu *v.i.* to become gluttonous, to be voracious, to have a voracious appetite.

zintzurkontrako *n.(anat.)* glottis.

zintzurkorapilo *n.(anat.)* Adam's apple.

zintzurluze *adj.(fig.)* talkative, loquacious. *adj.(fig.)* drunk, drinking a lot.

zintzurmihi *n.(anat.)* epiglottis.

zintzurmin *n.(med.)* angina, sore throat, laryngitis.

zintzurreri *n.(med.)* laryngitis.

zintzurreste *n.(anat.)* trachea.

zintzursagar *n.(anat.)* Adam's apple.

zintzurtu *v.i.* to choke.

zintzurzulo *n.* pharynx, trachea.

zinu *n.* sign. *n.* gesture.

zinuka *adv.* gesturing, making a sign.

zinuketa *n.* gesticulation, signing, pantomime.

zinulari *n.* gesticulator; mime.

zinuti *adj.* gesturing, signing.

zinutsu *adj.* gesturing, gesticulating.

zio *n.* reason, cause, motive.

zipli-zapla *n.* sound of slapping.

zipli-zaplaka *adv.* slapping.

ziplo *adv.* suddenly.

zipo *n.* provocation, incitement.

zipo egin *v.t.* to provoke, to incite.

zipokari *n./adj.* provoker; provoking, provocative.

zipote *adj.* unsociable, ill-tempered.

zipotz *n.* tap, stopper, cork, plug. *adj.* stubborn, hard-headed.

zipozkada *n.* pop (of a cork, stopper, etc.).

zipozkeria *n.* obstinacy, stubbornness, hard-headedness.

zipozketa *n.* stopping, corking, plugging.

zipozkile *n.* maker of corks, plugs, stoppers, caps, etc.

zipozkintza *n.* manufacture of corks, plugs, stoppers, caps, etc.

zipoztu *v.t.* to plug, to cork, to stop

(up).

zipristin n. splashing, splattering. adj. rascally, vile, mischievous.

zipristinaldi n. splashing, splattering.

zipristindu v.t. to splash, to splatter.

zipriztindura n. splattering, splashing.

zipunpa n. fireworks.

zira n. raincoat. n. shoe polish.

ziraun n.(zool.) glass snake. n.(fig.) snake, bad person, evil person.

zirdin n. rag, tatter, string hanging from clothing.

zirga n. towrope, towline.

zirgabide n. towpath.

zirgari n. tower, one who tows.

zirgatu v.t. to tow (boats).

ziri n. tire block or wedge; axletree pin (of a wheel). n.(fig.) wrong, difficulty, trick. n. dowel, cotter pin, plug, peg.

ziri(a) sartu v.t. to insert a cork or stopper. v.t. to deceive, to trick, to cheat, to defraud.

zirika adv. harassing, pestering, plaguing.

zirikada n. poking, jabbing. n. satire, biting commentary. n. temptation.

zirikadura n. temptation. n. poking, prodding, jabbing.

zirikagarri adj. exciting, stimulating. adj. tempting.

zirikaketa n. stimulus, provocation. n. temptation.

zirikakor adj. inducive, provocative; inciting.

zirikalari n. instigator, provoker. n. tempter. n. picador (bullfighting). adj. satirical, biting.

zirikaldi n. provocation, stimulation, incitement. n. temptation.

zirikamen n. provocation, stimulation, incitement. n. temptation.

zirikamendu n. provocation, stimulation, incitement.

zirikarazi v.t. to cause (someone) to poke or jab (something); to cause (someone) to tempt (someone).

zirikari n. instigator, provoker, tempter.

zirikatu v.t. to prod, to jab. v.t. to tempt.

zirikatzaile n. provoker, stimulator, inciter; tempter. n. picador (bullfighting). adj. bothersome, annoying.

ziriketa n. jabbing, poking, prodding.

ziriketan adv. poking, jabbing, pestering, plaguing.

ziriko n. silk.

zirikon n. batch of combed flax.

zirimola n. storm, tempest, squall.

zirimolatu v.i. to form whirls (water, wind, hurricanes, etc.).

zirin adj. uneasy, nervous, upset, hyperactive. n. diarrhea. n. bird excrement.

zirindu v.i. to be nervous, to be upset, to be fidgety, to be hyperactive. v.i. to have diarrhea.

zirineri n.(med.) dysentery.

zirisartzaile n. one who tricks, one who defrauds.

ziritu v.i. to become sturdy, to become tough (plants). v.t. to tap, to cork, to plug, to cap; to wedge (a tire), to block (a tire).

ziritxo n.(dim.) small stick.

ziriztatu v.t. to insert a plug, to cork, to tap; to wedge, to insert a block (under a tire).

zirkin n. movement.

zirkin egin v.t. to move.

zirkin eragin v.t. to make (someone) move.

zirku n. circus.

zirkuitu n.(elec.) circuit.

zirkuituitxi n. closed circuit.

zirkulapen n. circulation.

zirkular adj. circular.

zirkularki adv. circularly.

zirkulatu v.i. to circulate (traffic, blood, etc.).

zirkulazio n. circulation.

zirkulu n.(geom.) circle.

zirkuluerdi n.(geom.) semicircle.

zirkunferentzia n.(geom.) circumference.

zirkunstantzia n. circumstance.

zirpil n. thread, loose thread (from clothing), snag. n. rag, tatter.

zirpildu v.i. to unravel (thread from clothing), to snag (a thread from clothing). v.i. to wear out, to deteriorate.

zirpiltsu adj. frayed, ragged, in tatters.

zirrara n. emotion, feeling, impression.

zirraragarri adj. emotional, producing emotion, moving.

zirraratu v.i. to be moved (emotionally), to become emotional.

zirrarazko adj. emotional.

zirri n. touching between young people of different sexes. n. straw mat.

zirriborrapen n. sketch.

zirriborratu v.t. to scribble. v.t. to sketch; to draft, to make a rough draft.

zirriborro n. scribble, scribbling mark(s). n. sketch, rough draft.

zirriborrotsu adj. illegible, smudgy, smeared, blurred.

zirriborrotzaile n./adj. scribbler; scribbling.

zirri egin v.t. to touch (usually a boy touching a girl in a sexual way).

zirrikatu v.t. to incite, to plague, to pester, to harass. v.t. to open part way, to leave ajar (a door).

zirrikiton adj. crude, rough spoken (man). n. tartan, Scotch plaid.

zirrikitu n. crack, crevice, cranny, fissure, interstice. n. fly (in trousers).

zirriki-zarraka adv. dragging one's feet, listlessly, awkwardly.

zirrilari adj. fond of touching girls (in a sexual way).

zirrimarra n. sketch; draft; summary.
n. scribbling, illegible writing.
zirrimarraka adv. sketching; drafting;
scribbling.
zirrimarrari n. scribbler.
zirrimarratu v.t. to scribble, to write
illegibly.
zirrindola n. slice, slab.
zirrist n.(onomat.) splash. Sound of
rapidly running water. n.(onomat.)
sound of a slip or fall.
zirristada n. splash, torrent of water. n.
slipping, sliding.
zirristatu v.i. to slip, to slide, to skid.
zirrist egin v.t. to splash, to spurt
(water). v.t. to slip, to slide, to skid.
zirrito n. small crack, small opening.
zirritu n. small crack, small opening,
fissure. adj. loyal, faithful.
zirrituki adv. faithfully, exactly,
scrupulously.
zirritxo n.(dim.) small straw mat.
zirri-zarra n. scribbling, illegible
writing. n. split, rip, rent, tear,
laceration.
zirta n. spark.
zirt edo zart adv. decisively,
resolutely.
zirt edo zart egin v.t. to make a
decision.
zirt edo zarteko adj. decisive.
zirti-zarta adv. decisively, resolutely.
zirti-zarta egin v.t. to decide, to make
a firm decision.
zirti-zarta erabaki v.t. to make a firm
decision, to decide.
zirtzil adj. insignificant, useless, trivial.
adj. vile, disgusting, destitute. n. rag,
tatter.
zirtzildu v.i. to become vile, to become
evil, to go bad.
zirtzileria n. bunch of trinkets, group of
cheap or trivial items. n. trifle,
bagatelle. n. vileness, lowness,
meanness.
zirtzilkari n. peddler, street hawker.
zirtzilkeria n. filth, slovenliness. n.
meanness, baseness, pettiness.
zirtzilki adv. lowly, vilely, meanly,
viciously, despicably.
zirtzilsaltzaile n. peddler, street
hawker.
zital adj. mean, vile, infamous.
zitaldu v.i. to become vile, to turn
mean.
zitaldura n. degeneracy, corruption. n.
poisoning.
zitaleria n. band of villains, group of
base and vile men.
zitalgarri adj. degrading, debasing.
zitalkeria n. vilification, debasement,
degradation.
zitalki adv. meanly, basely, vilely,
abjectly, villainously.
zitalkiro adv. vilely, basely, meanly.
zitaltalde n. band of villains, group of
base and vile men.

zitaltasun n. vileness, baseness,
meanness, dishonesty.
zitara n.(mus.) zither.
zitarajole n. zither player.
zitori n.(bot.) white lily, Easter lily.
n.(bot.) iris.
zitroi n.(bot.) lemon.
zitu n. fruit (of a harvest).
ziur adj. sure, certain, indubitable. adv.
for sure, certainly, undoubtedly.
ziur egon v.i. to be sure, to be certain.
ziurgarri adj. assurable, certifiable,
certifying.
ziurpetu v.t. to prove, to demonstrate.
v.t. to put in a safe place.
ziurtagiri n. certificate.
ziurtapen n. confirmation, certification.
ziurtasun n. assurance, assuredness,
certainty.
ziurtatu v.t. to confirm, to assure, to
make certain.
ziurtu v.t./v.i. to certify, to assure, to
testify (to); to ascertain, to make
sure, to be sure (of).
ziza n.(bot.) mushroom (Di cardinali). n.
lisp, pronouncing s like th.
zizaka adv. lisping, pronouncing s like
th; stuttering, stammering.
zizakadura n. lisping; stuttering,
stammering.
zizakari adj. lisping; stuttering,
stammering.
zizakatu v.t. to lisp; to stutter, to
stammer.
zizalkaka n. small mound of earth
created by worm waste.
zizare n.(zool.) earthworm, worm.
zizarebelar n.(bot.) southernwood.
zizarehilkin n. vermicide.
zizareluze n.(zool.) tapeworm.
zizaretsu adj. wormy.
zizarezulo n. worm hole.
zizeilu n. long kitchen bench with a
back.
zizel n. chisel.
zizelatu v.t. to chisel, to sculpt using a
chisel.
zizeldu v.t. to chisel, to sculpt using a
chisel.
zizeldura n. chiseling.
zizelkari n. chiseler, one who uses a
chisel.
zizelkaritza n. sculpting, chiseling.
zizelkatu v.t. to chisel, to sculpt with a
chisel.
zizelketa n. chiseling.
zizipaza adj. lisping, lisper.
zizka-mizkak n.(pl.) assortment of
tidbits or appetizers.
zizkatu v.i. to become worm-eaten, to
be gnawed by worms.
zizki-mizki n. bagatelle, trifle.
zizkolatsu adj. strident.
zizpa n. blunderbuss.
zizpakada n. shot from a blunderbuss.
n. blow to the head with a
blunderbuss.

zizpuru *n.* sigh, moan, sob.

zizpuruka *adv.* sighing, moaning, sobbing.

zizpurutu *v.i.* to sigh, to moan, to sob.

zizt *n.(onomat.)* sound of an incision or injection.

zizta *n.* injecting, puncturing, piercing.

ziztada *n.* puncture, injection. *n.* insinuation.

ziztagarri *adj.* biting, piercing.

ziztailu *n.* scalpel, bistoury, surgical knife.

ziztaka *adv.* piercing, cutting, puncturing.

ziztakatu *v.t.* to pierce, to puncture, to jab, to poke.

ziztaketa *n.* puncturing, jabbing, poking; tattooing.

ziztakor *adj.* exciting, stimulating.

ziztatu *v.t.* to poke, to prod, to jab, to pierce, to puncture. *v.t.* to stimulate, to excite.

ziztatzaile *n.* poker, prodder, jabber. *adj.* pricking, stinging, poking, jabbing.

ziztor *n.* special sausage made for St. Thomas' day (December 21). *n.* icicle.

ziztorgile *n.* sausage maker.

ziztortegi *n.* sausage shop.

ziztrin *adj.* insignificant, useless, trivial. *adj.* malnourished, very weak, wasted away.

ziztrindu *v.i.* to become vile, to go bad, to become evil, vicious or wicked.

ziztrinkeria *n.* petty or insignificant thing, puny thing. *n.* pettiness, puniness, baseness, lowness, meanness.

ziztrinki *adv.* lowly, meanly, vilely, viciously, despicably.

ziztro *adj.* (sexually) impotent (men).

ziztrotasun *n.* sexual impotence in males.

ziztu *n.* great speed, alacrity, celerity. *n.* whistle.

ziztuan *adv.* quickly, at great speed.

-zki- *(gram.)* Infix usually indicating a plural direct object in transitive verb forms. Used in all dialects except Biscayan.

-zko *(gram.)* Suffix indicating material, made of. **Egurrezko etxea.** A wooden house.

zo *inter.* whoa!

zohar *adj.* clear (sky).

zohardi *adj.* clear. *n.* clear sky.

zohardura *n.* brilliance, radiance.

zohartu *v.i.* to be brilliant, to be radiant; to clear up (sky).

zohi *n.* clod of dirt with grass, piece of sod. *adj.* ripe, mature.

zohitsu *adj.* full of clods (of earth); covered with sod.

zohiztadura *n.* laying sod (for a lawn).

zohiztatu *n.* to lay sod.

zokil *n.* clod of earth. *n.* poorly

leavened bread.

zoko *n.* corner, secret place.

zokodun *adj.* concave, deep.

zokogune *n.* depression, hollow.

zokokari *adj.* withdrawn, anti-social, misanthropic.

zokokeria *n.* excessive fondness for one's local area.

zokoketari *adj.* withdrawn, anti-social, misanthropic.

zoko-mokoak *n.(pl.)* nook, out-of-the-way corner.

zokondo *n.* corner.

zokondoratu *v.t.* to corner, to put in a corner, to put in an out-of-the-way place.

zokor *n.* dirt clod.

zokoragarri *adj.* abandonable; laid aside.

zokoraketa *n.* setting aside, laying away, abandoning, relegating (something) to a corner.

zokoraldi *n.* relegating (something) to a corner, laying aside, abandoning; confinement.

zokoratu *v.t./v.i.* to corner, to put in a corner, to relegate (something) to a corner, to set aside, to put away; to confine; to be confined, to go to a corner.

zokorkada *n.* blow with a clod of dirt.

zokorrausketa *n.* breaking up clods of dirt.

zokortsu *adj.* full of clods or lumps of earth.

zokortu *v.i.* to turn over earth, to convert (a field, etc.) into clods of earth.

zokotsu *adj.* angular.

zokozale *adj.* misanthropic, antisocial.

zola *n.* sole (of the shoe). *n.* floor; pavement. *n.* foundation. *n.(anat.)* sole of the foot.

zolaberritu *v.t.* to resole (shoes).

zolaberrizte *n.* act of resoling shoes.

zoladura *n.* reflooring, laying a new floor; repaving.

zolaezarle *n.* cobbler, shoe repairman. *n.* one who lays floors; one who lays pavement.

zolagune *n.* depression, hollow, dale, dell.

zolaki *n.* leather used to sole shoes.

zolan *adv.* at the bottom.

zolatu *v.t.* to resole (shoes). *v.t.* to lay a floor; to lay pavement, to pave, to cover with planks.

zolatzaile *n.* one who lays pavement; one who lays floors.

zolda *n.* dandruff. *n.* dirtiness, filth.

zoldadun *adj.* dandruffy, having dandruff, full of dandruff.

zoldagabetu *v.t.* to get rid of dandruff.

zoldatsu *adj.* dandruffy, having dandruff, full of dandruff.

zolerdi *n.* half sole.

zolerditu *v.t.* to put a half sole on (a

shoe).

zoli adj. lively, energetic, agile, jumpy, nervous. adj. sharp, keen (ears, eyes, etc.); sharp, piercing (pain). adj. resonant, sonorous, pleasant sounding. adj. festered, infected, inflamed.

zoliki adv. keenly, sharply, lively.

zolitasun n. liveliness, agility, energeticness, nervousness, jumpiness. n. sharpness, keenness (of vision, hearing, etc.); sharpness (of pain), piercing quality. n. resonance, sonorous quality. n. festering, infection, inflammation.

zolitu v.i. to sharpen (one's wits, one's senses, etc.). v.i. to fester, to become infected, to become inflamed.

zomorro n. insect. n. mask used to frighten children.

zomorrojale adj. insectivorous.

zoologia n. zoology.

zoologiko adj. zoological.

zopa n. soup; soup pot, caldron. n. piece of bread (usually dunked in coffee and milk).

zopak egin v.t. to soak pieces of bread in a bowl of milk or milk and coffee.

zopazale adj. fond of soup.

zopontzi n. soup pot, caldron.

zor n. debt.

zora- Used in compound words. Derived from zoro, crazy; enchanted.

zorabiadura n. grogginess, befuddlement.

zorabiagarri adj. dizzying, maddening.

zorabiatu v.i. to be groggy, to be dazed, to be stunned; to be bewildered, to be confused, to be agitated. v.t. to make dizzy, to make sick.

zorabio n. delirium; dizziness, seasickness, motion sickness.

zorabiodun adj. delirious, dizzy.

zorabioketa n. fainting, passing out, losing consciousness.

zorabioz adv. groggily, in a daze, confusedly, bewilderedly.

zoradura n. confusion, bewilderment.

zoragarri adj. delightful, splendid, marvelous, wonderful, enchanting.

zoragarriki adv. delightfully, splendidly, marvelously, wonderfully.

zoragarriro adv. delightfully, splendidly, wonderfully, marvelously.

zoragarritasun n. delightfulness, splendidness, wonderfulness, marvelousness.

zoragarritu v.i. to fall in love.

zorakeria n. insanity, craziness, foolishness, stupidity, nonsense, folly.

zoraketa n. going crazy, going mad.

zorakila adj. slightly crazy (female).

zorakilo adj. slightly crazy (male).

zoralda n. confusion, bewilderment.

zoraldi n. delirium, passing madness.

zoramen n. great joy, jubilation, rapture. n. craziness, dementedness.

zorarazi v.t. to drive (someone) crazy. v.t. to fascinate, to enchant, to seduce, to charm.

zorarazle adj. maddening. adj. charming, fascinating, seductive.

zoratu v.i./v.t. to be crazy, to go crazy; to drive (someone) crazy. v.t. to charm, to enchant, to fascinate.

zoraxka adj. slightly crazy.

zordun n. debtor, one who goes into debt. adj. indebted.

zordundu v.i. to go into debt, to become indebted.

zordunkide n. joint debtor.

zorgabe adj. solvent, without debts.

zorgabetasun n. solvency, lack of debts.

zorgabetu v.i. to get out of debt, to be out of debt, to be solvent.

zorgin n. debtor, one who goes into debt.

zori n. luck, fortune, fate, destiny.

zorian egon v.i. to be about to, to be on the verge of, to be on the point of.

zoridura n. ripeness, maturity.

zorigabe adj. unfortunate, unhappy, misfortunate, unlucky. n. misfortune, adversity.

zorigabeki adv. unfortunately, unhappily, unluckily.

zorigabeko adj. unhappy, unfortunate, unlucky.

zorigabetasun n. misfortune, unhappiness, adversity, unluckiness.

zorigaitz n. misfortune, bad luck, adversity.

zorigaitzeko adj. unfortunate, unhappy, misfortunate, unlucky.

zorigaitzez adv. unhappily, unfortunately, unluckily.

zorigaizki adv. unfortunately, unhappily, unluckily.

zorigaiztasun n. misfortune, adversity, unluckiness.

zorigaizto n. bad luck, misfortune, adversity.

zorigaiztoko adj. unfortunate, unhappy, unlucky.

zorigaiztotu v.i. to be unfortunate, to be unlucky, to be disastrous.

zorigaiztoz adv. unfortunately, unluckily.

zorigaiztu v.i. to suffer misfortune, to suffer adversity, to have bad luck.

zorigogor n. bad luck, misfortune, adversity.

zorigogorreko adj. unfortunate, unlucky.

zorijoko n. game of chance.

zorion n. happiness, good luck, good fortune.

zorionagur n. congratulations. Usually used in plural.

zorionagurtu *v.t.* to congratulate; to wish (someone) good luck.

zorionak *n.(pl.)* congratulations, best wishes, happy birthday, etc.

zorionak eman *v.t.* to congratulate, to offer best wishes.

zorionaldi *n.* time of prosperity or happiness, good time.

zorionbideak *n.(pl.)* Beatitudes of Christ's Sermon on the Mount.

zoriondu *v.t.* to make (someone) happy; to congratulate.

zoriondun *adj.* lucky, fortunate, happy.

zorionean *adv.* fortunately, happily, luckily.

zorioneko *adj.* lucky, fortunate, happy. Often used ironically with a negative meaning of blasted, confounded.

zorionez *adv.* fortunately, happily, luckily.

zoriongabe *adj.* luckless, unfortunate, unhappy.

zoriongarri *adj.* pleasing, cheering.

zoriontasun *n.* happiness, good luck, good fortune.

zoriontsu *adj.* happy, fortunate, lucky.

zoritasun *n.* ripeness, maturity.

zoritu *v.i.* to ripen, to mature.

zoritxar *n.* misfortune, bad luck, adversity.

zoritxarkoi *adj.* fateful, ominous.

zoritxarreko *adj.* unhappy, unfortunate.

zoritxarrez *adv.* unfortunately, unluckily, unhappily.

zoriz *adv.* by chance, by luck.

zorizka *adj.* half ripe, partially ripe.

zorizko *adj.* chance, fortuitous, lucky, coincidental.

zorketa *n.* debt.

zorki *n.* recourse, resort.

zorkide *n.* joint debtor.

zorkontu *n.* bill, invoice.

zorna- Used in compound words. Derived from *zorne*, pus, infection.

zornabelar *n.(bot.)* groundsel.

zornagaitz *n.(med.)* abscess.

zornakor *adj.* suppurative, suppurant, discharging pus, pussy.

zornarazle *adj.* suppurant, suppurative.

zornatsu *adj.* ulcerous, full of pus, purulent, suppurant.

zornatu *v.i.* to fester, to form pus, to discharge pus, to become infected with pus, to make purulent.

zornazorro *n.(med.)* abscess, sore.

zorne *n.* pus, infection.

zornedun *adj.* purulent, suppurant, discharging pus.

zornejario *n.* purulence, suppuration, forming or discharging of pus.

zornegabetu *v.t./v.i.* to remove pus; to drain (pus from a wound).

zoro *n./adj.* crazy. *adj.(fig.)* stupid, irresponsible.

zoroa izan *v.i.* to go crazy.

zoroetxe *n.* mad house, insane asylum.

zorogaizto *adj.* evil and crazy.

zoroki *adv.* crazily, foolishly, stupidly.

zoronga *n.* coiffure, hairdo.

zorongo *adj.* harebrained, slightly crazy.

zoroska *adj.* slightly crazy, harebrained.

zorotasun *n.* craziness, dementedness, insanity.

zorozain *n.* one who cares for the insane.

zorpe *n.* debt, debit.

zorpeko *n.* debtor, one who goes into debt.

zorpetu *v.i.* to be in debt, to go into debt, to fall into debt.

zorragiri *n.(econ.)* I.O.U., statement of one's account, etc.

zorra(k) garbitu *v.t.* to pay off debts, to settle debts, to liquidate debts.

zorra(k) kitatu *v.t.* to pay off debts, to settle debts, to liquidate debts.

zorralde *n.* accumulation of debts.

zorretan *adv.* on credit.

zorretan eman *v.t.* to loan. (lit.) to give in debt.

zorretan hartu *v.t.* to buy on credit.

zorreztatu *v.i.* to go into debt.

zorri *n.(zool.)* louse.

zorridun *adj.* pedicular, lousy, of or relating to lice.

zorrieri *n.* pediculosis, state of being infested with lice.

zorrigabetu *v.t.* to delouse.

zorrikari *adj.* delousing.

zorrikatu *v.t.* to delouse.

zorrikatzaile *adj.* delousing.

zorrikeria *n.* filth, dirtiness, lousiness.

zorriketa *n.* delousing, ridding of lice. *n.* act of preening (birds' feathers).

zorriketan *adv.* killing lice, delousing.

zorriketari *adj.* delousing.

zorrino *n.(dim.)* nit, egg of a louse.

zorriteria *n.* lice, group of lice, bunch of lice.

zorritoki *n.* delousing station.

zorritsu *adj.* lousy, full of lice.

zorritza *n.* lice, bunch of lice.

zorrizko *adj.* pedicular, lousy, of or relating to lice.

zorriztatu *v.i.* to become infested with lice.

zorrizto *adj.* lousy, covered with lice.

zorro *n.* sack, bag, leather pouch, game bag. *n.* sheath, scabbard. *n.* bramble bush.

zorroalde *n.* sackful, contents of a sack.

zorroilo *adj.* rough, rough hewn, poorly made. *n.* belly. *adj.* big-bellied, pot-bellied.

zorroratu *v.t.* to put in a sack, to put in a case; to sheath, to scabbard.

zorrotu *v.t.* to put in a sack; to sheathe, to scabbard.

zorrotz *adj.* sharp, biting, piercing, acute, keen. *adj.* profound, deep.

adj. severe, harsh, demanding. *adj.* exact.

zorrotzaile *n.* sharpener, knife sharpener.

zorrotzaldi *n.* sharpening. *n.* severity, moment of harshness.

zorrotzarazi *v.t.* to have (something) sharpened.

zorrotzarri *n.* whetting stone.

zorrotzegi *adj.* overbearing, too demanding, rigid, overly strict or severe. *adj.* too sharp.

zorrozkailu *n.* pencil sharpener, any kind of sharpener.

zorrozkeria *n.* severity, inflexibility, excessive demandingness.

zorrozketa *n.* sharpening, grinding.

zorrozki *adv.* keenly, sharply (in a mental sense). *adv.* severely, rigorously.

zorrozkile *n.* sharpener, knife sharpener.

zorrozkiro *adv.* keenly, sharply.

zorroztaile *n.* sharpener, knife sharpener.

zorroztarri *n.* whetting stone, grindstone.

zorroztasun *n.* keenness of mind, mental sharpness, cleverness, intelligence. *n.* severity, harshness, rigorousness, rigidity.

zorroztatzaile *n.* sharpener, knife sharpener.

zorrozte *n.* act of sharpening, act of filing.

zorroztu *v.t./v.i.* to sharpen (points or senses), to grind (to a sharp edge or point).

zorroztura *n.* knife sharpening, sharpening of any cutting edge.

zorte *n.* luck, chance.

zorteatu *v.t.* to draw lots, to throw dice.

zortzi *adj./n.* eight.

zortzigarren *adj.* eighth.

zortzikatu *v.t.* to divide by eight, to put in groups of eight.

zortziko *n.* eight-line stanza (in Basque poetry). *n.(mus.)* traditional Basque musical rhythm; traditional Basque dance. *n.* octet, eight-member group (choir, etc.). *n.* eight (in cards).

zortzikote *n.* octet, group of eight singers.

zortzina *adj./adv.* eight apiece, eight to each one.

zortzinaka *adv.* of eight, eight by eight, by eights, in groups of eight.

zortzinakatu *v.t.* to divide into groups of eight, to put into groups of eight.

zortzinan *adv.* in groups of eight, by eights, eight by eight.

zortzirehun *adj./n.* eight hundred.

zortziren *adj.* eighth, one eighth.

zortzisilabadun *adj.* octosyllabic.

zortziurren *n.(eccl.)* festival celebrated in an octave.

zortzizkatu *v.t.* to divide into groups of eight, to put into groups of eight.

zoru *n.* floor, ground. *n.* hold (of a ship).

zoruezarketa *n.* paving, tiling, laying a new floor.

zoruezarle *n.* paver, one who lays new flooring.

zor ukan *v.t.* to owe.

zorupe *n.* underfloor, subflooring.

zot- Used in compound words. Derived from *zohi*, clod of dirt and grass.

zotal *n.* clod of dirt.

zotaldu *v.t.* to break up clods of dirt, to turn over earth.

zotarrain *n.* earthen floor.

zotazal *n.* lawn, grass sod.

zotin *n.* hiccup(s).

zotindun *adj.* having the hiccups.

zotin egin *v.t.* to have the hiccups, to hiccup.

zotinka *adv.* hiccupping.

zotintsu *adj.* hiccupping.

zotz *n.* stick, branch, small piece of a stick; chopstick; toothpick.

zotzabar *n.* pieces of small branches, twigs.

zotzegiketa *n.* game of chance, drawing lots, raffle.

zotzegile *n.* raffler.

zotz egin *v.t.* to leave to chance, to toss a coin, to raffle (off), to draw lots.

zozkatu *v.t.* to leave to chance, to toss a coin, to raffle (off).

zozketa *n.* drawing lots, game of chance. *n.* gathering twigs.

zozketagarri *adj.* capable of being left to chance, capable of being raffled off.

zozketari *n.* raffler, one who organizes the drawing of lots.

zozketatu *v.t.* to raffle (off), to draw lots.

zozkide *n.* raffle participant, bingo player.

zozkile *n.* toothpick maker.

zozo *n.(zool.)* blackbird (*Turdus merula*). *adj.* imbecilic, stupid, foolish.

zozoaldi *n.* grogginess, dazedness.

zozoar *n.(zool.)* male blackbird.

zozodura *n.* foolishness, stupidity, imbecility.

zozoeme *n.(zool.)* female blackbird.

zozoilo *adj.* foolish, stupid, imbecilic.

zozoilokeria *n.* stupid act or expression.

zozoiloki *adv.* foolishly, stupidly.

zozoilotasun *n.* foolishness, stupidness, imbecility.

zozoilotu *v.i.* to become foolish, to be silly.

zozokeria *n.* foolishness, stupid act.

zozoki *adv.* stupidly, foolishly.

zozokume *n.* small blackbird.

zozotasun *n.* stupidity, foolishness.

zozotu *v.i.* to become a fool, to be stupid, to be an imbecile.

zoztor *n.* obstacle, impediment, stumbling block, hindrance.

zoztor egin *v.t.* to trip, to stumble.

zoztor eragin *v.t.* to trip (someone), to make (someone) stumble.

zoztorgabetu *v.t.* to remove an obstacle.

zoztorzale *adj.* obstructing, impeding.

zoztu *v.t.* to tap, to put a faucet in.

-ztatu *(gram.)* Verbal suffix which denotes action, act of anointing, act of filling with, etc. **Koipeztatu.** To oil, to grease.

zu *pron.* you. Formerly considered a plural subject but now used as a singular.

-zu- Verbal infix meaning you, used as indirect object with aux. verbs. **Hiru sagar emango dizkizut.** I will give you three apples.

Zubero *n.(geog.)* One of the three provinces of the northern Basque country. Its capital is Mauleon.

zuberoera *n.* Basque dialect spoken in Zuberoa.

zuberotar *n./adj.* native of Zuberoa.

zubi *n.* bridge.

zubibegi *n.* archway under a bridge, space under a bridge.

zubibide *n.* road or path on a bridge, bridge where it forms part of a road.

zubibular *n.* pillar of a bridge, buttress of a bridge.

zubiburu *n.* bridgehead.

zubigile *n.* builder of bridges.

zubigin *n.* builder of bridges.

zubigintza *n.* bridge building.

zubisaihets *n.* pillar of a bridge.

zubisari *n.* bridge toll.

zubito *n.(dim.)* small bridge; planks used for crossing rivers or streams.

zubitu *v.t.* to bridge, to build a bridge over.

zubixka *n.(dim.)* small bridge.

zubizain *n.* toll collector, keeper of the bridge.

zubizulo *n.* archway under a bridge, space under a bridge.

-zue- Verbal infix meaning you all, used with aux. verbs as indirect object.

zuek *n.(nom.)* you (active pl.).

zuhain *n.* forage, fodder, straw.

zuhaindegi *n.* grain loft where fodder is stored, hay loft, straw loft.

zuhaitz *n.* tree.

zuhaitzain *n.* arboriculturist, one who grows trees.

zuhaitzale *n.* arborist.

zuhaitzantzeko *adj.* arboriform, tree-shaped.

zuhaitzazkuntza *n.* arboriculture.

zuhaitzulo *n.* small irrigation ditch around a tree.

zuhaixka *n.(dim.)* little tree, bush.

zuhaizpide *n.* tree-lined road.

zuhaizti *n.* forest, woods, plantation or grove of trees.

zuhaiztu *v.t.* to plant trees.

zuhamu *n.* tree. *n.* grapevine that climbs a tree trunk.

zuhamuki *n.* wood, piece of a tree.

zuhandor *n.(bot.)* dogwood tree (*Cornus sanguinea*).

zuhar *n.* elm tree. *adj.* strong, robust, hardy.

zuhur *adj.* wise, sensible, cautious, prudent. *adj.* observant, perspicacious, shrewd, keen. *adj.* stingy; economical, thrifty.

zuhur egon *v.i.* to be cautious, to take precautions.

zuhurgabe *adj.* careless, not cautious.

zuhurgabekeria *n.* carelessness, lack of caution.

zuhurgabetasun *n.* carelessness, lack of caution.

zuhurgabezia *n.* carelessness, lack of caution.

zuhurkeria *n.* stinginess, miserliness, niggardliness. *n.* shrewdness, cunning.

zuhurki *adv.* cautiously, carefully, wisely, prudently. *adv.* shrewdly, perspicaciously.

zuhurragin *n.(anat.)* wisdom tooth.

zuhurrezko *adj.* sensible, judicious, prudent, cautious, wise.

zuhurtasun *n.* wisdom, discretion.

zuhurtasunez *adv.* with discretion, cautiously.

zuhurtu *v.i.* to become wise, to become prudent, to become shrewd, to become cautious. *v.i.* to become thrifty.

zuhurtzia *n.* prudence, caution, discretion.

zuin *n.* ridge between the furrows of a field.

zuinarri *n.* boundary stone, landmark.

zuindu *v.t.* to mark with range poles (surveying).

zuinketa *n.* marking with range poles.

zuk *pron.* you (active subject, used with transitive verbs).

zuka *adv.* using the formal (form of) you.

zuketa *n.* use of the formal form of you, *zu*.

zuku *n.* soup. *n.* gravy, sauce. *n.* juice.

zukugailu *n.* juicer.

zukutsu *adj.* juicy.

zukutu *v.i.* to overcook, to cook down, to reduce to paste, to thicken.

zula- Used in some compound words. Derived from *zulo*, hole.

zuladura *n.* perforation, making holes, punching holes.

zulagailu *n.* perforator, hole puncher.

zulagaitz *adj.* impenetrable, impermeable.

zulagaiztasun *n.* impenetrability, impermeability.

zulagarri adj. puncturable, pierceable, penetrable, drillable.
zulakada n. perforation.
zulakaitz n. chisel, burin.
zulakaiztu v.t. to chisel, to carve; to engrave with a burin.
zulakatu v.t. to perforate, to make a hole (in), to punch a hole (in), to drill, to bore.
zulaketa n. perforation, making holes, punching holes, drilling, boring.
zulape n. shaft, tunnel.
zulapen n. perforation; excavation, hole, dig.
zulapetu v.t. to mine, to excavate, to dig under, to undermine; to perforate.
zulapetzaile n. miner, excavator, digger of holes.
zulatu v.t. to dig a hole, to make a hole, to burrow (under), to drill, to bore, to perforate. v.i. to prick, to stick, to poke (a hole in), to puncture.
zulatzaile n. digger of holes, miner, excavator. n. conductor, ticket-taker, ticket collector.
zulo n. hole, orifice, opening, perforation. n. den, lair, burrow.
-zulo (gram.) Noun suffix which indicates fondness or affection for. Aitazulo. Fond of father.
zulodun adj. holey, perforated, having holes.
zulo egin v.t. to dig a hole, to make a hole (in), to mine, to excavate, to perforate.
zulogile n. digger of holes, miner, excavator. n. gravedigger.
zulogune n. pothole, hole; cavity, hollow.
zulondo n. bottom (of a hole or hollow object).
zuloraketa n. ensilage, storage in a silo.
zuloratu v.i. to enter a hole, to go to ground, to burrow in, to enter a burrow.
zulotsu adj. full of holes, perforated, porous.
zuma- Used in compound words. Derived from zume, osier willow.
zumalakar n.(bot.) alder buckthorn.
zumar n.(bot.) English elm (Ulmus procera).
zumardi n. grove of elm trees.
zumarkide adj./n. ulmaceous; ulmaceous plant.
zumarrondo n.(bot.) elm tree.
zume n.(bot.) osier, osier willow.
zumeki n. wicker, piece of willow or wicker.
zumel n.(bot.) holm oak.
zumetsu adj. abundant in osier willows.
zumesare n. wicker lattice, woven wicker.
zumezko adj. wicker, made of wicker, made of willow.

zumintz n.(bot.) aloe.
zumintzatu v.t. to make bitter with aloes.
zumitz n.(zool.) bedbug. n. iron hoop, iron strap, iron band. n. cheese hoop, cheesemold.
zumo n. juice.
zumotsu adj. juicy.
zunburrun n. buzzing.
zunburrunka adv. buzzing.
zunda n. sounding, probing, fathoming. n. plot, lot, parcel (of ground).
zundaezin adj. unfathomable, unsoundable.
zundagarri adj. soundable, fathomable.
zundaketa n. sounding, fathoming.
zundako adj. parceling; pertaining to parceled lands.
zundaldi n. sounding, fathoming.
zundatu v.t. to sound, to probe, to fathom. v.t.(fig.) to sound (someone) out, to find out how (someone) feels about (something).
zuntz n. fiber, filament, thread.
zuntzetsu adj. fibrous, full of threads, stringy.
zuntzun adj. foolish, stupid.
zuntzundu v.i. to become foolish, to lose one's senses.
zuntzunkeria n. foolishness (word or deed).
zur n. wood, timber, lumber.
zurabe n. wooden beam.
zurbeltz n.(bot.) kermes oak.
zurbeso n. wooden framework, baywork.
zurbil adj. pale, faded.
zurbildu v.i. to turn pale, to pale, to lose color. v.t. to make (someone) pale, to leave (someone) pale.
zurbildura n. paleness.
zurbiltasun n. paleness, pallor.
zurda n. mane. n. fishing line. n.(anat.) tendon.
zurdaki n. horse's hair, hair of a mane.
zurdatsu adj. hairy, mane-like, full of hair.
zurdatu v.t. to make a fishing line.
zurdaztatu v.t. to decorate a horse's mane.
zurdile n. mane hair.
zurdoihal n. rough fabric made of horsehair used for sacks, such as burlap.
zure adj./pron. your; yours.
zurekiko adj. your, pertaining to you, relating to you.
zureria n. framework (used in construction).
zuresi n. wooden fence.
zurezko adj. wooden, wood, made of wood.
zureztaketa n. building a plank molding (for cement, etc.).
zureztatu v.t. to build a plank molding

(for cement, etc.).

zureztu *v.t.* to cover with wood, to make with wood.

zurgai *adj.* woody, ligneous.

zurgin *n.* carpenter; joiner.

zurgindegi *n.* carpenter's shop.

zurgingo *n.* carpenter's trade.

zurginlan *n.* carpenter's work, carpentry.

zurginmahai *n.* carpenter's bench.

zurginmutil *n.* carpenter's apprentice.

zurgintza *n.* carpentry, woodwork.

zurgoiko *n.(naut.)* topgallant.

zuri *adj./n.* white. *n.* sycophant, brown-noser, flatterer. *adj.* lazy, good-for-nothing. *pron.(dat.)* to you. *n.* small (glass of) white wine.

zurialdi *n.* whitening, bleaching, whitewashing. *n.* excuse, explanation.

zuribeltz *n.* mulatto.

zuribide *n.* excuse.

zuribizi *adj./n.* bright white.

zuribizitasun *n.* perfect whiteness, pure whiteness.

zurigailu *n.* peeler.

zurigarbi *n.* laundry, wash.

zurigarri *adj.* explainable, excusable, justifiable.

zurigintza *n.* job of a whitewasher.

zurigorri *adj.* rose, pinkish. *adj.* red and white.

zurigorritu *v.t./v.i.* to paint pink, to color (something) pink; to turn pink.

zurikail *adj.* whitish, off-white.

zurikari *n./adj.* sycophant, flatterer, brown-noser; flattering, brown-nosing.

zurikatu *v.t.* to flatter excessively, to offer false flattery.

zurikatzaile *n./adj.* sycophant, flatterer; flattering, brown-nosing.

zurikeria *n.* adulation, cajolery, false flattery. *n.* laziness.

zurikeriaz *adv.* flatteringly.

zurikeriazko *adj.* flattering.

zuriketa *n.* bleaching, whitewashing. *n.* peeling (fruit, vegetables). *n.* flattery, adulation.

zuriketari *n.* sycophant, flatterer.

zuriki *adv.* whitely. *adv.* flatteringly.

zurikin *n.* peel.

zurimin *adj.* very white. *n.* pure whiteness.

zurimindura *n.* whiteness.

zurimintasun *n.* perfect whiteness.

zuringo *n.* egg-white, white of the egg. *n.(anat.)* white of the eye.

zurirudi *n.* wooden statue.

zuriska *adj.* whitish, off-white.

zuritasun *n.* whiteness.

zuritu *v.t.* to bleach, to whiten, to whitewash. *v.t.* to peel (fruit), to shuck (corn). *v.t.* to flatter, to adulate. *v.t.* to excuse, to make an excuse, to justify.

zuritzaile *n.* whitewasher. *n.* flatterer,

sycophant. *n.* excuser, excuse maker.

zuriune *n.* blank space.

zuriurdinska *adj.* bluish-white, whitish-blue.

zuri-zuri *adj.(superl.)* very white, stark white.

zurkaitz *n.* plant stake, supporting pole or stake. *n.(fig.)* support.

zurkaiztatu *v.t.* to stake up a plant, to provide support for climbing plants.

zurkaiztu *v.t.* to stake up plants, to provide support for climbing plants.

zurketari *n.* woodworker; wood dealer, lumber dealer; lumberjack.

zurlan *n.* woodwork, woodworking, carpentry.

zurlandu *v.t.* to work with wood, to do woodworking.

zurlangile *n.* woodworker, carpenter.

zurlanketa *n.* woodworking.

zurlantza *n.* woodworking, carpentry.

zurlantzaile *n.* carpenter, woodworker.

zurmaila *n.* wooden step, wooden stair, wooden rung.

zurmailu *n.* wooden hammer, mallet.

zurmami *n.* medulla, pith (of a tree).

zurmin *n.* flavor given to wine by wooden barrels.

zurmindu *v.i.* to be bitter, to be sour, to turn bitter or sour. *adj.* sour, bitter. *v.i.* to go numb; to become painful.

zurmindura *n.* numbness, stiffness.

zurmingarri *adj.* capable of souring, capable of turning bitter.

zurminkor *adj.* easily soured.

zurmintasun *n.* numbness, stiffness.

zurmolde *n.* wood framework for cement.

zurra *n.* beating (carpets, etc.). *n.(fig.)* punishment, castigation.

zurraldi *n.* act of beating (a carpet, etc.), time spent beating (something).

zurrategi *n.* tannery.

zurratu *v.t.* to tan (hides).

zurratzaile *n.* tanner.

zurru *n.* snoring.

zurruburru *n.* murmuring, rumor. *n.* confusion, disorder, jam, mess, imbroglio.

zurrukalari *adj.* snoring.

zurrukutun *n.* soup made of codfish and potatoes. *n.* preferred, predilect, favorite.

zurruma *n.* heel of a shoe.

zurrumurru *n.* rumor, murmuring, whispering, gossip, empty talk.

zurrumurrutu *v.i.* to be rumored, to be said.

zurrun *adj.* stiff, taut, rigid. *n.* thick pole, shaft (of a cart).

zurrunba *n.* channel conducting water in a water mill, including the dam. *n.* waterfall, cascade.

zurrunbilo *n.* storm, tempest, squall; tornado.

zurrunbilotsu *adj.* stormy, tempestuous; whirling (as in a tornado).

zurrunbilotu *v.i.* to form whirls (in water or air).

zurrundu *v.i.* to go stiff, to stiffen, to become rigid.

zurrundura *n.* going stiff, becoming rigid, stiffening.

zurrunga *n.* snoring. *n.* purring of a cat.

zurrunga egin *v.t.* to snore.

zurrungaka *adv.* snoring.

zurrungari *n.* snorer, one who snores.

zurrungatu *v.t.* to snore.

zurruntasun *n.* rigidity, inflexibility, tautness, stiffness.

zurruntza *n.* disagreeable sensation or feeling, disagreeable impression.

zurrupa *n.* slurping, sucking, glugging, slug, sip.

zurrupada *n.* noisy swallow, gulp, sip, slug.

zurrupaka *adv.* gulping, sipping, in sips, by sips, swallowing noisily.

zurrupakari *n.* big drinker, one who drinks a lot. *n.(fig.)* moocher, parasite.

zurrupaketa *n.* imbibing.

zurrupari *n.* gulper, swallower, sipper.

zurrupatu *v.t.* to gulp, to slurp, to drink noisily, to sip. *v.t.(fig.)* to swallow up, to use up.

zurrupita *n.* torrential rain.

zurrust *n.(onomat.)* sound of a swallow or gulp.

zurrusta *n.* gulp, noisy swallow. *n.* spring, fountain, spurt (of water).

zurrustada *n.* swallow, gulp.

zurrustadaka *adv.* gulping, in gulps.

zurrustailu *n.* sprinkler.

zurrustatu *v.t.* to decant, to pour from one vessel to another.

zurrust egin *v.t.* to gulp down, to drink in gulps.

zurrut *n.(onomat.)* sound of a gulp, small swallow, sip.

zurruta *n.* stream of water (from a brook or a faucet).

zurrutada *n.* small swallow, gulp, sip.

zurrutaka *adv.* gulping, by gulps, in gulps. *adv.* in torrents, torrentially.

zurrutaka edan *v.t.* to gulp, to gulp down, to drink by gulping.

zurrutaldi *n.* gulp, swallow, sip.

zurrutari *n.* gulper, one who drinks in gulps. *n.* big drinker, one who drinks a lot (of alcohol).

zurrutatu *v.i.* to flow abundantly, to gush, to stream.

zurrut egin *v.t.* to gulp, to drink in gulps.

zurrutero *n.* big drinker, drunkard.

zurru-zurru *adv.* gulping, in gulps.

zurrutzaile *n.* big drinker, heavy drinker.

zurtegi *n.* timberyard, lumberyard.

zurtoin *n.(bot.)* stalk (of a plant).

zurtu *v.i.* to sharpen, to whet, to prick up (one's ears). *v.i.* to be surprised, to be astonished.

zurtz *adj.* orphan.

zurubi *n.* staircase, stairway.

zurzizel *n.* wood chisel.

zurztasun *n.* state of being an orphan.

zurzubi *n.* wooden bridge.

zurzuri *n.(bot.)* white poplar.

zut *adj.* vertical, upright. *adj.* svelte.

zutabe *n.* column, pillar, post.

zutargi *n.* torch.

zutarri *n.* stone pillar, stone column.

zutasun *n.* verticalness, uprightness.

zutidura *n.* standing up.

zutierazi *v.t.* to set upright, to stand (something) up.

zutierazle *n.* erector, one who sets (things) upright.

zutik *adv.* standing (up), upright.

zutikaketa *n.* act of standing up, act of getting on one's feet.

zutikako *adj.* vertical, upright.

zutikatu *v.t.* to prop up, to brace, to set upright. *v.i.* to straighten up.

zutik egon *v.i.* to be standing, to stand up.

zutiketa *n.* standing up, getting on one's feet, straightening up.

zutiko *n.* support, brace.

zutikor *adj.* erectile, causing (someone) to stand up straight.

zutikortasun *n.* erectness, uprightness, verticalness. *n.* quality of making someone or something stand up straight; capacity to be raised to an erect position.

zutitasun *n.* stiffness, standing at attention, erectness, straightness.

zutitu *v.i.* to stand up, to get erect, to get on one's feet.

zutitzaile *n.* erector.

zutoihal *n.* standard, banner.

zutoihaldun *n.* standard bearer.

zutoin *n.* pedestal, column, pillar, post.

zutoinbe *n.* base of a pillar or column.

zutoindu *v.t.* to mark with poles or posts.

zuzen *adj.* straight, direct. *adj.* right, correct, proper. *adj.* nice, honest, good. *adv.* straight, directly. *n.* right, legal right.

zuzenbide *n.* right, justice. *n.* address. *n.* rule, regulation.

zuzenbideketa *n.* taking up residence, residing, moving in.

zuzenbideko *adj.* legitimate, rightful.

zuzenbidetu *v.t.* to drive, to conduct, to guide. *v.i.* to dwell, to take up residence, to reside.

zuzenbidez *adv.* justly, rightly.

zuzenbidezko *adj.* just, fair, equitable.

zuzendari *n.* manager, director, conductor.

zuzendarikide *n.* codirector.

zuzendarikidetza *n.* codirection.

zuzendariorde *n.* vice-director, vice-coordinator, assistant director.

zuzendaritza *n.* direction, management, directorate, directorship.

zuzendu *v.t.* to correct, to rectify, to remedy. *v.t.* to straighten (something crooked). *v.i./v.t.* to point toward, to aim for, to orient oneself toward, to head for. *v.t.* to determine; to direct, to guide. *v.i.* to be aimed at, to be intended for, to be directed at.

zuzendura *n.* correcting, rectifying, straightening out.

zuzenean *adv.* directly, straightly.

zuzen egon *v.i.* to be right. (lit.) to be straight.

zuzeneko *adj.* direct, straight. *adj.* legal, legitimate.

zuzenespen *n.* justification.

zuzenetsi *v.t.* to justify, to consider (something) fair.

zuzenez *adv.* by rights, according to justice, justly.

zuzenezin *adj.* incorrigible, not correctible, not straightenable.

zuzengabe *adj.* unfair, unjust.

zuzengabekeria *n.* injustice, inequity, unfairness.

zuzengabeki *adv.* unfairly, unjustly. *adv.* incorrectly, irrationally.

zuzengabeko *adj.* unfair, unjust. *adj.* irrational.

zuzengabetasun *n.* dishonesty, lack of integrity.

zuzengaitz *adj.* incorrigible, not correctible, not reformable.

zuzengarri *adj.* correctible, reformable, rectifiable.

zuzengune *n.* straight stretch of road.

zuzenka *adv.* straight(ly), directly.

zuzenketa *n.* rectification, correction, adjustment.

zuzenki *adv.* straight(ly), directly. *adv.* justly, fairly, honestly.

zuzenkontra *adv.* unjustly, unfairly.

zuzenkontrako *adj.* unjust, unfair.

zuzenkor *adj.* correcting, rectifying.

zuzenpen *n.* correction, rectification.

zuzentasun *n.* straightness. *n.* justice, rightness, honesty.

zuzentezin *adj.* incorrigible, not correctible.

zuzentiar *adj.* favoring justice.

zuzentza *n.* justice, rectitude.

zuzentzaile *n.* corrector, reformer, rectifier. *n.* guide, advisor, counselor.

zuzi *n.* torch. *n.(bot.)* larch tree.

zuzika *adj.* fickle, inconstant.

zuzikakeria *n.* fickleness, instability.

zuzikatasun *n.* fickleness, instability.

zuzimutil *n.* candelabrum, large candlestick.

zuzitu *v.t.* to destroy, to undo, to ruin. *v.t.* to stomp, to squash, to tread underfoot.

zuzper *adj.* recovered, revived, better.

zuzperdura *n.* recovery.

zuzpergarri *adj.* renewing, reviving, invigorating. *adj.* recuperable, retrievable.

zuzperraldi *n.* convalescence, period of recovery.

zuzpertu *v.i.* to recover, to convalesce, to recuperate, to get better.

zuzter *n.* root, stalk.

zuztertu *v.i.* to sprout, to grow shoots.

English-Basque
Dictionary

A

a *n.* Ingeles alfabetoko letra.
abandon *v.t.* utzi, etsi, babesgabetu, zapuztu.
abandonment *n.* babesgabezia, uztasun, uzketa; zokoraketa.
abate *v.t./v.i.* gutiagotu, murriztu, beheragotu.
abbey *n.* abatetxe.
abbot *n.* abata.
abbreviate *v.t.* laburtu, laburragotu, moztu.
abbreviated *adj.* laburgarri, murrizgarri, txikigarri.
abbreviation *n.* laburpen, laburketa; hizlabur, kontrakzio. **Abbreviation by initials.** Laburritz.
ABC's *n.* agaka, alfabeto; alfabeta.
abdicate *v.i./v.t.* erregetza edo nagusitza utzi.
abdomen *n.* errai.
abdominal *adj.* sabeleko, erraietako.
abduct *v.t.* emarrapatu, bahitu.
abduction *n.* emarrapaketa, bahiketa.
abductor *n.* harrapatzaile, harrapakari, bahitzaile.
aberration *n.* zeihardura, okerkuntza.
abet *v.t.* lagundu (gaizkerian).
abeyance *n.* geraldi, etenaldi, pausarte.
abhor *v.t.* higuin izan, gorrotatu.
abhorrent *adj.* gaiztetsigarri, higuinkor, nazkakor.
abide *v.i.* geratu. *v.i.* iraun. *v.i.* bizi. *v.t.* itxaron. *v.t.* jasan.
abiding *adj.* irauteko.
ability *n.* abilezia, ahalmen, ahalpide, artezia, gaitasun, taxu; -men. **Teaching ability.** Maisutasun.
abject *adj.* doilor, zital.
ablative *adj. (gram.)* ablatibo.
ablaze *adj.* sutsu.
able *adj.* moldedun, moldetsu, taxudun, on.
ably *adv.* moduz, trebeki, trebekiro, artezki.
abnormal *adj.* anormal, eznormal. *adj.* araugabeko.
abnormality *n.* anormaltasun, eznormaltasun.
abnormally *adv.* eznormalki.
aboard *adv.* ontzian.
abolish *v.t.* deuseztatu, deuseztu, ezereztatu, kendu.
abolition *n.* legekenketa, deslegekuntza. *n.* ezeztapen, ezeztadura.
abominable *adj.* gorrotagarri, gaitzezkor, higuingarri, nazkakor, nardagarri, herragarri, hastangarri.
abominably *adv.* higuingarriki, higuingarriro, gaitzesgarriki, gaitzesgarriro.
abomination *n.* higuinkeria, narda.
aboriginal *adj.* jatorrizko, bertako.
aborigine *n.* lehenengo biztanle;

bertako.
abort *v.t.* haurregozi, egotzi, umea galdu, haurra bota.
abortion *n.* haurregoizte, haurbotatze.
abortive *adj.* porrot egindako, azken gaizto egindako, huts egindako.
abound *v.i.* ugaritu, ugari izan, narotu, jori izan, askotu.
about *adv.* edo, inguru, -ren bat. **About twenty.** Hogeiren bat. *prep.* -z, -taz, -(r)i buruz. *prep.* inguruan. *adv.* (*to*) zorian. **He is about to die.** Hil zorian dago.
above *prep.* gain, gainean. **Above all.** Batez ere. *adv.* gora. **Above average.** Neurrigorako.
abrasive *adj.* urragarri.
abreast *adv.* lerro batean, alboan.
abridge *v.t.* laburtu, labur egin.
abroad *n.* erbeste. **To go abroad.** Erbesteratu. *adv.* Atzerriratu.
abrupt *adj.* ebazkor.
abscess *n. (med.)* zornazorro, zornagaitz.
absence *n.* kanpoaldi, kanporaldi; huts.
absent *adj.* aldegin(a), desagertu(a), ezdagoen(a). **To be absent.** Huts egin.
absenteeism *n.* kanpokeria.
absent-minded *adj.* ahaztukor, adigabe.
absent oneself *v.i.* kanporatu, urruneratu.
absinthe *n. (bot.)* azantzio.
absolute *adj.* guzti, garbi, oso.
absolutely *adv.* guztiz, guztiro, oroz, osoki.
absoluteness *n.* osotasun, biribiltasun.
absolution *n.* barkamen.
absolve *v.t.* barkatu.
absorb *v.t.* zurgatu, xurgatu, irentsi.
absorbable *adj.* irensgarri, xurgagarri, xurgakari, hurrupagarri.
absorbency *n.* irespen, xurgagarritasun.
absorbent *adj.* irensgarri, xurgakari.
absorption *n.* irenstura, xurgaketa, xurgapen, hurrupaketa. *n.* barnelilura, norberaldi.
abstain *v.t.* haratutzi. *v.t.* botu ez eman.
abstention *n.* abstenzio.
abstinence *n.* gabetasun. *n.* haragiuzte, haratuzte, barau.
abstinent *adj.* uzle, uztaile.
abstract *n.* bildupen. *adj.* abstraktu.
abstraction *n.* abstrakzio.
abstruse *adj.* ulergaitz.
absurd *adj.* arrazoingabeko, zentzugabeko, itxuragabeko.
absurdity *n.* itxuragabekeria, zentzugabekeria, funtsgabekeria.
absurdly *adv.* arrazoingabeki.
abundance *n.* ugalketa, ugaritasun, multzo, naharotasun, oparotasun, ainiztasun, joritasun, parrasta.

abundant *adj.* ugari, ugaritsu, naharo, oparo, jori, parrastatsu; ugal-.

abundantly *adv.* ugari, jori, naharo, eskubeteka, farra-farra, erruz.

abuse *v.t.* gaizki erabili, gaizki hartu. *v.t.* nagusikeritu.

abuse *n.* nagusikeria, soberakeria.

abuser *n.* gaizkierabiltzaile.

abusive *adj.* gaizkierabilgarri. *adj.* gehiegizko. *adj.* iraingarri, laidogarri.

abusively *adv.* gehiegikeriaz, neurriz kanpo.

abysmal *adj.* lezeko; sakon.

abyss *n.* leze, osin, troka.

academic *n.* akademikide. *adj.* akademiko; akademi-.

academy *n.* akademia, ikastetxe. **Academy of the Basque Language.** Euskaltzaindi.

accede *v.i.*(**to**) baieztu, ados egon, baietza eman.

accelerate *v.i./v.t.* arinagotu, lasterrarazi, agurotu.

acceleration *n.* arinketa, azkarketa; azelerazio.

accelerator *n.* (*mech.*) azeleragailu; lastergailu.

accent *v.t.* azentuatu.

accent *n.* azentu. **Acute accent.** Azentu zorrotz.

accented *adj.* azentudun.

accentuate *v.t.* azentuatu.

accentuation *n.* azentuapen, azentuketa.

accept *v.t.* baietsi, ontzat eman, onartu, oneritzia eman, ontzat hartu, oneritzi, abegi egin.

acceptability *n.* hargarritasun, onargarritasun.

acceptable *adj.* hargarri, onargarri, oneskarri, onerizgarri.

acceptably *adv.* oneskarriki, onerizgarriro.

acceptance *n.* onarketa, onespen, onarpen, harrera, oneritzi, harkortasun; abegi.

accepting *adj.* onesle, harrerakor.

access *n.* helbide.

accessible *adj.* eskuragarri, hurbilerraz, sargarri, helgarri.

accessory *n.* errukide, gaizkide, gaiztakide. *n.* gainerako, gainontzeko, gainerantzeko, gehigarri.

accident *n.* istripu; ezbehar, zorigaitz. **Accident insurance.** Ezbehar-aseguru.

accidental *adj.* ustekabe, ustekabeko, apikako.

accidentally *adv.* ustekabe, ustekabez, alabeharrez, ezustez.

· **acclaim** *v.t.* gorakaitu.

acclamation *n.* goraketa.

acclimate *v.i.* girotu, herrikotu.

acclimatization *n.* giroztapen.

acclimatize *v.t.* bertakotu, girotu, lurrak hartu.

accommodate *v.t.* doitu.

accommodating *adj.* etorkor, ezargarri, moldaerraz, moldakor, erakor.

accommodation *n.* egokiera, moldakoitasun. *n.* (*pl.*) egoitza, egonleku; logela.

accompaniment *n.* lagungo. *n.* (*mus.*) musika-laguntza.

accompany *v.t.* lagun egin, lagundu.

accomplice *n.* gaizkide, errukide, ezkutari, ohoinkide.

accomplish *v.t.* egin, bete, gauzatu, lortu.

accomplishment *n.* lorpen, egite, burutzapen.

accord *n.* akordio, hitzarmen, konponbide.

accordance *n.* araberatasun.

accordingly *adv.* dagokionez.

according to *prep./adv.* arauz, -(ar)en arabera, arauera, eredura, -(ar)i dagokionez, eraz; -z.

accordion *n.* (*mus.*) akordeoi, ausposoinu, eskusoinu, trikitixa.

accordionist *n.* trikitilari, akordeoilari.

account *v.t.* (**for** edo **of**-**ekin**) kontu eman.

account *n.* kontu; kontaketa. **Checking account.** Erabilkontu. *n.* kontaketa, istorio.

accountable *adj.*(**for** edo **to**-**rekin**) erantzule.

accountant *n.* kontulari, kontugile.

accounting *n.* kontabilitate, kontugintza, kontularitza. **Final accounting.** Kontuak egitea.

accredit *v.t.* kreditatu.

accredited *adj.* aipuoneko.

accrue *v.t.* pilatu, multzatu, metatu, gehitu.

accumulate *v.t./v.i.* multzatu, metatu, pilakatu, bildu, mordoskatu.

accumulation *n.* metaketa, multzaketa, pilaketa, mukurru.

accumulator *n.* metatzaile, pilatzaile. *n.*(*mech.*) akumulagailu.

accuracy *n.* zehaztasun, xehetasun.

accurate *adj.* zuzen, akatsgabe.

accursed *adj.* madarikagarri, madarikatu(a).

accusation *n.* salaketa, salakuntza.

accusative *adj.*(*gram.*) akusatibo.

accusatory *adj.* salakor.

accuse *v.t.* salatu, aurpegira bota, auzitaratu, gainezkarri, aurpegiratu, errutatu.

accused *adj.* salatu(a), auzipeko.

accuser *n.* salatzaile, salatari.

accusing *adj.* salatari, salati, salakor.

accustom *v.t.* ohituarazi.

accustomed *adj.* ohiturazko, ohizko. **To become accustomed (to).** Ohitu. Ekandu.

ace *n.* bata, bateko.

acephalous *adj.* burugabe.

acerbity *n.* garraztasun. *n.* laztasun.

acetic *adj.* ozpinezko, azetiko.
acetone *n.(chem.)* azetona.
acetosity *n.* ozpintasun.
ache *v.i.* mindu.
ache *n.* sormin, min.
achieve *v.t.* burutu, lortu, erdietsi.
achievement *n.* lorpen, burutzapen, irispen, erdiespen.
aching *adj.* minbera, minberatsu, mingor.
achoo! *int.* atxis!
acid *n.* azido, garrazkin. *adj.* min, minkor, garratz, mikatz. **Acid indigestion.** Bihotzerre.
acidic *adj.* garratz, gazi, mikatz, min.
acidify *v.t./v.i.* mingartu.
acidity *n.* garraztasun, mikaztasun, azidotasun, ozpintasun, samintasun, minkortasun.
acknowledge *v.t.* aitortu. *v.t.* ezagutu.
acolyte *n.* mezalagun, mezamutil, elizmutil.
acorn *n.* (bot.) ezkur.
acoustics *n.* akustika.
acquaint *v.t.* (with) trebatu, jabetu; ezagutu.
acquaintance *n.* ezagun. *n.* ezagutza, ezagupen, ezaguera.
acquiesce *v.i.* (askotan in-ekin) amore eman, esanera etorri.
acquiescence *n.* amore, amoregite.
acquiescent *adj.* baiesle, amoregile.
acquire *v.t.* eskuratu, lortu, jabetu, erdietsi.
acquisition *n.* erospen, eskurapen, eskuraketa, erdiespen.
acquisitive *adj.* eskurakor, erdieskor.
acquisitiveness *n.* eskurakortasun, erdieskortasun.
acquit *v.t.* errugabetu.
acre *n.* akre (lur-azala neurtzeko).
acrimonious *adj.* garratz, latz, zorrotz.
acrobat *n.* itzulipurdikari, iraulkalari, jauzkalari, sokagainkari.
across *prep.* zehar, trabes.
act *v.i.* ibili, jo, egitaratu, aritu, portatu. *v.t./v.i.* antzeztu.
act *n.* egina, egite, egipen. **Act of (doing something).** -tze, -te. *n.* aktu, aldi, zati.
acting *n.* antzezlaritza.
action *n.* ekintza, egipen, egite, jardunketa, jardunaldi; -era, -men.
actionable *adj.* auzigarri, auzitara eramangarri.
activate *v.t.* eragin. *v.t.* abiarazi, martxan jarri.
activated *adj.* eraginezko.
activation *n.* eragite.
activator *n.* mugitzaile, eragile.
active *adj.* bizkor, azkar; eginkor, eraginkor, egintzaile.
actively *adv.* azkarki, azkarki, erneki.
activist *n.* ekintzaile, ekintzari, eragintzale.
activity *n.* ekintza, ihardun, ariketa, mugimendu, higidura, eragiketa.

actor *n.* antzerkilari, antzezlari (gizon).
actress *n.* antzerkilari, antzezlari (emakume).
actual *adj.* benetako, egiazko.
actually *adv.* egiaz, arean.
actuate *v.t.* eragin, abiarazi, martxan jarri.
acuity *n.* gogoargitasun, zorroztasun.
acumen *n.* gogoargitasun.
acute *adj.* begizorrotz, zorrotz, zoli.
acutely *adv.* gogoernez.
ad *n.* iragarki.
adage *n.* esaera, erranki.
adamant *adj.* zurrun, gogor, burugogor.
Adam's apple *n.* (anat.) zintzur, zintzurkorapilo.
adapt *v.i./v.t.* egokitu, moldatu, hartarakotu, apropostu, araberatu.
adaptability *n.* moldamen, moldagarritasun, egokitasun.
adaptable *adj.* moldagarri, moldakor, erakor, taxukor, taxugarri, ezargarri.
adaptation *n.* moldaketa, moldapen, eraketa, taxuketa, egokiera, gertapen, prestapen, kera.
adapted *adj.* taxuzko.
adapter *n.* egokitzaile, moldatzaile.
adaptive *adj.* egokitzaile, moldatzaile.
add *v.t.* gaineratu, gainezarri, erantsi, gehitu. **To add up.** Orotu. *v.t.* (arith.) batu.
addable *adj.* batugarri, erasgarri.
addend *n.* (arith.) batugai.
addendum *n.* gehigarri, itsaski, osakizun. *n.* eranskin.
adder *n.* (zool.) sugegorri, bipera. *n.* kopuratzaile.
addict *n.* drogazale; -zale.
addiction *n.* atxekimendu, drogazalekeria.
addition *n.* (arith.) batuketa. *n.* eranskin, eranspen, erasketa, gehigarri, gehiketa, itsaski, osakin. **In addition to.** Gainetik.
additional *adj.* gehigarri, gehikor, gaineratiko.
additive *n.* osagarri. *adj.* batukor, gehigarri.
addle *v.t./v.i.* nahastu, itsutu.
address *v.t.* pertsona bati hitz egin. *v.t.* eskutitzaren azalean helbidea jarri.
address *n.* helbide, zuzenbide.
address book *n.* oharliburu.
addressee *n.* hartzaile, jasotzaile.
adept *adj.* kide; -kide.
adequate *adj.* egoki, apropos, araberazko, hartarako.
adequately *adv.* egoki, egokiro, eraz, beharbezala.
adequateness *n.* egokitasun.
adhere *v.i.* erantsi, iratsi, itsatsi, atxiki.
adherence *n.* atxikimendu.
adherent *adj.* eranskor, itsaskor, atxikigarri. *n.* eranskailu.
adherible *adj.* itsasgarri, atxikigarri.
adhesion *n.* itsasketa, atxikimendu,

atxikidura, erasketa, eransketa.
adhesive adj. atxikigarri, itsasgarri,
itsaskor, eraskor, eransgarri. n.
eranskailu.
adhesiveness n. atxikitasun,
itsaskortasun.
adipose adj. gantzadun.
adjacent adj. aldeko, aldameneko,
alboko, ondoko.
adjective n. izenlagun, izenondoko.
Demonstrative adjective. Izenlagun
erakusle. **Possessive adjective.**
Izenlagun jabekor.
adjoining adj. ondoko, alboko.
adjourn v.t./v.i. gerokotu.
adjournment n. luzaketa, gerorapen.
adjudge v.t. esleitu.
adjudicate v.t./v.i. epaitu.
adjunct n./adj. ondoko, laguntzaile.
adjust v.t. araberatu, araupetu, doitu,
egokitu, eraratu, idekotu, taxutu. v.i.
laketu.
adjustable adj. graduagarri, taxugarri,
taxukor, moldaerraz, moldagarri.
adjusted adj. gradudun.
adjustment n. graduapen, moldaketa,
moldaera, taxu, taxuketa, zuzenketa,
egokidura, konpondura.
administer v.t. aministratu, ardura izan.
v.i. lagundu.
administrate v.t./v.i. aministratu,
gobernatu.
administration n. aministralgo,
aministrazio. n. arduraldi.
administrative adj. aministral-.
administrator n. aministratzaile,
aministrari, kudeatzaile,
ekonomo.
admirable adj. ikusgarri, ikusgarrizko,
begiragarri, miragarri, miresgarri.
admirableness n. miragarritasun.
admirably adv. miragarriki, miragarriro,
ikusgarriro.
admiral n. almirante.
admiration n. harrigarritasun,
mirespen, mireskunde.
admire v.t. miretsi, mirestu,
harrigarritu.
admirer n. miresle.
admiring adj. mireskor.
admissibility n. onargarritasun,
hargarritasun.
admissible adj. onargarri, hargarri,
oneskarri, oneskor.
admission n. onarpen, onarketa. n.
erru-aitorpen.
admit v.t. sartzen utzi. v.t. onartu,
onetsi, v.t. utzi, baimendu, baimena
eman. v.t. aitortu.
admittance n. onartze, sartze. **No
admittance.** Debekatua sartzea.
admonish v.t. ohartu, oharrarazi. v.t.
gogor egin, agirakatu.
admonition n. iratzarmendu. n.
agiraka, murrunga.
ado n. zalapartada, arrapalada.
adolescence n. nerabetasun,

nerabezaro, nerabetza,
morrointasun.
adolescent n. nerabe.
adopt v.t. umetzakotu, semetzat hartu,
alabatzat hartu, semeordekotu. v.t.
berekotu, bereganatu, jabetu.
adopted adj. -tzako, -orde, -ordeko.
adoption n. semeordekotza,
semetzakotza, alabatzakotza,
umetzakotza.
adoptive adj. -orde, -tzako. **Adoptive
parent.** Gurasotzako.
adorable adj. gurgarri. adj. xarmant,
zoragarri.
adorably adv. xarmantki, zoragarriro.
adoration n. gurketa, gurtza,
gurtzapen, gurtasun, jauresketa,
jaurespen.
adore v.t. gurtu, jauretsi.
adorer n. gurkari, jauresle.
adorn v.t. apaingarriztu, dotoretu,
ederreztatu, edertu, politu, adeiatu,
apaindu.
adornment n. dotoreketa, edertzapen,
apain.
adrift adv./adj. jitoan, nora ezean.
adroit adj. trebe, moldatsu, bitore.
adulate v.t. lausengatu, losindu,
losintxatu, balakatu.
adulation n. ahozurikeria, ahozuriketa,
balaku, eztikeria, koipekeria,
lausengu, limurkeria, losintxa.
adult n. adineko, nagusi.
adulterate v.t. faltsuztatu, faltsutu.
adulteration n. faltsuztapen.
adulterer n. adulteriogile (gizon).
adulteress n. adulteriogile (emakume).
adultery n. adulterio, ezkontza-
nahaste.
adulthood n. gizaro.
advance v.t./v.i. aurreratu, aitzineratu,
aurrera jo.
advance n. aurrerakada, aurrerapen,
aurrerapide. n. aintzinapen,
aintzipen. n. (econ.) aurrerakin.
advanced adj. goiztar, aurreratu(a).
advancement n. aurreraketa,
aurreraldi, aurrerapen, aurrerapide.
advantage n. abantaila, atarramendu,
hobari.
advantageous adj. abantailezko,
onuratsu, onuragarri, komenigarri,
aurreragarri.
advantageously adv. abantailatuki,
gaindiro.
Advent n. abendu.
adventure n. abentura, mentura. n.
pasadizu, ipuin, istorio.
adventurer n. abenturari, abenturazale
(gizon).
adventuress n. abenturari,
abenturazale (emakume).
adventurous adj. menturazale,
abenturazale.
adverb n. (gram.) adizlagun,
aditzondoko.
adverbial adj. (gram.) adizlagunezko.

adversary n. aurkalari, aurkari, aurkagile, kontrako, jarkitzaile.
adversative adj. (gram.) kontrazko.
adverse adj. jarkitzaile, kontrajarle, aurkazko.
adversely adv. ezbeharrez.
adversity n. eragozpide, ezbehar, okerraldi, zorigaitz, zorigaizto, zoritxar, malura.
advertise v.t./v.i. iragarri, aditzera eman, jakinerazi.
advertisement n. iragarki, iragarpen.
advertiser n. iragarlari, iragarle.
advertising n. propaganda, publizitate.
advice n. oharbide, aholku, jakinarazpen, erakuspide, kontsulta, burubide. **To give advice.** Oharkarazi. n. mezu.
advisability n. komenientzia.
advisable adj. aholkugarri, kontseilagarri, komendagarri. **To be advisable.** Komeni izan.
advise v.t./v.i. aholkatu, aholku eman, oharrarazi. v.t. ezagutarazi, jakinarazi.
advisement n. aholkatze.
adviser n. oharrarazle, kontseilari, aholkulari, aholkuemale.
advocate v.t. -(r)en alde egin, aldeztu.
advocate n. abokatu.
adz n. zeio.
aerate v.t. aireberritu, airetu, airestatu, haizeztatu.
aeration n. airealdi, aireketa, haizeztaketa.
aerial adj. aireko, haizezko. n. antena.
aerialist n. orekari.
aerie n. arranoen habia.
aeronautics n. hegazkintza.
aerosol n. (chem.) aerosol.
aesthetic adj. ederbera, edergarri, estetiko, apaingarri.
aesthetics n. estetika.
affability n. laztankortasun, harreratasun, laguntzaletasun, lainotasun.
affable adj. harrerakor, lagunkor, gisako, jendekiko, xalo, laino.
affably adv. lainoki.
affair n. eginkizun. n. gertaera, jazoera. n. gauza. n. arazo. n. epe laburreko bikote baten barneko sexu-harremanak. n. gaizbide, eskandalu.
affairs n. kontuak; arazoak.
affect v.t. erasan, ukitu. v.t. hunkitu.
affect n. ondorio.
affectation n. itxurakeria, polikeria.
affected adj. mirgitsu; -keri. adj. ukitu(a).
affection n. maitasun, begikotasun, maitajoera, begion, eraspen, xera.
affectionate adj. bihozkoi, maitabera, maitakor, laztankor, amodiotsu, bihozti, amultsu.
affectionately adv. bihotzez, laztanki,

maiteki, xeraz.
affidavit n. idaz-testigantza, lekukotasun.
affiliate v.t./v.i. elkartetu, kidetu.
affiliation n. kidetza.
affinity n. kidetasun, kidekotasun, ahaidetasun, antzekotasun, kidego, parekidetasun.
affirm v.t. baieztatu, baieztu, baietz esan.
affirmation n. baietza, baiezpen.
affirmative adj. baikor, baiezko. **Affirmative sentence.** Baiezko esaldi.
affirmatively adv. baiezka.
affirmer n. baieztari.
affix v.t. atxeki, erantsi.
affix n. hizki.
afflict v.t. atsekabetu, lazeriatu, samindu.
afflicted adj. nahigabedun, nahigabetsu, oinazedun, atsekabedun.
affliction n. atsekabe, bihozmin, mindura, nahigabe, samin, dolu, dolamen.
affluence n. diruketa, aberastasun. n. ugaritasun, oparotasun.
affluent adj. aberats, dirudun.
afford v.t. zerbait erosteko dirua ukan.
affront v.t. laidokatu, laidoztatu, iraindu.
affront n. laido, laidogarrikeria, lotsagaizto. n. kontrajarketa.
afield adv. kanpoan.
afoot adv. oinez. adv. gertueran, prestaeran.
aforesaid adj. jakineko.
afraid adj. beldurkor, beldurti, ikaradun. **To be afraid.** Ikara izan. Beldur izan. Beldurtu.
after prep. ondoan, gero, -(r)en buruan, ezkero; -oste.
afterbirth n. karen.
afternoon n. arratsalde. adj. eguerdiondoko.
aftertaste n. kutsu, edanondoko.
afterward(s) adv. geroz, gero, geroztikan.
afterword n. hitzate, gibelsolas.
again adv. berriz, berriro.
against prep. aurka, kontra.
age v.i/ v.t. zahartu, zaharkitu.
age n. adin. **School age.** Eskoladin. Eskolaro. **Legal age.** Adin-nagusitasun. n. (geol.) aro.
aged adj. adintsu, zahar, urtetsu, adineko.
ageless adj. betiko, betidaniko.
agency n. agentzia.
agenda n. gaizerrenda.
agent n. egile, egintzaile; -kin, -gile. n. kudeatzaile, igorle; artekari.
agglutinate v.t./v.i. erantsi, lotarazi.
agglutination n. eransketa.
aggrandize v.t. handitu, handiagotu.

aggravate *v.t.* gaizkiagotu. **To become aggravated.** Okerragotu.

aggravating *adj.* nekarazle, sumingarri. *adj.* txarkor, gaizkor.

aggravation *n.* larrikuntza, txarketa. *n.* ezerosotasun.

aggregate *v.t/v.i.* erantsi.

aggregation *n.* eraspen.

aggression *n.* erasoaldi, erasoketa, oldar, kolpaldi.

aggressive *adj.* erasokor, erasotzaile, oldarkor, odolbero.

aggressively *adv.* erasoz, oldarrez, oldarka.

aggressiveness *n.* erasotasun, gerrazaletasun, oldarkortasun.

agile *adj.* bizkor, azkar, lirain, zoli, zalu.

agilely *adv.* lirainki, zaluki.

agility *n.* bizkortasun, azkartasun, zalutasun.

aging *n.* zahardura, zaharketa, zahartzapen. *adj.* zahargarri; zahartzaile.

agitate *v.t.* erabilkatu, higitu, inarrosi, inarroskatu.

agitated *adj.* eragin, higitsu, egonezin; estu, kezkatsu, larri, urduri.

agitation *n.* eragin, eraginaldi, asaldaketa, inarrosketa, inarrospen, kitzikadura.

agitator *n.* iskanbilari, nahastari, nahastekari, nahastero, zalapartari, asaldatzaile.

aglow *adj.* gori, distiragarri.

agnostic *n./adj.* agnostiko.

ago *adv.* duela, orain dela, aspaldi. **A long time ago.** Aspaldi. **Not so long ago.** Ez hain aspaldi. **Two years ago.** Duela bi urte.

agog *adj.* jakingale, begirakoi.

agonize *v.i.* izularritu, nahigabetu.

agony *n.* nekelarri. *n.* hilordu, herioaldi, azkenats, azkenarnasa, heriotzordu, hilzori.

agrarian *adj.* nekazaritzako.

agree *v.i./v.t.* baietsi, baietz esan, batera egon, bat etorri, elkar hartu, irizkidetu, gogaidetu, hitzartu, ados egon, akordiotu, bat izan, konforme egon.

agreeable *adj.* atsegingarri, atsseginkor, begietako, gogoko, atsegintsu, gustoko, laket, gogobetegarri. *adj.* baiesle, gogaidegarri, akordiogarri, adostasunezko, baterakoi.

agreeably *adv.* atsegingarriro, gozoki, gustora, eztiro.

agreed *adj.* hitzarmenezko.

agreement *n.* baiespen, baietza, baiezko, baieztapen, gogaidego, gogaidetasun, adostasun, iriskidego. *n.* akordio, konponketa, itun, tratatu, hitzarmen.

agricultural *adj.* nekazaritzako, nekazal.

agriculture *n.* nekazaritza, laboraritza, laborantza, lurlangintza.

aground *adj./adv.* lurrean, lurrera.

aha *exclam.* ujuju.

ahead *adv.* aurrera. *adv.* gerokoan.

aid *v.t.* lagundu, esku luzatu, esku eman, faboretu.

aid *n.* laguntasun, laguntza, lagungarri, lagunketa, fabore.

AIDS *n.* HIES, SIDA.

ail *v.t./v.i.* min egin; gaisorik egon.

ailing *adj.* erikor, gaisokor, eribera, erikoi.

ailment *n.* gaisoaldi, gaiso, eritasun, gaitz.

aim *v.t.* jo, zuzendu, norabidetu. *v.i.* saiatu.

aim *n.* punteria, begizizta. *n.* helburu, xede, jomuga.

aimlessly *adv.* noragabe, noraezean.

ain't "am + not"-aren laburpena.

air *v.t. (batzutan* **out***-ekin)* egurastu, airetu, haizeztatu, haizatu.

air *n.* aire, egurats. *n.* aire, taiu, itxura. *adj.* aireko.

air conditioner *n.* girogailu, haizegailu, haizemaile.

air conditioning *n.* haizaberrizte, haizaketa.

aircraft *n.* hegazkin. **Manufacture of aircraft.** Hegazkintza.

aircraft carrier *n.* hegazkinontzi.

air force *n.* aire-armada.

airily *adv.* txairoki, lerdenki, lirainki.

airline *n.* airebide.

airliner *n.* airebideko hegazkin.

airmail *n./adj.* aire-posta.

airplane *n.* hegazkin, abioi, aireontzi, aireplanu.

airport *n.* aireportu.

air-raid signal *n.* sirena.

air route *n.* airebide.

airship *n.* aireontzi, zepelin, haizontzi.

airway *n.* hegazkinen ibilbideak. *n.* haize egokitua igarotzen den hodia; aire-hodi. *n.* komunikabide(ak).

airy *adj.* aire-antzeko, aireko. *adj.* txairo, txanbelin.

aisle *n.* barnebide, pasabide.

aitch *n.* hatxe.

ajar *adv.* erdizabalik.

akimbo *adj./adv.* eskuak gerrian jarriaz.

akin *adj.* antzeko. *adj.* odolkide, ezkontzahaide.

Alabama *n. (geog.)* Estatu Batuetako estatu bat.

alabaster *n.* hartzuri.

alacrity *n.* ziztu, lastertasun, bizkortasun, bizitasun, ernetasun.

alarm *v.t.* beldurtu. **To become alarmed.** Koldartu.

alarm *n.* asaldura, ikara, izu, beldur. *n.* deiadar. *n.* sirena, alarma, iratzargarri.

alarm clock *n.* esnaerloju, esnagailu, iratzargailu.

alarming *adj.* asaldagarri, iratzargarri, iratzarle, kexarazale.

alarmingly adv. asaldagarriki.
alas int. aiene!
Alaska n.(geog.) Estatu Batuetako estatu bat.
Alava n. (geog.) Araba.
albeit conj. arren.
albino n. pertsona zuriska.
alchemy n. alkimia.
alcohol n. alkohol.
alcoholic n. mozkortzale, hordiputz, alkoholtzale. adj. mozkorgarri, alkoholdun, alkoholezko, alkoholtsu, hordigarri.
alcoholism n. alkoholkeria, mozkorkeria, mozkorreria, hordikeria.
alcove n. nitxo.
alderman n. (pol.) kontzejal, zinegotzi, kontseilari.
ale n. garagardo mota bat.
alert v.t. ernejarri.
alert adj./adv. erne, itzarri, erlantz, begi-belarri, gogoerne.
alertness n. ernetasun, ohartasun.
alfalfa n. (bot.) argibelar, frantzesbelar. **Alfalfa field.** Argibelardi.
alga n. (bot.) aloka, alga.
algae n. (pl.) alokak, algak.
algebra n. aljebra.
alias n. ezizen; izenorde, gaitzizen, goitizen, izengoiti.
alien n. kanpotar, arrotz. n. beste planetako pertsona.
alienate v.t. inorenganatu, deszaletu.
alienated adj. inorendu. **To become alienated.** Inorendu.
alienation n. inorenganaketa, alienazio, besteraketa.
alienist n. erosendagile.
alight v.i. kokatu, pausatu.
align v.t./v.i. herronkatu, lerrokatu, lerrotu.
alignment n. lerrokadura, lerrokapen.
alike adv./adj. antzeko, bezalako, gisako, itxurako, moduko, pareko.
alimentary canal n. (anat.) hodi.
alimony n. dibortzio ondoren senarrak emazteari ordaindu behar izaten dion dirua.
alive adj. bizi, arimadun, bizidun, bizitiar; bizirik. adj. erne.
all adj./pron. guzti(ak), oro, dena(k). adv. guztiz. **In all.** Guztira. Denera. **At all.** Nehola. Inolako. Inola ere ez.
allegation n. argudio, arrazoinbide.
allege v.t. egiaztatu.
allegorical adj. alegorizko, alegiazko.
allegorically adv. alegiaz, irudibidez.
allegory n. alegia, irudibide, alegoria.
allegro n. (mus.) aire-arin, alegro. adj. alegro.
allergic adj. alergiko.
allergy n. alergia.
alleviate v.t. bigundu, arindu, gozatu, eztitu.
alleviating adj. arintzaile.
alleviation n. arinaldi, arinketa, arindura, lasaidura, lasotasun.

alleviator n. arintzaile.
alley n. kaletarte, karrika, zeharkale.
alliance n. elkartasun, elkargo.
alligator n. (zool.) kaiman.
alliteration n. hitzerrepika, aliterazio.
all-knowing adj. orojakitun, orojakin.
allocate v.t. nori berea eman, banandu.
allocation n. banapen, banaketa.
allot v.t. banandu.
allotment n. banaketa.
allow v.t./v.i. baimendu, utzi, zilegi izan, haizutu, laketu.
allowable adj. zilegigarri, uzkarri.
allowance n. haurren sari, haurren alokairu.
allowed adj. zilegi, haizu, sori.
alloy n. aleazio.
all-powerful adj. guztiahaltsu.
all together adv. orotara.
allude v.i. (to) aipatu, ukitu.
allure n. lilurapen.
alluring adj. lilurakor.
allusion n. hitzerdi, zeharresan, zeharritz, aipamen, aipaldi, aipuera.
allusive adj. dagoki-, doaki-.
ally v.t./v.i. (with) elkartu; elkarfederatu.
ally n. konfederatu.
almanac n. almanaka.
almighty adj. ahalguztidun, guztiahaldun.
almond n. (bot.) almendra.
almost adv. kasik, ia, erdi.
alms n. limosna, erremusina, limosnatxo, eskari.
almsgiver n. erremusinagile, erremusinari, limosnari.
aloe n. (bot.) zumintz.
aloft adv. airean, goian.
alone adj./adv. bakar, lagungabe, soil, bakarrean, bakarrik.
along prep./adv. luzeran, luzeraz, luzez.
alongside prep./adv. ondoan, aldean.
aloof adj. muzin, mukerbera, zaputz, zapuzkor, zapuzti.
aloofly adv. zapuzki, mukerki.
aloofness n. mukertasun, zaputzaldi.
aloud adv. ozenki, goraki.
alphabet n. agaka, abeze, alfabeto.
alphabetize v.t. alfabetatu.
alpine adj. alpesetako, alpestar.
already adv. jadanik, lehendik; ba-.
also adv. ere, baita, baita . . . ere, halaber. conj. eta.
altar n. aldare, aldaremahai, elizmahai. **Portable altar.** Eskualdare.
alter v.t./v.i. aldatu, bestetu.
alteration n. aldakuntza, aldaketa.
altercation n. kontrajarketa.
alternate v.i./v.t. txandatu, txandakatu, aldizkatu.
alternate adj. txandako, aldikako. n. ordezkari, ordezko.
alternately adv. aldizka, txandaka.
alternating n. aldizkatze. adj. txandako. adj. (elec.) alterno.

alternation n. txandaketa.
alternative n. hautamen, aukera, hautabide, aukerabide. adj. aldizko, aldikako, txandako, hautabidezko.
although conj. hala ere, halere, baina, arren, nahiz eta, nahiz, halabaina; - gatik.
altimeter n. goibeheneurkin.
altitude n. goratasun, goitasun, goialde.
altogether adv. erabat, arras, guztiz, osoki, zeharo.
altruism n. gizakortasun.
altruistic adj. gizaldeko.
aluminum n. aluminio.
alumni n. (pl.) unibertsitateko ikasle izanak.
always adv. beti, betiere, betidanik.
am Cf. be.
amateur n. amateur.
amaze v.t. harritu, miretsi, zurtu.
amazement n. harridura, harritasun, harrimen, txundidura.
amazing adj. harrigarrizko, txundigarri, erdiragarri.
ambassador n. enbaxadore, enbaxadari, enbaxadarisa.
ambassadorship n. enbaxadorego.
amber n./adj. anbare.
ambidextrous adj. ezker-eskuin, ezker-eskuindar.
ambience n. giro, girorapen.
ambiguity n. zalantzagarritasun, lainotasun.
ambiguous adj. zalantzagarri, lainotsu.
ambiguously adv. itzulinguruka, hitzerdika.
ambition n. handinahitasun, handinahikeria, handizaletasun, handinahi, goranahi, irrits.
ambitious adj. handinahiko, handizale, askonahiko, goranahi(ko), orozale, goizale.
ambivalent adj. baliobikun, baliobikoizdun.
ambulance n. eriauto, anbulantzia.
ambush v.t. kukutu, zelatu, zelatatu.
ambush n. zelatadura, zelataldi, zelatarte. n. eraso.
ameliorate v.t. hobetu, hobeagotu.
amen int. halabedi, amen.
amenable adj. eskurakoi, molderraz. adj. harbera.
amend v.t. zuzendu, hobetu.
amends n. ordainbide.
amenity n. (pl.) aieru atseginak. n. adikortasun, harreratasun.
America n. (geog.) Amerika, Indiak.
American n./adj. estatubatuar, amerikanu, amerikar.
amiability n. harreratasun, atseginkortasun.
amiable adj. atseginkor, harrerakor, harreratsu, lagunartekor, lagunkor, lagunkoi, laino, amoltsu, txerati.
amiably adv. lagungisa.
amicability n. lagunkoitasun, lagunzaletasun.
amicable adj. adiskidetsu, lagunkor.
amicably adv. adiskideki, adiskidegisa, begionez.
amid(st) prep. arte, artean.
ammonia n. amoniako.
ammunition n. munizio.
ammunition dump n. balaketa.
amnesia n. (med.) oroitezin, amnesia.
amnesty n. barkamendu, amnistia.
among prep. arte, artean.
amoral adj. moralgabe.
amorous adj. maitatzaile, maitazale, maitezko, maitati.
amorously adv. maitasunez, maitekiro, maiteki.
amorphous adj. taxugabe, eragabe.
amortization n. (econ.) kitapen, garbiketa, amortizazio.
amortize v.t. amortizatu.
amount n. kopuru, zenbatasun, kantitate; -keta, -pilo. **The same amount.** Beste hainbeste.
amphibian adj./n. urlehortar.
amphibious adj. urlehortar.
amphitheater n. anfiteatro.
ample adj. hedatsu, zabal.
amplifier n. ozengailu.
amplify v.t. ozendu.
amplitude n. zabaldura, hedadura.
amputate v.t. ebaki, moztu.
amputation n. mozketa, ebaketa, mozte.
amulet n. kutun.
amuse v.t. jostatu, olgatu.
amusement n. jostadura, jostaketa, olgeta.
amusement park n. jolasleku, jolastoki.
amusing adj. jostalari, jostagarri, txantxetako, pozekarle, pozarazle, moñoño.
an art. bat.
anachronism n. anakronismo; zaharkeria.
anal adj. ipurtzuloko, uzkiko.
analagous adj. kidekotsu, kidetsu, berdintsu.
analogy n. analogia.
analysis n. azterkaldi; analisi.
analyst n. aztertzaile.
analytical adj. azterbidezko.
analytically adv. aztertuaz.
analyze v.t. aztertu, arakatu, ikertu, txerkatu.
anarchical adj. legegabe(ko), anarkiko.
anarchism n. anarkismo.
anarchist n. legeaurkari, anarkista.
anarchy n. anarkia, desgobernu, gobernugabezia.
anathema n. anatema.
anatomy n. anatomia.
ancestor n. arbaso, asaba, lehenguraso, aitalehen, aintzineko, aurreko.
ancestral adj. arbasoengandiko,

aintzinakoen, asaben.
ancestry n. sorterro, jatorri.
anchor v.t./v.i. ainguratu.
anchor n. aingura, arlanka.
anchovy n. (zool.) antxoa.
ancient adj. aintzinako, behinolako, lehenaroko.
anciently adv. aintzina, behinola.
and conj. eta, ta.
anecdotal adj. gertaerazko.
anecdote n. istorio, pasadizu, xelebrekeria.
anemia n. (med.) odolahuldura, anemia.
anemic adj. odolgabe, odolgabeko, odolustu, odolahul.
anesthesia n. anestesia.
angel n. aingeru.
angelic adj. aingeru-antzeko, aingeruzko.
angelically adv. aingeru-antzera, aingerugisa, aingeruki.
anger v.t./v.i. haserretu, haserrerazi, ernegatu, ernegarazi.
anger n. haserre, haserredura, arnegu, muturkeria, amorrubizi, ernegamendu, sumin, sumindura.
angina n. (med.) zintzurmin, zintzurreri; bihotzestu.
angle n. (geom.) angelu. **Acute angle.** Angelu zorrotz. **Obtuse angle.** Angelu kamuts. **Right angle.** Angelu zuzen. n. kikimako, bihurgune. n. ikuspide, ikuspuntu; alderdi, alde.
angler n. arrantzale. n. (zool.) zapo, itsasapo.
Anglican adj. anglikar.
Anglo-American adj. ingeles-amerikar.
angrily adv. haserrez, amorruz, subizian.
angry adj. haserre, haserreti, kopetilun, sumin, amorruzko. **To get angry.** Haserretu.
anguish n. atsekabe, bihotzestura, arrenkura, itomen, larritasun, larrialdi.
anguished adj. atsekabetsu, estutalarri, atsekabedun, kexu, izutu.
angular adj. angeluar, angelutsu, angeluzko; zokotsu.
angularly adv. angeluarki.
animal n. abere, piztia, animalia, kabale.
animate v.t. biziarazi, bizieragin. v.t. adoretu, azkortu, gogoberotu, piztu.
animated adj. gogoberotsu, sinokari, sinolari.
animated cartoon n. marrazki bizidun.
animator n. bizkortzaile, piztaile, gogoberotzaile, ernarazle. n. marrazki bizidunen egile(a).
animosity n. ikusezin, ezinikusi, elkarrezin, elkarrikusiezin.
anisette n. anis.
ankle n. orkatila, aztalbeharri, txorkatila, kabila.
annex n. pabeloi.
annexation n. iratxekidura.

annihilate v.t. birrindu, deuseztatu, deuseztu, ezereztatu, hauts egin, erraustu.
annihilation n. ezereztapen, deusestapen, suntsidura.
annihilator n. funditzaile, suntsitzaile.
anniversary n. urteburu, urteurren, urtemuga. **Wedding anniversary.** Eztei. **Silver wedding anniversary.** Zilarrezko ezteiak. **Golden wedding anniversary.** Urrezko ezteiak.
annotate v.t./v.i. ertzohartu.
announce v.t./v.i. (v.i.,for) deadar egin, iragarri, azaldatu, aldarrikatu, deitu, dei egin.
announcement n. iragarbide, iragarki, iragarpen, irratimezu, mezu. n. adierazgai, adierazgailu.
announcer n. irratigorle, irratimezulari, irratizlari, irratalbistari; telealbistari, iragarle. **News announcer.** Berriemaile.
annoy v.t. nekarazi, gogait eragin, gogaitarazi, asperterazi, nazkarazi, ozpindu, erretxindu.
annoyance n. gogaitaldi, unadura; zirikapen; kitzikapen.
annoyed adj. haserretsu, haserrekoi. **To be annoyed.** Gogaikarritu.
annoying adj. gogaikarri, nazkagarri, ernegagarri, gogobetegarri, zirikatzaile.
annoyingly adv. gaitzigarriki, unagarriki, nekegisaz.
annual adj. urteko, urteroko. **Annual publication.** Urtekari.
annually adv. urtero, urteka.
annuity n. pentsio, urtesari, urteko.
annul v.t. indargabetu, kendu, baliogabetu, indargetu. v.t. ezabatu, ezereztatu, ezeztatu, ezgaitu.
annullable adj. kengarri, ezerezkor.
annulment n. deslegekuntza. n. ezeztapen, ezereztapen, ezeztaketa, ezabapen.
Annunciation n. (eccl.) deikunde (martxoaren 25), iragarkunde.
anoint v.t. gantzutu, oliotu, lardatu.
anointer n. gantzulari, gantzutzaile.
anointing n. gantzualdi, gantzudura, gantzuketa, gantzupen.
anointment n. gantzadura.
anomalous adj. araugabeko.
anomalously adv. araugabeki.
anomaly n. araugabetasun, araugabezia, anomalia.
anonymity n. izengabetasun.
anonymous adj. izengabe, izengabeko, ezezagun, anonimo.
anonymously adv. izengabeki.
anorak n. anoraka.
another adj. beste; ezberdin. pron. beste bat.
answer v.t./v.i. erantzun, ihardetsi. v.i. (for) arduradun izan.
answer n. erantzun, erantzunbide, ihardespen, ihardetsaldi, jardespen.

answerable *adj.* erantzungarri, ihardesgarri. *adj.* arduradun.
answerer *n.* erantzule, ihardesle.
ant *n.* zinaurri, inurri, txingurri, xinaurri.
antagonism *n.* aurkakotasun, kontrakotasun, oposaketa.
antagonist *n.* aurkari, aurkagile, aurkalari.
antagonistic *adj.* kontrako, aurkako.
antagonize *v.t.* etsaiarazi.
antecedent *n./adj.* aurrelehen, lehenagoko, aurrekari.
antechamber *n.* gelaurre, aurregela, aretoaurre.
antediluvian *adj.* uholdeaurreko.
antelope *n.* antilope.
antemeridian *adj.* eguerdiaurreko.
antenna *n.* antena.
antepenultimate *adj.* azkenirugarren.
anterior *adj.* aurrelehen, aurreko.
anteroom *n.* gelaurre, ikusgelaurre, aretoaurre.
anthem *n.* ereserki; goratzarre.
ant hill *n.* inurritegi, txingurritegi.
anthology *n.* idazbilduma, idaz-sorta, lorategi, antologia.
anthracite *n. (min.)* lurrikatz.
anthrax *n. (med.)* lipu.
anthropoid *adj.* gizonantzeko.
anthropological *adj.* antropologiko.
anthropologist *n.* antropologari, antropologo.
anthropology *n.* antropologia.
anthropomorphous *adj.* gizaitxurako.
anthropophagous *adj.* gizajale.
anthropophagy *n.* gizajalekeria.
anti- *(gram.)* kontra-.
antibiotic *n./adj.* antibiotiko.
antibody *n.* antigorpuzki.
Antichrist *n.* antikristo.
anti-Christian *adj.* kristaukontrako.
anticipate *v.t./v.i.* aintzindu, aurrebegiratu, aurreikusi, lehendu.
anticipated *adj.* garaiaurreko.
anticipation *n.* aurrezte, aitzinapen, aldeaurre.
anticlerical *adj.* apaizkontrako, apaizetsai.
anticorrosive *n./adj.* herdoilkontrako.
antidote *n.* sendagarri, eztitu, kontrapozoi, osagarri, osakizun.
antifreeze *n.* izozketaren kontrako isurgai(a).
antimonarchic *adj.* erregekontrako.
antipathetic *adj.* kontrako, aurkako.
antipathy *n.* gaizkigura, gaizkinahi, higuintza, higuin.
antipolitical *adj.* politikaurkako, politikakontrako.
antiquarian *n.* aintzinkari. *adj.* aspaldizale.
antiquary *n.* aintzinkari.
antiquated *adj.* modaz kanpo dagoena.
antique *n.* zaharki, zaharkin. *adj.* lehenaroko, aintxinako.
antiquity *n.* zaharkitasun, aintzinatasun. *n.* aintzinate.

antiregulatory *adj.* araukontrako.
antireligious *adj.* erlijioetsai, erlijiokontrako.
antisemite *n.* juduetsai.
antisemitism *n.* juduetsaikeria.
antiseptic *n.* deskutsakin. *adj.* kutsugalgarri.
antisocial *adj.* zokokari, zokoketari, zokozale, gizartetsai.
antitetanus *adj.* tetanoaurkako.
antithesis *n.* antitesi.
antitoxic *adj.* pozoikontrako, pozoiaurkako.
anti-war *adj.* gerrakontrako, gudukontrako.
antler *n.* adarberri (orein).
antonym *n.* antonimo.
anus *n. (anat.)* ipurtzulo, uzki.
anvil *n.* ingude.
anxiety *n.* larritasun, larrialdi, artegatasun, urduritasun, kezka, estutasun, kexutasun, itobehar. *n.* irrika, irrikitasun, lehia.
anxious *adj.* egonezin, kexatiar, larri, hersturadun, estu. *adj.* gogoberotsu, irrikatsu. **To be anxious.** Irrikitu.
anxiously *adv.* kezkaz, larri, ezinegonik, estu, larriki, kexuki, urduri. *adv.* irriketan, lehiatsuki.
anxiousness *n.* kexadura. *n.* irritasun.
any *adj.* edozein, edozer. *(gram.)* -(r)ik.
anybody *pron.* edonor, edozein, nornahi, zeinnahi, inor.
anyhow *adv.* nolanahi, edozela, inola, edonola. *adv.* dena dela.
anyone *pron.* inor, edozein, nehor, zeinnahi.
anything *n./pron.* zernahi, edozer, ezer, deus(ik), tutik.
anytime *adv.* edonoiz, noiznahi.
anyway *adv.* nolanahi, edonola, edozelan. *adv.* dena den, dena dela, nolanahi ere.
anywhere *adv.* nonnahi, nonbait, noranahi, inora, inon, nehon.
aorta *n. (med.)* aorta.
apace *adv.* laster, presaki.
Apache *n.* apatxe, Ameriketako indio mota bat.
apart *adv.* aparte.
apartheid *n.* enda-bereizketa (Hegoafrikan).
apartment *n.* etxebizitza, apartamendu.
apathetic *adj.* epel, odolgabe, odolgabeko, desarduratsu, gogogabeko, geldo.
apathy *n.* gogogabetasun, gogogabekeria, gogogabezia, nahigabetasun, odolgabetasun, hiltasun, geldotasun.
ape *n.* ximio, mono.
aperture *n.* irekiera, irekigune, idekidura.
apex *n.* goien, erpin.
aphorism *n.* atsotitz.
apiarist *n.* erladun, erlajaun, erlazain.

apiary *n.* erlategi, erlatoki.
apiculture *n.* erlazaintza.
apiece *adv.* bakoitzean, banaka.
aplomb *n.* gogoberdintasun.
apogee *n.* gorenaldi, goimaila, goraldi.
apolitical *adj.* politikagabe.
apologetic *adj.* aitzakirik bete, desenkusik bete.
apologize *v.i. (batzutan for-ekin)* irainordaindu.
apology *n.* desenkusa. *n.* aldezketa, aldezpen, apologia.
apoplexy *n. (med.)* odolkolpe, sorreri, apoplegia.
apostasy *n.* fedehausketa, fedeukapen.
apostate *adj./n.* fedegalduko; ukoegile.
apostle *n.* apostolu, bidali.
apostrophe *n.* apostrofe.
apothecary *n.* botikari.
appall *v.t.* izularritu, ikaratu.
apparatus *n.* -gailu, -kailu.
apparel *n.* jantzi, janzkera.
apparent *adj.* nabari, bistako, ageri, ageriko. *adj.* azaleko, itxuradun, itxurako, itxurazko.
apparently *adv.* dirudienez, itxuraz, iduriz, itxura denez.
apparition *n.* agerkunde; mamu. *n.* agerkera, ageri, agerkuntza, agerraldi, agertaldi.
appeal *v.i.* laguntza eskatu. *v.i.* atsegindu, atsegin izan. *v.t.* jo, gora jo.
appeal *n.* gorabide. *n.* lilurapen, sentipen.
appealing *n./adj.* gorajole. *adj.* gogagarri, irrikagarri, tirriagarri.
appear *v.i.* ageri izan, azaldu, agertu, aurkeztu, iduri, iruditu. *v.i.* sortu.
appearance *n.* agertualdi, agertuera. *n.* itxura, itxurapen, planta, taiu. *n.* auzian aurkezte.
appease *v.t.* desaserretu, deskezkatu, desgorrotatu, emarazi, balakatu.
appeasement *n.* desgorroto, bakerazpen.
appellation *n.* izen.
append *v.t.* gaineratu, erantsi.
appendage *n.* gainerako, osagarri. *n.* beso; hanka.
appendix *n.* eranskin, gehigarri. *n. (anat.)* hestemutur, hestesobre.
appertain *v.i. (to)* -rena izan. *v.i. (to)* -kiko izan.
appetite *n.* jangogo, jangura. **Lack of appetite.** Gosegabezia.
appetizer *n.* bazkalaurreko.
appetizing *adj.* ahobeteko, janbera, jangogotsu.
applaud *v.t./v.i.* txalokatu, txalo egin, txalotu, eskuzartatu. *v.t.* gorakatu.
applaudable *adj.* txalogarri. *adj.* laudagarri, goresgarri, aupagarri, goragarri.
applauder *n.* txalojole, txalokari,

txalotzaile.
applause *n.* txalo, txaloaldi, eskuzarta, eskuzartada, eskuzafla.
apple *n.* sagar.
appliance *n.* tresna, gailu.
applicability *n.* gaurkotasun, egokitasun.
applicable *adj.* egoki, dagokion; -(re)kiko.
applicant *n.* eskatzaile.
application *n.* eskabide, eskari. *n.* eskariorri; idazki. *n.* saiapen.
apply *v.t.* erabili. *v.t.(for)* eskatu, arrenkatu (lanpostua edo laguntza). *v.t.* ipini, jarri. *v.i.* egoki izan.
appoint *v.t.* izendatu.
appointment *n.* izendapen (lanpostua hartzeko). *n.* lanpostu, ogibide, lanbide. *n.* ikustordu, txanda.
apportion *v.t.* hainbanatu.
apportionable *adj.* zatigai, zatigarri, partigarri, banagarri, hainbanagarri.
appraisal *n. (econ.)* tasaketa, tasa; balioztapen. *n.* ebaluaketa, ebaluapen.
appraise *v.t.* balioztatu, balio eman, ebaluatu, tasatu.
appraiser *n.* tasatzaile, balioztatzaile, taiutzaile. *n.* ebaluatzaile.
appreciable *adj.* estimagarri, onerizgarri, onesgai. *adj.* begiztagarri, ikusgarri, ikusgai, nabari, agiri.
apreciate *v.t.* estimatu, onetsi. *v.i.* balioa gehitu, birbaliotu, preziatu.
appreciated *adj.* estimagarri.
appreciation *n.* estimu, estimagarritasun, ondonahi. *n.* onerizte. *n.* eskerron, ezagutza. *n. (econ.)* plusbalio, gainbalio, birbaliodura, birbalioketa, birbaliopen.
appreciative *adj.* onerizle, estimatzaile. *adj.* eskerdun, eskerroneko, eskertsu.
apprehend *v.t.* harrapatu, atzeman.
apprehendable *adj.* harrapagarri, atxikigarri, heldugarri, atzemangarri.
apprehensible *adj.* ulergarri, adigarri, konprenigarri.
apprehension *n.* larrialdi, hestura, urduritasun. *n.* ulerkuntza, adikuntza, ulerketa. *n.* harrapaldi, harrapaketa, atzemate.
apprehensive *adj.* urduri, larri, herabeti.
apprentice *n.* ikasberri; -mutiko, -mutil.
apprenticeship *n.* lanbide berria ikasteko garaia.
approach *v.t./v.i.* inguratu, hurbildu, hurreratu, gerturatu, alboratu, ondoratu, alderatu.
approach *n.* hurreraketa, hurbilpen, hurbilketa, alboraketa, alborapen. *n.* hurbilbide, sarbide. *n.* ikuspuntu, ikusbide.
approbation *n.* baieztapen, baiezko,

onespen, oneritzi.
appropriate *v.t.* nori berea eman. *v.t.*
beretu, jabetu, hartu, bereganatu,
beregaindu, eskuperatu.
appropriate *adj.* egoki, erako, erazko,
hartarako, aukerako.
appropriately *adv.* egoki, eraz.
appropriateness *n.* egokitasun,
idekotasun.
appropriation *n.* berekuntza,
eskurantza, jabeketa, jabetzapen,
jabekuntza, gureganaketa,
bereganaketa. *n.* gauza berezi bat
egiteko laguntza, batez ere
gobernuak ematen duen dirua.
approvable *adj.* baiezgarri, onirizgarri,
oneskor.
approval *n.* onarketa, onespen,
onarpen, onesmen, onirizte, oniritzi,
baieztapen.
approve *v.t./v.i. (v.i., gehienetan
of-ekin)* baieztu, onartu, onetsi,
baietsi, onespena eman, ontzat
eman, ontzat hartu.
approving *adj.* onesle.
approximate *v.t./v.i.* hurbildu. *v.t.*
igarri, uste izan.
approximate *adj.* gorabeherako,
gutigorabeherako.
approximately *adv.* inguru, edo, bat,
gutigorabehera.
approximation *n.* kalkulu, taxu. *n.*
hurbilpen.
apricot *n. (bot.)* albarikoke.
April *n.* apirila, jorraila.
apron *n.* amantal.
apronful *n.* altzokada, amantalbete.
apropos *adv. (of-ekin)* -(r)i buruz. *adj.*
egoki.
apse *n. (archit.)* elizbular.
apt *adj.* joerabateko, emana, jarria;
-bera. *adj.* gertagarri, egiantzeko.
adj. argi, zorrotz, trebe, modutsu,
moldatsu. *adj.* egoki, gai, hartarako
gauza.
aptitude *n.* doitasun, gaitasun,
edozertarakotasun, egokitasun.
aptly *adv.* moduz.
aptness *n.* egokitasun, gaitasun;
trebetasun.
aquarium *n.* akuario.
aquatic *adj.* uretako.
aqueduct *n.* ubide, urbide.
aqueous *adj.* urtar, urezko.
aquiline *adj.* kako (sudur).
Arab *n./adj.* arabiar; musulman.
arable *adj.* iraulgarri, itzulgarri,
laboragarri, langarri, luberrigarri,
landugarri.
arbiter *n.* ebazle.
arbitrarily *adv.* nahikeriaz, nolanahika.
arbitrariness *n.* nahikeria.
arbitrary *adj.* nahikerizko, bidegabeko,
arrazoigabeko. *adj.* nagusikeria.
arbitration *n.* epaiketa, epaikunde,
epaikuntza.
arbitrator *n.* irizpidetzaile.

arboreal *adj.* zuhaitzantzeko.
arc *v.i.* uztaitu.
arc *n.* arku, uztai.
arch *n.* arku.
archaeological *adj.* arkeologiko.
archaeologist *n.* arkeologari.
archaeology *n.* arkeologia.
archaic *adj.* behinolako, aspaldiko,
modaz kanpo dagoena.
archangel *n. (theol.)* goiaingeru.
archbishop *n.* artzapezpiku,
apezpikuburu, gotzainburu,
goigotzain.
archbishopric *n.* artzapezpikutegi,
goigotzainbarruti.
archduke *n.* artxiduke.
arched *adj.* bizkarrantzeko, kakodun,
arkudun.
archer *n.* gezilari, gezitari.
archetype *n.* leheneredu, lehenmolde.
archiepiscopal *adj.* artzapezpikutar.
archipelago *n. (geog.)* uhartedi,
uharteta, irlategi.
architect *n.* arkitekto.
architecture *n.* arkitektura.
architrave *n. (archit.)* erlaizpe.
archive *n.* artxibo.
archivist *n.* artxibari, artxibozain.
archpriest *n. (eccl.)* artxipreste,
artzapez.
archstone *n. (archit.)* arkuharri.
archway *n.* zubibegi, zubizulo.
arctic *n.* izotz-iparralde. *adj.* izotz-.
ardent *adj.* gartsu, suhar, sutsu, bero,
gogobero, susper. *adj.* bizi.
ardently *adv.* gartsuki, beroki, jo ta ke,
jo ta su, sutsuki, gori-gori, suminki,
goriki.
ardor *n.* suhartasun, suminketa,
sutsutasun, gar, joran.
arduous *adj.* zail.
are *Cf.* be.
area *n.* alde, lekugune, barruti, eremu,
eskualde, esparru, tokialde, lurralde.
n. sail.
arena *n.* estadio, jolas-zelai.
aren't "are + not"-aren laburpena.
argot *n.* lanbide jakin batean erabili ohi
den hiztegi berezia.
arguable *adj.* eztabaidagarri,
gezurtagarri, ihardukigarri.
argue *v.i./v.t.* aharratu, erronkatu,
gatazkatu, iharduki, liskartu,
mokokatu.
arguer *n.* eztabaidatzaile, liskarremaile,
ahakartzaile, liskarrari, liskargile,
argudiatzaile, mokokari.
argument *n.* argudio, errieta, liskar,
ahakar, liskarkeria, iskanbila, istilu,
mokoketa.
argumentative *adj.* ahakarzale,
ezeztakor, liskarrari, mokokatzaile,
liskarti.
argumentatively *adv.* eztabaidaka.
aria *n. (mus.)* aria.
arid *adj.* idor, lehor, agor, ihar, siku.
aridity *n.* idortasun, lehortasun.

aridness *n.* lehortasun, idortasun, idorte, agortasun.
arise *v.i.* sortu. *v.i.* igo, igon. *v.i.* jaiki.
aristocracy *n.* aristokrazia.
aristocrat *n.* handiki, handizki, handi-mandi(ak), jauntxo.
aristocratic *adj.* handiki, aristokrata.
arithmetic *n.* aritmetika.
arithmetical *n.* aritmetikako.
Arizona *n. (geog.)* Estatu Batuetako estatu bat.
ark *n.* ontzitzar. *n.* kutxa.
Arkansas *n. (geog.)* Estatu Batuetako estatu bat.
arm *v.t./v.i.* armatu.
arm *n. (anat.)* beso, besa-.
armada *n.* ontzidi.
armament *n.* armateri.
armchair *n.* besaulki.
armed *adj.* armadun.
armful *n.* besakada, besaldi.
armhole *n.* galtzarbegi.
armistice *n.* gerlarte, gudarte.
armless *adj.* mantxu.
armor *n.* soinburdin, izterburdin, altzairujantzi, izterbabes, soinbabes.
armory *n.* iskilotegi, armategi.
armpit *n. (anat.)* besape, besazpi, galtzarpe, galtzarbe.
arms *n.* armak, armateri.
army *n.* gudaroste, soldadugo, soldadutza.
aroma *n.* usaingozo, usaingarri, lurrinusain.
aromatic *adj.* usaingarri, usaingozodun, lurrintsu, usaintsu.
around *adv./prep.* inguru, inguruan.
arouse *v.t.* bizitu.
arraign *v.t.* epaimahai aurrera deitu.
arraignment *n.* epaimahai aurrera deitze(a).
arrange *v.t.* disposatu, egokitu, atondu. *v.t.* antolatu, antzatu, moldatu, arautu, prestatu, taiutu.
arrangement *n.* antolabide, antolakizun, gertuera, konponketa, moldaketa, taiuketa. *n.* gertapen, prestapen, antolapen, prestakuntza, disposaketa. *n.* akordio, hitzarmen. *n. (mus.)* konponketa.
arranger *n.* antolatzaile, atontzaile, disposatzaile. *n. (mus.)* musika-konpontzaile, doinu-konpontzaile.
arrant *adj.* nabari; goren(a).
array *v.t.* antolatu, sailkatu. *v.t.* apaindu.
array *n.* antolaketa, sailkapen. *n.* jantzi dotore.
arrears *n. (pl.)* ordaindu beharreko atzerapenak.
arrest *v.t.* harrapatu, atxilotu, atzeman. *v.t.* aurrerapena geldiarazi.
arrest *n.* atxiloketa.
arrival *n.* etorraldi, etorrera, helduera.
arrive *v.i.* heldu, tokiratu, lekuratu, iritsi.

arrogance *n.* handinahikeria, handikeria, harropuzkeria, harrokeria, oilarkeria.
arrogant *adj.* harro, handinahiko, harroputz, handiusteko, hanpurutsu, oilar. **To be arrogant.** Harrotu.
arrogantly *adv.* harroki, harropuzkeriaz, harrokeriaz.
arrow *n.* gezi, azkon.
arsenal *n.* polborategi, armatoki, armategi.
arsenic *n.* arseniko.
arson *n.* nahita sorturiko sute(a).
arsonist *n.* suteak nahita eragiten dituena.
art *n.* arte, erti.
arterial *adj.* zaingorriko, zainetako.
arteriole *n.* zaingorritxo.
arteriosclerosis *n. (med.)* zainsormindura.
artery *n. (anat.)* arteria, zain, zaingorri.
arthritis *n.* artritis, hezueri.
artichoke *n. (bot.)* alkatxofa, orriburu.
article *n.* idazlan, artikulu. *n.* merkatalgai; -ki. *n. (gram.)* artikulu, mugizki. *n.* idaztxatal.
articulate *v.t.* artikulatu; ahoskatu, ogusi.
articulate *adj.* ulergarri.
articulately *adv.* ulergarriki.
articulation *n. (anat.)* giltzadura. *n.* ahoskatze, artikulazio.
artifice *n.* zuhurtasun, azerikeria. *n.* trebetasun, eskuaire.
artificial *adj.* egindako, artifizial.
artificially *adv.* artifizialki.
artillery *n.* artileria.
artilleryman *n.* kainoilari.
artisan *n.* eskulangile.
artist *n.* artista, artelari, edertilari.
artistic *adj.* artezko.
artistically *adv.* artez, artelegez.
artistry *n.* arte, artezia, abilidade.
arts *n. (pl.)* ederti.
arts and crafts *n.* eskulangintza.
as *adv./conj.* gisa, bezala, moduan, legez.
ascend *v.i./v.t.* igan, igo.
ascendancy *n.* nagusitza, aginte.
ascendant *adj.* goranzko, gorunzko.
ascension *n.* igoera, igonaldi, gorakaldi; igokunde, zeruratze.
ascent *n.* gorabide, iganaldi.
ascertain *v.t.* ziurtu, iragarri.
ascetic *adj.* aszetiko.
asexual *adj.* sexugabe(ko).
ash *n. (bot.)* lizar. *n.* hauts, hausterre, errauts, geldo.
ashamed *adj.* lotsati, lotsa. **To be ashamed.** Lotsatu.
ashamedly *adv.* lotsaz.
ashcan *n.* zaramontzi.
ashen *adj.* hautsezko. *adj.* zurbil, hits.
ashore *adv.* itsasertzera, lurrera. **To go ashore.** Desontziratu.
ashtray *n.* hautsontzi, errautsontzi.
ash tree *n. (bot.)* lizar.

Ash Wednesday n. (eccl.) hausterregun, hausterre.
ashy adj. hautsezko, errautsezko, erraustun.
aside adv. alboan, ondoan, aldean, aldamenean; aparte. n. bazter-solas.
ask v.t./v.i. galdetu, galde egin (G,LN,U). v.t. **(for)** eskatu.
askance adv. mesfidantzaz. adv. zeharka, zeharbidez, zeharki, zeharretara.
askew adv. zeharka, zeharbidez, zeharki, zeharretara. adj. oiher.
asleep adj. lo, lotan. **To fall asleep.** Loak hartu.
asp n. (zool.) sugegorri.
asparagus n. (bot.) frantsesporruondo; frantsesporru, zainzuri.
aspect n. itxura, itxurapen, taxu, planta (c), eite, aire. n. puntu, tankera. n. albo.
aspen n. (bot.) lertxun, orrikara.
asperity n. mokortasun, laztasun, lazdura.
aspersion n. ihiztadura.
asphalt n. asfalto.
asphyxia n. itodura.
asphyxiate v.t./v.i. ito arazi, ito.
asphyxiation n. itoaldi, itobehar, itodura.
asphyxiator n. itoarazle.
aspirate v.t. arnasgoratu, haskoititu.
aspirated adj. haskoitu(a), arnasgoratu(a). **Aspirated h.** H arnasgoratu(a).
aspiration n. arnasgora.
aspirin n. (med.) aspirina.
ass n. (zool.) asto; asta-. n. (anat.) ipurdi. n. astakilo.
assail v.t. erasan, eraso, oldartu.
assailable adj. erasogarri.
assailant n. erasotzaile.
assassin n. hiltzaile, heriogile, gizahiltzaile, gizaeraile, eraile.
assassinate v.t. hilarazi, sarraskitu.
assassination n. sarraski, hilketa, erailketa, gizahilketa, hiltzarre.
assault v.t. eraso, oldartu.
assault n. eraso, erasoaldi, erasoketa, oldargune, oldarketa, oldarraldi.
assay v.t. metalak aztertu.
assayer n. metalikerle; urreikertzaile, zilarrikertzaile.
assemble v.t./v.i. elkartu, bildu, batzartu. v.t. muntatu, eraiki.
assembler n. muntatzaile.
assembly n. batzarre, bilera, biltzarre, topaketa. n. muntaketa, muntaia. n. (mil.) soldaduak biltzen dituen deia.
assent v.i. (gehienetan **to**-ekin) ados egon, baietza eman, baietz esan, baieztu.
assent n. baiezko.
assert v.t. baieztatu.
assertion n. baieztapen.
assertive adj. baieztakor.

assertively adv. baietz, baiezka.
assess v.t. zergabanatu, zergatu, tasatu.
assessable adj. zergagarri, tasagarri.
assessment n. balioztadura, tasaketa.
assessor n. talulari, tasatzaile, neurtzaile.
asset n. (pl.) ondasun, hartzeko.
assiduous adj. jarraikor, jarraile, iraunkor.
assiduously adv. jarraikiro, jarraituki.
assiduousness n. jarraikitasun, iraunaldi, iraunketa.
assign v.t. eman, ezarri. v.t. izendatu.
assignable adj. ezargarri.
assignation n. maitelagunen isilpeko ikustordu(a).
assignment n. ikasgai, ikaskai, arieta. n. lanpostu.
assimilate v.t./v.i. haragitu; kidekotu, bereganatu.
assimilation n. bereganaketa.
assist v.t./v.i. lagundu, faboretu.
assistance n. laguntza, laguntasun, lagungarri.
assistant n. laguntzaile; -lagun. adj. -orde, behe-.
assistantship n. Ameriketako unibertsitateko ikasleek ikerketak edo ikasketak egiteko jasotzen duten dirulaguntza.
associate v.t./v.i. bat egin, bateratu, elkargotu, lagunartetu, elkarganatu.
associate n. lagunkide, kide, lagunarteko, elkarkide, erkide. adj. urgazle. **Associate member of the Basque Academy.** Euskaltzain urgazle.
associated adj. elkartu(a).
association n. elkarte, elkargo, lagunbatza. n. elkarketa, bategite. n. erkidego, erkidetasun. n. ideien-elkarlotze, adimenezko elkarlotze(a).
associative adj. elkarkor, elkarkoi.
assonance n. asonantzia.
assorted adj. nahasitako.
assortment n. askotariko gauzak; sorta, bilduma.
assume v.t. gainulertu, balizkatu. v.t. hartu, bereganatu, gureganatu.
assumed adj. ustezko, delako.
assumption n. ieru, susmo, errezelu, goganbehar. n. (eccl., cap.) jasokunde, zeruratze.
assurable adj. ziurgarri.
assurance n. ziurtasun, segurantza, segurtasun; birbaiezpen.
assure v.t. ziurtatu, ziurtu. v.t. fidarazi, seguratu, segurtatu.
assured adj. ziur, irmo, segur.
assuredly adv. seguraski.
assuredness n. ziurtasun, segurantza, segurtasun.
assurer n. seguratzaile.
asterisk n. izartxo.
asteroid n. (astron.) izarraide.

asthma n. (med.) hatsneke, arnasneke.

asthmatic adj. hatsnekedun, arnasnekedun.

astigmatism n. astigmatismo.

astonish v.t. kolokarazi, harritu, txunditu.

astonished adj. harrituta, ahozabalik.

astonishing adj. harrigarri, izugarri, miragarri, txundigarri.

astonishment n. harridura, harritzapen, txundidura, txundiketa.

astound v.t. kolokarazi, txunditu, harritu.

astounded adj. txundituta.

astounding adj. harrigarri, izugarri, miragarri, txundigarri, txundikor.

astraddle adj. zangalatraba.

astray adj./adv. bidegabe. **To go astray.** Okerbidetu. **To lead (someone) astray.** Okerrarazi.

astride adv./adj. zangalatraba.

astringent adj. estukor; idorgarri. n. gauza idorgarri, gauza lehorgarri.

astrologer n. astrologo.

astrological adj. astrologiko.

astrology n. astrologia.

astronaut n. astronauta.

astronautics n. astronautika.

astronomer n. astrologari.

astronomical adj. astronomiko.

astronomy n. astronomia.

astute adj. amarrudun, bihurri, maltzur, luki, azeri, zaharketo.

astutely adv. bihurriz, maltzurki.

astuteness n. azerikeria, amarru.

asylum n. zoroetxe; umezurtzetxe. n. babesetxe, babesleku, babestoki.

at prep. -(a)n, -(eta)n, -ean.

atheism n. fedegabekeria, jainkogabetasun, ateismo.

atheist n. fedegabe, jainkogabe.

atheistic adj. fedegabeko.

athlete n. kirolari, atleta.

athletic adj. kirolezko, kirolzale, jolaszale.

athletics n. kirolak, atletismo.

Atlantic adj. Atlantiko.

atlas n. (geog.) atlas, mapasorta.

atmosphere n. egurats; aire. n. giro, girorapen, ingurugiro, bizigiro.

atmospheric adj. airezko.

atoll n. atoloi.

atom n. (phys.) atomo.

atomic adj. atomiko, atomozko.

atomizer n. lurringailu.

atonal adj. (mus.) giltzagabeko, klabegabeko.

atonality n. soinugabetasun.

atone v.t./v.i. (v.i., for-ekin) lege haustea ordaindu.

atrocious adj. izugarri, izugarrizko, izigarri.

atrociously adv. izugarriro, izugarriki, lazgarriki.

atrociousness n. lazgarritasun.

atrocity n. izugarrikeria, lazgarrikeria,

izigarrikeria, otsokeria.

atrophy v.t./v.i. endurtu, enuldu, atrofiatu.

atrophy n. atrofia.

attach v.t. lotu, lokarriztatu. v.t. desjabetu.

attachment n. atxikimendu, itsasketa, atxikidura, eraspen.

attack v.t./v.i. erasan, eraso, oldartu, jazarri.

attack n. eraso, erasoaldi, erasoketa, gudaldi, oldar, jazarraldi.

attacker n. erasotzaile, oldartzaile.

attain v.t. gauzatu, lortu.

attainable adj. helgarri, eskuragarri.

attainment n. lorpen, erdiespen.

attempt v.t. saiatu, ahalegina egin, ahalegindu.

attempt n. ahalegin, saiakera, saialdi, saio, ekinaldi. n. eraso, erasoaldi.

attend v.t. joan; etorri. v.i. (to) aiutatu, laguntza eman, zaindu.

attendance n. joate; etortze.

attention n. aditasun, someketa, oharkera, oharmen, jaramon, kasu. **To pay attention.** Jaramon egin. n. (exclam.) entzun!

attentive adj. adikor, arretadun, arretatsu, begirakor, entzunkor, erne, zuhur. adj. axolati, axolatsu.

attentively adv. erneki, adi-adi, arduraz, arretaz, kontuz, buru-belarri. adv. axolaki, axolaz.

attentiveness n. adikortasun, ernetasun.

attenuate v.t./v.i. bigundu, ematu, ahuldu, mehetu.

attenuated adj. mehe, ahul.

attenuation n. ahuldura, leunketa.

attest v.t./v.i. (v.i. to-ekin) baieztu, zineztu, aitor egin, testifikatu.

attestation n. testigutza.

attic n. ganbara, sabai, teilatupe.

attire n. jantzi, jantziera.

attitude n. adimeneko jokabide(a). n. jarrera, jokabide, portaera, jokaera. n. jarrera, egoera.

attorney n. legegizon.

attorney general n. Estatu Batuetako justizi-ministrari(a).

attract v.t. erakarri, etorrarazi; bereganatu, norberaganatu, norberagana erakarri.

attraction n. erakarpen, erakarketa, erakarmen. n. liluraketa, lilurapen, liluramendu.

attractive adj. lilurakor, lilurazko, liluratzaile, polit, galant; tirriagarri; xarmant. adj. erakarkor, erakargarri, erakarle.

attractively adv. xarmanki, xarmaz, liluraz.

attractiveness n. liluragarritasun, xoramen, politasun. n. erakargarritasun, erakarpen.

attributable adj. egozkarri, ezargarri.

attribute v.t. egotzi, leporatu.

attribute *n.* nolakotasun, kalitate. *n.*
(*gram.*) atributo.
attributive *n.* (*gram.*) atributo. *adj.*
leporagarri, egozkarri.
attrition *n.* (*eccl.*) beldurdamu.
attune *v.t.* musika-tresnak afinatu.
auburn *n./adj.* gaztainikara.
auction *v.t.* (*askotan* **off**-*ekin*)
subastatu, enkantatu.
auction *n.* subasta, enkante.
auctioneer *n.* subastari.
audacious *adj.* izukaitz, beldurgaitz,
kopetadun, oldakor, ikaragaitz.
audaciously *adv.* ausarki, ausarkiro,
oldarki.
audaciousness *n.* oldarkoitasun,
ausartasun, izukaiztasun.
audacity *n.* ausarpen, kopeta, balore,
bipildura.
audible *adj.* entzungarri.
audibly *adv.* entzungarriro.
audience *n.* entzulego, entzuleria,
entzulesail. *n.* ikustaldi, elkarrikuste.
audio-visual *adj.* ikusentzuteko.
audit *v.t.* diru-kontuak egiaztatu.
audit *n.* diru-kontuen egiaztapen.
audition *n.* entzunaldi, entzute. *n.*
abeslariek eta antzezlariek lana lortu
aurretik eskeini behar izaten duten
emanaldia.
auditive *adj.* entzumenezko.
auditor *n.* diru-kontuen egiztalari.
auger *n.* zaztagin, ginbelet.
aught *n.* zerbait, ezer; ezer ez.
augment *v.t./v.i.* gehiagotu, gehitu,
handitu, ugaldu, gaineratu, ainiztu,
areagotu.
augmentable *adj.* gehigarri, ugalgarri.
augmentation *n.* gehikuntza, emendio,
berretura.
augmentative *adj.* gehikor, handigarri.
n. (*gram.*) handikari.
augur *v.t.* aurresan, auguratu.
augury *n.* hegaztiaztikeria, asmakeria,
aztiketa.
August *n.* abuztua, agorril.
aunt *n.* izeba.
aura *n.* pertsona batek bere inguruan
sortzen duen dirdaidura berezia.
aural *adj.* entzumenezko.
auricular *adj.* belarriko.
auriferous *adj.* urretsu, urredun.
aurora *n.* egunsenti, egunabar.
auspices *n.* (*pl.*) babespen.
auspicious *adj.* faboragarri.
austere *adj.* zorrotz, latz, garratz,
gogor. *adj.* larderiatsu.
austerity *n.* gogortasun, garraztasun.
authentic *adj.* jator, egitazko, egiazko.
authenticate *v.t.* benetakotasuna
frogatu.
authenticity *n.* benetakotasun,
egiazkotasun, jatortasun.
author *n.* liburugile; egile, idazle.
authoritarian *adj.* larderiatsu,
larderiadun.
authoritarianism *n.* nagusikeria,

agintzalekeria, jabekeria.
authoritative *adj.* agintezale.
authoritatively *adv.* eskubidez.
authority *n.* aginpide, aginte,
eskumen, mende, agintaritasun,
eskukotasun, jauntasun, agintaritza;
nagusigo, nagusitza, manu,
eskubide. *n.* agintari, agintaritalde. *n.*
(*pl.*) gobernu(a), jaurlaritza. *n.*
pertsona aditu(a), pertsona jantzi(a).
authorizable *adj.* baimengarri, uzkarri,
haizugarri.
authorization *n.* baimen, haizugo,
baimendura, lagapen.
authorize *v.t.* ahalmendu, eskubidea
eman, eskubidetu, zilegitu, baimena
eman, esku eman, utzi.
authorized *adj.* haizu, lagagarri.
authorship *n.* egiletasun; liburu-idazle,
liburugile.
auto *n.* kotxe.
auto- (*gram.*) auto-, buru-.
autobiographical *adj.* autobiografiko.
autobiography *n.* autobiografia.
autocracy *n.* autokrazia.
autocrat *n.* autokrata.
autocratic *adj.* autokratiko.
autograph *v.t.* eskuz izenpetu.
autograph *n.* izenpe, izenpeko.
automate *v.t./v.i.* automatizatu.
automated *adj.* automatizatu(a).
automatic *adj.* automatiko. *adj.*
oharkabeko, konturagabeko.
automatically *adv.* automatikoki. *adv.*
oharkabeki, konturagabeki.
automation *n.* automatizapen. *n.*
ordenagailuen erabilpen(a).
automobile *n.* auto, kotxe.
autonomous *adj.* berjabe, burujabe,
autonomo.
autonomy *n.* autonomia, berjabetasun,
berjabetza, burujabetza.
autopsy *n.* gorpuebaketa,
gorpuazterketa.
autosuggestion *n.* burulilurapen,
autosugestio.
autumn *n.* udazken, udazkenaldi,
udagoien.
autumnal *adj.* udazkeneko.
auxiliary *adj.* laguntzaile. **Auxiliary
verb.** Aditz-laguntzaile. *n.* laguntzaile;
talde-laguntzaile(a).
avail *v.t./v.i.* gauza izan, -az baliatu.
availability *n.* baliagarritasun.
available *adj.* baliagarri.
avalanche *n.* elurlauso.
avarice *n.* zekenkeria, zikoizkeria,
diruzalekeria, dirukoikeria, dirugose,
xuhurkeria.
avaricious *adj.* zeken, zikoitz, xuhur.
avariciously *adv.* zekenki, zikoizki,
xuhurki.
avenge *v.t.* mendekatu, aspertu.
avenger *n.* aspertzaile, mendekari,
mendekatzaile.
avenging *adj.* mendekagarri,
mendekatzaile, mendekuzko,

asperbera, asperkoi.
avenue *n.* bidezabal, bidehandi, bidenausi. *n. (fig.)* -bide; -era.
average *adj.* batez-besteko, ertain. *n.* erdineurri, erdimaila.
averse *adj.* kontrako, aurkako.
aversion *n.* nazka, higuin, narda, enpagu, higuindura, nakaitz, nakaizgo, ikusiezin.
avert *v.t.* (begirada) aldendu. *v.t.* (hondamendiari) aurrea hartu.
aviary *n.* txoritoki.
aviation *n.* hegazkintza.
aviator *n.* hegazkilari, hegazkari.
aviculture *n.* hegaztihazkuntza, hegaztizaintza, txorizaintza.
avid *adj.* gale.
avocado tree *n. (bot.)* aguakate.
avoid *v.t.* saihestu, zehartu, itzuri.
avoidable *adj.* alderagarri, baztergarri, itzurgarri.
avow *v.t.* esan, aitortu.
avowable *adj.* aitorgarri, aitorbidezko.
await *v.t./v.i.* itxaro, itxoin, igurikatu, zain egon.
awake *adj.* iratzarri, esnai, ernai. **To be awake.** Esnai egon.
awaken *v.i./v.t.* esnatu, iratzarri, itzarri, itzartu, ixartu.
awakener *n.* iratzarle, esnaerale.
awakening *n.* iratzarpen.
award *n.* sari.
aware *adj.* jakitun. **To be aware of. To become aware of.** Konturatu. Ohartu. Sumatu. Jakitun egon.
awareness *n.* konorte. *n.* ezaguera, jakite.
away *adv.* urrun, urrutik, urrundik, lekutan. *adv.* etengabe, etengabeki. *adv.* bapatean, berehala, behingoan. *adj.* aldegin, urrutiko. *adj.* kanpoko (kirol).
awe *n.* beldurrikara, begiramendu beldurgarri(a), mirespen beldurgarri(a).
awful *adj.* harrigarrizko, beldurgarrizko, izugarri, ikaragarri. *adj.* lazgarri. *adj.* itzel, handitzar, eskerga; itsusl.
awfully *adv.* beldurgarriro, izugarriro, izugarriki, ikaragarriki.
awfulness *n.* beldurgarritasun, ikaragarritasun, izugarritasun.
awkward *adj.* baldar, trakets, dorpe, moldagaitz, moldagabeko, artekaitz. *adj.* kankailu, troskote. *adj.* taxugabe, ezegoki. *adj.* ezatsegin, eragozkarri, gaitzikor, trabakor.
awkwardly *adv.* dorpeki, baldarki, trakeski, airegabeki, zirriki-zarraka, ganoragabeki.
awkwardness *n.* dorpetasun, moldagaiztasun, trakestasun, taxugabekeria, baldartasun.
awl *n.* ezten, puntzoi.
awning *n.* itzaloihal, toldo, olana. *n.* aterpe.
ax *n.* aizkora.

axilla *n. (anat.)* besape, besazpi, galtzarpe.
axillar *adj.* hegazpiko.
axiom *n.* esana, axioma.
axis *n.* ardatz; ehunardatz.
axle *n.* ardatz, gurtardatz, txabeta.
axletree *n.* ziri, kabila.
aye *adv.* bai.

B

b *n.* Ingeles alfabetoko letra.
baa *n.* me.
babble *v.i./v.t.* erdimintzatu.
babble *n.* kalamatrika, berritsukeria, hitzontzikeria.
babbler *n.* zezel.
babbling *n.* hitzontzikeria, berritsukeria, solaskeria. *adj.* berritsu, hitzontzi, kalakari, eleketari, berrijario, hitzjario.
babe *n.* haurtxo.
baboon *n. (zool.)* babuino.
baby *n.* haur, haurtxo, sein, umetxo.
babyhood *n.* lehen haurtzaro.
babysitter *n.* haurtzain, umezain, umezaintzaile.
bachelor *n.* emaztegabe, senargai, mutilzahar.
bachelorhood *n.* ezkongabetasun, ezkongabezia, ezkongetasun.
bacillus *n. (med.)* bazilo.
back *v.t.* lagundu. *v.t./v.i. (askotan up-ekin)* gibeldu, gibelatu, gibelalderatu. *v.i. (down edo off)* atzeratu, atzera joan, atzera egin. *v.i. (out)* hitzik ez bete.
back *n. (anat.)* bizkar, bizkarralde, lepo. *n.* bizkar, atze, oste, atzealde, gibel. *n.* liburuaren azken orrialdeak. *n.* atzelari (kirol). *adj.* atzeko, atzekaldeko, bizkarraldeko, bizkarreko. *adj.* atzeratu, aintzinako, zahar. *adv.* atzera, atzerantza.
backache *n.* bizkarmin, lepokomin.
backbiter *n.* ausikilari.
backbone *n. (anat.)* bizkarrezur.
backdoor *adj.* izkutuko, isileko.
back door *n.* atzeko ate, gibeleko ate.
backfield *n.* atzeko sail. *n.* jokalari-atzelariak.
background *n.* hondo.
backhand *n./adv.* errebeska (kirol).
backing *n.* sostengu.
backlight *n.* kontrargi.
backpack *n.* bidezorro, bizkarzorro, motxila.
backside *n.* ipurdi.
backsliding *adj.* erorbera, erorti. *n.* berrerorpen, berretura, berrerortzi.
backward(s) *adv.* atzezka, atzez, atzera, gibelka, alderantziz, aldrebes, atzekoz aurrera. *adj.* atzerakoi, alderantzizko, atzerakor. *adj.* atzeratu(a).
backwoods *n.* urrun dagoen zuhaitzez betetako ingurua.
backwoodsman *n.* baso urrunetan bizi

den pertsona.
backwoodsy *adj.* mendirakoi.
bacon *n.* urdai-giharre, urdaiki.
bacteria *n.* bakteria.
bacterial *adj.* bakteriako.
bacteriology *n.* baktereologia.
bad *adj.* txar, gaizto, gizagaizto, gaizkile, oker, makur. **To go bad.** Gaiztotu. Txartu. *adv.* txarto, gaizki. *adj.* gaiso. *adj.* gorri, txar, gogor (eguraldi).
badge *n.* ezaugarri.
badger *n. (zool.)* azkonar.
badly *adv.* gaizki, txarki, txarto, makur.
badness *n.* txartasun, gaiztasun.
bad-tempered *adj.* haserre, haserrekor, sukoi, suminkor.
baffle *v.t.* kolokarazi.
bag *v.t.* zakuratu. *v.t.* hil; harrapatu (ehiza).
bag *n.* fardel, zorro, zaku.
bagful *n.* zakukada, zakutada.
baggage *n.* fardeleria, maletak.
baggage check *n.* aireportuan edo trenbidean maletak hartzea.
baggage counter *n.* maletegi.
baggy *adj.* lasai, laxo (frakak).
bagpipe *n.* Eskoziako gaita.
bagpiper *n.* gaitajotzaile, gaitari.
bah *int.* ba.
bailiff *n.* Estatu Batuetako auzitegietako polizia.
bail *n.* espetxeko fiantza, fidantza.
bait *n.* garnata, beita, mazi.
bake *v.t./v.i.* erre.
baked *adj.* erreta.
baker *n.* ogigile, okin, okintsa.
bakery *n.* ogitegi, okindegi.
baking *n.* ogigintza, okintza, okingo; errealdi.
baking soda *n.* legami-ordeko(a).
balance *v.t./v.i.* kordokatu, orekatu, zabukatu, kolokatu. *v.t.* kontu(ak) egin, kontu(ak) atera.
balance *n.* balantza, pisu, pisagailu. *n.* oreka, orekatasun.
balcony *n.* balkoi.
bald *adj.* ilesoil, burusoil, kaskasoil.
baldness *n.* ilegabezia, burusoildura, kaskasoildura, burusoileri, ileri.
bale *v.t.* fardoztatu.
bale *n.* fardo, haxe.
baleful *adj.* zorigaiztoko.
baler *n.* fardoztagailu.
balk *v.i.* gelditu. *v.i.* **(at)** kontrajarri, oposatu.
ball *v.t.* harildu, harilkatu, mataza egin. *v.t.* (-ezko) bolak egin. *v.i.* opildu.
ball *n.* baloi, pelota, pilota, bola, girla. *n.* dantza; aldi atsegingarri. *n. (colloq.)* barrabil, potro.
ballad *n.* balada.
balladeer *n.* erromantzari; koblari, koblakari.
ballast *n.* lastra, itsasontziak azpikaldean daraman zama.
ballet *n.* ballet.

balm *n.* gantzugailu, baltsamo.
balmy *adj.* eder (eguraldi). *adj.* gantzudun, gantzuzko.
balloon *n.* globo, haizontzi.
ballot *n.* hauteskundeko txartela. *n.* hautabide.
ballot box *n.* atabaka.
ball player *n.* pelotari, pilotari.
ball-point pen *n.* boligrafo.
ballroom *n.* dantzareto.
balls *n. (colloq.)* potro, barrabilak.
balsam *n.* balsamo, gantzugailu.
balustrade *n.* baranda, kalostra.
bam *n.* tupust.
bamboo *n.* banbu.
ban *v.t.* debekatu, galerazi.
ban *n.* debeku.
banana *n. (bot.)* banana, platano.
band *n.* talde; -teria, -talde. *n.* banda. *n.* zinta, zerrenda; uztaigailu.
bandage *v.t./v.i.* bendatu.
bandage *n.* esparadrapu, benda.
bandanna *n.* margozko zapi handi(a).
banderilla *n.* zezenziri.
bandit *n.* lapur, ohoin, ebasle; gaizkile.
bandy *v.t.* kirol-zelaian pilota batetik bestera jaurti.
bandy-legged *adj.* hankazabal, hankoker, zangoker, zangomakur.
bane *n.* hondamendi edo atsekabearen arrazoia.
bang *v.t./v.i.* panpakatu, panpatu.
bang *n.* tirots, zart, punpa, daunba, danba, zanpa. *n.* punpada. *n.* kopetile.
banish *v.t.* atzerriratu, arroztu.
banishment *n.* atzerriraketa, atzerrirapen.
banister *n.* baranda.
banjo *n. (mus.)* banjo.
bank *n.* banku, banketxe, diruetxe. **Bank account.** Bankukontu. **Piggy bank.** Itsulapiko. *n.* hondarpila, hondarmeta, hodeite; -pila, -meta. *n.* guren, ibaiertz, urbazter, urertz, uhalde. *n.* gordeleku; odol-banku. *n.* itsaspeko hondarmeta. *n.* erreskada, lerroak.
banker *n.* bankari.
banking *n.* banka-iharduera, banka-negozio.
bank note *n.* banku txartel.
bankrupt *adj.* ordainezin, porrot. **To go bankrupt.** Porrot egin. Hondatu.
bankruptcy *n.* bankuporroketa.
banner *n.* zutoihal.
bannister *n.* eskudel, baranda, kalostra.
banns *n. (pl.)* ezkondeiak, deiagiriak.
banquet *n.* janaldi, janedan, oturuntza.
banter *n.* irrijolas, irri, trufa.
baptise *v.t.* bataiatu.
baptism *n.* bataio.
baptismal *adj.* bataioko.
baptist *n./adj.* baptista.
baptistery *n.* bataiategi.
baptize *v.t./v.i.* bataiatu, bateatu,

kristautu.
baptizer n. bataiari (G,L), bataiatzaile.
bar v.t. trangatu, atagatu.
bar n. taberna, edaritegi. n. listoi (kirol).
Bar Association n. legegizon-elkargo.
barb n. garranga, suster.
barbarian n./adj. basati, anker.
barbaric adj. anker, gizagabeko.
barbarism n. basatasun, gizagabetasun. n. erderakada.
barbarity n. mairukeria, izukeria, ankerkeria, basakeria.
barbarously adv. mairuki.
barbecue n. erretegi.
barbed adj. burdinarizko arantzadun hesi(a).
barber n. ileapaintzaile, ilemozkin, ilemozle; barberu, bizargile, bizargin.
bard n. koblari, koblakari.
bare adj. murritz, soil.
barefoot adj./adv. hankuts, hankutsik, oinuts, oinutsik, hankagorri.
bare-headed adj. buruts, burutsik, kaskutsik.
barely adv. ozta-ozta, eskaski, urriki, ia, doi-doi. adv. biluzik, larrugorriz.
bareness n. larrugorritasun. n. murriztasun.
bargain n. tratu, eginkunde. n. eroseketa abantailatsu(a).
bargainer n. tratulari. n. merkatari.
barge n. gabarra, ontzitzar.
baritone n./adj. baritono.
bark v.i. zaunka egin, zaunkatu, ahausi egin, erausi. v.t. haserrez esan.
bark n. ahausi, zaunka. n. azal.
barker n. ferietako oihulari, jaietako erausle.
barking n. erausi, zaunka, ahausi. adj./adv. ahausikari, zaunkari; zaunkaka.
barley n. (bot.) garagar.
barmaid n. tabernari (emakume).
barman n. tabernari (gizon), txiribogin.
barn n. bihitegi, aletegi, garautegi, belartegi, sapai.
barnacle n. (zool.) lanperna.
barn owl n. hontza, ontza, gauhontza.
barnyard n. gortatze.
barometer n. gironeurkin.
baron n. baroi, haundiki.
baroness n. baronesa.
baronial adj. baroiaren.
barrack(s) n. barrakoi(ak), kuartel, goarditoki, gudaletxe.
barrage n. kainoiez eginiko erasoaldia(a). n. kopuru handi(a).
barrel n. upel, barrika, pipa.
barren adj. soil, soilgorri, murritz; igor, agor. **Barren mountains.** Mendi soilak. adj. haurgabe; antzu.
barrenness n. murriztasun. n. haurgabetasun.
barricade n. barrikada.
barrier n. langa. n. oztopo.
barrister n. legegizon.
barrow n. orgatxo, karretila.

bartender n. tabernari, tabernandre.
barter n. truke.
Bascologist n. euskalari.
Bascophile n. euskaltzale, euskozale.
Bascophilia n. euskaltzaletasun.
base v.t./v.i. (on) funtsatu, oinarritu. v.t./v.i. ezarri, ipini.
base n. oin, oinarri, hondo, funts, azpiharri, zimendu, zimentarri. adj. doilor, zirtzil, zital. n. (pl.) beisbol zelaiko lau bazterrak.
baseball n. beisbol.
baseboard n. hormoin.
baseless adj. funtsgabeko, funtsgabe.
basely adv. doilorki, zitalki, zitalkiro.
basement n. etxazpi, etxabe; soto.
baseness n. famatxar, zirtzilkeria, doilortasun, zitaltasun.
bash v.t. gogorki jo.
bash n. zartada. n. jai, besta.
bashful adj. lotsakor, lotsati, ahalkedun, ahalketi, herabeti.
bashfully adv. lotsaz, ahalkegarriki.
bashfulness n. lotsakortasun, lotsatasun, lotsakizun.
basic adj. oinarrizko, oineko, funtsezko, errozko. n. (cap.) ordenadorearen oinarrizko hizkuntza.
basically adv. oinarriz, funtsez, funtsean.
basil n. albahaka.
basilica n. basilika.
basin n. konketa. n. arro, haran. n. itsas-hondoko zulogune, itsasondo.
basis n. oinarri, sustrai, zimendu, zimentarri, funts.
bask v.i. eguzkia hartu. v.i. (in) atsegin ukan, laket izan.
basket n. otar, saski. n. xistera.
basketball n. saskibaloi.
basketful n. saskikada, zareta, otarkada.
Basque n. euskara. **Unified Basque.** Euskara batua. **Basque is spoken here.** Hemen euskaraz mintzatzen da. adj. euskal-, eusko-. **Basque festivals.** Euskal-jaiak.
Basque Academy n. Euskaltzaindi.
Basque Country n. Euskal Herri, Euskadi.
Basqueness n. euskalduntasun.
Basque Nationalist Party n. E.A.J.-P.N.V.
bass adj. lodi, n. bozlodi, baxu. n. (zool.) izokin mota bat.
bassinet n. zumezko seaska.
bassoon n. (mus.) fagota.
bass viol n. (mus.) kontrabaxu.
basswood n. (bot.) ezku.
bastard n. sasikume, sasiko, bort, herriume. n. lotsagabeko pertsona. adj. sasiko; lotsagabeko.
baste v.t. albaindu. v.t. koipez busti.
basting n. albain, albainu.
bastion n. hesibabes.
bat n. (zool.) saguzar, gauenara (L).
batch n. labekada, labealdi, errealdi.

bate v.t. gutxiagotu, arnasari eutsi.

bath n. bainu, mainu, bustialdi.

bathe v.i. bustialdi bat hartu. v.t. bustialdi bat eman.

bather n. bainulari.

bathing suit n. bainujantzi.

bathrobe n. bata.

bathroom n. komun, pixtoki, kakategi, txizatoki, pixategi. n. apaingela, bainugela, garbigela.

bathtub n. bainuontzi.

baton n. makila; batuta.

battalion n. batalioi.

batter v.t./v.i. uspelkatu, zanpakatu.

batter n. nahasketa irabiatu(a). n. bateatzaile (beisbol).

batterer n. zanpatzaile.

battering-ram n. ahariburu.

battery n. pila.

battle v.t./v.i. (v.i., with) borrokatu, burrukan egin, borrokan egin, gudakatu, gatazkatu, gerlatu.

battle n. gudaldi, guduketa, gudaketa, borroka, burruka, gatazka, gerla.

battle-ax n. Erdi Aroan borrokan erabili ohi zen aizkora luzea. n. emakume sendo eta marmartia.

battlefield n. gudaleku, gudategi, gudatoki.

battlement n. almena.

battleship n. gudontzi, gudarontzi, gerrontzi.

bauble n. girgileria, purtxileria, merkekeri(ak).

bawl v.i./v.t. oihu egin, oihuka negar egin, arrantzaka negar egin.

bay n. itsasgolko, badia. **Bay of Biscay.** Bizkaiako Golkoa.

bayonet n. baioneta.

bayou n. ubide estu(a).

bazaar n. tonbola.

B.C. (Before Christ) K.a. (Kristo aurreko). **That happened in 300 B.C.** Hori K.a. 300 urtean jazo zen.

be v.i. izan. v.i. egon. v.i. ibili.

beach v.t./v.i. hondoa jo, hondartu.

beach n. hondartza, hareatza, hondarreta.

beacon n. gauargi. n. baliza.

bead n. gargantila. n. burbuila.

beagle n. (zool.) belarrihandidun ehizazakur txiki(a).

beak n. moko.

beaker n. laborategiko pipeta.

beakless adj. mokogabe.

beam n. habe, aga, zurabe. n. argizpi, arraio, argisorta.

bean n. baba, babarrun, indaba.

bean pod n. (bot.) leka.

bear v.t./v.i. haurra egin, umea egin. v.t./v.i. eman. v.t. eutsi, sostengatu. v.t. iraun, iragan, pairatu. v.t. jasan, ekarri; eraman. v.i. joan, leku aldatu. v.i. (down on) zapaldu. v.i. (out) egiztatu, baietsi. v.i. (with) jasankor izan, eramankor izan.

bear n. (zool.) hartz. **Female bear.**

Hartzeme.

bearable adj. eramangarri, jasangarri, pairagarri, eroangarri.

bearably adv. jasangarriro.

beard n. bizar.

bearded adj. bizardun, bizarti.

beardless adj. bizargabe, bizargabeko.

bearer n. eramale, eramantzaile.

bearing n. (mech.) ardatzeusle. n. ibilkera, jokera.

bearskin n. hartz-larru.

beast n. abere, piztia, animalia. n. astopotro.

beast of burden n. zamabere, zamal, zamari.

beat v.t./v.i. (batzutan up-ekin) berotu, astindu, makilatu, jipoindu, jo, kolpatu, zaflatu. v.t. azpiratu, gailendu, garaitu. v.t. irabiatu. v.t. pilpiratu, pilpil egin, taupadatu.

beat n. taupada, pilpira. n. (mus.) pondu. n. egunkari edo aldizkarietako gai berezia.

beaten p. part. of beat.

beater n. astinkari, astindari, jipoiemale, zanpatzaile, zafratzaile. n. eragitailu, malats. n. ehizibiltzaile.

beating n. joaldi, astinaldi, jipoi, kolpaketa, makilaldi, astinketa, zanpaldi, zafraldi. n. irabiamen. n. zurra. n. taupada, pilpira.

beatitudes n. (pl.) zorionbideak.

beauteous adj. eder.

beautiful adj. eder, polit, panpoxa (L,LN,Z), galant.

beautifully adv. ederki, ederto, poliki.

beautify v.t./v.i. apaindu, ederreztatu, liraindu.

beauty n. edertasun, politasun, eder.

beauty parlor n. ileapaindegi.

beaver n. (zool.) kastore.

becalm v.t. lasaitu.

because conj./adv. -lako, bait-, -eta, arren, -gatik, -gaitik, zeren.

beck n. dei-keinu.

beckon v.t. keinuz deitu.

become v.i. zerbait izatera heldu, bilakatu, heldu, bihurtu. v.t. egokitu, egoki izan, ondo joan.

bed n. ohe, etzauntza; oha-. **To go to bed** Oheratu. n. -ondo, -tegi (landareak).

bedbug n. tximitxa.

bedchamber n. logela.

bedclothes n. ohe-aldagarri, ohe-gain.

bedding n. estalkiak, maindirak eta burukoak.

beddy-bye n. lolo.

bedeck v.t. apaindu.

bedlam n. istilu, iskanbila, nahaste.

bedpost n. oheadar.

bedraggled adj. lurdun, kutsakoi.

bedroom n. logela, ohetegi, ohetoki.

bedside n. ohe-alde, ohe-ondo.

bedspread n. ohazal, ohegaineko, ohestalki.

bedstead n. ohezur.

bedtime n. loaro, logiro.
bee n. erle, erla-.
beech tree n. *(bot.)* fago, fagondo, bago.
beef n. behiki.
beefsteak n. xerra.
beefy adj. mamitsu.
beehive n. erlategi, erlauntza, erletxe.
beekeeper n. erlazain, erlajaun, erladun.
beekeeping n. erlazaintza.
been p.part. of be.
beep n. tutuhots.
beer n. garagardo.
beet n. *(bot.)* erremolatxa, frantzesarbi.
beetle n. kakarraldo.
befall v.i./v.t. gertatu, jazo, pasatu.
befallen p. part. of befall.
befell pret. of befall.
befit v.t. egoki izan.
befitting adj. egoki, dagokion.
before adv./prep. aitzinean, aurretik, lehenago, lehendik. conj. -(e)nerako, aurre, baino lehen, lehen, orduko.
beforehand adv. lehendik, aurretik.
befriend v.t. langundu, laguntasuna eskeini.
befuddlement n. zorabiadura.
beg v.t./v.i. *(v.i., for)* eskatu, eskean egin, eskean ibili.
began pret. of begin.
beget v.t. sortu.
beggar n. eskale, eskeko, ateko.
beggarly adj. behartsu, arlote.
begging n. eskaletza, eskaletasun, eske.
begin v.i./v.t. hasi, hasiera eman.
beginner n. hasle, hasberri.
beginning n. hasiera, haseraldi, hastapen, haskunde. n. jatorri, sorrera, iturburu, jatorburu.
begone v.i. *(gehienetan agintekeran)* aldegin.
begonia n. *(bot.)* begonia.
begot pret./p. part. of beget.
begrudge v.t. gogo txarrez eman edo jaso.
beguile v.t. iruzur egin, gezurrezko aginduz liluratu.
begun p. part. of begin.
behalf n. irabazi, etekin. On behalf of. Norbaiten izenean.
behave v.i./v.t. jokatu, portatu, zentzatu.
behavior n. jokabide, jokamolde, jokera, portaera, jarrera.
behead v.t. burugabetu, desburutu, lepamoztu, buru moztu, buru kendu.
beheading n. burumozketa, lepamozketa, lepamozte.
beheld pret. of behold.
behest n. agindu, mandamendu.
behind adv./prep. atzean, gibelean; atzetik. adj. atzeko.
behold v.t. begiratu.
behoove v.t. beharrezkoa izan. v.t. tokatu.

beige n./adj. beis.
being n. izaki; izate.
bejewel v.t. bitxitu.
bejeweled adj. bitxidun.
belated adj. beranduko, berantiar.
belch v.i./v.t. poker egin, kokada egin, korrok egin.
belch n. ahopats, korrokada, gorakada.
beleaguer v.t. inguratu, setiatu. v.t. nekarazi, nazkatu, higuindu.
belfry n. ezkiladorre, ezkilategi, kanpandorre.
belie v.t. gezurtatu, ezeztatu.
belief n. sinesmen, fede, sineste, kredo. **False belief.** Sineskeria. n. uste.
believable adj. sinesgarri.
believe v.t. uste ukan, sinestu, hitzartu; -lakoan egon. v.i. *(in)* fidatu, sinetsi.
believer n. fededun, fedeaitortzaile, sinesle, fedeaitorle.
bell n. kanpai, arran, joare, ezkila, zintzarri, txilin. **Fire bell.** Sukanpai.
belle n. emakume gazte eta polit(a).
bellflower n. *(bot.)* txilinbelar, txilinlore.
bellicose adj. borrokazale, gerrazale, burrukalari, gatazkari, gudazale, gerlazale, gudatiar.
bellicosity n. gerrazaletasun, gudazaletasun, gudakortasun.
belligerence n. borrokakortasun, gerlazalekeria, gudakortasun, gudazalekeria, gudazaletasun.
belligerent adj. borrokazale, gerrazale, gudazale, gerragile, gudatiar; liskarti, liskartsu.
bellow v.i./v.t. oihu egin, txilio egin.
bellow n. oihu, txilio, orroe.
bellows n. hauspo, puzkailu, labehauspo, garrauspo. **To pump the bellows.** Hauspotu.
bellows pole n. hauspohaga.
belly n. sabel, tripa; urdail.
bellyache n. tripakomin.
bellyband n. sabelestalki.
bellybutton n. *(anat.)* zilbor.
bellyful n. sabelbete, tripakada, asealdi, betekada, sabelkada.
belong v.i. bazkide izan, elkartetu. v.i. *(to)* -(r)ena izan, -koa izan, -(r)i egon.
belongings n. ondasunak, trasteria.
beloved adj. maite, maitagarri, kuttun, begiko, laztan, maiteño, bihotzeko.
below adv. behean, behera. prep. -pean, azpi, azpian.
belt v.t. gerrikotu, inguratu. v.t. jo.
belt n. gerriko, uhal. **To buckle a belt.** Gerrikoa lotu.
bemoan v.t. arrenguratu, arrenguraz aritu.
bench n. banku, jarleku, jartoki. n. epaiaulki; epaitalde. n. tosta. n. lanmahai.
bend v.t./v.i. bihurkatu, bihurtu, gakotu, okertu, makurtu. v.t./v.i. *(over)* beheratu, beheititu.

bend *n.* ibaibira, ibaizoko, itzulinguru, inguru-minguru, makurgune, bihurgune.
bendable *adj.* makurgarri, bihurkoi.
bender *n.* okertzaile; okergailu. *n.* mozkorra, mozkorraldi.
beneath *adv./prep.* azpi, -pean.
benediction *n.* bedeinkapen.
benefaction *n.* onegite.
benefactor *n.* onegile, ongile, faboretzaile.
benefice *n. (rel.)* prebenda, eliz-sari.
beneficence *n.* ongintza, ontasun, ongiegite.
beneficent *adj.* onegitezko; eskuzabal, ongile.
beneficial *adj.* ongarri, onuragarri, onurakor, mesedegarri, probetxugarri.
beneficially *adv.* onuraz.
beneficiary *n.* onuradun.
benefit *v.t./v.i.* on egin.
benefit *n.* irabazi, onura, probetxu, etekin. *n.* ongintza-emanaldi. *n.* aseguru-diru(a).
benevolence *n.* ongura.
benevolent *adj.* bihozleun.
benign *n.* berati, onbera.
benignant *adj.* xalo, onbera, bihozpera.
benignity *n.* ontasun, ongura, onginahi.
bent *adj.* bihurri, bihur, oker, makur, gakodun.
bequeath *v.t.* utzi.
bequest *n.* uzkuntza.
berate *n.* gaizkitu, gaizki esan.
bereave *v.t.* nahigabetu, atsekabetu, samindu.
bereaved *adj.* nahigabetu(a), atsekabedun, samindun.
bereavement *n.* dolu; nahigabe.
bereft *adj.* -gabe, gabetu(a).
beret *n.* txapel.
berg *n.* izozmendi, iceberg.
berth *v.t./v.i.* atrakatu.
berry *n.* baia.
beseech *v.t.* erregutu, arren eskatu.
beset *v.t.* enbarazu egin, nekarazi, haizatu. *v.i.* **(with)** -z josi, -z bete.
beside *prep./adv.* alboan, ondoan, aldean, ondora.
besides *adv./prep.* gainera, gainerakoan, gainerantzean, aparte. **Besides that.** Hortaz gainera.
besiege *v.t.* hesinguratu, ingurukatu.
besought *pret./p. part. of beseech.*
best *adj.* onen(a), hoberen(a), egokien(a). **Best seller.** Gehien saldua. *adv.* ondoen, hobekien. *n.* onena, onenak.
bestial *adj.* astopotro; piztiantzeko.
bestiality *n.* aberekeria, mandakeria, basakeria. *n.* gizaki eta animalien arteko haragizko harremanak.
bestir *v.t.* mugitu, mugierazi, zirikatu.
bestow *v.t.* **(on, upon)** eman.

bet *v.t./v.i.* dematu, postura egin, jokatu, trabesa egin.
bet *n.* apostu, dema, postura, trabes.
betray *v.t.* azpijokatu, saldu, azpilan egin, iruzurrez saldu.
betrayal *n.* saldukeria, iruzurkeria.
betrayer *n.* traidore, saltzaile, azpisuge, judas.
betroth *v.t.* ezkon-hitza eman.
betrothal *n.* ezkonagintza.
better *v.t.* bikaindu, hobeagotu.
better *adj.* hobe. *adv.* hobe, hobeki, hobeto, hobekiago.
betterment *n.* hobealdi, hobekuntza.
bettor *n.* apostugile, dirujokalari.
between *prep./adv.* artean, arte, tartean.
beverage *n.* edari.
bevy *n.* talde; multzo.
bewail *v.t.* negar egin, arrenguratu.
beware *v.t./v.i. (v.i., of-ekin)* kontu izan, ernai egon, begiratu.
bewilder *v.t.* txunditu, harri eta zur utzi, zorabiatu.
bewildered *adj.* harri eta zur, zorabiatu(a).
bewilderedly *adv.* zorabioz.
bewilderment *n.* zoradura, zoralda, harridura, itsualdi.
bewitch *v.t.* sorgindu. *v.t.* liluratu.
bewitched *adj.* sorgindun, sorginkerizko. *adj.* liluratuta.
bewitcher *n.* sorgintzaile.
beyond *prep./adv.* bestaldean, haindi.
bi- *(gram.)* bis, ber-, bir-, birr-.
biannual *adj.* seihileko, seihilabeteko. *adj.* biurteko, biurteroko.
biannually *adv.* seihilabetero. *adv.* biurtero.
bias *v.t.* bultzatu, hartaratu, aurrezbultzatu, eragin.
bias *n.* alderakoikeria, aurreiritzi, aurreritzi, aldebatekokeria. *n.* zehardura. *adj.* zehar, zeharkako. *adv.* zeharka, sieska.
biased *adj.* alderdikor.
biaxial *adj.* ardazbiko.
bib *n.* adurzapi, eldorzapi, lerdezapi, adurretako, kokospeko. *n.* bularbabes. *n. (zool.)* faneka; palanka.
Bible *n.* Biblia.
biblical *adj.* bibliako.
bibliographer *n.* bibliografo; liburulari, liburuzain.
bibliography *n.* bibliografia.
bibliophile *n.* liburuzale, idaztizale.
bicentennial *n.* bimendeurren. *adj.* bimendeurreneko.
biceps *n.* bizeps.
bicker *v.i.* arazo arinez eztabaidatu, liskartu.
bicolor *adj.* margobidun, margobiko.
bicycle *n.* bizikleta, txirrindula.
bicycler *n.* ziklista, txirrindulari, bizikletari.
bicycling *n.* ziklismo.

bicyclist *n.* bizikletari, txirrindulari.
bid *v.t./v.i. (v.i.,* **for***)* eskaini. *v.t./v.i.*
agindu, manatu. *v.t.* esan. *v.i. (up)*
gehiagokatu.
bidder *n.* eskaintzaile, enkanterosle.
bide *v.t.* zain egon.
biennial *adj.* biurteko, biurteroko.
biennially *adv.* biurtero.
biennium *n.* biurtealdi.
bier *n.* hilkutxa, zerraldo; hiltronu.
bifocal *adj.* bifokal. *n.(pl.)* betaurreko
bifokalak.
big *adj.* haundi, handi.
bigamist *n.* emaztebiko; senarbiko.
bigamous *adj.* emaztebiko; senarbiko.
bigamy *n.* emaztebitasun,
senarbitasun.
bigger *adj. (comp.)* handiago.
biggest *adj.* -(r)ik handien(a).
bigness *n.* handitasun.
bigot *n.* aurreiritziz jokatzen duen
pertsona.
bigoted *adj.* jasangaitz, eramangaitz.
bigotry *n.* eramangaiztasun,
jasangaiztasun.
bike *n.* bizikleta, txirrindula. *n.* motor,
motorbizikleta.
biker *n.* motolari *n.* txirrindulari,
bizikletari.
bikini *n.* bikini.
bilateral *adj.* aldebiko, bialdeko,
aldebitako.
bilateralism *n.* aldebitakotasun.
Bilbao *n. (geog.)* Bilbo.
bile *n.* behazun.
bilingual *adj.* elebidun, bimintzairadun.
bilingualism *n.* elebitasun, elebitza,
bimintzotasun.
bilious *adj.* behazuntsu.
bill *v.t.* fakturatu.
bill *n.* kontu, faktura, zorkontu. *n.*
dirupaper, paperdiru. *n.* legegai. *n.*
iragarki, kartel. *n.* moko.
billboard *n.* karteldegi.
billet *n.* militar egoitzetatik kanpoko
bizileku(a). *n.* militar egoitzetatik
kanpo bizitzeko ahozko edo idatzizko
agindu(a).
billfold *n.* kartera, txartelzorro.
billiards *n.* bilare.
billing *n.* fakturaketa, fakturapen,
fakturazio.
billion *n./adj.* bilioi.
billow *v.i.* uhindu, kulunkatu. *v.i.*
haizatu, puztu.
billow *n.* uhin, olatu.
billowy *adj.* kulunkari.
billy club *n.* idizil.
billy goat *n.* aker.
bimonthly *adj.* hamabosteroko;
bihilabeteko. *adv.* hamabostero;
behin bihilabetero. *n.* bihilabetekari.
bin *n.* kutxa.
binary *adj.* bitar.
bind *v.t.* hertsi, lokarritu, lotu,
kordaztu. *v.t.* azaleztatu, larruztatu,
azpibabestu.

binder *n.* lotzaile, uztartzaile. *n.* lotura,
estekadura. *n.* liburu-josle. *n.*
aseguru behin-behingo dokumentu.
binding *n.* azaleztapen, azaleztadura,
azalerazpen.
binge *n.* asebete, asekaldi.
bingo *n.* bingo; erlo, tonbola.
binoculars *n.* urrutikuskin, begitako,
ikuskailu.
biochemical *adj.* biokimiko.
biochemistry *n.* biokimika.
biographer *n.* biografo, bizitz-idazle.
biography *n.* biografia.
biologist *n.* biologari, bizitzalari.
biology *n.* biologia.
biped *n./adj.* hankabidun, hankabiko,
zangobiko.
birch tree *n. (bot.)* urki. **Forest of
birch trees.** Urkidi.
bird *n.* txori.
bird droppings *n.* txorigorotz,
txoriongarri.
birdseed *n. (bot.)* txoribelar; alpiste.
birth *n.* jaiotza, jaioera, sorkura. **To
give birth.** Haur ukan. Erditu. *n.*
sabelaldi, umaldi, haurgintza,
erditzapen, seingintza. *n.* etorki,
jatorri, sorketa. *n.* leinu, azkazi.
birth control *n.* jaiotze-kopuru
kontrola. *n.* kontrol-era, kontrol-bide.
birthday *n.* urtebetetze, urtegun,
jaiotegun, urtebetegun.
birthplace *n.* jaioleku, sorleku.
birthright *n.* jaiotza-eskubideak.
Biscay *n. (geog.)* Bizkaia.
Biscayan *n.* bizkaiera. *n./adj.* bizkaitar.
biscuit *n.* opil.
bisect *v.t. (geom.)* bitan banatu, bitan
zatitu.
bisexual *n./adj.* arreme, sexubiko.
bishop *n. (eccl.)* apezpiku, gotzai(n).
bishopric *n.* apezpikugo,
gotzainburugo.
bison *n. (zool.)* basazezen, bisonte.
bit *n.* zatitxo, zatixka, apur. *n.* alditxo.
n. daratulu. *n.* balazta, aho-burdin.
adv. samar, zertxobait.
bitch *n.* txakurreme, zakurreme. *n.*
emagaldu, urdanga, maribidetako;
emakume maltzur eta handinahikoa.
bite *v.t./v.i.* hozka egin, haginkatu,
horzkatu. *v.t.* heldu (arrainak), ausiki.
v.t. pikatu.
bite *n.* haginkada, horzkada,
horzkadura, ausiki; graskada,
grauskada, klaskada. *n.* ahokada. *n.*
otamen, hamarretako, ahamen. *n.*
sarkortasun, zorroztasun,
suspertasun, zolitasun.
biter *n.* haginkari, horzkalari, horzkari,
ausikari, aginkari.
biting *n.* horzkadura, ausikidura,
horzkaketa. *adj.* erremingarri,
mingarri, minkor, zorrotz. *adv.*
haginka.
bitingly *adv.* mingarriki, mingarriro,
erreminez.

bitten *p. part. of bite.*
bitter *adj.* samin, mikats, mingaitz, mingots, garratz.
bitterly *adv.* saminki, saminkiro, mingoski.
bitterness *n.* garraztasun, garrazkeria, samintasun, mindura, samindura, mingostasun.
bittersweet *adj.* gazigozo, gezagozo, gezamin.
bivalve *n./adj. (zool.)* bioskoldun (molusko).
bivouac *n. (mil.)* bibak.
biweekly *adj.* astebiko, biasteko. *adj.* astean bitan gertatzen den gauza bat. *adv.* biastero, hamabostero. *adv.* bi aldiz astean.
bizarre *adj.* arraro, zarpail, arlote, barregarri.
black *n./adj.* beltz. *n.* iluntasun, ilunbe, ilundura. *n. (pl.)* beltz(ak). *adj.* ilun, argigabe, goibel, itzal. *adj.* ezkor, etsikor. *adj.* doilor, gaizto, zital. *adj./adv.* huts, hutsik (kafe). *adj.* ubel.
blackberry *n. (bot.)* masusta.
blackbird *n. (zool.)* zozo.
blackboard *n.* idaztola, oholbeltz, arbel.
blacken *v.t./v.i.* belztu.
black eye *n.* gando.
black fly *n. (zool.)* eulibeltz, mandeuli, eulitzar.
blackhead *n.* pikort.
black-hearted *adj.* bihotzbeltz.
blackish *adj.* beltziska.
black magic *n.* aztikeria, deabrukeria.
blackmail *v.t.* txantaia egin.
blackmail *n.* txantaia.
black market *n.* estraperlo.
blackness *n.* belztasun, beltzura.
blacksmith *n.* errementari, burdingile.
blade *n.* aizto-aho, ezpata-aho; ezpata. *n. (bot.)* belartxo. *n.* arraun-zali, arraun-pala. *n.* turbinako palaxka. *n.* errota-gurutze.
bladder *n. (anat.)* puxika, gernupuxika, maskuri.
blamable *adj.* errudun, hobendun.
blame *v.t.* gaitzetsi, erru ezarri, erruztatu, hobena egotzi.
blame *n.* hoben, erru, kulpa.
blameless *adj.* hobengabe, errugabe, gaizkabe, okergabe.
blamelessly *adv.* errugabeki.
blamelessness *n.* errugabetasun, gaizkabetasun.
blanch *v.t.* zuritu, marguldu.
bland *adj.* motel, geza, gazkabeko.
blandishment *n.* lausengu, lausengukeria, losintxa, zuriketa.
blank *n.* hutsune.
blanket *n.* burusi, ohestalki.
blare *v.i./v.t.* zarataka jo, turutatu.
blaspheme *v.t./v.i.* biraokatu, juramendu egin, arnegu egin.
blasphemer *n.* biraotzaile,

arneguegile, biraolari.
blasphemous *adj.* biraodun, madarikatzaile.
blasphemy *n.* birao, arnegu, juramendu.
blast *v.t./v.i.* eztandatu, lehertu.
blast *n.* bunbada, iraizpen, bunpada. *n.* bonbaketa, bonbaleherketa.
blasted *adj.* madarikatu(a).
blast furnace *n.* labe garai.
blatant *adj.* agiri, nabarmen, agirizko.
blaze *n.* su.
blazon *v.t.* erakutsi, ezagutarazi, begitaratu. *v.t.* apaindu, dotoretu.
bleach *v.t./v.i.* zuritu, lisibatu, desmargotu.
bleach *n.* lixiba, ehe.
bleachers *n. (pl.)* mailadi.
bleak *adj.* soil, inorgabe. *adj.* ilun, itzal, goibel, gogoilun.
bleat *v.i.* marraskatu, bee egin.
bleat *n.* marraka, be.
bled *pret./p. part. of bleed.*
bleed *v.i./v.t.* odoldu, odoleztatu, odolgabetu, odolustu.
bleeding *n.* odolusketa, odolisuri, odolisurketa, odoljario.
blemish *n.* orban, laido, izentxar, akats. *n.* pikort, pinporta.
blend *v.t./v.i.* nahastu, nahasi.
blend *n.* nahaste-mahaste, nahaski.
bless *v.t.* bedeinkatu, donetsi, onetsi.
blessed *adj.* bedeinkatu(a), bedeinkagarri. *adj.* santu. *adj.* dohatsu, dontsu. *adj. (fig.)* madarikatu(a).
blessedness *n.* zoriontasun. *n.* saindutasun.
blesser *n.* bedeinkatzaile.
blessing *n.* bedeinkapen, bedeinkazio, onespen.
blew *pret. of blow.*
blight *n.* herdoil, gorrina.
blind *v.t.* itsutu, itsuerazi.
blind *n./adj.* itsu. *n.* leiho-oihal. *n.* ihizitegi, ehizitoki.
blindfold *n.* betestalki.
blindfolded *adj.* betestalkidun.
blinding *adj.* itsugarri, lausogarri. *n.* itsumustu.
blindly *adv.* itsuki, itsumustuka, itsutuki, itsuka.
blind man's bluff *n.* itsu-itsuka (joko).
blindness *n.* itsukeria, itsualdi, itsutasun.
blink *v.t./v.i.* begikaratu; keinu egin.
blink *n.* ñirñir, keinu.
bliss *n.* zoriontasun.
blissful *adj.* zoriontsu.
blissfully *adv.* pozez, zorionez.
blister *v.t./v.i.* babatu.
blister *n.* baba, babalarru.
blithe *adj.* alai, pozdun, pozkor, alegera.
blithely *adv.* pozik, pozez, pozkiro, alaiki, alegeraki.
blizzard *n.* bisuts.

bloat *v.i./v.t.* haizatu, puztu.
block *v.t./v.i.* hesinguratu. *v.t.* ziritu. *v.t.* oztopatu.
block *n.* tako. *n.* etxalde, etxesail. *n.* xorta (joko).
blockade *v.t.* hesinguratu.
blockade *n.* blokeo. *n.* inguraketa. *n.* hesiketa.
blond *adj.* kirru, horail (gizon).
blonde *adj.* kirru, horail (emakume).
blood *n.* odol. **Blood relative.** Odolkide. **To lose blood.** Odolgabetu. **Blood type.** Odol mota.
blood clot *n.* odolguri, odoluri, odolbatu, odolbide.
blood-curdling *adj.* erdiragarri.
bloodhound *n.* ehizizakur mota.
bloodily *adv.* odoljarioz, odolez.
bloodless *adj.* odolgabe, odolgabeko, odolustu.
bloodletting *n.* zainebaki.
bloodline *n.* odoljatorri.
blood sausage *n.* odolki, odoloste.
bloodshed *n.* odol isurki.
bloodthirsty *adj.* odolkoi, odolisurle, odolzale.
bloody *adj.* odoldun, odolezko, odoltsu. *adj.* odolisurle, odolkoi, odoltzale.
bloom *v.i.* loratu, loraburutu, garatu, muskildu.
bloom *n.* (*bot.*) pipil.
blooming *n.* lilialdi, loraldi. *n.* lilitze. *adj.* loredun.
blossom *v.i.* loratu, muskildu.
blossom *n.* lore.
blot *v.t.* zikindu, lohitu, kutsatu. *v.t.* tinta paperez xukatu.
blot *n.* orban, lohidura.
blotch *v.t.* zetakatu, orbaindu.
blotch *n.* zetaka, orbain.
blotter *n.* xurgapaper, xukapaper.
blouse *n.* ator, mantar.
blow *v.t.* futz egin, hauspotu, haizeman, ufatu. *v.i.* haizatu, haizeztatu. *v.t./v.i.* (**up**) eztanda egin, eztandatu, lehertu, leher egin, leherrarazi, zartatu. *v.t./v.i.* (**out**) itzali. *v.i.* (**over**) ekaitzaren indarra gutxitu.
blow *n.* ukaldi, kolpe, muturreko, belarrondoko, plastada, masaileko, zartada, zaplazta, zanpako. *n.* ezbehar, zorigaitz, gaitzaldi. *n.* futz, putzaldi. *n.* haizebolada, haizete, haizeketa. *n.* turutots, tronpetaldi.
blower *n.* haizegile, putzegile. *n.* hauspo.
blowfly *n.* mandeuli.
blowout *n.* zapart.
blubber *n.* balegantza.
blubbering *n.* negarmuxin.
blue *v.t.* urdineztu, urdinskatu, urdindu.
blue *n./adj.* urdin, ubel, urdintsu.
blue-collar worker *n.* eskulangile.
blue humor *n.* berdekeria.

blueness *n.* urdintasun.
bluff *v.t.* itxura egin.
bluff *n.* planta(k) inkario.
bluish *adj.* urdinska, urdinzuri, zuriurdinska, ubelurdin.
blunder *n.* aldrebeskeria, hutsaldi, errakuntza.
blunderbuss *n.* zizpa.
blunt *v.t.* deszorroztu, kamustu, moztu, ahomoztu.
blunt *adj.* motz, amotz, kamuts, lanputs. *adj.* zakar, latz; bipil.
bluntly *adv.* bipilki.
bluntness *n.* kamustasun, lanpustasun. *n.* zakartasun, lazkeria.
blur *v.i./v.t.* zirriborratu.
blurt *v.t.* (**out**) zakarki esan.
blush *v.i.* gorritu, lotsagorritu, aurpegi gorritu.
blush *n.* gorritasun, gorrialdi, lotsa.
blushingly *adv.* lotsaz.
bluster *n.* haize-bolada, haize-burrunda, zirimola. *n.* harropuzkeria, hitzarro, erronka.
boa constrictor *n.* boasuge, sugetzar.
boar *n.* basurde ar.
board *v.t./v.i.* ostatu eman, ostatatu. *v.t.* (**up**) oholeztatu, oholeztu, taulatu, taulaztatu, zolatu. *v.t.* sartu, igon (hegazkinean, trenean, etab.).
board *n.* hurtsa, ohol. *n.* kontseilu, batzorde; -burugo.
boarder *n.* apopilo.
boarding *n.* abordaia. *n.* pentsio batetan bizitze(a).
boardinghouse *n.* pentsio.
boarding school *n.* barnetegi.
boast *v.i.* (*batzutan* **of** *edo* **about**-*ekin*) harropuztu, hantustu.
boast *n.* harropuzkada, farranda, gizonkada.
boastful *adj.* harroputz, hanpurutsu.
boastfully *adv.* harroki, harropuzkeriaz, burgoiki.
boastfulness *n.* harropuzkeria, handikeria, burgoitasun, handipuzkeria, harrokeria.
boat *n.* itsasontzi, ontzi, untzi.
boatman *n.* txalupari, ontzilari, txalupazain.
bob *v.t./v.i.* kulunkatu. *v.t.* moztu.
bob *n.* buru-zirkina. *n.* kaskamotz. *n.* kulubiz.
bobbin *n.* bobina, txirrika, harilgailu, txaratila.
bobcat *n.* (*zool.*) Estatu Batuetako basakatu.
bobolink *n.* (*zool.*) Estatu Batuetako txori mota bat.
bobsled *n.* kirol-lera.
bobwhite *n.* (*zool.*) Estatu Batuetako galeper antzekoa.
bode *v.t./v.i.* iragarri, aurresan.
bodice *n.* gerruntze.
bodily *adj.* gorputzeko, gorputzezko. *adv.* gorputzez, soinez.
body *n.* gorputz, soin. **Body and soul.**

Gorputz eta arima. *n.* gorpu, hilotz. *n.*
elkarte, elkargo, lagunarte, lagundi.
n. sorta, bilduma. *n.* sendotasun,
tinkotasun, lauspeapen, lauspeaketa.
bodyguard *n.* lepazain, bizkarzain.
bog *n.* istinga, lupetza, lokatza, zingira,
aintzira.
bog down *v.t./v.i.* lupeztu.
bogey man *n.* mamu, mozorro,
mamarro.
boggy *adj.* zingiratsu, aintziratsu.
bogus *adj.* faltsu.
boil *v.t.,v.i.* egosi, irakin, pilpil egin,
borborka egin, borborkatu. *v.i. (over)*
gainez egin, gainezka egin.
boil *n.* zaldar. *n.* egosketa, irakinaldi,
irakidura.
boilable *adj.* egosgarri, irakingarri.
boiled *adj.* egosi. **Easily boiled.**
Egosbera. Egoserraz.
boiler *n.* egosgailu, galdara.
boilermaker *n.* galdaragile, galdaragin.
n. whisky eta garagardoaren
nahastura.
boiling *adj.* irakin, gori.
boisterous *adj.* zaratatsu, zaratari.
boisterously *adv.* zarataz.
bold *adj.* ausarti, oldarkoi. *adj.*
lotsagabe, ahalkegabe,
aurpegihandi, mutiri, kopetadun. *adj.*
irudikor, irudipentsu, gogoetatsu.
adj. kontrastedun (margoak edo
marrazkiak).
boldly *adv.* ausarki, ausarkiro.
boldness *n.* kopeta, ausardia,
oldarkoitasun, balore.
boll *n.* leka, algodoi-leka.
bologna *n.* Boloniar saltxitxoi(a).
bolster *v.t.* tinkatu, indartu,
sendoagotu.
bolt *v.t.* morroildu, torlojotu, krisketatu.
v.i. ihes egin, ihieska joan, korrikan
egin. *v.t.* lasterka jan, presaka jan.
bolt *n.* morroilo, krisket, mihi. *n.* torlojo.
n. iheste, ihesaldi. *n.* ehunbilgu,
oihalbilgu.
bolt of lightning *n.* tximistaketa,
tximista, oinaztarri.
bomb *v.t.* bonbakatu, bonbaztatu. *v.i.*
porrot egin (antzerkian).
bomb *n.* leherkin, lehergailu,
eztandagailu, bonba. **Bomb blast.**
Bonbaleherketa.
bombard *v.t.* bonbardatu, bonbaz jo.
v.t. nekarazi (galderaz, eskabidez).
bombardment *n.* kainoiketa.
bombastic *adj.* zaratandiko.
bomber *n.* lehertzaile, bonbakari,
bonbardari.
bombing *n.* bonbaketa, bonbaztapen.
bonanza *n.* meatz, baliotsu.
bonbon *n.* gozoki, bonboi.
bond *n.* lokarri, lotura. *n. (econ.)*
fiantza, fidantza, kaudimen. *n.*
(econ.) balore. *n. (pl.)* kateak.
bondage *n.* joputasun, jopukeria. *n.*
menpetasun, menpekotasun,

menpekeria.
bondsman *n.* erantzule, berme.
bone *v.t.* hezurgabetu.
bone *n.* hezur. *adj.* hezurrezko.
boneless *adj.* hezurgabe,
hezurgabeko.
bone marrow *n.* hezurmuin,
hezurmami.
bonfire *n.* suhandi, sutzar, sumeta.
bonnet *n.* boneta.
bonus *n.* hobari, eskusari, sari,
gainordain.
bony *adj.* hezurdun, hezurrezko,
hezurraire, hezurrantzeko. **Very**
bony. Hezurtsu.
boo *v.t./v.i.* eup egin.
boo *n.* eupada, eup.
boob *n.* inozo, tentel, ergel.
boo-boo *n.* pupu, min. *n.* oker,
errakuntz, akats.
boobs *n. (pl., colloq.)* ditiak.
booby *n.* inozo, tentel, ergel.
book *n.* liburu.
bookbinder *n.* liburujosle.
bookbinding *n.* liburujospen,
liburujoskura, liburujostura.
bookcase *n.* araseria, apaleria,
apalategi.
bookkeeper *n.* kontulari, kontugile.
bookkeeping *n.* kontabilitate,
kontugintza, kontularitza.
booklet *n. (dim.)* liburutxo, liburuxka,
liburuño.
bookmaker *n.* liburugile. *n.* apostulari,
apostugile.
bookseller *n.* liburusaltzaile.
bookshelf *n.* liburuapal.
book stand *n.* liburuzaldi.
bookstore *n.* liburudenda.
bookworm *n.* liburuzale. *n.* liburu-sitsa.
boom *v.i./v.t.* ozendu, ozenki azaldu;
burrunbatu, trumoiak jo. *v.i.* arin
handitu, azkar hazi.
boom *n.* zart, zanpa. *n.* goraldi.
boomerang *n.* bumerang.
booming *adj.* dunbadatsu. *adj.*
gehigarri, handigarri.
boon *n.* dohai, bedeinkapen.
boor *n.* zakar, trakets, baldar,
moldagaitz.
boorish *adj.* saskar.
boorishly *adv.* saskarki.
boorishness *n.* saskarkeria.
boot *n.* bota.
bootblack *n.* zapatagarbitzaile,
oskigarbitzaile.
boot camp *n.* kanpamendu.
bootee *n.* zapatatxo, oskitxo.
booth *n.* txosna, kiosko. *n.* etxetxo,
etxano.
bootleg *v.t./v.i.* edari alkoholikoak
egin, garraiatu edo saldu.
bootleg *n.* botazango. *n.* kontrabanduz
lortutako edari(a).
bootlegger *n.* edari alkoholikoen
kontrabandari.
booty *n.* harrapakin, ebaskin,

zakurapen, harrapaketa.

booze n. pattar, likore.

boozer n. hordiputz, hordizale, mozkortzale.

bordello n. putetxe, emagaletxe, ematxartegi.

border v.t. muga egin, muga izan, mugakidetu, aldameneko izan, azpildu. v.t. **(on)** zorian egon.

border n. ertz, hegal, hegi. n. muga, zede, mugalde, mugarri. adj. mugako, mugondoko, mugaldeko. n. liburuetako azal-ertzetan ipini ohi diren apaingarriak.

border guard n. mugazain, mugaldezain.

borderless adj. mugagabe, ezmugatu.

border pass n. pasatxartel, pasagiri.

bore v.t./v.i. ginbeletatu, zulatu, zulakatu. v.t. asperterazi, gogaitarazi, gogaitu, aspertu.

bore n. ginbel. n. barne-diametro. n. pertsona aspergarri(a).

bored adj. aspertu. **To get bored.** Gogaitu. Aspertu.

boredom n. asperdura, asperketa, gogaiketa, gogait, gogaitasun.

borer n. zulagailu, sastagailu, sakongailu, puntzoi. n. sastagin, sondalari, zulatzaile.

boric adj. (chem.) boriko.

boring adj. gogaikarri, gogaitsu, aspergarri. n. zulaketa.

boringly adv. aspergarriro, gogaikarriro.

born adj. jaio, sortu. adj. jaiotzetiko, berezko, sortzetiko. adj. -tar, -dar, -ar.

borough n. herri. n. New York-eko hauteskunde barruti.

borrow v.t./v.i. mailegatu.

borrower n. mailegatzaile, mailegari.

bosom n. golko, kolko, bular.

boss n. nagusi, bulegoburu, buru, ugazaba. n. buru politiko(a). n. jauntxo, aitzindari.

bota bag n. zahato.

botanical adj. botanikako.

botanist n. belarkari.

botany n. botanika.

both adj./pron. biak, biek, biok; bata-besteak.

bother v.t. samindu, nekarazi, kezkarazi, zirikatu, gaitzerazi. v.i. arduratu.

bother n. neke, ongieza, asaldu.

bothersome adj. nekarazle, trabagarri, zirikatzaile, haserregarri, nahaspilari, debeiagarri.

bottle v.t. botilatu, ontziratu, bonbileratu.

bottle n. botila, bonbila; biberoi.

bottle cap n. iturri, tapoi.

bottleful n. botilakada.

bottler n. botilari, botilatzaile, ontziratzaile.

bottling n. botilaketa.

bottom n. hondo, azpialde, zulondo. n. hondo (itsaso), ibaiondo. n. ipurdi, atzekalde; ipurt-. n. behe, funts, oinarri. adj. azken, azkeneko. adj. hondoko, oineko, azpiko, beheko. adj. behen(a), beheren(a). adj. oinarrizko, funtsezko.

bottomless adj. hondogabe.

bottom line n. (econ.) azkenitz.

bough n. adar.

bought pret./p. part. of buy.

bouillon n. salda.

boulder n. harritzar biribil(a).

boulevard n. ibilbide, hiribide.

bounce v.i./v.t. jauzi egin. v.i./v.t. itzuli. v.i. **(back)** indarra berreskuratu.

bouncy adj. bizi (pilota).

bound v.i. jauzi, saltatu, salto egin.

bound adj. **(for)** leku batetara zuzenduta. n.(pl.) mugak. n. jauzi, salto. pret./p. part. of bind.

boundary n. muga, zede, mugalerro, zedarri.

boundless adj. mugagabe; bukagabe.

bounteous adj. ugari, jori, kopurutsu.

bountiful adj. ugari, jori. adj. eskuzabal.

bounty n. eskuzabaltasun. n. opari, erregali. n. sari.

bounty-hunter n. lapurketari.

bouquet n. lorasorta, lorazorro, lilitxorta.

bourgeois adj./n. burges.

bourgeoisie n. burgesia.

bout n. -aldi; txanda. n. gaisoaldi, erialdi. n. burrukaldi.

boutique n. denda txiki.

bovine adj. idiaire, idizko. n. idikide.

bow v.i./v.t. gorputz erdia makurtu, buru beheratu, kilimusi egin.

bow n. kilimusi, buruagur. n. jaurtigailu. n. makurdura, okertasun. n. lokarri, apaingarri. n. (mus.) arku. n. (naut.) branka.

bowed adj. makur.

bowel n. (anat.) errai.

bowl v.i./v.t. birlatu. v.t. **(over)** eraitsi, lurrera bota; harritu.

bowl n. katilu.

bowlegged adj. hankazabal, zangozabal, zangoker, zangomakur.

bowler n. bolari, birlari.

bowlful n. katilukada.

bowling n. bolajoku, bolaketa, bola, girla.

bowling alley n. bolatoki, bolaleku, birlaleku, bolategi.

bowling ball n. girla, bola.

bowling pin n. birla.

bowman n. (naut.) brankako, brankari. n. gezilari, gezitari.

bowwow n. au-au.

box v.t. kutxaratu. v.t./v.i. zaplaztakotu, zaplaztatu, masailekotu. v.i. boxeatu, ukabilkatu.

box n. kutxa, kutxatila, kaxa. n. postakutxa, kartakutxa. n. palku, antzoki-gela, aurregela. *n.* etxetxo, etxano, txosna.

boxer *n.* ukabilkari, borrokari, boxealari.

boxing *n.* boxeaketa, ukabilketa, boxeo.

boxing arena *n.* borrokategi, borrokatoki.

boy *n.* mutil, mutilkoskor, mutiltxo.

boycott *v.t./v.i.* boikot egin.

boycott *n.* boikot.

boy crazy *adj.* mutilzale.

boyfriend *n.* gizongai, senargai, mutil-lagun.

boyhood *n.* mutiltasun.

boyish *adj.* mutilantzeko.

boyishly *adv.* mutilki.

boy scout *n.* scout (mutil).

bra *n.* bularretako, bularreko, ditizorro.

brace *v.t.* zutikatu.

brace *n.* uztagailu. *n.* tirakin. *n.* gogorgarri. *n.* errefortzu, euskarri, sostengailu, indargarri.

brace and bit *n.* birabarki.

bracelet *n.* eskuturreko, eskumuturreko, besoko, besuztai.

bracket *n.* uztaigailu.

brag *v.i./v.t.* hantustu, buru erakutsi, harropuztu.

brag *n.* harropuzkada, gizonkada, farranda.

braggart *n.* harroputz, ahobero.

braid *v.t.* ilekordatu, txirikordatu.

braid *n.* txirikorda. *n.* xingola.

Braille *n.* itsuidazkera.

brain *n. (anat.)* garun, burumuin.

brake *v.t./v.i.* frenatu, galgatu.

brake *n.* frenu; galga, txarrantxa. *n. (bot.)* sasi; iratze mota bat. *n.* garba.

brakeman *n.* trenak zaintzeaz arduratzen den gizona.

bramble bush *n. (bot.)* sasi, sastar, lahar, sastraka, sasitza.

bramble thicket *n.* sasiarte, sasitegi.

brambly *adj.* lahartsu, sasitsu, sasizko.

bran *n.* birrin, zahi.

branch *n.* abar, adar. *n.* sail, adar. *n.* -orde, adar. *n.* ibaibeso, ibaiadar.

branch *v.i./v.t.* (off) adarbanatu. *v.i./v.t.* (out) zabaldu, gehitu; negozioa hedatu.

branchia *n.* zakatz.

branchial *adj.* zakatzeko.

brand *n.* marka. *n.* aberemarka. *n.* abereak markatzeko burdin goria. *n.* ilenti.

brandish *v.t.* astindu.

brand-new *adj.* guztiz berri, berri-berri.

brandy *n.* koinak, pattar.

brass *n. (chem.)* latoi, burdinori.

brass band *n.* txaranga.

brass knuckles *n.* eskutako.

brassiere *n.* bularretako, bularreko.

brat *n.* haurtxar, haurgaizto.

bratty *adj.* gaizto, oker.

bravado *n.* hantustekeria, harropuzkeria, hantuste.

brave *adj.* ausarta, zangar, adoretsu, kementsu, frakadun, bihoztun. *n.* pertsona ausarta. *n.* Iparrameriketako indio borrokolari(a).

bravely *adv.* ausarki, ausartki, kementsuki.

bravery *n.* ausarpen, ausartasun, ausartzia, zangartasun, balentria.

bravo *int.* bravo!

brawl *v.i.* zalapartaz borrokan egin.

brawl *n.* borroka zalapartatsu, borroka zaratatsu.

brawn *n.* gihar-indar.

brawny *adj.* gihartsu, indartsu.

bray *v.i.* arrantza egin, marraska egin.

bray *n.* arrantza, arrantzaldi, astoarrantza.

braying *n.* arrantzaldi, astoarrantza, arrantza.

braze *v.t.* soldatu.

brazen *adj.* lotsagabe, lotsagaiztoko, lotsagalduko, kopetadun, ahalkegabe. *adj.* burdinoridun, latoidun.

brazenly *adv.* lotsagabeki.

brazier *n.* suontzi, sutontzi.

breach *v.t.* (-n) zuloa egin. *v.t.* legea hautsi.

breach *n.* hausketa, puskaketa, etendura. *n.* lege-hausketa.

bread *n.* ogi.

breadth *n.* zabalera, zabaltasun.

break *v.t./v.i.* apurtu, hautsi, urratu, eten, puskatu, txikitu. *v.i. (down)* matxuratu. *v.i. (out)* sortu, hasi. *v.i. (up)* desbateratu, zatikatu; harremanak bukatu; harrotu. *v.t.* egundu, egunargitu.

break *n.* hauste, hausketa, puskaketa, apurketa; urraketa, etenaldi, etendura; arrakala, arrail, pitzaketa. *n.* lainotarte, aterrarte, aterrune. *n.* atsedenaldi, langeldiketa, lanarte, etenaldi. *n.* bat-bateko aldaketa. *n.* lasterketaren hasiera. *n.* ihes, ihesaldi, ihesketa. *n.* eten (olerki).

breakable *adj.* hauskor, puskagarri, zatikor, etenkor, etengarri, pitzakor, apurkor, urragarri.

breakableness *n.* hauskortasun, zatikortasun.

breakage *n.* hausketa, hauste, puskaketa, etendura, apurketa.

break down *v.i.* aberiatu.

breakdown *n.* aberia, matxura.

breaker *n.* hausle, apurtzaile, puskatzaile; etengailu. *n.* uhin urratu(a); olatu hautsi(a).

breakfast *v.i.* barautsi, gosaldu.

breakfast *n.* gosari; gosal-.

breakwater *n.* uhinurrategi.

bream *n. (zool.)* urkula.

breast *n. (anat.)* diti, bular, ugatz. **To breast-feed.** Ditia eman. *n.* ditialde; golko.

breastbone *n. (anat.)* bularrezur.

breast-feed *v.t.* bulartu, ditia eman,

bularra eman.

breath *n.* hats, arnasa, arnasaldi.

breathable *n.* arnasgarri.

breathe *v.t./v.i.* arnasa hartu, hats egin, hatsartu.

breathing *n.* arnasketa.

breathless *adj.* arnas-estudun. *adj.* harrituta, harri eta zur, sor eta lor, txundituta.

bred *pret./p. part. of* breed.

breech *n.* ipurdi, atzekalde, gibelalde. *n.* errekamara.

breed *v.i./v.t.* ernaldu, ernarazi.

breed *n.* arraza, kasta, enda, leinu, askazi. *n.* mota.

breeding *n.* hezkuntza, heziera. *n.* hazkuntza, hazketa. **Horse breeding.** Zaldihazkuntza.

breeze *n.* haizetxo, haizexka, firi-firi, haizeño.

breezy *adj.* haizetsu.

brethren *n.* haurride. **My beloved brethren!** Ene haurride maiteok!

Breton *n.* bretainiar. *n.* bretainiera.

brevity *n.* laburtasun, laburrera, murriztasun; iheskortasun.

brew *v.t.* garagardoa egin. *v.t.* edakin beroa prestatu.

brewer *n.* garagardogile.

brewery *n.* garagardotegi.

briar *n. (bot.)* txilar.

bribe *v.t.* sobornatu, erosi.

bribe *n.* eskuazpikeria, tongo.

bribery *n.* eroskeria.

brick *v.t. (over edo up)* adreiluztatu.

brick *n.* adreilu, buztinarri.

bricklayer *n.* adreilatzaile, hargin, igeltsari, igeltsero.

bricklaying *n.* igeltsaritza.

bridal *adj.* ezkontzako.

bride *n.* emaztegai, ezkonkide, ezkonlagun, ezkontide (emakume).

bridegroom *n.* senargai.

bridesmaid *n.* andragaiaren ohorezko dama.

bridge *v.t.* zubitu.

bridge *n.* zubi. *n.* ontzizubi. *n.* sudurgain. *n. (mus.)* musika tresnaren zubi. *n.* karta joko mota bat. *n.* hortzetako, hortz zubitxo.

bridle *v.t.* ahosokatu, balaztatu.

bridle *n.* ahosoka, hede.

bridle path *n.* zaldibide.

brief *adj.* labur, motz. *n.* txosten, laburpen, eskema, idazkitxo.

briefcase *n.* kartera.

briefing *n.* txosten.

briefly *adv.* labur, laburki, laburkiro, mozki, murrizki, iheskorki.

brig *n. (naut.)* bergantin, bimasta. *n. (naut.)* espetxe-militar(ra).

brigade *n. (mil.)* brigada.

brigadier *n. (mil.)* brigadier.

brigand *n.* bide-lapur, bide-ohoin.

brigandage *n.* bidelapurkeria, bidelapurketa.

bright *adj.* argi, argidun, argitsu,

distiragile, distirakor, dizdiztsu, arraiotsu, dirdizkari. *adj.* buruargi, burutsu, azkar, adimendun, ulermendun. *adj.* min (margo).

brighten *v.t.* bizitu.

brighter *adj. (comp.)* argiago. *adj.* adimentsuago.

brightly *adv.* dizdizka. *adv.* buruargiz.

brightness *n.* argitasun, dirdiratasun, arraitasun, argidura, argialdi, dirdirapen, dirdiradura. *n.* azkartasun, buruargitasun. *n.* mintasun (margoak).

brilliance *n.* distiratasun, dirdiratasun, dirdiradura, distirapen, dirdirapen, zohardura. *n.* buruargitasun, azkartasun. *n.* mintasun (margoak).

brilliant *adj.* argi, argidun, argitsu, distiragile, distiratsu, distirakor, dizdiztsu, arraiotsu, dirdizkari, zohar, aratz. *adj.* buruargi, burutsu, azkar, adimendun, ulermendun. *adj.* min (margo).

brilliantly *adv.* dirdiraz, distiraz, dizdizka.

brim *n.* ertz, hegal (amildegi, ontzi, etab.) *n.* kapela-hegal.

brimful *adj.* goraino beteta.

brine *n.* gatzun, gatzur, gezal. *n.* itsaso.

bring *v.t.* ekarri, erakarri; helduarazi; etorrerazi. *v.i. (up)* aipatu; hezi, hazi. *v.i. (about)* sortarazi, gertarazi; birakatu, itzulerazi, jirabiratu. *v.i. (forth)* erditu, ume egin, sortu. *v.i. (off)* arrakastara eraman. *v.i. (down)* lurreratu, gainazpikatu; prezioak erori. *v.t. (around, to)* berbiztu. *v.t. (out)* nabarmendu.

bringing up *n.* hazketa, hazkunde, hazkuntza. *n.* hezkuntza.

brink *n.* ertz, hegal.

brisk *adj.* bizkor; azkar, arin.

bristle *v.i.* ilea laztu.

bristle *n.* zurda.

Britain *n. (geog.)* Britania.

Britisher *n.* ingeles, britaniar.

brittle *adj.* hauskor, apurkor, zatikor. *n.* gozoki mota.

brittleness *n.* hauskortasun, apurkortasun, apurgarritasun.

broach *v.t.* lehen aldiz aipatu.

broad *adj.* zabal. *n. (colloq.)* emakume.

broad bean *n. (bot.)* baba.

broadcast *v.t./v.i.* irratsaiotu, telesaiotu, irratiz igorri; telebistaz eman, telebisatu.

broadcast *n.* transmisio, emankizun, irrati-emanaldi, telesaio. *adj.* hedatu, zabaldu.

broadcloth *n.* oihal.

broaden *v.t./v.i.* zabaldu, handitu.

broadly *adv.* zabalki. *adv.* liberalki, askatasunez. *adv.* orokorki.

broadness *n.* zabaltasun, zabalgo.

broadside *n.* ontzisaihets. *n.* eraso. *adv.* saiheska.

broadsword n. ezpatatzar, ezpatandi.
broccoli n. (bot.) brokoli.
brochure n. liburuxka, liburutxo, liburuño.
broil v.t./v.i. labean erre.
broiled adj. erre(a).
broiler n. txigorgailu.
broke adj. dirugabe, sosgabe, jota.
broken adj. etenda, pusketazko. adj. mordoilo.
broken-down adj. zaharkilo, zaharkote, matxuradun. adj. deserabilgarri.
broken-hearted adj. pozgaitz.
brokenly adv. etenka.
broker n. artekari, trukatzaile.
brokerage n. artekaritza.
bromide n. (chem.) bromuro.
bronchial tube n. (anat.) bronkio.
bronchitis n. (med.) bronkitis.
bronchus n. (anat.) bronkio.
bronze v.t. brontzeztu.
bronze n. brontze. adj. brontzezko.
brooch n. paparreko, orratz, zarrailu.
brood n. ohekada, txitatalde, umaldi.
brook n. erreka.
broom n. (bot.) erraiz, isats. n. erratz, isats, eskoba.
broth n. salda, zuku.
brothel n. emagaletxe, putetxe, ematxartegi.
brother n. anaia, haurride, senide.
brother-in-law n. ezkonanaia, anaigiarreba, koinatu.
brotherhood n. anaitasun, anaigo, senidego, anaiartekotasun, ahaidetasun, haurridetasun. n. anaitegi.
brotherly adj. anaitiar, senidegarri, anaikor, senidezko.
brought pret./p. part. of bring.
brow n. betarte.
brown n./adj. marroi, beltzaran.
brownie n. intxaur eta txokolatezko bizkotxoa. n. scout neska gazte(a). n. lamia.
brownish adj. marroixka.
brown-nose v.i./v.t. ferekatu, elexuritu.
browse v.t./v.i. larratu, bazkatu, alatu. v.i. orrikatu, ikusmiran ibili, ikuskatu, gainbegiratu.
bruise v.i./v.t. uspeldu, uspelkatu, maspildu, mailatu, zafardatu.
bruise n. beltzune, ubelune, uspel, zanpaketa, mailatune, zanbro.
brunette adj. ilebeltz.
brunt n. talka, elkarjoaldi, danbateko.
brush v.t. eskuilatu, zepilatu. v.t./v.i. bigunki ukitu. v.t. (aside) desezagutu, baztertu. v.t. (off) arbuiatu, etsi. v.t. (up on) berrikasi.
brush n. eskuila, zepilu; pintzel. n. txapardi, txapar. n. azeriaren buztan(a). n. elkarketa labur(ra), topaketa labur(ra).
brushwood n. sastraka.
brusque adj. gozagabe, gozagaitz, zakar, butoi.

brusquely adv. zakarki, abereki, aberekiro, mokorki.
brusqueness n. lazkeria, laztasun, mokortasun, zakarraldi, zakarkeria.
brutal adj. aberetsu, aberezko, basati, basa.
brutality n. aberekeria, aberetasun, basakeria, astakeria.
brutally adv. abereki, aberekiro, zakarki.
brute n. abere, astapotro, asto.
brutish adj. aberezko, astapotro, aberetsu, astotzar, astoko.
brutishness n. aberekeria, astakeria, mandaketa.
bubble v.i./v.t. burbuilatu, burbuileztatu.
bubble n. anpulu, burbuila, gurguilu, puspulu, anpulo.
bubbly adj. irakingai; gurguiludun, puspuludun. n. txanpain, champagne.
buccaneer n. itsaslapur, itsas-ohoin.
buck v.t. iraulikatu.
buck n. -ar. n. aztalka. n. (colloq.) dolar.
bucket n. garbiontzi, ikuztontzi, bertz, suil.
bucketful n. berzkada.
buckle v.t. gerrikoa lotu. v.i. belaunikatu; makurtu, makotu, konkortu. v.i. (down) saiatu, ahalegindu.
buckle n. ixtailu.
buckskin n. antelarru.
buckwheat n. (bot.) gari mota.
buckshot n. perdigoi.
buckthorn n. (bot.) karraskila.
bud v.i./v.t. loraburutu, muskildu, ninikatu, kimatu, garatu, ernamuindu.
bud n. (bot.) begi, ninika. n. (bot.) ernamuin, kimu, txerto, muskil.
budding n. muskildura, ninikadura, kimuketa, erneketa. adj. bizkor, azkar.
Buddhism n. budismo.
buddy n. lagun, laguntxo.
budge v.i./v.t. mugitu.
budget v.t. aurrekontu(a) egin.
budget n. (econ.) aitzinkontu, aurrekontu, presupostu.
budgetary adj. aurrekontuzko.
buff v.t. leundu, findu.
buff n. antelarru, bufalo-larru. n. (colloq.) giza-larru. n. (colloq.) amorratu(a).
buffalo n. (zool.) basazezen.
buffer n. amortiguadore, indargailu. n. leungailu.
buffet v.t. masailekoa eman, alderdikoa eman.
buffet n. masaileko, alderdiko. n. jan-edariak. n. bufet.
buffoon n. bufoi, barreragile.
bug n. zomorro, mamarro. n. kokotxo. n. (mech.) akats. n. gartsu, sutsu; -zale, -koi (pertsona). n. elkarrizketak

isilka entzuteko mikrofono ezkutua.
buggy n. zaldi bakarreko gurdi(a). n.
haur-kotxe. adj. zomorroz josi(a).
bugle n. turuta.
bugler n. turutajole, turutari.
bugloss n. (bot.) idimihi, idimingain.
build v.t./v.i. eraiki, altxatu, jaso,
goititu.
builder n. etxegile, etxegin, eraikile,
eraikitzaile; -gile.
building n. etxe, obra, eraikin; -tegi,
-degi. n. eraiketa, eraikidura,
eraikintza.
bulb n. (bot.) erraboila. n. bonbila. n.
neurkinaren erraboila.
bulbous adj. erraboiladun,
erraboilatsu.
bulge v.i. konkortu, handitu.
bulge n. konkor, handitune.
bulk n. lodiera. n. zatirik handiena.
bulkhead n. (naut.) itsasontzi barrua
zatikatzeko trenkada.
bulky adj. handikote.
bull n. (zool.) zezen.
bull calf n. idigai, zekor, zezenko,
idisko.
bull's-eye n. jopuntu.
bulldog n. (zool.) zezentxakur.
bullet n. bala.
bulletin n. iragarki, iragarpen. n.
hilabetekari, aldizkari, boletin.
bulletin board n. karteldegi.
bullfight n. zezengudu, zezenketa,
zezenlaster, zezenjai.
bullfighter n. zezenkari, toreatzaile,
zekorkari; burtzikari.
bullfighting n. toreaketa, zezenka.
bullfighting ring n. zezenplaza.
bullfinch n. (zool.) menditxonta.
bullfrog n. zezen-igel.
bullion n. zilar-totxo, urre-totxo.
bullock n. (zool.) zezentxo, zezenko.
bull pen n. zezendegi, zezentoki. n.
jokalariek beroketak egiten dituzten
beisbol zelaiko leku berezia.
bullshit int. kakazaharra!
bully n. liskarti, mokokari, zezioti.
bulrush n. (bot.) urezpata.
bulwark n. hesibabes.
bum n. alfer, alfertzar, jantxakur(ra). n.
(anat.) ipurdi.
bumblebee n. (zool.) erlamando.
bump v.t./v.i. (v.i., into) jo, mankatu,
itsumustu egin.
bump n. txoke, talka, tope, topekada.
n. koskor, konkor, tontor.
bumper n. kolpeleungailu.
bumpy adj. konkordun, mokordun,
koskordun. adj. haize zakarrez
astindu(a).
bun n. opil. n. motots.
bunch v.t./v.i. multzokatu, pilakatu,
sortatu.
bunch n. mordo, sorta, mulko. n. talde,
elkarte. n. eskukada, ahurkada; pilo;
kopuru.
bunchy adj. molkodun, mordodun,

mulkotsu.
bundle v.t. fardeldu. v.i./v.t. (up)
erropa asko jantzi.
bundle n. sorta, txorta. n. fardel, haxe.
n. diruketa, dirupilo, dirumoltso.
bungalow n. etxetxo.
bungle v.t./v.i. lardaskatu.
bungling adj. lardaskontzi.
bunk n. kamaina, kamantza, ohekutxa.
n. txorakeria, zorakeria, tentelkeria,
ergelkeria.
bunny n. untxitxo.
buoy n. bonbil; baliza.
buoyancy n. igerikakortasun,
igerikapen.
buoyant adj. igerikakor. adj. zoridun,
zorihandiko, zorioneko.
bur n. kirikiño, lakatz.
burden v.t. zamatu.
burden n. zama, besakada.
burdensome adj. zamadun, zamagarri,
astungarri.
burdock n. (bot.) lapabelar.
bureau n. komoda. n. agentzia,
gobernu-agentzia; bulego.
bureaucracy n. burokrazia.
bureaucrat n. burokrata.
burglar n. lapur, ebasle, ohoin,
eskuluze, harrapakari.
burglar alarm n. antilapurkin.
burgundy n. ardangorri.
burial n. lurremate, ehorzketa,
hilobiratze, ehorzpen, lurperaketa.
burlap n. muilo, amelu.
burlesque n. iseka, karikatura.
burly adj. gihartsu, sendokote,
indartsu.
burn v.t./v.i. erre, sumindu, kiskaldu,
erremindu, erraustu.
burn n. errezauri, sumindura. n.
erredura, erretasun. n. suziria
pizteko erabiltzen ohi den sugarra.
burnable adj. erregarri, errebera,
sukoi, sukor.
burned adj. kiskal, erreta, garmindu(a).
burner n. erregailu; errelari, erretzaile.
burning n. erreketa, erretzapen,
errealdi, kiskalketa, kiskalpen. n.
zanbro; erremindura, erremin. adj.
kiskalgarri, gori. adj. bero, oldartsu,
suhar, sutsu, bizi.
burnish v.t. leundu, findu, labaindu,
distirazi.
burnt adj. erreta, erretxin.
burp v.i./v.t. kokada egin, korrok egin,
poker egin.
burp n. ahopats, korrokada, poker.
burr n. lakatz, kirikiño.
burro n. (anat.) asto; asta-.
burrow v.i./v.t. zulatu, ziloratu,
zuloratu.
burrow n. piztizulo.
burst v.i./v.t. apurtu, hautsi, puskatu;
lehertu.
burst v.i. eztanda egin, lehertu.
bury v.t. hilobiratu, hobiratu, lurperatu,
lurra eman, ehortzi.

bus *n.* autobus.
busboy *n.* mahaimutil, mahaigarbitzaile (jatetxe).
bush *n.* zuhaixka, zuhamuxka. *n.* sasi, mulu. *n.* azeriaren buztan iletsu(a).
bushel *n.* Estatu Batuetako 35,23 litroko neurria.
bushy *adj.* mulutsu.
busier *adj. (comp.)* lanpetuago.
busily *adv.* gogoz, arduraz, axolaz.
business *n.* lanbide, ogibide, irabazpide, dirubide. *n.* salerosi, salerosketa, salerospen, salerosgo, merkatalgo. *n.* enpresa, negozio. *n.* denda, bulego, lantegi. *n.* lan, eginkizun, zeregin, betebehar, arazo, iharduketa. *n.* ardura, erantzunkizun, erantzunbehar.
businesslike *adj.* eraginkor, sistematiko, eginkor.
businessman *n.* salerosle, salerosketari, merkatari, tratulari, negozio-gizon.
businesswoman *n.* negozio-emakume.
bust *n.* soin (eskultura). *n.* bular, soin-gain. *n.* porrot, molokot. *n.* mozkorraldi, hordialdi. *n.* kolpe, ukabilkada. *n. (econ.)* eroraldi, beheraldi. *n.* espetxeraketa, atxiloketa, espetxeratze, atxilotze.
bustard *n. (zool.)* basoilo.
bustle *n.* arrapalada.
busy *v.t./v.i.* **(oneself)** aritu, ari izan, ihardun.
busy *adj.* lantsu, lanpetu(a), arazopetu(a). *adj.* hartuta, okupatuta (telefono). *adj.* zehatz, xehe.
busybody *n.* nahasketari, nahastaile, nahastero, usnakari.
but *conj.* baina, berriz, ordea, aldiz, ostera. *prep.* ezik, salbu, kanpo, baizik, baino, ez beste. *conj.* besterik baino. *conj.* izan ezik. *n.* oztopo, eragozpen.
butane *n.* butano.
butcher *n.* harakin, haragisaltzaile. *n.* aberehiltzaile. *n.* sarraskitzaile, hiltzaile.
butcher shop *n.* harategi, harakintegi, okelategi.
butchery *n.* harakintza. *n.* odolkeria, odolketa.
butler *n.* etxezain.
butt *v.t./v.i.* talkatu, talka egin, adarkatu. *v.i.* **(in)** usnatu, sudurra sartu. *v.i.* **(out)** muturrik ez sartu.
butt *n. (anat.)* ipurdi. *n.* topekada, talka, adarkada. *n.* kulata; -ipurdi. *n.* zigarrokin. *n.* farregarri, irrigarri. *n.* upel.
butte *n.* muino, bizkartontor, mendixka.
butter *n.* gurin.
butter dish *n.* gurinontzi.
buttercup *n. (bot.)* urrebotoi.
buttered *adj.* gurinezko.
butterfly *n.* tximeleta, pinpilinpauxa.
buttery *adj.* gurinezko, gurintsu.

buttock(s) *n.* ipurmasail, ipurtalde, ipurdi, mokor; ipurt-. *n.* aberipurdi.
button *n.* botoi, botoin. *n. (mech.)* eragingailu.
buttonhole *n.* botoizulo, begite.
buttress *n. (archit.)* hormabular, zubibular.
buxom *adj.* bular handidun (emakume).
buy *v.t.* erosi.
buyer *n.* erosle, erostari.
by *prep.* ondoan, alboan, aldean, aldamenean, inguruan. *prep.* -z. **He arrived by horse.** Zaldiz heldu zen. *prep.* -etako, -etan. **I'll finish by five o'clock.** Bukatuko dut bostetako. *prep.* legez, arauera. *prep.* bidez. *prep.* egin(a), idatzi(a). *prep.* ondorioz. *prep.* -n. *prep.* izenean, aldez. *prep./adv.* bestaldean. *prep.* -gandik sortu(a).
by-and-by *n.* etorkizunean, gero, geroaldi.
bye-bye *int.* adio.
bygone *adj.* zahar, lehenaldiko, aintzinako. *n.* lehena; egindako irainak.
bylaw *n.* araudi, barne-araudi.
bypass *n.* bihotz-ebakuntza.
by-product *n.* bigarren mailako produkto(a).
bystander *n.* alabeharrezko ikusle, alabeharrezko lekuko.
byway *n.* norabide-aldaketa. *n.* bide aldendu(a)
buzzing *n.* burrunbada, burrundara, zunburrun, burrunba.

C

C *n.* Ingeles alfabetoko letra.
cab *n.* taxi.
cabal *n.* azpikeria, azpilan, azpijoko, satorkeria. *n.* alderdikeria.
cabalistic *adj.* sorginkerizko.
cabaret *n.* kabaret.
cabbage *n. (bot.)* aza, azalandare. **Head of cabbage.** Azaburu. **Cabbage leaf.** Azosto.
cabin *n.* txabola, etxola, borda. *n. (mar.)* ontzigela.
cabinboy *n.* ontzimutiko, untzimutil.
cabinet *n. (pol.)* ministrari-kontseilu. *n.* arasa, ontzitegi. *n.* apalategi.
cable *n.* kable. *n.* kablegrama, harigrama.
cablegram *n.* kablegrama, harigrama.
caboose *n.* trenaren azken bagoi(a).
cache *n.* gordailu, gordeleku.
cachet *n.* usainontzi.
cackle *v.i.* kakarakatu, kakaraka egin, karraka egin, kolokatu.
cackle *n.* kakara, kakaraka, karranka, karraskari.
cacophony *n.* kalapita, soinu-zurruburru.
cactus *n. (bot.)* kaktus.
cad *n.* gizatxar.
cadaver *n.* hilotz, gorpu, gorputzil.

cadaverous *adj.* gorpuaire.
cadence *n.* eresneurri, dantzaneurri.
cadet *n.* soldadu, kadete.
caducity *n.* zaharreria, zaharkeria. *n.* joankortasun; galkortasun.
caecum *n.* *(anat.)* esteitsu.
caesura *n.* eten.
cafe *n.* kafetegi.
cafeteria *n.* kafeteria, kafetegi.
caffeine *n.* kafeina.
cage *v.t.* kaiolaratu, kaiolatu.
cage *n.* kaiola, txoritoki.
cajole *v.t.* ahozuritu, balakatu, lausengatu, losintxatu.
cajolery *n.* balaku, lausengu, losintxa, zurikeria, lausengukeria.
cake *n.* tarta.
calamitous *adj.* hondagarri, kalteko.
calamity *n.* ezbehar, zorigaitz, zoritxar, lazeri.
calcify *v.t./v.i.* kaltzio bilakatu, kaltzifikatu.
calcium *n.* *(chem.)* kaltzio.
calculable *adj.* kalkulagarri, zenbakarri.
calculate *v.t./v.i.* kalkulatu, kontatu, hainbatu. *v.t.* *(colloq.)* sinetsi, uste izan, suposatu.
calculating *adj.* kalkulatzaile.
calculation *n.* kalkulapen, zenbaketa, kontaketa.
calculator *n.* kalkulagailu, zenbagailu, kontagailu.
calculus *n.* *(arith.)* kalkulu. *n.* *(med.)* pixarri.
caldron *n.* lapikotzar, eltzetzar, zopontzi.
calendar *n.* egutegi.
calf *n.* *(zool.)* behikume, txahal, xexenko, idisko, zekor. *n.* *(anat.)* zangoaztal, zangosagar, berna.
caliber *n.* kalibre.
calibrate *v.t.* neurtu, lodineurtu.
calibration *n.* lodineurketa.
California *n.* *(geog.)* Kalifornia, Estatu Batuetako estatu bat.
Californian *n./adj.* kaliforniar. *adj.* kaliforniako.
calk *n.* kaskal (zamarien perretarako).
call *v.t./v.i.* dei egin, deitu, deadar egin, hots egin. *v.t.* erran. *v.t./v.i.* telefonatu. *v.i.* *(for)* behar izan. *v.i.* *(off)* geldiarazi; (batzarra, jai, etab.) ezeztatu, bilera ezereztatu.
call *n.* dei, deiera; eupada; -dei. *n.* ikustaldi labur. *n.* txori eta hegaztien kantu. *n.* erreklamo. *n.* arrazoi, zio, zergati. *n.* eskari, eskaera.
calla lily *n.* *(bot.)* urlili.
called *adj.* izeneko, izendun.
caller *n.* deitzaile, hotsegile, deilari, deiegile. *n.* ikustari.
calligraphy *n.* idazkera, kaligrafia.
calling *n.* deika, deiera. *n.* dei, Jainkoaren dei(a), bokazio.
calling card *n.* ikustxartel.
callous *adj.* maskurdun. *adj.* gogor, sor.

callus *n.* maskur.
calm *v.t./v.i.* *(askotan* **down**-*ekin)* baretu, lasaitu, trankildu, isilarazi, mantsotu, gozatu, eztitu.
calm *adj.* baketi, baketsu, lasai, mantso, patxadatsu, trankil, otzan. *adj.* baretsu, ezti, eztitsu, bare, aterri. *n.* baretasun, lasaitasun, lasaidura, patxada, trankiltasun, mantsoaldi.
calmable *adj.* lasaigarri, otzangarri, mantsogarri.
calmative *adj.* sorgarri, baregarri.
calmer *n.* eztiarazle. *adj.(comp.)* lasaiago, bareago.
calming *adj.* eztigarri, mantsogarri, otzankor, trankiltzaile, baregarri.
calmly *adv.* bare-bare, bareki, eztiki, eztikiro, patxadaz, trankilki, mantsoki.
calmness *n.* otzantasun, trankiltasun, eztitasun, mantsotasun.
calorie *n.* kaloria.
calumnious *adj.* gezurlaidozko.
calumny *n.* gezurlaido, gaizkiesate, desizenketa.
calve *v.i.* behiak umea egin.
calypso *n.* Antilletako indioen doinu(a).
camel *n.* *(zool.)* gamelu.
camellia *n.* *(bot.)* kamelia.
camera *n.* argazkimakina. **Movie camera.** Zinegailu.
camomile *n.* *(bot.)* idibegi, kamamila.
camouflage *n.* ezkutapen, kamuflaia.
camp *n.* kanpamendu.
campaign *n.* kanpaina.
camper *n.* kanpinlari. *n.* rulota.
camphor *n.* kanfor.
camping *n.* kanping.
campus *n.* kanpus.
can *v.i./v.aux.* ahal izan, ezan. *v.t.* ontziratu, potoratu.
can *n.* latontzi, lata, poto.
canal *n.* biderreten, erreten, ubide, kanale.
canary *n.* *(zool.)* kanario.
cancel *v.t./v.i.* ezeztatu, ezereztatu, indargetu. *v.t.* kitatu, barkatu (zorrak). *v.t.* seilu(a) baliogabetu *v.t./v.i.* *(batzutan* **out**-*ekin)* pisuberdindu; ordainbaztu.
cancellation *n.* ezabapen, ezeztadura, ezeztaldi, ezeztapen.
cancer *n.* *(med.)* kantzer, minbizi. *n.* *(cap.)* karramarro.
cancerous *adj.* minbiziantzeko, minbizidun.
candelabrum *n.* zuzimutil.
candid *adj.* xalo.
candidacy *n.* kandidatura.
candidate *n.* kandidatu, hautagai.
candidly *adv.* tolesgabeki, xaloki.
candidness *n.* tolesgabetasun, xalotasun.
candied *adj.* azukrezko, azukreztatu(a).
candle *n.* argizagi, kandela, kriseilu.

candleholder *n.* argimutil, argileku, argitoki.
candlelight *n.* kandelargi.
candlemaker *n.* kriseilugin, ezkoegile, kandelagile, argizarigile.
Candlemas *n. (R.C.Ch.)* kandelario.
candlestick *n.* kandelgailu.
candor *n.* xalotasun.
candy *n.* gozoki, gozo, gozokari, goxo, karamelu.
cane *n. (bot.)* kainabera, seska. *n.* makila, eskumakila, makulu. *adj.* kainaberazko.
canful *n.* potokada.
canine *n.* txakur, zakur. *adj.* zakurkide, zakurrezko.
canine teeth *n. (anat.)* letagin.
canker *n.* ahozauri.
canned food *n.* kontserba, kontserbakin.
cannibal *n.* kanibal. *adj.* gizajale.
cannibalism *n.* gizajalekeria, kanibalkeria.
canning *n.* kontserbaketa.
cannon *n.* kainoi.
cannonade *v.t./v.i.* kainoikatu.
cannonade *n.* kainoiketa.
cannot *v.i./v.aux.* ezin izan, ezin ukan.
canny *adj.* zuhur, zentzudun. *adj.* maltzur, azeri.
canoe *n.* kanoa, piragua.
canon *n. (eccl.)* kalonje; elizarau.
canonic *adj.* elizarauzko.
canonical *adj.* elizlegezko, elizarauzko.
canonization *n.* donekuntza.
canonize *v.t.* saindutu, santu egin, santutu, donetu, gurendu.
Canon Law *n. (eccl.)* elizaraudi, elizlege.
canonry *n.* kalonjego, kalonjetza.
canopy *n.* toldo, olana; ohezeru.
can't *v.i./v.aux.* ezin izan, ezin ukan.
canteen *n.* txiriboga. *n.* kantinplora.
canticle *n.* kantika.
cantilever *n.* habe.
cantina *n.* edaritegi.
canvas *n.* belaki.
canvass *v.t.* hauteskundetako botoak zenbatu. *v.t.* eritziak eskatu.
canyon *n.* haizpitarte.
cap *v.t.* ziritu; estali.
cap *n.* buruko, ginbailtxo, kapelu.
capability *n.* taxu, trebaketa, ahalduntasun, ahalmen, artezia. *n.* apropostasun, doitasun, gaitasun.
capable *adj.* ahaldun, moldatsu, moldetsu, moduzko, taxudun, gauza, iaio, trebe; -garri.
capably *adv.* trebeki, trebekiro.
capacious *n.* zabal, lekutsu, zabalote.
capacitate *v.t.* gauzatu.
capacity *n.* kokamen, edukiera, edukitasun. *n.* ahalmen, doitasun, gaitasun.
cape *n.* gainjantzi, jantzigain, soingaineko. *n.* lurmutur.
caper *n.* saltu, jauzi.

capercaillie *n. (zool.)* basoilar.
capillary *n.* ilehodi.
capital *n.* hiriburu. *n. (econ.)* dirumoltso, dirupilo, dirutza, kapital.
    Fixed capital. Kapital finko. *n.* hizki handi, hizki nagusi.
capitalism *n.* kapitalismo.
capitalist *n.* kapitalista.
capitalizable *adj.* kapitalizagarri, kapitalgarri.
capitalization *n. (econ.)* kapitaleztapen, kapitalizazio.
capitalize *v.t.* hizkinagusiz idatzi. *v.t.* kapitaleztatu, kapitalizatu, kapitaldu. *v.i.* (**on**) probetxatu, profitatu.
capital punishment *n.* heriozigor.
capitol *n.* etxegarai; kapitolio.
capitulate *v.i.* amor eman, errendatu, makurtu.
capon *n. (zool.)* kapoi(n).
caprice *n.* apeta, nahikeria, berekeria, apetaldi, kasketeria. *n.* eguraldiaren batpateko aldaketa.
capricious *adj.* kasketadun, kasketatsu, apetatsu.
capriciously *adv.* plazerez, fantasioski.
capsize *v.i./v.t.* tirabira egin, tirabiratu, zanbulukatu.
capsule *n.* kapsula. *n.* txosten.
captain *v.t.* ontzigidatu.
captain *n.* ontziburu; kapitain.
captaincy *n.* kapitaintza.
caption *n.* idazpuru, irakurburu. *n.* azpidatzi (zine), azpititulu.
captivate *v.t.* liluratu; erakarri, xarmatu.
captivation *n.* xarmaldi, xarmaketa, lilurapen.
captive *n.* gatibu, uztarpeko. *adj.* gatibu. *adj. (fig.)* liluratu, zoratu.
captivity *n.* gatibualdi, uztarpekotasun, uztarpe.
captor *n.* harrapatzaile, harrapakari.
capture *v.t.* atzeman, harrapatu, jabetu.
capture *n.* harrapaldi, atzemate, eskuraketa, harrapaketa.
capturer *n.* harrapatzaile, harrapakari.
car *n.* kotxe, auto. **Car accident.** Autoezbehar. **Car parts.** Autoaldakin. **Car race.** Autolasterketa. *n.* bagoi, trengurdi.
carafe *n.* pitxer.
caramel *n.* azukrerre(a).
carat *n.* kilate.
caravan *n.* karabana, jendetaldearen ibilaldi(a).
carbide *n. (chem.)* karburo.
carbohydrate *n.* karbohidrato.
carbon *n. (chem.)* ikazki, karbono.
carbonate *v.t.* gaseztatu, gaseztu.
carbonate *n. (chem.)* karbonato.
carbonated *adj.* gasdun, gasezko. **To be carbonated.** Gaseztatu.
carbonation *n.* gaskuntza, gaseztapen.
carboniferous *adj.* ikaztun.
carbonize *v.t.* ikaztu.

carbon paper *n.* ikazpaper, ikazki.
carbuncle *n. (med.)* lipu.
carburetor *n.* karburagailu.
carcass *n.* hezurruts. *n. (fig.)* gorpu.
carcinoma *n. (med.)* minbizikoskor.
card *v.t.* kardatu.
card *n.* karta (joko). *n.* fitxa. *n.* karnet, zedula. *n.* txarrantxa.
cardboard *n.* kartoi. *adj.* kartoizko.
carder *n.* txarrantxari, gardari, garbari.
card game *n.* kartajoko, truke.
cardiac *adj.* bihotzeko.
cardinal *n. (eccl.)* kardenal. *n. (gram.)* kardinal. *n. (zool.)* kardinal.
cardinalship *n. (eccl.)* kardenalgo, kardenaltza.
cardiologist *n.* bihozkari, kardiologari.
cardiology *n.* kardiologia.
care *v.i.* axola izan. *v.i.* **(for)** gainartu, begiratu, zaindu, gorde; gustatu, laket izan. *v.i.* nahi izan.
care *n.* arrangura, arreta, grina, axola. *n.* tentu. *n.* antsia, ardura, arduratasun, kezka, grina. *n.* kontu, zaintza. **To take care of.** Zaindu.
career *n.* karrera.
carefree *adj.* lasai, axolagabetsu, arduragabe, gibelaundi.
careful *adj.* arduradun, ardurati, arduratsu, arretadun, axoladun, axolati, tentudun, begirakor. **Be careful!** Kontuz! *adj.* zehatz.
carefully *adv.* arduraz, arretaz, kontuz, tentuz, zuhurki. *adv.* zehazki, zeharo, xeheki, zehatz-mehatz.
carefulness *n.* arreta, ardura, kontu, begirakortasun.
careless *adj.* axolagabe, axolagabeko, desarduratsu, arduragabeko.
carelessly *adv.* axolagabeki, arduragabeki, kontugabeki.
carelessness *n.* arduraeza, arduragabekeria, axolagabekeria, tentugabezia, zabartasun, ezaxola.
caress *v.t.* ferekatu, laztandu, laztan egin, xeratu, balakatu.
caress *n.* fereku, losin, xera; laztan.
caresser *n.* ferekari, ferekatzaile.
caressingly *adv.* laztanki.
caretaker *n.* zaindari; -(t)zain.
careworn *adj.* urduritsu, urduri, kezkati, kezkatsu.
cargo *n.* ontzikada, ontzikarga, ontzizama, kargamendu.
caribou *n. (zool.)* karibu.
caricature *n.* karikatura.
caries *n.* txantxar.
Carlism *n. (pol.)* karlismo.
Carlist *n./adj.* karlista.
Carlist War *n.* karlistada.
carload *n.* trenzama.
carmine *n./adj.* gorri-bizi, gorri-gorri.
carnage *n.* hilkuntza, odolkeria.
carnal *adj.* haragikoi, haragizko. **Carnal excesses.** Haragizko gehiegikeriak. *adj.* zentzukor.
carnally *adv.* haragiz, gorputzez.

carnation *n.* krabelin.
carnival *n.* ihauteri, zanpantzar.
carnivore *n.* abere haragijale(a).
carnivorous *adj.* haragijale, haragikor.
carob bean *n. (bot.)* algarroba, xingil.
carol *n.* gaukanta, gabon-abesti.
caroler *n.* gabonkantari.
carouse *v.i.* iskanbilan ibili, zalaparta egin.
carousel *n.* zaldi-maldiko(ak).
carp *v.i.* maiseatu, marmari egin.
carpenter *n.* arotz, zurgin, zurlangile.
carpentry *n.* arotzeritza, arozkintza, zurgintza, zurlantza; zurginlan, zurlan.
carpet *v.t.* moketatu, oinoihaldu, oinzapitu.
carpet *n.* oinoihal, oinzapi.
carriage *n.* gurdi.
carrier *n.* ekarle; eramale; garraialari, garraiatzaile, lorketari, soinkari, zamaketari. *n.* garraigailu.
carrion *n.* hiliki.
carrot *n. (bot.)* azenario, pastana.
carry *v.t.* eraman, jasan, garraiatu, erakarri. *v.i.* hedatu (ahots). *v.i.* **(on)** jarraitu, aurrera ekin. *v.i.* **(out)** burutu, kunplitu, bete. *v.i.* **(over)** iraun.
cart *v.t.* gurdizkatu, gurdikatu. *v.t.* eraman, erakarri.
cart *n.* gurdi; gurt-. **By cart.** Gurdiz.
cartage *n.* lor, lorreta.
cartilage *n. (anat.)* hezurlokarri.
cartload *n.* gurkada, gurdibete.
cartographer *n.* mapagile.
cartography *n.* mapagintza, kartografia.
carton *n.* kartoizko kutxa.
cartoon *n.* marrazki bizidun(ak). *n.* komiki.
cartoonist *n.* marrazki bizidun egile(a).
cartridge *n.* kartutxo.
cartwheel *n.* kirrinka.
cartwright *n.* orgagile, gurdigile.
carve *v.t./v.i.* zulakaiztu, harlandu, zizelkatu, zizeldu. *v.t.* ebaki (haragi), jaki(a) zatitu, zatikatu.
carver *n.* jakizatitzaile. *n.* irudigile, zizelkari.
carving *n.* egurrezko eskultura.
cascade *n.* zurrunba.
case *n.* kasu; gertaera, gertakizun. **In any case.** Dena dela. Nolanahi ere. **Just in case.** Badaezpadan. *n. (gram.)* kasu. *n.* gai, arrazoi. *n.* auzi, auzibide. *n.* kutxa, kutxatto, kutxatila. *n.* molditz.
casement window *n.* lehiorri.
cash *n.* eskudiru; tanka-tanka. **To pay cash.** Eskudiruz erosi.
cashier *n.* kaxari, kutxazain, diruzain.
casing *n.* estalki.
casino *n.* jokoetxe, kasino.
cask *n.* upel, pipa.
casket *n.* hilkutxa, zerraldo. *n.* kutxatila.

casserole *n.* kazola. *n.* kazolakada.
casserole dish *n.* kazola.
cassette *n.* kaxete.
cassock *n. (eccl.)* sotana.
cast *v.t./v.i.* bota, jaurtiki, iraitzi. *v.t./v.i.* kaldatu, galdatu; moldekatu, moldeztatu. *v.t. (out)* bidaldu, bidali. *v.t. (off)* utzi; aingura altxatu, aingura jaso.
cast *n.* jaurtaldi, iraitzi. *n.* moldazka. *n.* moldelan. *n.* itxura, antz, tankera. *n.* ñabardura, tindu. *n. (med.)* igeltsuki, igeltsu. *n.* erreparto, aktore-talde.
castanet *n.* kaskaineta, kriskitin.
caste *n.* kasta, etorki, enda.
caster *n.* botari, botatzaile, jaurtikitzaile.
castigate *v.t.* zigortu; gaitzetsi, zigorkatu.
castigation *n.* zurra, zigor, zigorketa.
castigator *n.* zigorlari.
Castile *n. (geog.)* Gaztela.
Castilian *n./adj.* gaztelaniar, gaztelar. *n.* gaztelania, gaztelania.
cast iron *n.(min.)* tupiki, burdingalda, burdingori, galdaburni, burniurtu.
castle *n.* gaztelu.
castor oil *n.* errizinolio, purgaolio.
castrate *v.t.* irendu, zikiratu, antzutu.
castrated *adj.* irendu(a), zikiro, iren.
castration *n.* irenaldi, irenketa, zikiraketa, zikirapen.
casual *adj.* ohizko, arrunt (jantzi). *adj.* ustegabeko, baezpadako.
casually *adv.* alabeharrez, ezustean, ustekabean.
casualty *n.* istripuan hildako pertsona; gudan hildako soldadu(a).
cat *n.* katu, katar, kateme; katu-, kata-.
cataclysm *n.* gainberaldi, uholde, lurrikara.
catacomb *n.* lurpeko hilobi, katakunba.
catafalque *n.* hilmahai, hiltronu.
Catalan *adj/n.* katalan, kataluniar. *n.* katalanera.
catalog *v.t.* katalogatu, klasifikatu, sailkatu, erroldatu.
catalog *n.* izendegi, izenlerro, errolda, katalogo.
cataloguer *n.* sailkatzaile.
Catalonia *n. (geog.)* Katalunia.
Catalonian *n./adj.* kataluniar.
catapult *n.* harrijaurtailu.
cataract *n. (med.)* begilauso, lanbro, lauso.
catastrophe *n.* hondamendi, hondamen, galera.
catcall *n.* eupada.
catch *v.t.* harrapatu, atzeman, atxiki, heldu. **To catch fire.** Su hartu. *v.t.* erantsi, izurreztatu, izurritu. *v.t.* arraintzatu, arrantzatu.
catch *n.* harrapaketa (kirol). *n.* arrantzu. *n.* maratila, kisket, txaramel. *n.* eragozpen, gako, koska, iltze, korapilo. **There's the catch.** Hor dago gakoa. *n.* iruzur, zipotz, ziri. *n.*

garatz.
catchable *adj.* harrapagarri.
catcher *n.* harrapatzaile, atzemaile, heltzaile. *n.* hartzaile (beisbol).
catechism *n.* kristau ikasbide, dotrina, katexima.
catechize *v.t.* katekizatu, erlijio(a) irakatsi.
categorical *adj. (fig.)* biribil.
categorically *adv.* biribilki.
category *n.* kategoria, maila.
cater *v.i./v.t.* hornitu. *v.i. (to)* atsegin eman.
caterpillar *n.* mamarro.
catfish *n. (zool.)* itsaskatu.
catharsis *n.* hestegarbiketa.
cathartic *n./adj.* hestegarbigarri.
cathedral *n.* katedrale.
cathode ray tube *n.* katodo-izpien hodi(a).
Catholic *adj./n.* katoliko.
Catholicism *n.* katolikutza.
catholicize *v.t./v.i.* katolikotu.
catholicness *n.* katolikotasun.
cattail *n. (bot.)* ezpatabelar, ezpatalore, zintabelar.
cattle *n.* ganadutza, ele, abelgorri, kabal.
cattleman *n.* abeldun.
Caucasian *n./adj.* kaukasiar.
caucus *n.* alderdi politikoaren agintarien bilera.
caught *pret./p.part. of catch.*
cauliflower *n. (bot.)* azalore.
caulk *v.t.* mastikatu, istinkatu, iztupatu, zuloak estali.
caulker *n.* iztupalari, istinkari.
cause *v.t.* gertarazi, sortu, erakarri, ekarri; -arazi.
cause *n.* zio, kari, zergati, zergatiko, gertabide; sorbide, erro, jatorri, sorburu, iturbide. *n.* eragile. *n.* auzibide. *n.* helburu, xede, jomuga.
caustic *adj.* ozpin, ozpintsu, minkor. *n. (chem.)* sosa.
caustically *adv.* mingarriki, mingarriro, pikoka.
causticness *n.* ozpinkeria, sumintasun, pikoketa.
cauterize *v.t.* suziztatu.
caution *n.* kontu, begiratasun, arreta, zuhurtasun. *n.* ohar, oharpen.
cautious *adj.* zuhur, oharkor, begirakor. **To be cautious.** Zuhur egon.
cautiously *adv.* begirakorki, zuhurki.
cautiousness *n.* oharkortasun.
cavalcade *n.* zaldiketa.
cavalier *n.* zaldun. *adj.* alai. *adj.* harro.
cavalry *n.* zaldieria, zalduntalde.
cave *n.* haitzulo, haizpe, harpe, koba, kobazulo.
cave in *v.i./v.t.* lurreratu, hondatu.
cave man *n.* haitzuloetako gizon, lezetar.
cavern *n.* haitzulo, haizpe, kobazulo, leizezulo.

cavernous adj. leizetsu.
caviar n. arrauki, kabiar.
cavil n. gaizkiesan, esamesa, hizki-mizki.
cavity n. hutsune, zulogune, sakonune, barrunbe. n. hortzulo.
cavort v.i. itzulipurdikatu. v.i. jolastu, dibertitu, atsegin hartu, jostatu.
caw v.i. karraka egin.
caw n. karranka, karraskada.
cease v.i./v.t. etsi, utzi, amor eman. v.i./v.t. geldilu, geratu, atertu.
cease fire n. bakeune, bakete, bakealdi, gerlarte.
ceaseless adj. etengabe, geldiezin, geraezin.
ceaselessly adv. geldigabeki.
ceaselessness n. etengabetasun.
cedar n. (bot.) zedro.
cede v.t. eman, utzi, laga.
ceiling n. goi, sabai, tronadura. n. goi, azkensari.
celebrate v.t./v.i. ospatu. v.t./v.i. jai egin, jaitu. v.t. meza eman. v.t. goratu, goretsi.
celebrated adj. famatsu, famatu, izenandiko, ospatsu, entzutetsu.
celebration n. jai, jaialdi, ospaketa, ospakizun, besta.
celebrity n. izar, pertsona famatu(a).
celerity n. berehalatasun, ziztu.
celery n. (bot.) apio.
celestial adj. zeruko, zerutar, ortzeko, zeruetako.
celibacy n. zelibato.
cell n. gela. n. adar, taldetxo. n. (biol.) zelula.
cellar n. etxabe, behealde, etxazpi; soto.
cello n. (mus.) biolontxelo.
cellophane n. zelofan.
cellular adj. zelular.
celluloid n. zeluloide.
cellulose n. (chem.) zelulosa.
cement v.t./v.i. porlaneztatu, espaloiztatu.
cement n. espaloi, hormigoi, porlan, zementu.
cemetery n. hilerri, kanposantu, hiltoki, lursaindu, hobitegi.
censer n. intsentsontzi.
censor v.t. zentsuratu.
censor n. maisealari. n. zentsuratzaile.
censorable n. zentsuragarri.
censorship n. zentsura.
censure v.t./v.i. gaizki esan, maiseatu, kritikatu, txarretsi.
censure n. maiseaketa, zentsura.
census n. biztanle-lerrokada, errolda.
cent n. (econ.) xentimo, zentimo.
centaur n. zentauro.
centenary n. ehunurteburu, mendemuga, mendeurren. adj. ehunurtedun, ehunurteko.
centennial n. ehunurteburu, mendemuga, mendeurren. adj. ehunurteko, ehunurtedun.

center n. erdi; erdi-, -erdi, ert-. n. erdiune, erdigune, erditoki, erdi. n. erdilari, erdiko (kirolak).
centigrade adj. zentigrado.
centiliter n. zentilitro.
centimeter n. zentimetro.
centipede n. (zool.) ehunoindun, ehunzango, ehunzangodun.
central adj. erdialdeko, erdi-erdiko, erdiko.
centralism n. erdikoitasun, erdirakoitasun. n. (pol.) zentralismo.
centralization n. erdiraketa, erdirapen. n. (pol.) zentralizaketa, zentralizapen.
centralize v.t./v.i. erdibildu, zentraldu, erdiratu.
centrifugal force n. ihesindar, indar kanporakoi.
centuple v.t. ehunkoiztu.
centuple n. ehunkoitz.
centurion n. ehunburu, ehuntari.
century n. gizaldi, ehunurte, mende. **Down through the centuries.** Mendez mende.
ceramic adj./n. zeramikazko, zeramika. **Ceramic pots.** Zeramikazko ontziak. n. (pl.) bustingintza.
cereal n. labore, zitu.
cerebellum n. (anat.) garuntxo.
cerebral adj. garunetako, burumuineko. adj. jakintsu.
cerebrum n. (anat.) zerebru, burumuin, garun.
ceremonial n. zeremonia. adj. zeremoniatsu.
ceremonious adj. adeitsu.
ceremony n. zeremonia. **Religious ceremony.** Elizkizun.
certain adj. dudagabeko, ziur, segur, zalantzagabeko, ezbaigabeko. adj. zenbait, hainbat.
certainly adv. dudagabeki, dudagabez, alafede, seguraski, segurki, ziur, egiazki. adv. jakina, noski.
certainty n. segurtasun, ziurtasun, segurantza.
certifiable adj. zineztagarri, ziurgarri.
certificate n. agerbide, egiaztagarri, ziurtagiri, zertifikatu, zedula.
certification n. zertifikapen, ziurtapen.
certified adj. egiztatu(a).
certifier n. egiztatzaile.
certify v.t./v.i. egiztatu, zertifikatu, ziurtu, idatziz ziurtatu.
cervix n. (anat.) garondo, lepondo.
cessation n. geldimen.
cession n. utziera, uzte.
cetacean adj./n. zetazeo.
chafe v.t. igurtzi. v.i. haserretu, haserre izan.
chaff n. ahotz, galtzu, galondar.
chaffinch n. (zool.) neguta, txonta, elurtxori.
chafing dish n. irakinontzi.
chagrin n. kezkazko larrialdi, apalkuntza lotsagarri(a).
chain v.t. (batzutan up-ekin) kateatu,

katetu, kateztatu, katigatu.
chain *n.* kate. *n. (pl.)* menpekotasun, katibutasun, joputasun, mirabetza. *n.* mendilerro, mendikate, mendizerra. *n.* sail, talde.
chain link mesh *n.* katesare.
chair *v.t.* mahaiburu izan, buru izan (batzarretan).
chair *n.* aulki, eserleku, kadira, jarleku. *n.* mahaiburu.
chairman *n.* mahaiburu, biltzarburu, batzarburu.
chairmanship *n.* mahaiburutza.
chairperson *n.* mahaiburu, biltzarburu, batzarburu.
chairwoman *n.* mahaiburu (emakume), biltzarburu, batzarburu.
chalet *n.* txalet.
chalice *n. (eccl.)* kaliza, mezontzi.
chalk *n.* klera, tuparri, igeltsu.
chalkboard *n.* idaztola, arbel.
chalky *adj.* igeltsutsu, kleratsu; klerazko.
challenge *v.t.* aupakatu, aurka egin, aupa egin.
challenge *n.* desafio, aupada, erronka.
challenger *n.* aupakari, aurkatzaile, desafiatzaile, kontrakari.
challenging *adj.* aurkatzaile, desafiatzaile. *adj.* kilikagarri.
chamber *n.* ganbara, gela. *n. (pol.)* ganbara. *n. (pl.)* epailearen bulego(a). *n.* (iskiluen) errekamara.
chamber pot *n.* gernuntzi, pixontzi, txizontzi, garnuontzi.
chameleon *n.* kamalehoi.
chamois *n. (zool.)* orkatz, sarrio.
champ *n.* txapeldun.
champagne *n.* txanpain, champagne.
champion *n.* txapeldun, garaile, garaitzaile, irabazle.
championship *n.* txapelketa, lehiaketa, sariketa.
chance *n.* mentura, zori, zorte. **Game of chance.** Zozketa. *n.* alabehar. **By chance.** Alabeharrez. *n.* une, abagadune, aukera, era, erreztasun, aldarte. *n.* kanore; posibilitate. *n.* arrisku. *adj.* alabeharrezko.
chancellor *n.* kantziler.
chancy *adj.* menturazko.
chandelier *n.* sapaian eskegita egon ohi den argi ugaridun lanpara.
change *v.t./v.i.* aldatu, bestelakotu, aldizkatu, itxuraldatu, antzaldatu,eraldatu, nolakotu.
change *n.* aldaketa, aldakuntza, bihurketa. *n.* berritura, berrikuntza, berrizte, aldarte. *n.* jantzi-erantzi, jazkiberrizte. *n.* aldakin, atzerako, kanbio, txanpon.
changeable *adj.* aldagarri, aldakor, bihurkor. *adj.* haizakor, itzulerraz.
changeless *adj.* aldakaitz, aldaezin, iraunkor.
changer *n.* aldatzaile.
channel *v.t.* kanaleztatu.

channel *n.* itsasodi; erreten. *n.* telebista-kate(a).
chant *n.* abesti, kanta.
chaos *n.* nahaspila, nahasketa, nahaste.
chaotic *adj.* nahaspilezko.
chaparral *n.* txapardi.
chapel *n.* kapera, otoiztegi, otoiztoki.
chaperone *n.* andere lagun.
chaplain *n.* kaperau, ministrari.
chaplaincy *n.* kaperautza.
chaplet *n.* errosario.
chapter *n.* atalburu, kapitulu. *n.* erlijiosoen bilera. *n.* erakunde baten aldaxka.
char *v.t./v.i.* ikaztu, kiskail. *v.t.* garbitu. *v.i.* neskame bezala lan egin.
character *n.* izaera, mendu, funts, jite. *n.* pertsonaia.
characteristic *n.* ezaugarri, bakoiztasun, berezitasun, nolakotasun. *adj.* berezi, beregisako.
characteristically *adv.* ezaugarriro, bereziki.
characterization *n.* deskribaketa.
characterize *v.t.* ezagungarritu, izaeratu, zeindu; deskribatu.
charcoal *n.* egurrikatz, ikatz.
chard *n. (bot.)* zerba, azelga.
charge *v.t./v.i.* erasan, eraso, oldartu. *v.t. (with)* zamatu, gainezarri. *v.t./v.i.* kendu, eskatu (diru). *v.t.* kredituz erosi. *v.t.* elektrindarrez bete. *v.t.* heriotza edo lapurketa leporatu.
charge *n.* zama, pisu. *n.* kargu, eginkizun, betebehar, eginbehar, arazo, zeregin. *n.* ardura, arreta, kontu. *n.* oldarraldi, erasoaldi, eraso. *n.* salaketa, salakuntza. *n.* agindu, gomendio. *n.* kauta; pertsona babestu(a). *n.* kontu, gastu. *n.* elektrindar.
chargeable *adj.* ezargarri, salagarri.
charger *n.* elektrika betegailu. *n.* gudazaldi.
charisma *n.* karisma.
charitable *adj.* eskuzabal, eskuluze, eskuzabaleko.
charity *n.* ongiegite, karitate, goimaitasun. *n.* karitatezko erakunde. *n.* erresumina, limosna.
charlatan *n.* sasisendagile; sasimaisu.
charm *v.t.* maitaxarmatu, zoratu, xarmakatu, zorarazi.
charm *n.* xarma, lilura, lilurapen, xarmagarritasun, grazi, zoragarritasun. *n.* kutun.
charming *adj.* xarmagarri, xarmant, zoragarri, zorarazle, grazidun, grazios.
charmingly *adv.* xarmanki, zoragarriro, grazioski.
charred *adj.* ikaztu, kiskal.
chart *n.* taula, ohol.
charter *n.* politik erakunde eta gizaeskubideak ezartzen dituen idazki konstituzionala.

chase *v.t./v.i.* -(r)i jarraiki, -(r)i segitu, -(r)en atzetik joan. *v.t.* **(away)** ohildu, uxatu.

chasm *n.* amiltegi, amiltoki, leze, malkortegi, osin.

chassis *n.* kotxearen armazoi(a), txasis.

chaste *adj.* garbi, bihozgarbiko.

chastely *adv.* garbi, oneski.

chasten *v.t.* zigortu, zuzendu, astindu.

chastise *v.t.* gogor egin, gogor hartu, zigorpetu.

chastisement *n.* zigor, zigorraldi.

chastity *n.* bihozgarbitasun, kastitate, garbitasun.

chat *v.i.* berriketan ari, berriketatu, hizketatu, jardun, solasketatu, hitz egin.

chat *n.* berriketaldi, hizketaldi, solasaldi, hizketa, solaseria, kalaka, mintzo, solasketa.

chateau *n.* gaztelu.

chattel *n.* *(pl.)* ondasunak. *n.* uztarpeko, esklabu.

chatter *v.i.* kalakatu, karraskots egin. *v.i.* berriketan ari, solasketatu.

chatter *n.* berriketari, elekari. *n.* ele-mele, erran-merran, hizki-mizki, hitz-mitz, hitzaspertu.

chatterbox *n.* hitzontzi, berritsu, hitzjario, kalakari, hiztun.

chattiness *n.* hitzjariokeria.

chatty *adj.* hitzontzi.

chauffeur *n.* txofer.

chauvinism *n.* abertzalekeria, txobinismo.

chauvinist *n.* txobinista.

cheap *adj.* merke.

cheapen *v.t./v.i.* merketu, merkeagotu, beheratu. *v.t./v.i.* arrunt bilakatu, arruntatu.

cheaply *adv.* merke.

cheapness *n.* merketasun, merkedura.

cheat *v.t./v.i.* iruzurtu, atzipetu.

cheat *n.* iruzurle, iruzurgile. *n.* iruzurkeria, atzipe.

cheater *n.* iruzurlari, iruzurle, gezurti.

cheating *n.* iruzurkeria, azpikeria, gibeljoko.

check *v.t.* kontrolatu, gelditu, bukatu. *v.i.* **(in)** hotelera heldu eta izena eman. *v.i.* **(out)** hoteletik irten ordaindu ondoren; miatu, arakatu, aztertu, ikertu. *v.t.* **(up on)** egiaztatu.

check *n.* kontrol, egiaztapen, frogaketa, frogantza, azterketa. *n.* txeke, taloi. *n.* jantokiko kontu(a). *n.* bapateko geldialdi, bapateko egonaldi. *n.* xake mate.

checker board *n.* damataula.

checkered *adj.* laukizko. *adj.* askotariko.

checkers *n.* damajoko.

checking account *n.* *(econ.)* erabilkontu.

checkmate *n.* xake mate.

checkup *n.* sendagilearen miaketa.

cheek *n.* *(anat.)* masaila. *n.* ipurtmami. *n.* lotsagabekeria, ozarkeria.

cheekbone *n.* *(anat.)* masailalbo, masailezur.

cheep *v.i.* pio egin, txio egin, piokatu.

cheep *n.* pio.

cheer *v.i.* gorakatu. *v.t./v.i.* **(up)** pozarazi, adoretu, bizkortu.

cheer *n.* umore.

cheerful *n.* pozgarri, pozkor, pozarazle, gogoalai, iaio.

cheerfully *adv.* pozgarriki, alaiki, pozik.

cheerfulness *n.* gogoalaitasun, poztasun, bozkario.

cheerily *adv.* pozgarriki, alaiki.

cheerleader *n.* berotzaile, hotsemaile.

cheerless *adj.* pozgabe(ko), itzal.

cheery *adj.* pozgarri, pozkor.

cheese *n.* gazta; gaztan-.

chemical *n.* kimikagai. *adj.* kimiko.

chemically *adv.* kimikoki.

chemist *n.* kimikari.

chemistry *n.* kimika.

cherish *v.t.* preziatu, estimatu.

cherished *adj.* kutun, laztan.

cherry *n.* *(bot.)* gerezi.

cherub *n.* aingerutxo.

chess *n.* xake. **Chess match.** Xakejoko.

chest *n.* kaxa, kutxa. *n.* kolko, papar, bular.

chest cavity *n.* *(anat.)* bularringuru.

chestnut *n.* gaztaina.

chest of drawers *n.* komoda, jantzikutxa.

chew *v.t./v.i.* mastekatu, murtxikatu, karraskatu.

chewing gum *n.* txikle.

chic *adj.* apain, dotore, pinpirin.

Chicano *n./adj.* txikanu.

chick *n.* *(zool.)* txita, txito. *int.* furra!. *n.* *(colloq.)* neska.

chicken *n.* *(zool.)* oilasko. *n.* oilaskoki, oilaki. *adj.* oilo, beldurti, koldar.

chicken coop *n.* oilategi.

chickenpox *n.* barizela.

chickpea *n.* *(bot.)* garbantzu, txitxirio.

chide *v.t.* llskar egin, mokokatu.

chief *n.* buruzagi, nagusi, aitzindari, agintari. *n.* *(mil.)* gudalburu. *n.* indioen nagusia(a). *adj.* garrantzitsuen, lehen, gailen.

chiefly *n.* batez ere, bereziki.

chieftain *n.* indio nagusi(a).

chigger *n.* *(zool.)* lapazorri.

chilblain *n.* ospel, azkordin. **To be covered with chilblains.** Ospeldu.

child *n.* ume, haur, sein; uma-.

childbirth *n.* haurgintza, erditzapen, ertaldi. **Difficult childbirth.** Haurgaizto.

childcare *n.* haurtzaintza.

childhood *n.* haurtzaro; haurtasun, umetasun. **To enter one's second childhood.** Umetu.

childish *n.* haurrantzeko, haurtzaroko, haurraire.

childishly *adv.* haurgisa, haurrantzera, umeki.
childishness *n.* haurkada, haurkeria, umekeria, ninikeria.
childless *adj.* haurgabe.
childlike *adj.* haurraire, haurrantzeko.
children *n. (pl.)* haurrak, seme-alabak.
chili pepper *n. (bot.)* bipermin.
chill *v.t./v.i.* hoztu, hotzarazi.
chill *n.* hotzikara, hozketa, hozkirri.
chilled *adj.* hotzik, hotzikaradun.
chilliness *n.* hoztasun.
chilly *adv.* hotzik, hozkirri.
chime *v.i./v.t.* kanpai(a) jo. *v.i.(in)* bere eritzia ezagutarazi, bere eritzia azaldu.
chime *n.* txilina, kanpai(a), ezkila. *n.* ezkila-errepika, ezkilots.
chimera *n.* ameskeria, ametsuts.
chimney *n.* kebide, kezulo, tximinia.
chimneysweep *n.* tximinigarbitzaile, kedarkentzaile, kedargarbitzaile.
chimpanzee *n.* txinpantze.
chin *n. (anat.)* kokots; okoz-.
china *n.* mahaiontzi, mahaiontziteria.
china hutch *n.* baxerategi.
Chinese *n./adj.* txinatar. *n.* txinera.
chink *n.* arrakala.
chip *v.t./v.i.* apurkatu, koskatu, akastu.
chip *n.* ezpal, brintza, samar, izpi. *n. (pl.)* patata prijitu(ak); zatitxo (janari). *n.* fitxa (joko). *n.* akats, hozka, koska. *n.* bekorotz siku(a).
chipmunk *n.(zool.)* urtxintxa.
chipped *adj.* akastsu, koskatu(a).
chiropodist *n.* oinsendagile, maskurlari.
chiropractor *n.* kiropraktore.
chirp *v.i.* txio egin, txiokatu, pio egin, piokatu.
chirp *n.* pio, txio.
chirping *n.* txio, tiuta, txiruliru, txorrotxio.
chisel *v.t./v.i.* zizelkatu, zulakaiztu. *v.t./v.i.* engainatu.
chisel *n.* trintxa, zizel, zurzizel.
chiseler *n.* zizelkari. *n.* iruzurgile, gezurtari, iruzurti.
chivalrous *adj.* adeitsu, adeibera, adeikor.
chivalry *n.* zalduneria.
chives *n. (bot.)* tipulin.
chloride *n. (chem.)* kloruro.
chlorinate *v.t.* kloroztatu.
chlorinated *adj.* klorotsu.
chlorine *n. (chem.)* kloro.
chloroform *n.* kloroformo.
chlorophyll *n.* klorofila.
chock *n.* tako; taket.
chocolate *n.* txokolate; mokolo. *n.* bonboi.
choice *n.* aukera, aukerabide, hautaketa, hautabide. *adj.* hoberen, aukeratu(a).
choir *n.* abesbatza, abestalde, kantaritalde, koru.
choke *v.i./v.t.* kok egin, arnasestutu,

zintzurtu, kontraeztarriratu.
choke *n.* haize-neurgailu.
cholera *n.* kolera.
choleric *adj.* haserretsu, haserrekoi, haserredun.
choosable *adj.* aukeragarri, hautagarri.
choose *v.t./v.i.* aukeratu, hautetsi, hautatu, hautu, berezi, begiz jo, begia bota.
chooser *n.* hautatzaile, hautari, aukeratzaile.
choosiness *n.* mizkinkeria, mokozurikeria.
choosy *adj.* mizkin, miliki, mokozuri.
chop *v.t.* izpikatu, xehekatu, zati-zati egin, zehetu.
chop *n.* txuleta.
chopstick *n.* zotz.
choral *adj.* koruko.
chord *n. (mus.)* akorde.
chore *n.* eginkizun, eginbehar, zeregin.
choreography *n.* koreografia.
chorizo *n.* lukainka, txorizo.
chortle *v.i.* ixilka barre egin.
chortle *n.* barre ito(a).
chorus *n.* kantaritalde, abesbatza, abestalde. *n.* lelo.
chosen *adj.* aukerako, begipeko, aukeratu(a), hautatu(a).
chow *n.* janari.
chowder *n.* arrainzopa.
Christ *n.* Kristo.
christen *v.t.* bataiatu, izena ezarri.
Christendom *n.* kristauherri.
christening *n.* bateo.
Christian *n./adj.* kristau. **Group of Christians.** Kristautalde. **To become a Christian.** Kristautu. *adv.* kristauki.
Christianity *n.* kristautasun. *n.* kristautalde; kristauherri.
Christianization *n.* kristaupen.
Christianize *v.t.* kristautu.
Christmas *n.* eguberri, gabonak. **Christmas holidays.** Gabonjaiak. **Christmas day.** Gabon-egun. **Christmas tree.** Eguberri zuhaitza. *adj.* gabonetako, eguberritako.
Christmas carol *n.* gabon-abesti, gabonkantu.
Christmas Eve *n.* gabon-gau.
chromatic *adj.* kolorezko.
chrome *n. (chem.)* kromo.
chromosome *n. (biol.)* kromosoma.
chronic *adj.* errotsu, iraunkor, aspaldiko.
chronically *adv.* ohituraz, ekanduz.
chronicle *n.* kronika.
chronicler *n.* kronikari.
chronological *adj.* kronologiko.
chronologically *adv.* kronologikoki.
chronology *n.* kronologia.
chronometer *n.* kronometro.
chrysalis *n. (zool.)* krisalida.
chrysanthemum *n. (bot.)* urrelili.
chubby *adj.* lodikote, potolo, pottolo, totolo.
chuck *v.t.* kokots azpian kolpetxoak

eman. *v.t.* bota, jaurti.
chuck *n.* kokots azpian eman ohi diren kolpetxoak. *n. (colloq.)* janari, elikagai. *n.* xerra.
chuckle *v.i.* furrust egin, barrez ito.
chuckle *n.* furrust, barrez itotze.
chug *v.i.* binbilikatu.
chug *n.* zalaparta labur eta eztandagarria.
chum *n.* lagun.
chunk *n.* atal, zati.
chunky *adj.* mamijario, gizen, lodi.
church *n.* eliza; eliz-. *adj.* elizako.
churchyard *n.* elizinguruak, elizalde.
churl *n.* pertsona zakar(ra).
churlish *adj.* zakar, latz.
churn *v.t./v.i.* bizitu. *v.t.* eragin, irabiatu. *v.i.* *(out)* ideia asko sortu.
churn *n.* gurina egiten duen tresna.
chute *n.* hodi, erreten. *n.* jausgailu, erorgailu.
cicada *n. (zool.)* txirrita.
cicatrice *n.* zaurimarka.
cider *n.* sagardo. **Cider shop.** Sagardotegi.
cigar *n.* puru, zigarropuru, txokor.
cigarette *n.* zigarreta, zigarro. **Cigarette butt.** Zigarrokin.
cigarette lighter *n.* pizgailu, metxero.
ciliary *adj.* betazaleko.
cinch *v.t.* petraldu, zingilatu.
cinch *n.* petral, zingila. *n.* ziurtasun; gauza erraz(a).
cinder *n.* herrauts.
cinema *n.* zine; zinegintza.
cinematography *n.* zinematografia.
cinerary *adj.* errautsezko.
cinerary urn *n.* errauskutxatila.
cinnamon *n. (bot.)* kanela.
cipher *n.* zenbaki. *n.* giltza, gako.
circa *prep.* inguru, inguruan (urteak).
circle *v.t./v.i.* biribildu, ingurukatu.
circle *n.* ingurubira, zirkulu, birunda, korru.
circuit *n.* jirabide. **A closed circuit.** Jirabide itxia. *n.* zirkuitu. *n.* inguru, lekune.
circuitous *adj.* oker, makur, okertsu, bihurri.
circular *n.* adierazia, idazki. *adj.* zirkular, biribil.
circularly *adv.* zirkularki.
circulate *v.i.* ibili, zirkulatu. *v.i.* jende artean nahasi. *v.t.* iraganarazi. *v.t.* barreiatu, hedatu.
circulation *n.* odolbilketa.
circumcise *v.t.* erdaindu.
circumcision *n.* erdainketa, erdainkuntza.
circumference *n. (geom.)* zirkunferentzia.
circumlocution *n.* hitzinguru, inguru-minguru, itzulinguru, estalki.
circumnavigate *v.t.* itsasbiratu, -(ar)i bira eman.
circumnavigation *n.* itsasbiraketa, itsasitzulbira.

circumscribe *v.t.* mugatu, laburtu, urritu.
circumspect *adj.* zuhur, sotil, urguri.
circumspection *n.* zuhurtasun, zentzutasun, sotiltasun.
circumstance *n.* gertaera, gertakizun, jazoera. *n. (pl.)* kondizio(ak), baldintza. *n.* kasu.
circumstantial *adj.* orduko.
circumvent *v.t.* galerazi; alderatu.
circus *n.* zirku.
cistern *n.* urontzi, uhaska, urtegi.
citadel *n.* babestoki.
citation *n.* aipamen.
cite *v.t.* aurkeztu. *v.t.* aipatu.
citer *n.* aipari, aipatzaile.
citizen *n.* hiritar, herritar.
citizenship *n.* hiritargo, hiritartasun, herritargo.
citric *adj.* zitriko.
city *n.* hiri. **Capital city.** Hiriburu.
city council *n.* udal.
city dweller *n.* hiritar, kaletar.
city hall *n.* udaletxe, aiuntamentu.
city limits *n.* herrimuga, udalbarruti.
city planner *n.* hirigin.
civic *adj.* hiriko.
civil *adj.* zibil. *adj.* adeitsu, gizatsu. *adj.* laiko.
civilian *n./adj.* zibil.
civility *n.* gizabidetasun, zibiltasun.
civilization *n.* zibilizazio.
civilize *v.t.* zibilizatu, gizabideratu.
civilized *adj.* gizabidetsu. **To become civilized.** Gizabideratu.
civilly *adv.* zibilki. *adv.* gizabidez, begirunez, itzalez.
civil war *n.* anaiguda.
clack *v.i.* karraskots egin.
clad *pret./p.part.* of *clothe*.
claim *v.t.* erreklamatu. *v.t.* baieztu, alegatu.
claim *n.* eskakizun, eskabide. *n.* meatze baten jabegoaren errejistrapena.
claimant *n.* auzilari. *n.* erregegai. *n.* meatz-jakinerazle.
clairvoyance *n.* argikuste.
clairvoyant *n.* barrenikusle, argikusle.
clam *n. (zool.)* txirla.
clamber *v.i.* lauzkatu, igo.
clammy *adj.* hotz-busti.
clamor *n.* zarataldi, zaratots, deiadar, astrapalada, hoszarata, aldarri.
clamorous *adj.* deadartsu, deadarti, danbadatsu, burrundaratsu.
clamorously *adv.* zarataka, aldarrika.
clamp *v.t.* grapatu.
clamp *n.* euskailu, euskarri, uztaigailu, finkagailu.
clan *n.* askazgo.
clandestine *adj.* isileko, isilpeko, gordekari.
clandestinely *adv.* isilgordeka, isilpean, gordeka.
clandestineness *n.* isilpetasun.
clang *v.i.* arranak jo.

clang *n.* metal-hots, arran-hots.

clank *v.i.* metal-hotsa egin.

clank *n.* metal-hots.

clap *v.t./v.i.* txalokatu, txalo egin, txalotu.

clap *n.* txalo; bapateko zarata. **Clap of thunder.** Trumoi. Ostots.

clapper *n.* txalotzaile. *n.* mihi, mingain, ezkilamihi, kanpaimihi.

clapping *n.* eskuzartaka, txaloketa.

clarification *n.* azalbide, azaldaketa, azaldura, argitzapen.

clarify *v.t./v.i.* argi egin, argierazi, argiztatu, argitu.

clarinet *n.* (mus.) klarintxo, klarinete.

clarion *n.* (mus.) turuta.

clarity *n.* argitasun, gardentasun, argialdi. *n.* gogoargitasun.

clary *n.* (bot.) zauribelar.

clash *v.i.* talka egin *v.i.* aurrez-aurre egon, bat ez etorri.

clash *n.* talka. *n.* liskar, eztabaida, haserre.

clasp *v.t.* besartu. *v.t.* grapatu.

clasp *n.* kakotxa, kortxete. *n.* bosteko, eskutinka.

class *n.* mota, talde, sail. *n.* gradu, maila, klase. *n.* ikastalde, ikaslego, ikasleria. *n.* ikastaro. *n.* klase, ikasgela. *n.* kalitate, bikaintasun. *n.* maila, klase (hegazkinetan, trenetan). *n.* gizalerro, klase, gizasail.

classic *adj.* klasiko.

classical *adj.* klasiko.

classically *adv.* klasikoki.

classicism *n.* klasizismo.

classifiable *adj.* sailkagarri, motagarri.

classification *n.* sailketa, sailkapen, sailkaketa, kidekapen, klasifikapen.

classifier *n.* kidekatzaile, sailkatzaile.

classify *v.t.* klasifikatu, sailkatu, mailakatu, motatu, kalifikatu, kidekatu.

classmate *n.* ikaskide, eskolalagun.

classroom *n.* ikasareto, ikasgela, ikastegi.

clatter *n.* burrundara, burrunba, burrunbada.

clause *n.* perpaus(a), esaldi.

clavicle *n.* (anat.) giltzezur, soinezur, lepauztai.

claw *v.t./v.i.* erpekatu, atzaparkatu.

claw *n.* azkazal, hatzazal.

clay *n.* buztin. **Red clay.** Buztingorri. **Piece of clay.** Buztinki. **Clay pot.** Buztinontzi. **Clay pit.** Buztintoki.

clean *v.t./v.i.* garbitu, xahutu, ikuzi, txukundu.

clean *adj.* garbi, txukun, xahu.

cleaner *n.* garbitzaile, garbikin, garbikari, ikuzle, xahutzaile.

cleaning *n.* txukunketa.

clenliness *n.* txukuntasun, xahutasun, araztasun, garbitasun.

cleanly *adv.* garbiki, txukunki, xahuki.

cleanness *n.* garbitasun, xahutasun, txukuntasun.

cleanse *v.t.* garbitu, xahutu, ikuztu.

clear *v.t./v.i.* argitu. *v.i.* (up) atertu, oskarbitu, goiargitu, deslainotu. *v.i.* (out) irten, alde egin, joan.

clear *adj.* zohar, argi, argitsu; garbi. *adj.* dirdiratsu, dirdiradun, dir-dir, dis-dis. *adj.* argi (margoak). *adj.* orbaingabe. *adj.* ageri, agerizko, agiriko. *adj.* garden. *adj.* adigarri, ulergarri, ulerterraz. *adj.* zohardi, aterri.

clearance *n.* kitapen.

clearing *n.* oskarbiarte, ostarte; aterrune.

clearly *adv.* argiki, argiro, argi ta garbí, garbi-garbi, garbiro, zehatz- mehatz, garbiki, gardenki. *adv.* agerian, bistan.

clearness *n.* argitasun, garbitasun.

cleat *n.* listoi. *n.* tako (kirol-oinetakoak). *n.* ziri, taket.

cleavage *n.* arrailgune, arrailadura, arrakala. *n.* bulartarte.

cleave *v.i.* (to) itsatsi. *v.t./v.i.* arrailatu, arrakalatu, hirrikatu.

cleaver *n.* arrakalatzaile. *n.* harakinaren aizto(a).

clef *n.* (mus.) giltza.

cleft *n.* brintza, zirrikitu.

clemency *n.* barkakoitasun, barkazaletasun.

clench *v.t.* estutu, hertsitu.

clench *n.* hertsidura, hertsipen.

clergy *n.* apezeria.

clergyman *n.* elizgizon.

cleric *n.* elizgizon.

clerical *adj.* apezkoi, klerikal.

clerk *n.* idazmutil, notarimutil, bulegari.

clever *adj.* buruargi, burudun, jakintsu, burutsu. *adj.* azkar, bizkor, mainatsu.

cleverly *adv.* buruargiz.

cleverness *n.* txera, zorroztasun.

cliche *n.* klitxe.

click *n.* idazmakinaz egiten den zaratatxoa; joaldi.

client *n.* bezero.

clientele *n.* bezeria.

cliff *n.* erortoki, malkortegi, malkor, amildegi, jausleku.

climate *n.* aro, egutaro; -aro. *n.* giro, klima.

climatic *adj.* klimaren; klima-.

climatology *n.* klimatologia.

climax *n.* gorenaldi, klimax.

climb *v.t./v.i.* igo, eskalatu, lauzkatu.

climb *n.* igonaldi, igoera.

climber *n.* igokari, igotzaile, gorakari; mendizale.

clime *n.* giro, klima; egutaro.

clinch *v.t.* gogorki estutu. *v.t.* amaitu, bukatu. *v.t.* irabazi, eskuratu. *v.i.* aurrez-aurre borrokan egin.

clinch *n.* euskarri.

cling *v.i.* itsatsi, heldu.

clinic *n.* sendategi, eritegi, gaisotegi.

clinical *adj.* grinagabe.

clink *n.* klink.

clip *v.t.* artaziz moztu, guraizez moztu. *v.t.* hitza laburtu.
clip *n.* matxarda, gako, papelgako. *n.* guraizekada, artazikada.
clipper *n.* itsasontzi laster(ra).
clippers *n. (pl.)* mandaguraizak, mandartazi.
clique *n.* laguntalde.
clitoris *n. (anat.)* emazakil.
cloak *n.* kapa.
cloakroom *n.* jantzileku, jantzitoki, kakotegi, aldagela.
clock *n.* ordulari, erloju, orenlari. **Alarm clock.** Iratzargailu. Esnaerloju. **Wall clock.** Hormaerloju.
clockwork *n.* erlojuerraiak, erlojuaren itzulika.
clod *n.* lurkoskor, lurmutur, zotal, mokor, zokil, zokor. *n.* ergeltzar, iñozo.
clodhopper *n.* zapataundi.
clog *n.* trasko.
cloister *v.t.* konbenturatu.
cloister *n.* herstegi. *n.* komentu. *n.* ezparru, barruti, barrendegi.
closable *adj.* itxigarri.
close *v.t./v.i.* itxi, hertsi.
close *n.* amaiera, amai, azken, bukaera. *adj.* alboko, aldeko, hur, gertu, hurbil, hurreko, ondoko, gertuko. *adj.* min, mami, kuttun, bihotzeko. *adj.* zehatz. *adj.* guztizko, oro, bete. *adj.* itogarri, itotzeko. *adj.* estu, hertsi, mehar. *adv.* hurbil, hurrean, ondoan, gertu, hur.
closed *adj.* itxita, hertsirik, itxi(a).
closely *adv.* hurbil, hurrean, ondoan, gertu, hur. *adv.* zehazki.
closeness *n.* hurbiltasun, hurkotasun, gertutasun, hurretasun.
closer *adj. (comp.)* hurbilago. **To get closer.** Hurbilagotu. *n.* itxitzaile.
closet *n.* kakotegi. *n.* ontzitegi, arasa.
close-up *n.* argazkiaren lehen plano(a).
closure *n.* itxialdi, itxiera.
clot *v.t./v.i.* odoluritu, odolguritu, odola bildu.
clot *n.* odolguri, odolbatu, odolbildu.
cloth *n.* oihal, trapu, ehun. *n.* zapi.
clothe *v.t.* soinekotu, jantzi.
clothes *n.* jantzi, erropa.
clothes closet *n.* jantziaraza, kakotegi.
clothes hanger *n.* zintzilgailu, kako.
clothesline *n.* idortegi, idortoki.
clothespin *n.* pintza.
clothing *n.* jantzi, janzki, soineko.
clottable *adj.* mamigarri.
cloud *v.t./v.i. (batzutan* up*-ekin)* hodeitu, hodeiztatu, goibeldu, hodeimordotu. *v.i.* **(up, over)** lausotu, lanbrotu, gandutu, lainoztatu.
cloud *n.* hodei (LN,Z,U).
cloudburst *n.* euri jasa.
cloudiness *n.* hodeitasun, goibeltasun.
cloudless *adj.* oskarbi, hodeigabeko.
cloudy *adj.* hodeitsu, ilunbetsu, goibel, hodeidun. **To get cloudy.** Hodeitu.

adj. hondartsu.
clout *n.* indar, ahalmen, eskubide (politika).
clove *n. (bot.)* iltze-belar. *n.* atal; -atal.
clover *n. (bot.)* hirusta, sekulabelar, pagotxa.
clown *n.* barregile, barrekari, pailaso.
club *n.* berga, ildoki. *n.* golf-eko makila. *n.* basto. *n.* lagunbatz, klub.
clubhouse *n.* klub (etxe).
cluck *v.i.* kolokatu, kakarakatu.
cluck *n.* kakara.
clue *n.* ezagubide.
clump *n.* pilo, zotil, zokor. *n.* zapaldura; oinetako hots(a).
clumsily *adv.* baldarki, ganoragabeki, trakeski, dorpeki.
clumsiness *n.* taxugabekeria, trakestasun, baldartasun, dorpetasun, ganoragabekeria.
clumsy *adj.* taxugabe, baldar, ganoragabe(ko), trakets, moldagaitz. **To be clumsy.** Trakestu, dorpetu.
cluster *v.t./v.i.* mulkokatu, mulkotu.
cluster *n.* luku, molko, mordo, pilo, multzo.
clutch *n. (mech.)* enbrage. *n.* orakada, oraldi.
clutter *n.* nahaste, nahasketa.
co- *(gram.)* -kide, -ide.
coach *n.* saiaketari, entrenadore (kirolak). *n.* gurdi; karroza. *n.* bagoi. *n.* bigarren klaseko eserleku(a).
coachman *n.* gurtzain.
coagulable *adj.* mamigarri.
coagulant *adj.* gatzatzaile.
coagulate *v.t./v.i.* odolguritu, odolgogortu.
coagulated *adj.* batu(a), guritsu.
coagulation *n.* gatzaketa, gatzapen, odolbatu, odolbildu.
coal *n.* ikatz, harrikatz.
coalesce *v.i.* batu, bildu, elkartu, bat egin.
coalition *n.* elkarketa, koalizio.
coarse *adj.* zakar, latz, trauskil; zarpail, lakar, lakatz. *adj.* astaputz, zakar; arrunt.
coarsely *adv.* oiheski.
coarseness *n.* oiheskeria, oihestasun, zakardura, zakarkeria, zarpailkeria, arrunkeria, trauskiltasun.
coast *n.* itsasalde, itsasbazter, kostalde.
coastal *adj.* itsasaldeko, itsasbazterreko, itsasertzeko, itsasondoko, kostako. **Coastal village.** Itsaserri. **The coastal fish.** Itsasbazterreko arrantza.
coast guard *n.* kostazain.
coastline *n.* kostalde, itsasalde, itsasbazter.
coat *n.* jantzigaineko. **Coat of armor.** Altzairujantzi.
coat hanger *n.* jantzigako.
coating *n.* eskualdi, margoaldi, emanaldi.

coat-of-arms n. erradola, armarri.
co-author n. eginkide.
coax v.t./v.i. (batzutan **into** edo **to**-rekin) zuriketaz sinestarazi; jasapenez lortu.
cob n. artamukutz.
cobalt n. (chem.) kobalto.
cobble v.t. oinetakoak egin. v.t. harlanduz estali.
cobbler n. oinetakogile, oskigile, zapatagin, zapatari. n. fruituz egindako pastel mota bat.
cobblestone n. harlandu.
cobra n. kobrasuge.
cobweb n. amarausare.
cocaine n. (chem.) kokaina.
coccyx n. ipurkonkor, ipurtezur, ipurtxuntxur.
cock n. oilar. **Cock's crow.** Oilarraren kukurruku.
cock-a-doodle-doo n. kikiriki, kukurruku.
cockeyed adj. begizehar.
cockfight n. oilargudu, oilarjoko.
cockiness n. oilarkeria.
cockpit n. pilotoaren kabina. n. oilarren burrukaleku(a).
cockroach n. (zool.) labazomorro, mamurio.
cockscomb n. kukula.
cocktail n. koktel.
cocky adj. harroxka, harro, handiputz, harroputz.
cocoa n. (bot.) kakao.
coconut n. (bot.) koko.
coconut tree n. (bot.) kokondo.
cocoon n. zetakuzku, zetazorro.
cod n. (zool.) makailo.
C.O.D. adj. postordain.
coddle v.t. mainatu.
code n. araudi, arautegi, legesorta, arausail, legebilduma, legeria. **Penal code.** Zigorlege. n. giltza.
codfish n. (zool.) makailo.
codification n. legebilketa.
codify v.t. sailkatu, arautu. v.t. kodetu, kodifikatu.
co-ed n. unibertsitateko ikasle (neska).
co-education n. neska-mutilen hezketa.
coefficient n. koefiziente.
coerce v.t. bortxatu, indarkatu, behartu, derrigortu.
coercion n. bortxa, bortxaketa, bortxakeria.
coercive adj. beharkor, bortxagarri, bortxari.
coercively n. beharrez.
coeval n./adj. adinkide.
coexist v.i. elkarrekin izan.
coexistence n. elkarbizitza, bizikidetasun, bizikidego, izankidego, izankidetasun.
coffee n. kafe.
coffee plant n. (bot.) kafetondo.
coffee pot n. kafegailu, kafetontzi.
coffee shop n. kafetegi, akeitetxe.

coffer n. dirukutxa.
coffin n. hilkutxa, zerraldo.
cog n. (mech.) hagin.
cogent adj. sinistarazle.
cogitate v.i./v.t. gogartu, pentsatu, ausnartu.
cogitation n. gogaketa, gogarpen, gogorakizun.
cognac n. koinak.
cognate n. gauza berdintsu(ak), pertsona berdintsu(ak). adj. antzeko; odoleko, odolkide.
cognitive adj. ezagukor.
cognizance n. ezaguera, ezaupen, jakite; ulerketa.
cognizant adj. ikastun, ikasi(a), jakintsu.
cognoscibility n. ezagungarritasun, ezaugarritasun.
cohabit v.i. elkarrekin bizi, bizikidetu.
cohabitation n. bizikidetza, elkarbizitza, bizikidetasun, bizilaguntza.
cohere v.i. itsatsi, batu, elkartu.
coherence n. barnelotura, barrenlotura.
coherent adj. barrenloturazko.
cohesion n. itsaspen, atxikitasun, elkartasun.
cohort n. erromatarren soldadu talde(a). n. lagunkide.
coif n. kapela, txano.
coiffure n. zoronga.
coil v.t./v.i. biribilkatu, kiribildu, kiribilatu.
coil n. kiribil.
coilable adj. biribilgarri, biribilkakor.
coin v.t. diru moldetu, txanpondu. v.t. asmatu, sortu.
coin n. txanpon, dirutxo.
coinage n. dirugintza. n. diru-sistima.
coincide v.i. (batzutan **with**-ekin) doitu, une berean gertatu.
coincidence n. ustekabe, ezuste, kasualitate.
coincident adj. adosgarri.
coincidental adj. zorizko.
coincidentally adv. alabeharrez, ezustez, alabeharrean.
coitus n. sexujoketa, estaldura.
coke n. (cap.) Coca-Cola. n. kokaina. n. ikatz erre(a).
colander n. iragazkin, iragazontzi, iragazgailu.
cold n. hotz, hozdura, hozketa, hozkirri. n. katarro. adj. hotz, hozdun. adj. odolgabe(ko), sentigabe, geldo. adv. bapatean, tupustean. adv. osoro, zeharo, osoki, erabat, guztiz. adv. oso ondo, ezin hobeki, bikainki.
coldly adv. hozki.
coldness n. hozdura, hoztasun.
cold snap n. hozgiro, hormate, hozte, hotzaldi, hotzaro.
coleric adj. amorruzko.
colic n. sabeleko, berazko, kakeri, sabelmin.

collaborate *v.i.* *(on edo* **with***)* lankidetu.
collaboration *n.* elkarlaguntza, elkarrekintza, lankidego, lankidetasun. *n.* elkarlan.
collaborator *n.* lagunkide.
collapse *v.i.* erori, gainbeheratu, zarbaildu. *v.i./v.t.* porrot egin.
collapse *n.* porrokaldi, porrotaldi, porroketa. *n.* erorketa, jausketa.
collar *n.* alkondaridun, alkondara-idun. *n.* garranga.
collar bone *n.* *(anat.)* giltzezur.
collateral *n.* berme, herresa.
colleague *n.* lagun, lagunkide, kide.
collect *v.t./v.i.* bilduma egin, bildumatu, kobratu, bildu.
collectable *n.* kobragarri, bilgarri.
collection *n.* bilduma, bilduketa, bilketa, sorta; -sorta, -keta, -tza. **Collection of books.** Liburu-sorta. *n.* kobraketa, kobrantza, eskebilketa; -keta, -tza.
collective *adj.* guztiekiko, multzozko, taldeko.
collectively *adv.* batez, mordoan.
collector *n.* dirubazaile, dirubiltzaile, kobratzaile, eskebatzaile, eskebiltzaile. *n.* batzaile, bildumari (L,U), bildumatzaile, bilketari, biltzaile.
college *n.* unibertsitate, ikastetxe.
collegiate *adj.* unibersitateko.
collide *v.i.* *(batzutan* **with***-ekin)* topo egin, tupust egin, jo egin, talkatu, talka egin, elkar jo.
collie *n.* *(zool.)* eskoziar artzainzakur.
collier *n.* ikatzmeatzari.
collision *n.* talka, tope, txoke, zanpa, topaldi.
colloquial *adj.* herrikoi (hizkuntza).
colloquy *n.* mintzaldi.
collusion *n.* elkarkeria.
cologne *n.* kolonia.
colon *n.* *(anat.)* hestelodi. *n.* bi puntu.
colonel *n.* *(mil.)* koronel.
colonial *adj.* koloniako, koloniar.
colonialism *n.* kolonialismo.
colonist *n.* kolonitar, populatzaile.
colonizable *adj.* koloniazagarri.
colonization *n.* koloniakuntza, koloniazaketa.
colonize *v.t./v.i.* kolonizatu.
colony *n.* kolonia.
color *v.t./v.i.* margotu, koloreztu, koloreztatu. *v.i.* lotsagorritu.
color *n.* margo, kolore.
Colorado *n.* *(geog.)* Estatu Batuetako estatu bat.
coloration *n.* koloretasun, koloraketa, kolorapen.
colored *adj.* koloredun, koloretsu, kolorezko, margodun, margozko. *adj.* beltz (pertsona).
colorful *adj.* koloredun, kolorezko, koloretsu.
coloring *n.* koloraketa, kolorapen,

koloretasun.
colorless *adj.* koloregabe, margogabe, margul.
colossal *adj.* handitzar. *adj.* bikain.
colossus *n.* erraldoi.
colt *n.* *(zool.)* moxal, zaldiko, zaldikume, zalditxo, pottoka.
column *n.* habe, zutabe, zutoin. **Stone column.** Zutarri.
columnist *n.* kazetari, artikulari.
coma *n.* *(med.)* koma; hilaldi.
Comanche *n.* Komantxe, Ameriketako indio mota bat.
comb *v.t.* orraztu, ilea apaindu.
comb *n.* orrazi.
combat *v.t./v.i.* *(v.i.* **with***)* borrokan egin, borrokatu.
combat *n.* borroka, borrokaldi, gudaketa.
combatant *n.* borrokagile, borrokalari.
combative *adj.* burrukalari.
comber *n.* orrazle, orraztaile, orraztari.
combination *n.* konbinaketa, konbinapen.
combine *v.t./v.i.* *(v.i. batzutan* **with***-ekin)* bat egin.
combustible *n.* errekin, erregai, sugai. *adj.* erregarri, sugarri.
combustion *n.* erretura, erretzapen, errekuntza.
come *v.i.* etorri. *v.i.* *(about)* gertatu. *v.i.* *(across)* topo egin. *v.i.* *(after)* zerbaiten bila ibili, jarraitu, zerbaiten atzetik ibili. *v.i.* *(along)* aurreratu. *v.i.* *(around, to)* bere senera itzuli. *v.i.* *(by)* -z etorri; lortu. *v.i.* *(clean)* dena aitortu. *v.i.* *(up with)* ideia bat eman.
comeback *n.* kontraerantzun. *n.* galdutako izen onaren berreskuraketa.
comedian *n.* barreragile, komedilari.
comedy *n.* komedia.
comeliness *n.* politasun, lerdentasun, txairotasun, edertasun, liraintasun.
comestible *n.* janari, jaki. *adj.* jangarri.
comet *n.* *(astron.)* kometa.
comfort *v.t.* kontsolatu.
comfort *n.* erosotasun, aisetasun (L,U). *n.* gozagarri, kontsolamendu.
comfortable *adj.* eroso, patxadazko, laso.
comfortableness *n.* erosotasun.
comfortably *adv.* eroso, eroski, aiseki, lasai.
comforter *n.* kontsolatzaile. *n.* ohestalki, ohegaineko.
comforting *adj.* kontsolagarri, gozogarri, alaigarri.
comfortless *adj.* itzal, atxekabendun, pozgabe, kontsolagabe.
comfy *adj.* eroso.
comic *n.* komiki, komiko. *n.* komedilari. *adj.* komiko.
comical *adj.* komiko.
comically *adv.* komikoki.
comic book *n.* komiki.
coming *n.* etorrera, helduera, etorraldi.

comma *n. (gram.)* koma.
command *v.t./v.i.* agindu, agintaritu, sailburutu, manatu.
command *n.* nagusitasun, nagusitza, nagusigo, aitzindarigo. *n.* agindu. *n.* hizkuntzaren menperatasun(a).
commandant *n. (mil.)* komandante.
commander *n. (mil.)* komandante, manatzaile.
commandment *n.* manu, agindu, aginte. **The ten commandments.** Hamar aginduak.
commemorate *v.t.* oroitarazi, ospatu.
commemoration *n.* oroitzaldi.
commemorative *adj.* oroikarrizko.
commence *v.i./v.t.* hasi.
commencement *n.* hastapen, hasiera. *n.* graduazio, ikasketen bukaeran egiten den zeremonia.
commend *v.t.* goietsi.
commendable *adj.* goragarri, goresgarri, laudagarri, txalogarri.
commendation *n.* laudorio.
commensurate *adj.* araberako, erazko.
comment *n.* ohar.
commentary *n.* ohar, adierazpen, azalpen.
commentator *n.* azaldari, azaltzaile.
commerce *n.* merkatalgo, salerosi, salerosketa, salerospen, merkataritza.
commercial *adj.* merkatal, merkagarri. **Commercial law.** Merkatal legetza. *n.* iragarki (telebista, irrati).
commercialization *n.* komertzialpen.
commercialize *v.t.* merkaturatu, merkataleztu, komertzialdu.
commercially *adv.* merkalegez, merkatalki.
commiserate *v.t./v.i. (v.i.* **with-***ekin)* errukitu, urrikal izan.
commiseration *n.* erruki, urrikalmendu, kupida.
commissariat *n.* komisartegi.
commissary *n.* jantegi, kafetegi. *n.* komisari.
commission *n.* mandataritza, mandatu.
commissioner *n.* komisari. *n.* udaletxeko batzarkide.
commit *v.t.* egin, bete. *v.t.* kargu eman. *v.t.* sartu (eritegian). *v.t.* beregain hartu, hitz eman.
commitment *n.* konpromisu, hitz.
committee *n.* batzorde.
commode *n.* arasa. *n.* pixontzitegi.
commodity *n.* merkatalgai.
common *adj.* arrunt, nolanahiko, soil, xume, guztitariko, xehe. *adj.* askoren, denen, orotar, guztien. *adj.* sarriko, noiznahiko, ohizko, ohiturazko. *adj.* elkar. *adj.* edozelako, saileko. *n. (pl.)* herrilurrak.
commoner *n.* herrixumeko, plebeio.
commonly *adv.* arruntki, eskuarki.
common market *n.* elkarmerkatu.
commonplace *adj.* badaezbadako, arrunt.

common sense *n.* sen, zentzu.
commonwealth *n.* herribatze.
commotion *n.* barnemugida, barrenmugida, zauzkada.
communal *adj.* herriko.
commune *v.i.* **(with)** hitz egin. *v.i.* Jaun(a) hartu.
commune *n.* komuna.
communicability *n.* komunikagarritasun.
communicable *adj.* komunikagarri.
communicate *v.t./v.i.* komunikatu, iragarri, jakinerazi, aditzera eman.
communication *n.* komunikazio, komunikapen. *n.* mezu. *n.* sarrera, igarobide, iraganleku. *n. (pl.)* komunikabideak.
communicative *adj.* komunikatzaile, komunikakor, kidegarri.
communicator *n.* komunikatzaile.
communion *n. (eccl.)* Gurejaun, jaunartze, komunio. *n.* komunikazio, komunikapen.
communism *n. (pol.)* komunismo.
communist *n. (pol.)* komunista, gorri.
community *n.* komunitate, erkidego.
commute *v.t.* zigorra laburtu.
commuter *n.* egunero lanerako bidean 30-40 mila egin behar izaten dituen langilea.
compact *v.t.* gorpuztu, gauzatu, trinkotu.
compact *adj.* trinko, tinko.
compactness *n.* trinkotasun.
companion *n.* adiskide, kideko.
companionable *adj.* gizakoi, adiskidetsu, lagunarteko.
companionship *n.* adiskidetasun, kidetasun, kidego.
company *n.* lagunarte, laguntalde. *n.* adiskidetasun, kidetasun, adiskidego. *n.* ikusle(ak), deitu(ak). *n. (econ.)* merkataletxe, enpresa. *n. (mil.)* ehuneko.
comparable *adj.* paregarri, parekide, gonbaragarri, pareko, erkagarri.
comparative *adj.* gonbaraziozko.
compare *v.t./v.i. (v.i., batzutan* **with-***ekin)* gonbaratu, berdinkatu, parekatu, erkatu.
comparison *n.* berdintza, gonbarabide, gonbaraketa, konparazio.
compartment *n.* tokibakan.
compass *n.* itsasorratz, iparrorratz, konpas(a).
compassion *n.* erruki, bihozberatasun, bihozbiguntasun, urrikalmendu, kupida.
compassionate *adj.* errukior, errukitsu, bihozdun, gupidatsu, samurbera, urrikalkor.
compassionately *adv.* errukiz.
compaternity *n.* aitakidego, aitakidetasun.
compatibility *n.* bateragarritasun, elkargarritasun, gogaidego, gogaidetasun.

compatible *adj.* bateragarri, baterakor, elkargarri, gogaide. **To be compatible with.** Gogaide izan.

compatriot *n.* herkide.

compel *v.t./v.i.* derrigortu, beharrarazi, behartu, bortxatu.

compelling *adj.* bultzegile.

compendium *n.* laburrera.

compensate *v.t./v.i. (batzutan for edo with-ekin)* irainordaindu, kalteordaindu, indemnizatu, ordaindu.

compensation *n.* ordain, ordaindiru, ordainketa, pagu, indemnizazio, irainorde, kalteordain.

compensator *n.* irainordainle, kalteordaintzaile.

compensatory *adj.* kalteordaintzaile.

compete *v.i.* lehiatu, dematu.

competence *n.* gaitasun, trebetasun.

competency *n.* gaitasun, trebetasun.

competent *adj.* ganoradun, gai.

competition *n.* lehiaketa, desafio, txapelketa, norgehiagoketa, sariketa, dema.

competitive *adj.* lehiakor, lehiagarri.

competitively *adv.* norgehiagoka, lehiaka, zeingehiagoka.

competitiveness *n.* lehiakortasun.

competitor *n.* lehiaketari, lehiakide, desafiatzaile; probalari.

compilation *n.* batuketa, bilketa, pilaketa, multzoketa.

compile *v.t.* batu, bildu, pilatu; bildumatu.

compiler *n.* bildumari, gordetzaile.

complacency *n.* ederrespen, laketasun.

complacent *adj.* atseginkor.

complain *v.i. (askotan about-ekin)* kexatu, deitoratu, arranguratu, hileta jo.

complainer *n.* auhendari.

complaint *n.* auhen, deitore, arrenkura, kexa, kexadura.

complement *v.t.* osatu.

complement *n.* gehigarri, osakin, osagarri, betegarri.

complementariness *n.* osatasun, osabidetasun.

complementary *adj.* osatzaile, osabidezko, osagarri, osagarrizko, osakor.

complete *v.t.* osatu, bete, kunplitu. *v.t.* azkendu, amaitu, bukatu, burutu.

complete *adj.* oso, erabateko.

completely *adv.* guztiz, erabat, arras, biziki, oso, zeharo.

completeness *n.* osatasun, guztikotasun.

completion *n.* betedura, betealdi, egiketa.

complex *adj.* askotariko, korapilotsu. *n.* bazkun, pilo.

complexion *n.* larrugain.

complexity *n.* zailtasun.

compliance *n.* menpetasun, menekotasun.

complicate *v.t.* mordoildu, mordoilatu, katramildu, lardakatu, lardaskatu.

complicated *adj.* korapilotsu, bihurri.

complication *n.* korapilo, xurruburrukeria.

complicity *n.* elkarkeria, ohoinkidetasun, gaizkidego, gaizkidetasun, errukidetasun.

compliment *v.t./v.i.* losintxatu, lausengatu, balakatu, laudoriotu.

compliment *n.* losintxa, balaku, lausengu, hitzerditxo. *n. (pl.)* eskumuinak, goraintziak.

complimentary *adj.* goresmenezko. *adj.* dohako.

comply *v.i. (batzutan with-ekin)* konformatu, begiratu.

component *n.* osagai, osaki, osagarri; gaiki. *adj.* eratzaile, osatzaile.

comportment *n.* jokabide, jokaera.

compose *v.t./v.i.* konposatu, soinu egin.

composed *adj.* lasai, trankil. *adj.* osatutako.

composer *n.* soinuegile, musikagile, konposatzaile.

composite *adj.* konposatu(a).

composition *n.* egitura, konposaketa. *n.* osaera. *n.* idazketa, idazkuntza, idazlan. *n. (mus.)* konposizio; konposaketa.

compost *n.* ongarri, zabarrak.

composure *n.* erabide, eratasun.

compote *n.* konpota.

compound *n.* nahasketa, nahastura, nahaste. *n.* inguru mugatu batean dagoen jabe baten etxe-multzoa. *adj.* nahastu(a), nahasi(a). *adj.* konposatu(a).

compound word *n.* hitzelkartu.

comprehend *v.t.* konprenitu, ulertu, aditu.

comprehensibility *n.* ulergarritasun, konprenigarritasun, adierreztasun, adigarritasun.

comprehensible *adj.* ulergarri, adigarri, konprenigarri, adikor, gogagarri.

comprehension *n.* ulerbide, ulerkuntza, ulerketa.

comprehensive *adj.* guztizko.

comprehensiveness *n.* guztizkotasun.

compress *v.t.* hertsarazi, hertsatu, zapatu, trinkotu.

compress *n. (med.)* konpresa, txaplata. *n.* trinkagailu (paketeak egiteko).

compressible *adj.* estukoi.

compression *n.* hersketa, zapaketa.

compressor *n. (mech.)* konprimagailu.

comprise *v.t.* besartu.

compromise *v.i.* arazo bat konpondu bi aldeek amore emanez.

compromise *n.* konponbide, erdibide.

compulsion *n.* bortxaketa, bortxaldi, hertsapen.

compulsive *adj.* bultzarazle, bultzeragile, porrokatu.
compulsively *adv.* behar-beharrez, premiaz, eginbestez.
compulsorily *adv.* behar-beharrez, premiaz, bortxaz, derrigorrez.
compulsoriness *n.* derrigortasun.
compulsory *adj.* beharrezko, derrigorrezko, bortxagarri, nahitaezko, ezinbesteko, betebeharreko.
compunction *n.* damu, garbai.
computability *n.* konputagarritasun.
computable *adj.* konputagarri.
computation *n.* kontaketa, zenbaketa.
compute *v.t./v.i.* kontatu, zenbatu.
computer *n.* konputagailu, konputadore, ordenadore, programailu.
comrade *n.* lagun, kide, erkide.
comraderie *n.* adiskidetasun.
con *n.* aldetxar. *n.* giltzapeko, espetxeko.
concatenation *n.* kateamendu.
concave *adj.* zokodun, ahur.
concavity *n.* ahurtasun, hutsune.
conceal *v.t.* ezkutarazi, ezkutatu, gorde, ostendu, itzalpetu.
concealable *adj.* izkutagarri, gordegarri.
concealer *n.* estaltzaile, ezkutatzaile, gordetzaile.
concealment *n.* estalpen, ezkutapen, kukukeria.
concede *v.t./v.i.* baietz esan.
conceit *n.* harropuzkeria, handikeria, harrokeria, haizepuzkeria. *n.* burutapen, burutazio. *n.* kasketaldi, nahikeria.
conceited *adj.* harroputz, handinahiko, handinahi.
conceitedly *adv.* harrokeriaz, harroki, harropuzkeriaz.
conceivable *adj.* irudigarri, pentsagarri.
conceivably *adv.* baliteke.
conceive *v.t./v.i.* asmatu, iruditu. *v.t./v.i.* erne, sortu.
concentrate *v.t./v.i.* kontzentratu, barneratu.
concentrated *adj.* kontzentratu(a) *adj.* bortitz.
concentration *n.* kontzentrazio.
concentric *adj.* erdirakor.
concept *n.* burutapen, burutazio, gogai.
conception *n.* burutapen, burutazio, gogorapen. *n.* sorkunde, sortze. *n.* sorketa, sorrera. *n.* ulerkuntza, adikuntza, ulerketa.
concern *v.t.* **(oneself with** *edo* **about-***ekin)* arduratu, egoki izan. *v.t.* egoki izan, egokitu.
concern *n.* axola, arreta, arrangura.
concerned *adj.* kezkadun.
concerning *prep./adv.* -(a)ri buruz, -z, buruzko, -(a)ri dagokionez, bederen.
concert *n.* akordio, itun, hitzarmen. *n.*

(mus.) kontzertu, kantaldi, musikaldi, abestaldi.
concerted *adj.* kidetu(a), bateratu(a), parekatu(a).
concession *n.* lagapen.
concierge *n.* giltzain, giltzari.
conciergerie *n.* etxezaindegi, etxezaingela.
concierto *n.* konzertu.
conciliate *v.t.* desaserretu.
conciliation *n.* adiskidepen, elkartze.
conciliator *n.* bakearazle, adiskidetzaile.
conciliatory *adj.* bakegarri, bakekor, etorkor.
concise *adj.* labur, murritz, motz.
concisely *adv.* laburki.
conciseness *n.* laburrera, laburtasun, murriztasun.
conclave *n.* bilera, batzar, biltzar; kardinal bilera.
conclude *v.t./v.i.* ondoretu.
conclusion *n.* azken, buru; hitzaldioste, azkenburu. *n.* ondorio, ondoren, aterakizun. *n.* erabaki.
conclusive *adj.* erabateko.
conclusively *adv.* azkenez.
concoct *v.t.* nahasi, nahastu. *v.t.* gezurrak asmatu.
concoction *n.* nahaste, nahasketa, nahastura.
concord *n.* gogaidego, gogaidetasun.
concordance *n.* irizkidetasun.
concourse *n.* bide zabal(a), kale zabal(a), leku zabal(a).
concrete *n.* hormigoi, zementu. *adj.* tinko, trinko, gogor, gotor. *adj.* zehatz; benetako. *adj.* berezi, konkretu. *adj.* hormigoizko.
concretely *adv.* zehatz-mehatz, zehazki, konkretuki.
concretion *n.* zehazpen, zehazketa.
concubine *n.* ohaide, ohekide, ohelagun, sasiemazte.
concupiscence *n.* haragi.
concur *v.i.* adostu, bateratu. *v.i.* une berean gertatu, batera gertatu. *v.i.* elkarlanean aritu, lagundu.
concurrence *n.* bateratasun. *n.* adostasun.
concurrent *adj.* bateratsu, aldibereko. *adj.* lankide.
concussion *n.* shock.
condemn *v.t.* kondenatu, txarretsi, gaitzetsi.
condemnable *adj.* gaitzesgarri, erdeinagarri, arbuiagarri, kondenagarri.
condemnation *n.* gaitzezpen.
condemnatory *adj.* gaitzezko.
condemned *adj.* hilerrudun, heriotz-zigordun.
condemner *n.* gaitzesle, kondenatzaile.
condensable *adj.* kondentsagarri.
condensation *n.* kondentsapen, kondentsazio, langar. *n.* laburpen,

laburtza.
condense *v.t./v.i.* kondentsatu,
ihinztatu. *v.t.* laburragotu, labur egin.
condenser *n.* kondentsagailu.
condescend *v.i.* amor egin, amor
eman.
condescending *adj.* amoremale.
condescension *n.* amoregite.
condiment *n.* adoba, gozagarri, ongai,
ongarri.
condition *v.t.* kirol-txapelketa
denboraldia baino lehen
gorputz-prestaketa burutu. *v.t.*
kondizionatu, baldintzatu,
baldintzapetu.
condition *n.* baldintza, baldintzapen,
kondizio. *n.* hitzarmenaren zati
berezia. *n.* gizamaila.
conditional *adj.* baldinkor,
baldintzezko, kondiziozko,
baldinezko, baldinpeko. *n. (gram.)*
baldintzera.
conditioning *n.* baldintzazkotasun.
conditioning *n.* kondizionamendu. *n.*
kirolariek txapelketa denboraldia
baino lehen burutzen duten
gorputz-prestaketa.
condole *v.i.* **(with)** dolu eman.
condolence *n.* *(pl.)* dolumin,
garbaikide.
condominium *n.* kondominio,
apartamentu.
condone *v.t.* barkatu; eraman, pairatu.
v.t. ezikusi egin.
conducive *adj.* aldeko, faboragarri.
conduct *v.t.* zuzenbidetu, eraman,
gidatu. *v.t.* ubideratu, ubidetu,
hodiratu. *v.t./v.i.* orkesta zuzendu.
conduct *n.* jokabide, portaera, jokaera,
gizalege. *n.* erabilketa, erabilaldi,
eginbide.
conductible *adj.* eramangarri.
conduction *n.* uroditza.
conductivity *n.* eramankortasun.
conductor *n.* gidari. *n.* eramale. *n.*
zuzendari. *n.* txartelketari, zulatzaile,
kobratzaile, trenzain.
conduit *n.* hodieria, tutueria.
cone *n. (geom.)* kono.
confection *n.* antolaketa, eraketa,
antolamendu, prestakuntza,
prestaketa, egindura. *n.* gozoki,
gozokari.
confectioner *n.* gozogile, gozokigile.
confectionery *n.* gozotegi, gozotoki.
Confederacy *n.* Estatu Batuetako
hegoaldeko estatuen konfederazioa
guda zibilean.
confederate *v.t./v.i.* elkarfederatu.
confederate *adj.* konfederatu.
confederation *n. (pol.)*
elkarfederaketa, konfederazio.
confer *v.i.* *(batzutan* **with**-*ekin)*
kontseilu eskatu, kontsultatu,
aholkatu. *v.i.* *(on edo* **upon**-*ekin)*
eman.
conference *n.* batzarre, kongresu,

bilera; batzaldi.
confess *v.t./v.i.* aitortu, barrenustu. **To
make (someone) confess.**
Aitorrarazi. Esanarazi.
confession *n.* aitormen, aitor, aitorpen.
n. (eccl.) aitortza.
confessional *n.* aitorleku, aitortegi.
confessor *n.* aitorregile, aitortzaile. *n.*
aitorrentzule. *n.* fedeaitorle,
fedeaitortzaile.
confetti *n.* konfeti.
confidant *n.* isilmandatari.
confidante *n.* isilmandatari (emakume).
confide *v.i./v.t.* *(v.i.,* **in**-*ekin)* fidatu,
usteon izan.
confidence *n.* fidagarritasun, fidaketa,
konfidantza. *n.* ziurtasun,
segurtasun. *n.* isilmandatu,
mandatuisil, ahopeko.
confident *adj.* fidakor; ziur, segur.
confidential *adj.* sekretuzko,
ezkutuko, ahopeko.
confidentially *adv.* isilka, sekretuan,
isilean.
confidently *adv.* fidakorki, uste onez.
configuration *n.* itxurapen, egitura,
itxura, konfigurazio.
configure *v.t.* itxuratu.
confine *v.t.* zokoratu, alboko izan.
confinement *n.* bazterraldi, zokoraldi.
confines *n. (pl.)* mugak.
confirm *v.t.* egiztatu, segurtatu,
ziurtatu, baieztu.
confirmation *n.* baieztapen, egiztapen,
ziurtapen. *n. (eccl.)* sendotza.
confiscate *v.t.* bahitu.
confiscation *n.* bahipen, konfiskazio.
conflagration *n.* sualdi, suketa,
suminaldi.
conflict *v.i.* borrokatu, mokokatu,
gatazkatu. *v.i.* **(with)** moldagaitz izan,
bateraezin izan.
conflict *n.* gatazka, burrukaldi. **Internal
conflict.** Barnegatazka.
confluence *n.* ibaibiltoki, ibaigurutze,
urbieta; bateratasun.
confluent *adj.* baterakide.
conform *v.i.* *(askotan* **to**-*ekin)*
konformatu, erakidetu, hartaratu.
conformation *n.* egitura.
conformity *n.* araberatasun,
gogaidego, gogaidetasun, baietza.
confound *v.t.* lardakatu.
confront *v.t.* aurrea eman, aurre egin,
aurpegiratu, buru eman, buruz jarri.
confrontation *n.* kontrajarketa,
aurkaketa.
confuse *v.t.* nahastu, nahastatu,
nahaspilatu, itsutu, lardaskatu.
confused *adj.* nahasitako, ilun.
confusedly *adv.* nahaski,
nahas-mahaska, nahasteka, ilunki,
goibelki, zorabioz.
confusing *adj.* nahastagarri,
nahasgarri, nahaspilatsu, aztoragarri.
confusion *n.* mordoilo, nahasketa,
nahaspila, nahaste, nahastura. *n.*

zoradura, buruhauste, ezbai, itsupen. *n.* lotsa, ahalke, lotsari.
congeal *v.i./v.t.* loditu, mamitu.
congenial *adj.* atsegingarri, begiko, jendekoi, elkargarri.
congenital *adj.* jaiotzako, sortzetiko, sortzezko.
conger eel *n. (zool.)* itsasaingira.
congested *adj.* marranta.
congestion *n.* marranta.
conglomerate *v.t.* multzotu, pilatu, metatu.
conglomerate *n. (econ.)* beste maila bateko elkarte txikiz eraturiko elkarte ekonomikoa.
conglomeration *n.* multzoketa, pilaketa, metaketa.
congratulate *v.t.* zorionak eman, zoriondu.
congratulations *n. (pl.)* pozagur, zorionak, zorionagurrak.
congregate *v.i./v.t.* baturazi.
congregation *n.* elkarte. *n.* anaigo, anaiarte, elizelkarte.
congregational *adj.* anaiarteko, elizelkarteko.
congress *n.* kongresu, batzar, bilera.
congressional *adj.* kongresuko.
congressman *n.* Estatu Batuetako Kongresuko batzarkidea (gizon).
congresswoman *n.* Estatu Batuetako Kongresuko batzarkidea (emakume).
conical *adj.* koniko.
conjecture *v.t./v.i.* asmatu; igarri.
conjecture *n.* susmo, errezelu, aieru, antzemate, igartzapen.
conjugal *adj.* ezkontzako.
conjugally *adv.* ezkonarauz, ezkonlegez.
conjugate *v.t./v.i.* adizjokatu, jokatu.
conjugation *n.* adizjoko.
conjunction *n. (gram.)* elkarritz, konjuntzio.
conjure *v.t./v.i.* arao egin, araokatu.
connatural *adj.* izatezko.
connect *v.t./v.i.* elkar lotu, lotarazi, ahokatu, mihiztatu.
connectability *n.* elkargarritasun.
connected *adj.* bategin(a), elkartu(a).
connectible *adj.* lotugarri, elkargarri.
Connecticut *n. (geog.)* Estatu Batuetako estatu bat.
connection *n.* elkarlotura, lotura, elkartasun. *n.* itsaspen, atxikitasun. *n. (pl.)* harremanak. *n.* sexujoketa, sexuketa. *n.* ahokadura.
connective *adj.* loturazko.
connivance *n.* elkarkeria.
connive *v.i.* **(at)** ezikusi egin. *v.i.* **(with)** azpijokatu, azpilandu.
connoisseur *n.* ezagule, perito (arte).
connotation *n.* sortarazpen.
connote *v.t.* zeharka adierazi.
conquer *v.t./v.i.* azpiratu, menperatu, menderatu, irabazi, nagusitu.
conquerable *adj.* garaigarri, menderagarri, menperagarri,

erasogarri, gainkor.
conqueror *n.* menderatzaile, menperatzaile.
conquest *n.* menderapen, menperapen.
conscience *n.* barru, barren, kontzientzia.
conscientious *adj.* eginbidetsu, kontzientzidun.
conscientiously *adv.* eginahalean, eginahalez.
conscientiousness *n.* kontzientziapen.
conscious *adj.* ezagueradun. **To be conscious.** Senera etorri. Konortera itzuli. **To be conscious of.** Jakinaren gainean egon. **To become conscious of.** Konturatu.
consciousness *n.* konorte, ezaguera, kontzientzia, zentzu, sen. **To regain consciousness.** Berera etorri.
consciously *adv.* oharrez, ohartuki, jakinez, jakitez.
conscript *v.t.* izen hartu, zerrendaratu, lerrokatu (gudari).
conscript *n.* soldadu berri, errekluta, kinto.
conscription *n.* soldaduketa, soldadubilketa.
consecrate *v.t.* sagaratu, gurendu.
consecrated *adj.* sagaratu(a).
consecration *n. (eccl.)* sagarapen, sagaraketa, sagarakuntza.
consecutive *adj.* jarraidun.
consecutively *adv.* jarraikiro.
consensual *adj.* adostasunezko.
consensus *n.* adostasun.
consent *v.i. (askotan to-rekin)* akordiotu, baimena eman, baimendu.
consent *n.* baiezko, baimen, oniritzi.
consequence *n.* ondoren, ondorio, atze. *n.* garrantzi. *n.* gizamaila.
consequent *adj.* ondoriozko.
consequential *adj.* ondoriozko. *adj.* garrantzitsu.
consequently *adv.* ondorioz, beraz, hortaz.
conservation *n.* kontserbazio.
conservative *adj.* eratsu. *n./adj. (pol.)* eskumako, eskuindar, eskumatar, kontserbadore.
conservatism *n.* kontserbadurismo.
conservatory *n. (mus.)* musikeskola, kontserbatorio.
conserve *v.t.* kontserbatu, iraunarazi.
conserver *n.* iraunarazle.
consider *v.t./v.i.* buruan hartu, begira egon, gogotan hartu, kontuan hartu, -tzat ukan.
considerable *adj.* kopurutsu. *adj.* garrantzitsu.
considerably *adv.* asko, biziki, guztiz.
considerate *adj.* fin, adeitsu.
considerately *adv.* adeitsuki.
consideration *n.* gogapen, gogoramen, gogoeta, hausnarketa, oharkuntza, pentsakizun. **To take into consideration.** Aintzakotu.

Gogotan hartu. *n.* begiramen,
begirune, itzal. *n.* ordainketa, ordain,
sari. *n.* adeitasun, arraitasun.
considered *adj.* kontutan hartu(a).
considering *prep.* kontuan harturik,
ikusirik.
consign *v.t.* igorri, bialdu, bidali.
consignment *n.* igorgai, bialgai.
consist *v.i. (of)* osatu, zer izan.
consistency *n.* gogortasun,
tinkotasun, sendotasun. *n.* iraupen,
jarraipen, iraute. *n.* adostasun,
akordio.
consistent *adj.* erabereko; adosgarri.
consistently *adv.* jarraituki.
consolable *adj.* kontsolagarri.
consolation *n.* kontsolabide,
kontsolamendu, gozagarri, pozbide.
console *v.t.* kontsolatu, dolu eman.
consoler *n.* pozekarle, kontsolatzaile,
poztzaile.
consolidate *v.t./v.i.* batu, elkartu.
v.t./v.i. indartu.
consolidation *n.* finkapen, finkaketa,
sendotasun, elkarketa, elkartasun,
batasun.
consonant *n.* kontsonante.
consort *n.* ezkonlagun, ezkontide;
-kide.
consortium *n.* partzuergo, erkidetza.
conspicuous *adj.* nabarmen, ikusgai,
agiri, nabari.
conspicuously *adv.* nabariki,
nabarmenki.
conspicuousness *n.* nabarmendura.
conspiracy *n.* azpijoko, azpilan,
matxinada, satorlan, satorkeria.
conspirator *n.* azpisapo, zinaide.
conspiratorial *adj.* matxinadazko.
conspire *v.t./v.i.* azpijokatu, azpilandu,
azpilan egin.
constable *n.* herrimutil, herrizain,
udaltzain.
constancy *n.* iraunketa, iraupen,
jarraitza. *n.* zintzotasun, leialtasun. *n.*
etengabezia.
constant *adj.* aldagabe, aldagaitz,
atergabe(ko), etengabe, iraunkor,
lehiati. *adj.* tinko, firme, leial. *n.*
(math.) konstante.
constantly *adv.* atergabeki, etengabe,
jarraikiro, iraunkorki.
constellation *n.* izarketa, izarmoltzo,
izarpilo.
consternation *n.* izualdi, ikaraldi.
constipate *v.t.* idortu.
constipated *adj.* sabelehor, sabelidor.
To be constipated. Idorreritu.
constipation *n.* idorketa, idorreri,
sabelehortasun, sabelidortasun.
constituency *n.* bozemale-talde.
constituent *n.* osagai, osagarri. *n.*
hautari, bozemale, hautatzaile. *adj.*
osagarri.
constitute *v.t.* konposatu, osatu, zer
izan.
constitution *n. (pol.)* konstituzio,

oinlegedi.
constitutional *adj.* konstituziozko.
constitutionality *n.*
konstituzionaltasun.
constitutionally *adv.* konstituzionalki.
constrain *v.t.* behartu, beharrarazi,
zedarritu, mugarritu.
constraint *n.* bortxaketa, bortxaldi,
hertsapen.
constrict *v.t.* hertsi, hertsitu.
constricting *adj.* hertsagarri,
hertsakor, kuzkur, murritz.
constriction *n.* murriztura, hertsapen.
construct *v.t.* eraiki, jaso.
constructed *adj.* egindako, egina,
eraiki(a).
construction *n.* eraiketa, etxagintza,
eraikidura. *n.* konstruzio, obra. *n.*
(gram.) eraiketa, konstruzio.
constructive *adj.* baikor, positibo.
constructively *adv.* baikorki,
positiboki.
construe *v.t./v.i.* azaldu, adierazi.
consul *n.* kontsul.
consular *adj.* kontsul-; kontsularen.
consulate *n.* kontsuletxe.
consulship *n.* kontsulaldi, kontsulgo.
consult *v.t./v.i.* kontsultatu.
consultant *n.* kontsultari.
consultation *n.* kontsulta.
consulting room *n.* ikusgela,
konsultagela, konsulta.
consume *v.t.* erosi; jan, kontsumitu.
consumer *n.* erosle; kontsumitzaile.
The consumer society.
Kontsumo-gizartea.
consumer goods *n.* kontsumogai.
consummate *v.t.* amaierara eraman,
azkendu, burutu. *v.t.*
ezkontza-harremanak burutu.
consummate *adj.* burutu(a), osatu(a),
biribildu(a).
consummation *n.* kontsumazio,
osotasun, bukaera, amaiera.
consumption *n.* kontsumo. *n. (med.)*
tisis.
consumptive *adj. (med.)* tisiko.
contact *v.t.* ukitu. *v.t.* zerbaitekin topo
egin, norbaitekin harremanetan jarri.
contact *n.* ukiketa, ukipen, kontaktu.
contact lens *n.* lentila.
contagion *n.* kutsapen, izurridura.
contagious *adj.* izurrigarri, izurrikor,
kutsagarri, kutsakor, eranskor,
itsaskor.
contagiously *adv.* izurriz.
contagiousness *n.* kutsakortasun,
itsaskortasun.
contain *v.t.* eduki, euki.
container *n.* ontzi, edukigailu.
containment *n.* euspen, eustura.
contaminable *adj.* kutsakoi.
contaminant *adj./n.* kutsagarri,
kutsakor.
contaminate *v.t.* kutsarazi, kutsatu,
izurritu, erantsi.
contaminated *adj.* izurritu(a).

contamination *n.* kutsaketa, kutsadura, satsudura.
contemn *v.t.* erdeinatu.
contemner *n.* erdeinari.
contemplate *v.t./v.i.* begira egon, begietsi.
contemplation *n.* kontenplazio, soegite, soaldi, begiraldi.
contemplative *adj.* soaldiko. *n.* kontemplalari.
contemplator *n.* begiesle.
contemporaneity *n.* mendekidetasun.
contemporaneous *adj.* adineko, garaikide, garaibereko, mendekide.
contemporary *adj./n.* adinbateko, adinkide, urtekide, mendekide, adinbereko, garaibereko, garaikide, kideko.
contempt *n.* gutiespen, arbuio, erdeinu, mesprezu.
contemptible *adj.* erdeinagarri, mesprezagarri, baztergarri.
contemptuous *adj.* arbuiakor, mesprezatzaile.
contemptuously *adv.* arbuioz, erdeinuz.
contend *v.i.* **(with)** borroka egin, borrokan egin, borrokatu. *v.i.* **(for)** lehiakatu, konpetitu. *v.t.* argi azaldu.
content *n.* mami, eduki, edukin, idazkai. *n.* **(pl.)** liburu baten aurkibide(a). *n.* kokamen. *n.* poz, poztasun, gozaldi. *adj.* alai, pozkor, pozdun. **To be content.** Atsegin izan.
contented *adj.* poz, pozgarri, zoriontsu.
contentedly *adv.* pozik.
contention *n.* mokokaldi, liskar, gatazka.
contentious *adj.* liskarti, liskartsu.
contentment *n.* pozkari, gozagarri.
contents *n.* edukin; -kada. *n.* argibide. **Table of contents.** Aurkibide.
contest *n.* lehiaketa, txapelketa, sariketa, jokaldi. *n.* borrokaldi, liskar, eztabaida.
contestant *n.* sariketari, kontrako, aurkako.
context *n.* hitzinguru, idatzinguru, textuinguru.
contiguous *adj.* alboko, aldeko, hurbileko, ondoko, aldameneko.
continence *n.* garbitasun, kastitate; eratasun, neurritasun.
continent *n.* **(geog.)** kontinente, lurrandi. *adj.* garbi, zintzo, orbaingabe, bihozgarbidun.
continental *adj.* kontinentar, lurrandiko.
contingency *n.* gertakizun, badaezbada.
contingent *adj.* badaezbadako, atergabeko.
continual *adj.* etengabe.
continually *adv.* segidan, etengabeki.
continuance *n.* jarraialdi, etengabezia, jarraipide.
continuation *n.* jarraialdi, jarraipide, jarraipen, segidura, segida.
continue *v.i./v.t.* ekin, iraun, jarraitu, segitu.
continuer *n.* jarraile, jarraitzaile.
continuity *n.* jarraiera, jarraitasun, iraupen.
continuous *adj.* artegabeko, atergabeko, epegabeko, etengabeko, segidazko.
continuously *adv.* etengabe, jarraikiro, atergabeki, etengabeki.
continuousness *n.* etengabetasun, jarraipen.
contort *v.t.* uzkurtu, kuzkurtu.
contortion *n.* bihurkada, bihurkaketa.
contour *n.* inguru.
contra- **(gram.)** kontra-, aurka-.
contraband *n.* gaulan, kontrabandu.
contraception *n.* antisorpen, antisorketa.
contraceptive *n./adj.* antiernari, antisorgarri.
contract *v.t./v.i.* kizkurtu. *v.t.* laburtu. *v.t.* erantsi, gaitz hartu, izurriztatu. *v.t.* akordiotu, kontratatu.
contract *n.* akordio, hitzarmen, itun, tratu, konbenio, kontratu.
contraction *n.* kizkurtzapen, kontrakzio. *n.* **(med.)** kontrakzio. *n.* **(gram.)** laburpen, laburtzapen, kontrakzio.
contractor *n.* kontratatzaile, kontratugile. *n.* kontratista.
contractual *adj.* ituneko, akordiozko.
contradict *v.t./v.i.* gezurtatu.
contradiction *n.* kontradikzio, kontraesan.
contradictor *n.* aurkagile, aurkalari, ezezkari, kontraesale.
contradictory *adj.* ezezkor, kontraesankor, kontraesanezko, ezezkari.
contralto *n.* **(mus.)** kontralto.
contraposition *n.* kontraezarketa.
contrarily *adv.* bestera.
contrary *adj.* ezezkor, kontrako, kontresankor, kontrajarle.
contrast *n.* kontraste.
contribute *v.t./v.i.* ekarri, eman, lagundu.
contribution *n.* erakarketa, erakarpen. *n.* dohai, emai, laguntza (diru). *n.* zama(k).
contributor *n.* emaile, laguntzaile.
contrite *adj.* garbaidun, damudun.
contrition *n.* barrendamu, damu, dolu, garbai.
contrivance *n.* lanabes, tresna.
contrive *v.t./v.i.* artetu.
control *v.t.* kontrolatu, menpetu, hezi, erabidetu, neurriak hartu.
control *n.* kontrol, eustura, esku. *n.* **(pl.)** kontrolgailu, gobernagailu.
controllable *adj.* gobernagarri, menderagarri, menperagarri,

kontrolagarri.
controller *n.* kontrolatzaile. *n.*
zuzendari, nagusi.
control panel *n.* kontrolgailu.
control room *n.* gidagela.
controversial *adj.* eztabaidatsu.
controversially *adv.* argudioka.
controversy *n.* eztabaida.
contumacy *n.* burugogorkeria,
kaskagogorkeria, setakeria, kasketa.
contumely *n.* laido.
contusion *n.* hanpatune, zanpaketa.
conundrum *n.* igerkizun.
convalesce *v.i.* zuzpertu.
convalescence *n.* eriondo, gaisondo,
gaitzondo, minondo, sendabitarte,
zuzperraldi.
convalescent *n.* eriondo. *adj.*
eriondoko, zuzperti.
convene *v.i./v.t.* elkartu, bildu,
batzartu.
convenience *n.* egokitasun, egokiera,
komenientzia. *n.* elektrika-aparailu.
convenient *adj.* egoki, erako, bidezko,
komeni.
conveniently *adv.* egoki, egokiro.
convent *n.* komentu, lekaimetxe,
mojetxe, serorategi; lekaidetxe,
fraidetxe. **To enter a convent.**
Komenturatu.
convention *n.* batzarre, kongresu.
conventional *adj.* ohizko, ohiturazko;
konbentzional.
conventionality *n.* konbentzionalismo.
converge *v.i.* bidebateratu, bat etorri.
convergence *n.* baterakuntza,
bateratasun; hurbilpen.
convergent *adj.* baterakor, bilkor,
hurbilkor.
conversant *adj.* ezagutzaile, ikasi(a).
conversation *n.* elkarrizketa, mintzaldi,
solasaldi, eleketa, jardun, hizketaldi.
conversational *adj.* elkarrizketako.
converse *v.i. (batzutan with-ekin)*
hizketatu, solastatu, eleztatu,
berriketatu, jardun, hitz egin,
mintzatu.
conversely *adv.* alderantziz.
converser *n.* hizketakide, hizketalagun,
mintzalagun, solaskide, mintzaide,
mintzalari, elekari, elkarrizketari.
conversion *n.* konbertzio, onbide,
eraldaketa, bihurketa.
convert *v.t./v.i.* itzuli, itzulikatu, bihurtu,
bilakatu.
convert *n.* kristauberri.
convertibility *n.* bihurgarritasun.
convertible *n.* sabai-kengarridun
kotxe(a). *adj.* bihurgarri.
convex *adj.* ganbil, konbexu.
convexness *n.* ganbiltasun.
convey *v.t.* eraman. *v.t.* ulertarazi,
edierazi. *v.t.* jabealdatu, eskuz
aldatu.
conveyable *adj.* eramangarri.
conveyance *n.* garraio, gidaketa.
convict *v.t.* kondenatu, gaitzetsi.

convict *n.* preso, giltzapeko.
conviction *n.* konbentzimendu,
sineste. *n.* gaitzespen, gaitzeste.
convince *v.t.* konbentzitu, buruan
sartu.
convincible *adj.* konbentzigarri.
convincing *adj.* egiztarazle,
konbentzigarri, sinestarazle.
convincingly *adv.* konbentzigarriki,
usteindarrez.
convivial *adj.* alai, lagunkoi, lagunkor.
convocation *n.* dei, deialdi. *n.* biltzar,
batzar.
convoke *v.t.* dei egin, hots egin, deitu.
convoker *n.* hotsegile.
convoy *n.* itsasontzisail, konboi.
convulse *v.t./v.i.* dardaratu,
dardarikatu.
convulsion *n.* gorputzikara,
dardarketa.
convulsive *adj.* dardaradun, dardarati,
dardarazko.
convulsively *adv.* dardaraka, dardaraz.
coo *v.i./v.t.* urrumakatu.
cooing *n.* urruma, urrumaka.
cook *v.t.* sukaldu, apailatu, zukutu.
cook *n.* sukaldari, eltzezain,
maneatzaile.
cookbook *n.* sukaldaritzako liburu.
cook stove *n.* sutegi.
cookie *n.* gaileta.
cooking *n.* sukaldaritza.
cool *v.i./v.t.* freskatu, hozkirritu,
hotzildu. *v.i. (off, down)* hotzagotu;
lasaitu.
cool *n.* fresku. *adj.* hozkirri.
cooler *n.* hoztegi, hozkailu. *adj.*
(comp.) hozkirriago.
coolly *adv.* hozki.
coolness *n.* freskutasun, hoztura,
hozkura.
coop *n.* oilatoki, oilategi. **To fly the
coop.** Ihes egin.
co-op *n.* kooperatiba.
cooper *n.* upagile, upagin.
cooperate *v.i.* lankidetu, lagundu.
cooperation *n.* elkarrekintza,
lankidego, lankidetza, elkarlaguntza.
cooperative *n.* kooperatiba, lankidego.
adj. laguntzaile.
coordinate *v.t./v.i.* koordinatu.
coordination *n.* elkarkuntza,
koordinaketa, koordinazio.
coordinator *n.* elkartzaile,
koordinatzaile.
co-owner *n.* jabekide.
cop *n.* ertzain, polizia. **Traffic cop.**
Trafikozain.
cope *v.i. (batzutan with-ekin)* ederki
moldatu, ederki konpondu.
copier *n.* berridazle; kopiatzaile. *n.*
kopiagailu.
copious *adj.* ugari, ugaritsu, oparotsu,
jori, joritsu.
copiously *adv.* ugari, jori, naharoki,
parra-parra.
copiousness *n.* ugaritasun,

oparotasun, naharotasun, joritasun.
copper n. *(min.)* burdingorri, tupiki, kobre. *adj.* kobreantzeko, kobredun, kobrezko.
coppery *adj.* kobretsu.
coprophagous *adj.* gorozjale.
copse n. baso txiki.
copulate *v.i.* larru jo.
copulation n. sexujoketa, estaldura.
copy *v.t./v.i.* kopiatu, berridatzi.
copy n. kopia, berridazki, antzirudi. n. ale (liburu) , iheki. n. idazki.
copyright n. idazlearen eskubideak, egilearen eskubideak.
coquetry n. txatxankeria, irtirinkeria.
coquette n. irtirin.
coquettish *adj.* goizoilanda.
coral n. koral, koralarkaitz. *adj.* koralezko, koraltsu, koraldun.
cord n. soka, kordel, kordoi; lokarri. Umbilical cord. Zilborreste. Zileste. n. soka (neurri mota bat).
cordial n. alkoholezko edari goxo bat. *adj.* bihotzeko, maitetsu, alaigarri, pozgarri.
cordiality n. bihoztasun, berotasun.
cordially *adv.* bihotzez.
corduroy n. pana.
core n. muskil, mutxikin. n. erdimuin.
cork *v.t.* kortxoztatu, ziritu, zipoztu, tapoindu.
cork n. zipotz, kortxo. n. *(bot.)* tortotx.
corkscrew n. irekailu, irekigailu, ginbalet.
cormorant n. *(zool.)* ubarroi, potorro.
corn n. *(bot.)* arto, artalandara.
cornea n. *(anat.)* betzuringo.
corner *v.t./v.i.* baztertu, bazterreratu, txokoratu, zokondoratu.
corner n. bazter, zoko, kantoin, txoko, zokobazter, zokondo.
cornerstone n. zimentarri, lehenarri, oinarri.
cornet n. turuta, turutu.
corn husk n. artamaluta, artazorro, maluta.
cornice n. *(archit.)* erlaitz, harriapal.
corn silk n. artabizar.
corn stalk n. lastaki, mailasto.
corolla n. lorosto.
corollary n. ondorio.
corona n. eguzki-eztun, ilargi-eztun. n. haginburu, hortzburu.
coronation n. koroaketa, koroapen.
coroner n. heriotzaren zehaztasunen ikertzaile(a).
corporal n. *(mil.)* kabu. n. *(eccl.)* oihalsakratu. *adj.* gorputzeko, gorputzezko, soineko.
corporate *adj.* taldeko, elkarteko.
corporation n. batzalde, erkidego.
corporeal *adj.* gorputzeko, gorputzezko, soineko.
corporeally *adv.* gorpuzki, soinez.
corps n. soldadutalde. n. laguntalde.
corpse n. hil, hilotz, sarraski, gorpu.
corpulence n. galantasun.

corpulent *adj.* lodi; -kote.
corpuscle n. *(anat.)* gorpuño, gorpuzki, globulu.
corral *v.t.* ukuiluratu, estutu, inguratu.
corral n. abeltegi, gorta.
correct *v.t.* zuzendu, oneratu, zentzatu, ondu.
correct *adj.* zuzen, eraoneko, jator. The correct sentence. Esaldi jatorra.
correctible *adj.* zuzengarri.
correction n. zuzenketa, zuzenpen, zentzadura; orrazketa.
corrective *adj.* zentzarazle, zentzagarri.
correctly *adv.* beharbezala, propioki, jatorki.
correlate *v.i./v.t.* elkarkidetu.
correlation n. elkar-harreman, elkarkidetasun.
correspond *v.i. (to)* egoki. *v.i. (with)* elkarri idatzi.
correspondence n. elkarkizun, korrespondentzia.
correspondent n. berriemaile. n./*adj.* elkarrekiko.
corresponding *adj.* elkargarri.
correspondingly *adv.* elkargarriki, elkargarriro.
corridor n. barrenbide, iragabide, ataka.
corroborate *v.t.* egiztatu, sendotu.
corroboration n. egiztaketa, egiztapen.
corroborator n. egiztatzaile.
corrode *v.t./v.i.* bipiatu, bipi jo, jan (herdoilak).
corrosive *adj.* errekor, erregarri, korrosibo. n. errekin, errekai.
corrugated *adj.* horzdun (kartoi, etabar), hagindun.
corrupt *v.t./v.i.* makurrarazi, okerrarazi, gaiztatu, galdu, lizunarazi. *v.i.* haratusteldu.
corrupt *adj.* likits, zabar, gizatxar. *adj.* makur.
corruptible *adj.* ustelgarritasun, ustelkortasun, andeakortasun, galkortasun. n. salkortasun, salkoitasun.
corruptible *adj.* ustelgarri, ustelkor, ustelbera, andeakor. *adj.* salkoi, salkor.
corruption n. ustelketa, ustelkeria, gaizkintasun, andeamendu.
corruptive *adj.* ustelarazle.
corruptor n. okerrarazle, makurrarazle, okertzaile, umegaltzaile, andeatzaile, gaiztotzaile.
corsair n. pirata, itsaslapur.
corset n. kortse.
cortege n. jarraigo, segitalde. Funeral cortege. Dolutalde.
cosmetic n./*adj.* azalapaingarri, kosmetiko.
cosmic *adj.* kosmiko.
cosmology n. kosmologia.

cosmopolitan adj. kosmopolita, edonongo.
cosmopolitanism n. kosmopolitasun, edonongotasun.
cosmos n. ortzune, kosmo.
cost v.t./v.i. balio izan, balio ukan, kostatu.
cost n. kostu, balio, eralki; gastu.
costliness n. garestitasun.
costly adj. garesti, kario.
costume n. kokojantzi, mozolojantzi, mozorrojantzi, mamujantzi.
cot n. bideohe, kamaina, ohantze, ohetxo, ohexka.
cottage n. borda, etxetxo; txabola, etxola.
cottage cheese n. gaztanbera.
cotter pin n. ziri, ardatziri.
cotton n. kotoi, algodoi.
cotton plant n. (bot.) kotoin-landare.
couch n. etzauntza.
cough v.i. eztul egin. v.t. (up-ekin) eztulaz bota; eman.
cough n. eztul. **Whooping cough.** Eztul-kukurruku.
could pret. of can.
couldn't "could + not"-aren laburpena.
council n. kontseilu, aholkularitza. **Town council.** Herrikontseilu. Udal-. **Town council meeting.** Udalbatzar. n. elizbatzar, kontzilio. n. herribatzar.
councillor n. kontseilari. n. zinegotzi.
councillorship n. zinegotzigo.
councilman n. (pol.) kontseilari. n. zinegotzi.
councilwoman n. (pol.) kontseilari (emakume). n. zinegotzi (emakume).
counsel v.t./v.i. kontseilatu, burubidetu, aholkatu, aholku eman.
counsel n. aholku, burubide.
counseling n. aholkaketa, kontseilaketa, kontsulta.
counselor n. aholkatzaile, aholkulari, kontseilari.
count v.t./v.i. kontatu, zenbatu. v.i. (gehienetan for-ekin) balio ukan, garrantzitsu izan.
count n. konde. n. kontu, zenbaketa. n. salakuntza, salakizun.
countability n. zenbakuntza.
countable adj. zenbakarri, kontagarri, zenbakizun, zenbakor. **Not countable.** Zenbatezin.
countenance n. begitarte, aurpegi.
counter n. kontatzaile, zenbatzaile. n. erakusmahai, salmahai. adj./n. kontrako, aurkako. adv. bestera, ostera.
counter- (gram.) kontra-.
counteract v.t. indarra kendu, buru eman, aurka egin; eragotzi, galarazi.
counterattack v.t./v.i. berreraso.
counterattack n. berrerasoketa, kontraerasoaldi.
counterbalance v.t. pisu berdindu.
counterbalance n. kontrapisu.

counterespionage n. kontraespionaia.
counterfeit v.t./v.i. faltsutu, faltsuztatu.
conterfeit adj. faltsu. **The counterfeit money.** Diru faltsua.
counterfeiter n. faltsutzaile.
counterfeiting n. faltsuztapen.
countermand v.t. desagindu, desmezutu, ezeztatu.
countermarch n. kontraibilaldi.
counteroffensive n. kontraeraso.
counteroffer n. kontraeskaintza.
counterorder n. kontragindu.
counterpane n. ohestalki.
counterpart n. osagarri, bikoizkin.
counterpoint n. (mus.) kontrapuntu.
counterrevolution n. kontrairaultza.
counterrevolutionary n. kontrairaultzaile.
countersign n. kontraezaugarri.
counterspy n. kontraespioi.
counterweight n. kontrapisu.
countess n. kondesa.
counting n. zenbaketa, kontaketa.
countless adj. kontaezin, zenbatezin.
countlessly adv. kontaezinez.
country n. lur, lurralde, herrialde. n. herri, aberri. n. landa, baserri. adj. landako, larreko, nekazal.
countryman n. herrikide, aberkide.
countryside n. landazabal, zelaieta.
countrywoman n. herrikide, aberkide (emakume).
countship n. kondego, kondetza.
county n. konderri, konterri.
coup n. kolpe, kalamatrika.
couple v.t./v.i. binakatu. v.i. larru jo.
couple n. bikote, pare, biko.
coupled adj. binako.
coupler n. parekatzaile.
couplet n. kopla.
coupling n. binaketa, lotune. n. sexujoketa. n. mihiztadura, mihiztaketa, mihiztapen. n. kako (tren).
coupon n. kupoi.
courage n. adore, adoretasun, ausardia, ausartasun, kemen, oldar.
courageous adj. adoretsu, ausarditsu, ausarta, kementsu, bihoztun, bipil.
courageously adv. ausartki, gizonki, adorez.
courier n. mezulari berezi, karta-eramaile.
course n. bide, igarobide, lasterleku. n. ikastaro, ikaskuntza, klase, ikastaldi. **The intensive course.** Ikastaro trinkoa. n. urlaster. n. jaki, jateko.
court v.t./v.i. maitaxarmatu.
court n. gorte. n. epaiaulki, auzitegi, epaitegi. **Supreme Court.** Auzitegi Nagusi. **Day in court.** Auziegun. **To take (someone) to court.** Auzitara eraman.
court clerk n. izkribau.
courteous adj. begirunedun, adeitsu, erabideko, gizabidetsu, eraoneko, gizabidezko, gizalegezko.

courteously adv. erabidez, eraonez, gizabidez.

courtesan n. gortelari.

courtesy n. adeitasun, begiramen, gizabide, jendetasun, sotilasun, erabidetasun, fintasun.

courthouse n. epaietxe, epaitegi, auzijauregi.

courting n. maitaxarma, maitaketa.

courtly adj. adeitsu. adv. adeitsuki.

court-martial n. guda-auzitegi.

courtroom n. auzitegi.

courtship n. ezkongaialdi.

courtyard n. atalondo, atari.

cousin n. lehengusina, lehengusu. **Male second cousin.** Lehengusutipi. **Female second cousin.** Lehengusintipi.

cove n. itsasarte, portutxo, portuxka, itsaszoko.

covenant n. elkargo, itun.

cover v.t. (batzutan up-ekin) estali, estalpetu, azpibabestu, gerizatu, gaineztatu. v.i. (for) ordeztu.

cover n. azal, estalki, gainestalki, azpibabes.

coverage n. telebista edo irratiko emanaldien antolaketa. n. eriaseguruaren babesa.

covered adj. estali. adj. azaldun, estalkidun.

coverlet n. ohestalkitxo.

covert adj. isileko, izkutuko, ezkutu.

covertly adv. isilkeriaz.

cover-up n. isilkeria.

covet v.t./v.i. gutiziatu, arrakastatu, irritsatu.

covetous adj. diruzale, gutiziagarri, gutiziatsu.

covetously adv. gutizioski.

covetousness n. gutiziamendu, nahikeria.

cow v.t. koldartu, kikildu.

cow n. behi, ganadu; bet-; mu.

coward n. pertsona koldarti(a), oilo.

cowardice n. oilakeria, beldurkeria, txepelkeria, koldarkeria.

cowardliness n. txepeltasun, koldarkeria.

cowardly adj. koldar, kikil, oilobusti, txepel; beldurti. adv. txepelki, beldurti, koldarki.

cowbell n. joare, txilintxa, bulunba, dunba, zintzarri.

cowboy n. behizain, betzain, abelari, unain.

cower v.i. kuzkurtu.

cowering adj. kuzkurkor.

cowhide n. behilarru.

cowl n. txano, txoto.

coy adj. lotsakor, lotsati, txepel. adj. goizoilanda, irtirin.

coyote n. (zool.) koiote.

cozy adj. epel eta eroso (leku).

crab n. (zool.) karramarro.

crab apple n. sagarmakatz.

crack v.i./v.t. arrrailatu, brintzatu, hirrikatu, kraskatu, pitzatu, zartatu. v.i. (up) bere onetik atera; zoratu; algara egin. v.i. (down on) neurri gogorrak hartu. **Crack a joke.** Adarra jo. **Crack a smile.** Irrifarre egin.

crack n. arrailadura, arrailakadura, arrakala, kraskadura, hirrikadura, pitzadura, zirrikitu.

crackable adj. arrailagarri, arrakalagarri, pitzagarri, pitzakor, zartagarri.

cracked adj. arrail, arrakalatu(a), printzatu, zartatsu.

cracker n. gazdun gaileta txiki(a).

crackle v.i./v.t. txinpartatu, txingartu, krakada egin.

crackle n. karrakada, krakada.

cradle n. ohako, kuma, sehaska.

craft n. eskulan. n. trebetasun.

crafted adj. landu(a).

craftiness n. azkerikeria.

craftsman n. ofiziale.

craftsmanship n. eskulangintza, eskulan.

crafty adj. maltzurkote, bihur.

crag n. malkor.

cragginess n. malkardura, malkartasun.

craggy adj. malkartsu, malkar, muger.

cram v.t. bete, gaineztu. v.i. arin ikasi.

cramp n. kalanbre, zurmindura.

cranberry n. (bot.) ahabi, abi.

crane n. (zool.) kurrilo. n. garabi.

cranium n. kaskar, kaskezur, garezur, kasket.

crank n. eragingailu. n./adj. txoriburu, zoroska.

cranky adj. kexukoi.

cranny n. zirrikitu.

crap n. kaka.

crash v.t./v.i. krak egin, tupust egin, puskatu. v.i. jo, elkar jo (hegazkin).

crash n. blaustada, tope, zanpa. n. dunbadaldi, punpa, tupust, danbada. n. hegazkinaren erorketa; txoke (kotxe). n. porrot, molokot. adj. trinko (ikastaro).

cross adj. zentzugabe, ergel. adj. zakar, zarpail, latz.

crate v.t. fardoztatu.

crate n. oholezko estalki kutxa.

crater n. krater, sumendiaho, sumendizulo.

cravat n. gorbata.

crave v.t. irrikatu, bortizki nahi ukan.

craven adj. koldar.

craving adj. asegaitz, asezkor. n. gurari asezin(a).

craw n. papo.

crawfish n. zigala, otarrainska.

crawl v.i. lauhankaka ibili, laukatu.

crawl n. lauhankaka ibiltzea.

crawler n. narrazkari.

crayfish n. zigala, otarrainska.

crayon n. margo-lapitz.

craze n. berrikuntza herrikoi(a).

crazily adv. zoroki, eroki, burugabeki.

craziness *n.* erokeria, zorakeria, zorotasun, burugalketa, erotasun, zentzugabekeria.

crazy *adj.* ero, zoro, sinotsu, zentzugabe.

creak *v.i.* kirrinka egin, kirrinkatu, karrankatu, krakada egin.

creak *n.* karrakada, krakada, irrintzi.

cream *n.* esnemami, esnegurin, esnegain. *adj.* kipurrezko, kipurrantzeko.

creamery *n.* gurindegi, esnedenda.

creamy *adj.* gurintsu.

crease *v.t./v.i.* tolestatu, tolestu.

crease *n.* zimur, tolestasun, tolestura.

create *v.t./v.i.* kreatu, egin, sortu.

creation *n.* kreapen, sortzapen, kreazio. *n.* izadi, kreazio. *n.* asmakuntza; egitura.

creative *adj.* ustetsu, sortzaile, kreatzaile, sormenezko.

creativity *n.* asmamen, kreamen, sormen.

creator *n.* kreatzaile, sortzaile.

creature *n.* izaki, sorkari.

creche *n.* portale.

credence *n.* sinestura, sineste, sinesmen, fede.

credential *n.* sinestagiri, noragiri.

credibility *n.* fidagarritasun, sinesgarritasun.

credible *adj.* sinesgarri, sinestagarri.

credit *n.* hartzeko, kreditu. **Credit cards.** Kreditu-txartelak. **On credit.** Epeka.

creditable *adj.* agurgarri, hitzalgarri, errespetagarri.

creditor *n.* hartzaile, hartzekodun.

credo *n.* (*rel.*) kredo.

credulity *n.* sinesberatasun, sineskortasun.

credulous *adj.* sinesbera, sineskor.

credulously *adv.* sineskorki.

credulousness *n.* sineskortasun; sinesterrazkeria.

creed *n.* (*rel.*) kredo.

creek *n.* erreka.

creep *v.i.* lauhankaka ibili.

creep *n.* pertsona nazkagarri(a).

creeping *adj.* herrestatzaile, narraztari.

creepy *adj.* beldurgarri, ikaragarri.

cremate *v.t.* erraustu.

cremation *n.* errausketa, errauspen.

cremator *n.* errausle.

crematorium *n.* errelabe, erreleku, sulabe.

Creole *n.* krioilo. *n.* Krioilo hizkuntza (Louisiana-n mintzatzen den frantzes dialektoa).

crepe *n.* krespoi.

crept *p.part. of creep.*

crepuscular *adj.* ilunbarreko.

crescent *n./adj.* ilgora.

crest *v.t./v.i.* tontortu.

crest *n.* gailur, tontor. *n.* gandor, motots, gangar. *n.* olatugain. *n.* armarrien gainean ipinten zen ezaugarria.

crestfallen *adj.* buruapal.

crevasse *n.* arrailgune, zirrikitu, arrail.

crevice *n.* arrailgune, zirrikitu, arrail, arrakala.

crew *n.* ontzilaguntalde, tripulazio, tostarteko.

crewman *n.* ontzilagun, ontzikari, untzilari.

crib *n.* sehaska, ohako. *n.* aska, ganbela. *n.* bihitegi, aletegi.

cricket *n.* kilkir, lakasta.

crier *n.* deiegile, deilari, hotsegile, oihukari, oihulari. **Town crier.** Aldarrikari. *n.* negarregile.

crime *n.* gizerailketa, gaiztakeria.

criminal *n.* gaizkile, gaizkin, gaiztagile, legeaurkari. *adj.* legeaurkako, gaizkin.

criminality *n.* gaizkiletasun, gaizkintasun.

criminology *n.* kriminologia.

crimson *n./adj.* gorri-bizi.

crimp *v.t.* kizkurtu. *v.t.* (*colloq.*) eragotzi, oztopatu, trabatu.

cringe *v.i.* beldurrez atzeratu; uzkurtu, kuzkurtu.

crinkle *v.t./v.i.* zimurtu. *v.t./v.i.* karrakada egin.

cripple *v.t.* herrendu, elbarritu.

cripple *n.* herren, txanket, hebain, zangomotz; maingu, hankamotz.

crippled *adj.* elbarri, elbarridun, hankabihur, zangoker, zangomakur; maingu. **To become crippled.** Maingutu. Herrendu.

crisis *n.* krisis, larri.

crisp *adj.* kizkur.

crisscross *n.* ezaugarri gurutzatu(a). *adj.* gurutzatu(a). *adv.* gurutzaduraz.

criteria *n.* (*pl.*) erizpideak.

criterion *n.* erizpide.

critic *n.* kritikalari, irizle. *n.* kritikatzaile, maiseatzaile, maisealari.

critical *adj.* mihiluze, mingainluze. *adj.* kritiko. *adj.* larri, erabateko. *adj.* arriskutsu.

critically *adv.* larri; arriskuz.

criticism *n.* kritika; maiseaketa.

criticize *v.i./v.t.* kritikatu, maiseatu, marmar ari.

criticizer *n.* kritikatzaile; maisealari.

croak *v.i.* kroa egin.

croak *n.* karranka, karraskada.

crochet *v.t./v.i.* gantxilo(a) egin.

crock *n.* lurrezko ontzi(a).

crockery *n.* ontziteria.

crocodile *n.* kokodrilo.

crocodile tears *n.* gezurnegar.

cromlech *n.* kromlech, harrespil.

crone *n.* atso.

crony *n.* adiskide.

crook *n.* iruzurtzaile.

crooked *adj.* bihur, makur, oker, azpisapo, bihurri.

crookedly *adv.* okerretara.

crookedness *n.* gaiztakeria,

makurkeria, okerkeria, txarkeria.
croon *v.t.* abestu.
crooner *n.* abeslari.
crop *v.t.* soildu; moztu.
crop *n.* uzta. *n.* papo. *n.* zartagailu.
croquette *n.* kroketa.
cross *v.t.* gurutzatu, aitaren egin.
v.t./v.i. zeharkatu, zehartu, pasatu,
iragan, igaro.
cross *n.* gurutze, habe. **Red Cross.**
Gurutze gorri. *adj.* haserre.
crossable *adj.* iragaiteko, iragangai,
iragangarri.
crossbow *n.* balezta.
cross-country *adj.* landa-zeharka.
cross-examination *n.* galdealdi.
cross-eyed *adj.* ezkel, begioker,
begiezkel.
crossing *n.* gurutzedura,
gurutzelkardura, gurutzaketa,
iragaitza, iraganketa. *n.* iraganleku,
igarobide, igaroleku, iraganbide.
crossroads *n.* bidegurutze, bidebieta,
karrikagurutze, gurutzagune.
crosswalk *n.* oinbide, oinpasabide,
zebrabide.
crossword puzzle *n.* gurutzegrama,
hitz-gurutzaketa.
crotch *n.* hankarte.
crouch *v.i.* kukutu, kukubilkatu.
croup *n.* (*med.*) zintzurmin, pintzelde.
crow *v.i.* kukurruku egin, kukurruku jo.
crow *n.* (*zool.*) bela, belatxinga, erroi.
crowbar *n.* balanka.
crowd *v.i.* samaldatu. *v.t.* bultz egin,
bultzatu.
crowd *n.* gizatalde, gizateria,
jendetalde, jendetza, jendeketa,
laguntalde.
crowded *adj.* jendetsu, laguntsu.
crowing *n.* kakara.
crown *v.t.* koroatu, burestundu.
crown *n.* koroa, burestun. *n.* burugain,
kaskagain. *n.* hortzburu. *n.* tontor,
gailur. *n.* monarkia, erregetza,
erregego.
crowned *adj.* koroidun.
crucial *adj.* garrantzitsu, funtsezko.
crucible *n.* arrago.
crucifix *n.* gurutze, gurutzirudi.
crucifixion *n.* gurutziltzapen.
crucify *v.t.* gurutzean josi,
gurutziltzatu, gurutzatu.
crucigram *n.* hitz-gurutzaketa.
crude *adj.* itsusi, baldar, saskar,
trakets, zatar, gozagaitz. *adj.* gordin.
Crude oil. Petrolio gordina.
crudely *adv.* itsuski, saskarki, zakarki,
gordinki, zatarki.
crudeness *n.* trauskilkeria, zakardura,
zakarkeria, zakarraldi, laztasun. *n.*
gordintasun.
crudity *n.* saskarkeria, zatarkeria,
itsuskeria, gordintasun.
cruel *adj.* bihozgogor, gupidagabe,
krudel, odoltzale, barrugogor,
bihozgabe, errukigabe.

cruelly *adv.* bihozgabeki, errukigabeki,
krudelki, gogorki.
cruelty *n.* bihozgabekeria,
bihozgogorkeria, errukigabekeria,
odoltzalekeria, bortizkeria.
cruet *n.* oilozpinontzi, ozpinandel.
cruise *n.* itsasbidaia.
cruller *n.* txurro.
crumb *n.* ogiapur, apur. *n.* pixka, pizka,
apurtxo, pusketa. *n.* mami.
crumble *v.i.* zarbaildu. *v.t./v.i.*
papurkatu, apurkatu, xehatu, zehatu.
crumbly *adj.* papurgarri.
crumple *v.t./v.i.* zimurtu. *v.i.* **(up)** -z
pilota egin.
crunch *n.* kosk.
crunchy *adj.* kraskari.
crusade *n.* gurutzgudaldi, gurutzada.
crusader *n.* gurutzgudari.
crush *v.t.* hankapetu, zapaldu,
oinazpitu, trinkatu. *v.t.* menperatu,
zanpatu.
crush *n.* maitemin, maitemindura. *n.*
herstura, hertsapen, tinkaketa,
tinkadura. *n.* jendetza, jendeketa,
gizatalde, lagunpilo.
crushable *adj.* puskagarri, birringarri,
ehogarri.
crusher *n.* zapalgailu, zanpagailu. *n.*
apurtzaile, puskatzaile.
crust *n.* ogiazal. *n.* lurrazal, lurgain,
geruza. *n.* zakardura; elurgeruza.
crustacean *adj.* oskoldun.
crusty *adj.* azaldun. *adj.* zakartsu.
crutch *n.* trikimako, txanka, besapeko,
makulu.
cry *v.i.* negar egin, negarmuxinkatu.
v.i./v.t. deadar egin, oihu egin,
garrasi egin, txilio egin, oihukatu.
cry *n.* deiadar, oihu, garrasi, intzirina,
txilio. *n.* negar.
crybaby *n.* negarti, negargile.
crypt *n.* elizpe.
cryptic *adj.* isileko.
crystal *n.* kristal; izarrarri; beira mota
bat. *n.* erlojuaren kristal(a). *adj.*
kristalezko.
crystalline *adj.* kristalezko.
crystallization *n.* beirakuntza,
kristaldura.
crystallize *v.i./v.t.* beiratu.
cub *n.* -kume (hartz, azeri, lehoi).
cube *n.* kubo.
cubic *adj.* kubiko.
cubism *n.* kubismo.
cuckoo *v.i.* kuku egin.
cuckoo *n.* (*zool.*) kuku.
cucumber *n.* (*bot.*) kuia, kuiluze,
pepino.
cud *n.* hausnarlariek bigarren aldiz
irensten duten janaria. **To chew
one's cud.** Hausnar egin.
cuddle *v.t./v.i.* besarkatu eta ferekatu.
cudgel *n.* eskumakila.
cue *n.* zantzu.
cuff *n.* bezazulo, mahukaburu.
cuirass *n.* bularreko, koraza.

cuisine *n.* sukalde.
cul-de-sac *n.* kaleitxi.
culinary *adj.* sukaldeko.
cull *v.t.* hautatu, aukeratu; bildu, batu.
culminate *v.i./v.t. (v.i., gehienetan in-ekin)* bukatu, amaitu.
culmination *n.* gorentasun, gorengotasun.
culpability *n.* hobendura, errutasun, hoben, okertasun.
culpable *adj.* hobendun, errudun, hobentsu.
culprit *n.* errudun, hobendun.
cult *n.* elizkizun. *n.* erlijio faltsu(a), gezurrezko erlijio.
cultivate *v.t.* irauli, landu, lurlandu.
cultivated *adj.* eskolatu(a), ikasi(a), jakitun, landu(a).
cultivation *n.* lurlantza, lurgintza, lurlan, nekazaritza.
cultural *adj.* kultur.
culture *n.* kultura, eskola.
culvert *n.* iroloditza, zikinodi.
cumbersome *adj.* eragozkarri.
cumulable *adj.* metagarri, pilagarri.
cumulative *adj.* metakor, pilakor.
cunning *n.* azerikeria, maltzurkeria. *n.* zuhurkeria. *adj.* azpikari. *adj.* bitxi, moñoño.
cunningly *adv.* malmuzki.
cunt *n.* potorro, alu.
cup *n.* kikara; gatilu. *n. (eccl.)* kaliza, mezontzi. *n.* kopa (kirol).
cupbearer *n.* kopari.
cupboard *n.* arasa, ontzitegi, untzitegi.
cupful *n.* kopakada; gatilukada.
cupidity *n.* dirugose, dirumin, diruegarri, dirunahi; nahikeria.
cupola *n.* ganga, kupula.
cur *n.* txakur xinitre(a). *n.* alproja.
curable *adj.* sendagarri, osagarri.
curate *n.* erretor-lagun, apaiz-laguntzaile.
curative *adj.* sendakor, osasungarri.
curator *n.* museoko zaindari(a).
curb *n.* espaloiertz.
curd *n.* gatzagi, gatzatu, mami.
curdle *v.t./v.i.* lapastu, bikortatu.
cure *v.t./v.i.* sendatu, sendarazi, osatu. *v.t.* ondu; gazitu; keztatu.
cure *n.* osabide, sendabide, erremedio, osagarri, sendakuntza, sendapen. *n.* gazialdi, kealdi.
curfew *n.* geldi-dei, gera-hots.
curiosity *n.* jakinnahi, jakingura, entzunahi, ikusmin, ikusnahi.
curious *adj.* entzungale, ikusgale, jakingale, begirazale, behazale. *adj.* belarriluze, begiluze. *adj.* ikusgarri, jakingarri; interesgarri.
curiously *adv.* entzunminez, ikusminez, jakinguraz, jakinminez.
curl *v.t./v.i.* kizkurtu, kuzkurtu, kiribildu, kurubilkatu, kiribilatu.
curl *n.* kiribilo, izur.
curled *adj.* izurdun, kirru.
curler *n.* kizkurgailu.

curliness *n.* kizkurberatasun, kizkurtasun, izurdura.
curling iron *n.* kizkurgailu.
curly *adj.* kizkur, kizkurbera, kizkurtsu.
currency *n.* diru.
current *n.* urlaster, haizelaster; elektrakorronte, elektraindar. *adj.* gaurko, gaurreguneko, orainaldiko, oraingo.
currently *adv.* gaurregun.
curriculum *n.* kurrikulun.
curry *v.t.* zaldiorraztu.
curry comb *n.* zaldiorrazi.
curse *v.t./v.i.* madarikatu, arnegatu, biraokatu, gaiztetsi, birao bota.
curse *n.* birao, maldizio, madarikazio, arnegu.
cursed *adj.* madarikatu(a).
curser *n.* gaizkiesale, madarikatzaile, biraolari, arneguegile.
cursive *n./adj.* kurtsiba.
cusory *adj.* azaleko, gaineko.
curt *adj.* zakar, latz.
curtail *v.t.* laburtu, txikitu, murriztu.
curtain *n.* oihal, leihoihal, gortina.
curtly *adv.* zakarki.
curtsy *n.* kilimusi (emakume).
curvature *n.* konkortasun.
curve *v.t./v.i.* gakotu, oihertu, okerrarazi, okertu, makurkatu.
curve *n.* bihurgune, okergune, makurgune, kikimako.
curved *adj.* bihur, bihurri, gakodun, makur.
curviness *n.* makurtasun, okertasun, oihestasun.
curvy *adj.* oker, okertsu, zeharkako.
cushion *v.t.* kolpea gerarazi, ematu (kolpe bat). *v.t.* zerbait bururdi batean ipini, kuxinan ipini.
cushion *n.* burukitxo, bururdi, kuxin; belaunpeko (aulki).
cushy *adj.* erraz eta atsegin.
cuspidor *n.* listuontzi.
cuss *v.i.* madarikatu, biraokatu, birao bota, juramendu egin, gaiztetsi.
cusser *n.* gaizkiesale.
custard *n.* flan.
custodian *n.* zaindari, zaintzaile, zain.
custody *n.* zaintza.
custom *n.* ohitura, usario, ekandu, aztura. *n. (pl.)* errenteri, aduana.
customarily *adv.* ohituraz.
customary *adj.* ohiko, ohiturazko, ohituzko.
customer *n.* bezero; erosle, erostun.
customs house *n.* aduana, aduanagela, errenderi, zergabildegi, zergaetxe.
cut *v.t./v.i.* moztu, trenkatu, ebaki, hautsi, zatitu. **To cut with scissors.** Guraizkatu. Artazikatu. **To cut in two.** Erdibitu. **To cut hair.** Ilea ebaki. *v.t.* txikitu, laburtu.
cut *n.* ebakune, ebaki, ebaketa, aiztokada, epai, moztura, sakaildura, trenkadura, zarrasta, mozketa, zauri.

n. zati, zerra, pusketa, ebakin, mozkin. *n.* ilemozte. *n.* jazkera. *n.* laburpen, laburtzapen. *n.* sasieskola, piper egite. *n.* esaldi-zorrotz. *n.* igarobide. *adj.* motz, ebaki(a), moztu(a). *adj.* labur.
cutaneous *adj.* larruko.
cute *adj.* moñoño, polit.
cuticle *n.* larrumintz.
cutlass *n.* txarrantxa.
cutlery *n.* aiztomoltzo, aiztosail.
cuttable *adj.* ebakigarri, epaigarri.
cutter *n.* moztutzaile, erdibitzaile, pikatzaile, epaile, ebakitzaile, zatitzaile.
cut-throat *n.* hiltzaile.
cuttlefish *n. (zool.)* pota, potta.
cyanide *n. (chem.)* zianuro.
cybernetics *n.* zibernetika.
cycle *n.* aldi, ziklo. **Lunar cycle.** llargialdi.
cyclist *n.* txirrindulari, bizikletari.
cyclone *n.* zikloi.
cylinder *n. (geom.)* zilindro. *n. (mech.)* zilindro (kotxe).
cylindrical *adj.* zilindriko.
cymbal *n. (mus.)* platillo.
cynic *n.* ziniko.
cynical *adj.* ahalkegabe, lotsagaldu.
cynically *adv.* lotsagabeki, ahalkegabeki.
cynicism *n.* lotsagaizto, zinismo.
cypress *n. (bot.)* alzifre.
cyst *n. (med.)* kiste.
czar *n.* tsar.

D

d *n.* Ingeles alfabetoko letra.
dab *v.t.* ukitu laburrez margotu.
dab *n.* ukitu laburrez margotze(a).
dabble *v.i.* (**in**) zerbaitean gaingiroki saiatu.
dad *n.* aita.
daddy *n. (dim.)* aitatxo.
daffodil *n. (bot.)* anbulo, lilipa.
dagger *n.* sastakai.
dahlia *n. (bot.)* dalia.
daily *adj.* eguneroko, eguneko. *adv.* egunero, egunoroz.
daintily *adv.* fin, estitasunez.
daintiness *n.* fintasun.
dainty *adj.* fin.
dairy *n.* esnetegi, gurindegi, esnedenda, gaztandegi. **Dairy product.** Esneki. *n.* esne-etxalde.
dais *n.* oholtza.
daisy *n. (bot.)* bitxilore.
dale *n.* haran; zolagune.
dam *v.t.* urbildu; oztopatu.
dam *n.* urbiltoki, urezi, urlingirda.
damage *v.t./v.i.* kalte egin, gaitz egin.
damage *n.* gaitz, kalte, galera, galketa, hondamen, hondamendi. *n. (pl.)* gaitzak eta okerrak.
damaged *adj.* kaltedun, kaltiar.
damaging *adj.* kaltegarri, kaltetsu, kaltekor, kaltegarrizko,

gaitzegingarri, kaltegile.
dame *n.* emakume.
damn *v.t.* madarikatu, kondenatu, gaitzetsi.
damn *int.* madarikatua, demonioa.
damnable *adj.* madarikagarri.
damnation *n.* kondenamendu.
damned *adj.* madarikatu(a), madarikagarri.
damning *adj.* kondenatzaile, gaitzesko.
damningly *adv.* gaizkiesaka.
damp *adj.* heze, erdibusti(a), hezetsu.
dampen *v.t.* hezetu, erdibusti.
damper *n.* indargetzaile.
dampness *n.* hezetasun, hezedura.
damsel *n.* neskatila.
dance *v.i./v.t.* dantzan egin, dantzatu.
dance *n.* dantza, dantzaldi. **Dance partner.** Dantzakide. Dantzalagun. **Dance group.** Dantzaritalde.
dancer *n./adj.* dantzari, dantzarisa.
dandelion *n.* sorginbelar, txikoribelar.
dandruff *n.* burukozahi, ezkabia, zolda.
dandruffy *adj.* zoldadun, zoldatsu.
dandy *n.* kriket. *adj.* bikain.
danger *n.* arrisku, galbide, galzori, erorbide. **To be in danger.** Galbideratu.
dangerous *adj.* arriskutsu, galbidegarri, galbidetsu, galbidezko, arriskugarri, erorgarri.
dangerously *adv.* arriskuz, erorgarriki.
dangerousness *n.* arriskugarritasun.
dangle *v.i.* eskegi, zintzilikatu, zintzilika ezarri.
dank *adj.* busti.
dapper *adj.* dotore, apain (gizonak).
dare *v.i./v.t.* ausartu, benturatu.
daring *n.* kopeta, oldarkoitasun, ausartasun, ausardia. *adj.* izugaitz, beldurgaitz, ikaragaitz, ausarta, kopetadun.
dark *n.* ilun. **To get dark.** Ilundu. Itzaldu. *adj.* ilun, ilunpeko, argigabe, goibel, itzal, itzaltsu; -ilun.
darken *v.t./v.i.* belztu, ilundu, ilunpetu, itzalcztatu, itzalpctu, goibeldu, gautu.
darkly *adv.* ilunpean.
darkness *n.* ilun, ilunbe, iluntasun, belztasun, goibeltasun.
dark-skinned *adj.* beltzaran.
darling *adj.* bihotzeko, laztan, maitagarri, maitetxo, moñoño, kutun, maite, pottolo, maiteño.
darn *v.t.* sareztatu.
darn *int.* madarikatu(a).
darner *n.* sareztari.
dart *n.* gezitxo, azkon.
dash *v.t.* bota, jaurtiki, egotzi. *v.i.* batpatean iragan, korrika egin.
dash *n.* marra, lerrotxo. *n.* abiada.
dashing *adj.* apain, dotore.
dastardly *adj.* petral.
data *n. (pl.)* datu(ak).
date *v.t./v.i.* epea jarri, eguna ipini. *v.i./v.t.* (*v.i.*, askotan **from**-ekin)

noizkotu. **To be up to date.**
Gaurkotu. *v.t./v.i.* mutil edo neska
lagunarekin irten.
date *n.* egun, noiz. *n.* elkarraldi. *n.*
(bot.) datil.
date stamper *n.* noizgailu.
dating *n.* noizkotasun. *n.* elkarraldi.
dative *n. (gram.)* datibo.
datum *n. (sing.) of data.*
daub *v.t.* lokaztu, lohiztatu.
daughter *n.* alaba.
daughter-in-law *n.* errain.
dauntless *adj.* ikaraezin, ikaragabe,
ikaragaitz, beldurgaitz.
davenport *n.* lozizeilu.
dawdle *v.i.* berandutu.
dawn *v.i.* egundu, egunabartu,
egunargitu, goizargitu, oskorritu. *v.i.*
hasi.
dawn *n.* egunsenti, goizalde,
egunabar, egunargite, egunurratze,
goiznabar, argibegi, goiztiri,
argihaste, oilarite.
day *n.* egun; egu-; aldi. **On the same
day.** Egun berean. **During the day.**
Egun argiz. **Every day.** Egunero. **Day
by day.** Egunetik egunera. **By day.**
Egunez. *adj.* egunezko.
day after tomorrow *n.* etzi.
day before yesterday *n.* herenegun.
daybreak *n.* egunabar, egunsenti,
goizalde.
daydream *v.i.* esnaturik amets egin.
daydream *n.* esnaturik eginiko
amets(a).
daydreaming *adj.* ameskor, ameskoi.
day laborer *n.* eskulangile, soldatari,
egunlangile.
daylight *n.* eguargi, egunargi.
day off *n.* oporregun, jaiegun, jai. **To
take a day off.** Jai egin.
daytime *n.* egunaldi. *adj.* egunezko.
daze *v.t.* txorabiatu, sorgortu.
daze *n.* txorabio.
dazzle *v.t./v.i.* liluratu; dirdiratu.
deacon *n. (eccl.)* diakono.
deaconship *n. (eccl.)* diakonotza.
dead *n.* hil(ak), hildako. *adj.* hil, hildako,
zerraldo. **To drop dead.** Zerraldo
erori. *adj.* sor, sor eta lor, minsor,
mingor. *adj.* bizigabe, geldi. *adj.* igar
(adarrak). *adj.* itzali (su, garmendi).
adj. ahitu, akitu, nekatu. *adj.* geldi
(ur). *adj.* hil (bateria, hizkuntza).
adj./adv. guztiz; guztizko (isiltasuna).
adj. batpateko (geldialdi).
deaden *v.t.* moteldu, erdihil.
dead end *n.* irtenezin, kaleitxi.
deadline *n.* epemuga, epebete,
mugaegun, azkenegun.
deadliness *n.* hilgarritasun.
deadly *adj./adv.* hilkor.
deaf *adj.* entzungor, gor. **To turn a
deaf ear (to).** Gor egin. Entzungor
egin.
deaf and dumb *adj.* gormutu.
deafen *v.t.* gortu.

deafening *adj.* gorgarri, sorgarri,
burrunbatsu.
deaf-mute *n.* gormutu.
deafness *n.* gorreri, gortasun, sorreri,
sogordura. **Slight deafness.**
Gorraize.
deal *v.t.* negoziatu, tratatu, tratu egin.
v.t. esku izan (kartajoko).
deal *n.* hitzarmen, akordio, itun, tratu.
n. esku (kartajoko).
dealer *n.* merkatari, salerosle, tratulari.
n. banatzaile (kartajoko).
dealt *p.part. of deal.*
dean *n.* dekano.
dear *adj.* bihotzeko, kutun, maite,
laztan, maiteño, moñoño, pottolo,
maitagarri, maitatu(a), begiko, min.
adj./adv. garesti, kario.
dearly *adv.* bihotzez, biziki,
maitagarriki, maitagarriro. *adv.* kario.
dearth *n.* eskasaldi, urrialdi,
gabetasun.
death *n.* heriotze, herio. *adj.* hil.
deathbed *n.* hilohe.
death knell *n.* hiljoaldi, hilkanpai,
hilezkila, hilots.
deathly *adj.* hilkor, zorigaiztoko,
zoritxarreko. *adv.* gaizki, hilbizian.
death sentence *n.* heriotzepai.
debase *v.t.* doilortu.
debasing *adj.* doilorgarri, zitalgarri,
lotsarazle.
debatable *adj.* eztabaidagarri,
zalantzagarri.
debate *v.i./v.t.* eztabaidatu.
debate *n.* eztabaida.
debauch *v.t.* lasaikerian eror arazi.
debauchery *n.* lasaikeria.
debilitate *v.t.* indargabetu, ahuldu.
debilitating *adj.* makalgarri, ahulgarri.
debilitation *n.* ahultasun, makalaldi.
debility *n.* ahuleria, makaltasun,
indargabetasun.
debit *n.* zor, zorpe.
debonair *adj.* dotore, lirain.
debone *v.t.* hezurgabetu.
debranch *v.t.* desadartu.
debris *n.* sastar.
debt *n.* zor, zorketa, zorpe,
ordainbehar.
debtor *n.* zordun, zorpeko.
debut *v.i./v.t.* estreinatu.
debut *n.* estreinaldi.
debutante *n.* estreinari (ia beti
emakumea).
decade *n.* hamarrurte, hamarrurtealdi.
decadence *n.* beheraldi,
gainbeheraldi, jaitsialdi, gainbehera.
decadent *adj.* jauskor, beherakor.
decaffeinate *v.t.* deskafetu.
decant *v.t.* zurrustatu, turrustatu.
decanter *n.* garrafoi.
decapitate *v.t.* burugabetu, burua
kendu, kokota kendu, kokota ebaki.
decapitated *adj.* burugabe.
decapitation *n.* burumozketa,
lepamozketa, lepamozte.

decasyllabic adj. hamarsilabadun.
decay v.i. usteldu, haratusteldu. v.i. gainbeheratu.
decay n. usteldura, ustelkeria, usteltasun. n. beheraldi, jaitsialdi.
deceased adj. hildako, hil(a).
deceit n. azpikeria, iruzurbide, iruzur, iruzurketa, maltzurkeria, atzipe, bihurrikeria.
deceitful n. maltzurkeriazko, iruzurkeriazko, gezurti, gezurzale.
deceitfully adv. maltzurki, atzipez, malmuzki, bihurriki.
deceitfulness n. malmuztasun.
deceive v.t./v.i. engainatu, iruzur egin, iruzurtu, atzipetu, ziria sartu.
deceiver n. iruzurle, iruzurgile.
December n. abendua.
decency n. onestasun, zintzotasun, prestutasun, erabidetasun.
decent adj. itxurazko, mazal, zintzo.
decently adv. oneski, erabidez.
decentralize v.t. deserdiratu, deszentralizatu.
deception n. iruzur, iruzurkeria, etsipen.
deceptive adj. iruzurrezko, iruzurti, faltsu, gezurti, engainagarri.
deceptively adv. iruzurrez, etsipenez.
decide v.t./v.i. erabaki, zirti-zarta egin.
decided adj. erabakitako.
decidedly adv. zirt edo zart.
deciduous adj. jauskor, erorbera, erorkor.
deciduousness n. erorkortasun.
decimal adj./n. hamartar.
decimate v.t. hamarnakotu, hamarkatu, hamarretik bat hil.
decimeter n. dezimetro.
decipher v.t. argi egin, tankera eman, tankeratu, igerri.
decision n. erabaki, erabakikuntza. n. epai.
decisive adj. erabakikor, erabakitzaile, erabakteko, zirt edo zarteko.
decisively adv. erabakiz, zirt edo zart, zirti-zarta.
decisiveness n. erabakikortasun.
deck n. ontzigain.
declarable adj. aitorbidezko.
declaration n. aitor, aitorpen, aitormen, aitorkizun, azalpen, adierazpen, aldarrikapen. n. ageri.
declarative adj. azalbidezko, agerbidezko.
declare v.t./v.i. aitortu, azaldu, erakutsi, ageri, agertu.
declarer n. azaltzaile.
declension n. (gram.) deklinabide, deklinazio.
declinable adj. deklinagarri.
decline v.t./v.i. ukatu, uko egin. v.t./v.i. gainbeheratu. v.t./v.i. (gram.) deklinatu. v.i. gaizkoatu.
decline n. gainbeheraldi, gainbeheraketa. n. ahuldura, makaldura, beherakada, eroraldi. n.

ekonomi-beheraldi.
decompose v.i./v.t. usteldu, kirastu.
decomposition n. usteldura.
decontaminate v.t. desizurritu, deskirastu, deskutsatu.
decontamination n. deskutsadura.
decorate v.t. apaindu, dotoretu, edertu, politu. v.t. kondekoratu.
decoration n. apaindura, apainketa, ederketa; apaingarri. n. kondekorapen, paparreko.
decorative adj. apaingarri, edergarri.
decorator n. edertzaile, dotoretzaile, apaintzaile.
decorous adj. apaingarri, edergarri.
decorum n. lotsa, erabide, eratasun.
decoy n. erakargailu.
decreasable adj. gutigarri.
decrease v.i./v.t. beheratu, jaitsi, gutitu, eskastu, txikitu, murriztu, urritu.
decrease n. gutiketa, urripen, beherapen.
decreasing adj. gutikor, urritzaile, beherakor. n. urridura.
decree v.t. dekretu.
decree n. manu, aginduagiri.
decrepit adj. zaharko, zaharkote.
decrepitude n. zaharreri.
decry v.t. gaitzetsi.
dedicate v.t. dedikatu. v.t. (oneself) saiatu, ahalegindu.
dedicated adj. saiatu(a). adj. dedikatu(a).
dedication n. dedikapen, eskaintza. n. saiapen.
deduce v.t. ondoretu, eratorri, atera.
deduct v.t. deskontatu, kendu.
deductible adj. kengarri.
deduction n. aterakizun, eratorpen, ondoriokunde. n. kenkari, kenketa.
deductive adj. ondorezko.
deed n. egintza, egite. n. jabetza-titulu, jabego-agiri.
deem v.t. gogartu, pentsatu, uste izan, uste ukan.
deep n. itsasondo, itsaspe. adj. sakon, hondodun; barne, barnekor, barreneko.
deepen v.t./v.i. barrendu, sakondu, barnetu.
deepening n. sakonketa.
deeply adv. sakonki, barrenki, barneki.
deepness n. sakontasun.
deep-sea diver n. itsaspekari, urpekari.
deer n. (zool.) orein, orkatz, basahuntz.
deerskin n. oreinlarru.
deface v.t. itsusitu, itsustu, ezaindu.
defamation n. famakenketa, gaizkiesate, izenkenketa.
defamatory adj. izenlohigarri, desizenezko, laidotzaile.
defame v.t. gaizki esan, gaitz esan, fama kendu, laidoztatu, izengabetu.
defamed adj. izentxarreko.

defamer n. famakentzaile, izenkentzaile, gaitzesale, gaizkiesale.
default v.i. eginkizun bat ez bete, kontratu bat ez bete.
defeat v.t. suntsitu, azpiratu, zanpatu, goibeheratu, menperatu.
defeat n. galtze, galera, galketa, lurjoaldi; hondamen.
defeated adj. lurjota.
defecate v.i. kaka egin, sabelustu, gorotz egin, sats egin.
defecation n. sabelustutze.
defect v.i. erbesteratu.
defect n. akats, huts, hutsune.
defection n. fedeukamen, zinauste. n. erbesteraketa.
defective adj. akastun, okerdun, hutsegingarri, urri. **Defective verb.** Aditz urri.
defectiveness n. narriotasun, huskortasun.
defend v.t. defenditu, babestu, babes egin, aldeztu, aldezkatu.
defendable adj. defendagarri.
defendant n. salatua; hauzipeko.
defended adj. babesdun, babestu(a).
defender n. defendatzaile, aldezlari, babesle.
defense n. aldezketa, gerizagarri, magalpe, babesgarri, babespe, defentsa.
defenseless adj. babesgabe, laguntzagabe.
defenselessness n. babesgabetasun, babesgabezia.
defensible adj. defendagarri.
defensive adj. babesezko, babeskor.
defer v.t./v.i. geroratu, gerorakotu, atzeratu, gibeleratu.
deference n. begirune, begiramen, begirapen.
deferent adj. begiramentsu.
deferential adj. begirunetsu, adikor.
deferment n. gerorapen, atzerabide.
deferrable adj. epegarri, berangarri, luzagarri.
deferral n. berandupen.
deferred adj. atzeratu, luzagarri.
defiance n. aupada.
defiant adj. buruemaile.
defiantly adv. etsaiki.
deficiency n. eza.
deficient adj. urri, eskas. adj. adimen laburreko.
deficit n. (econ.) dirufalta, dirueza.
defier n. aupagile, aupakari, aupari, desafiatzaile.
defile v.t. zikindu, kutsatu. v.i. lerroz joan, andanan ibili.
definable adj. definigarri.
define v.t. definitu, zertu. v.t. mugatu, zedatu.
definite adj. erabateko, irme, irmo, sendo. adj. (gram.) mugarazle, mugatu(a).
definitely adv. irmoki.
definition n. definizio, zerketa.

definitive adj. behinbetiko, erabateko.
definitively adv. erabakiz.
deflate v.t./v.i. hustu, despuztu, haizea galdu.
deflation n. haizegalketa.
deflect v.t. alderazi, alderatu.
defloration n. desloraketa, desloramendu. n. mintzurradura, mintzurraketa.
deflower v.t. desloratu, loregabetu. v.t. emakumeari birjintasuna kendu.
defog v.t./v.i. deslurrindu.
defoliate v.t. hostogabetu, desorritu.
defoliation n. desorridura, desostoketa.
deform v.t. desitxuratu, deseratu, itsustu, eragabetu, itxuragabetu.
deformed adj. deserazko, desitxurazko, itxuragabe(ko), eragabeko.
deformity n. deseraketa, desitxurapen, itxuragabetasun, eragabetasun, itsusketa.
defraud v.t. engainatu, iruzur egin, ebatsi, atzipetu, ziria sartu.
defrost v.t./v.i. desizoztu.
deft adj. moldetsu.
deftly adv. moldetsuki.
defunct adj. zen(a), hil(a).
defy v.t. aupaka egin, aurka egin.
degeneracy n. zitaldura.
degenerate v.i. desjatortu, endekatu.
degenerate adj. endekatu(a).
degeneration n. desjatortasun, desjatorketa.
deglutition n. irenste, irespen.
degradation n. doilorkeria, zitalkeria.
degrade v.t. desohoretu, kaxkartu, doilortu.
degrading adj. doilorgarri, zitalgarri, desohoregarri, lotsarazle.
degree n. gradu, beromaila. n. gradu, maila. n. gradu, titulu; doctoradutza, lizentzia.
dehumanize v.t. desgizartetu, gizagabetu.
dehydrate v.t./v.i. urgabetu.
deification n. jainkotze.
deify v.t. jainkotu, jaungoikotu.
deign v.t./v.i. baimena eman, utzi; amor eman.
deity n. jainko, jaungoiko. n. jaungoikotasun, jainkotasun.
dejected adj. lurjota.
dejection n. beherapen, lurjoaldi.
delay v.t./v.i. geroratu, berandutu, atzeratu, luzarazi.
delay n. luzabide, luzapen, atzerapen, atzerabide, atzerakuntza, luzaketa, luzamen, gibelamendu, luzakortasun.
delayed adj. berantiar, gerotiar.
delaying adj. luzatzaile, gerozale, luzagarri. n. atzeratze.
delectable adj. atsegingarri, gozo, zaporetsu, gozagarri.
delegate v.t. ordezkotu, eskubidetu, eskubidea eman.

delegate *n.* agintariorde, ordezkari; diputatu, mandatari.
delegation *n.* mandataritza, ordezkaritza, ordezkotasun.
delete *v.t.* kendu, ezegin.
deleterious *adj.* kaltegarri.
deletion *n.* kenketa, ezegite.
Delaware *n. (geog.)* Estatu Batuetako estatu bat.
deliberate *v.t.* pentsatu, gogoratu, gogoan erabili.
deliberate *adj.* xedatsu. *adj.* motel.
deliberately *adv.* ohartuki, nahita, jakinez. *adv.* astiro, poliki-poliki.
deliberation *n.* gogaketa, gogarpen, pentsaketa.
delicacy *n.* fintasun.
delicate *adj.* fin.
delicately *adv.* bigunki, bigunkiro.
delicatessen *n.* maneatutako janariak saltzen diren denda.
delicious *adj.* ahogozagarri, gozo, zaporetsu.
delight *v.t./v.i. (v.i., askotan in-ekin)* atsegindu, gozarotu, gozartu, plazer egin.
delight *n.* atsegin, atsegindura.
delighted *adj.* atsegindu(a).
delightful *adj.* atsegingarri, atsegintsu, laketgarri, zoragarri, gozatsu.
delightfully *adv.* zoragarriki, zoragarriro.
delightfulness *n.* zoragarritasun, xoragarritasun.
delimit *v.t.* mugarritu, xedatu, zedarritu, mugatu.
delimitation *n.* mugapen, mugarriketa, xedaketa, zedarriketa, zedarriztapen.
delimiter *n.* mugatzaile.
delimiting *adj.* mugarazle, mugatzaile.
delineate *v.t.* lerrotu, xedatu.
delineation *n.* mugaketa, lerroketa.
delinquency *n.* gaizkintza, gaizkiletasun, luzakeria.
delinquent *n.* gaizkin, gaizkile. *adj.* gaizkile.
delirious *adj.* zorabiodun.
delirium *n.* zoraldi, zorabio, burunahasketa, ameskoikeria.
deliver *v.t.* helarazi, partitu, banatu. *v.i.* haur egin, haur ukan.
deliverance *n.* banaketa. *n.* libraketa.
delivery *n.* emanaldi. *n.* erditzapen.
dell *n.* ziloka, zolagune.
delouse *v.t.* zorriak kendu, zorrigabetu.
delta *n.* delta.
delude *v.t.* iruzur egin, atzipetu, ziria sartu, zipotza sartu.
deluge *n.* uholde, uraldi.
delusion *n.* ameskeria, ametsuts. *n.* iruzurkeria.
deluvial *adj.* uholdezko.
deluvian *adj.* uholdetar.
deluxe *adj.* sekulako, bikainen(a).
delve *v.t.* industu. *v.t.* ikertu.
demagogue *n.* demagogo.

demagogy *n.* demagogia.
demand *v.t./v.i.* eskatu, erreklamatu; galdetu.
demand *n.* eskabide, eskakizun, eskari, eske, manamendu, erregu.
demanding *adj.* eskabidezko, eskaerazko, eskakor.
demarcate *v.t.* mugatu.
demarcation *n.* mugatasun.
demarcator *n.* mugarritzaile.
demeanor *n.* jokaera, jokabide, portaera, gizabide.
demented *adj.* erokeriazko, ero.
dementia *n.* erokeria, erotasun.
demerit *n.* gaitzesbide, ezmerezimendu.
demigod *n.* erdijainko.
demigoddess *n.* erdijainkosa.
demijohn *n.* garrafoi.
demilitarized *adj.* desmilitartu(a).
demise *n.* galera, heriotze.
democracy *n.* demokrazia.
democrat *n. (pol.)* demokrata.
democratic *adj.* demokratiko.
demographic *adj.* demografiko.
demography *n.* demografia.
demolish *v.t.* desegin, azpirakatu, eror arazi, jausiarazi, amildu, eraitsi, beherarazi.
demolition *n.* azpiraketa, desegite, hondaketa, desegintza, erauzketa.
demon *n.* gaizkin, deabru, galtzagorri.
demoniacal *adj.* deabruzko.
demonology *n.* deabrugurtza.
demonstrable *adj.* erakusgarri. *adj.* frogagarri.
demonstrate *v.t.* erakutsi, agertu. *v.t.* egiztatu, frogatu, ziurpetu. *v.i.* manifestatu.
demonstration *n.* erakuste. *n.* froga, frogaketa, ikuspide. *n.* manifestaldi, manifestazio.
demonstrative *adj. (gram.)* erakusle. *adj.* erakuskor, frogagarri.
demonstrator *n.* aurkezlari, aurkezle, agerkide. *n.* frogatzaile. *n.* manifestari.
demoralize *v.t.* desadoretu.
demoralized *adj.* desadoretu(a).
demoralizing *adj.* desadoregarri, kikilgarri.
demur *v.t.* kontra egin, kontra jarri.
demure *adj.* eratsu, eraoneko, modu oneko, lotsakor.
demurely *adv.* erabidez, apalki, apalkiro.
den *n.* ohatze, zulo. **Wolf's den.** Otsazulo.
denaturalize *v.t.* desjatortu.
denature *v.t.* desnaturaldu.
deniable *adj.* ezeztagarri, ukagarri.
denial *n.* ezeztapen, ukamen, gezurtapen, uko.
denier *n.* ezeztaile, ezeztatzaile, gezurtatzaile.
denigrate *v.t.* desohoretu, itsusitu, laidokatu, izengabetu.

denigrating *adj.* desohoregarri, izenlohigarri, mihizikin, mingainzikin.
denigration *n.* laidogile.
denizen *n.* biztanle.
denominate *v.t.* izena eman, izendatu, izeneztatu.
denomination *n.* deitura, izendapen, izeneztapen. *n.* sail, talde. *n.* elkarte-erlijioso. *n.* balio.
denominator *n.* izendatzaile. *n.* (math.) beheko.
denounce *v.t.* salatu.
dense *adj.* zarratu.
density *n.* (phys.) dentsitate.
dent *v.t./v.i.* akastu, maspildu, konkatu.
dent *n.* akasdura.
dental *adj.* hagineko, hortzeko.
dented *adj.* akastsu.
dentist *n.* haginateratzaile, haginlari, hortzateratzaile.
dentures *n.* (pl.) hortzordeko.
denude *v.t.* desapaindu.
denunciation *n.* salaketa, salakuntza.
deny *v.t.* ezeztu, ukatu, uko egin, gezurtatu, ezeztatu.
deodorant *n.* desusaingailu, desusaingarri.
deodorize *v.t.* desusaindu.
depart *v.i./v.t.* irten, abiatu, atera, jalgi.
departed *adj.* joandako. *n./adj.* hildako.
department *n.* sail, departamentu.
departmental *adj.* departamentuko.
departure *n.* joan, abialdi, jalgitza, joate, irteera. **Day of departure.** Irtenegun.
depend *v.i.* (gehienetan on-ekin) beragan egon, eskuan egon, mende egon, baldinpetu.
dependability *n.* seriostasun.
dependable *adj.* ganorazko, serios.
dependably *adv.* ganoraz, serioski.
dependence *n.* -(en) premia; eskuko. *n.* konfidantza. *n.* menpetasun, menpe.
dependency *n.* menpekotasun, agindupe. *n.* kolonia.
dependent *adj.* eskuko, aginpeko, meneko, menpeko.
depict *v.t.* marraztu. *v.t.* azaldu.
depilatory *n.* ilesoilgailu.
deplete *v.t.* gutitu, agortu, urritu.
deplorable *adj.* deitoragarri, auhengarri, negargarri.
deplore *v.t.* dolutu.
deploy *v.t.* zabaldu.
deployment *n.* zabalketa.
depopulate *v.t.* jendegabetu, despopulatu.
depopulation *n.* desjendeketa, despopulaketa.
deport *v.t.* deportatu, erbesteratu, atzerriratu, kanporatu. *v.t.* (oneself) portatu, jokatu.
deportation *n.* deserriraketa, erbesteraketa.
deportment *n.* gizalege, jokaera.

depose *v.t.* desaulkitu, desezarri, kenarazi.
deposer *n.* kenarazle.
deposit *v.t./v.i.* ezarri, ipini, jarri, diru ezarpena egin.
deposit *n.* (econ.) fidantza, diruezarketa, dirusarketa, ezarpen.
deposit book *n.* (econ.) libreta.
deposition *n.* testigutza; desaulkidura.
depositor *n.* diruezarle.
depository *n.* gordailu, gordetegi.
depot *n.* geraleku, geltoki.
depraved *adj.* galdu, oker, bihurri, gaizto, ustel.
deprecate *v.t.* gaitzetsi. *v.t.* gutietsi.
deprecatory *adj.* gutiespenezko, laidogarri, laidoztatzaile.
depreciate *v.t./v.i.* beheratu, merketu, ezbaliotu.
depreciation *n.* (econ.) desbalioketa, desbalioztapen, ezbalio, diru beheratze.
depredation *n.* harrapakeria, lapurketa, harrapaketa.
depress *v.t.* adoregabetu. *v.t.* markatu, sakatu.
depressed *adj.* atsekabekor, goibel. *adj.* (econ.) goibeheratu(a).
depressing *adj.* desadoregarri, nahigabetzaile, goibelgarri.
depression *n.* makalaldi, adoregabetasun, apalaldi, goibeheraldi, ahulaldi. *n.* (econ.) depresio ekonomiko. *n.* sakonune, zokogune, zulogune, sakonalde, malkargune.
deprivation *n.* gabezia, eztasun, eza.
deprive *v.t.* gabetu, murritu, kendu.
deprived *adj.* -gabe, -gabeko.
depth *n.* sakonera, sakontasun, barnatasun; barnetasun, barne, hondotasun.
depths *n.* (pl.) hondo, itsasbarne, itsasondo, itsasosin, osin, itsasleze.
deputation *n.* diputazio.
deputize *v.t./v.i.* ordezkotu.
deputy *n.* (pol.) diputatu; mandatari. *n.* Estatu Batuetako sheriffaren laguntzaile.
derail *v.i./v.t.* karrile galdu.
derailment *n.* karrilgalketa.
deranged *adj.* zoro.
deride *v.t.* farre egin, adarra jo, lotsagarritu, irrigarritu, trufatu.
derision *n.* irrigaizto.
derisive *adj.* irrigarri, laidogarri, isekagarri.
derisively *adv.* laidoz.
derivation *n.* eratormen, eratorpen.
derivative *adj.* eratorkor, eratorle.
derive *v.t./v.i.* (gehienetan from-ekin) eratorri.
derived *adj.* eratorri(a). **A derived word.** Hitz eratorria.
dermatologist *n.* larruerizain, larrusendagile.
dermatology *n.* larruerizaintza.

dermis *n.* *(anat.)* larruazal, larruarte.
derogatory *adj.* arbuiozko, ezezko.
descend *v.i./v.t.* jaitsi, jetxi, beheratu.
descendant *n.* ondorengo, geroko.
descent *n.* beherapen, beheraketa, apalaldi.
describable *adj.* kalifikagarri, kontagarri.
describe *v.t.* deskribatu, kontatu.
description *n.* azalpen, deskribapen.
desecrate *v.t.* desagaratu.
desecration *n.* desagarakunde, profanazio.
desert *v.t./v.i.* laga, oldartu; ihes egin.
desert *n.* basamortu, eremu, desertu. *adj.* basamortuko.
deserted *adj.* inorgabeko, auzogabe, inorgabe.
deserter *n.* iheslari (soldadu), iheskari.
desertion *n.* soldaduaren iheseta.
deserve *v.t./v.i.* merezi, merezi ukan, merezi izan, duin izan.
deserved *adj.* merezitako.
deservedly *adv.* irabaziz, mereziki.
deserving *adj.* merezidun, merezigarri, nor; -garri.
deservingly *adv.* mereziz.
desiccation *n.* agorketa, ihartasun, lehorketa, agorpen.
design *v.t.* diseinatu, gogotan erabili.
design *n.* marrazki, zirrimarra. *n.* asmo.
designate *v.t.* izendatu,izeneztatu, aipatu.
designated *adj.* izeneko.
designation *n.* izendapen, izeneztapen.
designator *n.* izendatzaile.
designer *n.* marrazlari, marrazkigile, marrazkilari, irudigile. *n.* jostun.
desirable *adj.* atsegingarri, guragarri. *adj.* bikain. *adj.* haragikor. *adj.* gomendagarri.
desire *v.t.* nahi izan, gogo ukan, irrikatu, opa izan, opatu, nahi ukan.
desire *n.* gogo, nahi, gurari, gutizia, irrika, tirria, apeta, grina.
desirous *adj.* guratsu, irrikatsu, gogotsu, gutiziatsu, gutizios; -gale, nahi.
desist *v.i.* etsi, gelditu, geratu, amor eman.
desk *n.* idazmahai, ikasmahai.
desolate *adj.* soil, lehor, inorgabe. *adj.* gogobehera, nahigabedun, atsekabedun.
desolation *n.* hondamen; suntsiketa.
despair *v.i.* desitxarotu, itxarogabetu, etsitu.
despair *n.* etsipen, desitxaropen.
despairingly *adv.* desitxaroz, etsigarriki.
desperado *n.* gaizkin, gaizkile.
desperate *adj.* desitxarokor, etsita.
desperately *adv.* desitxaroz, etsipenez, etsigarriki.
desperation *n.* desitxaropen, etsipen, etsi.

despicable *adj.* gaitzesgarri, arbuiagarri, bilau, erdeinagarri, alproja, purtzil, zirtzil.
despicably *adv.* landerki, zakurki, zirtzilki.
despisable *adj.* gorrotagarri.
despise *v.t.* gorrotatu, higuindu, gorroto ukan, arbuiatu.
despised *adj.* gorrotozko.
despite *prep.* arren, nahiz eta.
despoil *v.t.* desjabetu, lapurtu, larrutu, orraztu.
despoliation *n.* ebasketa, ebaste, lapurreta.
despondency *n.* goibeltasun, uzkurdura.
despondent *adj.* gogobehera, goibel.
despot *n.* jauntxo, jauntzar.
despotic *adj.* larderiadun, agintezale, larderiatsu.
despotically *adv.* agintekeriaz, larderiaz.
despotism *n.* nagusikeria, agintekeria, larderialdi.
dessert *n.* postre, bazkalburuko, bazkalazkeneko.
destination *n.* helbide, helburu, norako.
destine *v.i.* destinatu.
destined *adj.* patuzko.
destiny *n.* gertabehar, alabehar, zori, jazobehar, patu, ezinbeste, asturu.
destitute *adj.* ezergabe, lander, behartsu.
destitution *n.* landerreria.
destroy *v.t./v.i.* desegin, deuseztu, errautsi, suntsitu, hondatu, ezeztatu, xahutu.
destroyable *adj.* deuseztagarri, ezeztagarri.
destroyer *n.* deuseztatzaile, ezeztatzaile, errausle, puskatzaile, apurtzaile. *n.* ontzisuntsitzaile.
destructible *adj.* deuseztagarri, ezeztagarri, suntsikor, desegingarri, ezerezkor.
destruction *n.* desegite, ezereztapen, suntsiketa, errausketa, porrokaldi, hondamendi, xahupen, sarraski, sakaila.
destructive *adj.* suntsitzaile, desegile, ezeztatzaile, hondagarri, suntsigarri, suntsikor, errausle, hondamenezko, irestzaile.
destructively *adv.* hondagarriro.
destructiveness *n.* suntsigarritasun, hondagarritasun.
desultory *adj.* ustegabeko, jarraigabeko. *adj.* noizbehinkako.
detach *v.t.* desitsasi, aldaratu.
detachable *adj.* aldaragarri.
detachment *n.* aldarakunde.
detail *v.t.* zehaztu.
detail *n.* zertzelada, xehetasun, zehazkizun. **In great detail.** Zeharo.
detailed *adj.* zehatz, zehatzale.
detailedness *n.* zehaztasun,

xehetasun.
detain v.t. gerarazi, geldiarazi.
detainable adj. geldigarri.
detainer n. gerarazle, geratzaile.
detainment n. harrapaldi, geldierazte, geldierazpen.
detect v.t. detektatu.
detective n. detektibe.
detention n. geldiarazpen, gerarazpen, geraldi.
deter v.t. oztopatu, eragotzi, debekatu.
detergent n. garbikari, garbikin.
deteriorate v.t./v.i. higatu, txarkitu, zirpildu, narriatu.
deteriorated adj. narriodun.
deterioration n. gaizkialdi, beherakada, higadura, narriapen.
determination n. buruzbide. n. zehaztapen.
determine v.t./v.i. erabaki, ebatzi. v.t./v.i. zertu, zehaztu, zuzendu.
determined adj. adoretsu, prestu, setatsu. adj. erabakitzaile.
determining adj. erabakitzaile.
detest v.t. gorrotatu, gorroto ukan, higuindu, herratu.
detestable adj. gorrotagarri, gorrotakor, higuingarri, gaitzesgarri, nardagarri.
detestably adv. gorrotagarriro, higuingarriki, higuingarriro, gaitzesgarriki, gaitzesgarriro.
detestation n. higuindura, nazkadura, okaztadura.
detester n. gorrotalari, gorrotatzaile, higuintzaile.
dethrone v.t. desaulkitu, deserregetu, tronugabetu.
dethronement n. deserregeketa, desaulkidura.
detonate v.i./v.t. danba egin, lehertu.
detonating device n. lehergailu, lehergai, eztandagailu.
detonation n. leherketa, eztanda.
detonator n. lehergailu, eztandagailu.
detour v.i./v.t. zeharkatu, okerrarazi.
detour n. desbideraketa, desbiderapen, zeharbide, norabide-aldaketa.
detoxicate v.t. pozoigabetu.
detoxify v.t. pozoigabetu.
detract v.i. (batzutan from-ekin) gutxitu, ezgaitu.
detraction n. gezurgaizto, gezurbeltz, gezurlaido, kalumnia.
detractor n. atzejaile, gutiarazle, gaitzerasle.
detriment n. kalte, hondamen, galera.
detrimental adj. galgarri, galkor, hondagarri, kaltegarri.
deuce n. biko.
devaluate v.t. desbalioztatu, ezbaliotu, hutsalarazi, balioa gutitu, balioa gainbera erori.
devaluation n. (econ.) desbalioketa, desbalioztapen, ezbalio, baliogalera, debaluazio.

devastate v.t. sarraskitu, suntsitu, porrokatu.
devastating adj. suntsigarri, suntsikor, suntsitzaile, hondagarri.
devastation n. suntsiketa, suntsigarritasun, porrokaketa, soilketa.
devastator n. porrokatzaile.
develop v.t./v.i. eboluzionatu, garatu, nagusitu, hazi. v.t. errebelatu.
developer n. argazki errebelagailu(a). n. Estatu Batuetako hirigile.
development n. hazkuntza, aurrerabide, bilakaera, eboluzio, bilakabide.
deviate v.i. desbideratu, desbidetu, saihestu.
deviation n. zeharketa, bidegalketa, desbideraketa, desbiderapen, noragabezia, desnorabide. n. desiritzi.
device n. gailu, aparailu. n. maneaketa.
devil n. deabru, galtzagorri, txerren.
devilish adj. deabruzko, deabrukoi.
devilishly adv. deabrukeriaz, deabruki, deabrukiro.
devilry n. deabrukeria.
devious adj. oker, desbidetu, noragabetu, bidegabetu. adj. iruzurgarri, iruzurgile.
devise v.t./v.i. asmatu, gogotan erabili.
devoid adj. (of) -gabe(ko).
devolution n. bihurketa, bihurrera, itzulera, berritzulketa.
devote v.t. eskaini, eman; -zaletu. v.t. dedikatu. v.t. (oneself) saiatu, ahalegindu.
devoted adj. -koi, -zale.
devotion n. eraspen, debozio. n. jainkozaletasun, jainkotiartasun.
devotional adj. deboziozko.
devour v.t. irentsi, klaskatu.
devourer n. irensle.
devouring adj. irensle, irenskor.
devout adj. jainkotar, jainkotiar, jainkozale, jaungoikozale, otoizbera, otoiztiar.
devoutness n. debozio.
dew n. ihintz, garo.
dewdrop n. ihintz-tanta.
dewfall n. ihintzaldi.
dewlap n. kokotsazpi, kokospe, kontrokots.
dexterity n. trebetasun, taxu, iaiotasun.
dextrous adj. eskuoneko, taxudun, iaio, jeinutsu.
dextrously adv. taiuz, moldetsuki.
diabetes n. (med.) diabete, gozoeri.
diabetic adj. diabetiko.
diabolical adj. deabruzko, gaizto.
diagnose v.t. eriaztertu, gaitza aztertu.
diagnosis n. (med.) eriazterpen, eriazterketa.
diagonal n./adj. diagonal.
diagram n. diagrama.
dial v.t. telefono-zenbakia markatu.

dialect n. hizkelgi, dialekto.
dialogue n. elkarrizketa.
dialysis n. dialisi.
diameter n. *(geom.)* diametro.
diamond n. diamante, bitxi.
diaper n. haurroihal, haurzapi, ipuroihal, ipurtzapi, pixoihal, txizoihal.
diaphragm n. diafragma.
diarrhea n. kakeri, kakajario, lasterreri, sabeleri, sabeljario, kakapirri, beruzko, berazko.
diary n. egunkari.
dice n. *(pl.)* xorta, seiko.
dictate v.t./v.i. iradatzi, diktatu. v.t./v.i. agindu, larderiatu.
dictation n. diktaketa.
dictator n. diktadore, zapaltzaile, jauntzar, oinperatzaile.
dictatorial adj. diktadore, larderiatsu, larderiazko.
dictatorially adv. larderiaz.
dictatorship n. diktadura, uztarri.
diction n. ahosketa.
dictionary n. hiztegi.
did pret. of do.
didactic adj. irakaskor, irakaspidezko, irakasteko, didaktiko.
didactically adv. irakasbidez.
didacticism n. didaktika.
didn't "did + not"-aren laburpena.
die v.i. hil, azkenarnastu, zendu. v.i. **(down)** jabaldu, haizeztitu.
die n. altzairumolde; -molde.
dierisis n. dieresi.
diesel engine n. diesel.
diesel fuel n. gasoil.
diet v.t./v.i. janeurritu.
diet n. janarau, janeurri, dieta.
differ v.i. ezberdin izan. v.i. akorgabetu.
difference n. ezberdintasun, besteiritzi, desberdintasun, diferentzia. n. alde. n. bereiztasun, ezaugarri. n. liskar, mokoketa.
different adj. ezberdin, desberdin, bestelako.
differentiate v.t./v.i. berezkatu, ezberdindu, berezitu.
differentiation n. ezberdintzapen, desberdintzapen.
differentiator n. ezberdintzaile, berezgarri.
differently adv. desberdinki.
differentness n. berdineztasun.
difficult adj. zail, gaitz, oztopatsu, eragozpenezko, gogor.
difficulty n. eragozpen, oztopo, zailtasun, gaiztasun, behaztopa; buruhauste, katramila.
diffidence n. kikilduria.
diffident adj. kikil, geldo.
diffuse v.t. hedatu.
diffusion n. hedamen, hedapen, zabalkunde.
diffusive adj. hedakor, zabalkor.
diffusiveness n. zabalkortasun.
dig v.i./v.t. (askotan **up**-ekin) zulatu,

zulo egin, desehortzi, aitzurtu.
dig n. ukondokada. n. irri-ohar. n. arkeologi zulaketa.
digest v.t./v.i. egosi, liseritu, eho.
digestibility n. egosgarritasun.
digestible adj. egosgarri, egosbera.
digestion n. digestio, egosketa, egostaldi, liseriketa.
digestive tract n. *(anat.)* egosgailu.
digger n. zulatzaile, aitzurlari. n. hondeagailu, induskailu.
digit n. hatzamar; behatz, hatz. n. zenbaki (zerotik bederatzira).
digital adj. behatzeko.
digitalis n. *(bot.)* kukubelar, kukufraka.
dignified adj. duingarri, eratsu, neurridun.
dignify v.t. duindu.
dignitary n. kargudun, handiki.
dignity n. duintasun.
digress v.i. bestetaratu.
digression n. desbideraketa, desbideraren.
dike n. kaimutur, urezi, murrutzar.
dilapidated adj. lurjota (etxe).
dilate v.t./v.i. zabalagotu.
dilation n. zabalkuntza, zabalpen, zabalketa, dilatazio.
dilatory adj. luzakor, luzagarrizko.
dilemma n. katramila, buruhauste.
diligence n. lankortasun.
diligent adj. langile, lankor, lanzale, grinatsu, fin, maratz.
diligently adv. ekinez.
dilute v.t. ureztatu, ureztu.
dim v.t. ilundu, ilunarazi, erditzali.
dime n. *(econ.)* Estatu Batuetako txakurrandi(a).
dimension n. izari, dimentsio.
dim headlights n. gurutzargi.
diminish v.t./v.i. gutiagotu, gutitu, murriztu, urritu.
diminishable adj. gutigarri, urrigarri.
diminishing adj. gutxigarri, txikigarri, txikitzaile.
diminution n. gutimen(du), eskasketa, urripen.
diminutive n. *(gram.)* diminutibo. adj. xehe, ttipitzaile.
dimly adv. ilun, ilunki, goibelki.
dimple n. masaileko zulotxo(a).
dim-witted adj. inozo, ergel, zozo, girten.
din n. iskanbila, zalaparta.
dine v.i. janaririk nagusiena jan. v.i. **(out)** jatetxean jan.
diner n. jantegi, jantoki. n. jankide, afaldar.
ding v.i. tilin egin, tilinkatu.
ding-dong n. dilin, dilin-dalan, din-dan, dindan-boleran.
dinner n. afal, afari. **Dinner time. Dinner hour.** Afalordu.
dinnerware n. mahaiontzi.
dining room n. jantoki, janleku.
dinosaur n. *(zool.)* dinosaurio.
diocesan adj. elizbarrutiar.

diocese *n. (eccl.)* elizbarruti, apezpikutegi.
dioxide *n. (chem.)* dioxido.
dip *v.t.* sakondu, murgildu.
dip *n.* sakongune.
diphtheria *n.* difteria, pintzelde.
dipthong *n.* diptongo.
diploma *n.* diploma, sinestagiri.
diplomacy *n. (pol.)* diplomazia.
diplomat *n. (pol.)* diplomari, diplomatiko.
diplomatic *adj.* diplomatiko.
diplomatically *adv.* diplomatikoki.
dipper *n.* burduntzali.
dire *adj.* izugarri, ikaragarri.
direct *v.t./v.i.* gidatu, zuzendu, norabidetu.
direct *adj.* zuzen, zuzeneko, xuxen.
direction *n.* bide, banda, norabide. *n.* zuzendaritza, gidaritzape, gobernu. *n.* argibide.
directional *adj.* norabidezko.
directly *adv.* zuzenki. *adv.* bapatean. *adv.* hain zuzen, hain zuzen ere.
director *n.* zuzendari, gerente, artezkari. *n.* komunikabideen gainbegiratzaile(a).
directorate *n.* zuzendaritza.
directorship *n.* zuzendaritza, gidaritza, buruzagitza.
directory *n.* telefono listin(a), telefono liburu.
dirge *n.* negarkantu, hiletasoinu, hilkantu.
dirigible *n.* haizontzi, aireuntzi, zepelin.
dirt *n.* lur. *n.* zikin. *n.* likistasun, lotsagabekeria, lizunkeria, lohikeria, urdekeria, zikinkeria.
dirtily *adv.* zikinki, zikinkiro. *adv.* likiski, lohiki, urdeki.
dirtiness *n.* zikinkeria, lohitasun. *n.* lohikeria, lizuntasun, likiskeria.
dirty *v.t./v.i.* zikindu, likistu, lohitu, satsutu.
dirty *adj.* zikin, lohi, kakazto, lohitsu. **To get dirty.** Zikindu. Lohitu. *adj.* maripurtzil, likits, lohi, satsu. *adv.* lohiki.
disability *n.* ezbaliapen, gaieztapen, gaieztasun.
disable *v.t.* ezgauzatu, gaieztu, desprestatu, ezbaliatu, ezindu.
disabled *adj.* elbarri, elbarridun; ezindu.
disadvantage *n.* desabantaila, gutiagotasun, aldetxar.
disadvantageous *adj.* desabantailatsu.
disaffect *v.t.* deszaletu.
disagree *v.i.* akorgabetu, gaizki etorri.
disagreeable *adj.* gozagaitz, gozagabe, izterbegiko.
disagreeableness *n.* gozagaiztasun, gozagaizkeria, gozagabekeria.
disagreeably *adv.* gozagaizki.
disagreement *n.* desadostasun, adiezin, adostezin, akorgabezia,

besteiritzi.
disappear *v.i.* desagertu, ezabatu, ezeztatu, itzalperatu.
disappearance *n.* desagerpen, desagerketa, itzaldura, ezabapen.
disappoint *v.t.* huts eman, desliluratu.
disappointment *n.* deslilura, desliluraketa.
disapproval *n.* gaitzespen, maiseaketa.
disapprove *v.t./v.i.* *(v.i. gehienetan of-ekin)* ezetsi, gaitzetsi, txarretsi, ezeztatu, txartzat eman.
disapproving *adj.* ezezle.
disapprovingly *adv.* ezetsiz.
disarm *v.t.* desarmatu, iskilo(ak) kendu, armagabetu.
disarmament *n.* armagabetze, ezarmaketa.
disarrange *v.t.* deskonpondu, aldrebestu.
disarranged *adj.* desegoki, galpartsu.
disarrangement *n.* deskonponketa.
disarray *n.* nahasmen, zabarkeria, arloteria, ilezutidura.
disaster *n.* hondamen, hondamendi, leherpen.
disastrous *adj.* hondagarri, hondamenezko, suntsigarri, galgarri, galkor.
disastrously *adv.* hondagarriro, suntsigarriz.
disastrousness *n.* hondagarritasun, suntsigarritasun.
disband *v.t./v.i.* banatu, barreiatu, banandu (taldeak).
disbelief *n.* sinesgabetasun; fedegabetasun.
disbelieve *v.t.* sinestegabetu.
disc *Cf. disk.*
discard *v.t.* baztertu, utzi. *v.t.* bota (kartajokoan).
discern *v.t.* ezagutu, argi ikusi.
discerner *n.* berezitzaile.
discernible *adj.* ikusgarri.
discerning *adj.* begizorrotz.
discernment *n.* argikusmen, adikuntza, asmamen, zolitasun, zorroztasun.
discharge *v.t.* lizentziatu. *v.t.* deskargatu.
discharge *n.* lizentziamendu, lizentziapen. *n.* altagiri. *n.* danbada, punpada. *n. (med.)* jario. *n. (elec.)* elektrika hustura.
disciple *n.* jarraitzaile; ikasle.
discipleship *n.* ikasletza.
disciplinary *adj.* araupezko. *adj.* zigorrezko, zentzabide.
discipline *n.* araubide. *n.* zigor, zentzabide.
disclaim *v.t.* ukatu, uko egin.
disclaimer *n.* uko.
disclose *v.t.* agertarazi, ezagutarazi, jakinarazi.
disclosure *n.* azalpen.
disco *n.* diskategi.

discolor *v.t./v.i.* desmargotu, tindugabetu, marguldu.
discoloration *n.* desmargoketa, marguldura.
discolored *adj.* margul, koloregabe.
discomfort *n.* deserosotasun.
disconcerting *adj.* aztoragarri.
disconnect *v.t.* deskonektatu.
disconnected *adj.* loturagabe, lotezin. *adj.* jarraigabe, ulergaitz.
discontent *n.* pozgabe.
discontented *adj.* pozgabe(ko), kontentagaitz.
discontinue *v.t.* segidagabetu.
discontinued *adj.* segidagabe.
discontinuity *n.* eten, segidagabetasun.
discontinuous *adj.* jarraigabe, iraungabe(ko).
discord *n.* bateztasun, desbatasun, banakuntza.
discordant *n.* ezakort. *n. (mus.)* abesgaitz, belarrimingarri.
discotheque *n.* diskategi.
discount *v.t.* deskontatu.
discount *n.* beherapen, deskontu.
discountable *adj.* kengarri.
discourage *v.t.* adoregabetu, desgogatu, gogogabetu, bihozkabetu.
discouraged *adj.* adoregabe, bihozgabe, gogogabe, desgogozko, lurjota, kikilduta.
discouragement *n.* adoregabetasun, bihozgabetasun, bihozgabezia, desgogo, makaldura, makurraldi.
discouraging *adj.* desadoregarri, gogogalgarri, kikilgarri.
discouragingly *adv.* etsigarriki.
discourse *n.* mintzaldi, hizketaldi.
discourteous *adj.* gisagabe, gizabidegabe.
discourteously *adv.* eragabeki, nabarmenki, nabarmenkiro.
discourtesy *n.* gisagabekeria, eragabekeria.
discover *v.t.* ezjakina jakin, ezjakina ezagutu, aurkitu, azaldu, agertu.
discoverable *adj.* sumagarri, jakingarri.
discoverer *n.* aurkitzaile, idorotzaile, agertzaile; asmalari.
discovery *n.* aurkiketa, azterketapen, aurkikuntza, idoroketa, agerpen.
discredit *v.t.* aipugabetu, aipu galdu, izengabetu, omengabetu, ospegabetu.
discredit *n.* aipugalketa, izentxar.
discredited *adj.* omengabeko, aipugabe.
discreet *adj.* zentzudun, begirakor, sotil.
discreetly *adv.* sotilki, begiramenez.
discrepancy *n.* adiezin, besteiritzi, adostezintasun.
discrepant *adj.* besteiritziko.
discrete *adj.* banandu, berezi.
discretion *n.* begirapen, zentzutasun, sotiltasun, zuhurtasun, zuhurtzia, begiramendu.
discriminate *v.i./v.t.* diskriminatu, berezi.
discriminated *adj.* banandu(a). *adj. (against)* diskriminatu(a).
discrimination *n.* berezketa, banaketa, berezkeria, barreiapen, diskriminazio.
discriminator *n.* alderatzaile.
discus *n.* disko.
discuss *v.t.* eztabaidatu, eztabaida egin, iharduki.
discusser *n.* eztabaidakari, eztabaidatzaile, eztabaidari.
discussible *adj.* eztabaidagarri. *adj.* mintzagarri, solasgarri.
discussion *n.* eztabaida, ezbai. *n.* elkarrizketa, hitzaldi.
disdain *v.t.* mesprezatu, arbuiatu, erdeinatu, muzin egin, txarretsi.
disdain *n.* arbuio, erdeinu, mesprezu, zaputzaldi, destaina, txarretsi.
disdainable *adj.* erdeinagarri.
disdainful *adj.* arbuiakor, arbuiotsu, erdeinatzaile, mesprezakor, mesprezagarri, zaputzkarri.
disdainfully *adv.* arbuioz, erdeinuz, mesprezuki, zaputzki.
disdainfulness *n.* esmoilkeria.
disease *n.* gaiso, gaisotasun, eri, gaitz, erikortasun.
diseased *adj.* gaisobera, gaizpera.
disembark *v.i./v.t.* desontziratu, lehorreratu.
disembarkation *n.* lehorrerapen, desontziraketa.
disembowel *v.t.* deserraindu.
disenchantment *n.* deslilura, desliluraketa.
disengage *v.t.* askatu.
disentail *v.t.* ezamortizatu.
disentailment *n.* desamortizazio, ezamortizazio.
disentangle *v.t./v.i.* desnahasi, desnahaspilatu, askatu.
disentery *n.* lasterreri.
disfavor *n.* omengabe, aipugaltze.
disfiguration *n.* itsusdura.
disfigure *v.t.* itxuragabetu, desitxuratu, itsusitu.
disfigured *adj.* desitxurazko, itxuragabe(ko).
disfigurement *n.* deseraketa, desitxurapen.
disfiguring *adj.* deserakor, desitxurakor.
disgrace *v.t.* izengabetu, aipu galdu, itsusitu.
disgrace *n.* aipugalketa, ezohore, laidogarritasun, laidogarrikeria, lotsa, dohakabetasun. *n.* dohakabe, dohakaitz, ezbehar.
disgraced *adj.* izengabe(ko), izentxarreko.
disgraceful *adj.* desohoretsu, lotsagarri, izenlohigarri,

lotsagabe(ko).
disgracefully adv. ezbeharrez.
disguise v.t. txantxotu, mozorrotu,
ezkutatu.
disguised adj. mozorrodun.
disgust v.t. nazkatu, nazka eman,
nazkarazi, gogaitu, higuindu.
disgust n. higuin, higuinaldi, nazka,
nazkadura, okaztadura, gogaindura.
disgusted adj. nazkatuta, nazkatu(a).
disgusting adj. higuin, higuingarri,
nazkagarri, okaztagarri, gogaingarri.
disgustingly adv. higuingarriki,
higuingarriro, nazkagarriro.
dish n. plater, jatontzi, azpil. **To do the
dishes.** Harrikoa egin. n. (pl.)
baxera.
dishcloth n. landerki, espartzu,
mustuka.
dishearten v.t. desgogatu,
gogogabetu, bihozkabetu.
disheartened adj. desgogozko,
adoregabe.
disheartening adj. gogogalgarri.
dishes n. ontziteria, mahaiontziteria,
mahaiontzi.
dishevel v.t. galpartu.
disheveled adj. tximadun, tximajario,
galpartsu.
dishonest adj. eskuzikin, gezurti,
maltzur, iruzurti, faltsu.
dishonestly adv. maltzurki, iruzurrez,
gezurrez, faltsuki, azpikeriaz.
dishonesty n. zintzogabetasun,
zuzengabetasun, doilortasun.
dishonor v.t. omengabetu,
ospegabetu, itsusitu, desohoratu.
dishonor n. ezohore, desohore,
izentxar, laidogarrikeria, lotsakizun.
dishonorable adj. desohorezko,
laidogarri, laidotsu.
dishonorably adv. desohoregarriki,
laidogarriro, laidogarriki.
dishonored adj. ohoregabe,
ospegabe, omengabeko,
izentxarreko.
dish rag n. landerki, espartzu,
mustuka.
dishtowel n. sukaldezatar.
dishwasher n. ikuzgailu, ikuztailu,
ontzigarbigailu.
disillusion v.t. desliluratu.
disillusionment n. deslilura,
desliluraketa, etsimen.
disinfect v.t. desizurritu, deskirastu,
deskutsatu, kutsugabetu.
disinfectant n. deskutsakin.
disinherit v.t. desoinordekotu,
ondoregabetu.
disinherited adj. oinordegabe,
ondoregabe.
disintegrate v.i./v.t. zatitu, deuseztatu.
disintegration n. desbateraketa,
elkarbanakuntza.
disinter v.t. desehortzi, deslurpetu.
disinterest n. interesgabezia.
disinterested adj. interesgabe.

disinterment n. deslurperaketa.
disjoint v.t./v.i. desorpotu.
disjointed adj. jarraigabe.
disjunction n. deselkarketa.
disjunctive adj. desbaterakor,
bai-ala-ezko.
disk n. diska.
dislike v.t. begitan hartu, higuindu.
dislocate v.t. lokatu, kolokatu, trokatu.
dislocation n. (med.) hezurlokadura,
lokadura, bihurri.
dislodge v.t./v.i. deslekutu, destokitu,
hutsarazi, leku aldatu.
disloyal adj. ezleial, azpisuge, judas.
disloyally adv. desleialki, fedegaiztoz.
disloyalty n. desleialkeria, ezleialtasun,
zintzogabetasun, fedegaizto,
salkeria, judaskeria.
dismal adj. zorigaiztoko, zorigabeko,
zoritxarreko. adj. txar, gogor
(eguraldi).
dismally adv. atsekabez, zorigabeki.
dismantle v.t. desegin, zatikatu,
zatitan banandu.
dismay v.t. gogogabetu, bihozkabetu.
dismay n. hebaindura.
dismiss v.t. kaleratu, kanporatu.
dismissal n. kaleratze. n. kargukentze,
kargugabetze.
dismount v.i. zalditik jaitsi, zaldijaitsi.
disobedience n. managaiztasun,
mendegabetasun, ezmenpekotasun.
disobedient adj. managaitz,
mendegabeko, manugaitz,
ezesaneko, esantxarreko.
disobey v.t./v.i. esanik ez bete, esanik
ez egin, agindua hautsi, ezobeditu,
esanetik irten.
disorder v.t. lardaskatu, deskonpondu,
nahastatu.
disorder n. nahaste, nahasketa,
desantolaketa, deskonponketa. n.
iskanbila, istilu. n. eri, gaiso,
gaisotasun.
disordered adj. lardaskatu,
antolagabe.
disorderly adv. harrapaka, zalapartaka,
zalapartan, iraulka.
disorganization n. desantolaketa,
nahas-mahas, desgobernu.
disorganize v.t. desantolatu,
antolagabetu, eragabetu,
nahas-mahastu.
disorganized adj. nahasi, eragabeko,
nahaspilatu.
disorient v.t. desnorabidetu.
disorientation n. desnorabide,
aztorapen.
disoriented adj. sorgor,
desnorabidetu(a).
disown v.t. ezezagutu, ezonartu.
disparage v.t. mesprezatu, erdeinatu,
arbuiatu, gutxietsi.
disparageable adj. mesprezagarri,
arbuiagarri, erdeinagarri.
disparaging adj. mesprezakor.
disparity n. paregabetasun,

desadostasun.
dispassionate *adj.* grinagabe(ko).
dispatch *v.t.* igorri, bidali, bialdu.
dispatch *n.* igorpen.
dispel *v.t.* barreiatu.
dispensary *n.* erigaldetegi,
gaisoikustegi.
dispensation *n.* barreiaketa. *n. (eccl.)*
libraketa, salbuespen.
dispense *v.t.* partitu, banatu, zabaldu,
sakabanatu, banandu, eman. *v.t.*
aministratu. *v.t.* xortatu. *v.i. (with)*
iraitzi, egotzi, eliminatu.
dispersable *adj.* barreiagarri.
disperse *v.t./v.i.* desbateratu,
sakabanatu, barreiatu.
dispersed *adj.* banakatu(a),
barreiatu(a).
dispersion *n.* barreialdi, barreiaketa,
sakabanaketa, zabalkunde.
displace *v.t.* leku aldatu, toki aldatu,
deslekutu, destokitu.
displacement *n.* deslekuketa,
deslekuraketa, destokiraketa,
lekualdaketa.
display *v.t.* nabarmendu, argitaratu,
argitara atera, argitara eman,
erakutsi, azaldu.
display *n.* erakusketa.
display case *n.* salmahai.
displease *v.t.* atsekabetu, gogaitarazi.
displeasure *n.* atsekabetasun,
gogaipen.
disposable *adj.* botagarri, botakor.
disposal *n.* banaketa, banapen. *n.*
zamar kenketa.
dispose *v.t.* disposatu, gertu, antolatu.
v.t. -kor izan, -bera izan. *v.i.* xedatu,
erabaki. *v.i. (of)* egotzi, iraitzi,
deuseztatu.
disposed *adj.* joeratsu; -bera.
disposition *n.* izaera. *n.* joera. *n.*
disposaketa, prestaketa, prestaera.
dispossess *v.t.* jabegabetu, hutsarazi,
kendu.
dispossession *n.* desjabeketa,
desjabekuntza, desjabetzapen.
disproof *n.* gezurtapen.
disproportionate *adj.* proportziogabe.
disprove *v.t.* gezurtarazi, gezurtatu.
disprover *n.* gezurtatzaile.
disputable *adj.* eztabaidagarri,
gezurtagarri.
disputant *n.* borrokalari.
dispute *v.i./v.t.* eztabaidakatu,
eztabaida egin, mokokatu, iharduki,
liskartu.
dispute *n.* eztabaida, liskar, errieta.
disputer *n.* eztabaidari, errietari,
eztabaidakari.
disqualify *v.t.* deskalifikatu.
disqualification *n.* deskalifikazio.
disquieting *adj.* kexagarri, larrikor.
disregard *n.* itzalgabekeria,
mesprezakizun.
disrespect *n.* desbegirune,
itzalgabekeria, mesprezu.

disrespectful *adj.* begirunegabe,
mesprezakor, errespetugabeko,
mesprezuzko.
disrespectfully *adv.* lotsagarriro,
lotsagarriki, mesprezuki, mesprezuz.
disrespectfulness *n.* itzalgabetasun.
disrobe *v..t./v.i.* biluztu, erantzi.
disrupt *v.t.* hautsi, eten, apurtu,
puskatu.
disruption *n.* haustura, etendura.
dissect *v.t.* gorputz(a) zatitu, atalkatu.
dissection *n.* gorputzatalketa,
gorputzatiketa, ebadura.
dissector *n.* atalkatzaile.
dissemble *v.t./v.i.* txurizkatu.
disseminate *v.t.* sakabanatu,
barreiatu, purrustatu.
dissemination *n.* banaketa,
sakabanaketa, barreiaketa.
disseminator *n.* banatzaile.
dissension *n.* desbatasun,
banakuntza.
dissent *v.i.* bat ez etorri, ados ez egon.
dissertation *n.* tesia, ihardunaldi.
dissidence *n.* zatikeria, alderdikeria.
dissimilar *adj.* ezberdin, antzgabeko.
dissimilarity *n.* antziketa,
berdineztasun, paregabetasun,
ezberdintasun.
dissimulation *n.* gainzurikeria,
gainzuriketa, isilkeria, izkutakeria.
dissipate *v.t./v.i.* barreiatu (laino,
hodei, jende).
dissipation *n.* barreiaketa, barreiapen.
dissociate *v.t./v.i.* deselkartu,
banandu.
dissociation *n.* deselkarketa,
banaketa.
dissolute *adj.* andrekoi.
dissolution *n.* desegite, deuseztapen,
suntsidura.
dissolvable *adj.* urtugarri.
dissolve *v.i./v.t.* urtu.
dissonance *n.* soinugaizto,
soinugaiztasun.
dissonant *adj.* gozagaitz, soinugaitz.
dissuade *v.t.* atzearazi, atzeragin,
desaholkatu.
dissuasion *n.* desaholku.
dissuasive *adj.* desaholkuzko,
atzeratzaile.
distaff *n.* goru, kilo. *n.* emakume. *adj.*
eme, emakumezko.
distance *v.t.* urrutiratu, urrundu.
distance *n.* tartegune, tarte, bidetarte,
urruntasun. **From a distance.**
Urrundik.
distant *adj.* urrutiko, urrun. **Distant**
relative. Urruneko ahaide.
distantly *adv.* urruti, urrun.
distasteful *adj.* higiungarri, nazkagarri,
nardagarri.
distemper *n.* zakurren gaisotasun mota
bat.
distill *v.t./v.i.* destilatu.
distillable *adj.* destilagarri.
distillery *n.* lurrindegi, lurrintoki,

destilategi.
distinct *adj.* ezberdin, berezi.
distinction *n.* berezkuntza, berezketa.
distinctive *adj.* ezaugarri.
distinctness *n.* berezitasun.
distinguish *v.t./v.i. (askotan* from *edo* **between**-*ekin)* berezikatu. *v.t.* ezagutu, argi ikusi.
distinguishable *adj.* berezgarri. *adj.* ikusgarri.
distinguished *adj.* aipuoneko, agurgarri, goragarri.
distort *v.t.* bihurdikatu, itxuragabetu.
distortion *n.* bihurdura. *n.* hitzaldaketa.
distract *v.t.* gogoa barreiatu.
distracted *adj.* adigalkor, oharkabe.
distractedly *adv.* oharkabez.
distraction *n.* adigabezia.
distraught *adj.* artega, urduri.
distress *v.t.* atsekabetu, larritu.
distress *n.* bihotzestura, nahigabe, estualdi, larrialdi.
distressed *adj.* kexu, larritsu.
distressing *adj.* larrigarri, larritsu, nahigabetzaile.
distressingly *adv.* larriturik.
distribute *v.t.* banakatu, banatu, partitu, hainbanatu.
distribution *n.* banaketa, hainbanaketa, partiketa, partimen. *n.* sailkapen.
distributive *adj.* banakor.
distributor *n.* banatzaile, partitzaile.
district *n.* barruti, eskualde, herrialde.
district attorney *n.* fiskal.
distrust *v.t.* mesfidatu, errezelatu, susmarazi.
distrust *n.* errezelu, mesfidantza, fidagaiztasun.
distrustful *adj.* mesfidakor, fidagaitz, susmabera.
distrustfully *adv.* mesfidantzaz.
distrustfulness *n.* fidakaizkortasun.
disturb *v.t./v.i.* aztoratu, asaldatu, larritu, artegarazi.
disturbance *n.* larrikuntza. *n.* nahastaldi, nahasketa. *n.* zalaparta, istilu, iskanbila.
disturbed *adj.* txoro, eroska, erohaize, zorohaize.
disturber *n.* asaldatzaile, iskanbilari.
disturbing *adj.* kexarazle, kezkagile, larrikor.
disunion *n.* desbatasun.
disunite *v.t./v.i.* desbateratu.
ditch *n.* erreten, pezoin.
ditty *n.* kantutxo, lelo.
diuretic *adj./n.* pixeragile.
diurnal *adj.* egunezko, egunargitako.
divan *n.* sofa.
dive *v.i./v.t.* urperatu, pulunpatu, murgildu, dzanga egin.
dive *n.* murgil, murgilaldi, dzangada, pulunpada, urperaldi.
diver *n.* urpekari, buzo, murgilari, pulunpatzaile.
divergence *n.* elkarretenketa.

divergent *adj.* ezberdin.
diverse *adj.* askotako, askotariko, bestelako.
diversely *adv.* desberdinki.
diversification *n.* desberdintzapen, ezberdintzapen.
diversify *v.t.* ezberdindu, desberdindu.
diversion *n.* joko, jolas, jostaketa, jolasketa, olgeta. *n.* desbideketa; desiritzi, besteiritzi.
diversity *n.* askotarikotasun, askotarikotza, askotasun. *n.* banatasun, bestelakotasun, bestetasun.
divert *v.t.* desbidetu, desbideratu.
divest *v.t.* erantzi, biluztu, larrugorritu, desapaindu. *v.t.* desjabetu, gabetu.
dividable *adj.* atalgai, atalgarri.
divide *v.t./v.i.* zatikatu, zatitu, banakatu, ataldu, txikitu.
divided *adj.* banakatu(a).
dividend *n. (math.)* zatigai, zatikizun.
divider *n.* atalkatzaile, erdibitzaile, bakantzaile, zatitzaile.
dividing *adj.* atalgarrizko, atalkor, zatigarrizko, zatikor.
divinable *adj.* sumagarri.
divination *n.* asmakeria, aztikeria, aztiketa.
divine *v.t./v.i.* igarri, iragarri, asmatu.
divine *adj.* jainkotar, jainkozko, jaungoikozko.
divinely *adv.* jainkoki.
diviner *n.* asmatzaile, asmakari.
diving *n.* urperaketa, urperaldi, murgildura, murgilketa, pulunpa.
divinity *n.* jainkotasun, jaungoikotasun.
divisibility *n.* zatigaitasun, atalgaitasun, atalgarritasun.
divisible *adj.* atalgai, atalgarri, banagarri, partigarri, sailkagarri, zatigarri.
division *n.* banakuntza, partiketa, zatiketa. *n.* adar, sail. *n.* deselkarketa, desakordio, alderdikeria. *n. (math.)* banaketa, dibisio. *n. (mil.)* dibisio.
divisional *adj.* atalgarrizko.
divisive *adj.* mokokari, liskarti. *adj.* banagarri.
divisor *n. (math.)* zatitzaile.
divorce *v.t./v.i.* desezkondu, ezkontzautsi, dibortziatu.
divorce *n.* ezkontzauste, desezkontza, dibortzio.
divorce *n.* ezkontzausle (gizon).
divorced *adj.* dibortziatu(a), ezkontzautsi(a).
divorcee *n.* ezkontzausle (emakume).
divulgation *n.* barreiaketa, zabalkunde.
divulge *v.t.* agertarazi, ezagutarazi, jakinarazi, zabalerazi. *v.t.* zabaldu (berriak).
divulgeable *adj.* barreiagarri, zabalgarri (berriak).
Dixie *n.* Estatu Batuetako hegoaldeko estatuak.

dizziness *n.* burubira, txorabio, txoradura.

dizzy *adj.* txorabiodun, zorabiodun. **To be dizzy.** Zorabiatu.

dizzying *adj.* txorabiagarri.

do *v.t.* egin, jardun.

docile *adj.* esanoneko, manakor, men, otzan, molderrez, eskurakoi, sotil.

docilely *adv.* otzanki, sotilki.

docility *n.* otzantasun, mentasun, mendetasun, molderreztasun, sotiltasun.

dock *v.t.* atrakatu, lehorreratu, lurreratu. *v.t.* desbuztandu.

dock *n.* atrakaleku, kai, nasa, barra.

docking *n.* lehorreraketa, lehorrerapen. *n.* animalien buztanaren ebaketa. *n.* bi espaziontziren elkarketa.

dockyard *n.* untzitegi, ontzitegi.

doctor *n.* sendagile, sendagin, mediku, osagile.

doctorate *n.* doktoradutza, doktorego.

doctrine *n.* ikasbide, doktrina.

document *n.* idazki, ageri, dokumentu.

documentary *adj.* agirizko.

documentation *n.* dokumentazio.

dodder *n. (bot.)* zaingorri.

doddering *adj.* dardarti, dardartsu.

dodecasyllabic *adj.* hamabisilabadun.

dodge *v.i./v.t.* zehartu.

doe *n.* basauntzeme, oreineme.

doer *n.* egile, eginkari; -gile, -gin, -kin.

does *pres. of do.*

doesn't "does + not"-aren laburpena.

doff *v.t.* kendu (txapela).

dog *n.* zakur, txakur, or; ora-.

dog days *n.* udabihotz, udamin.

dogfish *n. (zool.)* mielga.

dogma *n.* dogma, sineskai.

dogmatic *adj.* dogmatiko.

dogmatically *adv.* dogmatikoki.

dogmatism *n.* dogmakeria.

dogmatize *v.i./v.t.* dogmatizatu.

do-gooder *n.* onegile.

dogwood tree *n. (bot.)* zuhandor.

doing *pres. part. of do.*

doleful *adj.* itzal, ilun, triste.

doll *n.* panpina, andrakila.

dollar *n. (econ.)* dolar.

dolly *n.* eskorga.

dolmen *n.* jentilarri, trikuharri.

dolphin *n. (zool.)* gizurde, izurde.

dolt *n.* ergel, inozo, tentel.

domain *n.* jaurerri, eskuera, barruti.

dome *n.* kupula.

domestic *adj.* etxatiar, etxeko. *adj.* nazional; nazio-. *n.* zerbitzari, otsein, morroi, ogipeko, sehi.

domestically *adv.* nazionalki.

domesticate *v.t./v.i.* etxekotu, eskuperatu, hezi, otzandu, mantsotu.

domestication *n.* zebadura. *n.* hezkunde, hezkuntza.

domesticator *n.* hezilari, hezitzaile.

domesticity *n.* etxekotasun.

domicile *n.* bizileku, egongu.

dominance *n.* nagusitasun.

dominant *adj.* gaineko, meneratzaile.

dominatable *adj.* menperagarri, uztargarri.

dominate *v.t./v.i.* menderatu, aginpetu, jabetu, nagusitu.

domination *n.* menderapen, eskumen, menderaketa. *n.* jauntxokeria, azpiraketa.

dominator *n.* menderatzaile, menperatzaile.

domineer *v.t.* menperatu, menderatu, azpiratu.

domineering *adj.* menperatzaile.

dominical *adj.* igandeko.

dominion *n.* jauntasun, nagusitasun, nagusitza, jabego. *n.* menperatasun, menpe. *n.* mendelur, menderri.

domino *n.* domino.

don *v.t.* jantzi.

donate *v.t.* eman.

donation *n.* emari, erregali, opari, erregalu, dohain, emaitza.

done *adj.* egina. *p. part. of do.*

donkey *n. (zool.)* asto, astakilo; asta-.

donor *n.* emaile.

don't "do + not"-aren laburpena.

doom *n.* heriotza; hondamendi.

doomsday *n.* munduaren azken egun(a).

door *n.* ate; ata-, atal-.

doorbell *n.* txirrin, tirrin.

doorkeeper *n.* atezain, atezaintzaile, giltzain.

doorknob *n.* kisket.

doorman *n.* atemorroi, atezain.

doorstep *n.* ataurre.

doorway *n.* atari, etxate.

dope *n.* drogak. *n.(colloq.)* ergel, kirten.

dormitory *n.* logela handi(a).

dormouse *n. (zool.)* muxar.

dorsal *adj.* bizkarraldeko, bizkarreko, bizkargaineko.

dose *v.t./v.i.* neurtu (medizina).

dose *n.* dosi, neurri.

dot *n. (gram.)* puntu, izpil. *n. (mus.)* puntutxo.

dotage *n.* sentontasun.

dote *v.i.* **(on, upon)** gehiegi maitatu.

dotted *adj.* izpildun.

dotty *adj.* zorakilo.

double *v.t./v.i.* bikoiztu, doblatu. *v.t./v.i.* izurtu. *v.i.* **(for)** ordeztu.

double *n.* bikundu. *adj.* bikun, bikoitz.

double chin *n.* kokotsazpi, gorgoilo, kokospe.

doubt *v.t./v.i.* zalantzatu, dudatu.

doubt *n.* zalantza, ezbai, kolokadura, duda.

doubtful *adj.* zalantzagarri, zalantzatsu, ezbaiezko, dudagarri.

doubtfully *adv.* zalantzan, zalantzaz.

doubtfulness *n.* zalantzagarritasun.

doubting *adj.* zalantzakor, dudakor.

dough *n.* ore, irinore; ora-, oretzar.

doughboy n. soldadu.
doughiness n. oratasun.
doughnut n. erroskila mota bat.
doughy adj. oretsu.
douse v.t. busti, blaitu, ura isuri. v.t. urez sua itzali.
dove n. (zool.) uso; usa-.
dovecote n. usategi, usapaltegi.
dowel n. ziri.
down adv. beheruntz, behera. adj. atsekabekor, goibel. prep. behean; zehar. n. lumatxa. n. erorketa, erorpen. n. porrotketa, molokot. n. futbol amerikanoan pilota lurrean ipintzea.
downcast adj. itzal, goibel, ilun, triste.
downfall n. erorketa, erorpen, jausketa.
downhearted adj. adoregabe, bihozgabe, gogogabe.
downhill adv. gainbehera, maldan behera. adj. beheratsu, makur. n. maldabehera, aldapabehera.
downpour n. eurizaparrada, zaparrada.
downright adv. argi, argiro, argi eta garbi, erabat. adj. oso, erabateko.
downstairs adv. behean. adj. beheko.
downtown n. herribarru.
downward adv. beheruntz.
dowry n. ezkontsari, dote.
doze v.i. lokuluxkatu. v.i. (off) loak hartu, lo geratu.
dozen n. dozena, hamabiko.
drab adj. nabar, arre.
draft v.t. marraztu. v.t. idatzi, idatziz asmoak egin.
draft n. zirrimarra, zirriborro.
draftsman n. lerrogile, marratzaile.
drag v.t./v.i. herrestatu, narraztu, atoitu, tatarrez eraman. v.t. dragatu.
dragon n. herensuge, dragoi.
dragonfly n. (zool.) sorginorratz, txitxiburduntzi.
drain v.t./v i. xukatu, ubideratu, lehortu, agortu.
drain n. erreten, kainu, iroloditza, zikinodi.
drainage n. urbidegintza, ubideketa.
drainer n. xukagailu.
drainpipe n. kainu, saneamendu.
drake n. ahate.
drama n. antzerki, drama.
dramatic adj. dramatiko.
dramatist n. antzerkigile, dramagile.
dramatize v.t. dramatizatu.
drape n. leihoihal handi(a).
drapery n. leihoihal handi(a).
drastic adj. gogorrezko, bortxazko, indarrezko.
draughts n. damajoko.
draw v.t./v.i. herrestatu. v.t. (out) iradoki. v.t./v.i. marraztu. v.t. deszorrotu. v.t./v.i. (near) hurbildu, hurreratu, gerturatu, inguratu, ondoratu.
drawback n. aldetxar.
drawbridge n. altxazubi, zubi altxagarri(a).
drawer n. kaxoi. n. marrazkigile, marrazkilari.
drawing n. marrazketa, marrazki.
drawn p. part. of draw.
dray n. narra.
dread n. beldur, ikara.
dreadful adj. beldurgarri, izugarri, gaizto.
dreadfully adv. beldurgarriro.
dream v.i./v.t. amets egin, amestu.
dream n. amets.
dreamer n. ameslari.
dreamland n. irudizko mundu.
dreamy adj. ameskor, ameskoi, amesti.
dreary adj. aspergarri eta kikilgarri.
dredge v.t./v.i. dragatu, karramarroztu, hondokatu, karrakatu.
dredge n. draga, karramarro.
dregs n. zabor, hondar.
drench v.t. iragazi, guztiz busti, blaitu.
dress v.t./v.i. jantzi, beztitu. v.t./v.i. (up) igandetu, panpinatu, panpoxtu.
dress n. soineko, jantzi.
dressed up adj. apain, dotore.
dresser n. komoda, jantzikutxa.
dressing n. lotura. n. ongarri (janarientzat).
dressmaker n. jostun, andrajostun, joskile.
drew p. part. of draw.
dribble v.t./v.i. adurra bota, adurra jausi, lerdezkatu.
dried adj. agorkoi, lehor.
drier n. lehortzaile, agortzaile, lehorketari; lehorgailu. adj. (comp.) lehorrago, agorrago.
drift v.i. urazalean korronteak eraman.
driftwood n. zakar, zabor.
drill v.t./v.i. daratulutu, ginbeletatu.
drill n. zaztagin, daratulu. n. ariketa.
drily adv. idorki, idorkiro.
drink v.i./v.t. edan.
drink n. edanaldi; edari, edateko; edal-. n. hurrupa, hurrupada, dzangada, klinkada, zurrupa. n. edan. n. kopa.
drinkable adj. edangarri, hurrupagarri, edateko.
drinker n. edalari, edale, edantzaile, hurrupatzaile. **Heavy drinker.** Hordi. Mozkor.
drinking n. edate. adj. edal-.
drip v.i./v.t. tantakatu, xortakatu, jario.
drip n. jario, jarioaldi, itaizur.
drive v.t./v.i. zuzenbidetu. v.t./v.i. gidatu (kotxe). v.t. (away, back, off, out) ohildu, uxatu, aienatu.
driven p. part. of drive.
driver n. txofer, autogidari.
driver's license n. gidabaimen, gidakarnet.
driveway n. garaje-aurreko maldatxo.
drizzle v.i./v.t. sirimiri egin, langar egin.
drizzle n. eurilanbro, sirimiri, eurixka, langar.
droll adj. farregarri.

dromedary *n.* dromedari.
drone *v.i.* burrunbatu, burrunba egin.
　v.i. hots bakarrez hitz egin,
　aldagabeki mintzatu.
drone *n. (zool.)* erlalfer, erlamando.
drool *v.i.* lerdezkatu, adurreztatu,
　eldertu.
drool *n.* adur, elder, lerde.
droop *v.i./v.t.* zintzilikatu, eskegi. *v.t.*
　bertan behera utzi, erori (loreak,
　etab).
drop *v.i./v.t.* tantakatu. *v.i./v.t.* erori,
　utzi.
drop *n.* eroraldi, jaitsialdi. *n.* tanta, istil,
　xorta; -tanta.
dropper *n.* tantakontailu.
droppings *n. (pl.)* abelongarri,
　abelgorotz.
dropsy *n. (med.)* ureri, urmin.
dross *n.* zabar, zepa.
drought *n.* lehorte, agorte, idorte,
　sikate, lehorraldi.
drove *n.* zekorketa, xexenketa.
drover *n.* abelzain.
drown *v.i./v.t.* ito, ito arazi, murgilarazi.
drowned *adj.* ito(a).
drowsiness *n.* lozorro, loeri.
drowsy *adj.* lozorrodun.
drub *v.t.* zaflatu, zafratu.
drubbing *n.* zaflaldi, zafraldi, zapalaldi.
drudgery *n.* lan neketsu(a).
drug *n.* droga, botika, medikamendu.
druggist *n.* botikari, drogalari.
drugstore *n.* botika, farmazia,
　botikategi.
drum *n. (mus.)* atabal, danbolin,
　danbor, tuntun. *n.* bidoi.
drummer *n.* atabalari, danborjole,
　danbolindari, txanbolin.
drum roll *n.* tarrapatada, tarrapata.
drumstick *n.* atabalmakila.
drunk *n.* mozkor. *n.* mozkorraldi,
　hordialdi. *adj.* mozkor, hordi,
　mozkorti.
drunkard *n.* hordiputz, hordi, mozkor,
　zurrutero.
drunken *adj.* hordi, mozkor, mozkorti.
drunkenly *adv.* hordirik, horditurik.
drunkenness *n.* hordialdi, hordikeria,
　mozkor, mozkorraldi.
dry *v.t./v.i. (v.i., askotan* **out** *edo*
　up*-ekin)* agortu, ihartu, lehortu,
　elkortu, idortu. *v.t.* **(off)** xukatu,
　txukatu.
dry *adj.* lehor, ihar, agor, elkor, idor,
　eihar.
dryable *adj.* lehorgarri.
dry cleaner *n.* tindategi.
dry dock *n.* kaiburu, arlanpa.
dryer *n.* lehorgailu, xukagailu, idorgailu.
dry-goods store *n.* kinkiladenda,
　mertzeria.
dry land *n.* lehor.
dryly *adv.* lehorki.
dryness *n.* lehorte, agorte, idorte;
　elkortasun, eihartasun, lehortasun.
dual *adj.* biren, biko.

dualism *n.* bitasun.
duality *n.* bitasun, bikoiztasun.
dub *v.t.* bikoiztu (zinema).
dubbing *n.* bikoizketa.
dubious *adj.* zalantzadun, ezbaiko,
　eztabaidazko, ezbaikor, ezbaiezko,
　badaezbadako.
dubiously *adv.* zalantzan, zalantzaz,
　ezbaiean.
dubiousness *n.* ezbaitasun.
ducat *n. (econ.)* dukat.
duchess *n.* dukesa.
duchy *n.* dukerri.
duck *v.i./v.t.* murgildu, murgil egin,
　urperatu. *v.i./v.t.* zehartu; burua
　beheratu.
duck *n. (zool.)* ahate.
duckling *n. (zool.)* ahatekume,
　ahatetxo.
duct *n.* tutu; -bide.
dude *n.* Estatu Batuetako ekialdetik
　denbora laburrerako errantxoak
　ikustera etortzen den pertsona.
due *adj.* epegainditu(a). *adj.* merezi(a).
　adj. nahiko. *adj.* igurikatu(a),
　iguriki(a).
due date *n.* epemuga, mugaegun.
duet *n. (mus.)* bikote, duo.
dug *p. part. of dig.*
dugout *n.* beisbol jokalarien egonleku
　estalia.
duke *n.* duke.
dukedom *n.* dukerri.
dull *v.t./v.i.* kamustu, lanpustu,
　ahomoztu.
dull *adj.* inozo, ergel, tentel, kirten. *adj.*
　muturmotz, kamuts, motz,
　puntamotz. *adj.* hil, itsu, motel (argia).
　adj. sor. *adj.* gazkabeko, gogaikarri,
　grazigabeko, motel, aspergarri.
dullness *n.* kirtenkeria. *n.* kamustasun,
　lanpustasun. *n.* motelkeria,
　moteltasun. *n.* aspergarritasun.
dully *adv.* ergelki, tentelki. *adv.*
　aspergarriro.
duly *adj.* gisaz, taiuz.
dumb *adj.* kirten, inozo, ergel,
　adigogor. *adj.* mutu.
dumbness *n.* ergeltasun. *n.* mutukeria,
　mututasun.
dumbwaiter *n.* jasogailu, platergorailu.
dummy *adj.* inozo. *n.* txoripitto.
dump *v.t.* bapatean hustu, bapatean
　zamagabetu. *v.t. (econ.)* merkatua
　zerbaitez bete, merke saldu.
dump *n.* zakartegi, zabortegi.
dumpster *n.* zaborrontzi,
　hondakindegi.
dun *n.* nabar.
dunce *adj./n.* inozo, kirten, ergel,
　tentel.
dune *n.* hondarmuino, aremeta.
dung *n.* gorotz, bekorotz, abelongarri,
　abelgorotz, gorozki.
dungeon *n.* ziega, presondegi.
dung heap *n.* goroztegi, simaurtegi.
dunk *v.t./v.i.* edarian (zerbait) sartu eta

atera. *v.t./v.i.* murgilarazi, murgildu.
duo *n.* bikote.
duodenum *n. (anat.)* hestemehe.
duplicate *v.t.* bikoiztu.
duplicate *n.* kopia. *adj.* bikundu(a).
duplication *n.* bikoizte, bikoizpen; ber-, bir-, birr-.
duplicity *n.* bikoiztasun. *n.* faltsukeria, nabarkeria.
durability *n.* egonkortasun, iraunkortasun, finkotasun, iragangaiztasun.
durable *adj.* iragangaitz, iraunkor, luzaroko.
durably *adv.* iraunki, iraunkiro, iraunkorki.
duration *n.* iraunaldi, iraupen.
duress *n.* bortxa, gogorkeria, indarkeria.
during *prep.* -(e)nean; bitartean, artean.
dusk *n.* gaualde, ilunsenti, iluntze. **At dusk.** Iluntzean.
dust *v.t./v.i.* hauskabetu, hautsa(k) kendu. *v.t./v.i.* hautsez estali.
dust *n.* hauts. **To be covered with dust.** Hautseztu. **To get dusty.** Hautsez bete.
dusty *adj.* haustun, hautsezko.
Dutch *n./adj.* holandar(rak). *adj.* Holanda-ko.
Dutchman *n./adj.* holandar.
duty *n.* eginkizun, betebehar, eginbehar, zeregin. *n.* zerga, petxa.
dwarf *v.t.* gauza bat berez dena baino txikiago eginarazi.
dwarf *n.* epotx, epo.
dwarfism *n.* epokeria.
dwell *v.i.* biztandu, bizi.
dweller *n.* biztanle, bizilagun, egoiliar. **City dweller.** Hiritar.
dwelling *n.* egoitza, bizileku, bizitoki, etxebizitza.
dwelt *p. part. of dwell.*
dwindle *v.i./v.t.* urritu, urriagotu, gutxitu, murriztu, bakandu, eskastu.
dye *v.t./v.i.* tindatu, tinduztatu, margotu, ilundu.
dye *n.* koloragailu, koloratzaile, tindagai.
dyer *n.* tindalari, tindatzaile.
dynamic *adj.* eragile.
dynamics *n.* dinamika.
dynamite *n. (chem.)* dinamita.
dynamiter *n.* dinamitari.
dynamo *n. (elec.)* dinamo.
dynamometer *n. (mech.)* indarneurkin.
dynasty *n. (pol.)* dinastia.
dysentery *n.* kakajario, berazko, zirineri, kakapirri.

E

e *n.* Ingeles alfabetoko letra. *n. (mus.)* mi.
each *pron./adj.* bakoitz, bat-bedera, bana.
each other *pron.* elkar.

eager *adj.* gogatsu, lehiatsu, borondatetsu.
eagerly *adv.* lehiatsuki.
eagerness *n.* gogamen, grina, irrika.
eagle *n. (zool.)* arrano.
eaglet *n. (zool.)* arranume.
ear *n. (anat.)* belarri. **Inner ear.** Belarribarne. Belarribarru. *n.* buru, artaburu. *adj.* belarriko.
eardrum *n. (anat.)* belarrimintz.
earl *n.* konde.
earldom *n.* kondego, kondetza.
earlobe *n.* belarrimami.
early *adj.* goiztar. *adj.* aintzinako. *adj.* lehen, lehentsu. *adj.* hurbil, hurreko, aldameneko, gertuko. *adv.* goiz, goizetik.
earn *v.t./v.i.* irabazi.
earned *adj.* irabazitako, irabazizko.
earner *n.* irabaztun, irabazle.
earnest *adj.* benetako, egiazko, tolesgabe.
earnestly *adv.* jo ta ke.
earnestness *n.* tolesgabetasun.
earnings *n. (pl.)* irabazi, irabazkin, irabazketa, mozkin.
earphone *n.* entzungailu.
earring *n.* zintzilikario, belarritako.
earshot *n.* entzumen maila.
earth *n. (astron., cap.)* Lur. *n.* lur, lurbira, mundu. *adj.* lurtar.
earthen *adj.* lurrezko.
earthenware *adj.* lurrezko.
earthling *n.* lurbizilagun, lurtar, mundutar.
earthly *adj.* lurtiar, lurreko, lurtar.
earthquake *n.* lurrikara.
earthworm *n. (zool.)* zizare.
earthy *adj.* lurdun, lurtsu. *adj.* zakar, trakets, zarpail. *adj.* atsegingale.
ease *v.t./v.i.* erraztu, aisatu, lasaitu, aiseatu. *v.t./v.i.* gutitu (min). *v.t./v.i.* kontuz mugitu.
ease *n.* aisetasun, aise.
easel *n.* hiruoineko, zurkaitz, asto.
easily *adv.* erraz, lasaiki, aiseki, aise, erosoki.
easiness *n.* erraztasun, errazpide, aisatasun.
east *n.* sortalde, ekialde. *adj.* sortaldeko, ekialdeko.
Easter *n.* bazko, pazko. *adj.* pazkoaldiko.
Easter lily *n. (bot.)* zitori.
eastern *adj.* ekialdeko, sortaldeko.
easternize *v.t.* ekialdetu.
East Germany *n. (geog.)* Aleman Errepublika Demokratiko(a).
east wind *n.* eguzkihaize, sortaldehaize.
easy *adj.* erraz. **Easy to do.** Egiterraz. *adv.* aise.
easy chair *n.* besaulki.
easygoing *adj.* tratagarri, kontentakor, haserregaitz, moldakor.
eat *v.t./v.i.* jan, janaritu.
eaten *p. part. of eat.*

eater n. -jale.
eating n. jate.
eave n. teilatuhegal.
ebb v.i. beheratu (itsaso).
ebb tide n. itsasbehera, marebehera.
ebony n. beltz.
eccentric adj. eroska, erohaize.
eccentrically adv. barregarriro, eroki, zoroki.
eccentricity n. kasketaldi, nabarmenkeria; barregarrikeria, xelebrekeria.
ecclesiastic adj. elizako.
ecclesiastical adj. elizako.
ecclesiastically adv. elizarauz.
echo v.i./v.t. durundatu, durunda egin, oihartzundu.
echo n. durundi, oihartzun, burrunba.
eclipse v.t. ilundu, ilunpetu, itzaldu.
eclipse n. (astron.) ilunaldi, itzalaldi.
ecologist n. ekologari, ekologista.
ecology n. ekologia.
economic adj. ekonomiko.
economical adj. zuhur, elkor.
economically adv. ekonomikoki, merke.
economics n. ekonomia.
economic slump adj. (econ.) lurjotze.
economist n. ekonomilari, ekonomista.
economization n. ekonomizaketa.
economize v.t./v.i. ekonomizatu, mozkindu, gerokoratu.
economy n. ekonomia.
ecosystem n. ekosistema.
ecstasy n. sorgorraldi, estasi. n. poztasun handi(a).
ecstatic adj. sorgor. adj. bozkariotsu.
ecstatically adv. xoraturik, liluraturik.
ecumenical adj. unibertsal, nagusi.
eczema n. ekzema.
-ed (gram.) lehenaldia egiten duen atzizkia.
edelweiss n. (bot.) elurlili.
edge n. hegi, hegal, kantoi(n), ertz; koska, akats -egi.
edged adj. hegidun.
edgeless adj. hegigabe, hegalgabe.
edible adj. jangarri.
edict n. aldarri.
edifice n. eraikuntza, etxe, konstruzio.
edify v.t. onbideratu.
edifying adj. onbidegarri, onbiderako, onbidezko, oneragile.
edit v.t. berridatzi, argitaratzeko zerbait antolatu, izkiriatu.
edition n. argitarapen, argitaldi, argitalpen. **The second edition.** Bigarren argitalpena.
editor n. argitaldari, argitaltzaile, argitaratzaile, argitarazle.
editorial n. egunkari edo aldizkari bateko editoreak idatzitako funtsezko artikulua.
editorship n. argitaldariaren lan(a).
educate v.t./v.i. irakatsi; hezi.
educated adj. ikasi(a), eskoladun, eskolatu(a), jakitun.

education n. hezkuntza, irakaskintza, irakasketa, heziera, eskola, irakaspen.
educational adj. hezikor, irakaskor, irakasgarri.
educationally adv. irakasbidez.
educator n. hezilari, hezitzaile, irakasle.
eel n. (zool.) aingira.
eerie adj. beldurti, mamukeriazko.
effect v.t. egin.
effect n. ondorio. **In effect.** Izan ere.
effective adj. eragile, eragintsu, eraginkor, ondoriotsu.
effectively adv. eraginez, eragitez.
effectiveness n. eraginkortasun.
effectual adj. eragile, eragintsu, eraginkor.
effeminacy n. andragizonkeria, emagizonkeria, emakumekeria, maritxukeria.
effeminate adj. emeti, andereantzeko, maritxu.
effervesce v.i. burbuilatu, burbuileztatu.
effervescence n. burbuileztapen, irakidura.
effervescent adj. burbuileztakor, irakingai.
efficacious adj. eraginkor.
efficacy n. eraginkortasun, eragidura, eragimen.
efficiency n. eraginkortasun, eragintasun, errendimendu.
efficient adj. eginkor, eragile, eraginkor, eginkari, egintzaile, eragintsu.
efficiently adv. eragitez.
effigy n. irudi.
effort n. ahalegin, eginahal, esfortzu.
effortless adj. ahalegingabe, esfortzugabeko.
effortlessly adv. esfortzu gabe.
effuse v.t./v.i. isuri.
effusion n. isurdura, isurpen.
effusive adj. isurkor, isurbera.
egalitarian adj. berdinzale.
egg n. arraultza, arraultze.
egg on v.t. akuilatu.
eggshell n. arrautzazal, kusku.
egg white n. arrautzuringo, zuringo.
egg yolk n. gorringo.
eglantine n. (bot.) otsalar.
ego n. ego.
egoist n. pertsona berekoi(a).
egoistic adj. berekoi.
egotism n. berezkeria, norberekeria, bakoizkeria.
egotist n. pertsona berekoi(a).
egotistic adj. berekoi.
egotistical adj. berekoi, buruzale, nerekoi.
egotistically adv. berekoiki.
egregious adj. izugarri, ikaragarri, handi.
eh int. e!, eup!
eight n./adj. zortzi.

eighteen n./adj. hemezortzi.
eighteenth adj. hemezortzigarren.
eighth adj. zortzigarren, zortziren.
eightieth adj. larogeigarren.
eighty n./adj. larogei.
either adj./pron. bat edo beste; biak. conj. edo, ere, nahiz, ezta ere. adv. ere ez.
ejaculate v.t. isuri.
ejaculation n. isurketa.
eject v.t. egotzi, iraitzi.
ejectable adj. egozkarri.
ejection n. iraizketa.
ejector n. botari, botatzaile, iraitzale.
eke out v.t. bizitza nekez irabazi.
elaborate v.t./v.i. landu.
elaborate adj. landu(a).
elaborately adv. landuz; zehazkiro, xeheki.
elaboration n. egintza, elaborazio.
elapse v.i. amaitu, bukatu.
elastic n./adj. elastiko, malgu.
elasticity n. (phys.) bultzagarritasun. n. elastikotasun, malgudura.
elate v.t. bozkariatu, poztu.
elated adj. bozkariotsu, poz-pozik.
elation n. poztasun handi(a).
elbow v.t. ukondoz emekiro jo.
elbow n. (anat.) ukondo, ukondoko, ukondohezur.
elder n./adj. nagusi; nagusiago.
elderly adj. zahar.
elderberry n. (bot.) intsusa.
eldest adj. (superl.) zaharren(a), nagusien(a), nagusi.
elect v.t./v.i. hauteman, hautatu, hautetsi, aukeratu.
electable adj. hautemangarri, hautagarri, aukeragarri.
elected adj. aukerako.
election n. hauteskunde, bozketa, hautaketa.
elective adj. hautapenezko, hautespenezko, aukerazko.
elector n. hautesle, hautatzaile, hautari.
electoral law n. hautalege.
electorate n. hautatzaileria, hautesleria.
electric adj. elektrika, elektrikazko, elektriko; elektra-.
electrical engineer n. elektronikari.
electrical outlet n. entxufe.
electrical switch n. argigiltza.
electrical wire n. elektrahari.
electric circuit n. elektrabide, elektrakorronte.
electric current n. elektraindar, argindar.
electrician n. argizain, argikari, argidun.
electricity n. argindar, elektrizitate.
electric light socket n. foku.
electrifiable adj. elektragarri.
electrification n. elektrapen, elektrindarpen, elektrizazio.
electrify v.t. elektrizatu, elektrindartu.

electrifying adj. elektratzaile.
electrocute v.t. elektrahilarazi.
electrocution n. elektrokuzio, elektraherio.
electrode n. (elec.) elektrodo.
electromagnet n. elektroiman.
electromagnetic adj. elektromagnetiko.
electrometer n. (elec.) elektraneurkin.
electrometry n. (phys.) elektraneurketa.
electron n. elektroi.
electronic adj. elektroniko.
electronics n. elektronika.
elegance n. dotoretasun, dotorezia.
elegant adj. dotore, galant, apain, pinpirin.
elegantly adv. apain, dotoreki, galanki, galankiro, dotore, aberaski.
elegiac adj. negarkantuzko.
elegibility n. hautagarritasun.
elegy n. negarkantu, hiletasoinu, hilkantu.
element n. elemendu. n. osagai.
elemental adj. funtsezko, oinarrizko.
elementary adj. hasierako, oinarrizko, hastapeneko.
elephant n. (zool.) elefante.
elevate v.t. goratu.
elevated adj. garaitsu, goitar, goidun.
elevation n. gainalde, goiera, garaitasun, bizkargune, gorapen.
elevator n. igogailu.
eleven n./adj. hamaika.
eleventh adj. hamaikagarren.
elf n. lamia, iratxo.
elicit v.t. atera, eragin, iradoki.
eligibility n. aukeragarritasun, hautagarritasun.
eligible adj. aukeragarri, hautagarri, hautemangarri.
eliminate v.t. eliminatu, egotzi, iraitzi, bazterreratu.
elimination n. kanporaketa.
elision n. (gram.) hizkenketa.
elk n. (zool.) oreinandi.
elm n. (bot.) zumarrondo, zumar.
elocution n. mintzakera.
elongate v.t. luzatu.
elongated adj. luzexka.
elope v.i. ihes egin eta ezkondu elizezkontza gabe.
eloquence n. erretolika, hitzetorri, hizjario, etorri.
eloquent adj. ahoeder, mintzodun, eleder, hitzeder.
else adj. beste; gehiago. adv. ez bada. adv. beste erara.
elsewhere adv. beste lekuan.
elucidate v.t. argierazi, adierazi.
elucidation n. argitapen, argiarazpen, adierazpen.
elude v.t. saihestu, txiri egin.
elusive adj. itzurkor, itzurti.
elves n. (pl.) of elf.
emaciated adj. argal.
emaciation n. argaltasun.

emanate *v.i./v.t.* isuri, jario; bota, jaurti.
emanation *n.* jario.
emancipate *v.t.* desmenpetu, askatu.
emancipated *adj.* menpegabe, askatu(a).
emancipation *n.* askapen.
embalm *v.t.* gantzutu, igortzi.
embalmer *n.* gantzutzaile, gantzulari.
embankment *n.* lubeta.
embarcation *n.* untzirapen, ontziraketa.
embargo *n.* bahitura.
embark *v.t./v.i.* ontziratu.
embarrass *v.t./v.i.* lotsatu, lotsagarritu, apalerazi.
embarrassed *adj.* lotsor, lotsakor.
embarrassedly *adv.* herabez, lotsaz.
embarrassing *adj.* lotsarazle, lotsazko, apalgarri.
embarrassment *n.* lotsa, apalketa, larridura, ahalke.
embassy *n.* enbaxada.
embellish *v.t.* apaindu, apaingarriztu, dotoretu, edertu, politu, ederreztatu, liraindu.
embellishment *n.* apaindura, dotoreketa, ederdura, ederketa.
ember(s) *n.* txingar, txingarrauts, sugeldo.
embitter *v.t.* samindu, garraztu.
emblem *n.* paparreko.
embodiment *n.* pertsonifikapen, nortzapen; gizantz.
embody *v.t.* gorputzeratu.
embrace *v.t.* besarkatu, laztandu.
embrace *n.* besarka, besarkada, besarkaldi.
embracer *n.* besarkatzaile.
embrasure *n.* kainozulo; gezileiho; leihobarren.
embroider *v.t./v.i.* bordatu.
embroiderer *n.* bordatzaile.
embroidery *n.* bordaketa.
embroil *v.t.* lardaskatu.
embryo *n. (anat.)* ernaberri, ernamuin.
embryonic *adj.* ernaberrizko.
emerald *n.* esmeralda.
emerge *v.i.* -tik etorri, agertu, jalgi.
emergency *n.* larriune, larrialdi, larriordu.
emeritus *adj.* ospagarri, ospatsu.
emery *n.* eskuharri, harlatz.
emetic *n.* purgagarri, gorakoi. *adj.* okagarri, okarazle.
emigrant *n.* joale, migrari.
emigrate *v.i./v.t.* atzerriratu, erbesteratu.
emigration *n.* herrialdaketa, erbesterapen.
eminent *adj.* goiko, garaitsu.
emir *n.* emir.
emissary *n.* mezulari, mezudun, mandatari.
emission *n.* emankizun, emanaldi.
emit *v.t.* jaurtiki, bota, egotzi. *v.t.* azaldu (eritziak).

emotion *n.* bihotzikara, bihotzirrara, hunkipen, sentipen, zirrara.
emotional *adj.* sentigarri, sentibera, sentikor, hunkibera, hunkigarri, erdirakor, zirrarazko, zirraragarri. **To become emotional.** Zirraratu.
emotionality *n.* sentiberatasun, hunkiberatasun.
emotionally *adv.* hunkigarriro, sentipenez, sentimenduz, biziro, biziki.
emotionalness *n.* sentiberatasun, hunkiberatasun.
emperor *n.* enperadore.
emphasis *n.* azpimarraketa, azpimarra.
emphasize *v.t.* azpimarratu.
emphatic *adj.* hanpurutsu.
emphatically *adv.* deblauki, gogorki.
empire *n.* enperadoretza; enperadorearen lurrak.
employ *v.t.* enplegatu, lana eman, jardunarazi. *v.t.* erabili.
employee *n.* mendeko pertsona, aginpeko, meneko.
employer *n.* kontratari, kontratatzaile, kontratugile; ugazaba.
employment *n.* beharkintza, lanpostu, irabazpide.
emporium *n.* denda handi(a).
empower *v.t.* ahalmendu, eskubidea eman, eskubidetu.
empowered *adj.* eskubidedun, eskudun.
empress *n.* enperadoresa.
emptier *n.* hustzaile. *adj. (comp.)* hutsago.
emptiness *n.* husketa, hustasun.
empty *v.t.* hustu.
empty *adj.* huts, hutsik; hus-.
emulate *v.t.* lehiakatu, zeingehiagoka ari.
enable *v.t.* gaitu, gai egin, trebatu, gauzatu; ahalmendu.
encampment *n.* kanpamendu.
encase *v.t.* kutxan sartu.
enchain *v.t.* kateatu, kateztatu, katigatu.
enchant *v.t.* xarmatu, liluratu, zorarazi, zoratu.
enchanting *adj.* zoragarri, liluragarri, xarmagarri.
enchantingly *adv.* liluragarriki.
enchantment *n.* xarma, xarmantasun, lilura, liluraketa, xoradura, xoragarritasun, xoraldi; xora-.
encircle *v.t.* inguratu, inguruestutu.
encirclement *n.* inguraldi.
enclose *v.t.* inguratu, kokatu, barrutu, hesiztatu.
enclosure *n.* hesi, hesibarruti. *n.* tokibakan, esparru.
encompass *v.t.* ingurukatu, inguratu. *v.t.* euki, eduki, hartu.
encore *n.* berriro, berriz, beste bat!, errepikapen eskaera (antzerkian).
encounter *v.t./v.i.* topatu, topo egin, bidetorri, itsumustu egin.

encounter *n.* topaldi, topo, topaketa.
encourage *v.t.* adoretu, berbizkortu, gogoa berotu, sustatu.
encouragement *n.* eragin, bultzapen, adore, kemen.
encouraging *adj.* adoretzaile, adoregarri, kemengarri.
encroach *v.t.* mugautsi.
encumber *v.t.* oztopatu.
encyclopedia *n.* entziklopedia.
end *v.t./v.i.* amaitu, bukatu, azkendu, burutu. *v.i.* **(up)** gelditu, halakatu.
end *n.* bukaera, azken, azkenalde, amai, azkenburu. *n.* punta. *n.* jomuga, helburu, xede.
endanger *v.t.* arriskatu, irriskatu.
endear *v.t.* maitarazi.
endearment *n.* laztan, balaku.
endeavor *v.i.* ahalegindu, saiatu.
endeavor *n.* ahalegin, saialdi.
ending *n.* bukaera, amaiera. *n. (gram.)* hitzamai.
endless *adj.* bukaezin, bukagaitz, amaigabe, amaigabeko, amaiezin, azkengabe, amaibako.
endlessly *adv.* azkengabeki. *adv.* kontaezinez.
endlessness *n.* amaigabetasun.
endodermis *n. (anat.)* barrenazal.
endorse *v.t.* txekea izenpetu. *v.t.* onartu, baieztu.
endorsement *n.* onespen, baiespen, baieztapen. *n.* izenpe. *n. (econ.)* besteganaketa.
endow *v.t.* diru eman.
endowment *n.* diru emanketa.
endurance *n.* eramankortasun, pairakortasun, pazientzia, jasapen. *n.* iragangaiztasun, iraunketa, iraunkortasun.
endure *v.t.* eraman, jasan, pairatu. *v.i.* iraun, luze izan.
enduring *adj.* iraunkor, iraungarri. *adj.* eramankor.
enema *n.* labatibaz egiten den gorputzaren garbiketa.
enemy *n.* etsai, arerio, izterbegi, kontrako.
energetic *adj.* kemendun, kementsu, odoldun, bizkor, zoli, zuhar.
energetically *adv.* kementsuki.
energeticness *n.* zolitasun.
energize *v.t.* bizkortu.
energy *n.* kemen, bizkortasun, indar.
enforce *v.t.* behartu, eragin.
enfranchise *v.t.* eskubideak eman, botu-eskubidea eman.
engage *v.t./v.i.* ari izan, ihardun. *v.t./v.i.* enplegatu. *v.t.* mihiztatu, ahokatu.
engaged *adj.* ezkongaitu(a).
engagement *n.* ezkongaialdi, ezkonagintza. *n.* konpromisu.
engender *v.t.* sortu, erne. *v.t./v.i.* gertarazi; -arazi.
engine *n.* motore. *n.* tren.
engineer *n.* injineru. *n.* trengidari,

makinazain, bultzigidari.
engineering *n.* injinerutza.
England *n. (geog.)* Britania, Ingalaterra.
English *n.* ingeles (hizkuntza).
Englishman *n.* ingeles (gizon).
Englishwoman *n.* ingeles (emakume).
engrave *v.t.* zulakaiztu, grabatu.
engraver *n.* zizelari.
engraving *n.* grabatu, lanketa.
engulf *v.t.* irentsi.
enhance *v.t.* biziagotu.
enigma *n.* asmagai.
enigmatic *adj.* asmagaitz, ezkutari.
enjoy *v.t.* atsegin hartu, gozatu, on egin, poz hartu.
enjoyable *adj.* jostalari, pozatsu, alaitsu, atsegingarri, laketgarri.
enjoyably *adv.* atsegingarriro, atseginez, gostuz.
enjoyment *n.* gozamen, laketkuntza.
enlarge *v.t./v.i.* handitu, handiagotu.
enlargeable *adj.* emendagarri.
enlargement *n.* handikuntza, handikunde, zabalketa, hedapen.
enlighten *v.t.* argitu, biztu, argi egin.
enlist *v.i./v.t.* gudaritu, soldadutu; lerrokatu, erroldatu.
enlistment *n.* lerrokaldi.
enliven *v.t.* sutarazi, ernatu, bizkortu, suspertu.
enlivener *n.* gogoberotzaile.
enlivening *adj.* ernatzaile, kemengarri, suztatzaile, suspertzaile.
enmity *n.* etsaigo, etsaitasun, areriotasun, gaizkinahi, ikusiezin.
ennui *n.* gogait, gogaiketa, gogaitasun, aspertasun.
enormity *n.* galantasun, izugarritasun.
enormous *adj.* handitzar, eskerga, izugarrizko, neurrigabe.
enough *adj./adv.* nahiko, aski.
enrage *v.t.* sumindu.
enraged *adj.* haserrekor.
enraging *adj.* haserrekor, irakingarri, sukoi, suminkor.
enrich *v.t.* aberastu, joritu.
enriching *adj.* aberasgarri.
enrichment *n.* aberasketa.
enroll *v.t./v.i.* matrikulatu.
enrollment *n.* matrikula.
en route *adv.* bidean zehar; bidean.
ensemble *n.* talde, multso, bilduma.
ensign *n.* itsas-armadako subteniente(a).
ensilage *n.* zuloraketa.
enslave *v.t.* mirabetu, uztarpetu.
enslavement *n.* esklabutzapen.
ensure *v.t.* baieztu.
entangle *v.t.* desorraztu, lardakatu, katramildu, korapilatu.
entanglement *n.* katramila, lardaska.
enter *v.i./v.t.* sartu, barneratu, barruratu.
enterprise *n.* enpresa.
enterprising *adj.* saiatsu, ahalegintsu, ekile, porrokatu(a).

entertain *v.t./v.i.* jostatu, jostarazi, jolas eragin, atsegindu.
entertainer *n.* jostalari, jostarazle.
entertaining *adj.* jolasgarri, jostagarri, jostalari.
entertainment *n.* jolasketa, josta, jostaketa, olgeta.
enthrall *v.t.* xarmatu.
enthrallment *n.* xarmaldi.
enthrone *v.t.* tronuratu, bakaulkitu.
enthuse *v.i./v.t.* sutarazi.
enthusiasm *n.* suhardura, suhartasun, sutsutasun, gogobero, goieragin, gar, goritasun.
enthusiast *n.* -zale.
enthusiastic *adj.* gartsu, sutsu, suhar, gogatsu.
enthusiastically *adv.* gartsuki, sutsuki, gogoberoz, su ta gar.
entice *v.t.* tentatu, iradoki, liluratu, gaitzeratu, zirikatu.
enticement *n.* zirikapen, zirikaldi, zirikamen, iradokizun.
enticer *n.* zirikatzaile, iradokitzaile.
enticing *adj.* iradokor.
entire *adj.* oso, osorik, atalgabeko.
entirely *adv.* osorik, guztiz, erabat, zeharo, arras, biziki.
entirety *n.* osotasun.
entitle *v.t.* eskubidea eman, eskubidetu.
entity *n.* izan, izaki, izadi.
entomb *v.t.* hobiratu, hilobiratu, lurperatu, ehortzi, lurra eman.
entourage *n.* lagungo.
entrails *n. (pl.)* erraiak, erraiki.
entrance *v.t.* sorgortu; liluratu.
entrance *n.* sarleku, sarrera, sarbide; -aho. *n.* sarkunde, sarraldi, sarreraldi.
entrap *v.t.* lakiotu, lakiopetu.
entreat *v.t.* otoitz egin.
entreaty *n.* arren, otoi, otoitz, erregu.
entrepreneur *n.* lanburuzagi, enpresari.
entrust *v.t.* arduratu, kargu eman.
entry *n.* sarleku, sarrera, sartune. *n.* sarkunde, sarkuntza.
entwine *v.t./v.i.* karakoildu.
enumerate *v.t.* zenbatu, zerrendatu.
enumeration *n.* kontaketa, zenbaketa, zerrendaketa.
enumerative *adj.* zenbakor.
enunciate *v.t.* ahoskatu. *v.t.* aipatu.
enunciation *n.* ahoskaketa. *n.* aipaketa.
envelop *v.t.* estali, paketatu, fardeldu.
envelope *n.* gutunazal, eskutizzazal, kartazal.
enviable *adj.* bekaizgarri, gutiziagarri.
envious *adj.* bekaizkor, bekaizti, gutiziagarri.
enviously *adv.* bekaizki.
environment *n.* bizigiro, ingurumen, bizinguru, ingurugiro. *n.* inguru, ingurune.
environs *n. (pl.)* inguru, inguralde, ingurumariak.
envoy *n.* mezulari, mandatari.
envy *v.t.* bekaiztu.
envy *n.* bekaizkeria, jelosia.
enzyme *n. (biol.)* entzima.
eon *n.* epe luze, aldi luze.
epaulet *n.* sorbaldako, soingaineko.
ephemeral *adj.* iragankor, igarokor, joankor, pasakor, funtsgabeko.
epic *n.* epika.
epidemic *n.* izurrite, izurrialdi, izurri.
epidermal *adj.* larruazaleko.
epidermis *n. (anat.)* azalmintz, larrumintz, mintz.
epiglottis *n. (anat.)* zintzurmihi.
epigram *n.* epigrama.
epigraph *n.* irakurburu.
epilepsy *n. (med.)* erormin.
epileptic *adj.* erorminezko.
epilogue *n.* hitzatze, gibelsolas.
Epiphany *n. (eccl.)* agerkunde, erregegun.
episcopal *adj.* apezpikuaren; gotzain.
Episcopalian *adj./n.* episkopalianu.
episcopal see *n.* gotzainaulki.
episode *n.* gertaera, gertakari, jazoera.
epistle *n.* gutun, eskutitz.
epistolary *n.* gutunsorta, eskutizsorta. *n. (eccl.)* irakurliburu.
epitaph *n.* hilobizkribu.
epithet *n.* izenlagun.
epitome *n.* laburpen, laburki.
epoch *n.* sasoin, aldi, aro, garai.
equable *adj.* gogoberdin, aldaezin, egonkor.
equal *v.t.* berdin izan, berdindu.
equal *adj.* berdin, pare, paregarri, pareko, hainbateko, erabateko.
equalitarian *n./adj.* berdinzale.
equality *n.* berdintasun, parebide, paretasun, paretza.
equalize *v.t.* parekatu, berdindu.
equalizer *n.* berdintzaile, paretzaile.
equally *adj.* berdin, berdinki, berebat, berdinzki.
equalness *n.* parebide, paretasun.
equanimity *n.* gogoberdintasun, orekatasun.
equation *n.* ekuazio.
equator *n. (geog.)* ekuadore, lurgerri.
equatorial *adj.* lurgerriko.
equestrian *n.* zaldidun. *adj.* zaldizko.
equidistant *adj.* tartekide, biderdiko.
equilateral *adj.* aldeberdin, aldekide, aldekideko.
equilateralness *n.* aldeberdintasun.
equilibrium *n.* orekatasun, oreka.
equine *adj.* zaldikide.
equinoctial *adj.* udaberriburuko; udazkenburuko.
equinox *n.* udaberriburu; udazkenburu.
equip *v.t.* trebatu, gaitu, tresnatu, hartarakotu, hornitu.
equipment *n.* tresneria, hornidura, material(ak).
equitable *adj.* berebateko, zuzenbidezko; legezko.

equitably *adv.* zuzenki.
equitation *n.* zaldiketa.
equity *n.* gogokidetasun; zuzentasun.
equivalence *n.* hainbestetasun, baliokidetza.
equivalency *n.* hainbatasun, baliokidetasun.
equivalent *n./adj.* baliokide, zenbakide, balioberdineko.
equivocal *adj.* nabar, bitariko, ilun, halaholako. *adj.* zalantzagarri, dudazko, ezbaiezko.
equivocate *v.i.* bihurdikatu, gezurra esan.
equivocation *n.* bihurdikapen, errakuntza.
era *n.* aro, etapa.
eradicable *adj.* deserrogarri, desustraigarri, erauzgarri.
eradicate *v.t.* deuseztatu, eliminatu. *v.t.* deserrotu, desustraitu.
eradication *n.* desustraiketa, deserroketa, erauzketa, erauztaldi.
eradicator *n.* desustraitzaile.
erasable *adj.* ezabagarri.
erase *v.t.* ezabatu, borratu.
eraser *n.* ezabailu, ezabagoma, borragoma.
erasure *n.* ezabapen.
ere *prep.* baino lehenago.
erect *v.t.* eraiki. *v.t./v.i.* goititu, goratu.
erect *adj.* tentekor, zutikor. *adv.* tente, zutik.
erectile *adj.* tentekor, zutikor.
erection *n.* zutiketa, tenteketa (sexual). *n.* eraiketa.
erectness *n.* tentekortasun, zutikortasun, tentetasun, zutitasun.
erector *n.* tenterazle, zutierazle, zutitzaile.
ergo *adv.* ergo.
erode *v.t./v.i.* higatu, urratu, erosionatu.
erosion *n.* erosio, lurrigadura, higadura.
erotic *adj.* erotiko.
eroticism *n.* erotismo.
err *v.i.* erru egin.
errand *n.* errekadu, mandatu.
errant *adj.* ibilkari.
erratic *adj.* aldakor, desiraunkor; txoriburu, buruarin.
erroneous *adj.* okerreko.
erroneously *adv.* oker, okerretara, okerrez, okerki.
error *n.* huts, hutsaldi, oker, makur, akats, errakuntza, falta.
eruct *v.t./v.i.* korrok egin, kokada egin.
eructation *n.* kokada.
erudite *adj.* jakintsu, ikastun.
eruditely *adv.* jakintsuki.
erudition *n.* jakituria, jakinduria.
erupt *v.i.* zapartatu, lehertu.
eruption *n.* lehertzapen.
escalate *v.t.* igotu, goratu; gehiagotu.
escalation *n.* igoaldi.
escalator *n.* eskilara mekaniko(a).

escape *v.i./v.t. (v.i., askotan from-ekin)* ihes egin, hanka egin, alde egin.
escape *n.* ihesaldi, ihes, aldegite, ihesbide.
escapee *n.* ihesgile, iheslari.
escarpment *n.* itsasezponda.
eschew *v.t.* utzi, baztertu, zaihestu, alderatu.
escort *v.t.* pertsona bat eraman.
escort *n.* jagoletalde, eskolta.
escudo *n. (econ.)* eskutu.
escutcheon *n.* erredola.
Eskimo *n./adj.* eskimale.
esophagus *n.* hestegorri.
especially *adv.* batez ere, bereziki, baitipat, gehien bat.
Esperanto *n.* esperanto.
espionage *n.* zelatakuntza, barranda, espioitza.
essay *n.* saiakera, saioaldi, entseiu.
essayist *n.* saiolari, saioidazle.
essence *n.* izatasun, mami, esentzia.
essential *adj.* oinarrizko, funtsezko, erroko, errozko, mamizko. *n.* behar-beharrezko gauza.
essentially *adv.* oinarriz, izatez, mamiz.
establish *v.t.* funtsatu, finkatu, fundatu, jaso, ezarri, errotu, sustraitu.
establishment *n.* agintari. *n.* ezarpen.
estate *n.* ondasun. *n.* ondasun higigarriak, diru. *n.* maila, klase. *n.* testamendu-ondasunak. *n.* hazienda.
esteem *v.t.* preziatu, estimatu, onetsi, begiramen izan, oneritzi.
esteem *n.* begiramen, errespetu, estima, oneritze, eder, ohore, preziamendu.
esteemed *adj.* estimagarri, preziagarri, preziatu(a), aupagarri, goragarri.
estimable *adj.* estimagarri, preziagarri, goragarri, aupagarri, txalogarri.
estimate *v.t./v.i.* tankeratu, tankera eman, hainbatu, aitzinkontu.
estimate *n.* aitzinkontu.
estimation *n.* aitzinkontu. *n.* irizpide, estimu.
estimator *n.* hainbatzaile.
estrange *v.t.* urrundu, hoztu.
estranged *adj.* hotz (harreman pertsonalak).
estrangement *n.* hozkeria.
estrus *n.* azkara.
estuary *n.* ibaiondo.
etc. etab.
et cetera abar eta abar, etabar.
eternal *adj.* betiko, sekulako, beti-betiko, betidaniko.
eternally *adv.* sekulakoz, sekulan, amaigabeki, betikoz.
eternity *n.* betikotasun, sekulatasun, betiere.
ether *n. (chem.)* eter.
ethic *n.* etika.
ethical *adj.* etikoa, etikazko.

ethics *n.* etika.
ethnic *adj.* etniko.
ethnically *adv.* arrazaz.
ethnography *n.* etnografia.
ethnologist *n.* etnologo.
ethnology *n.* etnologia.
etiquette *n.* etiketa, gizabide.
etymological *adj.* hitzerrozko.
etymologically *adv.* hitzerroz.
etymologist *n.* hitzsorkunlari.
etymology *n.* hitzerro, hitzsustrai.
eucalyptus *n. (bot.)* eukalitu.
eucharist *n.* eukaristia, aldareko Jaun.
eulogist *n.* goraipatzaile, goratzaile,
  goresle.
eulogistic *adj.* goresmenezko.
eulogize *v.t.* goraipatu, goretsi, goratu.
eulogizer *n.* goratzaile, goresle.
eulogy *n.* gorazarre, goraipu,
  gorespen, goraipamen, laudorio,
  handiespen.
eunuch *n.* gizonerdi.
euphemism *n. (gram.)* itzestali,
  eufemismo.
Europe *n. (geog.)* Europa.
European *n./adj.* europar. *adj.*
  Europako.
euthanasia *n.* eutanasia.
evacuate *v.t./v.i.* -tik joan, alde egin.
  v.t. iraitzi.
evacuation *n.* husketa. *n.* kakaldi,
  kakegite.
evacuator *n.* hustzaile.
evaluate *v.t.* balioztatu, baloratu,
  tasatu.
evade *v.t./v.i.* zehartu, ihes egin.
evaded *adj.* ihesi(a).
evaluatable *adj.* baloragarri.
evaluate *v.t.* baloratu, ebaluatu.
evaluation *n.* ebaluaketa, ebaluapen,
  balioztapen, balorazio.
evaluator *n.* ebaluatzaile.
evangelical *adj.* ebanjeliozko.
evangelist *n.* berrionlari, ebanjelari.
evangelistic *adj.* ebanjeliozko.
evangelize *v.t./v.i.* ebanjeliotu.
evaporate *v.i./v.t.* lurrindu, lurrineztatu.
evaporated *adj.* lurrineztatu(a),
  lurrindun.
evaporation *n.* lurrindura,
  lurrinkortasun, lurrineztapen,
  lurrinketa, lurrunketa.
evasion *n.* ihesbide, iheseketa,
  ihespide, ihesaldi, itzurpen, itzuraldi.
  n. ingurukeria, inguru-minguru.
evasive *adj.* ihesbidezko, iheskor,
  itzurgarri.
evasively *adv.* zeharka-meharka,
  itzulinguruka.
evasiveness *n.* ingurukeria.
eve *n.* aurregun, bezpera.
even *v.t. (batzutan out edo up-ekin)*
  laundu, lauzatu, galgatu. *v.i.*
  berdindu.
even *adj.* leun, labain. *adj.* parekide.
  adj. etengabe(ko), artegabeko,
  geldigabeko. *adj.* baketsu, lasai. *adj.*

(math.) pare. *adv.* baita, ere.
evening *n.* ilunabar, ilunsenti, arrats.
  adj. arratsaldeko, arratseko.
evenly *adv.* leunki, leunkiro.
evenness *n.* leuntasun. *n.* berdintasun.
event *n.* gertaldi, gertakari, gertaera,
  jazoera.
eventful *adj.* gogoragarri, oroikarri.
even though *conj.* arren.
eventual *adj.* badaezbadako,
  gertagarri.
eventuality *n.* badaezbada,
  gertagarritasun.
eventually *adv.* azkenean, azkenik.
ever *adv.* beti. *adv.* etengabeki. *adv.*
  inoiz, nehoiz, behinere. *adv.* inola.
everlasting *adj.* betiko, betiraun.
every *adj.* guzti, oro; -ero, -oro. **Every
  day.** Egunero.
everybody *pron.* denok, denak, denek,
  guztiak, oro.
everyday *adj.* eskuarteko; eguneroko.
everyone *pron.* nornahi; denok, denak,
  denek, guztiak, edonor.
everything *pron.* dena, guzti, oro,
  zernahi, edozer.
everywhere *adv.* nonnahi, edonon,
  orotan.
evict *v.t.* desmaiztertu, etxetik bota.
eviction *n.* lekugabetze.
evidence *n.* agergarri, argi, argibide,
  argigarri, nabaritasun.
evident *adj.* ageri, argi-argi, nabari,
  nabarmen, begietako, ezagun, jakin.
evidently *adv.* agerian, ageriz,
  nabarian, garbiro.
evil *n.* gaizkeria, gaitz, gaiztakeria,
  bihurrikeria, makurkeria, okerkeria,
  txarkeria, malezia. *adj.* gaizto,
  gaizkin, makur, oker, txar,
  gaiztoarazle.
evildoer *n.* gaiztagile, gaiztagin.
evilly *adv.* gaizki, makur, txarki.
evilness *n.* txartasun, gaiztotasun,
  gaiztakeria.
evince *v.t.* erakutsi, azaldu, agertu.
eviscerate *v.t.* deserraindu.
evocation *n.* gogarazpen.
evocative *adj.* gogarazle, gogoragarri.
evoke *v.t.* gogarazi, oroitarazi.
evolution *n.* bilakaketa, bilakaera,
  eboluzio.
evolutionary *adj.* bilakakor.
evolutionism *n.* eboluzionismo.
evolve *v.t./v.i.* hazi, garatu, bilakatu.
  v.t./v.i. eboluzionatu.
ewe *n. (zool.)* ardi.
ex- *(gram.)* -izana.
ex *n.* senar-izana, emazte-izana.
exacerbate *v.t.* gaizkitu; sumindu.
exact *v.t.* eskatu, behartu, eragin.
exact *adj.* zehatz, justu, konkretu,
  zuzen.
exacting *adj.* zehatz.
exactitude *n.* funts.
exactly *adv.* justu, zehazki,
  zehatz-mehatz.

exactness n. zehastasun, zehetasun, justutasun.
exaggerate v.t./v.i. ederra sakatu, ederrak bota, gehiegitu.
exaggerated adj. gehiegizko, sinokari.
exaggeratedly adv. gehiegikeriaz, gehiegizka, gehiegiz.
exaggeration n. gehiegikeria, ahoberokeria(L,U), neurrigabekeria.
exaggerative adj. ahozabal, ahohandiko.
exalt v.t. goraipatu, goratu, goretsi, handietsi, laudorioztatu, ohoratu.
exaltation n. goraipaketa, goraipamen, goraldi, handiespen, laudorio, gorespen.
exalted adj. goralgarri.
exalter n. handiesle.
exam n. azterketa, azterpen.
examinable adj. arakagarri.
examination n. azterketa, azterpen, ikermen, ikerpen, araketa. n. begiraketa, ikuskapen.
examine v.t. aztertu, arakatu, ikertu, galdezkatu.
examiner n. azterlari, aztertzaile, azterkari, ikerle, ikertzaile, txerkatzaile.
example n. adibide, exenplu. n. eredu, ikasbide, erakusbide, jarraibide, ikuspide.
exasperate v.t. haserrerazi, gainez eragin.
exasperated adj. haserredun.
exasperating adj. haserregarri, sumingarri.
exasperation n. haserrekeria, suminaldi, erretxindura.
excavate v.t. zulo egin, zulapetu, azpizulatu, hondeatu.
excavation n. azpizulo, hondalan, zulapen.
excavator n. hondeatzaile, zulapetzaile, hondalangile, zulatzaile, zulogile.
exceed v.t./v.i. gainpasatu, gainditu, gehiegitu, goititu.
excel v.t./v.i. gain hartu, nabarmendu, gailurtu, besteak baino hobea izan.
excellence n. bikaintasun, gailentasun, goitasun, goratasun.
excellent adj. bikaina, goren, gailen, paregabeko, berdingabeko, aparta.
excellently adv. ezinobeki, garaiki.
except v.t. salbuetsi, lekoratu.
except prep./conj. ez beste, ezik, izan ezik, kanpo, landa, salbu.
exception n. salbuespen, exzepzio.
exceptional adj. paregabe, salbuespenezko, berdingabeko, aparta.
exceptionally adv. exzepzionalki.
excerpt n. pasarte, textu.
excess n. gehiegikeria, neurrigabekeria, gaindidura, larregikeria.
excessive adj. gehiegitsu, gehiegizko,

neurrigabeko, gaindizkako.
excessively adv. gehiegiz, gehiegi, neurrigabeki, sobera, gainezka.
excessiveness n. gehiegikeria, neurrigabekeria, neurrigabetasun, lartasun.
exchange v.t./v.i. (v.i., batzutan for-ekin) truke egin, trukatu, elkartrukatu; ordeztatu.
exchange n. truke, trukaketa, truk, elkartrukaketa, ordeztapen. n. (econ.) ganbio.
exchangeability n. trukagarritasun, ordeztagarritasun.
exchangeable adj. trukagarri, trukakor, ordezkagarri, ordeztagarri.
excise v.t. deserrotu, erauzi, errotik atera.
excitability n. kilikortasun, kitzikaberatasun, kilimakortasun.
excitable adj. subera, kitzikabera.
excitation n. kitzikapen.
excite v.t. sustatu, berotu, piztu, ernarazi (sentipenak). v.t. kitzikatu; narritatu.
excited adj. grinatsu, grinati, bero-bero.
excitedly adv. grinaz, erreminez.
excitement n. beroaldi, kitzika, asaldaketa, kitzikapen; narritadura.
exciter n. gogoberotzaile, kitzikatzaile, kitzikari.
exciting adj. bizkorgarri, biztugarri, bizikor, kilikagarri, kitzikagarri, suhargarri, susperkor, ziztakor, narritatzaile.
exclaim v.t. oihu egin, oihukatu.
exclamation n. oihu, hots.
Exclamation mark. Harridura ikur.
exclude v.t. baztertu, lekatu, salbuetsi, aldebateratu, alboratu.
excluder n. baztertzaile, alderatzaile.
exclusion n. salbuespen, kanporaketa, bazterketa.
exclusive adj. bakar, soil; berezi. n. aldizkarietako artikulu.
exclusively adv. soilik, soilki.
excommunicate v.t. (eccl.) eskomunikatu.
excommunication n. (eccl.) eskomuniku, exkomunio.
ex-convict n. espetxetik irtendako pertsona.
excrement n. bekorotz, gorozki, kaka.
excremental adj. ongarritsu.
excretion n. iraizpen, iraizketa.
excretory adj. iraizkor.
excruciating adj. mingarri, neketsu, nekegarri.
exculpate v.t. garbitu, zuritu, errua kendu.
excursion n. ibilaldi, txango, ateraldi, irtenaldi.
excusable adj. barkagarri, desenkusagarri, zurigarri.
excuse v.t. errugabetu, barkatu, desenkusatu, zuritu, gainzuritu.

excuse *n.* aitzakia, zurialdi, desenkusa, zuribide.
excuser *n.* zuritzaile.
execrate *v.t./v.i.* gaizki esan; madarikatu.
execration *n.* gaizkiesaka.
execute *v.t.* egitaratu. *v.t.* fusilatu, urkatu.
executed *adj.* hil(a), garbitu(a). *adj.* beteriko, eginda.
executive *n./adj.* administrari.
execution *n.* urkamendu, fusilamendu. *n.* egintza, egite, betekizun.
executioner *n.* heriotzemale, borrero.
executor *n.* eginkari, beterazle. *n.* testamenduzain.
executrix *n.* testamenduzain (emakume).
exemplariness *n.* eredutasun, jarraigarritasun.
exemplary *adj.* ered-uzko, jarraigarri, eredugarri, onbiderako, oneragile, imitagarri.
example *n.* adibide, exenplu, ikasbide. **To set a good example.** Onbideratu. **For example.** Esate baterako.
exemplify *v.t.* adibidetu, argitu.
exempt *v.t.* lekatu.
exempt *adj.* lekatu(a), salbuespenezko.
exemption *n.* salbuespen. **Tax exemption.** Zergagabezia.
exercise *n.* ariketa, eragiketa, jarduketa. **Physical exercise.** Gorputz eragiketa.
exerciser *n.* jardule.
exert *v.t.* erabili (aginpide), jardun, ari izan. *v.t.* ahalegindu, lehiatu.
exertion *n.* ahalegin.
exfoliate *v.t./v.i.* hostogabetu, orrigabetu.
exfoliation *n.* orrierorketa.
exhalation *n.* arnasbehera, arnasemaldi.
exhale *v.i./v.t.* arnasa bota, arnaseman.
exhaust *v.t.* ahitu, nekatu. *v.i.* abaildu. *v.t.* porrokarazi, leher egin, pot egin, akiarazi.
exhaust *n.* ihesgas(ak).
exhausted *adj.* indargabe, etenda, hebain, herbal, nekatu(a).
exhaustible *adj.* agorgarri, ahitugarri.
exhausting *adj.* nekagarri, nekarazle, lehergarri, ahulgarri, makalkor.
exhaustion *n.* nekaldi, nekebizi, leherbehar, hebaindura.
exhaustive *adj.* porrokatu(a).
exhaustively *adv.* sakonki, osorik.
exhaust pipe *n.* ihestutu.
exhibit *v.t./v.i.* erakutsi, nabarmendu, aurkeztatu, azaleratu.
exhibit *n.* erakustaldi.
exhibition *n.* erakusketa, aurkezpen, agerkaldi.
exhibitionism *n.* agerzalekeria, nabarmenkeria, erakuskeria. *n.* biluzkeria.
exhibitionist *n.* nabarmenzale.
exhibitionistic *adj.* agerzale.
exhibitor *n.* erakusle, erakustari.
exhilarate *v.t.* alaitu, poztu.
exhorbitance *n.* gehiegikeria, neurrigabekeria.
exhorbitant *adj.* gehiegitsu.
exhorbitantly *adv.* neurrizgain.
exhort *v.t.* aholkatu, oharrarazi.
exhortation *n.* aholku, ohar.
exhumation *n.* deslurperaketa.
exhume *v.t.* deslurpetu, desehortzi.
exhumer *n.* lurkentzaile.
exigency *n.* eskakizun, beharkuntza.
exigent *adj.* eskakor.
exile *v.t.* atzerriratu, erbesteratu, deserritu.
exile *n.* atzerri, desterru, atzerriraketa, erbesteraketa, erbesterapen. *n.* atzerriratu.
exiled *adj.* erbesteratu(a), atzerriratu(a).
exist *v.i.* izan, bizi, geratu.
existence *n.* izate.
existing *adj.* izatedun.
exit *v.i.* irten, jalgi, atera.
exit *n.* aterabide, irteera, irtenbide.
exodus *n.* atzerriraketa, atzerrirapen.
exonerate *v.t.* barkatu, desenkusatu.
exorbitant *adj.* gehiegi, neurrigabe.
exorcise *v.t.* exorzizatu, arao egin, araokatu.
exorcism *n.* araoketa, exorzismo.
exorcist *n.* araolari, exorzista.
exotic *adj.* erbestetar, exotiko.
exoticism *n.* exotismo.
expand *v.t./v.i.* handiagotu, hedatu, zabaldu.
expandability *n.* hedakortasun.
expandable *adj.* hedagarri, hedakor, zabalkor, zabalgarri.
expandableness *n.* hedakortasun.
expander *n.* hedatzaile, zabaltzaile.
expanse *n.* hedadura.
expansion *n.* hedadura, hedapen, hedaketa, zabalkuntza, zabalpen.
expansive *adj.* hedatsu, zabalkor, hedakor. *adj.* tokitsu, tokidun.
expansiveness *n.* zabalkortasun, hedakortasun.
expatriate *v.t.* deserritu, erbesteratu, atzerriratu.
expatriate *n.* pertsona atzerriratu(a).
expatriated *adj.* atzerriratu(a), erbesteko.
expatriation *n.* atzerriraketa, atzerrirapen, atzerrialdi, erbesterapen, erbesteraketa.
expect *v.t.* espero ukan. *v.t.* itxaron, iguriki. *v.i.* haurdun izan, haurdun egon.
expectant *adj.* itxarodun. *adj.* haurdun.
expectantly *adv.* zain. *adv.* itxaropenez.
expectation *n.* itxaropen, iguripen,

igurikapen.
expecting *adj.* umadun, haurdun. *adj.* aiduru, igurika, zain.
expectorant *n.* tuegile.
expectorate *v.t./v.i.* listu bota, listu egin, listukatu.
expectoration *n.* listuketa, karkaisaldi, gorroaldi.
expedient *adj.* abantailatsu, onuratsu, ongarri.
expedite *v.t.* arinarazi, bidetu.
expedition *n.* bidaritalde.
expel *v.t.* kanporatu, kaleratu, itzulerazi.
expend *v.t.* gastatu; erabili.
expendable *adj.* iraungikor, galkor.
. **Expendable assets.** Ondasun iraungikorrak. *adj.* aienagarri.
expenditure *n.* gastu.
expense *n.* gastu, eralki.
Expense-account. Gastu-kontu.
expensive *adj./adv.* garesti, kario.
expensively *adv.* kario, garesti.
expensiveness *n.* garestitasun.
experience *n.* esperientzia, trebaketa; eskarmentu.
experienced *adj.* trebe, askoikusi(a).
experiment *v.i. (batzutan with-ekin)* saiatu, experimentatu, entsegutu.
experiment *n.* esperimentu, experimentazio.
experimental *adj.* entseguzko, experimentuzko, saiozko.
. **Experimental method.** Saiozko bide.
experimentally *adv.* experimenduz, saioz.
experimentation *n.* ikerbide.
experimenter *n.* saiolari, experimentatzaile.
expert *n.* berezilari, perito, maixu. *adj.* aditu(a), askoikasi(a), trebe.
expertise *n.* maixutasun.
expertly *adv.* trebeki, trebekiro, taiuz.
expertness *n.* trebetasun, molde, moldadura.
expiate *v.t.* ordaindu, garbitu.
expiation *n.* bakearazpen.
expiration date *n.* mugaegun, epemuga.
expire *v.i.* epe galdu; amaitu, bukatu. *v.i.* hil.
explain *v.t./v.i.* agertu, azaldu, erakusten eman, ezagutarazi, argiarazi, jakinerazi.
explainable *adj.* azalgarri, adieragarri, zurigarri.
explainer *n.* agertzaile, argierazle, azaltzaile.
explanation *n.* azalpen, adierazpen, azalbide, azalketa, erakusaldi, zurialdi, argitasun.
explanatory *adj.* azalbidezko, erakusbidezko, argigarri, argibidezko.
expletive *n.* birao, arnegu.
explicit *adj.* garbi, ageriko, argi.

explicitly *adv.* agerki, garbiki, argiro.
explodable *adj.* lehergarri, eztandagarri.
explode *v.i./v.t.* eztanda egin, eztandatu, lehertu, leher egin, danba egin.
exploder *n.* lehertzaile.
exploit *v.t.* baliatu, probetxatu.
exploitation *n.* explotazio.
exploiter *n.* hurrupatzaile.
explorable *adj.* aztergarri, ikergarri.
exploration *n.* bilaketa; ikerketa; ikusketa.
exploratory *adj.* ikerkor, aztergarri, ikergarri.
explore *v.t./v.i.* miatu, ikuskatu, ikertu, aztertu.
explorer *n.* bilakari, ikustari, ikuskatzaile, ikusketari.
explosion *n.* lehertzapen, leherketa, eztanda.
explosive *n.* lehergailu, leherkin, eztandagailu. *adj.* leherkor, lehergarri, eztandagarri.
explosiveness *n.* lehergarritasun.
export *v.t.* kanporatu, gauzak beste herrietara bidali sal daitezen.
export *n.* exportazio, kanporaketa.
exportable *adj.* kanporagarri.
exportation *n.* kanporaketa, exportazio.
exporter *n.* kanporatzaile.
exporting *n.* kanporaketa.
expose *v.t.* menturatu, erakutsi. *v.t.* desestali.
exposed *adj.* gerizagabe.
exposition *n.* agerkaldi, erakustaldi, erakusketa, adierazpen. *n.* planteamendu.
exposure *n.* erakusketa. *n.* argitaldi (argazki).
express *v.t.* adierazi.
express *n.* trenlaster, express. *adj.* ageriko, argi, garbi. *adj.* laster.
expression *n.* esaera, mintzaera, esamolde. *n.* erakutsi, adierazpen. *n.* aurpegi-keinuz edo ahotsez sentipenak azaltzea. **Facial expression.** Aurpegiera.
expressive *adj.* esankor. **An expressive greeting.** Agur esankorra. *adj.* adierazkor.
expressively *adv.* adierazkorki, biziro.
expressiveness *n.* adierazkortasun, bizitasun.
expressly *adv.* asmoz, nahita, ohartuki. *adv.* agerkiro.
expropriate *v.t.* besteganatu, besterendu, desjabetu.
expropriation *n.* desjabeketa, desjabetzapen, besteganaketa.
expropriative *adj.* kentzaile.
expropriator *n.* desjabetzaile, kentzaile, kenarazle.
expulsion *n.* botaketa, egozketa.
exquisite *adj.* on-on, bikain.
exquisitely *adv.* bikainki.

extend v.t./v.i. hedatu, hedabanatu, luzatu.
extendable adj. luzagarri.
extender n. hedatzaile, zabaltzaile, luzarazle.
extendible adj. hedagarri, zabalgarri.
extension n. hedaketa, hedapen, luzapen, luzaketa.
extensive adj. hedatsu, zabal. adj. luze. adj. oso.
extensively adv. luzaro, luzaroan, luzeki, luzaz.
extent n. hein. n. zabalera.
extenuate v.t. arindu, ematu.
extenuating adj. aringarri, emagarri.
exterior n. etxaurre; kanpo; itxura. adj. ateko, kanpoko.
exterminate v.t. sakailakatu, deuseztatu, ezereztatu.
extermination n. sarraski, sakaila, triskantza.
exterminator n. sarraskitzaile, garbitzaile.
external adj. kanpoko, kanpotikako, ateko.
externally adv. azaletik, azalez.
extinct adj. hil(a), hildako, zen.
extinction n. itzalketa, iraungipen.
extinguish v.t. itzali, iraungi, hil. v.t. deuseztu, ezereztu.
extinguishable adj. iraungigarri, iraungikor, itzalgarri.
extinguished adj. hil(a), hildako. adj. itzaldu(a), itzali(a).
extinguisher n. itzaltzaile; itzalgailu, suitzalgailu.
extirpate v.t. ezereztu, deuseztu. v.t. deserrotu, desustraitu.
extirpation n. desustraidura, desustraiketa.
extol v.t. goietsi, goratu, jaso, handietsi.
extort v.t. indarkeriaren bitartez dirua lortu.
extortion n. indarkeriaren bitartezko diru-lorpena.
extortionist n. eragozle.
extra adj./n. gehigarri.
extract v.t. ateratu, atera, kanpora atera, erautzi.
extract n. aterakin.
extraction n. ateraketa, ateraldi, erauzketa. n. leinu.
extractor n. erauzgailu. n. erauzle.
extradite v.t. erbesteratu.
extradition n. extradizio.
extrajudicial adj. auzikanpoko.
extramarital adj. ezkontza kanpoko.
extraordinarily adv. harrigarriro. adv. bikainki.
extraordinary adj. harritzeko, harrigarri. adj. bikain, paregabe, berdingabe, egundoko, aparteko.
extravagance n. nabarmenkeria, parrastada.
extravagant adj. parrastatsu, parrastatzaile; nabarmenkor, sakats.

extravagantly adv. parrastaka, parra-parra, arruntki.
extreme n. mutur, punta. adj. ertzeko, muturreko.
extremely adv. gehiegi, larregi, neurrizgain.
Extreme Unction n. oleazio.
extremism n. erradikalismo.
extremist n./adj. ertzerakoi, erradikal.
extremity n. muga, mustur. n. soinadar, gorputzadar. n. arrisku; premia.
extricate v.t. desnahasi, desnahaspilatu.
extroversion n. kanporakoitasun.
extrovert n. pertsona kanporakoi(a).
extroverted adj. kanporakoi.
exuberance n. alaitasun, bizitasun.
exuberant adj. alai, bizi. adj. mardul.
exude v.t. jario.
exult v.i. pozdardartu.
exultation n. pozikara, pozdardara.
eye v.t. gainbegiratu, begiratu, ikuskatu.
eye n. (anat.) begi; be-.
eyeball n. begi-nini.
eyebolt n. granpoi.
eyebrow n. (anat.) bepuru, bekain, begiburu.
eye doctor n. begisendagile, begisendatzaile.
eyedropper n. tantakontagailu.
eyeglasses n. betaurreko(ak), begiaurrekoak.
eyelashes n. (anat.) betile.
eyelid n. (anat.) betazal.
eyesight n. bista.
eyetooth n. (anat.) letagin, betagin, betortz.
eyewitness n. lekuko, ikuslari, ikustaile, ikusle.

F

f n. Ingeles alfabetoko letra.
fable n. alegia; ipuin.
fabled adj. ipuinezko.
fabric n. oihal ehun.
fabricate v.t. fabrikatu.
fabrication n. gezur; irudikeria. n. fabrikaketa; -gintza.
fabulist n. alegilari.
fabulous adj. bikain, sekulako.
facade n. aurrekalde, aintzinalde, aurpegi. n. itxura.
face v.t./v.i. (v.i., askotan **toward** edo **to**-ekin) aurpegi eman, aurre egin, buru egin, aurre eman. v.i. (**up to**) aurre egin, aurpegi eman. **Face the music.** Ondorioei aurre egin. **To keep a straight face.** Barreari eutsi. **To lose face.** Izen ona galdu. **To save face.** Itxurak gorde.
face n. aurpegi, begibitarte, begitarte, musu. n. gainalde. n. aurrekalde, aintzinalde. n. itxura. n. ohore, ospe.
facet n. fase. n. alderdi.
facetious adj. umoretsu.

face to face *prep.* Aurpegiz-aurpegi, aurrez-aurre, buruz-buru, begiz-begi.
facial *adj.* aurpegiko, begitarteko.
facile *adj.* erraz.
facilitate *v.t.* erraztu, erreztu.
facility *n.* erraztasun, aisetasun, errazpide.
facing *prep.* aurrez, buruz.
facsimile *n.* fakzimil, antzantzeko.
fact *n.* gertakari, datu. **In fact.** Izan ere. Egitez.
faction *n.* talde.
factor *n.* (arith.) biderki, zatitzaile, faktore.
factory *n.* lantegi, ola, fabrika, lantoki, enpresa.
factotum *n.* oroegile.
factual *adj.* datudun, benetako, egiazko.
faculty *n.* irakaslego, maisutalde, maisuteria, fakultate, irakasleria. *n.* ahalmen, men. *n.* buruahalmen (ikusmen, entzumen, ezaumen).
fad *n.* zaletasun iheskor(ra).
fade *v.i./v.t.* desmargotu, koloregabetu, tindugabetu, margoldu, zurbildu.
faded *adj.* koloragabe, margul, zurbil.
fadedness *n.* histasun, moteltasun (margoak).
faggot *n.* egursorta. *n.* (colloq.) atzelari.
fail *v.i./v.t.* porrot egin, hondatu, lur jo.
failure *n.* porrot, porrotaldi, lurjotze, hutsegite.
faint *v.i.* zorabiatu, ahitu, mareatu, aldigaiztu.
faint *n.* zorabio, konorte-galketa, konorte-galtze. *adj.* zurbil, margul. *adj.* indargabe(ko), ahul. *adj.* beldurti.
fainthearted *adj.* ikarati.
faintly *adv.* ahulki.
faintness *n.* margultasun, zurbildura. *n.* anu.
fair *n.* feria, azoka. *adj.* bidezko, zuzenbidezko, garbi, artez, zuzen. *adj.* eder, polit. *adj.* pasagarri. *adj.* nahiko, handi. *adj.* arauzko. *adj.* zurigorri. *adj.* on (eguraldi).
fairgoer *n.* ferialari.
fairground *n.* jolasparke; ferientzako leku berezi(a).
fairly *adv.* garbiro, zuzenki, bidezki. *adv.* nahiko, aski. *adv.* pasagarriki. *adv.* osoki.
fairness *n.* zuzentasun.
fairy *n.* iratxo.
fairy tale *n.* ipuin, sorgin ipuin.
faith *n.* fede, sineste, sinesmen. **To have faith in.** Fidatu. **To lose faith.** Fedegabetu. **To renounce one's faith.** Fedea ukatu. *n.* uste. *n.* konfidantza.
faithful *adv.* fededun, fedezko, sinesmendun. *adv.* leial, iraunkor, zintzo.
faithfully *adv.* leialki, leialkiro, zintzo,

zintzoki.
faithfulness *n.* leialtasun.
faithless *adj.* sinestegabe, fedebako.
fake *v.t.* faltsutu.
fake *n.* gauza faltsu(a). *n.* gezurti. *adj.* faltsu, gezurrezko, sasizko.
faker *n.* gezurti, itxuralari.
falcon *n.* (zool.) aztore.
fall *v.i.* erori, jausi, trumilkatu. *v.i.* **(back)** atzeratu, gibeleratu. *v.i.* **(back on)** laguntza eskatu. *v.i.* **(behind)** atzean gertatu. *v.i.* **(down)** lur jo, erori. *v.i.* **(due)** ordaingarri izan. *v.i.* **(flat)** erabat porrot egin. *v.i.***(for)** norbaitek norbait iruzurtu. *v.i.* **(off)** murriztu, gutxitu. *v.i.* **(through)** porrot egin. *v.i.* **(to)** ekigi; hasi; borrokatu.
fall *n.* eroraldi, erorketa, beherakada, gainbeheraldi, jausketa. *n.* udazken, udazkenaldi, udagoien. *adj.* udazkeneko.
fallacious *adj.* iruzurti, gezurti.
fallacy *n.* sasiarrazoin, marrokeria.
fallen *adj.* erori.
fallibility *adj.* huskortasun.
fallible *adj.* huskor.
falling out *n.* elkarretenketa.
fallout *n.* nuklear eztanda ondoren eguratsean jausi ohi diren erradiaktibo zatikiak.
fallow land *n.* laboreondo, larraki, lugorri.
false *adj.* faltsu, gezurrezko, iruzurrezko, iruzurti, sasizko, azalutsezko; sasi-, -izun.
falsehood *n.* gezur, gezurkeria.
falsely *adv.* faltsuki, gezurkiro, iruzurrez, engainamenduz, itxurakeriaz.
falseness *n.* faltsutasun, iruzur, itxurakeria, engainu.
falsetto *n.* faltsete.
falsification *n.* faltsuztapen, faltsuketa, faltsupen.
falsifier *n.* faltsutzaile.
falsify *v.t.* faltsuztatu. *v.i.* gezurtu.
falter *v.i.* kolokan egon, zalantzatu.
fame *n.* fama, aipu, aipamen, ospe, hots, entzute, ohore, izen; ospa-.
familial *adj.* etxeko, familiako.
familiar *adj.* ezagun, jakin; barreneko. *adj.* arin. *adj.* aurpegihandi, lotsagabe, muturrandi. *n.* adiskide. *n.* sorginen abere laguntzaile(a).
familiarity *n.* kuttuntasun, barrukotasun; trebetasun. *n.* lotsagabekeria, lotsagabetasun.
familiarize *v.t.* trebatu; ohitu.
familiarly *adv.* familiarki.
family *n.* familia, senitarte, sendi, mainada, etorki.
famine *n.* gosete, gosealdi.
famished *adj.* goseti, gosezto.
famous *adj.* famatu(a), famatsu, famadun, omendun, ospedun, ohoredun, aipagarri, aipatu(a),

izenandiko, entzutetsu.
famously *adv.* ospez.
fan *v.t.* aireztatu.
fan *n.* haizagailu, haizemale, airegailu, aireztailu. *n.* fanatiko; -zale.
fanatic *n./adj.* fanatiko, alderdikeritsu, burubero.
fanatical *adj.* fanatiko, burubero, itsu.
fanatically *adv.* itsuki, itsu-itsuan.
fanaticism *n.* sineskeria, buruberokeria, fanatismo, garbizalekeria.
fancier *n.* -zale. **Bird fancier.** Hegaztizale.
fanciful *adj.* ameskeriazko, ameskile. *adj.* apetatsu.
fancifully *adv.* ameskeriaz.
fancy *v.t.* begitandu; amestu. *v.t.* atsegindu, atsegin izan, laket izan.
fancy *n.* ameszoro. *n.* apeta, apetaldi. *adj.* apain.
fandango *n.* fandango.
fang *n.* *(anat.)* letagin, hortzagin (abere).
fanny *n.* *(anat.)* atzekalde, ipurdi.
fantastic *adj.* egundoko, miresgarri, zoragarri, harritzeko. *adj.* fantasiatsu, irudimenezko.
fantastically *adv.* fantasioski.
fantasy *n.* ameslilura, irudiketa, fantasia, begitazio.
far *adv.* urruti, urrun. *adj.* urrutiko, lekutako. *adj.* guztiz, guztizko.
far away *adv.* lekutan, urrun, urruti. *adj.* urrutiko.
farce *n.* komedia.
farcical *adj.* komediako, barregarri, zentzugabe.
fare *n.* pasaia, uhasari.
farewell *n.* azkenagur, agurraldi. *int.* adio, agur.
farm *v.t.* laboratu.
farm *n.* baserri, borda.
farmer *n.* baserritar, nekazari, laborari, bordari, lurlantzaile.
farmhouse *n.* baserri, etxalde, landetxe; borda.
farming *n.* nekazaritza, laborantza, laboraritza, lugintza, nekazalgo.
farmland *n.* bordalde.
farrier *n.* ferratzaile, ferraezarle.
fart *v.i.* puzkar egin, uzker egin, uzkerra bota.
fart *n.* uzker, haize, sabelaize, puzkar.
farter *n.* haizeti.
farther *adv.* harago, aitzinago. *adj.* urrunago, urrutiago.
farthest *adj./adv. (superl.)* urrunen, urrutien.
fascinate *v.t./v.i.* liluratu, lilurarazi, xorarazi, zoratu, xarmatu, xarmarazi.
fascinating *adj.* liluragarri, liluratzaile, lilurakor, xoragarri, zorarazle, xarmagarri, xarmakor.
fascinatingly *adv.* liluragarriki, liluraz, xoragarriro.
fascination *n.* lilura, liluraldi, xarmaldi,

xarmaketa, xoraketa, xoraldi.
fascism *n.* faxismo.
fascist *n./adj.* faxista.
fashion *v.t.* ereduztatu, egin, moldatu.
fashion *n.* janzkera, moda, menta. *n.* era.
fashionable *adj.* mentadun, mentatsu.
fashion designing *n.* modagintza.
fashion model *n.* modelo.
fast *v.i.* barau egin, barautu, mehe egin. **To break the fast.** Barau hautsi.
fast *n.* barau, janeza. *adj.* azkar, bizkor, bizi, laster. *adj.* egonkor, iraunkor, finkagarri, tinko, iraun. *adj.* leial, zintzo. *adj.* lizun, haragikor, zantar, likits, lohi, zikin. *adj.* hunkigarri (filma). *adv.* azkar, arin, bizkor, laster, agudo. *adv.* tinko, iraunkiro, iraungarriro.
fasten *v.t./v.i.* estekatu, finkatu, lotu.
fastener *n.* finkatzaile, lokarri, estugarri, estekagailu.
fastening *n.* estekadura, estekaldi, lotura. *n.* estekailu, lokarri.
fastidious *adj.* kontentagaitz, asegaitz.
fastidiously *adv.* gogaikarriro.
fat *n.* gantz, gantzu, koipe, ziho, urin. *adj.* lodi, gizen, totolo. **To get fat.** Gizendu. Loditu.
fatal *adj.* herioekarle, herioemale, heriogarri, heriotzemale, erailkor, hilgarri.
fatalist *adj.* patukoi.
fatality *n.* heriozkortasun.
fatally *adv.* alabeharrez. *adv.* hilzoriaz, hilbidez.
fate *n.* alabehar, jazobehar, zori, patu, ezinbeste, zorte.
fated *adj.* patuzko.
fateful *adj.* zoritxarkoi.
father *v.t.* ernarazi, sortarazi. *v.t.* aitatu.
father *n.* aita. **Like father, like son.** Hazitik dator landarea. *n.* abade jauna.
father-in-law *n.* aitaginarreba.
fatherhood *n.* aitatasun.
fatherland *n.* aberri.
fatherly *adv.* aitakiro.
fathom *v.t.* barrenaztertu, barneratu, itsasoaren sakontasuna neurtu, zundatu. *v.t.* ulertu.
fathomable *adj.* zundagarri. *adj.* ulergarri.
fatigue *v.t.* akiarazi, nekarazi.
fatigue *n.* neke, nekadura, nekaketa, akidura, akialdi. *n. (pl.)* soldaduen jantzi(a).
fatiguing *adj.* neketsu, nekegarri, akigarri.
fatness *n.* loditasun, gizentasun.
fatten *v.t./v.i.* guritu, gizendu, gizenarazi, lodiarazi.
fattener *n.* gizentzaile.
fattening *n.* gizenketa, lodiketa. *adj.* loditzaile, gizentzaile.

fatty *adj.* gantzadun, gantzatsu, gizendun, gizentsu, koipetsu, koipejario. *n.* pottolo, potxolo.
fatuous *adj.* gangar, tentel.
faucet *n.* turru, txorrota.
fault *n.* akats, huts, makur, oker. *n. (geol.)* koska. *n.* erru, kulpa; hoben. *n.* falta, huts (kirolak).
fault line *n.* pasamarra.
faulty *adj.* faltatsu, husdun, narriotsu.
faun *n.* fauno.
fauna *n.* fauna.
favor *v.t.* begipetu, magalperatu, onberatu, hegapetu.
favor *n.* mesede, fabore, onegite. *n.* begikotasun. *n.* dohain, esker.
favorable *adj.* faboragarri, aldezko, alderakoi.
favorably *adv.* bihotzonez.
favored *adj.* faboredun.
favorite *n.* zurrukutun, kuttun. *adj.* kuttun, begipeko, gogoko, gustoko, aldeko.
favoritism *n.* kutunkeria, aldekeria, aldekoikeria, bihozmintasun; bereizkeria.
fawn *v.i.* (**over**) ferekatu, koipetu, elexuritu.
fawn *n.* (*zool.*) oreinkume.
fawner *n.* ferekatzaile, ipurgarbitzaile.
fear *v.t./v.i.* beldur izan, beldurtu, larde izan.
fear *n.* beldur, ikara, ikaraldi, izualdi, izudura. **In fear of.** Beldurrez.
fearful *adj.* beldurti, beldurkor, ikarati, izubera, izuti.
fearfully *adv.* beldurrez, ikaraz, izuz.
fearfulness *n.* beldurgarritasun, beldurkoitasun, ikaragarrikortasun, izuberatasun, izukortasun.
fearless *adj.* beldurgabe, ikaraezin, ikaragabe, ikaragaitz, izuezin, izugabe, ausartsu.
fearlessly *adv.* beldurgabeki.
fearlessness *n.* ausartzia, beldurgabetasun, ausartasun.
feasibility *n.* eginkortasun, egingarritasun, bideragarritasun.
feasible *adj.* eginkor, egingarri, bideragarri, betegarri.
feast *v.t./v.i.* jan.
feast *n.* jan, orrits, oturuntza. *n.* festa, besta, jai, bestaldi, bestaegun.
feat *n.* ekintza, balentria.
feather *v.t./v.i.* lumaztatu.
feather *n.* luma. *adj.* lumazko.
feather bed *n.* lumakoltxoi.
feather-brained *adj.* txoriburu, kaskarin, buruarin, txolin.
feather duster *n.* mustuka.
feathered *adj.* lumadun, lumatsu; lumazko.
featherless *adj.* lumagabe.
feathery *adj.* lumatsu, lumadun.
feature *n.* aurpegiera, nolakotasun, ezaugarri. *n.* filma nagusi(a); kronika. *n. (pl.)* aurpegi.

February *n.* otsaila.
fecal *adj.* hondakintsu.
feces *n.* kaka.
fecund *adj.* aberaskarri, emankor, ernalgarri, ernarazle, jori, ugalkor, erdikor.
fecundity *n.* emankortasun, ernalindar, ernalmen, ugalkortasun, ugalmen.
fecundly *adv.* emankorki.
fed *n.* Estatu Batuetako agente federala. *p. part. of feed.*
federal *adj.* federakor, federal.
federalism *n. (pol.)* federalismo.
federalist *adj.* federalista.
federalize *v.t.* federatu.
federate *v.t./v.i.* federatu.
federated *adj.* federakor.
federation *n.* federazio, federakuntza.
fee *n.* bideordain, bidesari, atesari.
feeble *adj.* ahul, makal, mengel.
feebleness *n.* ahuldura, ahuleria, herbaldura, makaldura, mengeltasun, mirrintasun.
feebly *adv.* ahulki, makalki, mengelki, herbalki, herbalkiro.
feed *v.t./v.i.* janarazi, janaritu, jaten eman, elikatu, alatu, asetu, janari(a) eman.
feed *n.* pentsu, bazka, ganadujanari.
feeder *n.* alatzaile, elikatzaile, mantenzaile.
feeding *n.* janaldi.
feel *v.t./v.i.* sentitu, hunkitu. *v.t.* ukitu.
feeler *n.* adar (insekto), garro, erro.
feeling *n.* sentipen, sentimendu, bihotzaldi, hunkipen, zirrara, bihotzikara. *n.* bihozsusmo, bihozkada.
feet *n. (pl.)* oinak.
feign *v.t./v.i.* itxuratu, gainzuritu, itxura egin, planta egin.
feigned *adj.* itxurati, plantati, ipuinezko, azalutsesko.
feisty *adj.* borrokalari, borrokari, gatazkari.
felicity *n.* poztasun, zoriontasun.
feline *adj.* katukide, katuaire.
fell *v.t.* basamoztu, moxkindu, moztu (zuhaitzak). *pret. of fall.*
felling *n.* basamozketa.
fellow *n.* kide, kideko; mutil.
fellowman *n.* lagunurko, gizakide.
fellowship *n.* adiskidetasun, adiskidego. *n.* beka.
felon *n.* lapur; hiltzaile.
felony *n.* lapurketa; hilketa.
felt *n.* feldro. *p. part. of feel.*
female *n.* eme. *adj.* andrazko, emakumezko; eme.
feminine *adj.* emezko, eme.
femininity *n.* emakumetasun, emetasun.
feminism *n.* feminismo.
feminist *adj.* emakumealdeko, feminista.
femur *n. (anat.)* izterrezur.
fen *n.* urtza.

fence *v.t.* hesitu, hesinguratu, hesiztatu, harresitu. *v.i.* ezpatatu.
fence *n.* hesi, hesibarruti, langa.
fenced *adj.* hesidun, hesi-, -mugatu.
fenceless *adj.* hesigabe.
fencer *n.* ezpataketari, ezpatari, ezpatalari.
fencing *n.* ezpatajoko, ezpataketa, esgrima. *n.* ingurapen.
fend *v.t.* babestu, itzalpetu, gerizatu.
fender *n.* lohiestalki.
ferment *v.t./v.i.* fermentatu, hartzitu, muztiotu, samindu.
ferment *n.* hartzigarri, altxagarri.
fermentable *adj.* hartzigarri, fermentagarri, muztiogarri, jaikigarri.
fermentation *n.* legamidura, fermentapen, hartzidura, muztiopen.
fern *n. (bot.)* iratze, ira.
fern bog *n.* legizamon.
ferocious *adj.* odoltzale, odolkoi, odolisurle, basati, piztitsu.
ferociously *adv.* abereki, mokorki, zakarki.
ferocity *n.* odolzalekeria, odolkeria, piztitasun, izukeria.
ferret *n. (zool.)* hudo.
ferrous *adj.* burdindun.
ferruginous *adj.* burdintsu.
ferry *n.* ibaiontzi, aldauntzi.
ferry toll *n.* iragansari.
fertile *adj.* aberaskarri, emankor, erdikor, ernalgarri, jori, ugalkor, gizen, gozatsu.
fertilely *adv.* emankorki, ugalkorki.
fertileness *n.* ernalindar.
fertility *n.* emankortasun, joritasun.
fertilizable *adj.* jorigarri, simaurgarri.
fertilization *n.* ongarriztadura.
fertilize *v.t.* ongarritu, ongarriztatu, goroztu, simaurtu, joritu.
fertilizer *n.* ongarri, gorotz.
fervent *adj.* gartsu, suhar, sutsu.
fervently *adv.* gartsuki, sutsuki, jo ta su, jo ta ke.
forvor *n.* suhardura, sugar.
fester *v.i./v.t.* gaiztatu, zolitu, zornatu.
festered *adj.* zoli.
festival *n.* erromeria, festa, jai, jaialdi. **Village festival.** Herrijai.
festive *adj.* jaitsu.
festivity *n.* jaialdi, bestaldi, bestaegun.
festoon *n.* lore-ustai, girlanda.
fetch *v.t.* ekarri.
fetid *adj.* kiraskarri, kirastsu, kiratsezko, kerudun.
fetidness *n.* kirats, kirastasun, kirastura.
fetish *n.* fetitxe, jainkorde.
fetishism *n.* fetitxismo.
fetter *v.t.* girgiluztu, kateatu.
fetter *n.* girgilu.
fetus *n. (anat.)* ernaberri, haurgaldu, umeki.
feud *n.* familien arteko borroka.
feudal *adj.* feudal.
feudalism *n.* feudalismo.

fever *n.* sukar. **High fever.** Sukarraldi. *adj.* sukarrezko.
fevered *adj.* sukardun, sukartsu.
feverish *adj.* sukardun, sukarrezko, sukartsu.
feverishly *adv.* sutsuki, sukarki.
few *n.* zenbait; batzuk, bizpahiru. *pron./adj.* zenbait, guti, bakan.
fewer *adj.(comp.)* gutiago.
fiance *n.* senargai, ezkongai.
fiancee *n.* andregai, emaztegai, ezkongai.
fiasco *n.* porrotaldi.
fib *n.* gezurtxo.
fiber *n.* biru, firu, hari, zuntz.
fibber *n.* gezurti, gezurtero.
fibrous *adj.* firudun, zuntzetsu, haritsu.
fickle *adj.* aldakor, haizakor, zuzika.
fickleness *n.* hutsalkeria, zuzikakeria, zuzikatasun, haizakortasun.
fiction *n.* asmakeria, fikzio.
fictional *adj.* fikziozko.
fictitious *adj.* itxurazko, itxurapenezko.
fiddle *n. (mus.)* bibolin, arrabita.
fiddler *n.* arrabitari.
fidelity *n.* zintzotasun, zintzoera, leialtasun.
fidget *v.i.* urduritu, larritu, kezkatu.
fidgety *adj.* urduri.
field *n.* belardi, zelai, soro, landa. **Playing field.** Kirol zelai. *n.* esparru, arlo.
field marshal *n. (mil.)* mariskal.
field mouse *n. (zool.)* satsuri, sorosagu.
fiend *n.* deabru.
fiendish *adj.* deabruzko.
fierce *adj.* begimakur, anker.
fiercely *adv.* ankerki, bortxaz.
fierceness *n.* ankerkeria.
fieriness *n.* sugardura.
fiery *adj.* gartsu, susper, suhar, sutsu.
fife *n.* txistu.
fifteen *n./adj.* hamabost.
fifteenth *adj.* hamaboskarren.
fifth *adj.* boskarren, boskarrengo.
fiftieth *adj.* berrogeitamargarren.
fifty *n./adj.* berrogeitamar.
fifty-fifty *adv./adj.* erdizka.
fig *n.* biku, piku.
fig tree *n. (bot.)* bikondo, fikondo.
fight *v.i./v.t.* borrokatu, borrokan egin, gudukatu, eskukatu, gatazkatu.
fight *n.* borroka, borrokaldi, haserraldi, liskar. *n.* topeka. **A ram fight.** Aharitopeka.
fighter *n.* borrokalari, borrokari, gatazkari.
figurative *adj.* irudizko, irudibidezko, irudikor.
figuratively *adv.* irudibidez, irudipenez.
figure *v.t./v.i. (askotan up-ekin)* kontatu. *v.i.* agertu, izan. *v.i.* arrazoizkoa izan. *v.i. (out)* asmatu, ulertu, burutu.
figure *n.* gizairudi. *n.* zifra, zenbaki.
figurehead *n.* sasiagintari. *n. (naut.)*

itsasontzien brankako irudi(a).
filament *n.* hari, harizpi, izpi, zuntz.
filamentous *adj.* haritsu.
filch *v.t.* litxartu, xixkatu.
filcher *n.* xixkari, litxarrero.
file *v.t.* artxibatu, karpetaratu, sailkatu, katalogatu. *v.i.* lerroka ibili. *v.t.* marruskatu, limatu.
file *n.* herronka, erreskada, ilara, lerro. *n.* fitxategi; agiritegi. *n.* lima, karraskailu.
filer *n.* fitxalari, artxibalari. *n.* limatzaile, marruskatzaile.
filet *n.* xerra (haragi edo arrain).
filial *adj.* semezko.
filibuster *n.* Estatu Batuetako parlamentuan egiten diren hitzaldi luze- luzeak.
filigree *v.t.* zilarrariztu.
filing *n.* marrusketa, marruskaketa, marruskaldi.
fill *v.t./v.i.* bete, gaineztu; oreztu, oreztatu. *v.t.* okatu, asetu.
fill *n.* ase, aseketa, kok, okaldi.
filler *n.* asetzaile.
filling *n.* aginore, oreztapen. *adj.* asegarri, betegarri.
filly *n.* (*zool.*) behorkume.
film *v.t./v.i.* (*batzutan* over-*ekin*) lausotu, lanbrotu. *v.t.* filmatu, filma egin.
film *n.* filma. *n.* pelikula, zinema. *n.* mintz.
filmy *adj.* hodeitsu, mintzadun.
filter *v.t./v.i.* iratzi, irazi, filtratu.
filter *n.* iragazgailu, iragazkin, iragaztontzi, filtro.
filterable *adj.* iragazkor, iragazkarri, filtrakor.
filth *n.* zikin, zakarreria, urdekeria, zerrikeria, satsukeria, mantar, kaka. *n.* lohikeria, lizunkeria, likistasun.
filthily *adv.* zikinkiro, urdeki, lohiki, likiski.
filthiness *n.* zikinkeria, satsutasun, likistasun.
filthy *adj.* mantartsu, zikin, zikinontzi, likits, tortikatsu, satsu.
filtration *n.* filtrapen, irazpen, iragazdura.
fin *n.* hegats, arrainegal.
final *adj.* azken, azkeneko, azkenaldeko, bukaerako, buru-buruko, amaierako. *n.* azken azterketa.
finale *n.* azken (musika eta antzerki).
finality *n.* aldaezintasun.
finalist *n.* azkeneko, azkenaldiko.
finalize *v.t.* azkendu, bukatu, amaitu.
finally *adv.* azkenez, azken batez, azkenean.
finance *v.t.* finantzatu.
finance *n.* finantzak.
financer *n.* finantzari, finantzatzaile.
finances *n.* (*econ.*) finantzak.
financial *adj.* diruzko; diru-.
financially *adv.* diruari buruz.

financier *n.* diruketari.
financing *n.* finantzaketa, finantzapen.
finch *n.* (*zool.*) txonta, neguta.
find *v.t.* aurkitu, kausitu, topatu, ediren. *v.t./v.i.* epaitu. *v.i.* (out) jakin, jakintsutu, arakatu, barrenaztertu.
find *n.* aurkipen, idoroketa, idoropen.
finder *n.* aurkitzaile, idorotzaile, topatzaile.
finding *n.* aurkikunde, aurkipen, aurkintza.
fine *v.t.* isundu.
fine *n.* multa, isun. **To impose a fine.** Isuna ezarri. *adj.* fin; mirrizka. *adj.* on, bikain; apain. *adv.* ontsa, ondo, ongi. *adv.* dotore.
finely *adv.* finki. *adv.* dotore.
fineness *n.* fintasun, findura.
finery *n.* ederjantzi.
finesse *n.* fintasun, tentu, abilezia.
finger *n.* (*anat.*) hatz, hatzamar, atzamar, behatz, eri.
fingernail *n.* (*anat.*) hatzazal.
fingerprint *n.* hatzamarratz.
fingerstall *n.* atzandel.
fingertip *n.* eripunta, erimami.
finickiness *n.* mizkinkeria, mokozurikeria.
finicky *adj.* mokozuri.
finish *v.t./v.i.* burutu, amaitu, bukatu, konplitu, azkena eman, iraungitu.
finishable *adj.* bukagarri, amaigarri.
finished *adj.* kito.
finisher *n.* bukatzaile, amaitzaile.
finite *adj.* amaikor. *adj.* mugatu(a).
finned *adj.* hegatsu.
fiord *n.* fiordo.
fir *n.* izai.
fire *v.t./v.i.* su eman, biztu, irazeki. *v.t./v.i.* tiro eman, tirokatu, tiro egin. *v.t.* lanpostutik bota, kanporatu.
fire *n.* su, sute, suketa, sutzar, sualdi, erreketa.
firearm *n.* arma, zizpa.
firebrand *n.* ilinti.
fire engine *n.* suzainen kotxe.
firefly *n.* (*zool.*) ipurtargi.
fireman *n.* suhiltzaile, suponpari, suzain.
fireplace *n.* sutondo, subazter, sutegi.
fireproof *n.* erregaitz.
fireside *n.* subazter, sutondo.
fire station *n.* suzaintoki.
firewood *n.* adarki, egur.
fireworks *n.* sujokoak, sujolasak, sugurpil, suziriak, txapligu, zipunga.
firm *n.* enpresa. *adj.* tinko, trinko, gotor. *adj.* iraunezko, iraunkor. *adv.* tinkoki, gotorki.
firmament *n.* ortzi, zerusabai, izartegi.
firmly *adv.* tinkoki, tinko, gotorki.
firmness *n.* finkadura, finkotasun, gotortasun, trinkotasun, sendotasun, gogortasun, tinkotasun. *n.* iraundura, iraupen, egonkortasun, iraute.
first *adj.* lehen, lehenbiziko, lehenengo, aurren. *adv.* lehenbizi,

lehenengo, lehenik.
first aid *n.* lehen-sendabide, lehen-osabide.
first-aid kit *n.* botikakaxa.
first-aid station *n.* zaurietxe.
first-class *adj.* bikain, oso ona. *adj.* lehen maila.
firsthand *adj.* zuzen, lehen eskuko. *adv.* zuzenki, artez.
fir *n. (bot.)* izai.
fiscal *adj.* zerga-. *adj.* diruzko.
fish *v.t./v.i.* arrantzatu, arrantzan egin, arrainetan ibili.
fish *n.* arrain, arrantza. *n.* arrainki, arraiki.
fishbone *n.* arrainezur.
fisherman *n.* arrantzale, marinel, arraintzari, itsasgizon.
fishhook *n.* amu.
fishing *n.* arrainketa, arrantzaldi, arrantza.
fishing tackle *n.* apailu.
fishmonger *n.* arrainsaltzaile, arraindun.
fissure *n.* arrailadura, arrail, zirrikitu, hirrikadura, pitzadura, brintza.
fist *n. (anat.)* ukabil.
fistful *n.* eskukada.
fit *v.t./v.i.* egoki, egokitu. *v.t./v.i.* doitu, ereduztatu. *v.t.v.i.* kabitu.
fit *n.* mokorraldi, odolberoaldi, ernegaldi, ernegamendu. *n.* erorminaldi, suminaldi. *adj.* egoki, gai, gauza. *adj.* duin. *adj.* zuzen. *adj.* gertu, prest. *adj.* osasun oneko, osasun onez.
fitful *adj.* aldiarteko, aldizkako.
fitness *n.* doitasun, egokitasun, duintasun, gaitasun, gauzatasun. *n.* osasun on.
fitter *n.* muntatzaile.
fitting *n.* kokadura, muntaia. *n.* taiadura, taiaketa. *adj.* dagokion , egoki.
fittingly *adv.* dagokionez, gisaz, propioki.
fitting room *n.* aldatoki, jantzigela, aldagela.
five *n./adj.* bost; bos-, bost-. *n.* bosteko (kartajoko).
five-fold *adj.* boskoitz, boski.
fix *v.t./v.i.* finkatu, tinkatu. *v.t.* konpondu. *v.t.* maneatu (janari), antolatu. *v.t.* zikiratu, irendu. *v.t.* tongo egin.
fix *n.* zailtasun, larritasun. *n.* tongo. *n.* droga xiringada.
fixation *n.* finkaketa, finkamendu, finkapen.
fixative *adj.* finkatzaile.
fixed *adj.* tinko, trinko, ibilge. *adj.* konponduta.
fixedly *adv.* errozki.
fixer *n.* finkatzaile, konpontzaile.
fixture *n.* eraskin, osagarri, tresna tinko(a).
flabby *adj.* mengel, bigun.

flaccid *adj.* mengel.
flag *n.* bandera, ikurrin.
flagellate *v.t.* hilduratu.
flagellation *n.* hilduraketa, hildura.
flagrant *adj.* nabari, nabarmen, ageri.
flagstaff *n.* ikurrinmakila, banderamakila.
flagstone *n.* harrizabal, lauza.
flail *v.t.* trailukatu.
flail *n.* trailu.
flailer *n.* idaburlari.
flair *n.* dotoretasun, apaintasun. *n.* gaitasun.
flake *n.* maluta.
flame *n.* gar, sugar.
flamenco *n.* flamenko, andaluzkantu.
flaming *adj.* gardun, gartsu, garrezko.
flamingo *n. (zool.)* flamenko.
flammability *n.* sukoitasun.
flammable *adj.* sugarri, erregarri, subera, sukoi.
flank *n.* alderdi.
flap *v.t./v.i.* hegazkatu; mugitu, astindu.
flap *n.* estalki. *n.* abioiaren hegoetako balazta.
flare *v.i.* erre, sugartu. *v.i. (up)* sutan egon; su hartu. *v.i.* hedatu, zabaldu.
flare *n.* sugarraldi, sutaldi, garraldi. *n.* bengala. *n.* hedapen, zabalketa.
flare up *n.* garraldi.
flash *n.* argiñirñir. *n.* tximistaldi, oinaztargi, tximistaketa, tximistargi.
flash fire *n.* sugarraldi, sutaldi, garraldi.
flashlight *n.* eskuargi, gauargi, gauargiño, linterna.
flashy *adj.* azalkor.
flask *n.* flasko.
flat *n.* zelai. *n.* errubera despuztua. *adj.* aldapagabe, berdin, lau, zelai. *adj.* motel, indargabe. *adj. (mus.)* bemol. *adj.* etzanda. *adj.* zapal. *adj.* erabakizko. *adj.* tinko, mugiezin. *adj.* hits, margul. *adj.* arrunt, orokor (zerga). *adv.* horizontalki.
flatly *adv.* lauki. *adv.* motelki.
flatness *n.* zelaitasun. *n.* moteltasun.
flatten *v.t./v.i.* plaundu, leundu, zelaitu, zapaldu.
flattenable *adj.* zelaigarri.
flatter *v.t./v.i.* ahozuritu, balakatu, koipetu, laudoriotu, losintxatu, lausengatu.
flattered *adj.* lausengutsu.
flatterer *n.* balakari, zurikari, ahozuri, zuri, lausengari, losintxari.
flattering *adj.* balakagarri, balakari, koipetsu, laudoriotsu, lausengatzaile, losintxari, limurkari.
flatteringly *adv.* balakuz, lausenguz, zurikeriaz.
flattery *n.* ahozuriketa, balaku, lausengu, zurikeria, limurketa, losintxa, zuriketa, lausengaldi. **False flattery.** Zuriketa. Koipekeria. Balaku.

flatulence *n.* sabelaize.
flatulent *adj.* uzkerti, uzkerrontzi.
flaunt *v.t.* nabarmendu, agertarazi, azaldu.
flautist *n.* txirulari, xirulari, flautajole.
flavor *v.t.* ontarazi, zaporeztatu.
flavor *n.* gustu, zapore. *n.* saltsa. *n.* kutsu, grazi.
flavorful *adj.* gozatsu, zaporagarri, zaporetsu.
flavoring *n.* saltsa; zapore, gustu.
flavorless *adj.* geza.
flaw *n.* akats, gaitz, huts.
flawed *adj.* husdun, akasdun.
flawless *adj.* huskabe, akatsgabeko.
flax *n. (bot.)* linu, liho.
flaxen *adj.* linuzko, lihozko.
flaxseed *n.* lihohazi, linazi.
flay *v.t.* larrutu.
flea *n. (zool.)* kukuso.
fleck *n.* izpi.
fled *p. part. of* flee.
flee *v.i./v.t.* ihes egin, alde egin, hanka egin, ospa egin.
fleece *v.t.* larrutu.
fleece *n.* ardile, artile.
fleecy *adj.* ardiletsu, artiletsu.
fleet *n.* itsasontzisail.
fleeting *adj.* eziraunkor, iragaitzazko, iraunpengabe.
fleetingly *adv.* iheskorki.
flesh *n.* haragi, okela; -mami. **Human flesh.** Gizaragi.
fleshiness *n.* txitxi, mamitasun.
fleshy *adj.* haragitsu, haragidun, haragizko.
flew *pret. of* fly.
flexibility *n.* malgudura, malgutasun, malguera, moldakoitasun, moldakortasun, moldamen, zalutasun.
flexible *adj.* malgu, bihurkor, zalu, moldakor, toleskor. *adj.* guziekilako.
flexibleness *n.* malguera.
flexibly *adv.* malguki, zaluki.
flick *v.t.* doi-doi ukitu.
flicker *v.i.* ñirñir egin.
flicker *n.* ñirñirkada.
flickering *adj.* ñirñirkari, ñirñirlari. *n.* ñirñira.
flier *n.* hegazkilari, hegalari, abiadore.
flight *n.* hegaketa, hegaldi. *n.* aire-bidaia. *n.* abioiaren ibilbide(a). *n.* denboraren igaroketa laster(ra). *n.* eskilaragune. *n.* etxebizitza. *n.* ihes, ihesaldi, iheseketa.
flightiness *n.* gangarkeria.
flighty *adj.* gangar, ganoragabe(ko).
flimsy *adj.* hauskor. *adj.* ziztrin.
flinch *v.i.* atzera egin.
fling *v.t.* bota.
fling *n.* maitemin, maitemindura.
flint *n. (min.)* suharri, sukarri, sutarri.
flinty *adj.* suharrizko.
flip *v.t.* zotz egin.
flirt *v.i.* maitaxarmatu, maitajokatu, txatxandu.

flirt *n.* maitajokatzaile.
flirtation *n.* maitajoko.
flirtatious *adj.* goizoilasko, goizoilanda.
flirtatiousness *n.* txatxankeria, xarmakeria.
flirter *n.* maitarazle.
flirting *n.* maitaxarma, maitaketa, xarmakeria.
flit *v.i.* pinpilinpauxatu.
float *v.i./v.t.* urgaindu, urgaineratu, urazaleratu, urazalean egon.
float *n.* kulubiz, buia, flotagailu. *n.* karroza.
floatability *n.* flotagarritasun.
floatable *adj.* flotagarri.
flock *n.* artalde, abeltalde; hegaztimordo, hegaztisail, txorimordo, txoritalde; txitalde; oilateria; bildostalde, arkumetalde; aharitalde.
floe *n.* itsaso edo lakuetako izozmendia; izoztontor.
flog *v.t.* astindu, berotu.
flogger *n.* astintzaile.
flogging *n.* astinaldi.
flood *v.t./v.i.* uholdetu, uralditu, urpetu, urgaineztatu.
flood *n.* uhol, uholde, uraldi.
floodgate *n.* uhate.
floor *n.* behe, lur, zola, zoru. *n.* etxebizitza, bizitza, estai, solairu.
floorboard *n.* taula.
flop *n.* porrotketa, frakasu.
flora *n.* landaredi, landaretza, landareria, loradi.
floral *adj.* lorezko.
floriculture *n.* loragintza, lorazaintza.
floriculturist *n.* loralari.
florid *adj.* lilitsu. *adj.* gorri (aurpegia).
Florida *n. (geog.)* Estatu Batuetako estatu bat.
florist *n.* lorasaltzaile.
floss *n.* hortzari.
flotation *n.* igerikakortasun, igerikapen, flotapen.
flotilla *n.* flota.
flounder *v.i. (about)* mugimendu traketsez saiatu.
flounder *n. (zool.)* mihiarrain.
flour *v.t.* irindatu, irineztatu.
flour *n.* irin.
flourish *v.i.* joritu, gurendu. *v.t.* apaindu.
flourish *n.* keinu zeremoniatsu. *n.* izenpe, errubrika. *n.* ahoeder.
flour mill *n.* irindegi, errota.
floury *adj.* irintsu, irundun.
flow *v.i.* jario, isuri, isurikatu, zurrutatu.
flow *n.* isurdura, jarioaldi, jariokin; -isuri, -jario, -isketa.
flowable *adj.* jariogarri, eriongarri.
flower *v.i.* loratu.
flower *n.* lore; lora-.
flowering *adj.* loratsu.
flower petal *n. (bot.)* lorosto.
flowery *adj.* loratsu.
flowing *adj.* isurbera, isurle, jariodura,

isurgarri, isurkor.
flown *p. part. of fly.*
flu *n.* gripe.
fluctuate *v.i.* kolokatu.
fluctuating *adj.* gorabeherakor.
fluctuation *n.* gorabehera.
flue *n.* kebide.
fluency *n.* hitzerraztasun, hitzetorri.
fluent *adj.* ahoeder.
fluently *adv.* ahoederrez.
fluff *v.t./v.i. (batzutan* up-*ekin)* harrotu, arrotu, guritu.
fluffiness *n.* harrotasun, astintasun.
fluffy *adj.* harrotsu, astintsu.
fluid *n.* isurgai. *adj.* isurki, isurgarri, isurkai, jariokor.
fluidity *n.* jariotasun, isurtasun, jariokortasun.
fluidness *n.* isurtasun, jariotasun.
flume *n.* ubide. *n.* egurbide.
flung *p. part. of fling.*
fluorescent *adj.* fluoreszente, fluorkoi.
fluorescent light *n.* fluorargi.
flurry *n.* elurbolada.
flush *v.t./v.i.* gorritu, lotsagorritu. *v.t./v.i.* ehizi uxatu, hots eman.
flush *n.* urkorronte, urlaster (komuna). *n.* urgarbiketa. *n.* gorritasun (aurpegia). *adj.* ugaritsu, bete. *adj.* eskuzabal. *adj.* maila berean.
flushed *adj.* gorritsu.
fluster *n.* aztorapen.
flute *n.* txilibitu, flauta; txistu; txirula, xirula. *n.* koskadura (metal).
flutter *v.i./v.t.* hegazkatu, hegaldakatu, pinpilinpauxatu.
fluvial *adj.* ibaiko.
flux *n.* gorabehera.
fly *v.i./v.t.* hegan egin, hegaz egin, hegaldatu, hegakatu, airez joan.
fly *n. (zool.)* euli. *n.* zirrikitu, brageta. *n.* beita, amuzki.
flycatcher *n. (zool.)* eulitxori, otatxori.
flyer *n.* hegazkari, hegazkilari, hegalari, abiadore.
flying *n.* hegazketa. *adj.* hegalari; hegazkor.
foal *n.* zaldikume.
foam *n.* bits, hagun, afar, ahobits.
foamy *adj.* apartsu, bitsu.
focal *adj.* erdiko.
focus *v.t.* enfokatu.
focus *n.* foku. *n.* galdegai, galdekizun.
fodder *n.* bazka, sorobelar, lasto; pentsu.
foe *n.* etsai, arerio.
fog *v.t./v.i. (batzutan* up-*ekin)* lainoztatu, lanbrotu, lainotu.
fog *n.* laino, lanbro, lauso; laina-. **Low lying fog.** Urlaino. **What a fog!** Hau bai lainoa!
fogginess *n.* lainotasun, lanbrotasun.
foggy *adj.* laino, lainotsu, lanbrotsu. **To get foggy. To become foggy.** Lainotu.
foghorn *n.* adar.
foible *n.* ahultasun, makaltasun.

foil *n.* sukaldeko zilarrezko papera.
fold *v.t./v.i.* tolestu, azpildu, malgurazi.
fold *n.* azpil, azpildura, toles. *n.* artalde.
foldable *adj.* tolesgarri, toleskor, malgugarri, zalu.
folder *n.* paperzorro, kartoizorro. *n.* tolesgailu.
folding chair *n.* tolesaulki.
folding screen *n.* ateorde.
foliaceous *adj.* hostokide.
foliage *n.* hostomordo, hostotza, orritza.
foliation *n.* orrialdi. *n.* hostadura.
folio *n.* paperorri, orri.
folk *n.* jende. *n. (pl.)* gurasoak; senideak, etxekoak. *adj.* herri, herrikoi.
folklore *n.* folklore.
folkloric *adj.* folklorezko, folkloriko.
folklorist *n.* folklorista, folklorezale.
folksong *n.* kopla.
follow *v.t./v.i.* jarraitu, segitu.
follower *n.* jarraitzale, segilari.
following *adj.* hurren, hurrengo, ondorengo, *n.* segitalde.
folly *n.* ergelkeria, zorakeria, burugabekeria.
foment *v.t.* bultzarazi, zirikatu, eztenkatu, probokatu.
fond *adj.* **(of)** zalekor; -zale, -zulo.
fondle *v.t.* laztandu, marruskatu.
fondness *n.* zaletasun, ondonahi, onginahi, eraspen; -koi.
font *n.* iturri.
food *n.* janari, jateko, jaki.
foodstuff *n.* janari, jateko.
fool *v.t.* ederra sartu, ederra sakatu. *v.i.* **(around)** gaztekeriak egin, denbora galdu.
fool *n.* burugabeko, kaiku, kirten, inozo, tentel.
foolhardy *adj.* arriskutsu. *adj.* ausarta, beldurgabe.
foolish *adj.* burugabe, ergel, inozo, tentel, zozo, astapotro, txoriburu, txotxolo, tonto.
foolishly *adv.* burugabeki, ergelki, zoroki, eroki, inozoki, tentelki, zozoki, tontoki.
foolishness *n.* ergelkeria, inozotasun, tontotasun, zentzugabekeria, zorakeria, zozokeria.
foot *n. (anat.)* oin, hanka, zango. **On foot.** Oinez. *n.* oin (30,48 zentimetro). *n.* hondo, behe.
football *n.* amerikar futbola. *n.* amerikar futboleko pilota.
footbridge *n.* oinzubi, zubito.
footfalls *n.* oinots, pausots.
foothill *n.* mendi ondoko tontor(ra).
foothold *n.* harkaitzetako oinleku seguru(a).
footing *n.* oinleku seguru(a).
footnote *n.* ohartxo, ertzohar.
footprint *n.* oinatz, zangohatz, zantzu.
foot race *n.* korrikaldi, korriketa.
foot soldier *n. (mil.)* oinezko.

footstep n. urrats, oinots, oinzapaldi, pauso, pausots.
footstool n. oinaulki.
fop n. kriket, handiputz, pinpirin.
foppish adj. kriket.
foppishness n. kriketasun.
for prep. -tzeko, -teko, -ko. **For tomorrow.** Biharko. prep. -gaitik. prep. -entzat, -tzat, -tzako. **For you.** Zuretzat. prep. truke. prep. alde. prep. gisa, ordez; -tzat. prep. arren. prep. -erako (denbora); -an, -etan. prep. bila. prep. -rantz. prep. ikusirik. conj. -lako.
forage v.t./v.i. (v.i., **for**) bazkatu; bila ibili.
forage n. sorobelar, zuhain.
foray n. erasoketa, erasoaldi.
forbear v.i. eraman, pairatu, jasan.
forbearance n. eramantasun, eramanpen, jasapen, pazientzia.
forbearing adj. eramankor, jasankor, pairakor.
forbid v.t. debekatu, galerazi.
forbiddable adj. debekagarri.
forbidden adj. debekatu(a).
forbidding adj. galerazle.
force v.t. bortxatu, derrigortu, behartu, indar egin.
force n. indar, indarraldi, kemen, derrigor. n. errazoi. n. indarkeria, indarketa, bortxa. n. esku, aginte, aginbide. n. (mil.) soldadutalde, gudaritalde.
forceful adj. indarrezko, kemendun.
forcefully adv. beharrez, gogorrean.
forceps n. pintza.
forcible adj. indarkeriazko, bortxazko. adj. konbentzigarri.
forcibly adv. bortxaz, txarrez, derrigor, derrigorrez, beharrez.
ford v.t. ibitu.
ford n. urmehe, ubide, ubehera, ibi.
fordable adj. ibiragankor, ibidedun, ibigarri.
fore- (gram.) aitzin-, aurre-.
forearm n. besaurre.
foreboding n. bihozsusmo, bihotzaldi, aurreuste. adj. iragarpentsu.
forecast v.t. aurreadierazi, aurreikusi, iragarri.
forecast n. aurreadierazpen, aurreikuste, aurreikuspen, iragarkizun, iragarpen. n. giroezagupen, giroiragarpen.
forecaster n. aurresale, iragarle, aurreratzaile. n. giroiragarle.
foreclosure v.t. ordainketa ezagatik hipoteka kitatzeko eskubidea galdu.
forefather n. lehenguraso, aitalehen.
forego v.i. aurre joan.
foregoing adj. aitzinagoko.
foregone adj. lehen. adj. nahitaezko, ezinbesteko, alabeharrezko.
foreground n. aurre, aurrekalde.
forehead n. (anat.) bekoki, kopeta.
foreign adj. atzerriko, arrotz, erbestetar, erdarazko, kanpoko, kanpotar; kanpo-.
foreign country n. erdalerri, erdal herri, atzerri, erbeste.
foreign currency n. (econ.) dibisa.
foreigner n. arrotz, atzerritar, erbesteko, kanpoko, kanpotar, erdaldun.
foreign language n. erdera.
foreignness n. arroztasun, erbestetasun.
foreknowledge n. aurrejakituria, aitzinjakite, aurrezaguera.
foreleg n. aurreko hanka.
forelock n. zaldiaren bekoki gaineko adatsa.
foreman n. kontramaisu, langileburu, langilezain.
foremost adj. lehen, aurren. adv. lehen aldiz.
forensic adj. auzitegiko.
foreordain v.t. aurreaukeratu.
foresaw p. part. of foresee.
foresail n. (mar.) trinket.
foresee v.t. aurreikusi, aurresusmatu, iragarri, aitzindu.
foreseeable adj. somagarri, aurreikusgarri.
foreseen adj. aurreikusi.
foreshadow v.t. iragarri, azaldu.
foresight n. aurreikuspen, aurreikuste, aurresusmo, aurreuste.
foreskin n. zilmutur.
forest n. baso, oihan, arboladi, zuhaizti, landabaso; oihar-. adj. basoko, oihaneko.
forestal adj. oihaneko, basoko.
forestall v.t. oztopatu, galerazi, eragotzi, debekatu. v.t. aintzindu.
forested adj. oihantsu. **To be forested.** Oihandu.
forester n. oihanlangile, mendilangile, oihartzain.
forestry n. oihanazkuntza, oihangintza.
foretell v.t./v.i. aurresan, aurreadierazi, iragarri.
forethought n. aurreasmo, aurregogarpen.
forethoughtful adj. begidun.
foretold p. part. of foretell.
forever adv. betiko, betirako, sekulako, sekulakoz, orain eta beti, orain eta sekulako.
forewarn v.t. oharterazi, aurretik esan, jakinaren gainean jarri.
foreword n. hitzaurre, aitzin solas, idatzaurre.
forfeit v.t. zigor gisa ondasun eta eskubideak galdu.
forfeiture n. ondasun eta eskubide galketa zigor gisa.
forgave pret. of forgive.
forge v.t. mailukatu. v.t./v.i. faltsutu, gezurtatu.
forge n. sutegi, burdinola.
forger n. mailukatzaile, mailulari. n. dirufaltsutzaile, faltsutzaile.

forgery *n.* dokumentuen faltsuztapena.
forget *v.t./v.i.* ahantzi, ahaztu.
forgetful *adj.* ahanzkor, ahaztukor. **To be forgetful.** Desoroitu.
forgetfulness *n.* ahanztura.
forget-me-not *n. (bot.)* oroilore.
forgettable *adj.* ahazgarri.
forgivable *adj.* barkagarri.
forgive *v.t./v.i.* barkatu, barkamen(a) eman.
forgiven *p. part. of* forgive.
forgiveness *n.* barka, barkamen, askespen.
forgiving *adj.* barkabera, barkakoi, barkatzaile, barkatiar.
forgo *v.t.* utzi.
forgotten *p. part. of* forget.
fork *n.* lauhortzeko, sardeska, tenedore. *n.* karrikarte.
forlorn *adj.* atsekabedun, atsekabetsu, goibel, ilun, triste. *adj.* despopulatu, huts.
form *v.t./v.i.* moldatu, itxuratu, konposatu, eratu.
form *n.* eite, tankera, itxura, taxu, forma. *n.* jokabide, portaera. *n.* arau. *n.* jardunbide. *n.* mota. *n.* sasoi. *n.* molde, orkoi.
formal *n.* jantziapain, jantziluze. *adj.* itxurazale. *adj.* arauzko, formal.
formalism *n.* formalismo.
formality *n.* etiketa.
formally *adv.* eraz. *adv.* zeremoniarauz.
formation *n.* aurrerabide, hazketa. *n.* egitura. *n.* disposapen, disposaketa, ezarketa, prestakuntza. *n.* hezkuntza, eraketa.
formative *adj.* hezikor, eragarri.
former *adj.* leheneko, aurreragoko, aurretiko, lehengo.
formerly *adv.* lehenago, lehenagotik.
formidable *adj.* izugarri, beldurgarri, ikaragarri.
formless *adj.* formagabeko, itxuragabe(ko).
formlessness *n.* itxuragabetasun.
formula *n.* formula, erabide.
formulate *v.t.* moldatu, prestatu.
formulation *n.* formulapen.
fornicate *v.i.* haragikeria egin, larru jo, likistu, lizundu.
fornication *n.* haragikeria, lizunkeria, likiskeria, lohikeria, zantarkeria.
fornicator *n.* larrujole.
forsake *v.t.* utzi, babesgabetu.
fort *n.* babestoki, gordeleku, gotorleku.
forth *adv.* aurrera.
forthcoming *adj.* aurrerantzeko, datorren.
fortieth *adj.* berrogeigarren.
fortification *n.* indardura, sendokuntza. *n.* gaztelu, gotorleku.
fortified *adj.* babesdun, harresidun.
fortify *v.t./v.i.* gazteluztatu, dorreztatu, berrindartu, indar eman.
fortifying *adj.* azkargarri, bizkorgarri,

indargarri, sendagarri; gogorgarri.
fortitude *n.* tenkortasun, sendotasun.
fortnight *n.* hamabostaldi.
fortnightly *adv.* hamabostero, hamabostaldiko, hamabosteroko.
fortress *n.* babestoki, gordeleku, gotorleku, babesiri.
fortuitous *adj.* zorizko, ustekabeko.
fortuitously *adv.* ustekabean.
fortunate *n.* zoriontsu, zoriondun, dohatsu.
fortunately *adv.* zorionez, zorionean.
fortune *n.* dirumoltso, diruketa, dirupilo, dirutza. *n.* mentura, zori, zorte, patu.
fortuneteller *n.* hegaztiazti.
fortunetelling *n.* aztiketa, hegaztiaztikeria.
forty *n./adj.* berrogei.
forward *v.t.* berbidali, berrigorri.
forward *adv.* aurrera.
forwarding *n.* berbidalketa.
fossil *n.* fosil.
fossilization *n.* fosileztapen.
fossilize *v.i./v.t.* fosildu.
foster *v.t.* zaindu, jagon.
foster brother *n.* ditianaia, bular-anaia.
foster child *n.* haurrorde.
foster father *n.* hazaita.
foster mother *n.* hazama.
foster parent *n.* gurasorde.
fought *p. part. of* fight.
foul *adj.* kirastsu. *adj.* nahasi, maltzur, iruzurti. *adj.* txar (eguraldi). *adj.* lizun, lohi.
foul-mouthed *adj.* ahogaizto, mihigaizto.
found *v.t./v.i.* fundatu, funtsatu, jaso. *v.t.* galdatu, urtu. *pret., p. part. of* find.
foundation *n.* hasiera. *n.* oinarri, zimentarri, zimendu. *n. (econ.)* diruondo, baltsa, eskuarte. *n.* erakunde, instituzio, fundazio. *n.* funts, oinarri.
founder *v.i./v.t.* zanbulukatu (ontzi), hondatu. *v.i.* porrot egin.
founder *n.* lehenezarle, zimendatzaile, fundatzaile, hasle, sortzaile.
founding *n.* haskunde. *adj.* aitzinako, lehen.
foundling *n.* umezurtz.
foundry *n.* ola. **Foundry worker.** Olagizon.
fount *n.* iturri, urgune.
fountain *n.* iturri, iturbegi, urbegi.
fountainhead *n.* iturburu.
four *n./adj.* lau.
fourscore *n./adj.* larogei.
fourteen *n./adj.* hamalau.
fourteenth *adj.* hamalaugarren.
fourth *adj.* laugarren.
fowl *n.* hegazti.
fox *n. (zool.)* azeri. **Female fox.** Azerieme. **Fox kit.** Azeriko. Azerikume.
foxglove *n. (bot.)* kukufraka, kukubelar.

foxiness *n.* azerikeria.
foxtail *n. (bot.)* azeribuztan.
foxy *adj.* bihurri, azeriantzeko.
foyer *n.* atari, atalondo.
fracas *n.* muturketa.
fraction *n. (math.)* zatiki, behezatiketa.
fractionary *adj.* zatizko.
fracture *v.t./v.i.* hautsi, pusketatu, apurtu, puskatu (normalki, hezurrak).
fracture *n.* haustura, hauste.
fractured *adj.* apurtu. *adj.* mordoilozko (hizkuntza).
fragile *adj.* hauskor, hauskarri, apurkor, apurgarri, deuseztakor, zatikor, puskagarri.
fragileness *n.* hauskortasun.
fragility *n.* hauskortasun, zatikortasun.
fragment *v.i./v.t.* atalkatu, atalbanatu.
fragment *n.* izpi, atal, puxketa, zatiko.
fragmentary *adj.* pusketazko, zatikako, zatizko.
fragmentation *n.* atalketa, zatiketa, apurketa, atalbanaketa.
fragrance *n.* lurrinusain.
fragrant *adj.* lurrintsu, usaingarri.
frail *adj.* ahul, indargabe, herbal, erkin, makal. *adj.* deuseztakor, mengel.
frailly *adv.* ahulki, herbalki.
frailness *n.* erkinaldi, ahuleria, ahultasun.
frailty *n.* herbaldura, ahultasun.
frame *v.t.* moldatu. *v.t.* laukitu. *v.t.* azpikeriaz jokatu norbaiten aurka.
frame *n.* lauki, marko.
framework *n.* armazoi, zureria, erakusleku.
franc *n.* libera.
France *n. (geog.)* Frantzia.
franchise *n.* hautespide. *n.* frankizia.
francophile *adj.* frantzeszale.
frank *adj.* barruzabal, laino, tolesgabe.
frankfurter *n.* Alemaniako lukainka.
frankly *adv.* zabalki, deblauki, xaloki.
frankness *n.* lainotasun, xalotasun, zabaltasun, zintasun.
frantic *adj.* amorratu, sutsu.
fraternal *adj.* anaikoi, anaitar, anaitiar, anaizale, senidegarri, senidezko.
fraternally *adv.* anaiki.
fraternity *n.* anaitasun, anaiarte, senidetasun. *n.* mutil ikasleen elkarte.
fraternization *n.* anaiketa.
fraternize *v.i.* **(with)** adiskidetu.
fratricide *n.* anaieraile, anaihiltzaile, anaihilketa.
fraud *n.* iruzur, iruzurkeria, maltzurkeria, azpikeria.
fraudulent *adj.* iruzurti, iruzurrezko, atzipetsu, engainakor.
fraudulently *adv.* iruzurrez, engainamenduz, atzipez, azpikeriaz, malmuzki.
fray *v.t./v.i.* zirpildu.
fray *n.* guduxka.
frayed *adj.* zirpiltsu.
freak *n.* beregisako pertsona, pertsona arraro(a). *n.* munstro.
freckle *n.* peka, orizta.
freckled *adj.* pekatsu, orezto.
free *v.t.* askatu, libratu, askarazi.
free *adj.* aske, berjabe, askatu(a). *adj.* dohako. *adj.* mugagabe, oztopogabe. *adj.* lotugabe, deslotu(a). *adv.* dohan, debalde. **Free of charge.** Dohan. *adv.* mugagabeki, oztopagabe.
freeable *adj.* askagarri.
freedom *n.* askatasun, askamen; berjabetasun.
freely *adv.* askatasunez. *adv.* debalde, dohain.
freeway *n.* bidezabal, bidehandi, autopista.
free will *n.* nahiera, aukeramen.
freeze *v.i./v.t.* izoztu, hormatu, jelatu, elurtu.
freeze *n.* izozketa, izozte.
freezer *n.* izoztontzi, izozkailu, jelagailu.
freight *n.* zama, karga, lor, garraio.
freighter *n.* gabarra, ontzitzar.
French *n./adj.* frantzes. *n.* frantziera, frantsesa.
Frenchman *n.* frantzes.
frenum *n. (anat.)* mihiazpiko, mihipeko, mingainazpiko.
frenzy *n.* erokeria; suminaldi.
frequency *n.* sarritasun, maiztasun, usutasun. **To increase the frequency of.** Sarritu. *n.* irratiko frekuentzia.
frequent *v.t.* usutu, maiztu, sarritu.
frequent *adj.* sarritako, sarrizko, noiznahiko, maizezko.
frequently *adv.* sarritan, sarri, maiz, askotan.
fresh *adj.* fresku, zindo, bizi. **Fresh apples.** Sagar zindoak. *adj.* gaurko. *adj.* garbi. *adj.* berri, beste. *adj.* erdiberri (behi). *adj.* lotsagabe.
freshen *v.t./v.i.* (v.i., **up**-ekin) freskatu, bizkortu, zuperzatu.
freshman *n.* unibertsitate eta goieskoletako lehen urteko ikasle.
freshness *n.* freskutasun, gordintasun.
fret *v.t./v.i.* urduritu. *v.t./v.i.* hortzikatu, karraskatu.
fretful *adj.* pairugabe, kexukoi, kakalarri.
fretfully *adv.* umoretxarrez.
friar *n.* fraide, fraidemotz, lekaide, erlijioso.
fricative *adj. (gram.)* igurtzaile.
friction *n.* igurtzi, igurzpen, igorzpen, marruskadura. *n.* desakordio, desadostasun.
Friday *n.* ostiral, bariku.
fridge *n.* izozkailu, hozkailu.
fried *adj.* frijitu.
friend *n.* lagun, adiskide.
friendliness *n.* laztankortasun, bihoztasun.
friendly *adj.* lagunkoi, lagunkor, adiskidetsu, bihozkoi. *adv.* begionez.

friendship *n.* laguntasun, adiskidetasun, adiskidantza, lagunartetasun.
frigate *n.* fragata.
fright *n.* ikara, ikaraldi, beldur, izu.
frighten *v.t.* beldurtu, izutu, ikaratu, beldurrarazi, ikararazi, izuarazi.
frightened *adj.* ikaradun, beldurti, kikil, izubera, beldurkoi.
frightener *n.* izuarazle, beldurrarazle, izutzaile.
frightening *adj.* ikaragarri, beldurgarri, beldurrarazle, izugarri.
frighteningly *adv.* beldurgarriro, asaldagarriki.
frightful *adj.* beldurgarri, ikarazle, izugarri.
frightfully *adv.* ikaragarriki, ikaragarriro, izugarriki.
frightfulness *n.* beldurgarritasun, ikaragarrikortasun.
frigid *adj.* hotz. *adj.* sexuhotz.
frigidity *n.* hoztasun.
frill *n.* apainkeria.
fringe *n.* zerrenda.
frisk *v.i.* saltokatu, salto egin. *v.t.* poliziak jendea arakatu.
frisky *adj.* saltari, jauzilari, jostakor.
fritter *n.* txurro.
frivolity *n.* aldakeria, arinkeria.
frivolous *adj.* txolin, txatxo.
frivolousness *n.* txolinkeria, txolintasun.
fro *adv.* atzeruntz.
frock *n.* jantzi.
frog *n. (zool.)* igel.
frogman *n.* itsaspekari, urpekari.
frolic *v.i.* saltokatu.
frolicker *n.* jostalari.
frolicsome *adj.* jostalari, jostari, saltari, jauzilari, jostakor.
from *prep.* -dik, -tik, -gandik, -etatik; -ko, -go. **From here.** Hemendik. Hemengo. **From there.** Handik. Hango. **From the house.** Etxetik. *prep.* -gaitik. *prep.* -ri.
from now on *adv.* gaurdanik, aurrerakoan, aitzina, aurrerantzean, hemendik aurrera, gaurtik aurrera. **From then on.** Harrezkero.
frondy *adj.* hostotsu, orritsu.
front *n.* aitzinalde, aitzin, aurrekalde; aurre-. **In front of.** Aurrean. Aitzinean.
frontage *n.* aurrekalde.
frontal *n. (anat.)* bekokiko, kopeteko. *n.* aitzinako.
frontier *n.* muga. *adj.* mugaldeko, mugondoko.
frontiersman *n.* Estatu Batuetako aintzinako exploratzailea.
fronton *n.* pelotatoki, frontoi.
frost *v.t./v.i.* intzigarra egin.
frost *n.* lantzurda, antzigar.
froth *n.* ahobits, hagun.
frown *v.i./v.t.* beltzuritu, kopetilundu, betilundu, zimurtu.

frown *n.* kopetabeltz, betondoilun.
frozen *adj.* izotzeko, izozkarri.
fructiferous *adj.* ernegarri.
fructification *n.* fruitupen.
fructify *v.i./v.t.* fruitutu, fruitu eman.
frugal *adj.* aurreratzaile, eskulabur, zeken, elkor, eskuitxi.
frugality *n.* zikoizkeria.
frugally *adv.* oraka.
fruit *n.* fruita, igali; garau. *n.* fruitu, ernari.
fruitful *adj.* fruitekarle, fruitukor, fruitutsu, emankor, ugalkor.
fruitfully *adv.* fruituz, fruitukorki, emankorki.
fruitfulness *n.* ugaritasun, ugalkortasun, ugarikortasun.
fruition *n.* egite.
fruitless *adj.* fruitugabe. *adj.* onuragabeko.
fruitlessly *adv.* alferrik.
fruitstand *n.* fruitadenda.
frustrate *v.t.* frustratu, zapuztu.
frustration *n.* frustrazio, zapuzketa, zapuzte.
fry *v.t./v.i.* frijitu.
fry *n.* frijialdi.
fryer *n.* txigorgailu.
frying pan *n.* zartagina, padera, frijigailu. *(Prov.)* **Out of the frying pan, into the fire.** Otsoari ihesi eta hartzak atzeman.
ft. "foot" edo "feet"-aren laburpena. Oin, oinak (neurria).
fuck *v.t.* larru jo.
fudge *n.* txokolatezko gozoki(a).
fuel *n.* errekin, karburagai.
fuel gauge *n.* gasolin-neurgailu.
fuel oil *n.* biztugarri.
fugacity *n.* iheskortasun, galkortasun.
fugitive *n.* iheslari, itzurle. *adj.* iheskor.
fulfill *v.t.* kunplitu, bete, gauzatu, gogoa bete.
fulfillment *n.* betetasun, betealdi, betekizun.
full *adj.* beterik, beteta, ase. **Half-full.** Erdibete. *adj.* okitu.
full-grown *adj.* heldu(a).
full-length *adj.* gorputz osoko (argazkia). *adj.* luzemetraia.
fullness *n.* asetasun, asekada, betedura, betetasun.
fully *adv.* bete-betean, betean; guztiz, osoro.
fumble *v.i./v.t.* baldarki erabili.
fume *v.t.* ketu; gasa jario.
fume *n.* gasjario; ke.
fumigate *v.t.* intsektizidaz keztatu.
fumigation *n.* kedura (intsektizidaz).
fun *n.* solasaldi, jolasaldi. *adj.* jostagarri, jostalari, pozekarle.
function *v.i.* funtzionatu, ibili.
function *n.* funtzio.
functionally *adv.* funtzionalki.
functionary *n.* funtzionari.
functioning *n.* funtzionamendu.
fund *v.t.* diruz josi.

fund *n.* dirumoltso, diruketa, dirupilo.
    Fund raising. Dirueske. *n. (pl.)*
    fondo.
fundamental *adj.* funtsezko, errozko,
    oinarriko.
fundamentally *adv.* funtsean, funtsez,
    mamiz, oinarriz, errotik.
fund raising *n.* dirubilketa, dirueske.
funeral *n.* ehortzetak, hileta.
funeral parlor *n.* ehorztetxe.
funereal *adj.* hilezko, ilunbetsu.
fungus *n. (bot.)* onddo, onto.
funnel *n.* onil.
funniness *n.* barregarritasun,
    irrigarritasun, irrikortasun.
funny *adj.* barregarri, farregarri,
    irrieragile, grazidun, umoretsu,
    txantxetako.
fur *n.* ilaje, larru, ehizilarru.
furious *adj.* haserre, haserrekoi,
    sumin, amorratu(a). **To be furious.**
    Sutan egon. Suztatu.
furiously *adv.* haserrez, amorruz,
    haserregorritan, haserrebizian.
furlong *n.* berrehun bat metro.
furnace *n.* sutegi.
furnish *v.t.* hornitu, jantzi. *v.t.*
    haltzaritu, erredizatu.
furnishings *n.* trasteria.
furniture *n.* haltzari.
furrier *n.* larrulantzaile, larruontzaile,
    larrugin.
furrow *v.t./v.i.* azalurratu, ildokatu.
furrow *n.* ildo.
furry *adj.* iletsu.
further *adj.* gainerako, gainontzeko.
    adv. haruntzago.
furthermore *adv.* bestalde, gainera,
    gainerakoan.
furtive *adj.* lapurretako, itzalpekari.
furtively *adv.* itzalka, itzulinguruka,
    ezkutuki, ezkutuan, isilean.
fur trade *n.* larrutegi.
fur trader *n.* larruketari.
furuncle *n. (med.)* zaldar.
fury *n.* amorro, amorrubizi,
    haserregorri, haserre, sumin.
furze *n. (bot.)* ote.
fuse *v.t.* galdatu, urtu. *v.t.* bat egin,
    elkartu.
fuse *n.* metxa. *n. (elec.)* fusible.
fusible *adj.* galdagarri.
fusilier *n.* fusilari.
fusion *n.* elkarketa.
fuss *n.* zalapartada.
futile *adj.* kaskar.
futility *n.* fitskeria, huskeria.
future *n.* gero, etorkizun, geroko. *n.*
    (gram.) geroaldi. *adj.* geroko.
futurist *n.* geroaldizale.
futuristic *adj.* etorkizuneko.
futurity *n.* gerotasun.
fuzzy *adj.* iletsu, bilotsu. *adj.* ilun,
    lauso.

G

g *n.* Ingeles alfabetoko letra.

gab *v.i.* hitz egin, mintzatu, solas egin.
gabbiness *n.* elekeria.
gadfly *n. (zool.)* ezpara.
gadget *n.* tresna.
Gaelic *n.* irlandera.
gag *v.i./v.t.* goragaletu, nazkatu, larritu,
    higuin izan. *v.t.* bozatu.
gag *n.* muturreko, muturlokarri. *n.*
    amarru. *n.* txiste.
gaiety *n.* poztasun.
gaily *adv.* pozik.
gain *v.t.* irabazi, garaitu, lortu. *v.i.*
    aurreratu.
gain *n.* irabazpen.
gainful *adj.* irabazkor, irabazgarri.
gainsay *v.t.* ukatu, uko egin, gezurtatu.
gait *n.* ibilera.
gaiter *n.* oinbabes, zangazorro.
gala *n.* jai.
galaxy *n.* galaxia.
gale *n.* mendebal, zurrunbilo.
gall *n.* behazun.
gallant *adj.* galanteder.
gallantly *adv.* galanki, galankiro.
gallantry *n.* adeitasun.
gall bladder *n.* behazun-maskuri,
    behaztun xixku.
galleon *n.* galeoi.
gallery *n.* barrenbide, meazulo. *n.*
    erakusareto, museo.
galley *n.* itsasontziko sutondo(a). *n.*
    galera. *n.* galeraki.
gallon *n.* galoi.
gallop *v.i./v.t.* lauoinkatu, lauoinka ibili.
gallop *n.* arrapalada.
galloper *n.* lauoinkari (zaldi).
gallows *n.* urkamendi, urkabe.
gallstone *n. (med.)* harri, gibelarri. *n.*
    (pl.) pixarri.
galore *adv.* asko, ainitz.
galvanize *v.t.* galbanezatu.
gamble *v.i.* diru jokatu, apostu egin.
gambler *n.* dirujokalari, jokalari.
gambling *n.* dirujoko. *adj.* jokozale.
game *n.* joko, jokaldi, jolas, partidu. *n.*
    ehizi.
gamekeeper *n.* basazain, mendizain.
gander *n. (zool.)* antzar.
gang *n.* hanpa; -talde.
ganglion *n. (anat.)* ganglio, gongoil.
gangly *adj.* luzanga.
gangplank *n.* pasabide, zubixka.
gangrene *n.* haratustel, pasmo.
gangrenous *adj.* ustel.
gangster *n.* gangster.
gap *n.* hutsune, irekidura, tarte, bitarte,
    tartegune.
gape *v.t.* begiratu, so egin.
garage *n.* autotegi, autotoki, kotxetegi,
    garaje.
garb *n.* jantzi.
garbage *n.* sastar, zamar, zabor,
    zaborreria.
garbanzo *n. (bot.)* garbantzu, txitxirio.
garble *v.t.* nahasi, nahastu.
garden *v.i.* baratzean lan egin,
    lorategian lan egin.

garden n. baratze, ortu; lorategi.
gardener n. landarezain, baratzain, lorazain, mindegizain.
gardenia n. (bot.) gardenia.
gardening n. lorazaintza.
garfish n. (zool.) akula.
gargantuan adj. handi-handi, erraldoizko.
gargle v.t./v.i. gurgurkatu, gargar(ak) egin.
gargling n. gargara, urgargara.
garish adj. nabarmen, puntako.
garland n. girlanda.
garlic n. (bot.) baratxuri. **Clove of garlic.** Baratxuriatal. **String of garlic.** Baratxurikorda.
garment n. soineko.
garner v.t. batu.
garnish v.t. apaindu, edertu. v.t. soldata bahitu.
garret n. sabaigela, teilatupe.
garrulity n. berritsutasun.
garrulous adj. berritsu.
garter n. liga.
gas n. gas. n. gasolina. n. laztergailu, azeleragailu.
gaseous adj. gasdun, gasezko.
gash n. labainada.
gasification n. gaseztapen, gaskuntza.
gasify v.t./v.i. gaseztatu, gaseztu.
gasoline n. gasolina.
gasometer n. gasneurkin.
gasp n. arnasestu, arnasbehar.
gas station n. gasolindegi.
gassy adj. gasdun, gasezko.
gastric adj. urdaileko.
gastritis n. (med.) urdaileko, gastritis, urdaileri.
gastronomical adj. gastronomiko.
gastronomy n. gastronomia, sukaldaritza.
gate n. hesiate.
gather v.t./v.i. bildu, multzokatu, batzartu, elkartu.
gatherer n. batzaile, biltzaile, bildumatzaile.
gathering n. bilera, biltzarre, jendeketa.
gauche adj. zakar, gaizkikasi.
gaucho n. gautxo.
gaudily adv. apainkeriaz.
gaudy adj. bizi, min (margoak).
gauge v.t. neurtu.
gauge n. neurgailu; -neurkin.
gauger n. ontzineurtzaile.
gaunt adj. erkin.
gauntlet n. eskubabes, eskuestalki, eskularru.
gauntness n. erkintasun.
gauze n. gasa.
gave pret. of give.
gavel n. epailearen zurezko mailu txikia.
gay adj. alai, pozkor. n./adj. atzelari.
gaze v.i. (at-ekin) so egin, begiratu.
gaze n. begirada, begiraldi, so, begirakune.

gazelle n. (zool.) gazela.
gazette n. egunkari.
gazetteer n. tokizendegi.
gazpacho n. gazpatxo.
gear n. (mech.) engranaia. n. hortz. n. gauza pertsonalak.
geese n. (pl.) antzarak.
gee up int. arre; aida.
geld v.t. irendu, zikiratu.
gem n. harribizi, harriargi.
gender n. jenero.
gene n. gen.
genealogical adj. etorkizko, genealogiko, leinuko.
genealogist n. genealogari.
genealogy n. genealogia, jaioterro.
general n. (mil.) jeneral. adj. orokor, orotar, denen, guztien, askoren.
generality n. orokortasun, jeneraltasun.
generalization n. orokorpen, jeneralizazio, jeneralizapen.
generalize v.t./v.i. orokortu, jeneralizatu.
generally adv. orokorki, gehienbat, gehienetan.
generalship n. (mil.) jeneralgo.
generate v.t. sortu.
generating adj. ernatzaile, sortarazle.
generation n. belaunaldi, leinu. n. sorkuntza.
generative adj. sortzaile, kreatzaile.
generator n. (elec.) dinamo. n. ernagarri, sorkailu.
generic adj. guztitariko.
generosity n. bihotzanditasun, eskuzabaltasun, bihozberotasun, emankortasun.
generous adj. bihotzandi(ko), eskuzabal, emankor.
generously adv. bihotzandiz, eskuzabalki.
genesis n. sorrera, etorki, jatorri, sorketa.
genet n. (zool.) katamuturluze.
genetic adj. genetiko. n. (pl.) genetika.
genetics n. genetika.
genial adj. atseginkor, adikor.
genie n. arabiatar iratxo(a).
genital adj. ernalbidezko; ernal-.
genitalia n. (anat.) ernalbide, ernalkin.
genitive n. (gram.) genitibo.
genius n. jeinu, buruzolitasun.
genocide n. genozidio.
genre n. literatur mota.
gent n. zaldun, gizon.
gentile n. jentil.
gentility n. adeikortasun, jendetasun.
gentle adj. ezti, bihozleun. adj. otzan, bihozpera, manakor. adj. adeitsu, harrerakor, harreratsu. adj. neurrizko.
gentleman n. zaldun, zamaldun.
gentlemanliness n. gizontasun.
gentlemanly adv. zaldungisa, zaldunki, zaldunkiro.
gentleness n. eztitasun, samurtasun,

emetasun. *n.* bihozperatasun, otzantasun. *n.* adeitasun, harreratasun.

gentlewoman *n.* andrauren (andra + guren).

gently *adv.* bihotzonez, bigunki, samurki, samurkiro. *adv.* emeki, astiro, geldiro, patxadaz.

genuflect *v.i.* belaunikatu (elizan).

genuflection *n.* belaunikaketa, belaunikaldi.

genuine *adj.* egiazko, egitazko, benetako, jator.

genuinely *adv.* jatorki, benetan.

genuineness *n.* egiazkotasun, jatortasun.

genus *n.* jenero.

geo- *(gram.)* lur-.

geocentric *adj.* lurrerdiko.

geographer *n.* geografari, geografo.

geographical *adj.* geografiko.

geography *n.* geografia.

geological *adj.* geologiko.

geologist *n.* geologari, geologo.

geology *n.* geologia.

geometrical *adj.* geometriko.

geometry *n.* geometria.

Georgia *n. (geog.)* Estatu Batuetako estatu bat.

geranium *n. (bot.)* geranio, mokobelar.

geriatrics *n.* zaharsendagintza.

germ *n.* mikrobio. *n.* ernamuin, hozi. *n.* jatorri, hasera.

German *n.* alemaniar. *n.* alemaniera.

germane *adj.* dagokion, buruzko.

Germany *n. (geog.)* Alemania.

germinal *adj.* ernaldizko, ernamuinezko.

germinate *v.i./v.t.* erne, ernatu, kimatu, ninikatu.

germination *n.* ernakuntza, ernarazpen, kimuketa, ernaldi.

gerund *n. (gram.)* gerundio.

gestate *v.t.* haurra sabelbarnean eraman. *v.t.* ideia bat bururatu.

gestation *n. (med.)* ernaldi, haurraldi.

gesticulate *v.i./v.t.* keinukatu, esku eraginl.

gesticulation *n.* keinuketa, zeinuketa.

gesticulator *n.* keinukari, zinulari.

gesture *v.i./v.t.* keinukatu, esku eragin.

gesture *n.* keinukada, keinu, zeinu, zinu.

get *v.t.* hartu, lortu, eskuratu, erdietsi. *v.t.* ekarri; bila ibili. *v.t.* -arazi, -erazi. *v.t.* entzun, ulertu. *v.t.* harrapatu. *v.t.* konbentzitu, sinestarazi. *v.t.* prestatu, antolatu. *v.t.* hunkitu; nekarazi; haserrarazi. *v.t.* ukitu, jo. *v.t.* mendekatu. *v.t.* gaisotu. **To get the measles.** Elgorriaz gaisotu. *v.t.* sortu. *v.i.* heldu. *v.i.* bihurtu, bilakatu. *v.i. (batzutan* (**out-ekin**) joan. *v.i.* (**out of**) jaitsi (kotxetik); iradoki. *v.i.* (**in, into**) barrendu, sartu. *v.i.* (**on**) gainean eseri; zahartu. *v.i./v.t.* (**up**)

jaiki, altxatu. *v.i.* (**along with**) konpondu, moldatu, aditu (harreman pertsonaletan), ondo hartu.

get *n.* ume, kume. *n.* sorketa, umeketa.

get away *v.i.* ihes egin, alde egin, hanka egin, ospa egin. *v.i.* (**from**) -gandik aldendu, urrundu, urrutiratu.

getaway *n.* ihesketa, iheste.

get drunk *v.i.* mozkortu, horditu.

get sick *v.i.* gaitz hartu, gaizkitu, eritu, gaisotu.

get together *v.i./v.t.* batu, batzarreratu; bildu.

get used to *v.t.* ohituratu, ohitu, zebatu.

get well *v.i.* osatu, sendatu.

geyser *n.* geiser.

ghastly *adj.* izugarri, ikaragarri.

gherkin *n. (bot.)* kuiluzetxo.

ghetto *n.* ghetto.

ghost *n.* mamu, mamutzar, iratxo.

giant *n.* erraldoi.

giantess *n.* erraldoi (emakume).

gibberish *n.* erderamordoilo; kalamatrika.

gibbet *n.* urka, urkamendi.

gibe *v.t./v.i.* iseka egin.

gibe *n.* eztenkada, iseka.

giblets *n.* barruki.

giddiness *n.* burubira.

giddy *adj.* zorabiatu.

giddy up *int.* arre!

gift *n.* erregali, erregalu, emaitza, opari. *n.* dohain; doha-.

gifted *adj.* talentadun.

gigantic *adj.* handitzar.

giggle *v.i.* maltzurki farre egin.

giggle *n.* haurren farre txiki(a).

gild *v.t.* urreztu, urreztatu.

gilder *n.* urreztatzaile.

gilding *n.* urreztadura.

gill *n.* zakatz.

gilthead *n. (zool.)* urraburu.

gimlet *n.* ginbelet, zaztagin.

gimmick *n.* jendearen arreta erakartzeko ideia berritzailea.

gin *n.* ginebra. *n.* kartajoko mota.

ginger *n. (bot.)* zingiber, epuru. *adj.* horigorri.

gingivitus *n. (med.)* oimin.

giraffe *n. (zool.)* jirafa.

gird *v.t.* gerrikotu.

girder *n.* haga.

girdle *n.* faxa. *n.* gerriko, zingulu.

girl *n.* neska, neskatxa, neskatila.

girlish *adj.* haurrantzeko, haurraire, neskantzeko.

girth *v.t.* petraldu; gerrikotu.

girth *n.* zingila.

gist *n.* mami.

give *v.t.* eman. *v.t.* oihukatu, esan. *v.t.* eskaini, opatu. *v.t.* hornitu. *v.t.* egin. *v.t./v.i.* (*v.i., batzutan* **up**-*ekin*) laga. *v.t.* eragin; -arazi, -erazi. *v.t.* aurkeztu, aurrejarri. *v.i.* aurrean egon. *v.i.* akordiotu. *v.i.* erori; puskatu. *v.i.* zabaldu (berriak). *v.i.*

samurtu. *v.i.* **(away)** oparitu, opari
egin; azaldu. *v.i.* **(ground)** atzera
egin; leku egin. *v.i.* **(in)** amor eman,
etsi. *v.i.* **(off)** usain eta lurrunak jario.
v.t. **(oneself up)** eskuetan jarri. *v.i.*
(up) borrokan amore eman. *v.i.* **(way)**
atzera egin. *v.i.* **(out)** amaitu, ahitu.
To give a hand to. Lagundu. **To
give a lift to.** Norbait kotxez eraman.
To give notice. Lanari uko egin;
norbait lanetik kanpora bota. **To give
up the ghost.** Hil. **To give up for
lost.** Galdutzat eman.
give *n.* elastikotasun.
give birth *v.i.* **(batzutan to-ekin)** haur
egin, haur ukan, ume(a) egin, erditu.
given *p. part. of give.*
giver *n.* emaile.
giving *adj.* emaile. *n.* emanaldi, emate.
gizzard *n.* (anat.) arandoi.
glacial *adj.* izozmendiko, izozpiloko,
izozkarri, hormagarri.
glacially *adv.* izozki.
glaciation *n.* izozte.
glacier *n.* izozpilo.
glad *adj.* pozik, atsegin.
gladden *v.t.* poztu, alaitu.
glade *n.* agerrune.
gladiator *n.* gladiadore, ezpatari.
gladiolus *n.* (bot.) urezpata.
gladly *adv.* atseginez, gustora, pozez,
pozgarriro, pozik, pozkarioz.
gladness *n.* poztasun, alaitasun.
glamorous *adj.* apain, dotore;
liluragarri, xarmagarri.
glamour *n.* xarma, lilurapen.
glance *v.i.* begiz joan, begiztatu. *v.i.* **(off)**
errebotatu, punpatu. *v.i.* **(over)** arinki
irakurri.
glance *n.* begiraldi, ikusaldi, so,
begirada, begirakada.
gland *n.* (anat.) glandula, guruin.
glanders *n.* murmu, okaila.
glandular *adj.* glandulatsu,
glandulazko.
glare *v.i.* dirdiratu, distiratu. *v.t.*
haserrez begiratu.
glare *n.* arraitasun, erlantz. *n.* begirada
haserrekor(ra).
glass *n.* beira. *n.* edalontzi, baso. *n.*
basokada. *n.* ispilu.
glasses *n.* betaurreko(ak).
glassful *n.* basokada, kopakada.
glassware *n.* beireria.
glassy *adj.* beirazko.
glaucoma *n.* glaukoma.
glaze *v.t.* beiraztatu. *v.t.* haragi gainean
saltsa ipini.
gleam *v.i.* dirdiratu, distiratu.
gleam *n.* dirdirapen, disdisera, printz.
gleaming *adj.* dirdiratsu, dirdirazko.
glean *v.t./v.i.* galburutu, burutu.
gleanings *n.* buruxka, galburuxka.
glee *n.* poztasun, alaitasun.
gleeful *adj.* alai, pozdun, pozbera.
glen *n.* haran luze eta estua.
glib *adj.* hiztun, hizjario, berritsu,

kalakari.
glide *v.i./v.t.* etengabeki eta esfortzurik
gabe mugitu, ibili edo hegaz egin.
glider *n.* hegabiko.
glimmer *v.i.* ñirñir egin.
glimmer *n.* dir-dir, ñirñirkada.
glimpse *v.t.* begiztatu, erdikusi.
glimpse *n.* begikolpe, begiraldi,
begikada, so.
glisten *v.i.* dirdiratu.
glitter *v.i.* dirdiratu.
glitter *n.* urreantz, dirdira.
gloat *v.i.* maltzurkeriaz poztu, gaiztoki
alaitu.
global *adj.* munduko; oso, osorik.
globe *n.* mundu.
globular *adj.* globulantzeko, globular.
globule *n.* (anat.) globulu.
gloom *n.* ilunpe.
gloomily *adv.* goibelki.
gloomy *adj.* goibeltsu, ilunbeltz,
ilunbetsu.
glorifiable *adj.* ospagarri, aintzagarri,
aintzalgarri.
glorification *n.* handiespen, aintzapen.
glorify *v.t.* aintzaldu, aintza eman,
laudorioztatu, goraipatu, handietsi.
glorifying *adj.* aupatzaile; aintzaka.
glorious *adj.* aintzagarri, aintzalgarri,
goragarri, goresgarri, aupagarri,
aintzadun.
gloriously *adv.* goragarriki,
goragarriro, aintzaz.
glory *n.* aintza, ospe, goraldi.
gloss *n.* distira. *n.* ohar, oharpen.
glossary *n.* izendegi.
glossiness *n.* limurtasun.
glossitis *n.* (med.) mingaineri.
glossy *adj.* distiratsu.
glottis *n.* (anat.) zintzurkontrako.
glove *n.* eskubabes, eskuestalki,
eskularru.
glow *v.i.* dirdiratu, distiratu, dizdiz egin.
glow *n.* dirdai, dirdirapen, distirapen.
glower *v.i.* kopetilundu.
glowing *adj.* dirdaitsu, dirdiratsu,
distiratsu.
glowingly *adv.* gorl-gorl, goriki.
glowworm *n.* (zool.) ipurtargi.
glucose *n.* glukosa.
glue *v.t.* likatu, kolatu.
glue *n.* kola.
glum *adj.* triste, itzal, ilun, betilun,
goibel, kopetilun.
glut *n.* ase, hestebete.
glutton *n.* tripandi, tripontzi, asezin.
gluttonous *adj.* irestzaile, sabelandiko,
sabelkoi, jatun, tripandi, tripontzi,
ezinase.
gluttonously *adv.* mauka-mauka,
asezinez, zanpa-zanpa.
gluttony *n.* tripontzikeria, asekeria,
jatunkeria, sabelkeria, sabelkoikeria.
glycerin *n.* glizerina.
gnarled *adj.* korapilotsu, adabegitsu,
begitsu.
gnash *v.t./v.i.* kirrika egin,

horzkarraskatu.
gnat *n.* eltxo.
gnaw *v.t./v.i. (v.i., on)* karraskatu, marraskatu, hortzikatu.
gnawer *n.* karraskari, hortzikari, marraskari.
gnome *n.* lamia.
go *v.i.* joan. *v.i.* funtzionatu, ibili. *v.i.* bukatu, amaitu. *v.i.* bere lekua izan, egokitu. *v.i.* egoki izan. *v.i. (in)* sartu, barruratu. *v.i. (in, around)* kabitu. *v.i.* gastatu. *v.i.* esan, hots egin. *v.i.* erori, hondatu, lur jo, gainbeheratu. *v.i. (out)* irten, atera; itzali; mutil edo neska lagunarekin irten. *v.i. (together)* egokitu. *v.i. (away)* urrutiratu, urruneratu. *v.i. (up)* igan, goratu. *v.i. (down)* beheratu. **To go bald.** Buru soildu. **To go blind.** Itsutu. **To go broke.** Behea jo. Porrot egin. **To go to sleep.** Lo hartu. Lotara joan. **To go wrong.** Gaiztatu.
goad *v.t.* akuilatu, akuilukatu.
goad *n.* eztenmakila, akuilu. *n.* akulukada.
goal *n.* helburu, jomuga, xede, helmuga. *n.* gol (futbol).
goalie *n.* atezain (kirol), ateko.
goalkeeper *n.* atezain, ateko (kirol).
goat *n.* ahuntz.
goatee *n.* ahunzbizar.
goatherd *n.* ahuntzain.
gobble *v.t.* irentsi, arin jan. *v.i.* indioilarraren zarata egin.
go-between *n.* bitartekari, bitarteko.
goblet *n.* kopa, gopor. **The goblet dance.** Godalet dantza.
gobletful *n.* kopakada.
goblin *n.* iratxo.
go-cart *n.* goitibehera, kotxetxo.
God *n.* Jainko. *n.* kreatzaile, oroegile.
godchild *n.* besoetako, ponteko.
goddamn *adj.* madarikatu(a).
goddaughter *n.* alabaponteko, alabatxi.
goddess *n.* jainkosa.
godfather *n.* aitabesoetako, aitabitxi.
godhead *n.* jainkotasun.
godless *adj.* jainkogabe.
godliness *n.* jainkotasun.
godly *adj.* jainkozale; otoizbera.
godmother *n.* amabesoetako, amabitxi.
godson *n.* semebitxi, semeponteko.
goes *pres. of go.*
goggle *v.i./v.t.* liluraz begiratu, harriduraz so egin.
goggle-eyed *adj.* begiharro.
goggles *n.* urbetaurrekoak.
goiter *n. (med.)* golo, bozio.
gold *n.* urre, urregorri; urra-. *adj.* horibizi, urreantzeko.
golden *adj.* urreaire, urregorrizko, urrezko.
gold fever *n.* urrezalekeria.
gold filling *n.* urreztaldi.
goldfinch *n. (zool.)* gardantxilo,

gardantxori.
goldfish *n. (zool.)* urre-arrain.
gold plate *v.t.* urreztatu.
gold plate *n.* urrebits, urrexafla.
goldsmith *n.* urregile.
goldsmithing *n.* urregintza.
golf *v.i.* golfean jokatu.
golf *n.* golf.
golly *int.* arranopola!
gondola *n.* gondola.
gondolier *n.* gondolari.
gone *p. part. of go.*
gong *n.* gong.
gonorrhea *n.* gonorrea, hazijario.
good *n.* on; on-. *adj.* on, zintzo, zuzen, prestu. **Good morning.** Egun on. **For good.** Betiko. *adj.* trebe. *adj.* atsegintsu, atsegingarri, atsegin.
good-bye *int.* agur, adio. *n.* azkenagur, diosale.
good-for-nothing *adj.* zuri.
good-hearted *adj.* bihotzoneko.
good-humored *adj.* iaio.
good-looking *adj.* galant, itxurederreko.
good-natured *adj.* onkote.
goodness *n.* onberatasun, zintzotasun, onzaletasun.
good night gabon.
goods *n.* ondasunak, merkagai, merkantzia.
good will *n.* borondate on(a); onginahi.
goody *n.* gozoki. *int.* arranopola!
goofy *adj.* inozo, tentel, txoriburu.
goose *n. (zool.)* antzar. *n.* antzarki.
goosebump *n.* ospel, azkordin.
gore *v.t.* adarkatu, adarka egin, adarra sartu, adartu.
gore *n.* odolbatu. *n.* odolkeria, odolisurketa (filmetan).
gorge *v.t./v.i.* larjan.
gorge *n.* leze, amildegi, malkortegi, osin, troka. *n.* eztarri.
gorged *adj.* ase-ase, asebetean.
gorgeous *adj.* bikain.
gorilla *n. (zool.)* gorila.
gorse *n. (bot.)* ote; ota-.
gory *adj.* odoleztatu, odolez estali(a).
gosh *int.* kontxo, orratio, arraio.
goshawk *n. (zool.)* miru, aztore.
gosling *n.* antzarkume.
gospel *n.* Berrion, Ebanjelio. **To spread the gospel.** Berriona zabaldu.
gossip *v.i.* erausi, kalakatu. *v.i.* gaitzesan.
gossip *n.* berriketa, esamesa, hizki-mizki, ele-mele.
gossiper *n.* autulari.
gossipy *adj.* berritsu, mihiluze, marmarti, mihigaizto.
got *pret. of get.*
Goth *n.* godo.
Gothic *adj.* gotiko.
gotten *p. part. of get.*
gouge *v.t.* zurzizelez egurra landu.
gouge *n.* zurzizel.

gourd n. kuia mota bat.
gourmand n. ahozuri.
gourmet n. ahozuri. adj. ahoneko.
gout n. (med.) hezueri.
govern v.t./v.i. gobernatu, kontrolatu, aministratu.
governable adj. gobernagarri.
governess n. etxeirakasle, haurzain, umezain.
government n. (pol.) gobernu, jaurlaritza. **The Basque Government.** Eusko Jaurlaritza.
governmental adj. gobernuko, jaurlaritzako.
governor n. gobernadore, gobernari. **Lieutenant governor.** Gobernariorde.
governorship n. gobernaritza.
gown n. jantziluze.
grab v.t. harrapatu, atxiki, heldu, atzeman, oratu.
grabber n. heltzaile, atzemaile.
grace n. airosketa. n. mesede, fabore, dohain. n. erruki. n. (theol.) esker, goieskar, grazia.
graceful adj. lirain, txairo.
gracefully adv. lirainki, txairoki.
gracefulness n. liraintasun, txairotasun.
gracious adj. maitagarri, adikor, abegikor. adj. grazios, grazidun. int. errekontxo.
graciously adv. grazioski.
grad n. graduatu, lizentziatu.
gradate v.i./v.t. mailatu.
gradated adj. gradudun.
gradation n. mailaketa.
grade v.t. mailakatu. v.t. galgatu. v.t. ikasleei notak eman.
grade n. klase, gizartemaila. n. malda. n. maila, gradu. n. nota.
gradient n. malda. n. desberdindura.
gradual adj. mailazko.
gradually adv. geldi-geldi, geldiro, mailaka, pizkanaka, poliki, gutika.
gradualness n. gelditasun.
graduate v.i./v.t. graduatu, irakasletu, llzentzlatu.
graduate n. ikasle graduatu(a). adj. graduatu(a), lizentziatu(a).
graduated adj. mailazko. adj. graduatu(a).
graduation n. graduapen, lizentziapen, graduazio.
graffiti n. (pl.) graffiti.
graft v.t./v.i. eztitu, txertatu, mendu.
graft n. txerto, mendu. n. (pol.) eroskeria, koipekeria.
graftable adj. txertagarri.
grafter n. txertatzaile.
graham cracker n. gari irinaz egindako gaileta.
grail n. azken afarian Kristok erabili zuen edalontzia.
grain n. ale, bihi. n. labore, zitu.
gram n. gramo.
grammar n. gramatika.

grammarian n. gramatikari.
grammar school n. oinarrizko heziketa orokor(ra).
grammatical adj. gramatikako.
grammatically adv. gramatikalki.
gramophone n. gramofono.
granary n. bihitegi, aletegi.
grand adj. handi. adj. garrantzitsu. adj. eder. adj. bikain.
granchild n. iloba.
granddaughter n. iloba (neska).
grandeur n. handigo.
grandfather n. aitona.
grandiloquence n. goimintzo, hitzandidura.
grandiloquent adj. hitzandiko.
grandiose adj. handiairezko.
grandiosely adv. handiki, handikiro.
grandly adv. handikiro, handiro.
grandma n. amona.
grandmother n. amona.
grandpa n. aitona.
grandparents n. (pl.) aiton-amonak.
grandson n. iloba (mutil).
grandstand n. palku, tribuna.
grange n. baserri, borda.
granger n. baserritar, nekazari.
granite n. (min.) granito. adj. granitozko.
granny n. amona.
grant v.t. eman.
grant n. beka, dirulaguntza.
grantable adj. baiezgarri.
granular adj. bikordun.
granulate v.t./v.i. birrindu, bikortu.
granulated adj. bikordun.
granulation n. bikorketa.
granule n. bikor.
granulous adj. bikordun, bikortsu.
grape n. (bot.) mahats; mahatsale.
grapefruit n. (bot.) arabi-sagar, pomelo.
grapevine n. mahatsondo, mahatsadar.
graph n. taula.
graphic n. marrazki, grafiko. adj. irudizko.
graphically adv. marrazkiz, grafikoki.
graphite n. (min.) grafito.
graphologist n. idazikerle, grafologo.
graphology n. grafologia.
grapple v.i. eskuz-esku burrukatu.
grapple n. gatazka, eskuz-esku egindako burruka.
grasp v.t./v.i. harrapatu, itsatsi, eutsi, heldu, oratu.
grasp n. atxekigailu, euskarri, helduleku. n. irispide. n. ulermen.
grass n. belar. n. belartza. n. marihuana, droga.
grasshopper n. (zool.) matxinsalto, txirrita.
grassland n. belartza.
grassy adj. belarrezko, belartsu.
grate v.t. burdinsaretu. v.i./v.t. karraka egin, karrakatu. v.i. (on, upon) haserretu, haserrerazi.
grate n. burdinsare, burdinesi.

grateful *adj.* eskerroneko, eskertsu.
gratefully *adv.* eskerronez.
gratefulness *n.* esker, eskerron.
grater *n.* karrakagailu, karraskailu.
gratification *n.* atsegin, plazer. *n.* sariordain, sarigarri.
gratify *v.t.* atsegindu, atseginarazi.
gratifying *adj.* atsegin, laket.
gratis *adv.* dohan.
gratitude *n.* eskerron, esker.
gratuitous *adj.* dohako. *adj.* hutsezko.
gratuitously *adv.* dohain.
gratuity *n.* eskupeko.
grave *n.* hilobi, hobi, ehorzleku. *adj.* hilkor, astun, axolazko.
gravedigger *n.* ehorzle, hobiratzaile, lurremaile, lurrematzaile.
gravel *v.t.* legartu, legarztatu.
gravel *n.* harrikoxkor, hartxirri, legar.
gravelly *adj.* legardun.
gravely *adv.* hilgarriro; bene-benetan.
grave marker *n.* hilarri.
gravestone *n.* hilarri, hobiharri.
graveyard *n.* hilerri, hobitegi, hiltoki.
gravitate *v.i.* grabitatu. *v.i.* **(to, toward)** zuzendu.
gravitation *n.* *(phys.)* grabitazio, grabitapen.
gravity *n.* *(phys.)* erakartasun, grabitate, erakar-indar. *n.* benetasun; eratasun, zentzutasun.
gravy *n.* zuku, saltsa.
gravy boat *n.* saltsontzi.
gray *adj.* arre, nabar.
gray matter *n.* *(biol.)* garuneko kirio-ehun. *n.* *(colloq.)* adimen.
grayness *n.* ileurdinketa, ilezuritasun. *n.* arretasun.
graze *v.i./v.t.* larreratu, alatu, bazkatu.
grease *v.t.* gantzutu, koipetu, koipeztatu, koipeztu, lardatu.
grease *n.* gantzu, gurin, koipe.
greaser *n.* koipetzaile, urindatzaile, koipemale, koipeztatzaile.
greasiness *n.* gantzutasun, koipetasun.
greasy *adj.* gantzutsu, kolpejarlo, koipetsu, gurintsu, gizendun. **Greasy meat.** Haragi koipetsu.
greasy spoon *n.* *(colloq.)* jantoki zikin eta merkea.
great *n.* txapeldun. *adj.* handi, haundi. *adj.* asko, franko, makina bat. *adj.* luze. *adj.* bikain, miragarri, egundoko, sekulako. *adv.* guztiz ondo, bikainki.
Great Basin *(geog.)* Estatu Batuetako mendebaldeko Arro Zabala.
Great Britain *n.(geog.)* Britania.
great-grandchild *n.* biloba.
great-grandfather *n.* berraitona.
great-grandmother *n.* berramona.
great-great-grandchild *n.* hereniloba.
great-great-grandfather *n.* herenaitona.
great-great-grandmother *n.* herenamona.

Great Lakes *(geog.)* Estatu Batuetako Laku Handiak.
greatly *adv.* handiro, handiki.
greatness *n.* handitasun, handiera, handigo.
Great Plains *(geog.)* Rocky Mendien ekialdean kokaturik dauden Zelai Zabalak.
Great Salt Lake *(geog.)* Laku Gazi Handi(a).
greed *n.* diruegarri, dirugose, dirunahi, nahikeria, gutizia.
greedily *adv.* asezinez, asezinik, asegabeki.
greediness *n.* asezintasun, dirugose, diruzalekeria.
greedy *adj.* dirukoi, diruzale, asezin, asegaitz, betezin, askonahiko; zeken, zikoitz.
green *adj.* orlegi, berde, musker. *adj.* heze, helgabe.
greenback *n.* dolar paper(a).
greenery *n.* landaretegi.
greenhorn *n.* *(colloq.)* ikasberri.
greenhouse *n.* mindegi.
greenness *n.* hezetasun, berdetasun.
greet *v.t.* agurtu, agur egin.
greeter *n.* agurgile, agurregile.
greeting *n.* agur, agurketa; agurritzak.
greetings *n.* goraintzi(ak), eskumuin(ak).
gregarious *adj.* taldekoi, elkarkoi, harremankor, jendekoi.
gregariously *adv.* taldean.
gregariousness *n.* jendekoitasun.
gremlin *n.* iratxo maltzur(ra).
grenade *n.* granada.
grenadier *n.* granadari.
grew *p. part.* of *grow.*
grey *adj.* arre, nabar, gris.
greyhound *n.* *(zool.)* galgo.
grid *n.* burdinsaretxo.
griddle *n.* burdinuntzi.
grief *n.* pena, bihotzestura, barrenatsekabe. *n.* atsekabe, mindura.
grievance *n.* kexa, arrengura.
grieve *v.i./v.t.* *(v.i.,* **over, for)** negarreztatu, aiene egin, egon, aika ari. *v.t.* penatu, oinazeztatu.
grievous *adj.* zamagarri.
grill *v.t.* parrilan erre, erreburdinean erre. *v.t.* luzaroan eta sakonki galdetu.
grill *n.* parrila, erreburdina.
grim *adj.* kopetilun.
grimace *v.i.* imintzioak egin, muzinkeinuak egin.
grimace *n.* muzinkeinu, muzin, keinu.
grime *n.* mantar, tortika.
griminess *n.* zikintasun.
grimy *adj.* ugertsu, tortikatsu.
grin *v.i.* hortzak erakutsiz irrifarre isila egin.
grin *n.* keinukada, hortzak erakutsiz egiten den irrifarre isila.

grind v.t./v.i. haustu, hauts egin, irindu, ehotu, eho, zehetu, birrindu. v.t. karraskots egin, horzkarraskatu.
grindable adj. ehogarri, birringarri, xehegarri.
grinder n. birringailu, ehogailu, errota.
grindstone n. errotarri, ehotarri.
grip v.t. trukesatu.
grip n. helduleku, atxekigailu, euskarri.
gripe v.i./v.t. kexatu, arrenkuratu.
gripe n. kexadura.
grisly adj. izugarri, ikaragarri, ilezutigarri.
grist n. alepilo, alemordo.
gristle n. kartilago, kurruska.
grit n. hondar aleak.
grits n. garimami.
grizzly bear n. (zool.) grizzly hartza.
groan v.i. aiene egin, intzirikatu, kurrinkatu, aienekatu.
groan n. intziri, oihumin.
grocer n. hornigile, hornitzaile.
groceries n. (pl.) jan-edariak, jangaiak.
grocery store n. hornitegi, janaritegi, hornidenda, janaridenda.
groggily adv. zorabioz.
groggily adv. zorabioz.
grogginess n. zorabiadura, zozoaldi.
groggy adj. ia konorterik gabe.
groin n. (anat.) izterrondo, iztai.
grommet n. txirrindolatxo.
groom v.t. zaldiak zaindu, zaldiak apaindu.
groom n. ezkonlagun, ezkontide (gizon). n. zaldimutil, zaldizain, zamaltzain.
groove v.t. hozkatu, koskatu.
groove n. hozka, hozkadura, koskadura.
grope v.i. haztatu, eskuztatu.
gross n. guztia. n. hamabi dozena. adj. erabateko, oso. adj. lizun, zakar. adj. lodi; zarratu.
grossly adv. zatarki, itsuski.
grossness n. zarpailkeria, zatarkeria, zarpailtasun.
grotesque adj. irrigarri. adj. itsusi.
grotesquely adv. itsuski. adv. farregarreki, farregarriro.
grotesqueness n. itsustasun arraro(a). n. barregarrikeria, farregarrikeria.
grotto n. mendizulo, haizpe, haitzulo.
grouch n. umoretxarreko pertsona.
grouchy adj. purrustari, marmarati, erremuskalari.
ground v.t./v.i. funtsatu, oinarritu. v.t. norbaiti hegaz egitea eragotzi.
ground n. lur, sola; zoru, behe. n. (pl.) alor. n. zio, errazoi. n. hondar. n. (elec.) lurretiko entxufe(a). adj. haustu, birrintsu. p. part. of grind. **From the ground up.** Hasieratik. Erabat. **Well grounded.** Ondo oinarritua.
ground floor n. behetxe.
groundless n. funtsgabe(ko).
groundlessly adv. funtsgabeki.

groundlessness n. funtsgabekeria, funtsgabetasun.
grounds n. (pl.) hondarrak, hondakin. n. (pl.) arrazoi, arrazoinketa, funts, argudio, oinarritze. n. (pl.) haziendako lurrak.
groundskeeper n. landazain, haziendazain.
groundwork n. zimendu.
group v.t./v.i. taldetu, taldekatu, kidekatu, multzokatu, saildu.
group n. talde, multzo, gizatalde, andana; sail; -talde.
grouper n. (zool.) meru.
grouping n. taldekapen, taldebilketa, kidekapen, sailketa.
grouse n. (zool.) basoilar.
grove n. arboladi, zuhaizti.
grovel v.i. doilortu, zitaldu.
grow v.i./v.t. handitu, hazi, koskortu. v.i. Ugaldu, gehitu, areagotu. v.i. (up) nagusitu, gizondu, koskortu, hazi.
grower n. hazle.
growl v.i./v.t. erremuskatu, erremuska egin.
growl n. purrust, erremuskada, furrustada.
grown adj. heldu, hazi. p. part. of grow.
grown-up n. pertsona heldu(a).
growth n. gehipen, gorakada, handikuntza, hazaldi, hazkuntza. n. landaretza. n. (med.) handidura, handitu.
grub n. (zool.) gurgurio, kotxorro, zeden. n. (colloq.) janari.
grubworm n. (zool.) babazorri, babakoko.
grudge n. ezinikusi.
grudgingly adv. ezinikusiaz.
gruel n. oloaz egindako janari urtsua.
grueling adv. lehergarri.
gruesome adj. ikaragarri, izugarri.
gruff adj. zakarrote, trauskil.
gruffness n. zakartasun, trauskiltasun.
grumble v.i./v.t. erremuskatu, marmar egin, purrustatu.
grumble n. marmar, erremuskada.
grumbler n. purrustari, murruzkari.
grumbling n. purrustada, erremuskada.
grumpy adj. purrustari.
grunt v.i./v.t. kurrinkatu, marraska egin.
grunt n. kurrinkada, marraska.
guano n. txorigorotz.
guarantee v.t. bermatu, fidarazi.
guarantee n. berme, fidantza, finkapen, bermatasun.
guaranteed adj. bermatu, bermendun.
guarantor n. bahiemale, bermatzaile.
guard v.t./v.i. (v.i., gehienetan against-ekin) zaindu, gorde, defenditu, itzalpetu.
guard n. zaintzaile, gordetzaile, zelatari, zaintzaile. **Tower guard.** Dorrezain. **The Civil Guard.** Goardia

Zibila. **Prison guard.** Gartzelari.
guard dog n. atezakur.
guardhouse n. espetxeko zaindariaren etxetxo(a).
guardian n. zaindari, zaintzaile, begirale, gordelari.
guardianship n. zaindaritza; aitordetza, gurasordetasun.
guerrilla fighter n. basagudari, gerrilari.
guess v.t./v.i. igarri, tankeratu, tankera eman, antzeman. v.t./v.i. usnatu, susmatu, asmatu.
guess n. antzemate, igarpen, usmo, aurresan, iragarpen.
guessable adj. usnagarri, asmagarri, somagarri.
guesser n. asmalari, asmatzaile, asmari.
guessing game n. ikusi-makusi.
guesstimate v.t./v.i. (colloq.) aitzinkontu.
guesswork n. igartzapen, igarpen.
guest n. gonbidatu, gomit; -liar. **Wedding guest.** Ezteiliar. Ezteilagun. **Guest of honor.** Ohorezko gonbidatu(a).
guff n. (colloq.) mutirikeria.
guffaw v.i. barrealgarak egin.
guffaw n. barrealgara, algara.
guidance n. gidaritza, gidaritzape, gidaketa.
guide v.t. gidatu, zuzendu, bidegidatu, bideratu.
guide n. gidari, bidegidari, biderakusle; zuzentzaile. **Guide for the blind.** Itsumutil. Itsuaurreko. n. gidaliburu.
guidebook n. oharliburu, gidaliburu.
guided missile n. misil telegidatu(a).
guideline n. gidabide, burubide.
guild n. elkarte, elkargo.
guile n. iruzur, engainu, maltzurkeria.
guileful adj. azpizale.
guileless adj. laino, tolesgabe.
guillotine n. gilotina.
guilt n. erru.
guiltily adv. erruz.
guiltiness n. hobendura.
guiltless adj. gaizkabe, faltagabe, errugabe.
guiltlessness n. gaizkabetasun, errugabetasun.
guilty n. errudun, hobendun, faltadun.
guinea pig n. (zool.) akuri.
Guipuzcoa n. (geog.) Gipuzkoa.
Guipuzcoan n. gipuzkera. adj./n. gipuzkoar.
guise n. itxura, itxurapen.
guitar n. gitarra.
guitarist n. gitarrari, kitarjole.
guitarmaker n. gitargile.
gulch n. amildegi, leize.
gulf n. itsasgolko, golko. **The Gulf of Mexico.** Mexikoko Golkoa.
gull v.t. iruzur egin, atzipetu, ziria sartu, zipotza sartu.
gull n. (zool.) kalatxori. n. inozo, tentel.

gullet n. (anat.) samazulo, zintzur.
gullibility n. sinesterrazkeria, sinesberatasun.
gullible adj. sinesterrazi, sinesbera, inozo.
gully n. uholdebide, sakan.
gulp v.i./v.t. hurrupatu, hurrupa egin, zurrupatu.
gulp n. hurrupada, tragu, zurrutada.dzangada.
gulpable adj. hurrupagarri.
gulper n. hurrupatzaile, hurrupari, zurrutari.
gum n. goma. n. muki. n. haginoi. n. txikle.
gumboil n. flemoi.
gummy adj. gomatsu.
gums n. (anat.) haginoi.
gun v.i. (for) norbaiten atzetik hiltzeko asmoz ibili. v.i. (down) tirokatu, tiroz hil. v.t. autoa erabat azeleratu.
gun n. arma, eskopeta, pistola, kainoi.
gunboat n. itsasontzi kainolari(a).
gunfighter n. pistolari.
gunman n. pistolari.
gunner n. kainoilari.
gunport n. kainoileiho, kainoizulo.
gunpowder n. polbora, sutauts.
gunsmith n. armagile, armagin, eskopetagile, eskopetari.
gurgle v.i. gurgurkatu.
gush v.i./v.t. jario, borborkatu, zurrutatu.
gusher n. petrolio-zurrusta, petrolio-zirrizta.
gust n. haizebolada, haizaldi, haizeburunda.
gusto n. gozaldi, atseginaldi.
gusty adj. haizakor.
guts n. (pl.) erraiak, haltsarrak; heste. n. ausartasun, adore, ausardia.
gutter n. erreten.
guttural adj. eztarriko.
gutturally adv. eztarriz.
guy n. mutil.
gym n. indarketaleku.
gymnasium n. indarketaleku.
gymnastics n. gimnasia.
gynecologist n. ginekologo.
gynecology n. ginekologia.
gypsum n. igeltsu, kisu, igeltsuharri.
gypsy n. buhame, ijito, motzaile. **Band of gypsies.** Ijiteria. Ijitotalde. **Gypsy language.** Ijitoera. Ijitohizkera.
gyrate v.i. jirabiratu, jiratu, birakatu.
gyration n. itzulbira, jirabira, biraketa.

H

h n. Ingeles alfabetako letra.
ha int. ene!
habit n. ohi, ohitura, ohitasun, ekandu, usario. n. lekaime-jantzi, fraile-jantzi. n. drogazaletasun, drogazalekeria.
habitable adj. bizigarri.
habitableness n. bizigarritasun.
habitat n. bizileku, habitat.
habitation n. egoitza, etxe,

etxebizitza.
habitual adj. ohizko, ohitzko, ohiturazko, sarrizko, azturazko.
habitually adv. ohituraz.
habitualness n. maiztasun, maiztapen, usutasun.
hack v.t./v.i. (v.i, at-ekin) aihozkatu. v.i. estul egin.
hack n. (colloq.) taxi. n. azkar eta erdipurdi idazten duen idazlea.
had pret./p. part. of have.
hadn't "had + not"-aren laburpena.
hag n. atsosorgin.
haggard adj. betzulodun, zurbil, margul.
haggle v.i. errekardaritu.
ha-ha int. ajaja.
hail v.t./v.i. agurtu. v.t. goratu, laudatu, aintzaldu. v.i. txingor egin, harria egin.
hail n. txingor, harri, babazuza. n. agur. **Hail Mary.** Agur Maria.
hailstorm n. txingor, txingorrada, babazuza, harri.
hair n. ile, ilaje, bilo. **Long tangled hair.** Txima. **Head of hair.** Ileadats.
hairbrained adj. memelo, ergel, inozo, tentel.
hair clasp n. ilelokarri.
haircut n. ilemozte.
hairdo n. ileapainketa, orrazkera, zoronga.
hairdresser n. ilemozkin, ilemozle, ileapaintzaile.
hairless adj. ilesoil.
hairpin n. burukorratz.
hairy adj. iletsu, iledun, bilotsu, zurdatsu.
hake n. (zool.) legatz.
hale adj. sano, sendokote.
half n. erdikin, erdi, erdika; erdi-. **In half.** Erdibana. **Half an hour.** Ordu erdi. adj. erdi. adv. erdizka.
half-day off n. jaierdi, jaiarin.
halfway adv. bidenabar, biderdi, biderdiko.
halfway house n. landerretxe.
hall n. atalondo, iragabide.
hallow v.t. sainduarazi.
hallowed adj. santu.
Halloween n. domusantu egunaren bezpera (urriaren azken eguna), bereziki haurrei zuzendutako jai(a).
hallucinate v.i. itsutu, liluratu.
hallucination n. irudikeria, itsukeria.
hallway n. iragabide.
halo n. argikoroa.
halt v.i./v.t. geldi, gelditu, geratu. v.i. durduzatu, zalantzatu.
halt n. geldiune, geldialdi; bukaera, amaiera. int. geldi!
halve v.t. erdibitu, erdibi egin.
ham n. (anat.) belaunpe, belaunzulo. n. pernil, xingar, urdaiazpiko.
hamburger n. hanburgesa.
hamlet n. herritxo, herrixka.
hammer v.t./v.i. mailukatu, mailuka

egin.
hammer n. mailu, pikotx.
hammerhead n. (zool.) mailuarrain.
hammock n. hamaka, ohasare.
hand v.t. eskuz eman.
hand n. esku; bosteko; esku-. **At hand.** Esku-eskuan. **By hand.** Eskuz. **To lend a hand.** Esku luzatu. Esku eman. **To shake hands.** Bostekoa eman. **To have a hand in.** Eskuak sartu. **Right hand.** Eskuin. **Left hand.** Ezker. **On one hand ... on the other hand.** Batetik.. bestetik. n. erlojorratz.
handbag n. boltsa.
handball n. pilota, eskupilota.
handbarrow n. anda, angaila.
handbook n. eskuliburu.
handcart n. eskugurdi, eskuorga, orgato.
handcuff v.t. girgiluztu.
handcuffs n. (pl.) eskuburdinak, girgilu.
handful n. eskubete, eskukada, ahurkada.
hand grenade n. eskubonba.
handicap n. handikap.
handicraft n. eskulan.
handkerchief n. mukizapi, sudurzapi.
handle v.t. eskuztatu, eskuz hartu, haztakatu. v.t. aministratu.
handle n. gider, girten, euskarri, heltoki.
handlebar n. eskuleku.
handleless adj. kirtengabe(ko).
handler n. maneatzaile.
handmade adj. eskuzko.
handout n. limosna. n. orritxo.
handprint n. eskudel.
handrail n. baranda.
handsaw n. zerrote.
handshake n. bostekoa emate(a).
handsome adj. aurpegieder, galant.
handsomely adv. ederki, galanki. adv. eskuzabalez, oparo, ugari.
handsomeness n. galantedertasun, edertasun.
hand truck n. eskorga.
handwrite v.t. eskuz idatzi.
handwriting n. idazkera.
handwritten adj. eskuz idatzi(a).
handy adj. eskuoneko, eskutrebe; erabilkor.
hang v.t./v.i. zintzilikatu, urkatu.
hangable adj. urkagarri.
hangar n. hangar.
hanger n. zintzilgailu, gako, pertxa.
hangman n. borrero, urkatzaile.
hangover n. aje, bestondo, oste, mozkorrondo.
hank n. mataza, haril; ilemordo, ilemataza.
haphazard adj. ustekabe, ustekabeko.
haphazardly adv. ustekabean.
hapless adj. zorigaiztoko, zoritxarreko.
happen v.i. gertatu, jazo, suertatu, pasatu. v.i. (along) ustekabean

igaro.
happening n. gertaera, gertakizun, jazoera.
happier adj. zoriontsuago, alaitsuago.
happiest adj. -(r)ik zoriontsuen(a).
happily adv. alaiki, pozez, pozgarriro, pozik, bozkarioz, zorionez, dohatsuki.
happiness n. zorion, zoriontasun, poz, poztasun, alaitasun, bozkario.
happy adj. zoriontsu, zoriondun, zorioneko. adj. alai, alaigarri, alaitsu, pozdun, pozgarri, pozkor, dohatsu, bozkariozko.
harangue v.t./v.i. sumintzatu, sutsuki mintzatu.
harangue n. hitzaldi sutsu, jardun bero.
harass v.t. aurrean erabili, aurrean hartu, zirrikatu.
harasser n. gaizkiarazle.
harassment n. jazarpen, esespen.
harbinger n. susmo, zantzu. n. mezulari.
harbor n. kai, itsasportu, itsasontzitegi.
hard adj. gogor; bortitz. adj. zail, gaitz; neketsu. adj. barrugogor, odolgaitz. adv. gogorki, sendoki, buru-belarri, sendo. **To get hard.** Gogortu. **Hard-of-hearing.** Entzungor. **To do (it) the hard way.** Erarik zailena aukeratu. **Hard by.** Hurbil. Ondoan.
hard-boiled adj. egosi(a) (arraultza).
hardcovered adj. gotor.
harden v.t./v.i. gogorrarazi, gogortu, mukertu.
hard-headed adj. setati, kaskagogor, burukoi.
hard-headedness n. kaskagogorkeria.
hard-hearted adj. bihozgogor, gupidagabe.
hard-heartedness n. sorgorkeria, sortasun.
hardly adv. doi-doi, ozta-ozta, eskaski, ia.
hardness n. gogortasun, gogordura. n. gogorkeria.
hard-of-hearing adj. belarrigogor, entzungor.
hardship n. eskasia, urri, urrialdi.
hardware n. tresneria. n. konputagailuak, ordenagailuak; konputagailuko gainerakoak (inprimagailuak, modemak, etab.).
hardworking adj. langile, lankor, lehiatsu, fin.
hardy adj. zuhar.
hare n. (zool.) erbi.
harebrained adj. zoroska, zorongo.
harem n. andrategi.
hark v.i./v.t. entzun, aditu.
harken v.i./v.t. entzun, aditu.
harlot n. emagaldu, urdanga, maripurtzil, maribidetako.
harm v.t. kalte egin, min hartu, kaltetu, min egin, min eman, minberatu.
harm n. gaitz, kalte, oker, min.

harmful adj. kaltegarri, kaltegarrizko, kaltegile, kalterako, gaizkile, okergile, galkor, galgarri, hondagarri.
harmfully adv. kaltegarriro, kaltez, galgarriro.
harmfulness n. kaltegarritasun, kaltekortasun, galgarritasun.
harmless adj. kaltegabe, gaizkabe.
harmlessness n. kaltegabetasun, kaltegabezia.
harmonic adj. harmoniko.
harmonica n. (mus.) ahosoinu, musukitarra.
harmonious adj. harmoniatsu.
harmonize v.i. (mus.) harmonizatu. v.t. konbinatu.
harmony n. (mus.) harmonia. n. batasun, gogaidego, gogaidetasun.
harness v.t. tresnatu; lauzkatu.
harness n. zaldiedergailu, zalditresna, zaldiuztarri, aberetresnak.
harp n. (mus.) harpa.
harpist n. harpajole.
harpoon v.t. arpoindu.
harpoon n. arpoi.
harpooner n. arpoilari.
harrow n. mokormailu.
harrower n. zokorrausle.
harsh adj. latz, zakar; bortitz.
harshly adv. gogorki, lazki, garrazki, bortizki.
harshness n. gogortasun, gogorkeria, gozagaiztasun, laztasun, garraztasun, bortizkeria.
hart n. (zool.) orein.
harvest v.t./v.i. segatu, uztatu, buruxkatu.
harvest n. uzta, igita, labore.
harvestable adj. segagarri, igitagarri.
harvester n. uztabilgailu, igitagailu, segagailu. n. segalari, igitalari, uztatzaile.
has pres. of have.
hasn't "has + not"-aren laburpena.
haste n. arinketa, azkartasun.
hasten v.i./v.t. arinarazi, azkartu, arinagotu.
hastily adv. berehala, itobeharrez, itobeharrean, zarrapastaka.
hastiness n. lasterdura.
hasty adj. laster, presati, lehiatsu.
hat n. kapela, sonbrero, ginbail, buruko.
hatch v.t./v.i. berotu (oiloak).
hatch n. ataska.
hatchery n. arrainleku.
hatchet n. aizkoratxo.
hate v.t./v.i. begitan hartu, gorrotatu, herratu, higuindu, ezin ikusi. **To hate each other.** Elkar gorrotatu.
hate n. gorroto, higuin, herra, hisi; gorrota-.
hated adj. gorrotozko.
hateful adj. gorrotagarri, gorrototsu, gorrotakor, herragarri.
hatefully adv. gorrotoz, gorrotagarriro.
hatefulness n. gorrotagarritasun.

hatpin *n.* burukorratz.
hat rack *n.* ginbailgako.
hatred *n.* gorroto, gaizkinahi, herra, aiher, ezinikusi. **Mortal hatred.** Gorroto gorri.
hatter *n.* kapelagin, kapelari, sonbrerogile.
haughtily *adv.* handikeriaz.
haughtiness *n.* haizepuzkeria, handikeria, harropuzkeria.
haughty *adj.* harro, haizaputz.
haul *v.t./v.i.* erremolkatu, herrestatu, narraztu, arrastakatu. *v.t./v.i.* eraman, erakarri. *v.t.* (**down**) erriatu, beheratu.
haul *n.* erremolkatzen den zama; eramaten den zama.
hauling *n.* lorreta, farraiaketa, narraketa.
haunch *n.* hankagain.
haunt *v.t.* maiztu, sarriztatu. *v.t./.v.i.* mamu itxuraz agertu.
haunted *adj.* mamuztatu(a).
have *v.t./v.i.* eduki. *v. aux.* ukan, izan. *v.t.* (**to edo infinitiboarekin**) behar, behar ukan, behar izan. **To have it in for (someone).** Begitan hartu. **To have it out with (someone).** Bereak eta bi entzunerazi. **To have to do with.** Zerbaiti buruz izan. **To have had it.** Ez gehiago jasan. **To let (someone) have it.** Jo. Egurra eman. Astindu. **You have been had.** Ziria sartu zizuten.
haven *n.* babesleku, babestoki.
havoc *n.* hondamendi, galera, galmen, kalte.
Hawaii *n.* (*geog.*) Hawai.
Hawaiian *n.* hawaiar.
hawk *n.* (*zool.*) aztore, belatz. **Sparrow hawk.** Zapelaitz.
hawthorn *n.* (*bot.*) arantza, elorri.
hay *n.* lasto, zuhain, belarsiku. **Make hay while the sun shines.** Dagonean bon-bon, ez dagonean egon.
hayfork *n.* urka, burdinsarde.
hayloft *n.* lastategi, zuhaindegi.
haystack *n.* belarmeta.
hazard *v.t.* arriskuratu.
hazard *n.* arrisku, galzori.
hazardous *adj.* arrikudun, arriskugarri, arriskutsu. **Hazardous waste.** Hondakin arriskutsuak.
hazardously *adv.* arriskuz.
hazardousness *n.* arriskugarritasun.
haze *n.* lanbrodura.
hazel *adj.* urrantzeko.
H-bomb *n.* H-lehergailu, hidrogeno bonba.
he *pron.* harek, hark, hura, bera, berak.
head *v.t.* burutu, mahaiburu izan. *v.t./v.i.* zuzendu, gidatu; leku jakinera joan, -ra jo. *v.i.* (**off**) geldiarazi. *v.i.* (**for**) zuzendu, -ra jo.
head *n.* buru, kasko, kaskar; bur-,

kaska-. **From head to toe.** Buruz-buru. Burutik burura. *n.* nagusi, agintari. *n.* abelburu. **Head on.** Mokoz-moko. **Head over heels.** Hankazgora.
headache *n.* burukomin, buruhauste.
headboard *n.* oheburu, bururki.
headdress *n.* indioen buruko(a). *n.* zoronga.
heading *n.* izenburu, titulu, idazpuru, irakurburu. *n.* (*naut.*) norabide; itsasbide.
headland *n.* lurmutur.
headless *adj.* burugabe.
headlight *n.* autoargi. **Dim headlights.** Gurutzargi. **High beam of a headlight.** Argi luze.
headline *n.* adierazburu.
headphones *n.* belarriko.
headquarters *n.* komandantzia.
headset *n.* belarriko.
headstone *n.* hilarri, hobiharri.
headstrong *adj.* setati, burugogor, kaskagogor, temati, kasketadun.
headway *n.* aurrerapen.
heady *adj.* mozkorgarri, hordigarri. *adj.* sutsu, suhar.
heal *v.t./v.i.* sendarazi, sendatu, azalbildu.
healable *adj.* sendagarri, sendakizun.
healer *n.* sendagile, sendagin, mediku.
healing *n.* sendabide, sendapen, haragikuntza.
health *n.* osasun.
healthful *adj.* sendagarri.
healthily *adv.* sanoki, osasungarriro.
healthiness *n.* osasungarritasun, sanotasun.
health spa *n.* bainuetxe.
healthy *adj.* osasungarri, osasuntsu, osasundun, indargarri, guren, mardul, sano.
heap *v.t./v.i.* pilakatu, pilatui, metakatu, multzatu.
heap *n.* meta, moltso, pila; -meta.
heapable *adj.* metagai, metagarri, pilagarri.
hear *v.t./v.i.* entzun, aditu, belarriratu.
heard *p. part. of* hear.
hearing *n.* entzumen, entzupen, entzute, adiera. **Worth hearing.** Entzungarri. *n.* auziaurre.
hearing aid *n.* entzungailu.
hearsay *n.* esamesa, zurrumurru.
hearse *n.* hilgurdi.
heart *n.* bihotz; bihoz-. **To learn by heart.** Buruz ikasi. **From the bottom of my heart.** Bihotz-bihotzez. **Soft-hearted.** Bihozbera.
heartache *n.* atsekabe, bihozmin, larrialdi.
heartbeat *n.* bihozkada, bihozpilpira, bihoztaupada.
heartbreaking *adj.* arrailagarri, atsekabetzaile, bihozmingarri.
heartbroken *adj.* triste, nahigabetsu.
heartburn *n.* bihotzerre.

heart disease *n. (med.)* bihozmin.
heartfelt *adj.* egiazko, benetako. *adj.* bihotzeko.
hearth *n.* subazter, sutondo.
heartiness *n.* sanotasun.
heartless *adj.* amodiogabe, bihozgabe.
heartrending *adj.* erdiragarri.
   Heartrending memories. Oroitzapen erdiragarriak.
hearty *adj.* indartsu, sendo.
heat *v.t./v.i.* berotu, zerrepeldu.
heat *n.* berotasun, bero. *n.* argose, arkara. *n.* -kara, susal-, giri.
heated *adj.* bero, sudun, suhar, sutsu.
heater *n.* berogailu, beroeragile, sutontzi.
heath *n.* ilarduia, txilardegi, linaza.
heathen *n.* fedegabe, sinesgabe.
heather *n. (bot.)* inarra, txilar.
heave *v.t.* indarrez jaso. *v.t.* arnaska egin. *v.t./v.i.* goragaletu.
heaven *n.* goi, zeru, izartegi; paradisu, ortz, ortzi; ost.
heavenly *adj.* zeruko, ortzeko, zerutar.
   Heavenly Father. Zeruetako Aita.
heavily *adv.* pisuki, astunki.
heaviness *n.* astunketa, astuntasun, pisutasun.
heavy *adj.* astun, astungarri, zamadun, zamagarri, pisudun, pisutsu.
Hebrew *n./adj.* hebraitar, hebreotar. *n.* hebraiera.
hectare *n.* hektarea.
hectic *adj.* lanpetsu, higitsu, neketsu.
hecto- *(prefix.)* hekto-.
hectogram *n.* hektogramo.
hectoliter *n.* hektolitro.
hectometer *n.* ehunmetro, hektometro.
hedge *v.t. (batzutan in-ekin)* larresitu. *v.i.* zeharka hitz egin.
hedge *n.* larresi.
hedgehog *n. (zool.)* kirikiño, triku.
hedonism *n.* hedonismo.
hedonistic *adj.* hedonista.
heed *v.t.* kasu egin; entzun.
heedless *adj.* entzungor, axolagabe, axolagabeko.
heedlessly *adv.* axolagabekl.
heedlessness *n.* axolagabetasun.
heel *n. (anat.)* orpahezur, orpo, ostiko. *n.* takoi, zurruma.
heeled *adj.* takoidun.
hefty *adj.* guri, mardul, gizen.
hegemony *n.* garaitasun, nagusigo, nagusitasun.
heifer *n.* bigantxa.
height *n.* goi, goialde, goratasun, garaitasun, altuera, goimaila.
heighten *v.t.* gehitu.
heinous *adj.* gaiztotzar.
heir *n.* oinorde, oinordeko, etxaseme, primu, etxalaba.
heiress *n.* prima.
heirloom *n.* ondorezhartutako bitxia edo ondasuna.
held *p. part. of hold.*
helicopter *n.* helikoptero.

hell *n.* infernu, suleze, gaiztoki. **Go to hell!** Zoaz infernura! *int.* arraio. **What the hell!** Zer arraio! **To tell (someone) to go to hell.** Pikutara bidali. Pikutara bota.
hellish *adj.* infernueko, ifernutar.
hello *int.* kaixo. *n.* diosale.
helm *n. (naut.)* lema.
helmet *n.* burubabes, burubabeskin, kasko.
helmsman *n.* lemadun, lemari, lemazain.
help *v.t./v.i.* lagundu, esku eman, esku luzatu, urgatzi, mesede egin.
help *n.* laguntza, laguntasun, lagunketa, laguntzabide, fabore.
helper *n.* laguntzaile, eskuemaile, urgazle.
helpful *adj.* lagungarri, laguntzaile, laguntari.
helping *adj.* laguntzile, urgazle.
helpless *adj.* laguntzagabe.
helplessness *n.* babesgabezia.
helter-skelter *adv.* samaldan, multzoka.
hem *v.t. (in)* hesinguratu. *v.t.* azpildu, azpilduratu.
hem *n.* azpildura.
hematoma *n.* odolbatu.
hematophagous *adj.* odoljale.
hematuria *n. (med.)* odolgernu, pixagorri.
hemisphere *n. (geog.)* hemisferio.
hemlock *n. (bot.)* astaperrexil.
hemorrhage *n. (med.)* odoljario, odolaldi, odolisuriketa.
hemorrhoid *n. (med.)* odoluzki, anburu.
hemp *n. (bot.)* espartzu, kainamo, kalamu.
hen *n.* oilo.
henceforth *adv.* aurrerantzean.
hendecasyllabic *adj.* hamaikasilabadun.
henhouse *n.* oilategi.
henpecked *adj.* emaztearen indarkeriaz zapaldua.
hepatitis *n. (med.)* gibelmin, gibeleko.
heptasyllabic *adj.* zazpisilabadun.
her *pron.* hura, bera; -o-. *adj. (genit.)* haren, bere.
herald *v.t.* iragarri, aldarrikatu, oihukatu.
heraldry *n.* heraldika.
herb *n.* belar (usaintsu edo osasuntsu).
herbaceous *adj.* belarrezko.
herbalist *n.* belarkari.
herbivorous *adj.* belarjale.
herd *v.t.* gidatu, joan arazi. *v.i./v.t.* abereak batu.
herd *n.* abeltalde, saldo, samalda; -talde, -keta.
herder *n.* -zain.
herding *n.* -zaingo.
herdsman *n.* abeltzain, aberezain.
here *n.* leku hau, toki hau. *adv.* hemen; hona. **Here and there.** Han eta

hemen. **Right here.** Hementxe.
Come here! Zatoz hona! **From here
on out.** Hemendik aurrera.
hereafter *n.* heriotzondo.
hereditarily *adv.* ondorez.
hereditary *adj.* herentziazko,
ondorezko, jaraunspenezko.
heredity *n.* herentzia.
herein *adv.* hemen.
heresy *n.* fedehausketa, herexia.
heretic *n.* fedehausle, herexe.
heretical *adj.* fedehauskor.
heretofore *adv.* orain arte.
heritage *n.* seniparte, herentzia.
hermaphrodite *n.* arreme.
hermetic *adj.* hermetiko, itxi.
hermit *n.* ermitari, eremutar.
hermitage *n.* ermita.
hero *n.* heroe.
heroic *adj.* heroiko.
heroin *n.* heroina.
heroine *n.* heroesa.
heroism *n.* heroizitate.
heron *n. (zool.)* gartza, koartza.
herpes *n.* herpe.
herring *n. (zool.)* sardintzar.
hers *pron.* haren.
herself *pron.* norbera, bere buru(a).
hesitant *adj.* eztabaidatsu, ezbaiti.
hesitantly *adv.* ezbaian.
hesitate *v.i.* ezbaian egon.
hesitation *n.* ezbaialdi, ezbaidura.
heterodox *adj.* heterodoxo.
heterodoxy *n.* heterodoxia.
heterogeneity *n.* askotarikotasun.
hew *v.t./v.i.* harlandu, harmailutu;
aizkoraz ebaki.
hexagon *n.* hexagono.
hexagonal *adj.* hexagonal.
hexahedron *n. (geom.)* hexaedro.
hey! *int.* to, no, eup, txo, tira.
heyday *n.* gorenaldi.
hi *int.* kaixo!
hibernate *v.i.* hibernatu.
hibernation *n.* hibernazio.
hiccup *v.i.* zotin egin.
hiccup(s) *n.* zotin. **To have the
hiccups.** Zotin egin.
hick *n.* baserritar ezjakin(a).
hidden *p. part. of hide. adj.* ezkutu,
ezkutuko, isilpeko.
hide *v.t./v.i.* ezkutatu, ezkutarazi,
estali, itzalpetu, gorde. *v.t.* larrutu.
hide *n.* larru, aberelarru, ehizilarru,
zezenlarru.
hide-and-seek *n.* kirika, kukumiku.
hideaway *n.* ezkutaleku, ezkutune.
hideous *adj.* desitxurazko.
hideously *adv.* izugarriki, izugarriro.
hideousness *n.* desitxuratasun.
hide-out *n.* ebaskindegi, lapurtegi,
ohointegi.
hider *n.* ezkutari, ezkutatzaile.
hiding place *n.* ezkutaleku, gordeleku.
hierarchy *n.* hierarkia.
hieroglyphics *n.* hieroglifiko.
hi-fi *n.* hifi.

high *adj.* garai, goi, gaineko, altu,
goitar.
high beam *n. (eccl.)* argiluze.
higher *adj. (comp.)* goragoko,
garaiago. *adv.* gorago.
highest *adj. (superl.)* goren, gorengo,
goien.
highlander *n.* menditar.
highly *adv.* goraki.
highness *n.* goidura, goiera. *n.* goren,
handi (errege).
high school *n.* Batxilergo
Batu-Polibalioduna eta
Unibertsitateko Orientabide
Ikastaroen pareko ikasketak;
goieskola.
high sea *n.* itsaszabal, itsasbarren,
itsasoste.
high tide *n.* itsasgora, maregora.
highway *n.* autobidezabal, bidezabal,
autopista.
highwayman *n.* bidelapur, bidebasle.
highway robber *n.* bidebasle,
bidelapur.
high wire walker *n.* sokadantzari,
sokagainkari.
hike *v.i./v.t.* mendira joan, mendira
igon.
hike *n.* ibilkunde, ibilaldi.
hiker *n.* zangokari, ibilkari, oinezko.
hiking trail *n.* ibiltoki, ibiltegi.
hilarious *adj.* barregarri, barregarrizko.
hilarity *n.* barregarritasun,
barregarrikeria.
hill *n.* muino, mendiska; aldapa.
hilliness *n.* menditsutasun.
hillock *n.* lurtontor, bizkartontor.
hillside *n.* aldapa, aldats.
hilly *adj.* bizkartsu, menditsu.
hilt *n.* girten.
him *pron.* hura, bera; -o-.
himself *pron.* norbera, bere buru(a).
hind *n.* atzealde, bizkarralde.
hinder *v.t./v.i.* eragozpidetu, eragotzi,
galarazi.
hindrance *n.* behaztopa,
behaztopagarri, eragozpen, oztopo.
hinge *n.* orpo, ateorpo.
hint *n.* hitzerdi.
hip *n. (anat.)* hankagain.
hip joint *n. (anat.)* hankagiltza.
hippodrome *n.* zaldilasterleku,
hipodromo.
hippopotamus *n. (zool.)* hipopotamo.
hire *v.t.* kontratatu, lan(a) eman,
arazopetu, alogeratu. *v.t.* alogeratu,
akuratu.
his *adj.* haren, beraren, bere.
Hispanic *adj.* hispaniar.
hispanicization *n.* gaztelaniaztapen.
Hispanicize *v.t.* gaztelaniatu,
gaztelartu.
hispanist *n.* hispanizale, gaztelanizale.
Hispano-American *adj./n.*
espainiamerikar.
hiss *v.i./v.t.* txistukatu.
hiss *n.* txistada.

historian *n.* historialari, historigile.
historic *adj.* historiko.
historical *adj.* historiko.
historically *adv.* historikoki.
history *n.* historia, edesti. **Prehistory.** Aitzin-historia. Historiaurre. **Bible History.** Edesti Deuna.
hit *v.t./v.i.* jo, jo egin, kolpatu, zaflatu.
hit *n.* kolpe, zartada, zanpako; -kada.
hitch *v.t.* lotu, gakotu; uztartu, uztarpetu.
hitchhike *v.i.* autostop egin.
hitch-hiker *n.* autostopista.
hitchhiking *n.* autostop.
hitching post *n.* txirrindola, txinga.
hither *adv.* honuntz.
hitherto *adv.* orain arte, gaur arte, gaurdaino, egundaino.
hitter *n.* jole, jotzaile, zafratzaile, jipoiemale.
hive *n.* erlauntza, erletxe.
hives *n.* *(med.)* azmin.
ho *int.* geldi!
hoard *v.t./v.i.* orobildu, altxortu.
hoard *n.* altxor.
hoarfrost *n.* lantzurda.
hoarse *adj.* eztarlatz, lakar (ahots).
hoarseness *n.* garrazpera.
hoary *adj.* ilezuri.
hobble *v.i.* maingu egin. *v.t.* zaldien hankak lotu.
hobby *n.* denboraemateko, astiemateko, hobby.
hobgoblin *n.* iratxo.
hobo *n.* hanemenkari.
hockey *n.* jokei.
hodgepodge *n.* nahaste-borraste.
hoe *v.t./v.i.* jorratu.
hoe *n.* aitzur.
hog *n.* urdetzar, zerrikote, zerritzar.
hoist *v.t.* motoiz altxatu, txirrikaz jaso. *v.t.* bandera jaso.
hoist *n.* garabi.
hold *v.t.* eutsi, eduki, heldu. *v.i.* *(back)* gelditu. *v.i.* *(down)* ogibide bati eutsi. *v.i.* *(in)* sentipenik ez azaleratu; egonarria izan. *v.i.* *(off)* etsaiari urreratzen ez utzi. *v.i.* *(on)* erantsi, itsasi; itxaron. *v.i.* *(out)* iraun, tinko egon. *v.i.* *(out on)* egia osoa agertu ordez egoeraren alderdi onak bakarrik azaldu. **Hold everything!** Geldi! **Hold it!** Geldi! **To hold one's tongue.** Isilik egon.
hold *n.* *(naut.)* zoru, zola.
holder *n.* euskailu, eskuleku; eusle, euslari.
hold up *v.t.* ebatsi, lapurtu, ohostu, ohoindu. *v.t.* jaso.
holdup *n.* atraku.
hole *n.* zulo, zulogune; irekidura, irekigune. **To punch a hole (in).** Zulakatu. **To dig a hole.** Zulatu. Zulo egin. *n.* hutsune.
holiday *n.* jai, jaiegun, festegun.
holiness *n.* donetasun, santutasun.
hollow *n.* hutsune, zokogune, zulogune.
hollow out *v.t.* zulatu.
holly *n.* *(bot.)* gorosti.
holm oak *n.* *(bot.)* arte, zumel.
holocaust *n.* erreopari.
holster *n.* pistolazorro.
holy *adj.* guren, santu, done, bedeinkatu(a).
holy ground *n.* elizlur.
Holy Land *n.* *(geog.)* Lursaindu.
Holy Rosary *n.* *(R.C.Ch.)* agurtza donea.
holy week *n.* Aste Saindu, Aste Santu.
homage *n.* gorazarre, omenaldi. **To pay homage.** Omendatu. Omen egin.
home *n.* etxe, bizitetxe, bizileku, egoitzar, baita. **Old folk's home.** Zaharren egoitza.
homebody *n./adj.* etxezulo, etxekoi, etxezale.
homeless *adj.* etxegabe.
home-loving *adj.* etxetiar, etxekoi, etxezale.
homely *adj.* itsusi.
homemaker *n.* etxekoandre.
homeowner *n.* etxejaun.
homesick *adj.* herrimindu(a).
homesickness *n.* herrimin, herriminaldi.
homestead *n.* baserri.
home town *n.* jaioterri, sorleku, sorterri.
homework *n.* eskolalanak.
home wrecker *n.* ezkontzausle.
homey *adj.* etxekoi, etxezale, etxetiar.
homicide *n.* gizahilketa, erailkintza. *n.* gizahiltzaile, gizaeraile.
homily *n.* mezitzaldi.
homogeneity *n.* idekotasun.
homogeneous *adj.* idekotsu.
homologous *adj.* eraubereko, homologo.
homonym *n.* izenkide, tokaio.
homonymic *adj.* izenbereko.
homonymous *adj.* izenberdin.
homonymy *n.* izenkidetasun.
homosexual *adj.* sexuberekoi, maritxu.
homosexuality *n.* maritxukeria.
honest *adj.* zintzo, zuzen, fin, artez, egiazko, prestu, garbi, leial.
honestly *adv.* zintzo, zintzoki, zuzenki, zinez, prestuki, garbiro, leialki.
honesty *n.* zintzotasun, zuzentasun, arteztasun, prestasun, onestasun, leialtasun.
honey *v.t.* eztiztu, eztiztatu.
honey *n.* ezti.
honeycomb *n.* abaraska. *adj.* eztizko.
honeyed *adj.* eztidun, eztitsu.
honeymoon *n.* ezteibilaldi, ezteibidaia.
honk *v.i.* karraka egin. *v.t.* bozina jo.
honor *v.t.* ohoratu, ohore eman, ohorarazi, omendu, omen egin, gur egin, laudatu, aintzaldu.
honor *n.* ohore, omen, ospe; gorespen, fama, entzute.

honorable adj. ohoretsu, ohoredun, omentsu, omenezko, gurgarri, itzaldun.
honorableness n. omengarritasun.
honorably adv. ohorezki, prestuki, laudagarriki.
honorary adj. ohorezko.
honored adj. lausengutsu.
hood n. txano, txoto. **Little Red Riding Hood.** Txano Gorritxo. n. kotxearen kapota.
hoodlum n. alproja, gizatxar.
hoodwink v.t. iruzur egin, atzipetu, ziria sartu.
hoof n. apo, hatzazal.apatx. **Horse's hoof.** Zaldiapo.
hoofed adj. apodun.
hook v.t./v.i. gakotu, gakoz harrapatu.
hook n. amu. n. gako, mako.
hooked adj. gakodun, makodun.
hooker n. emagaldu, maripurtzil, lilitxo, maribidetako.
hooky n. piper egite(a). **To play hooky.** Biper egin. Sasieskola egin.
hoop n. uztai, txirrindola.
hoot v.i. uhukatu, uhu egin.
hoot n. uhu. adv. tut, tautik.
hop v.i. saltoka ibili.
hop n. saltu, jauzi, jauzketa, saltaketa. n. (colloq.) dantzaldi.
hope v.t./v.i. (v.i., **for**) itxaro, espero ukan, uste ukan.
hope n. itxaropen, esperantza, itxaro.
hopeful adj. itxarogarri, itxarokor, esperantzagarri.
hopefully adv. itxaropenez.
hopeless adj. itxarogabe, itxaroezin, esperantzagabe, etsita.
hopelessly adv. itxarogabez.
hopelessness n. etsipen.
hops n. (bot.) otsahien.
hopscotch n. txintxirrinka.
hop vine n. (bot.) otsahien.
horde n. jendetza, jendemultzo, jendepilo.
horizon n. ikusmuga, zeruertz, zerumuga.
horizontal adj. horizontal.
hormone n. hormona.
horn n. adar. n. turutu, bozina. n. tronpa.
horned owl n. (zool.) gauhontz.
hornet n. liztortzar.
horny adj. adardun. adj. gogor. adj. emagale, haragikoi, gizakoi, emajoera.
horoscope n. horoskopo.
horrendous adj. izugarrizko.
horrible adj. beldurgarri, ikaragarri, izugarri, ikaragarrizko.
horribleness n. beldurgarritasun, lazgarritasun.
horribly adv. ikaragarriki, ikaragarriro, izugarriro.
horrid adj. ikaragarri, izugarri.
horrify v.t. izuarazi, ikararazi.
horrifying adj. izuikarakor.

horror n. izu, izuikara.
horse n. zaldi. adj. zaldizko.
horseback adj. zaldigain.
horseback rider n. zaldigaineko.
horseback riding n. zaldiketa.
horse blanket n. zaldiestalki, zaldigaineko.
horse collar n. zaldiuztarri.
horse fly n. (zool.) mandeuli, zamaleuli.
horsehair n. zurda. adj. zurdazko.
horseman n. zaldidun.
horsepower n. lurrinzaldi, zaldindar.
horse race n. zaldilaster, zaldilasterketa.
horseshoe n. ferra.
horseshoer n. ferratzaile.
horse soldier n. zaldungudari.
horse trader n. zaldiketari.
horticulture n. barazkintza, baratzelan.
hosanna int. hosanna.
hose n. hodi, garastodi. n. galtzerdi.
hosiery n. galtzerdiak.
hospitable adj. harrerazko, harkor, abegikor, arroztiar.
hospital n. sendategi, gaisotegi, erietxe, eritegi, ospitale.
hospitality n. harkortasun, abegion, abegikortasun.
hospitalize v.t. ospitaleratu, gaisoetxeratu.
host n. gonbidatzaile (gizon). n. (eccl.) hostia, gurejaun.
hostage n. bahituri.
hostel n. ostatu.
hostess n. gonbidatzaile (emakume).
hostile adj. borrokagile, etsaiezko.
hostilely adv. etsaiki.
hostility n. areriotasun, etsaigo, ikusezin.
hostler n. zaldimutil, zaltzain.
hot adj. bero, sukardun. adj. biperdun.
hot-blooded adj. odolbero.
hot chocolate n. txokolate.
hotel n. ostatu, hotel.
hotelkeeper n. ostalari, ostatari, hotelari.
hotheaded adj. burubero, haserrekor.
hothouse n. mindegi.
hot pepper n. bipermin.
hot springs n. urberoaga.
hound n. ehizatxakur.
hour n. ordu, tenore.
hourglass n. hondarrerloju.
hour hand n. orenorratz.
hourly adv. orduz-ordu, orduro.
house n. etxe; etxa-.
houseboy n. etxemutil.
housecoat n. etxejantzi.
household n. etxea eta etxekoak.
household goods n. trasteria.
housekeeper n. etxezain.
houseless adj. etxegabe.
housewife n. etxekoandre, andere.
housework n. etxelan, etxezeregin.
housing n. egoitza.
hovel n. bordatxo.

hover *v.i.* hegabiratu.
how *adv./conj.* nola, nolatan.
however *adv./conj.* hala ere, berriz, halere, ordea.
howl *v.i.* arrama egin, ulu egin, intziri egin.
howl *n.* intziri, ulu, arrama.
howler *n.* ululari.
how many *adv.* zenbat.
how much *adv.* zenbat.
how often *adv.* noizero.
hub *n.* gurdi-ardatz.
hubbub *n.* zarataldi.
hubby *n.* senar.
hue *n.* margo, kolore.
hug *v.t./v.i.* besarkatu.
hug *n.* besarkada, besarkaldi.
huge *adj.* handitsu, handitzar, eskerga, galant, egundoko.
hugeness *n.* handitasun, eskergatasun, galantasun.
hugging *n.* besarketa.
hula *n.* Hawai-ko dantza.
hulk *n.* gizon handi.
hull *n.* ontziazal.
hum *v.t.* kanta marmaritu, ahopetik kantatu.
human *adj.* gizaerazko, gizako, gizatiar. *n.* gizaki.
human being *n.* gizaki, gizon.
humane *adj.* gizalegezko, gizatar, gizazale. *adj.* errukior, errukitsu, gupidatsu, bihozpera.
humanely *adv.* gizalegez, gizabidez. *adv.* errukiz, gupidaz.
humanism *n.* gizakoitasun, humanismo.
humanist *n.* humanista.
humanistic *adj.* gizatar, gizakoi, gizazale.
humanitarian *adj.* gizalegezko, gizabidezko.
humanitarianism *n.* gizakortasun.
humanity *n.* gizatasun. *n.* gizateria, gizadi. *n.* ontasun, errukitasun.
humanization *n.* gizagintza, gizakuntza.
humanize *v.t./v.i.* gizatu, gizatartu.
humankind *n.* gizadi, enda, gizateria.
humanly *adv.* gizonki.
human nature *n.* gizatasun.
humble *v.t.* umildu, beheratu, apaldu.
humble *adj.* apal, umil, xume.
humbleness *n.* apaltasun, xumetasun, umiltasun.
humbling *adj.* apalgarri.
humbly *adv.* apalki, apalkiro, umilki.
humbug *n.* iruzur, iruzurkeria.
humdrum *adj.* aspergarri, doinubakar.
humerus *n. (anat.)* besondohezur, besahezur.
humid *adj.* busti, umel.
humidify *v.t.* umeldu, busti.
humidity *n.* bustitasun, umeltasun.
humidor *n.* pipontzi.
humiliate *v.t.* lotsagarritu, desohoretu, apalerazi.

humiliating *adj.* lotsarazle, desohoregarri, apalgarri, umilgarri.
humiliation *n.* apalketa, apaldura, umildura.
humility *n.* apaltasun, umiltasun, xumedura.
humor *n.* umore, grazi, biper.
humorist *n.* barreragile.
humorous *adj.* umoretsu, barregarrizko, gazdun.
hump *n. (anat.)* bizkarkonkor, korkoitz, konkor.
humpbacked *adj.* konkordun, korkoizdun, bizkarmakur.
humped *adj.* konkordun, korkoizdun.
humus *n.* lubeltz.
hunch *v.t./v.i. (over)* konkortu.
hunch *n.* bihotzaldi, susmaketa.
hunchback *n. (anat.)* korkoitz, bizkarkonkor, konkor, ttontor.
hunchbacked *adj.* korkoizdun, bizkarmakur, konkordun, lepoker.
hunched *adj.* makur, bihur, oker.
hundred *n./adj.* ehun.
hundredth *adj.* ehungarren, ehundar.
hung *p. part. of* hang.
hunger *n.* gose, tripazorri, sabelzorri.
hungrily *adv.* gosez.
hungry *adj.* gose, goseti, gosebera. **To be hungry for money.** Diru gosez egon.
hunk *n.* zati handi.
hunt *v.t./v.i.* ehizatu.
hunt *n.* ehizaldi.
hunter *n.* ehiztari.
hunting *n.* ehiza, ehizaketa. **To go hunting.** Ehizan ibili. **Fond of hunting.** Ehizazale.
hurl *v.t.* bota, jaurti, egotzi.
hurrah *int.* gora!
hurray *int.* gora!
hurricane *n.* haizeketa, tifoi, zirimola.
hurried *adj.* lastertsu, presadun, zarrapastada.
hurriedly *adv.* presaz, presaka, lasterka, lehiatuki, itobeharrez.
hurry *v.i./v.t.* azkartu, presatu, presakatu, lasterkatu, lastertu, lasterrarazi, presaz ibili.
hurry *n.* arineketa, presa, lasterdura.
hurt *v.t./v.i.* min izan, min ukan, min eman, min egin, minberatu, zauriztatu, kalte egin.
hurt *n.* kalte, min, atsekabe.
hurtful *adj.* mingarri, kaltegarri.
husband *n.* senar, emaztedun.
husbandry *n.* laboraritza, nekazaritza.
hush *v.t./v.i.* isilarazi, isildu.
hush money *n.* isilsari.
husk *v.t.* artazuritu.
husk *n. (bot.)* artazorro, ahotz, teka, leka.
husky *n.* eskimal txakur(ra). *adj.* sendo.
hustle *v.i.* presa izan, presatu.
hut *n.* txabola, etxola, borda.
hutch *n.* untxitegi. *n.* arasa.

hybrid n./adj. hibrido.
hydrate n. (chem.) hidrato.
hydraulic adj. hidraulika.
hydrocarbon n. hidrokarburo.
hydrochloric adj. klorhidriko.
hydroelectricity n. urelektrika.
hydroelectric power n. urindar.
hydrogen n. (chem.) hidrogeno.
hydrometer n. urneurkin.
hydrometry n. urneurketa, urneurkintza.
hydrophobia n. amorru. n. urgorroto, urfobia.
hydroplane n. uregazkin.
hydroxide n. (chem.) urerdoil.
hygiene n. osasunbide.
hygienic adj. osasunkor, garbikor.
hygienically adv. osasungarriro.
hygienist n. osasunlari.
hymen n. (anat.) emamintz.
hymn n. ereserki, goratzarre.
hyperactive adj. geldiezin, geldigaitz.
hypersensitive adj. goisentibera.
hypertension n. (med.) hipertentsio.
hyphen n. elkarziri, marratxo, gioi.
hypnosis n. hipnosis.
hypnotist n. loeragile.
hypnotize v.t. hipnotizatu, lo eragin.
hypocrisy n. azalkeria, itxurakeria, azaluskeria, toleskeria.
hypocrite n. itxuralari, azaluts.
hypocritical adj. azalzuri, itxurazale.
hypocritically adv. itxurakeriaz.
hypodermic adj. azalazpiko.
hypotenuse n. hipotenusa.
hypothesis n. hipotesi.
hypothetic(al) adj. baldinezko, baldinkor.
hysteria n. histeria.
hysterical adj. histeriko.

I

i n. Ingeles alfabetoko letra.
I pron. ni, nik, neu, neuk.
ice n. izotz, jela, horma, lei.
iceberg n. izozmendi, iceberg.
icebox n. hozkailu, izozgailu.
icebreaker n. izotzauskailu.
ice cream n. izozki.
ice cube n. izotz-koxkor.
ice pick n. puntzoi.
icicle n. ziztor.
icily adv. izozki.
icing n. pastelek daramaten azukrezko geruza.
icon n. iruditxo.
iconoclast n. irudihausle.
icterus n. (med.) minori, lauremin.
icthyology n. iktiologia.
icy adj. izotzeko, izozkarri, jelatsu.
I.D. n. karnetagiri, noragiri.
I'd "I + should," "I + had," "I + would"-en laburpena.
Idaho n. (geog.) Estatu Batuetako estatu bat.
idea n. bururapen, burutazio, gogamen, uste, asmo, pentsamentu,
ideia.
ideal n. eredu, eredugarri. adj. ereduzko.
idealism n. idealismo.
idealist n. ideialtzale, ameslari.
idealistic adj. ideialtzale.
idealize v.t./v.i. ideializatu, ametsetsi.
ideally adv. ideialki.
identical adj. hainbateko, orobateko, berdin.
identifiable adj. antzemangarri, identifikagarri.
identification n. identifikapen, identifikazio. n. karnetagiri, noragiri.
identify v.t. identifikatu, ezagutu, antzeman. v.t./v.i. (with) bat egin, bat etorri.
identity n. izate, identitate, izan.
ideologist n. ideologari.
ideology n. pentsaera, pentsakera, pentsamolde.
idiocy n. kaikukeria, tutulukeria, tentelkeria, kirtenkeria, lelokeria.
idiom n. hizkuntza, mintzaera. n. esaera.
idiomatic adj. esaerazko.
idiosyncrasy n. jite.
idiot n. kaiku, inozo, tentel, zozo.
idiotic adj. ergel, tontolapiko, inozo, tentel, burugabe, memelo, zozo.
idiotically adv. kaikuki.
idle adj. alfer, nagi.
idleness n. nagikeria, nagipen, langabezia.
idler n. alfer, nagitzar, erlamando.
idly adv. alferki, nagiki.
idol n. jainkoizun, jainkorde, sasijainko, idolo.
idolater n. idolgurtzaile, sasijainkozale.
idolatry n. sasijainkokeria, idolokeria.
idolize v.t. itsumaitatu. v.i. idolatratu.
idyll n. maitamindura, amorio.
i.e. esaterako, esate baterako, adibidez.
if conj. ba-, baldin; ezkero, -(e)nez gero, -tekotan. n. baldintza.
igloo n. Eskimalen izotzezko etxe(a).
igneous adj. suzko.
ignite v.t./v.i. irazeki, biztu, su eman.
ignition n. sutasun.
ignoble adj. ttattar, doilor.
ignominious adj. laidogarri, iraingarri.
ignominiously adv. laidogarriki, laidoki, laidogarriro.
ignominy n. laido, laidogarrikeria, lotsakizun.
ignorance n. ezjakintza, ezjakite, ezjakin, jakinez(a), jakingabezia.
ignorant adj. jakingabe, ezjakin, eskolagabe.
ignorantly adv. ezjakinean, ezjakinez, ezjakitez.
ignore v.t. ezikusi egin, ezaxolatu, gor egin, ezezagutu.
ill adj. eri, gaiso, gaizdun, osasungabe. adv. ondoezik, minez.
I'll "I + will"-aren laburpena.

ill-bred adj. gizabidegabe.
illegal adj. legekontrako, legeaurkako, bidegabeko.
illegality n. bidegabetasun, deslegetasun.
illegally adv. legezkanpo, legezkontra.
illegible adj. irakurgaitz, zirriborrotsu, irakurtezin.
illegibly adv. irakurtezinez.
illegitimacy n. bidegabetasun, sasikotasun, ezlegetasun.
illegitimate adj. bidegabeko, deslegezko; sasi-.
illegitimately adv. ezlegez.
ill-fated adj. zoritxarreko, zorigaitzezko.
illicit adj. deslegezko, eragotzi, debekatu(a).
illicitly adv. desbidez.
Illinois n. (geog.) Estatu Batuetako estatu bat.
illiteracy n. kulturgabetasun, ezjakintza, ezjakite, ezjakituria.
illiterate adj. ezjakin, kulturgabe, alfabetagabe, eskolagabe, ezikasi.
ill-mannered adj. gaizkikasi, gizabidegabe.
illness n. gaiso, eri, gaisoaldi, erialdi, eritasun, gaitz, ondoez, ondoezaldi, makalaldi; eri-. **Minor illness.** Gaitzarin. **Serious illness.** Gaitz larri.
illogic n. gisagabekeria.
illogical adj. zentzugabe, zentzugabeko.
ill-tempered adj. zipote, prakestu, saltakor.
ill-treat v.t. gaizki erabili.
illuminate v.t./v.i. argitu, argi egin.
illuminating adj. argiztagarri.
illumination n. argialdi, argikuntza, argiztapen, argiztadura, goiargi.
illumine v.t./v.i. argitu, argi egin.
illusion n. irudikeria, ameslilura; begitazio.
illusive adj. ametsezko, ametsutzezko.
illusively adv. ametsutzez.
illusorily adv. lilurabidez.
illusory adj. irudimenezko.
illustrate v.t./v.i. adibideekin argitu. v.t. iruditzatu, irudiztu.
illustrated adj. irudidun.
illustration n. irudi. n. argitasun, argitzapen.
illustrative adj. argigarri.
illustrator n. marrazlari.
illustrious adj. izendun, omentsu, ohoredun, ohoretsu, ospatsu, aintzatsu, gailen.
ill will n. gaitzuste, azpildura, gaizkinahi, ezinikusi, gogogaizto, tirria.
I'm "I + am"-aren laburpena.
image n. irudi, itxura, antzirudi, imajina.
imagery n. irudimenak.
imaginable adj. asmagarri, irudigarri.
imaginary adj. ameskeriazko, irudimenezko, ustezko, ipuinezko.

imagination n. irudimen, irudipen, asmamen.
imaginative adj. asmakor, irudikor, irudimentsu.
imaginatively adv. irudipenez.
imagine v.t./v.i. irudikatu, iruditu, amestu.
imbecile adj. kaiku, astakilo, kirten, zozo.
imbecilic adj. ergel, zozo, burugabe, inozo, kokolo, memelo, tentel.
imbecility n. xorakeria, ergeltasun, lelotasun, tenteltasun.
imbed v.t. txertatu.
imbibe v.t./v.i. edan.
imbricate v.t./v.i. ahokatu.
imbroglio n. zurruburru.
imbue v.t. burutaratu.
imitable adj. imitagarri, jarraigarri, irudikakor, irudikagarri.
imitate v.t. imitatu, antzekotu, antzera egin, antzeratu, parodiatu, -ren plantak egin.
imitation n. imitapen, irudiketa, jarraipen, antzirudi, antzarpen.
imitative adj. jarraipenezko, jarraibidezko.
imitator n. jarraile, antzegile, imitatzaile.
immaculate adj. garbi-garbi, kutsugabe, orbaingabe.
immaterial adj. materigabe.
immature adj. helgabe.
immaturity n. helgabezia, ondugabetasun, ondugabezia.
immeasurable adj. neurgaitz, neurtezin, kontaezin.
immeasurably adv. kontaezinala.
immediacy n. hurretasun.
immediate adj. arartegabeko, berehalako, bapateko, kolpeko.
immediately adv. arinki, berehalaxe, hitzetik hortzera, lasterki.
immemorial adj. gogoraezin, oroitaurreko.
immense adj. handi-handi, mugagabeko, neurrigabeko.
immensely adv. mugagabeki.
immenseness n. mugagabetasun.
immensity n. neurgabetasun, mugagabetasun.
immerse v.t. urperatu.
immersion n. urperaldi, urperaketa, murgilaldi, pulunpaldi, murgilketa.
immigrant n. erbesteko.
immigrate v.t./v.i. herriratu, inmigratu.
immigration n. inmigraketa, inmigrazio.
immigratory adj. inmigraketazko.
imminent adj. berehalako, hurbil.
immobile adj. mugiezin, mugigabe, mugigaitz, geldikor, gerakor, higiezin.
immobility n. mugiezintasun, geldiegote, geldotasun.
immobilization n. geldiarazpen, gerarazpen, geldierazte, geraldi.
immobilize v.t. geldiarazi, gerarazi,

ibilgetu.
immoderate *adj.* neurrizgaineko, eragabeko.
immoderately *adv.* gehiegitxo, eragabez, neurrigabez.
immodest *adj.* lotsagabe(ko), lotsagarri.
immodesty *n.* lotsagabetasun, lotsagabekeria.
immolate *v.t.* bizi opatu.
immolation *n.* biziopari.
immolator *n.* biziopatzaile.
immoral *adj.* lotsagabe, lotsagalduko; lizunkoi, lohi.
immorality *n.* moralgabekeria, moralgabetasun, lohikeria, lotsagabekeria.
immorally *adv.* lizunki, gordinki.
immortal *adj.* hilezkor, betiraungarri, hilezin.
immortality *n.* hilezintasun, hilezkortasun.
immortalize *v.t.* hilezkorreztatu, betikotu.
immovable *adj.* higiezin, higigaitz, mugiezin.
immune *adj.* kutsagaitz.
immunity *n.* kutsagaiztasun. *n.* libraketa.
immutability *n.* desaldakortasun, aldaezintasun, aldagaiztasun.
immutable *adj.* desaldagarri.
immutably *adv.* aldaezinez, aldagaizkiro.
imp *n.* iratxo.
impact *v.t./v.i.* jo.
impact *n.* elkarjoaldi. *n.* zerikusi, ondorio.
impair *v.t.* indargetu, okerragotu, gaizkitu.
impairment *n.* indargabezia, ahuldura, ahulezi, gaizkialdi.
impale *v.t.* paldotu.
impart *v.t.* jakinarazi. *v.t./v.i.* eman.
impartial *adj.* alderdigabeko, gogoberdin.
impartiality *n.* alderdigabetasun, gogoberdintasun.
impartially *adv.* alderdigabeki, impartzialki.
impassable *adj.* iragangaitz, pasaezin, iraganezin.
impasse *n.* eragozpen handi(a).
impassioned *adj.* grinadun.
impassive *adj.* geldo, nagitsu, sor.
impassively *adv.* soraioki.
impassivity *n.* pairugabetasun, soraiokeria.
impatience *n.* ezinegon, jasangaizkeria, jasangaiztasun, pairugabekeria, pairugabetasun.
impatient *adj.* pairugabe, pairugabeko, astigabe, zazpiki.
impatiently *adv.* arrenkuraz, pairugabeki, kexuki, arranguraz.
impeach *v.t.* gobernuko agintariak auzitaratu.

impeachment *n.* gobernuko agintariak auzitaratze(a).
impeccability *n.* bekatugabezia.
impeccable *adj.* bekatuezin.
impede *v.t.* oztopatu, galarazi, trabatu, eragotzi.
impediment *n.* eragozpen, galarazketa, oztopaketa, oztopo.
impel *v.t.* bultzatu, aurrerarazi.
impend *v.i.* hurbil egon, gerturatu (denbora).
impending *adj.* berehalako, hurbil.
impenetrability *n.* zulagaiztasun, irazgaiztasun, sartezintasun.
impenetrable *adj.* barrengaitz, zulagaitz, sargaitz, sartezin.
impenitence *n.* damugabekeria, damugabezia.
impenitent *adj.* damugabe.
imperative *n.* (*gram.*) aginkera, agintaldi. *n.* agindu. *adj.* ezinbesteko, beharrezko, premiazko; presazko.
imperceptible *adj.* ohartezin, sumagaitz, sumaezin.
imperceptibly *adv.* sumaezinez, sumaezinik.
imperfect *adj.* akasdun, narriodun. *adj.* bukagabe, osagabe. *n.* (*gram.*) lehenaldi bukagabe(a).
imperfection *n.* gaitz, makur.
imperfectly *adv.* ezondo, ezongi, gaizki.
imperial *adj.* enperadorearen. *adj.* aginkor.
imperialism *n.* inperialismo.
imperialist *n.* inperialista.
imperil *v.t.* arriskuan jarri, arriskuratu.
imperious *adj.* aginkor.
imperishable *adj.* hilezkor, hilezin, iraunkor.
impermanence *n.* igarokortasun.
impermeability *n.* iragazkaiztasun, iragaztezintasun, zulagaiztasun.
impermeable *adj.* iragazkaitz, iragaztezin, zulagaitz.
impersonal *adj.* norgabe, norgabeko.
impersonalize *v.t.* norgabetu.
impersonally *adv.* norgabeki.
impersonalness *n.* norgabetasun.
impersonate *v.t.* imitatu, antzeratu, irudikatu.
impersonation *n.* antzarpen, imitapen.
impertinence *n.* milikeria, ozarkeria, mutirikeria.
impertinent *adj.* nekarazle, ozar.
impertinently *adv.* ozarki, mutiriki.
imperturbability *n.* izukaiztasun.
imperturbable *adj.* lasai, ikaraezin, ikaragabe, izuezin, izugabe.
impervious *adj.* sartezin, sargaitz, barrengaitz.
impetuous *adj.* gogobero, gogoberotsu, suhar, oldarkor, oldartsu, bultzakari, bultzakor.
impetuously *adv.* oldarka, oldarki, oldarrez, zarrapastaka.
impetuousness *n.* oldarkortasun,

bultzadatasun, odolberotasun, oldartasun.
impetus *n.* indar, oldar, oldarpen.
impiety *n.* erlijiogabetasun, erlijiogabezia.
impious *adj.* fedegabe, erlijiogabe.
impishly *adv.* pikaroki, gaizki, petralki.
implacable *adj.* bihozgabe, bihozgogor.
implant *v.t.* *(med.)* txertatu. *v.t.* burutaratu.
implant *n.* *(med.)* txertaketa.
implement *v.t.* egitaratu.
implement *n.* tresna, erreminta, lanabes.
implicate *v.t.* sartu, barruan egon (gizerailketan); errutatu.
implication *n.* iradokizun.
implicit *adj.* aipagabeko, isilbidezko.
implicitly *adv.* isilbidez, aipagabe.
implicitness *n.* aipagabetasun.
implore *v.t./v.i.* arrendu, arrenkatu, erregutu.
imply *v.t.* barrenartu. *v.t.* adierazi, jakinarazi.
impolite *adj.* adeigabeko, eragabe, gizabidegabe, begirunegabe.
impolitely *adv.* eragabez, nabarmenki, eragabeki, nabarmenkiro.
impoliteness *n.* eragabekeria, eragabetasun, nabarmentasun.
import *v.t.* *(econ.)* barneratu, inportatu.
import *n.* *(econ.)* inportazio. *n.* ganora, kanore.
importance *n.* garrantzi, burutasun, munta.
important *adj.* garrantzitsu, garrantzidun, garrantzizko.
importantly *adv.* garrantziz.
importation *n.* *(econ.)* inportaketa, barneraketa.
importer *n.* inportatzaile.
importunate *adj.* nazkagarri, nekagarri, mutirikor.
importune *v.t.* erregutu, arrenka eskatu.
importunity *n.* desegokirotasun.
impose *v.t./v.i.* inposatu, ezarri, jarri.
imposing *adj.* egundoko, itzelezko.
imposition *n.* larderialdi, inposaketa.
impossibility *n.* ezin, ezintasun.
impossible *adj.* ezin, ezinezko, gertaezin, izangaitz; -ezin.
impossibly *adv.* ezinez, ezinik.
imposter *n.* iruzurgile, azpilangile, engainatzaile, iruzurti.
imposture *n.* gezurketa.
impotence *n.* ahalgabetasun, ezin, ezintasun.
impotency *n.* ezinkizun.
impotent *adj.* ahalezin, ahalgabe, ezinkor.
impoverish *v.t.* behartsutu.
impoverished *adj.* txiro, behartsu.
impractical *adj.* ezeginkor.
imprecation *n.* madarikazio, birao.

imprecatory *adj.* madarikaziozko.
imprecise *adj.* zehazkabe.
imprecisely *adv.* zehazkabeki.
impreciseness *n.* zehazkabetasun.
imprecision *n.* zehazkabezia, goibeltasun.
impregnable *adj.* erasogaitz, erasoezin.
impregnate *v.t.* izorratu, haurdundu, ernaldu, ernaritu.
impregnation *n.* ernalketa, ernalkuntza.
impress *v.t.* hunkitu, mugidatu.
impression *n.* inpresio, zirrara. *n.* irarketa, inprimaketa.
impressionable *adj.* eraginbera, sentibera.
impressionableness *n.* sentiberatasun, minberatasun.
impressionism *n.* inpresionismo.
impressive *adj.* erdiragarri, itzelezko.
impressively *adv.* handikiro, hunkigarriro.
imprint *v.t.* inprimatu.
imprint *n.* hatz, lorratz.
imprison *v.t.* espetxeratu, espetxetu, gartzelatu, gartzelaratu, giltzapetu.
imprisonment *n.* gatibualdi, katigualdi.
improbability *n.* gertagaiztasun, sinesgaiztasun, itxuragabetasun.
improbable *adj.* itxuragabe(ko), kanoragabeko, gertagaitz.
improbably *adv.* itxuragabeki.
impromptu *adj.* gertugabe, ustekabe. *adv.* ustekabean, ustekabeki.
improper *adj.* desegoki, ezegoki.
improperly *adv.* desegokiro, ezegokiro.
impropriety *n.* desegokitasun, ezgizakotasun.
improvable *adj.* hobegarri.
improve *v.t./v.i.* hobetu, ondu.
improvement *n.* hobealdi, hobekuntza.
improvise *v.t./v.i.* asmatu, hitzetik-hortzera prestatu.
improvised *adj.* gertugabe.
improviser *n.* asmalari, asmatzaile.
imprudence *n.* zentzugabetasun, zuhurgabezia, txoriburukeria.
imprudent *adj.* zentzugabe, zentzugabeko, sengabeko.
imprudently *adv.* zentzugabeki.
impudence *n.* lotsagabekeria, mutiritasun, mutirikeria.
impudent *adj.* lotsagabe(ko), ahalkegabe, ahogaizto, ahozikin, mutirikor.
impudently *adv.* lotsagabeki, mutiriki.
impulse *n.* biztagarri. *n.* bultzadura, bultz.
impulsion *n.* eragikuntza, eragimen.
impulsive *adj.* odolberoko, oldarkor, oldarti. *adj.* bultzakari, bultzakor.
impulsively *adv.* oldarka, oldarki, oldarrez.
impulsiveness *n.* odolberotasun, oldarkortasun, oharkabekeria.

impunity n. zigorgabetasun, zigorgabezia.
impure adj. lohi, zantar, likits, zikin. adj. mordoilo (hizkuntza).
impurely adv. lohiki.
impurity n. lohikeria.
impute v.t. leporatu, gainezarri.
in prep. -n, -etan, barru, barruan. prep. -z. **Written in ink.** Tintaz idatzia.
in- (gram.) ez-.
in. Cf. inch.
inability n. ezin, ahalezin, ahalgabetasun, ezintasun, gaieztasun.
inaccessible n. helgaitz, eziniritsizko.
inaccurate adj. akasdun, okerdun, ezuzen, faltsu.
inaction n. geldotasun, geldiegote.
inactive adj. geldo, geldi.
inactively adv. geldiro.
inactivity n. ezeragite, geldiegote, geldotasun, ekingabezia.
inadequacy n. desegokitasun.
inadequate adj. desegoki, ezegoki, kontrabideko.
inadequately adv. eragabeki, desegokiro; gutiegi.
inadequateness n. ezegokitasun.
inadmissibility n. onartezintasun.
inadmissible adj. onartezin, oneskaitz.
inadvertence n. ustekabezia, oharkabetasun.
inadvertent adj. konturagabe(ko), oharkabe.
inadvertently adv. konturagabez, ustekabean.
inalienable adj. debekaezin.
inane adj. tentel, zoro, burugabe.
inanely adv. burugabeki.
inanimate adj. bizigabe.
inanity n. elezoro.
inappropriate adj. kontrabideko, bidegabeko, desegoki, ezgisako.
inappropriately adv. desegokiro, eragabeki, desegoki.
inappropriateness n. desegokitasun, eragabekeria.
inarticulate adj. adierazmen urriko, hiztotel.
inasmuch as -lako, bait-, eta.
inattention n. adigabetasun, entzungogortasun.
inattentive adj. adigabe, adigalkor, begiragabe, entzungogor.
inaudible adj. entzunezin.
inaugural adj. estreinaldizko, hasierako.
inaugurate v.t. inauguratu, estreinatu.
inauguration n. estreinaldi, agertualdi, zabalkunde.
inauthenticity n. desjatortasun.
inborn adj. jaiotzako, izatezko.
inc. L.I. (Lagunarte Izengabe). Cf. incorporated.
incalculable adj. kalkulezin, kontaezin, neurtezin, zenbatuezin, kalkulagaitz.
incalculably adv. kontaezinez,

neurtezinez.
incandescence n. goritasun.
incandescent adj. gori.
incandescently adv. gori-gori, goriki.
incantation n. sorginen hitz majikoak.
incapability n. ahalgabetasun, ezin, ezintasun.
incapable adj. ahalezin, ezgai, ezgauza, ahalgabe, moldegaitz, taxugabe.
incapably adv. ahalezinez, taxugabeki.
incapacitate v.t. gaieztu, ezindu, ezgaitu.
incapacitated adj. ezindu(a), ezindun.
incapacity n. ahalgabetasun, ezereza, ezgaitasun, gaieztapen, gaieztasun, ahalezin.
incarcerate v.t. giltzaperatu, giltzapetu, gartzeleratu, espetxeratu.
incarnate v.t. haragitu, haragiztatu, gizondu.
incarnation n. gizakunde, haragikuntza, haragipen.
incendiary adj. erregarri, subera, sukor. n. erretzaile, suemaile.
incense v.t./v.i. intsentsatu.
incense n. intsentsu.
incenser n. intsentsatzaile.
incentive n. bizigarri, biztugarri, aurrerabide, bultzagarri, eragingarri.
inception n. haskunde.
incessant adj. atergabe, aterrezin, atergabeko, epegabeko, etengabeko, geldigabe(ko).
incessantly adv. atergabeki, etengabeki, geldigabeki.
incest n. ahaide-haragikeria.
incestuous adj. ahaidekerizko.
inch n. hatz, hazbete.
incidence n. sarritasun, maiztasun.
incident n. jazokuntza.
incidental adj. gertaerazko.
incidentally adv. bidenabar. adv. iraganki.
incinerate v.t. erraustu.
incineration n. errauspen, errausketa.
incinerator n. errausle; errausgailu.
incipient adj. hasgarri, hasberri.
incision n. (med.) zarrastada, epai, epaite, sakaildura. n. ebakidura, ebakune, moztura.
incisive adj. sarkor, ebakor, ebatzaile.
incisively adv. sarkorki.
incisiveness n. sarkortasun.
incisor n. (anat.) hortz sarkor.
incitation n. kitzikadura.
incite v.t. zirikatu, sustatu, akuilatu, buru berotu.
incitement n. eragiketa, zirikaldi, zirikamen.
inclement adj. gogor, txar (eguraldi).
inclination n. aiher, joera, zaletasun, apeta, eroritasun.
incline v.i./v.t. makurtu. v.i. -kor izan, -bera izan.
incline n. maldabehera, maldagora, mendialdapa.

inclose v.t. inguratu, hesiztatu, barrutu.
inclosure n. hesibarruti.
include v.t. barrutu, barnesartu, sartu, eduki.
including prep. barne; baita ere.
inclusion n. barneketa, barneraketa.
inclusive adj. barnekor.
incoherence n. loturaezin.
incoherent adj. lotezin, loturagabe.
incohesive adj. ezingogortuzko.
income n. soldata.
incoming adj. sarkor.
incommunicability n. komunikaezintasun.
incommunicable adj. komunikaezin.
incommunicado adj. bakartu.
incommunication n. bakarketa.
incomparable adj. berdingabe, gonbaraezin, paregabeko.
incomparably adv. paregabeki, berdingabeki.
incompatibility n. adostezintasun, elkargaiztasun, elkartezintasun, bateraezintasun.
incompatible adj. elkartezin, elkargaitz, bateraezin, adostezin. n. adiskidegaitz.
incompetence n. gauzaeztasun, ezgaitasun.
incompetent adj. antzegabeko, ezgauza.
incomplete adj. osagabe, osabehar.
incompletely adv. ezosoki.
incompleteness n. osagabetasun.
incompletion n. ezbetekizun.
incomprehensibility n. adiezintasun, ulerkaiztasun.
incomprehensible adj. ulerkaitz, adiezin, adigaitz, konprenigaitz, ulertezin.
incomprehension n. adigaiztasun, ulerkaiztasun, ulertezintasun.
inconceivable adj. asmagaitz, asmakaitz, pentsaezin, burutaezin, iritzezin.
inconceivably adv. pentsaezinez, burutaezinez.
inconclusive adj. deserabakigarri.
incongruently adv. desegokiro, desegoki.
incongruity n. desegokitasun, gisagabekeria.
incongruous adj. desegoki.
inconsequential adj. ondoriogabe.
inconsiderable adj. txiki, kaxkar.
inconsiderate adj. eragabe, gisagabe, adeigabe, itzalgabeko.
inconsistency n. desiraupen, aldakoikeria, aldakoitasun, iraupengabetasun.
inconsistent adj. alditsu, aldakor, iraupengabe, desiraunkor.
inconsistently adv. aldakorki, iraupengabeki.
inconsolable adj. kontsolaezin.
inconspicuous adj. ikusgaitz,

aztergaitz, nabarmengaitz.
inconstancy n. aldakortasun, aldi, iraupengabetasun.
inconstant adj. iraupengabe, aldagarri, aldakor.
incontestable adj. ezbaiezin, argudiaezin, ukagaitz.
incontrovertible adj. argudiaezin.
inconvenience n. deserosotasun, eragabetasun.
inconvenient adj. eragaitz. adj. ezorduko, ordutxarreko, orduzkanpoko.
inconveniently adv. erakaizki, ezorduz.
incorporate v.t./v.i. lagunartetu, elkartu, elkarganatu. v.t. barrukotu. v.i. gorputzeratu.
incorporated adj. lagunartetu(a). adj. (cap.) Izengabeko Elkargo, Lagunarte Izengabe.
incorporation n. gehitzapen.
incorporeal adj. gorpuzkabe(ko).
incorrect adj. zuzengabe; mordoilozko.
incorrectly adv. zuzengabeki, desegokiro, makur.
incorrigible adj. onduezin, zuzengaitz, zuzentezin.
incorrupt adj. ustelgabe.
incorruptibility n. ustelgabetasun.
incorruptible adj. ezustelkor, andeakaitz, ustelgaitz.
increasable adj. ugalgarri, emendagarri.
increase v.t./v.i. gehitu, handitu, ugaldu, aniztu, askotu, gaineratu, naharotu, ugaritu.
increase n. handitasun, hazkuntza, goraldi, zabalkuntza, gehikuntza, gehigarri, gurentasun.
increasingly adv. gero eta gehiago.
incredibility n. sinestezintasun.
incredible adj. sinesgaitz, sinestezin.
incredibly adv. sinestezinez.
incredulity n. fedegabekeria, sinesgogortasun, sinestegabetasun.
incredulous adj. fedegabe, fedegabeko, sinesgabe, sinesgogor, sinesgaitz.
incredulously adv. fedegabeki.
increment n. gehikuntza.
incriminate v.t. aurpegira bota, erruztatu, errutatu.
incrimination n. auzitaraketa.
incubate v.t./v.i. txitatu, xitatu, berotu.
incubation n. xitatze, xitaketa.
incubation period n. lokaldi.
incubator n. txitagailu.
inculcate v.t. ekinarazi, saiatu.
inculpate v.t. errutatu, erruztatu.
inculpation n. auzitaraketa.
incumbent n./adj. kargadun. adj. beharrezko.
incur v.t. jautsi, erori (zor, erru, etab.).
incurable adj. sendagaitz, osasungaitz, medikaezin, sendaezin.

incursion *n.* eraso, erasoaldi, sarreraldi.
indebted *adj.* zordun.
indebtedness *n.* zorreztaketa, zorpe.
indecency *n.* lotsagabekeria, lotsagarrikeria.
indecent *adj.* gordin, lotsagarri, ahalkegarri, lohi.
indecent exposure *n.* biluzkeria.
indecipherable *adj.* ulertezin, igarrezin, irakurgaitz, adierazgaitz.
indecision *n.* ezbaialdi, ezbaidura, erabakiezintasun.
indecisive *adj.* erabakiezin, erabakigabe, eztabaidatsu, ezbaikor, gereino.
indecisively *adv.* kordokan.
indecisiveness *n.* kordoka, kolokaldi.
indeclinable *adj.* deklinaezin.
indeed *int.* alabaina; bai.
indefatigability *n.* aspergaiztasun.
indefatigable *adj.* aspergaitz.
indefensible *adj.* babesgaitz, babestezin.
indefinable *adj.* definigaitz.
indefinite *adj.* zehazkabe, mugagabe.
indefinitely *adv.* epegabeki, mugagabeki, mugagabekiro.
indelible *adj.* ezabaezin, ezabagaitz.
indemnification *n.(econ.)* kalteordain, ordainorde, ordaintzapen, indemnizazio.
indemnify *v.t.* indemnizatu, ordaindu, ordainzkatu, ordainordetu.
indemnity *n.* ordaindiru, indemnizazio, indemnizapen.
indent *v.t./v.i.* hozkatu.
indentation *n.* akats, hozkadura. *n.* pasarte hasierako tarte idatzigabea.
indented *adj.* akastun.
indenture *n.* kontratu.
independence *n.* berjabetasun, berjabetza, independentzia, askatasun, burujabetza.
independent *adj.* berjabe, burujabe, aske.
independently *adv.* askatasunez.
indescribable *adj.* ezinesanezko, izendaezin.
indescribably *adv.* kontaezinez.
indestructibility *n.* suntsiezintasun.
indestructible *adj.* suntsiezin, hautsezin, hondaezin, porrokaezin.
indeterminable *adj.* erabakiezin, erabakiezinezko; zehatzezin.
indeterminate *adj.* mugagabe; zehazkabe.
index *n.* agerbide, aurkibide.
index finger *n. (anat.)* erkin.
Indiana *n. (geog.)* Estatu Batuetako estatu bat.
indicate *v.t.* ezaguerazi, ezagurgarritu.
indication *n.* ezagubide, ezagungarri; susmo.
indicative *adj.* zantzuzko, adierakor. *n. (gram.)* indikatiboera, indikatibo.
indicator *n.* adierazkailu.

indict *v.t.* salatu.
indictment *n.* auzilabur.
indifference *n.* ezaxola.
indifferent *adj.* desarduratsu, ezaxolati, gogogabe.
indifferently *adv.* berezgabeki.
indigence *n.* erromestasun, behargorri, premia, eza.
indigenous *adj.* herriko, herritar.
indigent *adj.* behartsu, txiro.
indigestible *adj.* egosgaitz.
indigestion *n.* egosgaiztasun, oka.
indignant *adj.* sumindu, haserre.
indignation *n.* gaitzidura, sumindura.
indignity *n.* ezduintasun.
indigo *n. (bot.)* anil. *n./adj.* anil, urdinilun.
indirect *adj.* zeharbidezko, zeharkako.
indirectly *adv.* zeharka, zeharka-meharka; hitzerdika.
indiscreet *adj.* ahohandi, zentzugabeko, ahobero, mihiluze.
indiscreetly *adv.* zentzugabeki, sengabeki.
indiscretion *n.* kaskarinkeria, mihiluzekeria.
indiscriminate *adj.* berezgabe.
indiscriminately *adv.* berezgabeki.
indispensable *adj.* premiazko, premiatsu, ezinbesteko, behar-beharrezko, beharrezko, nahitaezko.
indisposed *adj.* ezongi, gaisoka.
indisposition *n.* larritasun, txarraldi, eritasun, gaisotasun, ondoez, larrialdi. *n.* desprestasun.
indisputable *adj.* dudaezin, dudagabeko, ezbaiezin, iritzezin, ukagaitz, gezurtaezin.
indissoluble *adj.* haustezin(ezko), urtezin.
indistinct *adj.* zehazkabe, lainotsu, ikuskaitz.
indistinctly *adv.* berezgabeki.
indistinguishable *adj.* ohartezin, oharkaitz, sumaezin.
indistinguishably *adv.* sumaezinez, ohartezinez.
individual *n.* gizaki, lagun. *adj.* beregisako, beregizko, norberekor.
individualism *n.* norberekoitasun.
individualist *n.* norberekoi.
individuality *n.* gizabakartasun, bakoiztasun, beregaintasun.
individualize *v.t.* nortu, bakoiztu.
individually *adv.* banaka, bat-banaka, gizabakarka.
indivisibility *n.* zatiezintasun, zatigaiztasun.
indivisible *adj.* atalgaitz, zatiezin, zatigabe.
indivisibly *adj.* zatigabeki.
indoctrinate *v.t.* eskolatu, ikaserazi.
indoctrination *n.* irakaspen.
Indo-European *adj.* indoeuropar.
indolence *n.* nagikeria, nagitasun, alferkeria.

indolent *adj.* nagi, alfer, geldo, fardel, soraio.
indolently *adv.* nagiki, nagikiro, alferki, soraioki.
indomitable *adj.* heziezin, hezgaitz, eskuragaitz, menperagaitz, menperaezin.
indomitableness *n.* heziezintasun.
indoor *adj.* barruko, etxebarruko, barneko.
indoors *adv.* barruan, etxebarruan.
indorse *v.t.* txekea izenpetu. *v.t.* onartu, ontzat hartu, baieztu.
indorsement *n.* izenpe. *n.* baieztapen.
indubitable *adj.* dudaezin, ezbaiezin, zalantzaezin, zalantzagabeko.
indubitably *adv.* ezbaigabez.
induce *v.t.* hartaratu, eragin, zirikatu.
inducement *n.* erreklamo.
inducive *adj.* zirikakor.
induction *n.* eragin, eragipen.
indulge *v.t.* mizkindu, balakatu, lausengatu. *v.t.* amor eman.
indulgence *n.* etorkortasun, amore. *n.* barkaberatasun, barkaldi.
indulgent *adj.* bihozdun, baimenkor, guri. *adj.* barkabera, barkazale.
indulgently *adv.* guriki, guriro.
industrial *adj.* industri, industrigintzako, lantegitsu.
industrialist *n.* industriari.
industrialization *n.* industrialeztapen, industrigintza.
industrialize *v.t./v.i.* industrialeztatu, lantegiztatu.
industrially *adv.* industrialki.
industrious *adj.* lankor, lanzale, langile.
industriously *adv.* arduraz.
industriousness *n.* langose, lankortasun, lanzaletasun.
industry *n.* industria.
inebriated *adj.* mozkorti, hordi, mozkor.
inebriation *n.* mozkorkeria, mozkorkeria.
inedible *adj.* janezin, jangaitz.
ineducable *adj.* heziezin.
ineffable *adj.* ezlnesan.
ineffective *adj.* alferreko, eragingabe, indargabe.
ineffectiveness *n.* eragingabetasun, indargabetasun.
ineffectual *adj.* ondoriogabe.
inefficiency *n.* ondoregabezia.
inefficient *adj.* ondoregabe.
inelegant *adj.* zangu-mangu.
inelegibility *n.* hautaezintasun.
inelegible *adj.* hautaezin.
inept *adj.* ezgai, moldagaitz, moldegabe.
ineptitude *n.* ezgaitasun, moldagaizkeria, moldagaiztasun, gauzaeztasun.
ineptly *adv.* moldagaizki, moldegabeki.
ineptness *n.* moldegaiztasun, moldegabetasun.
inequality *n.* ezberdintasun, berdineza.

inequity *n.* bidegabekeria, zuzengabekeria.
inequivocable *adj.* erauztezin.
inert *adj.* bizigabe, arimagabeko.
inertia *n.* *(phys.)* inertzia, ezeragite.
inestimable *adj.* baloraezin.
inevitability *n.* gertabehar.
inevitable *adj.* ezinbesteko, alabeharrezko, nahitaezko, derrigorrezko.
inevitably *adv.* ezinbestean, ezinbestez, nahitaez.
inexact *adj.* zehazkabe. *adj.* faltsu.
inexactness *n.* zehazkabetasun, zehazkabezia.
inexcusable *adj.* desenkusagaitz.
inexhaustible *adj.* agorgaitz, agortezin, ahigaitz.
inexorable *adj.* tinko, malguezin.
inexorably *adv.* gogorki.
inexpensive *adj.* merke.
inexpensively *adv.* merke.
inexperience *n.* trebegabezia, experientzigabezia.
inexperienced *adj.* ezohitu(a), experientzigabe.
inexplicable *adj.* azalgaitz, erakusgaitz.
inexpressible *adj.* esanezin, esanezinezko, ezinesandako.
inexpressive *adj.* adierazkaitz, adieragabe, bizigabe, motel.
inexpressiveness *n.* adieragabetasun, bizigabetasun, molteltasun.
inextinguishable *adj.* iraungigaitz, itzalezin, iraungiezin.
inextricably *adv.* nahas-mahas, nahasian.
infallibility *n.* hutsezintasun, okertezintasun.
infallible *adj.* okerrezin, hutsezin.
infamous *adj.* izentxarreko, laidogarri, doilor, zital.
infamously *adv.* laidogarriro, laidogarriki.
infamy *n.* izentxar, famatxar, laidogarrikeria.
infancy *n.* haurtzaro, haurketa, umetza, umetasun.
infant *n.* haur, sein, bularretako. **Newborn infant.** Haurberri.
infanticide *n.* haurrilketa.
infantile *adj.* haurrantzeko, haurtzaroko.
infantry *n.* oinezkoak (gudari).
infantryman *n.* oinkari (gudari).
infatuate *v.t.* liluratu, lelotu.
infatuation *n.* lilurapen, xarmadura, xoradura.
infect *v.t./v.i.* izurritu, izurreztatu, erantsi.
infected *adj.* izurridun, zoli.
infection *n.* zolitasun, zorne, infekzio.
infectious *adj.* kutsakor, izurridun.
infer *v.t./v.i.* ondoretu, ondorioztatu, antzeman.

inference *n.* antzemate.
inferior *adj.* azpiko, behemailako, beheragoko. *adj.* txarrago.
inferiority *n.* txarragotasun, txikiagotasun. *n.* mendekotasun, azpikotasun, behetasun.
infernal *adj.* infernuko.
inferno *n.* infernu.
inferred *adj.* ondorezko.
infertile *adj.* antzu, emangaitz, ezemankor; idor.
infertility *n.* antzutasun; idortasun.
infest *v.t.* ugaritu, okitu.
infestation *n.* ugaritasun, oparotasun, joritasun, naharotasun.
infested *adj.* ugaritu(a), okitu(a).
infidel *n.* fedegabe, sinesgabe.
infidelity *n.* fedegabetasun, zintzogabetasun.
infield *n.* beisboleko jolaslekuaren zati berezi bat.
infinite *adj.* amaigabe, amaigabeko, azkengabe, mugagabe.
infinitely *adv.* mugagabeki.
infinitesimal *adj.* txiki-txiki.
infinitive *n. (gram.)* infinitibo.
infinity *n.* azkengabetasun, amaigabetasun.
infirm *adj.* gaiso.
infirmary *n.* gaisotegi, erizaindegi, eritegi.
infirmity *n.* gaisotasun, eritasun.
infix *n.* (gram.) artizki.
inflame *v.t./v.i.* su hartu, su eman. *v.t./v.i.* beroarazi, garreztatu, gartu.
inflamed *adj.* garrezko, zoli.
inflammability *n.* garkortasun.
inflammable *adj.* garkor.
inflammation *n. (med.)* gorritune, handidura, erresumindura, gaiztodura, zolitasun.
inflammatory *adj.* subera, suztagarri.
inflatable *adj.* puzgarri.
inflate *v.t./v.i.* puztu, haizatu, airez edo gasez handitu.
inflation *n. (econ.)* inflazio, prezio gorakada.
inflationary *adj.* garestigarri, garestitzaile.
inflection *n.* ahoskatze.
inflexibility *n.* gotortasun, zurruntasun.
inflexible *adj.* amoregaitz, gotor, gotorgarri, malguezin.
inflict *v.t.* inposatu.
infliction *n.* inposaketa.
influence *v.t.* erasan, bultzatu, eragin.
influence *n.* eragin, eragipen, eskuharmen, parteharmen.
influential *adj.* itzaldun, itzalandiko, eragingarri.
influenza *n.* gripe.
influx *n.* jendetorri. *n.* urbieta, urgurutze.
inform *v.t./v.i.* jakinarazi, ezagutarazi, berri eman, argitu.
informal *adj.* informal.

informant *n.* informatzaile, berriemaile, jakinarazle.
information *n.* argibide, informazio.
informative *adj.* informatzaile.
informed *adj.* jakitun, berridun.
informer *n.* jakinarazle, informatzaile. *n.* salatzaile, salatari.
infra- *(gram.)* azpi-.
infraction *n.* arauhauspen, arauhauste, legehauste, legehausketa.
infrastructure *n.* azpiegitura, oinegitura.
infrequent *adj.* noizbehinkako, noizbehingo.
infrequently *adv.* bakanki, bakanka.
infringe *v.t./v.i. (v.i., batzutan on-ekin)* hautsi, urratu, zapaldu, eten (eskubideak, etab.).
infringement *n.* arauhauste.
infuriate *v.t.* haserrerazi.
infuriating *adj.* haserrekor, sumingarri, ahakargarri.
infuse *v.t.* ekinarazi, burutaratu.
infusion *n.* infuzio.
ingenious *adj.* jeinutsu, burutsu, mainatsu, susper, argi.
ingeniously *adv.* buruargiz, jeinuz, mainaz.
ingeniousness *n.* buruargitasun, jeinutasun.
ingenuity *n.* buruargitasun, jeinutasun.
ingenuous *adj.* sineskor, oso.
ingenuousness *n.* lautasun, osotasun, xalokeria, lainokeria.
ingest *v.t.* ahoratu, jan.
inglorious *adj.* aintzagabeko.
ingot *n.* totxo.
ingratiate *v.t. (gehienetan with-ekin)* norbaiten ederra irabazi.
ingratitude *n.* eskertxar, eskergabekeria, eskergaizto, eskergabetasun.
ingredient *n.* osagarri, osakin.
infuriate *v.t.* haserrerazi.
inhabit *v.t.* biztandu, bizi.
inhabitable *adj.* bizigarri.
inhabitant *n.* biztanle, herritar, lagun, egoiliar; -tar.
inhalation *n.* arnasgora.
inhale *v.t./v.i.* arnasgoratu.
inhaler *n.* arnasgailu; arnasgoratzaile.
inharmonious *adj.* abesgaitz.
inherent *adj.* barneko, barruko.
inherit *v.t./v.i.* heredatu, primutu, oinordeko izan, oinordetu, jaruntsi.
inheritable *adj.* jaraunsgarri, heredagarri.
inheritance *n.* seniparte, herentzia, jaraunspen.
inheritor *n.* oinorde, etxaseme, primu.
inhibit *v.t.* oztopatu, galerazi, debekatu.
inhibition *n.* inibizio.
inhospitable *adj.* harreragabe, biziezin, bizigaitz.
inhospitableness *n.* harreragabezia.
inhuman *adj.* bihozgogor,

barrengaizto, ezgizakor, basati.
inhumane *adj.* gizakontrako.
inhumanity *n.* ankertasun,
bihozgabekeria, bihozgogorkeria,
bihozgogortasun,, gizagabetasun.
inhumanly *adv.* desgizonki.
inimical *adj.* etsaiezko.
inimically *adv.* etsaiki.
inimitable *adj.* paregaitz, imitaezin,
irudikagaitz.
iniquity *n.* okertasun, bidegabe.
initial *adj.* haserako, hastapeneko,
lehendabiziko. *adj.* lehenengo letra.
initially *adv.* lehenbizi, lehendabizi,
lehenengotan.
initiate *v.t.* aitzindu, abiarazi.
initiation *n.* sarbidapen-errito,
iniziazio-errito, sarbide-ohikune. *n.*
hasiera, hastapen.
initiative *n.* kabu.
initiator *n.* hasle, abiarazle, hasberri.
inject *v.t.* xiringatu, ziztatu.
injectable *adj.* txertagarri, xiringarri.
injection *n.* xiringada, indizio, txerto,
ziztada.
injunction *n.* auzitegiko agindu(a),
epai-debeku(a).
injure *v.t.* gaizki egin, zauritu,
zauriztatu, kalte egin.
injured *adj.* zauritsu.
injurious *adj.* gaizkor, iraingarri,
iraintsu, laidotsu, galtzegingarri,
galtzikor.
injury *n.* zauri, gaitz, irain, okerkeria,
oker, sakaila.
injustice *n.* bidegabe, bidegabekeria,
makurkeria, okerkeria,
zuzengabekeria, injustizia.
ink *n.* tinta.
inkling *n.* susmo.
inkstand *n.* tintontzi.
inkwell *n.* lumontzi, tintontzi.
inky *adj.* tintadun.
inland *adj.* barneko, barruko. *adv.*
barruan, barnean.
in-law *n.* ezkontzahaide.
inlet *n.* itsasarte, itsasbeso, itsaszoko.
inmate *n.* kide; -kide (espetxean edo
zoroetxean).
inmost *adj.* barrukoen(a).
inn *n.* ostatu, bideostatu, ostaletxe,
benta.
innate *adj.* berezko, jaiotzako,
sortzetiko, jitezko, jatorrizko.
inner *adj.* barne, barrenaldeko,
barren-barrengo, barreneko,
barruko.
innermost *adj.* barne-barneko,
barru-barruko, barrukoen(a).
inning *n.* beisbol taldearen txanda.
innkeeper *n.* ostalari, bentari, ostatari,
ostatuzain.
innkeeping *n.* ostalaritza, ostalgintza.
innocence *n.* errugabetasun,
errugabezia, gaizkabetasun,
hobengabetasun.
innocent *adj.* errugabe, errugabeko,

gaizkabe, hobengabe, okergabe.
innocently *adv.* errugabeki.
innocuous *adj.* kaltegabe.
innocuousness *n.* kaltegabetasun,
kaltegabezia.
innovation *n.* berrikuntza, berrikunde,
berritasun.
innovative *adj.* berri, aurrerakoi,
aldakor.
innovator *n.* berrikuntzari, berritzaile.
innuendo *n.* itzerdi, zeharresan.
innumerable *adj.* kontaezin,
kontagaitz, kontaezinbesteko,
zenbatezin.
inoculate *v.t./v.i.* txertatu, gaiztxertatu,
xiringatu.
inoculation *n.* gaiztxertaketa.
inoffensive *adj.* kaltegabeko,
laidogabeko.
inoperable *n.* ebakiezin. *n.* erabilgaitz.
inoperative *adj.* ekintzagabe.
inopportune *adj.* eragaitz, ezorduko,
ordutxarreko, orduzkanpoko.
inopportunely *adv.* ezorduz.
inopportuneness *n.* desegokitasun,
ezgaraitasun.
inordinate *adj.* gehiegizko.
inordinately *adv.* gehiegi, larregi.
inorganic *adj.* inorganiko, ezorganiko.
inquest *n.* aztarnaketa, inkesta.
inquire *v.t./v.i.* galdetu, aztertu,
inkestatu.
inquirer *n.* galdetzaile, galdegile,
azterkari, inkestalari, inkestatzaile.
inquiring *adj.* galdezka.
inquiringly *adv.* galdezka.
inquiry *n.* aztarnaketa, inkesta,
miaketa.
inquisition *n.* inkisizio.
inquisitive *adj.* azterkor, galdeontzi,
galdetsu, arakakor, miakor.
inquisitively *adv.* jakinguraz.
inquisitor *n.* inkisidore.
inroad *n.* erasoaldi, erasoketa.
insane *adj.* erokeriazko, zoro.
insane asylum *n.* zoroetxe, erotegi,
eroetxe.
insanely *adv.* eroki.
insanity *n.* erotasun, erokeria,
zorakeria, burunahasketa, zorotasun.
insatiability *n.* irenskortasun,
asezintasun, asegabetasun.
insatiable *adj.* asegaitz, asezkor,
betezin, ezinase, sabeldarraio,
sabelkoi.
insatiableness *n.* asegabetasun,
asezintasun, irenskortasun.
insatiably *adv.* asezinik.
inscribe *v.t.* zizelatu, zizeldu. *v.t.*
dedikatu. *v.t.* lerrokatu, lerrotu.
inscription *n.* izenburu, titulu. *n.*
liburuetako eskeintza hitzak.
inscrutable *adj.* barneragaitz,
aztergaitz, barrengaitz, ikergaitz.
insect *n.* zomorro, mamutz, insektu,
mamarro.
insect bite *n.* zimiko.

insecticide n. insektizida.
insectivorous adj. zomorrojale.
insecure adj. seguragaitz.
inseminate v.t. ernamindu, ernaritu, ernarazi.
insensibility n. sorgorkeria, hiltasun.
insensible adj. sengabe, zentzugabe.
insensibly adv. zentzugabeki.
insensitive adj. barrugaizto, sorgor, idor.
insensitively adv. sentiezinik, idorki.
insensitivity n. sorgorkeria, sorgortasun.
inseparable adj. zatigaitz, bakanezin, berezgaitz.
insert v.t. sartu, barneratu, artera sartu, barrensartu, kokatu, tarteratu.
insertion n. artejarrera, artekadura, artezarketa, sarkunde, sarkuntza,sartzapen, tartekapen.
inset n. artejarrera, artezarketa.
inside prep./adv. baitan, barren, barru, barruan, barnean. n. barnetasun, barren, barru, barrualde, barne, barnealde. adj. barruko, barne.
insidious adj. azpizale.
insight n. zuhurtasun, zorroztasun.
insignia n. ezaugarri, domina.
insignificance n. ezerezkeria, txikikeria, huskeria.
insignificant adj. kaskar, purtzil, zirtzil, ttattar.
insincere adj. azalzuri, azaluts.
insincerely adv. toles, toleskeria, tolestasun.
insinuate v.t./v.i. erdiadierazi, berberdi esan.
insinuation n. berberdi, ziztada.
insipid adj. geza, motel, gazkabe, zaporegabe.
insipidity n. gezatasun.
insipidly adv. gazkabeki, gezaki.
insipidness n. motelkeria, moteltasun, gezatasun.
insist v.i./v.t. sar erazi, ekin.
insistence n. ekiera, lehiadura, ekinaldi.
insistent adj. ekile, lehiakor, jardunkor.
insistently adv. lehiaka, lehiatsuki.
insister n. lehiatzaile.
insole n. txantiloi.
insolence n. lotsagabekeria, mutirikeria, ozartasun.
insolent adj. aurpegihandi, mutiri, buruharro, ozar.
insolently adv. handikeriaz, mutiriki, ozarki.
insolubility n. urtuezintasun.
insoluble adj. urtuezin, urtugaitz.
insolubly adv. konponezinik.
insolvency n. kaudimengabezia, ordainezintasun.
insolvent adj. kaudimengabe.
insomnia n. loezinaldi, logabezia, logabetasun.
insomuch adv. (gehienetan as-ekin) -lako, eta, bait-.

inspect v.t. ikusmiratu, ikustatu, miatu.
inspection n. fiskalizapen, inspekzio, ikerketa, ikerpen, miaketa.
inspector n. inspektore, ikerlari, ikerle, miatzaile.
inspiration n. barrendei, goieragin, etorri.
inspire v.t./v.i. isuri, iradoki.
instability n. ezegonkortasun, egongaiztasun, tinkogabezia.
install v.t. kokatu, ezarri.
installation n. ezarketa, ezarpen, muntaia, muntaketa, instalazio.
installer n. ezarlari, ipintzaile, muntatzaile, ezartzaile.
installment n. (econ.) letra.
instance n. gertakizun, gertakari, kasu. n. adibide.
instant n. oldar, aresti, une. adj. berehala prestatzen diren elikagaiak.
instantaneous adj. berehalako, bapateko, kolpeko, uneko.
instantaneously adv. mementoan.
instantly adv. berehalaxe, unean.
instead adv. (batzutan of-ekin) beharrean, lekuan, ordez, orde.
instep n. (anat.) oingain, hankagain, zangabizkar, oingainalde, oinbular.
instigate v.t. narritatu, zirikatu.
instigation n. kitzikadura, narritadura.
instigator n. gaitzeragile, zirikalari, narritatzaile; -erazle, -arazle.
instill v.t. sar erazi, ekin, sorterazi.
instinct n. sen, jite. **The instinct for self-preservation.** Iraupen sena.
instinctive adj. senezko, jitezko.
instinctively adv. jitez, berez.
institute v.t. jaso, ipini, ezarri.
institute n. institutu, instituzio.
institution n. instituzio, erakunde.
institutional adj. erakundezko.
institutionalization n. erakundetze.
institutionalize v.t. erakundetu. v.t. pertsona bat zoroetxera eraman.
instruct v.t. irakatsi, ikaserazi, eskolatu.
instructed adj. eskolatu(a), ikasi(a), jakitun.
instruction n. irakaskintza, irakaspen, eskola, eskolaketa, eskolapen, irakaste.
instructive adj. hezikor, irakasgarri, irakaskor.
instructively adv. irakasbidez.
instructor n. irakasle, irakaslesa.
instrument n. tresna. n. musikatresna, soinugailu.
instrumental adj. erabilgarri, lagungarri, baliagarri. n. (mus.) musika-tresnaz jotako doinua.
instrumentalist n. soinulari, musikalari.
insubordinate adj. managaitz, mendegabea.
insubordination n. desmenderapen, managaiztasun, mendegabetasun.
insubstantial adj. mehe, mengel, iraungabeko.

insufferable adj. pairaezin, pairagaitz, eramanezin, eramangaitz, jasanezin.
insufferably adv. jasanezinez.
insufficiency n. gutiegitasun, gutitasun.
insufficient adj. eznahiko, gutiegi.
insufficiently adv. gutiegi.
insular adj. irlako.
insulate v.t. (elec.) isolatu. v.t. isolatu, bakartu.
insulation n. xingola isolagarri, isolagailu.
insulator n. bakargailu, isolagailu.
insulin n. (med.) intsulina.
insult v.t. iraindu, laidotu.
insult n. irain, laido, lotsagaizto.
insulter n. iraintzaile, laidogile, laidoztatzaile.
insulting adj. iraingarri, iraintzaile, irainkor, laidogarri, lotsagaiztoko.
insultingly adv. laidogarriro, laidoki.
insuperable adj. ezingehiagoko, gaindiezinezko.
insupportable adj. jasangaitz, eramangaitz, eramanezin.
insurance n. asegurantza, aseguru.
insure v.t. aseguratu.
insured adj. asegurudun.
insurer n. aseguratzaile.
insurgent adj. altxatzaile.
insurmountable adj. gaindigaitz, gaindiezinezko.
insurrection n. matxinada, altxamendu.
insurrectional adj. matxinadazko.
intact adj. osorik, oso.
intangible adj. ezinikutuzko, ukiezinezko, ukigaitz.
integer n. zenbaki.
integral adj. osatzaile.
integrate v.t./v.i. integratu.
integration n. integrakuntza, integrazio.
integrity n. osotasun, tenkortasun, sendotasun, orotasun. n. garbitasun, zintzotasun, prestutasun.
intellect n. adimen, ulermen.
intellectual adj. buruzko, intelektual. n. pertsona intelektual(a).
intelligence n. adimen, buruargitasun, gogamen, pentsamen, talentu, ulermen, endelgu, azkartasun.
intelligent adj. buruargi, burutsu, burudun, adimentsu, kaskodun, gogoargi.
intelligently adv. jakintsuki, jakinduriaz, zuhurki.
intelligentsia n. intelektualgo.
intelligibility n. adierreztasun, adigarritasun, ulergarritasun.
intelligible adj. adigarri, gogagarri, ulergarri, ulerterraz, adierazkor, adiezkarri.
intelligibly adv. adigarriki.
intemperance n. eragabekeria, neurrigabekeria (bereziki alkoholdun edariekin).

intemperate adj. gozagabe, gozagaitz.
intend v.t./v.i. asmo izan.
intense adj. min, gorri, bizi.
intensely adv. biziki, azkarki.
intensify v.t./v.i. biziagotu, areagotu.
intensity n. bizidura.
intensive adj. trinko. **The intensive course.** Ikastaro trinkoa.
intensively adv. biziki, bizikiro.
intent adj. lehiadun.
intention n. asmo, nahi; helburu.
intentional adj. nahizko.
intentionally adv. apropos, asmoz, nahita, ohartuki.
intently adv. burubelarri.
inter v.t. hilobiratu, lurperatu, lurra eman, hobiratu.
inter- (gram.) elkar-; -arte.
interaction n. elkarrekintza, elkarreragin.
intercede v.i. bitarteko izan, bitartekotu.
intercept v.t. bideragotzi, ateragotzi.
interception n. arteragozpen.
intercession n. arartekotasun, bitartekotasun, bitartekotza.
interchange v.t./v.i. trukatu, truke egin, elkarraldatu.
interchange n. elkarraldaketa.
interchangeable adj. trukagarri, aldagarri.
intercontinental adj. kontinentarteko, lurrandiarteko.
intercourse n. haragilotura.
interdependence n. lagunaro.
interdependency n. elkarmenderapen, elkarmenpekotasun.
interdict n. (eccl.) elizdebeku.
interdigital adj. behatzarteko.
interest v.t. interesatu.
interest n. (econ.) interes, irabazkin, korritu. n. axola.
interested adj. interesdun.
interesting adj. interesgarri, arduragarri, ardurazko, deigarri.
interfere v.i. (askotan with edo in-ekin) artetu, artenahasi, esku hartu, tartean sartu, tarteratu.
interference n. usnaketa, artenahaste, sarkeria. n. interferentzia.
interim n. tarte, bitarte.
interior adj. barneko, barne, barren, barrenaldeko, barreneko. n. barnatasun, barru, barrualde.
interiorization n. barneratze, barruratze, barrurapen.
interjection n. (gram.) hitzasperen.
interlace v.t./v.i. gurutzelkartu.
interlinear adj. lerroarteko.
interlock v.t./v.i. elkartu, lotu.
interlocutor n. hizketalagun, mintzaide, solaskide.
interloper n. barrendari.
interlude n. tarteko.
intermarriage n. erlijio edo enda ezberdineko pertsonen ezkontza.
intermarry v.i. ezkondu (gehienetan

erlijio edo arraza ezberdineko
pertsonak).

intermaxillary *adj.* masailarteko.

intermediary *n.* ararteko, bitarteko,
artekari.

intermediate *adj.* erdiarteko, erdiko,
tarteko.

interment *n.* ehorzketa, hilobiratze,
lurperaketa, lurremate.

interminable *adj.* bukaezin, bukagaitz,
azkengabe, amaiezin.

interminably *adv.* azkengabeki,
etengabeki, atergabeki.

intermingle *v.t./v.i.* elkartu;
tartenahasi.

intermission *n.* geldiarte, pausarte,
tarte, tartegune.

intermittence *n.* aldiartekotasun,
aldizkotasun, geldiarte, geldiune.

intermittent *adj.* eten, aldiarteko,
aldizkako.

intermittently *adv.* etenka, geldiarteka.

intermix *v.t./v.i.* tartenahasi.

intern *n.* erizain, gaisozain; sendagile
berri(a).

internal *adj.* barne, barnetiko,
barrutiko, barren.

internally *adv.* barnekiro, barrenetik,
baitan, barnez.

international *adj.* nazioarteko,
herrialdearteko.

internationalism *n.* nazioartekotasun.

internationality *n.* nazioartego.

internationalize *v.t.* nazioartekotu.

internationally *adv.* nazio artean,
nazioarteki, nazioarte mailan.

interpenetration *n.* barnekidetasun.

interpersonal *adj.* pertsonarteko.

interplanetary *adj.* planetarteko.

interpose *v.t./v.i.* tartean sartu,
tartekatu.

interpret *v.t./v.i.* adierazi. *v.t.* itzuli.

interpretation *n.* adierazpen, argipen,
adiera, adierazkizun.

interpreter *n.* itzultzaile; adierazle,
irizle.

interracial *adj.* arrazaskotako,
arrazarteko.

interregional *adj.* herrialdearteko,
erregioarteko.

interrelate *v.t.* elkargotu.

interrogate *v.t./v.i.* galdekatu, galde
egin.

interrogation *n.* galdeketa, galdekizun.

interrogative *adj.* galdegarri,
galdetzaile, itaunezko.

interrogator *n.* galdegile, galdekari,
galdetzaile.

interrupt *v.t./v.i.* eten, etenkatu,
geldiarazi, gerarazi.

interrupted *adj.* eten, etenda,
jarraigabe.

interruption *n.* eten, etenaldi,
etendura, geldialdi, geldiune.

intersect *v.t./v.i.* gurutzetu.

intersection *n.* gurutzagune,
gurutzelkardura, kalegurutze,

bidegurutze.

intersperse *v.t.* tartekatu.

interstate *adj.* estatuarteko. *n.*
autobidezabal, autopista.

interstellar *adj.* izarrarteko.

interstice *n.* kraskadura, zirrikitu.

intertwine *v.t./v.i.* gurutzelkartu.

interval *n.* bitarte, tarte, aldiune,
geldiarte, geldialdi.

intervene *v.i. (batzutan in-ekin)* artetu,
bitarteu, tartekatu, tartetu. *v.i.* esku
hartu, esku sartu.

intervention *n.* eskuharmen,
eskusarketa, bitartekotasun,
bitartekotza.

interview *v.t.* elkar ikusi.

interview *n.* elkarrikuste,
elkarrikusketa.

interviewer *n.* elkarrizketari.

interweave *v.t./v.i.* gurutzelkartu.

intestate *adj.* testamentugabeko.

intestinal *adj.* hesteko.

intestine *n. (anat.)* heste, errai.

intimacy *n.* kuttuntasun,
barrengotasun, barrentasun.

intimate *adj.* barnekor, min, barreneko,
begiko.

intimately *adv.* barrenki, minki,
barneki, kuttunki.

intimidate *v.t.* koldartu, kikildu,
txepeldu.

intimidated *adj.* kikil.

intimidating *adj.* izuarazkor, kikilgarri,
larderiazko.

intimidation *n.* larderia, ikaraketa,
izuarazpen.

into *prep.* barrura; -ra.

intolerable *adj.* eramanezin, jasanezin,
jasangaitz, pairaezin, pairagaitz.

intolerably *adv.* jasanezinez,
eramanezinez.

intolerance *n.* eramangaiztasun,
jasangaiztasun.

intolerant *adj.* jasangabe.

intonation *n.* tonuera, doinuera.

intone *v.t./v.i.* doinutu.

intoxicate *v.t.* mozkortu, horditu.

intoxicated *adj.* hordi, mozkor,
mozkorti.

intoxication *n.* horditasun,
mozkortasun.

intra- *(gram.)* -barne, barneko.

intracellular *adj.* zelulabarneko,
zelularteko.

intracranial *adj.* garezurbarneko.

intractable *adj.* tratagaitz.

intramural *adj.* ikastetxebarneko.

intramuscular *adj.* giharbarneko,
giharrarteko.

intransigence *n.* amoregaiztasun,
eramangaiztasun.

intransigent *adj.* jasangabe,
amoregaitz.

intransitive *adj. (gram.)* iragangaitz.

intransmissible *adj.* emanezin,
emangaitz.

intravenous *adj.* zainbarneko,

zainpeko.
intrepid adj. ikaraezin, ikaragaitz, ausarditsu, izukaitz.
intricate adj. korapilatsu.
intrigue n. maneaketa, satorlan.
intrinsic adj. barneko, barru-barruko.
introduce v.t. presentatu, aurkeztu, ezagutarazi. v.t. barneratu.
introduction n. aurkezpen. n. hitzaurre, sarrera, artekadura.
introductory adj. hitzaurreko, sarrerako.
introspection n. barneazterpen, barneikusketa, barrenazterpen.
introvert n. pertsona barrukoi(a). adj. barnekor, barrukor, barrenkoi.
introverted adj. barnekoi, barrukoi, barnerakoi.
intrude v.t./v.i. artean sartu edo esku hartu baimenik gabe.
intruder n. barrendari.
intrusion n. sarkoikeria.
intuit v.t./v.i. barnesusmatu, barrensusmatu.
intuition n. bihozkada, barnesusmaketa, intuizio.
intuitive adj. barrensusmakor.
inundate v.t. murgilarazi, uralditu, uholdetu.
inundation n. uholde, uraldi, uhol.
inure v.t. ohitu.
invade v.t./v.i. gaineraso.
invader n. gainerasotzaile.
invalid adj. baliogabe, ezindu. n./adj. erizahar, herbal.
invalidate v.t. baliogabetu.
invalidation n. ezereztatze.
invalidity n. baliogabetasun, balioeza, baliogabezia.
invaluable adj. baloraezin.
invariability n. aldagaiztasun, desaldaketa, aldaezintasun.
invariable adj. aldaezin, aldagaitz, desaldagarri, betibateko.
invariably adv. aldaezinez, aldagaizkiro, aldaezinik, desaldakorki.
invasion n. gainerasoketa, inbasio.
invent v.t. asmatu, ideiatu, sortu.
invention n. asmaketa, asmakizun, asmapen.
inventive adj. asmodun.
inventiveness n. asmamen.
inventor n. asmakari, asmalari, asmatzaile.
inventory n. gaizerrenda, ondasunak, hornigai.
inverse n. alderantziketa. adj. alderantzizko.
inversely adv. alderantziz.
inversion n. alderantziketa, gainazpiraketa, iraulketa, alderanzketa.
invert v.t./v.i. alderantzitu, azpigoratu, gainbeheratu, itzulikatu.
invertebrate adj. hezurgabeko, ornogabe. **Invertebrate beings.**

Hezurgabeko izakiak. n. abere hezurgabe(a).
invest v.t./v.i. (econ.) (v.i., in) inbertitu.
investigable adj. aztergarri, ikergarri, arakagarri, inkestagarri.
investigate v.t./v.i. galdezkatu, ikertu, ikuskatu, miatu, txerkatu, aztertu, arakatu.
investigation n. araketa, azterketa, ikerketa, inkesta; mintegi, miaketa.
investigative adj. ikerkor.
investigator n. ikertzaile, ikerketari, ikerle, arakatzaile, azterlari, inkestatzaile, azterkatzaile.
investment n. (econ.) inbertsio.
investor n. inbertitzaile.
invigorate v.t. indartu, indarztatu, indarberritu.
invigorating adj. biziarazle, bizkortzaile, bizkorgarri, zuzpergarri.
invincibility n. garaiezintasun.
invincible adj. garaiezin, menderaezin.
invincibly adv. garaiezinez, menderaezinez.
inviolate adj. ukigabe.
invisibility n. ikusezin, ikusezintasun.
invisible adj. ikuskaitz, ezikuskor, ikusezin.
invitation n. dei.
invite v.t./v.i. gonbidatu, gomitatu, deitu, dei egin.
invited adj. deitu(a); -tiar, -liar.
inviter n. deitzaile, gonbidatzaile.
inviting adj. atsegingarri, xarmangarri, tiragarri.
invocation n. oles.
invoice n. faktura, zorkontu.
invoke v.t. oles egin, dei egin.
invoker n. deitzaile, deiegile, hotsegile.
involuntarily adv. indarka, desgogoz.
involuntary adj. desgogozko, guraezezko, nahigabeko.
involve v.t. mordoildu, nahasi.
involved adj. nahasi(a), mordoildu(a).
involvement n. konpromisu, nahaspila.
invulnerable adj. zauriezin.
inward adv./adj. barrura, barnera.
iodine n. (chem.) iodo.
ion n. (phys., chem.) ion.
I.O.U. n. ordainagindu, ordainagiri, ordainbide, ordaintxartel, zorragiri.
Iowa n. (geog.) Estatu Batuetako estatu bat.
irascibility n. haserrekoitasun, haserrekortasun, suminkortasun, sumintasun.
irascible adj. haserrekoi, haserrekor, suminkoi, suminkor, kakerre.
irate adj. sukoi, sukor, haserrekor.
ire n. haserre, sumin.
Ireland n.(geog.) Irlanda.
iridescent adj. islatu(a), disdiratsu.
iris n. (anat.) beginini. n. zitori, lirio.
Irish n./adj. irlandar n. irlandera.
irk v.t. nekarazi, gogaitarazi, ernegatu.
irksome adj. ernegagarri.
iron v.t./v.i. lisatu, plantxatu.

iron *n.* burdina. *n.* lisakin, plantxa. *adj.* burdinazko.
ironclad *adj.* burdinez babestu(a).
ironic *adj.* ironiatsu, ziztakari.
ironically *adv.* ironiaz.
ironing *n.* lisaldi, plantxaldi, lisaketa.
irony *n.* ironia, eztenkada.
irradiate *v.t./v.i.* irradiatu.
irradiation *n.* arraiobihurtza, irradiazio.
irrational *adj.* adimengabe, zentzugabeko, arrazoingabeko.
irrationality *n.* arrazoingabekeria, desarrazoin, zentzugabetasun.
irrationally *adv.* arrazoingabeki, zuzengabeki.
irreconcilable *adj.* adiskidegaitz, baketuezin, bateraezin, bateragaitz.
irrecoverable *adj.* berreskuraezin.
irredeemable *adj.* berrerosezin.
irrefutable *adj.* gezurtaezin, erantzunezin, ezeztaezin.
irregular *adj.* eragabe, gisagabe, itxuragabeko, malkartsu. *adj.* araugabeko.
irregularity *n.* eragabetasun, gisagabetasun. *n.* araugabetasun, araugabezia.
irregularly *adv.* araugabeki, segidagabeki.
irrelevant *adj.* desegoki.
irreligious *adj.* erlijiogabe, erlijiogabeko.
irremediable *adj.* erremediaezinezko.
irreparable *adj.* konponezin.
irreparably *adv.* konponezinik.
irreplaceable *adj.* ordezkaezin, ordeztezin.
irrepressible *adj.* eskuragaitz, managaitz, kontrolgaitz. *adj.* pozkor.
irreproachable *adj.* errugabe, akaskabe.
irresistible *adj.* kontraezin, euskaitz, jarkiezin.
irresistibly *adv.* jarkiezinez, kontraezinez.
irresponsibility *n.* txoriburukeria.
irresponsible *adj.* burugabe, txoriburu, kaskarin, ergel, inozo.
irresponsibly *adv.* burugabeki.
irretrievable *adj.* berreskuraezin, kobraezin.
irreverence *n.* itzalgabekeria, desbegirune.
irreverent *adj.* itzalgabe, lotsagabe, begirunegabe.
irreverently *adv.* desbegirunez, lotsagabeki.
irreversible *adj.* itzulezin, atzeraezin, bihurtezin.
irrevocable *adj.* atzeraezin, etenezin.
irrigatable *adj.* ureztagarri.
irrigate *v.t.* garastatu, ureztatu.
irrigation *n.* ureztaketa.
irritability *n.* haserrekortasun, suminkortasun.
irritable *adj.* suminbera, errebera, frakerre, haserrekor.

irritably *adv.* suminki.
irritableness *n.* suminkortasun.
irritant *n.* samurrarazle.
irritate *v.t.* haserrerazi, suminarazi, amorrarazi, erresumindu.
irritated *adj.* haserretsu, haserrekoi.
irritating *adj.* haserregarri, sumingarri, erresumingarri, saminkor, erremingarri.
irritation *n.* erresumindura, erretxindura, sumindura.
irritator *n.* haserrerazle, samurrarazle.
is *pres.* da, dago. *Cf. be.*
Islam *n.* islam, mairuerlijio.
Islamic *adj.* islamiar.
island *n.* irla, uharte, izaro. *adj.* uharteko.
islander *n.* irlatar.
isle *n.* irlatxo, irla, uharte.
islet *n.* irlatxo.
isn't "is + not"-aren laburpena.
isolatable *adj.* bakangarri, isolagarri.
isolate *v.t.* isolatu, bakartu, banandu, bakarreratu, banakatu.
isolated *adj.* bakar, bakartu(a), banandu(a).
isolation *n.* bakarketa, bakartasun, isolamendu.
isothermal *adj.* beroberdindun.
issue *v.t.* eman, hornitu. *v.i.* irten; isuri, jario. *v.i.* (**from**) etorri, sortu. *v.t.* argitaratu.
issue *n.* arazo. *n.* banaketa. *n.* ale (aldizkari), zenbaki. *n.* ondorengo, umeteria.
isthmus *n.* istmo, lurzintzur.
it *pron.* hura, bera. *n.* kirikari.
itch *n.* hazgale, hazkura, haznahi.
itching *n.* hazkura, zanbro, errasumin. *adj.* hazkuratsu.
itchy *adj.* hazkuratsu.
item *n.* gauza.
itemizable *adj.* zehaztagarri.
itinerary *n.* ibilkizun, ibilbide.
its *pron.* bere, haren.
it's "it + is"-aren laburpena.
itself *pron.* bere buru; berbera.
itsy-bitsy *adj.* ttipitto, txikitxo.
I've "I + have"-aren laburpena.
ivory *n.* boli, marfil. *adj.* bolizko, marfilezko.
ivy *n.* (*bot.*) huntzadar, huntz.

J

j *n.* Ingeles alfabetoko letra.
jab *v.t./v.i.* ziztatu, ziztakatu, zirikatu.
jab *n.* ukabilkada, ukaldi.
jabber *v.i.* mintzatu, hitz egin.
jabber *n.* ziztatzaile. *n.* zentzugabeko hizketa.
jabbering *adj.* kalaka.
jack *n.* txanka.
jackal *n.* (*zool.*) txakal.
jackass *n.* (*zool.*) asto.
jacket *n.* jaka, txamarra.
jackhammer *n.* urragailu.
jack-of-all-trades *n.* oroegile.

jacks n. tortolos.

jade n. (min.) jade.

jagged adj. koskadun, hortzdun.

jaguar n. (zool.) jaguar.

jai alai n. zezta, zezta-pilota.

jail v.t. gartzelaratu, espetxeratu, itzalperatu.

jail n. espetxe, gartzela, presondegi, ilunpe.

jailer n. espetxezain, presondegizain, presozain, gartzelari.

jalopy n. kotxe zahar.

jam n. nahaste-borraste, itobehar, nahaspila, nahastakeria. n. mermelada.

jamb n. atezango.

jamboree n. festa, jai.

jangle v.t./v.i. giltz-zarata egin, arranak jo.

jangle n. giltzots.

janitor n. labairu.

January n. urtarrila, ilbeltz.

jar n. pitxer, pegar.

jarful n. pitxerkada.

jargon n. erderamordoilo.

jasmine n. (bot.) krasmin.

jasper n. (min.) harrinabar.

jaundice n. (med.) minori, larumin.

jaundiced adj. lauremindun, minoridun.

jaunt n. ibilaldi.

jaunty adj. adoretsu.

javelin n. txabalina.

jaw n. matela, matelezur.

jawbone n. (anat.) masailezur, matelezur.

jay n. (zool.) bela antzeko txori bat.

jazz n. (mus.) jazz.

jealous adj. jelos, jeloskor, bekaizti, bekaizkor.

jealously adv. bekaizki.

jealousy n. jelosia, bekaitz.

jeans n. Levi's frakak, fraka bakeroak.

jeep n. jeep.

jeer v.i./v.t. txistukatu.

jeer n. iseka, trufa.

jelly n. mermelada.

jellyfish n. (zool.) marmoka.

jenny n. -eme; asteme.

jeopardize v.t. arriskuan jarri.

jeopardy n. arrisku.

jerk v.t./v.i. bapatean teink egin; bapatean mugitu, zirkin egin.

jerk n. iharrausaldi.

jerky n. gatzartu, zezin.

jest v.i. trufatu, trufa egin.

jest n. irri, iseka, trufa, txantxa.

jester n. irrigile.

jet n. jet (hegazkin).

jetty n. uhinurrategi.

Jew n. judu.

jewel n. harribizi, harribitxi.

jeweler n. bitxigile, bitxisaltzaile.

jewelry n. zilarreria, zilarteria, bitxiteria.

Jewish adj. judu, judutar.

jew's-harp n. (mus.) tronpa.

jiffy n. unetxo.

jig n. dantza arin eta bizia.

jingle v.i./v.t. giltz-zarata egin, arranak jo.

jingle n. giltzots. n. iragarki merkagarrietan erabiltzen den kanta labur bat.

jinx n. suerte txarra ekartzen duen pertsona edo gauza.

jitteriness n. urdurikeria, urduritasun.

jittery adj. urduri, frakerre, pirri.

job n. lanpostu, lanbide, ogibide, irabazbide, bizibide, lan.

jockey n. zaldilasterkari, zaldigaineko, zaldikari, zamaldun.

jocular adj. irrieragile.

jocularity n. irrikortasun, barregarritasun.

jog v.i. poliki korrika egin.

john n. komuna. n. putazale.

join v.t./v.i. batu, lokarritu, bateratu, mihiztatu. v.t./v.i. elkarbatu, elkarbildu, elkarganatu, elkar lotu, elkartu, elkarkidetu, partzuertu, lagunartetu, taldekatu.

joinable adj. lotugarri.

joined adj. bategin(a), batuta.

joiner n. elkartzaile.

joint n. (anat.) giltza, giltzadura, hezurgiltza, hezurgiltzadura. n. elkarrune; lotune.

jointly adv. batera, elkarki, elkarturik.

joist n. gapirio.

joke v.i./v.t. trufatu, trufa egin, txantxatu, iseka egin, turrut egin.

joke n. irri, iseka, txantxa, trufa, trufakeria, xelebrekeria.

joker n. irrigile, irrilari, isekari, trufari, txantxari.

joking adj. txantxetako, txantxetan, olgetan.

jokingly adv. farregarriro, barregarriro, isekaz, trufaka, txantxetan.

jolly adv. barrezale, barretsu, airos, irrigura.

jolt v.t./v.i. binbilikatu.

jostle v.t./v.i. bultzatu, bultz egin.

jot v.t. azkar idatzi.

jota n. jota.

journal n. kazeta, egunkari.

journalism n. kazetalgo, kazetaritza.

journalist n. kazetari.

journalistic adj. kazetarizko, kazetazko.

journey n. bidaia, ibiltaldi.

joust v.i. burrukatu (zaldun), jostagudu egin.

joust n. zaldunborroka, zaldungudu, jostagudu.

jovial adj. gogoalai, iaio, irrieragile, jostazale.

joviality n. gogoalaitasun.

jovially adv. pozik, alaiki, pozez.

jowl n. masail.

joy n. poz, atsegin, bozkario, loria, poztasun, alaitasun, gozamen.

joyful adj. alai, alaitsu, alaigarri, bozkari, bozkariogarri, bozkariotsu, pozkor.

joyfully adv. alaiki, alaikiro, bozkarioz, pozez, pozgarriro, pozik.
joyfulness n. alaitasun.
joyless adj. pozkabe.
joyous adj. alaitzaile, alaitsu.
joyously adv. alaiki, alaikiro, pozik.
joyousness n. alaitasun, poztasun.
Jr. Cf. junior.
jubilant adj. pozezko.
jubilation n. pozikara, pozaldi, pozbizi, zoramen.
jubilee n. (eccl.) barkamenurte.
judge v.t./v.i. epaitu, epaipetu, jujatu.
judge n. epaile, auziepaile, juje. n. iritzemale, irizle, erabakitzaile.
judgement n. ezagumen, zentzu. n. epai, epaiketa, epaikuntza, epaierabaki, jujamendu. n. iritzi, irizpide.
judicable adj. epaigarri.
judicial adj. epaiezko, epaibidezko, legezko.
judicially adv. epaibidez.
judiciary adj. epaiezko. n. epaikaritza; epailetalde.
judicious adj. burudun, burutsu.
judiciously adv. arrazoinbidez, zentzuz, zentzuzki.
judiciousness n. begiratasun.
jug n. pegar, pitxer.
juggle v.i./v.t. malabar-jolasak egin.
juggler n. malabarista.
jugular n. (anat.) lepazain.
juice n. zuku, zumo, ur.
juicer n. zukugailu.
juiciest adj. -(r)ik urtsuen(a).
juiciness n. urtsutasun.
juicy adj. urtsu, zukutsu, zumotsu.
July n. uztaila.
jumble n. txokorreria, murgil, nahaste-borraste.
jump v.i./v.t. saltatu, salto egin, saltokatu, jauzi, jauzi egin.
jump n. jauzi, salto, saltaketa.
jumper n. jauzilari, saltari. n. emakumeen soineko mota bat.
jumpiness n. urduritasun, zolitasun.
jumpy adj. urduritsu, zoli, odolbizi.
junction n. bidegurutze, bidarte.
juncture n. elkargune, elkarpide.
June n. ekaina.
jungle n. oihan.
junior adj./n. gazte. n. unibertsitate eta goieskoletako hirugarren urteko ikaslea.
juniper n. (bot.) ipuru.
junk n. txatar.
junket n. atseginezko bidaia.
junkyard n. txatxartegi.
Jupiter n. (astron.) Jupiter.
juridical adj. legearauzko.
jurisdiction n. eskuera, eskubidetasun, eskubidetza, legemende. n. barruti.
jurisprudence n. legejakintza, legetza.
jurist n. legelari.
juror n. Estatu Batuetako hamabi kidez

osaturiko epaimahaiko lagun bat.
jury n. Estatu Batuetako auzitegietan hamabi kidez osaturiko epaimahia.
just adj. eskubidezko, zuzenbidezko. adj. justu, zuzen. adv. unealditxo bat aurrera, goiztxoago. adj. doi-doi, ozta-ozta.
justice n. justizia, zuzentasun, zuzenbide.
justifiable adj. zurigarri.
justification n. egiztabide, zuzenespen.
justify v.t. zuzenetsi, gainzuritu, edertu.
justly adv. zuzenbidez, zuzenki.
juvenile adj. gaztaroko.
juxtaposition n. elkarjarrera.

K

k n. Ingeles alfabetoko letra.
kale n. (bot.) aza.
kaleidoscope n. kalidoskopio.
kangaroo n. kanguru.
Kansas n. (geog.) Estatu Batuetako estatu bat.
kaolin n. toska.
karate n. karate.
kayak n. eskimalen kanoa.
keel n. gila.
keen adj. zoli, gogoerne, zorrotz.
keenly adv. zoliki, zorrozki, zorrozkiro.
keenness n. gogoargitasun, zorroztasun.
keep v.t. gorde, zaindu, mantendu, eduki, bete. v.i. (at edo on-ekin) jarraitu, segitu, ekin. v.t. begiratu, babestu. **To keep a promise.** Hitz emana eduki. **To keep it up.** Ez eten. **Keep out!** Ez sartu! **To keep tabs on.** Begiratu. Begira egon. **For keeps.** Betirako. **To earn one's keep.** Bizia atera. Bizibidea atera. **To play for keeps.** Benetan jokatu.
keeper n. begirale, begiratzaile, zain, zaindari, zaintzaile.
keg n. upeltxo.
kennel n. txakurtoki, zakurtegi.
Kentucky n. (geog.) Estatu Batuetako estatu bat.
kept adj. zainpeko. pret./p.part. of keep.
kerchief n. mukizapi, sudurzapi.
kernel n. mihuri, artale.
kerosene n. keroseno.
ketch n. bateltxo.
kettle n. lapiko.
key n. giltza, gako. **Master key.** Giltza nagusi. n. (mus.) gako, giltza; tekla; tonuera. n. giltzarri.
keyboard n. teklatu.
keychain n. giltzuztai, giltzatako.
keyhole n. sarrailtzulo.
keystone n. gainarri, arkugiltza, harrigiltza.
khaki n. kaki.
kick v.t./v.i. ostikatu, ostikokatu.
kick n. zangokada, hankapuntako,

ostiko, ostikada.
kicker *n.* ostikalari, ostikari,
ostikatzaile.
kid *v.t./v.i.* adarra jo, txantxatu,
txantxetan egon.
kid *n.* ahuntzume. *n.* haur, sein, ume.
kidnap *v.t.* bahitu (pertsona).
kidnapper *n.* gizebasle, bahitzaile.
kidnapping *n.* bahikuntza, bahimendu,
bahitura (pertsona).
kidney *n. (anat.)* giltzurrun.
kill *v.t./v.i.* hil, hilarazi, sarraskitu.
killer *n.* gizahiltzaile, hiltzaile,
gizaeraile.
killer whale *n. (zool.)* orka.
killing *n.* hilketa.
kiln *n.* labe.
kilogram *n.* kilo.
kilometer *n.* kilometro.
kilowatt *n. (elec.)* kilobatio.
kilt *n.* eskoziar gona.
kimono *n.* kimono.
kin *n.* ahaidego.
kind *adj.* bihotzoneko, bihozbigun,
onbera, onzale. *n.* klase, mota, era.
kindergarten *n.* haurlilitegi, haurtegi,
umetegi, haurreskola.
kindle *v.t./v.i.* su eman, su hartu.
kindling *n.* sorta.
kindly *adj./adv.* bihotzonez, onean.
kindness *n.* harreratasun, onginahi,
onzaletasun, ontasun.
kindred *n.* ahaidego, ahaideria. *adj.*
antzeko.
kinetic *n.* zinetiko.
kinfolk *n.* senitarte.
king *n.* errege, bakaldun.
kingdom *n.* erreinu, erresuma.
kingfisher *n. (zool.)* martinarrantzale.
kinglet *n. (zool.)* erregetxo,
txorierrege.
kinky *adj.* kirru, kizkur.
kinship *n.* ahaidego, ahaidetasun,
odolkidego, odolkidetasun, askazgo.
kiosk *n.* kiosko.
kiss *v.t./v.i.* musu eman, pot eman,
laztan egin, laztandu.
kiss *n.* laztan, musu, apa.
kisser *n.* musuemaile, musukari, potari.
kit *n.* -kume. *n.* erreminta-kutxa.
kitchen *n.* sutondo, sukalde, ezkaratz.
kitchenette *n.* sutondotxo, sukaldetxo.
kite *n. (zool.)* miru. *n.* kometa.
kitten *n.* katakume.
kitty *n.* katakume, katu. *int.* biz-biz!
miz!
kleptomania *n.* lapurzalekeria.
kleptomaniac *adj.* lapurzale.
knack *n.* maina.
knapsack *n.* fardel, saka, motxila.
knapweed *n. (bot.)* mandabelar.
knave *n.* txanka. *n.* gizon gaizto.
knavery *n.* gizatxarkeria, okerreria.
knead *v.t.* oratu; eskuztatu.
knee *n. (anat.)* belaun.
kneecap *n. (anat.)* belaunburu,
belaunezur, belaunkonkor.

kneel *v.i.* belaunikatu, belauniko egon.
kneepad *n.* belaunetako, belaunbabes.
knell *n.* kanpaihots. **Death knell.**
Hilkanpai. Hilezkila.
knife *n.* aizto, ganibet(a), labaina,
sastakai.
knifer *n.* sastakari.
knight *v.t.* zaldundu.
knight *n.* zaldun.
knighthood *n.* zalduneria.
knit *v.t./v.i.* trikotatu, puntu egin,
oihaldu.
knit *n.* trikota.
knitting *n.* trikota.
knob *n.* kisket.
knock *v.t./v.i.* jo, atejo. *v.t.* **(over)**
eratzan, uzkail. *v.t.* **(down)** eragotzi,
eraitsi. *v.t.* **(out)** K.O. utzi;
lekugabetu, atera.
knock *n.* joaldi, kisketots. **Knock,
knock!** Dan, dan!
knocker *n.* atejoki, kisket, aldaba.
knocking *n.* kisketots.
knock-kneed *adj.* hankoker, zangoker.
knockout *n.* K.O.
knoll *n.* bizkartontor, lurtontor,
lurbizkar.
knot *v.t./v.i.* korapilatu.
knot *n.* korapilo, lokarrimendu. *n.*
adabegi, lakar, araka.
knottiness *n.* korapiltasun.
knotty *adj.* korapilotsu. *adj.*
adarbegidun.
know *v.t./v.i.* jakin. *v.t.* ezagutu.
knowingly *adv.* jakinean, jakinik,
jakitez.
know-it-all *adj.* sasijakitun, sasijakintsu.
knowledge *n.* jakinduria, jakintza,
jakite; ezaguera.
knowledgeable *adj.* jakintsu, jakile.
known *adj.* ezagun, jakin.
knuckle *n.* eribizkar.
koala *n. (zool.)* koala.
kosher *adj.* rabinoak bedeinkatutako
(janaria).

L

l *n.* Ingeles alfabetoko letra.
lab *n.* laborategi.
label *v.t.* etiketatu.
label *n.* etiketa.
labial *adj.* ezpaineko.
labiodental *adj.* hortzezpaineko.
labor *n.* lan. *n.* haurgintza, erditzapen,
haurmin.
laboratory *n.* laborategi.
laborer *n.* langile. *n.* lurlangile,
lurlantzaile.
laborious *adj.* lehiati, zailtsu.
laboriously *adv.* eginahalez.
laboriousness *n.* lehia, joran.
labor party *n. (pol.)* langile alderdi.
labor union *n.* sindikato.
Labourd *n. (geog.)* Lapurdi.
Labourdin *n./adj.* lapurtar. *n.* lapurtera.
labyrinth *n.* galgune, irtenezin.
lace *v.t./v.i.* josi, amarratu.

lace n. lokarri. n. sare, burukosare.
lacerate v.t. zauritu.
laceration n. zirri-zarra.
lachrymal adj. negarrezko.
lachrymose adj. negarreragile.
lack v.t./v.i. falta izan, faltatu, gabetu.
lack n. eza, gabekeria, gabetasun, gabezia, eskastasun, gutiezia.
lackadaisical adj. galtzandi, galtzajario.
lackey n. zerbitzari, mendeko.
lacking adj. gabezko.
laconic adj. hizgutiko.
lacquer v.t. txaroldu.
lacquer n. txarol.
lactation n. esneketa, edoskitzaro.
lacy adj. burusareantzeko.
lad n. mutil, mutilkoskor.
ladder n. eskilara.
laden adj. zamadun, kargadun.
ladle n. zali. **Iron ladle.** Burduntzali.
lady n. andre, emakume.
ladybug n. (zool.) amona mantalgorri, amona gonagorri.
lag v.i. astiro joan, atzeratu, gibeleratu.
laggard adj. gibelkoi.
laggardliness n. gibelkoitasun.
laggardly adv./adj. atzerakoi, gibelkoi.
lagoon n. itsasaintzira.
laicism n. laizismo.
laid p. part. of lay.
lain p. part. of lie.
lair n. zulo, ohatze.
laity n. laikotasun.
lake n. zingira.
lamb n. bildots, arkume, atxuri; bildos-. n. bildoski.
lame adj. mainger, herren, zangomotz.
lamely adv. mainguka, herrenka.
lameness n. herrenketa, herrenkura, herrentasun, maingutasun.
lament v.t./v.i. aienekatu, auhendatu, deitoratu, zinkurinatu, aika ari.
lament n. aiene, deitore.
lamentable adj. negargarri, tamalgarri, deitoragarri, penagarri.
lamentably adv. penagarriro.
lamentation n. deitore, aiene.
laminable adj. xaflagarri.
laminate v.t./v.i. xaflatu.
lamination n. xafladura, xaflaketa, xaflalan.
laminator n. xaflagile.
lamp n. argizuzi, argiontzi, lanpara.
lamplighter n. farolari, piztaile.
lance v.t. lantzakatu.
lance n. lantza.
lancer n. lantzari.
lancet n. odolustailu.
land v.t./v.i. lehorreratu, lurreratu, lurra hartu.
land n. lur, lehor. adj. lurtar.
landed adj. ondasundun, ondasuntsu.
landing n. lurrerakela, lehorrerakela, lehorrerapen. n. mailadiburu, mailarte.
landing strip n. aireportuko pista.
landlady n. errentazaile, lurjabe

(emakume).
landlord n. errentazaile, lurjabe (gizon).
landlubber n. lehortar.
landmark n. harrimuga, mugarri, mugarrieta, zedarri.
landowner n. lurjabe, lurdun.
landscape n. ikuspegi, paisaia.
landslide n. lurjausi, luperia, lurreten.
landward adv./adj. lehorreraruntz.
lane n. kalestu, zeharkale.
language n. hizkuntza, hizkera, mintzaira, mintzo. **Foreign language.** Erdara.
languid adj. alfer, nagi, ahul, makal.
languidly adv. alferki, nagikiro, nagiki.
languidness n. nagitasun.
languish v.i. ahuldu, makaldu, indargabetu.
languor n. makaltasun, ahultasun, herbaltasun.
lanky adj. luzanga.
lantern n. gauargi, linterna, farol.
lap n. magal, altzo.
lapel n. mendel.
lapful n. altzokada.
lapse n. tarte. n. beherapen. n. iraungipen.
lapwing n. (zool.) hegabera.
larceny n. litxarreria.
lard v.t. urindu, urineztatu, urdaiztatu.
lard n. gantz, gantzu.
larder n. jakitegi.
larder beetle n. (zool.) zeden.
large adj. handi, ikaragarri.
largely adv. handiki, handikiro.
largeness n. handiera.
larger adj. (comp.) handiago.
largess(e) n. eskuzabaltasun.
largest adj. -(r)ik handien(a).
lark n. (zool.) larretxori, pirripio.
larva n. (zool.) beldar.
larval adj. eltxar ituxrazko.
laryngitis n. (med.) eztarmin, zintzurmin, zintzurreri.
larynx n. (anat.) eztarri.
lascivious adj. haragikor, lizun, lizunbera, likits.
lasciviously adj. lizunki, zantarki, gordinki.
lasciviousness n. lizunkeria, haragikeria, haragizalekeria, lizunkoikeria, likiskeria.
laser n./adj. laser.
lash v.t./v.i. hagakatu, zanbrotu, zartakatu. v.t. lotu.
lash n. zanbro, zartagailu.
lass n. neska.
lasso n. zaldiak harrapatzeko soka luzea.
last v.i./v.t. (askotan out-ekin) iraun.
last adj. azken, azkenengo, hondar. **Next to the last.** Azkenurren.
lasting adj. iraunkor, irauti, iragangaitz, luzaroko.
lastly adv. azkenik.
last name n. abizen, deitura,

izenondoko.
last night *adv.* bart, barda.
last rites *n. (eccl.)* elizakoak,
azkenigurtzi.
last will and testament *n.* azkenahi,
azkenagiri.
latch *n.* kalaka, kisket, maratila.
late *adj.* berankor, beranduko,
berantiar. *adj.* zen. *adv.* berandu,
berant.
lately *adv.* aspaldion.
lateness *n.* berandutasun.
latent *adj.* ezkutuko.
later *adv.* gero, geroago. **A little later.**
Gerotxoago. *adj.* geroagoko.
lateral *adj.* aldeko.
laterally *adv.* alboko, aldameneko;
albotik, aldamenetik.
lath *n.* listoi.
lathe *n.* tornu, estoka.
lathe operator *n.* estokari, tornulari.
lather *v.t./v.i.* xaboitu.
lather *n.* xaboibitsa.
Latin *n.* latin, latinera. *adj.* latindar,
latinezko.
Latin America *n.* Hegoamerika,
Latinamerika.
Latin American *adj.* hegoamerikar,
latinamerikar.
latitude *n. (geog.)* latitude. *n.* zabalgo.
latter *adj.* azken, bigarren. *adj.*
gerozko, ondorengo, arrezkeroko.
latrine *n.* komun, kakategi.
Latvia *n. (geog.)* Letonia.
laud *v.t.* laudatu, laudoriotu.
laudable *adj.* laudagarri, ospagarri,
ohoragarri.
laudably *adv.* laudagarriki.
laudatory *adj.* laudoriotsu.
lauded *adj.* lausengutsu.
laudibly *adv.* goragarriki, goragarriro.
laugh *v.i./v.t.* barre egin, irri egin.
laugh *n.* barre.
laughable *adj.* barregarri, irrigarri.
laughableness *n.* barregarrikeria,
irrigarritasun.
laughably *adv.* barregarriro, irrigarriro.
laughing *n.* barre. *adj.* barrez,
barrezale.
laughingly *adv.* barrez, farrez,
barreka.
laughter *n.* barre, irri, algara.
launch *v.t.* uretaratu, bota, jaurti.
v.t./v.i. hasi.
launch *n.* botaketa. *n.* txalupa,
itsasontzitxo, untzixka.
launching *n.* botaketa.
launder *v.t.* jantziak garbitu, erropak
garbitu, lisiba egin.
launderette *n.* ikuztegi, garbitoki.
laundress *n.* latsari.
laundry *n.* lisiba, erropa. *n.* garbileku,
ikuzleku, zapigarbitegi.
laureate *adj.* saritu, ereinostun.
laurel *n. (bot.)* erramu, ereinotz.
lava *n.* laba, garmendiko harriurtu(a).
lavatory *n.* komun.

lavender *n. (bot.)* izpiliku.
lavish *adj.* bonbontzaile.
lavishly *adv.* bonbonka, parra-parra.
lavishness *n.* diruhondaketa, dirujario,
diruxahuketa, bonbonkeria.
law *n.* lege, erregela. **Old Basque
laws.** Foruak. **To break the law.**
Legea hautsi. **Under the law.**
Legepean. *n.* legegizontza,
legejakintza, abogadutza.
law-abiding *adj.* legegordetzaile,
legebetetzaile.
lawbreaker *n.* legehausle.
lawful *adj.* legezko, legebidezko,
araubidezko, zilegi.
lawfully *adv.* legebidez, legez,
araubidez, zilegiki.
lawfulness *n.* legebidetasun,
arauzaletasun, zilegitasun.
lawgiver *n.* legemale.
lawless *adj.* legegabe, legegabeko. **To
be lawless.** Legegabetu.
lawlessness *n.* legegabezia.
lawmaker *n.* legegile.
lawn *n.* belardi.
lawsuit *n.* auzi.
lawyer *n.* legegizon, abogadu.
lax *adj.* lasai, lasaiegi.
laxative *n.* hestegarbikin, garbigai,
libragarri. *adj.* lasagarri, aringarri.
laxity *n.* errazkeria, lasaikuntza.
laxly *adv.* lazoki.
laxness *n.* lasaitasun, lazokeria.
lay *v.t.* eratzan, utzi, ipini. *v.i.* errun,
arrautza egin. *pret. of lie (*etzan*)*
lay *adj.* laiko, seglar.
layer *n.* geruza.
layered *adj.* geruzadun.
layette *n.* jaioberriaren atu(a).
laying hen *n.* oilo errule.
layman *n.* laiko.
layoff *n.* lantegiko botaketa,
kargukentze.
layout *n.* eskema; antolaketa;
banaketa.
laywoman *n.* laiko.
lazily *adv.* alferki, nagiki, nagikiro.
laziness *n.* alferkeria, nagikeria,
geldotasun, nagitasun, zurikeria.
lazy *adj.* alfer, nagi, nagitsu, zuri,
geldo, fardel.
lb. *Cf. pound.*
lea *n.* belardi, larre, belartza.
lead *v.t./v.i.* gidatu, bideratu. *v.t./v.i.*
buru izan, buru egin.
lead *n.* aurreko leku. *n.* berun, plomu.
n. hede, uhal. *n.* antzerkiaren rolik
garrantzitsuena. *adj.* berunezko,
berundun.
leaden *adj.* berunezko, berundun,
berunantzeko.
leader *n.* buru, buruzagi; aurrelari,
aitzindari. *n.* biderakusle, bidegidari.
leadership *n.* buruzagitza, nagusigo,
nagusitza; aurrendaritza,
aitzindaritza, aurrelaritza.
leaf *n.* hosto, orri. **Fallen leaf.** Orbel.

To lose leaves. Hostagabetu.
Orrigabetu. **Deciduous leaf.** Hosto
erorkor. **Evergreen leaf.** Hosto
iraunkor.
leafage n. hostotza, orritza.
leafiness n. hostotasun, orritasun.
leafless adj. hostogabe, orrigabe.
leaflet n. orrialdetxo, panfleto. n.
orriska, orritxo.
leafy adj. hostoaskodun, hostodun,
hostotsu, orridun, orritsu.
league n. legua. n. liga.
leak v.i./v.t. erion.
leak n. itaizur, erion.
leakage n. itaizur, isurialdi.
leaky adj. itogintsu.
lean v.i./v.t. alboratu, makurtu. v.i.
joera izan, jo. v.i./v.t. (against, on)
euskarritu, sostengatu.
lean adj. gihartsu. n. urdaigizen,
zerrigiharre, giharre.
leanness n. gihartasun.
lean-to n. txabolatxo.
leap v.i./v.t. salto egin, jauzi, jauzkatu,
saltakatu, saltatu.
leap n. jauzi, saltaketa, salto.
leapfrog n. txorromorro, asto-astoka.
leapt p. part. of leap.
leap year n. bisestu.
learn v.t./v.i. ikasi. v.i. (of) jakin,
entzun.
learnable adj. ikasgarri.
learned adj. ikastun, jakitun,
eskolatu(a), ikasi(a).
learning n. ikaskuntza, ikaskintza,
ikasgo.
leasable adj. errentagarri.
lease v.t./v.i. akuran hartu, akuran
eman.
lease n. maizterkuntza, maizterketa.
leash n. hede, uhal.
least adj./n. gutienezko. adv. gutien.
At least. Gutxienez. Behintzat.
Bederen. n. gutxientasun.
leather n. larru. adj. larruzko.
leathery adj. larruantzeko.
leavable adj. uzkarri.
leave v.i./v.i. irten, urrundu, -tik joan,
aldaratu. v.t. utzi, iraitzi. v.t. (out)
utzi, ezegin, lekatu, baztertu. v.i. (off)
gelditu, geratu, eten.
leaven v.t. legamiatu.
leavening n. orantza, legamia.
lecherous adj. linburkoi.
lecherousness n. linburkoitasun.
lechery n. likisdura.
lectern n. irakastoki.
lecture n. hitzaldi, irakasaldi.
lecturer n. txostenemaile.
led p. part. of lead.
ledge n. koska, mailagune.
ledger n. kontuliburu.
leech n. (zool.) odoledale, izain.
leek n. (bot.) porru.
leer v.i. lizunki begiratu.
left adj. ezkerreko, ezkertiar. n. ezker,
ezkerkada. adv. ezkerrera.

left-hand adj. ezkerreko, ezkertiar.
left-handed adj. ezkerra, ezker,
ezkerti.
leftist n. ezkertiar. adj. ezkerreko,
ezkertiar, ezker.
leftover adj. hondakinezko,
kondarrezko.
leftovers n. kondar, hondakin, hondar,
zabar, soberakin.
leg n. (anat.) hanka, zango. n. etapa.
legacy n. oinorde, ondore. n. emaitza,
donazio.
legal adj. legezko, legearauzko.
legalistic adj. legezale.
legality n. legetasun, legeztasun.
legalization n. legeketa, legeztapen.
legalize v.t. legezkotu, legeztu,
legeztatu.
legally adv. legearauz, legez.
legalness n. legebidetasun.
legend n. ipuin, kontu, leienda.
legendary adj. ipuinezko.
legged adj. hankadun. **Long-legged.**
Hankaluze. **Two-legged.** Hankabiko.
Hankabidun. **One-legged.**
Hankabakar.
legging n. azmantar.
legibility n. irakurgarritasun.
legible adj. irakurgarri.
legion n. (mil.) legio. n. talde handi(a).
legionary n. (mil.) legionari.
legionnaire n. (mil.) legionari.
legislate v.i./v.t. legetu, araueratu,
arautu.
legislation n. legegintza, legeaginte.
legislative adj. legegintzako.
legislator n. legegile, legelari.
legislature n. legetxe, ganbara. n.
legealdi, legegintzaldi.
legitimacy n. legezuzentasun,
legebidetasun, legezkotasun.
legitimate v.t. legezkotu.
legitimate adj. legebidezko,
zuzenbideko, bidezko, zuzeneko.
legitimately adv. araudiz, legebidez.
legitimize v.t. legezkotu, legeztatu,
legeztu.
legless adj. hankagabe, zangogabeko.
legume n. (bot.) lekari, barazki.
leguminous adj. lekadun, lekari.
leisure n. asti. adj. astitsu.
lemon n. (bot.) limoi.
lemonade n. limoiedari, limonada.
lend v.t./v.i. aurreratu, prestatu,
zorretan eman, aurrez eman.
lender n. mailegukari.
length n. luzera, luzetasun, hedadura,
hedakuntza.
lengthen v.t./v.i. luzatu.
lengthening n. luzaketa, luzapen. adj.
luzatzaile.
lengthwise adv./adj. luzeran, luzeraz;
luzezko.
lengthy adj. luzetsu, luze.
leniency n. bihozberatasun,
bihozleuntasun.
lenient adj. bihozdun, leunkor.

lens *n.* lente. *n.(pl.)* betaurrekoak, lentilak.
Lent *n. (eccl.)* garizuma.
lentil *n. (bot.)* dilista.
leopard *n. (zool.)* lehoinabar.
leper *n.* legendun, legenardun.
lepidopterous *adj.* hegalezkatadun.
leprechaun *n.* Irlandako iratxo.
leprosy *n. (med.)* legen, legenar.
leprous *adj.* legendun, legenardun, legenarti, soraio.
lesbian *n.* sexuberekoi (emakume), lesbiana.
lesion *n.* zauri, zauridura, sakaila, saki.
less *adv./adj.* gutiago. *n.* guti. *prep. (arith.)* ken.
-less *(gram.)* -gabe.
lessee *n.* maizter, errentadore.
lessen *v.i./v.t.* gutitu, eskastu, murriztu.
lesser *adj.* txikiago, gutxiago.
lesson *n.* ikaskai, ikaskizun.
let *v.t.* utzi, baimena eman. *v.i.* akuran izan, maiztertu. *v.t.* **(down)** deszintzilikatu; huts eman.
lethal *adj.* hilgarri, hilkor, heriogarri.
lethargic *adj.* lozorrodun.
lethargy *n.* lozorro, loeri.
let's dezagun. "let + us"-aren laburpena. **Let's do it.** Egin dezagun.
letter *n.* gutun, eskutitz, karta. *n.* letra, hizki. **Capital letter.** Hizki nagusi. **Small letter.** Letra tipi.
lettered *adj.* letradun.
letterhead *n.* idazpuru.
lettering *n.* errotulazio.
lettuce *n. (bot.)* letxu, uhaza.
leukemia *n. (med.)* leuzemia.
levee *n.* kaimutur.
level *v.t./v.i.* zelaitu, berdindu, lauzatu, galgatu, plaundu.
level *n.* galga, nibelgailu. *n.* maila. *adj.* mailabereko. *adj.* horizontal.
leveler *n.* berdintzaile, galgatzaile.
lever *n.* palanka, balanka.
levitation *n.* jaikiera.
levity *n.* kaskarinteria. *n.* arintasun.
levy *v.t.* inposatu; bildu; gainzergatu.
lewd *adj.* lizun, lizunbera, zantar.
lewdly *adv.* lizunki, zantarki.
lewdness *n.* haragikeria, lizunkeria, zantarkeria.
lexicographer *n.* hiztegigile, hiztegilari.
lexicography *n.* hiztegigintza.
lexicon *n.* hitz zerrenda.
liability *n.* zor; desabantaila. *n.* aurreprestaera, aurredisposapen.
liable *adj.* -bera, -kor. *adj.* arduradun.
liaison *n.* lotura, lokarri.
liar *n.* gezurti, gezurjario.
libation *n.* edanaldi, edanketa.
libel *n.* gezurlaido.
libeler *n.* atzejale.
liberal *adj.* liberal.
liberalism *n. (pol.)* liberalismo.
liberality *n.* liberaltasun.

liberally *adv.* liberalki.
liberate *v.t.* libratu, askatu, askarazi.
liberation *n.* askapen, librantza.
liberator *n.* askatzaile.
libertine *adj.* likits, lizun, andrekoi, zabar, zantar, limuri.
libertinism *n.* askakeria, lasakeria.
liberty *n.* askatasun, askamen.
librarian *n.* liburuzain.
library *n.* liburutegi. **Serials library.** Egunkaritegi.
libretto *n.* gioi (musika), libreto.
lice *n.(pl.)* zorriteria, zorritza.
license *n.* eskahalmen. *n.* gidakarnet, gidabaimen.
license plate *n.* kotxearen matrikula.
licentious *adj.* andrekoi, zantar, lizunkoi, haragikoi, linburkoi.
licentiously *adv.* lizunki.
licentiousness *n.* haragizalekeria, lohikeria, zikinkeria.
lichen *n. (bot.)* liken.
lick *v.t.* lamikatu, miazkatu, milikatu.
lick *n.* miazketa.
licorice *n.* erregaliz.
lid *n.* estalgarri, tapa, lapikogain.
lie *v.i.* gezurra esan. *v.i. (batzutan* **down**-*ekin)* etzan.
lie *n.* gezur.
lieutenancy *n. (mil.)* tenientetza.
lieutenant *n. (mil.)* teniente.
life *n.* bizi, bizitza, bizitzaldi.
lifeboat *n.* salbamendu itsasontzi, soros-ontzi.
life-giving *adj.* bizierazle, biziemangarri, azkargarri, biztukor.
life jacket *n.* flotagailu, salbajazki.
lifeless *adj.* bizigabe.
lifelike *adj.* ia benetako bizi(a).
lifelong *adj.* biziguztiko, bizirako.
life preserver *n.* igergailu, igerigailu.
lifesaver *n.* sorosle.
lifetime *n.* bizitzaldi, bizialdi. *adj.* bizialdiko.
lift *v.t./v.i.* jaso, jasoarazi, altxatu, igo arazi.
lift *n.* jasoaldi, jasoketa, altxaldi. *n.* igogailu.
liftable *adj.* jasokor.
ligament *n. (anat.)* lokarrimendu.
light *v.t./v.i.* biztu, sutu, bizitu. *v.t./v.i. (v.i., gehienetan* **up**-*ekin)* argitu, argiztatu, argi egin. *v.i. (from)* zaldijaitsi, (kotxetik) atera. *v.i. (on)* pausatu.
light *n.* argi, argitasun. **Electric light.** Elektrargi. **Beam of light.** Argizpi. **Set of lights.** Argiteria. **Dim light.** Argilabur. **Small light.** Argitto. **Group of lights.** Argitza. **Funerary light.** Argizariohol. **Firelight.** Suargi. *adj.* astungabe, pisugabe, arin.
light bulb *n.* bonbila.
lighten *v.i./v.t.* argitu, argiztatu, argieman; argiagotu. *v.t./v.i.* pisugabetu, arindu, arinagotu. *v.t./v.i.* alaitu.

lighter *n.* argitzaile, argiemale, subizle; pizgailu. *adj.* argiago. *adj.* arinago.
light-hearted *adj.* alai.
lighthouse *n.* itsasargi, faro, kaiargi.
lightly *adv.* airoski, arin. *adv.* azaletik, gain-gainetik, gainetik.
lightness *n.* astungabezia, pisugabezia, arintasun.
lightning *v.i.* tximista bota, tximista egin.
lightning *n.* tximist, tximistargi, tximistaldi, oinaztargi.
lightning rod *n.* tximistorratz.
lightweight *n.* pisu arin.
light-year *n.* argi-urte.
likable *adj.* maitagarri, atsegingarri.
like *v.t.* gustatu, atsegin izan, eder izan, gogoko izan, begiko izan. *v.i.* nahi ukan, gura izan. **To not like (someone).** Begi onetik ez sartu. Ezkerreko begitik ukan.
like *adj./prep.* kideko, bezalako, bezala, erako, antzeko, itxurako, moduko; - lako. *adv.* antzera, erara, bezala, gisara, moldera, eraz, ereduz, gisa. **Like this. Like that. Like so.** Hola. Honela. Horrela. *n.* mota.
likelihood *n.* egitxura, kanore.
likely *adj.* egitxurako, egiantzeko, kanorezko. *adv.* egiantzez, kanorez.
likeness *n.* antzekotasun, antz, itxurapen.
likewise *adv.* halaber. *adv.* eraberean, antzera, gisa-berean.
liking *n.* xera, joera.
lilac bush *n. (bot.)* amatxilili.
lily *n. (bot.)* lili, lirio.
limb *n. (anat.)* soinatal, soinzati, alderdi.
limber *adj.* malgu.
limbo *n. (eccl.)* linbu.
lime *n.* kare. *n. (bot.)* limoi itxura duen fruitu txiki eta orlegia.
limerick *n.* bost lerroko bertso barregarri(a).
limestone *n. (min.)* gisuharri, kareharri.
limit *v.t.* mugatu, murriztu, hertsi, zedarritu, zedarriztatu.
limit *n.* muga, mugalerro, zede; mukuru.
limitable *adj.* mugagarri.
limitation *n.* mugapen.
limited *adj.* mugatu(a).
limiting *adj.* mugakor, mugatzaile, murritzaile. *n.* mugaketa.
limitless *adj.* neurgabe, mugagabe.
limousine *n.* limusin, kotxe handi eta ederra.
limp *v.i.* herrenkatu, herren egin, maingutu.
limp *n.* herrenketa, herrenkura. *adj.* lasai.
limpet *n. (zool.)* lapa.
limpid *adj.* garden, garbizi.
limy *adj.* karedun, karezko, karetsu, kareharritsu.

linden tree *n. (bot.)* ezki, ezku.
line *v.t./v.i.* **(up)** lerrotu, herronkatu, lerroztatu. *v.t.* **(up)** aurkitu, lortu. *v.t.* marraztu; marrakatu.
line *n.* lerro, marra. *n.* ilara, errenkada, herronka. *n.* idazlerro.
lineage *n.* leinu, etorki, sorterro.
linear *adj.* lerroko, marrazko.
linearity *n.* lerrozkotasun.
lined *adj.* lerrodun, lerrozko, marrazko, marradun, marratsu.
linen *n.* liho, linu, hari. *adj.* harizko.
lingerie *n.* andreen barruko erropa(k).
linguist *n.* hizkuntzalari.
linguistics *n.* hizkuntzalaritza.
liniment *n.* gozagai, gozagailu, linimentu.
lining *n.* marradura, marraketa. *n.* forru.
link *v.t./v.i.* elkar lotu, kateatu, lotarazi, lokarritu, mihiztatu.
link *n.* lokarri, lotura, ahokadura. *n.* katebegi, gartza.
linkable *adj.* lotugarri.
linoleum *n.* linolio.
linotype *n.* linotipia.
linseed *n.* linazi.
lint *n.* zirpil.
lintel *n.* ataburu.
lion *n. (zool.)* lehoi.
lioness *n. (zool.)* lehoieme.
lip *n. (anat.)* ezpain.
lipstick *n.* ezpainpintura.
liquefaction *n.* urkuntza.
liquefiable *adj.* urtugarri, urkoi.
liquefication *n.* urdura.
liquefy *v.t./v.i.* likidotu.
liquefying *adj.* gesalkor.
liqueur *n.* likore.
liquid *n.* isurki, isurkai, likido.
liquidate *v.t./v.i. (econ.)* garbitu. *v.t.* hil, deuseztu.
liquidation *n.* kitaketa, kitapen, kontugarbiketa, kontuzuriketa. *n.* merkealdi.
liquidator *n.* garbitzaile.
liquidity *n.* isurkortasun, urtasun, isurkitasun. *n.* dirubihurkortasun.
liquidness *n.* isurkitasun, isurkortasun.
liquor *n.* likore.
lisp *v.t./v.i.* zizakatu, zizipaza egin.
lisp *n.* ziza, zizipaza.
list *v.t.* zerrendatu. *v.i.* alderatu (ontziak).
list *n.* zerrenda, lerrokada.
listen *v.i.* entzun. *v.i. (askotan* **to**-*rekin)* aditu, kasu egin, jaramon egin.
listener *n.* entzule, aditzaile.
listing *n.* zerrendaketa.
listless *adj.* grinagabe, odolgabe, zaingabeko.
listlessly *adv.* zirriki-zarraka.
listlessness *n.* odolgabetasun.
lit *p. part. of* light.
litany *n. (eccl.)* letania.
liter *n.* litro.
literacy *n.* irakurri eta idazteko

ahalmena.
literal adj. literal.
literally adv. hitzez-hitz, literalki.
literarily adv. elertiz.
literary adj. literatur.
literate adj. eskoladun.
literature n. elerti, literatura.
lithe adj. lerden, lirain, pertxenta.
lithely adv. lerdenki, txairoki, lirainki.
litheness n. lerdentasun, liraintasun, txairotasun.
lithography n. litografia.
litigant n. auzikide, auzilagun, auzilari.
litigate v.t./v.i. auzikatu.
litigation n. auzi, auzigai, auziketa.
litter n. sabelaldi. n. angaila, anda. n. zabor, zaborreria.
little adj. txiki, txikitxo, xehe, koskor; -ska, -ko, -ño, -tila, -tto, - txa, -xka, -sko, -skila. adv. guti, pixka, pixka bat. **Little by little.** Pixkaka. Gutxika.
littleness n. gutitasun, txikitasun.
littoral n. kostalde, itsasalde.
liturgical adj. liturgiko; liturgi-.
liturgy n. liturgia.
livable adj. bizigarri.
live v.i./v.t. bizi, biztandu. **To live off (someone).** Inoren bizkarretik bizi. **To live from hand to mouth.** Eguneroko premiak betetzeko adina irabazi. **To live high.** Nabarmenki bizi. **To live it up.** Errege bezala bizi.
livelihood n. hornigai, bizigarri.
liveliness n. bizitasun, zolitasun.
livelong adj. oso, bete.
lively adj. bizikoi, airos, saltakor, saltari, zoli. adv. biziki, bizikiro, biziro, zoliki.
liven up v.t. suztatu.
liver n. (anat.) gibel. **To move into the liver.** Gibeleratu.
livery n. librea.
livestock n. ganadutza, eletalde.
livid adj. ubel.
lividness n. ubeltasun.
living n. ofizio, bizibide, lanbide, ogibide, bizimodu. **To earn a living.** Bizimodua atera. **Standard of living.** Bizimaila. **Living together.** Bizikidego. Bizikidetza. adj. bizi, bizidun, arimadun.
living room n. egongela.
lizard n. (zool.) musker, sugelandara.
llama n. (zool.) llama.
load n. zama, karga; -keta, -zama.
load v.t./v.i. zamatu, kargatu, sortatu. v.t. munizioztatu.
loading n. kargaketa, lepaketa, zamaketa.
loaf v.i. (batzutan **around**-ekin) baldartu, alfertu.
loaf n. ogi biribil edo luze.
loafer n. alfer, alferzama. n. lokarrigabeko oinetako mota bat.
loam n. lur beltz.
loan v.t./v.i. aurrez eman, aurreratu,

prestatu, zorretan eman, gerotan eman, mailegatu.
loan n. mailegu, prestamo, aurrediru. **On loan. As a loan.** Maileguz. Prestamoz. **To ask for a loan.** Maileguz eskatu.
loanable adj. prestagarri.
loathe v.t. gorrotatu.
loathing n. gorroto, higuin, higuindura, okazadura.
loathsome adj. gorrotogarri, higuingarri, nazkagarri.
loathsomely adv. higuingarriki, higuingarriro.
loathsomeness n. gorrotogarritasun, higuingarritasun.
loaves n.(pl.) loaf.
lobby n. oldartalde. n. hall, atalondo.
lobe n. (anat.) gingila.
lobster n. (zool.) otarrain.
local adj. bertako, lekuko, tokiko.
locality n. leku, toki.
localize v.t./v.i. lekutu, ezarri, kokatu.
locate v.t. kokatu; aurkitu.
location n. leku, lekune, une.
lock v.t./v.i. giltzatu, giltzapetu.
lock n. sarraila. n. kopetile, iledi, ileadats.
locker n. arasatxo. n. izozkutxa.
locket n. kutun.
lockjaw n. (med.) tetano.
locksmith n. sarrailari, sarrailgin.
locksmithing n. sarrailgintza.
locomotive n. lokomotore, trenmakina.
locust n. (zool.) txirrita.
locution n. mintzaera.
locutory n. mintzaleku, mintzatoki, solastegi, solastoki.
lode n. meadar, zerrenda.
lodge v.i./v.t. ostatu, ostaturatu, etxerakotu.
lodge n. bideostatu.
lodger n. bideostatari, ostatukari.
lodging n. ostatuketa, ostaturaketa, ostatutza.
loft n. ganbara, sabai.
lofty adj. gorati.
log n. subil.
logarithm n. logaritmu.
logging n. zuhaitz mozketa.
logic n. logika.
logical adj. zentzuzko, logiko.
logically adv. logikoki, logikaz.
loincloth n. gerripeko.
loins n. (pl.) (anat.) solomo.
loiter v.i. kikili-makala ibili.
lollipop n. azukrezko txupete.
lone adj. soil.
loneliness n. bakartasun, bakarte.
lonely adj. bakartsu, bakartar.
loner n. bakartzale.
lonesome adj. bakartsu, bakartar.
long v.i. (for edo infinitiboarekin) aiher izan, bakarmindu, irrikitu.
long adj. luze; luza-. adv. luzaz. **How long?** Zenbat denbora? Noiz arte?
longevity n. biziluze.

longing *n.* gutizia, nahikari.
longitude *n. (geog.)* luzera.
longitudinal *adj.* luzezko.
longitudinally *adv.* luzeraz, luzez,
luzetara.
long-legged *adj.* hankaluze, hankandi,
zangoluze.
long-lived *adj.* biziluzeko, urtetsu,
zaharkoi.
long-term *adj.* luzaroko, epeluzeko.
look *v.i./v.t. (v.i.,* **at, toward)** begiratu,
behatu, begitu, ikusi, so egin. *v.i.*
(batzutan **like-***ekin)* iruditu, irudi;
antzekotu. *v.i. (after)* zaindu,
arduratu. *v.i. (for)* bilatu, arrakastatu,
bila ibili. *v.i. (into)* arakatu, aztertu,
ikertu. **To look good.** Itxura ona izan.
look *n.* begikada, begirakada,
begirada, so, begirakune. *int.* begira!
hara! *n. (batzutan* **looks)** itxura,
aurpegiera.
look-alike *n.* iduriko.
lookout *n.* talaiari, talaiero; talaia, tala.
loom *n.* ehungailu.
loop *n.* katebira, bigizta.
loophole *n.* gezileiho. *n.* itzurpide.
loose *adj.* lasai, lazo. *adj.* lotugabe,
solte, aske.
loosely *adv.* lazoki, kili-kolo.
loosen *v.t./v.i.* lasaitu, askatu,
desestutu.
loosenable *adj.* askagarri, lasaigarri.
looseness *n.* lasaiera, lasaitasun,
lazotasun.
loot *v.t.* lapurtu, harrapakatu.
loot *n.* ebaskin, harrapakin.
looter *n.* harrapakari, lapur, ebasle.
looting *n.* harrapakeria, harrapaketa.
lope *v.i.* zaldia trostaka ibili.
loquacious *adj.* hitzjario, hitzontzi,
hiztun, berritsu, mintzalari, solasti,
kalakari.
loquaciousness *n.* hitzjariotasun,
berriketontzi.
loquacity *n.* hitzjariotasun,
elejariotasun, solaskeria,
berriketontzi.
lord *n.* jaun, jaunandi, jauntxo; jaur-.
lore *n.* herri jakituria.
losable *adj.* galgarri.
lose *v.t./v.i.* galdu. **To lose one's
mind.** Burugabetu.
loser *n.* galtzaile.
loss *n.* galera, galmen, hondamen;
gal-. *n.* kaltekeria, xahupen.
lost *adj.* galdu(a), herratu(a). *pret./p.
part. of lose.*
lot *n.* zotza (zoztaketan). **To draw lots.**
Zotz egin. Zozkatu. *n.* zati. *n.* lurzati,
eremu, arlo, sail. **A lot (of).** Asko. **A
lot.** Askotan.
lotion *n.* gantzugarri, baltsamo.
lottery *n.* erlo, errifa, loteria.
loud *adj.* burrunbatsu, danbadatsu,
hotsandiko.
loudly *adv.* hotsandiz, bortizki, ozenki.
loudness *n.* arrabostasun. *n.*

ahotsindar, zaratindar.
loudspeaker *n.* ozengailu, bozgorailu.
Louisiana *n. (geog.)* Estatu Batuetako
estatu bat.
lounge *n.* areto.
louse *n. (zool.)* zorri.
lousiness *n.* zorrikeria.
lousy *adj.* zorridun, zorritsu.
lovable *adj.* maitagarri, maitakor,
maitabera, laztangarri, maitasamur.
lovableness *n.* maitagarritasun,
maitakortasun.
love *v.t.* maitatu, maite izan, maite
ukan. **To fall in love.** Maitemindu. **To
fall out of love.** Maitegabetu.
love *n.* maitasun, maitetasun, amodio;
maita-.
loved *adj.* maitatu(a).
loveless *adj.* maitegabe.
loveliness *n.* liraindura.
lovely *adj./adv.* polita, eder, begionez.
lover *n.* maitale, maitarazle, maitekide,
maitalari.
loverly *adj./adv.* maitezko.
loving *adj.* maitakor, maitemindu,
maitatzaile, amodiotsu, amodiozko,
laztankor, laztantsu.
lovingly *adv.* maitagarriki, maitagarriro,
maitekiro, maiteminez, laztanki,
amodiozki, maiteki, bihotzez.
lovingness *n.* laztantasun.
low *v.i.* mu egin.
low *adj./adv.* behe, beheko; behean.
adj. baxu. *n.* behe, puntu behe.
lower *v.t./v.i.* beheratu, beheragotu,
jaitsi, eraitsi.
lower *adj.* behe, beheko. *adj.* beheago,
beherago.
lowering *n.* beheradura, jaitsiera.
lowest *adj.* behereneko, beherengo.
lowing *n.* marruma.
lowland *n.* ibar, haran, beterri.
lowly *adj.* apal. *adv.* baxuki. *adv.*
ziztrinki. *adv.* behean, behe.
Low Navarra *n. (geog.)* Behe-Nafarroa,
Nafarroa Beherea
lowness *n.* behetasun. *n.* ziztrinkeria,
zirtzileria, purtzilkeria.
low tide *n.* marebehera, itsasbehera.
loyal *adj.* leial, zintzo.
loyally *adv.* leialki, leialkiro, zintzo,
zintzoki.
loyalty *n.* leialtasun, zintzotasun.
lubricant *n.* labaingai, labanerazgai.
lubricate *v.t.* koipeztatu.
lubrication *n.* labaindura, labainketa,
koipeztadura.
lubricator *n.* koipeztatzaile,
labanerazle.
lubricity *n.* labaintasun.
luck *n.* zori, zorte, mentura.
luckily *adv.* zorionez, zorionean.
luckless *adj.* zoriongabe.
lucky *adj.* zoriondun, zoriontsu.
lucrative *adj.* irabazkor, irabazteko.
lucre *n.* diru, irabazpen, etekin.
ludicrous *adj.* irribidezko.

lug *v.t.* nekez eraman.
luggage *n.* fardeleria, bidefardeleria.
lugubrious *adj.* itzaltsu, ilunbera, ilungarri.
lukewarm *adj.* epel, zerrepel.
lullaby *n.* loabesti, lokantu.
lumbago *n. (med.)* lumbago, gerrikomin, gerrimin.
lumbar *n.* gerrialde. *adj.* gerrialdeko.
lumber *n.* oholeria, zur, ohol.
lumberjack *n.* oholketari, zurketari.
lumberyard *n.* oholdegi, zurtegi.
luminescence *n.* argikortasun.
luminescent *adj.* distirakor, distiragile.
luminosity *n.* dirdiratasun, distiratasun, argitasun.
luminous *adj.* argikor, argitsu, dirdiratsu, dirdiratzaile, brintzatsu.
lump *n.* hanpatune, bikor, koskor, konkor.
lumpy *adj.* bikortsu.
lunacy *n.* erotasun, zorotasun.
lunar *adj.* ilargiko.
lunatic *n./adj.* alditsu, haizejo.
lunch *v.t./v.i.* bazkaldu.
lunch *n.* bazkari. **To have lunch.** Bazkaldu.
lung *n. (anat.)* birika.
lunge *v.i.* bapatean aurrera abiatu.
lure *n.* erakargailu.
lurk *v.i.* zelatatu, zelatan egon.
lushness *n.* mardotasun.
lush *adj.* mardul, guren.
lust *n.* haragikeria, haragirrits, haragigrina, atseginkeria, emagose, emajoera, likisdura.
lustful *adj.* haragikoi, haragikor, haragizale, lizunarazle, lizunbera, lizunkoi, likitsu, likits, linburkor, limuri, zantar. **To become lustful.** Haragikortu.
lustfully *adv.* haragiz.
lustfulness *n.* lizunzalekeria, lizunkeria, likistasun.
lusty *adj.* haragizko, likits, lohi.
lute *n. (mus.)* arrabita.
luxation *n. (med.)* lokadura, bihurri.
luxuriance *n.* mardultasun.
luxuriant *adj.* mardo, guri, mardul.
luxuriantly *adv.* mardulki.
luxurious *adj.* luxozko, luxotsu.
luxuriously *adv.* luxoki.
luxury *n.* luxo.
lye *n.* latsa, lixiba.
lying-in *n.* haurgintzondoren.
lymph *n. (anat.)* linfa.
lynch *v.t.* urkatu.
lynx *n. (zool.)* katamotz.
lyre *n. (mus.)* lira.
lyric *n.* lirika, liriku.
lyrical *adj.* liriku.
lyricism *n.* lirismo.

M

m *n.* Ingeles alfabetoko letra.
ma *n.* ama.
ma'am *n.* andre.

macadam *n.* makadan.
macaroni *n.* makarroi.
mace *n.* porra. *n. (cap.)* poliziek manifestarien eta emakumeek erasotzaileen aurka erabili ohi duten sustantzi kimiko itsutzaile eta azal-larrutzailea.
machete *n.* aihotz.
machine *n.* makina.
machine gun *n.* metrailadore.
machinery *n.* makineria.
machinist *n.* makinari, makinlari.
mackerel *n. (zool.)* berdel.
macrocosm *n.* makrokosmo, mundutzar.
mad *adj.* haserre, haserretsu. *adj.* ero, erokeriazko. *adj.* amorratu(a).
madam *n.* andre.
madden *v.t./v.i.* haserretu. *v.t.* zoratu, erotu.
maddening *adj.* ahakargarri, sumingarri. *adj.* burugalgarri, erogarri, zorabiagarri, zorarazle.
made *adj.* egina, egindako. *pret./p. part.* of **make**.
madhouse *n.* eroetxe, erotegi, zoroetxe.
madly *adv.* zoroki, eroki.
madman *n.* zoro.
madness *n.* zorotasun, erotasun, erokeria, zorakeria, burunahasketa.
Madrid *n. (geog.)* Madril.
madrigal *n.* madrigale.
magazine *n.* kaseta, egunkari, aldizkari. *n.* armagordailu, polborategi.
maggot *n. (zool.)* beldar.
magic *n.* asmagintza, sorginkeria, magia. *adj.* sorginkerizko.
magical *adj.* magiko.
magically *adv.* magikoki.
magician *n.* aztigaizkile, mago.
magistrate *n.* auzigizon, epaile, magistratu.
magnanimity *n.* bihotzanditasun, eskuzabaltasun.
magnanimous *adj.* bihotzandi(ko), gogohandi(ko).
magnanimously *adv.* bihotzandiz.
magnanimousness *n.* gogohanditasun.
magnate *n.* handiki, jauntxo.
magnesium *n. (chem.)* magnesio.
magnet *n.* burdinbizi, iman.
magnetic *adj.* imandun, magnetiko.
magnetism *n.* magnetismo, magnetindar.
magnetization *n.* imandura, imanezpen, imanketa.
magnetize *v.t.* imandu, imaneztatu.
magnification *n.* handiagotze.
magnificence *n.* ospagarritasun.
magnificent *adj.* ikusgarri, munduko.
magnificently *adv.* bikainki, ezinobeki.
magnify *v.t./v.i.* handiagotu.
magnitude *n.* neurri. *n.* handitasun. *n.* garrantzi.

magpie *n. (zool.)* mika.
mahogany *n. (bot.)* kaobondo, kaoba.
  n. kaobazur.
maid *n.* neskame.
maiden *n.* neskaso.
mail *n.* posta.
mailbox *n.* postontzi, kartakutxa,
  gutunontzi, idazkikutxa.
mailman *n.* postari, kartero.
maim *v.t.* elbarritu.
main *adj.* nagusi. *adj. (superl.)*
  nagusien, behinen.
Maine *n. (geog.)* Estatu Batuetako
  estatu bat.
mainland *n.* lur, lehor.
mainly *adv.* gehienbat, nagusiki,
  nagusiro.
maintain *v.t.* mantendu, eutsi, eduki,
  eutsarazi, iraunarazi.
maintenance *n.* euspen, iraunarazte.
maize *n. (bot.)* arto.
majestic *adj.* handiairezko, itzelezko.
majestically *adv.* handikiro, ospetsuki.
majesty *n.* ospetasun.
major *n. (mil.)* komandante. *n.* Estatu
  Batuetako unibertsitatean
  ikasgai-kopuru nagusia. *adj.*
  handiago. *adj.* nagusien(a).
majordomo *n.* etxegizon.
majority *n.* gehiengo, gehientasun.
make *v.t.* egin. *v.t.* eragin; -arazi,
  -erazi. *v.i.* **(for)** -rantz joan. *v.i.* **(of)**
  eritzia ukan. *v.i.* **(up for)** kitatu. *v.i.*
  (up to) lausengatu, norbaiti belarria
  gozatu, mingaina leun erabili. **To
  make a face.** Keinu egin. **To make a
  living.** Bizibidea atera. Bizimodua
  atera. **To make a mistake.** Huts
  egin. **To make friends.** Lagunak
  egin. **To make it.** Irabazi, garaitu. **To
  make up.** Bakeak egin. Adiskidetu.
  To make sense. Zentzu ukan. **To
  make up one's mind.** Erabakia
  hartu, zirt edo zart egin.
make-believe *n.* itxuramendu.
maker *n.* egile; -gin, -kin, -gile.
make-up *n.* azalapainketa, kosmetiko.
maladjusted *adj.* moldagabe,
  desegoki.
maladjustment *n.* desegokidura,
  desdoikuntza, moldagabezia.
maladroit *adj.* ganoragabe(ko).
malady *n.* gaiso, eritasun, gaitz.
malaise *n.* ondoez, gaitz.
malaria *n. (med.)* malaria.
malcontent *n.* kontentagaitz. *n.*
  matxinzale, zalapartari.
male *adj.* ar. *n.* gizaseme, gizonezko.
malediction *n.* gaizkiesaka.
malefactor *n.* gaiztagile, gaiztagin.
maleness *n.* gizonezkotasun.
malevolence *n.* ezinikusi, gogogaizto.
malevolent *adj.* bihoztxarreko,
  gaizkinahiezko, gogotxarreko.
malevolently *adv.* asmotxarrez,
  gogotxarrez, bihurriki, ezinikusiaz.
malformation *n.* gaizkierapen.

malformed *adj.* deserazko, markets.
malice *n.* gaitzuste, malezia.
malicious *adj.* bihoztxarreko, gaizto,
  makur, txar, bihurri, maltzurkeriazko.
maliciously *adv.* maltzurkiro, maltzurki,
  bihurriki.
maliciousness *n.* maltzurreria,
  okerkeria, gaiztotasun, txarkeria.
malign *v.t.* gezurrez gaitz esan, izena
  lohitu.
malignancy *n.* maltzurkeria.
malignant *adj.* gaiztorazle.
maligner *n.* gaizkiesale.
mall *n.* galeria, dendez beteriko leku
  luze eta itxia.
mallard *n. (zool.)* basahate.
malleability *n.* malgutasun.
malleable *adj.* malgugarri, malgukor,
  xaflakor.
mallet *n.* zurmailu.
malnourished *adj.* ziztrin.
malnutrition *n.* deselikadura.
malpractice *n.* arduragabeko ekintza.
maltreat *v.t.* gaizki erabili, gaizki hartu.
maltreatment *n.* gaizkierabilketa.
mama *n.* ama.
mamma *n.* ama.
mammal *n.* ugaztun.
mammalian *adj.* ditidun.
mammary *adj.* bularreko, ugatzeko.
mammiferous *adj.* ugaztun.
mammoth *n. (zool.)* mamut.
man *n.* gizon, gizaseme, gizakume,
  gizonezko; giza-.
manacle *v.t.* esku lotu.
manage *v.t./v.i.* konpondu, erabili.
manageability *n.* erabilkortasun.
manageable *adj.* erabilkor,
  erabilterraz, eskurakoi. *adj.* gidagarri,
  molderrez.
management *n.* erabilketa, erabilkizun.
  n. zuzendaritza, aministrazio,
  aministralgo.
manager *n.* aministratzaile, arduradun,
  enpresari, zuzendari.
managerial *adj.* aministralgoko,
  aministrazioko.
man-crazy *adj.* gizakoi.
mandarin orange *n. (bot.)*
  mandarinondo; mandarina.
mandate *n.* agindu.
mandatory *adj.* derrigorrezko,
  ezinbesteko, nahitaezko,
  eginbeharrezko.
mandible *n. (anat.)* masailezur,
  matelezur.
mandibular *adj.* masailezurreko.
mandolin *n. (mus.)* bandolina.
mandragora *n. (bot.)* urrilo.
mandrake *n. (bot.)* urrilo.
mane *n.* zurda.
maneuver *n.* egiketa; lemaketa.
mange *n. (med.)* ezkabia, sarna.
manger *n.* aska, harriaska, abelaska.
mangle *v.t.* zauritu, trenkatu.
mangy *adj.* ezkabiatsu.
manhandle *v.t.* haztakatu.

manhole cover *n.* erretenarri.
manhood *n.* gizontasun, artasun.
mania *n.* burugalketa.
maniac *n.* zoro, ero.
manicure *n.* eskuartezia, manikura, eskuardura.
manifest *v.t.* agertu, agerrarazi, azalkeratu, azaleratu. *v.t.* frogatu.
manifest *adj.* nabarmen, nabari, ageri, jakin.
manifestable *adj.* azalgarri.
manifestation *n.* aitorkunde, agermen, azalpen, erakusmen.
manifestly *adv.* agerian.
manifesto *n.* agiri, deiagiri.
manifold *adj.* ugari.
manikin *n.* jantzimaistra, maniki.
manioc *n.* *(bot.)* mandioka.
manipulate *v.t.* eskukatu, erabili. *v.t.* moldatu, aldatu.
manipulating *adj.* eskutatzaile. *n.* eskusarketa.
manipulation *n.* eskukaketa, erabilketa.
mankind *n.* gizadi.
manliness *n.* gizatasun.
manly *adj.* gizongisako, gizontsu.
manna *n.* mana.
mannequin *n.* maniki, jantzimaestra.
manner *n.* era, gisa, modu, molde; -era. **In a different manner.** Bestela. **In this manner.** Era honetan. **In the same manner.** Eraberean. *n.(pl.)* era onak.
mannerism *n.* berezitasun, ohitura berezi(a).
mannerly *adj.* erabidetsu, gisatsu.
mannish *adj.* zargasta.
manor *n.* jauretxe.
manservant *n.* morroi.
mansion *n.* jauretxe.
manslaughter *n.* ustekabeko hilketa.
mantel *n.* beheko-suaren gainean dagoen apala.
mantle *n.* estalki. *n.* mantu.
manual *n.* gidaliburu. *adj.* eskuko, eskuarteko, eskuzko.
manually *adv.* eskuz.
manufacture *v.t.* fabrikatu, eskulandu, eskuz egin.
manufacture *n.* fabrikaketa.
manufactured *adj.* eskulanezko.
manufacturer *n.* fabrikatzaile, fabrikante.
manufacturing *n.* fabrikazio, fabrikapen.
manure *n.* gorotz, lastongarri, simaur, ongarri.
manuscript *n.* eskuidazki, eskuidatzi, eskuizkribu.
many *adj.* asko, hamaikatxo, hamaika, frango, ainitz, hainbat. **How many?** Zenbat? *n./pron.* makina bat, asko. **So many.** Hainbat. Hainbeste. **As many.** Horrenbeste. **Not many.** Guti.
map *n.* mapa.
maple *n.* *(bot.)* astigar.

maquette *n.* maketa.
mar *v.t.* itsusitu, itsustu.
maraud *v.i./v.t.* ondasunak ebatsi eta sarraskitu.
marble *n.* haitzurdin, marmol. *n.* kanika.
march *v.i./v.t.* herrenkatu.
March *n.* martxoa.
march *n.* ibilaldi, kaleibilketa.
Mardi Gras *n.* zanpantzar, ihauteri.
mare *n.* *(zool.)* behor. **Herd of mares.** Behorketa. Behortalde.
margarine *n.* margarina.
margin *n.* ertz.
marginal *adj.* ertzeko.
marigold *n.* *(bot.)* aingerulili, aingerulora.
marihuana *n.* *(bot.)* marihuana.
marinate *v.t.* olio eta ozpinetan beratu.
marine *n.* itsastar.
mariner *n.* marinel.
marionette *n.* marioneta, txotxongilo.
marital *adj.* ezkontzako.
maritally *adv.* senargisaz, ezkonlegez.
maritime *adj.* itsasoko, itsastar; itsas-.
    Maritime law. Itsas-legetza.
    Maritime commerce. Itsas-merkataritza.
marjoram *n.* *(bot.)* mendaro.
mark *v.t.* markatu, marratu; zedatu. *v.i.* adi egon, konturatu. *v.i.* **(down)** prezioa beheratu. *v.i.* **(up)** prezioa goratu.
mark *n.* ezagubide, ezaugarri, aztarna, marka.
marker *n.* markatzaile, markagailu. *n.* zedarri, mugarri.
market *v.i./v.t.* salerosi.
market *n.* merkatu, saltoki, plaza, azoka.
marketable *adj.* salgarri, merkatalgarri, salerosgarri, salkoi, salkor.
marketing *n.* komertzialpen, salerosgo.
marksmanship *n.* punteria.
marmalade *n.* mermelada.
marquee *n.* markagailu.
marquis *n.* markes.
marquise *n.* markesa.
marriable *adj.* ezkongarri, ezkontadineko.
marriage *n.* ezkontza, ezkontze.
marriageable *adj.* ezkongarri, ezkontadineko.
married *adj.* senardun, emaztedun, ezkondu. **Just married.** Ezkonberri. **To get married.** Ezkondu.
marrow *n.* *(anat.)* barnemuin, mami.
marry *v.t./v.i.* ezkondu, ezkontarazi.
Mars *n.* *(astron.)* Martitz.
marsh *n.* zingira, aintzira, istinga.
marshal *n.* *(mil.)* mariskal. *n.* sherif.
marshland *n.* zingiradi, aintziradi.
marshmallow *n.* gozoki mota bat.
marshy *adj.* paduratsu; zingiratsu, aintziratsu.
marsupial *n.* *(zool.)* marsupial,

sakeldun.
martial adj. gudatsu.
martially adv. gudagisaz.
Martian n./adj. martiztar.
martin n. (zool.) txirritxori.
martyr v.t. martiri egin, nekaldu.
martyr n. martiri.
martyrdom n. martiritza, odolaitortza.
marvel v.t./v.i. (askotan **at**-ekin)
  harrigarritu, harritu, miretsi.
marvel n. harrigarritza, mirari.
marvelous adj. ikusgarri, miragarri,
  miresgarri, zoragarri, miragarrizko,
  miragarritsu.
marvelously adv. miragarriki,
  miragarriro, miresgarriki,
  miresgarriro, zoragarriki, zoragarriro.
marvelousness n. miragarritasun,
  miresgarritasun, zoragarritasun.
Maryland n. (geog.) Estatu Batuetako
  estatu bat.
marzipan n. mazapan.
mascot n. maskota.
masculine adj. gizonezko, maskulino.
masculinity n. artasun,
  gizonezkotasun.
mash v.t. janaria xehetu, xehekatu.
mask v.t./v.i. maskaratu, musu estali.
mask n. aurpegimozorro,
  aurpegiordeko, mozorro. **To wear a
  mask.** Mozorrotu.
masked adj. mozorrodun, maskaradun.
masochism n. masokismo.
masochist n. masokista.
mason n. hargin, harlangile, hormagin,
  igeltsari.
masonry n. hormagintza, igeltserotza,
  harlangintza.
masquerade n. maskarada.
mass n. (eccl.) meza. **Solemn mass.**
  Mezanagusi. **Requiem mass.**
  Hilmeza. n. kopuru, pilo, meta.
Massachusetts n. (geog.) Estatu
  Batuetako estatu bat.
massacre v.t. sakailakatu.
massacre n. sarraski, hilkintza, sakaila.
massage v.t. igurzkatu, igurtzi.
massage n. igurtzialdi, lgurtzlketa.
masses n. (pl.) jendalde, jendeteria.
masseur n. igurtzaile, ferekari, masaiari
  (gizon).
masseuse n. igurtzaile, masaiari
  (emakume).
massive adj. astun, trinko, handi.
mast n. ontzitantai, tantai.
master v.t. menperatu.
master n. ugazabe, jaunandi.
masterfully adv. maisuki, maisukiro.
masterpiece n. maisulan.
mastery n. maisutasun.
mastic n. mastika, txertore.
masticate v.t./v.i. murtxikatu,
  mastekatu, mamurtu.
mastication n. murtxikapen.
mastiff n. (zool.) mastin zakur.
mastitis n. (med.) ditimin.
mastodon n. (zool.) mastodonte.

masturbate v.i./v.t. masturbatu.
mat n. oinoihal.
matador n. zezenkari, zezenketari,
  toreatzaile.
match v.t./v.i. berdindu. v.t./v.i.
  pareiatu, paretu, kidetu.
match n. poxpolo, misto. n. kide. n.
  partidu.
matchable adj. parekide.
matcher n. parekatzaile.
matchless adj. berdingabe.
matchmaker n. ezkongile,
  ezkontzagile, ezkontzalari.
matchmaking n. ezkontzagintza.
mate v.t./v.i. parekatu, paretu,
  elkarbatu; estaldu, idiskotu.
mate n. kide, lagun.
material n. gai, gaiki, materiale; -gai.
  Reading material. Irakurgai. n. oihal.
materialism n. materialismo.
materialist n. materialista.
materialistic adj. materialista.
materialization n. materialkuntza.
materialize v.t./v.i. materializtatu.
materially adv. materialki.
maternal adj. amatar, amazko.
maternally adv. amagisa.
maternity n. amatasun.
mathematic(al) adj. matematiko.
mathematically adv. matematikoki.
mathematician n. matematikari.
mathematics n. matematika.
mating n. estalketa.
matins n. (eccl.) goizotoitz.
matricide n. amaerailketa, amaerailtza,
  amahilketa.
matriculate v.t./v.i. matrikulatu.
matriculation n. matrikula.
matrimonial adj. ezkontzako.
matrimonially adv. ezkonarauz,
  ezkonlegez.
matrimony n. ezkontza.
matron n. andraundi.
matte adj. hits, zurbil.
matter n. arazo. n. arlo, gai. n. (phys.)
  materia.
mattress n. koltxoi.
maturate v.i. heldu, umatu, zoritu.
maturation n. heldura, umodura.
mature v.i. gizondu, umatu, heldu,
  zoritu; aleztatu.
mature adj. heldu(a), zohi, zori.
maturely adv. tankeraz.
maturity n. heldutasun, heltasun,
  heltzaro, gizaro, umotasun,
  zoritasun.
maudlin adj. minbera, samur.
maudlinism n. minberakeria,
  samurkeria.
maul v.t. zanpatu, makilkatu.
mausoleum n. jaunobi, mausoleo.
maw n. papo.
mawkish n. minkunkerizko.
mawkishly adv. minkunki.
maxillary adj. masailezurrezko,
  mateleko.
maxim n. esaera, ikurritz.

maximum *adj.* gehien, gehienezko.
May *n.* maiatza.
may *v. aux.* zilegi izan, utzi. *v.i.*
  baliteke.
maybe *adv.* agian, beharbada,
  menturaz.
mayonnaise *n.* maionesa.
mayor *n.* alkate.
mayoralty *n.* alkatetasun, alkatetza.
maze *n.* laberinto.
me *pron.* ni, niri; nau-; -da-. **About me.**
  Nitaz. **For me.** Niretzat. **In me.**
  Nigan. **Come with me!** Zatoz
  nirekin! **They have brought it to**
  me. Ekarri didate. **They love me.**
  Maite naute.
mead *n.* urezti fermentatu(a).
meadow *n.* belardi, belarzelai, zelai.
meager *adj.* urri, eskas, murritz.
meal *n.* otordu, jatordu.
mealtime *n.* jatordu, otordu.
mealy bug *n. (zool.)* koko.
mean *v.t./v.i.* saiatu, ahalegindu. *v.t.*
  esan nahi, adierazi.
mean *adj.* doilor, zital, alproja. *adj.*
  behe, beheko. *n.* erdi.
meander *v.i.* norgabetu, noraezean
  ibili.
meaning *n.* esanahi, esangura,
  adierapen, zentzu.
meaningful *adj.* esankor, esanguratsu,
  adieragarri, adierazkor.
meaningless *adj.* gisagabe.
meanly *adv.* doilorki, zitalki, gaizki,
  krudelki, petralki.
meanness *n.* doilortasun, zitaltasun,
  krudelkeria, petralkeria.
means *n. (pl.)* baliakizun, eginbide,
  moldabide; -bide. **By means of.**
  Bidez. Bitartez.
meant *pret./ p. part. of mean.*
meanwhile *adv./n.* bitartean, artean,
  bizkitartean.
measles *n. (med.)* elgorri, mingorri.
measurable *adj.* neurgarri.
measure *v.t./v.i.* neurtu, kanakatu,
  hagazneurtu.
measure *n.* neurri, hein.
measured *adj.* neurrizko, erabidezko.
measureless *adj.* neurrigabe.
measurement *n.* neurri, neurketa.
measurer *n.* neurtzaile.
meat *n.* haragi; harat-.
meatball *n.* albondiga, amandogila.
meatiness *n.* mamitasun.
meaty *adj.* haragidun, haragizko,
  mamizko, haragitsu, mamitsu.
mechanic *n.* makinari, makinazain,
  mekanikari, motorlari.
mechanical *adj.* mekaniko.
mechanically *adv.* mekanikoki.
mechanics *n.* mekanika.
mechanism *n.* mekanismo.
mechanization *n.* mekanikaketa,
  mekanikapen.
mechanize *v.t.* mekanikatu.
medal *n.* domina.

meddle *v.i.* esku sartu.
meddlesome *adj.* sarkoi, sudurluze,
  usnakari, lepaluze.
meddling *n.* eskusarketa, usnaketa,
  nahastero.
media *n.* komunikabide.
median *n.* erdibideko. *n. (geom.)*
  erdiko.
mediate *v.t./v.i.* artetu, bitartetu,
  bitartekotu, bitarteko izan.
mediation *n.* bitartekotasun,
  bitartekotza, arartekotasun.
mediator *n.* bitarteko, artekari,
  ararteko.
medical *adj.* senda-, osa-.
medicate *v.t.* botikatu, sendagaitu.
medication *n.* osasunbide, sendagai,
  sendagailu, sendaki, medikamendu.
medicinal *adj.* sendakor, osasungarri,
  osasunkor.
medicinally *adv.* sendabidez.
medicine *n.* botika, sendagai,
  sendagailu, sendaki. *n.* medikuntza.
  Preventive medicine. Aurretiazko
  medikuntza.
medieval *adj.* erdi aroko.
mediocre *adj.* halaholako, nolabaiteko,
  hits.
mediocrity *n.* kaskarkeria, txatxarkeria.
meditate *v.t./v.i.* hausnartu, hausnar
  egin, gogoetak egin, bururatu.
meditation *n.* gogarketa, gogarpen,
  gogoeta, pentsakizun, gogoketa,
  meditazio.
meditative *adj.* gogartetsu, pentsakor.
meditator *n.* gogoetari.
medium *n.* baliakizun, eginbide. *n.*
  artekari. *adj.* bitarteko, tarteko,
  ertain. *adj.* gordinska.
medlar *n. (bot.)* mizpirondo; mizpira,
  mizpila.
medulla *n. (anat.)* hezurmami,
  hezurmuin; muin. **Spinal medulla.**
  Bizkarrezurmuin. *n. (bot.)*
  landaremami, zurmami.
medullar *adj.* muineko.
meek *adj.* mantso, otzan, sotil,
  mantsobera.
meekly *adv.* mantsoki, otzanki, sotilki.
meekness *n.* mantsotasun,
  otzantasun, sotiltasun.
meet *v.t./v.i.* ezagutu, topatu, topo
  egin, aurkitu. *v.i.* bildu, biltzarreratu,
  elkarganatu, elkartu, batu.
meeting *n.* batzarre, bilera; bilketa;
  kongresu; batzar-. **To attend a**
  meeting. Batzarreratu. **To hold a**
  meeting. Batzarre egin. *n.* topaketa.
megalomania *n.* handinahikeria.
megaphone *n.* deigailu.
melancholic *adj.* itun, iluntsu.
melancholy *n.* tristura, goibelaldi,
  ilunaldi. *adj.* gogoilun, goibelgarri.
melee *n.* liskar, errieta, borrokaldi.
mellification *n.* eztiegite.
mellifluous *adj.* eztitsu, eztijario.
mellow *adj.* gibelandi.

melodic adj. meloditsu.
melodically adv. melodioski.
melodious adj. meloditsu.
melodrama n. melodrama.
melody n. (mus.) doinu, soinu, musika.
melon n. (bot.) meloi.
melt v.i./v.t. urtarazi, urtu, gesaldu. v.t. funditu, galdatu, goritu.
meltable adj. gesalgarri, urkor, urtugarri. adj. fundigarri.
member n. kide, atalkide, partaide, taldekide, bazkide.
membership n. barrukotasun.
membrane n. mintz, azal.
membranous adj. mintzantzeko, mintzatsu, mintzezko.
memento n. oroikarri, oroigailu, gomutaki.
memoirs n. bizitzako oroitzapenak.
memorable adj. gogoragarri, gogangarri, oroikarri, oroimengarri.
memorably adv. aipagarriro, gogoangarriro, oroikarriki.
memorandum n. oharridazti.
memorial n. oroialdi, oroigailu, oroikarri. adj. oroimengarri.
memorize v.t. buruz ikasi, buruan hartu.
memory n. oroimen, oroipen, oroitzapen, gogo, gogorapen, gogarazpen, gomutapen.
men n. (pl.) gizonak, gizonek.
menace v.t. mehatxatu, larderiatu, zemaitu, keinatu.
menace n. mehatxu, zemai.
menacing adj. mehatxagarri, zematzaile, mehatxakor, mehatxuzko.
menacingly adv. mehatxuka, mehatxuz, larderiatsuki, zemaika.
menagerie n. zoo.
mend v.t. adobatu, birjosi, adabakitu, birkonpondu.
mender n. adabakitzaile, konpontzaile.
mendicancy n. eskalego, eskaletasun.
mendicant n. eskale.
mendicity n. eskaletasun, eske, eskekotasun, erromeskeria.
mending n. adabaketa, birjoste, birjosketa.
menial adj. apal, umil; mirabe-, morroi-, morroin-.
meningitis n. (med.) burutik-berako.
menopause n. odolgeldimen.
menstruation n. hileroko, emalege.
menstrual adj. emalegezko.
mensual adj. hilabeteko, hileko, hileroko.
mental adj. buruzko, gogozko.
mentality n. pentsaera.
mentally adv. gogoz.
mention v.t. aipatu, ukitu, ahotan erabili, izendatu, ikutu.
mention n. aipamen, aipaera, izendapen, aipabide, aipakizun, kontaera.
mentionable adj. aipagarri, aipatzeko, izendagarri, kalifikagarri.

mentioned adj. aipatu(a), aipatutako, aitatutako.
mentor n. eskuemale.
menu n. jakitxartel.
meow v.i. miau egin, miaukatu.
meow n. miau.
mercantile adj. merkatal.
mercenary n. sarigudari, mertzenari.
merchandise n. erosgai, merkagai, saleroski, merkantzia.
merchant n. salerosle, saltzaile, azokalari, merkatari.
merciful adj. barkatzaile, errukidun, errukior, errukitsu, bihozbera, gupidatsu.
mercifully adv. errukiz.
mercifulness n. barkazaletasun, errukitasun.
merciless adj. bihozgabe, bihozgogor, gupidagaitz, gupidagabe, krudel.
mercilessly adv. bihozgabeki, gupidagabeki, krudelki, ankerki, gogorki.
mercilessness n. bihozgogorkeria, bihozgogortasun, errukigabekeria, gupidagabekeria, krudelkeria.
Mercury n. (astron.) Merkurio.
mercury n. (min.) merkurio.
mercy n. erruki, gupida, barka, barkamen.
mere adj. huts, soil.
merely adv. hutsik, soilik, soilki.
merge v.t./v.i. bat egin, elkartu.
merger n. bategite.
meridian n. meridiano.
meridional adj. hegoko, hegoaldeko.
merit v.t. merezi.
merit n. merezimendu, meritu, merezi.
meritorious adj. meritudun, merezigarri, sarigarri.
meritoriously adv. mereziz.
mermaid n. sirena, itsasneska, arrainandre.
merrily adv. alaiki, alaikiro, pozgarriro, bozkarioz.
merriment n. poztasun, bozkario.
merry adj. alai, alaitsu, pozkor, bozkariotsu, airos.
merry-go-round n. tiobibo, zaldi-maldiko(ak).
mesh n. saremaila.
mesoderm n. (anat.) erdiazal.
mess v.t. (askotan (up-ekin) nahastu, nahasi, mordoilotu.
mess n. deskonponketa, murgil, nahas-mahas, nahaspila, nahasteka. n. istilu, iskanbila, mordoilo.
message n. errekadu, mezu.
messenger n. mandatari, berrieramaile, mezulari.
Messiah n. Mesias.
messily adv. nahasiz, nahaspilaz, mordoiloka, zalapartaka.
messy adj. nahaspilezko, nahastagarri, zabar.
met pret./p. part. of meet.

metabolism n. metabolismo.
metacarpus n. (anat.) eskuenbor, eskubarne.
metal n. metale. adj. metalezko.
metallic adj. metalantzeko, metaldun.
metallurgic adj. metalgintzako.
metallurgist n. metalgile, metalgin.
metallurgy n. metalgintza.
metamorphosis n. itxuraldapen, itxuraldaketa.
metaphor n. metafora.
metaphoric adj. irudizko, metaforazko.
metaphorically adv. irudiz, metaforaz.
metaphysical adj. metafisiko.
metaphysically adv. metafisikaz.
metaphysicist n. metafisikari.
metaphysics n. metafisika.
metatarsus n. (anat.) oinenbor.
meteor n. (astron.) meteoro.
meteorite n. (astron.) meteorito.
meteorological adj. meteorologiko.
meteorologist n. giroasmatzaile, meteorologari.
meteorology n. meteorologia.
meter n. metro. n. hizneurri, neurri, erritmo. n. kontadore.
methane n. metano.
method n. irakasbide, erabide, metodo.
methodical adj. metodozko, metodiko.
methodically adv. metodoz, neurrieraz.
Methodist n. (eccl.) metodista.
methodology n. egitarau, metodologia.
meticulous adj. miliki, xehezale.
meticulousness n. xehezaletasun.
metric adj. metriko.
metrics n. neurtzeko sistema hamartar(ra).
metropolis n. metropoli, hirinagusi.
mew v.i. miau egin, miaukatu.
mew n. miau.
mewing n. marmar, miau. adj. miaulari.
miaow v.i. miau egin.
miasma n. kirats.
miasmatic adj. kiratsezko, kiraskarri.
mice n. (pl.) saguak.
Michigan n. (geog.) Estatu Batuetako estatu bat.
microbe n. mikrobio.
microbiology n. mikrobiologia.
microcosm n. mikrokosmo, mundutxo.
microfilm n. mikrofilme.
microphone n. mikrofono.
microscope n. mikroskopo.
mid- ert-.
midday n. eguerdi, eguerdian. adj. eguerdiko.
middle n. erdi, gerri.
middle age n. berrogeitabost eta hirurogeitabost urte arteko epea.
middle-aged adj. berrogeitabostetik hirurogeitabost urteko (pertsona).
Middle Ages n. Erdi Aro.
middle class n. burgesia.
middleman n. bitarteko, bitartekari.
midget n. pertsona oso txiki(a).

mid-morning n. goizerdi. adj. goizerdiko.
midnight n. gauerdi, gaumin. adj. gauerdiko.
midsection n. erdialde.
midway n. biderdi. adv. bidenabar.
midwife n. emagin, erditzaile.
mien n. taiu, itxura, tankera.
might pret. of may. baliteke; ote.
mightily adv. ahalmenez, ahaltsuki.
mighty adj. ahaldun, ahaltsu.
migraine n. (med.) burukomin handi(a).
migrate v.i. larraldatu, lekuz aldatu, migratu.
migration n. iraganaldi, kanporaldeketa, migrakuntza, migrazio, pasaia.
migratory adj. lekualdakor, iragaile, pasaiako, paseko.
mild adj. mantso, geza, gozo.
mildew v.t./v.i. lizundu.
mildew n. lizun.
mildly adv. emeki, eztiro, gozoki.
mild-mannered adj. gozatsu.
mile n. mila.
mileage n. mila-kopuru.
milestone n. harrimuga.
militancy n. ekinkidetasun.
militant n. ekinkide.
militarily adv. militarki.
militarism n. militarkeria, militarismo.
militarize v.t. militartu.
military n./adj. militar. n. soldadutza, soldaduska.
military draft n. soldaduketa.
militia n. herritarrez egindako gudaroste.
milk v.t./v.i. eraitsi, bildu (behia).
milk n. esne. Powdered milk. Esne hauts(a). Mother's milk. Diti. Bular.
milking n. eraisketa.
milkmaid n. esne eraisle (emakume).
milkman n. esnedun, esnesaltzaile, esneketari.
milk of magnesia n. (med.) magnesio.
milky adj. esnezko.
Milky Way n. Santio-bide.
mill v.t. irindu. v.i. (about, around) zurrunbildu.
mill n. errota, errotaetxe, eihera.
millenary adj. milurteko.
millenium n. milaurte, milurteburu.
miller n. errotari, eiherari.
millet n. (bot.) artatxiki, artaxehe.
milliary n. milarri.
milligram n. miligramu.
millimeter n. milimetro.
milliner n. kapelari, kapelagin.
milling n. errotaldi, ehieraldi.
million n./adj. milioi.
millionaire n./adj. milioidun.
millionth adj. milioigarren.
millrace n. ubide.
millstone n. ehotarri, errotarri, eiheraharri.
mime n. zinulari.
mimic v.t. idurikatu.

mimic *n.* zinulari.
mimicry *n.* mimika.
minaret *n.* mairudorre.
mince *v.t.* izpitu, izpikatu.
mincemeat *n.* txikitutako sagar eta mahaspasez egindako nahasketa.
mind *v.t./v.i.* obeditu, kasu egin. *v.t.* zaindu. *v.t./v.i.* kontuz ibili.
mind *n.* adimen, gogo, sen. **To be in one's right mind.** Senean egon. **To change (someone's) mind.** Burutik kendu. **To bring to mind.** Oroitarazi. Gogora ekarri. Gogoratu. **To lose one's mind.** Burugabetu. **To be out of one's mind.** Zentzugabetu. **To have (something) in mind.** Gogoan ukan.
mine *v.t.* minatu. *v.i./v.t.* zulapetu, zulo egin.
mine *pron.* nire, neure. *n.* mea, meatze, meategi, meatoki. *n.* mina. **Mine sweeper.** Minabiltzaile.
miner *n.* meatzari, meagizon.
mineral *n.* mea, mineral, minerale; metal-. **Mineral water.** Metalur.
mineralize *v.t./v.i.* meaztu.
mineralogy *n.* mineralogia.
miniature *n.* miniatura.
minicourse *n.* ikasalditxo.
minimal *adj.* gutxienezko, beheren, behereneko.
minimize *v.t.* garrantzia kendu; txikitu, gutitu.
minimum *n.* txikien, tipien, gutienezko, beheren, behereneko.
mining *n.* mealangintza, meagintza, meatzagintza.
miniscule *adj.* ñimiño.
miniskirt *n.* gonamotz.
minister *n.* *(pol.)* ministro, ministrari. *n. (eccl.)* pastore.
ministerial *adj.* ministral.
ministry *n.* *(pol.)* ministergo, ministeritza, ministraritza. *n. (eccl.)* ministeritza, ministraritza.
minium *n.* *(chem.)* minio.
mink *n.* *(zool.)* bisoi.
Minnesota *n.* *(gcog.)* Estatu Batuetako estatu bat.
minnow *n.* *(zool.)* ezkailu.
minor *n./adj.* adingabeko. *adj.* arin, xume, kaskar.
minority *n.* gutxiengo, minoria.
minstrel *n.* koblakari.
mint *v.t.* txanponeztatu, txanpondu, moldeztatu, diru moldetu.
mint *n.* *(bot.)* mende. *n.* paperdirua eta txanponak egiten diren egoitza.
minuend *n.* *(arith.)* kengai.
minus *n.* *(arith.)* ken.
minute *n.* minutu. *adj.* txiki-txiki, izpi, xehe, zehatz.
minutely *adv.* xeheki, zeheki.
minuteness *n.* txikitasun, xehadura.
minutes *n.* *(pl.)* batzarragiri, bileragiri.
miracle *n.* mirari, mirakulu.
miraculous *adj.* miraritsu, mirarizko.

miraculously *adv.* mirariz, mirakuluz.
mirage *n.* isladura. *n.* ameskeria, irudikeria.
mire *n.* istinga.
mirror *n.* ispilu, mirail.
mirth *n.* pozkari.
misadministration *n.* diruhondaketa.
misanthrope *n.* bakarti.
misanthropic *adj.* bakartzale, zokokari, uzkur.
misbehave *v.i./v.t.* gaizki jardun, gaizki jokatu.
misbehavior *n.* jokaera gaizto(a).
miscalculate *v.t./v.i.* gaizki kalkulatu.
miscarriage *n.* haurbotatze, umegaltze, haurregoizte.
miscarry *v.i.* haurra galdu, umea galdu.
miscellaneous *adj.* nahas-mahaseko, askotariko.
miscellany *n.* nahas-mahas, nahasketa.
mischief *n.* bihurrikeria, maltzurkeria, zapokeria.
mischievous *adj.* bihurri, maltzur, gaizto.
mischievously *adv.* bihurriki, gaizki.
mischievousness *n.* bihurritasun.
miscible *adj.* nahaskor.
misconception *n.* ideia faltsu(a), ideia oker(ra).
misconduct *n.* okerbide.
miscreant *n.* pertsona bihurri(a), pertsona zital(a).
miser *n.* lukur, lukurari, lukurrero.
miserable *adj.* lander, ondikotsu, urri.
miserably *adv.* landerki.
miserliness *n.* zekenkeria, zikoizkeria.
miserly *adj.* zeken, zikoitz.
misery *n.* gabezia, premiagorri, eza. *n.* zorigaitz, zoritxar.
misfit *v.t./v.i.* desegokitu.
misfortunate *adj.* zorigaitzeko, zorigabe, tamalezko.
misfortune *n.* zorigaitz, zorigaiztasun, zoritxar, zorigaizto, ezbehar, gaitz.
misgiving *n.* susmo, errezelu.
mishandle *v.t.* gaizki erabili.
mishap *n.* makurraldi.
misjudge *v.t.* oker gogartu. *v.t.* oker epaitu.
mislay *v.t.* galdu.
mislead *v.t.* okerreratu, gaiztatu.
mismanagement *n.* bonbonkeria.
mismatch *v.t.* desegokitu, gaizki pareiatu.
misnomer *n.* izendapen oker(ra).
misogamist *n.* ezkonetsai.
misogamy *n.* ezkonetsaigo.
misogynist *n.* andretsai.
misogyny *n.* andretsaigo, andre-higindura.
misplace *v.t.* galdu.
misrepresentation *n.* erakuspen oker(ra).
miss *v.t./v.i.* faltatu, huts egin, galdu, ez lortu. *v.t.* hutsetsi, -(r)en falta hartu.

miss *n.* huts. *n. (cap.)* andrea (emakume ezkongabeentzat). *n.* emakume ezkongabea(a).
missal *n.* mezaliburu.
misshapen *adj.* itxuragabe(ko).
missile *n.* iraizkin.
missing *adj.* mantxu; galdu(a).
mission *n.* misio. *n.* enkargu.
missionary *n.* misiolari.
missis *n. (colloq.)* emazte.
Mississippi *n. (geog.)* Estatu Batuetako estatu bat.
missive *n.* gutun, eskutitz, mezu.
Missouri *n. (geog.)* Estatu Batuetako estatu bat.
mist *v.i./v.t.* lurrineztatu, gandutu, sirimiri egin.
mist *n.* laino, lanbro.
mistake *n.* huts, oker, makur, falta.
mistaken *adj.* herratu, okerreko.
mistakenly *adv.* oker, hutseginez, okerrez, okerretara.
mister *n.* jaun, on.
mistiness *n.* lanbrotasun.
mistletoe *n. (bot.)* mihura.
mistreat *v.t.* gaizki erabili, gaizki hartu.
mistreatment *n.* gaizkierabilketa.
mistress *n.* amorante, ohaide, emaztorde (emakume).
mistrust *v.t./v.i.* susmarazi; mesfidatu.
mistrust *n.* errezelu, aieru, susmo.
mistrustful *adj.* goganbehartsu.
mistrustfully *adv.* goganbeharrez.
misty *adj.* lainodun, lanbrotsu.
misunderstand *v.t./v.i.* gaizki ulertu, txarto aditu.
mite *n. (zool.)* zeden.
miter *n. (eccl.)* mitra.
mitigate *v.t./v.i.* gozatu, bigundu, eztitu.
mitigating *adj.* emagarri, arintzaile, bigungarri, eztigarri.
mitigation *n.* arindura, arinaldi, arinketa, gozadura, eztidura.
mitigator *n.* arintzaile.
mitten *n.* haurren eskularru.
mix *v.t./v.i.* nahasi, nahastu, nahastatu.
mix *n.* nahasketa.
mixable *adj.* nahaskor, nahastagarri, nahasgarri.
mixableness *n.* nahaskortasun.
mixed *adj.* nahasi(a).
mixer *n.* nahasgailu, irabiagailu.
mixing *n.* nahaste.
mixture *n.* nahasketa, nahaste, nahaste-mahaste.
mix-up *n.* nahastapen, nahaskeria.
mnemonics *n.* mnemoteknia.
moan *v.i./v.t.* intziri egin, intzirikatu, zizpurutu.
moan *n.* zizpuru, hasperen, zinkurin, intziri.
moat *n.* osin, putzu.
mob *n.* jendaila.
mobile *adj.* higikor, higigarri, mugikor, mugigarri.
mobility *n.* higikortasun, mugikortasun, ibilkortasun.
mobilization *n.* higiketa, mugiketa.
mobilize *v.t./v.i.* mugitu, prest jarri.
moccasin *n.* mokasin.
mock *v.t./v.i. (v.i., askotan at-ekin)* isekatu, iseka egin, irri egin, murrikatu.
mocker *n.* barrelari, isekagile, isekari, irrigile.
mockery *n.* irri, iseka.
mocking *adj.* isekagarri, isekagile.
mockingly *adv.* irrika, isekaz.
mock-up *n.* itxurantz.
mode *n.* gisa, moda.
model *v.t./v.i.* ereduztatu. *v.t.* molde egin, moldatu.
model *n.* maketa, eredulan. *n.* eredu, erakuspen, eredugarri, ikasbide. *n.* modelo.
moderate *v.t./v.i.* ematu, erabidetu, bigundu. *v.t./v.i.* mahaiburu izan.
moderate *adj.* erabidetsu, erabidezko, eratsu, neurridun, ematsu, eztitsu.
moderately *adv.* begiramenez, erabidez.
moderation *n.* eratasun, gozadura, neurritasun, begiramendu.
moderator *n.* irizpidetzaile, neurriemale, moderatzaile.
modern *adj.* gaurko, gaurreguneko, orainaldiko, oraingo, eguneko, moderno.
modernism *n.* modernismo.
modernist *n.* berrikizale.
modernity *n.* gaurkotasun, egungotasun.
modernization *n.* oraingoera, gaurkoraketa, zaharberrizte, eraberrizte.
modernize *v.t./v.i.* gaurkoratu, gaurkotu, oraingotu, eraberritu, eguneratu.
modernizer *n.* zaharberritzaile.
modernly *adv.* berriki, modernoki.
modernness *n.* egunekotasun, gaurkotasun, oraingotasun, modernotasun.
modest *adj.* apal. *adj.* erabidezko, eratsu, neurrizko.
modestly *adv.* oneski.
modesty *n.* lotsakizun, lotsa, ahalke.
modification *n.* aldaerazpen, aldakera.
modify *v.t./v.i.* hartarakotu, aldatu.
modulation *n.* bozgorabehera, ahoskatze.
moist *adj.* busti, heze.
moisten *v.t./v.i.* busti.
moistness *n.* hezedura, hezetasun.
moisture *n.* hezetasun.
molar *n. (anat.)* ehortz, matrailagin.
mold *v.t.* molde egin, moldekatu, ereduztatu.
mold *n.* lizun. *n.* molde, orkoi.
molder *n.* moldekari.
moldiness *n.* lizuntasun.
moldy *adj.* lizuntsu. **To get moldy.** Lizundu.

mole n. (zool.) sator. n. (anat.) orein.
molecular adj. molekular.
molecule n. molekula.
molehill n. satorlur, satormeta.
molest v.t. amorrarazi, mindu, asperrarazi. v.t. bortxatu.
molestation n. asperraldi, gogaitaldi. n. bortxaketa.
mollify v.t. eztitu.
mollifying adj. eztikor, emagarri, eztitzaile.
mollusk n. (zool.) molusko, hezurgabe.
molt v.i./v.t. lumaldatu, lumaberritu.
molten adj. gori. **To become molten.** Gori-goritu.
moltenly adv. goriki, gori-gori.
moltenness n. goritasun.
molting n. lumaberrizte.
mom n. ama.
moment n. aresti, une, memento.
momentary adj. behingo, mementoko.
momentum n. oldar.
momma n. ama.
mommy n. (dim.) amatxo.
monarch n. errege, erregina.
monarchic adj. erregealdeko, monarkiko.
monarchism n. erregezaletasun.
monarchist n./adj. erregealdeko, erregezale, erregetiar.
monarchy n. monarkia, erregetza.
monastery n. fraidetxe, lekaidetxe, komentu, serorategi.
Monday n. astelehen.
monetary adj. diruzko, txanponezko.
money n. diru, koroa, sos.
moneylender n. prestatzaile.
money-loving adj. diruzale, dirukoi.
mongrel n. txakur xinitre.
monied adj. dirudun, sosdun.
monitor n. oharkari.
monk n. fraide, erlijioso, lekaide.
monkey n. (zool.) tximino, zimino.
monkey business n. tximinokeria.
monochromatic adj. kolorebakarreko, kolorebakar.
monocle n. lentebakar.
monogamous adj. emabakar, senarbakar.
monogamy n. emaztebakartza, senarbakartza.
monograph n. monografia.
monographic adj. monografiko.
monolith n. monolito.
monologue n. bakarrizketa.
monopolize v.t. monopolizatu, beretzakotu, orobatu.
monopolizer n. bereganatzaile, orobiltzaile.
monopoly n. monopolio.
monosyllabic adj. silababakardun.
monosyllable n. silababakar.
monotone n. doinubakar.
monotonous adj. aldagabeko.
monotonously adv. doinuberez, hots bakarrez; aldagabeki.
monotony n. aldagabetasun,

doinubakar.
monsoon n. montzoi.
monster n. mamutzar, munstro.
monstrosity n. mamutzarkeria, mamukeria, izugarrikeria.
monstrous adj. izugarri.
monstrousness n. izugarritasun.
Montana n. (geog.) Estatu Batuetako estatu bat.
month n. hil, hilabete. **Half a month.** Hilerdi.
monthly adj./adv. hileroko; hilero.
monument n. oroitarri, oroigailu.
moo v.i. mu egin, marraska egin (behiak).
moo n. mu.
mooch(er) n. jantxakur, zurrupakari.
mood n. giro, umorealdi.
moodily adv. umoretxarrez.
moody adj. umoretxar.
moon n. ilargi.
moonbeam n. ilargiaren izpi(a).
moonlight n. ilargiaren argi(a).
moonshine n. artoz egindako edari alkoholikoa.
Moor n. mairu, mairutar.
moor n. eremu, basamortu.
mooring n. (mar.) ditxo, aihen.
Moorish adj. mairuaire, mairuantzeko, mairutar.
moose n. (zool.) oreinandi.
moot adj. irizkarri, eztabaidagarri.
mop v.t. xukatu, idortu, lehortu (zapi batez).
mop n. landerki, iztripu, traputzar.
mope v.i./v.t. adoregabetu, kikildu.
moped n. motordun txirrinda.
mopper n. lanbasketari.
moral n. ipuinondore, moral. adj. moralezko.
morale n. adore.
moralist n. moralista, moralzale.
morality n. moral, moraltasun.
moralize v.i./v.t. moralizatu.
morally adv. moralki.
morass n. lizundi.
moratorium n. luzamendu, luzamen, luzabide.
morbid adj. gaisokor, gaizkor, gaitzekarle.
morbidity n. erikortasun.
mordacity n. mingarritasun, mintasun.
mordant adj. pikokari, mokokari.
mordantly adv. pikoka, mokoka.
more adj./adv. areago, gehiago, zenbat, haboro; -ago. n. gehiago.
moreover adv. honezaz gainera, gainerakoan, gainerantzean.
morgue n. gorpugela, gorputegi.
moribund adj. hilurren.
Mormon n./adj. mormoi.
morning n. goiz. adj. goizetiko, goiztar, goizeko. **Good morning!** Egun on!
morose adj. itzal, atsekabekor.
morpheme n. (gram.) morfema.
morphine n. morfina.
morphological adj. morfologiko.

morphology n. (gram.) morfologia.
morrow n. bihar, hurrengo egun.
morsel n. ahokada, kopau.
mortal adj. heriogarri, hilkor, hilgarri. adj. astun.
mortality n. hilbehar, hilkortasun.
mortally adv. hilzoriaz.
mortar n. espaloi, morteiru.
mortar and pestle n. birringailu.
mortgage n. bahi, bahikuntza, bahitura.
mortgageable adj. bahigarri.
mortgager n. bahitzaile.
mortician n. hiljazle.
mortification n. hildura, mortifikapen.
mortify v.t./v.i. hilduratu, mortifikatu.
mortise n. elkarrune.
mortmain n. eskualda ezin daiteken jabetasuna. **To free from mortmain.** Ezamortizatu.
mortuary n. hildegi.
mosaic n. mosaiko.
Moslem n./adj. musulman.
mosque n. mezkita.
mosquito n. (zool) eltxo.
moss n. goroldio, mihura.
mossy adj. goroldiozko, goroldiotsu.
most adj./adv. gehien. **At the most.** Gehienez. n. gehien(ak).
mostly adv. gehienik.
motel n. motela, gaua pasatzeko ostatu mota (Estatu Batuetan).
moth n. (zool.) sits.
motheaten adj. sitsadun.
mother n. ama.
motherhood n. amatasun.
mother-in-law n. amaginarreba.
motherland n. Ama-Lur.
motherless adj. amagabe.
motherly adj./adv. amatiar, amarekiko; ama-; amagisa, ama legez.
mother-of-pearl n. nakare, perlama.
motif n. gai.
motion n. mugida, higidura, mugimendu.
motionless adj. geldi.
motivate v.t. eraiki, bideman.
motivation n. eragikuntza, eragingarri, eragiketa.
motive n. zio, zergati, zergatiko.
motley adj. nabar, pintarkatu. adj. ezberdin, askotariko.
motor n. (mech.) mugindar, motore.
motorboat n. motordun batela.
motorcycle n. moto, motor, motorzikleta.
motorcyclist n. motolari.
motorist n. autogidari.
motto n. ikurritz.
mound n. lurbizkar, bizkartontor.
mount v.t./v.i. lauzkatu, igo. v.t. zamaritu. v.i. (up) gehiagotu; zaldira igo.
mountain n. mendi. adj. mendiko.
mountaineer n. mendigoizale, mendizale, menditar.
mountaineering n. mendizaletasun.
mountainous adj. mendiskatsu, menditsu.

mounted adj. zaldizko.
mourn v.i./v.t. negarreztatu, mindurikatu.
mourner n. hiletari, hiletajole.
mournful adj. dolugarri, negarrarazle.
mournfully adv. arrenguraz, goibelki, itunki.
mourning n. lutu, dolu. adj. hiletasun; dolu-.
mouse n. (zool.) sagu, xagu.
mouser n. sagukari.
moustache n. bibote, ezpaingaineko.
mouth n. aho, mutur. n. bokale.
mouthful n. ahokada, ahamen, ahobete, otaman.
mouth-to-mouth resuscitation ahoz-ahozko arnasaldi(a).
movable adj. higigarri, higikor, mugigarri, mugikor.
movableness n. higikortasun, mugikortasun.
move v.i./v.t. mugitu, higitu, ibili, erabili, eragin. v.i./v.t. etxaldatu, auzogabetu. v.t. -arazi, -erazi, eragin. v.t. hunkitu, bihotza irauli, bigundu, iharrosi. v.i. (along) bide egin, joan. v.i. (aside) albora egin, alboratu. v.i. (away, away from) urrundu, urrutiratu. v.i. (back) atzeratu. v.i. (forward) aitzinaratu, aurreratu. v.i. (out) destokitu, deslekutu; etxe batetik irten (gehienetan gurasoen etxetik); leku aldatu. v.t./v.i. (over) baztertu, albora egin.
movement n. higidura, mugidura, mugimendu, mugida, ibilketa; eraiketa.
mover n. higitzaile, mugitzaile.
movie n. zinema, pelikula.
moviegoer n. zinemazale.
movies n. (pl.) zine.
moving adj. hunkigarri. n. etxaldaketa.
mow v.t./v.i. belarra ebaki. v.t. (down) deuseztatu, pertsona asko hil.
mowable adj. igitagarri.
mower n. segalari, segari.
Mr. n. jauna.
Mrs. n. andre ezkondu(a).
Ms. n. andre(a).
much adj./adv. asko(z), ainitz, hainbat, hamaikatxo, frango, makina bat. n. asko. **As much as.** Beste. Bezainbat. Hainbat. **So much.** Hainbat. Hainbeste. **So much the better.** Hainbat hobe. **That much.** Horrenbeste. **Too much.** Gehiegi. **How much?** Zenbat?
mucous adj. mukidun.
mucus n. muki.
mud n. lokatz, basa, basatza, lupetza.
muddiness n. lokaztasun, lohitasun, uhertasun.
muddle n. nahasteka, nahastakeria, korapilo.
muddled adj. nahasitako.
muddy v.t./v.i. lohitu, lohiztatu, lokaztu.

muddy adj. lokazti, lokaztsu, lupetsu, basatsu, uher.
mudhole n. zikinzulo, zikintza.
mudslide n. lurjausi, luperia, lurreten.
muffin n. bizkotxo mota bat.
muffler n. indargetzaile.
mug v.t. kalean pertsona bati zerbait lapurtu.
mug n. pitxer, gandola.
mugger n. kalelapur.
mugging n. kalelapurreta.
muggy adj. umel. **Muggy weather.** Eguraldi umela.
mulatto n./adj. zuribeltz, erdibeltz.
mulberry n. (bot.) masustondo; masusta.
mulch n. simaur, sats.
mule n. (zool.) mando; manda-.
muleteer n. mandazain, mandaketari.
mulish adj. mandotar.
mullet n. (zool.) korkoin, lasun.
multi- (gram.) -askodun, -tsu.
multicellular adj. zelulatsu, zelulaskodun.
multicolored adj. koloreaskodun, koloreanitz, margoaskodun, margotsu, nabar.
multilateral adj. aldeanitz, aldeaskotako, aldeaskodun.
multilingual adj. hizkuntzaskodun.
multimillionaire n./adj. milioiaskodun, milioitsu.
multinational adj. nazioaskotako, nazioaskodun.
multiple n. (arith.) anizkoitz. adj. askozko, askotako.
multipliable adj. ugalgarri, anizkarri.
multiplicand n. (arith.) bidergai.
multiplication n. (arith.) biderkaketa, biderketa, multiplikazio. **Multiplication table.** Biderkaketa-taula.
multiplicator n. (arith.) bidertzaile.
multiplicity n. askotarikotasun, anizkoiztasun.
multiplier n. bidertzaile, biderkatzaile, multiplikatzaile.
multiply v.t./v.i. biderkatu, aniztu, gehitu, ugaritu; -koiztu.
multiracial adj. arrazaskotako.
multitude n. jendalde, jendetza, jendetalde, gizaketa, gizatalde.
multivalve adj. oskoltsu.
mum adj. isil, isilkoi.
mumble v.i./v.t. hitzak jan, ahomoteldu, purrustatu.
mummy n. momia.
mumps n. (med.) umorotz, paperak.
mundane adj. mundukoi, mundutar, mundutiar, munduko.
mundaneness n. mundutasun.
municipal adj. udaleko, herriko, munizipal.
municipality n. udalbarruti.
munitions n. munizio(ak).
mural n. ormirudi.
murder v.t./v.i. hilarazi, hil.

murder n. hilketa, gizerailketa, erailketa, sarraski, gizahilketa.
murderer n. gizahiltzaile, gizeraile, eraile, hiltzaile, sarraskitzaile.
murderess n. gizaeraile (emakume).
murderous adj. eraile, hiltzaile.
murky adj. itzal, ilun, goibel.
murmur v.i./v.t. marmar egin, murmurikatu.
murmur n. marmar, murmur, murmurrots.
murmurer n. murmurikari.
muscat n. (bot.) moskatel.
muscle n. (anat.) giharre.
muscular adj. gihartsu, gihartza.
musculature n. (anat.) giharreria.
muse v.i./v.t. hausnar egin, hausnartu.
museum n. museo, erakustetxe.
mush n. morokil.
mushiness n. fardotasun.
mushroom v.i. arin handitu, laster zabaldu.
mushroom n. (bot.) perretxiko, ziza, txanpinoin.
mushy adj. marruskari, bigun.
music n. musika, soinu, solfeo. **To read music.** Solfeatu.
musical adj. musikazko; musika-.
musicaiity n. musikaltasun, soinutasun.
musically adv. musikalki.
musicalness n. musikaltasun.
musician n. musikagile, soinulari, musikalari.
musk n. amizkla.
musket n. fusil.
Muslim n./adj. mahomatar.
muslin n. muselin, musulehun.
mussel n. (zool.) muskuilu.
must v.aux./v.i. behar, behar ukan, behar izan.
must adj. beharrezko. n. behar, beharrezko. n. muztio.
mustache n. bibote, ezpaingaineko.
mustard n. ziape.
mutate v.t./v.i. aldaerazi, aldatu.
mutation n. aldaketa.
mute n. mutu. n. motelgailu. adj. mintzogabe, hitzgabe(ko).
muteness n. mutudura, hizkabezia.
mutilate v.t. gorputz(a) ebaki.
mutilation n. gorputz-ebaketa, mozketa.
mutineer n. asaldari, matxino.
mutiny v.t. oldartu, asaldatu, bihurritu.
mutiny n. asaldakuntza, bihurrialdi.
mutism n. mutukeria, mututasun.
mutter v.i./v.t. murdurikatu, hitzak jan.
mutton n. ahariki, ardiki.
mutual adj. elkar, elkarren, bienarteko.
mutuality n. elkarkidego, elkarkidetasun.
mutually adv. elkar.
mutualness n. elkarganakotasun.
muzzle v.t. musu estali, musukoa ezarri.
muzzle n. mutur. n. musuko,

muturlokarri.
my *pron.* nire.
myocardium *n. (anat.)* bihozmami.
myopia *n. (med.)* miopia, begimoteltasun.
myopic *adj.* begigaizto, begimotel, miope.
myriad *adj.* zenbagaitz, zenbaezin, kontagaitz, kontaezin.
myrrh *n.* mirra.
myself *pron.* neu, neuk, nerorek, neroni.
mysterious *adj.* isilkari, ezkutuzko.
mysteriously *adv.* ezkutuan, ezkutuz.
mystery *n.* ezkutuki, misterio, ezkutapen. *n.* polizi-nobela, polizi-elaberri.
mystic *n./adj.* mistiko.
mystical *adj.* mistiko.
mystically *adv.* mistikoki.
mysticism *n.* mistika; mistizismo.
myth *n.* mito.
mythic *adj.* mitiko, mitozko.
mythical *adj.* mitiko, mitozko.
mythological *adj.* mitologiko.
mythologist *n.* mitologari.
mythology *n.* mitologia.

N

n *n.* Ingeles alfabetoko letra.
nab *v.t.* lapurretan harrapatu.
N.A.B.O. *n. (North American Basque Organizations, Inc.)* Ipar-Ameriketako Euskal Amerikar Elkarte.
nag *v.t.* gogaitarazi, nekarazi.
nail *v.t.* josi, iltzatu.
nail *n.* iltze. *n.* hatzazal.
naive *adj.* inozo, geldo, gizagaiso.
naivety *n.* inozotasun, geldokeria, lainokeria.
naked *adj.* biluzi, biluzik, larrugorri.
nakedly *adv.* biluzik, larrugorrian, larrutsik.
nakedness *n.* larrugorritasun, larrugorrikeria.
name *v.t.* izena jarri, izendatu, deitu, erltzl. *v.t.* alpatu.
name *n.* izen. **Middle name.** Bigarren izena. **Christian name.** Bataioizen. **Last name.** Deitura. Abizen. **First and last names.** Izen-deiturak.
named *adj.* izendun, izeneko.
nameless *adj.* izengabe.
namely *adv.* hots, bereziki.
namer *n.* izendatzaile.
namesake *n.* izenkide.
nanny *n.* haurtzain.
nap *v.i./v.t. (v.t., askotan away-kin)* lokuluxkatu.
nap *n.* loaldi, lokuluxka.
nape *n. (anat.)* lepagain, garondo, lepondo.
napalm *n. (chem.)* napalm.
naphtha *n. (chem.)* nafta.
napkin *n.* ezpainzapi.
narcissus *n. (bot.)* lilipe, nartziso.

narcotic *n.* loeragile, loeragingarri, loerazle, narkotiko.
nark *n.* narkotiko-, poliziarentzat lan egiten duen espioia.
narratable *adj.* kontagarri, jaulkigarri.
narrate *v.t./v.i.* kontatu, jaulki.
narration *n.* kontaketa, kontakizun, istorio.
narrative *n.* ipuingintza.
narrator *n.* kontalari, kontari, jaulkitzaile.
narrow *v.i./v.t.* estutu, mehetu, mehartu, hertsitu.
narrow *adj.* mehar, estu, hertsi.
narrowly *adv.* estuki, hertsiro, hertsiki.
narrowness *n.* estugune, estuera, mehartasun, hertsitasun.
nasal *adj.* sudurkari, sudurreko.
nasality *n.* sudurtasun.
nasalization *n.* sudurmintzo.
nasalize *v.t./v.i.* sudurkatu.
nasally *adv.* sudurrez, sudurmintzoz.
nastily *adv.* zikinki.
nastiness *n.* nazkagarritasun, higuingarritasun. *n.* lizunkeria.
nasty *n.* nazkagarri, higuingarri, zikin. *n.* lizun, zantar.
natal *adj.* jaiotzazko; jaio-.
natatorium *n.* igerietxe.
nation *n.* herri, aberri, nazio. **The United Nations.** Nazio Batuen Erakundea.
national *adj.* nazional.
nationalism *n.* nazionalismo, abertzaletasun.
nationalist *adj./n.* abertzale, nazionalista.
nationalistic *adj.* abertzale, nazionalista.
nationality *n.* naziotasun, nazionalitate, herritargo.
nationalization *n.* nazionalizazio, nazionalkuntza, nazionalpen.
nationalize *v.t./v.i.* nazionaldu, nazionalizatu.
nationally *adv.* nazionalki.
nationless *n.* herrigabe(ko).
nationwide *adj.* nazio guztiko; nazio guztian.
native *n./adj.* sorterriko, herritar, herriko. **Native son.** Herriko seme. **Native of.** -ar, -tar, -dar. **Native of Gernika.** Gernikar.
native tongue *n.* jaiotizkera, jaiotizkuntza, lehenizkuntza.
nativity *n.* jaiotze, jaiokunde.
natural *n.* berezko, izatezko, jitezko; natur-.
naturalist *n.* naturazale, naturalista.
naturalization *n.* herritarketa, naturalizapen.
naturalize *v.t./v.i.* naturalizatu, hartaratu, bertakotu.
naturally *adv.* bereziki, naturalki. *adv.* jakina.
naturalness *n.* naturaltasun, berezkotasun.

nature *n.* izaera. *n.* natura.
naught *n.* bapeza.
naughty *adj.* bihurritxo, deabru, gaizto.
nausea *n.* goragale, okanahi, botagale, egozgale.
nauseate *v.t./v.i.* goragaletu, larritu; okaztatu.
nauseating *adj.* okarazle, goralegarri, goitikagarri.
nauseous *adj.* okagile, egozgale. **To be nauseous.** Goragaletu.
nautical *adj.* itsasoko, itsastar.
Navaho *n./adj.* navajo.
naval *adj.* ontzi-.
Navarra *n. (geog.)* Nafarroa, Nafarra.
Navarrese *n./adj.* nafar, nafartar; Nafarroako. *n.* nafarrera.
nave *n.* elizbarne.
navel *n. (anat.)* zilbor, zil.
navigable *adj.* itsasgarri, nabigagarri.
navigate *v.t./v.i.* itsastatu, nabigatu.
navigation *n.* itsasketa, itsasibilketa.
navigator *n.* untziko.
navy *n.* marina.
nay *adv.* ez.
near *adv.* hurbil, hurrean, gertu. **To draw near.** Hurbildu. *adj.* hurbileko. *prep.* aldamenean, hurbil, ondoan.
nearby *adj.* hur, hurbil, hurre, hurreko. *adv.* hurbil, hurrean, ondoan.
nearer *adj./adv.* hurbilago.
nearly *adv.* ia, kasik.
nearness *n.* hurbiltasun, hurkotasun.
near-sighted *adj.* begimotel, begigaizto, miope, itsusko, begilabur.
near-sightedness *n.* begimoteltasun, miopia.
neat *adj.* txukun.
neatly *adv.* txukunki.
neatness *n.* txukuntasun.
Nebraska *n. (geog.)* Estatu Batuetako estatu bat.
nebula *n. (astron.)* izarlaino.
nebular *n.* izarlainotsu.
nebulous *adj.* goibel, ilun. *adj.* lainotsu.
necessarily *adv.* behar-beharrez, ezinbestean, alabeharrez, nahitaez, premiaz.
necessary *adj.* beharrezko, nahitanahiezko, alabeharreko, premiazko, premiatsu.
necessitate *v.t.* behar izan. *v.t.* behartu.
necessity *n.* behartasun, behar, beharrizan, premia. **Out of necessity.** Ezinbestez. Nahitaez.
neck *n.* lepo, idun; lepa-. *n.* zintzur.
neckerchief *n.* lepozapi.
necklace *n.* gargantila, iduneko.
neckline *n.* eskote, golkohuts.
necktie *n.* gorbata.
necrological *adj.* hilen, nekrologiko.
necrology *n.* nekrologia.
necromancy *n.* hilaztikeria.
nectar *n.* eztigai.
need *v.t./v.i.* behar izan, behar ukan,

premia ukan.
need *n.* behar, beharrizan, gabetasun, premia. **To be in need of.** -(r)en premian egon.
needful *adj.* beharrezko.
needle *n.* orratz, jostorratz.
needless *adj.* ezbeharrezko, premiagabeko.
needlessly *adv.* ezbeharrez, premiagabeki.
needlework *n.* orrazlan.
needn't "need + not"-aren laburpena.
needy *adj.* behartsu, dirugabe, gabe, txiro, pobre, premiadun.
ne'er *adv.* inoiz ere ez, nehoiz.
nefarious *n.* gaiztotzar.
negate *v.t./v.i.* ezeztu, ukatu.
negation *n.* ukamen, ezeztaketa, eza.
negative *adj.* ezkor, ezezkor, ukakor, ukatzaile.
negatively *adv.* ukoz, ezezka.
negativism *n.* ezkortasun.
negativity *n.* ezezkotasun.
neglect *v.t.* ezaxolatu, desarduratu, arduragabetu.
neglect *n.* ezaxola, desardura, axolakabekeria.
neglectful *adj.* arduragabeko.
neglectfulness *n.* arduragabezia, arduragabetasun.
negligee *n.* etxejantzi, bata.
negligence *n.* arduraeza, arduragabezia, axolakabezia, lazotasun, nagitasun.
negligent *adj.* arduragabe, desarduratsu, ezaxolati, adigabe, axolagabeko, lazo.
negligently *adv.* axolagabeki, arduragabeki, lazoki, zabarki.
negligible *adj.* zirtzil, kaskar, xume.
negotiable *adj.* merkagarri, negoziagarri, tratugarri.
negotiate *v.i./v.t.* negoziatu, gestionatu.
negotiation *n.* negoziaketa, negoziazio.
negotiator *n.* negoziari, negoziatzaile.
Negro *n./adj.* beltz, negro.
neigh *v.i.* irrintzina egin.
neigh *n.* irrintzi, irrintzina.
neighbor *n.* auzakide, auzo, bestaldeko; auza-.
neighborhood *n.* auzo, etxadi.
neighboring *adj.* auzoko, aldameneko, bestaldeko.
neighborly *adj.* lagunkor, adiskidetsu, lagunarteko.
neither *conj./adj.* ere, ezta, ezta ere, ez . . . ez. **Me, neither.** Ni ere ez. *pron.* ez bat ez beste, ez batak ez besteak.
nemesis *n.* lehiakide menderaezin(a).
neo- *(gram.)* berri-. neo-.
neoclassical *adj.* neoklasiko.
neolithic *adj.* neolitiko.
neological *adj.* neologiko.

neologism *n.* neologismo, hizperri.
neology *n.* neologia.
neon *n.* *(chem.)* neon.
neon sign *n.* argirudi.
nephew *n.* iloba, loba (mutil).
nephritis *n.* *(med.)* giltzurrineri.
nepotism *n.* ahaidezalekeria, ilobakeria.
Neptune *n.* *(astron.)* Neptuno.
nerve *n.* *(anat.)* kirio, zain, nerbio.
nerveless *adj.* bare, lasai, patxadazko. *adj.* koldar, beldurti.
nervewracking *adj.* hertsagarri, hertsakor, hertsu, urdurigarri.
nervous *adj.* artega, kexu, hersturadun, urduri, pairugabe, larri, kezkati.
nervous breakdown *n.* nerbioaldi.
nervously *adv.* ezinegonik, larri, kexurik, urduriki, estu.
nervousness *n.* estutasun, urduritasun, ezinegon.
nest *v.t./v.i.* habia egin.
nest *n.* habia.
nestle *v.i.* kuxkurtu, kukubilkatu.
net *v.t.* sareratu, saretaratu.
net *n.* sare. *n.* *(econ.)* garbi, huts, soil.
netful *n.* sarekada.
nether *adj.* beheko, azpiko.
nettle *n.* *(bot.)* asun.
net weight *n.* pisugarbi.
network *n.* sare. *n.* telebista kate(ak).
neuralgia *n.* *(med.)* nerbiomin, neuralgia.
neurasthenia *n.* *(med.)* neurastenia.
neuritis *n.* *(med.)* nerbioeri.
neurologist *n.* *(med.)* neurologo.
neurology *n.* neurologia.
neuron *n.* neurona.
neurosis *n.* neurosi.
neurotic *adj.* neurotiko.
neuter *v.t.* zikiratu, irendu, antzutu.
neuter *n.* *(gram.)* neutro.
neutered *adj.* zikiro.
neutral *adj.* neutral, alderdigabeko.
neutrality *n.* alderdigabetasun, neutraltasun.
neutralizable *adj.* neutralgarri.
neutralization *n.* neutralpen.
neutralize *v.t./v.i.* neutraldu.
neutrally *adv.* neutralki.
neutron *n.* neutroi.
Nevada *n.* *(geog.)* Estatu Batuetako estatu bat.
never *adv.* inoiz ere ez, inoiz ez, egundaino, behinere ez.
nevermore *adv.* inoiz ere ez gehiago.
nevertheless *adv.* hala ere, halere, halabaina.
new *adj.* berri.
newborn *n./adj.* haurberri, jaioberri, ernaberri.
newcomer *n.* etorberri.
newfangled *adj.* berri-berri.
New Hampshire *n.* *(geog.)* Estatu Batuetako estatu bat.
New Jersey *n.* *(geog.)* Estatu Batuetako estatu bat.
newly *adv.* berriki.
newlywed *n./adj.* ezkonberri.
New Mexico *n.* *(geog.)* Estatu Batuetako estatu bat.
newness *n.* berritasun.
news *n.* berri, albiste.
newsboy *n.* aldizkaria saltzen duen mutila.
newscast *n.* teleberri, teleguneko, telegunkari.
newscaster *n.* telealbistari.
newspaper *n.* egunkari, kazeta, aldizkari. **Sunday paper.** Igandekari.
news reporter *n.* albistalari.
news stand *n.* kiosko.
New World *n.* Mundu Berri.
New Year's Day *n.* urteberri.
New Year's Eve *n.* gabonzahar, urtezahar.
New York *n.* *(geog.)* Estatu Batuetako estatu bat.
New Zealand *n.* *(geog.)* Zelanda Berria.
next *adj.* hurren, hurrengo, datorren. **Until next time.** Hurren arte. Hurrengoarte. **Next week.** Datorren astean. **Next time.** Hurrengoan. *adv.* **(to)** ondoan, aldean, alboan, ondoko.
next-door *adv.* parean, kontra. *adj.* auzoko.
next-door neighbor *n.* etxeondoko.
nexus *n.* lotura.
nibble *v.i./v.t.* gozokatu.
nice *adj.* onzale, prestu, zintzo, zuzen, on.
nicely *adv.* formalki.
niceness *n.* onberatasun.
nicety *n.* fintasun.
niche *n.* hormaune.
nick *v.t.* koskatu, akastu, hozkatu.
nick *n.* akats, hozkadura, koska, hozka.
nickel *n.* *(chem.)* nikel. *n.* Estatu Batuetako bost zentimoko txanpona.
nickname *v.t.* izengoititu, gaitzizendatu.
nickname *n.* ezizen, gaitzizen, goitizen, izengoiti, izenorde.
nicotine *n.* *(chem.)* nikotina.
niece *n.* iloba, loba (neska).
nifty *adj.* bikain, oso on.
niggardliness *n.* eskaskeria, zuhurkeria.
niggardly *adj./adv.* zeken, eskulabur.
night *n.* gau, arrats. *adj.* gaueko.
nightcap *n.* txano. *n.* lotara joan baino lehen hartzen den edaria.
nightfall *n.* gautze.
nightgown *n.* atorluze, kamisoi.
nightingale *n.* *(zool.)* txindor, erresinul, urretxindor.
nightjar *n.* *(zool.)* zata.
nightly *adj./adv.* gauero.
nightmare *n.* ameskaitz, ameskaizto, amestxar.
night owl *n.* gautxori, gauzale.

nightshirt n. atorluze.
nightstand n. gaumahai.
nighttime n. gaualdi.
nighty n. atorluze, kamisoi.
nimble adj. bizkor.
nimbleness n. bizkortasun.
nimbly adv. bizkor, bizkorki.
nincompoop n. inozo, tentel.
nine n./adj. bederatzi.
ninefold adj./adv. bederatzikoitz.
nineteen n./adj. hemeretzi.
nineteenth adj./n. hemeretzigarren, hemeretzi.
ninetieth adj./n. larogeitamargarren.
ninety n./adj. larogeitamar.
ninety-year-old adj. larogeitamardun.
ninth adj./n. bederatzigarren, bederatzi.
nip v.t./v.i. tximakatu.
nipple n. (anat.) dituburu, bularmutur.
nit n. zorriño.
nit-picking adj. xehezale, hutsikusle, okerrikusle.
nitrate n. (chem.) nitrato.
nitrogen n. (chem.) nitrogeno.
nitwit n. inozo, tentel.
no adj. ez, ezetz, ezezka. n. eza, ezetza. **Yes or no?** Baietza ala ezetza?
nobility n. aitoren semetasun, zalduntasun, urentasun.
noble adj. odolgarbiko, printzetar; noble, prestu, zintzo, sotil. n. noble, zamaldun.
nobleman n. zamaldun, noble, aitoren seme.
nobleness n. urentasun.
noblewoman n. aitorralaba.
nobly adv. zaldungisa, zaldunki, zaldunkiro.
nobody pron. inor(k) ere ez, nehor(k).
nocturnal adj. gaueko, gauzale, gautar; gau-. **Nocturnal animal.** Gaupizti.
nocturnalness n. gaukotasun.
nod v.i./v.t. buru behetu, buru makurtu. v.i. (off) lotara joan, kuluskatu.
nod n. buruagur.
nodding off n. kuluska, lokuluska.
node n. (anat.) konkor.
Noel n. eguberri(ak), gabon(ak).
noise n. hots, zalaparta, zarata, zaratots.
noiseless adj. zaratagabe, isil.
noiselessly adv. isilean, isilik.
noisemaker n. karrakagailu, karraka.
noisily adv. hotsandiz, zalapartaz, zarataz, zarataka, dunbadaka.
noisome adj. zaratatsu, zalapartatsu.
noisy adj. zaratatsu, zalapartatsu.
nomad n./adj. nomada.
nomadic adj. ibildari, larraldatzaile, nomada.
nomadism n. larraldaketa, nomadismo.
nomenclature n. izendegi, nomenklatura.
nominal adj. izenezko.

nominally adv. izenez.
nominate v.t. izendatu.
nomination n. izendapen.
nominative adj. (gram.) nominatibo.
nominee n. kandidatu; -gai.
non- (gram.) ez-; -ezin.
nonadhesive adj. atxikiezin.
nonagenarian n./adj. larogeitamarrurteko.
nonbelieving adj. fedegabe, fedegabeko, sinesgabe.
nonchalance n. arduragabezia, axolakabezia.
nonchalant adj. arduragabe, axolagabe.
nonchalantly adv. arduragabeki, axolagabeki.
noncombustible adj. erreezin, erregaitz.
nonconformist adj./n. konformagaitz.
noncountable adj. zenbatezin.
nondescript adj. ezinesaneko, zehazkaitz.
none pron. inor(k) ere ez. adv. batere ez.
nonessential adj. gainerako, gainontzeko.
nonetheless adv. hala ere, halere.
nonexistence n. ezizate.
nonexistent adj. izategabe.
nonextendible adj. hedaezin, hedagaitz.
nonnegotiable adj. negoziaezin.
nonpayment n. ezordainketa.
nonperishable adj. ezingalduzko.
nonpotable adj. edanezin, edangaitz.
nonproductive adj. ezemankor.
nonsense n. ergelkeria, zorakeria, burugabekeria, eragabekeria, tontakeria.
nonsensical adj. itxuragabeko.
nontoxic adj. pozoigabe.
nontransferable adj. pasaezin.
nonunion adj. sindikatogabe. adj. sindikatokontrako.
nonviolent adj. odolotz.
noodle n. makarroi-zerrenda.
nook n. hormaune, zoko-moko, zurkulu.
noon n. eguerdi. adj. eguerdiko.
no one pron. bat ere ez, inor(k) ere ez.
noose n. sokalaster.
no place adv. inon, inora ere ez.
nor adv. ez.
Nordic adj./n. iparreko; nordiko.
norm n. arau, jarraibide.
normal adj. neurriko, normal.
normality n. normaltasun.
normalization n. normaleztapen, normalkuntza.
normalize v.t./v.i. normaldu.
normally adv. normalki, normalean.
normative adj. arauemaile.
north n. ipar. **North Sea.** Ipar itsaso. adj. iparreko, ipartar.
North America n. (geog.) Iparramerika.

North American n./adj. iparramerikar.
North American Basque
Organizations, Inc. n. (N.A.B.O)
Ipar-Ameriketako Euskal Amerikar
Elkarte.
North Carolina n. (geog.) Estatu
Batuetako estatu bat.
North Dakota n. (geog.) Estatu
Batuetako estatu bat.
northeast n. iparrekialde, iparsortalde.
adj. iparrekialdeko. adv.
iparrekialdetik, iparrekialdera.
northeaster n. enbataldi.
northeastern adj. iparrekialdeko.
northerly adj/adv. iparralderuntz,
iparraldetik.
northern adj. ipar, ipartar.
northerner n. ipartar.
Northern Ireland n. (geog.) Eire.
North Pole n. (geog.) iparburu,
izotz-iparralde, goiko-polo.
North Star n. (astron.) iparrizar.
northward adv. iparralderuntz.
northwest n. iparmendebalde,
iparsartalde. adj. iparmendebaldeko,
iparsartaldeko. adv.
iparmendebaldetik,
iparmendebaldera.
northwestern adj. iparmendebaldeko.
nose n. (anat.) sudur, mutur. **To blow**
one's nose. Zintz egin.
nosebleed n. sudurrodol.
nostalgia n. herrimin, bakarmin; -min.
nostril n. (anat.) sudurzulo, musuzulo.
nosy adj. lepaluze, muturluze,
begiluze.
not adv. ez. **If not.** Ezezkoan. **Of**
course not. Ez horixe.
notable adj. nabarigarri,
nabarmengarri.
notableness n. nabarigarritasun.
notably adv. nabarigarriro, nabariki,
nabariro.
not any adv. batere.
not anywhere adv. inon ere ez.
notary n. eskribau. **Notary public's**
office. Eskribautegi.
not at all adv. batere ez.
notation n. ohar, oharketa.
notch v.t. akastu, hozkatu, koskatu.
notch n. akats, hozka, hozkadura.
notched adj. akastun.
notcher n. horzkari, horzkalari.
note v.t. ohartu, sumatu, hauteman.
note n. oharpen, oharketa.
notebook n. kuaderno.
noteworthy adj. ikusgarri, aipagarri,
adigarri.
nothing n. ezer, ezdeus. adv. ezerez,
batere ez, tut.
nothingness n. ezerezkeria, ezereza,
ezdeustasun.
notice v.t. nabaritu, sumatu, ohartu,
konturatu, igarri, hauteman.
notice n. oharkera, kasu.
noticeability n. oharkarritasun.
noticeable adj. nabarigarri, nabarmen,

oharkarri.
noticeableness n. nabarigarritasun.
noticeably adv. oharki.
notification n. jakinarazpen, ohar.
notify v.t. jakinarazi, azaldatu.
notion n. nozio. n. purtxileria,
merkekeri(ak).
notoriety n. agiritasun, nabaritza.
notorious adj. entzutetxarreko,
izentxarreko. adj. ager, ageriko,
jakin.
notoriously adv. entzutetxarrez,
famatxarrez, lotsagarriro. adv.
nabariki, nabarmenki.
notoriousness n. entzutetxar,
famatxar.
nonwithstanding adv./prep. arren,
nahiz eta.
nougat n. turroi.
nought n./adj. huts, ezer, ezdeus.
noun n. izen. **Common noun.** Izen
arrunt. **Determinate noun.** Izen
mugatu. **Indeterminate noun.** Izen
mugagabe.
nourish v.t. jaten eman, janaritu,
janarazi, elikatu, mantendu.
nourisher n. mantentzaile, elikatzaile.
nourishing adj. elikagarri, gizenkor.
nourishment n. elikadura, hazkurri,
jangai.
novel n. elaberri, nobela. **Novel**
writing. Elabergintza.
novelist n. elabergile, nobelari.
novelty n. berrikitasun, berritasun.
November n. azaroa.
novena n. (eccl.) bederatziurren.
novice n. fraidegai, mojaberri,
lekaidegai, nobizio. n. hasberri,
sarberri.
novitiate n. nobizialdi, nobiziatu.
now adv. orain. **By now.** Honez gero.
For now. Oraingoz. **Every now and**
then. Noiz edo noiz. **From now on.**
Hemendik aurrera. **Right now.**
Oraintxe. **Until now.** Orain arte.
nowadays adv. gaurregun,
gaurregunean.
noway adv. inola ere ez, ezelanbere
ez.
nowhere adv./n. inon, inora. **Nowhere**
at all. Inon ere ez.
noxious adj. erigarri, galgarri, gaisokor.
noxiously adv. galgarriro.
noxiousness n. galgarritasun,
heriozkortasun.
nozzle n. mangera-mutur.
nuance n. ñabardura.
nuclear adj. nuklear.
nuclear reactor n. erreaktore.
nucleus n. erdimuin, gune.
nude n./adj. larrugorri, biluzi, biluzgorri.
nudely adv. biluzik.
nudge v.t. ukitu eta sakatu emekiro.
nudism n. biluzkeria, biluztasun,
larrugorritasun.
nudity n. larrugorritasun,
biluzgorritasun.

nugget n. urrepipitta.
nuisance n. nekaldi, gauza nekagarri.
null adj. baliogabe, ezdeus, indargabe.
nullification n. ezeztapen, ezeztadura.
nullify v.t. indargabetu.
nullity n. baliogabezia, ezdeustasun, ezereztasun, baliogabetasun.
numb v.t. mangutu, sormindu. **To go numb.** Minsortu.
numb adj. sormindun, mangu.
number v.t./v.i. zenbatu.
number n. (math.) zenbaki, zifra. **Whole number.** Zenbaki oso.
numbering n. zenbaketa.
numberless adj. zenbakigabe.
numbness n. sortasun, sorrera, mangutasun.
numeral n. (math.) zenbaki. adj. zenbakizko.
numerator n. (math.) zatigai.
numeric adj. zenbakizko, kopuruzko.
numerical adj. zenbakizko.
numerically adv. zenbakiro.
numerous adj. kopurutsu, zenbatsu.
numismatics n. numismatika.
nun n. lekaime, serora, moja.
nunciate n. (eccl.) nuntziatura.
nuncio n. (eccl.) nuntzio.
nunnery n. lekaimetxe, mojetxe, komentu.
nuptial adj. ezkontzazko, ezteietako.
nurse v.t./v.i. gaisoak zaindu. v.t./v.i. ditia eman, elikatu, edoski.
nurse n. erizain, gaisozain. n. haurtzale.
nursemaid n. seintzain.
nursery n. haurtegi, haurtzaindegi, umetegi. n. hazleku, mindegi.
nursery school n. haurreskola, haurlilitegi.
nurseryman n. landarezain.
nursing n. erizaintza. n. edoskialdi.
nurture v.t. elikatu, mantendu.
nut n. ur(ra).
nutcracker n. kraskagailu.
nut meat n. mihuru, ale.
nutrient n. janari elikagarri(a).
nutrition n. hazkurri, elikapen.
nutritious adj. indargarri, gizenkor, elikagarri.
nutritive adj. elikagarri, gizenkor.
nutshell n. intxaurroskol.
nutty adj. intxaurrantzeko. adj. zoro.
nuzzle v.i./v.t. musturkatu, musuritu.
nylon n. (chem.) nylon.
nymph n. maiteder. n. (zool.) kusku.

O

o n. Ingeles alfabetoko letra.
oaf n. tentel, ergel; trakets.
oafish adj. trakets, baldar.
oak n. (bot.) haritz, harizti.
oaken adj. haritzezko.
oakum n. iztupa, kirru.
oar n. arraun, erramu.
oarlock n. (naut.) tolet.
oarsman n. arraunlari.

O.A.S. n. (Organization of American States) Amerikar Estatuen Erakunde.
oasis n. oasis.
oath n. zin, juramendu.
oatmeal n. gosaltzeko jaten den zereal mota bat.
oats n. (bot.) olo.
obdurate adj. damugabe, garbaigabe.
obdurateness n. damugabekeria, damugabezia.
obedience n. manukortasun, menekotasun, esanekotasun, mentasun.
obedient adj. esaneko, esanoneko, meneko, manakor.
obediently adv. menpez, obedituz.
obeisance n. begirune, itzal, begiramen. n. burumakurketa, kilimusi.
obelisk n. obelisko.
obese adj. lodi, gantzadun, gizen.
obesity n. lodiera, gizentasun, loditasun.
obey v.t./v.i. obeditu, esana egin, men egin, meneratu.
obeyable adj. obedigarri.
obituary n. hilberri, hildei, hiltxartel.
object v.i./v.t. ezetsi.
object n. gauza, gauzaki.
objection n. erreparu.
objectionable adj. agiragarri. adj. iraingarri, nazkagarri, higuingarri.
objective n. helburu, jomuga, xede.
oblation n. (eccl.) elizdiru.
obligate v.t. hertsatu, behartu, bortxatu.
obligation n. betebehar, eginkizun, beharkizun.
obligatorily adv. premiaz, ezinbestean.
obligatoriness n. derrigortasun.
obligatory adj. beharrezko, nahitaezko, ezinbesteko, manuzko.
oblige v.t. beharrarazi, behartu.
obliging adj. amoregile, moldakoi.
obligingly adv. emankortasunez.
oblique adj. zehar.
obliquely adv. zeharka, trabeska.
obliqueness n. zehardura, zehartasun.
obliterate v.t. deuseztatu, suntsitu, desegin.
oblivion n. ahasdura, desgogorazio, ahanzdura.
obnoxious adj. nazkagarri, higuingarri, gorrotagarri, iraingarri.
oboe n. (mus.) oboe.
obscene adj. lizun, lohi, likits, gordintzale, zantar.
obscenely adv. lizunki, zantarki, gordinki, likiski.
obsceneness n. lizunzaletasun, linburkortasun.
obscenity n. lizunkeria, zantarkeria, likiskeria, linburkeria, urdakaria.
obscurantism n. kulturgabekeria. n. ilunkeria, ilunzalekeria.
obscurantist n. ilunzale.
obscure v.t. itzalpetu, itzali, itsuerazi.

obscure adj. ilun, ilunbetsu, ilunbezko. adj. entzutegabe.
obscurely adv. ilunki, ilunpean.
obscurity n. iluntasun, ilunbe.
obsequious adj. lausengatzaile, mihizuri.
obsequiously adv. adeitsuki.
observable adj. sumagarri, oharkarri, hautemangarri.
observance n. zeremonia; ohitura; betekizun.
observant adj. oharti, zuhur, hautemale.
observation n. soegite, oharketa, ohar, behaketa.
observatory n. behatoki, ohartoki.
observe v.t./v.i. ohartu, oharrarazi, hauteman, hautetsi, zelatu. v.t./v.i. esan. v.t. obeditu. v.t. ospatu.
observer n. begirale, behatzaile, soegile, oharrarazle, ohartzaile.
obsession n. obsesio, itsumen, buruhauste.
obsessive adj. kezkabiziko.
obsessively adv. itsuki.
obsolete adj. ezohizko, ohigabe.
obstacle n. behaztopa, oztopo, eragozpen. **To pose obstacles.** Oztopatu. Eragotzi.
obstetrician n. emagin, sortzain.
obstetrics n. emagintza, tokologia.
obstinacy n. burugogorkeria, kasketaldi, seta, temakeria, itsukeria.
obstinate adj. burugogor, temakor, temati, hisikor, sinesgogor.
obstinately adv. burugogorki, temaz, setatsuki.
obstreperously adv. dunbadaka.
obstruct v.t. oztopatu, eragotzi, behaztopatu.
obstruction n. oztopo, oztopaketa.
obstructive adj. galarazkor, baldargarri.
obtain v.t. lortu, erdietsi, eskueratatu. v.i. modan egon.
obtainable adj. eskurakor, lorgarri.
obtrude v.t./v.i. sakatu, saka egin, bultzatu.
obtuse adj. (geom.) kamuts. **Obtuse angle.** Angelu kamuts.
obverse n. aldegain.
obviate v.t. alderatu.
obvious adj. ageri, nabari, argi, nabarmen.
obviously adv. nabariki, nabarmenkiro.
obviousness n. nabaritasun, nabarmentasun.
occasion v.t. erakarri, gertarazi.
occasion n. abagadune, aldi.
occasional adj. noizbehinkako, inoizkako, aldizko.
occasionally adv. noizean behin, noiz edo noiz, noizbehinka, lantzean behin, tarteka.
occident n. mendebalde.
occipital adj. garondoko. n. kokotezur.
occult adj. izkutuko, isileko. n. isileko jakituria.

occupancy n. etxetiargo, maiztergo, maiztertasun.
occupant n. maizter.
occupied adj. hartuta. adj. lantsu, arazotsu.
occupation n. arazo, eginkizun; irabazpide, lan, lanbide, lanpostu, bizibide, ogibide. n. atzemate, jabeketa.
occupy v.t. ihardun, jardunarazi. v.t. bete (leku edo denbora). v.t. kontrolatu (militar).
occur v.i. gertatu, suertatu. v.i. (to) burura etorri, bururatu, gogoratu, kasketak eman, otu, ahoratu.
occurred adj. gertatutako.
occurrence n. gertakizun, gertakari, gertaldi, jazoera.
ocean n. itsasandi, itsaszabal, urandi, ozeano. adj. ozeaniko.
oceanic adj. itsasandiko, urandiko.
oceanography n. ozeanografia.
o'clock adv. -ak izan; erlojuaren, ordulariaren.
octagon n. oktogono.
octagonal adj. oktogonal.
octet n. zortziko, zortzikote.
October n. urrila.
octogenarian adj./n. larogeiurteko, larogeitsu.
octopus n. (zool.) olagarro.
octosyllabic adj. zortzisilabadun.
ocular adj. begiko.
oculist n. begikari, okulista.
ocurrence n. gertaera.
odd adj. bakotxi. adj. arraro.
oddity n. bitxikeria.
odds n. abantaila. n. posibilitate; kanore.
ode n. oda.
odontology n. odontologia.
odious adj. gorrotagarri, gorrotakor, herragarri.
odiously adv. gorrotagarriro, gorrotagarriz.
odiousness n. gorrotagarritasun.
odometer n. (mech.) kilometrokontagailu.
odor n. usain.
odorless adj. usaingabe(ko).
odorous adj. usainemaile, usaingarri.
o'er Cf. over.
oestrus n. argose, ohara.
of prep. -ko, -etako, -tariko.
off prep./adv. kanpo, landa, at; -tik, gainetik, gaindik. prep./adv. urruti, urrun. adv. itzali(a). prep. inoren bizkarretik bizi. prep. guttiago, gutxiago. **Off days.** Ondoezik igarotzen diren egunak. **Off key.** Soinugaiztu. **Off limits.** Debekatuta. **Off season.** Garaiz kanpo(ko). **Off shore.** Itsasandi. Itsaszabal.
offal n. pikatxa, barruki, tripaki.
offend v.t./v.i. laidotu, laidoztatu, iraindu, gaitzitu, mindu, min eman.
offender n. iraintzaile, kaltegile,

laidotzaile.
offense n. irain, gaitzegite, oker.
offensive n. erasoaldi, oldarraldi. adj.
oldartzaile, erasotzaile. adj. iraingarri,
irainkor, mingarri, laidogarri.
offensively adv. erasoz. adv. minduz,
minki.
offer v.t. eskaini, opa izan, opari egin,
opa ukan, presentatu.
offer n. eskaintza.
offerer n. eskaintzaile, opatzaile.
offering n. eskaintza, opari, oparigai,
eskain, eskainaldi.
offertory n. (eccl.) eskainaldi.
offhand adj./adv. bapatean, berehala,
oldez.
office n. bulego. **Office hours.** Bulego
orduak. **Office clerk.** Bulegolari.
officer n. ofiziale. n. polizia.
official n. ofiziale. adj. ofizial.
officially adv. ofizialki.
officialness n. ofizialtasun.
officiate v.i./v.t. jardun, aritu; meza
eman. v.i. arbitratu.
offprint n. separata.
offshoot n. errokimu.
offspring n. ume, semetalde,
ondorengoak; abelkume.
off-white adj./n. zuriska.
oft adv. sarritan, askotan.
often adv. sarritan, sarri, maiz,
askotan, usu, ainitzetan, frangotan.
How often? Noizero?
ogle v.t./v.i. lotsagabeki begiratu.
ogre n. haurjale.
oh int. o, ai.
Ohio n. (geog.) Estatu Batuetako
estatu bat.
oil v.t. koipetu, koipeztatu, gantzutu,
urineztatu.
oil n. (chem.) petrolio; olio.
oilcloth n. hule.
oiler n. koipeztatzaile.
oiliness n. oliotasun, koipetasun,
gantzutasun.
oiling n. oliodura, olioztadura,
gantzuketa, koipeketa.
oilskin n. hule.
oil tanker n. petroliontzi.
oily adj. petroliozko, petroliotsu;
oliozko, oliotsu, oliodun, koipezko.
ointment n. gantzu, gantzuki,
gantzugailu.
O.K. Cf. okay.
okay v.t. baietsi.
okay adj. on, zuzen. adv. ondo, ongi.
n. baiezpen.
Oklahoma n. (geog.) Estatu Batuetako
estatu bat.
old adj. zahar, adintsu, zaharkote. adj.
aspaldiko, behinolako.
oldest adj. nagusien(a).
old-fashioned adj. modaz kanpoko.
oldness n. zahartasun. n. aspalditasun,
aspaldikotasun.
old saying n. errefrau, atsotitz, esaera
zahar.

olfaction n. usnadura.
olfactory adj. usainmenezko; usain-.
oligarchy n. (pol.) oligarkia.
olive n. (bot.) oliba.
olympic adj. olinpiar.
Olympics n. olinpiada.
ombudsman n. ararteko.
omelet n. arrautzopil, tortila.
omen n. zori.
ominous adj. zoritxarkoi.
ominously adv. zorigaitzez,
zorigaiztoan.
omission n. ezaipaketa, ezegite,
uzketa.
omit v.t. ezegin, utzi.
omitted adj. aipatugabe.
omni- guzti, oro.
omnipotence n. ahalguzti.
omnipotent adj. ahalguztidun.
omnipotently adv. ahalguztiz.
omnipresence n. nonnahikotasun,
orotan egote.
omnipresent adj. nonnahiko.
omniscience n. guztijakintza.
omniscient adj. orojakin, orojakitun,
guztijakitun.
omnivorous adj. guztijale, orojale.
on prep. gain, gainean. adv. piztu(a),
pizturik. prep. -z; (-ari, -ei), buruzko.
On foot. Oinez. prep./adv. -runtz,
-rantz. prep. -n. **On time.** Garaiz.
Come on! Goazen! **From that time
on.** Handik aurrera. **On credit.**
Epeka. **On purpose.** Nahita.
once adv. behin, behinola, ezkero, -z
gero. **At once.** Berehalaxe. **Once
upon a time.** Behin batean. **More
than once.** Behin baino gehiagotan.
Once and for all. Behingoz.
one n./adj. bat. **One at a time.**
Banaka. **One by one.** Bat-banaka.
One hour. Ordu bete. pron.
pertsona bat.
one-armed adj. besobakar, maingu.
one-eyed adj. begibakar.
one-fourth n./adj. laurden.
oneness n. bakuntasun.
onerous adj. zamadun.
oneself pron. norbera, norbere.
one-third n./adj. heren, hirugarren.
onion n. (bot.) tipula, tipulaburu.
onlooker n. ikusle.
only adv. soilik, soilki, bakarrik,
besterik. adj. bakar. conj. baina.
onomastic adj. izenezko.
onomatopoeia n. hotsizen,
onomatopeia.
onset n. hastapen, hasiera.
onslaught n. eraso gogor, oldarketa.
on time adv. orduz, tenorez, sasoiz,
garaiz.
onto prep. gainean.
ontological adj. ontologiko.
ontologist n. ontologilari.
ontology n. ontologia.
onward adv. aurreruntz.
ooze v.i./v.t. poliki jario, poliki isuri.

opal n. *(min.)* opalo, opalarri.
opaque adj. opaku.
open v.t./v.i. ireki, zabaldu. v.t./v.i. inauguratu, hasiera eman.
open adj. ireki(a), irekita, zabalik, zabal. adj. xalo, zabal, harbera.
openable adj. irekigarri.
opened adj. ireki(a), irekita.
opener n. irekigailu, irekitzaile.
opening n. zulo. n. irekidura, zabalketa, zabalaldi.
openly adv. agerian, zabalki, xaloki, ahobetean, argi ta garbi.
openness n. irekitasun, zabaltasun, xalotasun.
open sea n. itsaszabal.
opera n. opera.
operable adj. ebakigarri, operagarri.
operate v.i. ibili, funtzionatu. v.i./v.t. makina erabili. v.t. *(med.)* operatu, ebaki.
operatic adj. operako.
operating room n. kirofano.
operation n. jarduneta, eragiketa, erabilaldi. n. *(med.)* ebaketa, operazio.
operator n. maneatzaile. n. telefonari.
operetta n. operatxo, operaxka.
opthalmologist n. begisendagile, begisendatzaile.
opthalmology n. begisendagiletza.
opiate n. narkotiko, loarazle, droga, lobelar. adj. narko-.
opine v.t./v.i. uste izan, eritzi, iritzi, pentsatu.
opinion n. uste, eritzi, aburu.
opinionable adj. erizgarri.
opinionated adj. burugogor, temati, hisikor, temakor, burukoi. **To be opinionated.** Burukoitu.
opium n. *(bot.)* opio.
opossum n. *(zool.)* zarigueia.
opponent n. aurkalari, kontrakari, jarkitzaile, kontrezarle.
opportune adj. garaizko, orduoneko, aldezko, erazko.
opportunely adv. orduonez, garaionez.
opportunism n. egokikeria.
opportunistic adj. guziekilako.
opportunity n. abagadune, era.
opposable adj. jarkigarri.
oppose v.t./v.i. oposatu, aurka egin, kontrezarri, kontrajarri, kontraeragin, gogor egin.
opposed adj. aurkako, aurrezko, kontrazko.
opposing adj. kontrajarle, kontrako, aurkagarri.
opposite adj./n. aurkako, jarkitzaile, kontrako.
opposition n. kontrajarrera, kontrakotasun, kontrajoera, kontraezarketa, aurkakotasun, oposizio.
oppress v.t. zanpatu, zapaldu, oinperatu, aurrean erabili, aurrean hartu.

oppressed adj. zanpatu(a).
oppression n. zapalkuntza, zapalketa.
oppressive adj. zapalkor, bortxatzaile.
oppressor n. azpiratzaile, zapaltzaile, oinperatzaile, bortxatzaile.
opt v.i. *(for)* begiz jo, aukeratu, hautatu.
optical adj. begi-.
optimal adj. ezinobe.
optimally adv. ezinobeki.
optimism n. baikortasun.
optimist n. baikor.
optimistic adj. baikor.
optimum adj. hoberen, hobezin, egokien.
option n. hautabide, aukerabide, aukera.
optional adj. ahalezko, aukerazko, hautapenezko, aukerabidezko.
opulence n. diruketa.
opulent adj. ondasuntsu, aberats.
opulently adv. bapo.
opus n. lan, idazlan, musika-lan.
or conj. edo, nahiz, zein, ala. **This or that.** Hau edo hori.
oracle n. igarle; orakulu.
oracular adj. igarlearen; igarle-.
oral adj. ahozko, hitzezko, mintzozko, ahokari.
orally adv. ahoz, hitzez, mintzoz.
orange n. *(bot.)* laranja. n./adj. laranja, laranjaire.
orangutan n. *(zool.)* orangutan.
oration n. hitzaldi.
orator n. hizlari, mintzalari.
oratory n. hizlaritza. n. otoiztegi, otoiztoki.
orbit n. *(astron.)* birabide, urtebira. n. *(anat.)* betzulo.
orchard n. fruitategi.
orchestra n. *(mus.)* orkesta.
orchestral adj. orkestazko.
orchestrate v.t./v.i. orkestatu.
orchestration n. orkestapen.
orchid n. *(bot.)* orkidea, orkibelar.
ordain v.t. abade egin, apeztu. v.t./v.i. agindu, manatu.
ordeal n. proba gogor, esperientzia neketsu.
order v.t./v.i. agindu, agintaritu, manatu. **In order to.** -tzeko. -teko. v.t. *(econ.)* eskabidea egin.
order n. agindu, aginduagiri, manamendu, manu; araubide. **By order of.** -(r)en aginduz. n. jarraikera. n. eskabide. n. mota, sail. n. lagundi.
ordered adj. agindutako, araubidezko. adj. gisaonezko.
orderly adv. gisaonez. adv. araubidez, arauz. n. eritegiko laguntzaile (gizon).
ordinance n. araudi, legedi.
ordinarily adv. eskuarki, gehienetan.
ordinary adj. ohizko, ohiturazko. adj. ximple, edonolako, nolanahiko, arrunt.
ordination n. *(eccl.)* ordenketa.

ore n. minerale.
oregano n. (bot.) loragiño.
Oregon n. (geog.) Estatu Batuetako estatu bat.
organ n. (mus.) organo. n. (med.) soinzati.
organic adj. organiko.
organism n. erakunde, organismo.
organist n. organojole, organista.
organization n. erakuntza, prestakuntza, antolaketa, antolamendu, gertuera. n. erakunde, organizazio.
organize v.t./v.i. antolatu, prestatu, taiutu, egituratu, eratu.
organized adj. taiuzko.
organizer n. antolatzaile, apaintzaile, eratzaile.
orgasm n. orgasmo.
orgy n. jaizoro, bestakeria.
orient v.t./v.i. noratu, norabidetu, zuzendu. v.t. ohitu.
orient n. ekialde, eguzkialde.
oriental adj. ekialdeko, sortaldeko.
orientalism n. sortaldezaletasun.
orientation n. norabide, jokamolde, biderapen.
orifice n. zulo, zilo.
origin n. iturri, etorbide, sustrai, erro, sorrera. n. jatorri, sorburu, sorrera.
original adj. etorkizko, jatorrizko, lehendabiziko. **Original sin.** Jatorrizko bekatu. adj. asmakor.
originality n. asmakortasun. n. jatortasun, berebizikotasun.
originally adv. izatez, jatorriz, lehendanik, sortzez, lehenengotik.
originate v.i./v.t. sortu, sorterazi.
originator n. kreatzaile, egile.
oriole n. (zool.) urretxori.
ornament v.t. apaindu, dotoretu, edertu.
ornament n. apain, apaindura, apaingarri, edergailu, edergarri.
ornamental adj. apaingarri, edergarri.
ornamentally adv. apainki.
ornamentation n. apaindura, dotoredura, apainketa.
ornate adj. apaindu(a), edertu, bitxi.
ornithologist n. hegaztilari, ornitologo.
ornithology n. ornitologia.
orography n. orografia.
orphan n. umezurtz.
orphanage n. umezurtzetxe, umezurztegi.
orphanhood n. umezurtza.
orthodox n. ortodoxo.
orthodoxy n. ortodoxia.
orthography n. ortografia.
orthopedics n. (med.) hezurlaritza, ortopedia.
orthopedist n. (med.) hezurlari.
oscillate v.i./v.t. zabukatu, kolokatu.
oscillating adj. kolokari.
oscillation n. gorabehera(k).
osier n. (bot.) zume, mihimen.
osmosis n. (chem.) osmosi.

osprey n. (zool.) arrano arrantzale.
osseous adj. hezurrezko.
ossification n. hezurketa, hezurtzapen.
ossify v.t./v.i. hezurtu.
ossuary n. hezurtegi, hezurtoki.
ostensible adj. nabari, agiri, nabarmen.
ostensibly adv. agerki.
ostentation n. handi-mandikeria, handipuzkeria, nabarmenkeria.
ostentatious adj. handinahiko, handi-mandi, nabarmenkor.
ostentatiously adv. handiki, nabarmenkiro, nabariki.
ostrich n. (zool.) ostruka, hegalfer.
other adj. beste.
otherwise adv./adj. bestela, osterantzean.
otitis n. (med.) belarrimin.
otter n. (zool.) ugabere.
ouch int. ai.
ought v. aux. behar ukan, behar izan.
ounce n. ontza.
our pron. gure, geure.
ours pron. gurea.
Our Lady n. Ama Birjina, Andra Mari.
ourselves pron. gu, geu.
oust v.t. desaulkitu.
out adv./prep. kanpora, at, landa; -tik, -dik. adj. kanpoko.
outbid v.t. gehiagokatu.
outbreak n. izurritearen hastapena; guda-hasiera.
outbuilding n. etxeorde.
outburst n. suminaldi; indarraldi; negarraldi.
outcast n./adj. erratzaile, noragabe.
outcome n. ondorio, emaitza.
outcrop n. harburu.
outcry n. arrantza.
outdated adj. modaz kanpoko.
outdo v.t. norbere garaipenak gainditu; markak hautsi, markak gainditu.
outdoor adj. kanpoko, lekoreko. n. (pl.) kanpo, kanpoalde.
outer adj. kanpo, kanpotar.
outermost adj. urrunen(a), urrutikoen(a).
outer space n. ortzune, ortzeune.
outfit n. ekipo, ekipaia.
outgoing adj. kanporakoi. adj. lagunzale, harremankor, gizarteko.
outgrow v.t. gehiegi hazi.
outhouse n. kanpoko komun(a).
outing n. ateraldi, bidaia.
outlandish adj. eroska, zoroska, arlote.
outlaw n. legetsai.
outlet n. isurzulo. n. irteera. n. (elec.) hormako entxufe. **Electrical outlet.** Entxufe.
outline v.t. planteatu, eskemaztu.
outline n. eskema. n. laburpen.
outlive v.t. denbora gehiago bizi, gehiago iraun, gainbizi.
outlook n. ikuspegi.
out loud adv. ozenki, mintzoz, goraki.

outlying adj. urruti, urrun.
outnumber v.t. gehiago izan.
outpost n. mugako gotorleku.
output n. produkzio orokor.
outrage n. irain, laido.
outrageous adj. iraingarri, lotsagarri.
outrageously adv. krudelki, lotsagarriro, ankerki, gogorkiro.
outset n. hasiera, hastapen.
outside n. kanpo. adv./prep. kanpoan, kanpora, kanpotik; at, landa. adj. kanpoko, lekoreko.
outsider n. kanpotar, arrotz, kanpoko.
outskirts n. aldamenak, hiringuru, herribazter, inguru.
outspoken adj. karpanta.
outstanding adj. goren, hobezin, bikain, puntako, garai, goieneko, aparta.
outward adj. kanpoko, kanpotiko. adj. itxurazko, azaleko.
outwardly adv. azalez, itxuraz.
outwit v.t. beste(ak) baino argiago izan.
ovary n. (anat.) arraultztegi.
ovation n. txaloaldi, eskuzartaldi, txaloketa.
oven n. labe, labetxo. **Oven door.** Labe-ate.
ovenful n. labealdi, labekada.
over prep./adv. gain, gainean, gainetik; gain-. adj. kitto.
over- gain-; gehiegi.
overabundant adj. gaindizko.
overabundantly adv. gaindizka, gaindizki.
overalls n. (pl.) gaineko-frakak.
overbearing adj. zorrotzegi.
overboard adv. itsasontzitik itsasora edo uretara (erori).
overburden v.t. gainkargatu.
overcast adj. hodeitsu.
overcharge v.t. garestiegi ipini.
overcoat n. gainjantzi, beroki, gainestalki, jantzigaineko.
overcome v.t./v.i. gainditu, goititu, menderatu, menperatu.
overconfident adj. fidakorregi.
overcook v.t. zukutu.
overdo v.t./v.i. larregitu; gehiegi egin.
overeat v.i. larjan, gainelikatu, asearazi.
overeating n. asealdi, sabelaldi, betekada, tripakada, kokaldi.
overestimate v.t. gainetsi, soberetsi.
overfeed v.t./v.i. gainelikatu.
overfill v.t./v.i. gainbete, larbete.
overflow v.i./v.t. gainditu, gainezkatu, gainbete, urgaineztatu, gainez egin.
overflow n. isurialdi, gaindidura.
overflowing adv. gaindizka, gainezka.
overgrown adj. sasitsu.
overgrowth n. gehiazkuntza.
overhaul v.t. konpondu.
overhead adv.adj. burugainean. n. (econ.) gastu orokorrak.
overhear v.t. ustekabean entzun.
overheat v.i./v.t. larberotu, largoritu.

overjoyed adj. poz-pozik.
overland adv.adj. lehorrez; lehorrezko.
overlap v.t./v.i. ahokatu.
overload v.t. gainkargatu, gainzamatu.
overload n. gehizama, gainkarga.
overlook v.t. desarduratu; ez ikusi.
overly adv. gehiegi, larregi, sobera.
overnight adv. gauerako, gauez. adv. bapatean.
overpower v.t. indarrez menperatu.
overpopulate v.t. gainpopulatu.
overpopulation n. gainpopulaketa.
overrate v.t. gehiegi preziatu, gainpreziatu.
override v.t. ezereztu. v.t. ostikopetu, hankapetu.
overripe adj. umel.
overrule v.t. kontra erabaki.
overrun v.t. ostikopetu, hankapetu.
oversaturate v.t. gainase.
oversea adj. itsasarunzko.
overseas adv. itsasaruntz, itsasosteruntz.
overseer n. gainbegirari.
oversensitive adj. minkun.
overshadow v.t. beste(ak) baino garrantzitsuagoa izan.
overshoe n. txanklo, eskalaproin.
oversight n. husketa, oharkabezia, ustekabezia.
overt adj. nabarmen, nabari, ageri.
overtake v.t. atzeman, harrapatu.
overthrow v.t. iraultzatu, eragotzi, egin, eratzan, agintegabetu, deserregetu.
overthrow n. iraultza, deserregeketa.
overthrower n. erorarazle, iraultzaile.
overtime n. gainordu.
overture n. eskeintza, proposapen. n. (mus.) obertura.
overturn v.t. gainbeheratu, irauli, gainazpikatu.
overweight n. gainpisu, lodiegi.
overwhelm v.t. ezereztu, deuseztatu, suntsitu.
overwhelming adj. sekulako.
overwork v.t./v.i. porrokarazi; gehiegi lan egin.
overworked adj. lantsu.
oviduct n. (anat.) arraultzpide.
ovoid adj. arraultzantzeko.
ovulation n. arraultzaldi.
owe v.t./v.i. zor ukan.
owl n. (zool.) gauhontza.
own v.t. jabe izan, jabetu.
own adj. berekiko, beretsu. **One's own.** Norbere. **On (one's) own.** (Nire, zure, bere) gain. **To each his own.** Bakoitzari berea zor zaio.
owner n. jabe, ugazaba. **To be the owner of.** Eskuko izan.
ownership n. jabetasun, jabetza, ugazabatasun, jabego.
ox n. (zool.) idi; it-.
oxen n. (pl.) idiak.
oxeye n. (bot.) idibelar, idibegi.
oxidation n. herdoilketa, herdoil, herdoildura.

oxide n. (chem.) oxido.
oxidizable adj. herdoilgarri, herdoilkoi.
oxidize v.t./v.i. herdoildu, ugertu.
oxidized adj. herdoildun.
oxtongue n. (bot.) idimihi, idimingain
oxygen n. oxigeno.
oxygenate v.t. oxigenatu, aireztatu.
oyster n. (zool.) ostra.
oyster bed n. ostrategi, ostraleku.
oysterman n. ostrari.
oz. Cf. ounce.
ozone n. (chem.) ozono.

P

p n. Ingeles alfabetoko letra.
pa n. aitatxo, aita.
pace n. abiada.
pachyderm n. (zool.) pakidermo.
pacific adj. bakezko, baketi.
pacification n. bakerazpen, mantsoketa, eztidura.
Pacific Ocean n. (geog.) Itsasandi Bare.
pacifier n. bakerazle, baketzaile, baretzaile, eztitzaile. n. txupete.
pacifism n. bakezaletasun.
pacifist n. baketiar, bakezale.
pacifistic adj. bakezale.
pacify v.t. baketu, bakerazi, eztiarazi, baretu.
pack v.t./v.i. fardeldu, jantziz bete (bereziki maletak). v.t. zamatu, kargatu. v.t. erakarri, eraman. v.t. (down) zanpatu.
pack n. talde (otsoak, txakurrak), zakurtalde, zakurteria, zakurketa.
package v.t. fardeldu, paketatu.
package n. fardel, pakete.
packaging n. paketaketa, paketapen.
packer n. fardelkari, paketari, paketegile.
packet n. pakete.
packsaddle n. basta, txalma.
pact n. akordio, elkargo, itun, tratu.
pad n. behatzmami, erimami.
paddle n. pala.
paddock n. bazkalarre, angio.
paddy n. arrozsoro.
padlock n. giltzarrapo.
padre n. apaiz, apez, abade.
pagan n./adj. jentil.
paganism n. jentiltasun.
page n. orrialde.
pageant n. ikuskizun, ikuskari; jantzi-erakusketa.
paginate v.t. orrialdeztatu.
pagination n. orrialdeztapen, orrizenbaketa.
pagoda n. pagoda.
paid pret./p. pret. of pay.
pail n. bertz, pertz.
pailful n. berzkada.
pain v.t./v.i. samindu, min eman, nahigabetu, oinazeztatu.
pain n. min, pena, dolore, neke, oinaze; neka- , -min. **Labor pain.** Erdimin.

pained adj. oinazetsu.
painful adj. minbera, minberatsu, mingarri, samingarri, nekegarri, oinazegarri.
painfully adv. atsekabeki, nahigabez, oinazez, minez.
painless adj. mingabe(ko).
painlessness n. mingabetasun, mingabezia.
painstaking adj. maratz.
painstakingly adv. arretaz, arduraz, axolaz.
paint v.t./v.i. pintatu, margoztatu, koloreztatu.
paint n. pintura.
paintbrush n. txispoi, pintzel.
painter n. margolari, pintore, pintatzaile.
painting n. pintura, margo.
pair v.t./v.i. (batzutan up edo off-ekin) parekatu, kidetu, binakatu.
pair n. bikote, lagun, pare.
pajamas n. (pl.) pijama.
pal n. laguntxo.
palace n. jauregi.
palatable adj. zaporetsu, gozatsu.
palatalize v.t./v.i. ahosabaitu.
palate n. (anat.) ahogain, ahosabai, ahozeru.
palatial adj. jauregiko. adj. sekulako.
palaver n. hitz-mitz.
pale v.i./v.t. zurbildu, koloregabetu.
pale adj. zurbil, hits.
paleface n. zuri, aurpegi zurbil.
paleness n. histasun, zurbiltasun, zurbildura.
paleology n. paleologia.
paleontology n. paleontologia.
palette n. pintatzailearen paleta.
palisade n. hesoholbarruti.
pall n. hilkutxa. n. hilzapi.
pallbearer n. andari.
pallet n. oholtza.
palliative adj. izkutabide.
pallid adj. zurbil.
pallidness n. zurbildura.
pallor n. zurbiltasun, hisdura.
palm n. (bot.) erramu, ercinotz. **Palm Sunday.** Erramu egun. n. (anat.) zehe, eskubarne, eskubarru, ahur.
palpable adj. ukigarri.
palpably adv. nabariro, nabariki, agirian.
palpate v.t. ukitu, eskuz aztertu.
palpitate v.i. taupadatu, pilpiratu.
palpitation n. bihozkada, bihoztaupada, bihozpilpira.
palsy n. (med.) elbarritasun, perlesi.
paltry adj. kaskar, ziztrin, ttattar.
pampas n. (pl.) panpa(k).
pamper v.t. mainatu.
pampered adj. mainati, mainatsu, mainadun.
pamphlet n. idaztiño.
Pamplona n. (geog.) Iruñea.
pan n. zartagina.
panacea n. panazea.

pancake *n.* Estatu Batuetan jaten den talo antzeko opila.
pancreas *n. (anat.)* are.
pancreatic *adj.* areko.
pander *v.t./v.i. (v.i., to)* lupu egin.
pane *n.* leihar, beira.
panegyric *n.* goratzarre, handiespen.
panel *n.* mahaiko. *n.* taula.
pang *n.* min bizi, oinaze.
panic *v.t./v.i.* izuikaratu.
panic *n.* izu, izuikara, beldurrikara.
panicky *adj.* izutu(a), ikaratua(a).
panic-stricken *adj.* izutu(a), ikaratu(a).
panorama *n.* ikuskizun, ikuspegi.
panoramic *adj.* ikuspegizko.
pansy *n. (bot.)* papantze. *n. (colloq.)* atzelari, sexuberekoi (gizon), marikoi.
pant *v.i./v.t.* arnasgabetu, arnasestutu, arnaska egin.
pantaloons *n. (pl.)* frakak
pantheon *n.* panteoi.
panther *n. (zool.)* pantera.
panties *n.* pantaloi.
pantomime *n.* zinuketa.
pantry *n.* janaritegi, jakitoki, jakigela, sukaldeatze.
pants *n.* galtzak, prakak.
papa *n.* aitatxo.
papacy *n.* aitasaindutza, aitasaindugo, aitasaindutasun.
papal *adj.* aitasainduaren.
papal bull *n. (eccl.)* bulda.
paper *v.t.* papereztatu.
paper *n.* paper. **Writing paper.** Idazpaper. **Toilet paper.** Komuneko paper. *n.* egunkari.
paperweight *n.* paperpisu, papergaineko.
papoose *n.* Estatu Batuetako indioen haurtxoa.
paprika *n.* biperrauts.
papyrus *n.* papiro.
par *n.* berdintasun, berdintza, paretza.
parable *n.* alegia, parabola.
parabola *n.* parabola.
parachute *n.* erorgailu, jausgailu.
parachutist *n.* jauzikari, saltalari.
parade *v.t./v.i.* kalejiran ibili, desfilatu.
parade *n.* kalejira.
paradigm *n.* paradigma.
paradise *n.* paradisu.
paradisiacal *adj.* paradisutar.
paradox *n.* paradoxa.
paradoxical *adj.* paradoxiko.
paragon *n.* eredu, jarraibide, modelo.
paragraph *n.* lerroalde.
parakeet *n. (zool.)* papagaitxo.
parallel *v.t.* idetu, parekatu, erkatu, gonbaratu.
parallel *adj.* parekide. *n.* paralelo.
parallelism *n.* paralelismo.
paralysis *n. (med.)* elbarritasun, hebaintasun.
paralytic *adj.* elbarridun, elbarri, hebain.
paralyzation *n.* ezindura.
paralyze *v.t.* ezindu.

paralyzed *adj.* ezindu(a), ezindun.
parameter *n.* parametro.
paramount *adj.* goren, goreneko, garrantzitsuen(a).
paramour *n.* ohaide, amorante.
parapet *n.* babeski.
paraphernalia *n.* bakoitzaren gauzak.
paraphrase *v.t./v.i.* hitzingurukatu.
paraphrase *n.* hitzinguru.
parasite *n.* zurrupakari, bizkarkoi.
parasitic *adj.* bizkarroi.
parasol *n.* eguzkitako.
paratrooper *n. (mil.)* jauskari, parakaidista.
parboil *v.t.* erdiegosi.
parboiled *adj.* egosarin, erdiegosi(a).
parcel *v.t. (gehienetan out-ekin)* sailkatu, lurzatitu, zatitu.
parcel *n.* fardel. *n.* lurzati, arlo, zunda.
parch *v.t./v.i.* ihartu.
parchment *n.* pergamino, larruki.
pardon *v.t.* barkatu, asketsi, zigorgabetu.
pardon *n.* barka, barkamen, askespen.
pardonable *adj.* barkagarri, desenkusagarri.
pardoner *n.* barkatzaile.
pare *v.t.* zuritu, azala kendu.
parent *n.* guraso.
parentage *n.* senitarte.
parental *adj.* gurasoen.
parenthesis *n. (gram.)* parentesi, gako.
parenthood *n.* aitatasun, amatasun.
pariah *n.* paria.
parish *n. (eccl.)* parrokia.
parishioner *n.* elizkide, eliztar.
parity *n.* kidego, parekotasun.
park *v.t./v.i.* aparkatu.
park *n.* parke.
parka *n.* kapusai, zamarrote.
parking lot *n.* aparkaleku.
parlance *n.* hizkera.
parley *n.* hizketa, hitzaldi.
parliament *n. (pol.)* parlamentu.
parliamentary *adj.* parlamentuko.
parlor *n.* jardundegi.
parochial *adj.* parrokiko.
parody *v.t.* parodiatu.
parody *n.* parodia.
parole *n.* baldintzapeko askatasun.
paroxysm *n.* sumindura.
parricide *n.* aitahilketa, aitaerailtza.
parrot *n. (zool.)* papagai, loro.
parry *v.t.* kolpea gerarazi.
parsimoniously *adv.* zuhurkeriaz.
parsley *n. (bot.)* perrezil.
parsnip *n. (bot.)* txiribi.
parson *n.* erretore.
part *n.* zati, zatiko, parte. *n.* une, gune, toki, leku.
partake *v.i.* (**in** edo **of**-ekin) parte hartu.
partial *adj.* zatikako. *adj.* alderdikoi.
partiality *n.* alderdikeria, alderdikoitasun.
partially *adv.* erdizka, erdiz. *adv.*

aldebatez.
participant *n.* partaide, partehartzaile, eskuhartzaile.
participate *v.i./v.t. (gehienetan in-ekin)* parte hartu, parte ukan, partaide izan, esku hartu.
participation *n.* parteharmen, eskuharmen.
participatory *adj.* eskuhartzaile.
participle *n.* partizipio.
particle *n.* zatiki.
particular *adj.* norberaren, bakoitzaren. *adj.* berezi, aparte. *adj.* miliki.
particularist *n.* berezizale.
particularly *adv.* bereziki, batez ere, batik-bat.
partier *n.* parrandari.
partisan *n.* alderdikide, aidekide, aldezkari; -kilako. *adj.* aldekor, alderdikoi, alderditar.
partisanship *n.* alderdikoitasun.
partition *n.* zatiketa, erdibiketa.
partitionable *adj.* sailkagarri.
partitive *n./adj. (gram.)* partitibo, zatikari.
partly *adv.* aldebatez.
partner *n.* erdikide, partaide, laguntzaile.
partnership *n.* jabekidetza, partaliergo, partzuergo.
partook *pret./p. part. of* partake.
partridge *n. (zool.)* eper.
parturition *n.* ertaldi.
party *v.i.* parranda egin, gaubesta egin.
party *n.* festa, jai. *n. (pol.)* partidu. *n.* auzilagun.
party pooper *n.* pozeragozle, jaihondatzaile.
paschal *adj.* pazkoaldiko.
pass *v.t./v.i.* aitzinaratu, aurre hartu. *v.t./v.i.* igaro, iragan, pasatu. *v.t. (on to)* besterenganatu, inorenganatu. *v.i. (out)* mareatu. *v.i. (through)* zehartu, zeharkatu.
pass *n.* ibilgune, igarobide, pasagune, pasaleku. *n.* igaroagiri, igarotxartel, iragantxartel. *n.* dubako txartel. *n.* jaurtiketa.
passable *adj.* pasagarri, iragangarri. *adj.* egoki, erazko, aukerako.
passably *adv.* pasagarriki, erdipurdizka.
passage *n.* pasabide, pasagune, iraganleku, pasaleku, pasatoki. *n.* pasarte.
passageway *n.* pasabide, pasaia.
passe *adj.* modaz kanpoko.
passenger *n.* bidaiari, pasaiari.
passenger liner *n.* bidaiontzi.
passer *n.* igarotzaile, iragaile, pasatzaile.
passer-by *n.* iragale.
passion *n.* gogomin, grina, irrits, gogobizi, maitagrina. *n. (eccl.)* pasio, nekaldi.
passionate *adj.* grinatsu, gartsu,

suhar, sutsu.
passionately *adv.* gartsuki, sutsuki, maiteminez, grinaz.
passive *adj.* pasibo, jasale. **Passive verb.** Aditz jasale.
passively *adv.* pasiboki, jasanbidez.
passiveness *n.* jasanbehar, pasibotasun.
passivity *n.* jasanbehar, pasibotasun.
Passover *n. (rel.)* israeldarren bazko(a).
passport *n.* ibilbide, mugatxartel, pasagiri, pasaporte.
password *n.* kontraezaugarri.
past *n.* lehenaldi, iragan, iraganaldi, lehen. *adj.* joandako, leheneko, lehengo.
pasta *n.* makarroi.
paste *v.t.* likatu, oreztatu.
paste *n.* cola. *n.* ore.
pasteboard *n.* kartoi.
pastel *n./adj.* kolore zurbil.
pasteurize *v.t.* kutsua kendu, pasteurizatu.
pastime *n.* olgura.
pastiness *n.* oratasun.
pastor *n. (rel.)* pastore.
pastoral *adj.* landako.
pastorale *n. (mus.)* artzainsoinu. *n.* Euskal antzerki zahar.
pastorally *adv.* artzaineraz, pastoralki.
pastry *n.* pastel.
past tense *n. (gram.)* lehenaldi.
pasture *v.t.* larreratu, bazkatu, alatu.
pasture *n.* belartegi, larre.
pasty *adj.* oretsu.
pat *n.* xera.
patch *v.t.* adobatu, adabatu.
patch *n.* adabaki, adoba, txaplata.
patched *adj.* ataldun.
patcher *n.* adabakitzaile.
patchwork quilt *n.* koloreaskodun estalki.
paten *n. (eccl.)* patena.
patent *v.t.* patentatu.
patent *n.* patente. *adj.* ageri, nabari, nabarmen.
patentable *adj.* patentagarri.
patented *adj.* patentedun.
patent leather *n.* txarol.
patently *adv.* nabariki, nabariro, nabarmenki, nabarmenkiro.
paternal *adj.* aitazko, aitaren, aitagandiko.
paternalism *n.* paternalismo.
paternally *adv.* aitakiko.
paternity *n.* aitatasun, aitasun.
path *n.* basabide, bidexka, bidetxo, bidezidor. **Bridle path.** Zaldibide.
pathetic *adj.* hunkigarri, zirraragarri.
pathetically *adv.* hunkigarriro.
pathogenic *adj.* eriekarle, erisortzaile, erigarri.
pathological *adj.* patologiko.
pathologist *n.* patologo.
pathology *n.* patologia.
pathos *n.* bihotzunkigarritasun.
pathway *n.* bideska, bidetxo.

patience n. eramankortasun, aidakortasun, jasankortasun, pairakortasun, pazientzia.
patient n. gaiso (eritegian). adj. eramankor, jasanbera, jasankor, pairakor, pairatsu.
patiently adv. jasanbidez, eramanez.
patio n. patio.
patriarch n. lehenguraso, aitalehen, aitagoi.
patriarchal adj. aitagoiaren.
patriarchy n. aitagoigo.
patricide n. aitahilketa, aitaerailtza.
patrimonial adj. gurasoengandiko, ondarezko.
patrimony n. seniparte, etxeogasun, ondare.
patriot n. abertzale.
patriotic adj. aberkoi, aberrikoi. **To become patriotic.** Herrizaletu.
patriotism n. aberritasun, abertzaletasun.
patrol n. gudaritaldetxo.
patrolman n. polizia.
patron n. bezero. n. babestaile, babestzaile. n. (eccl.) zaindari, patroi.
patronage n. zaindaritza, patrointza.
patroness n. bezero (emakume).
patronize v.t. bezero izan; sarri erosi denda batean. v.t. laidoki jokatu. v.t. zainpetu, babespean hartu.
patter n. hitz-mitz.
pattern n. eredu, modelu (jostun). n. adibide.
paucity n. eskasia, gabezia, urrialdi, lazeria.
paunch n. sabelzorro.
paunchy adj. sabeltsu.
pauper n. errumes, txiro.
pauperism n. eskaleria.
pause v.i. geldigu, pausatu.
pause n. geldiune, egonaldi, geldialdi, egotaldi, isilune.
pave v.t. harriztatu, harriztu, adreilatu, tronatu, zolatu.
pavement n. espaloi, zola.
paver n. harriztatzaile, lauzari, zoruezarle, mundrunatzaile.
pavilion n. pabilioi, kiroltegi.
paw v.t./v.i. haztakatu, marruskatu, maspildu (bereziki txakurrek edo beste abereek hankez baliatuz).
paw n. oin (txakur, otso, lehoi, etab.).
pawn v.t. bahitu.
pawn n. peoi.
pawnable adj. bahitugarri.
pawnbroker n. prestatzaile.
pawnshop n. bahitegi, bahituretxe.
pay v.t. ordaindu, pagatu, kitatu. v.t. (back) eskerrordaindu. v.t. (off) amortizatu.
pay n. lansari. **To pay cash.** Eskura ordaindu.
payable adj. ordaingarri, ordaintzeko, pagagarri.
payee n. edukitzaile, hartzaile.

payer n. ordaintzaile, kitatzaile.
paymaster n. ordainlari.
payment n. ordainketa, pagu, kontugarbialdi, kitaketa, pagamendu.
payoff n. ordainketa; isilsari.
payroll n. langileen soldatak zehazten dituen zerrenda. n. ordainsari.
pea n. (bot.) ilar.
peace n. bake.
peaceable adj. bakedun, bakezko, baketsu.
peaceably adv. bakez, bareki.
peaceful adj. bakedun, bakezko, baketsu, trankil.
peacefully adv. bakez, bareki, onez.
peacefulness n. baketasun, trankildura.
peacemaker n. baketzaile, bakegile.
peach n. (bot.) melokotoi, muxika.
peacock n. (zool.) pauma.
peak n. gailur, tontor. n. goien, goigain.
peal n. ezkilots, ezkilasoinu.
peanut n. (bot.) kakahuete.
pear n. madari, udare.
pearl n. perla.
pearly adj. perlantzeko.
peasant n. nekazari, baserritar, laborari, nekazarisa, laborarisa, lurlangile.
peasantry n. nekazaritza, nekazalgo.
pebble n. harrikaskar, harrixka, hartxirri, legar, errekarri.
pebbly adj. legardun.
pecan n. (bot.) pekan.
peck v.t./v.i. mokokatu, pikokatu.
peck n. pikokada, mokokada. n. musu arin, musu txiki. n. lakari.
pecker n. mokokari, mokokatzaile.
pectoral adj. (anat.) bularreko, paparreko.
peculiar adj. beregisako.
peculiarity n. bakoiztasun, bereizgarri.
peculiarly adv. bitxiki.
pecuniary adj. diruzko.
pedagogical adj. irakasteko, irakaspidezko, pedagogiko.
pedagogically adv. irakasbidez, pedagogikoki.
pedagogue n. pedagogari.
pedagogy n. irakasbide, irakaspide, pedagogia.
pedal n. pedal.
pedantic adj. sasijakitun, maisukeriazko, sasijakintsu.
pedantically adv. maisukeriaz.
peddle v.t./v.i. girgilak saldu.
peddler n. girgilari, zirtzilsaltzaile.
pedestal n. oinpeko, zutoin.
pedestrian n. oineztari, zangokari, ibiltari. adj. arrunt, askotako.
pediatrician n. haursendagile.
pediatrics n. haurgintza, haursendagintza.
pedicure n. oinsendagintza.
pedicurist n. oinsendagile.
pedigree n. pedigre.
pee v.i. pix egin, txiza egin.

pee *n.* pix, txiza, gernu.
peek *v.i.* zeharka begiratu.
peekaboo *n.* mamuka.
peel *v.t./v.i.* azalkatu, azalzuritu.
peel *n.* azal. *n.* labehaga, endai.
peeled *adj.* azalgabe.
peeler *n.* zurigailu.
peep *v.i./v.t.* kirik egin, txiokatu. *v.i.* zeharka begiratu.
peepee *n.* pipi.
peephole *n.* ataleiho, kirikazulo.
peer *v.i.* zeharka begiratu.
peerless *adj.* paregabe.
peevish *adj.* umoretxarreko, haserrekor.
peg *n.* ziri, larako.
pejorative *adj.* gutiespenezko.
pelican *n.* (*zool.*) pelikano, sanga.
pellet *n.* perdigoi.
pell-mell *adv.* nahas-mahas, nahasiki.
pelota *n.* pilota.
pelt *n.* larru, ehizilarru.
pelvis *n.* pelbis, azpilezur.
pen *n.* idazluma, idazkortz, luma. *n.* hesibarruti, behitegi, eskorta.
penal *adj.* zigorrezko.
penalize *v.t.* zigorpetu.
penalty *n.* penalti (kirol); zigor.
penance *n.* (*eccl.*) penitentzia. **To do penance.** Penitentzia egin.
pencil *n.* arkatz, lapitz.
pendant *n.* dominandi, domina.
pending *prep./adv.* bukatugabe, erabakigabe.
pendulum *n.* zintzilikari.
penetrable *adj.* iragazkarri, zulagarri, sargarri, sondagarri.
penetrant *n./adj.* barrenkor.
penetrate *v.t./v.i.* barnatu, barrendu, barruratu.
penetrating *adj.* barnakor, sarkor. *adj.* oharti.
penetration *n.* sarpen. *n.* argialdi, adimen.
penetrative *adj.* barrenkor.
penguin *n.* (*zool.*) pinguino.
penicillin *n.* (*med.*) penizilina.
peninsula *n.* (*geog.*) penintsula, lurbeso.
peninsular *adj.* penintsulako, lurbesoko.
peninsularity *n.* peninsulartasun.
penis *n.* (*anat.*) zakil; berga.
penitence *n.* damutasun, garbai.
penitent *n.* penitentzigile. *adj.* damuzko.
penitential *adj.* damuzko.
penitentiary *n.* kartzela, espetxe, presondegi.
penknife *n.* lumaizto.
penmanship *n.* idazkera.
pennant *n.* banderatxo.
penniless *adj.* dirugabe.
Pennsylvania *n.* (*geog.*) Estatu Batuetako estatu bat.
penny *n.* zentimo, xentimo.
pension *n.* urtediru, pentsio.

pensioner *n.* pentsiodun.
pensive *adj.* pentsakor, gogartetsu, gogartzaile, gogoetazale.
pensively *adv.* gogartuz.
pentagon *n.* (*geom.*) pentagono. *n.* (*cap.*) Estatu Batuetako Pentagonoa.
pentagram *n.* (*mus.*) pentagrama.
pentahedron *n.* (*geom.*) bostaldeko.
Pentecost *n.* (*eccl.*) mendekoste.
penthouse *n.* goren etxebizitza, aterpe, azken solairu.
penultimate *adj.* azkenaurreko, azkenurren.
penury *n.* eskasia, behargorri, ezeria, eskasgo, lazeria.
people *n.* (*pl.*) jende, herri, populu.
pep *n.* indar, kemen.
pepper *v.t.* biperztatu.
pepper *n.* (*bot.*) biper.
peppermint *n.* menta, peldo.
peppery *adj.* biperrezko.
per *prep.* bakoitzeko, bakoitzarentzat. *prep.* arauz, arabera; -z.
percale *n.* perkal.
perceivable *adj.* hautemangarri.
perceive *v.t.* ohartu, konturatu, nabaritu, igarri, sumatu.
perceiver *n.* somakari.
percent *n.* ehuneko. **One percent.** Ehuneko bat.
percentage *n.* ehuneko, ehuneko honenbeste, portzentaia.
perceptibility *n.* oharkarritasun.
perceptible *adj.* oharkarri, hautemangarri.
perceptibly *adv.* oharki.
perception *n.* oharmen, oharpen, somaketa.
perceptive *adj.* hautemale, sumakor, nabarikor.
perceptively *adv.* oharrez.
perch *v.i./v.t.* kokatu, pausatu, ezarri.
perch *n.* txoria pausatzen den leku.
perchance *adv.* agian, beharbada.
percheron *n.* (*zool.*) zalditzar.
percolate *v.t./v.i.* iragazi, filtratu.
percussion *n.* atabaljoaldi.
percussionist *n.* atabalkari, atabalari.
perdition *n.* galera, galmen, galketa, hondamendi, okerbide.
peremptory *adj.* ukaezin, ukagaitz; premiazko, beharbeharrezko; erabakizko, erabateko.
perennial *adj.* betiereko, aldioroko, egundainoko.
perfect *v.t.* burutu, osatu. *v.t.* bikaindu, hobetu.
perfect *adj.* hobezin, onuts. *adj.* oso.
perfection *n.* hobezintasun.
perfectionist *n.* zehatzale.
perfectly *adv.* guztiz, ezinobeki, oso ondo, osoki.
perfidious *adj.* gaitz.
perfidy *n.* fedegaizto.
perforate *v.t./v.i.* zulapetu, zulatu, zulo egin.
perforated *adj.* zulodun, zulotsu.

perforation *n.* zulaketa, zulapen, zulo.
perform *v.t./v.i.* egin, egitaratu, kunplitu. *v.t./v.i.* antzeztu, antzertu.
performance *n.* eginaldi, emanaldi, saio. *n.* antzerkialdi.
perfume *v.t.* usainztatu, lurrineztatu, lurrinkatu.
perfume *n.* usaingozo, lurrinusain, usaingarri.
perfumed *adj.* usaingozodun, lurrintsu.
perfumer *n.* lurringailu.
perfumery *n.* lurrindegi.
perfunctory *adj.* desarduratsu, axolagabe, azaleko, azalutseko.
perhaps *adv.* agian, beharbada, menturaz.
pericardium *n. (anat.)* bihozsare.
perigee *n. (astron.)* ilargihurbil.
perihelion *n. (astron.)* eguzkihurbil.
peril *n.* arrisku.
perilous *adj.* arriskutsu.
period *n.* garai, sasoi, epe. *n. (gram.)* puntu, kulatz. *n.* hilekoaldi, hileroko.
periodic *adj.* noizbehingo.
periodical *n.* aldizkari, agerkari. *adj.* aldizko.
periodically *adv.* aldian-aldian.
periodicity *n.* aldizkotasun.
peripheral *adj.* azalaldeko, inguraldeko, ertzaldeko.
periphery *n.* azalalde, ertzalde.
periphrasis *n.* hitzinguru.
periphrastic *adj.* hitzinguruko.
periscope *n.* periskopio.
perish *v.i.* hil, usteldu, zendu, ahitu.
perishability *n.* iraungikortasun, ustelkortasun.
perishable *adj.* ustelbera, ustelerraz, ustelgarri, galkor, zimelgarri.
perishableness *n.* ustelgarritasun, galkortasun.
peritoneal *adj.* sabelsareko.
peritoneum *n. (anat.)* sabelsare.
peritonitis *n. (med.)* sabelsaremin.
perjure *v.t.* zingezur egin, zinoker egin.
perjured *adj.* zingezurti.
perjurious *adj.* zingezurti.
perjury *n.* zingezur.
permanence *n.* iraunkortasun, iraunaldi, iraute, iraunketa.
permanent *adj.* iraunkor, iragangaitz, iraungarri.
permanently *adv.* betiro, iraungarriro, iraunki, iraunkiro, iraunkorki.
permanent wave *n.* huin iraunkor.
permeability *n.* iragazkortasun.
permeable *adj.* iragazkarri, iragazkor, irazgarri.
permeate *v.t./v.i.* sartu, sondatu.
permissible *adj.* baimengarri, baiezgarri.
permissibly *adv.* soriki.
permission *n.* baimen, baiespen, zilegidura, zilegitasun.
permissive *adj.* baimenkor.
permit *v.t./v.i.* baimena eman, zilegi

izan, baimendu, esku eman, utzi.
permitted *adj.* zilegi. **That is permitted.** Zilegi da hori.
pernicious *adj.* kaltegarri, hilkor, suntsigarri, hondagarri, galgarri. *adj.* bidegabetsu.
perniciously *adv.* kaltegarriro.
perpendicular *adj.* elkarzut, perpendikular.
perpetrate *v.t.* egin; gaizki egin.
perpetrator *n.* egile.
perpetuable *adj.* betiraungarri.
perpetual *adj.* betiko, betiereko, egundainoko, aldioroko.
perpetually *adv.* sekulakoz, betiraunez.
perpetualness *n.* etengabetasun, jarraipen.
perpetuate *v.t.* iraunarazi, luzarazi, betiraun, betikotu.
perpetuation *n.* betiraunpen, iraunarazte.
perpetuator *n.* iraunarazle.
perpetuity *n.* betikotasun, betitasun, sekulatasun.
perplex *v.t.* larritu, nahastu.
perplexed *adj.* zalantzako.
perplexity *n.* ezbai, zalantza.
persecute *v.t.* jazarri, aurrean erabili, gaizki erabili.
persecution *n.* jazarketa, jazarpen.
persecutor *n.* jazartzaile, jazarle, gaizkierabiltzaile.
perseverance *n.* iraupen, euskortasun.
perseverant *adj.* euskor, iraukor.
persevere *v.i./v.t.* jarraitu, segitu, gogor egon, ekin.
persist *v.i.* iraun, ekin, lehiatu.
persistence *n.* ekite, ekin, ekinaldi, iraunaldi, iraupen, lehiadura.
persistent *adj.* ekile, irauti, jardunkor, jarraikor, lehiati.
persistently *adv.* ekinez, lehiatsuki, setatsuki, jo ta ke.
person *n.* gizaki, lagun, pertsona.
personage *n.* pertsonaia.
personal *adj.* pertsonal, norberakiko, norbereganako.
personality *n.* izakera, izaera, mendu, nortasun.
personalization *n.* nortzapen.
personalize *v.t.* bakoiztu, nortu.
personally *adv.* pertsonalki.
personification *n.* nortzapen.
personify *v.t.* nortu.
personnel *n.* pertsonal, plantila.
perspective *n.* ikuspegi, ikusmolde, ikuspuntu.
perspicacious *adj.* zuhur, gogoerne.
perspicacity *n.* argikusmen, gogoernetasun, gogoargitasun, zolitasun.
perspiration *n.* izerdi, izerketa.
perspire *v.i./v.t.* izerdikatu.
persuadable *adj.* konbentzigarri.
persuade *v.t.* limurtu, sinestarazi, ikusarazi, buruan sartu.

persuasion *n.* ikuserazpen, sinestarazpen.

persuasive *adj.* usteragikor, usteragile, konbentzigarri.

persuasively *adv.* usteragikorki.

persuasiveness *n.* usteragin, usteindar.

pert *adj.* bizi, erne, ponpox.

pertain *v.i.* -(r)ena izan, -koa izan.

pertinacity *n.* burugogorkeria, burugogortasun, hisikortasun, kaskagogorkeria, setakeria.

pertinent *adj.* dagokion; -rekiko.

perturb *v.t.* kezkarazi, haserrerazi.

perturbation *n.* asaldura.

peruse *v.t.* kontuz irakurri, arretaz leitu.

perverse *adj.* gaizkile, gaizto, gizagaizto.

perversely *adv.* gaiztoki, makurki, txarki.

perversion *n.* gaiztakeria, galkeria.

perversity *n.* gaiztotasun, makurkeria, okerkeria, gaiztakeria.

pervert *v.t.* okerreratu, okerrarazi, makurrarazi, gaiztoarazi, gaizkindu.

pervert *n.* okertzaile, gaiztatzaile, okerrarazle, makurrarazle, galtzaile.

pervertable *adj.* okergarri.

perverted *adj.* oker, makur.

peseta *n. (econ.)* pezeta, laurleko.

pessimism *n.* ezezkotasun, ezkortasun, etsipen.

pessimist *n.* ezkor, pesimista.

pessimistic *adj.* ezezkor, ukakor.

pest *n.* aspergarri, gogaikarri, nazkagarri. *n.* zomorro kaltegarri(a).

pester *v.t.* zirikatu, zirrikatu.

pestiferous *adj.* izurrizko, izurridun, kutsakor.

pestilent *adj.* izurrizko, kirastsu, itsaskor.

pestle *n.* mortairu.

pet *v.t.* eskuztatu, ferekatu, balakatu.

petal *n.* petalo, lorehosto.

petite *adj.* txiki.

petiteness *n.* txikitasun, xumedura.

petition *n.* eskari, erregu, eskablde, arren; idazki.

petitioner *n.* eskatzaile, arrenkari.

petrified *adj.* harritu(a).

petrify *v.t./v.i.* harri bihurtu.

petroleum *n. (chem.)* petrolio. *adj.* petroliodun.

petticoat *n.* azpikogona, gonazpiko.

pettiness *n.* txikikeria, huskeria, ziztrinkeria, xehekeria, zirtzilkeria, tipikeria.

petting *n.* ferekaldi, fereka.

petty *adj.* ziztrin, kaxkar, ttattar.

petty theft *n.* litxarreria, xixketa.

petty thief *n.* lapurtxo, litxarrero, karteralapur.

petulant *adj.* aurpegihandi, mutiri.

pew *n.* jarleku, banko.

phalanx *n. (anat.)* behatzezur.

phallic *adj.* zakilantzeko.

phantasm *n.* mamutzar.

phantom *n.* mamutzar.

pharmacist *n.* botikari, sendagaisaltzaile.

pharmacy *n.* botika, botikategi, sendagaitegi, farmazia.

pharynx *n. (anat.)* zintzurzulo, irensbide, faringe.

phase *n.* fase, aldi.

Ph. D. *n.* doktoradutza, doktorego.

pheasant *n. (zool.)* basoilanda, faisai.

phenomenal *adj.* bikain, sekulako, ezinobe.

phenomenon *n.* fenomeno.

philandering *n.* emakoitasun. *adj.* emagale, emakoi, gonazale.

philanthropic *adj.* gizatiar, gizakoi, gizazale.

philanthropist *n.* gizatiar.

philanthropy *n.* gizakoitasun, gizakortasun, gizatiartasun.

philately *n.* filatelia.

philharmonic *adj.* musikazale.

philologist *n.* hizkuntzalari, filologari.

philology *n.* hizkuntzalaritza, filologia.

philosopher *n.* pentsalari, filosofari, pentsatzaile.

philosophize *v.i.* filosofatu.

philosophy *n.* filosofia.

phlebitus *n. (med.)* zainera.

phlegm *n.* gorro, karkaisa.

phlegmatic *adj.* astikoi, patxadatsu.

phone *v.t./v.i.* telefonatu.

phone *n.* telefono.

phone booth *n.* telefongela.

phoneme *n.* fonema.

phonetics *n.* fonetika.

phonograph *n.* diskajogailu.

phonology *n.* fonologia.

phony *adj./n.* faltsu, gezurrezko.

phosphate *n.* fosfato.

phosphoresce *v.i.* fosforeztatu.

phosphorescence *n.* fosforargi.

phosphorous *n. (chem.)* fosforo.

photo *n.* argazki.

photocopy *n.* fotokopia.

photograph *v.t./v.i.* erretratatu, argazkia atera.

photograph *n.* argazki, erretratu, foto.

photographer *n.* argazkilari, erretratari.

photography *n.* fotogintza, argazkintza.

phrase *v.t.* esalditu.

phrase *n.* esaldi.

physical *adj.* gorputzeko, soineko, fisiko.

physically *adv.* soinez, fisikoki, gorputzez.

physician *n.* sendagile, sendagin, mediku, doktore.

physicist *n.* fisikari.

physics *n.* fisika.

physiognomist *n.* fisonomista.

physiognomy *n.* fisonomia.

physiologist *n.* fisiologari.

physiology *n.* fisiologia.

pianist *n.* pianojole.

piano n. (mus.) piano.
picaresque adj. pikarezko, jostagarri, barragarri.
pick v.t. (batzutan out-ekin) aukeratu, hautatu. v.t./v.i. pikatu, ziztatu. v.t. (up) jaso, altxatu.
pick n. pika.
pickaxe n. aitzurpikotx.
picket n. ziri luze, taket. n. pikete (grebetan). n. (mil.) soldadusail.
pickiness n. milikatasun, mizkinkeria, mokozurikeria, kontentagaiztasun.
pickle v.t. ozpineztatu, ozpindu.
pickle n. ozpinez ondutako kuia.
pickpocket n. lapurtxo, litxarrero.
pickup truck n. kamioixka, troka (USA).
picky adj. milika, miliki, mizkin, mokozuri, jakan.
picnic n. sasiburduntzi.
pictorial adj. irudizko, irudidun.
picture n. argazki, erretratu, foto; koadro, margoki, irudi.
picturesque adj. ikusgarri, bitxi.
pie n. Ameriketako pastel mota bat.
piece n. zati, atal, puska, pusketa.
pied adj. koloreaskodun.
pier n. atrakaleku, barra, kai, nasa.
pierce v.t./v.i. sastatu, barrundu, ziztatu.
piercing adj. sarkor, zoli, zorrotz, ziztagarri.
piety n. jainkozaletasun, debozio, erlijiozaletasun.
pig n. (zool.) txerri, zerri, urde; urdan-.
pigeon n. (zool.) usakume.
pigheaded adj. setati, burugogor, kaskagogor, temati.
pigheadedness n. setakeria.
piglet n. zerrikume, txerrikume, urdekume.
pigment n. koloregai.
pigpen n. txerrikorta, txerritegi, urdandegi, zerritoki.
pigskin n. txerri azal. n. Estatu Batuetako futbol-pilota.
pigsty n. txerritegi, zerritoki, txerrikorta, urdandegi.
pigtail n. ilekorda, ileisats.
pike n. (zool.) lutxo.
pikeman n. lantzari.
pilable adj. metagarri, pilagarri, multzogarri.
pile v.t./v.i. pilatu, metatu, multzokatu. v.i. (in, into, out of) nahas-mahas sartu edo irten.
pile n. meta, multzo, pila, pilo; -meta.
piler n. metatzaile, pilatzaile.
pilgrim n. erromes, saindulari.
pilgrimage n. erromesaldi, sainduralerio. **To go on a pilgrimage.** Erromes ibili.
pill n. sendagarri, pastila; antiernari, antikontzeptibo, antisorgailu.
pillage v.t./v.i. zakuratu, lapurtu, ebasti, harrapakatu.
pillage n. harrapaketa, harrapakeria,

lapurketa.
pillager n. harrapakari, harrapatzaile, lapur.
pillaging n. zakurapen.
pillar n. habe, zutabe, zutoin.
pillow n. burupeko, lumatza, ohaburuko.
pilot v.t. lematu, ontzigidatu.
pilot n. hegazkilari, abiadore, piloto. n. ontzizain, lemazain, pilotu.
pimp v.i. lupu egin.
pimp n. emazain, andraketari, putazain.
pimping n. emazaintza, lupukeria.
pimple n. suldar, pikort.
pimply adj. suldartsu.
pin v.t. urkilatu.
pin n. orratz, iskilinba; burukorratz. n. paparreko.
pincers n. (pl.) pintzak; trukesak.
pinch v.t./v.i. imurtxi egin, txatxamurka egin, zimiko egin.
pinch n. zimiko, imurtxikida, atximurkada.
pincher n. atximurkari, zimikokari.
pincushion n. orratzontzi, orraztoki, kutun.
pine n. (bot.) pinu.
pineapple n. (bot.) pinaburu (fruita jangarria).
pinecone n. (bot.) pinaburu.
pin feather n. lumatxo.
ping-pong n. ping-pong.
pink adj. gorrimotel, zurigorri.
pinko n. komunistazale.
pinky n. (anat.) eritxiki.
pinnacle n. erpin.
pinprick n. orrazkada.
pint n. pinta.
pioneer n. aurrelari, aitzindari.
pious adj. jainkozale, jainkotar, erlijiozale.
piously adv. sainduki, santuki.
piousness n. jainkozaletasun, jainkotiartasun.
pipe v.t./v.i. txilibitua jo. v.t. (batzutan in-ekin) hodiratu, tutukatu.
pipe n. pipa. n. tutu, hodi.
pipefish n. (zool.) orratz.
pipeline n. hodieria, tutueria, oliobide.
pipette n. pipeta.
pippin n. (bot.) gezagozo.
piracy n. itsaslapurreta, piratakeria.
pirate n. itsaslapur, pirata.
pirouette n. biradura.
piscatory adj. arrantzazko.
pisciform adj. arrainantzeko, arrainitxurako, arrainaire.
pissy adj. pixati, pixegale.
pistol n. pistola.
piston n. (mech.) pistoi.
pit v.t./v.i. zulatu. v.t. oposatu, kontrajarri, kontrezarri.
pit n. osin, putzu.
pitch v.t. prestatu, ezarri (kanpingo dendak, etab.). v.t./v.i. bota (bereziki beisbolean). v.i. aurrera erori. v.t. galipotatu.

pitch *n.* mundrun, bike, pike. *n.* aldapa, malda. *n.* doinu, ahozketa. *n.* beisboleko pilota-jaurtaldi.
pitcher *n.* pitxer, pegar. *n.* beisbol jokuan pilota-jaurtilari.
pitcherful *n.* pitxerkada.
pitchfork *n.* sarde, belarsarde, arbasta.
pitch pipe *n. (mus.)* doinugailu, diapasoi.
pitchy *adj.* biketsu.
piteous *adj.* dolugarri, errukarri.
pith *n.* mami.
pitiable *adj.* dolugarri, errukarri, urrikalgarri.
pitiful *adj.* gupidagarri, urrikalgarri, errukarri.
pitifully *adv.* tamalgarriro.
pitiless *adj.* gupidagabe, errukigabe, krudel, gupidagaitz.
pitilessly *adv.* errukigabeki.
pitilessness *n.* gupidagabekeria.
pitter-patter *n.* tipi-tapa.
pity *n.* erruki, gupida, urrikalmendu.
placard *n.* pankarta, hormakartel.
placate *v.t.* mantsotu, otzandu, balakatu.
place *v.t.* ipini, ezarri, jarri, lekutu, kokatu. *v.t.* **(before)** aurrejarri. *v.t.* **(beside)** saiheskatu. *v.t.* **(between)** tartekatu, tartean sartu.
place *n.* leku, toki, une; -gune.
placeable *adj.* ipingarri.
placed *adj.* jarritako.
placement *n.* ezarketa, ezarpen, jarpen.
placenta *n. (anat.)* umezorro.
placid *adj.* baretsu.
placidity *n.* eztitasun, gozatasun.
plagiarism *n.* kopiaketa, plagiaketa.
plagiarist *n.* plagiatzaile.
plagiarize *v.t.* plagiatu.
plagiary *n.* plagio.
plague *v.t.* zirikatu, zirrikatu.
plague *n. (med.)* izurri.
plaice *n. (zool.)* platuxa, xabalo.
plaid *n.* Eskoziako oihal mota bat.
plain *adj.* nabarmen, nabari, agiri. *adj.* huts(ik), garbi. *adj.* apaingabe; arrunt. *adj.* agirian. *n.* lautada, ordeka.
plainly *adv.* nabariki.
plainness *n.* sinpletasun, arruntasun, soiltasun.
plainsman *n.* beterriko.
plaint *n.* arrengura, aiene. *n.* auzieske.
plaintiff *n.* auzilari.
plaintive *adj.* arrenguratsu, kexati.
plaintively *adv.* arrenguraz.
plait *n.* txirikorda.
plan *v.t./v.i.* plan egin, plangintzatu, planifikatu.
plan *n.* asmo, plan, jardunbide.
plane *v.t./v.i.* urringatu.
plane *n.* hegazkin, aireplanu. **Jet plane.** Erreakzio hegazkin. *n.* urringa, garlopa, kurbi. *n. (geom.)*

plano.
planet *n.* planeta, lur.
planetary *adj.* planetako.
plank *n.* hurtsa, ohol.
planking *n.* oholeria.
planner *n.* plangile, planifikatzaile.
planning *n.* planifikapen, plangintza, programaketa, programakuntza.
plant *v.t.* landatu, landareztatu, zuhaiztu, oihandu.
plant *n.* landare. **Water plant.** Urlandare. *n.* instalazio.
plantable *adj.* landagarri.
plantain *n. (bot.)* zainbelar.
plantation *n.* landatoki, hazienda.
planter *n.* landatzaile.
plaque *n.* plaka.
plasma *n.* odolplasma.
plaster *v.t.* igeltsuztu, igeltsuztatu, kisutu, mantartu.
plaster *n.* enplasto, kisu, kare.
plastic *n.* plastiko. *adj.* plastikozko.
plastic explosive *n.* plastika.
plasticity *n.* plastikotasun.
plate *v.t.* zilartu, urreztu, brontzeztu, burdindu.
plate *n.* plater, aspil, jatontzi.
plateau *n.* sapalda, goizabaldi.
plateful *n.* platerkada.
platform *n.* oholtza, plataforma. *n. (pol.)* alderdi politiko baten oinarriak.
platinum *n. (min.)* platino.
platonic *adj.* platoniar.
platonically *adv.* platonikoki.
platoon *n. (mil.)* hogeitalau bat soldaduz osotutako gudaroste.
platter *n.* plater, aspil, jatontzi.
plausible *adj.* egitxurako, egiantzeko, sinesgarri.
plausibly *adv.* egiantzez.
play *v.t.* jokatu (antzerkian). *v.t./v.i.* jolastu, jostatu, olgetan egin, jokatu. *v.t./v.i.* jo. **He has played the guitar.** Kitarra jo du. *v.i.* **(around)** gaztekeriak egin, olgetan egin; ezkontza nahastu.
play *n.* antzerki, antzezpen, teatro. *n.* jolasaldi, jolasketa, josteta, jostabide.
playable *adj.* jokagarri.
player *n.* jolaskide, jostalari, jokalari. *n.* jole, jotzaile, soinujole.
playful *adj.* jostari, jostalari, jostakor.
playfully *adv.* txantxetan, jolasean, olgetan.
playground *n.* haur-jolastoki, haur-jolaseta.
playhouse *n.* haurrentzat eginiko jolas-etxetxoa.
playing card *n.* karta.
playing field *n.* jolastoki, jolasleku, jostaleku, kirolzelai.
playmate *n.* jolaskide, jolaslagun.
plaything *n.* jostailu.
playtime *n.* jolastordu.
playwright *n.* antzerkigile, dramagile, komedidazle.
playwriting *n.* dramagintza.

plaza n. plaza, enparantza.
plea n. erregu, eskari, arren.
plead v.i. otoikatu. v.t. auzikatu.
pleading adj. erreguzko, otoizko, otoigile.
pleasant adj. atsegin, atsegintsu, atsegingarri, harrerakor, gustagarri, bozkariozko, laketgarri, pozgarri.
pleasantly adv. atsegingarriro, gustora, gozaro, gozoki, goztuz, pozik.
pleasantness n. atsegingarritasun, gozotasun.
pleasantry n. ateraldi, umoraldi.
please v.t./v.i. atsegindu, atsegin izan, gogoko izan, laket izan, plazer ukan, ederretsi, begiko izan.
please int. faborez, mesedez, otoi, arren.
pleasing adj. atsegin, atseginezko, gogobeteko, gustagarri, gogobetegarri, xarmant.
pleasurable adj. gustagarri, gogozko.
pleasurably adv. gostura.
pleasure n. atsegin, atseginaldi, gozamen, laket, gustu.
pleat v.t. tolestu, izurtu, ximurtu.
pleat n. tximur, zimur, toles.
pleated adj. zimur, zimurtsu.
plebeian n./adj. herrixume; plebeio.
plebiscite n. hauteskunde, hautaketa.
pledge n. bermetasun, fiantza.
pleiad n. ospetsutalde.
plenteous adj. ugari, ugaritsu.
plentiful adj. ugari, ugaritsu.
plenty n. ugaritasun. adj. frango, ugari. adv. guztiz, oso.
pleurisy n. (med.) anderraieria.
pliable adj. zalu, malgu, zinbel.
pliant adj. zalu, malgu, zinbel.
pliers n. (pl.) aliketak.
plight n. larrialdi, estutasun.
plod v.i. geldiro ibili.
plot v.t. azpilan egin, azpilandu, isiljokatu, elkar hartu.
plot n. isiljoko, zimarku. n. gai (literatura). n. une, gune, zunda.
plotter n. zinaide.
plow v.t./v.i. goldatu, luberritu, irauli, urratu, ildokatu.
plow n. golde; golda-.
plowable adj. iraulgarri, laiagarri.
plowman n. goldalari, goldatzaile.
plowshare n. goldamutur.
pluck v.t./v.i. lumatu, bipildu.
plug v.t. (batzutan up-ekin) txantoldu, zipoztu, ziritu. v.t. (in) entxufatu, xiribistatu, ahokatu.
plug n. tapoi, ziri. n. entxufe.
plum n. (bot.) aran, okaran.
plumage n. lumaia.
plumb v.t. plomatu.
plumber n. berunkari, iturgin, iturrikari.
plumbing n. etxeko hodieria, etxeko hodiak.
plume v.t. tontortu.
plume n. lumagandor, motots.

plumed adj. lumadun.
plummet n. berun, sondagailu.
plump adj. lodikote, gizenkote.
plumpness n. gizentasun, loditasun.
plunder v.t./v.i. zakuratu, harrapakatu.
plunder n. harrapaketa, ebasketa, ebaskin.
plunderer n. ebasle.
plunge v.t./v.i. erroiztu.
plunge n. murgil, murgilketa.
plunger n. libragailu.
plural adj. askozko, plural.
pluralism n. aniztasun, pluralismo, pluralitate.
pluralist n. pluralista.
plurality n. pluraltasun, aniztasun.
pluralize v.t./v.i. pluralizatu; aniztu, askotu, ugaldu.
plus prep. gehi, eta, gehiago. adj. on, positibo. n. abantaila.
plush adj. luxotsu, dotore, aberats.
Pluto n. (astron.) Pluton.
plutonium n. (min.) plutonio.
ply v.t. arretaz erabili, arduraz lan egin.
p.m. arratsaldeko, eguerdiondoko.
pneumatic adj. neumatiko.
pneumonia n. (med.) albokomin, birikomin, alborengo.
poach v.t. geldiro egosi, zurbulutu. v.t. legez kanpo edo baimenik gabe arrantzan edo ehizean aritu.
pocket v.t. sakeleratu, poltsikoratu.
pocket n. sakela, poltsiko, patrikara.
pocketbook n. kartera, poltsa.
pod n. (bot.) leka.
podiatrist n. oinsendagile.
podium n. mintzaleku, irakastoki.
poem n. olerki, poema, poesia.
poet n. olerkari, poeta.
poetaster n. sasiolerkari.
poetess n. olerkarisa, poetisa.
poetic adj. poetiko, poesizko.
poetical adj. poetiko, poesizko.
poetically adv. olerkiro, poesiaz, poetikoki.
poetry n. olerki, poesia, olerti.
poignant adj. hunkigarri.
point v.t./v.i. hatzamarrez zuzendu. v.t. (out) ezaguarazi, ikusarazi.
point n. punta, mutur. n. puntu, pondu, tanto (kirolak). n. mami, pondu (hizketan). n. lurmutur.
point-blank adj./adv. zuzen; zuzenki, zuzenez.
pointed adj. puntazorrotz, muturdun, puntadun.
pointer n. ziritxo. n. (zool.) pointer (txakur).
pointless adj. zentzugabeko, alferrikako.
point of a compass n. ortzalde.
point of view n. ikuspuntu, iritzi.
pointsman n. orratzain.
pointy adj. muturtsu, puntazorrotz.
poise n. oreka. n. zentzutasun, tentu.
poison v.t. pozoitu, pozoindatu, edendu.

poison *n.* pozoi.
poisoned *adj.* pozoitu(a).
poisoner *n.* pozoitzale.
poisoning *n.* pozoiketa.
poisonous *adj.* pozoidun, pozoitsu.
poisonousness *n.* pozoitasun.
poke *v.t./v.i.* ziztatu, eztendu.
poker *n.* ziztatzaile, sumakila, suburdina. *n.* poker, kartajoko mota bat.
polar *adj.* lurburuko.
polar cap *n. (geog.)* poloinguru, lurburualde.
pole *n. (geog.)* polo, lurburu. **South Pole.** Hegoburu. **North Pole.** Iparburu. *n.* haga, pertika.
polecat *n. (zool.)* ipurtats.
polemicist *n.* eztabaidakari, eztabaidari.
police *n.* polizia, ertzain. **Secret police.** Isilpolizia.
policeman *n.* goardia, polizia, ertzain (gizon). **Basque police force.** Ertzaintza. **City policeman.** Hirizain.
policewoman *n.* polizia (emakume).
policy *n.* gobernu baten jokabide politikoa. *n.* poliza.
polio *n. (med.)* polio.
polish *v.t.* distirarazi, findu, leundu. *v.t.* margotu, pintatu (hatzazalak).
polish *n.* labaindura, leuntasun. *n.* distiraki.
polishable *adj.* labaingarri, leungarri.
polished *adj.* txarolezko; labaindu(a).
polisher *n.* leungailu, distirailu; leunkari, leuntzaile.
polite *adj.* fin, adeitsu, moduoneko, eraoneko.
politely *adv.* erabidez, finki.
politeness *n.* jendetasun.
political party *adj.* politiko.
politically *adv.* politikaz, politikoki.
political *n.* alderdi, partidu.
politician *n.* politikari, politiko.
politics *n.* politika.
polka *n.* polka.
poll *v.t./v.i.* inkestatu.
poll *n.* inkesta, azterbide, galdeketa.
pollen *n.* lorauts, lorairin, polen.
pollinate *v.t.* ernamindu, ernatu.
pollination *n.* poleneztapen.
pollster *n.* inkestalari, inkestatzaile.
pollute *v.t.* kutsatu.
pollution *n.* kutsadura, satsudura, kutsaketa, poluzio.
polo *n.* polo.
poltergeist *n.* iratxo zaratatsu, mozorro zaratatsu.
polychrome *adj.* koloreaskodun, koloreanitz.
polygamist *n.* poligamo, emazteanizko, emazteaskodun.
polygamy *n.* emazteanitz, poligamia.
polyglot *adj./n.* hizkuntzaskodun.
polyp *n. (zool.)* itsaslore.
polyphase *adj.* faseaskodun, fasetsu.
polysyllabic *adj.* silabaskodun.

pomade *n.* pomada.
pomegranate *n. (bot.)* granada, mingrana.
pomp *n.* handikeria, harropuzkeria.
pomposity *n.* handi-mandi, harrotasun.
pompous *adj.* handi-mandiko, harro, harroputz.
poncho *n.* pontxo.
pond *n.* urtzulo, itsasaintzira.
ponder *v.i./v.t.* hausnartu, gogoetak egin, gogartu.
pontificate *n.* aitasaindutza.
pontiff *n.* Aita Saindu.
pontoon bridge *n.* ontzizubi.
pony *n.* zalditxo, zaldixka.
pooch *n.* txakur, zakur.
poodle *n. (zool.)* zakur ilekizkur(ra).
pool *v.t./v.i.* istildu.
pool *n.* urbiltoki, urbildegi. *n.* igerileku, igertoki.
poop deck *n.* popa, txopa.
poor *adj.* behartsu, pobre, txiro, lander. *adj.* koitadu, gaixo, gizagaixo. *n.* pobreak.
poorhouse *n.* pobretxe, txirotegi.
poorly *adv.* pobreki.
pop *n.* zipozkada, tapoikada. *n.* gasdun edari.
popcorn *n.* palomitak.
Pope *n.* aitasaindu, aitasantu.
poplar *n. (bot.)* makal.
poppy *n. (bot.)* mitxoleta.
populace *n.* herrixehe, herrixume.
popular *adj.* herrikoi, herrialdeko, herriko, herritar; herri-. **To become popular.** Herrikoitu.
popularity *n.* entzute, izen, ospe.
popularize *v.t.* herrikoitu.
popularly *adv.* popularki.
populate *v.t.* populatu.
populated *adj.* jendetsu.
population *n.* biztanlego, biztanleria, herri.
populous *adj.* jendetsu.
porcelain *n.* portzelana.
porch *n.* etxaurre, ataurre.
porcupine *n. (zool.)* arantzurde.
pore *n. (anat.)* xularme.
pork *n.* zerriki, txerriki, urdeki.
pornographic *adj.* pornografiko.
pornography *n.* liburu, filma eta aldizkari pornografikoak.
porous *adj.* xularmetsu.
porous *adj.* zulotsu.
porpoise *n. (zool.)* mazopa.
porridge *n.* olo-ahi.
port *n. (naut.)* kai, portu, itsasontzitegi. *n. (naut.)* ezkerralde.
portable *n.* eramanerraz, molderraz, eskuko, lekualdagarri.
portal *n.* ate.
portent *n.* harrigarritza.
porter *n.* zamaketari, zamatzaile, bizkarkari, maletari.
portfolio *n.* karpeta, kartoizorro.
porthole *n.* argizulo (itsasontzi).
portico *n.* elizpe, elizatari, elizataurre.

portion n. parte, puska.
portly adj. mamijario, gizen, lodi.
portrait n. margozki; eskuz eta margoz eginiko irudia.
portray v.t. irudikatu, eskuz eta margoz irudia egin. v.t. -(ren) papera antzeztu.
pose v.i./v.t. ipini, jarri (bereziki artistaren modeloa).
position n. leku, lekune, nongotasun. n. lanpostu, bizibide, lanbide, ogibide. n. jarrera, jokabide.
positive adj. baikor, aurreragarri, positibo.
positively adv. baikorki, positiboki.
positiveness n. baikortasun.
positivism n. (phil.) positibismo.
posse n. Estatu Batuetan sherifari laguntzeaz arduratzen den hiritar taldea.
possess v.t. euki, jabe izan.
possessed adj. gaizkidun, deabrudun.
possession n. edukitza, jabekunde. n. deabrupekotasun, txerrenpekotasun. n. ondasun.
possessive adj. jabekor. **Possessive pronoun.** Izenorde jabekor.
possessor n. eukitzaile.
possibility n. ahalbide, posibilitate.
possible adj. gertagarri, ahalezko, ahalgarri, eginahal, posible.
possibly adv. agian, beharbada.
post n. poste, zutabe, zutoin. n. lanpostu. n. leku, ezartoki.
postage n. frankeo, gutunak zigilatzea.
postal service n. posta, postalgo.
postcard n. postal(e).
poster n. hormakartel, kartel.
posterior adj. atzeko, atzealde. adj. gerozko, geroztikako.
posterity n. gerokotasun.
postgraduate adj. graduatu ondorengo. n. graduatu ondorengo ikasle(a).
posthumous adj. hilondoko, hilosteko.
postiche n. ileorde.
postman n. postari.
postmeridional adj. eguerdiondoko, arratsaldeko.
post office n. postetxe.
postponable adj. epegarri, berangarri, luzakizun.
postpone v.t. atzeratu, atzezarri, berandutu, geroratu, epea luzatu.
postponed adj. atzeratu(a).
postponement n. berandupen, epeluzapen, atzezarketa, gerorapen, atzerapen.
postposition n. atzejarrera.
postscript n. azpiohar, gutunohar.
postulant n. lekaimegai.
postulate v.t. eskatu. v.t. egitzat eman, egitzat hartu.
posture n. jarrera.
postwar adj. gerraondoko, gerraosteko, gudondoko, gerlondoko.

pot n. lapiko, eltze, tupin(a); lurpoto. n. (colloq.) marihuana.
potability n. edangaitasun, edangarritasun.
potable adj. edangarri, edangai, edateko.
potash n. (chem.) potasa.
potassic adj. potasiko, potasiosko.
potassium n. (chem.) potasio.
potato n. patata, lursagar.
pot-bellied adj. sabelandi, zorroilo.
pot cheese n. gaztanbehera, zenbera.
potency n. indar, kemen.
potent adj. ernalgai; indartsu.
potentate n. errege, erregin.
potential mood n. (gram.) ahalmenera.
potentially adv. litekeena.
potentiate v.t. ahalmendu.
pothole n. zulogune, bidezulo, sabelune.
pothook n. laratz, larazkako.
potion n. botikaedari, edabe.
potpourri n. pupurri.
potter n. lurrontzigin, baxeragile, buztineratzaile, eltzegile, lapikogile.
pottery n. ontzigintza, lurrontzigintza.
pouch n. zakuto.
poultice n. plasto, enplasto, mantar.
poultry n. oilaskoki, oilaki.
pounce v.i. (on) -(r)en gainera salto egin, jauzi egin.
pound v.t./v.i. mailuskatu, astin-astindu.
pound n. libra, libera.
pounder n. astinkari, astindari.
pour v.t./v.i. erion; bota. v.i. euri asko egin.
pourable adj. eriongarri.
pout v.i./v.t. muturtu, muzindu.
poverty n. behartasun, premia, pobrezia, txirotasun, gabezia.
poverty-stricken adj. behartsu, txiro.
powder v.t./v.i. hauts egin, birrindu.
powder n. hauts, haur-hautsak, eder-hautsak. n. polbora, leherrauts.
powdered adj. birrintsu.
powder magazine n. sutaustegi.
powdery adj. haustsu, haustun.
power v.t. higiarazi, elektrindartu.
power n. ahal, ahalmen, indar, mende, aginte, botere, podere. **Power station.** Elektretxe. **Electric power.** Elektrindar. n. nagusitasun, nagusigo; eskumen.
powerful adj. ahaldun, ahaltsu, indardun, indartsu, aginbidedun, boteredun, boteretsu.
powerfully adv. ahalmenez, ahaltsuki, boteretsuki.
powerless adj. indargabe, ahul.
powerlessness n. ezinegin.
power saw n. zerramakina.
power station n. elektretxe.
practicable adj. egingarri.
practical adj. jardunbidezko, praktiko.
practicality n. praktikotasun.
practical joke n. jokotxar.

practically adv. jardunbidez, praktikoki.
practicalness n. praktikotasun.
practice v.t./v.i. praktikatu.
practice n. jarduketa, praktika.
prairie n. larre, belardi, landeta, landa.
praise v.t. goraipatu, goratu, goretsi, handietsi, laudatu, ohoratu, omendatu.
praise n. gorazarre, goraipaketa, gorespen, laudorio, handiespen.
praiser n. goraipatzaile, goresle, handiesle, laudatzaile.
praiseworthiness n. ospagarritasun.
praiseworthy adj. goragarri, laudagarri, txalogarri, omengarri.
praisingly adv. goraki.
prance v.i. saltoka ibili (zaldi).
prank n. okerreria, bihurrikada, jokotxar, mutikokeria.
prawn n. (zool.) otarrainska, otarraintxo.
pray v.t./v.i. otoitz egin, otoizkatu, erregutu, eskatu.
prayer n. erregutzaile; otoiketa, arren, otoitz. adj. otoitzezko.
prayerful adj. otoizle, otoizkile.
praying mantis n. (zool.) marisorgin.
pre- (gram.) aitzin-, aurre-.
preach v.t./v.i. predikatu, prediku egin, sermoi egin, ebanjeliotu.
preacher n. hizlari, predikatzaile, predikari, sermoilari.
preamble n. legeaurre.
precarious adj. eziraunkor.
precaution n. kontu, neurri, aitzineurri, oharkortasun.
precede v.t./v.i. aurrean joan, lehen izan, lehendu.
precedence n. aitzintasun, aurrekotasun, burutasun.
precedent adj. aurretiko. n. aurre, jarraibide.
preceding adj. aitzinagoko, aurrekari, aintzineko, aurreragoko, lehenagoko.
precept n. manu, aginketa, arau.
preceptive adj. arauzko.
preceptively adv. araueraz.
precinct n. egoitza.
preciosity n. finkeria, kulturkeria.
precious adj. balios, preziatu(a).
preciously adv. preziozki.
precipice n. erortoki, jaustegi, malkortegi, amildegi.
precipitate v.i./v.t. euria egin, euria ari ukan.
precipitately adv. zarrapastaka, arrapaladan.
precipitation n. euri egite; elur egite.
precipitously adv. zalapartaka, zalapartan, arrapastaka.
precise adj. justu, konkretu, zehatzezko.
precisely adv. konkretuki, zehatz-mehatz, zehazki, preseski, hain zuzen.
preciseness n. xehetasun,

zehaztasun, zehetasun.
precision n. zehazketa, zehaztasun.
precocious adj. goiztiar.
precociously adv. goizegi.
precociousness n. goiztartasun.
precocity n. goiz-.
preconceive v.t. aurreburutu, aurresortu.
preconsider v.t./v.i. aurregogartu.
precursor n. aurrelari, aurrendari.
predator n. harrapakari.
predatory adj. harrapakari.
predecessor n. aitzindari, aurreko, aurrelari.
predestination n. aurrehautaketa.
predestine v.t. hautetsi, aurrehautatu, aurreaukeratu.
predestined adj. hautetsi, zerurako.
predetermination n. aurrerabaki.
predetermine v.t. aurrerabaki.
predicament n. larrialdi, estualdi.
predict v.t./v.i. aurresan, iragarri, aurreadierazi.
predictable adj. asmagarri, igarterraz, susmagarri.
prediction n. aurresan, igarpen, iragarpen, aurreadierazpen.
predictor n. hegaztiazti.
predilect adj. gogoko, zurrukutun, gogozkoen(a).
predilection n. begikotasun, bihozmintasun, kuttuntasun.
predominance n. gainaginte.
predominant adj. gaineko, goiagintedun.
pre-election n. aurrehautaketa.
preeminence n. goiengo, lehengotasun, lehentasun.
preeminent adj. gorako.
preen v.t./v.i. txoriek beren lumak mokoaz txukundu.
preexistence n. aurreizate.
preface n. aitzin solas, hitzaurre.
prefect n. arduradun, prefekto.
prefer v.t. nahiago ukan, nahiago izan, hobetsi, lehenagotu, maitego izan.
preferable adj. hobe, nahiago.
preference n. begikotasun, lehentasun, aurretasun, lehenagotasun.
preferential adj. lehentasunezko.
preferred adj. gogoko, gogozkoen(a), zurrukutun, lehenagoko, begiko.
prefix v.t. aurrean ipini. v.t. aurrizkiztatu, aurrizkia ezarri.
prefix n. (gram.) aurrizki.
prefrontal adj. (anat.) kopetaurreko.
pregnancy n. ernaldi, haurraldi, sabelaldi.
pregnant adj. haurdun, umedun, izor.
prehensile adj. atziki.
prehistoric adj. historiaurreko, kondairaurreko.
prehistorical adj. historiaurreko.
prehistory n. historiaurre, kondairaurre.
prejudge v.t. aurrepaitu.

prejudgmental adj. epaiaurreko.
prejudice n. aurreritzi.
prejudiced adj. alderdikor.
preliminary adj. hasgarri, sarrerako;
aurre-. **Preliminary words.**
Sarrerako hitzak. **Preliminary work.**
Aurrelan.
prelude n. (mus.) aurremusika,
preludio.
premarital adj. ezkontzaurreko.
premature adj. zazpiki, goiztar,
garaiaurreko.
prematurely adv. goizik.
prematurity n. goiztartasun.
premeditate v.t./v.i. aurregogartu.
premeditation n. aurreasmo,
aurregogarpen.
premier n. lehen ministro, lehen
ministrari. adj. lehen, nagusien(a),
buru.
premise n. premisa.
premium n. sari.
premonition n. bihozsusmo,
bihozkada; aurreohar.
prenatal adj. jaioaurreko.
prenuptial adj. ezkontzaurreko.
preoccupation n. kexadura, kezka,
kezkaldi.
preoccupied adj. kezkati, kezkadun,
axolazko, kexati, kexukoi.
preoccupy v.t. kezkatu, artegatu.
prepaid adj. aurrez ordaindu(a).
preparation n. antolaketa, gertualdi,
atonketa, gertulan, moldapen.
preparatory adj. prestagarri.
prepare v.t./v.i. antolatu, prestatu,
gaitu, eratu, moldatu, gertu.
prepared adj. gertu(a), prest.
preparedness n. prestamen.
preparer n. atontzaile, gertarazle,
gertutzaile, prestatzaile.
preponderance n. gainditasun.
preponderant adj. gaindiko.
preposition n. (gram.) preposizio.
preposterous adj. arrazoingabeko,
desarrazoinezko, barregarri.
prerequisite n. aurrebaldintza.
prerogative n. abantaila, pribilegio.
Presbyterian n. presbiteriano.
preschool n. haurlilitegi, eskolaurre.
adj. eskolaurreko.
prescience n. aitzinjakite,
aurrejakituria.
prescient adj. aurrejakitun.
prescribable adj. errezetagarri.
prescribe v.t./v.i. errezetatu. v.t./v.i.
arautu.
prescriber n. errezetari.
prescription n. errezeta, sendaki,
sendatxartel.
prescriptive adj. aginduzko.
presence n. bista, agerre, presentzia.
present v.t. presentatu, aurkeztu. v.t.
(with) opari egin, erregalatu.
present n. gaurkotasun, gaur,
egungotasun, orain. n. (gram.)
orainaldi. **Present progressive.**

Orainaldi iraunkor. n. erregalu,
erregalia, opari. **To give a present
to.** Erregalatu. adj. gaurko,
oraintsuko.
presentable adj. aurkezgarri,
presentagarri.
presentation n. agertuera,
aurkezkunde, aurkezpen,
presentazio, agerpen, presentapen.
n. (theat.) antzezpen.
presenter n. aurkezlari, aurkezle,
aurkeztatzaile.
presentiment n. aurresusmo,
aurreuste, bihozsusmo.
presently adv. orain.
preservable adj. gordegarri, zaingarri.
preservation n. babesdura,
iraunarazte.
preservative adj. babeskor, zainkor.
preserve v.t. iraunarazi, begiratu,
babes egin. v.t./v.i. potoratu,
kontserbatu.
preserver n. iraunarazle.
preserves n. kontserbakin.
preside v.i. buru egon, maiburuan jarri.
presidency n. lehendakaritza.
president n. lehendakari, buru.
presidential adj. lehendakariaren;
lehendakari-.
press v.t./v.i. trinkatu, zapatu; azkartu.
v.t. lisatu. v.t. sakatu, bultz egin.
press n. herskin. n. inprimategi,
moldiztegi, prentsa. n. dolare.
press agency n. prentsagentzia.
press conference n. prentsaurreko,
prentsa mahai.
presser n. prentsatzaile, estutzaile.
pressing adj. presazko. n.
prentsaketa, tinkaketa, zapalaldi,
estukaldi, trinkaketa.
pressure n. hertsadura, hertsaketa,
hersketa, sakadura. n. tentsio,
presio. **Blood pressure.** Odolaren
tentsioa.
prestidigitator n. eskujokalari,
eskuketari.
prestige n. itzal, ospe, entzute, fama.
prestigious adj. Itzalandiko, ospetsu.
presto adv. laster.
presumable adj. susmagarri.
presumably adv. susmagarritasunez.
presume v.t./v.i. suposatu, uste izan.
presumed adj. susmozko, ustezko.
presumption n. harrokeria,
hantuzkeria, burgoikeria.
presumptuous adj. harroputz,
harroxka, farfailadun, handiuste.
presumptuously adv. hantzuzki.
presumptuousness n. handiustekeria,
handiuste.
pretend v.t./v.i. plantak egin, asmo
izan.
pretender n. erregegai. n. itxuregile.
pretense n. itxurantz, itxurapen,
itxurakeria, itxuramendu.
pretension n. asmobizi.
pretentious adj. arranditsu, handiputz,

pinpirin.
preterite n./adj. joandako, lehenaldi bukatu(a).
pretext n. aitzakia, txutxumutxu, estakuru.
pretrial adj. auziaurreko, epaiaurreko.
prettier adj. (comp.) ederrago, politago.
prettiest adj. politen(a), ederren(a).
prettily adv. poliki, lerdenki, lirainki.
prettiness n. politasun, liraintasun, liraindura.
pretty v.t. (batzutan up-ekin) politu, edertu.
pretty adj. polit, eder. adv. samar.
prevail v.i. nagusitu, gailendu, garaitu.
prevailing adj. gaindiko.
prevalence n. askotasun, maiztasun. n. gainditasun, nagusitasun.
prevalent adj. askotako.
prevalently adv. sarritan, askotan.
prevaricate v.i. gezurra esan.
prevarication n. gezur.
prevent v.t./v.i. eragozpidetu, arretatu, aitzindu, aurrebegiratu.
preventable adj. alderagarri, itzurgarri.
prevention n. aurrejarrera.
preventive adj. aurreosasunezko, aurretiazko.
preview n. hurrengo filmaren aurrerapen laburra; teleaurrekin.
previous adj. aurreko, aurretiko, lehenagoko, aldeaurreko.
previously adv. aitzinadanik, aurrez, lehenago, lehendanik, aitzinetik, aldeaurrez.
previousness n. lehengotasun.
prewar n. gerraurre. adj. gerraurreko.
prey n. harrapakin.
price n. balio, salneurri, prezio, kostu.
To go up in price. Garestitu. **To lower the price.** Merketu.
priceless adj. baloraezin, estimagaitz.
prick v.t./v.i. arantzatu, eztenkatu, sastakatu.
prick n. sastada, sastako.
prickle n. arantza. n. kilika.
prickly adj. izpidun.
pride n. harrotasun.
priest n. apez, abade.
priestess n. beretertsa.
priesthood n. apezkunde, apezgo, abadetza.
priestly adv. apezgisa, apezlegez.
prim adj. fazatu, estu.
primacy n. nagusitasun, burutasun, aurrelaritza.
primarily adv. gehienbat, funtsean, lehenengoz, nagusiki.
primary adj. lehen, lehengo, lehenbiziko. **Primary school.** Lehen irakaskintza.
primate n. (zool.) primate, lehendiko. n. (rel.) apezpikuburu.
primateship n. (rel.) apezpikuburutza.
prime n. gizonadin. adj. lehenengo. adj. bikain. adj. sasoiko.

primer n. katoi. n. eztandagailu.
primeval adj. aintzinako; lehen-.
primiparous adj. lehenumedun.
primitive adj. basa. adj. jatorrizko.
primogeniture n. primutasun, semeoinordetza, lehensemetza, semenagusitasun, lehentasun.
primordial adj. aintzinako; lehen-.
prince n. erregeseme, printze, tronukide.
princedom n. printzerri.
princehood n. printzego.
princely adj. printzetar.
princess n. erregealaba, printzesa.
principal adj. behinen, nagusien, goien, gehien. n. eskolako nagusi.
principally adv. gehienbat, gehienik, nagusiro, nagusiki.
principle n. arau. n. hasiera, jatorri.
print v.t./v.i. inprimatu, irarri. v.t. etenez idatzi.
printer n. liburugile, inprimatzaile, moldizkin.
printing n. inprimaketa, irarketa, prentsaketa, argitarapen.
printing press n. inprimailu, moldizkailu.
printout n. konputadora-zerrenda.
printshop n. inprimategi, moldiztegi.
prior adj. lehentasunezko.
priority n. aurrekotasun, aurretasun, lehengotasun, lehentasun, aitzintasun.
priory n. prioretxe.
prism n. prisma.
prison n. espetxe, presondegi, gartzela.
prisoner n. preso, katigu, giltzapeko.
prison guard n. espetxezain, gartzelazain, presondegizain, presozain.
privacy n. bakardade.
private adj. pribatu, bakarrezko, bakarreko. n. soldadu berri, soldadu xehe.
privately adv. bakarrik, bakarrean, bakarka.
privation n. kenketa, gabekeria; -gabeko.
privilege n. bereztasun.
privileged adj. abantailadun, faboredun.
privy n. komun.
prize n. sari, garaisari.
prize-winning adj. sarigarri, sarigai.
pro adv./n. alde, alderdi. n. profesional. n. jokalari bikain(a).
probability n. egitxura, gertagarritasun, gertakortasun.
probable adj. egiantzeko, egitxurako, itxuradun, kanorezko, gertagarri.
probably adv. egiantzez, bide, kanorez, edo.
probate v.t. azkennahia legeztatu, testamentua legeztatu.
probate n. azkennahiaren legeztapen.
probation n. probaldi.

probe *v.t./v.i.* zundatu.
probe *n.* bilakuntza.
probity *n.* prestasun, prestutasun.
problem *n.* buruhauste, arazo, kinka, korapilo.
problematic *adj.* buruhausgarri.
proboscis *n.* tronpa.
procedure *n.* eginbide, egitada, prozedura, jardunbide.
proceed *v.i.* aurrera joan, -ra jo.
proceeding(s) *n.* biltzar-txosten.
process *n.* aurrerabide, bilakaera, gertabide, prozedura.
procession *n.* elizbira, prozesio.
processional *adj.* elizbirako.
proclaim *v.t./v.i.* aldarrikatu.
proclamation *n.* aldarrikaketa, aldarrikapen.
procrastinate *v.i./v.t.* atzeratu, gerotatu, epetu.
procrastination *n.* luzagarri, luzakortasun.
procrastinator *n.* luzakari.
procreate *v.i.* umatu, sortu.
procreation *n.* sormen, umegintza, umeketa, ernaldura.
procreator *n.* sortzaile.
procure *v.t.* lortu. *v.t./v.i.* lupu egin.
procurer *n.* lupu.
prod *v.t.* zirikatu, ziztatu, akuilukatu.
prod *n.* akuilukada; eztenmakila, akuilu.
prodigal *adj.* bonbontzaile.
prodigality *n.* bonbonkada.
prodigious *adj.* jori, joritsu.
prodigiously *adv.* oparo, ugari.
prodigy *n.* harrigarritza.
produce *v.t./v.i.* ekoitzi, ekoiztu, fruitu eman.
product *n.* ekoizkin, ekoizpen, fruitu. *n.* ondorio, fruitu. *n.* (*math.*) emaitza.
production *n.* ekoizpen, ekarpen, produkzio.
productive *adj.* ekoizkor, ekoizle, emankor, fruitukor.
productively *adv.* fruitukorki.
productiveness *n.* ekoizkortasun.
productivity *n.* emankortasun, ekoizkortasun.
profane *v.t.* profanatu, narriotu.
profane *adj.* erlijiogabe, fedegabe.
profanity *n.* birao.
profess *v.t./v.i.* aitortu.
professed *adj.* botudun.
profession *n.* bizibide, bizimodu, irabazbide, lanbide, ogibide; -gintza, - ari, -lari. *n.* erlijio-aitormen.
professional *adj.* profesional.
professionalism *n.* profesionaltasun.
professionally *adv.* profesionalki.
professor *n.* irakasle, irakaslesa.
professorship *n.* katedra.
proffer *v.t.* eskaini.
proficient *adj.* trebe, jakintsu, moldetsu.
profile *n.* isla.
profit *v.i./v.t.* gainirabazi.
profit *n.* irabazi, etekin, gozamen,

probetxu, gainirabazpen, onura.
profitability *n.* errentabilitate, errentagarritasun.
profitable *adj.* onuragarri, probetxuzko, probetxugarri, abantailezko, errentagarri, irabazgarri.
profitableness *n.* irabazgarritasun.
profitably *adv.* onuraz, probetxuz.
profiteer *n.* orobiltzaile.
profiteering *n.* lukuru, lukurantza, lukurreria.
profits *n.* (*pl.*) irabazte.
profound *adj.* sakon, barna, barnakor.
profoundly *adv.* sakonki, barneki, barren-barrendik.
profuse *adj.* oparotsu, parrastatsu, ugaritsu.
profusely *adv.* parra-parra, burrustaka.
profusion *n.* parrasta, oparotasun, bala-bala.
progenitor *n.* aitalehen, guraso.
progeny *n.* semetalde, ondorengoak.
prognosis *n.* (*med.*) adierazpen erreserbatu(a), iragarpen, aurresan.
prognosticate *v.t.* iragarri, aurresan.
prognosticator *n.* aurresale.
program *v.t.* programatu.
program *n.* programa, egitarau, iragarki. **Television program.** Telemanaldi. Telesaio. *n.* programazio.
programming *n.* programaketa, programakuntza.
progress *v.i.* aurrerabidetu, aitzinatu, aitzinaratu.
progress *n.* aurrerapen, aurreraldi, aurrerakada, aitzinaldi, aintzinpen.
progression *n.* aurrerakuntza.
progressive *adj.* aurrelari, aurrerakoi, aurreragarri, aurrerakor.
progressively *adv.* aurrerabidez, gehiagoka.
progressiveness *n.* aurrerakortasun, aurrerazaletasun.
prohibit *v.t.* debekatu, galarazi, eragotzi.
prohibitable *adj.* debekagarri.
prohibited *adj.* debekatuta. **Entrance prohibited.** Debekatuta sarrera.
prohibition *n.* debeku, eragozketa, galerazpen, eragozbide.
prohibitive *adj.* galerazle, debekatzaile, eragozpenezko.
prohibitor *n.* debekatzaile.
project *v.t.* gogotan erabili, plan egin. *v.t.* bota.
project *n.* egitarau, egingai.
projectile *n.* granada, iraizkin, jaurtigai.
projection *n.* irtenune, mailagune. *n.* zine-proiektapen, proiekzio.
projector *n.* zinemagailu, proiektore.
proletarian *n.* proletari.
proletariat *n.* langileria, langilego, proletalgo.
proliferate *v.i./v.t.* ugaritu, aniztu,

askotu, gehitu, ugaldu.
prolific *adj.* emankor, ugalkor, umetsu, naharo, semetsu, umagile.
prolificly *adv.* naharoki, ugalkorki.
prolificness *n.* ugalkortasun, naharotasun, ugaritasun.
prologue *n.* aitzin solas, hitzaurre, solasaitzin.
prolong *v.t.* luzatu (denbora), luzarazi.
prolongable *adj.* luzagarri, hedagarri.
prolongation *n.* epeluzapen, hedaketa, hedakuntza, luzabide, luzakortasun, luzapen.
prom *n.* Estatu Batuetan unibertsitate aurreko lau urte ondoren burutzen den dantzaldi garrantzitsua.
promenade *n.* oinezaldi.
prominence *n.* gorentasun, begiramen, garaitasun. *n.* konkordura.
prominent *adj.* garai, goidun.
prominently *adv.* nabarmenki, garaiki.
promiscuous *adj.* lizun, haragikoi. *adj.* nahastatu.
promise *v.t./v.i.* hitz eman, promes egin, agindu.
promise *n.* promes, agindu, hitz, hitz eman(a).
promised *adj.* agindutako.
promiser *n.* hitzemaile, promesari, agintzaile.
promissory note *n.* *(econ.)* ordaintxartel, ordainagindu, ordainagiri.
promontory *n.* lurmutur. *n.* konkor, irtenune.
promote *v.t.* sustatu, sorterazi, aurreratu, eragin, aupatu.
promoter *n.* eginerazle, bultzatzaile, eragile.
promotion *n.* goraketa, promozio.
prompt *adj.* garaioneko.
promptly *adv.* garaionez.
promptness *n.* agudotasun, azkartasun, lastertasun, bizitasun.
promulgate *v.t.* aldarrikatu, manatu.
promulgation *n.* aldarrikaketa, aldarrikapen.
prone *adj.* -kor, -bera.
prong *n.* arantza.
pronominal *adj.* izenordeko.
pronoun *n.* *(gram.)* izenorde.
Possessive pronoun. Izenorde jabekor. **Demonstrative pronoun.** Izenorde erakusle.
pronounce *v.t./v.i.* ahoskatu.
pronouncement *n.* aldarrikapen, aldarrikaketa, iragarpen.
pronunciation *n.* ahoskaketa.
proof *n.* egiztabide, egiztapen, proba, sinesgarri, froga.
prop *v.t.* zutikatu, sardeztatu.
propaganda *n.* iragarketa, propaganda.
propagate *v.t./v.i.* hedabanatu.
propagation *n.* hedabanaketa.
propagator *n.* sortzaile.

propel *v.t.* bultzatu, eragin.
propeller *n.* helize.
propensity *n.* makurrera.
proper *adj.* zuzen, berekiko.
properly *adv.* beharbezala, egoki, taiuz, propioki.
propertied *adj.* jabedun.
property *n.* landasail, ontasun, ondasun.
prophecy *n.* igarpen, iragarpen, aurresan.
prophet *n.* iragarle, profeta.
prophetess *n.* iragarlesa.
prophetic *adj.* iragarpentsu.
prophetically *adv.* iragarpenez.
prophylactic *n.* aurreosasunezko.
prophylaxis *n.* *(med.)* aurreosasun.
propinquity *n.* gertutasun, hurbiltasun.
propitiate *v.t.* bakearazi.
propitiation *n.* bakearazpen.
propitiatory *adj.* bakegarri.
propitious *adj.* aldezko, lagungarri, onezko.
proportion *n.* hein, proportzio, arabera.
proportional *adj.* bataz-besteko.
proportionally *adv.* arauz, arauka, proportzionalki.
proportionate *adj.* araberako.
proposal *n.* proposapen, proposamen, proposamendu. *n.* ezkontitz.
propose *v.t./v.i.* proposatu. *v.i.* mandatu egin.
proposition *n.* proposamen, proposamendu.
proprietary *adj.* etxedun.
proprietor *n.* etxejabe, jabe, etxejaun.
proprietorship *n.* jabetasun, jabetza, ugazabatasun.
propulsion *n.* bultzaldi, bultzada, eragite.
prorate *v.i./v.t.* hainbanatu.
prosaic *adj.* arrunt, prosaiko.
pros and cons *n.* *(pl.)* ongaitzak, aldekontrakoak.
proscribe *v.t.* galarazi, arbuiatu, debekatu.
proscription *n.* galerapen, arbuio.
prose *n.* hitz lau, prosa.
prosecute *v.t./v.i.* auzitaratu, ari, auzitan sartu, auzibidetu, auzitan ibili.
prosecuted *adj.* auzipeko, auzipetu(a).
prosecuting attorney *n.* fiskal.
prosecution *n.* auzialdi, auzitaraketa.
prosecutor *n.* fiskal.
prose writer *n.* prosalari.
prospect *v.t./v.i.* mehatzak ikertu.
prospect *n.* itxarobide, arrakasta eta ondasunak areagotzeko aukera. *n.* hautagai izan litekeen norbait.
prospective *adj.* ustezko.
prospector *n.* bilaketari; -ketari. **Gold prospector.** Urreketari.
prosper *v.i./v.t.* joritu, gurendu.
prosperity *n.* aurrerakunde, joridura, oparoaldi, goratzapen.
prosperous *adj.* aurrerakor, aldezko.

prosperously adv. ongiroz.
prostate n. (anat.) prostata.
prostitute v.t. lizunarazi.
prostitute n. emagaldu, ematxar, maribidetako, maripurtzil, urdanga.
prostitution n. emagaldutza, emagalkeria, ematxarkeria, emalizunkeria.
prostrate v.t. ahozpeztu, ahoz beheratu, goibeheratu.
prostration n. eroraldi, eroritasun.
protect v.t./v.i. zaindu, babestu, gerizatu, defenditu, aldezkatu, gorde, estalpetu.
protectable adj. gordegarri, babesgarri.
protected adj. babesdun, babestu(a), babespeko.
protection n. babespen, laguntza, babes, magalpe, itzal, zaindaritza, geriza.
protective adj. babesezko, zainkor, gerizagarri, itzalpetzaile.
protector n. babesemale, babesle, defendatzaile. n. zaintzaile, faboretzaile, aldezkari, zaindari, patroi.
protectorate n. (pol.) babeslur.
protein n. (chem.) proteina.
protest v.i./v.t. protesta egin.
protest n. protesta.
Protestant n./adj. protestante.
protestation n. manifestazio.
protester n. manifestari, protestatzaile.
protest march n. manifestaldi, manifestapen, manifestazio.
proto- (gram.) aitzin-, lehen-.
protocol n. protokolo.
proton n. (chem.) protoi.
protoplasm n. protoplasma.
prototype n. leheneredu, lehenmolde.
protozoan adj./n. (biol.) lehenbizidun.
protract v.t. luzeagotu.
protruberance n. tontor, mokor, konkor.
protrusion n. mokor.
proud adj. harro, harrotsu.
proudly adv. harro, harroki, handiki.
provability n. frogagarritasun.
provable adj. frogagarri, egiztagarri.
prove v.t. egiztatu, frogatu, arrazoinketatu, ziurpetu. v.i. geratu.
proven p. part. of prove.
provender n. janari; bazka, sorobelar.
prover n. egiztalari, frogatzaile.
proverb n. atsotitz, zaharritz, errefrau.
proverbial adj. esaerazko.
proverbially adv. atsotitzez.
provide v.t./v.i. (v.i.), **for** edo **against**-ekin) hornitu, ornitu, ekarri.
providence n. probidentzia, Jainkoaren ardura.
provident adj. aurreikusle.
providential adj. onerako.
provider n. hornitzaile, hornilari.
province n. probintzia.
provincial adj. probintziar,

probintziako.
provision v.t. hornitu, ornitu.
provision n. horni.
provisional adj. behin-behineko, mementoko.
provisionally adv. oraingoz.
provisions n. jaki, jan-edariak, jatekoak, hornigai.
provocation n. aupada, kitzika, narritadura, zirikaldi.
provocative adj. narritagarri, zirikakor.
provoke v.t. zirikatu, tirritatu, kitzikatu, aupakatu, narritatu.
prow n. ontziaurre, branka. **Prow first.** Brankaz.
prowess n. balentria.
prowl v.i./v.t. ingurukatu, jirabiratu, inguruka ibili.
proximate adj. hurreneko, hurko, inguruko.
proximity n. hurbiltasun, hurbilgo, ondo, hurkotasun, gertutasun, hurrentasun.
proxy n. ordezkari, mandatari.
prude n. sasisaindu.
prudence n. zentzutasun, zuhurtzia, begiratasun, begirakortasun.
prudent adj. zuhur, zentzudun, begirakor, aurreikusle.
prudently adv. zentzuz, begirakorki, zuhurki.
prune v.t. adarrakatu, kimatu, inaustu, muskildu. v.t. murriztu, eskastu.
pruning n. inausketa, kimaketa.
prurient adj. lizun, haragikoi.
pry v.i. ikusmiratu. v.t. destokitu, altxatu.
P.S. azpiohar, gutunohar.
psalm n. salmo, salmokantu.
psalmist n. salmogile.
psalmody n. (eccl.) salmueresi.
psalter n. salmoliburu, salmotegi.
pseudo- (gram.) sasi-, -izun.
pseudonym n. izengoiti, ezizen, gaitzizen, izenorde.
pseudopoet n. sasipoeta.
psyche n. arima.
psychiatrist n. (med.) psikiatra.
psychiatry n. (med.) psikiatria.
psychic adj. psikiko.
psychoanalysis n. (med.) psikoanalisi.
psychological adj. psikologiko.
psychologist n. psikologari.
psychology n. psikologia.
psychopath n. psikopata.
psychosis n. (med.) psikosi.
psychotherapy n. (med.) psikoterapia.
pub n. taberna, ardandegi.
puberty n. nerabetza, nerabezero. **To enter puberty.** Nerabetu.
pubescence n. nerabetasun.
pubic adj. sabelpeko.
pubis n. (anat.) sabelpe.
public adj. ageri, herri, herriko, jendarteko, jendaurreko. **Public school.** Herri-eskola. **Public works.** Herrilan. n. jendarte, herri.

publication *n.* argitarapen, agermen, barreiaketa. **Annual publication.** Urtekari.
public figure *n.* herrigizon.
publicity *n.* agiritasun, iragarbide, iragarketa.
publicize *v.t.* deadar egin, publikatu.
publicly *adv.* nabarian, publikoki, argitan.
public school *n.* herri-eskola.
public works *n.* herrilan.
publish *v.t./v.i.* argitaratu, argitarazi, argitara eman, inprimatu, agerrarazi.
publishable *adj.* argitaragarri, argiragarri, agergarri.
publisher *n.* liburugile, argitaltzaile.
publishing *n.* liburugintza; barreiatze.
publishing house *n.* argitaletxe, argitaldari.
puddle *v.t./v.i.* istildu.
puddle *n.* urputzu, urtzulo, istil, putzu.
pudgy *adj.* trapalote, lodikote.
puerile *adj.* haurraren, haurrantzeko.
puerilely *adv.* haurgisa, umeki.
puerility *n.* ninikeria.
puff *v.i./v.t.* pufa egin, putz egin. *v.i.* **(up)** handitu, hanpatu.
puff *n.* buhako, putz.
puffer *n.* putzegile.
pugilism *n.* boxeaketa, ukabilketa.
pugilist *n.* ukabilkari.
pugnacious *adj.* liskarzale, errietazale.
pugnaciousness *n.* gudazaletasun.
pugnacity *n.* borrokagrina.
pug-nosed *adj.* sudurmotz, sudurzapal.
puke *v.i./v.t.* goragaletu.
pulchritude *n.* kriketasun.
pull *v.t./v.i.* tiratu, teinkatu, teink egin. *v.t.* **(back)** atzeratu. *v.t.* **(out)** atera. *v.i.* **(out)** irten. *v.i.* **(together)** orobatu, elkarrekin lan egin.
pull *n.* teinkada, tirakada.
puller *n.* teinkari, tiratzaile.
pullet *n.* *(zool.)* oilanda.
pulley *n.* txirrika, motoi, polea.
pulmonary *adj.* birikako, biriketako.
pulpit *n.* predikaleku, pulpitu.
pulse *n.* pultsu.
pulverization *n.* hausketa.
pulverize *v.t./v.i.* haustu, hauts egin, errautsi.
pulverized *adj.* haustu(a).
puma *n.* *(zool.)* puma.
pumice *n.* *(geol.)* pomezarri, harrigeldo.
pummel *v.t.* ukaldikatu.
pump *v.t.* **(out)** hustu. *v.t.* **(up)** puztu.
pump *n.* puzkailu.
pumpkin *n.* *(bot.)* kuia.
pun *n.* hizjoko.
punch *v.t./v.i.* ukabilkada eman, ukabilkatu. *v.t.* zulakatu.
punch *n.* daunba, danba. *n.* abarkaziri, puntzoi. *n.* edari goxo mota bat.
punctilious *adj.* xehezale.
punctual *adj.* orduko, garaioneko, tenoretsu.

punctuality *n.* ordukotasun, tenoretasun.
punctually *adv.* garaionez, orduz, orduonez.
punctuate *v.t.* puntu ezarri.
punctuation *n.* puntuezarketa.
puncturable *adj.* zulagarri.
puncture *v.t./v.i.* zulatu, ziztatu.
puncture *n.* ziztada.
puniness *n.* ziztrinkeria.
punish *v.t./v.i.* zigortu, zigorrarazi, zehatu.
punishable *adj.* zigorgarri.
punisher *n.* zigorkari, zigorlari.
punishment *n.* zigor, zigorraldi. **Capital punishment.** Heriozigor.
punitive *adj.* zigorkor.
punk *n.* ardai.
puny *adj.* sistrin.
pup *n.* txakurrume, zakurkume.
pupa *n.* *(zool.)* kusku.
pupil *n.* ikasle. *n.* begi-nini.
puppet *n.* gizonorde, giñol.
puppy *n.* *(zool.)* zakurkume, txakurkume.
purchasable *adj.* erosgarri.
purchase *v.t.* erosi.
purchase *n.* erosketa, erospen, eroskin.
purchaser *n.* erosle.
purchasing power *n.* lormen, eros-ahalmen.
pure *adj.* garbi, huts, soil.
puree *n.* pure.
purely *adv.* hutsik, jatorki, nahasgabeki.
pureness *n.* garbitasun, jatortasun. **Pureness of heart.** Bihozgarbitasun.
purgative *adj.* iraizkor, garbigai, libragarri.
purgatory *n.* garbitoki.
purge *v.t./v.i.* purgatu, garbitu, libratu.
purge *n.* garbialdi, garbiketa, garbipen, ikuzketa.
purifiable *adj.* garbigarri, ikuzgarri.
purification *n.* garbialdi, garbiarazpen, garbipen, ikuzketa.
purify *v.t./v.i.* garbitu, garbiarazi, xahutu.
purifying *adj.* garbigarri.
purism *n.* garbizaletasun.
puristic *adj.* garbizale.
purity *n.* garbitasun.
purple *n./adj.* ubel, more. **To turn purple.** Ubeldu.
purplish *adj.* ubelaire, moreantzeko.
purport *v.t.* azpijokoz norbere burua aurkeztu.
purpose *n.* gogo, asmo, xede, helburu.
purposeless *adj.* helburugabe.
purposelessly *adv.* firri-farra.
purr *v.i.* zurrunkatu (katuak).
purring *n.* zurrunga (katu).
purse *n.* poltsa, kartera, diruzorro. **Coin purse. Change purse.** Txanponzorro.

pursue *v.t./v.i.* -(r)i jarraiki, -(r)en atzetik joan.
pursuit *n.* jarraiketa.
purulence *n.* zornejario.
purulent *adj.* zornatsu, zornedun.
purvey *v.t.* hornitu.
purveyor *n.* hornitzaile.
pus *n.* zorne, materia, gerli.
push *v.t./v.i.* bultzatu, bultz egin, bultzakatu, bulkatu, saka egin.
push *n.* bultza, bultzakada, sakada. *n.* eragin, aurrerraketa.
pusher *n.* bultzatzaile. *n.* drogasaltzaile.
pushpin *n.* txintxeta.
pushy *adj.* bultzagile, bultzatzaile, ekile.
pussy *adj.* zornakor. *n.* katutxo.
pustule *n.* (*med.*) zakar, zakardura, suldar.
put *v.t.* ipini, jarri, ezarri, kokatu, lekutu. *v.t.* (**aside**) ertzatu, alboratu. *v.t.* (**away**) zokoratu, bazterreratu; espetxeratu. *v.t.* (**down**) apalerazi; etzan. *v.t.* (**near**) hurbildu, ondoratu. *v.t.* (**off**) geroratu. *v.t.* (**on**) jantzi, soineko ipini. *v.t.* (**out**) iraungi, amata egin. *v.t.* (**outside**) lekoreratu. *v.t.* (**up**) ostatatu. *v.t.* (**up with**) elkar eraman.
put *adj.* jarritako.
putrefaction *n.* ustelketa, andea.
putrefy *v.t./v.i.* usteldu, kirastu.
putrescence *n.* andeakortasun.
putrescent *adj.* ustelkor.
putrid *adj.* kirastun, kerudun.
putt *v.i./v.t.* golf-eko pilota geldiro jo zuloan sar dadin.
putt *n.* ukitu geldia(k).
putter *n.* ezartzaile, jartzaile.
putty *v.t.* mastikatu.
putty *n.* mastika, ore, txertore.
puzzle *v.t./v.i.* itsutu; kezkatu.
puzzle *n.* buruhauste, katramila, asmagai, asmakaitz.
pygmy *n.* pigmeo.
pyjama *n.* pixama.
pyramid *n.* piramide.
pyre *n.* sumeta.
Pyrenees *n.* (*geog.*) Pireneomendiak.
pyromania *n.* suzalekeria.
pyromaniac *n.* erreketari, suemaile.
pyrotechnics *n.* suzirigintza.
python *n.* (*zool.*) piton, sugetzar.

Q

q *n.* Ingeles alfabetoko letra.
quack *n.* ahateen zarata. *n.* (*colloq.*) sasisendagile, sasisendatzaile.
quadrangle *n.* lauki.
quadrant *n.* koadrante.
quadrilateral *adj.* laualdeko.
quadruped *n./adj.* lauhankadun, lauoindun, lauzangodun, lauhankako.
quadruple *v.t./v.i.* laukoiztu.
quadruple *adj./n.* laukoitz, laukote.
quadruplet *n.* laukoitz.

quaff *v.t.* gozamenez edan.
quagmire *n.* zikinzulo, zikintza.
quail *n.* (*zool.*) pospolin, Estatu Batuetako galeper antzeko txoria.
quaint *adj.* arraro, berezi.
quake *v.i.* dardar egin, dardarikatu.
quake *n.* lurrikara.
Quaker *n.* (*rel.*) kuakero.
qualification *n.* gaikuntza, kalifikazio.
qualified *adj.* gaitu(a).
qualify *v.t./v.i.* gaitu, trebatu, kalifikatu.
qualifying *adj.* (*gram.*) kalifikatzaile.
qualitative *adj.* kualitatezko, tasunezko.
quality *n.* nolakotasun, kalitate.
qualm *n.* barren kezka, bihotz-zimiko.
quantitative *adj.* kantitatezko, zenbanako.
quantity *n.* kopuru, multzo, zenbatasun, kantitate, multzotasun.
quarantine *v.t.* izurritea heda ez dadin agindu zorrotzak ezarri.
quarantine *n.* izurritea heda ez dadin ezartzen diren agindu zorrotzak.
quarrel *v.i.* errieta egin, eskatimatu, liskartu.
quarrel *n.* haserraldi, errieta, liskar, mokoketa, muturketa, eskatima.
quarreler *n.* errietari, eskatimari, liskargile, mokokari.
quarrelsome *adj.* errietazale, liskarti, liskarrari.
quarry *n.* harrobi.
quart *n.* galoi-laurden.
quarter *v.t.* laurdendu, laurdenkatu. *v.i.* gudaletxeratu.
quarter *n.* laurden. *n.* Estatu Batuetako hogeitabost xentimoko txanpona. *n.* (*pl.*) soldaduen egoitza.
quarterback *n.* Estatu Batuetako futboleko atzelaria.
quarterly *adv./adj.* hiruhilebetero; hiruhilebeteko.
quarter note *n.* (*mus.*) beltz.
quarterstaff *n.* makila luze(a).
quartet *n.* (*mus.*) laukote.
quartz *n.* (*min.*) sutarri, sukarri.
quasi *adj.* antzeko. *adv.* sasi-, erdi-.
quaver *v.i.* dardar egin, dardarikatu.
quay *n.* nasa, atrakaleku, lehorrerategi.
queasy *adj.* okagile, egozgale.
queen *n.* erregina.
queenly *adj.* erregina-gisako, erregina-antzeko.
queer *adj.* sinoti, sinotsu. *n.* (*colloq.*) marikoi, sexuberekoi.
queerness *n.* sino.
quell *v.t.* menperatu, oinperatu. *v.t.* baretu, eztitu, ematu, gozatu.
quench *v.t.* egarria asetu, egarria hil.
querulous *adj.* kexukoi, zinkuri.
query *n.* galdeagiri.
quest *n.* bilaketa.
question *v.t./v.i.* galdetu, galde egin, itaundu.
question *n.* galde, galdera, itaun.

questionable *adj.* zalantzagarri, irizkarri, ihardukigarri.

questioner *n.* galdegile, galderagile, galdetzaile.

questioningly *adv.* galdebidez.

question mark *n.* (*gram.*) galdemarka, galdeikur.

questionnaire *n.* galdesorta, galdebide, galdeliburu, galdeagiri.

quibble *v.i.* ihesbideka ibili.

quick *adj.* azkar, berehalako, laster, lasterkari, agudo, bizkor.

quicken *v.t./v.i.* arinagotu, lasterkatu, presakatu. *v.t./v.i.* biztu, bizkortu, suspertu, biziagotu.

quicklime *n.* gisubizi, karebizi.

quickly *adv.* arin, arinka, azkar, berehalaxe, bizkor, laster, zalu, agudoki.

quickness *n.* bizkortasun, lastertasun, azkartasun, agudotasun.

quicksand *n.* hondar mugikorrak.

quicksilver *v.t.* zilarbizitu.

quicksilver *n.* (*min.*) zilarbizi.

quick-tempered *adj.* suminkoi, haserrekor, odolbizi.

quiescent *adj.* bare, lasai, trankil.

quiet *v.t./v.i.* (*v.i.*, *askotan* **down**-*ekin*) isildu, isilarazi, mutuarazi; baretu.

quiet *n.* isiltasun; sosegamendu. *adj.* isil, isilkor; baretsu, baketsu, ekuru, geldi. *int.* ixo, isilik. **Be quiet!** Hago isilik!

quietly *adv.* isilik, isilka.

quietness *n.* baretasun, egonaldi, isilkoitasun, naretasun.

quill *n.* hegats.

quilt *n.* edredoi.

quince *n.* (*bot.*) irasagar.

quinine *n.* (*chem.*) kinina.

quintet *n.* (*mus.*) bosteko, bostekote.

quintuple *v.t/v.i.* boskoiztu.

quintuple *adj./n.* boskoitz, boski.

quintuplet *n.* boskoitz, boski.

quintuplication *n.* boskoizte.

quip *n.* ateraldi zorrotza.

quirk *n.* berezitasun.

quit *v.t./v.i.* utzi, gelditu. *v.t./v.i.* irten.

quite *adv.* samar, xamar, aski, nahiko.

quiver *v.t./v.i.* dardaratu, dardar egin.

quiver *n.* geziontzi.

quixotic *adj.* kixoteriazko.

quixotism *n.* kixotekeria, kixotekada.

quiz *n.* azterketa laburra.

quorum *n.* bilera bat burutu ahal izateko behar den gutxienezko kopurua.

quota *n.* ordainsari, kuota, pagu.

quotable *adj.* aipagarri.

quotation *n.* aipuera, aipatze. *n.* (*econ.*) kotizazio.

quotation marks *n.* (*gram.*) gakotxak.

quote *v.t.* aipatu. *v.t.* (*econ.*) kotizatu.

quote *n.* aipamen.

quoter *n.* aipatzaile, aipari.

quotidian *adj.* eguneroko.

quotient *n.* (*math.*) zatidura.

R

r *n.* Ingeles alfabetoko letra.

rabbi *n.* rabino.

rabbit *n.* (*zool.*) untxi, koneju.

rabble *n.* jendaila, gizatzar, alproja, alprojatalde.

rabid *adj.* amorratu(a).

rabidly *adv.* amorratuz.

rabies *n.* amorru.

raccoon *n.* (*zool.*) mapatxe.

race *v.i./v.t.* lasterka egin, lasterkatu, korrika egin.

race *n.* arineketa, korrika, lasterketa, lasterraldi. *n.* arraza, enda, abenda, etnia.

racecourse *n.* lasterleku.

race horse *n.* zaldiarin.

racer *n.* korrikalari, lasterkari, lasterketari, lasterlari.

racetrack *n.* lasterleku.

racial *adj.* arrazazko, arrazaren.

racially *adv.* arrazaz.

racism *n.* arrazakeria.

rack *n.* ganbela, aska. *n.* oinaze-zaldi.

racket *n.* burrundara, tarrapada, astrapalada, abarrots. *n.* legez kanpoko ekintza. *n.* raketa, xare.

racketeer *n.* estafatzaile, xantaiari.

racoon *Cf.* raccoon.

radar *n.* radar.

radial *adj.* erradioko.

radiance *n.* zohardura.

radiant *adj.* errainutsu.

radiate *v.i./v.t* irradiatu, errainutu.

radiation *n.* errainuketa, izpiketa.

radiator *n.* (*mech.*) erradiadore. *n.* beroeragile, berogailu.

radical *n./adj.* erradikal, ertzeko, sustraiko. *n.* (*bot.*) sustraixka.

radicalism *n.* erradikalismo.

radically *adv.* erradikalki.

radicle *n.* (*bot.*) buztan.

radio *n.* irratigailu, irrati, irratentzukin; irrat-.

radioactive *adj.* erradiaktibo.

radio broadcast *n.* irratialdi, irratsaio.

radio program *n.* Irratsaio.

radio station *n.* irratetxe, irratartegi.

radiotelegraphic *adj.* irratitelegrafiko.

radiotelegraphy *n.* irratitelegrafia.

radio transmitter *n.* irratemandegi.

radish *n.* (*bot.*) janarbi.

radium *n.* (*chem.*) erradio.

radius *n.* erradio.

raffle *v.t./v.i.* (*v.t.*, *askotan* **off**-*ekin*) errifatu, zotz egin, zozkatu.

raffle *n.* errifa, zotzegiketa, zozketa.

raffler *n.* zozketari, zotzegile.

raft *n.* almadi.

rag *n.* zatar, zirtzil, trapu, eskuzapi, eskuoihal, piltzar.

rage *v.i.* amorratu.

rage *n.* haserre, amorrubizi, ernegu, odolberoaldi.

ragged *adj.* zatardun, zatartsu, piltzartsu.

raggedly adv. traskilki.
raggedness n. trauskilkeria, zakarkeria.
raggedy adj. zatardun, zatartsu.
raging adj. amorratu(a).
raid v.t./v.i. gaineraso.
raid n. gainerasoketa.
raider n. gainerasotzaile.
rail n. errail, karrile. n. eskudel, baranda.
railing n. baranda, kalostra, eskudel.
railroad n. trenbide, trenbideko, bultzibide, burdinbide.
railway n. trenbide. adj. trenbideko.
raiment n. jantzi.
rain v.i. euria egin.
rain n. euri. adj. eurizko, euridun.
rainbow n. ostadar.
raincoat n. kurtako, gabardina.
raindrop n. euritanta.
rainstorm n. euribolada, euriketa, jasa.
rainy adj. euritsu, lorrin. **Rainy season.** Eurite.
raisable adj. hezigarri. adj. jasokor.
raise v.t. jaso, jasoarazi, goratu, altxatu, igo arazi. v.t. gehitu. v.t. hezi, hazarazi.
raise n. (econ.) soldata-gehikuntza.
raisin n. mahaspasa.
rake v.t./v.i. azalurratu, eskobaratu, areatu. v.t. (in) eskuaretu.
rake n. are, eskuare.
rally n. herrikoi biltzar, herri-biltzar.
ram v.t. talkatu.
ram n. (zool.) ahari, marro.
ramble v.i./v.t. noragabetu, hara-hona ibili.
ramification n. adarkadura.
ramp n. aldape.
rampant adj. erasokor, oldarkor.
rampart n. babeski.
ranch n. arrantxu.
rancher n. arrantxero, bordari.
rancid adj. mindu.
rancidness n. gardingadura, zaharmindura.
rancor n. gorroto, herra, hegigo, tirria, aiher.
rancorous adj. gorrotodun, herradun, herratsu.
random adj. adur, zorizko, ustekabeko.
range n. sutegi, sutalde, sutondo. n. larre, belardi. n. mendikate, mendilerro. n. sail, maila. n. tiro-zelai. n. tiramen.
ranger n. mendizain, basazain.
rank n. ozka, lerrun. n. ilada.
ransack v.t. harrapakatu, zakuratu.
ransom n. askasari, librasari.
rant v.i. gogorki hitz egin.
rap v.i. (at edo on-ekin) jo.
rapacious adj. harrapari.
rape v.t./v.i. bortxatu, neskabehartu.
rape n. bortxaketa, bortxapen.
rapid adj. azkarti, azkar.
rapidity n. agudotasun, lastertasun, azkartasun.

rapidly adv. azkarki, lasterki, arinki.
rapist n. bortxatzaile, neskabehartzaile.
rapture n. lilura, liluradura.
rapturous adj. sorgor.
rare adj. arraro, urri.
rarely adv. bakanki, gutitan, bakanka.
rareness n. bitxikeria.
rarity n. bakantasun, urritasun.
rascal n. oker, barrabas.
rascally adj. barrabas, bihurri, petral, pikaro, deabru.
rash n. gorriune. adj. sengabeko, oharkabe, ausarti.
rashly adv. oharkabeki.
rashness n. oharkabekeria.
rasp v.t./v.i. karrakatu, limatu.
rasp n. lima, karrakagailu.
raspberry n. (bot.) masustagorri.
rat n. (zool.) arratoi. **Female rat.** Arratoieme.
rate n. neurri; -neurri.
rather adv. samar, xamar. adv. hobe.
ratification n. baieztapen, birbaiezpen.
ratify v.t. baieztu, baieztatu, baitetsi (bereziki legeak Estatu Batuetako Kongresuan).
rating n. ebaluaketa, ebaluazio.
ratio n. proporzio, arabera.
ration v.t. eskastu.
ration n. otamen, errazio.
rational adj. ezagueradun, zentzuko, zentzuzko, adimenezko, arrazoizko.
rationalize v.t./v.i. arrazoizko azalpen bat eman.
rationing n. errazionamendu.
rattle n. matraka, txintxarri, txilintxa.
rattlesnake n. (zool.) kriskitinsuge.
raucous adj. burrunbatsu, zaratatsu; zakar.
ravage v.t./v.i. suntsitu, deuseztatu, hondatu.
ravage n. suntsiketa, deuseztapen.
rave v.i./v.t. burutik egin.
ravel v.t./v.i. altzitu.
raven n. (zool.) bela, bele.
ravenous adj. harrapari. adj. gose, betezin.
ravine n. amildegi, leze, malkortegi.
ravish v.t. bortxatu, bahitu.
raw adj. gordin, egosgabe.
rawhide n. iledun larru(a).
rawly adv. gordinik.
raw material n. lehengai.
rawness n. gordintasun.
ray n. (zool.) arrai. n. brintza, marra, errainu, izpi.
raze v.t. suntsitu, soildu, herrautsi, deuseztu.
razor n. labaina, bizarmoztailu. **Electric razor.** Bizarmakina.
re- (gram.) berr-, ber-, bir-.
reabsorption n. berrirespen, birxurgapen.
reach v.t./v.i. heldu, iritsi, lortu.
react v.i. (askotan to-rekin) erreakzionatu.

reaction *n.* erreakzio.
reactionary *adj.* atzerakoi, erreakzionari.
reactivate *v.t./v.i.* berrabiatu, berreragin.
reactivation *n.* berreragiketa, susperraldi.
reactive *adj.* erreakziozko.
reactor *n.* erreaktore.
read *v.t./v.i.* irakurri, leitu.
readability *n.* irakurgarritasun.
readable *adj.* irakurgarri.
reader *n.* irakurle. *n.* irakurliburu.
readily *adv.* presaka, lasterka, berehala. *adv.* erraz, aise.
readiness *n.* prestaera, prestapen.
reading *n.* irakurketa, irakurraldi, irakurgai.
readjust *v.t./v.i.* hartarakotu, egokitu, berregokitu.
readjustment *n.* konpondura.
ready *v.t.* prestatu, antolatu.
ready *adj.* gertu. *adv.* gerturik, prest.
reaffirm *v.t./v.i.* birbaieztu.
real *adj.* benetako, egiazko, zinezko.
real estate *n.* onibar, etxeondasun.
realism *n.* errealtasun, errealismo.
realist *n.* errealista, egizale.
realistic *adj.* errealista.
reality *n.* errealitate. **In reality.** Izan ere.
realization *n.* egite, burutzapen.
realize *v.t.* konturatu, nabaritu, ohartu, sumatu. *v.t.* gauzatu.
really *adv.* benetan, biziki, zinez, egiaz.
realm *n.* erreinu, erresuma.
realty *n.* etxeondasun.
ream *n.* paperketa (500 orrialde).
reanimate *v.t.* bizkortu, berbizkortu.
reanimation *n.* bizkordura, bizkorraldi, susperraldi, pizte.
reap *v.t.* igitaitu.
reaper *n.* segalari; segamakina.
reappear *v.i.* berrazaldu, berragertu.
reappearance *n.* berragerpen, berragerketa.
rear *v.t.* hezi. *v.i.* jaso, altxatu.
rear *n.* atzealde, ipurtalde.
rearrange *v.t.* berreratu.
rearrangement *n.* berrantolaketa, berrizte.
rearranger *n.* berrantolatzaile.
rearview mirror *n.* atzeispilu.
reason *v.i./v.t.* (*v.t., askotan* **out**-*ekin*) arrazoiak eman, hausnartu.
reason *n.* arrazoi, agerbide. **For that reason.** Hargatik. *n.* ezagumen, zentzu.
reasonable *adj.* bidezko, zentzudun.
reasonableness *n.* zentzutasun.
reasonably *adv.* arrazoinbidez, zentzuz, zentzuzki.
reasoner *n.* arrazointzaile.
reasoning *n.* arrazoinbide, arrazoinketa, arrazoinamendu.
reassemble *v.t./v.i.* berrelkartu.
reassert *v.t.* birbaieztu.

reassertion *n.* birbaiezpen.
reassurance *n.* berbaieztapen, konfidantza.
reassure *v.t.* birbaieztu, birbaietsi.
reassuring *adj.* lasaigarri.
rebate *n.* diruitzulpen. *n.* deskontu.
rebel *v.i.* altxatu, matxinatu, oldartu.
rebel *n.* altxaketari, altxatzaile.
rebellion *n.* altxaketa, altxaldi, matxinada, oldarraldi.
rebellious *adj.* matxinadazko, matxintzale.
rebelliousness *n.* bihurritasun, manugaiztasun.
rebirth *n.* berjaiotza, susperraldi.
rebloom *v.i.* birloratu.
rebound *v.i./v.t.* birjauzi. *v.i.* errebotatu, errebote egin.
rebuff *v.t.* agirika egin, agirakatu.
rebuff *n.* agirakatasun.
rebuild *v.t./v.i.* berreraiki, birjaso.
rebuke *v.t.* agirika egin.
rebuke *n.* agiraka.
rebuttal *n.* gezurtabide, jarkibide.
recalcitrant *adj.* burugogor, eskuragaitz.
recall *v.t.* oroitu, gogoratu, gogoan ukan, gomutatu, gogora ekarri, bururatu.
recall *n.* gogo.
recant *v.t./v.i.* ezeztatu, gezurtatu.
recap *v.t./v.i.* bildumatu, laburtu.
recapture *v.t.* berrartu, birjabetu.
recast *v.t.* birgaldatu, berrurtu.
recede *v.i.* urgutitu, ibitu; atzera egin, atzera jo, atzeraka egin.
receipt *n.* ordaingiri, diruagiri, errezibu.
receive *v.t./v.i.* hartu, jaso, kobratu. *v.t.* harrera egin, abegi egin.
received *adj.* hartu.
receiver *n.* hartzaile.
recent *adj.* berri, gertaberri, arestiko.
recently *adv.* arestian, oraintsu, berrikitan.
receptacle *n.* ontzi.
reception *n.* abegi, harrera. *n.* ezkontzondorengo jaia, eztei(ak).
receptionist *n.* harreragile.
receptive *adj.* harbera.
receptiveness *n.* harmen.
receptivity *n.* harmen.
recess *n.* jolastordu.
recession *n.* atzerakada, atzerapen.
recessive *adj.* atzerakor.
recipe *n.* errezeta.
recipient *n.* hartzaile. **Scholarship recipient.** Bekadun.
reciprocal *adj.* elkar, elkarganako, elkarrekiko, elkarren.
reciprocate *v.i.* elkarrerantzun.
reciprocity *n.* elkarganakotasun, elkarkidego, elkarkidetasun.
recital *n.* (*mus.*) kantaldi, orkestaldi.
recitation *n.* herriaren aurrean poema bat buruz errepikatzea.
recite *v.t.* herriaren aurrean poema bat buruz errepikatu.

reckless *adj.* arduragabe, axolagabe.
recklessly *adv.* arduragabeki, axolagabeki.
recklessness *n.* axolagabetasun, arduragabetasun.
reckon *v.t./v.i.* kalkulatu, zenbatu. *v.t./v.i.* pentsatu, gogartu.
reckoning *n.* zenbaketa, kalkulapen, kalkulu.
recline *v.i.* etzan, alboratu, atzeratu.
recliner *n.* bizkarraulki.
recluse *n.* bakartzale.
reclusive *adj.* bakarti, bakartiar.
reclusiveness *n.* gibelkoitasun.
recognition *n.* onarketa, onarpen.
recognizable *adj.* ezagugarri.
recognize *v.t.* ezagutu, antzeman.
recoil *v.i.* gibelalderatu.
recollect *v.t./v.i.* oroitu, gogoratu, gogoan ukan, gomutatu, gogora ekarri, bururatu.
recollection *n.* gogorazio.
recommend *v.t.* gomendatu, artamendatu.
recommendable *adj.* gomendagarri.
recommendation *n.* artamendu, gomendio. **Letter of recommendation.** Gomendiozko gutun.
recommended *adj.* gomendatu(a).
recommender *n.* gomendari.
recompense *n.* sari, ordain.
reconcilable *adj.* gogaldegarri.
reconcile *v.t.* berrelkartu, birbaketu, adiskidetu, eskuak eman.
reconciler *n.* baketzaile.
reconciliation *n.* adiskidetza, adiskidedura, bakearazpen, berrelkarketa.
reconnaissance *n.* (*mil.*) ikerpen-hegaldi.
reconnoiter *v.t./v.i.* (*mil.*) ikertu, aztertu, miatu.
reconquer *v.t.* berjabetu, bermenperatu.
reconquest *n.* birjabeketa.
reconsider *v.t./v.i.* birplanteatu.
reconsideration *n.* birplanteamendu.
reconstruct *v.t.* berreraiki.
reconstruction *n.* berreraiketa, berreraikuntza.
record *v.t.* idatziz ofizialki ipini, legez ezarri, inskribatu. *v.t./v.i.* grabatu.
record *n.* diska. *n.* txosten. *n.* marka.
recorder *n.* adierazkailu.
recording *n.* grabaketa, grabapen.
record player *n.* diskagailu.
recount *v.t.* kondatu. *v.t.* birzenbatu.
recount *n.* birzenbaketa.
recourse *n.* irtenbide, helbide, zorki.
recover *v.t.* berreskuratu, birjabetu, birlortu, berrartu. *v.i.* birsendatu, hobetu, zuzpertu.
recoverable *adj.* berreskuragarri.
recovered *adj.* susper.
recovery *n.* sendaketa, eriondo, gaisondo, susperraldi, minondo,

sendabitarte. *n.* berreskuratze, birlorpen.
recreate *v.t.* birsortu, berregin.
recreation *n.* joko, jolas, josta, jostaketa, jolastordu.
recreational *adj.* jolasgarri, jostagarri.
recruit *v.t./v.i.* erreklutatu, lerrokatu.
recruiter *n.* soldaduketari. *n.* langilebiltzaile.
recruiting *n.* lerrokaldi.
recruitment *n.* erreklutaketa.
rectal *adj.* ipurdiko.
rectangle *n.* (*geom.*) laukizuzen.
rectangular *adj.* anqeluzuzendun.
rectifiable *adj.* zuzengarri.
rectification *n.* zuzenketa, zuzenpen, zentzadura.
rectify *v.t.* zuzendu.
rectifying *adj.* zuzenkor.
rectitude *n.* zuzentza, onestasun, prestutasun, zintzotasun.
rector *n.* bikario, parroko, erretore.
rectory *n.* erretoretxe, apezetxe, abadetxe.
rectum *n.* (*anat.*) hondarreste, ipurteste.
recuperable *adj.* suspergarri; berreskuragarri.
recuperate *v.i./v.t.* birsendatu, onera egin.
recuperation *n.* birlorpen, berreskurapen. *n.* indarberrizte.
recur *v.i.* berriz gertatu.
recurrence *n.* gaizperrialdi; aldizkotasun.
recurrent *adj.* aldizko.
recycle *v.t.* berrerabili.
red *adj./n.* gorri. *n.* (*pl.*) komunistak.
redden *v.t./v.i.* gorritu, gorriztatu.
reddening *n.* gorritasun.
reddish *adj.* gorraire, gorriska, gorriantzeko.
redeem *v.t.* berrerosi, arrerosi.
redeemable *adj.* berrerosgarri, gaizkagarri.
redeemer *n.* berrerosle. *n.* (*cap.*) Jesukristo.
redemption *n.* berrerosketa, berrerospen.
red-headed *adj.* kaskagorri, ilegorri.
rediscover *v.t.* berraurkitu.
rediscovery *n.* berraurkikunde.
redness *n.* gorridura, gorritasun.
redo *v.t.* berregin, ostera egin.
redress *v.t.* zuzendu, konpondu.
Red Sea *n.* (*geog.*) Itsaso Gorria.
redskin *n.* Estatu Batuetako indio(a).
reduce *v.t./v..i* gutxitu, murriztu, txikitu, eskastu, urritu.
reducer *n.* gutitzaile.
reducible *adj.* laburgarri, txikigarri, gutigarri, murrizgarri, urrigarri.
reduction *n.* gutitasun, laburpen, murrizketa, tipiketa, urriketa, gutiketa.
redundance *n.* gaindidura.
redundancy *n.* gaindidura, hitzalfer.

redundant adj. gainezko, berrirozko.
redwing n. (zool.) birigarro.
redwood n. (bot.) sekuoia, pinugorri.
reed n. (bot.) kainabera.
re-educate v.t. berrezi.
re-education n. berreziera, berreziketa.
reef n. harkaizpuru, itsasaitz.
reek v.i. kirastu, ufaztu.
reel v.t. harildu, harilkatu, desmatazatu.
reel n. harilgailu, bobina, txaratila.
reelect v.t. berraukeratu, berrautatu.
reelection n. berraukeraketa, berrautaketa, berrautapen.
reeligible adj. berraukeragarri, berrautagarri.
reenter v.t./v.i. birsartu.
reestablish v.t. birjarri, berrezarri.
reestablishment n. birjarpen, berrezarpen.
reevaluate v.t. berrebaluatu, berbaloratu, birneurtu.
reevaluation n. birneurketa.
reexamine v.t. berraztertu.
refer v.t./v.i. norbait norbaitengana zuzendu, gidatu. v.i. **(to)** ukitu, ikutu, aipatu.
referee n. jokazain, marrazain.
reference n. aipamen, aipaldi, aipuera, erreferentzia.
referendum n. erreferendun.
refill v.t. berriro bete.
refine v.t. findu, garbiarazi, araztu.
refined adj. sotil.
refinement n. findura, garbiarazpen.
refinery n. iragaztegi, errefindegi.
reflect v.t. isladatu, islada egin. v.i. (batzutan upon-ekin) gogartu, gogoetatu, hausnartu.
reflected adj. zeharreko.
reflection n. islada, dirdira, isladapen. n. asmakizun, gogarketa, gogoeta, oharkuntza, pentsakizun.
reflective adj. isladatsu, isladatzaile, isladakor. adj. oharti.
reflectively adv. gogartuz.
reflector n. distirailu, dirdirailu.
reflex n. erreflexu.
reflexive adj. gogoetatsu, gogoetazko, pentsakor. adj. (gram.) norberekiko. **Reflexive verb.** Norberekiko aditza.
reforest v.t. oihaneztatu.
reforestation n. oihaneztaketa, oihaneztapen.
reform v.t. berriztatu, eraberritu, itxuraldatu. v.i. zintzotu, erreformatu.
reform n. berrikera, berriztadura, eraberri, eraberritzapen, eraldaketa.
reformable adj. zuzengarri, artezgarri, berrigarri, eraldagarri.
reformation n. eraberrizte, berriztasun.
reformatory n. erreformategi.
reformer n. berrikuntzari, berritzaile, zuzentzaile, eraberritzaile.
reformist n. eraberrizale, erreformista.

reform school n. erreformategi.
refractory adj. burugogor. adj. (phys.) pasagaitz.
refrain n. esaera, lelo, sautrela, zaharritz, errepika, errefrau.
refresh v.t./v.i. freskatu, bizkortu, berbiztu.
refreshing adj. freskatzaile, hozkarri, freskagarri.
refreshment n. freskadura, freskagarri.
refrigerant adj. freskakor.
refrigerate v.t. freskatu, izozkailuan ipini.
refrigeration n. freskaketa, hozketa.
refrigerator n. hozkailu, izozkailu, hoztegi.
refuge n. geriza, gordeleku, ihesleku, babes, babesetxe, babesleku, babespen, ihestoki, aterpe. **To take refuge.** Gerizatu. Babestu.
refugee n. ihesle, errefuxiatu.
refund v.t./v.i. diru itzuli, amortizatu.
refund n. diruitzulpen, amortizazio, amortizapen.
refundable adj. amortizagarri.
refusable adj. ukagarri.
refusal n. ezezpen, ezetza, ukamen, uko, ukapen, gaitzezpen.
refuse v.t./v.i. ukatu, ezetza eman, ezetsi, uko egin.
refuse n. zarama, zakar.
refutable adj. ezeztagarri, gezurtagarri.
refutation n. gezurtapen, jarkipen.
refute v.t. gezurtatu, gezurreztatu, ezeztatu.
regain v.t. birlortu.
regal adj. erregeren, printzetar.
regale v.t. ospatu, jostatu.
regally adv. erregeantzera, erregegisa, erregekiro.
regalness n. erregetasun.
regard v.t. begiratu. v.t. oneritzi.
regarding prep. -(r)i buruz.
regardless adv. hortaz kanpo, nahiz eta, arren.
regards n. goraintziak, eskumuinak.
regatta n. estropada, arraunketa.
regency n. erregeordego, erregeordetza.
regenerate v.t./v.i. birsortu, ernaberritu.
regeneration n. birsorketa, birsorkuntza.
regent n. erregeorde, erreginorde.
regicide n. erregehilketa.
regime n. gobernamendu.
regimen n. erregimen. n. (med.) janarau.
regiment n. (mil.) erregimendu.
region n. eskualde, herrialde, lurralde.
regional adj. herri, erregioko, herrialdeko, lurraldeko.
regionalism n. erregionalismo, herrialdezaletasun.
regionalist n./adj. erregiozale, herrialdezale.

regionalistic adj. herrialdezale.
register v.t./v.i. erregistratu, inskribatu, erroldatu. v.t./v.i. matrikulatu.
register n. erregistro.
registrar n. zerrendatzaile, izenartzaile.
registration n. izenartze, matrikula, inskripzio.
regression n. atzeraldi.
regressive adj. atzerakor.
regressiveness n. atzerakotasun.
regret v.t. damutu, damu izan, deitoratu.
regret n. damutasun, dolu, urrikimendu.
regretful adj. damudun, garbaidun.
regretfully adv. damuz.
regrettable adj. negargarri.
regular adj. neurriko, araberako, erregular. adj. etengabe, iraunkor.
regularity n. jarraikitasun, erregulartasun.
regularize v.t. erregularizatu.
regularly adv. erregularki; segidan.
regulate v.t. araupetu, erregulatu, kontrolatu, legepetu, neurriratu.
regulated adj. araupeko, arautu(a), graduagarri.
regulation n. arauketa, arau, lege, zuzenbide. adj. ohiko, usaiako.
regulative adj. arauzko.
regulator n. arautzaile, neurkari, neurriemaile; kontadore.
regurgitate v.t./v.i. goragaletu.
rehabilitate v.t. erreabilitatu, leheneratu.
rehabilitation n. leheneraketa, erreabilitazio.
rehearse v.t./v.i. entseiatu, aurresaiatu.
rehearsal n. saiakera, entseiu.
rehearse v.i./v.t. entsegutu, entseiatu.
rehearser n. entsegulari.
reheat v.t. birberotu.
reign v.i. agindu, nagusitu, errege izan.
reign n. erregego, erregetza, erreginaldi, printzealdi.
reimburse v.t. diru itzuli, birjaso.
reimbursement n. diruitzulpen, errenboltsu.
rein v.t. (batzutan in-ekin) balaztatu, galgatu.
rein n. txarrantxa, garranga.
reincarnate v.t. birgizondu.
reincarnation n. berraragipen.
reincorporation n. berrelkarketa.
reindeer n. (zool.) elurrorrein.
reinforce v.t. berrindartu, azpindartu, ostikoztu.
reinforcement n. gogorgarri, laguntza.
reinstate v.t. berrezarri, berrerakundetu.
reinstatement n. berrezarpen.
reiterate v.t. errepikatu, berrizkatu, berresan.

reiteration n. berrizkunde, berrizkuntza.
reiterative adj. berrizkakor, berrirozko, osterako.
reject v.t. alderazi, zapuztu, gaitzetsi, baztertu.
rejectable adj. iraizgarri.
rejection n. ezezpen, gaitzespen.
rejoice v.i./v.t. pozkaritu, poztu.
rejoin v.t. berbatu.
rejoinder n. kontraerantzun.
rejuvenate v.t. birgaztetu, gazteberritu, gaztetu.
rejuvenation n. gaztekuntza.
rekindle v.t. berriro biztu.
relapse n. berrerorketa, berrerorpen.
relate v.t. kontatu, esan. v.i. (to) erlazionatu, harreman izan.
related adj. elkartu(a). adj. ezkontzahaide, odolkide.
relation n. kidetza, senitarte, ahaide. n. zerikusi. n. (pl.) harremanak.
relationship n. harreman, bizikidetza, lotura, tratu; senitasun.
relative n. ahaide, odolkide, senide, odoleko. adj. dagokion; -rekiko. adj. (gram.) erlatibo, elkartzaile.
relatively adv. erlatiboki.
relativity n. (phys.) erlatibitate, erlatibotasun.
relax v.t./v.i. lasaitu, atsedendu, baretu, trankildu.
relaxation n. atseden, atsedenaldi, gozaldi, lasaidura, lasaipen.
relaxed adj. lasai, patxadazko.
relaxing adj. atsedengarri, lasaigarri, trankilgarri.
relay v.t. berreman, aurrera eraman.
relay station n. errepikagailu.
release v.t. libratu, askatu, largatu. v.t. utzi.
release n. norbait espetxetik aske uztea. n. arinketa. n. baimen.
relegate v.t. baztertu, zokoratu. v.t. eman.
relent v.i. bigundu, samurtu.
relentless adj. gogor, aldaezin, bihozgabeko.
relevance n. egokitasun; gaurkotasun.
relevant adj. egoki.
reliability n. zintzotasun leialtasun, prestutasun, fidagarritasun.
reliable adj. zintzo, leial, prestu, fidagarri.
reliance n. konfidantza.
relic n. erliki.
relief n. lasaitasun, lasotasun, kontsolabide, lagungarri, patxada. n. errelebu.
relieve v.t. bigundu, ematu, eztitu, gozatu, arindu.
relight v.t. birpiztu, berriro biztu.
religion n. erlijio. **Protestant religion.** Erlijio protestantea. **Catholic religion.** Erlijio katolikoa.
religiosity n. erlijiotasun.
religious adj. erlijiozko.

religious ceremony n. elizkizun.
religiously adv. erlijioski, erlijioz.
religiousness n. erlijiotasun, erlijiozaletasun.
religious order n. lekaidego, lekaimego, lekaidetza.
relinquish v.t. laga, utzi.
reliquary n. erlikikutxa, erlikitegi, erlikiontzi.
relish v.t. atsegina hartu, gozatu.
reload v.t. zamaberritu. v.t. bermunizioztatu.
reluctance n. gogogabetasun.
reluctant adj. gogogabe.
rely v.i. (gehienetan **on** edo **upon**-ekin) fidatu.
remain v.i. gelditu, egon, geratu, mantendu.
remainder n. (math.) hondar; -kin.
remains n. (pl.) hondakin, hondar, soberakin, gainerako. **Mortal remains.** Hilki.
remark v.i. ohartu, esan.
remark n. ateraldi. n. ohar.
remarkable adj. oharkarri, nabarmengarri, nabarigarri, nabarmen.
remedy v.t. erremediatu, zuzendu, konpondu. v.t. sendotu.
remedy n. erremedio, sendagai, sendaki, osagarri, sendagarri.
remember v.t./v.i. oroitu, gogoratu, gogoan ukan, gogora etorri, bururatu.
remembrance n. gogarazpen.
remind v.t. oroitarazi, gogarazi, burura ekarri.
reminder n. oroikarri, oroigailu, gomutapen, gomutagarri. **Written reminder.** Oroitagiri.
reminiscence n. oroitzapen, gogorapen.
reminiscent adj. oroitarazle.
remiss adj. ezaxol.
remit v.t./v.i. ordaindu. v.t. itzuli.
remittance n. igorketa, bidalpen.
remnant n. ebakin, oihalki. n. aztarna.
remodel v.t. birmoldatu; berritu, berriztatu, zaharberritu.
remodeler n. berritzaile, berriztatzaile.
remodeling n. berrikunde, berrikuntza, birmoldaketa, birmoldapen.
remorse n. barrendamu, damu, barrenkezka.
remorseful adj. damubera, damudun, damukor, garbaitsu.
remote adj. urruti, urrun, baztertu(a).
removal n. erauzketa, erauzpen, kenketa.
remove v.t. aldaratu, desezarri, kendu.
remover n. erauzle, kentzaile.
remunerate v.t. ordaindu, sariztatu.
remuneration n. ordain, ordainsari, ordainketa, honenbesteko.
remunerative adj. irabazpidezko, ordainkor, ordaintzaile.
Renaissance n. errenazimendu,

loraldi. adj. errenazentista.
renal adj. giltzurrinetako, giltzurrineko.
renal gland n. (anat.) giltzurrinzorro.
render v.t. egin, eman.
rendezvous n. batzar, bilera; batzartoki, biltoki.
rendition n. errendimendu.
renegade n./adj. ernegari, fedegalduko.
renew v.t./v.i. berritu, berriztatu.
renewable adj. berrigarri, eraldagarri.
renewal n. berrizte, eraldaketa, lehengoraketa.
renounce v.t. uko egin, ukatu. **To renounce one's faith.** Fedea ukatu.
renovate v.t. berritu, berriztatu, lehengoratu, zaharberritu.
renovation n. zaharberrizte, berretura, berriztaketa, eraberrizte, eraldapen, lehengoraketa.
renovator n. zaharberritzaile, eraberritzaile, berriztari.
renown n. ospe, entzute.
renowned adj. ospatsu, entzutetsu, famatsu, famatu(a).
rent v.t./v.i. errentatu, alokatu.
rent n. errenta, alokairu, maiztergo.
rentable adj. errentagarri.
rental n. errentapen.
rented adj. errentatsun.
renter n. maizter, alokari, errentadun, errentari.
renunciation n. ukapen; fedeukapen.
reorganization n. berrantolaketa, berregitura, berregiturapen.
reorganize v.t./v.i. berrantolatu, berregituratu, berreratu.
reorganizer n. berrantolatzaile, eraberritzaile.
repaint v.t. birmargotu, gainmargotu.
repair v.t. konpondu, berritu, berriztatu.
repair n. berrizte, birkonponketa, konponketa.
repairable adj. konpongarri, antolagarri.
repairman n. konpontzaile, berrantolatzaile.
reparable adj. antolagarri, konpongarri.
reparation n. kalteordain, irainordain. n. ordainsari, ordaintza.
repast n. janari, jaki.
repatriate v.t. herriratu, sorterriratu.
repatriated adj. herriratu(a).
repay v.t. diru itzuli; ordaindu.
repayment n. diruitzulpen, errenboltsu.
repeal v.t. legea kendu.
repeal n. legekenketa.
repealable adj. legekengarri, legekenkor, errepikagarri.
repeat v.t./v.i. berresan, errepikatu, berritu. v.t. berregin.
repeated adj. sarritako.
repeatedly adv. behin eta berriz, maizetan, behin eta berriro.
repeater n. errepikari, errepikatzaile.
repel v.t./v.i. iraitzi, itzulerazi.

repent *v.i./v.t.* damutu, damu izan, dolutu.

repentance *n.* damu, damutasun, dolu, dolamen.

repentant *adj.* garbaidun, damubera.

repercussion *n.* ondorio, zerikusi.

repertoire *n.* sorta, bilduma.

repetition *n.* berrizte, berregite, errepikapen.

repetitious *adj.* berrirozko, berrizkor, berrizkakor, osterakor.

repetitive *adj.* berrizko, errepikakor, errepikatzaile.

replace *v.t.* ordeztatu, ordeztu, ordezkatu. *v.t.* berrezarri, birjarri.

replaceable *adj.* ordegarri, ordezkagarri, ordezkakor.

replacement *n.* birjarpen, ordeztapen, berrezarketa, ordezko. *n.* lekuko, ordeztatzaile.

replant *v.t.* birlandatu, oihaneztatu.

replenish *v.t.* berriro bete.

replete *adj.* bete-bete, ase.

replica *n.* bigarren.

reply *v.i./v.t.* erantzun, ihardetsi.

reply *n.* erantzun, ihardespen.

repopulate *v.t.* jendeztatu, berpopulatu.

report *v.t./v.i.* kontatu, kontu eman.

report *n.* kontaketa, txosten, narrazio, istorio, erreportaia.

reporter *n.* berribiltzaile, berriemaile, kazetari.

repose *v.i.* etzan, lasaitu.

repose *n.* lasaialdi, patxadaldi, pausa.

reprehensible *adj.* agirakagarri.

represent *v.t.* errepresentatu, ordezkatu, irudikatu.

representable *adj.* errepresentagarri.

representation *n.* irudikapen, itxurapen. *n.* ordezkaritza, errepresentaketa, errepresentazio.

representative *n.* (*pol.*) diputatu, ordezkari, errepresentatzaile. *adj.* eredugarri, errepresentakor.

representativeness *n.* ordezkaritasun.

repress *v.t.* zapaldu, hertsatu.

repression *n.* zapalkuntza, errepresio, zigorraldi.

repressive *adj.* errepresio, zapalkor.

repressor *n.* hertsatzaile, oinperatzaile, zapaltzaile.

reprieve *v.t.* gaizkile baten heriotz-zigorra deuseztatu.

reprieve *n.* indultu.

reprimand *v.t.* agirika egin, gogor egin, gogor hartu, gaizki egin, murrungatu.

reprimand *n.* gaizki, astinaldi, erretolika, murrunga.

reprint *v.t.* berrargitaratu.

reprint *n.* berrargitarapen, berrargitaraldi.

reprisal *n.* mendeku, bengantza.

reproach *v.t.* agirika egin, gaizki egin.

reproach *n.* gaizki, agirakatasun.

reproachable *adj.* agirakagarri.

reproachful *adj.* desohoreki.

reproduce *v.t.* birsortu, bikoiztu. *v.i.* umatu, ugaldu.

reproducible *adj.* ugalgarri.

reproduction *n.* umeketa, ugalketa. *n.* birsorketa, berregintza.

reproductiveness *n.* ugalmen, ugaltasun.

reproductivity *n.* ugalmen.

reproof *n.* iroi.

reproval *n.* gaitzespen.

reprove *v.t./v.i.* gaitzetsi, iroiztatu.

reproving *adj.* ezezle.

reprovingly *adv.* ezetsiz.

reptile *n.* (*zool.*) herrestari, narraztari, narrazti.

republic *n.* errepublika.

republican *adj.* errepublikar.

repudiate *v.t.* ezonartu, iraitzi, furrustatu, zapuztu.

repugnance *n.* higuin, higuindura, nazka, okaztadura, herabetasun.

repugnant *adj.* higuingarri, higuinkor, nazkakor, okaztagarri, nazkagarri.

repugnantly *adv.* higuingarriki, nakaizkor, nazkagarriro, nardagarriro.

repulse *v.t.* iraitzi, itzulerazi. *v.t.* nazkatu.

repulsion *n.* gaitzespen, nakaiztasun, okaztadura, zapuzketa.

repulsive *adj.* higuinkor, nardagarri, nazkagarri, nazkakor, okaztagarri, higuingarri.

repulsiveness *n.* nardagarritasun, nardatasun.

repurchase *n.* berrerospen.

reputable *adj.* aipuoneko.

reputation *n.* aipu, fama, entzute, omen, ospe.

repute *n.* fama, aipu, entzute.

reputed *adj.* usteko, famadun.

request *v.t.* eskatu, otoikatu, galdezkatu.

request *n.* arren, erregu, eskabide, eskari, eske.

requiem mass *n.* hilmeza.

requirable *adj.* eskagarri.

require *v.t.* behartu, hertsatu, derrigortu.

required *adj.* eskakizunezko, galdezko.

requirement *n.* baldintza, betebehar, eskakizun.

requisite *adj.* galdezko, eskakizunezko, beharrezko.

requisition *n.* dei, aurkezkizun.

requisitory *adj.* eskakizunezko.

rescind *v.t.* ezeztatu, indargabetu, ezereztu, kendu (lege).

rescindable *adj.* kengarri.

rescue *v.t.* salbatu, berreskuratu.

rescue *n.* berreskuraketa, berreskurapen, berrerosketa, berrerospen, erospen, salbamen, salbamendu.

rescuer *n.* berrerosle, berreskuratzaile.

research *v.i./v.t.* ikertu, azterkatu.

research *n.* azterketa, ikerketa, ikerlan, azterlan, ikerpen, txerkaketa.

researcher *n.* inkestalari, azterlari, ikerketari, ikertzaile.

resemblance *n.* itxura, itxurapen, antz.

resemble *v.t.* antzekotu, antza izan, bezalakatu, iduri izan.

resent *v.t.* erremindu, minberatu, aihertu.

resentful *adj.* aiherti, aiherkor.

resentment *n.* barnemin, gaitzi, erremindura, erresumin.

reservation *n.* arreta, ardura. *n.* indioen erreserba. *n. (pl.)* erreserbak.

reserve *n.* isiltasun, uzkurtasun.

reserved *adj.* isil, hitzgutxiko.

reservoir *n.* urbiltoki, uhaska, presa.

reside *v.i.* bizi, biztandu, egon.

residence *n.* bizileku, bizitetxe, bizitoki, egoitza.

resident *n.* biztanle, lagun, egoiliar, bizilagun.

residential *adj.* egonlekuko.

residual *adj.* hondakintsu, hondarrezko, gainerako, hondakinezko.

residue *n.* hondakin, hondar, zakar, soberakin.

resign *v.i./v.t. (v.i., askotan* **from-***ekin)* laga, utzi (lanpostuak), dimititu.

resignation *n.* etsi, etsipen, egonarri. *n.* lan uzte, dimisio.

resigned *adj.* etsita.

resignedly *adv.* etsipenez.

resilient *adj.* iraunkor.

resin *n.* erretxin.

resinous *adj.* erretxinantzeko, erretxintsu.

resist *v.t./v.i.* kontra egin, kontrezarri, gogor egin, gogor egon, iharduki.

resistance *n.* kontrezarketa, kontrajoera, herabe, erresistentzia.

resistant *adj.* erasoezin, sostor, gotor.

resistible *adj.* jarkigarri.

resole *v.t.* zolaberritu, zolatu.

resolute *adj.* erabakidun, dzartadako, bipil.

resolutely *adv.* zirt edo zart, zirti-zarta.

resolution *n.* erabaki, ausardia, erabakikuntza.

resolve *v.t./v.i.* askabidetu; erabaki.

resolve *n.* ebazpen, erabaki.

resolved *adj.* zartadako.

resonance *n.* durundi, durunda, zolitasun, ozendura.

resonant *adj.* durundatsu, durunditsu, durundari, hotsandiko, zoli.

resort *n.* zorki. *n.* turismo gune(a).

resound *v.i./v.t.* durundatu, durundi egin, ozendu.

resounding *adj.* burrunbari, durundari, durundatsu, ozen.

resource *n.* baliabide, baliakizun, baliamendu. *n. (pl.)* ondasunak.

resourceful *adj.* burutsu, asmotsu.

resourcefulness *n.* zorroztasun, buru,

jeinu.

respect *v.t.* errespetatu, begiramen izan, lotsa izan.

respect *n.* begiramen, begirune, itzal, errespetu.

respectability *n.* agurgarritasun, errespetagarritasun.

respectable *adj.* agurgarri, itzalgarri, itzaldun, errespetagarri.

respectableness *n.* itzalgarritasun.

respected *adj.* itzalandiko, preziagarri, estimagarri, oneskarri.

respectedly *adv.* gurgarriro.

respectful *adj.* begirakor, begiramentsu, begirunedun, errespetutsu.

respectfully *adv.* agurgarriro, begirunez, errespetuz, itzalandiz, itzalgarriro.

respective *adj.* bakoitzaren.

respectively *adv.* bakoitzari buruz.

respiration *n.* hatsaldi, arnasaketa, arnasa.

respirator *n.* arnasgailu.

respiratory *adj.* arnasezko.

respiratory problem *n. (med.)* hatsneke.

respiratory tract *n. (anat.)* arnaspide.

respite *n.* atseden, sosegu, geraldi, etenaldi.

resplendence *n.* dirdiradura, distiradura, dotoretasun.

resplendent *adj.* dirdiratsu, izpitsu, distiratsu.

resplendently *adv.* dotoreki.

respond *v.i./v.t. (batzutan* **to-***ekin)* erantzun.

respondent *n.* erantzule.

responder *n.* ihardesle.

response *n.* erantzun, ihardetsaldi.

responsibility *n.* eginbide, erantzunkizun, kontu, ardura, kargu, nagusigo.

responsible *adj.* arduratsu, kargudun, arduradun, ardurati, kontzientziatsu, erantzule.

responsibly *adv.* ganoraz.

responsive *adj.* erantzunkor, erantzunzale.

responsory *n. (eccl.)* hilotoitz.

rest *v.i./v.t.* atsedenartu, atsedendu. *v.i.* pausatu.

rest *n.* atseden, lasaitasun, geldialdi, egotaldi, etzaldi. *n.* gainerako, gainontzeko, abar. *n.* pausa, pausaldi.

restaurant *n.* jatetxe, janedangei.

restful *adj.* atsedengarri.

resting *adj.* atsedengarri, pausagarri.

Rest in Peace Goian Bego.

restitution *n.* berritzulketa, bihurrera, itzulketa.

restless *adj.* artega, barruestu, egonezin, pausagabe.

restlessness *n.* artegatasun, larridura, egonezintasun, kexadura.

restorable *adj.* itzulgarri, berrizkagarri.

restoration *n.* berrezarketa, berrezarpen, berriztaketa, lehengoraketa, berrikuntza, birkonponketa.
restore *v.t.* birjarri, birjaso. *v.t.* berriztu, berritu, leheneratu. *v.t.* bihurtu.
restrain *v.t.* murriztu, mugatu, hertzatu.
restraint *n.* euspen.
restrict *v.t.* mugatu, zedatu, murriztu, hertsi.
restriction *n.* murrizketa.
restrictive *adj.* laburkor, murritzaile, mugakor, hertsikor.
restroom *n.* komun, pixatoki, txizaleku, kakatoki.
restructure *v.t./v.i.* berreratu, berregitaratu.
result *n.* ondorio, ondore, ondoren, aterapen, emaitza, fruitu. **As a result.** Ondorioz.
resultant *adj.* ondoriozko.
resume *v.t./v.i.* jarraitu, segitu, (-ri) ekin.
resume *n.* eskema, laburpen.
resumption *n.* jarraipen.
resurge *v.i.* sorberritu, berragertu.
resurgence *n.* berragertze.
resurrect *v.t./v.i.* berbiztu, berbizi, biztu.
resurrected *adj.* biztuberri.
resurrection *n.* berbizkunde, susperraldi, berbizketa, berbizte.
resuscitate *v.t.* berbiztu.
retail *v.t./v.i.* apurka saldu.
retail *n.* xehesalketa, xeherosketa. *adv.* xehean, xeheka.
retailer *n.* xehekari, xehesaltzaile, gutikasaltzaile.
retain *v.t.* gorde, atxiki.
retaliate *v.i.* mendekatu, ordainzkatu.
retaliation *n.* mendekatze, ordainkizun.
retard *v.t.* atzeratu.
retention *n.* eutsarazpen, atxekidura.
reticence *n.* uzkurkeria.
reticulate *adj.* saretsu.
reticulum *n.* *(anat.)* saretto.
retina *n.* *(anat.)* begisare, erretina.
retinitis *n.* *(med.)* begisaremin.
retinue *n.* segitalde.
retire *v.i./v.t.* jubilatu, erretiroa hartu. *v.i./v.t.* erretiratu.
retired *adj.* jubilatu(a), erretiratu(a).
retirement *n.* bazterketa, erretiro, jubilazio.
retiring *adj.* uzkur, uzle, bakartzale.
retort *n.* kontraerantzun.
retouch *v.t.* txukundu, berregin, berrukitu.
retrace *v.t.* berrirudikatu. *v.t.* norberaren bizitzako urratsetara itzuli.
retract *v.t./v.i.* desesan. *v.t./v.i.* atzera egin.
retreat *v.i.* atzera egin, atzeraka egin, gibeleratu.

retreat *n.* atzeraketa. *n.* gordeleku, bakantasun, bakartegi.
retribution *n.* ordain, ordainketa, pagu, pagamendu.
retrievable *adj.* berreskuragarri, zuzpergarri.
retrieve *v.t.* berreskuratu.
retroactive *adj.* atzeraeragineko.
retrogression *n.* atzerakuntza, atzerapen.
return *v.i./v.t.* bihurtu, itzuli, atzera ekarri, atzera jo, bihurrarazi.
return *n.* jira, itzulketa, bihurketa, itzulaldi, itzuli.
returnable *adj.* bihurgarri, itzulgarri.
reunion *n.* batzar, bilera, topaketa.
reunite *v.t./v.i.* berrelkartu, berbildu.
revaluation *n.* *(econ.)* birbalioztapen, balioberrizte.
revalue *v.t.* birbaliotu, birbalioztatu.
reveal *v.t.* erakutsi, ezagutarazi.
reveille *n.* diana.
revelation *n.* ageri, agerpen, agerkunde.
reveler *n.* parrandari.
revelry *n.* parranda.
revenge *n.* mendeku, aiher.
revengeful *adj.* mendekuzko, aiherkor, aiherti.
revengefully *adv.* aiherki.
revenue *n.* irabazpen, etekin, dirusarketa.
reverberate *v.i./v.t.* isladatu, islada egin.
reverberation *n.* islada.
revere *v.t.* gurtu, gurkatu, begiramen izan.
reverence *n.* begiramendu, gurkera, gurketa.
reverend *n.* pastore. *adj.* estimagarri, itzalgarri, agurgarri.
reverent *adj.* gurgarri.
reverential *adj.* gurgarri.
reverently *adv.* gurgarriro, begiramenez.
reverie *n.* amets.
reverse *v.t./v.i.* alderantzitu, berritzuli.
reverse *n.* azpikalde, alderantzi.
reversibility *n.* bihurgarritasun, itzulgarritasun.
reversible *adj.* itzulgarri, alderanzkarri.
revert *v.i.* berritzuli.
review *v.t.* berraztertu, berrikustatu. *v.t.* berrikasi. *v.i.* kritika egin, kritikatu.
review *n.* berrikuspen, berrikasketa, berrikusketa.
reviewer *n.* kritiko.
revile *v.t./v.i.* iraindu, laidotu.
revise *v.t.* aldatu, berridatzi.
revision *n.* berrazterketa, berrikuspen.
revitalize *v.t.* bizkortu, zuzpertu.
revival *n.* berbizkunde, berbizte, bizkorraldi, birlorpen.
revive *v.t./v.i.* berbizi, bizitu, bizkortu, zuspertu.
revived *adj.* zusper.

revocable adj. legekenkor, kengarri.
revocation n. deslegekuntza, ezeztapen.
revoke v.t. atzera egin, desagindu, desegin.
revolt v.i. iraultzatu, matxinatu, altxatu, bihurritu. v.t. nazkatu, higuindu.
revolt n. matxinada, bihurritza, asaldakuntza.
revolting adj. higuingarri, nazkagarri, arbuiagarri.
revolution n. iraultza, altxaketa, biraketa, bihurrialdi, matxinada.
revolutionary n. iraultzaile, altxaketari. adj. matxintzale, iraultzaile.
revolutionist n. iraultzaile, altxaketari.
revolutionize v.t. sakonki aldatu, sakonki eraberritu. v.t. iraultza egin.
revolve v.i./v.t. biratu, itzulikatu, itzulingurukatu.
revolver n. errebolber.
revulsion n. nazka, nazkadura, higuin, higuinaldi, narda.
reward v.t. saritu, saria eman.
reward n. sari, ordainsari. **Reward for finding something.** Bilasari.
rewardable adj. sariztagarri.
rewarded adj. saridun.
rewarding adj. ordainkor, saritzaile, sariztatzaile.
rhetoric n. hizlaritza, erretorika.
rhetorical adj. erretoriko.
rheumatic adj. erreumadun.
rheumatism n. (med.) erreuma, erreumatismo.
rhinoceros n. (zool.) errinozero.
Rhode Island n. (geog.) Estatu Batuetako estatu bat.
rhyme v.i./v.t. (v.i., askotan with-ekin) errimatu.
rhyme n. errima, oin. **rhymed** adj. amaiberdin. **rhymer** n. errimatzaile.
rhythm n. erritmo, neurri; konpas(a).
rhythmic adj. konpasezko.
rhythmically adv. neurkeraz.
rib n. (anat.) saiheski, saihetsezur, saihets.
ribbon n. ilelokarri. n. zinta, xingola.
ribcage n. saihetsezurreria.
rice n. (bot.) arroz.
rich adj. aberats, dirudun, ondasuntsu. adj. jori, joritsu, oparo, gizen.
richly adv. gizenki.
richness n. aberastasun. n. joritasun.
rickets n. (med.) hebaintasun.
rid v.t. libratu, kendu.
riddle n. asmagai, asmaketa, igarkizun. n. zetabe.
riddled adj. josirik.
ride v.t./v.i. zaldikatu, zamarikatu. v.t./v.i. ibilgailuz joan.
rider n. zaldidun, zamaldun, zaldizko.
ridge n. hegi, mailagune.
ridged adj. hegidun.
ridicule v.t. iseka egin, isekatu, irri egin, lotsagarritu, murrikatu.
ridicule n. irri, murrikaldi, isekaldi.

ridiculer n. irrilari, isekagile, barrelari, murrikari.
ridiculous adj. barregarri, irrigarri.
ridiculously adv. irrigarriro, barregarriro.
ridiculousness n. farregarrikeria.
rife adj. ugaritsu, jori, oparo.
riffraff n. alproja, alprojatalde, gizatzar.
rifle n. fusil.
rifleman n. fusilari, karabinari.
rift n. arrailadura, arrakala, pitzadura.
rig n. hornitu, tresnatu, jantzi.
right v.t. zuzendu, irainordaindu.
right n. eskubide, zuzen, zuzenbide. **Human rights.** Gizaeskubideak. n. eskuin, eskuma. adj. zuzen, on, eskubidezko. adj. eskuineko, eskumako.
right angle n. (geom.) angeluzuzen.
right away adv. berehala, berehalaxe, lehenbailehen.
righteous adj. zintzo, zuzen.
righteousness n. zuzentasun, zintzotasun.
rightful adj. zuzenbideko.
right-handed adj. eskuin, eskumati.
rightist n./adj. eskuindar, eskuineko, eskumako.
rightly adv. zuzenbidez.
rightness n. zuzentasun.
rigid adj. gogor, larderiatsu.
rigidity n. gogortasun, hertsikeria, zurruntasun.
rigidly adv. estuki.
rigor n. larderia.
rigorous adj. garratz, mikatz, gogor.
rigorously adv. gogorki, zorrozki, bortizki.
rigorousness n. gordintasun, gogortasun, garraztasun.
rill n. errekatxo.
rim n. ezpain, aro.
rind n. laranjazala; urdai-azala.
ring v.t./v.i. ingurukatu. v.i./v.t. tilin egin, tilinkatu, arranak jo, kanpai(a) jo.
ring n. eraztun; katebegi; uztai. **Wedding ring.** Ezkoneraztun. n. joaldi, txirrin, tilin-tilin. n. beta. n. betazpi. n. boxealeku, ring.
ringing n. tilinketa, txilinketa, tirrin, tilin.
ringleader n. jauntxo, buru.
ringworm n. ezkabia.
rink n. patin-pista.
rinse v.t. xafarratu.
riot v.i. asaldarazi, bihurri egin, asaldatu.
riot n. iskanbila, istilu, bihurrialdi, asaldapen, zalaparta.
rioter n. iskanbilari.
riotous adj. iskanbilatsu.
rip v.t./v.i. tarratatu, hautsi, zarratatu, urratu.
rip n. tarratada, zirri-zarra, zarrasta, urradura.
R.I.P. G.B., Goian Bego.
ripe adj. zori, heldu, lirin, umo.

ripen *v.t./v.i.* zoritu, sasoindu, heldu, umatu.
ripeness *n.* zoritasun, heldutasun, umotasun.
ripening *n.* heldura, umodura. *adj.* umogarri, umokor.
ripper *n.* gantzateratzaile, tripajale.
ripple *v.i./v.t.* izurkatu, uhindu.
ripple *n.* uhinkada, uhindura.
ripply *adj.* uhintsu.
rise *v.i.* goratu, gorendu, igan, jaiki, altxatu. **To rise from the dead.** Berbiztu. *v.i.* biztu.
rise *n.* gorakada, gorakaldi, igoera. *n.* bizkargune, muino.
risen *adj.* biztuberri, jaikigarri.
rising tide *n.* gorakaldi.
risk *v.t.* arriskatu, menturatu.
risk *n.* galbide, galzori, arrisku.
riskily *adv.* erorgarriki.
riskiness *n.* arriskugarritasun.
risky *adj.* arriskutsu, arriskugarri, galbidetsu, galbidezko.
risque *adj.* laban, lizun.
rite *n.* errito. **Last rites.** Elizakoak.
ritual *n.* errito.
ritualist *n.* erritozale.
rival *v.t.* lehiakatu.
rival *n.* lehiakide, desfiatzaile. *adj.* lehiagarri.
rivalry *n.* lehiakidetasun, elkarlehia, elkarlehiaketa, desafio.
river *n.* ibai, uhaitz. *adj.* ibaiko.
riverbank *n.* ibaiondo, ibar.
riverbed *n.* ibaibide, ibaiondo, errekabide, uharka.
riverboat *n.* ibaiontzi.
riverlet *n.* errekatxo, latsa.
riverside *n.* ibaiertz, errekondo, errekalde.
rivulet *n.* latsa.
road *n.* bide, autobide, zidor; bida-.
roam *v.i./v.t.* noragabetu, bestetaratu.
roar *v.i.* orrokatu, orroe egin.
roar *n.* marru, orroe, marruma.
roast *v.t./v.i.* erre.
roasted *adj.* erreta.
rob *v.t./v.i.* lapurtu, lapurretan egin, ebatsi.
robber *n.* lapur, ebasle, bidelapur.
robbery *n.* lapurkeria, bidelapurkeria, lapurreta, ohoinkeria. **Armed robbery.** Atraku.
robe *n.* etxejantzi.
robin *n.* (*zool.*) txantxangorri, papargorri.
robust *adj.* sendo, indartsu, sotil, gotor, mardul, guri. **To be robust.** Marduldu.
robustness *n.* mardultasun, sendotasun.
rock *v.i./v.t.* kulunkatu, kulunkarazi, kordokatu, sehaskatu.
rock *n.* haitz, haitzeta, harri, harkaitz. **Pile of rocks.** Harrimeta. Harripilo.
rocker *n.* kulunkari, kulunkaulki, kulunkatzaile.

rocket *n.* suziri, txapligu, bolandera.
rocking chair *n.* kulunkaulki.
rock-'n'-roll *n.* (*mus.*) rock.
rock quarry *n.* harrobi.
rockrose *n.* (*bot.*) berroja, berrondo, txara.
rock salt *n.* gatzarri.
rocky *adj.* harritsu, malkortsu, harriantzeko.
rococo *n./adj.* errokoko.
rod *n.* haga, berga.
rode *pret. of* ride.
rodent *n./adj.* (*zool.*) karraskari, hortzikari.
rogue *n.* gizatxar, alproja.
roguery *n.* gizatxarkeria.
roguish *adj.* mokoti, pikaro.
roguishly *adv.* pikaroki.
role *n.* rol, antzerkiko papera.
roll *v.i./v.t.* gurpildu. *v.i.* (**over, about**) ihauskatu, ihalozkatu. *v.i./v.t.* (**up**) kurubilkatu.
roll *n.* tutu, hodi. *n.* opil. *n.* zerrenda, zentsu, errolda.
rollable *adj.* biribilgarri, iraulkor.
roller *n.* zanpagailu.
Roman *n./adj.* erromatar, erromar.
romance *n.* erromantze. *n.* amodio, maitaldi. *adj.* (*cap.*) latinetiko. **Romance languages.** Latinetiko hizkuntzak.
Romanesque *adj.* (*arch.*) erromaniko.
romantic *adj.* erromantiku. *adj.* samurbera.
romanticism *n.* erromantizismo.
Rome *n.*(*geog.*) Erroma.
roof *n.* teilatu, etxegain; sabai, sapai; estalki.
roofer *n.* teilaezarle, teilaberritzaile.
rook *n.* dorre.
room *n.* gela; areto.
roommate *n.* gelalagun, gelakide, bizikide.
roomy *adj.* zabal, lekudun, lekutsu.
root *v.t./v.i.* itsatsi, industu. *v.i.* sustraitu, errotu.
root *n.* erreboil, sustrai, erro.
rootless *adj.* errogabe, sustraigabe.
rootlet *n.* (*bot.*) buztan, errokimu, zain.
rooty *adj.* erreboiltsu.
rope *n.* lokarri, soka, kordel.
rosary *n.* (*eccl.*) arrosario.
rose *n.* (*bot.*) arrosa. *n.* haizarrosa. *adj.* zurigorri, larrosantzeko, larrosazko.
rose *n./adj.* gorri, ardogorriska.
rosebud *n.* (*bot.*) lorakuzku, muskil.
rosebush *n.* (*bot.*) larrosadi.
rosin *n.* kolofon-erretxin.
rosiness *n.* gorridura.
rosy *adj.* arrosaire, arrosantzeko, gorriska.
rot *v.i./v.t.* usteldu, kirastu.
rot *n.* ustelketa.
rotary *adj.* itzulkari.
rotatable *adj.* jiragarri.
rotate *v.t./v.i.* biratu, jirabiratu, itzulikatu, itzulingurukatu.

rotation *n.* biraketa, jirabira, egunbira, biraldi.

rote *n.* ohitura, ekandu. **By rote.** Buruz.

rotgut *n.* pattar.

rotor *n.* biragailu.

rotten *adj.* ustel, kiratsezko, kirastun.

rottenly *adv.* ustelki.

rottenness *n.* usteltasun, ustelgarritasun, kirastura, harjodura.

rotunda *n.* biribilgu.

rough *v.t.* laztu.

rough *adj.* gozagabe, gozagaitz, latz, lakartsu. *adj.* zakar, zakarrote, zarpatsu. *adj.* nahasi (itsaso); malkar, malkortsu.

roughly *adv.* abereki, gordinki, lazki, malkarki, zakarki, zarpailki, gordinkiro.

roughness *n.* bortiztasun, gozagaizkeria, laztasun, malkartasun, zakarkeria.

roulette *n.* erruleta.

round *v.t./v.t.* biribildu.

round *n.* ingurualdi. *n.* eskualdi. *adj.* biribil, potolo, totolo.

roundabout *adv.* zaldiko-maldiko.

roundness *n.* biribiltasun, biribildura.

round trip *n.* joan-etorri, joan-itzuli.

roundup *n.* abeltaldearen bilketa.

rouse *v.t./v.i.* esnatu. *v.t./v.i.* kitzikatu.

rousing *adj.* kitzikagarri.

route *n.* bide, ibilbide, ibilketa; -bide. **Sea route.** Itsasbide.

routine *n./adj.* ohizko.

rove *v.i./v.t.* noragabetu, bestetaratu.

rover *n.* arlote.

row *v.i./v.t.* arraunatu, arraunean egin.

row *n.* lerro, lerroka, ilara. **In a row.** ilaran.

rowboat *n.* batel, arraununtzi.

rowdily *adv.* zarpailki, zalapartaz, zarataz.

rowdy *adj.* zaratari, zaratatsu, zarpailtsu. **To become rowdy.** Zarpaildu.

rowlock *n.* (*naut.*) tolet.

royal *adj.* erregezko, erregetiar, erregeren, erregetar.

royally *adv.* erregeantzera, erregegisa, erregekiro.

royalty *n.* erregetza, erregetasun, erregintasun.

rub *v.t./v.i.* ferekatu, igortzi, igorzkatu, xafratu, igurtzi, marruskatu.

rubber *n.* goma, kautxu. *n.* igorzle, igurtzaile. *adj.* gomadun, gomazko.

rubbery *adj.* gomadun, gomatsu.

rubbish *n.* zabor, zaborreria, zakar.

rubble *n.* zabor, zaborreria, zakar.

rubdown *n.* igurtzi, igurtzialdi, igurtziketa.

rubicund *adj.* gorrail.

rubicundity *n.* gorrailtasun.

ruby *n.* (*min.*) errubi.

rucksack *n.* motxila.

ruckus *n.* zalaparta, zalapartada, zarramar.

rudder *n.* lema.

rudderhole *n.* lemazulo.

ruddiness *n.* gorridura.

ruddy *adj.* gorriska, gorraire.

rude *adj.* gozagaitz, tratagaitz, zakarrote.

rudely *adv.* gozagaizki, baldanki.

rudeness *n.* adeigabetasun, zakartasun, gozagaizkeria, baserritarkeria.

rudimentary *adj.* hasimasizko, oinarriko, oinarrizko, funtsezko.

rudiments *n.* (*pl.*) hasimasiak.

rue *v.t.* damutu, arrenguratu, aiene egin.

rueful *adj.* ilun, itzal, pozgabe, triste.

ruffian *n.* lotsagabe, alproja, gizatxar.

ruffle *n.* gonabarren.

rug *n.* oinzapi, oinoihaltxo.

rugged *adj.* malkar, malkartsu, muger.

ruggedly *adv.* malkarki.

ruggedness *n.* malkartasun, lakartasun, laztasun.

ruin *v.t./v.i.* suntsitu, birrindu, deuseztatu, sakailakatu, zatartu. *v.t./v.i.* behea jo, porrot egin, hondatu.

ruin *n.* galera, eroraldi, erorpen, hondaketa, hondamen, hondamendi, sakaila, galmen; sarraski, suntsiketa.

ruinous *adj.* galgarri, hondagarri, suntsigarri, hondatzaile, suntsikor, suntsitzaile.

ruinously *adv.* hondagarriro.

rule *v.t./v.i.* gobernatu, jaundu, legeperatu, legepetu, nagusitu, jabetu.

rule *n.* arau, erregela, lege, zuzenbide. *n.* nagusitasun, aitzindarigo. *n.* lerroeta, lerrotza. *n.* neurgailu.

ruler *n.* neurgailu, erregla. *n.* agintedun, agintzale.

rum *n.* ron.

rumble *n.* burrunba.

ruminant *n.* hausnarkari, hausnartzaile. *adj.* hausnarti.

ruminate *v.i./v.t.* hausnartu, hausnar egin, mamurtu. *v.i./v.t.* pentsatu.

rumination *n.* hausnar, hausnarketa.

rumor *n.* esamesa, zurrumurru, marmario.

rump *n.* ipurtmami, aberipurdi.

rumple *v.t./v.i.* tximurtu, zimurtu. *v.t./v.i.* tximatu.

rumpled *adj.* tximajario.

run *v.i./v.t.* korrika egin, lasterkatu. *v.i.* funtzionatu. *v.t.* higiarazi. *v.i.* bulegorako kandidatu izan. *v.i.* (**into**) topo egin, tupust egin, topatu, jo. *v.i./v.t.* (**aground**) enkailatu. *v.i.* (**away**) alde egin, ihes egin, hanka egin, ospa egin *v.i.* (**out of**) eskastu, urritu, murriztu, bakandu.

run *n.* lasterketa, lasterka, korrika.

runaway *n.* ihesle.

rung *n.* maila.

run-in *n.* liskar, errieta, eztabaida.
runner *n.* korrikalari, lasterkari.
runny nose *n.* ureri.
runny-nosed *adj.* mukitsu, mokoti.
runt *n.* pertsona txiki(a); abere txiki(a).
runway *n.* aireportuko pista.
rupture *v.t./v.i.* trenkatu, ebaki, hautsi.
rupture *n.* hausketa, hauspen, trenkadura, urraketa.
rural *adj.* baserriko, nekazal, nekazaritzako, larreko, landako.
Rural migration. Nekazal irteera.
ruralization *n.* baserritargintza.
ruse *n.* kalamatrika, trikimailu.
rush *v.i./v.t.* laster egin, lastertu, lasterkatu, presakatu, presatu. *v.t.* eraso.
rush *n.* presatsu, presa, arrapalada. **Rush hour.** Jendetza-orduak. *n.* *(bot.)* ihi.
rushed *adj.* presadun, lastertsu.
rust *v.i./v.t.* herdoildu, ugertu.
rust *n.* herdoil; gorrina.
rustic *adj.* basati, larreko, mendiko, basa, nekazale.
rustically *adv.* artzaineraz.
rusticity *n.* baserrikeria, baserritarkeria.
rustle *n.* karrakada, murmurio.
rustler *n.* aberelapur.
rustling *n.* farfar, karrakadura. *n.* abereostutze.
rustproof *adj.* herdoilgaitz.
rusty *adj.* herdoildun, herdoiltsu, ugertsu.
rut *n.* giri, susara. *n.* ildo; gurdiek bidean uzten dituzten arrastoak.
ruthless *adj.* bihozgogor, bihozgabe.
ruthlessly *adv.* ankerki, bihozgabeki.
ruthlessness *n.* bihozgogorkeria, bihozgogortasun.
rye *n.* *(bot.)* zikirio, zekale.

S

s *n.* Ingeles alfabetoko letra.
Sabbath *n.* atsedenegun, jaiegun; larunbata; igandea.
saber *n.* sable.
sabot *n.* trasko.
sabotage *v.t.* saboteiatu.
sabotage *n.* sabotaia.
saboteur *n.* sabotaiari.
saccharin *n.* *(chem.)* sakarina.
sacerdotal *adj.* apezaren; apez-.
sack *v.t.* zakuratu, lapurtu.
sack *n.* zorro, zaku. **Sack race.** Zaku lasterketa. **To put in a sack.** Zorroratu.
sackcloth *n.* txarpa.
sackful *n.* zakutada, zakukada, zorroalde.
sacrament *n.* *(eccl.)* sakramentu.
sacramental *adj.* sakramentuzko.
sacramentally *adv.* sakramentalki.
sacraments *n.* *(pl.)* eleizakoak, sakramentuak.
sacred *adj.* sakratu, santu.

sacredly *adv.* gurgarriro, sakratuki.
sacrifice *v.t./v.i.* sakrifikatu, opari egin, bizi opatu.
sacrifice *n.* opari, biziopari, oparigai, sakrifizio.
sacrificer *n.* biziopatzaile, sakrifikatzaile.
sacrificial *adj.* hilgai.
sacrilege *n.* sakrilegio.
sacristan *n.* elizain, sakristau.
sacristy *n.* sakristi.
sacrum *n.* *(anat.)* erreinezur.
sad *adj.* goibel, gogoilun, itzal, kopetilun, triste, pozgabe, tristagarri, itun.
sadden *v.t./v.i.* tristatu, atsekabetu, dolutu, ilundu.
saddening *adj.* tristagarri, ilungarri, goibelgarri.
saddle *v.t.* zelatu, bastatu, txalmatu.
saddle *n.* zaldiaulki, txalma, zela.
saddlebag *n.* sakuta.
saddler *n.* txalmagile.
sadism *n.* sadismo.
sadistic *adj.* sadiko.
sadly *adv.* triste, goibelki, tristekiro.
sadness *n.* tristezia, tristura, pozgabetasun, goibeltasun.
safari *n.* safari.
safe *adj.* arriskugabe. *n.* dirukutxa.
safe and sound *adj./adv.* kaltegabe(ko), onik, mingabe(ko).
safeguard *n.* babesgailu.
safely *adv.* segurki, arriskurik gabe.
safety *n.* segurtasun, segurantza.
saffron *n.* azafran.
sag *v.i./v.t.* sabeldu.
saga *n.* leienda, saga.
sagacious *adj.* gogoerne, begizorrotz.
sagacity *n.* azkartasun, ohartasun, gogobizi, gogoernetasun.
sage *adj.* zuhur, zentzudun. *n.* jakitun.
sagebrush *n.* *(bot.)* artemisia.
sagely *adv.* zuhurki.
said *pret./p. part. of say. adj.* jakineko.
sail *v.i./v.t.* itsasbidetu, itsasontziz joan.
sail *n.* bela, haizoihal, ontzioihal.
sailboat *n.* belaontzi, oihalontzi.
sailor *n.* itsasgizon, ontzigizon, marinel.
saint *n.* santu, done, guren.
sainted *adj.* saindu, guren.
saintly *adj.* jainkozale, otoizbera.
sake *n.* zio, errazoi. *n.* probetxu, onura.
salacious *adj.* lizun, lohi.
salad *n.* entsalada.
salad bowl *n.* entsaladontzi.
salamander *n.* *(zool.)* arrubio.
salami *n.* saltxitxoi.
salaried *adj.* soldatadun.
salary *n.* soldata, aloger.
sale *n.* merkesalketa, merkealdi, salmenta.
sales *n.* erosalketa.
saleslady *n.* saltzaile (emakume).

salesman *n.* saltzaile (gizon).
salesmanship *n.* salketarako abilezia.
sales slip *n.* salduagiri.
sales tax *n.* plazasari.
saleswoman *n.* saltzaile (emakume).
salient *adj.* garai, nabarmen.
saline *adj.* gazdun, gaztun.
salinity *n.* gazitasun, gazidura.
saliva *n.* listu, txistu, tu.
salivary *adj.* listuzko.
salivate *v.i.* listukatu, listu egin, listu bota.
salivation *n.* listujario.
salivator *n.* listukari.
sallow *adj.* horiska, horibeltz.
salmon *n. (zool.)* izokin.
salmonoid *adj.* izokinkide.
salon *n.* areto.
saloon *n.* paitartegi.
salt *v.t.* gazitu, gatz eman.
salt *n.* gatz; gaz-. *adj.* gazi.
saltbox *n.* gatzontzi.
salt flat *n.* gazlur, gatzune.
saltiness *n.* gaztasun, gazitasun.
saltless *adj.* geza, motel.
salt marsh *n.* fadura.
salt mine *n.* gatzaga.
saltpeter *n. (chem.)* sodio nitrato.
salt shaker *n.* gatzontzi, gatzandel.
salt water *n.* gezal, itsasur, urgazi.
salty *adj.* gazdun, gazi.
salutary *adj.* osasungarri, sendakor.
salutation *n.* agurtze, agurtzapen, agurritz(ak).
salute *v.t./v.i.* agur egin, agurtu.
salute *n.* agur.
salvage *v.t.* gorde.
salvage *n.* gordeketa.
salvageable *adj.* gordegarri.
salvation *n.* salbabide, gaizkapen, salbamen, salbazio. **The road to salvation.** Salbazioko bidea.
salve *n.* gantzu, gantzuki.
same *adj./pron.* berdin, erabateko, berbera, bat, bera.
sameness *n.* berdintasun, erakidetasun, idekotasun.
sample *n.* erakusgarri, agerkin, ale.
sampler *n.* probatzaile. *n.* erakusgai.
sampling *n.* probaketa, erakuskarketa; dastapen.
sanatorium *n.* sendategi.
sanctifiable *adj.* santugarri.
sanctification *n.* donekuntza, santutze.
sanctifier *n.* saindutzaile.
sanctify *v.t.* santu egin, donetu.
sanctimonious *adj.* santujale, saindujale.
sanctimony *n.* elizkoikeria.
sanction *v.t.* legetu, baimendu, baietsi.
sanctionable *adj.* zigorgarri.
sanctity *n.* santutasun, donetasun.
sanctuary *n.* saindutegi, santutegi.
sanctum *n.* leku saindu. *n.* gela kuttun(a).
sand *v.t.* hondarreztu, harekatu. *v.t.*

lixatu.
sand *n.* hondar, harea. *adj.* hondarrezko.
sandal *n.* sandalia.
sand bar *n.* barra.
sand dab *n. (zool.)* oilar.
sand dune *n.* hondarmeta, hondarmuino, hondartza.
sander *n. (mech.)* igurtzailu.
sand flea *n. (zool.)* itsasarkakuso.
sandpaper *n.* paperlatz, lixagailu.
sand scorpion *n. (zool.)* hondarpeko.
sandstone *n.* harehaitz, hareharri.
sandwich *n.* sandwich, otarteko.
sandy *adj.* hondardun, hondarrantzeko, hondarrezko, hareatsu, hondartsu.
sane *adj.* sano, zentzudun.
sang *pret. of* sing.
sanitarium *n.* eritegi, erizaindegi, gaisotegi, osatetxe.
sanitary *adj.* garbikor.
sanitation *n.* saneamendu, saneaketa.
sanitize *v.t.* osasungarritu, garbitu.
sanity *n.* sen, sanotasun (burutik), zentzu.
sank *pret. of* sink.
sans *prep.* gabe.
San Sebastian *n. (geog.)* Donostia. **A native of San Sebastian.** Donostiar.
Santa Claus *n.* Santa Klaus.
sap *n. (bot.)* izerdi.
sapling *n.* zuhaitz gazte.
sapphire *n.* zafiro.
sarcasm *n.* mingarritasun, mintasun.
sarcastic *adj.* ozpin, eztenkari.
sarcastically *adv.* irrizkari, irrimaltzurrez.
sarcophagus *n.* sarkofago.
sardine *n. (zool.)* sardina.
sardonic *adj.* irrizurizko, eztenkari.
sardonically *adv.* eztenka, irrizuriz.
sash *n.* gerriko.
sat *pret./p. part. of* sit.
Satan *n.* Satan.
satchel *b.* bidezorro.
satellite *n.* satelite.
satiate *v.t.* asebete, asetu.
satiated *adj.* ase, beterik.
satiety *n.* ase, asetasun, ok, betekada.
satin *n.* orban.
satire *n.* zirikada, eztenkada, satira.
satirical *adj.* zirikalari, ziztakari, erremingarri, irrizurizko.
satirically *adv.* erreminez, satiraz.
satirist *n.* isekatzaile.
satirize *v.t.* satirizatu, isekatu.
satisfaction *n.* atsegin, atseginketa, betetasun, eder. *n.* irainorde, ordain, ordainbide.
satisfactorily *adv.* gogobetez.
satisfactory *adj.* ordainbidezko. *adj.* gogaragarri, gogobeterri.
satisfied *adj.* konforme, laso, beterik.
satisfy *v.t./v.i.* gogobete, gogoa bete, gogobetetu; asebete.
satisfying *adj.* betegarri, gogobeteko.

saturate *v.t./v.i.* asetu, bete.
saturation *n.* betealdi, asetasun.
Saturday *n.* larunbat, larunbateko.
Saturn *n. (astron.)* Saturno.
satyr *n.* akergizon.
sauce *n.* saltsa, zuku.
saucepan *n.* kazo.
saucer *n.* platertxo.
saucy *adj.* saltsadun. *adj.* erantzukoi.
sauerkraut *n.* ozpinetan beratutako aza.
sauna *n.* sauna.
sausage *n.* saltxitxa.
saute *v.t.* olio gutxiz frijitu.
savable *adj.* salbagarri, gaizkagarri.
savage *adj.* basati, ohil, hezgabe.
savagely *adv.* basaki.
savageness *n.* ankerkeria, krudelkeria, basakeria.
savagery *n.* basatikeria, basatasun.
savant *n.* jakitun.
save *v.t.* gaizkatu, salbatu, gorde. *v.i.* aurreratu, aldaratu, aurreztu, gorde (dirua).
save *prep./conj.* ezik, izan ezik, salbu.
saver *n.* aurreratzaile, aurrezlari.
savings *n.* aurrezki, aurrezpen.
   Savings account. Aurrezkikontu.
savior *n.* salbatzaile, salbagile, salbatore.
savor *v.t.* gozatu.
savory *adj.* gozo, gozatsu, ahobeteko.
saw *v.t./v.i.* zerratu.
saw *n.* zerra. **Chain saw.** Zerramakina. *pret. of see.*
sawdust *n.* zerrauts.
sawfish *n. (zool.)* zerrarrain.
sawmill *n.* zerrategi, zerratoki.
sawyer *n.* zerrari, zerratzaile.
saxhorn *n. (mus.)* bonbardin.
saxophone *n. (mus.)* saxofoi.
say *v.t./v.i.* esan, mintzo izan.
saying *n.* esaera, esamolde, esan, atsotitz.
scab *v.i.* ezkabiatu, azaleztu.
scab *n. (med.)* zakar, zakardura. *n.* grebausle.
scabbard *v.t.* zorrotu, zorroratu.
scabbard *n.* ezpatazorro, zorro.
scabby *adj.* zaragardun.
scabies *n. (med.)* sarna, zaragar.
scaffold *n.* aldamio. *n.* urkabe, urkamendi.
scaffolding *n.* aldamiotza.
scald *v.t./v.i.* urgoritu.
scale *v.t./v.i.* eskamak kendu. *v.t.* igo, eskalatu.
scale *n.* balantza, pisu. *n.* eskama, ezkata. *n. (mus.)* eskala. *n.* maila.
scale model *n.* maketa.
scales *n. (pl.)* pisaleku, balantza.
scalp *v.t.* buruko larruazala errotik kendu.
scalp *n.* buruko larruazala.
scalpel *n.* ziztailu, bisturi.
scaly *adj.* ezkatadun, ezkatatsu.
scamp *n.* bihurri, alproja.

scan *v.t.* kontuz aztertu, kontuz begiratu. *v.t./v.i.* bertsoneurtu.
scandal *n.* galbide, gaizpide, eskandalu; gaiz-.
scandalize *v.t.* eskandalizatu, galbideratu, gaizpideratu.
scandalmonger *n.* erorarazle.
scandalous *adj.* galbidezko, galbidetsu.
scandalously *adv.* galgarriro, gaizpidez.
scansion *n.* bertsoneurketa.
scant *adj.* eskas.
scanty *adj.* eskas.
scapegoat *n.* besteen erruak leporatzen zaizkion pertsona.
scapular *n. (eccl.)* kutun.
scar *v.t./v.i.* orbaindu, azaleztu.
scar *n.* orbain, zaurimarka.
scarce *adj.* eskas, bakan, urri.
scarcely *adv.* eskaski, doi-doi, urriki.
scarcity *n.* eskasia, eskastasun, urrialdi, urritasun, gabetasun.
scare *v.t./v.i.* beldurtu, izutu, izuarazi, ikaratu.
scare *n.* izu, izualdi, ikaraldi.
scarecrow *n.* kuso, txorimalo.
scarf *n.* estalki, buruko, buruzapi.
scarlet *n./adj.* gorri-gorri, gorrimin.
scarred *adj.* orbaindun, orbaintsu.
scary *adj.* beldurrarazle, izugarri, ikaragarri.
scatter *v.t./v.i.* sakabanatu, zabaldu, barreiatu.
scatterable *adj.* hedagarri.
scatterbrained *adj.* memela, goiarin, txolin.
scattered *adj.* nahas-mahas.
scavenger *n.* haratustelez elikatzen den piztia.
scenario *n.* antzezlaneko gaiaren laburpena.
scene *n. (theat.)* agerraldi.
scenery *n.* ikusbide, ikuspegi, bista.
scenic *adj.* ikusgarri, ikuspegizko.
scenically *adv.* ikusgarriki, ikusgarriro.
scent *v.t./v.i.* aztarnatu, usainztatu. *v.t.* lurrineztatu, lurrinkatu.
scent *n.* lurrinusain.
scented *adj.* lurrintsu.
scepter *n.* zetro. **Royal scepter.** Erregemakila.
sceptic *C.f. skeptic.*
schedule *n.* ordutegi, programa.
scheduling *n.* programaketa, programakuntza.
schematic *adj.* eskemazko. *n.* eskema.
scheme *v.t./v.i.* elkar hartu, isiljokatu.
scheme *n.* isiljoko.
schism *n.* zisma.
schizophrenia *n.* eskizofrenia.
scholar *n.* jakintsu, ikasle.
scholarly *adj.* ikaskoi, ikaskor.
scholarship *n.* beka.
scholastic *adj.* eskolastiko.
scholastically *adv.* eskolastikoki.
scholasticism *n. (phil.)* eskolastizismo.

scholastics n. eskolastika.
school n. ikastegi, ikastetxe, eskola,
  ikastola. n. arraintalde gorri, manjuba,
  sarda.
schoolbook n. eskolaliburu.
schoolboy n. eskolamutil, ikasle.
schoolchild n. eskolume.
schoolgirl n. eskolaneska, ikasle.
schoolhouse n. ikastegi, ikastetxe.
schoolmate n. ikaskide, eskolakide,
  eskolalagun.
schoolroom n. ikasgela.
schooner n. goleta.
sciatica n. (med.) iztermin.
science n. zientzia.
scientific adj. zientziazko, zientziaren,
  zientifiko.
scientifically adv. zientifikoki.
scientist n. zientzilari, zientzigizon.
scintillate v.i./v.t. pindartu.
scintillation n. dirdira.
scissors n. guraizeak, artaziak.
scoff v.i. (at) irri egin, trufatu, isekatu.
scoffer n. irrigile.
scold v.t./v.i. gogor egin, gogor hartu,
  sarramuskatu, gaizkitu, agirika egin.
scolder n. aharrari.
scolding n. murrunga, erretolika. adj.
  larderiatzaile.
scoop v.t. txikatu.
scoop n. tangart.
scooter n. goitibehera.
scope n. esparru, zabalera.
scorch v.t. kiskaldu, eguzki jo,
  gainerre.
scorched adj. kiskal.
scorcher n. eguzkigalda.
scorching adj. kiskalgarri. Scorching
  sun. Eguzki kiskalgarri.
score v.t./v.i. puntuatu.
score n. puntuazio, erresultatu, tanto.
scoreboard n. markagailu.
scorekeeper n. tantokari.
scoria n. txirta, zepa.
scoring n. puntuaketa.
scorn v.t./v.i. erdeinatu, mesprezatu,
  arbuiatu.
scorn n. arbuio, mesprezu, erdeinu,
  gaitzestasun.
scornable adj. arbuiagarri,
  erdeinagarri, gaitzesgarri.
scorner n. arbuiatzaile, mesprezatzaile,
  erdeinari.
scornful adj. ufakari, erdeinatzaile,
  arbuiagarri.
scornfully adj. erdeinuz.
scorpion n. (zool.) luhartz, lupu.
Scot n. eskoziar.
Scotch adj. eskoziar. n. eskoziera.
Scotchman n. eskoziar.
Scotland n. (geog.) Eskozia.
Scotsman n. eskoziar.
Scottish adj. eskoziar. n. eskoziera.
scoundrel n. gizatxar, barrabas.
scoundrelly adj. azpisapo, mokoti.
scour v.t./v.i. murruskaz deskoipetu,
  murruskaz garbitu.

scourge v.t. hilduratu, zartatu.
scourge n. usta.
scout n. scout.
scouting n. scoutismo, eskultismo.
scow n. gabarra.
scowl v.i./v.t. kopetilundu.
scowl n. kopetabeltz, betondo.
scowling adj. kopetilun.
scraggly adj. mirrin.
scramble v.t. nahasi, nahastu. v.t.
  arraultzak nahasi.
scrap n. oihalki. n. estualdi, esturaldi.
scrapbook n. ebakin-album.
scrape v.t./v.i. murruskatu, hatz egin,
  hazka egin, karraka egin.
scrape n. estualdi, estularri, estura.
scraped adj. haragigorri.
scraper n. karrakagailu,
  marruskatzaile.
scratch v.t./v.i. hazka egin, hatz egin,
  hatzamarkatu, urratu, karrakatu.
scratch n. hatzamarkada, urrakada.
scratcher n. aztergailu, urratzaile,
  aztarkari.
scrawl v.i./v.t. zirriborratu.
scream v.i./v.t. txilio egin, oihu egin,
  garrasi egin, oihukatu, orrokatu.
scream n. oihu, garrasi, txilio.
screamer n. oihulari, intzirikari,
  orrolari.
screech n. irrintzi.
screen v.t. galbahetu.
screen n. pantaila. n. zetabe, galbahe.
screenplay n. gidoi.
screw v.t./v.i. (on) torlojotu. v.t./v.i.
  (in) kiribilatu. v.t./v.i. (up) oker egin,
  huts egin.
screw n. torloju.
screwdriver n. bihurkin.
scribble v.t./v.i. zirriborratu,
  zirrimarratu.
scribble n. zirriborro, zirriborraketa,
  zirrimarraketa.
scribbling n. zirrimarra, zirriborro.
scribe n. notarimutil.
scrimmage n. iskanbila, errieta.
script n. gidoi.
scriptural adj. idazti sainduko,
  Bibliako.
scripture n. idazti. Holy scripture.
  Idazti Saindu.
scroll n. pergamu larrutxa.
scrooge n. lukur, lukurari, pertsona
  zeken(a).
scrotum n. (anat.) barrabilzorro.
scrub v.t./v.i. murruskatu, xafratu,
  zatarreztu, igurtzi.
scruple n. barrenkezka.
scrupulous adj. kezkati, kezkatsu,
  hertsi.
scrupulously adv. zirrituki.
scrutable adj. aztergarri.
scrutinize v.t./v.i. ikusmiratu, arakatu.
scrutinizer n. ikusmiratzaile.
scrutiny n. arakapen, azterraldi,
  bilaketa, ikerketa.
scuffle n. guduxka.

scullery *n.* sukalondo, sukaldeatze.
scullion *n.* eltzezain, sukalmorroin, sukalmutil.
sculpt *v.t./v.i.* zizelatu, zizelkatu.
sculptor *n.* marmolari, eskultore, irudigile.
sculptural *adj.* eskulturazko.
sculpture *n.* eskultura.
scum *n.* zabar, zabor.
scurrilous *adj.* desohoretsu.
scurrilously *adv.* desohoreki.
scurry *v.i.* irristatu, alde egin.
scurvy *n. (med.)* eskorbuto.
scythe *v.t.* aihozkatu.
scythe *n.* sega, kodaina.
sea *n.* itsaso, itsastar; itsas-.
seaboard *n.* itsasertz, itsasalde.
seacoast *n.* itsasbazter, itsasertz, kostalde, itsasondo.
seafaring *adj.* itsasoko; itsas-.
seagull *n. (zool.)* antxeta, kaio, kalatxori.
seahorse *n. (zool.)* zaldiarrain, itsaszaldi.
seal *n. (zool.)* itsastxakur.
sea lion *n. (zool.)* itsasotso.
seam *n.* jostura. **Double seam.** Birjostura.
seaman *n.* itsasgizon, marinel.
seamanship *n.* itsasjakintza, marinelgintza, nautika.
seamless *adj.* josgabe.
seamstress *n.* jostun, joskile, joskin, josle (emakume).
seaplane *n.* uregazkin.
seaport *n.* itsasgeltoki, itsasportu.
seaquake *n.* itsasikara.
sear *v.t./v.i.* gardostu, sugarastatu.
search *v.t./v.i.* bilatu, ikuskatu, ikusmiratu, barneratu, arakatu.
search *n.* bila, bilaketa, araketa.
searcher *n.* bilatzaile, ikuskatzaile, bilaketari, arakatzaile.
searchlight *n.* faru, distirailu.
seashore *n.* itsasalde.
seasick *adj.* itsasgaitz.
seasickness *n.* itsasmin.
seaside *n.* itsasertz, itsasalde.
season *v.t.* ontarazi, gozagarritu, adobatu.
season *n.* aro, garai, sasoi, denboraldi, tenore.
seasonably *adv.* ongiroz.
seasonal *adj.* sasoiko, sasoinezko, urtaroko.
seasoning *n.* gozagarri, ongarri.
seat *v.t.* jarrerazi, eseri.
seat *n.* jarleku, eserleku, kadira.
sea water *n.* itsasur, gezal, kresal.
seaweed *n. (bot.)* itsasbelar.
sebaceous *adj.* bilkordun, bilkortsu.
seborrhea *n. (med.)* bilgorjario, bilgorreria.
secant *n. (geom.)* ebatzaile.
secede *v.i.* banandu.
secession *n.* berezketa, banapen, bereizte. **War of Secession.** Estatu

Batuetako guda zibila.
secessionist *n.* bereiztiar.
seclude *v.t.* bakarreratu, baztertu, zokoratu.
seclusion *n.* bakartaldi, barruraketa, bazterdura, bazterketa.
second *adj.* bigarren, bigarrengo. *n.* segundu, une, lipar.
secondary *adj.* bigarreneko. *adj.* gainerako, gainerantzeko, gaineratiko, ondoko, gainetiko, gainontzeko.
second cousin *n.* birlehengusin (emakume), birlehengusu (gizon).
secondhand *adj.* berreskuko.
second hand *n.* segundari.
secondly *adv.* bigarrenez.
second-rate *adj.* halaholako.
secrecy *n.* isilpetasun, isilpe, kukukeria, misterio.
secret *n.* isilpe, isilmandatu, ahopeko, hitzisil. *adj.* ezkutuko, barreneko, isil, itzaleko, isileko.
secretary *n.* idazkari, izkribau, sekretari.
secrete *v.t.* jariotu.
secretion *n.* jario, jariokin, jariopen.
secretive *adj.* ezkutuko, isilgordelari, isilkari, itzalpekari.
secretively *adv.* izkutuki.
secretiveness *n.* isilketa, isiltasun.
secretly *adv.* isilean, ezkutuan, ezkutuki, ahopean, sekretuki.
sect *n.* sekta.
sectarian *adj./n.* alderdikor.
section *n.* sail, lakatz, sekzio. *n.* zati.
sectionable *adj.* zatikagarri, partigarri.
sector *n.* sail, eremu.
secular *adj.* laiko, sekular.
secularity *n.* laikotasun.
secularization *n.* sekulargintza, sekularpen.
secularize *v.t.* sekulartu.
secularly *adv.* sekularki.
secure *v.t.* lortu, tinkotu, irmotu. *v.t./v.i.* aseguratu.
secure *adj.* arriskugabe.
securely *adv.* errozki.
security *n.* segurtasun, finkapen, segurantza, ziurtasun. *n. (econ.)* fiantza, fidantza.
sedan *n.* sedan (kotxe).
sedate *adj.* erabidetsu.
sedately *adv.* patxadaz, soseguz, geldiro, astiro.
sedateness *n.* erabide.
sedation *n.* bareketa.
sedative *n.* lasaigarri, gozagailu, aringarri.
sedentarily *adv.* eserita, mugigabeki, egonez.
sedentary *adj.* lekuko.
sediment *n.* hondar, hondakin.
sedimentation *n.* jalkiera.
sedition *n.* bihurritza.
seduce *v.t.* gaizkiratu. *v.t.* liluratu, xarmarazi, zorarazi.

seduction n. liluraketa, limurkeria, lilurakeria.

seductive adj. lilurakor, liluratzaile, limurkor, xarmakor, xarmatzaile, xorarazle.

seductively adv. liluraz, limurki.

seductiveness n. limurkortasun.

see v.t./v.i. ikusi.

seed v.t. erein.

seed n. bihi, hazi, ale, garau, hozi.

seedbed n. erneleku, mindegi, hazitegi, mintegi.

seeder n. ereile, ereintzale.

seedless adj. bihigabe.

seek v.t./v.i. bilatu, arakastatu.

seeker n. bilakari, kirikatzaile.

seem v.i. iruditu, irudi, iduri izan, irudikatu, iduri, itxura egin, eman. **She seems young.** Gazte ematen du.

seemingly adv. itxuraz, dirudienez.

seemly adj. zuzen, erazko, begirazko.

seen p. part. of see.

seep v.i. (in) geldiro sartu (isurkai), iragazi.

seer n. igarle.

seesaw n. bilintzi-balantza.

seethe v.i. egosi, irakin.

segment n. zati, pusketa.

segregate v.t. aldebateratu, banakatu, banandu.

segregation n. berezketa, berezipen.

segregator n. berezitzaile, alderatzaile.

seignory n. jaurerri.

seismic adj. sismiko.

seismometer n. dardarneurkin.

seizable adj. harrapagarri.

seize v.t./v.i. harrapatu, jabetu, atzeman, erauzi, eskuak ezarri, eskuratu, heldu.

seizer n. harrapatzaile, heltzaile, atzemaile.

seizure n. harrapaldi, harketa, hatzemate. n. enbargo, bahitura. n. (med.) eraso, erasoaldi.

seldom adv./adj. bakan, bakanka, gutitan, gutxitan.

select v.t. hautatu, hautu, aukeratu, berezitu, berezi.

select adj. aukerako, bana-banako, aukeratu(a).

selectable adj. hautagarri, aukeragarri.

selected adj. hautatu(a), hautetsi, aukeratu(a).

selection n. hautaketa, berezketa, aukera.

selective adj. hautespenezko, aukerabidezko, hautakor.

selectivity n. hautespide.

self n. norbera, nortasun. adj. norbereganako. pron. neure buru, neu(k), neron(ek); zure buru; bere buru.

self-centered adj. berekoi, beretar.

self-centeredness n. norberekeria.

self-confidence n. norbereganako fidakortasun.

self-confident adj. norberarekiko, fidakor, autofidakor.

self-conscious adj. beldurti, lotsati, lotsakor.

self-contained adj. burujabe.

self-control n. autokontrol, norberaren kontrol(a), norbere menperatasun(a).

self-defense n. autodefentsa, norberaren defentsa.

self-denial n. burukapen.

self-determination n. jabetasun, autoerabaki.

self-government n. autoaginte, autogobernu.

self-hypnosis n. burulilurapen.

self-important adj. handikor, handi-mandi, puzkor.

selfish adj. berekoi, beretar, berekor.

selfishly adv. berekoiki, neurekoiki, zeurekoiki.

selfishness n. berekoitasun, berekoikeria, buruzalekeria.

self-pity n. autoerruki, norberaren erruki.

self-preservation n. biziraupen-sen, bizirik irauteko sena.

self-reliance n. berebaitako konfidantza.

self-reliant adj. bere buruaz konfidantza duena.

self-respect n. autobegirune, norberaren begirune, bereburuaren itzala.

self-sacrifice n. buru ukamen.

self-sacrificing adj. burukatzaile.

self-service n. autozerbitzu.

self-sufficiency n. autonahikotasun.

self-supporting adj. autoeusle, norberaren eusle.

sell v.t./v.i. saldu.

sellable adj. salgarri.

seller n. saltzaile.

seltzer n. seltza.

selvage n. oihalertz.

selves n. (pl.) self.

semblance n. itxurantz.

semen n. (anat.) hazi, semen.

semester n. seihilabete, urterdi.

semestral adj. seihilabeteko, seihileko, urterdiko.

semi- (gram.) erdi.

semiannual adj. seihilabeteroko.

semicircle n. (geom.) zirkuluerdi.

semicircular adj. erdibiribil.

semicolon n. puntu eta jarrai.

semiconscious adj. erdiohartu.

semiconsciousness n. erdioharmen.

semidry adj. erdilehortu.

seminar n. mindegi, azterlan.

seminarian n. apezgai, abadegai.

seminary n. apezgaitegi, seminario.

semitic adj. semitar.

semitone n. (mus.) doinuerdi.

semivowel n. erdibokale.

semolina n. garimami.

senate n. (pol.) senatu.

senator n. (pol.) senadore.

senatorial *adj.* senatuko.
send *v.t./v.i.* bidali, igorri.
sendable *adj.* bidalgarri, igorgarri.
sender *n.* igorle, igortzaile, bidaltzaile.
senile *adj.* txotxatuta, umetuta.
senility *n.* zaharmin, zaharreri.
senior *adj.* nagusi. *n.* senior, unibertsitate eta goieskoletako laugarren urteko ikaslea.
senior citizen *n.* pertsona zahar.
seniority *n.* aintzinatasun.
sensation *n.* sentsazio, sentipen, hunkipen.
sensational *adj.* ikusgarri, bikain, sekulako.
sense *n.* zentzu, zentzumen.
senseless *adj.* itxuragabe(ko), sengabe, zentzugabe.
senselessly *adv.* sengabeki.
senselessness *n.* zentzugabekeria, sengabekeria, eragabekeria.
sense of humor *n.* umore.
senses *n.* *(pl.)* sen, konorte, zentzu.
sensibility *n.* sentikortasun.
sensible *adj.* zentzudun, zuhur, senezko, zentzuko.
sensibleness *n.* umotasun.
sensibly *adv.* senaz.
sensitive *adj.* minbera, minberatsu, sentibera, sentikor, bihozbera, bigun, hunkibera, samur.
sensitively *adv.* hunkigarriro.
sensitiveness *n.* minberatasun, sentiberatasun, sentikortasun.
sensitivity *n.* minberatasun, sentiberatasun, hunkiberatasun.
sensorial *adj.* zentzuzko.
sensory *adj.* zentzuzko.
sensual *adj.* zentzukoi, zentzukor; atseginzale, sentsual, laketzale.
sensuality *n.* atsegingose, atsegintzalekeria, zentzukoitasun.
sensuous *adj.* atseginzale.
sent *pret./p. part. of send.*
sentence *v.t.* kondenatu, epaitu; erabaki.
sentence *n.* *(gram.)* esaldi, esanaldi, perpausa. *n.* epai, auziepai. **Death sentence.** Heriotzepai.
sentenced *adj.* epaipeko.
sentencer *n.* kondenatzaile.
sentient *adj.* jakitun, ohardun. *adj.* sentibera.
sentiment *n.* sentimendu, sentimen.
sentimental *adj.* bihozbera, minbera, minberakor, sentimenduzko, samurbera.
sentimentalism *n.* bihozberakeria, minberakeria.
sentimentality *n.* minberatasun, hunkiberatasun, sentiberatasun.
sentimentally *adv.* minkunki.
sentinel *n.* zelatari, zelatatzaile, behazale.
sentry *n.* behazale.
separable *adj.* banagarri, bereizgarri, zatigai, banangarri.

separableness *n.* banangarritasun, zatigaitasun.
separate *v.t./v.i.* banandu, berezi, deselkartu.
separate *adj.* berezi, banandu(a).
separated *adj.* banandu(a), banatutako, banakatu(a).
separately *adv.* bakoizka, bereziki, aparte.
separation *n.* berezipen, deselkarketa, banaketa.
separatism *n.* *(pol.)* separatismo.
separatist *n./adj.* banazale, bereiztiar, separatista.
separator *n.* bakantzaile, berezitzaile, alderazle; banagailu.
September *n.* iraila.
septic tank *n.* karkaba.
septicemia *n.* *(med.)* odolusteldura.
septum *n.* *(anat.)* sudurtarte.
septuple *adj.* zazpikoitz.
sepulcher *n.* hobi, hilobi, hildegi, ehorzleku.
sepulchral *adj.* hilobiko.
sequel *n.* jarraialdi.
sequence *n.* ondorio, sekuentzia.
sequoia *n.* *(bot.)* sekuoia.
serenade *n.* gaukanta, goizsoinu.
serendipity *n.* ezuste.
serene *adj.* bakezko, nare.
serenely *adv.* bakez, lasaiki.
serenity *n.* baretasun, lasaitasun, eztialdi.
serf *n.* mirabe.
sergeant *n.* sarjento.
serial *adj.* segidazko. *n.* telesail(ak).
series *n.* sail. **Television series.** Telesail.
serious *adj.* serios. *adj.* ganoradun, larri.
seriously *adv.* serioski, zinez, menaz.
seriousness *n.* seriotasun, benetasun.
sermon *n.* sermoi, hitzaldi, predikaldi, prediku. **To give a sermon.** Sermoi egin.
sermonizer *n.* predikatzaile, sermoilari.
serous *adj.* suerotsu.
serpent *n.* *(zool.)* narrazti, herrestari, suge.
serpentine *adj.* sugeaire, sugeantzeko.
serrated *adj.* koskadun.
serum *n.* *(med.)* suero.
servant *n.* morroi, etxemutil, ogipeko, otsein, zerbitzari.
serve *v.i./v.t.* zerbitzatu, morroindu. *v.i.* **(as)** balio ukan.
serve *n.* sake.
server *n.* sakegile, ateratzaile. *n.* zerbitzari, eradale.
service *n.* morroiketa, neskametza, otseinketa, otseintza, zerbitzu. *n.* gudaritza.
service station *n.* gasolindegi, zerbitzune.
servile *adj.* jopu, zital.
servility *n.* morroikeria, apalkeria.

servitude *n.* morroitza, menpetasun, mirabetza, sehigo, manupekotasuna, otseintza.

session *n.* saialdi, saio, aldi; batzar, batzarraldi.

set *v.t.* ipini, jarri, ezarri. *v.i.* tinkotu. *v.i.* txitatu. *v.t.* **(aside)** zokoratu, baztertu. *v.t.* **(back)** gibelatu. *v.i.* **(out)** irten. *v.t.* **(up)** muntatu, zutierazi; antolatu.

set *n.* sail, multzo, meta, pilo; talde. *adj.* tinko, trinko.

setback *n.* okerbehar, okerraldi, makurraldi, gibelamendu, arteragozpen.

setting *n.* inguru, ingurumari.

settle *v.t./v.i.* **(v.i., batzutan** **down-**ekin) finkatu, tinkatu, bertakotu, errokatu. *v.t./v.i.* konpondu, antolatu, erabaki. *v.t.* garbitu, kitatu (zorrak).

settlement *n.* antolabide, konponbide, antolamendu. *n.* ezarkuntza.

settler *n.* lehenezarle, populatzaile.

seven *n./adj.* zazpi; zazpiko.

sevenfold *adj.* zazpikoitz.

seventeen *n./adj.* hamazazpi.

seventeenth *adj.* hamazazpigarren.

seventh *adj.* zazpigarren, zazpiren.

seventieth *adj.* hirurogeitamargarren.

seventy *n./adj.* hirurogeitamar.

sever *v.t.* banandu, ebaki, zatitu.

several *adj./n.* zenbait, hainbat.

severe *adj.* barrugogor, bortitz, gogor, gupidagabe, zorrotz.

severely *adv.* gogorki, zorrozki, garrazki.

severity *n.* gogortasun, zorrotzaldi, garrazkeria, zorrozkeria, laztasun.

sew *v.t./v.i.* josi.

sewage *n.* hondakin-urak, ur-zikinak.

sewer *n.* jostun. *n.* zikinodi, estolda, saneamendu. **Sewer system.** Estolderia.

sewer drain *n.* kainu, zakarrodi.

sewing *n.* orrazlan.

sewn *p. part. of sew.*

sex *n.* sexu.

sexagenarian *n./adj.* hirurogeiko.

sexiness *n.* sexualtasun, sexutasun.

sexless *adj.* neutro.

sextet *n.* seikote, seinako.

sexton *n.* sakristau, ehorzle, lurremaile.

sextuple *v.t./v.i.* seikoiztu, seitu.

sextuple *adj.* seikoitz.

sexual *adj.* haragizko, haragizale, sexual.

sexuality *n.* sexutasun, sexualtasun.

sexually *adv.* haragiz, haragiki, sexualki.

sexual organ *n.* (anat.) ernalbide, ernalkin.

shabby *adj.* arlote, baldres.

shack *n.* txabola.

shackle *v.t.* girgiluztu, oinburdineztu.

shackle *n.* oinburdin, girgilu.

shad *n.* (zool.) kolaka.

shade *v.t.* gerizpetu, itzalpetu, itzaldu.

shade *n.* itzalpe, geriza, gerizpe, itzal, itzalgune.

shaded *adj.* ilunpeko, goibel.

shadow *n.* itzal, itzalpe, geriza.

shadowy *adj.* itzaltsu, ilunpeko.

shady *adj.* iluntsu, itzaldun, itzaltsu, goibel, ilun, itzalgarri.

shaft *n.* burtaket, gurdihaga, pertika. *n.* meabide, zulape.

shag *n.* (zool.) ubarroi.

shaggy *adj.* iletsu.

shake *v.i./v.t.* astindu, dardar egin, iharrausi, eragin.

shake *n.* dardaraldi, iharrausaldi, astinaldi.

shaken *adj.* higitsu.

shaker *n.* iharrausle, iharrozaile.

shakily *adv.* dardaraz.

shaky *adj.* dardartsu, dardaratsu.

shall *v. aux.* -go, -ko.

shallot *n.* (bot.) tipulatz.

shallow *adj.* azal; ibitsu.

shallowness *n.* hutsalkeria, harropuzkeria.

sham *n.* iruzur, azpikeria. *adj.* itxurati.

shambles *n.* leku nahasi(a).

shame *v.t.* lotsatu.

shame *n.* lotsa, ahalka.

shamefaced *adj.* lotsatuta, lotsagorritu(a).

shameful *adj.* lotsagarri, ahalkegarri, lotsagarrizko.

shamefully *adv.* ahalkegarriki, lotsagarriro.

shamefulness *n.* lotsagarritasun.

shameless *adj.* lotsagabe, lotsagaiztoko, lotsagalduko, gordintzale, ahalgegabe.

shamelessly *adv.* lotsagabeki, lotsagarriki, lotsagarriro, mutiriki,ahalkegabeki.

shamelessness *n.* lotsagabekeria, lotsagabezia, lotsagarrikeria, ahalkegabekeria, mutiritasun.

shampoo *n.* txanpu.

shamrock *n.* (bot.) hiruste, sekulabelar, pagotxa.

shank *n.* bernahezur.

shanty *n.* txabola.

shape *v.t./v.i.* itxuratu, moldatu.

shape *n.* itxura, egikera, moldura, eite.

shapeless *adj.* itxuragabe(ko), formagabeko.

shapelessness *n.* itxuragabetasun, moldegabetasun.

shapely *adj.* itxura oneko.

share *v.t./v.i.* erdibanatu.

share *n.* (econ.) balore, akzio. *n.* parte, banapen.

shareholder *n.* akziodun.

sharer *n.* erdikide, partaide.

shark *n.* (zool.) tiburoi, marraxo.

sharp *adj.* zorrotz, puntazorrotz. *adj.* zoli, sarkor, ozen. *adj.* mingarri. *adj.* doi-doi, zuzen.

sharpen *v.t./v.i.* zorroztu, zolitu, zurtu.
sharpener *n.* zorrotzaile, zorroztaile, zorroztatzaile; zorrozkailu.
sharply *adv.* zorrozki, saminki, saminkiro, sarkorki, zorrozkiro, zoliki.
sharpness *n.* zorroztasun. *n.* mingarritasun, sumintasun, sarkortasun.
sharpshooter *n.* tiratzaile.
sharp-tongued *adj.* mihizorrotz, mingainzorrotz.
shatter *v.t./v.i.* zazkildu, zati-zati egin, haustu.
shave *v.i./v.t.* bizarra moztu, bizargabetu; soildu.
shaven *adj.* motz, soilgorri.
shaver *n.* labaina, bizarmakina.
shaving *n.* bizarmozketa, bizarmoztaldi, bizarmozte. *n.* txirbil, txiri.
shawl *n.* txal, besana.
she *pron.* hura, hark, bera, berak.
sheaf *n.* azau.
shear *v.t.* ile(a) moztu (ardiak).
shearing *n.* mozketa, motzaldi, murrizdura. **Sheep shearing.** Ardi mozketa.
shears *n.* (*pl.*) ilemoztailu, aizturrak.
sheath *n.* ezpatazorro.
sheathe *v.t.* zorroratu, zorrotu, lekaratu.
sheave *v.t.* espaldu, espalkatu, azaukatu.
shed *v.t./v.i.* jario, isurikatu, erori.
shed *n.* estalpe, etxola.
she'd "she + would" edo "she + had"-en laburpena.
sheen *n.* disdira, dirdira.
sheep *n.* (*zool.*) ardi(ak); ardi-.
sheepdog *n.* ardizakur, arditxakur, artzanor.
sheepfold *n.* abeltegi, eskorta, artegi.
sheepherder *n.* artzain.
sheepherding *n.* artzaintza.
sheepish *adj.* beldurti; ezti, otzan.
sheepshearer *n.* ilemoztaile, ileapaintzaile.
sheepskin *n.* ardilarru.
sheer *adj.* fin, mehe. *adj.* malkartsu, maldatsu. *adj.* egiazko.
sheet *n.* maindire, izara. *n.* orri.
shelf *n.* apal, balda, arasa.
shell *v.t./v.i.* lekatu, garandu, alebanatu. *v.t.* kainoikatu.
shell *n.* maskor, oskol; kusku. *n.* kurkuilo.
she'll "she + will"-aren laburpena.
shellac *n.* laka.
shelled *adj.* maskordun.
shellfish *n.* itsaski.
shelter *v.t./v.i.* aterpetu, babestu, gerizatu, gerizpetu.
shelter *n.* aterpe, babesleku, estalpe, etzauntza, ihesleku.
shelve *v.t.* apaletan ipini.
shelving *n.* apalategi.
shepherd *n.* artzain, bazkatzaile (gizon).

shepherdess *n.* artzaineska, artzaintsa.
sherbet *n.* izozki.
sheriff *n.* sherif.
sherry *n.* jerez.
she's "she + is" edo "she + has"-en laburpena.
shield *v.t.* erredoleztatu, blindatu.
shield *n.* babeski, bularbabes, erredola.
shift *n.* txanda, aldi.
shimmer *n.* ñirñira.
shin *n.* (*anat.*) bernahezur, hankezur.
shinbone *n.* (*anat.*) hankezur.
shine *v.i./v.t.* dirdiratu, dirdirazi, distiratu, distirarazi, dizdiz egin. *v.i./v.t.* argitu, errainutu. *v.t.* leundu, labaindu.
shine *n.* dirdirapen, distira, erlantz, labaindura.
shingle *n.* teila.
shininess *n.* labaintasun.
shiny *adj.* dirdiratzaile, distiratzaile, distiratsu.
ship *v.t./v.i.* itsasontziz karreiatu, itsasontziz garraiatu, itsasontziz bidali. *v.i.* (**out**) herri batetik itsasontziz irten.
ship *n.* itsasontzi, ontzi, untzi.
shipbuilder *n.* untzigile.
shipbuilding *n.* untzigintza.
shipment *n.* igorketa, bidalpen, igorpen.
shipowner *n.* untzidun, untzijabe.
shipping *n.* igorketa, igorpen, ontzigarraio.
shipwreck *v.t./v.i.* hondoratu, ontzia galdu.
shipwreck *n.* hondoraketa, hondorapen, ontzigalera.
shipyard *n.* untzitegi.
shirk *v.t.* bazterratu, saihestu, alderatu.
shirt *n.* alkandora, ator.
shirtfront *n.* kolko.
shirtless *adj.* atorgabe.
shit *v.i.* kaka egin.
shit *n.* kaka.
shivaree *n.* intxarrots.
shiver *v.i.* hotzikaratu, dardaratu.
shiver *n.* gorputzikara, hotzikara, hozkirri.
shoal *n.* barra.
shock *v.t./v.i.* kalanbretu, kolokarazi, harritu.
shock *n.* ikaraldi, izualdi, izularri. *n.* kalanbre. *n.* talka.
shocked *adj.* izukor, izuti.
shocking *adj.* harritzeko, asaldagarri, harrigarrizko, izugarri.
shockingly *adv.* asaldagarriki.
shod *pret./p. part. of* shoe.
shoddiness *n.* lardaskeria.
shoddy *adj.* lardaskatzaile.
shoe *v.t.* ferratu, burdineztatu. *v.t.* oinetakoak eman.
shoe *n.* oinetako, zapata, oski.

shoelace *n.* kordel, kordoi, aiubeta.
shoemaker *n.* zapatagin, zapatagile, oskigile, oinetakogile.
shoestring *n.* kordel.
shoo *v.t./v.i.* (*v.t., batzutan* **away**-*ekin*) uxatu, ohildu, haizatu, hots eman.
shoo *int.* u!, xapi!
shoot *v.t./v.i.* tirokatu, tiro eman, tiro egin; gezikatu, gezitu.
shoot *n.* kimu, ninika, muskil. *int.* demonioa!, zer deabru!
shooter *n.* tirogailu.
shooting *n.* tiroaldi, tiroketa.
shop *v.i.* dendara joan, erosketak egin.
shop *n.* denda, erostetxe. *n.* lantoki, lantegi.
shopkeeper *n.* dendari, dendako.
shopper *n.* erosle.
shore *n.* kostalde, itsasalde, itsasbazter, itsasertz, ibaiondo.
shorn *adj.* kaskagorri, kaskamotz.
short *adj.* labur, motz, xume, txiki, baxu, murritz.
shortage *n.* eskasaldi, eskasia, urritasun.
short circuit *n.* zirkuitubakar.
shortcoming *n.* akats, huts.
shortcut *n.* bidelabur, bidelaster, bidezidor, laburbide, lasterbide.
shorten *v.t./v.i.* laburtu, moztu.
shortening *n.* laburketa, laburpen. *n.* urin, koipe.
shorthand *n.* takigrafia.
shortly *adv.* laster, azkar. *adv.* labur(ki), laburkiro, mozki. *adv.* zakarki.
shortness *n.* laburrera, laburtasun, murriztasun, moztasun.
shorts *n.* (*pl.*) galtzamotz, frakamotz.
short-sighted *adj.* begilabur, miope.
short-tempered *adj.* suminkor, haserrekor, sukoi.
short-temperedness *n.* sukortasun, suminkeria.
shot *n.* tiro, tirokada, danbada. *n.* indizio, iraizpen, xiringada. *pret./p. part. of shoot.*
shotgun *n.* eskopeta.
should *v. aux.* behar ukan, behar.
shoulder *v.t.* sorbaldaratu.
shoulder *n.* (*anat.*) besaburu, besagain, soingiltza, bizkargain, sorbalda. *n.* bidebazter, kalertz, bidertz.
shoulder blade *n.* (*anat.*) besaburu.
shouldn't "should + not"-aren laburpena.
shout *v.i./v.t.* oihu egin, dei egin, deadar egin, orrokatu.
shout *n.* deiadar, garrasi, oihu, txilio.
shouter *n.* hoslari, oihukari, oihulari.
shove *v.t.* bultz egin, bultzatu, saka egin, sakatu.
shove *n.* bultzada, bultz, sakada.
shovel *n.* pala.
shovelful *n.* palakada, palaldi.
show *v.t./v.i.* erakutsi, ikusarazi,

agerrarazi, argitara eman, ezagutarazi, nabarmendu, plazaratu. *v.i.* agertu, argitu.
show *n.* antzezpen. *n.* agerpen.
showable *adj.* agergarri.
showcase *n.* erakusleku, erakustapal, erakustoki, erakustegi.
shower *n.* aurkezlari, aurkezle, aurkeztatzaile. *n.* dutxa. *n.* ezkontzeko edo haurdun dagoen emakumeari egin ohi zaion festa.
shown *p. part. of show.*
show-off *n.* harroputz, hanpurutsu.
showy *adj.* azalkor, itxurandizko.
shrank *pret. of shrink.*
shrapnel *n.* metraila.
shred *v.t./v.i.* apurkatu, xehatu, zehatu.
shrew *n.* (*zool.*) sahatsuri.
shrewd *adj.* gogoargi, zuhur, zoli, amarruti, amarrutsu.
shrewdly *adv.* zuhurki, malmuzki.
shrewdness *n.* amarru, gogoernetasun, malmuztasun, gogoargitasun.
shriek *v.i./v.t.* oihu egin, garrasi egin.
shrike *n.* (*zool.*) antzandobi.
shrill *adj.* oihukari, karrankari.
shrimp *n.* izkira.
shrine *n.* erlikikutxa, erlikitegi.
shrink *v.i./v.t.* txikitu, kizkurtu, laburtu. *v.i.* (**back**) atzera eman.
shrink *n.* (*colloq.*) sikiatra.
shrinkage *n.* laburpen, gutxiketa, urriketa.
shrivel *v.t./v.i.* kizkurtu, igartu, ihartu, karkaildu, ximeldu.
shriveled *adj.* uzkur, mirrin, pirtxil.
shroud *v.t.* beztitu (gorpua).
shroud *n.* hiloihal, hiljazki, hiljantzi.
shrub *n.* mulu, txapar.
shrubbery *n.* txapardi.
shrug *v.i./v.t.* sorbaldak jaso.
shrug *n.* sorbalda jasoketa.
shrunk *p. part. of shrink.*
shrunken *adj.* uzkur.
shuck *v.t.* zuritu (artoa).
shudder *v.i.* dardar egin, hotzikaratu.
shudder *n.* dardar, hotzikara.
shuffle *v.i./v.t.* bihurdikatu.
shun *v.t.* alde egin, irristatu.
shut *v.t./v.i.* itxi, hertsi. *v.t./v.i.* (**up**) isildu, isilik egon, mututu. **Shut up!** Zaude isilik!
shut *adj.* itxita, hertsirik.
shutter *n.* kontraleiho.
shuttle *n.* hurbileko (hegazkin, izarrontzi, tren, autobus, etab.)
shy *adj.* lotsati, lotsakor, herabe, ahalkedun, ahalketi.
shyly *adv.* herabez, herabeki, txepelki.
shyness *n.* lotsa, lotsakortasun, txepeltasun, herabetasun.
sibilant *adj.* txistukari.
sibling *n.* haurride.
sic *v.t.* eraso. *v.t.* tirriatu, tirriarazi, xaxatu.

sick *adj.* eri, gaiso, herbal, minez, ondoezik, makal, ahul, indarge.
sicken *v.t./v.i.* eritu, gaisotu.
sickening *adj.* nazkagarri.
sickish *adj.* gaisoka.
sickle *n.* igitai.
sickly *adj./adv.* eribera, erikoi, gaisobera, herbal, gaisoti.
sickness *n.* eri, eritasun, gaiso, gaisoaldi, gaisotasun, gaitz; gaiz-, el-.
side *n.* alderdi, hegal, albo, aldamen, alde, ondo, saihets, eskualde. *adj.* alboko, aldameneko, zeharreko.
sideboard *n.* jakimahai. *n. (eccl.)* baztermahai.
sideburn *n.* masailbizar.
sided *adj.* hegaldun.
sideless *adj.* hegalgabe.
sidetrack *v.t.* desbideratu, alderatu.
sidewalk *n.* kalertz, espaloi, galtzada.
sideways *adv./adj.* zeharka, saiheska, zeharbidez; zeharreko.
siding *n.* bazterleku (trenbide).
siege *n.* inguraketa, hesiketa.
sierra *n.* mendizerra, mendieta, mendikate. *n. (zool.)* zerrarrain.
siesta *n.* biago, abaro.
sieve *v.t./v.i.* bahetu.
sieve *n.* galbahe, bahe, eskubahe.
sift *v.t.* eralki, bahestatu.
sifter *n.* zetabe, bahe.
sifting *n.* baheztadura, galbahaldi, baheztaketa.
sigh *v.i./v.t.* intziri egin, hasperen egin, zizpurutu, zinkurinatu.
sigh *n.* hasperen, zinkurin, zizpuru, ai, antzi, intziri.
sight *v.t.* ikusi.
sight *n.* ikusmen. *n.* bista, ikuskai, ikustapen. *n.* begiztabide, begiztailu.
sightless *adj.* itsu.
sightseeing *n.* leku interesgarrien ikustaldi(a).
sign *v.t./v.i.* izenpetu. *v.i.* **(up)** inskribatu, erroldatu.
sign *n.* adierazgai, agerbide, ezaugarri, seinale, lkur. *n.* kartel.
signal *v.t./v.i.* seinalatu, seinaleztatu, markatu.
signal *n.* ezagugailu, ezaugarri, seinale, agerbide, marka.
signaller *n.* seinalari, markatzaile.
signature *n.* izenpeko, izenpe, sinadura.
signed *adj.* izenpedun.
signer *n.* izenpetzaile.
significance *n.* esanahi, esangura. *n.* garrantzi.
significant *adj.* esanguratsu, adierazkor, adieragarri. *adj.* garrantzidun, garrantzizko.
significantly *adv.* adierazkorki.
signify *v.t.* adierazi, jakinerazi, ezaguterazi.
silence *v.t.* mututu, mutuarazi, isildu.
silence *n.* isilune, isiltasun, isilgune.

int. isilik!
silenceable *adj.* isilgarri.
silencer *n.* isilarazle, isiltzaile; motelgailu, isilgailu.
silent *adj.* isil, isileko, hitzgutxiko.
silently *adv.* isilean, isilki.
silentness *n.* isilkoitasun.
silex *n. (chem.)* silex.
silhouette *n.* isla.
silica *n.* muger.
siliceous *adj.* mugerrantzeko, mugertsu, mugerrezko.
silicon *n. (chem.)* silizio.
silicosis *n. (med.)* silikosis, mugerreri.
silk *n.* seda, sedehun, sedoihal, ziriko, zeta. *adj.* zetazko.
silken *adj.* zetatsu, sedantzeko.
silkworm *n. (zool.)* zetar, ingumar.
silky *adj.* zetatsu, sedantzeko.
sill *n.* atebarren; leihobarren.
silliness *n.* txotxolokeria, gazkabekeria, pellokeria.
silly *adj.* astakilo, burugabe, ergel, inozo, memelo, tentel, zozo.
silo *n.* silo.
silver *n. (min.)* zilar. *adj.* zilartsu, zilarrezko.
silversmith *n.* zilargile, zilargin.
silverware *n.* zilarrezko baxera.
silvery *adj.* zilarrantzeko, zilartsu.
simian *n. (zool.)* tximino.
similar *adj.* antzeko, itxuradun, berdintsu, bezalako, gisako, idekotsu, kideko, moduko, pareko, aireko.
similarity *n.* antz, kidekotasun, itxurapen, kidetasun, parekidetasun, antzekotasun.
similarly *adv.* berdinki, erdiberdin, berdinzki.
simile *n.* gonbarabide; ezaugarri.
similitude *n.* berdinkuntza.
simple *adj.* bakun, xehe, arrunt. *adj.* xinple, oso.
simpleminded *adj.* sinple.
simplemindedness *n.* sinplekeria.
simpleton *n.* inozo, ergel, tentel.
simplicity *n.* soiltasun, xalotasun, arruntasun, xumetasun.
simplifiable *adj.* bakungarri.
simplification *n.* errezketa, soilketa.
simplified *adj.* bakundu(a).
simplify *v.t.* bakundu.
simplistic *adj.* soiltzale.
simply *adv.* soilki, lainoki, arrunki.
simulate *v.t.* plantak egin, irudikatu, itxura egin.
simulated *adj.* itxurazko, alegiazko.
simulation *n.* alegia, itxurantz.
simultaneity *n.* aldikidetasun, aldiberetasun.
simultaneous *adj.* aldibereko, bat-bateko, baterako, unebereko.
simultaneously *adv.* batera, aldiberean, batean, bat-batera.
simultaneousness *n.* aldiberetasun.
sin *v.i./v.t.* bekatu egin.

sin *n.* bekatu, hoben, gaizpide.
since *adv./prep./conj.* harrezkeroz, ezen, ezkero, geroztik; -danik, -(e)nez gero.
sincere *adj.* zinezko, benetako, egizale, zabal, tolesgabe, egiazko.
sincerely *adv.* benetan, tolesgabeki.
sincerity *n.* egiberatasun, egizkotasun, lainotasun, tolesgabetasun, egizaletasun.
sine *n.* (math.) sinu.
sinecure *n.* lan gutxi eta diru askoko lanpostua. *n.* benefizio.
sinew *n.* zain.
sinewy *adj.* zaintzu.
sinful *adj.* bekatuzko, hobendun, hobenezko, hobentsu.
sing *v.i./v.t.* abestu, kantatu. *v.i.* txiruliru egin, txorrotxio egin.
singable *adj.* kantagarri.
singe *v.t.* gardostu, sugarastatu.
singer *n.* kantari, abeslari.
singing *n.* kantaldi. *n.* txioketa.
single *adj.* senargai, ezkongabe, ezkongai. *adj.* bakar, soil.
single file *adv.* lerroka, lerroan.
single-handed *adj.* bakar, bakarrik.
single-minded *adj.* asmobakarreko.
singleness *n.* ezkongabetasun, ezkongabezia.
singly *adv.* bakarrik.
singsong *n./adj.* doinubakar; doinubakarreko.
singular *adj.* bakar, bakan, banako.
singularity *n.* bakartasun, berezitasun.
sinister *adj.* txar, gaizto, alproja.
sink *v.i./v.t.* beheratu. *v.i./v.t.* hondatu, hondoratu, itsasperatu, urperatu.
sink *n.* konketa, ikuzleku, harri, sukaltarri.
sinkable *adj.* hondoragarri, hondagarri, murgilgarri, urperagarri.
sinless *adj.* hobengabe, errugabe.
sinlessness *n.* hobengabetasun.
sinner *n.* bekatari.
sinuous *adj.* zeharkako, bihurgunetsu, oker.
sinus *n.* (anat.,med.) sinus.
sinusitis *n.* (med.) sinusitis.
Sioux *n.* Estatu Batuetako indio tribu bat.
sip *v.t./v.i.* hurrupatu, hurrupa egin, zurrupatu.
sip *n.* hurrupada, zurrupada, zurrutada.
siphon *v.t.* hurrupatu (edangabe).
siphon *n.* hurrupaketa (edangabe).
sir *n.* jaun.
sire *n.* aita. *n.* handitasun, maiestate.
siren *n.* turuta, deiadar. *n.* itsasneska, uhandre, arrainandere.
sirloin *n.* solomo.
sirocco *n.* siroko.
sis *n.* ahizpa, arreba.
sissy *n.* maritxu.
sister *n.* ahizpa, arreba. *n.* serora, lekaime.
sisterhood *n.* ahizpatasun.

sister-in-law *n.* ezkonahizpa, ezkonarreba, arrebagiarreba, koinata.
sisterly *adj.* senidegarri.
sit *v.i./v.t. (askotan down-ekin)* eseri, jarri, mahaieratu, eserita egon.
site *n.* etxeleku, lekune, leku.
sitting *n.* jarrialdi, eseraldi.
situate *v.t.* lekutu, ezarri, kokatu, ingurakatu, tokitu.
situation *n.* egoera. *n.* lekutasun, nongotasun, egoitza, tokiera.
six *n./adj.* sei, seiko.
sixteen *n./adj.* hamasei.
sixteenth *adj.* hamaseigarren.
sixth *adj.* seigarren.
sixtieth *adj.* hirurogeiko, hirurogeigarren.
sixty *n./adj.* hirurogei.
sizable *adj.* handi, ugari, itzal.
size *v.t.* oreztu.
size *n.* tamainu, izari, neurri.
skate *v.i.* patinatu.
skate *n.* patina, irristailu. *n. (zool.)* arrai.
skater *n.* patinari, irristari.
skating rink *n.* patinatoki, irristaleku, lerrategi.
skating *n.* patinaketa, irristaketa.
skein *n.* mataza, haril.
skeletal *adj.* hezurrutsezko.
skeleton *n. (anat.)* hezurdura, hezurruts.
skeptic *n.* ezbaikor, dudakor.
skeptical *adj.* ezbaikor, fedegutxiko, dudakor.
skepticism *n.* ezbaikorkeria, eskeptizismo.
sketch *v.t./v.i.* zirriborratu, marraztu.
sketch *n.* zirriborro, zirriborrapen, zirrimarra.
skewer *n.* burruntzi.
ski *v.i./v.t.* skiatu.
ski *n.* ski.
skid *v.i./v.t.* zirristatu, zirrist egin, limurtu, lerratu, irrist egin.
skid *n.* lerra, limuri, irristaketa.
skier *n.* skiatzaile, skialari.
ski lift *n.* funikular.
skill *n.* trebetasun, artezia, maina, abilezia.
skilled *adj.* moldetsu, ikasi(a), moldedun.
skillet *n.* zartagina.
skillful *adj.* artetsu, mainadun, abil, eskuoneko, trebe, moldatsu.
skillfully *adv.* moldez, abilki, maisuki.
skillfulness *n.* trebetasun.
skim *v.t.* desgaindu. *v.t.* gainbegiratu.
skimmer *n.* bitsadera.
skimp *v.t./v.i.* urritu, gutxitu, aurreratu, ekonomizatu.
skin *v.t.* larrutu.
skin *n.* azal, mintz, larru.
skinner *n.* larrukentzaile, larrutzaile.
skinny *adj.* argal, sistrin, mehe.
skip *v.i.* saltoka ibili. *v.t.* ahaztu, ahantzi, huts egin, ezaipatu.

skipper *n.* patroi, atzeko, kapitain, pilotu, untzigidari.
skirmish *v.i.* guduxkatu.
skirmish *n.* guduxka.
skirt *n.* gona.
skull *n. (anat.)* buruhezur, kaskezur.
skunk *n. (zool.)* mofeta.
sky *n.* ortz, zeru.
skydiver *n.* jauzikari, saltalari.
skylab *n.* izarrontzi.
skylight *n.* gainleiho, goileiho, argizulo.
skyline *n.* ikusmuga.
skyscraper *n.* etxeorratz, etxerraldoi.
slab *n.* lauza.
slack *adj.* manu.
slacken *v.t./v.i.* desestutu, erriatu.
slackening *n.* lasaikuntza.
slacker *n.* bere lana edo betebeharra baztertzen duena.
slacks *n.* frakak.
slag *n.* zepa, zakar.
slain *p. part. of slay.*
slam *v.t./v.i.* indarrez eta zalapartaz itxi, erauntsi, panpatu.
slam *n.* panpakada.
slander *v.t./v.i.* gaitz esan, lohiztatu, murdurikatu, maiseatu.
slander *n.* gaizkiesate, famakenketa, gezurlaido, maiseaketa, murduri.
slanderer *n.* gaitzesale, murdurikari, famakentzaile.
slanderous *adj.* gezurlaidozko, murdurikari, maiseagarri.
slang *n.* argot.
slant *v.i./v.t.* oihestu.
slant *n.* alborapen, zehardura.
slanted *adv.* trabeska, zeharka.
slap *v.t.* zaflatu, zaplaztatu, eskuzartatu.
slap *n.* blaustada, zaflada, zartada, zaplaztako, eskuzartada.
slash *n.* zastada, labainada, aiztokada.
slate *n.* arbel, arbelaitz. **Slate roof.** Arbelteilatu.
slaughter *v.t.* sarraskitu.
slaughter *n.* odolketa, hilketa.
slaughterer *n.* aberehiltzaile.
slaughterhouse *n.* aberehiltoki.
slave *n.* uztarpeko, esklabu.
slaver *n.* lerdejario. *n.* belzketari.
slavery *n.* uztarpe, esklabutza, jopukeria, katigutasun.
slay *v.t.* hil.
slayer *n.* hiltzaile.
sled *n.* elurlera, narra.
sledge *n.* elurlera, narra.
sledge hammer *n.* mailutzar, baldar, olamailu, porra.
sleek *adj.* leun eta distiratsu.
sleep *v.i./v.t. (v.t., gehienetan away-ekin)* lo egin, lo egon, lotan egon, lokuluxkatu.
sleep *n.* lo. *n.* makar, pizta.
sleepily *adv.* logosez, loguraz.
sleep-inducing *adj.* logarri.
sleepiness *n.* loeri, logaletasun, logale, logura, logose.

sleeping bag *n.* lozaku.
sleepless *adj.* logabe.
sleeplessness *n.* logabetasun.
sleepwalker *n.* ametsibiltzaile.
sleepy *adj.* loegile, loti, erdiesna, loerdi, logale, logura, erdilo. *adj.* makartsu.
sleepyhead *n.* lobera, loti.
sleet *n.* elurreuri.
sleeve *n.* beso, mahuka.
sleeveless *adj.* mahukagabe.
sleigh *n.* lera.
sleight of hand *n.* eskujoko, eskuketa.
slender *adj.* argal, mehar, makar, erkin.
slenderness *n.* argaldura, mehetasun.
slept *pret./p. part. of sleep.*
slice *v.t.* zerrakatu, okelatu.
slice *n.* zerra, zafla.
slicer *n.* jakizatitzaile.
slick *adj.* labain, irristakor, lerrakor, limurkor.
slickly *adv.* labainki.
slickness *n.* labainkortasun, lerrakortasun, limurtasun.
slide *v.i./v.t.* zirristatu, zirrist egin, irrist egin, lerratu, limurtu, labaindu.
slide *n.* irristabide, irristaleku, labainbide, lerra, linburtegi, lerrabide. *n.* labanaldi. *n.* filmina, diapositiba.
slight *v.t.* min eman, mindu.
slight *n.* gaitzestasun. *adj.* txiki. *adj.* argal, mehe.
slightly *adv.* apur bat, apurtxo bat, pixka bat, pitin bat.
slim *v.t./v.i. (askotan down-ekin)* mehartu, mehetu.
slim *adj.* mehe, argal.
slime *n.* lingirda, lerdeliska.
sliminess *n.* lohitasun, zikinkeria.
slimness *n.* mehetasun, argaltasun.
slimy *adj.* lingirdatsu, lohibera, mukidun, mukijario, likitsu.
sling *n.* habaila.
slinger *n.* habailari.
slingshot *n.* tiragoma, habaila.
slip *v.i./v.t.* zirristatu, zirrist egin, irristatu, lerratu, limurtu, labaindu.
slip *n.* gonazpiko, azpigona, gonabarren. *n.* irristaldi, labanketa, lerraldi. *n.* akats, errakuntza. *n.* erorketa, erorpen.
slipper *n.* oskitxo, txinal.
slipperiness *n.* labainkortasun, labaintasun, lerrakortasun, limurtasun.
slippery *adj.* irristagarri, irristakor, labain, lerragarri, limurkor.
slipshod *adj.* lardaskatzaile.
slit *v.t.* ebaki.
slit *n.* ebakidura, ebaketa.
slither *v.i./v.t.* herrestatu, narraztu, narraz ibili.
slithery *adj.* narraztari.
sliver *n.* egurbrintz, erbatz.
slobber *v.i./v.t.* eldertu.
slobber *n.* adur, elder.

sloe *n. (bot.)* basaran.
sloe gin *n.* patxaran.
slogan *n.* goiburu, ikurritz.
slop *n.* xerribazka, zerrijan.
slope *n.* aldapa, aldats, beherabide, malda, muino, bizkar.
slopeless *adj.* aldapagabe(ko).
sloppy *adj.* arlote, lardaskontzi.
slop trough *n.* zerriaska.
slot *n.* zulo, aho.
sloth *n. (zool.)* nagi. *n.* nagikeria, gogaitza, ganoragabekeria.
slothful *adj.* nagitzar, alfertzar.
slothfully *adv.* nagiki, alferki.
slot machine *n.* sosbilgailu, txanponjale.
slovenliness *n.* narraskeria, narrasketa, arlotetasun, baldreskeria, zirtzilkeria.
slovenly *adj.* fardel, lander, baldres.
slow *v.t./v.i. (batzutan* **down***-ekin)* geldiagotu, baratu, geldiroago ibili.
slow *adj.* berankor, geldo, baratz, patxadatsu, geldi. *adj.* burumotel.
slowly *adv.* astiro, emeki, geldika, geldiro, poliki, eztiki, geldi.
slowness *n.* geldiera, astirotasun, patxada, luzakeria.
slug *n. (zool.)* bare. *n.* hurrupa, hurrupada.
sluggish *adj.* astidun, patxadatsu, baldan.
sluggishly *adv.* trakeski, baldarki, dorpeki.
sluggishness *n.* baldarkeria, baldartasun, trakeskeria, patxada.
slumber *v.i.* lo egin.
slumber *n.* lozorro, lokardura.
slump *n.* beherakada, motelaldi, beherapen. *n.* nagialdi, alferraldi.
slur *v.t.* nahas-mahas hitz egin. *v.t.* gezur iraindu, gaitzesan, izen ona kendu.
slur *n.* gaitzesate.
slurp *v.t./v.i.* zurrupatu.
slush *n.* elurbusti, elurbasa.
sly *adj.* begigaizto, maltzurkote, azpikari.
slyness *n.* makurkeria, maltzurkeria.
smack *n.* zaflada, plast.
small *adj.* txiki, xehe, koskor, ñimiño.
smallness *n.* gutitasun, txikitasun, xehadura, xumetasun.
smallpox *n. (med.)* nafarreri, baztanga.
smart *adj.* buruargi, argi, kaskodun, azkar, susper. *adj.* apain, dotore.
smarten up *v.t.* apaindu. *v.t.* ernarazi, bizkortu.
smartly *adj.* apain(ki).
smartness *n.* buruargitasun, goiargi.
smash *v.t./v.i.* tinkatu, suntsitu.
smattering *n.* ezagupen mugatu(a), azaleko ezaguera.
smear *v.t.* zikindu, lohitu, lokaztu.
smeared *adj.* lohi, zikin.
smell *v.t./v.i.* usaindu, usnatu, sumatu. *v.i.* ufaztu; lizunusaindu.

smell *n.* usain, suma, usaimen.
smeller *n.* usainkari, usmatzaile, usnatzaile.
smelt *v.t.* funditu, galdatu, urtu.
smidgen *n.* lipar.
smile *v.i./v.t.* irrikatu, irribarre egin, barre egin.
smile *n.* irribarre, irriño.
smiling *adj.* irrikor, irribera, irrikoi, barrebera.
smilingly *adv.* barrez, irribarrez.
smirch *v.t.* zikindu, lohitu.
smirk *v.i.* irrifarre harroa egin.
smirk *n.* irrifarre harro(a).
smite *v.t.* jo.
smith *n.* burdingile.
smithy *n.* burdindegi.
smitten *p. part. of* smite.
smog *n.* ke eta laino nahasketa.
smoke *v.i.* ketu. *v.t.* erre, pipatu. *v.t.* keztatu, kemindu.
smoke *n.* ke. *n.* pipaldi.
smoker *n.* erretzaile.
smokestack *n.* kebide, tximinia.
smoking *adj.* erretzaile, ketan. **No smoking!** Ez erre!
smoky *adj.* ketsu, kedun; kemin.
smolder *v.i.* zititrri.
smooth *v.t.* leundu, labaindu, lautu, lauzatu, guritu.
smooth *adj.* lau, leun, berdin, eztitsu, zelai.
smoothable *adj.* leungarri.
smoother *adj. (comp.)* leunago.
smoothly *adv.* leunki, leunkiro, lauki, emeki, eztiki, gozaro.
smoothness *n.* leuntasun, guritasun, labaintasun, ematasun, eztitasun, gozotasun.
smother *v.t./v.i.* ito, ito arazi.
smudge *n.* kedarketa.
smudged *adj.* gedartsu.
smudgy *adj.* zirriborrotsu.
smug *adj.* harro, harroputz, handiputz.
smuggle *v.t./v.i.* mugautsi.
smuggler *n.* kontrabandista, gaulangile.
smuggling *n.* gaulan, kontrabandu, mugausketa. **Smuggling operation.** Gaulan.
smut *n.* lizunkeria, gordinkeria, itsuskeria.
smutty *adj.* gedartsu.
snack *v.i.* krakada egin.
snack *n.* jaki, hamaiketako, otamen.
snack bar *n.* meriendatoki, askaldegi.
snag *v.t./v.i.* zirpildu.
snag *n.* zirpil.
snail *n. (zool.)* barraskilo.
snake *n. (zool.)* suge, narrazti; suga-.
snakebite *n.* mizto.
snap *v.i.* dzart egin, tart egin. *v.i.* azkar hozka egin. *v.i.* puskatu, apurtu. *v.i./v.t.* (**at, out**) haserrez esan. *v.t.* kriskitin egin.
snap *n.* zart.
snap fastener *n.* kortxeta.

snapshot n. argazki.
snare n. gako-mako, harrapagailu, zelatadura, lakio.
snarl v.i. haserrez hortzak erakutsi.
snatch v.t./v.i. dzapart egin, harrapatu.
sneak v.i. aldendu.
sneakily adv. isilkeriaz.
sneaky adj. lerrati.
sneer v.i. (at) musuriku egin.
sneer n. murrika.
sneeze v.i. usin egin.
sneeze n. dominístiku, urtzintz, usin.
sneezer n. urtzintzalari.
snicker v.i. isilkeriaz farre egin.
sniff v.i./v.t. usnatu, usmatu, usaindu, usainkatu.
snip v.t. guraizez ebaki, guraizez moztu.
snivel v.i. muxin egin, muxindu.
sniveling adj. muxin, maina.
snob n. pertsona harropuzt(a).
snobbishness n. modazalekeria.
snoop v.i. ikusmiratu, usnatu.
snooze v.i. lo egin.
snore v.i. zurrunga egin, zurrungatu, karrankatu.
snore n. loarrantza, zurrunga.
snorer n. zurrungari, karrankari.
snoring n. lozurrunga, karranka, karrankari.
snort v.i./v.t. furrust egin.
snot n. zintz, muki.
snotty adj. mukitsu, mokoti.
snout n. mutur.
snow v.i./v.t. elurra egin, elurtu.
snow n. elur.
snowball n. elurpilota.
snowdrift n. elurmeta.
snowfall n. elurraldi, elurte, elurtza.
snowflake n. elurluma, elurmaluta, elurmataza, elurketa.
snow flurry n. elurlauso, elurbolada, elurraldi.
snowless adj. elurgabe.
snowplow n. elurkengailu, lurmengailu.
snowshoe(s) n. elur gainean ibiltzeko oinazpian jarri ohi diren arrabila antzeko(ak).
snowy adj. elurrezko, elurtsu, elurbera.
snub-nosed adj. sudurmotz.
snuck pret./p. part. of sneak.
snuff n. sudurrauts.
snuggle v.i. elkarganatu, elkar estutu.
so adv. hala, hola, honela, horrela. adv./conj. beraz; ba. adv. hain, horren. adj. honelako, horrelako; egiazko.
soak v.i./v.t. urasetu, beratu, busti.
soaked adj. blai, busti.
soaker n. urtatzaile.
so-and-so n. zera.
soap v.t. xaboitu.
soap n. xaboi.
soapbox n. xaboiontzi.
soapsuds n. (pl.) burbuilak, punpuilak.
soapy adj. xaboitsu, xaboidun.
soar v.i. hegan egin, hegatu; gehiegi igo.

sob v.i./v.t. negarmuxinkatu, negarzotinkatu, zinkurinatu, zizpurutu.
sob n. zinkurin, negarzotin, zizpuru.
sober adj. ez hordi. adj. neurrizko, neurritsu, eratsu.
sobriety n. edanurritasun. n. seriotasun.
so-called adj. delako.
soccer n. futbol, hankapilota.
sociability n. elkarkoitasun, jendekoitasun, lagunkoitasun, lagunartetasun.
sociable adj. lagunarteko, kidegarri, lagunbera, gizartekoi, elkarkor, harremankor, jendekoi, lagunkoi, taldekoi.
sociableness n. jendekintasun, mintzaerraztasun.
social adj. gizarteko, gizatsu. **Social security.** Gizarte-aseguru.
socialism n. (pol.) sozialismo.
socialist n./adj. sozialista.
socialization n. sozializazio, sozializaketa.
socialize v.t./v.i. gizartetu, sozialdu, sozialeztatu.
socially adv. gizartean, gizarteaz.
societal adj. gizarteko.
society n. elkarte, lagunbatz. n. gizarte.
sociological adj. soziologiko.
sociologist n. soziologo.
sociology n. soziologia.
sock v.t. zaplaztatu, zaplaztakotu.
sock n. galtzerdimotz. n. muturreko, ukabilkada, ukaldi, zaplazteko, zartada.
socket n. (elec.) lanparaburu.
sod n. zohi, zotal. **To lay sod.** Zohiztatu.
soda n. (chem.) sosa. n. soda.
soda water n. soda, gasedari.
sodium n. (chem.) sodio.
sodomite n. marikoi, atzelari.
sodomy n. sodomia.
sofa n. sofa.
soft adj. leun, bigun, harro, ezti, malgu, samur. adj. gozo, ezti.
soften v.t./v.i. bigundu, guritu, leundu, harro-harrotu, astin-astindu, emetu.
softener n. leuntzaile, bigungarri, leunkari.
soft-hearted adj. bihozbigun, bihozbera.
soft-heartedness n. bihozberakeria.
softly adv. bigunki, emeki, eztiro, gozoki, samurki.
softness n. biguntasun, harrotasun, beratasun, eztitasun, leuntasun, samurtasun.
soil v.t./v.i. zikindu, lohitu, lohiarazi, likistu.
soil n. lur.
soiled adj. lurdun, kutsakoi.
sojourn n. egonaldi.

Sol n. eguzkiaren izena.
solace n. pozaldi, pozbide.
solar adj. eguzkitar, eguzki-.
solar eclipse n. (astron.) eguzkilune.
sold adj. saldu(a).
solder v.t./v.i. soldatu, berundu, iratxeki.
solder n. soldagai.
solderable adj. soldagarri.
soldering n. soldaketa, iratxekidura, soldadura.
soldering iron n. soldagailu.
soldier n. gudari, gudatzaile, armagizon, gerlagizon, soldadu.
soldiering n. gudaritza.
sole v.t. zolak ezarri.
sole n. (zool.) mihiarrain. n. oinazpi, oinzola, zola, azpizoru. adj. bakar.
solecism n. mordoilokeria, sasijoskera, joskeratxar.
solely adv. bakarrik, soilik.
solemn adj. itzaltsu, itzaleko, serios.
solemnity n. seriotasun.
solemnly adv. serioski.
solicit v.t./v.i. eskatu. v.i. emagalduak sexu-harremanetarako eskeintza egin.
solicitation n. eskaketa. n. emagalduaren sexu-harremanetarako eskeintza.
solicitor n. eskatzaile, eskale.
solicitous adj. eskatzaile, xolatsu, xolati.
solicitude n. axola, ardura, arrangura.
solid n. lehorki, solido. adj. gotor, irmo, trinko, gogor.
solidarity n. elkartasun.
solidify v.t./v.i. gotortu, sendartu, irmetu, lehorkitu, gorpuztu.
solidifying adj. gotorgarri.
solidity n. gogortasun, trinkotasun, sendotasun.
solidly adv. irmoki, sendoki, tinkoki.
solidness n. gotortasun, finkotasun.
soliloquy n. bakarrizketa.
solitaire n. bateko.
solitarily adv. bakarrik.
solitary adj. bakarti, bakartiar, baztertu(a), lagungabe.
solitude n. bakartaldi, bakartade.
solo n. pertsona bakar(ra).
soloist n. bakarlari.
solstice n. -muga.
solubility n. urgarritasun.
soluble adj. gesalgarri.
solution n. konponbide, irtenbide, konponketa, antolabide, erremedio, soluzio.
solvable adj. konpongarri, erabakigarri.
solve v.t. soluzionatu, konpondu, atondu.
solvency n. zorgabetasun, ordaingaitasun, kaudimen.
solvent adj. zorgabe, kaudimendun. n. disolbatzaile.
solver n. konpontzaile.
somatic adj. soineko.

somber adj. ilungarri, itzal, beltzilun.
some adj./pron. bat edo beste, hiruzpalau, hainbat, zenbait, batzuk, batzu; - ik. adv. pixka bat.
somebody pron. norbait, baten-bat, inor.
someday adv. egunen baten, noizbait.
somehow adv. nolabait, inolaz.
someone pron. norbait, inor, bat edo bat, nor edo nor.
somersault v.i. itzulipurdikatu, zilipurdikatu, gainazpikatu.
somersault n. iraulaldi, iraulketa, gainburuzketa, itzulipurdi.
something pron. zer, zertxobait, ezer, deus, zerbait, zer edo zer.
sometime adv. egunen baten, inoiz.
sometimes adv. batzutan, behin edo behin, behin edo beste, lantzean behin, noizbehinka, noizik behin, tarteka.
somewhat adv. samar.
somewhere adv. nonbait, norabait, noranahi, inora, inon, nora edo hara.
somnambulism n. ametsibilaldi, ametsibileria.
somnambulist n. ametsibiltzaile.
son n. seme. **Oldest son.** Seme nagusi. **First-born son.** Lehenseme.
sonata n. (mus.) sonata.
sonatina n. sonatatxo.
song n. abesti, kantika, kantu.
songwriter n. kantagile.
son-in-law n. suhi.
sonnet n. hamalauko, soneto.
son of a bitch n. putaseme, putakume.
sonority n. ozentasun, soinutasun.
sonorous adj. ozen, ozentsu, soinugarri, zoli, zolitasun, soinudun.
soon adv. berehala, laster, agudo. **As soon as possible.** Lehenbailehen.
soot n. gedar.
soothe v.t. eztitu.
soother n. baretzaile.
soothing adj. gozagarri, atsedengarri, baretzaile, gozatzaile, lasaigarri.
soothsayer n. errainazti.
sooty adj. gedartsu.
sop v.t./v.i. (batzutan **up**-ekin) xukatu; zopak egin, ardoztatu.
sophism n. sasiarrazoin.
sophisticated adj. kulturadun.
sophistication n. sofistikazio, jakinduria.
sophomore n. unibertsitate eta goieskoletako bigarren urteko ikaslea.
soporific adj. logarri, loeragile, loerazle, loeragingarri.
soprano n. (mus.) soprano, bozgoren.
sorcerer n. azti, sorgintzaile, aztigaizkile (gizon).
sorceress n. azti, aztigaizkile (emakume), sorgintzaile.
sorcery n. aztikeria, sorgingo, sorginkeria.

sordid adj. lohitsu.
sordidly adv. lohiki, zikinki, likiski.
sordidness n. zikintasun.
sore adj. minbera, minberatsu, mindun, mingor. **To get sore.** Minberatu. n. (med.) zornazorro.
soreness n. gaiztodura, mingortasun; -min.
sorority n. unibertsitateetan neskez osaturiko taldea.
sorrel n. (zool.) zaldigorri, belargazi, mingarratz.
sorrow n. atsekabe, nahigabe, damu, dolamen, dolu, pena, samindura.
sorrowful adj. atsekabetzaile, dolutsu, nahigabedun, atsekabetsu, penagarri, deitoragarri.
sorrowfully adv. atsekabeki, nahigabez, damuz, errukarriro.
sorry adj. damubera, damukor, urrikikor.
sort n. maila, mota.
sort of adv. erdipurdika, hala hola.
so-so adj. erdipurdiko, hala-holako. adv. erdipurdika, hala hola.
sought pret./p. part. of seek.
soul n. arima, izpiritu.
Soule n. (geog.) Zubero-.
soulful adj. maitabera.
sound v.i./v.t. hots egin, soinuztatu. v.t./v.i. zundatu.
sound n. joaldi, hots, soinu, zaratots. adj. sano, funtsezko, zentzudun. n. sondagailu.
sounding lead n. sondagailu, sondaneurri.
sounding line n. berun, sondagailu, sondasoka.
soundless adj. hoskabe, soinugabe.
soundlessness n. soinugabetasun.
soundly adv. sakonki. adv. gogorki, gogor.
soundness n. sendotasun, sanotasun.
soundproof adj. hoskabe.
soup n. salda, zopa, zuku.
soupy adj. saldadun, saldatsu, saldazko.
sour v.i./v.t. mikaztu, mingostu, mindu, garraztu, ozpindu.
sour adj. garratz, garraztu(a), mingots, mikatz, samin.
source n. iturri, iturburu, jatorri, sorrera.
sourness n. garrazkeria, garraztasun, mindura, mikaztasun, mingostasun.
soutane n. apaizsoineko, sotana.
south n. (geog.) hegoalde. adj. hegoko.
South Africa n. (geog.) Hegoafrika, Hegoafrikar Errepublika.
South African n./adj. hegoafrikar.
South America n. (geog.) Hegoamerika, Latinamerika.
South American n./adj. hegoamerikar, latinamerikar.
South Carolina n. (geog.) Estatu Batuetako estatu bat.

South Dakota n. (geog.) Estatu Batuetako estatu bat.
southeast n. (geog.) hegoekialde, hegosortalde.
southerly adj. hegoko.
southern adj. hegoaldeko.
southerner n. hegoar, betar.
southland n. hegoalde.
South Pole n. (geog.) hegoburu.
southwest n. hegosartalde, hegomendebalde. adj. hegosartaldeko, hegomendebaldeko.
souvenir n. oroikarri, gomutagarri.
sovereign n. errege, erregin.
sovereignty n. erregetza.
soviet n. (pol.) soviet. adj. sovietar.
Soviet Union n. (geog.) Sovietar Batasuna.
sow v.t. erein.
sow n. (zool.) zerrieme, txerrieme, urdama, urdanga.
sown p. part. of sow.
spa n. uretxe, bainuetxe.
space v.t. bakarkatu.
space n. eremu, une, lekune, zabalgune, tarteune. n. ortzi, ortzune; ortze-.
spaceship n. izarrontzi, ortzeontzi.
space shuttle n. hurbileko ortzeontzi.
spacious adj. tokidun, tokitsu, zabaltsu.
spaciously adv. zabalki, zabalkiro.
spaciousness n. zabalkortasun.
spade v.t. laiatu.
spade n. pala.
spadeful n. palakada.
spaghetti n. makarroi.
Spain n. (geog.) Espainia.
span n. (arch.) begi. n. arte, tarte. **Life span.** Bizitzaro.
Spaniard n. gaztelaniar, espainiar.
Spanish n./adj. espainiar, gaztelaniar. n. gaztelania, espainiera, gaztelera.
spank v.t. ipurdiak zaflatu.
spanking n. ipurdiko, zaflada.
spare v.t. barkatu. v.t. errukitu. v.t. utzi, salbuetsi.
spare adj. gehigarri, gaineratiko, osagarri. n. ordezko gurpil(a).
sparingly adv. urriki, eskaski.
spark v.i. txingartu, txinpartatu.
spark n. txinpart, zirta, brintza.
sparkle v.i./v.t. dizdiz egin, pindartu, ñirñir egin, distiratu.
sparkle n. dirdira, errainukada, distiraldi, pindar, ñirñira.
sparkling adj. dirdiragarri, distiragarri, ñirñirkari, ñirñirlari.
spark plug n. (mech.) buxia.
sparrow n. (zool.) txolarre, pardel, etxetxori.
sparrow hawk n. (zool.) gabirai, kabilara, zapelaitz.
sparse adj. eskas, urriki hedatu(a).
spasm n. giharrestura.
spasmodic adj. giharresturazko,

espasmodiko.
spat n. oinbabes, azmantar. n. iskanbila, haserraldi, mokokaldi.
spatial adj. lekuzko.
spatter v.t./v.i. zipristindu.
spawn v.i. errun (arrainak). v.t. sortu.
spawn n. arrainen errunketa.
speak v.i./v.t. hitz egin, mintzatu, solas egin, hizketatu.
speakeasy n. legezkanpoko taberna.
speaker n. hizlari, mintzatzaile, hitzegile, solasegile.
spear n. burtzi.
special adj. berezi, bestemunduko, aparteko, bat.
specialist n. berezlari.
speciality n. espezialitate, berezitasun.
specialization n. espezializapen, espezializazio.
specialize v.i./v.t. espezializatu, berezitu.
specially adv. bereziki.
specialty n. espezialitate, berezitasun.
species n. espezie, mota.
specifiable adj. berezgarri.
specific adj. konkretu, espezifiko.
specifically adv. zehazki, zehatz-mehatz, konkretuki.
specification n. zehazpen, zehazketa, espezifikazio.
specify v.t./v.i. konkretatu, espezifikatu, zehaztu.
specimen n. erakusgarri, erakuskin, eredu, modelu.
speck n. pikortadura, zetaka txiki.
spectacle n. ikuskizun, ikusketa.
spectacles n. (pl.) betaurrekoak.
spectacular adj. ikusgarri, ikusteko.
spectator n. ikusle, ikuslari.
specter n. zomorro, mamu.
speculate v.i. (askotan **on**-ekin) gogoetatu.
speculation n. teoria, baldintza, hipotesi. n. (econ.) dirujoko, espekulazio.
speculative adj. gogetari.
speech n. hitzaldi, mintzaldi, mintzo, solasaldi, berriketaldi. n. mintzaera, mintzaira, hizkuntza.
speechless adj. hizkabe, hitzgabe(ko), mintzogabe, mutu.
speechlessness n. ezinesana.
speed v.t./v.i. (askotan **up**-ekin) azeleratu.
speed n. abiadura, azkartasun, lastertasun.
speedily adv. laster, azkar, arin.
speedometer n. abiada-neurgailu.
speleologist n. leizeikerle.
speleology n. harpelaritza, leizeikerketa.
spell v.t./v.i. letrakatu.
spell n. begizko.
spellbound adj. liluratu(ta), xarmatu(a).
spelunker n. leizeikerle.
spelunking n. harpelaritza,

leizeikerketa.
spend v.t./v.i. gastatu, eralki, irazi. v.t. pasatu, iragan, igaro.
spendthrift n./adj. hondatzaile, parrastari, gastatzaile.
spent pret./p. part. of spend.
sperm n. (anat.) sortazi, esperma.
sperm whale n. (zool.) zeroi.
sphere n. globu, esfera.
spherical adj. esferadun, globudun.
spice n. espezia, ongailu.
spicy adj. biperdun.
spider n. (zool.) armiarma, armamio, lipu.
spiderweb n. armiarmasare.
spigot n. upazotz.
spike n. iltze luze. n. buruska.
spikenard n. (bot.) akara.
spill v.t./v.i. erion, jario, isuri.
spill n. erion, isurdura, isurketa.
spillable adj. jariogarri.
spillway n. isurtegi, isurtoki.
spin v.t. haritu, goruetan egin, ardaztu, irun. v.i. jiratu, biratu.
spinach n. (bot.) espinaka.
spinal cord n. (anat.) ornomuin.
spinal medulla n. (anat.) bizkarmuin, bizkarrezurmuin.
spindle n. ehunardatz.
spine n. (anat.) bizkarrezur.
spineless adj. bizkarrezurgabe. adj. zalantzako, koloka, indarge, txepel, beldurti.
spinner n. irule, ardazlari, gorulari.
spinning n. ardazketa, gorueta.
spinning top n. ziba, tronpa.
spinning wheel n. txirrika.
spinster n. neskazahar, mutxurdin.
spinsterhood n. ezkongabetasun, ezkongabezia.
spiny adj. elorritsu.
spiral v.i./v.t. kiribildu, kurubilkatu.
spiral n./adj. kiribil, kiribilo.
spire n. goi, gain, gailur.
spirit n. izpiritu, gogo.
spirited adj. suhar, zangar.
spiritual adj. izpirituzko, gogozko.
spiritualism n. izpiritismo. n. izpiritualitate.
spirituality n. izpiritutasun, izpiritualitate.
spiritualization n. izpiritualeztapen.
spiritualize v.t. izpiritualeztatu.
spiritually adv. gogoz, izpiritualki, izpirituz.
spiritualness n. izpiritutasun.
spit v.i./v.t. listu bota, listukatu, txistu egin, txistu(a) bota.
spit n. listu, ttu, txistu. n. burruntzi, erretegi.
spite n. hisi, gorroto, ezinikusi.
spiteful adj. herratsu.
spitefulness n. aiherkunde, herra, hegigo.
spittle n. adur, elder, lerde, lerderia.
spittoon n. tuontzi, listuontzi, txistuontzi.

splash *v.t./v.i.* txipristindu, zipristindu.
splash *n.* zirristada, plast, txipristin.
splashdown *n.* itsasoraketa.
splat *n.* zanpa, plaust.
splatter *v.t./v.i.* lohiztatu, zipristindu, txipristindu.
spleen *n. (anat.)* bare.
splendid *adj.* zoragarri.
splendidly *adv.* zoragarriki, zoragarriro.
splendidness *n.* zoragarritasun.
splendor *n.* handitasun, ospagarritasun. *n.* distira.
splice *n.* elkarrune, muturlotura.
splint *n. (med.)* oholtso.
splinter *v.t./v.i.* printzatu, izpikatu, izpitu.
splinter *n.* ezpal, brintza.
splintery *adj.* ezpalkor, ezpaltsu, printzatsu.
split *v.t./v.i.* erdibitu, erdibi egin, ezpaldu, ezpalkatu, arrakalatu.
split *n.* arrakala, arrail, arrailakadura, brintza.
spoil *v.t./v.i.* usteldu, kirastu, haratusteldu; zaharmindu. *v.t.* alferrikaldu, andeatu. *v.t.* mainatu.
spoilable *adj.* ustelerraz, ustelgarri, andeagarri.
spoilage *n.* andea, andeamendu, usteldura.
spoiled *adj.* ustel. *adj.* mainadun, mainati, mainatsu; mizkin.
spoiledness *n.* ustelkeria, usteltasun. *n.* milikeria.
spoiler *n.* andeari, andeatzaile, usteltzaile. *n.* hondatzaile, etxekalte.
spoils of war *n.* gudakin.
spoilsport *n.* jaihondatzaile, bestanahasle.
spoke *pret. of speak.*
spoken *adj.* mintzozko. *p. part. of speak.*
spokesman *n.* bozeramale (gizon).
spokesperson *n.* bozeramale.
spokeswoman *n.* bozeramale (emakume).
sponge *v.t. (askotan off-ekin)* belakiz garbitu. *v.i. (off)* jantxakur izan.
sponge *n.* belaki.
sponginess *n.* fardotasun.
spongy *adj.* harro, belakitsu.
sponsor *v.t.* babestu, lagundu.
sponsor *n.* babestzaile, eskuemale.
sponsored *adj.* babespeko.
sponsorship *n.* eskuemate, babeste.
spontaneity *n.* berezkotasun, olde.
spontaneous *adj.* berezko, oldezko, oharkabe.
spontaneously *adv.* berez, bereburuz, oldez, oldezki.
spook *n.* mamu, mozorro.
spooked *adj.* izukor, izuti.
spooky *adj.* izuti, izukor.
spool *v.t.* matazatu.
spool *n.* harigailu, hariltegi, hastari, bobina.

spoon *v.t.* goilarez atera.
spoon *n.* goilare, zalixka.
spoonful *n.* goilarekada.
sporadic *adj.* noizbehingo, noizbehinkako.
spore *n. (biol.)* espora.
sport *n.* joko, kirol(a), jolas.
sporting *adj.* kirolezko.
sportive *adj.* kirolzale.
sportiveness *n.* kiroltza.
sports *adj.* kirolezko. *n. (pl.)* kirolak.
sports-loving *adj.* kirolzale.
sportsman *n.* kirolari; ehizlari.
sportsmanship *n.* kirol etika.
sporty *adj.* jolaszale.
spot *v.t./v.i.* lohitu, narriotu, zetakatu, orbaindu. *v.t.* ikusi.
spot *n.* izpil, lohiune, zikin, lauso, orbain. *n.* toki, lekune, une.
spotless *adj.* kutsugabe, orbaingabe.
spotlight *n.* foku.
spottable *adj.* orbaingarri.
spotted *adj.* nabar, pikart, orbaindun, zikintsu. *adj.* izpildun.
spouse *n.* ezkontide, bizikide, bizilagun.
spout *n.* kafe edo teontziaren aho(a).
sprain *v.t.* trokatu, hankokertu.
sprain *n. (med.)* hezurbihurketa, trokaketa, zainbihurketa, bihurri, zaintiraketa.
spray *v.t./v.i.* pirrist egin.
sprayer *n.* ihinztailu, bustigailu.
spread *v.t./v.i.* zabaldu, hedanbanatu, sakabanatu, barreiatu.
spread *n.* hedapen, hedamen.
spreadability *n.* hedagarritasun, hedakortasun.
spreadable *adj.* barreiagarri, hedakor, zabalgarri, zabalkor.
spree *n.* parranda.
sprig *n.* erromuskil.
spring *n.* udaberri. *n.* iturbegi, iturritza, urbegi. *n. (mech.)* bultzagailu, eragingailu, malgugailu. *adj.* udaberriko, udaberritiar.
springboard *n.* saltagailu.
springtime *n.* udaberri.
springy *adj.* malgu.
sprinkle *v.t./v.i.* ihinztatu, garastatu, zipristindu.
sprinkler *n.* bustigailu, garastailu, ihinztailu.
sprint *n.* arinaldi.
sprite *n.* iratxo.
sprout *v.i./v.t.* kimatu, buztandu, erne, garatu, ninikatu, muskildu.
sprout *n.* kimu, kimetz, muskil, ninika, txerto.
spruce up *v.t./v.i.* panpinatu, panpindu, panpoxtu.
spud *n. (fam.)* patata.
spume *n.* ahobits.
spur *v.t./v.i.* ezproindu, akuilatu, akuilukatu.
spur *n.* akuilu, ezproin.
spurious *adj.* legezkanpoko, faltsu,

sasiko, bort.
spurn v.t. arbuiatu, mespreziatu,
erdeinatu.
spurt v.t./v.i. zirrist egin.
spurt n. zurrusta. n. bizkorraldi.
spy v.i./v.t. zelatatu, zelatan egon,
barrendatu, ikuskatu.
spy n. zelatari, barrendari, espioi.
spyglass n. kataloxa.
squabble n. liskar, mokokaldi,
mokoketa, muturketa.
squad n. gudaritaldetxo.
squalid adj. zikin.
squall n. zurrunbilo, zirimola,
itsasekaitz.
squalor n. arloteria.
squander v.t. irion, diru hondatu.
square v.t. (batzutan off-ekin) laukitu,
laukotu. v.i. (with) ados egon.
square n./adj. lauki, laukotu, koadratu.
n. plaza, enparantza.
squared adj. koadratu, laukotu,
laukizko. adj. (math.) ber bi.
squarely adv. aurrez-aurre. adv.
zuzenki, prestuki. adv. gogorki,
sendoki.
squareness n. laukitasun.
squash v.t./v.i. zuzitu, tinkatu.
squash n. (bot.) kuia, kalabaza. n.
squash.
squat v.i./v.t. kokorikatu, kukubilkatu,
uzkurtu.
squat n. kukubilkapen, uzkurpen. adj.
lodikote, potzolo.
squeak v.i./v.t. kirrinka egin, kirrinkatu,
karrankatu.
squeak n. kirrinka.
squeaking adj. kirrinkari. **The
squeaking door.** Ate kirrinkaria.
squeal v.i./v.t. kurrinkatu, kurrinka
egin.
squeal n. kurrinkada.
squeamish adj. okabera, okagarri.
squeeze v.t./v.i. hertsi, hertsitu,
prentsatu, trinkatu, eskuztatu,
maisatu.
squid n. (zool.) txipiroi.
squint v.i./v.t. ezkeldu.
squint n. (med.) ezkeltasun.
squint-eyed adj. begizehar.
squirm v.i. bihurka mugitu.
squirrel n. (zool.) urtxintxa, katagorri.
squirt v.t. zirriztarazi.
St. "saint"-aren laburpena; saindu.
stab v.t./v.i. sastakatu, sastatu,
aiztokatu.
stab n. sastada, sastako.
stability n. egonkortasun, finkotasun,
iraunkortasun.
stabilization n. egonkortzapen,
estabilizazio.
stabilize v.t./v.i. estabilizatu, finkatu,
egonkortu.
stabilizer n. egonkortzaile, finkatzaile.
stable v.t./v.i. ukuiluratu, gortaratu.
stable n. gorta, abeletxe, ikuilu, itegi,
abeldegi, zamaltegi. adj. egonkor,

iraugarri, irmo, finko.
stably adv. iraungarriro, iraunkorki.
staccato adj. (mus.) staccato.
stack v.t. pilatu, metatu.
stack n. meta.
stadium n. kiroldegi, kirolzelai.
staff n. eskuko, bidemakila,
eskumakila. n. pertsonal. n. (mus.)
pentagrama.
stag n. (zool.) orein, basahuntz, orkatz.
stage n. etapa, bilakaune. n.
antzeztoki, agertoki.
stagecoach n. Estatu Batuetako
aintzinako zaldigurdia.
stagger v.i./v.t. ganguren-manguren
ibili, zabu egin, zabukatu. v.t.
mailakatu.
stagger n. balantza, balantzaketa.
stagnant adj. geldi, hil. **Stagnant
water.** Ur hilak.
stagnate v.i. urbildu, urmindu.
stagnation n. urmindura.
stain v.t./v.i. likistu, likistatu, lohitu,
narriotu, odoleztatu.
stain n. kedarketa, lohiune, lohidura.
stainable adj. zikingarri.
stained adj. zikintsu.
stained glass n. beiraleiho, beirateria.
stainless adj. garbi, orbangabe. adj.
herdoilgaitz.
stair n. eskilara maila.
staircase n. eskilara, zurubi, mailadi.
stair landing n. eskilaraburu.
stairs n. eskilara, zurubi.
stairway n. eskilara, zurubi.
stake v.t. (out) taketez mugatu. v.t.
arriskutu.
stake n. taket, hesohol.
stalactite n. aitznegar, estalaktita.
stalagmite n. estalakmita.
stale adj. zahar, urtedun, gardinga. adj.
zikin (haize).
staleness n. gardingadura.
stalk v.i./v.t. isilpean segitu.
stalk n. (bot.) zurtoin, zuzter.
stall n. abeletxe, gorta.
stallion n. (zool.) kalano, zikiratu
gabeko zaldi(a).
stamen n. (bot.) lorazil.
stamina n. kemen, indar.
stammer v.i./v.t. erdimintzatu, toteldu,
zizakatu.
stammerer n. moteldura, toteldura.
stammerer n. zezel, motel.
stammering n. erdimintzo, zezel,
esanezina, zizaka, totel-motel.
stamp v.t./v.i. ostikatu, zanpatu,
lehartu. v.t. zigilatu, seilatu. v.t.
moldeztatu.
stamp n. seilu. n. tanpoi, zigilu.
stampede v.i./v.t. ohildu, uxatu.
stance n. egoera, jarrera. n. iritzi, uste,
joera, jokabide.
stanch v.t. odoljarioa gelditu.
stanchion n. besanga, abe.
stand v.i./v.t. (batzutan up-ekin) zutitu,
zutik egon, tentetu, jeiki. v.i. (out)

nabarmendu, buruzagitu, gailendu.
stand *n.* oinpeko.
standard *n.* zutoihal, bandera. *n.*
neurri, maila. **Standard of living.**
Bizimaila. *n.* arau. *adj.* arrunt.
standardization *n.* normaleztapen,
normalizazio.
standardize *v.t./v.i.* normaldu,
normalizatu.
stand-by *n.* konfidantzazko pertsona.
stand-in *n.* lagunorde.
standing *n.* egoera. *n.* aipu, entzute,
fama.
stand-offish *adj.* hotz.
standpoint *n.* ikuspuntu, ikuspegi.
standstill *n.* geldi, geldiune, geldialdi.
stanza *n.* ahapaldi, bertso.
staple *v.t.* grapatu.
staple *n.* grapa, granpoi.
stapler *n.* grapagailu.
star *n.* izar. *n.* astro.
starboard *n./adj. (naut.)* eskuinalde,
estibor, istribor.
starch *v.t.* almidoiztu.
starch *n.* almidoi.
stare *v.i./v.t. (v.i., askotan* at*-ekin)*
begi-begi egon, begiratu.
starfish *n. (zool.)* itsasizar.
starlight *n.* izarniadura.
starry *adj.* izarratu, izarti, izartsu.
starship *n.* izarrontzi.
start *v.i./v.t.* hasi. *v.t./v.i.* mugiarazi,
piztu.
start *n.* hasiera, hastapen. *n.* martxa.
starter *n. (mech.)* azeleragailu. *n.*
mugitzaile.
startle *v.t./v.i.* miretsarazi, sarrakiotu.
starvation *n.* gosemin, gosegorri.
starve *v.i./v.t.* gosez hil.
starving *adj.* goseti.
stash *n.* gordailu, gordeleku,
ebaskindegi.
state *n.* egoeraldi, egoera. *n. (pol.)*
estatu.
stateliness *n.* ospetasun.
stately *adj.* ospetsu.
statement *n.* planteamendu.
statesman *n.* estatugizon,
gobernugizon, estatari.
statesmanship *n.* estatariaren
abilidadea, estatugizonaren
ahalmena.
station *n.* geltoki, estazio.
stationary *adj.* geldikor, gerakor,
mugigabe, mugigaitz.
stationery *n.* idazpaper.
stationmaster *n.* geltokiburu,
geltokizain.
statistical *adj.* estatistikako.
statistician *n.* estatistikalari.
statistics *n.* estatistika.
statuary *n.* irudi-bilduma,
estatu-bilduma.
statue *n.* irudi, imajina, estatu.
stature *n.* gizaluzera.
status *n.* egoera, status. *n.* lerrun.
statute *n. (pol.)* estatutu.

statutory *n.* estatutuzko.
staunch *v.t.* odoljarioa geldiarazi.
staunch *adj.* zintzo, leial, hitzezko.
stave *v.i. (off)* gelditu, geratu, eragotzi,
galarazi. *v.i. (in)* upaoholak hautsi.
stave *n.* upohol.
stay *v.i.* egon, gelditu, geratu. *v.i.*
ostatatu. *v.t.* geldi, bertanbehera
utzi.
stay *n.* egote, euskarri, egonaldi.
stead *n.* ordezkariak hartzen duen
lekua.
steadfast *adj.* tinko, irmo.
steadfastness *n.* finkadura.
steadily *adv.* irmoki, tinkoki,
etengabeki.
steadiness *n.* atxikitasun.
steady *v.t./v.i.* tinkotu.
steady *adj.* etengabe, tinko, finko,
irmo.
steak *n.* xerra.
steal *v.t./v.i.* ebatsi, lapurtu, ostu,
lapurretan egin, ohoindu. *v.i.* kontuz
ibili, isilpean ibili.
stealth *n.* zelata.
stealthily *adv.* isilik, izkutuan.
stealthy *adj.* izkutuko, isileko.
steam *v.i./v.t.* lurrun egin. *v.t./v.i. (up)*
lainotu.
steam *n.* lurrin, lurrun.
steamboat *n.* lurrinontzi.
steamed *adj.* lurrintsu.
steamroller *n.* zapalgailu, alferrarri.
steamship *n.* baporontzi.
steamy *adj.* lurrintsu, lurrindun.
steed *n.* zaldi.
steel *n.* altzairu; altzairutsu. *adj.*
altzairuzko.
steely *adj.* altzairutsu.
steep *v.t./v.i.* urberatu, urtatu.
steep *adj.* maldatsu, aldapatsu.
steeple *n.* kanpandorre.
steeply *adv.* malkortsuki.
steepness *n.* patartasun.
steer *v.t./v.i.* gidatu, lematu.
steer *n.* ganadu.
steerable *adj.* gidagarri.
steering wheel *n.* gobernagailu.
stein *n.* garagardoa edateko pitxar(ra).
stellar *adj.* izarretako, izarren; izar-.
stem *n.* enbor.
stench *n.* kirats, hats, kirastasun.
stenographer *n.* takigrafari.
stenographic *adj.* takigrafiko.
stenographically *adv.* takigrafikoki.
stenography *n.* takigrafia.
step *v.i./v.t.* oinkada bat egin. *v.t. (on)*
hankapetu, zangopetu, oinazpitu. *v.i.*
(on it) presatu, lasterka ibili, laster
egin.
step *n.* maila, etapa. *n.* pauso, urrats,
oinkada.
step- *(gram.)* -orde.
stepchild *n.* ugazume.
stepbrother *n.* anaiorde, ugazanaia.
stepdaughter *n.* ugazalaba, alaborde.
stepfather *n.* aitorde, ugazaita.

stepladder *n.* eskueskilara.
stepmother *n.* ugazama, amorde.
steps *n.* eskailera, zurubi, mailadi.
stepsister *n.* ahizporde, ugazahizpa, ugazarreba.
stepson *n.* semeorde, ugazeme.
stereo *n.* estereo.
stereotype *n.* estereotipo.
sterile *adj.* elkor, idor, antzu. *adj.* haurgabe, agor, sabelehor.
sterility *n.* agortasun, antzutasun, elkortasun, idortasun.
sterilization *n.* agorketa, antzuketa.
sterilize *v.t.* esterilizatu. *v.t.* antzutu.
sterling *adj. (econ.)* esterlina.
stern *adj.* gogor, bortitz. *n.* popa, txopa.
sternly *adv.* gogorki, bortizki.
sternness *n.* gogorkeria, bortizkeria.
sternpost *n. (naut.)* koasta.
sternum *n. (anat.)* bularrezur.
stethoscope *n. (med.)* bularrikuskin.
stethoscopy *n. (med.)* bularrikuspen.
stevedore *n.* kargari, zamaketari, deskargatzaile.
stew *v.t./v.i.* erregosi.
stew *n.* eltzeko, lapikoko, menestra.
steward *n.* aeromutil, itsasmutil, txo.
stewardess *n.* aeroneska, azafata.
stewpot *n.* eltze.
stick *v.t./v.i.* likatu, iratxeki, itsatsi, erantsi.
stick *n.* makila, eskumakila, palu.
sticker *n.* eranskailu, eranskin.
stickiness *n.* itsaskortasun, likatasun, likinkeria, likits.
sticky *adj.* eranskor, itsaskor, likitsu, likiskor.
stiff *adj.* sor, sormindun, hilgogor, zurrun.
stiffen *v.t./v.i.* sormindu, zurrundu.
stiffness *n.* sortasun, zutitasun, zurmintasun, zurruntasun, larderia.
stifle *v.t./v.i.* ito. *v.t.* itzali.
stifling *adj.* itogarri, berogarri.
stigma *n.* izentxar. *n.* zaurimarka.
stigmatize *v.t.* zaurimarkatu. *v.t.* izenlohitu.
stiletto *n.* eztentxo.
still *adj.* geldi. *adv.* oraindik.
stillness *n.* baretasun, egonaldi, geldiera, patxada.
stimulant *n.* biztugarri, ernagarri, eragintza.
stimulate *v.t./v.i.* zirikatu, ziztatu, adoretu, esnatu, kilikatu, gogoa berotu, akuilatu.
stimulating *adj.* bizikor, bizkortzaile, ernagarri, iratzargarri, bizigarri, susperkor, ziztakor.
stimulation *n.* eragin, zirikaldi, bizikortasun, ernarazpen, kitzika.
stimulator *n.* zirikatzaile, eztenkatzaile, kilikari.
stimulus *n.* zirikaketa, eragite, aurrerabide.
sting *v.t./v.i.* pikatu, eztenkatu,

erremindu.
sting *n.* eztenkada, mizto, izpi.
stinger *n.* ezten, eztenkari, izpi.
stingily *adv.* zekenki, zikoizki, zimurki, zuhurkeriaz.
stinginess *n.* zekenkeria, zikoizkeria, zuhurkeria.
stingy *adj.* zeken, zikoitz, bekaitz, eskulabur. **To be stingy.** Zikoiztu. Zekendu.
stink *v.i./v.t. (v.t., batzutan up-ekin)* ufaztu, gaizki usaindu.
stink *n.* kirats, hats, kirastasun.
stinking *adj.* kirastsu, kirastun.
stint *v.t./v.i.* mugajarri, mugatu; neurtu.
stint *n.* muga, mugapen, neurri.
stipend *n.* mezasari, mezadiru.
stipulate *v.i./v.t.* baldintzatu, baldindu; derrigortu.
stipulation *n.* baldintza, baldintzapen.
stir *v.t./v.i.* higitu, mugitu, inarroskatu, kitzikatu.
stirrup *n.* oinburdin.
stitch *n.* jostura, puntu, puntada.
stock *v.t./v.i. (v.i., askotan up-ekin)* hornitu, ornitu.
stock *n. (econ.)* balore, akzio. *n.* hornigai.
stockade *n.* hesoholbarruti.
stockbreeder *n.* abeltzain.
stockholder *n.* akzionista.
stockings *n. (pl.)* galtzerdiak.
stocky *adj.* mozkote.
stoic *n./adj.* pairugabe, estoiko.
stoke *v.t./v.i.* su eragin, su bizitu.
stoker *n.* sugile, sugin, kaldatzaile.
stole *n. (eccl.)* estola. *pret. of steal.*
stolen *adj.* lapurretako. *p. part. of steal.*
stolid *adj.* ezsentibera, ezminbera.
stomach *n. (anat.)* sabel, sabelzorro, tripa, urdail.
stomp *v.t./v.i.* oinkatu, oinperatu, ostikopetu, zapaldu.
stomper *n.* oinkatzaile, oinperatzaile, zanpatzaile.
stone *v.t.* harrikatu, harrika egin.
stone *n.* harri, haitz, losa. *adj.* harrizko. *n. (med.)* pixarri.
stonecutter *n.* harlangile, harrigile, hargin.
stony *adj.* harritsu, harkaitsu, harriantzeko.
stood *pret./p. part. of stand.*
stooge *n.* inozo, tentel.
stool *n.* aulki.
stoop *v.i./v.t.* kukutu.
stop *v.t./v.i.* gelditu, geratu. *v.t. (askotan up-ekin)* tapoitu, tapoindu, zipoztu, txantoldu.
stop *n.* egonaldi, geldialdi, geraldi, geldiune; geltoki; stop.
stoppable *adj.* geldigarri.
stopper *n.* gelditzaile, geratzaile. *n.* tako, taket, zipotz, tapoi.
storable *adj.* zaingarri.
storage *n.* biltegiratze, bilkuntza.

store *v.t./v.i.* gorde, ganbaratu, sabairatu.
store *n.* denda.
storehouse *n.* zaindegi.
storekeeper *n.* dendari.
storeroom *n.* baztergela.
stork *n. (zool.)* zikoina, amiamoko.
storm *v.i.* ekaiztu. *v.t.* eraso.
storm *n.* ekaitz, zurrunbilo, zirimola.
stormy *adj.* ekaiztsu, zurrunbilotsu.
story *n.* ipuin, istorio, kontaketa, kontu.
storyteller *n.* kontalari, ipuinlari.
stout *adj.* mamijario, sendor, biribil.
stove *n.* sukalde, sutegi.
stow *v.t.* gorde, metatu, pilatu.
stowaway *n.* isil-bidazti,
• izkutuko-bidazti.
straggler *n.* ardigaldu.
straight *adj.* artez, zuzen, zuzeneko. *adv.* artez, zuzenki, zuzen, zuzenka.
straight ahead *adv.* artez-artez, bidez-bide.
straighten *v.t./v.i.* arteztu, zuzendu. *v.t./v.i.* **(up)** zutikatu.
straightenable *adj.* arteztu, zuzendu.
straightforward *adj.* egiazko, zuzen.
straightforwardly *adv.* bipilki.
straightly *adv.* zuzenean.
straightness *n.* zuzentasun, zutitasun, tentetasun.
strain *v.t./v.i.* tenk egin, tiratu. *v.t.* iragazi, irazi.
strain *n.* presio.
strainer *n.* iragazgailu, iragazkin, iraztontzi.
strait *n. (geog.)* itsasestu, mehargune, itsasarte. *n. (pl.)* estualdi, herstura, larrialdi.
strand *v.t.* galduta utzi.
strand *n.* piru, lits.
strange *adj.* arrotz, kanpotar, sinotsu, aldrebes.
strangely *adv.* harrigarriro.
strangeness *n.* sino.
stranger *n.* arrotz, atzerritar, kanpotar, ezezagun.
strangle *v.t./v.i.* ito arazi, ito.
strangler *n.* itoarazle, itotzaile.
strangulation *n.* itoketa, itodura.
strap *n.* hede, uhal.
strapping *adj.* sendo, gorputz-handiko.
strata *n. (pl.)* estratuak, geruzak, lurmailak.
stratagem *n.* gako-mako, kalamatrika.
strategic *adj.* estrategiko.
strategy *n.* estrategia.
stratification *n.* geruzapen.
stratum *n. (geol.)* geruza, estratu, lurmaila.
straw *n.* lasto, zuhain. *adj.* lastozko.
strawberry *n.* marrubi.
stray *v.i.* galdu, aldendu, desbidetu.
stray *n.* pizti galdu(a).
streak *n.* arrasto luze eta estua.
stream *v.i./v.t.* zurrutatu, isuri.
stream *n.* erreka, bidaso.
street *n.* kale, karrika. **Dead-end**

street. Kale itsu.
streetcar *n.* tranbia. **Streetcar conductor.** Tranbiari.
strength *n.* indar, gogortasun, kemen, sendotasun, irmotasun.
strengthen *v.t./v.i.* indartu, indar eman, gogortu, bizkorrerazi, kemendu, sendotu.
strengthener *n.* sendotzaile.
strenuous *adj.* zail, gaitz. *adj.* sendo, indartsu.
strenuously *adv.* sendo, sendoki.
stress *v.t.* azentuatu.
stress *n.* stress, tentsio. *n.* azentu.
stressed *adj.* azentudun. *adj.* stressdun, tentsiodun.
stressful *adj.* herstu, hertsi, larri.
stretch *v.t./v.i.* luzatu, luzarazi, tirakatu, teinkatu. *v.i.* **(out)** etzandu.
stretch *n.* nagibotaketa. *n.* etapa, bidegune, tarteune.
stretcher *n.* anda, angaila. *n.* luzatzaile.
stretchiness *n.* nasaitasun, elastikotasun.
strew *v.t.* sakabanatu, barreiatu, zabaldu.
strewn *p. part. of* strew.
striate *v.t.* koskatu.
striation *n.* koskadura.
stricken *adj.* zauritu(a); atsekabedun, penadun.
strict *adj.* amoregaitz, bortitz, hertsi, zehatz.
strictly *adv.* hertsiki, hertsiro, estuki.
strictness *n.* hertsitasun.
stride *n.* urrats, zangokada. **Long stride.** Urrats luze.
strident *adj.* karrankari, oihukari.
strife *n.* indarketa, indarkaldi.
strike *v.t./v.i.* jo, kolpatu, jipoitu. *v.t.* burura etorri. *v.i.* greba egin. *v.i.* tximista jausi.
strike *n.* greba, lanuzte. *n.* eraso, erasoaldi.
striker *n.* grebari.
striking *adj.* itzal, harrigarri, sekulako.
string *v.t./v.i.* kordatu, txirikordatu. *v.t.* musika-tresna bati kordak ipini.
string *n.* hari, korda, kordel.
stringy *adj.* haritsu, pirutsu, izpitsu.
strip *v.t./v.i.* biluztu, erantzi, larrugorritu.
strip *n.* zerrenda, listoi.
stripe *n.* zerrenda, marra, lerro.
striped *adj.* marradun, lerrodun, zerrendadun.
strive *v.i.* gogor saiatu, buru-belarri ahalegindu.
stroke *v.t.* ferekatu.
stroke *n.* fereka, lausengu. *n.* arraunaldi, arraunkada. *n. (med.)* sorreri.
stroll *v.i./v.t.* egurastu.
stroll *n.* oinezaldi.
strong *adj.* indartsu, kementsu, gotor, indardun, sotil. **To become strong.**

Indartu. *adj.* sano, sendo. *adj.* mutiri. *adj.* mardul. *adj.* bizi.

stronghold *n.* gotorleku, babestoki, gordeleku.

strongly *adv.* gogorki, indarrez. *adv.* sendo, sendoki, sanoki.

strophe *n.* ahapaldi.

strove *pret. of strive*

struck *pret./p. part. of strike*

structural *adj.* egiturazko.

structure *v.t.* estrukturatu, egituratu.

structure *n.* egitura, molde, plan, barnegitura.

struggle *v.i./v.t.* gogor egin, indarkatu, burrukatu, burrukan egin, borrokatu.

struggle *n.* borroka, indarketa, jazar.

struggler *n.* borrokalari, borrokagile.

strum *v.t.* kitarra zarrastatu.

stubborn *adj.* burugogor, kaskagogor, temakor, temati, setati. **To be stubborn.** Burukoitu.

stubbornly *adv.* burugogorki, temaz, setatsuki, setaz.

stubbornness *n.* burugogortasun, kaskagogorkeria, kasketaldi, seta, tema.

stubby *adj.* kamuts.

stucco *n.* iztuku.

stuck *pret./p. part. of stick.*

stuck-up *adj.* harroputz.

stud *n.* hazitarako.

student *n.* ikasle.

student body *n.* unibertsitalgo.

studies *n. (pl.)* ikaskuntza, ikasketa, karrera.

studio *n.* estudio. *n.* telebista estudio.

studious *adj.* ikasgale, ikaskor, ikaszale, jakintzale.

studiously *adv.* sendoki, tinkoki.

studiousness *n.* ikasnahai, ikaszaletasun.

study *v.i./v.t.* ikasi; ikertu.

study *n.* ikasketa, ikaspen, ikertzapen. *n.* etxeko ikasgela.

studying *n.* ikaskunde, ikaste.

stuff *v.t./v.i.* asearazi, janerazi, gaineztu. *v.t.* disekatu, lastoztu.

stuffable *adj.* disekagarri.

stuffed *adj.* ase-ase, okagarri. *adj.* disekatu.

stuffing *n.* betekin.

stuffy *adj.* itogarri.

stumble *v.i./v.t.* behaztopatu, behaztopa egin, oztopatu.

stumble *n.* oztopaldi, behaztopa.

stumbler *n.* behaztopatzaile, behaztopari.

stump *n.* motzondo; besondo.

stun *v.t.* sorgortu.

stung *pret./p. part. of sting.*

stunning *adj.* harrigarri, izugarri. *adj.* oso eder.

stunt *n.* gorputz-liraintasunaren erakustaldea.

stupefy *v.t.* txunditu.

stupefying *adj.* txundikor.

stupendous *adj.* harrigarri, miragarri.

stupendously *adv.* primeran, oso ondo.

stupid *adj.* buruhandi, geldo, inozo, tonto, zozo, tentel, ergel.

stupidity *n.* ergelkeria, burugabekeria, inozokeria, lelokeria, tentelkeria, tontakeria, zozotasun, geldokeria.

stupidly *adv.* tentelki, inozoki, zozoki, ergelki, tontoki.

stupidness *n.* ergeltasun, tentelkeria.

stupor *n.* lozorro.

sturdy *adj.* sendo, indartsu.

stutter *v.t./v.i.* erdimintzatu, ahomoteldu, toteldu.

stutterer *n.* ahomotel, totel, tartamutu.

sty *n. (med.)* txindor, begitxindor. *n.* zerrikorta, urdandegi.

style *n.* gisa, modu, era, molde. *n.* tankera, idazkera. *n.* apainkera.

stylish *adj.* apaindu(a).

stylistic *adj.* estilistiko.

suave *adj.* erabidetsu, gizatsu, modu oneko.

sub *n.* murgilontzi, urpeontzi.

sub- *(gram.)* azpi-, behe-.

subcommittee *n.* azpibatzorde.

subconscious *n.* behekonzientzia. *adj.* behekonzientziazko, behekonzientie.

subcutaneous *adj.* larruazpiko, azalazpiko, larruarteko, larrupeko.

subdivide *v.t./v.i.* behezatitu, birzatitu.

subdivision *n.* behezatiketa, birzatiketa.

subdue *v.t.* menderatu, azpiratu, azpikotu.

subgroup *n.* azpitalde.

subhuman *adj.* gizapeko.

subject *v.t.* (**to**) eskuperatu, oinazpitu, menperatu.

subject *n.* gai, pondu, idazkai. *n.* mendeko, manupeko, agindupeko. *n.* (*gram.*) sujetu. *adj.* meneko, aginpeko, mendeko.

subjected *adj.* mendeko.

subjection *n.* menperaketa, manupekotasun, azpirapen, menperaldi.

subjective *adj.* norberakiko, subjetibo.

subjectively *adv.* subjetiboki.

subjectiveness *n.* subjetibotasun.

subjectivism *n.* subjetibismo.

subjectivity *n.* norberakeria, norberekikotasun, subjetibotasun.

subjugable *adj.* menderagarri, menperagarri, uztargarri.

subjugate *v.t.* meneratu, menperatu, oinperatu, azpiratu, morroindu.

subjugated *adj.* azpiratu(a).

subjugation *n.* menderaketa, menderapen, menperapen.

subjugator *n.* menperatzaile, oinperatzaile, azpiratzaile.

subjunctive *n.* (*gram.*) subjuntiboera. *adj.* subjuntibo.

sublimate *v.t./v.i.* sublimatu.

sublime *adj.* goieneko, goi-goiko. *n.* goientasun, gorentasun, goratasun.

submachine gun n. metraileta.
submarine n. murgilontzi, urpeontzi.
  adj. itsaspeko.
submerge v.t./v.i. murgildu, urperatu,
  itsasperatu.
submergible adj. murgilgarri,
  urperagarri, hondoragarri.
submersible adj. murgilgarri,
  urperagarri, hondoragarri.
submersion n. pulunpaldi, urperaldi,
  murgildura.
submission n. agindupe,
  manupekotasun, menekotasun,
  azpirapen.
submissive adj. azpiko, eskupeko,
  mendeko, menperakoi, manupeko,
  meneragarri.
submissively adv. menpez.
submissiveness n. azpikotasun,
  manukortasun, menpetasun.
submit v.t. aurkeztu, azaldu, eskaini.
  v.t./v.i. (v.i., **to**-ekin) menpetu,
  menpekotu, meneratu.
subordinate v.t. (askotan **to**-ekin)
  behezarri, aginpetu, manupetu.
subordinate adj. eskupeko, azpiko,
  menpeko, aginpeko.
subordinately adv. eskupean,
  mendean.
subordination n. azpikotasun, eskupe,
  mendekotasun, menpe, menpetasun,
  menerapen.
suborn v.t. erosi, busti.
subornation n. eskuazpikeria.
suborner n. koipemale, erosle,
  bustitzaile.
subpoena n. auzitegiko dei(a).
subscribe v.t./v.i. harpidetu.
subscriber n. harpidedun, izenemaile.
subscription n. harpide, harpidetza.
subsection n. behezatiketa,
  birzatiketa.
subsequent adj. geroztikako,
  hurrenondoko, geroztiko.
subsequently adv. geroz, arrezkeroz,
  geroztikan.
subsequentness n. hurrentasun.
subservience n. morroikeria.
subservient adj. menperakoi,
  gizabidetsu; morroi-.
subserviently adv. morroigisa.
subside v.i. hondoratu, beheratu. v.i.
  baretu.
subsidiary adj. eskumenpeko.
subsidize v.t. diruz lagundu.
subsidy n. dirulaguntza.
subsist v.i. nekez bizi, iraun, jarraitu,
  izan.
subsistence n. iraupen.
substance n. muin, ekai, ganora.
substantial adj. mamidun, mamitsu,
  mamizko. adj. egiazko. adj. sendo,
  indartsu. adj. garrantzitsu. adj. handi.
substantially adv. handiki. adv.
  egiazki, egitan.
substitute v.t./v.i. (v.i., askotan
  for-ekin) ordezkatu, ordeztatu,

ordeztu, aldikatu, oinordetu.
substitute n. ordezkari, ordezkatzaile,
  ordezko, ordain, lekuko,
  ordeztatzaile.
substitution n. ordezkapen,
  ordezketa, ordeztapen.
substratum n. behestratu, substratu.
substructure n. azpiegitura,
  oinegitura.
subterfuge n. inguru-minguru,
  ingurukeria.
subterranean adj. lurpeko, lurrazpiko.
subtitle v.t. azpidatzi (filmetan).
subtitle n. azpizenburu, azpititulu.
subtle adj. mehe, mehar, fin.
subtlety n. mehetasun. n. zorroztasun.
  n. jite ona, samurtasun.
subtly adv. finki.
subtract v.t./v.i. kendu.
subtraction n. (arith.) kenketa,
  zenbakenketa.
subtractive adj. kentzaile.
subtractor n. kentzaile.
subtrahend n. (arith.) kenkari.
subtropical adj. tropikopeko.
suburb n. bailara, hiringuru, auzategi,
  auzune.
suburban adj. hiringuruko.
subvention n. dirulaguntza.
subversion n. gainazpikaldi,
  iraulkortasun, iraultza.
subversive adj. iraulkor.
subvert v.t. gainbeheratu, gainazpi
  egin.
subway n. azpibide, lurbarren. n.
  metro.
succeed v.i./v.t. burutu, arrakasta izan.
success n. arrakasta, aurrerakunde.
successful adj. arrakastatsu,
  aurrerakor.
succession n. jarraikera, oinordekotza,
  ondoretasun, lerro. n. ondorengotza,
  ondorengotasun.
successive adj. gaurgerozko,
  geroagoko.
successively adv. segidan.
successor n. jarraile, ondoko,
  ondorengo, oinordeko.
succinctly adv. labur.
succor n. laguntza, laguntasun.
succumb v.i. erori, hil.
such adj./pron. honelako, hain.
suck v.t./v.i. edoski, xurgatu,
  murdukatu, ditia hartu, irentsi.
sucker n. edoskitzaile, xurgari,
  xurgazaile. n. engainagarri,
  iruzurgarri.
suckle v.t./v.i. ditia eman, ditia hartu,
  egoski, eradoski.
suckling adj. esneko, bularretako.
suction n. xurgaketa, hurrupaketa.
sudden adj. bat-bateko, berehalako,
  kolpeko, oldarrezko, itsumustuko.
suddenly adv. bapatean, behingoan,
  hitzetik hortzera.
suddenness n. bapatekotasun.
suds n. (pl.) xaboi-burbuilak.

sudsy *adj.* xaboidun.
sue *v.t./v.i.* auzipetu, auzitan ari, auzitaratu.
suffer *v.i./v.t.* nahigabetu, pairatu, jasan, pena ukan, zorigaiztu, samindu, sufritu, nekaldu, oinazeztatu.
sufferable *adj.* pairagarri, jasanerraz.
sufferance *n.* baimen.
sufferer *n.* pairatzaile, eramale.
suffering *n.* atsekabe, jasate, nahigabe, neke, pena, pairamen, jasanbehar, oinaze, saminaldi. *adj.* nahigabetsu, pairatzaile, jasanbera, penadun.
suffice *v.i./v.t.* askitu.
sufficiency *n.* nahikotasun.
sufficient *adj.* ase, nahiko.
sufficiently *adv.* aski.
suffix *n. (gram.)* atzizki.
suffocate *v.t./v.i.* ito arazi, ito.
suffocated *adj.* ito(a).
suffocating *adj.* itogarri, sargoritsu.
suffocation *n.* itomen, itobehar, itoaldi, arnasestu.
suffrage *n.* aukeraketa, hautaketa.
sugar *v.t.* azukreztu, azukreztatu.
sugar *n.* azukre, pontxe, gozaki. **Sugar cube.** Azukrekoskor.
sugary *adj.* azukretsu, urazukretsu.
suggest *v.t.* sorterazi, gogorazi, bururatu, belarriratu.
suggestible *adj.* sugestionagarri.
suggestion *n.* iradokizun, bururapen, sugestio.
suggestive *adj.* gogarazle, iradokor.
suggestively *adv.* hitzerdika.
suicide *n.* buruhilketa, norberahilketa. *n.* burueraile, buruhiltzaile.
suit *v.t./v.i.* komeni, komeni izan, egoki, egoki izan.
suit *n.* jazki, traje. *n.* urre, ezpata, kopa, basto.
suitability *n.* egokitasun.
suitable *adj.* egoki, gai, ezargarri, dagokion.
suitably *adv.* dagokionez, egoki, taxuz.
suitcase *n.* maleta, maletatxo.
suite *n.* laguntalde. *n.* suite.
suitor *n.* gizon maitemindu(a).
sulfate *n. (chem.)* sulfato.
sulfide *n. (chem.)* sulfuro.
sulfur *n. (chem.)* sufre.
sulfuric *adj.* sulfuriko.
sulk *v.i.* sulk *v.i.* humoretxartu, mindu.
sulky *adj.* humoretxarreko, mindu, minbera.
sullen *adj.* humoretxarreko, zakar.
sullenly *adv.* humoretxarrez, zakarki.
sully *v.t./v.i.* zikindu, orbaindu, izenlohitu.
sulphur *Cf. sulfur.*
sultan *n.* sultan.
sultry *adj.* umel.
sum *n. (arith.)* batura, guztia, kopuru.
summarily *adv.* laburbidez.

summarize *v.t.* laburtu, moztu.
summarized *adj.* eskemazko.
summary *n.* laburpen, laburrera, sintesi, bildupen.
summation *n.* laburpen. *n. (arith.)* batuketa.
summer *n.* uda, udaldi, udaro; uda-. *adj.* udako.
summertime *n.* uda, udaldi, udaro. *adj.* udako, udamineko.
summit *n.* gailur, menditontor, mendigain; -egi.
summon *v.t.* deitu, dei egin, bilerazi.
summons *n.* oles, aurkezkizun, deialdi, etordei.
sumptuous *adj.* handizale.
sumptuously *adv.* aberaski, apainki.
sum up *v.t.* kopuratu, guztiratu, orotu.
sun *v.t./v.i.* eguzkiztatu, eguzkitaratu.
sun *n.* eguzki, eki. **Sun dial.** Eguzki ordulari.
sunbathe *v.i.* eguzki hartu, eguzki galdatu, eguzkiztatu.
sunbathing *n.* eguzkiztapen.
sunbeam *n.* dirdira, errainukada.
sunburn *v.t./v.i.* eguzki jo, eguzkikatu.
sunburn *n.* eguzkierre.
Sunday *n.* igande. *adj.* igandeko.
sundial *n.* eguzkierloju, eguzkiorratz.
sundown *n.* ilunabar.
sunflower *n. (bot.)* eguzkilore, ekilore.
sung *p. part. of sing.*
sunk *pret./ p. part. of sink.*
sunken *adj.* jota, hondatuta, murgilduta.
sunlight *n.* errainuketa, eguzkiargi.
sunny *adj.* eguzkitsu, eguzkitar.
sunrise *n.* arginabar, egunsenti.
sunset *n.* ilunabar, ilunsenti.
sunshine *n.* dir-dir.
sunspot *n. (astron.)* eguzkiaren beltzune(a).
sunstroke *n.* eguzkikolpe, eguzkikada.
suntanned *adj.* beztura.
sup *v.i.* afaldu.
super *adj.* bikain.
super- *(gram.)* -gain, super-.
superabundance *n.* gainugaritasun.
superabundant *adj.* gaindizko.
superb *adj.* gailen, goimailako.
superbly *adv.* ezinobeki, ezinobeto.
superciliary *adj.* bekaineko, betondoko.
supercilious *adj.* harroputz, hanpurutsu, harro.
superficial *adj.* gainetiko, azaleko.
superficiality *n.* azalkeria, azaltasun.
superficially *adv.* azaletik, gainetik, arinki, gain-gainetik.
superfluous *adj.* gainezko, gehigarrizko, premiagabeko, alferrikako.
superhuman *adj.* gizagaineko, gizagoitiko.
superimpose *v.t.* gainjarri.
superintendent *n.* kontramaisu, nagusiorde, begiztatzaile.

superior *n.* nagusi, buru, ugazaba. *adj.* goien, goiko, goimailako, goi, puntako; gehi-.

superiority *n.* gailentasun, gainditasun, garaitasun, goratasun, nagusitasun.

superlative *adj.* goien, superlatibo.

superlatively *adv.* superlatiboki.

superman *n.* goigizon.

supermarket *n.* goimerkatu, plaza, supermerkatu.

supernatural *n.* goinatura. *adj.* goinaturazko, naturgaindiko, naturgaineko.

superposition *n.* gainezarketa, gainezarpen, goiezarketa.

supersede *v.t.* ordezkatu, ordeztu.

supersonic *adj.* soinugaindiko.

superstition *n.* sineskeria, superstizio.

superstitious *adj.* aztizale, sineskeriazko, sineskeritsu.

superstitiously *adv.* sineskeriaz.

supervisable *adj.* fiskalizagarri.

supervise *v.t.* gainbegiratu, ikuskatu, kudeatu, fiskalizatu.

supervision *n.* fiskalizapen, gainbegiraketa, gainbegiraldi.

supervisor *n.* gainbegirari, nagusiorde, gainbegiratzaile; langilezain, kontramaisu.

supine *n.* *(gram.)* aditz-izen.

supper *n.* afari, afal.

suppertime *n.* afalordu.

supplant *v.t.* beste baten lekua azpijokoz lortu.

supple *adj.* zinbel, malgu, zalu.

supplement *n.* betegarri, eranskin, gehigarri.

supplementary *adj.* gaineratiko, laguntzazko, ordezkakor, ordezko.

suppliable *adj.* hornigarri.

suppliant *n.* erregugile, arrenkari.

supplicant *n.* erregugile, arrenkari.

supplicate *v.i./v.t.* otoitz egin, erregutu.

supplication *n.* erregu, otoi, otoiketa, arren.

supplicatory *adj.* erreguzko, eskabidezko, eskezko.

supplier *n.* hornigile, hornitzaile, hornilari.

supplies *n.* *(pl.)* hornigai.

supply *v.t./v.i.* hornitu.

supply *n.* hornigai, horni, eskaintza.

support *v.t.* jasan, eutsarazi; aldezkatu, aldeztu, urgaiztu, sostengatu.

support *n.* abe, euskarri. *n.* sostengu, aldezketa.

supporter *n.* aldekide, alderdikide, aldezkari, urgazle, babestzaile, eusle, indarremale, jarraitzaile.

supportive *adj.* aldekor.

suppose *v.t./v.i.* suposatu, balizkatu, somatu, uste ukan.

supposed *adj.* delako, ustezko.

supposition *n.* suposaketa, suposamendu.

suppress *v.t.* ezabatu.

suppression *n.* kenketa.

suppressor *n.* ezeztaile.

supra- *(gram.)* -gain, -gaindiko, -gaineko.

supremacy *n.* nagusitasun, garaitasun, gorentasun, gailentasun, gehientasun.

supreme *adj.* goren, goi-goiko, goien, nagusi, garaien.

supremely *adv.* goi-goian.

sur- *(gram.)* gain-.

surcharge *n.* gainzerga, errekargu, gehizama.

sure *adj.* segur, seguru, ziur. *adv.* aurki, bide, segur, segurki, irmoki.

surely *adv.* dudagabeki, ezbaigabez, egiazki.

surety *n.* finkotasun.

surf *v.i./v.t.* surf egin.

surf *n.* uhinaldi, olatualdi, surf.

surface *v.i.* urazaleratu.

surface *n.* gain, azal, gainalde, gaineko.

surfeit *n.* gehiegikeria, neurrigabekeria. *n.* ok, oka, okaldi, sabelbete, betekada.

surfing *n.* surf.

surgeon *n.* ebatzaile, operatzaile.

surgery *n.* ebaketa, ebakuntza.

surgical *adj.* kirurjiko; kirurji-.

surliness *n.* zakartasun, trauskiltasun.

surly *adj.* mozolo, zakarrote, zaputz.

surmise *v.t./v.i.* susmatu, usmatu, usnatu.

surmount *v.t.* gainditu.

surmountable *adj.* gaindigarri, konpongarri.

surname *n.* abizen, deitura.

surpass *v.t.* abantailatu, aintzindu, gain hartu, gehiegitu, gaindu, gailendu.

surpassable *adj.* gaindigarri.

surplice *n.* *(eccl.)* txaramel.

surplus *n.* gainerako.

surprise *v.t.* txundu, harritu, ustekabetu.

surprise *n.* txundidura, ustekabe, harridura, harrimen. **By surprise.** Ustekabez.

surprised *adj.* harrituta, izukor, izuti.

surprising *adj.* harrigarri(zko), harritzeko, ezusteko, txundigarri.

surprisingly *adv.* harrigarriro.

surrealism *n.* surrealismo.

surrender *v.t./v.i.* errenditu; makurtu.

surrender *n.* txil; uzketa.

surreptitiously *adv.* azpitik.

surround *v.t.* inguratu, hesinguratu.

surrounded *adj.* inguratu(a), inguraturik.

surrounder *n.* ingurukari, hesitzaile.

surrounding *adj.* inguruko.

surroundings *n.* *(pl.)* aldamenak, inguru, ingurumariak, ingurune.

surtax *n.* gainzerga.

surveillance *n.* begiraldi iraunkor(ra).

survey *v.t.* lurrak neurtu. *v.t.* aztertu,

arakatu, ikertu.
survey n. begiraketa, inkesta,
  galdeketa.
surveying n. lurneurketa.
surveyor n. lurneurgile, lurneurtzaile,
  basoneurle.
survival n. gainbizitza.
survive v.i./v.t. iraun, gainbizi.
survivor n. gainbizidun, bizirik
  gelditu(a).
susceptibility n. gaitzikortasun,
  minberatasun, sentiberatasun.
susceptible adj. minbera, minberakor,
  minberati.
suspect v.t./v.i. susmatu,
  goganbehartu, usmatu, usnatu, usain
  hartu.
suspected adj. susmagarri, susmozko.
suspend v.t./v.i. eskegi, zintzilikatu.
  v.t./v.i. geldi, gerarazi.
suspenders n. (pl.) tirakin, tirante.
suspense n. estutasun, larribizi.
suspension n. ezeztaketa, geldialdi.
suspicion n. susmo, aurresusmo,
  aurreuste, susmaketa, susmotxar,
  errezelo.
suspicious adj. susmabera, susmotsu,
  errezelagarri, goganbehartsu.
suspiciously adv. mesfidantzaz,
  susmoz, goganbeharrez.
suspiciousness n. aierukortasun.
sustain v.t. eutsarazi, eutsi.
sustenance n. janari, jaki, hornigai,
  bizigarri.
suture n. (med.) joskura.
svelte adj. lerden, lirain, pinpirin, txairo,
  pertxenta.
sveltely adv. lerdenki, lirainki, txairoki.
sveltness n. liraintasun, lerdentasun,
  txairotasun.
swab n. traputxar.
swaddle v.t. haurtxoa gerrikatu.
swaddling n. oihal, troxa, troxadura,
  faxa.
swag n. ebaskin.
swagger v.i. harroki ibili.
swallow v.t./v.i. irentsi, klaskatu,
  klikatu. **To swallow up.** Hurrupatu.
  Zurrupatu.
swallow n. hurrupa, klakada,
  zurrustada, hurrupako, klinkada. n.
  (zool.) enara.
swallowable adj. hurrupagarri,
  irensgarri.
swam pret. of swim.
swamp v.t./v.i. zingiratu. v.t./v.i. lanaz
  gainzamatu.
swamp n. zingira, aintzira, fadura,
  istinga.
swampy adj. zingiratsu, aintziratsu,
  zingirako.
swan n. (zool.) beltxarga.
swap v.t./v.i. trukatu, truke egin.
swarm v.i./v.t. erlaberritu.
swarm n. erlateria, erlepilo, erletalde.
swarthy adj. ilun, beltzeran.
swastika n. svastica.

swat n. jipoi, ipurdiko.
swathe v.t. gerribildu; bendatu.
sway v.i./v.t. binbilikatu, kulunkatu,
  tranbalatu.
swear v.i./v.t. madarikatu, biraotu,
  biraokatu. v.i./v.t. zin egin, zin egotzi,
  zineztatu, juramendu egin.
sweat v.i./v.t. izerditu, izerdikatu.
sweat n. izerdi, izertaldi; izer-.
sweater n. jertse.
sweatiness n. izerkoitasun.
sweating n. izerdidura, izerketa.
sweaty adj. izerditsu, izerterraz,
  izerbera.
sweep v.t./v.i. erraztatu, eskobatu.
sweeping n. errazketa. adj. orokor,
  hedatsu.
sweet adj. azukretsu, ezti, eztijario,
  eztitsu, gozo. n. gozoki, gozo.
sweetbread n. era, gera, arandoi.
sweeten v.t./v.i. azukreztu,
  azukreztatu, gozagarritu, gozakitu,
  gozatu, eztitu.
sweetened adj. azukreztu.
sweetener n. gozagai, gozakin.
sweetheart n. neskalagun.
sweetly adv. gozoki, gozaro, eztiki,
  eztiro.
sweetmeat n. gozoki.
sweetness n. eztitasun, gozotasun. n.
  emetasun, gozagarritasun.
sweets n. (pl.) gozokiak, goxoak.
swell v.i./v.t. hantu, handitu, konkortu.
swell n. itsaseraso.
swelling n. konkordura, handidura,
  hanpuru.
swelter v.i. beroz ito.
swept pret. p. part. of sweep.
swerve v.i. bapatean alboratu.
swift adj. azkar, azkarti. n. (zool.)
  txirritxori.
swiftly adv. azkarki, arin.
swiftness n. berehalatasun,
  azkartasun, arintasun.
swill n. zerrijan.
swim v.i./v.t. igeri egin, igerikatu.
swimmer n. igerlari, igerigile.
swimming n. igeri, igeriketa.
swimmingly adv. zoragarriki, arrakasta
  handiz.
swimming pool n. igerileku, igertoki.
swimsuit n. bainujantzi.
swindle v.t. azpilapurtu.
swindle n. azpilapurketa, ohoinkeria.
swindler n. gezurti, iruzurtzaile,
  azpilapur.
swine n. zerri, txerri. n.(fig.) alproja.
swineherd n. zerrizain, txerrizain,
  urdezain.
swing v.t./v.i. binbilikatu, kulunkatu,
  zalantzatu, zanbulukatu, tranbalatu,
  zabukatu.
swing n. bilintzi-balantza, kulunka,
  zabu.
swinger n. kulunkari.
swipe v.t./v.i. xixkatu.
swirl v.i./v.t. jirabiratu, biratu.

switch *v.t./v.i.* makilatu. *v.t./v.i.* truke egin. *v.t./v.i.* **(off)** itzaldu.
switch *n.* etengailu, bilaka. *n.* makila.
switchblade *n.* labaina mota bat.
switchman *n.* trenbidezain.
swivel *v.t./v.i.* jirabiratu, ardatzaren inguruan jira-bira egin.
swollen *adj.* hanpurudun, malgor, harro.
swoon *v.i.* zorabiatu, konortea galdu.
swoop *v.i.* **(down on)** gainbera etorri.
swoosh *n.* pirrist.
sword *n.* ezpata.
swordfish *n.* *(zool.)* ezpatarrain.
swordsman *n.* ezpatari.
swore *pret. of swear.*
sworn *adj.* sinestagarri. *p. part. of swear.*
swung *pret./p. part. of swing.*
sycamore *n.* *(bot.)* basabikondo.
sycophant *n.* zuri, balakari, mihizuri, ipurgarbitzaile.
syllable *n.* silaba.
syllogism *n.* silogismo.
sylvan *adj.* basotsu, oihantsu.
symbiosis *n.* bizikidetza, sinbiosi.
symbol *n.* irudi, goiburu, ikur, sinbolo, ezaugarri.
symbolic *adj.* irudizko, sinboliko.
symbolically *adv.* irudipenez, irudiz, sinboloz.
symbolism *n.* sinbolismo.
symbolize *v.t./v.i.* iruditu, irudipetu, antzitxuratu.
symmetric(al) *adj.* neurkide.
symmetrically *adv.* neurkeraz.
symmetry *n.* neurkera, berdindura, simetria.
sympathetic *adj.* doluzko, gogoko, onbera.
sympathetically *adv.* errukiz.
sympathize *v.i.* *(askotan with-ekin)* errukitu, deitoratu, lagundu.
sympathizer *n.* kontsolatzaile, lagunkide.
sympathy *n.* begion, dolumin, kontsolamendu. **To express sympathy.** Dolu eman.
symphony *n.* *(mus.)* sinfonia.
symposium *n.* batzarre, solasketa, hizketaldi.
symptom *n.* zantzu, gaitzaztarna.
symptomatic *adj.* zantzuzko, gaitzaurreko.
synagogue *n.* sinagoga.
synalepha *n.* sinalefa.
synchronize *v.i./v.t.* sinkronizatu, aldiberetu.
syncopate *v.t.* *(mus.)* sinkopatu. *v.t.* *(gram.)* hizlaburtu.
syncope *n.* *(gram.)* hizlaburpen, sinkope.
syndicate *v.t.* taldez edo gizabanakoz osaturiko elkartea. *n.* gangster talde(a).
syndication *n.* sindikapen.
syndrome *n.* sindrome.

synod *n.* sinodo.
synonym *n.* sinonimo.
synonymous *adj.* zentzubereko, esanahibereko.
synopsis *n.* laburpen.
syntax *n.* sintaxi, joskera.
synthesis *n.* sintesi.
synthesize *v.t.* sintetizatu.
synthetic *n.* tergal. *adj.* sintetiko, trinko.
syphilis *n.* *(med.)* frantzeseri, sifilis.
syphilitic *adj.* sifilidun.
syringe *n.* txiringa, xiringa.
syrup *n.* botikaedari. *n.* almibar.
system *n.* metodo, sistima, araubide.
systematic *adj.* araubidezko, araudun, arauzko.
systematically *adv.* araubidez.
systematization *n.* eraketa, sistimatizazio.
systematize *v.t.* araukatu.

T

t *n.* Ingeles alfabetoko letra.
tab *n.* kontu, zorkontu.
tabby *n.* tigre itxurako katu(a).
tabernacle *n.* sagrario. *n.* eliza handi(a).
table *n.* mahai. *n.* taula.
tableau *n.* ikuskizun.
tablecloth *n.* mahaiestalki, mahaigaineko, mahaioihal.
tableland *n.* sapalda.
table of contents *n.* aurkibide, agerbide.
tablespoon *n.* goilare.
tablespoonful *n.* goilarekada.
tablet *n.* ohar liburuxka, elkarri loturiko orri multzoa. *n.* pastila.
tableware *n.* mahaiontziteria.
taboo *n.* tabu.
tabulate *v.t.* sistematikoki ezarri.
tabulation *n.* botuazterraldi, botuzenbaketa, bozazterketa.
tacit *adj.* aipagabeko, isilbideko.
taciturn *adj.* hitzgutiko, isilkor, hitzurri.
taciturnity *n.* isiltasun, isilkoitasun.
tack *n.* iltzemotz, tatxet. *n.* hederia.
tackle *v.t.* abiatu, ekin, -ri lotu. *v.t.* Estatu Batuetako futbolean arerioa geldiarazi.
tackle *n.* tresnak. *n.* Estatu Batuetako futbolean arerioa geldiaraztea.
tacky *adj.* itsaskor, eranskor. *adj.* deigarri, nabarmen.
tact *n.* tentu, zuhurtzia. *n.* ukimen.
tactful *adj.* zuhur, adeitsu, modu oneko, erabidezko.
tactfully *adv.* zuhurki, erabidez.
tactical *adj.* taktiko.
tactics *n.* taktika.
tactile *adj.* ukikor, ukimenezko.
tactlessness *n.* kaskarinkeria, burugabekeria.
tadpole *n.* *(zool.)* zapaburu, apaburu.
tag *n.* etiketa. *n.* izen. *n.* harrapaketa (haur jolasa).

tail *n.* buztan, isats.
tailbone *n. (anat.)* ipurkonkor, ipurtezur.
tailless *adj.* buztangabe.
tailor *v.i./v.t.* taiatu.
tailor *n.* joskile, jostun, jantzigile.
tailoring *n.* jantzigintza, taiaketa.
taint *v.t.* usteldu. *v.t.* desohoretu, laidotu.
taint *n.* usteldura, kutsadura.
take *v.t.* hartu, eutsi, atzeman. *v.t.* eraman, eroan. **To take a step.** Pausoa eman. **To take after.** -ren antza ukan. **To take away.** Kendu. **To take back.** Atzera eraman. **To take care.** Kontu eduki. **To take care of.** Zaindu. Arduratu. **To take down.** Beheratu. Jaitsi. **To take in.** Estutu. **To take it easy.** Lasaitu. Trankildu. **To take it that.** Jo dezagun. Eman dezagun. **To take it upon oneself to (do).** Zerbait egiten hasi. **To take an oath.** Zin egin. **To take off.** Erantzi, kendu; aireratu; irten, joan. **To take on.** Lan baten erantzunkizuna hartu. **To take out.** Atera, kanporatu. **To take over.** Lan baten arduradun nagusia izan. **To take place.** Gertatu. **To take up with.** Elkartu. **Take it or leave it!** Har ala utz ezazu!
taken *p. part. of take. adj.* hartuta.
takeoff *n.* aireraketa.
taker *n.* hartzaile.
talc *n.* talko.
talcum *n.* talko.
tale *n.* ipuin, istorio, pasadizu, kontaketa.
talent *n.* abilezia, abilitate, jeinu, asmamen, etorri.
talented *adj.* jeinutsu, burutsu.
talisman *n.* kutun.
talk *v.i./v.t.* hitz egin, mintzatu, solas egin, solasketatu, elekatu, berriketan ari.
talk *n.* hizketa, hitzaldi, mintzaldi, berriketa, solas.
talkative *adj.* berritsu, hitzjario, berriketazale, solasti, kalaka, hitzontzi, hiztun.
talkativeness *n.* hizjariotasun, elejariotasun.
talker *n.* hizketari, mintzalari, solasegile, berriketari, mintzatzaile.
talkie *n.* ahotsdun filma.
tall *adj.* goi, altu, handi, garai.
tallow *n.* ziho.
talon *n.* erpe, hatzapar.
tamable *adj.* hezigarri, otzangarri, zebakor.
tamableness *n.* otzankortasun.
tamarisk *n. (bot.)* milazka.
tambour *n.* atabal.
tambourine *n.* pandero.
tame *v.t.* mantsotu, otzandu, eskuperatu, etxekotu, etxerakotu, hezi.

tame *adj.* mantso, otzan.
tamely *adv.* mantsoki, otzanki.
tameness *n.* mantsotasun.
tamer *n.* hezitzaile, hezle.
tamp *v.t.* zanpatu.
tamper *v.i. (gehienetan* **with***-ekin)* faltsutu, faltsuztatu.
tampering *n.* faltsuztapen.
tampon *n.* tapoi.
tan *v.t./v.i.* larruondu, larruapaindu, zurratu. *v.t./v.i.* beztu, beltzarandu, kiskaldu, ilundu.
tan *adj.* beltzaran, larruondu(a), larruapaindu(a).
tang *n.* edankutsu, kutsu.
tangent *n. (geom.)* ukitzaile, tangente.
tangentially *adv.* ukituz.
tangerine *n. (bot.)* mandarina mota bat.
tangible *adj.* ukagai, ukigarri.
tangle *v.t./v.i.* mordoildu, mordoilatu.
tangle *n.* korapilo, mordoilo, nahastakeria.
tangled *adj.* lardaskatsu, mordoilozko.
tango *n. (mus.)* tango.
tank *n.* uhaska, urbildegi, urbiltoki, urontzi. *n.* gudagurdi, tanke.
tankard *n.* pitxar.
tanker *n.* ontzitzar; petroliuntzi.
tanned *adj.* beltzaran. *adj.* larruapaindu(a).
tanner *n.* larruapaintzaile, larrulantzaile, larruontzaile.
tannery *n.* larruapaindegi, zurrategi.
tanning *n.* larruapaintza, larruapainketa, larruonketa, larrugintza.
tantalize *v.t.* zirikatu, eztenkatu.
tantalizing *adj.* kitzikatzaile.
tantrum *n.* erretxinaldi.
tap *v.t./v.i.* behin eta berriz leunki ikutu. *v.t./v.i.* zoztu, ziritu, ziriztatu.
tap *n.* kolpetxo. *n.* zipotz, upazotz.
tape *v.t./v.i.* grabatu. *v.t.* zelloz itsatsi.
tape *n.* zinta. *n.* itsasteko (paper), zello.
tape recorder *n.* grabagailu, magnetofono.
taper *n.* ezkoargi.
tapestry *n.* tapiz.
tapeworm *n. (zool.)* zizareluze, bizio.
tar *v.t.* bikeztatu, mundrunatu, galipotatu.
tar *n.* bika, mundrun, galipot.
tarantula *n. (zool.)* armiarmagaitz.
tardiness *n.* astirotasun, luzakeria, berandutasun, moteltasun; berant-.
tardy *adj.* astidun, beranduko, berankor, astikor, atzerakoi, gibelari, berant.
tare weight *n.* pisuhil.
target *n.* jopuntu. *n.* helburu, jomuga, xede.
tariff *n.* zerga, tarifa.
tarnish *v.t./v.i.* urregabetu, desargitu, zatartu.
tarpaulin *n.* mundrun-geruza.
tarred *adj.* bikedun, bikeztu.

tarry adj. biketsu, mundrunatsu.
tart n. frutaz eginiko opiltxo(a). adj. mikaztsu, minkor, garratz, gazi, mingar.
tartan n. zirrikiton.
tartar n. haginlariak hortzetatik kentzen duen zikina.
tartness n. mingostasun.
task n. eginkizun, eginbehar, arlo, zeregin, arazo, eginbide.
tassel n. buruka; -buru. n. borla.
taste v.t./v.i. dastatu, gozatu, gustatu, mihiztatu, zaporeztatu.
taste n. dastamen, gustu, gozamen. n. zapore, grazi, gustu. n. zentzu. n. zatitxo.
tasteful adj. dotore, itxura oneko.
tasteless adj. dastaezin, zaporegabe, gozagabe, gezamin, motel.
tastelessness n. moteltasun, zaporegabetasun, gezatasun, gozagabekeria.
taster n. ahozgozatzaile, dastari, dastatzaile, gozatzaile.
tastiness n. gozagarritasun, gozatasun.
tasty adj. gustagarri, zaporedun, gostudun, gozatsu, gozo, zaporetsu.
tatter v.t./v.i. zarrastatu, urratu.
tatter n. zirdin, zirpil.
tattered adj. zatardun, zatartsu, piltzartsu, zarpailtsu.
tattle v.i./v.t. sekretuak hedatu.
tattoo v.t. tatuatu, tatuaia(k) egin.
tattoo n. tatuaia.
taught pret./p. part. of teach.
taunt v.t. isekatu.
taunt n. iseka, trufa.
taut adj. zurrun, teinko.
tauten v.t./v.i. tenkatu, teinkatu, teink egin, tirakatu.
tautness n. zurruntasun, tiradura, teinkatasun, etenbehar.
tavern n. ardandegi, edaritegi, taberna.
tawdry adj. deigarri, nabarmen.
tawny n./adj. hori-marroixka.
tax v.t. zergatu, zergabanatu, gainzergatu.
tax n. zerga, legar, petxa, kontribuzio.
taxable adj. zergagarri.
taxation n. zergaketa, tasaketa.
taxi n. taxi.
taxidermist n. disekatzaile.
taxidermy n. disekapen.
taxi driver n. taxista, taxilari.
taxing adj. zamagarri.
taxpayer n. zergaemale, zergaordaintzaile, zergapeko.
tea n. (bot.) te.
teach v.t./v.i. irakatsi, ikaserazi, eskolatu, eskola eman, alfabetatu.
teachable adj. irakasgarri.
teacher n. irakasle, hezitzaile, maisu.
teaching n. irakaspen, irakasketa, irakaskuntza, irakatsi. n. irakaslego, irakasletza, maisugo, maisukintza, irakaslaritza, irakaskintza, maisutza.

teachings n. (pl.) ikasbide.
teacup n. tekatilotxo.
teakettle n. teontzi.
team n. ekipo.
teammate n. jolaskide.
teamster n. kamioi-gidari.
teamwork n. elkarlan, taldelan.
teapot n. teontzi.
tear v.i. malkoz betetu (begiak). v.t./v.i. urratu, tarrat egin, tarratatu, zarrastatu, eten. v.t. (down) lurreratu, azpirakatu.
tear n. negarmalko, malko. n. tarratada, zirri-zarra.
teardrop n. negarmalko, negartanta.
tear duct n. (anat.) negarbide.
tearful adj. malkojario, marrakari, negarrontzi.
teary adj. malkodun, malkojario, negarbera.
tease v.t./v.i. txantxatu, adarra jo, kitzikatu, berriketan egin, zirikatu.
teaser n. kilikari, txantxari, zirikatzaile.
teasing adj. adarjole, jostagarri; txantxetan, olgetan. n. isekaldi.
teasingly adv. txantxetan, olgetan.
teaspoon n. goilaretxo.
teaspoonful n. goilaretxokada.
teat n. ugatz, diti, titi.
technical adj. teknikazko, tekniko.
technicality n. teknizismo.
technically adv. teknikaz, teknikoki.
technician n. tekniko, teknikari.
technique n. teknika.
technological adj. teknikazko, tekniko.
technologically adv. teknikaz, teknikoki.
technologist n. teknikari.
technology n. teknika, teknologia.
teddy bear n. hartz-panpina.
tedious adj. gogaikarri, aspergarri, unagarri.
tediously adv. gogaikarriro, aspergarriro, unagarriki.
tediousness n. gogaikarritasun, asperketa, aspertasun, unatasun.
tedium n. gogaidura, gogaiketa, unadura.
tee n. belar gainean jartzen den pilota-eusgailu (golf). n. te (letra).
teem v.i. (gehienetan with-ekin) beteta egon, gainezkatu.
teenager n. nerabe, hamairu urtetik emeretzi urte bitarteko neska edo mutila.
teens n. (pl.) morrointasun, hamairu urtetik hemeretzi urte bitarteko adina. n. (pl.) hamairu urtetik hemeretzi urte bitarteko gazteak.
teeter v.i./v.t. kulunkarazi, kolokatu, zabukatu, zabu egin.
teeter-totter n. zanbulu, kulunka, zarabanda.
teeth n. (pl.) of tooth.
teethe v.i. agindu.
teething n. hortzazketa, hortzaro, haginazketa.

telecommunication *n.*
telekomunikabide.
telegram *n.* irratidazki, telegrama.
telegraph *v.t./v.i.* telegrafiatu.
telegraph *n.* urrutidazkin, telegrafo.
telegraphic *adj.* telegrafiko.
telegraphically *adv.* telegrafikoki.
telegraphy *n.* telegrafia,
urrutidazkintza.
telepathy *n.* telepatia.
telephone *v.t./v.i.* telefonatu, telefonoz
deitu.
telephone *n.* telefono, urrutizkin.
telescope *n.* teleskopio.
telescopic *adj.* teleskopiko.
teletype *n.* teletipo.
televise *v.t./v.i.* telebisatu, telebistaz
eman.
television *n.* telebista, teleikuskin.
telex *n.* telex.
tell *v.t./v.i.* esan, kontatu, mintzatu.
teller *n.* kutxazain, kontatzaile.
telltale *adj.* salatzaile.
temper *v.t./v.i.* ausitu.
temper *n.* zima, giro. *n.* zima txar.
temperament *n.* zima, tenperamendu.
temperamental *adj.* haserrekor,
suminkor, errebera.
temperate *adj.* ematsu. *adj.* epel.
Temperate zone. Epelalde.
temperature *n.* tenperatura. *n.* sukar.
tempest *n.* ekaitz, zirimola, zurrunbilo.
tempestuous *adj.* ekaiztun, ekaiztsu,
zurrunbilotsu.
temple *n.* eliza. *n. (anat.)* loki.
tempo *n.* erritmo, konpas(a).
temporal *adj.* aldizkako, aldiko.
temporarily *adv.* oraingoz,
behin-behinean.
temporary *adj.* aldiko, behin-behineko,
aldibateko, aldizkako.
tempt *v.t.* tentatu, zirikatu, gaitzeratu,
kilimatu.
temptation *n.* galbide, hondabide,
tentabide, tentazio, zirikaldi.
tempter *n.* tentatzaile, zirikalari,
zirikatzaile.
tempting *adj.* tentagarri, tentatzaile,
zirikagarri.
temptress *n.* tentatzaile, tentakari
(emakume).
ten *n./adj.* hamar, hamarreko.
tenacious *adj.* euskor, irauti, gogor,
setatsu.
tenaciously *adv.* lehiatsuki, jarraikiro.
tenacity *n.* euskortasun, atxikitasun.
tenancy *n.* maiztergo, maiztertasun.
tenant *n.* maizter, errentadore,
errentari.
tend *v.i.* **(to** edo infinitiboarekin)
aihertu, makurtu.
tendency *n.* joera, aiherkunde, apeta,
grina; -ti, -koi.
tender *adj.* samur, samurkor,
bigunbera, bihozbera, bihozdun,
laztanbera, guri. *n.* -zain.
tenderly *adv.* bigunki, bigunkiro,

samurki, samurkiro.
tenderness *n.* samurtasun,
bihozberatasun, samurkortasun,
laztantasun.
tendon *n. (anat.)* zain, zainzuri.
tenebrous *adj.* goibeltsu.
tenement *n.* hirigune ingurutako
apartamendu-etxea.
Tennessee *n. (geog.)* Estatu
Batuetako estatu bat.
tennis *n.* tenis.
tenor *n. (mus.)* tenore.
tense *n. (gram.)* -aldi. *adj.* hertsagarri,
hertsakor. *adj.* teinko.
tensely *adv.* hunkigarriki. *adv.* teinkoki.
tenseness *n.* etenbehar, teinkadura.
tension *n.* etenbehar, teinkadura,
hertsaketa. *n.* tiragailu.
tent *n.* kanpadenda.
tentacle *n.* erro.
tentative *adj.* mementoko, saialdiko.
tenth *adj.* hamargarren, hamarreko.
tenuous *adj.* mehe.
tenuousness *n.* mehetasun.
tenure *n.* eukite, eukipen. *n.* irakasle
bati bizi osorako lana ziurtatzen dion
statusa.
tepid *adj.* hotzepel.
term *n.* epe.
terminable *adj.* bukagarri, amaigarri.
terminal *adj.* bukaerako, azkenburuko,
amaierako. *n.* geltoki. *n.* terminal.
terminate *v.t./v.i.* bukatu, amaitu,
azkendu.
terminated *adj.* kito.
termination *n.* bukaera, amaiera.
terminology *n.* terminologia.
termite *n. (zool.)* termita.
terrace *n.* terraza, begiratoki.
terrain *n.* landa.
terrestrial *n./adj.* lurreko, lehortar,
mundutiar; lurbizilagun, lurtar.
terrible *adj.* beldurgarri,
beldurgarrizko, harrigarrizko,
ikaragarri, ikaragarrizko, izugarri,
sekulako, gorri.
terribleness *n.* ikaragarritasun,
lazgarritasun.
terribly *adv.* beldurgarriro, ikaragarriki,
ikaragarriro, izugarriro, lazgarriki.
terrier *n. (zool.)* terrier txakur(ra).
terrific *adj.* bikain, oso on(a), sekulako.
terrify *v.t.* ikara egin, ikaratu, izutu,
izuarazi.
terrifying *adj.* ikaragarri, ikarazle,
izutzaile.
territorial *adj.* lurraldeko, barrutiko.
territoriality *n.* lurraldetasun.
territorially *adv.* lurrez.
territory *n.* herrialde, lur, lurralde.
terror *n.* ikara, ikaradura, izudura,
beldurgorri.
terrorism *n.* indarrikara, terrorismo.
terrorist *n.* terrorista, ikaratzaile,
izuarazle.
terrorize *v.t.* indarkeritu, ikaratu.
terse *adj.* hizgutiko.

tersely *adv.* laburki.

terseness *n.* laburtzaletasun.

tertiary *adj.* hirugarren. *n.* hirugarren aro.

test *v.t./v.i.* probatu, saiatu, entsegutu, entseiatu.

test *n.* frogaldi, saiakuntza, entsegu, entseiu, proba.

testament *n.* itun, testamentu, hilburuko.

tester *n.* probatzaile.

testicle *n. (anat.)* barrabil, potro.

testifier *n.* aitorgile.

testify *v.i./v.t.* testigatu, aitortu, ageri, lekukotu. *v.i.* **(to)** ziurtu.

testimonial *adj.* sinespidezko, testiguzko.

testimony *n.* aitormen, aitorraldi, lekukotasun, testigutza, sinesgarri, testigantza.

testy *adj.* haserrekor, suminkoi.

tetanus *n. (med.)* tetano.

tether *n.* hede, uhal.

tetrasyllabic *adj.* lausilabadun.

Texan *n./adj.* texatar.

Texas *n. (geog.)* Estatu Batuetako estatu bat.

text *n.* textu.

textbook *n.* eskolaliburu, eskuliburu.

textile *n./adj.* ehun.

textual *adj.* textuko, doi.

texture *n.* egitura.

than *conj.* baino.

thank *v.t.* eskertu, eskerrak eman.

thankful *adj.* eskerroneko, eskertsu.

thankfully *adv.* eskerronez.

thankfulness *n.* eskerron, eskerrontasun, eskertza.

thank goodness *int.* beharrik.

thankless *adj.* eskergabe, eskerbeltzeko, eskergaitz, eskertxarreko.

thanklessness *n.* eskergaizto, eskergaitz, eskergabetasun, eskertxar, eskerbeltz.

thanks *n.* esker, mila esker.

Thanksgiving *n.* Estatu Batuetako eskertza eguna.

that *pron./adj.* hori, hura, horrek. *adv.* holako. *conj.* -n, -la, ezen.

thatch *n.* zarbasta.

that's "that + is"-aren laburpena.

thaw *v.i./v.t.* desizoztu, gesaldu, elurgabetu.

the *art.* -a, -ak, -ek, -ok.

theater *n.* antzoki, teatro. **Movie theater.** Zinematoki.

theatrical *adj.* antzerkiko, antzokiko.

theft *n.* lapurreta, ebasketa, ohoinkeria.

their *pron.* beren, beraien, haien.

theirs *pron.* beren, beraien, haien.

them *pron. (acc.)* haiek, heurak; -zki-.

theme *n.* gai, pondu, arlo.

themselves *pron.* beraiek.

then *adv.* orduan. *adv.* gainera. *adv.* bada, ba. *adj.* orduko. *n.* aro hura, denboraldi hura.

theologian *n.* jainkolari, teologari.

theological *adj.* teologiako.

theology *n.* jainkojakintza, teologia.

theorem *n.* teorema.

theoretical *adj.* gogoetazko, teoriko.

theoretician *n.* teorilari.

theorist *n.* teorilari.

theorization *n.* teorizazio.

theorize *v.i.* teorizatu, gogoetatu.

theory *n.* teoria.

therapeutic *adj.* terapeutiko, sendabidezko.

therapeutically *adv.* sendabidez.

therapeutics *n.* terapeutika.

therapy *n.* sendabide, osabide, terapia.

there *adv.* han, hor, hara, horra. **Right there.** Hantxe. *pron.* bada. *int.* begira!

therabout(s) *adv.* inguruan. *adv.* gutxigorabehera.

thereafter *adv.* aurrerantzean.

thereby *adv.* honela; horren bitartez.

therefore *adv.* beraz, hortaz.

therein *adv.* barruan; horretan.

thereof *adv.* hango, horko. *adv.* honen, horren.

thereon *adv.* gainean.

there's "there + is"-aren laburpena.

thermal *adj.* berozko, termiko.

thermic *adj.* berozko, termiko.

thermodynamic *adj.* beroindarrezko, termodinamiko.

thermodynamics *n.* termodinamika.

thermometer *n. (phys.)* beroneurkin, termometro.

thermos *n.* termo.

thermostat *n.* termostato.

thesaurus *n.* sinonimo eta antonimoen hiztegia.

these *pron./adj. (pl.)* hauek.

thesis *n.* tesi, tesina.

they *pron. (pl.)* haiek.

they'd "they + had" eta "they + would"-en laburpena.

they'll "they + will"-aren laburpena.

they're "they + are"-aren laburpena.

they've "they + have"-aren laburpena.

thick *adj.* lodi.

thicken *v.t./v.i.* loditu, zukutu, mamitu, gogortu.

thickenable *adj.* mamigarri.

thickening *n.* lodiketa, loditzaile.

thicket *n.* sapar, sasi.

thickly *adv.* lodiro.

thickness *n.* lodiera, loditasun.

thief *n.* lapur, ebasle, ohoin.

thievery *n.* lapurreria, lapurreta, ohointza.

thieves *n. (pl.)* Cf. thief.

thigh *n. (anat.)* izter, aztal.

thimble *n.* ditare.

thin *v.t./v.i.* **(down, out)** mehetu, mehartu, argaldu.

thin *adj.* argal, makar, mehar, mehe.

thing *n.* gauza.

think *v.t./v.i.* pentsatu, uste ukan, eritzi. *v.i.* **(of)** asmatu; gogoratu, gogoan ukan. *v.t.* **(over)** hausnartu, gogoetak egin, kontu(ak) atera.

thinkable *adj.* pentsagarri.

thinker *n.* pentsalari, gogoetari, pentsatzaile.

thinking *n.* pentsamolde, pentsaera.

thinly *adv.* meheki.

thinness *n.* argaltasun, mehetasun, mehartasun.

third *adj./n.* hirugarren, heren, hiruren.

thirdly *adv.* hirugarrenez.

thirst *n.* egarri, edagale; egar-.

thirstiness *n.* egarberatasun.

thirsty *adj.* egarri, egarbera, edagale, egarti, egartsu.

thirteen *n./adj.* hamahiru.

thirteenth *adj.* hamahirugarren.

thirtieth *adj.* hogeitamargarren.

thirty *n./adj.* hogeitamar.

this *pron.* hau, hauxe, honek. **In this way.** Honela.

thistle *n. (bot.)* gardu, gardabera, txorigardu.

thorax *n. (anat.)* bularralde, bular.

thoraxic *adj.* bularringuruko.

thorn *n.* elorri, arantza. *adj.* elorrizko.

thorny *adj.* elorritsu, arantzadun, arantzazko.

thorough *adj.* oso, bete, erabateko. *adj.* ardurati, axolatsu.

thoroughbred *n.* odolgarbiko lasterketa-zaldi(a). *adj.* odolgarbiko.

thoroughfare *n.* bide nagusi.

thoroughly *adv.* osoki, osoro, guztiz.

thoroughness *n.* osotasun, betealdi. *n.* arduratasun.

those *pron. (pl.)* haiek, horiek, hoiek.

though *conj.* baina. *adv.* ere, hala ere.

thought *n.* asmakizun, bururapen, pentsamentu, pentsaketa, gogo, gogoeta.

thoughtful *adj.* pentsakor, gogartetsu, burudun, gogoetatsu. *adj.* adeikor, eraoneko.

thoughtfully *adv.* gogartuz.

thoughtfulness *n.* ardura, arreta, axola. *n.* adeitasun.

thoughtless *adj.* konturagabeko; arin. *adj.* zabar.

thoughtlessly *adv.* axolagabeki, kontugabeki. *adv.* zabarkiro, zabarki.

thoughtlessness *n.* axolagabekeria, oharkabekeria. *n.* eragabetasun, begirunegabetasun, adigabezia.

thousand *n./adj.* mila; milako.

thousandth *adj.* milagarren, milaren.

thrash *v.t./v.i.* makilatu, zaflatu.

thrashing *n.* zaflaldi, makilkaketa, makilaldi.

thread *v.t.* haritu, hari(a) sartu, hariztatu.

thread *n.* hari, zirpil, biru, jostari.

threadbare *adj.* karraskatu.

threat *n.* mehatxu, zemai.

threaten *v.t./v.i.* mehatxatu, keinatu, mehatxu egin.

threatening *adj.* mehatxakor, mehatxatzaile, mehatxuzko, zematzaile.mehatxagarri.

threateningly *adv.* mehatxuka, mehatxuz, zemaika.

three *n./adj.* hiru.

threefold *adj.* hiruko, hiru aldiko.

threescore *n./adj.* hirurogei.

thresh *v.t./v.i.* garijo, eultzitu, trailukatu.

thresher *n.* eultzi; trailukari, garijotzaile.

threshold *n.* atalarri, alartze.

threw *pret./p. part. of throw.*

thrice *adv.* hiru aldiz, hiru bider.

thrift *n.* aurrezki, zuhurtasun.

thrifty *adj.* zuhur, elkor, zeken, zikoitz; aurreztaile.

thrill *n.* dardara, ikara.

thrive *v.i.* kozkortu, hazi; aberastu.

throat *n. (anat.)* zintzur, eztarri.

throaty *adj.* eztarriko.

throb *v.i.* pilpiratu.

throbbing *adj.* pilpiragarri, sor. *n.* pilpira.

thrombosis *n.* tronbosis.

throne *n.* erregeaulki, bakaulki, tronu.

throng *n.* jendetza, jendetalde.

throttle *v.t.* ito arazi.

throttle *n.* iratopen-balbula.

through *prep./adv.* zehar, bitartez, bidez, medio. *prep./adv.* hasieratik amaierara. *adj.* irteeradun. *adv.* horrenak egin du; bukatua da, amaitu da. *adj.* zuzen.

throughout *prep./adv.* zehar. *prep./adv.* edonon, nonnahi.

throw *v.t./v.i.* bota, egotzi, iraitzi, jaurtiki, besagainkatu. *v.t.* **(out)** kaleratu, kanporatu, bidaldu; farrastatu. *v.t./v.i.* **(up)** goitikatu, goragaletu, oka egin, okatu.

thrown *p. part of throw.*

thrush *n. (zool.)* birigarro.

thrust *v.t./v.i.* bultz egin, bultzakatu, saka egin.

thrust *n.* bultzaldi, tinkadura, bultzada, sakaldi.

thud *n.* dunbadaldi.

thumb *n. (anat.)* hatz, erpuru.

thumbtack *n.* txintxeta.

thump *n.* dunbadaldi.

thunder *v.i./v.t.* trumoitu, ostots egin, trumoiak jo.

thunder *n.* trumoi, ostots.

thunderbolt *n.* oinaztarri, tximista.

thunderclap *n.* ostosketa, trumoialdi, trumoihots.

thundercloud *n.* hodeimordo, hodeitzar.

thunderous *adj.* trumoitsu, ostostsu.

thunderstorm *n.* trumoialdi, ostotsaldi.

Thursday *n.* ostegun.

thus *adv.* honela, horrela, hala, honetara. *adv.* beraz.

thwart *v.t.* kontrajarri, eragotzi, galarazi.
thyme *n.* ezkai.
tiara *n.* tiara.
tibia *n.* (*anat.*) bernahezur, hankezur.
tick *v.i.* tik-tak egin.
tick *n.* (*zool.*) lapazorri.
ticker *n.* hargailu. *n.* (*colloq.*) bihotz.
ticket *n.* txartel, sarrera, igaroagiri.
tickle *v.t./v.i.* kili-kili egin, kilikatu, gilikatu, kitzikatu.
tickle *n.* kilika, hazkura, haznahi.
tickler *n.* kilikari.
ticklish *adj.* kilikadun, gilbera, kilikabera.
ticklishness *n.* kilikaberatasun, kilikortasun.
tidal *adj.* itsasaldiko, itsasgorabeherako.
tidbit *n.* kopau, ahamen.
tide *n.* itsasaldi, itsasgorabehera.
tidily *adv.* txukunki.
tidiness *n.* txukuntasun, laztantasun.
tidings *n.* berriak.
tidy *v.t./v.i.* (*askotan* **up**-*ekin*) txukundu, taiutu, taxutu.
tidy *adj.* txukun, laztan.
tie *v.t./v.i.* lotu, lokarriztatu, elkar lotu, estekatu.
tie *n.* lokarri. *n.* gorbata. *n.* lotura. *n.* hainbana, hainbanapen, berdin.
tier *n.* maila.
tiger *n.* (*zool.*) tigre.
tight *adj.* hertsi, estu, mehar.
tighten *v.t./v.i.* estutu, hertsatu, teinkatu, teink egin.
tight-fisted *adj.* xuhur, zuhur, eskuitxi.
tight-fitting *adj.* hertsi.
tightly *adv.* hertsiki, estuki, estukiro.
tightness *n.* estuera, hertsitasun, estutasun. *n.* teinkatasun.
tightrope *n.* orekarien soka.
tightwad *n.* pertsona zeken(a).
tile *v.t.* arbeleztatu, teilaztu, teilaztatu.
tile *n.* losa, lauza.
tiler *n.* lauzari, lauzatzaile.
till *v.t/v.i.* goldatu, irauli, luberritu, ildokatu.
tillable *adj.* landugarri, iraulgarri, luberrigarri.
tillage *n.* aitzurketa, lurlantza, goldalan.
tiller *n.* goldalari, goldatzaile. *n.* lemaren taketa.
tilt *v.t/v.i.* iraulkatu, irauli, makurtu.
timber *n.* zur, ohol. *n.* zuhaitzak.
time *v.t.* denbora neurtu.
time *n.* aldi, asti, garai, sasoi, tenore, denbora, arte; ordu. **On time.** Garaiz. **Free time.** Txolarte. **From time to time.** Noizbehinka. **What time is it?** Zer ordu da? *n.* (*pl.*) bider, aldiz. *n.* erritmo.
timekeeping *n.* kronometraketa.
timely *adj.* garaizko.
timepiece *n.* erloju, ordulari.
timetable *n.* ordutegi.

timid *adj.* ikarakor, ikarati, ahalkedun, gelbera, txepel. *adj.* lotsati, lotsor, herabe, kikil.
timidity *n.* izukortasun, kikildura, gelberatasun, txepeldura.
timidly *adv.* gelberaki, herabeki, txepelki, uzkurki.
timidness *n.* uzkurtasun, lotsakortasun, txepeltasun, izuberatasun, herabetasun.
timing *n.* une egokia aukeratzeko gaitasuna. *n.* erritmo-sena.
timorous *adj.* ikarati, beldurti.
timorously *adv.* ikaraz.
tin *n.* (*min.*) eztainu. *n.* hoxalata. *n.* latontzi. *adj.* eztainuzko.
tinder *n.* ardai.
tine *n.* arantza.
tinfoil *n.* aluminio-paper(a).
tinge *n.* nabardura.
tingle *v.i.* inurritu.
tininess *n.* ttipitasun.
tinker *n.* berzkin, tupinagile.
tinkle *v.i.* tilin egin.
tinkle *n.* tilinketa.
tinny *adj.* eztainutsu.
tinplate *n.* hoxalata.
tinsel *n.* zilarrezko hari, urrezko hari.
tinsmith *n.* eztainatzaile, eztainugile; hoxalatari.
tint *v.t.* tindatu, margotu, tinduztatu.
tint *n.* koloragailu.
tintable *adj.* koloragarri.
tiny *adj.* ttipi, ttipitto.
tip *v.t/v.i.* kili-kolo egin, irabiratu. *v.t./v.i.* eskupeko eman.
tip *n.* bazter, punta. *n.* eskupeko, eskusari. *n.* aholku, jakinarazpen, oharbide.
tipple *v.i./v.t.* xurrutada laburretan edan.
tipsiness *n.* mozkorraldi, hordialdi.
tipsy *adj.* txolin, bixibixi, moxkor.
tiptoe *v.i.* behatz puntetan ibili.
tirade *n.* hitzastun, hitzeraso.
tire *v.t./v.i.* abaildu, pot egin, akitu, nekatu, unatu.
tire *n.* gurpil, errubera, txirringa.
tired *adj.* nekatu(a), etenda, lehertuta.
tiredly *adv.* leherbeharrez.
tiredness *n.* neke, nekadura, nekaldi, akidura, abaildura, hebaindura.
tireless *adj.* nekaezin, nekagaitz.
tirelessly *adv.* nekaezinik.
tirelessness *n.* nekaezintasun.
tiresome *adj.* nekagarri, nekatzaile.
tiring *adj.* nekagarri, neketsu.
tiringly *adv.* nekez, nekagarriro.
'tis "it + is"-aren laburpena.
tissue *n.* zeta-ehun. *n.* zeta-paper. *n.* (*biol.*) ehun.
tit *n.* diti.
titanic *adj.* handitzar, izugarrizko.
tithe *n.* hamarren.
tither *n.* hamarrendun.
title *v.t.* idazpurutu, goiburutu.
title *n.* izenburu, adierazburu,

idazpuru. *n.* izenaurre, izenaurreko. *n.* titulu.
titled *n.* tituludun, izenaurredun.
titmouse *n. (zool.)* milotx.
titter *v.i.* isilka farre egin.
titter *n.* isilka farre egite(a).
to *prep./adv.* -ra, -runtz; -gana. *prep./adv.* -tzeko; -tera, -tzera. *prep.* Infinitiboa ezaguarazten du. **To go.** Joan. *prep.* Datiboa ezaguarazten du. **She gave it to me.** Eman zidan.
toad *n. (zool.)* apo, zapo, txantxiku.
toadstool *n. (bot.)* onddo, onto.
toady *v.t./v.i.* xaboi(a) eman.
toast *v.t./v.i.* errearindu, kiskaldu, txigortu. *v.t.* topa egin.
toast *n.* ogierre. *n.* topa egitean esaten diren hitzak.
toaster *n.* txigorgailu.
tobacco *n.* tabako.
tobacconist *n.* tabakari, tabakosaltzaile.
toboggan *n.* lera.
toccata *n. (mus.)* tokata.
today *n.* egun, gaurregun. *adv.* gaur.
today's *adj.* gaurko.
toddle *v.i.* taka-taka ibili.
to-do *n.* zalaparta, astrapalada, istilu.
toe *n. (anat.)* behatz. *n.* ostikopunta, oinpuntako.
toenail *n.* behatzazal.
toga *n.* toga.
together *adv.* batean, batera, elkarrekin.
togetherness *n.* elkarzaletasun.
toil *v.i.* gogor lan egin.
toil *n.* lan gogor, lan astun.
toilet *n.* komun, txizatoki, kakatoki, txizaleku. *n.* kakontzi.
token *n.* ezaugarri, irudi.
tolerable *adj.* eramangarri, jasanerraz, jasangarri.
tolerably *adv.* jasangarriro.
tolerance *n.* eramankortasun, jasamen, pazientzia, pairakortasun.
tolerant *adj.* amoremale, eramankor, jasankor, pairakor.
tolerate *v.t.* jasan, eraman, pairatu.
toll *v.t./v.i.* dangadatu.
toll *n.* atesari, bideordain, bidasari, peaia. *n.* danbada, dei, danga. *n.* gudu edo istripuan hilak.
tolling *n.* errepika, drangada, danbada.
tomahawk *n.* Estatu Batuetako indioen guda-aizkora.
tomato *n. (bot.)* tomate.
tomb *n.* hobi, hilobi, ehorzleku.
tombola *n.* tonbola.
tomboy *n.* neska-mutil, marimutiko, marimutil.
tombstone *n.* hilarri.
tomcat *n.* katar.
tome *n.* liburuki, tomo.
tomfoolery *n.* lelokeria.
tommy gun *n.* metraileta.
tomorrow *n./adv.* bihar. **See you tomorrow!** Bihar arte! **Day after**

tomorrow. Etzi.
tom-tom *n.* Estatu Batuetako indioen danborra.
ton *n.* tonelada.
tonal *adj.* doinuzko.
tonality *n.* doinutasun, tonuera.
tone *n. (mus.)* doinuera, tonu. **Half tone.** Tonuerdi.
tongs *n. (pl.)* trukesak.
tongue *n. (anat.)* mihi. *n.* hizkuntza. *n.* zapatagain.
tonic *n.* sendagarri, bizkorgarri.
tonight *n.* gau hau. *adv.* gau hontan, gaur gauean, gaur gauez.
tonnage *n.* tonelaia.
tonsil *n. (anat.)* amigdala.
tonsure *v.t.* kaskamoztu.
tonsure *n.* koroi, koroa.
tonsured *adj.* koroidun, kaskagorri.
too *adv.* ere, ere bai. **Me, too.** Ni ere bai. *adv.* baita, baita . . . ere. *adv.* -egi.
took *pret. of* take.
tool *n.* lanabes, tresna, erreminta.
toolbox *n.* erremintontzi, erreminkutxa.
toolshed *n.* erremintetxe, tresnategi.
toot *n.* tutuhots, fiit.
tooth *n.* hortz, hagin. *n.* zerragin. *adj.* hagineko.
toothache *n.* haginmin, horzkidura, haginetako min.
toothbrush *n.* hortzeskuila.
toothed *adj.* horztun, koskadun.
toothless *adj.* hagingabe, horzkabe.
toothpaste *n.* hortzore.
toothpick *n.* hortziri, zotz.
top *v.t.* gainditu. *v.t.* birmargotu. *v.t.* **(off with)** bukatu, amaitu; osotu.
top *n.* gailur, buru, gain, goi, tontor. **On top of.** -(r)en gainean. *adj.* goi, gaineko. *n.* mukuru. *n.* tronpa, ziba.
topic *n.* maiseabide, mintzagai. *n.* ikergai.
topographer *n.* topografari.
topographical *adj.* topografiko.
topography *n.* topografia.
topple *v.i./v.t.* erori, jausi.
topsy-turvy *adj.* nahas-mahas.
torch *n.* zuzi, eskuzuzi, argiegur, zutargi.
tore *pret. of* tear.
toreador *n.* toreatzaile.
torment *v.t.* minarazi, oinazetu, penatu.
tormented *adj.* oinazetsu, oinazedun.
tormentedly *adv.* oinazez.
tormentor *n.* minemale.
torn *p. part. of* tear.
tornado *n.* zurrunbilo.
torpedo *v.t.* torpedoztatu.
torpedo *n.* torpedo.
torpor *n.* girtenkeria.
torque *n.* bihurraldi.
torrent *n.* zirristada.
torrential *adj.* uholdezko.
torrentially *adv.* zurrutaka.
torrid *adj.* erre, kiskali, erregarri,

kiskalgarri. *adj.* sutsu.
torsion *n.* bihurraldi, bihurtza, bihurdura.
torso *n. (anat.)* soin.
torticollis *n. (med.)* lepagogordura, lepamin, lepokomin.
tortoise *n. (zool.)* dortoka.
tortuous *adj.* oker, zeharkako, oiher.
torture *v.t.* minarazi, oinazetu, penatu.
torture *n.* oinaze, zigordura.
  Instrument of torture. Oinazegailu.
torturer *n.* minemale, oinazemale, zigortzaile.
torturous *adj.* oinazezko.
toss *v.t.* bota, egotzi, jaurtiki, jaurti. *v.i.* inarrosi.
toss *n.* jaurtaldi, iraitzi.
tot *n.* haurtxo, sein.
total *v.t./v.i.* guztiratu, orotu.
total *n.* guztia, kopuru. *adj.* erabateko, guztizko, oso.
totalitarian *adj.* totalitario.
totalitarianism *n.* totalitarismo.
totality *n.* orotasun, osotasun, guztitasun, orobatasun.
totalize *v.t.* guztiratu, orotu.
totally *adv.* erabat, osorik, osoki, guztiz, denera, bete-betean, oroz, arras, biziki.
totalness *n.* guztikotasun.
totter *v.i.* balantzatu, kordokatu, zabukatu.
touch *v.t./v.i.* haztatu, ukitu, eskuztatu, zirri egin. *v.t.* hunkitu.
touch *n.* uki, ukimen, ukitu.
touchable *adj.* ukigai, ukigarri.
touched *adj.* samurkor, hunkitu(a).
touchiness *n.* sentikortasun, kilikaberatasun, minberatasun.
touching *adj.* hunki, hunkigarri, bihozmingarri, urragarri, samurkor. *n.* ukialdi, ukiera.
touchingly *adv.* hunkigarriro.
touchy *adj.* erretxin, erretxintsu, gaitzikor, minbera.
tough *adj.* bortitz, lakatz, karkail. *adj.* zail. *adj.* gogor.
toughness *n.* bortiztasun. *n.* zailtasun.
toupee *n.* ileorde, ileordeko.
tour *n.* bira, jira-bira.
tourism *n.* turismo.
tourist *n.* turista.
tournament *n.* lehiaketa.
tourniquet *n.* odol-gelditzeko.
tow *v.t.* atoitu, garraiatu, erremolkatu.
towage *n.* erremolke.
toward(s) *prep.* -runtz, -ganantz; aldera.
towel *n.* eskuoihal, xukadera, eskuzapi.   **Towel rack.** Eskuoihaltoki.
tower *n.* dorre. *n.* zirgari.
towing *n.* erremolke.
towline *n.* zirga.
town *n.* herri, hiri.
town hall *n.* udaletxe, alkatetxe, herrikoetxe.

townspeople *n.* herrixume, herrixehe.
towpath *n.* zirgabide.
towrope *n.* zirga.
toxic *adj.* pozoitsu, pozoizko, toxiko.
toxin *n.* pozoi, pozoigai, toxina.
toy *n.* jostailu.
trace *v.t.* aztarkatu, aztarnatu. *v.t.* kalkatu.
trace *n.* lorratz, aztarna, zantzu, arrasto.
tracer *n.* kalkagailu, kalkatzaile. *n.* marralari, marratzaile.
trachea *n. (anat.)* zintzur, zintzurreste, eztarrizulo.
track *v.t.* aztarkatu, aztarnatu.
track *n.* arrasto, aztarna, hatz, urrats, zantzu. *n.* errail.
tracker *n.* usmatzaile, usnatzaile, aztarkari, aztarnari.
tract *n.* lurzati, sail, arlo, eremu. *n.* -bide.
tractable *adj.* lagunbera.
traction *n.* trakzio. *n.* erakartze.
tractor *n.* traktore.
trade *v.t./v.i.* salerosi, merkataldu. *v.t./v.i.* truk(e) egin, trukatu.
trade *n.* truke, truk, trukaketa. *n.* negozio, salerosi, merkatalgo, merkataritza.
trademark *n.* marka.
tradesman *n.* merkatari, salerosle.
tradition *n.* tradizio, usario.
traditional *adj.* tradiziozko, ohizko.
traditionalism *n.* tradizionalismo.
traditionalist *n./adj.* tradiziozale.
traditionally *adv.* tradizionalki, tradizioz.
traffic *v.i. (askotan* **in**-*ekin)* merkataldu, salerosi.
traffic *n.* trafiko, zirkulazio.
tragedy *n.* tragedia.
tragic *adj.* tragiko.
tragically *adv.* tragikoki.
trail *v.t./v.i.* arrastaka eraman. *v.t.* aztarnatu. *v.t./v.i.* jarraiki, segitu.
trail *n.* aztarren, bide, hatz, zidor. **Cart trail.** Gurdibide.
trailer *n.* errulota, atoi.
train *v.t./v.i.* hezi, trebatu.
train *n.* tren, trenlerro, bultzi. *n.* tirrin.
trainable *adj.* hezigarri.
trainee *n.* ikasberri; -mutil.
trainer *n.* hezilari, hezitzaile.
training *n.* hezkuntza, entrenamendu, hezketa, trebaketa.
trait *n.* berezitasun.
traitor *n.* azpijokalari, azpisapo, azpijale, traidore, saltzaile, judas.
traitorous *adj.* azpizale, hitzustel, azpisuge, judas.
trajectory *n.* tirobide, ibilbide.
tram *n.* teleferiko, funikular, tranbia.
tramp *n.* arlote.
trample *v.i./v.t.* oinperatu, zanpatu, zapaldu, ostikopetu, zangopetu, hankapetu.
trampoline *n.* jauzleku, saltagailu,

saltaleku.

tranquil *adj.* bakezko, trankil, nare.

tranquility *n.* trankiltasun, baretasun, egonaldi, lasaitasun, naretasun, patxada.

tranquilize *v.t.* baretu, lasaitu, trankildu.

tranquilizer *n.* baretzaile, lasaigarri.

tranquilly *adv.* gozaro, lasaiki, lasai-lasai, patxadan, pausatuki.

trans- *(gram.)* zehar, beste aldera.

transact *v.t./v.i.* egitaratu, bete.

transaction *n.* negoziaketa, negoziapen, transakzio.

transalpine *adj.* alpesarunzko.

transatlantic *adj.* atlantikandiko, atlantikarunzko.

transcend *v.t./v.i.* gainditu.

transcendence *n.* orozgaintasun.

transcontinental *adj.* kontinentarteko.

transcribe *v.t.* idatzaldatu, idatzi.

transcriber *n.* berridazle, kopidazle, kopiatzaile.

transcript *n.* idatz-kopi.

transcription *n.* idatzaldaketa.

transfer *v.t./v.i.* bestetu, besteganatu, lekualdatu.

transfer *n.* lekualdaketa. *n. (econ.)* lagapen.

transferable *adj.* eskualdagarri, bestegangarri.

transference *n.* eskualdaketa, lekualdaketa.

transfiguration *n.* antzaldaketa, itxuraldaketa, irudialdaketa.

transfigure *v.t.* antzaldatu, itxuraldatu, irudiz aldatu, eraldatu.

transform *v.t./v.i.* itxuraldatu, antzaldatu, eraldatu, bestelakotu.

transformation *n.* eraldaketa, itxuraldaketa, antzaldaketa.

transformer *n. (phys.)* aldagailu, transformadore. *n.* bihurtzaile.

transfuse *v.t. (med.)* odolaldatu.

transfusion *n.* odolnahasdura, odolaldaketa, odolemate.

transgress *v.t.* agindu hautsi. *v.i./v.t.* igaro.

transgression *n.* aginduhausketa, saiheskeria, gaitzegite; legekalte.

transgressor *n.* hausle, lege hausle.

transhumance *n.* larraldaketa.

transhumant *adj.* larraldatzaile.

transient *adj.* iraungabeko. *n.* ibiltari.

transistor *n. (elec.)* transitore. *n.* irratigailu txiki(a).

transit *n.* iragaite.

transitable *adj.* ibilgarri.

transition *n.* iragaite, iraganaldi, igaroaldi, iragapen.

transitive *adj. (gram.)* iragankor.
  Transitive verb. Aditz iragankor.

transitorially *adv.* iragankorki, iraganez.

transitoriness *n.* igarokortasun, iragankortasun.

transitory *adj.* iragankor, iraganaldiko,

iragaile, igarokor, pasakor.

translatable *adj.* itzulgarri.

translate *v.t./v.i.* itzuli, irauli, bihurtu.
  To translate into Basque.
  Euskaratu. **To translate into**
  English. Ingeleseratu.

translation *n.* itzulpen, itzulaldi, itzulketa, itzulpenlan.

translator *n.* itzultzaile.

translucent *adj.* zeharrargitsu.

transmigration *n.* herrialdaketa.

transmissible *adj.* emangarri, bidalgarri, igorgarri, eskualdagarri.

transmission *n.* emanaldi, emankizun. *n.* transmisio.

transmit *v.t./v.i.* irratsaiotu, helarazi, bidali. *v.t.* izurriztatu.

transmittable *adj.* emangarri, igorgarri, komunikagarri. **Not transmittable.**
  Emangaitz. Emanezin.

transmitted *adj.* emandako.

transmitter *n.* bidalgailu, emangailu, igorgailu; igorle, igortzaile.

transoceanic *adj.* itsasosteko.

transom *n.* gurdilanga, ategainleiho.

transparency *n.* gardentasun.

transparent *adj.* garden.

transparently *adv.* gardenki.

transpire *v.i.* gertatu, jazo.

transplant *v.t.* birlandatu, lurraldatu, berraldatu.

transplant *n.* berraldaketa, birlandaketa. *n. (med.)* transplante.

transport *v.t.* erakarri, eraman, garraiatu.

transport *n.* garraio. *n.* garraigailu.

transportable *adj.* eramangarri, eramankor, garraigarri, lekualdagarri, ekargarri.

transportation *n.* eramate, garraiaketa, garraialdi, igorketa.

transporter *n.* garraialari, garraiatzaile; garraigailu, garraiontzi.

transpose *v.t.* leku aldatu. *v.t./v.i. (mus.)* doinu aldatu, doinu berritu.

transposition *n. (mus.)* doinualdaketa. *n.* lekualdaketa.

transverse *adj.* zeharreko, zeharkako.

transvestism *n.* andragizonkeria.

trap *v.t./v.i.* lakiotu, sareartetu, harrapatu.

trap *n.* harrapagailu, lakio, zelataldi, gako-mako, tranpa.

trapeze *n.* trapezio.

trapezoid *n. (geom.)* trapezio.

trapper *n.* harrapatzaile, lakiolari.

trapping *n.* larruketa.

trappings *n. (pl.)* deusak.

trash *n.* zabor, zakarkeria, zatarreria, zamar, zarama.

trashy *adj.* zakartsu.

trauma *n.* trauma.

traumatic *adj.* traumazko.

traumatism *n.* traumatismo, zauridura.

travel *v.i./v.t.* bidaia egin, piaiatu, ostera egin.

travel *n.* bidaldi, ibilaldi.

traveler *n.* bidalari, ibiltari, bidazti.
traverse *v.t./v.i.* zeharkatu.
travesty *n.* literatur lan zakar. *n.* parodia barregarri.
trawler *n.* ontziarrastari.
tray *n.* erretilu. *n.* hiruko.
treacherous *adj.* azpijale, saltzaile.
treacherously *adv.* salkeriaz, saldukeriaz, zakurki.
treachery *n.* zakurkeria, txakurkeria, salkeria, traizio, saldukeria.
tread *v.t./v.i.* hankazpiratu, lehartu, ostikatu, zuzitu, zanpatu, oinkatu.
tread *n.* oinots. *n.* gurpilaren hozkadura.
treason *n.* saldukeria, traizio, azpijan, azpilan, satorkeria, judaskeria.
treasonously *adv.* saldukeriaz, salkeriaz.
treasure *n.* altxor, ondasunketa.
treasurer *n.* altxorzain, diruzain.
treasury *n.* diruzaingela, dirugordailu, diruzaindegi.
treat *v.t.* tratatu.
treat *n.* goxo.
treatise *n.* tratatu.
treatment *n.* medikapen, tratamendu.
treaty *n.* elkargo, hitzarmen, itun.
treble *adj.* hiruko. *adj./n. (mus.)* soprano.
tree *n.* zuhaitz, arbola.
trefoil *n. (bot.)* hirusta, sekulabelar.
trek *n.* ibilkunde, ibilaldi.
tremble *v.i.* hotzikaratu, dildiratu, dardarikatu, dardar egin.
tremble *n.* gorputzikara.
trembling *n.* dardara, ikara. *adj.* dardarati, dardaradun, dardarka.
tremendous *adj.* izugarri, izugarrizko, ikaragarri, ikaragarrizko.
tremendously *adv.* izugarriro, ikaragarriro.
tremor *n.* dardarikara, dardara.
tremulous *adj.* dardarti, dardartsu, dardarati.
trench *n.* biderreten, erreten, ubide, luebaki.
trend *n.* joera.
trepanation *n. (med.)* buruzulaketa.
trepanning *n. (med.)* buruzulaketa.
trepidation *n.* kezkaldi, larrialdi.
trespass *v.i. (batzutan* on*-ekin)* galerazitako leku batetan sartu. *v.i.* legea hautsi. *v.i.* bekatu egin.
trespassing *n.* aginduhausketa.
tresses *n. (pl.)* ile luze.
triad *n. (mus.)* hiruko.
trial *n.* auzi, epaialdi; auzi-. *n.* ahalegin, frogaldi, saialdi, saiamen, entseiu. *adj.* frogagarri, saiagarri.
trial run *n.* saiaketa.
triangle *n. (geom.)* hiruangelu, hiruki.
triangular *adj.* hiruangeludun.
tribal *adj.* tribuko.
tribe *n.* tribu, leinu.
tribulation *n.* estualdi, lor.
tribunal *n.* auzitegi, epaileku, epaitegi.

tributary *n.* ibaiadar.
tribute *n.* gorazarre, omenaldi, goraipamen, gorespen, laudorio.
trick *v.t.* engainatu, iruzurtu, iruzur egin, ziri(a) sartu, zipotza sartu.
trick *n.* iruzur, bihurrikeria, engainu, ziri, judukeria.
trickery *n.* maltzurkeria, bihurrikeria, iruzurbide.
trickily *adv.* bihurriki, maltzurki, maltzurkiro.
trickiness *n.* maltzurkeria, malmuztasun.
trickle *v.i.* erion, tantakatu.
trickster *n.* engainari, iruzurgile.
tricky *adj.* iruzurtsu, maltzurkeriazko, malmutz.
tricolor *adj.* hirumargodun, hirumargoko.
tricolored *adj.* hirukoloreko, hirumargodun, hirumargoko.
tricycle *n.* hirugurpileko, triziklo.
trident *n.* hiruhortzeko.
triennial *adj.* hirurteko.
triennium *n.* hirurte.
trifle *n.* huskeria, fits, tipikeria, xehekeria.
trifling *adj.* txatxar, hutsal, purtzil.
trigger *n.* sugiltz, katu.
trigonometry *n.* trigonometria.
trillion *n./adj.* Estatu Batuetako trilioia (1,000,000,000,000).
trilogy *n.* hiruko, trilogia.
trill *v.t./v.i.* txinta egin.
trim *v.t.* kimatu, moztu, inaustu. *v.t.* murriztu.
trimester *n.* hiruhilabete, urtelaurden.
trimestral *adj.* hiruhileko, urtelaurdeneko.
trimmer *n.* murruztaile.
trinity *n.* hirutasun, trinitate.
trinket *n.* girgileria, purtxileria, bitxikeria.
trio *n.* hiruko, hirukote.
trip *v.i./v.t.* behaztopatu, oztopatu, zoztor egin.
trip *n.* ateraldi, ibilaldi, bidaia, txango. *n.* behaztopa, oztopaldi, oztopo.
tripartition *n.* hirurenketa, hiruzatiketa.
tripe *n.* hesteki, tripaki(ak), gibelerrai, tripakailu(ak), barruki.
triple *v.t./v.i.* hirutu, hirukoiztu.
triple *adj.* hirukoitz.
triplet *n.* hiruki, hirukoitz, hirukote. *n. (mus.)* hiruko.
triplicate *v.t.* hirutu, hirukoiztu.
triplicate *adj.* hirukoiztu(a).
tripod *n.* hiruoineko, trebera.
trite *adj.* arrunt, edonolako.
triumph *v.i. (askotan* over*-ekin)* irabazi, gailendu, garaitu, burutu.
triumph *n.* garaipen, garaitza, irabazpen.
triumphant *adj.* garaile, garaitiar, irabazle.
triumphantly *adv.* garaitsuki.
trivet *n.* trebera.

trivial *adj.* zirtzil, ziztrin.
triviality *n.* huskeria, xehekeria, arinkeria, tipikeria.
troll *n.* lamia.
trolley *n.* trolebus.
trombone *n. (mus.)* tronboi.
troop *n.* gudalsail, gudaltalde, soldadutalde.
trophy *n.* garaisari, kopa, trofeo.
tropic *adj.* tropiko.
tropical *adj.* tropikoko, beroaldeko.
tropics *n. (pl.)* beroalde, tropikoak.
trot *v.i./v.t.* takataka ibili.
trot *n.* takata.
troubadour *n.* koblakari, bertsolari.
troubadourism *n.* koblakaritza, bertsolaritza.
trouble *n.* iskanbila, istilu, estualdi, korapilo.
troubled *adj.* hersturadun.
troublemaker *n.* kezkarazle, nahastari, nahastero, nahasketari.
troublesome *adj.* buruhausgarri, trabagarri, eragozkarri, nahaspilari, nahaspilatzaile, nahastekari, kezkagarri, korapilotsu.
troubling *adj.* kexagarri, kezkagarri.
trough *n.* aspil.
troupe *n.* aktore-konpainia.
trousers *n. (pl.)* galtza(k), praka(k).
trousseau *n.* hatu, ostilamendu.
trout *n. (zool.)* amurrain, arrankari.
trowel *v.t.* azalurratu.
trowel *n.* palote. *n.* landare-erauzle.
truant *adj./n.* piperrero. *adj./n.* bere beharrari ihes egiten diona.
truce *n.* bakealdi, bakeune, gerlarte, gudarte.
truck *n.* kamioi, troka.
truckload *n.* kamioikada.
truculent *adj.* bihozkabe, bihozgogor, basa.
trudge *v.i.* nekez ibili.
true *adj.* benetako, egiazko, zinezko, egitazko.
truly *adv.* benetan, egiaz, egiazki.
trumpet *n. (mus.)* turuta, tronpeta.
trumpeter *n.* tronpetajole, turutajole.
trunk *n.* jantzikutxa, jazkikutxa, kutxa. *n.* tronpa, sudurradar. *n.* arbolagerri, enbor. *n. (anat.)* gorputzenbor.
truss *v.t.* lotu.
trust *v.i./v.t. (v.i., gehienetan* **in** *edo* **to**-*ekin)* fidatu, konfidantza ukan, sinetsi.
trust *n.* fidagarritasun, konfidantza, fidantza.
trusted *adj.* usteoneko.
trustee *n.* gordailuzain.
trusting *adj.* fidakor, sineskor.
trustingly *adv.* fidakorki, fidatuki, sineskorki.
trustworthy *adj.* fidagarri, sinesgarri.
trusty *adj.* fidagarri, sinesgarri.
truth *n.* egia.
truthful *adj.* egiati, egitazko, egizale, benetako.

truthfully *adv.* benetan, egiaz.
truthfulness *n.* egiberatasun, egitasun.
try *v.t./v.i.* saiatu, saio egin, ahalegindu, eginahalak egin. *v.t. (*on, out*)* probatu.
try *n.* ahalegin, saiakera, saialdi.
trying *n.* saiapen, saialdi. *adj.* nekagarri.
tryout *n.* gaitasun froga.
T-shirt *n.* kamiseta.
T-square *n.* laukigailu.
tub *n.* garbiontzi, ikuztontzi. *n.* upeltxo.
tuba *n. (mus.)* tuba.
tube *n.* hodi, tutu, tutulu, tubo.
tuber *n.* tuberkulu.
tubercular *adj. (med.)* tisiko.
tuberculosis *n. (med.)* hetika, birikeri, bularreri.
tubular *adj.* hodiantzeko, hodizko.
Tuesday *n.* astearte, martitzen.
tuft *n.* motots, gandor.
tug *v.i./v.t.* gogor teink egin.
tugboat *n.* atoiontzi, erremolkatzaile.
tug-of-war *n.* sokatira.
tuition *n.* matrikulatze-eskubideen ordainketa.
tulip *n. (bot.)* tulipa, idibihotz.
tumble *v.i./v.t.* lur jo, erori. *v.i.* zilipurdika ari, zilipurdikatu, itzulipurdikatu.
tumble *n.* iraulaldi, itzulipurdi, iraulketa, tirabira.
tumbler *n.* itzulipurdikari. *n.* edalontzi.
tumbling *n.* iraulaldi.
tummy *n. (colloq.)* sabel.
tumor *n.* hanpuru, minbizikoskor.
tumult *n.* asaldapen, iskanbila, istilu.
tumultuous *adj.* zaratari, zalapartatsu.
tumultuously *adv.* harrapaka, iskanbilka.
tuna *n. (zool.)* atun, atunki.
tune *v.t./v.i. (askotan* **up**-*ekin)* doinukidetu, gozatu, sintonizatu, musika-tresnak afinatu. *v.t./v.i. (irratia edo telebista)* doinukidetu.
tune *n. (mus.)* doinu, soinu, melodia.
tuneful *adj.* soinugarri, meloditsu.
tunefully *adv.* melodioski.
tunic *n.* soingaineko, tunika.
tuning *n.* sintonizapen, doinukidetasun, soinukidetasun.
tunnel *n.* lurpebide, tunel, zulape.
turban *n.* buruoihal.
turbid *adj.* uher, arre.
turbidity *n.* uhertasun, arretasun.
turbidness *n.* uherdura, uhertasun, arretasun.
turbine *n. (mech.)* turbina.
turbot *n. (zool.)* erreboilo.
turbulence *n.* uherdura, uhertasun, asaldaketa.
turbulent *adj.* uher.
turbulently *adv.* iskanbilka, zalapartaz.
turd *n.* kakamokordo, mokordo.
turf *v.t.* zohiztatu.
turf *n.* zohi, zotala.

turkey *n. (zool.)* indioilar, indioilo.
turmoil *n.* zalaparta, iskanbila.
turn *v.t./v.i. (batzutan* **around***-ekin)* itzuli, itzulinguratu, biratu, jirabiratu. *v.i.* orbeldu (hostoak). *v.t./v.i. (away)* desbidetu, desbideratu. *v.i./v.t. (back)* berribili, atzeratu. *v.t./v.i. (into)* bihurtu, bilakatu. *v.t. (off, out)* itzali, iraungi. *v.t. (on)* biztu, argi egin. *v.t./v.i. (over)* irauli, irabiratu, itzulikatu, alderantzikatu. *v.t. (over to)* eskuetaratu. *v.i. (up)* azaldu, agertu. *v.i. (down)* eragotzi; tolestu.
turn *n.* aldi, txanda, tornu. *n.* bihurgune, biragune, biraldi, itzuli, jirabira, itzulaldi.
turnip *n. (bot.)* arbi, nabo.
turnout *n.* bidebazter.
turnpike *n.* peaiezko bide.
turpentine *n.* aguarras.
turquoise *n./adj.* urdinberde.
turtle *n. (zool.)* dortoka.
turtldove *n. (zool.)* usatortola, usapal.
tusk *n.* betagin, betortz.
tussle *n.* errieta, mokokaldi.
tutelage *n.* tutorego.
tutelar *adj.* zainpeko.
tutor *n.* etxeirakasle, tutore.
tutorship *n.* tutorego.
TV *n.* telebista, teleikuskin.
twain *n./adj.* bi.
'twas "it + was"-aren laburpena.
tweet *v.i.* pio egin, tiutatu, txiokatu.
tweet *n.* pio, fiit.
tweeter *n.* piokari.
tweezers *n. (pl.)* pintzak.
twelfth *adj.* hamabiren, hamabigarren, hamabi.
Twelfth-day *n.* erregegun.
Twelfth-night *n.* erregegun bezpera.
twelve *n./adj.* hamabi.
twentieth *adj.* hogeigarren, hogeinako.
twenty *n./adj.* hogei.
'twere "it + were"-aren laburpena.
twice *adv.* bitan, bi aldiz, birritan, bi bider.
twig *n.* adaska, erromuskil.
twilight *n.* ilunalde, ilunsenti, ilunabar, arrats. *adj.* ilunabarreko.
twin *n./adj.* bikoitz, biki, sabelkide.
twine *n.* kordel, lokarri.
twinge *n.* min bizi. *n.* barrendamu.
twinkle *v.i./v.t.* izarniatu, ñirñir egin, pindartu, dis-dis egin.
twinkle *n.* distiraketa, izarniadura, ñirñira, pindar.
twinkling *adj.* ñirñirkari, distiratsu, kiñulari.
twirl *v.i./v.t.* jira-bira egin, jira-bira eragin, jirabiratu, bira eragin.
twist *v.t./v.i.* bihurritu, bihurtu, kiribildu, makurkatu, oihertu, okertu. *v.t./v.i. (away)* zehartu.
twist *n.* bihurkada, makurgune, okerrune, zaintiraketa, okergune.
twistable *adj.* bihurkoi, biribilkakor, makurgarri, okergarri, bihurgarri.

twisted *adj.* oker, bihur, makur, zeharkako, oiher, kiribil.
twistedly *adv.* kiribilka, okerki, okerretara.
twistedness *n.* okertasun, makurtasun.
twister *n.* okertzaile. *n.* zurrunbilo.
two *n./adj.* bi, biga.
twofold *adv.* biko.
tycoon *n.* handi-mandi.
tyke *n.* jatorri ezezaguneko txakur. *n.* haurtxo, umetxo.
tympanum *n. (anat.)* belarrimintz.
type *v.t./v.i.* makinidatzi, mekanografiatu. *v.t.* motatu.
type *n.* mota, klase, molde, moeta.
typewrite *v.t./v.i.* makinidatzi.
typewriter *n.* idazmakina, idazkailu.
typewriting *n.* makinidazkera, makinidazkintza, mekanografia.
typewritten *adj.* makinaz idatzi(a).
typhoid *n.* tifus. *adj.* tifusaire.
typhoon *n.* tifoi, traganarru, mangera.
typhus *n. (med.)* tifus.
typical *adj.* eredugarri, jator, tipiko.
typing *n.* makinidazkintza, makinidazkera, mekanografia.
typist *n.* makinidazle, makinidazlari, mekanografari.
typography *n.* tipografia.
tyrannical *adj.* bortxatzaile.
tyrannize *v.i./v.t.* nagusikeritu, indarkeritu.
tyranny *n.* nagusikeria.
tyrant *n.* jauntzar, behartzaile.
tzar *Cf. czar.*

U

u *n.* Ingeles alfabetoko letra.
ubiquitous *adj.* nonnahi.
udder *n.* errape.
ugh *int.* uf.
ugliness *n.* itsustasun, itsuskeria, ezaintasun.
ugly *adj.* itsusi, itxuragaiztoko, zatar, ezain.
ukulele *n. (mus.)* ukelele.
ulcer *n. (med.)* ultzera.
ulcerate *v.i./v.t.* ultzeratu.
ulcerated *adj.* zauritsu.
ulceration *n.* ultzeraketa, ultzerapen.
ulcerous *adj.* ultzeratsu, zaurikoi, zornatsu.
ulterior *adj.* gerozko.
ultimate *adj.* azkenaldeko, hondar, azkenengo.
ultimately *adv.* azkenez, azkenekoz, azken batez.
ultimatum *n.* ultimatum, azkenitz.
ultra *adj.* gehiegizko, neurrigaineko.
ultramarine *adj.* itsasarunzko, itsasurdin.
ultraviolet *adj.* ultramore.
umbilical *adj.* zileko, zilborreko.
umbilical cord *n. (anat.)* zileste, zilborreste.
umbrella *n.* euritako, aterkin.
umpire *n.* jokazain, arbitro.

un- *(gram.)* ez-.
unabated *adj.* etengabe, geldigabe, atergabe.
unable *adj.* ahalezin, ezgauza.
unaccentuated *adj.* azentugabe.
unacceptable *adj.* onartezin, onargaitz, hargaitz, harrezin.
unaccountable *adj.* adieragabe. *adj.* arduragabedun, axolagabe.
unaccustomed *adj.* ohigabe.
unachievable *adj.* lortezin.
unacquainted *adj.* **(with)** ezjakin. *adj.* inor ezagutzen ez duena.
unadaptable *adj.* egokiezin, egokigaitz, ezinmoldatuzko, desaldagarri.
unadorned *adj.* apaindugabe, bipil.
unadulterated *adj.* garbi, jator.
unaffected *adj.* berezko, xume. *adj.* aldagabe.
unafraid *adj.* ezbeldurti.
unaided *adj.* laguntasunik gabe.
unalterable *adj.* aldagaitz, aldaezin.
unalterably *adv.* aldaezinez, aldagaizkiro.
unanimity *n.* ahobatasun, erizkidetasun, gogaidetasun, gogobatasun, gogokidetasun.
unanimous *adj.* erizkide, ahobateko, ustebereko, gogobateko.
unanimously *adv.* elkarturik, ahobatez, gogo batez, bihozbatez.
unanimousness *n.* gogokidetasun.
unannounced *adj.* iragarrigabe(ko).
unanswerable *adj.* erantzunezin, erantzunezinezko.
unanswered *adj.* erantzungabe.
unappraised *adj.* baloragabe.
unapproachable *adj.* helgaitz, eskuragaitz.
unarmed *adj.* armagabeko.
unashamed *adj.* ezlotsati, ezlotsakor.
unassuming *adj.* erabidetsu, eraoneko, eratsu.
unattached *adj.* solte, aske, ezlotu.
unattainable *adj.* eskuraezin.
unattended *adj.* bakar. *adj.* huts. *adj.* zaindugabe(ko) (gaiso), baztertu(a). *adj.* zaindugabe (moralki), baztertu(a).
unattractive *adj.* ia itsusi(a).
unauthorized *adj.* baimengabetu(a), agintegabetu(a), deseskubidetu(a).
unavailing *adj.* alferreko, alferrikako, ezgauza.
unavoidable *adj.* utziezin(ezko), alabeharreko, aldezin, baztergaitz, bazterrezineko.
unavoidably *adv.* alabeharrez.
unaware *adj.* ezjakin.
unbalanced *adj.* ezegonkor, orekagabe.
unbearable *adj.* jasanezin, eramanezin, pairaezin.
unbearably *adv.* jasanezinez.
unbeatable *adj.* garaiezin.
unbeatableness *n.* garaiezintasun.

unbeaten *adj.* garaitugabe, gailendugabe.
unbecoming *adj.* desegoki, eragabe.
unbelievable *adj.* asmaezin, sinesgogor, sinestezin.
unbelievableness *n.* sinesgogortasun.
unbelievably *adv.* ezinsinetsiz.
unbeliever *n.* fedegabe, sinesgabe.
unbelieving *adj.* sinestegabe, fedegabe(ko), sinesgabe.
unbend *v.t./v.i.* desokertu.
unbendable *adj.* makurtezin, ezinmoldatuzko.
unbending *adj.* makurtezin.
unbiased *adj.* alderdigabe(ko), ezalderdikari, erdi-erdiko.
unblemished *adj.* akaskabe, lausogabe.
unborn *adj.* jaiogabe, sorgabe.
unbraid *v.t.* desehundu, ehungabetu.
unbraided *adj.* ehungabe.
unbreakable *adj.* haustezin(ezko), apurtezin, ezauskor, etenezin.
unbreakableness *n.* hauskaiztasun.
unbreathable *adj.* arnasezin, hatsezin.
unbridled *adj.* neurrigabe, grinati.
unbroken *ad.* zatigabeko.
unbuckle *v.t.* askatu.
unbutton *v.t.* botoiak askatu.
unburden *v.t.* lasotu; deskargatu.
uncage *v.t.* deskaiolatu.
uncalled for *adj.* ezbeharrezko.
uncanny *adj.* izkutuko, bitxi, adieragabe.
unceasing *adj.* geldiezin, atergabe, etengabe, geldigabe.
unceasingly *adv.* geldiezinik.
uncertain *adj.* noizbaiteko, zalantzagarri, eztabaidako, menturako, seguragaitz.
uncertainly *adv.* kili-kolo, kikilki.
uncertainty *n.* zalantza, zalantzagarritasun, ezbaitasun.
unchain *v.t.* deskateatu.
unchangeable *adj.* aldaezin, desaldagarri, betibateko, itzulezin.
unchangeableness *n.* itzulezintasun.
unchanged *adj.* aldagabe.
unchecked *adj.* neurrigabe.
uncircumcised *adj.* erdaingabe.
uncivilized *adj.* hezgabe.
unclad *adj.* biluzi, larrugorri, larruts.
unclassifiable *adj.* kalifikaezin.
uncle *n.* osaba.
unclean *adj.* zikin.
uncleanliness *n.* narrasketa.
uncollectable *adj.* kobraezin.
uncomfortable *adj.* deseroso, ezeroso.
uncomfortableness *n.* deserosotasun.
uncomfortably *adv.* ezerosoki, eratxarrean.
uncommon *adj.* bakan, ohigabe.
uncommonly *adv.* ohigabeki, ohi ez bezala.
uncomplaining *adj.* pairugabe, ezsentibera.

uncompromising *adj.* batezin, elkarrezin.
unconcealable *adj.* ezingordezko.
unconceivable *adj.* asmaezin.
unconcerned *adj.* kezkagabe, gibelandi, axolagabe.
unconditional *adj.* baldingabe, kondiziogabe.
unconditionally *adv.* kondiziogabeki.
unconfessed *adj.* aitorgabe.
unconnectable *adj.* lotezin.
unconnected *adj.* loturagabe.
unconquerable *adj.* erasogaitz, garaiezin, menderaezin.
unconscious *adj.* zentzugabe, konorterik gabe. *adj.* konturagabe.
unconsciously *adv.* konturagabez.
unconsciousness *n.* kordegabetasun.
unconsolable *adj.* pozgaitz.
unconstitutional *adj.* konstituzioaurkako.
uncontainable *adj.* kabiezin.
uncontaminated *adj.* kutsugabe.
uncontrollable *adj.* kontrolaezin, eustezin, gobernagaitz.
uncontrolled *adj.* kontrolgabe, menpegabe.
uncooked *adj.* gordin, egosgabe.
uncork *v.t.* desziritu, kortxogabetu.
uncorrupted *adj.* ustelgabe, andeagabe.
uncountable *adj.* zenbatezin.
uncourteous *adj.* gaizkikasi.
uncouth *adj.* zarpailtsu, eragabe, zakar.
uncouthness *n.* oiheskeria, zarpailkeria, zarpailtasun.
uncover *v.t.* estalgabetu, estalgetu.
uncovered *adj.* estalgabe, ageri.
uncrossable *adj.* ibiezin, ibilgaitz.
unction *n.* gantzudura, gantzuketa, gantzualdi.
unctuous *adj.* gantzutsu, koipetsu.
uncultivated *adj.* landugabe, basa.
uncultured *adj.* eskolagabe, ezikasi, ezjakin.
uncurl *v.t./v.i.* desokertu.
uncustomary *adj.* ohigabe.
uncut *adj.* ebakigabe, oso.
uncuttable *adj.* moztuezin.
undamaged *adj.* kaltegabe.
undaunted *adj.* ausart, izugaitz, ikaragaitz.
undecided *adj.* erabakigabe, aldakor, zalantzako.
undecipherable *adj.* argigaitz, irakurgaitz.
undeclarable *adj.* aitorrezin.
undefeatable *adj.* garaiezin.
undefined *adj.* mugagabe. *adj.* adieragabe.
undeniable *adj.* ezeztaezin, ukaezin, ukagaitz.
undeniably *adj.* ukaezin, ukagaitz.
under *prep./adv.* azpi, azpian, behean, behera; behe-, -peko. *adj.* beheko, azpiko.

under- *(gram.)* -peko, behe-, azpi-.
underarm *n. (anat.)* besape, galtzarpe.
underbrush *n.* sasitza, sastraka.
undercurrent *n.* itsas edo ibaiko urlaster. *n.* eritzi ezkutuko korronte.
underdeveloped *adj.* atzeratu(a).
  Underdeveloped countries. Lurralde atzeratuak.
underdevelopment *n.* atzeratasun.
underdog *n.* elkarlehian galtzaile izatea espero dena.
underestimate *v.t./v.i.* gutietsi, txikietsi, arbuiatu.
underestimated *adj.* gutiespenezko.
underestimation *n.* gutiespen.
underfed *adj.* deselikatu(a).
underfeed *v.t.* deselikatu.
underfeeding *n.* deselikadura.
underfloor *n.* zorupe.
underfoot *adv./adj.* oinazpian. *adj.* oztopatsu, eragosgarri, trabakor.
undergo *v.t.* jaso.
undergraduate *n.* unibertsitateko ikasle graduatugabe(a).
underground *n.* lurbarne, lurpe, lurrazpi. *adj.* lurpeko, lurrazpiko.
underhanded *adj.* izkutuko, isileko.
underhandedness *n.* nabarkeria, toleskeria.
underline *v.t.* azpimarratu.
underline *n.* azpimarra.
underling *n.* menpeko, aginpeko.
undermine *v.t.* zulapetu, azpijo, azpijan.
underneath *prep./adv.* azpian, behean. *adj.* azpiko, beheko.
undernourished *adj.* deselikatu(a).
underpants *n. (pl.)* pantaloi.
underpass *n.* azpibide.
underpin *v.t.* azpindartu.
underpriveleged *n./adj.* behartsu.
underrate *v.t.* gutietsi.
undersea *adj.* itsasazpiko.
undersecretary *n.* azpidazkari, beheidazkari.
underskirt *n.* gonabarren.
understand *v.t./v.i.* ulertu, konprenitu, endelgatu, aditu, tankeratu.
understandable *adj.* adikor, gogagarri, konprenigarri, ulerkor, adierrez, ulergarri.
understanding *n.* adikuntza, ulerketa, ulermen, ezaupide, endelgu. *adj.* ulertzaile.
understate *v.t.* gutietsi, apaletsi.
understatement *n.* xumetasun gehiegiz eginiko azalpena. *n.* ideia bat azalez agertzen duen baieztapena.
understood *pret./p. part. of* *understand.*
undertake *v.t.* ekin, aritu, ihardun.
undertaker *n.* hiljazle.
undertaker's *n.* ehorztetxe.
undertaking *n.* egintza, egite, ekintza.
undertook *pret. of undertake.*
undertow *n.* erresaka.

undervalue *v.t.* gutietsi, txikietsi.
underwater *adj.* urpeko, itsaspeko. *adv.* urpean, itsaspean.
underwear *n.* galtzontzilo, galtzazpiko, barruko erropak.
underwent *pret. of undergo.*
underworld *n.* hanpa.
underwriter *n.* aseguratzaile.
undeserved *adj.* merezigabe.
undeservedly *adv.* merezigaberik.
undeserving *adj.* merezigabe, gaiez.
undesirable *adj.* opaezin.
undid *pret. of undo.*
undies *n. (pl.)* emakumearen barruko erropak.
undigested *adj.* pisutsu, egosgabe.
undigestible *adj.* liserigaitz.
undiminished *adj.* iraunkor.
undisciplined *adj.* legegabe.
undiscovered *adj.* ikergabe, aurkigabe, asmagabe.
undisputed *adj.* ezbaiezin.
undistinguished *adj.* hits.
undivided *adj.* zatigabeko, atalgabeko.
undo *v.t.* desegin, zuzitu.
undocumented *adj.* argibidegabe.
undoing *n.* galera, hondamendi, hondamen.
undomesticated *adj.* larr-.
undone *p. part. of undo.*
undoubtedly *adv.* dudagabeki, dudagabez, segurki, ziur.
undress *v.t./v.i.* erantzi, biluztu, larrugorritu.
undrinkable *adj.* edanezin, edangaitz.
undue *adj.* debekuzko, desbidezko.
undulate *v.i./v.t.* karabilkatu, izurkatu, uhindu.
undulating *adj.* izurdun, izurtsu, uhinkari, uhinkor.
undulation *n.* uhindura.
unduly *adv.* okerbidez, desbidez.
undying *adj.* iraungigaitz.
unearth *v.t.* desehortzi, deslurpetu.
uneasily *adv.* kexuki, kezkaz, larriki, ezinegonik.
uneasiness *n.* kezka, kexadura, kexutasun, zimiko, ezinegon, ekurugaiztasun.
uneasy *adj.* kexu, zirin, barruestu, ezinegonezko, kexati, kezkati.
uneducable *adj.* hezgaitz, hezikaitz.
uneducated *adj.* ezikasi, ezjakin, hezgabe, kulturgabe, eskolagabe.
unemployed *adj.* langabe, zeregingabe.
unemployment *n.* langabezia, langabealdi.
unending *adj.* ahituezin, azkengabe, bukaezin, amaigabeko.
unequal *adj.* ezberdin, berdingabeko, desberdin.
unequaled *adj.* berdingabe, paregabe.
unequivocal *adj.* zalantzagabe, dudagabeko, ezbaigabeko.
unerasable *adj.* kenezin.
unerring *adj.* hutsezin, okerrezin.

uneven *adj.* desberdin, gainbeheratsu, malkartsu. **To make uneven.** Gainbeheratu.
unevenly *adv.* desberdinki, ezberdinki, paregabeki.
unevenness *n.* desberdindura, desberdintasun.
uneventful *adj.* baketsu, bare.
unexcusable *adj.* barkaezin.
unexpandable *adj.* hedaezin, hedagaitz.
unexpected *adj.* ustekabe, ustekabezko, kasual, susmagabeko, ezuste.
unexpectedly *adv.* ezustez, ustekabean, ustekabez, kasualki, prestagabeki.
unexplainable *adj.* adieraezin, azalduezin, azalgaitz, erakusgaitz.
unexplained *adj.* adieragabe, azaldugabe.
unexplorable *adj.* ikertezin.
unexplored *adj.* ikergabe.
unextinguishable *adj.* ezinitzalizko.
unfailing *adj.* amaigabe, bukagabe.
unfair *adj.* zuzengabe, zuzengabeko, bidegabe, zuzenkontrako.
unfairly *adv.* bidegabeki, oker, zuzengabeki, makurka.
unfairness *n.* bidegabekeria, zuzengabekeria.
unfaithful *adj.* ezleial, desleial.
unfaithfulness *n.* ezleialtasun, desleialtasun.
unfamiliar *adj.* ezezagun.
unfasten *v.t./v.i.* askatu.
unfathomable *adj.* zundaezin, barneragaitz.
unfavorable *adj.* kontrako, aurkako; kaltegarri.
unfavorably *adv.* kaltegarriki.
unfeasible *adj.* bideraezin, ezeginkor.
unfeeling *adj.* idor, soraio, sor.
unfeelingly *adv.* sentiezinik, soraioki, idorki.
unfeelingness *n.* gogordura, pairugabetasun.
unfertile *adj.* elkor, agor.
unfinished *adj.* osagabe, amaigabe, bukagabe.
unfit *adj.* desegoki, erabilgaitz, baliaezin, ezgai, ezgai.
unflappable *adj.* lasai.
unfold *v.t./v.i.* destolestu, tolesgabetu.
unfolding *n.* destolesketa.
unforeseen *adj.* ezusteko, ustekabe, bat-bateko.
unforgettable *adj.* ahantzezin, bazterrezineko.
unforgivable *adj.* barkaezinezko, barkagaitz.
unforgiving *adj.* aihertsu.
unfortunate *adj.* zorigabe, zorigaitzeko, zorigaiztoko, gizagaiso, dohakabe, zoritxarreko, tamalgarri.
unfortunately *adv.* zoritxarrez, zorigabeki, zorigaitzez, zorigaiztoz,

dohakabeki, tamalez.
unfounded adj. funtsgabe, oinarrigabe, eutsezin.
unfriendliness n. mukerkeria, muzinkeria, zapuzkeria.
unfriendly adj. mukerbera, muzin, zaputz, betilun.
unfruitful adj. agor, antzu.
unfulfillable adj. betezin.
unfulfilled adj. betegabe, egingabe.
unfurl v.t./v.i. destolestu.
unfurnished adj. deserredizatu.
ungainly adj. loditzar, trakets. adv. zangu-mangu.
ungenerous adj. eskuitxi.
unglue v.t. desitsasi.
ungodly adj. erlijiogabe, fedegabe.
ungovernable adj. gobernaezin.
ungrateful adj. eskergabe, eskerbeltzeko, eskergaitz, eskergaiztoko, eskertxarreko.
ungratefully adv. eskergabeki, eskergaiztoz, eskertxarrez.
ungratefulness n. eskergabekeria, eskergaizto, eskergaitz, eskergabetasun, eskertxar.
unguarded adj. zentzugabe(ko), seingabeko, kaskarin. adj. babesgabe.
unguent n. gantzu, gantzuki.
ungulate adj. apodun.
unhallowed adj. ezsakratu.
unhappily adv. zorigaitzez, zoritxarrez, zorigabeki.
unhappiness n. pozgabetasun, zorigabetasun, beltzura, zoritxar.
unhappy adj. zorigabe, kopetilun, zorigaitzeko, zorigaiztoko, zoritxarreko, goibel, pozgabe.
unharmed adj. kaltegabeko, okergabe, onik. **To escape unharmed.** Onik irten.
unharness v.t. desgakotu.
unhealthy adj. erigarri, gaisobera, gaisoti, gaitz, gaizkor, osasungabe.
unheard-of adj. aditugabe, entzungabe, ezentzun.
unhinge v.t. desorpotu, deserrotu.
unhitch v.t. desgakotu, askatu.
unholy adj. ezsakratu(a), erlijiogabe.
unhook v.t./v.i. desgakotu.
unhurriedly adv. patxadaz, astiro, geldiro, poliki.
unhurt adj. gaizkabe, kaltegabe, mingabe, mingabeko, zaurigabe.
unicorn n. adarbakar.
unicycle n. gurpilbakar.
unidentified adj. agirigabe.
unification n. batasun, bateraketa, bateratasun.
unified adj. bateratu, batu(a), batuta.
uniform n. uniforme, jantzi. adj. erabereko, eraberdineko, erakide, berebbateko.
uniformity n. erakidetasun, erabatasun.
uniformly adv. erabatez, eraberdinez.

unify v.t./v.i. bat egin, batu, orobatu, anaitu.
unifying adj. batugarri, batutzaile, loturakoi, batzaile.
unilateral adj. aldebakar, aldebateko, albobateko.
unimaginable adj. irudiezin, imajinezin.
unimportant adj. garrantzigabe(ko).
unimprovable adj. huskabe.
uninformed adj. ezjakin.
uninhabitable adj. biziezin, bizigaitz.
uninhabited adj. auzogabe, biztanlegabeko, inorgabe, jendegabe.
uninjured adj. gaizkabe, okergabe, zaurigabe.
unintelligibility n. ulerkaiztasun, adigaiztasun, ulertezintasun.
unintelligible adj. ulertezin, ulerkaitz, adiezin.
unintentional adj. asmogabeko, konturagabe(ko), oharkabe.
unintentionally adv. asmogabez, konturagabez.
uninterrupted adj. atergabeko, tartegabeko, etengabe, geldigabe(ko).
uninterruptedly adv. atergabeki, jarraika, etengabe.
uninvited adj. ezgonbidatu, gonbidatugabe.
union n. batasun, elkartasun, elkarte, bategite, elkargo, elkarketa, lotura. n. lantalde, sindikatu.
unionism n. sindikapen; batasunzaletasun.
unionize v.t./v.i. sindikatu.
unionizer n. sindikatzaile.
unique adj. bakar, banako, bat, berdingabeko, paregabe, bakarreko.
uniqueness n. bakartasun, berebizikotasun.
unisexual adj. sexubakar.
unison n. soinubakartasun, doinubakartasun.
unit n. gauza bat, pertsona bat, elemendu, bateko, ale, unitate. n. talde.
unite v.t./v.i. batu, bat egin, elkarbatu, anaitu, elkartu.
united adj. bateratu, bategina.
United States of America n. (geog.) Ameriketako Estatu Batuak. **Citizen of the United States.** Estatubatuar.
unity n. baterakuntza, batasun, elkartasun.
universal adj. unibertsal, orokor, ororen, orotar.
universalize v.t. orotu.
universally adv. orokorki, unibertsalki.
universe n. lurbira, mundu, unibertso.
university n. unibertsitate.
unjust adj. bidegabe, zuzenkontrako, zuzengabe.
unjustly adv. makurka, okerbidez, zuzenkontra, bidegabeki, oker, zuzengabeki.

unkempt *adj.* lazo, hartzi, tximadun.
unkind *adj.* ezatsegin.
unkindly *adv.* lazki.
unkindness *n.* bihozgabekeria, krudelkeria.
unknot *v.t.* deskorapilatu.
unknowable *adj.* ezaguezin, jakinezin.
unknowingly *adv.* ezjakitez, ezjakinez.
unknown *adj.* ezazagun, izengabe, famagabe, entzutegabe.
unlace *v.t.* deslokarritu.
unlawful *adj.* deslegezko, bidegabeko.
unleavened *adj.* legamigabe, jalkiezin.
unless *conj./prep.* ezik, salbu.
unlevel *adj.* gainbeheratsu.
unlike *adj.* ezberdin, antzgabeko, desberdin.
unlikelihood *n.* sinesgaiztasun.
unlikely *adj./adv.* kanoregabe, gertagaitz.
unlimitable *adj.* mugaezin, mugagaitz.
unlimited *adj.* mugagabe(ko), neurrigabe(ko), ezmugatu(a), epegabeko, azkengabe.
unlimitedly *n.* mugagabeki, neurrigabez, azkengabeki.
unload *v.t./v.i.* zamagabetu, desontziratu, deszamatu.
unlock *v.t.* atearen morroiloa ireki.
unloose *v.t.* askatu.
unloved *adj.* maitegabe.
unloyal *adj.* desleial, ezleial.
unluckily *adv.* zorigaitzez, zoritxarrez, zorigabeki, zorigaiztoz.
unluckiness *n.* zorigabetasun, zorigaiztasun.
unlucky *adj.* zorigaitzeko, zorigaiztoko, dohakaizdun, alditxarreko, zorigabe, zoritxarreko.
unmanageable *adj.* erabiltezin, managaitz.
unmanly *adj.* beldurti, txepel, oilo. *adj.* maritxu, emagizon.
unmarketable *adj.* salgaitz, salezin.
unmarriable *adj.* ezkonezin.
unmarried *adj.* ezkongabe, ezkongai.
unmask *v.t./v.i.* mozorroa kendu.
unmatched *adj.* ezpare.
unmeasurable *adj.* neurgaitz.
unmentionable *adj.* esanezin, aipaezin, izendaezin.
unmentioned *adj.* aipatugabe.
unmerciful *adj.* errukigabe, gupidagabe, gupidagaitz, errukigabeko, anker, bihozgabe, bihozgogor.
unmercifully *adv.* errukigabeki, gupidagabeki.
unmistakable *adj.* okerrezin, nahasezin.
unmistakably *adv.* nahasgabeki.
unmolested *adj.* eznekarazi.
unmovable *adj.* higiezin, kenezin, mugiezin.
unmoved *adj.* desarduratu, aldagabe.
unmoving *adj.* mugigabe, ibilge.
unnameable *adj.* izendaezin, izendagaitz.

unnatural *adj.* eznormal; artifizial.
unnavigable *adj.* itsasibilezin.
unnecessarily *adv.* beharrik gabe, premiarik gabe.
unnecessary *adj.* behargabe, premiagabeko, ezbeharrezko.
unnoticeable *adj.* oharkaitz, ohartezin.
unnoticed *adj.* oharkabe.
unobtainable *adj.* lorgaitz, lortezin.
unoccupied *adj.* zeregingabe. *adj.* huts.
unofficial *adj.* ezofizial.
unopenable *adj.* zabalezin.
unopened *adj.* ezireki(a).
unopposable *adj.* kontraezin.
unorganized *adj.* antolagabe, eragabe.
unpack *v.t./v.i.* desbildu.
unpaid *adj.* ordaindugabeko.
unpardonable *adj.* barkaezin, barkagaitz.
unpayable *adj.* ordainezin.
unperishable *adj.* ezinzimelduzko.
unpile *v.t.* desmetatu.
unplanned *adj.* asmogabeko.
unpleasant *adj.* gozagabe, gozagaitz, gustagaitz.
unpleasantness *n.* gozagabekeria, gozagaizkeria.
unpleasing *adj.* gustagaitz.
unplug *v.t./v.i.* desziritu, txantola kendu. *v.t. (elec.)* desentxufatu.
unpolished *adj.* basto.
unpolluted *adj.* kutsagabe, satsudura gabeko.
unpopular *adj.* herrikontrako.
unpopulated *adj.* jendegabe, auzogabe, biztanlegabeko.
unpotable *adj.* ezinedanezko.
unprecedented *adj.* aurregabeko.
unpredictable *adj.* igarrezin, susmaezin.
unprepared *adj.* gertugabe, gordin, prestagabe.
unpreservable *adj.* ezingordezko.
unproductive *adj.* agor, ezemankor, fruitugabe.
unproductiveness *n.* fruitugabetasun, fruitugabezia.
unprofitable *adj.* probetxugabe.
unprotected *adj.* gerizagabe, aterbegabe, babesgabe, itzalgabe(ko), laguntzagabe.
unpublished *adj.* argitaragabeko.
unpunished *adj.* zigorgabe.
unqualified *adj.* ezgai. *adj.* titulugabe, baimengabe. *adj.* oso.
unquestionable *adj.* zalantzaezin, zalantzagabeko.
unquestionably *adv.* ezbairik gabe, dudarik gabe, zalantzarik gabe.
unravel *v.t./v.i.* desarildu, desaritu, desehundu, zirpildu.
unraveled *adj.* ehungabe.
unreachable *adj.* eskuragaitz, eziniritxizko.
unreal *adj.* desegiazko, itxurazko,

asmautako.
unrealistic adj. itxuragabe(ko).
unrealistically adv. itxuragabeki.
unreality n. errealtasuneza, ezizate.
unrealizable adj. eginezin, gertaezin.
unreasonable adj. senbako, zentzugabe.
unreasonably adv. zentzugabeki.
unreasoning adj. zentzugabe.
unrecognizable n. ezagutezin.
unrecoverable adj. kobraezin.
unrefined adj. gordin, zikin. adj. trakets, arrunt.
unrelenting adj. euskor, iraunkor.
unreliable adj. funtsgabe. adj. ezfidakor, sinesgaitz.
unrepaired adj. konpongabe.
unrepentant adj. garbaigabe, damugabe.
unresolvable adj. askatuezin.
unrest n. larridura, kezka, larrialdi. n. iskanbila, nahastaldi, bakehauste.
unreturnable adj. ezinitzuliko.
unrewarded adj. sarigabeko.
unroll v.t. desbiribildu, hedatu, zabalerazi.
unruffled adj. lasai.
unruliness n. lasaikeria.
unruly adj. eskumenperagaitz, tarrapatari.
unsafe adj. arriskutsu.
unsaid adj. esangabeko.
unsalted adj. gazkabe.
unsatisfactory adj. ezegoki.
unsatisfied adj. betegabe, asegabe.
unsavory adj. dastaezin.
unscrupulous adj. eskrupulugabe, barnekezkagabe.
unseasonable adj. desgaraiko, desorduko.
unseasonableness n. desgiro.
unseasonably adv. desorduz, destenorez, desgaraiz.
unseasoned adj. geza. adj. heze.
unseemly adv. desegoki.
unseen adj. ikusigabe.
unselfish adj. eskuzabal, emankor.
unselfishness n. eskuzabaltasun, emankortasun.
unsettle v.t. antolagabetu.
unsettled adj. ezinegonezko, tinkogabe. **To become unsettled.** Tinkogabetu.
unsheathe v.t. deszorrotu.
unsheltered adj. atergabe, gerizagabe.
unsightly adj. itxuragaiztoko.
unsinkable adj. hondaezin.
unskilled adj. baldar, moldegabe, trakets.
unskillful adj. moldagaitz, dorpe, baldar.
unskillfully adv. dorpeki, baldarki, trakeski.
unsociable adj. gozagaitz, tratagaitz, zaputz, muzin, elkargaitz.
unsociableness n. gozagaizkeria,

mukertasun.
unsociably adv. mukerki, gozagaizki, zapuzki.
unsocial adj. zaputz, muker, gizartetsai.
unsolvable adj. askaezin, konponezin, erabakiezin, antolaezin.
unsolved adj. konpongabe.
unsophisticated adj. arrunt.
unsophisticatedly adv. arrunki.
unspeakable adj. esanezin, esanezgarri.
unspoiled adj. ustelgabe, andeagabe. adj. ezmainatsu.
unspoken adj. esangabeko.
unstable adj. geldiezin, geldigaitz, koloka, egongaitz, tinkogabe.
unstably adv. kili-kolo.
unsteadiness n. desiraupen.
unsteady adj. desiraunkor, eziraunkor.
unstoppable adj. geldiezin, geraezin.
unsuccessful adj. porrotatu(a), arrakastagabe.
unsuccessfully adv. arrakastarik gabe.
unsuitability n. desegokitasun, gaieza, gaieztapen, moldagaiztasun.
unsuitable adj. desegoki, debekuzko, egokiezin, egokigaitz.
unsuitably adv. desegoki, desegokiro, moldagaizki.
unsuited adj. moldagaitz, ezgisako.
unsupported adj. ezeuskor.
unsure adj. seguragaitz.
unswayable adj. makurrezin, makurtezin.
unswerving adj. zuzen; aldagabe.
untamable adj. eskuraezin, hezgaitz, heziezin, zebagaitz.
untamed adj. domagaitz, hezgabe, eskumenperagaitz.
untangle v.t./v.i. askatu, desmordoildu.
unthinkable adj. asmaezin, pentsaezin, ustezin.
unthinking adj. oharkabe, pentsagabe.
unthinkingly adv. ezustean, oharkabez, oharkabeki.
untidily adv. baldreski, fardelki.
untidiness n. arloteria, baldreskeria, narrasketa.
untidy adj. arlote, baldres, fardel, lander.
untie v.t./v.i. deslokarritu, deskoropilatu, deslotu, laxatu.
untied adj. solte, aske.
until conj./prep. arte, arik eta. **Up until now.** Egundaino.
untimeliness n. desgaraitasun.
untimely adj. ezorduko, ordutxarreko, orduzkanpoko, desgaraiko. adv. desgaraiz, ezorduz, desorduz, orduzkanpo.
untiring adj. aspergaitz, aspergabeko, nekatuezin.
unto prep. -raino; -runtz, -rantz.
untold adj. sekula ez esana.
untouchable adj. ezinikutuzko,

ikutuezin, ukigaitz.
untouched adj. ukigabe.
untranslatable adj. ezinitzulizko, itzulezin, emangaitz.
untransferable adj. itzulezin.
untreatable adj. medikaezin.
untrue adj. desegiazko.
untrustworthiness n. sinesgaiztasun, fidagaiztasun.
untrustworthy adj. fidagaitz.
untruth n. gezur.
untruthful adj. egigabe.
untruthfulness n. egigabezia.
untwist v.t./v.i. desokertu.
unusable adj. erabilgaitz, ezinerabilizko.
unused adj. erabilgabe.
unusual adj. bitxi, ohigabe.
unusually adv. ohi ez bezala.
unutterable adj. esanezin, esanezgarri, ezinesandako.
unveil v.t. agertarazi, ezagutarazi.
unverifiable adj. egiztaezin, frogaezin.
unwarily adv. kontugabeki, axolagabeki.
unwary adj. kontugabe, axolagabe.
unwashable n. garbiezin, ikuztezin, ikuzgaitz.
unwelcome adj. harreragabe.
unwell adj. ezongi.
unwilling adj. eznahiko, gogogabe.
unwillingly adv. gogotxarrez.
unwillingness n. eznahi, guraeza.
unwind v.t. desaritu; desokertu. v.i. lasaitu.
unwise adj. inozo, zentzungabe, sengabeko.
unworried adj. kezkagabe, larrigabe, axolagabetsu.
unworriedly adv. axolagabeki.
unworthily adv. merezigaberik.
unworthiness n. gaitzesbide.
unworthy adj. merezigabe, baliaezin, duingabe.
unwrap v.t. fardela askatu, lotura askatu.
unwritten adj. ezidatzi.
unyielding adj. menperagaitz.
unyoke v.t. desuztartu.
up adv./prep. gora, gorantza. adj. goiko, garaitiko, gorako. n. goi. n. gehiagotze.
upbringing n. hezikera, hezkuntza.
upcoming adj. etorkizuneko, gaurgerozko, gerokoan.
update v.t. oraingotu, gaurkotu, eguneratu, aldikotu.
upheaval n. nahastaldi, barnemugida.
upheld pret./p. part. of uphold.
uphill adj./adv. gorunzko. n. aldapagora, aldats.
uphold v.t. jasan.
upholstery n. tapiz, estali.
upkeep n. mantenu.
upon prep. gainean; -n, -ra. prep. -tean, -tzean.
upper adj. goiko, garaitiko, gaineko;

gain-.
uppermost adj. gaingoitiko, goieneko, goiengo.
uppity adj. gorati.
upright adj. tentekor, zutikako. adj. prestu, zintzo, duin. adv. zutik.
uprising n. altxaketa, altxaldi, istilu, oldarraldi.
uproar n. zaratots, iskanbila, algara.
uproarious adj. algaratsu.
uproariously adv. zarataka.
uproot v.t./v.i. desustraitu, deserrotu, deslandatu, sustraigabetu.
uprooted adj. sustraigabe.
ups and downs n. (pl.) gorabeherak.
upset v.t. iraili, itzulikatu, iraulkatu, irabiratu, artegarazi. v.t. haserretu.
upset adj. kezkatsu, larri, urduri, grinatsu, zirin. n. nahastaldi, iraulketa, gainazpikaldi.
upsetting adj. larrigarri, asaldagarri, ahakargarri, urdurigarri, kezkagile.
upshot n. ondorio.
upside down prep./adv. azpikozgain, azpikozgora, hankazgora, buruzbehera.
upstairs adv. goian, gora. adj. goiko. **Upstairs room.** Goiko gela. n. goi.
upstream adv./adj. errekan gora.
upswing n. gorakada.
uptight adj. urduri.
up-to-date adj. orainaldiko, oraintsuko.
upward adv. gorantza, gora, gorantz. adj. gorako.
uranium n. (chem.) uranio.
Uranus n. (astron.) Urano.
urban adj. hiriko, hiritar, kaletar.
urbanization n. hirigintza, hiritarpen, urbanizazio.
urbanize v.t. kaletartu, urbanizatu.
urchin n. mutiko.
urea n. gernuki, urea.
uremia n. (med.) odolgernu, uremia.
urethra n. (anat.) gernubide, pixabide, pixodi.
urge v.t./v.i. tirriatu, lasterkarazi, presa eman, azkartu.
urge n. joran.
urgency n. premiatasun, larri, urgentzia.
urgent adj. premiazko, prestatsu, presazko, beharrezko, larri, lasterreko.
urgently adv. presaz, premiaz.
urinal n. txizontzi, txizaleku, pixontzi, gernuntzi.
urinary adj. gernuzko, pixazko.
urinate v.i. pix egin, txiza egin.
urination n. pixaketa.
urine n. pix, txiza.
urn n. kutxatila.
urologist n. urologari.
us pron. gu; -gu-. **All of us.** Denok. **About us.** Gutaz.
U.S.A. n. (geog.) A.E.B., Ameriketako Estatu Batuak.
usable adj. erabilgarri, erabilkor.

usage *n.* usaia, erabilbide, erabilaldi, ohikuntza.
use *v.t.* erabili, baliatu, gozatu, usatu.
use *n.* erabilketa, erabilbide, erabilpen, erabilkuntza; probetxamendu.
useable *adj.* erabilkor.
used *adj.* bigarren eskuko, erabili(a). **To get used to. To be used to.** Ohitu.
useful *adj.* baliagarri, komenigarri, onuragarri, erabilgarri, ongarri.
usefully *adv.* onuraz, balioski.
usefulness *n.* baliagarritasun, erabilgarritasun, ongaitasun.
useless *adj.* ezinerabilizko, ezgai, baliaezin, gauzaez, ezbaliagarri, alferreko, alferrikako.
uselessly *adv.* ezdeuski. *adv.* alferrik.
uselessness *n.* ezbaliadura, ezgaitasun.
user *n.* erabiltzaile, baliatzaile.
usher *n.* ezarlari, ezarle, atezain.
usual *adj.* ohi, ohiturazko, ohizko.
usually *adv.* gehienetan, gehienbat, ohi, ohituraz, usaian.
usufruct *n.* erabilfruitu, gozamen.
usurer *n.* lukurari, lukur.
usurious *adj.* lukur, zeken, zikoitz.
usurp *v.t.* bortxaz harrapatu (gehienetan politiko lanpostu bat), indarlapurtu.
usurpation *n.* indarlapurketa.
usurper *n.* indarlapur, beregantzaile.
usury *n.* lukurantza, lukurreria, lukuru, dirukoikeria.
Utah *n.* *(geog.)* Estatu Batuetako estatu bat.
utensil *n.* tresna, erreminta.
uterine *adj.* sabeleko, umontziko, haurtokiko.
uterus *n.* *(anat.)* umetoki, umontzi, emasabel.
utilitarian *adj.* erabilgarri.
utilitarianism *n.* erabilgarritasun.
utility *n.* balioketa, baliagarritasun. *n.* zerbitzu-entrepresa publikoa (argi, telefono, etab.).
utilization *n.* baliaketa, baliakuntza, erabilbide, erabilera, erabilketa.
utilize *v.t.* baliatu, erabili.
utmost *n./adj.* gehien, goren.
utopia *n.* utopia.
utopian *adj.* utopiko, ametszale.
utter *v.t.* ahoskatu.
utter *adj.* erabateko, guztizko.
utterable *n.* esangarri.
utterance *n.* esaldi.
utterly *adv.* erabat, guztiz.
uttermost *n./adj.* gehien, goren.
uvula *n.* *(anat.)* gangaila, gargail.
uxoricide *n.* emaztehilketa. *n.* emaztehiltzaile.

V

v *n.* Ingeles alfabetoko letra.
vacancy *n.* hutsaldi.
vacant *adj.* inorgabe, huts, jabegabe,
hutsik, betegabe.
vacantly *adv.* ilunki, hala hola.
vacate *v.t./v.i.* hustu, auzogabetu, erantzi.
vacation *n.* opor(rak), oporraldi, bakantza(k). **To take a vacation.** Opor egin. **On vacation.** Oporretan.
vaccinate *v.t.* txertatu.
vaccination *n.* txerto, txertaketa.
vaccine *n.* eztitu, txerto.
vacillate *v.i.* kolokatu, koloka(n) egon.
vacillation *n.* kolokadura, eztabaida, kolokaldi.
vacuous *adj.* adimengabe(ko).
vacuum *n.* huts, husketa, hustasun.
vagabond *n.* noragabe, ibilkari, ardigaldu.
vagina *n.* *(anat.)* ematutu, emabide, emagina.
vaginal *adj.* emabideko.
vaginitis *n.* *(med.)* emabidemin.
vagrancy *n.* alferkeria.
vagrant *n./adj.* noragabe, hanemenkari.
vague *adj.* zehazgabe(ko), ilun, lainotsu.
vaguely *adv.* zehazgabeki, ilunki, lainoki, goibelki, hala hola, hitzerdika.
vagueness *n.* lainotasun, goibeltasun, zehazkabetasun.
vain *adj.* harroputz, handi-mandiko, handinahi, hanpurutsu. *adj.* alferrikako. **In vain.** Alferrik.
vainglorious *adj.* harroputz, haizetsu.
vainly *adv.* harroki, handikeriaz, harrokeriaz. *adv.* alferrik.
valentine *n.* San Balendin eguneko erregalia.
valet *n.* jantzizain, gelazain.
valiant *adj.* kementsu, zangar, potrodun, frakadun.
valiantly *adv.* kementsuki, kemenez.
valid *adj.* baliodun, balioko, indardun, indarrezko.
validity *n.* balio, baliotasun.
valise *n.* maleta.
valley *n.* ibar, bailara, haran.
valor *n.* kemen, adoretasun, kemendura, zangartasun.
valuable *adj.* baliodun, balios, baliotsu, baliogarri.
valuableness *n.* preziagarritasun, baliostasun.
valuation *n.* balorapen.
value *v.t.* balioztatu, balio eman, baloratu.
value *n.* meritu, merezimendu. *n.* balio, baliostasun.
valued *adj.* meritudun. *adj.* baliogarri.
valueless *adj.* gauzaez.
valve *n.* balbula.
vamoose *v.i.* *(colloq.)* joan, ihes egin, irten.
vamp *n.* sirena.
vampire *n.* odoledale, odolxurgalari, drakula.
van *n.* kamioneta, furgoneta.

vandal n. hondatzaile.
vandalism n. hondamenkeria, lapurkeria, ohoinkeria.
vane n. haizorratz.
vanguard adj. aurrelari.
vanilla n. (bot.) bainila.
vanish v.i. desagertu.
vanity n. hutsalkeria, handiustekeria, harropuzkeria, handikeria, handimandikeria.
vanquish v.t. gain hartu, uzkali.
vanquisher n. menderatzaile, menperatzaile.
vapid adj. geza, motel.
vapor n. lurrin, gandu.
vaporization n. lurrinketa, lurrindura.
vaporize v.t./v.i. lurrindu, lurrineztatu, lurrundu.
vaporized adj. lurrindun.
vaporizer n. lurringailu, lurrinmakina.
vaporous adj. lurrindu, lurrintsu, gandutsu.
variability n. aldaberatasun, aldagarritasun, aldakortasun.
variable adj. aldagarri, aldakor, aldabera, aldagai.
variance n. aldagai, aldaera; desberdintasun.
variant n./adj. aldagai, aldakin, aldaera.
variation n. aldaera.
varicose adj. odoluritsu.
varied adj. askotariko, askotsu.
variegated adj. nabar.
variety n. askotarikotza, askotasun, bestelakotasun, askotarikotasun.
various adj. motaskodun, askotariko; ugari, oparo, kopurutsu, jori.
variously adv. era askotara.
varlet n. alproja, bihurri, petral, pikaro, doilor.
varmint n. (colloq.) haur bihurri(a), aberetxo bihurri(a).
varnish v.t. berniztatu; txaroldu.
varnish n. berniz; txarol.
varnished adj. berniztatu(a).
varsity n. unibertsitateko kirol talde.
vary v.t./v.i. bestelakotu.
vascular adj. hodizko, hodiantzeko; hodi-.
vase n. liliontzi.
vasectomy n. basektomia.
Vaseline n. baselina.
vassal n. manupeko.
vast adj. tokitsu, lekutsu.
vastly adv. oso, guztiz, erabat.
vastness n. handitasun, neurrigabetasun.
vat n. upel.
Vatican n. Vatikano.
vaudeville n. vaudeville.
vault v.i./v.t. saltoka egin. v.t. sabaitu.
vault n. ganga, sabai. n. etxe edo bankuetan dirua eta baliozko gauzak gordetzen diren lekua. n. pertika-salto.
vaunt v.t. hantustu, harropuztu.
veal n. txahalki, zekorki.

veer v.i. desbideratu, bidealdatu.
vegetable n. barazki, lekari, ortuari, eltzekari.
vegetarian n./adj. barazkijale, landarejale, haragiuzle.
vegetarianism n. barazkijate.
vegetate v.i. adimen mailako ahaleginik egin gabe bizi.
vegetation n. landaretza, landaredi.
vehemence n. odolberotasun, oldartasun, suhartasun.
vehement adj. gartsu, gogobero, odoldun, erasokor, suhar, bero, oldarti.
vehemently adv. oldarrez, gartsuki, oldarki.
vehicle n. ibilgailu, ibiltresna.
veil n. estalki.
vein n. (anat.) zain. n. (min.) beta, zerrenda.
veined adj. zaindun.
veinous adj. zaintsu.
vellum n. pergamu, pergamino.
velocity n. arintasun.
velvet n./adj. ileguri, balusa.
velvety adj. ileguriantzeko, balusantzeko.
venal adj. salkoi, salkor.
venality n. salkoitasun, salkortasun.
vend v.t. saldu.
vendetta n. mendeku.
vendor n. saltzaile.
veneer n. haltzariei gainjazten zaien egurrezko estalki xumea. n. egoera.
venerable adj. agurgarri, gurgarri, itzalgarri.
venerate v.t. gurtu, gurkatu, gur egin.
veneration n. gurtasun, gurtza, gurtzapen.
venereal disease n. (med.) sexugaitz, emamin.
Venetian blind n. pertsiana.
vengeance n. asperkunde, mendeku.
vengeful adj. asperti, mendekati, mendekakor.
venial adj. arin.
venison n. orein-haragi.
venom n. pozoi, eden.
venomous adj. edendun, edentsu.
vent n. suateraldi, arnasbide.
ventilate v.t. haizeztatu, egurastu, aireztatu, aireberritu.
ventilation n. airealdi, aireberrizte, haizeztaketa.
ventilator n. haizagailu, haizemaile, aireztailu.
ventricle n. (anat.) bentrikulu.
ventriloquism n. sabeliztuntasun, sabelmintzo.
ventriloquist n. sabeliztun, sabelmintzari.
venture v.t./v.i. ausartu, benturatu.
venture n. negozio arriskutsu, ekintza arriskutsu.
Venus n. (astron.) Artizar.
veracious adj. egitazko, egizale.
veracity n. egitasun, egizkotasun.

verb n. (gram.) aditz.
verbal adj. hitzezko, mintzozko. adj. aditzezko.
verbally adv. hitzez, mintzoz.
verbatim adv. hitzez-hitz.
verbose adj. jarduntsu.
verboseness n. elejariotasun.
verbosity n. erretolika, hitzarrotasun, hizjario.
verdant adj. orlegi, berdeska. adj. oihantsu, landaretsu.
verdict n. epai.
verdigris n. gardinga.
verdure n. berdetasun. n. belar eta landare orlegiak. n. mardul.
verge n. ertz, hegal, kinka. **To be on the verge of.** Zorian egon. Kinkan egon.
verifiable adj. egiaztagarri, frogagarri.
verification n. egiztaketa, egiztapen, froga, frogaketa.
verify v.t. egiaztatu, egiaztu.
verisimilitude n. kanore, egitxura.
veritable adj. egiazko, benetako.
vermilion n./adj. gorri bizi.
vermin n. ziringilo, zomorro.
verminous adj. hardun, ziringilodun; zomorrodun.
Vermont n. (geog.) Estatu Batuetako estatu bat.
vermouth n. vermouth.
vernacular n. herrizkera, jaiotizkera, jaiotizkuntza.
vernal adj. udaberriko.
versatile adj. alditsu, itzulerraz, aldakor, itzulkor.
versatility n. itzulerraztasun, aldakortasun, itzulkortasun, aldakeria.
verse n. bertso, neurtitz. **To make verses.** Bertso(ak) egin.
versed adj. gai, ikasi(a).
versification n. bertsogintza, neurtizketa.
versifier n. bertsogile, neurtizlari.
versify v.t./v.i. bertso egin, hizneurtu.
version n. bertsio.
verso n. orrialdearen atzekalde.
versus prep. kontra, aurka. prep. (-kin) alderatuz, (-kin) gonbaratuz.
vertebra n. (anat.) orno.
vertebrae n. (pl.) of vertebra.
vertebrate adj. hezurdun, ornodun, bizkarrezurdun.
vertex n. goien, erpin, gandor.
vertical adj. zut, zutikako.
vertically adv. zutik.
verticalness n. zutikortasun, zutasun.
vertigo n. buruzoraldi, zorabio, txoradura.
very adv. guztiz, oso, erabat, biziki, arras, zeharo. **Very well.** Guztiz ondo. adj. zehatz, berbera. adj. huts, txiki, soil.
vespers n. (pl.) bezperak.
vessel n. ontzi, murko. **Blood vessel.** Odolodi. **Drinking vessel.** Edalontzi.

vest n. maripulis.
vested adj. legez babestua, legepean babestuta. adj. jantzita (apaiz).
vestibule n. atarte, atari, atalaurre.
vestige n. arrasto, aztarna.
vestment n. soineko.
vestry n. sakristi.
vet n. beterano. n. abelsendagile, aberesendatzaile, abelosagile, albaitari.
veteran adj. beterano. adj. trebe, ikasi(a), ohitu(a).
veterinarian n. abelsendagile, albaitari.
veterinary medicine n. albaitaritza, aberesendakintza.
veto v.t. betatu, beto(a) ipini.
veto n. ezezko, beto, debeku.
vex v.t. gaitziarazi, gaitzitu, erretxindu, gogaitu, gogait eragin.
vexation n. erretxindura, larritasun, ernegu, estularrialdi.
vexing adj. gaitziarazle, ernegatzaile.
via prep. bidez, bitartez.
viability n. bideragarritasun, egingarritasun.
viable adj. bideragarri, egiaztagiri.
viaduct n. zubibide.
vial n. bonbiltxo, flasko.
viand n. janari bat. n. (pl.) janariak.
vibrant adj. dardarakor. adj. bizikor, indartsu.
vibrate v.i./v.t. dardaratu.
vibration n. dardarketa, dardaraldi, dardara.
vibrator n. dardarazle.
vibratory adj. dardarazko.
vicar n. bikario.
vicarious adj. ordezko, ordezkari.
vicarship n. bikaritza.
vice n. galkeria, txarbide, galbide, bizio.
vice- (gram.) -orde.
vice-chairman n. lehendakariorde, buruorde.
vice-consul n. kontsulorde.
vice-governor n. gobernariorde.
vice-presidency n. lehendakariordetza.
vice-president n. lehendakariorde.
vice-rector n. erretororde.
viceroy n. erregeorde.
vice versa adv. alderantziz, bestera.
vicinity n. aldamen, inguralde, inguru, mugakidetasun.
vicious adj. biziotsu, odoltzale, odolkoi, zirtzil.
viciously adv. zirtzilki, ziztrinki.
viciousness n. odolzalekeria.
vicissitude n. goibehera.
victim n. hilgai.
victor n. garaile, garaitzaile, irabazle.
victorious adj. garaile, garaipenezko, irabazle, garaitiar.
victoriously adv. garaitsuki.
victory n. garaipen, garaitza, irabazpen, irabazketa.
victuals n. (pl.) bizikai, hornigai.

videocassette *n.* ikuskaseta.
vie *v.i.* **(for)** lehiakatu, zeingehiagotu.
view *v.t.* ikusi.
view *n.* ikusbide, ikusgune, ager. *n.* aburu, eritzi.
viewer *n.* ikusle, ikuslari, ikustaile.
viewfinder *n.* begiztailu.
viewpoint *n.* ikuspuntu, ikusmira, ikuspegi, erizpide.
vigil *n.* beila, hilbeila, gaubeila.
vigilance *n.* ernetasun, ohartasun, zaintza, begirapen.
vigilant *adj.* oharkor, itzarri, axolati.
vigor *n.* indar, indarraldi. *n.* bizkortasun, mardultasun, bizi, azkartasun. *n.* kemen, sendotasun.
vigorous *adj.* kementsu, sendo, indardun, sasoinezko, mardul.
vigorously *adv.* sendoki, bortizki, kemenez, mardulki.
Viking *n.* vikingo.
vile *adj.* azpisapo, bilau, doilor, gizagaizto, zital, laidozko.
vilely *adv.* doilorki, itsuski, landerki, zitalki.
vileness *n.* bilaukeria, doilortasun, itsuskeria, zatarkeria, zitaltasun.
villa *n.* landetxe.
village *n.* herritxo.
villager *n.* herritar, herrikide, herritxo bateko biztanle.
villain *n.* petral, pikaro, doilor, zital.
villainous *adj.* petral, pikaro.
villainously *adv.* petralki, bilauki, doilorki, zitalki.
villainy *n.* bihurrikada, bilautasun, doilortasun, petralkeria, zapokeria.
vim *n.* indar, kemen.
vindicate *v.t.* garbitu, burua zuritu, justifikatu.
vindication *n.* irainordain, irainorde.
vindicator *n.* irainordainle.
vindictive *adj.* mendekakor, mendekuzko, mendekati, aiherti.
vine *n. (bot.)* mahatsondo. *n. (bot.)* aihenbelar.
vinegar *n.* ozpin.
viney *adj.* aihentsu.
vineyard *n.* mahasti, ardantza.
vintage *n.* mahasbilketa. *adj.* zahar.
viola *n. (mus.)* biola.
violate *v.t.* urratu (legea), hautsi. *v.t.* bortxatu (emakumea).
violation *n.* arauhauspen, arauhauste. *n.* bortxakeria.
violator *n.* arauhausle, hausle, legehausle.
violence *n.* indarkeria, bortizkeria, bortxakeria, gogorkeria.
violent *adj.* bortxari, gogor, indarrezko, odolbero, odolgaitz, mutiri.
violently *adv.* bortizki, bortxaz, indarrez, indarka.
violet *n./adj.* more, ubel. *n. (bot.)* liliubel.
violin *n. (mus.)* bibolin, arrabita.
violinist *n.* arrabitari, bibolinjole.

viper *n. (zool.)* sugegorri.
virgin *n.* birjina. **Virgin Mother.** Ama Birjina.
virginal *adj.* birjinezko. *adj.* garbi, orbangabe.
Virginia *n. (geog.)* Estatu Batuetako estatu bat.
Virginian *n. (adj.* virginiatar.
virginity *n.* birjintasun.
virile *adj.* gizontsu.
virilely *adv.* gizonki.
virility *n.* gizontasun, gizatasun, gizakunde.
virtual *adj.* benetako, egiazko.
virtually *adv.* ia guztiz, ia osorik.
virtue *n.* bertute, onbide.
virtuoso *n.* artista trebe.
virtuous *adj.* bertutedun, onbidetsu.
virtuously *adv.* bertutez.
virulence *n.* pozoinkeria, pozointasun.
virulent *adj.* pozointsu.
virus *n.* birus.
visa *n.* ibilbide.
visage *n.* aurpegiera.
viscera *n. (anat.)* errai.
visceral *adj.* erraietako.
viscosity *n.* likits, lingirda.
viscount *n.* kondeorde.
viscountess *n.* kondesaorde.
viscountship *n.* kondeordetza.
viscous *adj.* likitsu, lingirdatsu.
vise *n. (mech.)* finkagailu, euskailu, herskailu, prentsa.
visibility *n.* ikusgarritasun, agiritasun, ikusgaitasun.
visible *adj.* ager, ikusgai, ikusgarri, ikuskor.
visibly *adv.* ikusgarriki, ikusgarriro.
vision *n.* ikusmen. *n.* agerpen, agerkera. *n.* aurreikuspen.
visionary *adj.* amesti. *n.* ameskile.
visit *v.t./v.i.* ikustatu, ikusi, ikertu.
visit *n.* ikustaldi, ikertaldi, ikustapen.
visitation *n.* ikustaldi, agerraldi. *n. (cap., eccl.)* ikerkunde.
visitor *n.* ikusle, ikusliar, ikusketari, ikuskatzaile.
vista *n.* ikuspegi.
visual *adj.* begiko, begietako, ikusmenezko.
visualize *v.t./v.i.* iruditu, asmatu.
visually *adv.* begiz.
vital *adj.* bizigarri. *adj.* funtsezko, garrantzitsu. *adj.* hilkor, heriozkor, hilgarri.
vitality *n.* bizkortasun, bizitasun, sendotasun, indar.
vitalize *v.t.* kemendu, indartu.
vitally *adv.* biziro, bizigarriro. *adv.* behar-beharrez, ezinbestez, nahitaez.
vitamin *n.* bitamina.
vitiate *v.t.* gaiztarazi.
Vitoria *n. (geog.)* Gasteiz.
vitreous *adj.* kristalezko, beirazko.
vitrification *n.* beirakuntza.
vitrify *v.t./v.i.* beiraztu, beiratu.

vitriol *n. (chem.)* bitriolo. *n.* eztenkada, irrizuri.

vituperable *adj.* gaitzesgarri.

vituperate *v.t.* gaizkitu.

vivacious *adj.* bizkor, bipi.

vivacity *n.* bizkortasun, bizitasun, bipildura.

vivid *adj.* bizi.

vividly *adv.* bizkorki.

vivify *v.t.* biziarazi, bizieragin, biztuerazi, biziagotu.

viviparous *adj.* biziemale.

vivisection *n.* biziebaketa.

vixen *n.* azerieme, lukieme. *n.* emakume marmarti.

viz. adibidez, esate baterako.

Vizcaya *n. (geog.)* Bizkaia.

vocabulary *n.* hitz-zerrenda, hiztegi, hiztegitxo.

vocal *adj.* ahokari, ahoko.

vocalize *v.t./v.i.* ahoskatu.

vocation *n.* Jainkoaren dei(a). *n.* ogibide, lanbide, irabazbide, bizibide.

vocational *adj.* ogibidezko, bizibidezko.

vociferate *v.i./v.t.* deadar egin.

vociferation *n.* hosketa.

vociferous *adj.* deadartsu, deadarti.

vodka *n.* vodka.

vogue *n.* moda, ohitura.

voice *v.t.* soinuztatu. *v.t.* ahoskatu, ozendu.

voice *n.* ahots, boz.

voiced *adj.* bozdun, ozen, ozentsu.

voiceless *adj.* bozgabe.

voicelessness *n.* bozgabezia, soinugabezia.

void *adj.* baliogabe. *adj.* alfer. *adj.* **(of)** huts. *n.* hutsune.

volatile *adj.* airagarri, hegazkor.

volatility *n.* hegazkortasun, lurrinkortasun.

volcanic *adj.* sumendiko, sumenditsu.

volcano *n.* sumendi, garmendi.

volition *n.* nahikunde, nahimen.

volley *n.* pilotaketa, iraitzaldi, bolea.

volleyball *n.* boleibol.

volt *n.* boltio.

voltage *n. (elec.)* boltaia.

voluble *adj.* haizakor, hizjario, hitzontzi.

volubly *adv.* hitzederrez, ahoederrez.

volume *n.* liburuki. *n. (phys.)* bolumen. *n.* ahotsaren indar, soinuaren indar.

voluminous *adj.* ugari, jori, oparo.

voluntarily *adv.* gogoz, borondatez, nahiz.

voluntariness *n.* nahitasun, gogozkotasun.

voluntary *adj.* nahizko, gogozko, gurazko, borondatezko.

volunteer *v.i./v.t.* norbere lana ezeren truke eskaini.

volunteer *n.* norbere lana ezeren truke eskaintzen duen pertsona.

voluptuous *adj.* atseginzale, limurkoi, lizunarazle.

voluptuously *adv.* limurki.

voluptuousness *n.* atseginkoitasun, atsegintzalekeria, limurkortasun, lizunkoikeria.

vomit *v.i./v.t.* goitikatu, goragaletu, okatu, oka egin, bota.

vomit *n.* goitika, gorale.

voodoo *n.* vudu.

voracious *adj.* betezin, irenskor, iresle, tripontzi.

voraciously *adv.* asezinez.

voraciousness *n.* zintzurkoikeria, zintzurkoitasun.

voracity *n.* irenskortasun, jaletasun.

vortex *n.* zurrunbilo, ubil.

vote *v.i./v.t.* botu eman, bozeman.

vote *n.* hautabide, botu, boz.

voter *n.* hautari, aukeratzaile, bozemale, hautesle, botari.

voting *n.* botazio, bozketa.

votive *adj.* zinezko.

vouch *v.i.* **(for)** garantizatu, berme izan.

voucher *n.* bono, gordekin, kupoi.

vow *n. (eccl.)* botu. *n.* agintza, promes, zin.

vowel *n. (gram.)* bokale.

voyage *n.* itsasbidaia.

voyager *n.* txangolari, ontzibidazti, ibilkari.

vulgar *adj.* purtzil, lanputs, arrunt, edozelako.

vulgarity *n.* purtzilkeria, arruntkeria, oiheskeria, zarpailkeria.

vulgarize *v.t.* herrikoitu.

vulgarly *adj.* purtzilki, oiheski.

vulgar tongue *n.* herrizkera.

vulnerable *adj.* zaurigarri, erasogarri.

vulpine *adj.* azeriko, azeriantzeko.

vulture *n. (zool.)* sai, arranobeltz, putre.

vulva *n. (anat.)* alu, tutu, motxin.

W

w *n.* Ingeles alfabetoko letra.

wad *n.* mordo, sorta (diru, papel, etab.).

waddle *v.i.* ahate antzera ibili.

wade *v.t./v.i.* **(ibaia)** igaro, uretan sartuta ibili, itsasertzean sartuta ibili.

wadeable *adj.* ibidedun, ibirangankor.

wader *n.* ibitzaile.

wafer *n.* gaileta mehe eta xigortua.

waffle *n.* opil mota bat.

wag *v.t./v.i.* buztana eragin.

wag *n.* buztana eragite(a). *n.* adarjole.

wage *n.* aloger, soldata, alokairu.

wager *v.t./v.i.* dematu, apostu egin.

wager *n.* dema, apostu, trabes.

wages *n. (pl.)* irabazi, etekin, egunsari, lansari.

wagon *n.* furgoi, bagoi, gurdi, orga.

waif *n.* haur galdu(a). *n.* etxe eta lagunik gabeko haurra.

wail *v.i./v.t.* intziri egin.

wail *n.* intziri, ulu, erosta.

wailer *n.* ululari, erostari.

waist *n.* gerri.

waistline *n.* gerri.

wait *v.i./v.t. (batzutan* **for***-ekin)* itxaro, itxaron, begira egon, zain egon, igurikatu. *v.i. (***on***)* zerbitzatu. *v.i. (***up, up for***)* itxaroten beilatu.

wait *n.* itxaroaldi, itxarote, igurikaldi.

waiter *n.* igurikitzaile. *n.* mahaimutil, zerbitzari (gizon).

waiting *n.* itxaronaldi. *adj.* itxaroten.

waitress *n.* gelandere, zerbitzari (emakume).

waive *v.t.* pertsona edo erakunde batek agiri baten bidez norbaiten alde, ezarritako arauen barne salbuespen bat egin.

waiver *n.* pertsona edo erakunde batek agiri baten bidez norbaiten alde, ezarritako arauen barne salbuespen bat egitea.

wake *v.i./v.t. (batzutan* **up***-ekin)* esnatu, itzarri, atzarri, iratzarri.

wake *n.* gaubeila, hilbeila. *n.* uhara.

wakeful *adj.* esnati, esnakor.

wakefulness *n.* logabetasun.

waken *v.t./v.i.* esnarazi, esnatu.

Wales *n. (geog.)* Gales.

walk *v.i./v.t.* ibili, bide egin, ostera egin. *v.i. (***in on***)* ustekabe hartu. *v.i. (***off***)* irten. *v.i. (***out***)* greba egin, grebara jo. *v.i. (***out, out of***)* ateratu. *v.i. (***out on***)* utzi.

walk *n.* ibilaldi, itzuli, ibilera.

walker *n.* bidari, ibiltari, oinezko, oinkari, zangokari.

walkie-talkie *n.* walkie-talkie.

walkout *n.* greba.

wall *v.t. (***in, off***)* hormatu, harresitu, hormaztatu.

wall *n.* horma, pareta; harresi, hesibarruti, hesi.

walled *adj.* harresidun, murrudun.

wallet *n.* diruzorro, kartera, txartelzorro, dirutoxa.

wallop *v.t.* jipoindu.

wallow *v.i.* ihalozkatu, ihauskatu, istingatu, iraulkatu.

wallpaper *v.t.* paperezтаtu.

wallpaper *n.* hormapaper.

walnut *n. (bot.)* intxaur.

walrus *n. (zool.)* itsasotso, mortsa.

waltz *v.i.* waltza dantzatu.

waltz *n.* waltza.

wampum *n.* Estatu Batuetako indioek txanpontzat erabiltzen zituzten maskorrezko kunder zilindrikoak. *n. (colloq.)* diru.

wan *adj.* zurbil.

wand *n.* makilatxo.

wander *v.i./v.t.* hara-hona ibili, haruntz-honuntz ibili, noragabetu, erratu, zehar-meharkatu.

wanderer *n.* erratzaile, hanemenkari.

wane *v.i.* gutitu, ilberatu.

wane *n.* beherapen.

waning *n.* beherapen. *adj.* gutikor.

wanly *adv.* hiski.

wanness *n.* zurbildura.

want *v.t./v.i. (v.i., askotan* **to***-ekin)* nahi

izan, nahi ukan, gura ukan.

want *n.* gurari, gura, nahitasun. *n.* gabezia, gabekeria, gabetasun.

wanton *adj.* doilor, anker. *adj.* grinatsu.

wantonly *adv.* doilorki, kruelki, ankerki. *adv.* grinaz.

wantoness *n.* grina, doilorkeria, ankerkeria.

war *v.i. (askotan* **with***-ekin)* gerla egin, gudukatu.

war *n.* gerla, gerrate, gudu, gatazka, borroka; -guda.

warble *v.i./v.t.* txorrotxio egin, txio egin, txinta egin.

ward *n.* auzo. *n.* eritegietako egoitzak. *n.* presondegiko gelaxka. *n.* babespean dagoen umezurtz(a).

warden *n.* gartzelari, presondegizain, presozain.

warder *n.* zaindari.

wardrobe *n.* jantziteria. *n.* armairu, arropategi.

ware *n.* -gai.

warehouse *n.* zaindegi, bildegi, gaitegi.

wares *n. (pl.)* erosgai.

warfare *n.* guda, gerla.

warily *adv.* arduraz, arretaz, axolaz, kontuz.

warlike *adj.* borrokagile, borrokazale, gerlazale, gerrazale, gudatzaile, gudukari.

warm *v.t./v.i. (batzutan* **up***-ekin)* epeldu, berotu, zerrepeldu. *v.i. (***up***)* korrikalariek lasterketa egin aurretik gorputz-prestaketak burutu.

warm *adj.* epel, hotzepel, zerrepel.

warmly *adv.* maitekiro, epelki, maiteki.

warmonger *n.* gudagile, gerlagile.

warmth *n.* epeltasun, epeldura, berotasun.

warm up *n.* kirolarien gorputz-prestaketa.

warn *v.t./v.i.* ohartu, ohartarazi, mezu egin.

warning *n.* iragarpen, ohar, jakinerazpen. **Last warning.** Azkenohar. *adj.* oharrezko.

warp *v.t./v.i.* irazi, irazki, irazkitu.

warp *n.* irazki, irazkin.

warrant *v.t.* bermatu.

warrant *n.* berma, zedula. *n.* baimenagiri. *n.* atxilotze-agindu(a).

warranted *adj.* bermatu(a),.

warren *n.* untxitegi.

warrior *n.* gudari, borrokalari, gerlari, gudulari, armagizon, gerrari, gudamutil.

warship *n.* gerrontzi, gudontzi.

wart *n.* garatxo, karetxa.

wartime *n.* gerrate, gudate, gerlate.

wary *adj.* arretatsu, tentudun.

was *pret. of* be.

wash *v.t./v.i.* uraz garbitu, ikuzi, uraz txukundu, xahutu.

wash *n.* ikuzketa, lixiba, xabonadura.

washable *adj.* garbigarri, ikuzgarri.

washbasin *n.* konketa, urazpil.

washboard *n.* ikuztohol, latsazur.
washer *n.* garbigailu, ikuztailu; ikuzle.
washerwoman *n.* ikuzle, latsari, zapigarbitzaile (emakume).
washing *n.* garbiketa, ikuzketa.
washing machine *n.* garbigailu, ikuzgailu.
Washington *n.(geog.)* Estatu Batuetako estatu bat.
Washington D.C. *n. (geog.)* Estatu Batuetako hiriburu(a).
washroom *n.* garbigela.
washtub *n.* konketa, lixibontzi.
wasn't "was + not"-en laburpena.
wasp *n. (zool.)* liztor.
waste *v.t./v.i.* galdu, parrastatu, hondatu. *v.i.* **(away)** higatu, irazi.
waste *n.* diruxahuketa, higadura, diruhondaketa, parrastada.
wasted *adj.* higatu(a).
wasteful *adj.* hondatzaile, galgarri, gastatzaile, barreiatzaile, xahutzaile, bonbontzaile.
wastefully *adv.* pirri-parra.
wasteland *n.* eremu, mortu.
wastepaper basket *n.* paperontzi, papersaski.
waster *n.* diruhondatzaile, diruxahutzaile, xahutzaile, etxekalte.
watch *v.t./v.i.* begiratu, so egon, so egin, adi egon, begira egon. *v.i.* **(out)** kontuz ibili. *v.i.* **(over)** goibegiratu, goardia egin, zaindu.
watch *n.* erloju, ordulari. **Pocket watch.** Sakelerloju.
watchdog *n.* ataritxakur, atezakur.
watcher *n.* begiratzaile, soegile, begiztatzaile, behatzaile, talaiari,zelatari.
watchful *adj.* zelatari, ikusbera, itzarri, kirikatzaile.
watchfulness *n.* begirapen, zaingo, ohartasun.
watchmaker *n.* erlojulari, erlojugile, erlojari.
watchman *n.* lantegizain, gakodun, jagole.
watchtower *n.* goibegiratoki, talaidorre, talaia.
watchword *n.* hitzezkutu.
water *v.t./v.i.* garastatu, ureztatu. *v.t.* edanarazi, edaratu.
water *n.* ur. **Boiled water.** Uregosi. **Stagnant water.** Mahel. **Fresh water.** Urgeza. **Warm water.** Urepel. **Salt water.** Urgazi. Gesal. **Potable water.** Ur edangarri. *adj.* uretako, urtar.
watercolor *n.* urmargo, akuarela. *n.* urmargolan.
waterfall *n.* zurrunba, urjauzi.
waterfront *n.* kai inguruak.
waterhole *n.* urtzulo.
wateriness *n.* urtasun, urtsutasun.
water line *n.* urezponda.
watermelon *n. (bot.)* angurri, sandia.
waterproof *v.t.* iragazkaiztu.

waterproof *adj.* iragaztezin.
water spout *n.* traganarru, mangera.
waterway *n.* errekabide.
watery *adj.* urezko, urtsu, urdun.
watt *n. (phys.)* batio.
wavable *adj.* kizkurgarri.
wave *v.i./v.t.* kizkurtu, uhindu. *v.t.* esku eragin.
wave *n.* olatu, uhin, olatualdi. *n.* izur.
waver *v.i.* kolokatu, koloka(n) egon.
wavering *adj.* koloka. *n.* kordoka, kordokadura.
waviness *n.* kizkurberatasun, kizkurtasun.
wavy *adj.* uhintsu. *adj.* izurdun, kizkurbera, kizkurtsu.
wax *v.t.* ezkoztatu.
wax *n.* argizari, ezko.
waxen *adj.* ezkozko, argizarizko.
waxing *n.* ezkoztadura, ezkodura.
waxy *adj.* ezkodun.
way *n.* era, modu, molde, eginbide, gisa, moldabide. **In this way.** Holaxe. *n.* bide, ibilbide, ibilgune. *prep.* erara, eraz.
wayfarer *n.* ibiltari, bidaiari.
waylay *v.t.* kukutu, zelatu, zelatatu.
way out *n.* irteera, aterabide, ihesbide, itzurpide.
wayside *n.* bidertz.
wayward *adj.* eskuragaitz, ezesaneko, managaitz.
we *pron.* gu, guk.
weak *adj.* ahul, indargabe, herbal, maskal, ahuleziadun, hebain, mendre.
weaken *v.t./v.i.* ahuldu, indargabetu, makaldu, indargetu, herbaldu, moteldu.
weakened *adj.* erkitu.
weakling *n.* pertsona ahul(a), pertsona indarge(a).
weakly *adv.* ahulki, herbalki, makalki.
weakness *n.* ahulezia, ahuleria, herbaltasun, indargabetasun, indargabezia, makalaldi, apalaldi, moteldura.
weal *n.* ubel, ubeldura.
wealth *n.* aberastasun, ontasun, diruketa, azienda.
wealthy *adj.* aberats, dirudun, dirutsu, sosdun.
wean *v.t.* desdititu, ditia kendu, esnegabetu.
weapon *n.* arma.
wear *v.t.* jantzi. *v.i.* **(out, off, away, down)** higatu, zarpaildu, erabildu, gastatu.
wear *n.* higadura.
wearily *adv.* leherbeharrez.
weariness *n.* abaildura, unadura.
wearisome *adj.* nekagarri; aspergarri.
weary *adj.* etenda, nekatuta, lehertuta.
weasel *n. (zool.)* erbinude, ogigazta.
weather *n.* eguraldi, aro, giro, denbora.
weatherman *n.* giroasmatzaile.
weave *v.t./v.i.* oihaldu, ehundu, irun,

eho, bilbatu. *v.i.* zabu egin.
weave *n.* ehun.
weaver *n.* irule, oihalgile, ehule, gorulari.
web *n.* sare. *n.* amaraun.
wed *v.t./v.i.* ezkondu.
we'd "we + had" edo "we + would"-en laburpena.
wedded *adj.* ezkondu(a).
wedding *n.* eztei(ak); eztei-. **Wedding day.** Ezteiegun. Ezkontegun. *adj.* ezteietako.
wedge *v.t./v.i.* ziritu, ziriztatu.
wedge *n.* geldigailu; taket, tako. *n.* ziri.
wedlock *n.* ezkontzondore.
Wednesday *n.* azteazken.
wee *adj.* txiki, ttipi.
weed *v.t./v.i.* jorratu.
weed *n. (bot.)* iraka.
week *n.* aste. **Every two weeks.** Hamabostero.
weekday *n.* astegun, lanegun.
weekend *n.* astebukaera, asteamai, asteburu.
weekly *adv.* astero. *adj.* asteko, asteroko.
weep *v.t./v.i.* negar egin.
weeper *n.* negarregile.
weeping *adj.* malkodun. *n.* negarjario, negarraldi.
weepy *adj.* malkojario, negarbera, negarti.
weevil *n. (zool.)* zeden.
weigh *v.t./v.i.* pisatu.
weight *n.* pisu, astunketa. **To lose weight.** Argaldu. **Net weight.** Pisugarbi. **Tare weight.** Pisuhil.
weightily *adv.* astunki, pisuki.
weightiness *n.* astuntasun, pisutasun.
weightless *adj.* astungabe.
weightlessness *n.* astungabezia.
weighty *adj.* pisutsu. *adj.* garrantzitsu.
weird *adj.* goinaturazko. *adj.* bakan, eznormal, beregizako.
welcome *v.t.* ongi-etorria eman, leku eman, abegi egin, onartu, harrera egin.
welcome *n.* onarketa, ongi-etorri, harrera. *adj.* ongietorri(a).
weld *v.t./v.i.* iratxeki, soldatu.
weldable *adj.* soldagarri.
welder *n.* soldatzaile.
welding *n.* iratxekidura, soldadura, soldaketa.
welfare *n.* dirulaguntza. *n.* ongizate, onegintza.
well *n.* osin, putzu. *adv./adj.* ondo, ongi, ontsa; egoki. **To get well.** Osatu. Sendatu. *int.* beno, ba, bada.
we'll "we + will"-aren laburpena.
well-behaved *adj.* formal.
well-being *n.* dohatasun, zorion, ongizate.
well-bred *adj.* gizabidetsu.
well-done *adj.* moldeoneko, ondo egin(a).
well-educated *adj.* eskolatu(a).

well-groomed *adj.* jaseko, kriket.
well-informed *adj.* kaskodun.
well-intentioned *adj.* asmoneko, onustez.
well-known *adj.* ezagun.
well made *adj.* moldeoneko.
well-mannered *adj.* gizabidetsu, moduoneko, erabideko, fin, itxurazko.
well-meaning *adj.* gogoneko, hobe-beharrez, asmoneko.
well-spoken *adj.* ahogarbi.
well-to do *adj.* aberats.
Welshman *n.* galestar.
welt *n.* ubel, ubeldura.
wench *n.* neska.
went *pret. of* go.
wept *pret./p. part. of* weep.
were *pret. of* be. **If I were.** Banintz.
we're "we + are"-aren laburpena.
weren't "were + not"-aren laburpena.
werewolf *n.* otso-gizon.
west *n.* mendebalde. *adj.* mendebaldeko.
western *n.* western, oesteko pelikula. *adj.* mendebaldeko, mendebaldar.
westerner *n.* mendebaldar.
westernize *v.t.* mendebaldu.
West Virginia *n. (geog.)* Estatu Batuetako estatu bat.
westward *adj./adv.* mendebalderuntz.
wet *v.t./v.i.* busti.
wet *adj.* busti(a), blai.
wetness *n.* bustitasun.
wet-nurse *v.t.* inudetu.
wet nurse *n.* inude.
wetsuit *n.* buzojantzi.
we've "we + have"-aren laburpena.
whack *v.t./v.i.* zarata eginaz jo.
whale *n. (zool.)* bale(a). **Killer whale.** Orka.
whalebone *n.* balebizar.
whaler *n.* baleatzale, baleakari.
whaling *n.* balea-harrapaketa.
wharf *n.* kargakentoki, nasa, kai.
wharves *n. (pl.) of* wharf.
what *pron./adj.* zer, zein, zertzu(k), zertan, zertaz.
whatever *pron./adj.* edozer, zernahi.
what's "what + is"-aren laburpena.
whatsover *adj.* inolako.
wheat *n.* gari, burudun; gal-. **Head of wheat.** Galburu.
wheedle *v.t./v.i. (v.t.,* out of, into*)* iradoki.
wheedler *n.* aitorrarazle, aterarazle, iradokitzaile.
wheel *n.* gurpil, errubera, txirringa.
wheelbarrow *n.* eskuorga, karretila, orgatila.
wheeled *adj.* gurpildun.
wheeze *v.i.* nekez arnasa hartu.
whelp *v.i./v.t.* jaio, erditu, ume izan, ume egin (txakurrak, otsoak, etab.).
whelp *n.* txakurkume, zakurkume.
when *adv.* noiz, noizko. *conj.* -enetan, -(e)nean. *n./pron.* noiz, ordu,

denbora.
whenever *adv./conj.* edonoiz, noiznahi; -(e)netan.
where *adv./conj.* non; nora. *n./pron.* non.
whereas *conj.* ezkero, -(en)ez gero.
whereby *conj./adv.* bitartez, -(r)i esker.
wherefore *conj./adv.* bitartez, -(r)i esker.
where's "where + is"-aren laburpena.
whereupon *conj.* eta gero, ondorioz.
wherever *adv./conj.* nonnahi, edonon.
wherewithal *n.* diru, bide, era.
whet *v.t.* zurtu, zorroztu.
whether *conj.* nahiz, zein, edo.
whetting stone *n.* zorroztarri, harlatz, labanarri.
whew *int.* pufa, uf.
whey *n.* gazur, gerli.
which *pron./adj.* zein, zeintzu; -n.
whichever *pron./adj.* zeinnahi, edozein.
whiff *n.* usain-bafada, usain-bolada.
while *n.* aldi, denbora, tarte. *conj.* artean, bitartean.
whim *n.* apeta, ameszoro, nahikari.
whimper *v.i./v.t.* muxindu, muxinkatu.
whimsical *adj.* apetatsu, ametsezko.
whine *v.i./v.t.* muxindu, muxinkatu, negarmuxinkatu.
whininess *n.* minkunkeria.
whining *n.* mina, muxinkada, negarmuxin. *adj.* kexati, minkun, muxin, mainadun.
whinny *v.i./v..t* irrintzina egin.
whinny *n.* irrintzi, irrintzina.
whiny *adj.* kexati, kexukoi.
whip *v.t.* astindu, hagakatu, zartakatu. *v.i.* **(into, around, out of)** arin-arin ibili, arin-arin mugitu. *v.t.* irabiatu.
whip *n.* usta, zartagailu, firrinda, zigor.
whipping *n.* astinaldi, zartakada.
whirl *v.i./v.t.* jirabiratu, jiratu, biratu.
whirlpool *n.* ubil, zurrunbilo.
whirlwind *n.* haizebihur, sorginaize.
whisker *n.* bizar-ile. *n.* katu-bibote.
whiskered *adj.* bizardun. *adj.* bibotedun.
whiskey *n.* whisky.
whisper *v.i./v.t.* xuxurlatu, txutxumutxu egin, murmurikatu, marmar egin, ahopekatu.
whisper *n.* marmar, murmur, murmurio. **In a whisper.** Isil-misilka.
whisperer *n.* murmurikari.
whistle *v.i./v.t.* txistu egin, txistu jo.
whistle *n.* txistuhots, txilibituhots, txistualdi, txistukada; txistu, txilibitu.
whistler *n.* txilibitulari, txistugile.
white *n./adj.* zuri. *n.* zuringo. *n.* pertsona zuri(a).
whitecap *n.* ardizuri.
white-haired *adj.* kaskazuri, buruzuri, ilezuridun.
White House *n.* Etxe-Zuri.
whiten *v.t./v.i.* zuritu.

whiteness *n.* zuritasun, zurimindura.
whitewash *v.t.* kareztatu, kisuztatu, gainzuritu, kisutu, zuritu.
whitewash *n.* karesne.
whitewasher *n.* zuritzaile, kisuztatzaile.
whitewashing *n.* etxezuriketa, kareztadura, kareztaldi, kisuztadura, kisuztaldi.
whither *adv./conj.* nora.
whittle *v.t.* egur printzatu, ezpaldu. *v.i.* **(away)** pixkanaka gastatu.
whiz *v.i.* **(by)** azkar igaro, tximistak eginean joan.
who *pron.* nor(k),nortzu(k); -n.
whoa *int.* so.
whoever *pron.* nornahi, edonor.
whole *adj.* guzti, oso, osorik, atalgabeko, zatigabe(ko). *n.* osotasun, guztitasun.
wholeness *n.* osotasun, guztitasun.
wholesale *n.* handika eginiko salmenta.
wholesaler *n.* askokari, handizkari.
wholesome *adj.* sano, sendo, osasungarri.
whole-wheat bread *n.* erresa, tremes.
who'll "who + will"-aren laburpena.
wholly *adv.* guztiz, osoki, erabat, zeharo.
whom *pron.* nori; -n.
whoop *v.i./v.t.* oihu egin, garrasi egin.
whooping cough *n.* eztulkukurruku.
whore *n.* urdanga, emagaldu, maribidetako, maripurtzil.
whorl *n.* espirale.
who's "who + is"-aren laburpena.
whose *pron. (genit.)* noren, nortzuren.
why *adv./conj.* zergatik, zertako, zeren, zer dela-ta. *n.* arrazoi, zergaitik. *int.* ba, bada.
wick *n.* metxa.
wicked *adj.* gaizto, gaizkin, galdu, makur, barrabas.
wickedly *adv.* gaiztoki, deabruki.
wickedness *n.* gaizkeria, txarkeria, okerkeria, makurkeria.
wicker *n. (bot.)* mihimen, zume, zumeki. *adj.* zumezko, mihimentsu, mihimenezko.
wicket *n.* ateleiho.
wide *adj.* zabal, zabaltsu.
wide-awake *adj.* ernai, guztiz esna.
widely *adv.* zabalki, zabalkiro, zabalera.
widen *v.t./v.i.* zabalagotu, zabaldu.
widenable *adj.* zabalgarri.
wideness *n.* zabaltasun, zabalgo.
widening *n.* zabalketa, zabalpen, zabalgune. *adj.* zabaltzaile.
widespread *adj.* hedatu(a), zabaldu(a).
widow *n.* alargun (emakume), alarguntsa. **Widow's weeds.** Dolu.
widowed *adj.* alargun.
widower *n.* alargun (gizon).
widowerhood *n.* alargungo, alarguntasun.
widowhood *n.* alargungo, alarguntasun.

width *n.* zabalera, zabalgo, zabaltasun.
wield *v.t.* (tresna bat) erabili.
wife *n.* emazte.
wig *n.* ileorde, ileordeko.
wiggle *v.i./v.t.* azkar mugitu.
wigwam *n.* Iparrameriketako indioen bizileku(a).
wild *adj.* basati, hezgabe, sasizko. *adj.* arlote.
wilderness *n.* eremu, mortu.
wildfire *n.* erreketa suntsigarri(a).
wildly *adv.* basatikeriaz.
wildness *n.* piztitasun.
wiliness *n.* maltzurkeria.
will *v. aux.* -go, -en. **She will do it.** Egingo du.
will *n.* azkenahi, azkenagiri, hilburuko, testamentu. *n.* gogo, nahi, gurari, borondate, nahikunde.
willfull *adj.* borondatetsu, gogozko. *adj.* burugogor, tematsu, setatsu.
willfully *adv.* borondatez. *adv.* burugogorki, temaz, setaz.
willing *adj.* ahalegintsu, borondatetsu, gogozko.
willingly *adv.* gogoz, nahiz, borondatez.
willingness *n.* gogozkotasun, nahitasun.
willow *n.* (bot.) mihimen, zume.
willy-nilly *adv.* fristi-frasta.
wilt *v.i./v.t.* zimeldu, txirpildu, ihartu.
wiltable *adj.* faungarri.
wilted *adj.* zimel, ihar.
wily *adj.* maltzur.
wimpy *adj.* txankil.
win *v.i./v.t.* irabazi, gain hartu, goititu.
wince *v.i.* uzkurtu, kuzkurtu.
wind *v.i./v.t.* karakoildu, oihestu, bobinatu. *v.i.* (**up**) halakatu; bukatu, amaitu.
wind *n.* haize. *n.* arnasa, hats. *n.* uzker, sabelaize.
windbreak *n.* haizababes, haizagordeleku, haizegeriza.
windiness *n.* haizetasun, haizakortasun.
winding *adj.* olher, makur, oker, zeharkako.
winding sheet *n.* hiljantzi, hiloihal, hilator.
wind instrument *n.* haizesoinu.
windmill *n.* haizerrota.
window *n.* leiho.
window blind *n.* barrenleiho.
windowpane *n.* leiho-beira.
window sill *n.* leiho-aurre.
windpipe *n.* (anat.) kontraeztarri, zintzurreste.
windshield *n.* haizetako.
windward *n./adj.* (naut.) haizalde.
windy *adj.* haizakor, putzeragile, haizeti, haizetsu.
wine *n.* ardo. *adj.* ardozko.
wineskin *n.* zahagi.
wing *n.* hego, hegal; hega-.
winged *adj.* hegadun, hegaldun.

wingless *adj.* hegalgabe.
wink *v.i./v.t.* begikeinu egin, kliskatu.
wink *n.* keinukada, begikeinu, keinu.
winker *n.* begikeinulari, keinugile.
winking *adj.* keinugile, keinuka.
winner *n.* garaile, irabazle.
winnings *n.* irabazkin.
winnow *v.t./v.i.* haizatu, bihikatu, bahetu, egurastu.
winsome *adj.* atsegingarri, erakargarri.
winter *n.* negu, negualdi. *adj.* neguko, negutar.
wintry *adj.* negutsu, negutar.
wipe *v.t./v.i.* ferekatu, igurtzi. *v.t.* (**off**) xukatu. *v.t.* (**out**) ezabatu.
wiper *n.* ezabailu.
wire *n.* alanbre, burdinari. **To fence with wire.** Burdinaritu.
wireless *n.* irratitelegrafia. *adj.* irratitelegrafiko. *adj.* harigabeko.
wiry *adj.* haritsu.
Wisconsin *n.* (geog.) Estatu Batuetako estatu bat.
wisdom *n.* jakintza, zuhurtasun, jakituria.
wisdom tooth *n.* adinagin, zuhurragin.
wise *adj.* jakintsu, zuhur, burutsu, gogoargi, ikastun, zentzudun, zentzuko.
wisely *adv.* tankeraz, zuhurki.
wish *v.t./v.i.* (v.i., askotan **for**-ekin) opa izan, opatu, opa ukan. **Best wishes!** Zorionak!
wish *n.* gogo, nahi.
wishful *adj.* guratsu.
wishy-washy *adj.* gangar, halaholako.
wistful *adj.* pentsakor eta triste.
wistfully *adv.* herriminez.
wistfulness *n.* irrikitasun, irrika, egarri; -min.
wit *n.* umore, grazi, gatz.
witch *n.* sorgin.
witchcraft *n.* sorginkeria, sorgingo, sorgintza.
witchery *n.* sorginkeria.
witchy *adj.* sorginezko.
with *prep.* -(re)kin; -z, -gaz.
withdraw *v.t.* kendu; -gabetu. *v.i.* atzera joan, alde egin.
withdrawal *n.* atzeraldi.
withdrawn *adj.* bakartu(a), zokokari, bakarti, bakartiar.
withdrawnness *n.* gibelkoitasun.
withdrew *pret. of* withdraw.
wither *v.i./v.t.* zimeldu, zapuztu, ihartu.
witherable *adj.* faungarri.
withered *adj.* faun, zimel.
withheld *pret./p. part. of* withhold.
withhold *v.t.* gelditu, geratu, eragotzi, galerazi. *v.t.* ukatu, uko egin.
within *prep./adv.* barnean, barru, barruan, barren. *n.* barru, baita.
without *prep.* gabe, ezik. *adv.* kanpoan; -at. *n.* kanpo.
withstand *v.t.* eraman, jaso. *v.t.* kontrajarri, oposatu, aurre eman.
withstood *pret./p. part. of* withstand.

witness *v.i.* testigatu, lekukotu, aitortu. *v.t.* ikusi, aurrean egon.
witness *n.* lekuko, testigu, aitorlari, aitorregile. **Eye witness.** Begizko.
witticism *n.* ateraldi.
wittily *adv.* gaziki.
witty *adj.* esaeratsu, grazidun.
wives *n. (pl.) of wife.*
wizard *n.* azti, aztigaizkile.
wizardry *n.* aztikeria.
wobble *v.i./v.t.* kili-kolo egin, kolokatu.
wobbly *adj.* kili-kolo, koloka.
woe *n.* atsekabe, nahigabe, bihozmin.
woeful *adj.* negargarri.
woke *pret. of wake.*
wolf *n.* otso; otsa-. **Male wolf.** Otsar. **She-wolf.** Otsanda. Otseme.
wolfsbane *n. (bot.)* irabelar.
wolves *n. (pl.) of wolf.*
woman *n.* andre, emakume, emazte, andere. **Old woman.** Atso.
womanhood *n.* andretasun.
womanish *adj.* andrazko, emakumezko.
womanizing *adj.* andrekari, emaztekoi.
womankind *n.* emakumeak mundu osoan.
womb *n. (anat.)* haurtoki, emasabel, umetoki.
women *n. (pl.) of woman.*
won *pret./ p. part. of win.*
wonder *v.i. (askotan* at-ekin) mirestu, miretsi, miraritu. *v.t.* jakin nahi izan; bere buruari galdetu.
wonder *n.* harrigarritza, miragarri, harritasun.
wonderful *adj.* zoragarri, miragarri, bapo.
wonderfully *adv.* zoragarriro, miresgarriki, zoragarriki.
wonderfulness *n.* zoragarritasun, miresgarritasun.
wonderland *n.* herrialde miragarri.
wondrous *adj.* miresgarri, miragarri, sekulako.
won't "will + not"-aren laburpena.
woo *v.t./v.i.* maitaxarmatu.
wood *n.* ohol, zur, egur. *adj.* zurezko.
woodcutter *n.* egurgile, egurtxikitzaile, egurxehatzaile, aizkolari.
woodcutting *n.* egurmozketa, egurmozte.
wooded *adj.* oihantsu.
wooden *adj.* zurezko; zur-, egurrezko.
woodland *n.* zuhaizti, baso, oihan.
woodpecker *n. (zool.)* okil.
woodpile *n.* egurketa, egurmeta, egurpilo, egurtza.
woods *n. (pl.)* oihan, baso, zuhaizti.
woodshed *n.* egurrola, egurtoki.
woodwork *n.* zurlan, zurgintza.
woodworker *n.* zurketari, zurlangile.
woodworking *n.* zurlan, zurlantza, zurlanketa.
woody *adj.* egurtsu, zurgai.
woof *n.* bilbe.
wool *n.* artile. *adj.* artilezko.

woolen *adj.* artilezko, artiletsu.
woolly *adj.* artiletsu, artiledun.
word *n.* hitz, ele, itz, berba. **Written word.** Idazlan. Idazki.
wordiness *n.* hitzjario, hitzontzikeria, hitzjariokeria.
wore *pret. of wear.*
work *v.i.* lan egin. *v.i.* ibili, funtzionatu. *v.t.* erabili, erabiltzen jakin. *v.t.* landu, maneatu.
work *n.* lan, lanketa; zeregin, arazo, egiteko; -lan. *n.* irabazbide, lanbide, langintza, lanpostu; -go.
workable *adj.* egingarri.
workday *n.* lanegun, astegun, lanaldi, ihardunaldi.
worked *adj.* landu(a).
worker *n.* langile.
working *n.* lanketa.
working class *n.* langilego, langileria.
working hours *n.* lanorduak.
workingman *n.* langile.
work of art *n.* artelan, ederlan.
work place *n.* lanleku, lantegi, lantoki.
workroom *n.* langela, bulego.
workshop *n.* lantegi, lantoki, lanleku.
world *n.* lur, mundu, lurbira, ludi. *adj.* munduko.
worldliness *n.* mundukoikeria, munduzalekeria, munduzaletasun.
worldly *adj.* sekular, munduzale, mundukoi. *adj.* lurkoi, lurreko, mundukoi, mundutar.
worldwide *adj.* lurguziko.
worm *n. (zool.)* har, mamutz, zizare. **Worm hole.** Zizarezulo.
worm-eaten *adj.* harjota.
wormy *adj.* hardun, hartsu, harjota, zizaretsu.
worn *p. part. of wear.*
worn out *adj.* higatu(a).
worried *adj.* kexu, kexati, kezkati, larri, axoladun, artega, urduri.
worriedly *adv.* kexagarriki, larri, kezkaz, urduriki.
worrisome *adj.* kezkagarri, larrigarri, urdurigarri, larritsu.
worry *v.i./v.t.* kezkatu, larritu, urdurltu, artegatu, estutu. **Don't worry!** Ez ezazu kezkarik izan!
worry *n.* kezka, larrialdi, larritasun, axola, kexadura, itoaldi, artegatasun, estutasun, urduritasun.
worse *adv. (comp.)* gaizkiago, gaiztoago, txarrago.
worsen *v.t./v.i.* gaizkiagotu, gaiztoagotu, gordindu.
worship *v.t./v.i.* gurtu, agur egin, jauretsi.
worship *n.* gurtza, gurtzaldi, jauresketa, jaurespen.
worshiper *n.* gurtzaile, jauresle.
worst *adj. (superl.)* txarren, okerren.
worth *n.* baliadura, balio, meritu, merezi.
worthily *adv.* merezkiri.
worthiness *n.* estimagarritasun,

merezimendu.
worthless *adj.* alferreko, baliagaitz.
worthlessness *n.* balioeza, gauzaez.
worthwhile *adj.* baliozko, balioko.
worthy *adj.* baliagarri, baliozko,
estimagarri, merezigarri, meritudun,
duin.
would *pret./p. part. of will.*
wouldn't "would + not"-aren
laburpena.
wound *v.t.* zauriztatu. *pret./p. part. of
wind.*
wound *n.* zauri, sakaila.
woundable *adj.* zaurigarri.
wounded *adj.* zauritsu, zauridun.
wove *pret. of weave.*
woven *p. part. of weave.*
wow *int.* kontxo, alajaina.
wrangle *v.t./v.i.* errieta egin,
mokokatu, liskar egin. *v.t.* behiak eta
zaldiak zaindu.
wrangler *n.* moxaltzain, abeltzain.
wrap *v.t./v.i.* (*v.i.*, *gehienetan* **up***-ekin*)
oihaleztu, batu, bildu, paketatu,
inguratu.
wrap *n.* gainjantzi.
wrapper *n.* lotzaile, gainjantzi.
wrapping *n.* bildukin, lotze, gainjantzi.
wrath *n.* suminkortasun, haserre,
haserrekortasun.
wrathful *adj.* amorruzko.
wreath *n.* girlanda.
wreck *v.t./v.i.* lauzkitu, deuseztatu. *v.i.*
ontzia galdu, hondoratu.
wreck *n.* hondoraketa, hondorapen,
ontzigalera.
wreckage *n.* deuseztapen. *n.* hondar.
wren *n.* (*zool.*) txepetx.
wrench *v.t.* bihurritu.
wrench *n.* (*mech.*) giltza zabalgarri.
wrestle *v.t./v.i.* gatazkatu, borroka
librean ihardun.
wrestler *n.* gatazkalari. **Arm wrestler.**
Pultsulari.
wretched *adj.* zarpazikin, gizajo,
zorigabeko.
wretchedness *n.* zoritxar.
wriggle *v.i.* gorputza astindu.
wring *v.t./v.i.* igortzi, bihurkatu,
maluskatu.
wrinkle *v.t./v.i.* zimurtu, pirtxildu.
wrinkle *n.* zimur, zimurdura.
wrinkled *adj.* zimur, zimurtsu, pirtxil.
wrinkledness *n.* izurdura.
wrist *n.* (*anat.*) eskutur, besamutur.
wristband *n.* eskuturreko.
wristwatch *n.* eskuerloju.
writ *n.* agindu-idatzi(a).
write *v.t./v.i.* idatzi, izkiriatu.
writer *n.* idazle, elertilari, literato,
liburugile.
writhe *v.i.* (oinazez) bihurrikatu.
writing *n.* idazlan, idazti, idazki,
idazketa. *n.* idazkera.
written *adj.* idatzi(a).
wrong *v.t.* iraindu.
wrong *n.* gaiztakeria, txarkeria,

makurkeria, okerkeria. *adj.* okerreko,
makur. **To go wrong.** Okertu.
Gaiztotu. *adv.* oker, gaizki.
wrongdoer *n.* gaizkile, gaiztagin.
wrongly *adv.* makur, oker.
wrongness *n.* gaiztotasun.
wrote *pret. of write.*
wrung *pret./p. part. of wring.*
Wyoming *n.* (*geog.*) Estatu Batuetako
estatu bat.

X

x *n.* Ingeles alfabetoko letra.
xenophile *n.* erdaltzale.
xenophobia *n.* erdalkeria, xenofobia.
xerox *v.t./v.i.* kopiak egin.
Xmas *n.* gabonak, eguberriak.
x-ray *v.t.* x-izpiez plaka bat atera.
x-ray(s) *n.* x-izpi(ak).
xylophone *n.* (*mus.*) xilofono.

Y

y *n.* Ingeles alfabetoko letra.
yacht *n.* iate.
yank *v.t./v.i.* teinkatu, teink egin,
tenkatu, tirakatu, tiratu.
yank *n.* teinkada, tenkada, tirakada,
tiraldi.
Yankee *n.* yanki.
yap *v.i.* zaunka egin, zaunkatu.
yard *n.* yarda. *n.* etxe inguruko zelai(a).
yardstick *n.* yardako neurgailu,
neurkin; haga.
yarn *n.* hari. *n.* ipuin.
yawn *v.i./v.t.* aharrausi egin,
ahozabaldu.
yawn *n.* aharrausi, ahozabalkada.
ye *pron.* zu.
yea *adv.* bai.
year *n.* urte, urtebete. **This year.**
Aurten. **New year.** Urteberri. **New
Year's Eve.** Gabonzahar.
yearbook *n.* urtekari.
yearling *n.* urtume. *adj.* urtedun.
yearly *adj./adv.* urteroko, urteko;
urtero.
yearn *v.i.* (askotan **for***-ekin*) irrikitu,
irritsatu, tirriatu.
yearning *n.* gogomin, gutizia.
yeast *n.* legamia, orantza, altxagarri.
yell *v.i./v.t.* oihu egin, garrasi egin,
txilio egin.
yell *n.* oihu, garrasi, txilio.
yellow *v.t./v.i.* horitu, horiztatu.
yellow *n./adj.* hori. **Golden yellow.**
Horigorri. **To turn yellow.** Horiskatu.
Horitu. *adj.* (*colloq.*) beldurti, oilo,
txepel, uzkur.
yellowish *adj.* horiska.
yellowness *n.* horitasun, horidura,
beilegitasun.
yelp *n.* zaunka, ahausi.
yen *n.* gura, gogo, guranahi. *n.* yen,
Japoiko diru(a).
yep *n.* (*colloq.*) bai.
yes *adv.* bai, baietz. *n.* baietza.
yesterday *adv.* atzo. **Day before**

yesterday. Herenegun.
yet *adv.* oraindik, oraindikan. *conj.* berriz.
yew *n. (bot.)* hagin.
yield *v.t./v.i.* errenditu, amore eman.
Y.M.C.A. *n. (Young Men's Christian Association)* Gizon gazteen kristau elkarte(a).
yodel *v.t./v.i.* tiroldarrek bezala abestu.
yogurt *n.* yogurt.
yoke *v.t.* uztartu.
yoke *n.* uztarri, uztai.
yokel *n.* larragizon.
yolk *n.* arraultzagorringo, gorringo.
yonder *adv.* han.
you *pron.* zu(k), zuek; hi(k); berori; -zu-. **You yourself.** Zerorrek. Zerori. **You yourselves.** Zeuek.
you'd "you + had" eta "you + would"-en laburpena.
you'll "you + will"-aren laburpena.
young *n.* gaztedi; ume, haur, sein. *n.* -kume. *adj.* gazte, gaztaroko.
youngster *n.* gaztetxo, gaztetto, gazteño.
your *pron./adj.* zure, zuen; hire; berorren.
you're "you + are"-aren laburpena.
yours *pron.* zure, zuen; hire.
yourself *pron.* zerorrek.
yourselves *pron. (pl.)* zuok.
youth *n.* gaztaro, gaztealdi. *n.* gazte; gazteria. *n.* gaztetasun.
youthful *adj.* gazte, gaztaroko.
youthfully *adv.* gaztegisa.
you've "you + have"-aren laburpena.
yowl *n.* marrao.
Yukon *n.* Kanada-ko herrialde bat.
yule *n.* gabonak.

Y.W.C.A. *n. (Young Women's Christian Association)* Emakume gazteen kristau elkarte(a).

Z

z *n.* Ingeles alfabetoko letra, zeta.
zany *adj.* arrazoigabeko, taxugabeko.
zarzuela *n. (mus.)* zartzuela.
zeal *n.* sugar.
zealot *n.* fanatiko.
zealous *adj.* sugartsu, lehiatsu.
zealously *adv.* sugarrez, lehiatsuki.
zebra *n. (zool.)* astanabar, zebra.
zed *n.* zeta.
zenith *n.* zenit.
zephyr *n.* haizetxo.
zeppelin *n.* zepelin.
zero *n./adj.* huts, zero.
zest *n.* azkortasun.
zigzag *adv.* zeharka, makurka. *adj.* zeharkako, zeharreko.
zinc *n. (chem.)* zink.
Zionism *n.* sionismo.
Zionist *adj.* sionista.
zip *v.t.* kremailera itxi.
zipper *n.* kremailera.
zither *n. (mus.)* zitara.
zodiac *n.* zodiako.
zone *n.* barruti, eremu; -alde.
zoning *n.* eskualdekapen.
zoo *n.* zoo.
zoological *adj.* zoologiko.
zoologist *n.* zoologo, abeliztilari.
zoology *n.* zoologia.
zoom *v.i.* zarataz eta azkar abiadura hartu (hegazkin, kotxe).
Zuberoa *n. (geog.)* Zubero.
Zuberoan *n./adj.* zuberotar. *n.* zuberoera.